T0190172

Lecture Notes in Computer Science 13436

More information about this series at https://link.springer.com/bookseries/558

Linwei Wang · Qi Dou · P. Thomas Fletcher ·
Stefanie Speidel · Shuo Li (Eds.)

Medical Image Computing and Computer Assisted Intervention – MICCAI 2022

25th International Conference
Singapore, September 18–22, 2022
Proceedings, Part VI

Springer

Editors
Linwei Wang
Rochester Institute of Technology
Rochester, NY, USA

Qi Dou 🆔
Chinese University of Hong Kong
Hong Kong, Hong Kong

P. Thomas Fletcher 🆔
University of Virginia
Charlottesville, VA, USA

Stefanie Speidel 🆔
National Center for Tumor Diseases
(NCT/UCC)
Dresden, Germany

Shuo Li 🆔
Case Western Reserve University
Cleveland, OH, USA

ISSN 0302-9743   ISSN 1611-3349 (electronic)
Lecture Notes in Computer Science
ISBN 978-3-031-16445-3   ISBN 978-3-031-16446-0 (eBook)
https://doi.org/10.1007/978-3-031-16446-0

This Springer imprint is published by the registered company Springer Nature Switzerland AG
The registered company address is: Gewerbestrasse 11, 6330 Cham, Switzerland

Preface

We are pleased to present the proceedings of the 25th International Conference on Medical Image Computing and Computer-Assisted Intervention (MICCAI) which – after two difficult years of virtual conferences – was held in a hybrid fashion at the Resort World Convention Centre in Singapore, September 18–22, 2022. The conference also featured 36 workshops, 11 tutorials, and 38 challenges held on September 18 and September 22. The conference was also co-located with the 2nd Conference on Clinical Translation on Medical Image Computing and Computer-Assisted Intervention (CLINICCAI) on September 20.

MICCAI 2022 had an approximately 14% increase in submissions and accepted papers compared with MICCAI 2021. These papers, which comprise eight volumes of Lecture Notes in Computer Science (LNCS) proceedings, were selected after a thorough double-blind peer-review process. Following the example set by the previous program chairs of past MICCAI conferences, we employed Microsoft's Conference Managing Toolkit (CMT) for paper submissions and double-blind peer-reviews, and the Toronto Paper Matching System (TPMS) to assist with automatic paper assignment to area chairs and reviewers.

From 2811 original intentions to submit, 1865 full submissions were received and 1831 submissions reviewed. Of these, 67% were considered as pure Medical Image Computing (MIC), 7% as pure Computer-Assisted Interventions (CAI), and 26% as both MIC and CAI. The MICCAI 2022 Program Committee (PC) comprised 107 area chairs, with 52 from the Americas, 33 from Europe, and 22 from the Asia-Pacific or Middle East regions. We maintained gender balance with 37% women scientists on the PC.

Each area chair was assigned 16–18 manuscripts, for each of which they were asked to suggest up to 15 suggested potential reviewers. Subsequently, over 1320 invited reviewers were asked to bid for the papers for which they had been suggested. Final reviewer allocations via CMT took account of PC suggestions, reviewer bidding, and TPMS scores, finally allocating 4–6 papers per reviewer. Based on the double-blinded reviews, area chairs' recommendations, and program chairs' global adjustments, 249 papers (14%) were provisionally accepted, 901 papers (49%) were provisionally rejected, and 675 papers (37%) proceeded into the rebuttal stage.

During the rebuttal phase, two additional area chairs were assigned to each rebuttal paper using CMT and TPMS scores. After the authors' rebuttals were submitted, all reviewers of the rebuttal papers were invited to assess the rebuttal, participate in a double-blinded discussion with fellow reviewers and area chairs, and finalize their rating (with the opportunity to revise their rating as appropriate). The three area chairs then independently provided their recommendations to accept or reject the paper, considering the manuscript, the reviews, and the rebuttal. The final decision of acceptance was based on majority voting of the area chair recommendations. The program chairs reviewed all decisions and provided their inputs in extreme cases where a large divergence existed between the area chairs and reviewers in their recommendations. This process resulted in the acceptance of a total of 574 papers, reaching an overall acceptance rate of 31% for MICCAI 2022.

In our additional effort to ensure review quality, two Reviewer Tutorials and two Area Chair Orientations were held in early March, virtually in different time zones, to introduce the reviewers and area chairs to the MICCAI 2022 review process and the best practice for high-quality reviews. Two additional Area Chair meetings were held virtually in July to inform the area chairs of the outcome of the review process and to collect feedback for future conferences.

For the MICCAI 2022 proceedings, 574 accepted papers were organized in eight volumes as follows:

- Part I, LNCS Volume 13431: Brain Development and Atlases, DWI and Tractography, Functional Brain Networks, Neuroimaging, Heart and Lung Imaging, and Dermatology
- Part II, LNCS Volume 13432: Computational (Integrative) Pathology, Computational Anatomy and Physiology, Ophthalmology, and Fetal Imaging
- Part III, LNCS Volume 13433: Breast Imaging, Colonoscopy, and Computer Aided Diagnosis
- Part IV, LNCS Volume 13434: Microscopic Image Analysis, Positron Emission Tomography, Ultrasound Imaging, Video Data Analysis, and Image Segmentation I
- Part V, LNCS Volume 13435: Image Segmentation II and Integration of Imaging with Non-imaging Biomarkers
- Part VI, LNCS Volume 13436: Image Registration and Image Reconstruction
- Part VII, LNCS Volume 13437: Image-Guided Interventions and Surgery, Outcome and Disease Prediction, Surgical Data Science, Surgical Planning and Simulation, and Machine Learning – Domain Adaptation and Generalization
- Part VIII, LNCS Volume 13438: Machine Learning – Weakly-supervised Learning, Machine Learning – Model Interpretation, Machine Learning – Uncertainty, and Machine Learning Theory and Methodologies

We would like to thank everyone who contributed to the success of MICCAI 2022 and the quality of its proceedings. These include the MICCAI Society for support and feedback, and our sponsors for their financial support and presence onsite. We especially express our gratitude to the MICCAI Submission System Manager Kitty Wong for her thorough support throughout the paper submission, review, program planning, and proceeding preparation process – the Program Committee simply would not have be able to function without her. We are also grateful for the dedication and support of all of the organizers of the workshops, tutorials, and challenges, Jianming Liang, Wufeng Xue, Jun Cheng, Qian Tao, Xi Chen, Islem Rekik, Sophia Bano, Andrea Lara, Yunliang Cai, Pingkun Yan, Pallavi Tiwari, Ingerid Reinertsen, Gongning Luo, without whom the exciting peripheral events would have not been feasible. Behind the scenes, the MICCAI secretariat personnel, Janette Wallace and Johanne Langford, kept a close eye on logistics and budgets, while Mehmet Eldegez and his team from Dekon Congress & Tourism, MICCAI 2022's Professional Conference Organization, managed the website and local organization. We are especially grateful to all members of the Program Committee for their diligent work in the reviewer assignments and final paper selection, as well as the reviewers for their support during the entire process. Finally, and most importantly, we thank all authors, co-authors, students/postdocs, and supervisors, for submitting and presenting their high-quality work which made MICCAI 2022 a successful event.

We look forward to seeing you in Vancouver, Canada at MICCAI 2023!

September 2022   Linwei Wang
                                                                          Qi Dou
                                                             P. Thomas Fletcher
                                                               Stefanie Speidel
                                                                        Shuo Li

Organization

General Chair

Shuo Li   Case Western Reserve University, USA

Program Committee Chairs

Linwei Wang   Rochester Institute of Technology, USA
Qi Dou   The Chinese University of Hong Kong, China
P. Thomas Fletcher   University of Virginia, USA
Stefanie Speidel   National Center for Tumor Diseases Dresden, Germany

Workshop Team

Wufeng Xue   Shenzhen University, China
Jun Cheng   Agency for Science, Technology and Research, Singapore
Qian Tao   Delft University of Technology, the Netherlands
Xi Chen   Stern School of Business, NYU, USA

Challenges Team

Pingkun Yan   Rensselaer Polytechnic Institute, USA
Pallavi Tiwari   Case Western Reserve University, USA
Ingerid Reinertsen   SINTEF Digital and NTNU, Trondheim, Norway
Gongning Luo   Harbin Institute of Technology, China

Tutorial Team

Islem Rekik   Istanbul Technical University, Turkey
Sophia Bano   University College London, UK
Andrea Lara   Universidad Industrial de Santander, Colombia
Yunliang Cai   Humana, USA

Clinical Day Chairs

Jason Chan	The Chinese University of Hong Kong, China
Heike I. Grabsch	University of Leeds, UK and Maastricht University, the Netherlands
Nicolas Padoy	University of Strasbourg & Institute of Image-Guided Surgery, IHU Strasbourg, France

Young Investigators and Early Career Development Program Chairs

Marius Linguraru	Children's National Institute, USA
Antonio Porras	University of Colorado Anschutz Medical Campus, USA
Nicole Rieke	NVIDIA, Deutschland
Daniel Racoceanu	Sorbonne University, France

Social Media Chairs

Chenchu Xu	Anhui University, China
Dong Zhang	University of British Columbia, Canada

Student Board Liaison

Camila Bustillo	Technische Universität Darmstadt, Germany
Vanessa Gonzalez Duque	Ecole centrale de Nantes, France

Submission Platform Manager

Kitty Wong	The MICCAI Society, Canada

Virtual Platform Manager

John Baxter	INSERM, Université de Rennes 1, France

Program Committee

Ehsan Adeli	Stanford University, USA
Pablo Arbelaez	Universidad de los Andes, Colombia
John Ashburner	University College London, UK
Ulas Bagci	Northwestern University, USA
Sophia Bano	University College London, UK
Adrien Bartoli	Université Clermont Auvergne, France
Kayhan Batmanghelich	University of Pittsburgh, USA

Hrvoje Bogunovic	Medical University of Vienna, Austria
Ester Bonmati	University College London, UK
Esther Bron	Erasmus MC, the Netherlands
Gustavo Carneiro	University of Adelaide, Australia
Hao Chen	Hong Kong University of Science and Technology, China
Jun Cheng	Agency for Science, Technology and Research, Singapore
Li Cheng	University of Alberta, Canada
Adrian Dalca	Massachusetts Institute of Technology, USA
Jose Dolz	ETS Montreal, Canada
Shireen Elhabian	University of Utah, USA
Sandy Engelhardt	University Hospital Heidelberg, Germany
Ruogu Fang	University of Florida, USA
Aasa Feragen	Technical University of Denmark, Denmark
Moti Freiman	Technion - Israel Institute of Technology, Israel
Huazhu Fu	Agency for Science, Technology and Research, Singapore
Mingchen Gao	University at Buffalo, SUNY, USA
Zhifan Gao	Sun Yat-sen University, China
Stamatia Giannarou	Imperial College London, UK
Alberto Gomez	King's College London, UK
Ilker Hacihaliloglu	University of British Columbia, Canada
Adam Harrison	PAII Inc., USA
Mattias Heinrich	University of Lübeck, Germany
Yipeng Hu	University College London, UK
Junzhou Huang	University of Texas at Arlington, USA
Sharon Xiaolei Huang	Pennsylvania State University, USA
Yuankai Huo	Vanderbilt University, USA
Jayender Jagadeesan	Brigham and Women's Hospital, USA
Won-Ki Jeong	Korea University, Korea
Xi Jiang	University of Electronic Science and Technology of China, China
Anand Joshi	University of Southern California, USA
Shantanu Joshi	University of California, Los Angeles, USA
Bernhard Kainz	Imperial College London, UK
Marta Kersten-Oertel	Concordia University, Canada
Fahmi Khalifa	Mansoura University, Egypt
Seong Tae Kim	Kyung Hee University, Korea
Minjeong Kim	University of North Carolina at Greensboro, USA
Baiying Lei	Shenzhen University, China
Gang Li	University of North Carolina at Chapel Hill, USA

Fuyong Xing   University of Colorado Denver, USA
Ziyue Xu   NVIDIA, USA
Yanwu Xu   Baidu Inc., China
Pingkun Yan   Rensselaer Polytechnic Institute, USA
Guang Yang   Imperial College London, UK
Jianhua Yao   Tencent, China
Zhaozheng Yin   Stony Brook University, USA
Lequan Yu   University of Hong Kong, China
Yixuan Yuan   City University of Hong Kong, China
Ling Zhang   Alibaba Group, USA
Miaomiao Zhang   University of Virginia, USA
Ya Zhang   Shanghai Jiao Tong University, China
Rongchang Zhao   Central South University, China
Yitian Zhao   Chinese Academy of Sciences, China
Yefeng Zheng   Tencent Jarvis Lab, China
Guoyan Zheng   Shanghai Jiao Tong University, China
Luping Zhou   University of Sydney, Australia
Yuyin Zhou   Stanford University, USA
Dajiang Zhu   University of Texas at Arlington, USA
Lilla Zöllei   Massachusetts General Hospital, USA
Maria A. Zuluaga   EURECOM, France

Reviewers

Alireza Akhondi-asl   Manas Nag
Fernando Arambula   Tianye Niu
Nicolas Boutry   Seokhwan Oh
Qilei Chen   Theodoros Pissas
Zhihao Chen   Harish RaviPrakash
Javid Dadashkarimi   Maria Sainz de Cea
Marleen De Bruijne   Hai Su
Mohammad Eslami   Wenjun Tan
Sayan Ghosal   Fatmatulzehra Uslu
Estibaliz Gómez-de-Mariscal   Fons van der Sommen
Charles Hatt   Gijs van Tulder
Yongxiang Huang   Dong Wei
Samra Irshad   Pengcheng Xi
Anithapriya Krishnan   Chen Yang
Rodney LaLonde   Kun Yuan
Jie Liu   Hang Zhang
Jinyang Liu   Wei Zhang
Qing Lyu   Yuyao Zhang
Hassan Mohy-ud-Din   Tengda Zhao

Yingying Zhu
Yuemin Zhu
Alaa Eldin Abdelaal
Amir Abdi
Mazdak Abulnaga
Burak Acar
Iman Aganj
Priya Aggarwal
Ola Ahmad
Seyed-Ahmad Ahmadi
Euijoon Ahn
Faranak Akbarifar
Cem Akbaş
Saad Ullah Akram
Tajwar Aleef
Daniel Alexander
Hazrat Ali
Sharib Ali
Max Allan
Pablo Alvarez
Vincent Andrearczyk
Elsa Angelini
Sameer Antani
Michela Antonelli
Ignacio Arganda-Carreras
Mohammad Ali Armin
Josep Arnal
Md Ashikuzzaman
Mehdi Astaraki
Marc Aubreville
Chloé Audigier
Angelica Aviles-Rivero
Ruqayya Awan
Suyash Awate
Qinle Ba
Morteza Babaie
Meritxell Bach Cuadra
Hyeon-Min Bae
Junjie Bai
Wenjia Bai
Ujjwal Baid
Pradeep Bajracharya
Yaël Balbastre
Abhirup Banerjee
Sreya Banerjee

Shunxing Bao
Adrian Barbu
Sumana Basu
Deepti Bathula
Christian Baumgartner
John Baxter
Sharareh Bayat
Bahareh Behboodi
Hamid Behnam
Sutanu Bera
Christos Bergeles
Jose Bernal
Gabriel Bernardino
Alaa Bessadok
Riddhish Bhalodia
Indrani Bhattacharya
Chitresh Bhushan
Lei Bi
Qi Bi
Gui-Bin Bian
Alexander Bigalke
Ricardo Bigolin Lanfredi
Benjamin Billot
Ryoma Bise
Sangeeta Biswas
Stefano B. Blumberg
Sebastian Bodenstedt
Bhushan Borotikar
Ilaria Boscolo Galazzo
Behzad Bozorgtabar
Nadia Brancati
Katharina Breininger
Rupert Brooks
Tom Brosch
Mikael Brudfors
Qirong Bu
Ninon Burgos
Nikolay Burlutskiy
Michał Byra
Ryan Cabeen
Mariano Cabezas
Hongmin Cai
Jinzheng Cai
Weidong Cai
Sema Candemir

Qing Cao
Weiguo Cao
Yankun Cao
Aaron Carass
Ruben Cardenes
M. Jorge Cardoso
Owen Carmichael
Alessandro Casella
Matthieu Chabanas
Ahmad Chaddad
Jayasree Chakraborty
Sylvie Chambon
Yi Hao Chan
Ming-Ching Chang
Peng Chang
Violeta Chang
Sudhanya Chatterjee
Christos Chatzichristos
Antong Chen
Chao Chen
Chen Chen
Cheng Chen
Dongdong Chen
Fang Chen
Geng Chen
Hanbo Chen
Jianan Chen
Jianxu Chen
Jie Chen
Junxiang Chen
Junying Chen
Junyu Chen
Lei Chen
Li Chen
Liangjun Chen
Liyun Chen
Min Chen
Pingjun Chen
Qiang Chen
Runnan Chen
Shuai Chen
Xi Chen
Xiaoran Chen
Xin Chen
Xinjian Chen

Xuejin Chen
Yuanyuan Chen
Zhaolin Chen
Zhen Chen
Zhineng Chen
Zhixiang Chen
Erkang Cheng
Jianhong Cheng
Jun Cheng
Philip Chikontwe
Min-Kook Choi
Gary Christensen
Argyrios Christodoulidis
Stergios Christodoulidis
Albert Chung
Özgün Çiçek
Matthew Clarkson
Dana Cobzas
Jaume Coll-Font
Toby Collins
Olivier Commowick
Runmin Cong
Yulai Cong
Pierre-Henri Conze
Timothy Cootes
Teresa Correia
Pierrick Coupé
Hadrien Courtecuisse
Jeffrey Craley
Alessandro Crimi
Can Cui
Hejie Cui
Hui Cui
Zhiming Cui
Kathleen Curran
Claire Cury
Tobias Czempiel
Vedrana Dahl
Tareen Dawood
Laura Daza
Charles Delahunt
Herve Delingette
Ugur Demir
Liang-Jian Deng
Ruining Deng

Yang Deng
Cem Deniz
Felix Denzinger
Adrien Depeursinge
Hrishikesh Deshpande
Christian Desrosiers
Neel Dey
Anuja Dharmaratne
Li Ding
Xinghao Ding
Zhipeng Ding
Ines Domingues
Juan Pedro Dominguez-Morales
Mengjin Dong
Nanqing Dong
Sven Dorkenwald
Haoran Dou
Simon Drouin
Karen Drukker
Niharika D'Souza
Guodong Du
Lei Du
Dingna Duan
Hongyi Duanmu
Nicolas Duchateau
James Duncan
Nicha Dvornek
Dmitry V. Dylov
Oleh Dzyubachyk
Jan Egger
Alma Eguizabal
Gudmundur Einarsson
Ahmet Ekin
Ahmed Elazab
Ahmed Elnakib
Amr Elsawy
Mohamed Elsharkawy
Ertunc Erdil
Marius Erdt
Floris Ernst
Boris Escalante-Ramírez
Hooman Esfandiari
Nazila Esmaeili
Marco Esposito
Théo Estienne

Christian Ewert
Deng-Ping Fan
Xin Fan
Yonghui Fan
Yubo Fan
Chaowei Fang
Huihui Fang
Xi Fang
Yingying Fang
Zhenghan Fang
Mohsen Farzi
Hamid Fehri
Lina Felsner
Jianjiang Feng
Jun Feng
Ruibin Feng
Yuan Feng
Zishun Feng
Aaron Fenster
Henrique Fernandes
Ricardo Ferrari
Lukas Fischer
Antonio Foncubierta-Rodríguez
Nils Daniel Forkert
Wolfgang Freysinger
Bianca Freytag
Xueyang Fu
Yunguan Fu
Gareth Funka-Lea
Pedro Furtado
Ryo Furukawa
Laurent Gajny
Francesca Galassi
Adrian Galdran
Jiangzhang Gan
Yu Gan
Melanie Ganz
Dongxu Gao
Linlin Gao
Riqiang Gao
Siyuan Gao
Yunhe Gao
Zeyu Gao
Gautam Gare
Bao Ge

Rongjun Ge
Sairam Geethanath
Shiv Gehlot
Yasmeen George
Nils Gessert
Olivier Gevaert
Ramtin Gharleghi
Sandesh Ghimire
Andrea Giovannini
Gabriel Girard
Rémi Giraud
Ben Glocker
Ehsan Golkar
Arnold Gomez
Ricardo Gonzales
Camila Gonzalez
Cristina González
German Gonzalez
Sharath Gopal
Karthik Gopinath
Pietro Gori
Michael Götz
Shuiping Gou
Maged Goubran
Sobhan Goudarzi
Alejandro Granados
Mara Graziani
Yun Gu
Zaiwang Gu
Hao Guan
Dazhou Guo
Hengtao Guo
Jixiang Guo
Jun Guo
Pengfei Guo
Xiaoqing Guo
Yi Guo
Yuyu Guo
Vikash Gupta
Prashnna Gyawali
Stathis Hadjidemetriou
Fatemeh Haghighi
Justin Haldar
Mohammad Hamghalam
Kamal Hammouda

Bing Han
Liang Han
Seungjae Han
Xiaoguang Han
Zhongyi Han
Jonny Hancox
Lasse Hansen
Huaying Hao
Jinkui Hao
Xiaoke Hao
Mohammad Minhazul Haq
Nandinee Haq
Rabia Haq
Michael Hardisty
Nobuhiko Hata
Ali Hatamizadeh
Andreas Hauptmann
Huiguang He
Nanjun He
Shenghua He
Yuting He
Tobias Heimann
Stefan Heldmann
Sobhan Hemati
Alessa Hering
Monica Hernandez
Estefania Hernandez-Martin
Carlos Hernandez-Matas
Javier Herrera-Vega
Kilian Hett
David Ho
Yi Hong
Yoonmi Hong
Mohammad Reza Hosseinzadeh Taher
Benjamin Hou
Wentai Hou
William Hsu
Dan Hu
Rongyao Hu
Xiaoling Hu
Xintao Hu
Yan Hu
Ling Huang
Sharon Xiaolei Huang
Xiaoyang Huang

Yangsibo Huang
Yi-Jie Huang
Yijin Huang
Yixing Huang
Yue Huang
Zhi Huang
Ziyi Huang
Arnaud Huaulmé
Jiayu Huo
Raabid Hussain
Sarfaraz Hussein
Khoi Huynh
Seong Jae Hwang
Ilknur Icke
Kay Igwe
Abdullah Al Zubaer Imran
Ismail Irmakci
Benjamin Irving
Mohammad Shafkat Islam
Koichi Ito
Hayato Itoh
Yuji Iwahori
Mohammad Jafari
Andras Jakab
Amir Jamaludin
Mirek Janatka
Vincent Jaouen
Uditha Jarayathne
Ronnachai Jaroensri
Golara Javadi
Rohit Jena
Rachid Jennane
Todd Jensen
Debesh Jha
Ge-Peng Ji
Yuanfeng Ji
Zhanghexuan Ji
Haozhe Jia
Meirui Jiang
Tingting Jiang
Xiajun Jiang
Xiang Jiang
Zekun Jiang
Jianbo Jiao
Jieqing Jiao

Zhicheng Jiao
Chen Jin
Dakai Jin
Qiangguo Jin
Taisong Jin
Yueming Jin
Baoyu Jing
Bin Jing
Yaqub Jonmohamadi
Lie Ju
Yohan Jun
Alain Jungo
Manjunath K N
Abdolrahim Kadkhodamohammadi
Ali Kafaei Zad Tehrani
Dagmar Kainmueller
Siva Teja Kakileti
John Kalafut
Konstantinos Kamnitsas
Michael C. Kampffmeyer
Qingbo Kang
Neerav Karani
Turkay Kart
Satyananda Kashyap
Alexander Katzmann
Anees Kazi
Hengjin Ke
Hamza Kebiri
Erwan Kerrien
Hoel Kervadec
Farzad Khalvati
Bishesh Khanal
Pulkit Khandelwal
Maksim Kholiavchenko
Ron Kikinis
Daeseung Kim
Jae-Hun Kim
Jaeil Kim
Jinman Kim
Won Hwa Kim
Andrew King
Atilla Kiraly
Yoshiro Kitamura
Stefan Klein
Tobias Klinder

Lisa Koch
Satoshi Kondo
Bin Kong
Fanwei Kong
Ender Konukoglu
Aishik Konwer
Bongjin Koo
Ivica Kopriva
Kivanc Kose
Anna Kreshuk
Frithjof Kruggel
Thomas Kuestner
David Kügler
Hugo Kuijf
Arjan Kuijper
Kuldeep Kumar
Manuela Kunz
Holger Kunze
Tahsin Kurc
Anvar Kurmukov
Yoshihiro Kuroda
Jin Tae Kwak
Francesco La Rosa
Aymen Laadhari
Dmitrii Lachinov
Alain Lalande
Bennett Landman
Axel Largent
Carole Lartizien
Max-Heinrich Laves
Ho Hin Lee
Hyekyoung Lee
Jong Taek Lee
Jong-Hwan Lee
Soochahn Lee
Wen Hui Lei
Yiming Lei
Rogers Jeffrey Leo John
Juan Leon
Bo Li
Bowen Li
Chen Li
Hongming Li
Hongwei Li
Jian Li

Jianning Li
Jiayun Li
Jieyu Li
Junhua Li
Kang Li
Lei Li
Mengzhang Li
Qing Li
Quanzheng Li
Shaohua Li
Shulong Li
Weijian Li
Weikai Li
Wenyuan Li
Xiang Li
Xingyu Li
Xiu Li
Yang Li
Yuexiang Li
Yunxiang Li
Zeju Li
Zhang Li
Zhiyuan Li
Zhjin Li
Zi Li
Chunfeng Lian
Sheng Lian
Libin Liang
Peixian Liang
Yuan Liang
Haofu Liao
Hongen Liao
Ruizhi Liao
Wei Liao
Xiangyun Liao
Gilbert Lim
Hongxiang Lin
Jianyu Lin
Li Lin
Tiancheng Lin
Yiqun Lin
Zudi Lin
Claudia Lindner
Bin Liu
Bo Liu

Chuanbin Liu
Daochang Liu
Dong Liu
Dongnan Liu
Fenglin Liu
Han Liu
Hao Liu
Haozhe Liu
Hong Liu
Huafeng Liu
Huiye Liu
Jianfei Liu
Jiang Liu
Jingya Liu
Kefei Liu
Lihao Liu
Mengting Liu
Peirong Liu
Peng Liu
Qin Liu
Qun Liu
Shenghua Liu
Shuangjun Liu
Sidong Liu
Tianrui Liu
Xiao Liu
Xingtong Liu
Xinwen Liu
Xinyang Liu
Xinyu Liu
Yan Liu
Yanbei Liu
Yi Liu
Yikang Liu
Yong Liu
Yue Liu
Yuhang Liu
Zewen Liu
Zhe Liu
Andrea Loddo
Nicolas Loménie
Yonghao Long
Zhongjie Long
Daniel Lopes
Bin Lou

Nicolas Loy Rodas
Charles Lu
Huanxiang Lu
Xing Lu
Yao Lu
Yuhang Lu
Gongning Luo
Jie Luo
Jiebo Luo
Luyang Luo
Ma Luo
Xiangde Luo
Cuong Ly
Ilwoo Lyu
Yanjun Lyu
Yuanyuan Lyu
Sharath M S
Chunwei Ma
Hehuan Ma
Junbo Ma
Wenao Ma
Yuhui Ma
Anderson Maciel
S. Sara Mahdavi
Mohammed Mahmoud
Andreas Maier
Michail Mamalakis
Ilja Manakov
Brett Marinelli
Yassine Marrakchi
Fabio Martinez
Martin Maška
Tejas Sudharshan Mathai
Dimitrios Mavroeidis
Pau Medrano-Gracia
Raghav Mehta
Felix Meissen
Qingjie Meng
Yanda Meng
Martin Menten
Alexandre Merasli
Stijn Michielse
Leo Milecki
Fausto Milletari
Zhe Min

Tadashi Miyamoto
Sara Moccia
Omid Mohareri
Tony C. W. Mok
Rodrigo Moreno
Kensaku Mori
Lia Morra
Aliasghar Mortazi
Hamed Mozaffari
Pritam Mukherjee
Anirban Mukhopadhyay
Henning Müller
Balamurali Murugesan
Tinashe Mutsvangwa
Andriy Myronenko
Saad Nadeem
Ahmed Naglah
Usman Naseem
Vishwesh Nath
Rodrigo Nava
Nassir Navab
Peter Neher
Amin Nejatbakhsh
Dominik Neumann
Duy Nguyen Ho Minh
Dong Ni
Haomiao Ni
Hannes Nickisch
Jingxin Nie
Aditya Nigam
Lipeng Ning
Xia Ning
Sijie Niu
Jack Noble
Jorge Novo
Chinedu Nwoye
Mohammad Obeid
Masahiro Oda
Steffen Oeltze-Jafra
Ayşe Oktay
Hugo Oliveira
Sara Oliveira
Arnau Oliver
Emanuele Olivetti
Jimena Olveres

Doruk Oner
John Onofrey
Felipe Orihuela-Espina
Marcos Ortega
Yoshito Otake
Sebastian Otálora
Cheng Ouyang
Jiahong Ouyang
Xi Ouyang
Utku Ozbulak
Michal Ozery-Flato
Danielle Pace
José Blas Pagador Carrasco
Daniel Pak
Jin Pan
Siyuan Pan
Yongsheng Pan
Pankaj Pandey
Prashant Pandey
Egor Panfilov
Joao Papa
Bartlomiej Papiez
Nripesh Parajuli
Hyunjin Park
Sanghyun Park
Akash Parvatikar
Magdalini Paschali
Diego Patiño Cortés
Mayank Patwari
Angshuman Paul
Yuchen Pei
Yuru Pei
Chengtao Peng
Jialin Peng
Wei Peng
Yifan Peng
Matteo Pennisi
Antonio Pepe
Oscar Perdomo
Sérgio Pereira
Jose-Antonio Pérez-Carrasco
Fernando Pérez-García
Jorge Perez-Gonzalez
Matthias Perkonigg
Mehran Pesteie

Jorg Peters
Terry Peters
Eike Petersen
Jens Petersen
Micha Pfeiffer
Dzung Pham
Hieu Pham
Ashish Phophalia
Tomasz Pieciak
Antonio Pinheiro
Kilian Pohl
Sebastian Pölsterl
Iulia A. Popescu
Alison Pouch
Prateek Prasanna
Raphael Prevost
Juan Prieto
Federica Proietto Salanitri
Sergi Pujades
Kumaradevan Punithakumar
Haikun Qi
Huan Qi
Buyue Qian
Yan Qiang
Yuchuan Qiao
Zhi Qiao
Fangbo Qin
Wenjian Qin
Yanguo Qin
Yulei Qin
Hui Qu
Kha Gia Quach
Tran Minh Quan
Sandro Queirós
Prashanth R.
Mehdi Rahim
Jagath Rajapakse
Kashif Rajpoot
Dhanesh Ramachandram
Xuming Ran
Hatem Rashwan
Daniele Ravì
Keerthi Sravan Ravi
Surreerat Reaungamornrat
Samuel Remedios

Yudan Ren
Mauricio Reyes
Constantino Reyes-Aldasoro
Hadrien Reynaud
David Richmond
Anne-Marie Rickmann
Laurent Risser
Leticia Rittner
Dominik Rivoir
Emma Robinson
Jessica Rodgers
Rafael Rodrigues
Robert Rohling
Lukasz Roszkowiak
Holger Roth
Karsten Roth
José Rouco
Daniel Rueckert
Danny Ruijters
Mirabela Rusu
Ario Sadafi
Shaheer Ullah Saeed
Monjoy Saha
Pranjal Sahu
Olivier Salvado
Ricardo Sanchez-Matilla
Robin Sandkuehler
Gianmarco Santini
Anil Kumar Sao
Duygu Sarikaya
Olivier Saut
Fabio Scarpa
Nico Scherf
Markus Schirmer
Alexander Schlaefer
Jerome Schmid
Julia Schnabel
Andreas Schuh
Christina Schwarz-Gsaxner
Martin Schweiger
Michaël Sdika
Suman Sedai
Matthias Seibold
Raghavendra Selvan
Sourya Sengupta

Carmen Serrano
Ahmed Shaffie
Keyur Shah
Rutwik Shah
Ahmed Shahin
Mohammad Abuzar Shaikh
S. Shailja
Shayan Shams
Hongming Shan
Xinxin Shan
Mostafa Sharifzadeh
Anuja Sharma
Harshita Sharma
Gregory Sharp
Li Shen
Liyue Shen
Mali Shen
Mingren Shen
Yiqing Shen
Ziyi Shen
Luyao Shi
Xiaoshuang Shi
Yiyu Shi
Hoo-Chang Shin
Boris Shirokikh
Suprosanna Shit
Suzanne Shontz
Yucheng Shu
Alberto Signoroni
Carlos Silva
Wilson Silva
Margarida Silveira
Vivek Singh
Sumedha Singla
Ayushi Sinha
Elena Sizikova
Rajath Soans
Hessam Sokooti
Hong Song
Weinan Song
Youyi Song
Aristeidis Sotiras
Bella Specktor
William Speier
Ziga Spiclin

Jon Sporring
Anuroop Sriram
Vinkle Srivastav
Lawrence Staib
Johannes Stegmaier
Joshua Stough
Danail Stoyanov
Justin Strait
Iain Styles
Ruisheng Su
Vaishnavi Subramanian
Gérard Subsol
Yao Sui
Heung-Il Suk
Shipra Suman
Jian Sun
Li Sun
Liyan Sun
Wenqing Sun
Yue Sun
Vaanathi Sundaresan
Kyung Sung
Yannick Suter
Raphael Sznitman
Eleonora Tagliabue
Roger Tam
Chaowei Tan
Hao Tang
Sheng Tang
Thomas Tang
Youbao Tang
Yucheng Tang
Zihao Tang
Rong Tao
Elias Tappeiner
Mickael Tardy
Giacomo Tarroni
Paul Thienphrapa
Stephen Thompson
Yu Tian
Aleksei Tiulpin
Tal Tlusty
Maryam Toloubidokhti
Jocelyne Troccaz
Roger Trullo

Chialing Tsai
Sudhakar Tummala
Régis Vaillant
Jeya Maria Jose Valanarasu
Juan Miguel Valverde
Thomas Varsavsky
Francisco Vasconcelos
Serge Vasylechko
S. Swaroop Vedula
Roberto Vega
Gonzalo Vegas Sanchez-Ferrero
Gopalkrishna Veni
Archana Venkataraman
Athanasios Vlontzos
Ingmar Voigt
Eugene Vorontsov
Xiaohua Wan
Bo Wang
Changmiao Wang
Chunliang Wang
Clinton Wang
Dadong Wang
Fan Wang
Guotai Wang
Haifeng Wang
Hong Wang
Hongkai Wang
Hongyu Wang
Hu Wang
Juan Wang
Junyan Wang
Ke Wang
Li Wang
Liansheng Wang
Manning Wang
Nizhuan Wang
Qiuli Wang
Renzhen Wang
Rongguang Wang
Ruixuan Wang
Runze Wang
Shujun Wang
Shuo Wang
Shuqiang Wang
Tianchen Wang

Tongxin Wang
Wenzhe Wang
Xi Wang
Xiangdong Wang
Xiaosong Wang
Yalin Wang
Yan Wang
Yi Wang
Yixin Wang
Zeyi Wang
Zuhui Wang
Jonathan Weber
Donglai Wei
Dongming Wei
Lifang Wei
Wolfgang Wein
Michael Wels
Cédric Wemmert
Matthias Wilms
Adam Wittek
Marek Wodzinski
Julia Wolleb
Jonghye Woo
Chongruo Wu
Chunpeng Wu
Ji Wu
Jianfeng Wu
Jie Ying Wu
Jiong Wu
Junde Wu
Pengxiang Wu
Xia Wu
Xiyin Wu
Yawen Wu
Ye Wu
Yicheng Wu
Zhengwang Wu
Tobias Wuerfl
James Xia
Siyu Xia
Yingda Xia
Lei Xiang
Tiange Xiang
Deqiang Xiao
Yiming Xiao

Hongtao Xie
Jianyang Xie
Lingxi Xie
Long Xie
Weidi Xie
Yiting Xie
Yutong Xie
Fangxu Xing
Jiarui Xing
Xiaohan Xing
Chenchu Xu
Hai Xu
Hongming Xu
Jiaqi Xu
Junshen Xu
Kele Xu
Min Xu
Minfeng Xu
Moucheng Xu
Qinwei Xu
Rui Xu
Xiaowei Xu
Xinxing Xu
Xuanang Xu
Yanwu Xu
Yanyu Xu
Yongchao Xu
Zhe Xu
Zhenghua Xu
Zhoubing Xu
Kai Xuan
Cheng Xue
Jie Xue
Wufeng Xue
Yuan Xue
Faridah Yahya
Chaochao Yan
Jiangpeng Yan
Ke Yan
Ming Yan
Qingsen Yan
Yuguang Yan
Zengqiang Yan
Baoyao Yang
Changchun Yang

Chao-Han Huck Yang
Dong Yang
Fan Yang
Feng Yang
Fengting Yang
Ge Yang
Guanyu Yang
Hao-Hsiang Yang
Heran Yang
Hongxu Yang
Huijuan Yang
Jiawei Yang
Jinyu Yang
Lin Yang
Peng Yang
Pengshuai Yang
Xiaohui Yang
Xin Yang
Yan Yang
Yifan Yang
Yujiu Yang
Zhicheng Yang
Jiangchao Yao
Jiawen Yao
Li Yao
Linlin Yao
Qingsong Yao
Chuyang Ye
Dong Hye Ye
Huihui Ye
Menglong Ye
Youngjin Yoo
Chenyu You
Haichao Yu
Hanchao Yu
Jinhua Yu
Ke Yu
Qi Yu
Renping Yu
Thomas Yu
Xiaowei Yu
Zhen Yu
Pengyu Yuan
Paul Yushkevich
Ghada Zamzmi

Ramy Zeineldin

Dong Zeng

Rui Zeng

Zhiwei Zhai

Kun Zhan

Bokai Zhang

Chaoyi Zhang

Daoqiang Zhang

Fa Zhang

Fan Zhang

Hao Zhang

Jianpeng Zhang

Jiawei Zhang

Jingqing Zhang

Jingyang Zhang

Jiong Zhang

Jun Zhang

Ke Zhang

Lefei Zhang

Lei Zhang

Lichi Zhang

Lu Zhang

Ning Zhang

Pengfei Zhang

Qiang Zhang

Rongzhao Zhang

Ruipeng Zhang

Ruisi Zhang

Shengping Zhang

Shihao Zhang

Tianyang Zhang

Tong Zhang

Tuo Zhang

Wen Zhang

Xiaoran Zhang

Xin Zhang

Yanfu Zhang

Yao Zhang

Yi Zhang

Yongqin Zhang

You Zhang

Youshan Zhang

Yu Zhang

Yubo Zhang

Yue Zhang

Yulun Zhang

Yundong Zhang

Yunyan Zhang

Yuxin Zhang

Zheng Zhang

Zhicheng Zhang

Can Zhao

Changchen Zhao

Fenqiang Zhao

He Zhao

Jianfeng Zhao

Jun Zhao

Li Zhao

Liang Zhao

Lin Zhao

Qingyu Zhao

Shen Zhao

Shijie Zhao

Tianyi Zhao

Wei Zhao

Xiaole Zhao

Xuandong Zhao

Yang Zhao

Yue Zhao

Zixu Zhao

Ziyuan Zhao

Xingjian Zhen

Haiyong Zheng

Hao Zheng

Kang Zheng

Qinghe Zheng

Shenhai Zheng

Yalin Zheng

Yinqiang Zheng

Yushan Zheng

Tao Zhong

Zichun Zhong

Bo Zhou

Haoyin Zhou

Hong-Yu Zhou

Huiyu Zhou

Kang Zhou

Qin Zhou

S. Kevin Zhou

Sihang Zhou

Tao Zhou
Tianfei Zhou
Wei Zhou
Xiao-Hu Zhou
Xiao-Yun Zhou
Yanning Zhou
Yaxuan Zhou
Youjia Zhou
Yukun Zhou
Zhiguo Zhou
Zongwei Zhou
Dongxiao Zhu
Haidong Zhu
Hancan Zhu

Lei Zhu
Qikui Zhu
Xiaofeng Zhu
Xinliang Zhu
Zhonghang Zhu
Zhuotun Zhu
Veronika Zimmer
David Zimmerer
Weiwei Zong
Yukai Zou
Lianrui Zuo
Gerald Zwettler
Reyer Zwiggelaar

Outstanding Area Chairs

Ester Bonmati   University College London, UK
Tolga Tasdizen   University of Utah, USA
Yanwu Xu   Baidu Inc., China

Outstanding Reviewers

Seyed-Ahmad Ahmadi   NVIDIA, Germany
Katharina Breininger   Friedrich-Alexander-Universität
                         Erlangen-Nürnberg, Germany
Mariano Cabezas   University of Sydney, Australia
Nicha Dvornek   Yale University, USA
Adrian Galdran   Universitat Pompeu Fabra, Spain
Alexander Katzmann   Siemens Healthineers, Germany
Tony C. W. Mok   Hong Kong University of Science and
                         Technology, China
Sérgio Pereira   Lunit Inc., Korea
David Richmond   Genentech, USA
Dominik Rivoir   National Center for Tumor Diseases (NCT)
                         Dresden, Germany
Fons van der Sommen   Eindhoven University of Technology,
                         the Netherlands
Yushan Zheng   Beihang University, China

Honorable Mentions (Reviewers)

Chloé Audigier   Siemens Healthineers, Switzerland
Qinle Ba   Roche, USA

Pulkit Khandelwal	University of Pennsylvania, USA
Andrew King	King's College London, UK
Stefan Klein	Erasmus MC, the Netherlands
Ender Konukoglu	ETH Zurich, Switzerland
Ivica Kopriva	Rudjer Boskovich Institute, Croatia
David Kügler	German Center for Neurodegenerative Diseases, Germany
Manuela Kunz	National Research Council Canada, Canada
Gilbert Lim	National University of Singapore, Singapore
Tiancheng Lin	Shanghai Jiao Tong University, China
Bin Lou	Siemens Healthineers, USA
Hehuan Ma	University of Texas at Arlington, USA
Ilja Manakov	ImFusion, Germany
Felix Meissen	Technische Universität München, Germany
Martin Menten	Imperial College London, UK
Leo Milecki	CentraleSupelec, France
Lia Morra	Politecnico di Torino, Italy
Dominik Neumann	Siemens Healthineers, Germany
Chinedu Nwoye	University of Strasbourg, France
Masahiro Oda	Nagoya University, Japan
Sebastian Otálora	Bern University Hospital, Switzerland
Michal Ozery-Flato	IBM Research, Israel
Egor Panfilov	University of Oulu, Finland
Bartlomiej Papiez	University of Oxford, UK
Nripesh Parajuli	Caption Health, USA
Sanghyun Park	DGIST, Korea
Terry Peters	Robarts Research Institute, Canada
Theodoros Pissas	University College London, UK
Raphael Prevost	ImFusion, Germany
Yulei Qin	Tencent, China
Emma Robinson	King's College London, UK
Robert Rohling	University of British Columbia, Canada
José Rouco	University of A Coruña, Spain
Jerome Schmid	HES-SO University of Applied Sciences and Arts Western Switzerland, Switzerland
Christina Schwarz-Gsaxner	Graz University of Technology, Austria
Liyue Shen	Stanford University, USA
Luyao Shi	IBM Research, USA
Vivek Singh	Siemens Healthineers, USA
Weinan Song	UCLA, USA
Aristeidis Sotiras	Washington University in St. Louis, USA
Danail Stoyanov	University College London, UK

Ruisheng Su	Erasmus MC, the Netherlands
Liyan Sun	Xiamen University, China
Raphael Sznitman	University of Bern, Switzerland
Elias Tappeiner	UMIT - Private University for Health Sciences, Medical Informatics and Technology, Austria
Mickael Tardy	Hera-MI, France
Juan Miguel Valverde	University of Eastern Finland, Finland
Eugene Vorontsov	Polytechnique Montreal, Canada
Bo Wang	CtrsVision, USA
Tongxin Wang	Meta Platforms, Inc., USA
Yan Wang	Sichuan University, China
Yixin Wang	University of Chinese Academy of Sciences, China
Jie Ying Wu	Johns Hopkins University, USA
Lei Xiang	Subtle Medical Inc, USA
Jiaqi Xu	The Chinese University of Hong Kong, China
Zhoubing Xu	Siemens Healthineers, USA
Ke Yan	Alibaba DAMO Academy, China
Baoyao Yang	School of Computers, Guangdong University of Technology, China
Changchun Yang	Delft University of Technology, the Netherlands
Yujiu Yang	Tsinghua University, China
Youngjin Yoo	Siemens Healthineers, USA
Ning Zhang	Bloomberg, USA
Jianfeng Zhao	Western University, Canada
Tao Zhou	Nanjing University of Science and Technology, China
Veronika Zimmer	Technical University Munich, Germany

Mentorship Program (Mentors)

Ulas Bagci	Northwestern University, USA
Kayhan Batmanghelich	University of Pittsburgh, USA
Hrvoje Bogunovic	Medical University of Vienna, Austria
Ninon Burgos	CNRS - Paris Brain Institute, France
Hao Chen	Hong Kong University of Science and Technology, China
Jun Cheng	Institute for Infocomm Research, Singapore
Li Cheng	University of Alberta, Canada
Aasa Feragen	Technical University of Denmark, Denmark
Zhifan Gao	Sun Yat-sen University, China
Stamatia Giannarou	Imperial College London, UK
Sharon Huang	Pennsylvania State University, USA

Anand Joshi	University of Southern California, USA
Bernhard Kainz	Friedrich-Alexander-Universität Erlangen-Nürnberg, Germany and Imperial College London, UK
Baiying Lei	Shenzhen University, China
Karim Lekadir	Universitat de Barcelona, Spain
Xiaoxiao Li	University of British Columbia, Canada
Jianming Liang	Arizona State University, USA
Marius George Linguraru	Children's National Hospital, George Washington University, USA
Anne Martel	University of Toronto, Canada
Antonio Porras	University of Colorado Anschutz Medical Campus, USA
Chen Qin	University of Edinburgh, UK
Julia Schnabel	Helmholtz Munich, TU Munich, Germany and King's College London, UK
Yang Song	University of New South Wales, Australia
Tanveer Syeda-Mahmood	IBM Research - Almaden Labs, USA
Pallavi Tiwari	University of Wisconsin Madison, USA
Mathias Unberath	Johns Hopkins University, USA
Maria Vakalopoulou	CentraleSupelec, France
Harini Veeraraghavan	Memorial Sloan Kettering Cancer Center, USA
Satish Viswanath	Case Western Reserve University, USA
Guang Yang	Imperial College London, UK
Lequan Yu	University of Hong Kong, China
Miaomiao Zhang	University of Virginia, USA
Rongchang Zhao	Central South University, China
Luping Zhou	University of Sydney, Australia
Lilla Zollei	Massachusetts General Hospital, Harvard Medical School, USA
Maria A. Zuluaga	EURECOM, France

Contents – Part VI

Image Reconstruction

Image Registration

SVoRT: Iterative Transformer for Slice-to-Volume Registration in Fetal Brain MRI

Junshen Xu[1]($\boxtimes$), Daniel Moyer[2], P. Ellen Grant[3,4], Polina Golland[1,2], Juan Eugenio Iglesias[2,4,5,6], and Elfar Adalsteinsson[1,7]

[1] Department of Electrical Engineering and Computer Science, MIT, Cambridge, MA, USA
junshen@mit.edu
[2] Computer Science and Artificial Intelligence Laboratory, MIT, Cambridge, MA, USA
[3] Fetal-Neonatal Neuroimaging and Developmental Science Center, Boston Children's Hospital, Boston, MA, USA
[4] Harvard Medical School, Boston, MA, USA
[5] Centre for Medical Image Computing, Department of Medical Physics and Biomedical Engineering, University College London, London, UK
[6] Athinoula A. Martinos Center for Biomedical Imaging, Massachusetts General Hospital and Harvard Medical School, Boston, USA
[7] Institute for Medical Engineering and Science, MIT, Cambridge, MA, USA

Abstract. Volumetric reconstruction of fetal brains from multiple stacks of MR slices, acquired in the presence of almost unpredictable and often severe subject motion, is a challenging task that is highly sensitive to the initialization of slice-to-volume transformations. We propose a novel slice-to-volume registration method using Transformers trained on synthetically transformed data, which model multiple stacks of MR slices as a sequence. With the attention mechanism, our model automatically detects the relevance between slices and predicts the transformation of one slice using information from other slices. We also estimate the underlying 3D volume to assist slice-to-volume registration and update the volume and transformations alternately to improve accuracy. Results on synthetic data show that our method achieves lower registration error and better reconstruction quality compared with existing state-of-the-art methods. Experiments with real-world MRI data are also performed to demonstrate the ability of the proposed model to improve the quality of 3D reconstruction under severe fetal motion.

Keywords: Slice-to-volume registration · 3D reconstruction · Fetal MRI · Transformer

Supplementary Information The online version contains supplementary material available at https://doi.org/10.1007/978-3-031-16446-0_1.

L. Wang et al. (Eds.): MICCAI 2022, LNCS 13436, pp. 3–13, 2022.
https://doi.org/10.1007/978-3-031-16446-0_1

1 Introduction

Volumetric reconstruction of fetal brain from multiple motion-corrupted stacks of MR slices is an important tool in studying fetal brain development [2,8,27]. Due to rapid and random fetal motion, fetal MRI are limited to fast acquisition techniques, such as the single-shot T2 weighted (SST2W) imaging that freezes in-plane motion. Even with such fast 2D sequences, fetal MRI is still vulnerable to inter-slice motion artifacts [19], leading to misalignment of slices in a stack. Moreover, the delay between slices due to safety constraints on specific absorption rate (SAR) [17] further worsen the situation. Therefore, Slice-to-Volume Registration (SVR) prior to 3D reconstruction of fetal brain is necessary. Manual SVR is usually infeasible in practice due to the magnitude of data involved. Although optimization-based SVR methods have successfully applied to 3D reconstruction of fetal brain [7,14,18], coarse alignment of slices is required to initialize the algorithm and the quality of reconstructed volume is highly dependent on the initial alignment. Hence, an automatic and accurate method for estimating slice transformations is crucial to 3D reconstruction of fetal brain.

In an attempt to speed up SVR of fetal MRI and improve its capture range, deep learning methods [11,23] have been proposed to predict rigid transformations of MR slices using Convolution Neural Networks (CNNs), which share similarity with camera pose prediction in computer vision [12,15]. Pei *et al.* [22] proposed a multi-task network to exploit semantic information in fetal brain anatomy which, however, requires annotations of segmentation maps. Moreover, these approaches process each slice independently, ignoring the dependencies between slices. Singh *et al.* [25] proposed a recurrent network to predict inter-slice motion in fetal MRI. In SVR of fetal ultrasound, Yeung *et al.* [31] tried to predict the 3D location of multiple slices simultaneously with an attention CNN.

Recently, Transformer models [28] and their variants have achieved astounding results in various fields [3,4]. The concept behind Transformers is to dynamically highlight the relevant features in input sequences with the self-attention mechanism, which demonstrates great capability of modeling long-distance dependencies and capturing global context. In SVR of fetal MRI, multiple stacks of slices are provided as inputs, which can also be modeled as a sequence of images. Multi-view information from stacks of slices with different orientations can be processed jointly to assist the SVR task.

Here, we propose a Slice-to-Volume Registration Transformer (SVoRT) to map multiple stacks of fetal MR slices into a canonical 3D space and to further initialize SVR and 3D reconstruction. As such, we present the following contributions: 1) We propose a Transformer-based network that models multiple stacks of slices acquired in one scan as a sequence of images and predicts rigid transformations of all the slices simultaneously by sharing information across the slices. 2) The model also estimates the underlying 3D volume to provide context for localizing slices in 3D space. 3) In the proposed model, slice transformations are updated in an iterative manner to progressively improve accuracy.

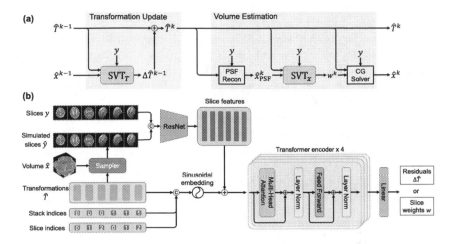

Fig. 1. (a) The k-th iteration of SVoRT. (b) The architecture of SVT.

2   Methods

Given n acquired slices of a scan, $y = [y_1, \ldots, y_n]$, the goal of SVoRT is to estimate the corresponding transformations $T = [T_1, \ldots, T_n]$, *i.e.*, rotations and translations of acquisition planes, in a 3D canonical atlas space. However, unlike SVR problems [5,9] where a 3D volume exists as a reference for matching 2D slices, high quality 3D references are usually unavailable in SVR of fetal MR due to fetal motion. Therefore, instead of predicting the transformations alone, we also estimate the underlying volume x from the input slices, so that the estimated volume $\hat{x}$ can provide 3D context to improve the accuracy of predicted transformations. In SVoRT, the estimated transformation $\hat{T}$ and the estimated volume $\hat{x}$ are updated alternately, generating a series of estimates, $(\hat{T}^0, \hat{x}^0), \ldots, (\hat{T}^K, \hat{x}^K)$, where $\hat{T}^0$ and $\hat{x}^0$ are the initial guesses, and K is the number of iterations. The estimated transformations of the last iteration $\hat{T}^K$ is used as the output of the model. Figure 1(a) shows the k-th iteration of SVoRT, which consists of two steps: 1) computing the new transformation $\hat{T}^k$ given $\hat{T}^{k-1}$ and $\hat{x}^{k-1}$ from the previous iteration, and 2) estimating volume $\hat{x}^k$ based on the new transformation $\hat{T}^k$.

2.1   Transformation Update

At the k-th iteration, the transformations are updated by $\hat{T}^k = \hat{T}^{k-1} + \Delta\hat{T}^k$. We propose a submodule named Slice-Volume Transformer (SVT) to regress the residual $\Delta\hat{T}^k$ given the set of input slice and the estimates from the previous iteration, $\Delta\hat{T}^k = \mathrm{SVT}_T^k(y, \hat{T}^{k-1}, \hat{x}^{k-1})$. SVT, whose architecture is shown in Fig. 1(b), aims to jointly extract features from stacks of slices and a 3D volume.

    To relate the volume $\hat{x}^{k-1}$ to the set of slices y with estimated transformations $\hat{T}^{k-1}$, SVT simulates slices from the volume following the forward model, $\hat{y}_i = DB\hat{T}_i^{k-1}\hat{x}^{k-1}$, $i = 1, \ldots, n$, where D and B are the operators for slice sampling and Point-Spread-Function (PSF) blurring respectively. The simulated slices $\hat{y}$ provide views of the estimated volume $\hat{x}$ at the estimated slice locations $\hat{T}^{k-1}$. The difference between $\hat{y}$ and the original slices y can be used as a proxy indicator of registration accuracy and guide models to update the estimated transformations. To this end, we concatenate $\hat{y}$ and y, and use a ResNet [10] to extract features $X^{\text{slice}} \in \mathbb{R}^{n \times d}$ from slices, where d is the number of features.

In addition to the image content, information about the position of the slice in the sequence and the estimated location in 3D space is injected for Transformers to encode spatial correlation of the input sequence, e.g., adjacent slices in the same stacks are usually highly correlated, while stacks with different orientations provide complementary information. Each slice in the input sequence is associated with two indices, the index of the stack that the slice belongs to, and the index of the slice in the stack. Positional embeddings $X^{\text{pos}} \in \mathbb{R}^{n \times d}$ are generated from the current estimated transformation $\hat{T}^{k-1}$, the stack indexes, and the slice indexes using sinusoidal functions [28].

The slice features and the corresponding positional embeddings are added and provided to a Transformer with four encoders [28]. Each Transformer encoder consists of a multi-head attention module, a feed forward network, and two layer normalization [1]. Let $X = X^{\text{slices}} + X^{\text{pos}}$ be the input matrix. The multi-head attention module first projects X into three different spaces, $Q_j = XW_j^Q, K_i = XW_j^K, V_j = XW_j^V, j = 1, \ldots, h$, where weights $W_j^Q, W_j^K, W_j^V \in \mathbb{R}^{d \times (d/h)}$ and h is the number of heads. Then, each head computes the output as $Y_j = \text{softmax}(Q_j K_j^T / \sqrt{d}) V_j$, where the softmax function is applied to each row. The outputs from all heads are aggregated and projected with a matrix $W^O \in \mathbb{R}^{d \times d}$, i.e., $Y = [Y_1, ..., Y_h] W^O$. The feed forward network is a fully connected network used to extract deeper features. At the end, a linear layer is applied to regress the residual transformations from the output of Transformer.

2.2   Volume Estimation

The next step is to compute the new estimate of volume $\hat{x}^k$ based on the updated transformations $\hat{T}^k$. One of the available methods is the PSF reconstruction [14], which aligns the slices in 3D space based on transformations $\hat{T}^k$ and interpolates the volume with the PSF kernel. However, there are two disadvantages of this approach. First, it over smooths the reconstructed volume and leads to a loss of image detail. Second, it fails to exclude slices with large transformation error during reconstruction, resulting in artifacts in the reconstructed volume.

To address these problems, we use another SVT in the volume estimation step to predict weights of slices, $w = [w_1, \ldots, w_n]$, where $w_i \in [0, 1]$ represents the image quality of the i-th slice. The SVT here shares the same architecture as the one in the transformation update step, but has different inputs. Specifically, in the inputs to SVT, $\hat{T}^{k-1}$ and $\hat{x}^{k-1}$ are replaced with the updated transformations $\hat{T}^k$ and the PSF reconstruction result $\hat{x}_{\text{PSF}}$ respectively, $w^k = \text{SVT}_x^k(\hat{T}^k, \hat{x}_{\text{PSF}}^k, y)$, where we denote the SVT in volume estimation as SVT_x^k. To compute the new estimated volume $\hat{x}^k$, we solve an inverse problem,

$$\hat{x}^k = \arg\min_x \sum_{i=1}^{n} w_i^k \|DB\hat{T}_i^k x - y_i\|_2^2, \tag{1}$$

where the weights help exclude outliers during volume estimation. Since the closed form solution involves inverting a very large matrix, we instead employ a conjugate gradient (CG) method to compute $\hat{x}^k$. Note that all operations (matrix multiplication, addition and scalar division) in CG are differentiable, so the gradient with respect to w can be computed via automatic differentiation.

2.3   Training

Data: Supervised learning of SVoRT requires the ground truth transformation of each slice. However, annotating the 3D location of a 2D MR slice is very challenging. Instead, we artificially sample 2D slices as training data from high quality MR volumes of fetal brain reconstructed from data with little fetal motion. The orientations of stack, *i.e.*, the normal vector and in-plane rotation, are randomly sampled as in [11] so that the dataset captures a wide range of rigid transformations. To Bridge the gap between the synthetic data and real MR scans and improve the generalization capability of networks, we also adopt various data augmentation and MR artifact simulation techniques [13], including image noise, bias field, signal void artifacts, and contrast jitter.

Representations of Transformations: Various representations are available for the describing the location of a plane in 3D space. For example, the Euler angles, the affine matrix, or the Cartesian coordinates of 3 points, called anchor points, within the plane. Previous works have demonstrated that the anchor point representation yields the highest accuracy for deep learning based SVR methods. Following [11], we use the center, the bottom right and left corners of a plane as the anchor points to define the rigid transformation.

Loss Functions: During training, we apply the L2 loss between the predicted and target anchor points for transformation prediction,

$$\mathcal{L}_T^k = \|\hat{P}_1^k - P_1\|_2^2 + \|\hat{P}_2^k - P_2\|_2^2 + \|\hat{P}_3^k - P_3\|_2^2,$$

where $\hat{P}_1^k, \hat{P}_2^k, \hat{P}_3^k$ are the predicted coordinates of the three anchor points in the k-th iteration, and P_1, P_2, P_3 are the ground truth locations. As for volume estimation, the L1 loss between the k-th estimated volume and the target volume is used, $\mathcal{L}_x^k = \|\hat{x}^k - x\|_1$. The total loss $\mathcal{L}$ is the sum of the losses in all iterations, $\mathcal{L} = \sum_{k=1}^{K} \mathcal{L}_T^k + \lambda \sum_{k=1}^{K} \mathcal{L}_x^k$, where λ is a weight determining the relative contribution of the L1 loss.

3   Experiments and Results

3.1   Experiment Setup

We evaluate the models on the FeTA dataset [21], which consists of 80 T2-weighted fetal brain volumes with gestational age between 20 and 35 weeks.

The dataset is split into training (68 volumes) and test (12 volumes) sets. The volumes are registered to a fetal brain atlas [8], and resampled to 0.8 mm isotropic. We simulate 2D slices with resolution of 1 mm × 1 mm, slice thickness between 2.5 and 3.5 mm, and size of 128 × 128. Each training sample consists of 3 image stacks in random orientations and each stack has 15 to 30 slices. Fetal brain motion is simulated as in [30] to perturb the transformations of slices. In the process of training, random samples are generated on the fly, while for testing, 4 different samples are generated for each test subject, resulting in 48 test cases.

To demonstrate SVoRT can generalize well to real-world data and help initialize SVR for cases with severe fetal motion, we test the trained models with data acquired in real fetal MRI scans. Scans were conducted at Boston Children's Hospital. MRI data were acquired using the HASTE sequence [6] with slice thickness of 2 mm, resolution of 1 mm × 1 mm, size of 256 × 256, TE = 119 ms, and TR = 1.6 s. The real MR dataset not only has different contrast, but also undergoes more realistic artifacts and fetal motion compared to the synthetic data. In the experiments, SVRnet [11] and PlaneInVol [31] ared used as baselines. SVRnet predicts the transformation of each slice independently with a VGGNet [24], while PlaneInVol uses an attention CNN which compares pairs of slices, and learns to map a set of slices to 3D space. For SVoRT, we set the initial estimates $\hat{T}^0$ and $\hat{x}^0$ to identity transformation and zero respectively and set $\lambda = 10^3$ and $K = 3$. All neural networks are implemented with PyTorch [20] and trained on a Nvidia Tesla V100 GPU with an Adam optimizer [16] for 2×10^5 iterations. We used an initial learning rate of 2×10^{-4} which linearly decayed to zero. The reference implementation for SVoRT is available on GitHub[1].

3.2 Simulated Data

To evaluate the accuracy of the predicted transformation for different models, we use the Euclidean Distance (ED) of anchor points, and the Geodesic Distance (GD) in $SO(3)$: ED $= \frac{1}{3} \sum_{j=1}^3 \|\hat{P}_j - P_j\|_2$ and GD $= \arccos(\frac{\mathrm{Tr}(R)-1}{2})$, where R is the rotation matrix from the predicted plane to the target, representing the rotation error. We also extract slices from the ground truth volume x according to the estimated transformations $\hat{T}$ and compare them to the original slices y. Comparison is performed via Peak Signal-to-Noise Ratio (PSNR) and Structural Similarity (SSIM) [29]. To further examine the model, we use the predicted transformations to initialize a 3D reconstruction algorithm [14] and compute PSNR and SSIM between the reconstructed volumes and the targets.

Table 1 reports the mean and standard deviations of quantitative metrics for different models on the test set of the simulated data. Our proposed method outperforms both SVRnet and PlaneInVol, which only leverage the intensity information of slices. As shown in Fig. 2(a), the transformation errors for SVRnet and PlaneInVol increase with the distance to the center of 3D space, since the slices near the boundary of fetal brain contain little content and can be ambiguous. However, by exploiting the positional information of slice in the input sequence, SVoRT is able to register such cases better and lead to lower errors.

---

[1] https://github.com/daviddmc/SVoRT.

Table 1. Mean values of quantitative metrics for different models (standard deviation in parentheses). ↓ indicates lower values being more accurate, vice versa. The best results are highlighted in bold.

Method	Transformation		Slice		Volume	
	ED(mm)↓	GD(rad)↓	PSNR↑	SSIM↑	PSNR↑	SSIM↑
SVRnet	12.82 (5.69)	.256 (.150)	20.53 (1.62)	.823 (.061)	19.54 (1.52)	.669 (.116)
PlaneInVol	12.49 (6.73)	.244 (.213)	19.96 (1.73)	.808 (.069)	18.98 (1.62)	.615 (.139)
SVoRT	**4.35** (0.90)	**.074** (.017)	**25.26** (1.86)	**.916** (.034)	**23.32** (1.42)	**.858** (.037)
w/o PE	9.97 (6.28)	.194 (.179)	21.44 (2.08)	.841 (.064)	20.74 (1.49)	.742 (.096)
w/o Vol	5.09 (1.05)	.088 (.020)	23.97 (1.68)	.894 (.040)	22.89 (1.37)	.844 (.043)
$K = 1$	5.99 (1.16)	.103 (.024)	23.02 (1.67)	.876 (.047)	22.57 (1.21)	.836 (.041)
$K = 2$	5.65 (1.07)	.097 (.022)	23.25 (1.84)	.878 (.048)	22.64 (1.50)	.837 (.043)

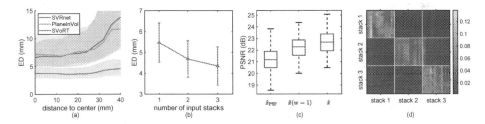

Fig. 2. (a) Medians of ED for slices sampled at different locations at the atlas space. Error bands indicate 25 and 75 percentiles. (b) Mean values of ED for SVoRT models with different numbers of input stacks. Error bars indicate standard deviations (c) PSNRs of different volume estimation methods. (d) An example heatmap of the self-attention weight matrix averaged over all the heads.

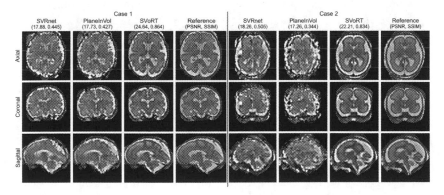

Fig. 3. Example reconstructed volumes and reference volumes of the test set.

Ablation studies are also performed by removing the positional embedding (w/o PE) and the volume estimation (w/o Vol), and using fewer iterations ($K = 1, 2$) in SVoRT. Results indicate that the positional embedding serves as a

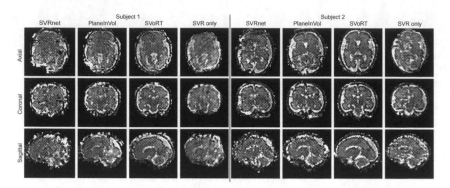

Fig. 4. Reconstructed volumes for different methods of real MR data.

prior for the relative locations of slices in a stack, which facilitates the registration process. The auxiliary volume estimation improves the accuracy of transformation prediction by providing 3D context. Moreover, the iterative update enable the model to progressively refine the predictions. We test SVoRT with different numbers of input stacks (Fig. 2(b)). With more input stacks, SVoRT receives more different views of the 3D volume, and therefore achieves lower registration error. We also compare different volume estimation methods: i) the proposed estimate $\hat{x}$, ii) the solution to the inverse problem in Eq. (1) with equal weight, $\hat{x}(w = 1)$, and iii) the PSF reconstruction, $\hat{x}_{PSF}$. As shown in Fig. 2(c), the proposed method achieves the highest PSNR. Figure 2(d) visualizes an example attention matrix generated by the last Transformer encoder. The 3D reconstruction results in Fig. 3 show that SVoRT also yields better perceptual quality compared with other state-of-the-art methods, in consequence of fewer slice misalignment in the initialization of SVR.

3.3 Real Fetal MR Data

We collect 3 orthogonal motion-corrupted stacks of MR slices from two subjects respectively. For preprocessing, bias fields are corrected [26], and the brain ROI is manually segmented from each slice. SVRnet, PlaneInVol and SVoRT are used to predict the transformations and initialize the SVR algorithm. For comparison, we also apply the SVR algorithm to the input stacks directly without deep learning based initialization (SVR only). Note that the results of "SVR only" are reconstructed in the subject space. We further register them to the atlas space for visualization. Fig. 4 shows that volumes reconstructed by SVR alone suffer from severe image artifacts due to slice misalignment caused by drastic fetal motion. SVRnet and PlaneInVol are incapable of generalizing to real MR data and fail to provide a useful initialization for SVR. In comparison, the estimated transformations of SVoRT are more accurate and the corresponding reconstructed volume presents better perceptual quality. Results indicate that SVoRT learns more robust features from synthetic data, and therefore generalizes well in the presence of real-world noise and artifacts. Moreover, the average inference time of SVoRT for each subject is 0.8 s, which is negligible compared with SVR algorithms that usually take minutes even on GPUs. SVoRT potentially enables high quality 3D reconstruction of fetal MRI in the case of severe fetal motion.

4   Conclusion

In this work, we propose a novel method for slice-to-volume registration in fetal brain MRI using Transformers. By jointly processing the stacks of slices as a sequence, SVoRT registers each slice by utilizing context from other slices, resulting in lower registration error and better reconstruction quality. In addition, we introduce an auxiliary task of volume estimation and update the transformation iteratively to improve registration accuracy. Evaluations show that SVoRT learns more robust features so that, by training on simulated data, it generalizes well to data acquired in real scans. SVoRT provides a robust and accurate solution to the initialization of 3D fetal brain reconstruction.

Acknowledgements. This research was supported by NIH U01HD087211, R01EB 01733, HD100009, NIBIB R01EB032708, NIBIB NAC P41EB015902, R01AG070988, RF1MH123195, ERC Starting Grant 677697, ARUK-IRG2019A-003.

References

1. Ba, J.L., Kiros, J.R., Hinton, G.E.: Layer normalization. arXiv preprint arXiv:1607.06450 (2016)
2. Benkarim, O., et al.: A novel approach to multiple anatomical shape analysis: application to fetal ventriculomegaly. Med. Image Anal. **64**, 101750 (2020)
3. Devlin, J., Chang, M.W., Lee, K., Toutanova, K.: Bert: pre-training of deep bidirectional transformers for language understanding (2019)
4. Dosovitskiy, A., et al.: An image is worth 16x16 words: transformers for image recognition at scale. arXiv preprint arXiv:2010.11929 (2020)
5. Esteban, J., Grimm, M., Unberath, M., Zahnd, G., Navab, N.: Towards fully automatic X-Ray to CT registration. In: Shen, D., et al. (eds.) MICCAI 2019. LNCS, vol. 11769, pp. 631–639. Springer, Cham (2019). https://doi.org/10.1007/978-3-030-32226-7_70
6. Gagoski, B., et al.: Automated detection and reacquisition of motion-degraded images in fetal haste imaging at 3T. Magn. Reson. Med. **87**(4), 1914–1922 (2021)
7. Gholipour, A., Estroff, J.A., Warfield, S.K.: Robust super-resolution volume reconstruction from slice acquisitions: application to fetal brain MRI. IEEE Trans. Med. Imaging **29**(10), 1739–1758 (2010)
8. Gholipour, A., et al.: A normative spatiotemporal MRI atlas of the fetal brain for automatic segmentation and analysis of early brain growth. Sci. Rep. **7**(1), 1–13 (2017)
9. Gillies, D.J., Gardi, L., De Silva, T., Zhao, S.R., Fenster, A.: Real-time registration of 3D to 2D ultrasound images for image-guided prostate biopsy. Med. Phys. **44**(9), 4708–4723 (2017)

10. He, K., Zhang, X., Ren, S., Sun, J.: Deep residual learning for image recognition. In: Proceedings of the IEEE Conference on Computer Vision and Pattern Recognition, pp. 770–778 (2016)
11. Hou, B., et al.: 3-D reconstruction in canonical co-ordinate space from arbitrarily oriented 2-D images. IEEE Trans. Med. Imaging **37**(8), 1737–1750 (2018)
12. Hou, B., et al.: Computing CNN loss and gradients for pose estimation with riemannian geometry. In: Frangi, A.F., Schnabel, J.A., Davatzikos, C., Alberola-López, C., Fichtinger, G. (eds.) MICCAI 2018. LNCS, vol. 11070, pp. 756–764. Springer, Cham (2018). https://doi.org/10.1007/978-3-030-00928-1_85
13. Iglesias, J.E., et al.: Joint super-resolution and synthesis of 1 mm isotropic MP-RAGE volumes from clinical MRI exams with scans of different orientation, resolution and contrast. Neuroimage **237**, 118206 (2021)
14. Kainz, B., et al.: Fast volume reconstruction from motion corrupted stacks of 2D slices. IEEE Trans. Med. Imaging **34**(9), 1901–1913 (2015)
15. Kendall, A., Grimes, M., Cipolla, R.: PoseNet: a convolutional network for real-time 6-DOF camera relocalization. In: Proceedings of the IEEE International Conference on Computer Vision, pp. 2938–2946 (2015)
16. Kingma, D.P., Ba, J.: Adam: a method for stochastic optimization (2017)
17. Krishnamurthy, U., et al.: MR imaging of the fetal brain at 1.5T and 3.0T field strengths: comparing specific absorption rate (SAR) and image quality. J. Perinat. Med. **43**(2), 209–220 (2015)
18. Kuklisova-Murgasova, M., Quaghebeur, G., Rutherford, M.A., Hajnal, J.V., Schnabel, J.A.: Reconstruction of fetal brain MRI with intensity matching and complete outlier removal. Med. Image Anal. **16**(8), 1550–1564 (2012)
19. Malamateniou, C., et al.: Motion-compensation techniques in neonatal and fetal MR imaging. Am. J. Neuroradiol. **34**(6), 1124–1136 (2013)
20. Paszke, A., et al.: Automatic differentiation in pytorch (2017)
21. Payette, K., et al.: An automatic multi-tissue human fetal brain segmentation benchmark using the fetal tissue annotation dataset. Sci. Data **8**(1), 1–14 (2021)
22. Pei, Y., et al.: Anatomy-guided convolutional neural network for motion correction in fetal brain MRI. In: Liu, M., Yan, P., Lian, C., Cao, X. (eds.) MLMI 2020. LNCS, vol. 12436, pp. 384–393. Springer, Cham (2020). https://doi.org/10.1007/978-3-030-59861-7_39
23. Salehi, S.S.M., Khan, S., Erdogmus, D., Gholipour, A.: Real-time deep pose estimation with geodesic loss for image-to-template rigid registration. IEEE Trans. Med. Imaging **38**(2), 470–481 (2018)
24. Simonyan, K., Zisserman, A.: Very deep convolutional networks for large-scale image recognition. arXiv preprint arXiv:1409.1556 (2014)
25. Singh, A., Salehi, S.S.M., Gholipour, A.: Deep predictive motion tracking in magnetic resonance imaging: application to fetal imaging. IEEE Trans. Med. Imaging **39**(11), 3523–3534 (2020)
26. Tustison, N.J., et al.: N4ITK: improved N3 bias correction. IEEE Trans. Med. Imaging **29**(6), 1310–1320 (2010)
27. Vasung, L., et al.: Exploring early human brain development with structural and physiological neuroimaging. Neuroimage **187**, 226–254 (2019)
28. Vaswani, A., et al.: Attention is all you need. In: Advances in Neural Information Processing Systems, vol. 30 (2017)
29. Wang, Z., Bovik, A.C., Sheikh, H.R., Simoncelli, E.P.: Image quality assessment: from error visibility to structural similarity. IEEE Trans. Image Process. **13**(4), 600–612 (2004)

30. Xu, J., Abaci Turk, E., Grant, P.E., Golland, P., Adalsteinsson, E.: STRESS: super-resolution for dynamic fetal MRI using self-supervised learning. In: de Bruijne, M., et al. (eds.) MICCAI 2021. LNCS, vol. 12907, pp. 197–206. Springer, Cham (2021). https://doi.org/10.1007/978-3-030-87234-2_19
31. Yeung, P.H., Aliasi, M., Papageorghiou, A.T., Haak, M., Xie, W., Namburete, A.I.: Learning to map 2D ultrasound images into 3D space with minimal human annotation. Med. Image Anal. **70**, 101998 (2021)

Double-Uncertainty Guided Spatial and Temporal Consistency Regularization Weighting for Learning-Based Abdominal Registration

Zhe Xu[1], Jie Luo[3], Donghuan Lu[2], Jiangpeng Yan[4], Sarah Frisken[3], Jayender Jagadeesan[3], William M. Wells III[3], Xiu Li[5], Yefeng Zheng[2], and Raymond Kai-yu Tong[1]([✉])

[1] Department of Biomedical Engineering, The Chinese University of Hong Kong, Shatin, Hong Kong, China
kytong@cuhk.edu.hk
[2] Tencent Healthcare Co., Jarvis Lab, Shenzhen, China
caleblu@tencent.com
[3] Brigham and Women's Hospital, Harvard Medical School, Boston, USA
[4] Department of Automation, Tsinghua University, Beijing, China
[5] Shenzhen International Graduate School, Tsinghua University, Shenzhen, China

Abstract. In order to tackle the difficulty associated with the ill-posed nature of the image registration problem, regularization is often used to constrain the solution space. For most learning-based registration approaches, the regularization usually has a fixed weight and only constrains the spatial transformation. Such convention has two limitations: (i) Besides the laborious grid search for the optimal fixed weight, the regularization strength of a specific image pair should be associated with the content of the images, thus the "one value fits all" training scheme is not ideal; (ii) Only spatially regularizing the transformation may neglect some informative clues related to the ill-posedness. In this study, we propose a mean-teacher based registration framework, which incorporates an additional temporal consistency regularization term by encouraging the teacher model's prediction to be consistent with that of the student model. More importantly, instead of searching for a fixed weight, the teacher enables automatically adjusting the weights of the spatial regularization and the temporal consistency regularization by taking advantage of the transformation uncertainty and appearance uncertainty. Extensive experiments on the challenging abdominal CT-MRI registration show that our training strategy can promisingly advance the original learning-based method in terms of efficient hyperparameter tuning and a better tradeoff between accuracy and smoothness.

Keywords: Abdominal registration · Regularization · Uncertainty

L. Wang et al. (Eds.): MICCAI 2022, LNCS 13436, pp. 14–24, 2022.
https://doi.org/10.1007/978-3-031-16446-0_2

1   Introduction

Recently, learning-based multimodal abdominal registration has greatly advanced percutaneous nephrolithotomy due to their substantial improvement in computational efficiency and accuracy [2,10,21,23–25]. In the training stage, given a set of paired image data, the neural network optimizes the cost function

$$\mathcal{L} = \mathcal{L}_{sim}\left(I_f, I_m \circ \phi\right) + \lambda \mathcal{L}_{reg}(\phi), \tag{1}$$

to learn a mapping function that can rapidly estimate the deformation field ϕ for a new pair of images. In the cost function, the first term $\mathcal{L}_{sim}$ quantifies the appearance dissimilarity between the fixed image I_f and the warped moving image $I_m \circ \phi$. Since image registration is an ill-posed problem, the second regularization term $\mathcal{L}_{reg}$ is used to constrain its solution space. The tradeoff between registration accuracy and transformation smoothness is controlled by a weighting coefficient λ.

In classical iterative registration methods, the weight λ is manually tuned for each image pair. Yet, in most learning-based approaches [2], the weight λ is commonly set to a fixed value for all image pairs throughout the training stage, assuming that they require the same regularization strength. Besides the notoriously time-consuming grid search for the so-called "optimal" fixed weight, this "one value fits all" scheme (Fig. 1(c)) may be suboptimal because the regularization strength of a specific image pair should be associated with their content and misalignment degree, especially for the challenging abdominal registration with various large deformation patterns. In these regards, HyperMorph [11] estimated the effect of hyperparameter values on deformations with the additionally trained hypernetworks [7]. Being more parameter-efficient, recently, Mok et al. [16] introduced conditional instance normalization [6] into the backbone network and used an extra distributed mapping network to implicitly control the regularization by normalizing and shifting feature statistics with their affine parameters. As such, it enables optimizing the model with adaptive regularization weights during training and reducing the human efforts in hyperparameter tuning. We also focus on this underexploited topic, yet, propose an explicit and substantially different alternative without changing any components of the backbone.

On the other hand, besides the traditional regularization terms, e.g., smoothness and bending energy [4], task-specific regularizations have been further proposed, e.g., population-level statistics [3] and biomechanical models [12,17]. Inherently, all these methods still belong to the category of *spatial regularization*. Experimentally, however, we notice that the estimated solutions in unsupervised registration vary greatly at different training steps due to the ill-posedness. Only spatially regularizing the transformation at each training step may neglect some informative clues related to the ill-posedness. It might be advantageous to further exploit such temporal information across different training steps.

In this paper, we present a novel double-uncertainty guided spatial and temporal consistency regularization weighting strategy, in conjunction with the Mean-Teacher (MT) [20] based registration framework. Specifically, inspired by

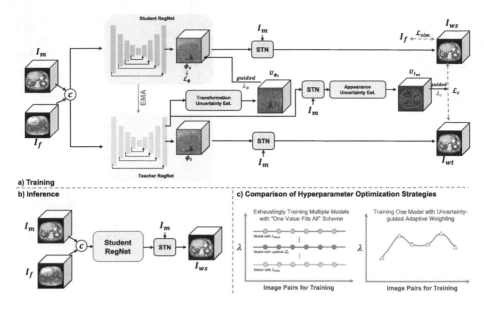

Fig. 1. Illustration of the proposed framework with (a) training process, (b) inference process and (c) comparison of hyperparameter optimization strategies.

the consistency regularization [20, 22] in semi-supervised learning, this framework further incorporates an additional *temporal consistency regularization* term by encouraging the consistency between the predictions of the student model and the temporal ensembling predictions of the teacher model. More importantly, instead of laboriously grid searching for the optimal fixed regularization weight, the self-ensembling teacher model takes advantage of the transformation uncertainty and the appearance uncertainty [15] derived by Monte Carlo dropout [14] to heuristically adjust the regularization weights for each image pair during training (Fig. 1(c)). Extensive experiments on a challenging intra-patient abdominal CT-MRI dataset show that our training strategy can promisingly advance the original learning-based method in terms of efficient hyperparameter tuning and a better tradeoff between accuracy and smoothness.

2   Methods

The proposed framework, as depicted in Fig. 1(a), is designed on top of the Mean-Teacher (MT) architecture [20] which is constructed by a student registration network (Student RegNet) and a weight-averaged teacher registration network (Teacher RegNet). This architecture was originally proposed for semi-supervised learning, showing superior performance in further exploiting unlabeled data. We appreciate the MT-like design for registration because the temporal ensembling strategy can (i) help us efficiently exploit the temporal information across different training steps in such a ill-posed problem (Sect. 2.1), and (ii) enable smoother uncertainty estimation [27] to heuristically adjust the regularization weights during training (Sect. 2.2).

2.1 Mean-Teacher Based Temporal Consistency Regularization

Specifically, the student model is a typical registration network updated by back-propagation, while the teacher model uses the same network architecture as the student model but its weights are updated from that of the student model via Exponential Moving Average (EMA) strategy, allowing to exploit the temporal information across the adjacent training steps. Formally, denoting the weights of the teacher model and the student model at training step k as θ'_k and θ_k, respectively, we update θ'_k as:

$$\theta'_k = \alpha\theta'_{k-1} + (1-\alpha)\theta_k, \tag{2}$$

where α is the EMA decay and empirically set to 0.99 [20]. To exemplify our paradigm, we adopt the same U-Net architecture used in VoxelMorph (VM) [2] as the backbone network. Concisely, the moving image I_m and the fixed image I_f are concatenated as a single 2-channel 3D image input, and downsampled by four $3 \times 3 \times 3$ convolutions with stride of 2 as the encoder. Then, corresponding 32-filter convolutions and four upsampling layers are applied to form a decoder, followed by four convolutions to refine the 3-channel deformation field. Skip connections between encoder and decoder are also applied. Given the predicted ϕ_s and ϕ_t from the student and the teacher, respectively, the Spatial Transformation Network (STN) [13] is utilized to warp the moving image I_m into I_{ws} and I_{wt}, respectively. Following the common practice, the dissimilarity between I_{ws} and I_f can be measured as the similarity loss $\mathcal{L}_{sim}(I_{ws}, I_f)$ with a spatial regularization term $\mathcal{L}_\phi$ for ϕ_s. To exploit the informative temporal information related to the ill-posedness, we encourage the temporal ensemble prediction of the teacher model to be consistent with that of the student model by adding an appearance consistency constraint $\mathcal{L}_c(I_{ws}, I_{wt})$ to the training loss. In contrast to $\mathcal{L}_\phi$ which spatially constrains the deformation field at the current training step, $\mathcal{L}_c$ penalizes the difference between predictions across adjacent training steps. Thus, we call $\mathcal{L}_c$ *temporal consistency regularization*.

As such, the cost function Eq. 1 can be reformulated as the following Eq. 3, which is a combination of similarity loss $\mathcal{L}_{sim}$, spatial regularization loss $\mathcal{L}_\phi$ and temporal consistency regularization loss $\mathcal{L}_c$:

$$\mathcal{L} = \mathcal{L}_{sim} + \lambda_\phi\mathcal{L}_\phi + \lambda_c\mathcal{L}_c, \tag{3}$$

where λ_ϕ and λ_c are the uncertainty guided adaptive tradeoff weights, as elaborated in the following Sect. 2.2. In order to handle multimodal abdominal registration, we use the Modality Independent Neighborhood Descriptor (MIND) [8] based dissimilarity metric for $\mathcal{L}_{sim}$. $\mathcal{L}_c$ is measured by mean squared error (MSE). Following the benchmark method [2], the choice of $\mathcal{L}_\phi$ is the generic L2-norm of the deformation field gradients for smooth transformation.

2.2 Double-Uncertainty Guided Adaptive Weighting

Distinct from the previous "one value fits all" strategy, we propose a double-uncertainty guided adaptive weighting scheme to locate the uncertain samples and then adaptively adjust λ_ϕ and λ_c for each training step.

Double-Uncertainty Estimation. Besides predicting the deformation ϕ_t, the teacher model can also serve as our uncertainty estimation branch since the model weight-averaged strategy can improve the stability of the predictions [20] that enables smoother model uncertainty estimation [27]. Particularly, we adopt the well-known Monte Carlo dropout [14] for Bayesian approximation due to its superior robustness [18]. We repetitively perform N stochastic forward passes on the teacher model with random dropout. After this step, we can obtain a set of voxel-wise predicted deformation fields $\{\phi_{t_i}\}_{i=1}^N$ with a set of warped images $\{I_{wt_i}\}_{i=1}^N$. We propose to use *the absolute value of the ratio of standard deviation to the mean*, which can characterize the normalized volatility of the predictions, to represent the uncertainty [19]. More specifically, the proposed registration uncertainties can be categorized into the transformation uncertainty and appearance uncertainty [15]. Formulating $\mu_{\phi_t}^c = \frac{1}{N}\sum_{i=1}^N \phi_{t_i}^c$ and $\mu_{I_{wt}} = \frac{1}{N}\sum_{i=1}^N I_{wt_i}$ as the mean of the deformation fields and the warped images, respectively, where c represents the cth channel of the deformation field (i.e., x, y, z displacements) and i denotes the ith forward pass, the transformation uncertainty map $U_{\phi_t} \in \mathbb{R}^{H \times W \times D \times 3}$ and the appearance uncertainty map $U_{I_{wt}} \in \mathbb{R}^{H \times W \times D}$ can be calculated as:

$$
\begin{cases}
\sigma_{\phi_t}^c = \sqrt{\frac{1}{N-1}\sum_{i=1}^N \left(\phi_{t_i}^c - \mu_{\phi_t}^c\right)^2} & \text{and} \quad U_{\phi_t}^c = \left|\frac{\sigma_{\phi_t}^c}{\mu_{\phi_t}^c}\right|, \\
\sigma_{I_{wt}} = \sqrt{\frac{1}{N-1}\sum_{i=1}^N \left(I_{wt_i} - \mu_{I_{wt}}\right)^2} & \text{and} \quad U_{I_{wt}} = \left|\frac{\sigma_{I_{wt}}}{\mu_{I_{wt}}}\right|.
\end{cases}
\tag{4}
$$

With the guidance of U_{ϕ_t} and $U_{I_{wt}}$, we then propose to heuristically assign the weights λ_ϕ and λ_c of the spatial regularization $\mathcal{L}_\phi$ and the temporal consistency regularization $\mathcal{L}_c$ for each image pair during training.

Adaptive Weighting. Firstly, for the typical spatial regularization $\mathcal{L}_\phi$, considering that unreliable predictions often correlate with biologically-implausible deformations [26], we assume that stronger spatial regularization can be given when the network tends to produce more uncertain predictions. As for the temporal consistency regularization $\mathcal{L}_c$, we notice that more uncertain predictions can be characterized as that this image pair is harder-to-align. Particularly, the most recent work [22] in semi-supervised segmentation combats with the assumption in [27] and experimentally reveals an interesting finding that emphasizing the unsupervised teacher-student consistency on those unreliable (often challenging) regions can provide more informative and productive clues for network training. Herein, we follow this intuition, i.e., more uncertain (difficult) samples should receive more attention (higher λ_c) for the consistency regularization $\mathcal{L}_c$. Formally, for each training step s, we update λ_ϕ and λ_c as follows:

$$\lambda_\phi(s) = k_1 \cdot \frac{\sum_v \mathbb{I}\left(U_{\phi_t}(s) > \tau_1\right)}{V_{U_{\phi_t}}} \quad \text{and} \quad \lambda_c(s) = k_2 \cdot \frac{\sum_v \mathbb{I}\left(U_{I_{wt}}(s) > \tau_2\right)}{V_{U_{I_{wt}}}}, \quad (5)$$

where $\mathbb{I}(\cdot)$ is the indicator function; v denotes the v-th voxel; $V_{U_{\phi_t}}$ and $V_{I_{wt}}$ represent the volume sizes of U_{ϕ_t} and $U_{I_{wt}}$, respectively; k_1 and k_2 are the empirical scalar values; and τ_1 and τ_2 are the thresholds to select the most uncertain predictions. Noteworthily, the proposed strategy can work with any learning-based image registration architectures without increasing the number of trainable parameters. Besides, as shown in Fig. 1(b), only the student model is utilized at the inference stage, which can ensure the computational efficiency.

3   Experiments and Results

Datasets. We focus on the challenging application of abdominal CT-MRI multimodal registration for improving the accuracy of percutaneous nephrolithotomy. Under institutional review board approval, a 50-pair intra-patient abdominal CT-MRI dataset was collected from our partnership hospital with radiologist-examined segmentation masks for the region-of-interests (ROIs), including liver, kidney and spleen. We randomly divided the dataset into three groups for training (35 cases), validation (5 cases) and testing (10 cases), respectively. After sequential preprocessing steps including resampling, affine pre-alignment, intensity normalization and cropping, the images were processed into sub-volumes of $176 \times 176 \times 128$ voxels at the 1 mm isotropic resolution.

Implementation and Evaluation Criteria. The proposed framework is implemented on PyTorch and trained on an NVIDIA Titan X (Pascal) GPU. We employ the Adam optimizer with a learning rate of 0.0001 with a decay factor of 0.9. The batch size is set to 1 so that each step contains an image pair. We set $N = 6$ for the uncertainty estimation. We empirically set k_1 to 5 since the deformation fields with maximum $\lambda_\phi = 5$ are diffeomorphic in most cases. The scalar value k_2 is set to 1. Thresholds τ_1 and τ_2 are set to 10% and 1%, respectively. We adopt a series of evaluation metrics, including Average Surface Distance (ASD) and the average Dice score between the segmentation masks of warped images and fixed images. In addition, the average percentage of voxels with non-positive Jacobian determinant ($|J_\phi| \leq 0$) in the deformation fields and the standard deviation of the Jacobian determinant ($\sigma(|J_\phi|)$) are obtained to quantify the diffeomorphism and smoothness, respectively.

Comparison Study. Table 1 and Fig. 2 present the quantitative and qualitative comparisons, respectively. We compare with several baselines, including two traditional methods SyN [1] and Deeds [9] with five levels of discrete optimization, as well as the benchmark learning-based method VoxelMorph (VM) [2] and its probabilistic diffeomorphic version DIF-VM [5]. As an alternative for adaptive weighting, we also include the recent conditional registration network [16] with the same scalar value 5 (denoted as VM (CIR-DM)). Fairly, we use the MIND-based dissimilarity metric in all learning-based methods. Although

Table 1. Quantitative results for abdominal CT-MRI registration (mean ± std). Higher average Dice score (%) and lower ASD (mm) are better. † indicates the best model via grid search. Best results are shown in bold. Average percentage of foldings ($|J_\phi| \leq 0$) and the standard deviation of the Jacobian determinant ($\sigma(|J_\phi|)$) are also given.

Methods	Dice [%] ↑			ASD [voxel] ↓			$|J_\phi| \leq 0$	$\sigma(|J_\phi|)$
	Liver	Spleen	Kidney	Liver	Spleen	Kidney		
Initial	76.23 ± 4.12	77.94 ± 3.31	80.18 ± 3.06	4.98 ± 0.83	2.02 ± 0.51	1.95 ± 0.35	-	-
SyN	79.42 ± 4.35	80.33 ± 3.42	82.68 ± 3.03	4.83 ± 0.82	1.62 ± 0.61	1.91 ± 0.44	0.07%	0.42
Deeds	82.16 ± 3.15	81.48 ± 2.64	83.82 ± 3.02	3.97 ± 0.55	1.44 ± 0.62	1.59 ± 0.40	0.01%	0.28
DIF-VM	83.14 ± 3.24	82.45 ± 2.59	83.24 ± 2.98	3.88 ± 0.62	1.52 ± 0.59	1.63 ± 0.41	<0.001%	0.12
VM ($\lambda = 1$)	85.21 ± 3.06	84.04 ± 2.52	83.12 ± 2.81	3.17 ± 0.59	1.34 ± 0.56	1.55 ± 0.37	0.03%	0.19
VM ($\lambda = 3$)†	85.36 ± 3.12	84.24 ± 2.61	83.40 ± 3.11	3.19 ± 0.53	1.31 ± 0.52	1.56 ± 0.42	0.001%	0.14
VM ($\lambda = 5$)	84.28 ± 2.93	83.71 ± 2.40	82.96 ± 2.77	3.83 ± 0.68	1.48 ± 0.59	1.65 ± 0.44	<0.0001%	0.08
VM (CIR-DM)	85.29 ± 3.39	84.17 ± 2.59	83.01 ± 3.06	3.32 ± 0.41	1.33 ± 0.47	1.49 ± 0.46	0.002%	0.17
VM (AS+ATC) (ours)	**87.01 ± 3.22**	**84.96 ± 2.55**	**84.47 ± 2.86**	**2.57 ± 0.48**	1.24 ± 0.49	**1.26 ± 0.43**	<0.0005%	0.13
Ablation Study								
VM (AS)	86.02 ± 3.02	84.75 ± 2.59	83.44 ± 2.96	3.21 ± 0.49	1.33 ± 0.50	1.45 ± 0.49	0.0007%	0.12
VM (S+TC)	86.32 ± 3.07	84.37 ± 2.53	83.95 ± 3.02	3.05 ± 0.50	1.26 ± 0.52	1.47 ± 0.47	0.001%	0.15
VM (AS+TC)	86.49 ± 3.13	84.87 ± 2.68	84.03 ± 2.89	2.88 ± 0.53	**1.20 ± 0.44**	1.32 ± 0.40	0.0005%	0.14

DIF-VM preserves better diffeomorphism properties, we find that its results are often suboptimal. Thus, we adopt VM as our backbone. For simplicity, we denote our adaptive spatial and temporal consistency regularization weighting strategy as VM (AS+ATC). Instead of training multiple models for finding the optimal fixed weight, only one model needs to be trained in both VM (CIR-DM) [16] and our VM (AS+ATC). Experimentally, training each VM model from scratch requires an average of 9.2h for this task. For the typical grid search scheme, five individual VM models are trained with varying fixed spatial regularization weights from 1 to 5, resulting in around 46h training time in total, wherein we observe that the overall best-performing VM model appears at $\lambda = 3$. As a comparison, the implicit control method, i.e., VM (CIR-DM), achieves comparable results with ~4.7x shorter total training time. Compared with VM (CIR-DM), our VM (AS+ATC) requires slightly longer training time due to the uncertainty estimation, yet, still resulting in ~4.2x faster than the grid search scheme. Distinct from VM (CIR-DM), we do not need to change any components in the network. Encouragingly, we find that VM (AS+ATC) further improves the registration accuracy in terms of Dice and ASD along with better properties of diffeomorphism and smoothness, implying that our strategy helps produce more desirable (smoother) solutions in this ill-posed problem. Visually, the structure boundaries registered by SyN and Deeds still have considerable disagreements, while the learning-based methods achieve more appealing boundary alignment. Besides, all trained models can infer an alignment in a second with a GPU.

Ablation Study. To better understand our training strategy, we perform an ablation study with three variants: (i) VM (AS): removing the adaptive temporal consistency term; (ii) VM (S+TC): using empirical fixed weights $\lambda_\phi = 3$ and $\lambda_c = 0.5$; (iii) VM (AS+TC): adaptively adjusting λ_ϕ while λ_c is fixed as 0.5. The quantitative results are also presented in Table 1. Especially, similar to

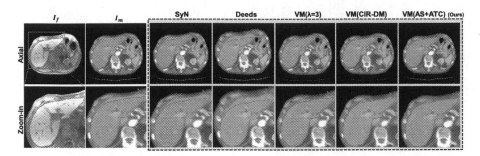

Fig. 2. Exemplar axial slice of an abdominal CT-MRI registration case. The segmentation contours of the liver (green), kidney (yellow) and spleen (blue) extracted from the fixed abdominal MRI I_f are overlaid on all images. Better alignment drives structures closer to the fixed contours of I_f. The red arrows indicate the registration of interest around the organ boundary. (Color figure online)

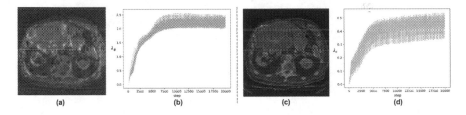

Fig. 3. (a) and (c) are the examples of U_{ϕ_t} and $U_{I_{wt}}$ (overlay on the moving image), respectively, where brighter areas denote more uncertain regions. (b) and (d) show the adaptive weighting process across the training steps for λ_ϕ and λ_c, respectively.

VM (CIR-DM), VM (AS) only adaptively adjusts λ_ϕ. We find that VM (AS) achieves even better performance compared with VM ($\lambda = 3$) and VM (CIR-DM), highlighting that our uncertainty-guided weighting scheme enables more precise control of the spatial regularization strength during training. It can be also observed that both VM (S+TC) and VM (AS+TC) achieve better performance than VM (AS), demonstrating that additionally exploiting the temporal information can be rewarding. When we integrate these components into our synergistic training scheme, their better efficacy can be brought into play.

Visualized Uncertainty Map and Weighting Process. Examples of two uncertainty maps U_{ϕ_t} and $U_{I_{wt}}$ are visualized in Fig. 3(a) and (c), respectively. We observe that high uncertainty often occurs in hard-to-align ambiguous areas. Note that at the early stage, the weights are relatively small since limited transformation has been captured. As the training goes, the weights of $\mathcal{L}_\phi$ and $\mathcal{L}_c$ are adaptively modulated after each step (Fig. 3(b) and (d)) assisted by the two uncertainties. Such scheme helps the model pursue a better tradeoff between accurate alignment and desirable diffeomorphism properties.

4   Conclusion

In this paper, we proposed a double-uncertainty guided spatial and temporal consistency regularization weighting strategy, assisted by a mean-teacher based registration framework. Besides temporal consistency regularization for further exploiting the temporal clues related to the ill-posedness, more importantly, the self-ensembling teacher model takes advantage of two estimated uncertainties to heuristically adjust the regularization weights for each image pair during training. Extensive experiments on abdominal CT-MRI registration showed that our strategy could promisingly advance the original learning-based method in terms of efficient hyperparameter tuning and a better tradeoff between accuracy and smoothness.

Acknowledgement. This research was done with Tencent Healthcare (Shenzhen) Co., LTD and Tencent Jarvis Lab and supported by General Research Fund from Research Grant Council of Hong Kong (No. 14205419) and the Scientific and Technical Innovation 2030-"New Generation Artificial Intelligence" Project (No. 2020AAA0104100).

References

1. Avants, B.B., Epstein, C.L., Grossman, M., Gee, J.C.: Symmetric diffeomorphic image registration with cross-correlation: evaluating automated labeling of elderly and neurodegenerative brain. Med. Image Anal. **12**(1), 26–41 (2008)
2. Balakrishnan, G., Zhao, A., Sabuncu, M.R., Guttag, J., Dalca, A.V.: An unsupervised learning model for deformable medical image registration. In: Proceedings of the IEEE Conference on Computer Vision and Pattern Recognition, pp. 9252–9260 (2018)
3. Bhalodia, R., Elhabian, S.Y., Kavan, L., Whitaker, R.T.: A cooperative autoencoder for population-based regularization of CNN image registration. In: Shen, D., et al. (eds.) MICCAI 2019. LNCS, vol. 11765, pp. 391–400. Springer, Cham (2019). https://doi.org/10.1007/978-3-030-32245-8_44
4. Bookstein, F.: Landmark methods for forms without landmarks: morphometrics of group differences in outline shape. Med. Image Anal. **1**, 225–243 (1997)
5. Dalca, A.V., Balakrishnan, G., Guttag, J., Sabuncu, M.R.: Unsupervised learning for fast probabilistic diffeomorphic registration. In: Frangi, A.F., Schnabel, J.A., Davatzikos, C., Alberola-López, C., Fichtinger, G. (eds.) MICCAI 2018. LNCS, vol. 11070, pp. 729–738. Springer, Cham (2018). https://doi.org/10.1007/978-3-030-00928-1_82
6. Dumoulin, V., Shlens, J., Kudlur, M.: A learned representation for artistic style. In: International Conference on Learning Representations (2016)
7. Ha, D., Dai, A., Le, Q.V.: Hypernetworks. arXiv preprint arXiv:1609.09106 (2016)
8. Heinrich, M.P., et al.: MIND: modality independent neighbourhood descriptor for multi-modal deformable registration. Med. Image Anal. **16**(7), 1423–1435 (2012)
9. Heinrich, M.P., Jenkinson, M., Brady, M., Schnabel, J.A.: MRF-based deformable registration and ventilation estimation of lung CT. IEEE Trans. Med. Imaging **32**(7), 1239–1248 (2013)

10. Hering, A., et al.: Learn2Reg: comprehensive multi-task medical image registration challenge, dataset and evaluation in the era of deep learning. arXiv preprint arXiv:2112.04489 (2021)
11. Hoopes, A., Hoffmann, M., Fischl, B., Guttag, J., Dalca, A.V.: HyperMorph: amortized hyperparameter learning for image registration. In: Feragen, A., Sommer, S., Schnabel, J., Nielsen, M. (eds.) IPMI 2021. LNCS, vol. 12729, pp. 3–17. Springer, Cham (2021). https://doi.org/10.1007/978-3-030-78191-0_1
12. Hu, Y., et al.: Adversarial deformation regularization for training image registration neural networks. In: Frangi, A.F., Schnabel, J.A., Davatzikos, C., Alberola-López, C., Fichtinger, G. (eds.) MICCAI 2018. LNCS, vol. 11070, pp. 774–782. Springer, Cham (2018). https://doi.org/10.1007/978-3-030-00928-1_87
13. Jaderberg, M., Simonyan, K., Zisserman, A., et al.: Spatial transformer networks. In: Advances in Neural Information Processing Systems, pp. 2017–2025 (2015)
14. Kendall, A., Gal, Y.: What uncertainties do we need in Bayesian deep learning for computer vision? arXiv preprint arXiv:1703.04977 (2017)
15. Luo, J., et al.: On the applicability of registration uncertainty. In: Shen, D., et al. (eds.) MICCAI 2019. LNCS, vol. 11765, pp. 410–419. Springer, Cham (2019). https://doi.org/10.1007/978-3-030-32245-8_46
16. Mok, T.C.W., Chung, A.C.S.: Conditional deformable image registration with convolutional neural network. In: de Bruijne, M., et al. (eds.) MICCAI 2021. LNCS, vol. 12904, pp. 35–45. Springer, Cham (2021). https://doi.org/10.1007/978-3-030-87202-1_4
17. Qin, C., Wang, S., Chen, C., Qiu, H., Bai, W., Rueckert, D.: Biomechanics-informed neural networks for myocardial motion tracking in MRI. In: Martel, A.L., et al. (eds.) MICCAI 2020. LNCS, vol. 12263, pp. 296–306. Springer, Cham (2020). https://doi.org/10.1007/978-3-030-59716-0_29
18. Qu, Y., Mo, S., Niu, J.: DAT: training deep networks robust to label-noise by matching the feature distributions. In: Proceedings of the IEEE/CVF Conference on Computer Vision and Pattern Recognition, pp. 6821–6829 (2021)
19. Smith, L., Gal, Y.: Understanding measures of uncertainty for adversarial example detection. arXiv preprint arXiv:1803.08533 (2018)
20. Tarvainen, A., Valpola, H.: Mean teachers are better role models: weight-averaged consistency targets improve semi-supervised deep learning results. In: Advances in Neural Information Processing Systems, pp. 1195–1204 (2017)
21. de Vos, B.D., Berendsen, F.F., Viergever, M.A., Sokooti, H., Staring, M., Išgum, I.: A deep learning framework for unsupervised affine and deformable image registration. Med. Image Anal. **52**, 128–143 (2019)
22. Wu, Y., Xu, M., Ge, Z., Cai, J., Zhang, L.: Semi-supervised left atrium segmentation with mutual consistency training. In: de Bruijne, M., et al. (eds.) MICCAI 2021. LNCS, vol. 12902, pp. 297–306. Springer, Cham (2021). https://doi.org/10.1007/978-3-030-87196-3_28
23. Xu, Z., Luo, J., Yan, J., Li, X., Jayender, J.: F3RNet: full-resolution residual registration network for deformable image registration. Int. J. Comput. Assist. Radiol. Surg. **16**(6), 923–932 (2021)
24. Xu, Z., et al.: Adversarial uni- and multi-modal stream networks for multimodal image registration. In: Martel, A.L., et al. (eds.) MICCAI 2020. LNCS, vol. 12263, pp. 222–232. Springer, Cham (2020). https://doi.org/10.1007/978-3-030-59716-0_22

25. Xu, Z., Yan, J., Luo, J., Li, X., Jagadeesan, J.: Unsupervised multimodal image registration with adaptative gradient Guidance. In: ICASSP 2021–2021 IEEE International Conference on Acoustics, Speech and Signal Processing (ICASSP), pp. 1225–1229. IEEE (2021)
26. Xu, Z., Yan, J., Luo, J., Wells, W., Li, X., Jagadeesan, J.: Unimodal cyclic regularization for training multimodal image registration networks. In: IEEE 18th International Symposium on Biomedical Imaging (ISBI), pp. 1660–1664. IEEE (2021)
27. Yu, L., Wang, S., Li, X., Fu, C.-W., Heng, P.-A.: Uncertainty-aware self-ensembling model for semi-supervised 3D left atrium segmentation. In: Shen, D., et al. (eds.) MICCAI 2019. LNCS, vol. 11765, pp. 605–613. Springer, Cham (2019). https://doi.org/10.1007/978-3-030-32245-8_67

Unsupervised Deformable Image Registration with Absent Correspondences in Pre-operative and Post-recurrence Brain Tumor MRI Scans

Tony C. W. Mok[✉] and Albert C. S. Chung

Department of Computer Science and Engineering, The Hong Kong University of Science and Technology, Kowloon, Hong Kong
{cwmokab,achung}@cse.ust.hk

Abstract. Registration of pre-operative and post-recurrence brain images is often needed to evaluate the effectiveness of brain gliomas treatment. While recent deep learning-based deformable registration methods have achieved remarkable success with healthy brain images, most of them would be unable to accurately align images with pathologies due to the absent correspondences in the reference image. In this paper, we propose a deep learning-based deformable registration method that jointly estimates regions with absent correspondence and bidirectional deformation fields. A forward-backward consistency constraint is used to aid in the localization of the resection and recurrence region from voxels with absence correspondences in the two images. Results on 3D clinical data from the BraTS-Reg challenge demonstrate our method can improve image alignment compared to traditional and deep learning-based registration approaches with or without cost function masking strategy. The source code is available at https://github.com/cwmok/DIRAC.

Keywords: Absent correspondences · Patient-specific registration · Deformable registration

1 Introduction

Registration of pre-operative and post-recurrence brain MRI images plays a significant role in discovering accurate imaging markers and elucidating imaging signatures for aggressively infiltrated tissue, which are crucial to the treatment plan and diagnosis of intracranial tumors, especially brain gliomas [11,26]. To better understand the location and extent of the tumor and its biological activity after resection, pre-operative and follow-up structural brain MRI scans of a patient

Supplementary Information The online version contains supplementary material available at https://doi.org/10.1007/978-3-031-16446-0_3.

first need to be aligned accurately. However, deformable registration between the pre-operative and follow-up scans, including post-resection and post-recurrence, is challenging due to possible large deformations and absent correspondences caused by tumor's mass effects [7], resection cavities, tumor recurrence and tissue relaxation in the follow-up scans.

Conventional registration methods mostly deal with the absent correspondence issue by (1) excluding the similarity measure of pathological regions [3,5], 2) replacing the pathological images with quasi-normal appearance [9,18,30] or 3) joint registration and segmentation framework [4,27]. Excluding the pathological regions often requires manual delineation [3] or initial seed [4,17] of the tumor regions in brain scans, which are often prohibitive and daunting to acquire in terms of labour cost and resources. Replacing the pathological image with the quasi-normal appearance, alternately, avoids the prerequisite of a prior pathological segmentation. However, modeling the tumor-to-quasi-normal appearance with a statistical model [9,18] often requires extra image scans, i.e., image scans from a healthy population. Moreover, existing approaches based on quasi-normal images require accurate registration to a common atlas space for quasi-normal reconstruction. Ironically, accurate alignment with images suffered from mass effect is very hard to achieve without reconstruction. Therefore, the registration and reconstruction problems with quasi-normal approaches need to be interleaved in a costly iterative optimization process. Alternatively, an unsupervised approach [27] to accommodate resection and retraction of tissue was proposed for registering pre-operative and intra-operative brain images. Their method alternates between registering the brain scans using the demons algorithm with an anisotropic diffusion smoother and segmenting the resection using the level set method in the space with high image intensity disagreement. Chitphakdithai *et al.* [4] extended this idea to a simultaneous registration and resection estimation approach with the expectation-maximization algorithm and a prior on post-resection image intensities. Nevertheless, these methods rely on the costly iterative optimization, which can be up to ~ 3.5 h per case [17].

While recent deep learning-based deformable registration (DLDR) methods have achieved remarkable registration speed and superior registration accuracy [2,6,10,13,15,23–25], these registration algorithms are incapable of accurately registering pre-operative and post-recurrence images due to the absent correspondence problem. A learning-based registration method for images with pathology was presented in [8] which dealt with missing correspondence by joint estimating the vector-momentum parameterized stationary velocity field (vSVF) and quasi-normal image to drive the registration. Nevertheless, the reconstruction of the quasi-normal image requires explicit tumor segmentation in the training phase. Moreover, the large deformation caused by the mass effect of tumor is difficult to model without resorting to complex multi-stage warping pipelines.

In this paper, we present an unsupervised joint registration and segmentation learning framework, in which a large deformation image registration network and a forward-backward consistency constraint are leveraged to estimate the valid and absent correspondence regions along with the dense deformation fields in a bidirectional manner, for pre-operative and post-recurrence registration. Instead of using

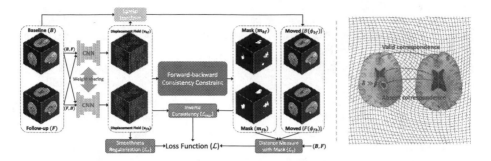

Fig. 1. Overview of the proposed method (Left) and the semantic representation of the forward-backward consistency constraint (Right). Our method jointly estimates the bidirectional deformation fields and locates regions with absent correspondence (denoted as mask). The regions with absent correspondence are excluded in the similarity measure during training. For brevity, the magnitude loss of the masks is omitted in the figure.

a manual delineation or image intensity disagreement to segment the pathological regions, our method leverages the forward-backward consistency constraint of the bidirectional deformation fields to explicitly locate regions with absent correspondence and excludes them in the similarity measure in an unsupervised manner. We present extensive experiments with a pre-operative and post-recurrence brain MR dataset, demonstrating that our method achieves accurate registration accuracy in brain MR scans with pathology.

2   Methods

Our goal is to establish a dense non-linear correspondence between the pre-operative scan and the post-recurrence scan of the same subject, where regions without valid correspondence are excluded in the similarity measure during optimization. Our method builds on the previous DLDR method [24] and extends it to accommodate the absent correspondence issue in the pre-operative and post-recurrence scans.

2.1   Bidirectional Deformable Image Registration

Let B and F be the pre-operative (baseline) scan B and post-recurrence (follow-up) scan defined over a n-D mutual spatial domain $\Omega \subseteq \mathbb{R}^n$. In this paper, we focus on 3D deformable registration, i.e., $n = 3$ and $\Omega \subseteq \mathbb{R}^3$ and assume that B and F are affinely aligned to a common space.

Figure 1 depicts an overview of our method. We parametrize the deformable registration problem as a bidirectional registration problem $\boldsymbol{u}_{bf} = f_\theta(B, F)$ and $\boldsymbol{u}_{fb} = f_\theta(F, B)$ with CNN, where θ is a set of learning parameters and $\boldsymbol{u}_{bf}$ represents the displacement field that transform B to align with F, i.e., $B(x + \boldsymbol{u}_{bf}(x))$ and $F(x)$ define similar anatomical locations for each voxel $x \in \Omega$ (except voxels with absent correspondence). The proposed method works with any CNN-based DLDR methods. In order to accommodate the large deformation and variation of anatomical structures caused by the tumor's mass effect, we parametrize an example of the function f_θ with the conditional deep Laplacian pyramid image registration network (cLapIRN) [24], which is capable of large deformation and rapid hyperparameter tuning for the smoothness regularization in a wide range of applications [12]. Despite the multi-resolution optimization strategy used in the cLapIRN, vanilla cLapIRN is incapable of accurately registering images with absent correspondence, i.e., missing correspondence caused by the tumor resection and recurrence, edema and cavity. Therefore, instead of measuring the similarity of B and F for every voxel $x \in \Omega$, our method estimates the regions with absent correspondence in both B and F domains using the bidirectional displacement fields and the forward-backward consistency constraint, and only measures the similarity on regions with valid correspondence during optimization.

2.2   Forward-Backward Consistency Constraint

Conventionally, regions with absent correspondence can be detected by comparing the appearance or image intensities of the warped scan to the target scan or an atlas [18,27]. However, corresponding regions in the pre-operative and post-recurrence scans may have different intensity profiles, which make their approaches less robust in practice. Therefore, we depart from approaches with spatial prior and extend the forward-backward consistency [19,21,28,29] instead. We design a forward-backward consistency constraint to locate regions with absent correspondence in the baseline and follow-up scans. The forward-backward (inverse consistency) error δ_{bf} from B to F is defined as:

$$\delta_{bf}(x) = |\boldsymbol{u}_{bf}(x) + \boldsymbol{u}_{fb}(x + \boldsymbol{u}_{bf}(x))|_2. \tag{1}$$

We estimate the regions with absent correspondence by checking the consistency of the forward and backward displacement fields. For any voxel x, if there is a significant violation of inverse consistency in x, i.e., $\delta_{bf}(x) > \tau_{bf}$, the voxel x is either without valid correspondence or the displacement field is not accurately estimated. τ_{bf} is the pre-defined threshold and is defined as follows:

$$\tau_{bf} = \sum_{x \in \{x | F(x) > 0\}} \frac{1}{N_f} \left(|\boldsymbol{u}_{bf}(x) + \boldsymbol{u}_{fb}(x + \boldsymbol{u}_{bf}(x))|_2 \right) + \alpha, \tag{2}$$

where the first term grants a tolerance interval that allows estimation errors to increase with the overall complexity of the registration and α is a constant. Then, we create a binary mask $\boldsymbol{m}_{bf}$ to mark voxels with absent correspondence as follows:

$$\boldsymbol{m}_{bf}(x) = \begin{cases} 1, & \text{if } (\boldsymbol{A} \star \delta_{bf})(x) \geq \tau_{bf} \\ 0, & \text{otherwise} \end{cases} \tag{3}$$

where $\boldsymbol{A}$ denotes an averaging filter of size $(2p+1)^3$ and $\star$ denotes a convolution operator with zero-padding p. Since the estimated registration fields will

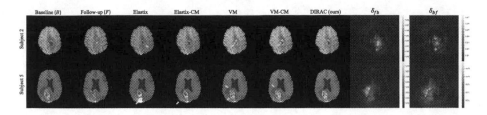

Fig. 2. Example axial T1ce MR slices of resulting warped images (B to F) from the baseline methods and our proposed method. Registration artefacts are highlighted with yellow arrows. The forward-backward errors (δ_{fb} and δ_{bf}) of our method are shown next to our result. The estimated regions with absent correspondence from our method are overlaid with the baseline and follow-up scans (in red). (Color figure online)

fluctuate during learning, we apply an averaging filter to the estimated forward-backward error to stabilize the estimation of the binary mask as well as to alleviate the effect of outliers to the mask estimation. For the mask $\boldsymbol{m}_{fb}$ in the backward to forward direction, we can define it in a symmetric way with $\boldsymbol{u}_{fb}$ and $\boldsymbol{u}_{bf}$ exchanged. We set $\alpha = 0.015$ and $p = 4$ in all our experiments. The values of α and p are determined by measuring the forward-backward error of the pathological regions from a vanilla cLapIRN model.

2.3   Inverse Consistency

Since the decision of regions with absent correspondence is highly dependent on the inverse consistency error in our method, we further enforce the inverse consistency on the regions with valid correspondence. Mathematically, the inverse consistency loss $\mathcal{L}_{\mathrm{inv}}$ is defined as:

$$\mathcal{L}_{\mathrm{inv}} = \sum_{x \in \Omega} (\delta_{bf}(x)(1 - \boldsymbol{m}_{bf}(x)) + \delta_{fb}(x)(1 - \boldsymbol{m}_{fb}(x))), \qquad (4)$$

where the measure of inverse consistency error δ is masked with the regions with valid correspondence $(1 - \boldsymbol{m})$ via elementwise multiplication.

2.4   Objective Function

Given the deformation fields $\phi_{bf} = Id + \boldsymbol{u}_{bf}$ and $\phi_{fb} = Id + \boldsymbol{u}_{fb}$, where Id is the identity transform. The objective of our proposed method is to compute the optimal deformation fields that minimize the dissimilarity measure of $B(\phi_{bf})$ and F as well as B and $F(\phi_{fb})$ in regions with valid correspondence. Specifically, we adopt the negative local cross-correlation (NCC) with masks to exclude the similarity measure of regions without valid correspondence as shown in Eq. 5.

$$\mathcal{L}_{\mathrm{s}} = -\mathrm{NCC}(F, B(\phi_{bf}), (1 - \boldsymbol{m}_{bf})) - \mathrm{NCC}(B, F(\phi_{fb}), (1 - \boldsymbol{m}_{fb})). \qquad (5)$$

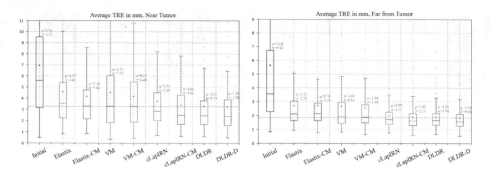

Fig. 3. Boxplots illustrate that the average target registration error (TRE) near tumor (left) and far from tumor (right). The mean (μ) and standard deviation (σ) are shown next to the 75th percentile of each box.

To encourage smooth solution and penalize implausible solutions, we adopt a diffusion regularizer:

$$\mathcal{L}_r = ||\nabla \boldsymbol{u}_{bf}||_2^2 + ||\nabla \boldsymbol{u}_{fb}||_2^2. \tag{6}$$

Hence, the complete loss function is therefore:

$$\mathcal{L} = (1 - \lambda_{reg})\mathcal{L}_s + \lambda_{reg}\mathcal{L}_r + \lambda_{inv}\mathcal{L}_{inv} + \frac{\lambda_m}{N}(|\boldsymbol{m}_{bf}|_1 + |\boldsymbol{m}_{fb}|_1), \tag{7}$$

where λ_{reg}, λ_{inv} and λ_m are the hyperparameters to balance the loss functions. N denotes the number of voxels in the mutual spatial domain Ω and the last term is to avoid the trivial solution where all voxels are marked in $\boldsymbol{m}_{bf}$ and $\boldsymbol{m}_{fb}$. During training, we follow the conditional registration framework in [24] to sample $\lambda_{reg} \in [0, 1]$ and set $\lambda_{reg} = 0.3$ in the inference phase. Formally, the optimal learning parameters θ^* is estimated by minimizing the complete loss $\mathcal{L}$ function using a training dataset D, as follows:

$$\theta^* = \arg\min_{\theta} \left[\mathbb{E}_{(B,F) \in D} \, \mathcal{L}\big(B, F, \boldsymbol{u}_{bf}, \boldsymbol{u}_{fb}, \boldsymbol{m}_{bf}, \boldsymbol{m}_{fb}\big) \right]. \tag{8}$$

3   Experiments

Data and Pre-processing. We evaluate our method on the brain tumor MR registration task using the 3D clinical dataset from the BraTS-Reg challenge [1], which consists of 160 pairs of pre-operative and follow-up brain MR scans of glioma patients taken from different timepoint. Each timepoint contains native T1, contrast-enhanced T1-weighted (T1ce), T2-weighted and FLAIR MRI. 140 pairs of scans are associated with 6 to 50 manual landmarks in both scans and 20 scans with landmarks in the follow-up scan only. All scans have carried out standard processing, including skull stripping, affine spatial normalization and resampled to the 1 mm^3 isotropic resolution. We use the DeepMedic [14] to segment the tumor core in each pre-operative scan. The tumor segmentation map is used in cost function masking for baseline methods. For learning-based methods, we further resample the scans to size of $160 \times 160 \times 80$ with $1.5 \times 1.5 \times 1.94$ mm^3 isotropic resolution in the training phase and upsample the solutions to 1 mm^3 isotropic resolution with bilinear interpolation in the evaluation. We perform 5-fold cross-validation and divide the 140 pairs of scans into 5 folds with equal size. In each group, we join 4 folds of data and the additional 20 pairs of scans as training set and validation set, and 1 fold as the test set. Specifically, for each group, we split the dataset into 122, 10, and 28 cases for training, validation and test sets.

Implementation. Our proposed method and the other baseline methods are implemented with PyTorch 1.9 and deployed on the same machine, equipped with an Nvidia Titan RTX GPU and an Intel Core (i7-4790) CPU. We build our method on top of the official implementation of 3-level cLapIRN with default parameters available in [22]. We set λ_{reg}, λ_{inv} and λ_m to 0.3, 0.5 and 0.01, respectively. We use Adam optimizer with a fixed learning rate 0.0001. All learning-based methods are trained from scratch.

Measurement. We register each pre-operative scan to the corresponding follow-up scan of the same patient, propagate the landmarks of the follow-up scan using the resulting deformation field and measure the mean target registration error (TRE) of the paired landmarks with Euclidean distance in millimetres. We divide the landmarks into two sets: 1) landmarks within 30mm from the tumor region (Near tumor), and 2) landmarks outside the 30mm tumor region (Far from tumor), using tumor segmentation maps and morphological dilation. We further measure the robustness of the registration. We follow [1] to define the robustness for a pair of scans as the relative number of successfully registered landmarks, i.e., 1 if the average distance of all the landmarks in the target and warped images is reduced after registration and 0 means none of the distances is reduced. As the local deformation at voxel p is invertible if and only if the Jacobian determinant of p ($|J_\phi|(p)$) is larger than zero, we also measure the number of percentage of the voxels with Jacobian determinant smaller or equal to 0 (denoted as $\%|J_\phi|_{\leq 0}$). We also measure the elapsed time in seconds for computations of each case in the inference phase (T_{test}).

Baseline Methods. We compare our method (denotes as DIRAC) with a conventional approach (denoted as Elastix [16]) and two cutting edge DLDR methods (denoted as VM [2] and cLapIRN [24]). For Elastix, we use the official implementation in the SimpleElastix library [20], which includes a 3-level iterative optimization scheme. For VM and cLapIRN, we use their official implementations with the best parameters reported in their papers. We also report the results of methods with cost function masking using the tumor core segmentation map for each method (denoted with postfix -CM). Note that the cost function masking strategy in learning-based methods is defined as excluding the similarity measure of the tumor region during the training phase, and the tumor

Table 1. Quantitative results of the pre-operative and follow-up brain MR registration. Results are provided as mean $\pm$ (standard deviation) Initial: spatial normalization. Runtime result highlighted with a asterisk (*) denotes runtime with CPU only. To our knowledge, Elastix does not have a GPU implementation. $\uparrow$: higher is better, and $\downarrow$: lower is better.

Method	Near Tumor			Far from Tumor			
	TRE$\downarrow$	Robustness$\uparrow$	$\%\|J_\phi\|_{\leq 0}\downarrow$	TRE$\downarrow$	Robustness$\uparrow$	$\%\|J_\phi\|_{\leq 0}\downarrow$	T_{test}(sec)$\downarrow$
Initial	6.94 ± (5.22)	–	–	5.64 ± (5.10)	–	–	–
Elastix-CM	4.19 ± (3.46)	0.71 ± (0.34)	0.16 ± (0.89)	2.73 ± (3.15)	0.72 ± (0.31)	0.08 ± (0.48)	120.17*±(6.31)
VM-CM	4.19 ± (3.08)	0.82 ± (0.27)	0.32 ± (0.42)	2.56 ± (1.98)	0.82 ± (0.23)	0.27 ± (1.53)	0.069 ± (0.001)
cLapIRN	3.73 ± (2.85)	0.80 ± (0.30)	0.51 ± (0.45)	2.03 ± (1.18)	0.80 ± (0.25)	0.21 ± (0.10)	0.023 ± (0.004)
cLapIRN-CM	3.40 ± (2.66)	0.82 ± (0.28)	0.83 ± (0.67)	1.92 ± (1.13)	0.82 ± (0.24)	0.32 ± (1.59)	0.024 ± (0.005)
DIRAC	3.31 ± (2.77)	0.82 ± (0.28)	0.18 ± (0.20)	1.91 ± (1.04)	0.82 ± (0.24)	0.12 ± (0.24)	0.023 ± (0.005)
DIRAC-D	**3.26** ± (2.78)	**0.83** ± (0.27)	**0.13** ± (0.16)	**1.86** ± (0.98)	0.82 ± (0.25)	0.08 ± (0.15)	0.025 ± (0.005)

segmentation is hidden during the inference phase, as opposed to conventional methods. All DLDR methods are trained from scratch with T1ce MR scans as input, except for our variant (denoted as DIRAC-D), which employs both the T1ce and T2-weighted scans of each case as input.

Results and Discussions. Figure 3 illustrates the box-and-whisker plots of average TRE of registered landmarks based on landmarks inside the 30 mm tumor boundary (Group 1) in the left graph as well as the one for the remaining landmarks in the right graph across the 140 subjects (Group 2). Among deformable image registration methods with single MR modality as input, our method DIRAC has the lowest mean registration error of 3.31 and 1.91 mm in groups 1 and 2, respectively, which improves the registration error of our baseline method cLapIRN significantly by 0.42 mm (-11%) and 0.17 mm (-8%) in groups 1 and 2, respectively. Among the alternative methods, methods with cost function masking (-CM) show significant improvement over their baseline method in group 1 and the improvement gain in group 2 is less significant, suggesting that implicitly or explicitly enforcing the smooth deformations inside the masked tumor regions is effective to the registration near the tumor regions. Table 1 shows a comprehensive summary of the registration error, robustness, local invertibility and runtime results across the 140 subjects. As opposed to the alternative methods using cost function masking, our methods (DIRAC and DIRAC-D) have achieved the best overall results in a fully unsupervised manner without sacrificing the runtime advantage of learning-based methods. Comparing the results of DIRAC and DIRAC-D, our variant DIRAC-D, which leverages additional MR modality, slightly improves the registration error by 1.5% and 2.6% in groups 1 and 2, respectively. Figure 2 shows qualitative examples of the registration results for each method and the estimated regions with absent correspondence by our method. The results demonstrate our method is capable of accurately locating the regions without valid correspondence, i.e., the tumor and cerebral edema in the baseline scan of subject 2, and explicitly excluding these regions in similarity measure during the training phase further reduces artefacts in the patient-specific registration.

4   Conclusion

We have proposed a unsupervised deformable registration method for the pre-operative and post-recurrence brain MR registration, which capable of joint registration and segmentation of regions with absent correspondence. We introduce a novel forward-backward consistency constraint and a pathological-aware symmetric loss function. Compared to existing deep learning-based methods, our method addresses the absent correspondence issue in patient-specific registration and shows significant improvement in registration accuracy near the tumor regions. Compared to conventional methods, our method inherits the runtime advantage from deep learning-based approaches and does not require any manual interaction or supervision, demonstrating immense potential in the fully-automated patient-specific registration.

References

1. Baheti, B., et al.: The brain tumor sequence registration challenge: establishing correspondence between pre-operative and follow-up MRI scans of diffuse glioma patients. arXiv preprint arXiv:2112.06979 (2021)
2. Balakrishnan, G., Zhao, A., Sabuncu, M.R., Guttag, J., Dalca, A.V.: An unsupervised learning model for deformable medical image registration. In: Proceedings of the IEEE Conference on Computer Vision and Pattern Recognition, pp. 9252–9260 (2018)
3. Brett, M., Leff, A.P., Rorden, C., Ashburner, J.: Spatial normalization of brain images with focal lesions using cost function masking. Neuroimage 14(2), 486–500 (2001)
4. Chitphakdithai, N., Duncan, J.S.: Non-rigid registration with missing correspondences in preoperative and postresection brain images. In: Jiang, T., Navab, N., Pluim, J.P.W., Viergever, M.A. (eds.) MICCAI 2010. LNCS, vol. 6361, pp. 367–374. Springer, Heidelberg (2010). https://doi.org/10.1007/978-3-642-15705-9_45
5. Clatz, O., et al.: Robust nonrigid registration to capture brain shift from intraoperative MRI. IEEE Trans. Med. Imaging 24(11), 1417–1427 (2005)
6. Dalca, A.V., Balakrishnan, G., Guttag, J., Sabuncu, M.R.: Unsupervised learning for fast probabilistic diffeomorphic registration. In: Frangi, A.F., Schnabel, J.A., Davatzikos, C., Alberola-López, C., Fichtinger, G. (eds.) MICCAI 2018. LNCS, vol. 11070, pp. 729–738. Springer, Cham (2018). https://doi.org/10.1007/978-3-030-00928-1_82
7. Dean, B.L., et al.: Gliomas: classification with MR imaging. Radiology 174(2), 411–415 (1990)
8. Han, X., et al.: A deep network for joint registration and reconstruction of images with pathologies. In: Liu, M., Yan, P., Lian, C., Cao, X. (eds.) MLMI 2020. LNCS, vol. 12436, pp. 342–352. Springer, Cham (2020). https://doi.org/10.1007/978-3-030-59861-7_35

9. Han, X., Yang, X., Aylward, S., Kwitt, R., Niethammer, M.: Efficient registration of pathological images: a joint PCA/image-reconstruction approach. In: 2017 IEEE 14th International Symposium on Biomedical Imaging (ISBI 2017), pp. 10–14. IEEE (2017)

10. Heinrich, M.P.: Closing the gap between deep and conventional image registration using probabilistic dense displacement networks. In: Shen, D., et al. (eds.) MICCAI 2019. LNCS, vol. 11769, pp. 50–58. Springer, Cham (2019). https://doi.org/10.1007/978-3-030-32226-7_6

11. Heiss, W.D., Raab, P., Lanfermann, H.: Multimodality assessment of brain tumors and tumor recurrence. J. Nucl. Med. **52**(10), 1585–1600 (2011)

12. Hering, A., et al.: Learn2Reg: comprehensive multi-task medical image registration challenge, dataset and evaluation in the era of deep learning. arXiv preprint arXiv:2112.04489 (2021)

13. Hu, X., Kang, M., Huang, W., Scott, M.R., Wiest, R., Reyes, M.: Dual-stream pyramid registration network. In: Shen, D., et al. (eds.) MICCAI 2019. LNCS, vol. 11765, pp. 382–390. Springer, Cham (2019). https://doi.org/10.1007/978-3-030-32245-8_43

14. Kamnitsas, K., et al.: Efficient multi-scale 3D CNN with fully connected CRF for accurate brain lesion segmentation. Med. Image Anal. **36**, 61–78 (2017)

15. Kim, B., Kim, J., Lee, J.-G., Kim, D.H., Park, S.H., Ye, J.C.: Unsupervised deformable image registration using cycle-consistent CNN. In: Shen, D., et al. (eds.) MICCAI 2019. LNCS, vol. 11769, pp. 166–174. Springer, Cham (2019). https://doi.org/10.1007/978-3-030-32226-7_19

16. Klein, S., Staring, M., Murphy, K., Viergever, M.A., Pluim, J.P.: Elastix: a toolbox for intensity-based medical image registration. IEEE Trans. Med. Imaging **29**(1), 196–205 (2009)

17. Kwon, D., Niethammer, M., Akbari, H., Bilello, M., Davatzikos, C., Pohl, K.M.: PORTR: pre-operative and post-recurrence brain tumor registration. IEEE Trans. Med. Imaging **33**(3), 651–667 (2013)

18. Kwon, D., Zeng, K., Bilello, M., Davatzikos, C.: Estimating patient specific templates for pre-operative and follow-up brain tumor registration. In: Navab, N., Hornegger, J., Wells, W.M., Frangi, A.F. (eds.) MICCAI 2015. LNCS, vol. 9350, pp. 222–229. Springer, Cham (2015). https://doi.org/10.1007/978-3-319-24571-3_27

19. Liu, P., Lyu, M., King, I., Xu, J.: Selflow: self-supervised learning of optical flow. In: Proceedings of the IEEE/CVF Conference on Computer Vision and Pattern Recognition, pp. 4571–4580 (2019)

20. Marstal, K., Berendsen, F., Staring, M., Klein, S.: Simpleelastix: a user-friendly, multi-lingual library for medical image registration. In: Proceedings of the IEEE Conference on Computer Vision and Pattern Recognition Workshops, pp. 134–142 (2016)

21. Meister, S., Hur, J., Roth, S.: Unflow: unsupervised learning of optical flow with a bidirectional census loss. In: Thirty-Second AAAI Conference on Artificial Intelligence (2018)

22. Mok, T.C., Chung, A.: Official implementation of conditional deep laplacian pyramid image registration network. http://github.com/cwmok/Conditional_LapIRN. Accessed 01 Mar 2021

23. Mok, T.C., Chung, A.: Fast symmetric diffeomorphic image registration with convolutional neural networks. In: Proceedings of the IEEE/CVF Conference on Computer Vision and Pattern Recognition, pp. 4644–4653 (2020)

24. Mok, T.C.W., Chung, A.C.S.: Conditional deformable image registration with convolutional neural network. In: de Bruijne, M., et al. (eds.) MICCAI 2021. LNCS, vol. 12904, pp. 35–45. Springer, Cham (2021). https://doi.org/10.1007/978-3-030-87202-1_4

25. Mok, T.C.W., Chung, A.C.S.: Large deformation diffeomorphic image registration with laplacian pyramid networks. In: Martel, A.L., et al. (eds.) MICCAI 2020. LNCS, vol. 12263, pp. 211–221. Springer, Cham (2020). https://doi.org/10.1007/978-3-030-59716-0_21

26. Price, S.J., Jena, R., Burnet, N.G., Carpenter, T.A., Pickard, J.D., Gillard, J.H.: Predicting patterns of glioma recurrence using diffusion tensor imaging. Eur. Radiol. **17**(7), 1675–1684 (2007)

27. Risholm, P., Samset, E., Talos, I.-F., Wells, W.: A non-rigid registration framework that accommodates resection and retraction. In: Prince, J.L., Pham, D.L., Myers, K.J. (eds.) IPMI 2009. LNCS, vol. 5636, pp. 447–458. Springer, Heidelberg (2009). https://doi.org/10.1007/978-3-642-02498-6_37

28. Sundaram, N., Brox, T., Keutzer, K.: Dense point trajectories by GPU-accelerated large displacement optical flow. In: Daniilidis, K., Maragos, P., Paragios, N. (eds.) ECCV 2010. LNCS, vol. 6311, pp. 438–451. Springer, Heidelberg (2010). https://doi.org/10.1007/978-3-642-15549-9_32

29. Wang, Y., Yang, Y., Yang, Z., Zhao, L., Wang, P., Xu, W.: Occlusion aware unsupervised learning of optical flow. In: Proceedings of the IEEE Conference on Computer Vision and Pattern Recognition, pp. 4884–4893 (2018)

30. Yang, X., Han, X., Park, E., Aylward, S., Kwitt, R., Niethammer, M.: Registration of pathological images. In: Tsaftaris, S.A., Gooya, A., Frangi, A.F., Prince, J.L. (eds.) SASHIMI 2016. LNCS, vol. 9968, pp. 97–107. Springer, Cham (2016). https://doi.org/10.1007/978-3-319-46630-9_10

On the Dataset Quality Control for Image Registration Evaluation

Jie Luo[1(✉)], Guangshen Ma[2], Nazim Haouchine[1], Zhe Xu[3], Yixin Wang[4],
Tina Kapur[1], Lipeng Ning[1], William M. Wells III[1], and Sarah Frisken[1]

[1] Brigham and Women's Hospital, Harvard Medical School, Boston, USA
jluo5@bwh.harvard.edu
[2] Department of Mechanical Engineering and Material Science,
Duke University, Durham, USA
[3] Department of Biomedical Engineering, Chinese University of Hong Kong,
Hong Kong, Hong Kong
[4] Department of Bioengineering, Stanford University, Stanford, USA

Abstract. Current registration evaluations typically compute target registration error using manually annotated datasets. As a result, the quality of landmark annotations is crucial for unbiased comparisons because registration algorithms are trained and tested using these landmarks. Even though some data providers claim to have mitigated the inter-observer variability by having multiple raters, quality control such as a third-party screening can still be reassuring for intended users. Examining the landmark quality for neurosurgical datasets (RESECT and BITE) poses specific challenges. In this study, we applied the *variogram*, which is a tool extensively used in geostatistics, to convert 3D landmark distributions into an intuitive 2D representation. This allowed us to identify potential problematic cases efficiently so that they could be examined by experienced radiologists. In both the RESECT and BITE datasets, we identified and confirmed a small number of landmarks with potential localization errors and found that, in some cases, the landmark distribution was not ideal for an unbiased assessment of non-rigid registration errors. Under discussion, we provide some constructive suggestions for improving the utility of publicly available annotated data.

Keywords: Image registration · Public datasets · Quality control

1 Introduction

With the increasing availability of new image registration approaches, unbiased and task-specific evaluation methods are necessary so that researchers and clinicians can choose the most suitable approaches for their applications.

In early work, researchers used image similarity metrics, such as the sum of squared intensity differences, to evaluate the registration results [26,28]. Later, the "Retrospective Image Registration Evaluation" (RIRE) project [8,27,31] introduced Target Registration Error (TRE) and Fiducial Registration Error

L. Wang et al. (Eds.): MICCAI 2022, LNCS 13436, pp. 36–45, 2022.
https://doi.org/10.1007/978-3-031-16446-0_4

(FRE). TRE is the true error of registered target points in physical space, while FRE represents the error of registered annotated fiducial markers (landmarks) in image space. Although Fitzpatrick pointed out that TRE and FRE are uncorrelated [9]. In practice, TRE is approximated by FRE. The Vista [10] and NIREP [5] projects included additional registration error measures, e.g., the region of interest (ROI) overlap, the average volume difference and the Jacobian of the deformation field. These metrics can provide insight for understanding a particular aspect of the registration quality [12–16,19,21,30,34,35]. Due to its simplicity and the reliability issues of other criteria [23], TRE has become the predominant registration error measure. However, using TRE has certain limitations: (1) Because landmarks are annotated by localization algorithms (manual, automatic or semi-automatic methods), they may contain a localization Error (FLE) [27]. (2) The TRE only estimates the error at specific landmark locations, thus a dense population of landmarks is preferred. If landmarks are sparse or are not distributed evenly across the entire ROI, it may introduce bias that favors regions with landmarks to the registration evaluation.

Recently, landmark-annotated datasets are becoming publicly available and used to evaluate new algorithms in various registration challenges [3,4,11,33]. The quality of the landmarks is crucial not only to provide an unbiased evaluation, but also to the clinical applicability of these new algorithms. For example, many learning-based registration algorithms are trained using these landmarks. With poor annotation quality, test results can look good if the models can learn to reproduce the inaccurate labels from the training data, but the actual clinical performance of these algorithms will be poor. Although some public datasets have claimed to have mitigated FLEs and inter-observer variability by averaging the results of landmark locations localized by multiple raters [1,26], the development process, strength and weakness of the datasets are not sufficiently detailed in the description. Nevertheless, the registration community has over looked the importance of the quality control in annotation in public datasets, and a *third-party screening* could be reassuring for users.

In this study, we perform a third-party screening on the landmarks of two benchmark neurosurgical datasets, RESECT [32] and BITE [18]. Both datasets have manually annotated corresponding landmarks on pre-operative Magnetic Resonance (p-MR) and intra-operative Ultrasound (i-US) images [17,18,22,32],. Due to the nature of image-guided neurosurgery, validating the landmarks on RESECT and BITE poses specific challenges:

1. Expert visual inspection is usually the preferred method for checking the quality of annotations, e.g., segmentation labels [2,20]. However, when there are large numbers of landmarks, manually checking landmark coordinates in a 3D rendering or simultaneously displayed axial, sagittal and coronal planes are time-consuming.
2. Registering two images using a plausible deformation model and visually inspecting the landmark pairs which yield particularly large errors is a feasible strategy to examine the annotation quality for thoracic and Lung images [19]. However, because of tumor resection and retraction, the structure of the

brain on two images differs significantly and thus it is not trivial to choose the appropriate deformation model for RESECT and BITE.

The *Variogram* is used extensively in geostatistics to describe the spatial dependence of mineral distributions. We use the Variogram to convert the distribution of 3D landmark coordinates into an intuitive 2D representation and in turn efficiently identify potential problematic cases. Potential problematic cases were then examined by experienced radiologists. The rest of the paper is organized as follows: In Sect. 2, we review how to use the Variogram to (1) detect any obvious FLEs; and (2) examine the distribution of landmarks. In Sect. 3, we share our findings on the RESECT and BITE datasets. Finally, we give constructive discussion about our findings in Sect. 4.

2 Method

Our datasets consist of pairs of 3D images, each of which are manually annotated with corresponding landmark points. We compute displacements between pairs of corresponding landmarks to generate a sparse 3D vector field $\mathcal{D}$. By analyzing $\mathcal{D}$, we can assess the quality of the annotations. The variogram characterizes the spatial dependence of displacment vectors in $\mathcal{D}$ and provides an intuitive 2D representation for visual inspection [6].

We first review constructing the variogram for a vector field and using the variogram to flag potential FLEs and problematic landmark distributions.

2.1 Constructing the Variogram

For image registration, let $\Omega \subset \mathbb{R}^3$, $I_f : \Omega \to \mathbb{R}$ and $I_m : \Omega \to \mathbb{R}$ be the fixed and moving images. $(\mathbf{x}, \mathbf{x}') \in \Omega$ represents a pair of manually labeled corresponding landmarks in I_f and I_m. $\mathbf{d}(\mathbf{x}) = \mathbf{x}' - \mathbf{x}$ is the displacement vector from $\mathbf{x}$ to $\mathbf{x}'$. For K pairs of landmarks, we have a set of displacement vectors $\mathcal{D} = \{\mathbf{d}(\mathbf{x}_k)\}_{k=1}^K$.

Given a landmark location $\mathbf{s}$, let h represent the distance to $\mathbf{s}$. The theoretical variogram $\gamma(h)$ is the expected value of the differences between $\mathbf{d}(\mathbf{s})$ and other $\mathbf{d}$'s whose starting points are h away from $\mathbf{s}$:

$$\gamma(h) = \frac{1}{2} E[(\mathbf{d}(\mathbf{s}) - \mathbf{d}(\mathbf{s} + h))^2], \tag{1}$$

here $\gamma(h)$ describes the spatial dependence of displacement vectors as a function of the distance. Since $\gamma(h)$ is a continuous function and we only have discrete samples, we use the empirical variogram cloud $\hat{\gamma}(h)$, which is an approximation of $\gamma(h)$, to compute the pairwise spatial dependence of all displacement vectors. For conciseness, In the rest of this article, we call $\hat{\gamma}(h)$ variogram. Given a vector field $\mathcal{D}$, $\hat{\gamma}(h)$ can be constructed as follows:

1. For each pair of vectors $(\mathbf{d}(\mathbf{x}_i), \mathbf{d}(\mathbf{x}_j))$, compute $\epsilon_{ij} = \|\mathbf{d}(\mathbf{x}_i) - \mathbf{d}(\mathbf{x}_j)\|^2$;
2. Compute $h_{ij} = \|\mathbf{x}_i - \mathbf{x}_j\|$;
3. Plot all (h_{ij}, ϵ_{ij}) to obtain $\hat{\gamma}(h)$.

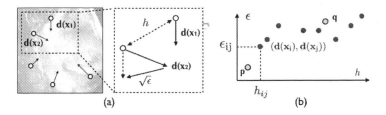

Fig. 1. (a) An Illustration of how to compute ϵ and h. $\mathbf{d}(\mathbf{x}_1)$ and $\mathbf{d}(\mathbf{x}_2)$ are displacement vectors for landmarks $\mathbf{x}_1$ and $\mathbf{x}_2$ respectively. $h = \|\mathbf{x}_1 - \mathbf{x}_2\|$ is the distance between $\mathbf{x}_1$ and $\mathbf{x}_2$, and $\epsilon = \|\mathbf{d}(\mathbf{x}_1) - \mathbf{d}(\mathbf{x}_2)\|^2$ measures the displacement difference; (b) A hypothetical $\hat{\gamma}(h)$ generated from the vector field in (a). Since the vector field has 5 displacement vectors, $\hat{\gamma}(h)$ has $\frac{5(5-1)}{2} = 10$ value points. p and q are two value points that demonstrate the typical increasing trend of $\hat{\gamma}(h)$: epsilon tends to increase as h increases.

Figure 1(a) illustrates computing ϵ and h for two vectors. Figure 1(b) shows a hypothetical variogram cloud generated from the vector field in Fig. 1(a). The horizontal and vertical axes represent h and ϵ respectively. Given K displacement vectors, each $\mathbf{d}(\mathbf{x})$ has $K - 1$ pairs of corresponding (h_{ij}, ϵ_{ij}), thus $\hat{\gamma}(h)$ contains $\frac{K(K-1)}{2}$ value points.

A common dependency assumption is that landmarks that are close to each other (i.e., smaller h) typically have smaller differences in their displacement vectors (i.e., smaller ϵ) than landmarks that are further apart. As a result, a typical $\hat{\gamma}(h)$ tends to exhibit an increasing trend.

2.2 Potential FLEs

A corresponding pair of annotated landmarks $(\mathbf{x}, \mathbf{x}')$ determines a displacement vector $\mathbf{d}(\mathbf{x})$, which should represent the deformation at $\mathbf{x}$. If $\mathbf{d}(\mathbf{x}) \in \mathcal{D}$ lies outside the general trend of the variogram, it could indicate FLE for $(\mathbf{x}, \mathbf{x}')$. We call these abnormally behaved vectors *outliers*. In general, there are global outliers λ_{G} and local outliers λ_{L}:

λ_{G}: are significantly different from the majority of displacement vectors in $\mathcal{D}$.
λ_{L}: do not have extreme values, but are considerably different from their neighbors.

Vector outliers tend to have different spatial dependence from other landmarks, which can be captured by the values of (h, ϵ), hence we can use $\hat{\gamma}(h)$ to identify λ_{G} and λ_{L}. In the example of Fig. 2(a), we deliberately added two problematic landmarks, one with global error λ_{G} (blue) and one with local error λ_{L} (green), to a vector field. In Fig. 2(b), all blue points in $\hat{\gamma}(h)$ belong to λ_{G}, which can be easily identified because all of its corresponding points have distinctively higher ϵ values. In Fig. 2(c), all green points in $\hat{\gamma}(h)$ belong to λ_{L}. We can also distinguish λ_{L} at the bottom-left corner of $\hat{\gamma}(h)$, because some of its points yield small h while having unusually large ϵ.

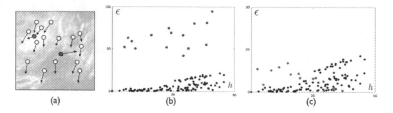

Fig. 2. (a) Manually added displacement vector outliers. The blue point is a global outlier λ_G, the green point is a local outlier λ_L (b, c) Colorized global and local outliers identified in $\hat{\gamma}(h)$. Each point represents the difference between a pair of displacement vectors, e.g., blue points are vector pairs that involve the global outlier. (Color figure online)

Some valid displacement vectors that indicate large tissue deformation may share the same features as outliers. Therefore, $\hat{\gamma}(h)$ is only used to flag suspicious λ_G and λ_L for further examination by experienced radiologists.

2.3 Atypical Variogram Patterns

The distribution of annotated landmarks can also be reflected in the pattern of $\hat{\gamma}(h)$. Figure 3(a) shows the smoothly increasing relationship between h and ϵ for an evenly distributed vector field $\mathcal{D}$. Other variogram patterns may indicate undesirable distributions of the vector field. Two undesirable patters are clustered landmarks and isolated landmarks:

1. If landmarks are clustered into two (or more) distinct groups, the clustering is evident in $\hat{\gamma}(h)$ as illustrated in Fig. 3(b).
2. If a landmark is isolated from other landmarks, its points in $\hat{\gamma}(h)$ only exist in areas where h is large. Fig. 3(c) shows an isolated landmark and its values in $\hat{\gamma}(h)$.

We construct $\hat{\gamma}(h)$ for all data and manually flag cases with the above atypical patterns for further examinations.

3   Experiments

RESECT [32] and BITE [18] are two clinical datasets that contain p-MR and i-US images of patients with brain tumors. They are widely used to evaluate registration algorithms for image-guided neurosurgery. RESECT includes 23 patients with each having p-MR (pMR), before-resection US (bUS), during-resection US (dUS) and after-resection US (aUS) images. Four image pairs, i.e., pMR-aUS, pMR-bUS, bUS-aUS and bUS-dUS, have been annotated with corresponding landmarks. For BITE, pre- and post-operative MR, and i-US images have been acquired from 14 patients. These images were further annotated and put into three groups (1) Group 1: bUS and aUS; (2) Group 2: pMR-bUS; (3) Group 4: pMR and post-MR.

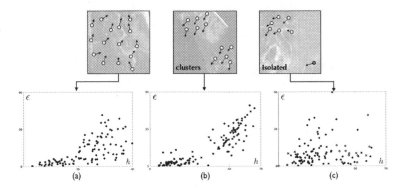

Fig. 3. (a) $\hat{\gamma}(h)$ of an evenly distributed vector field; (b) $\hat{\gamma}(h)$ of a vector field that has clusters; (c) $\hat{\gamma}(h)$ of a vector field that has an isolated landmark.

To provide a thrid-party screening of the annotations in these two datasets, we generated $\hat{\gamma}(h)$ for all 700+ landmark pairs and flagged those landmark pairs with potential FLE issues. Two operators visually inspected the flagged landmark pairs and categorized them into three categories: (1) They are certain that the landmark pair is problematic; (2) $\hat{\gamma}(h)$ looks atypical, but they are unsure whether the landmark pair is problematic; (3) $\hat{\gamma}(h)$ looks normal. In addition, they also flagged cases with clusters or isolated landmark $\hat{\gamma}(h)$ problems.

It's noteworthy that the variogram screening is a time-efficient process. With the help of the variogram, the average screening time on a pair of landmarks is approximately 15 s. In comparison, visual inspecting a pair of landmarks using simultaneously displayed axial, sagittal and coronal planes takes about three minutes.

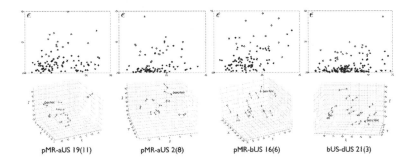

Fig. 4. Examples of category one atypical landmark pairs (red). The first row shows their $\hat{\gamma}(h)$'s while the second row displays their 3D displacement vectors.

Findings. After screening, we found that $\hat{\gamma}(h)$ for the vast majority of landmarks appeared to be normal. This indicates that both datasets have high-quality annotations. In total, we identified 29 pairs of landmarks with potential

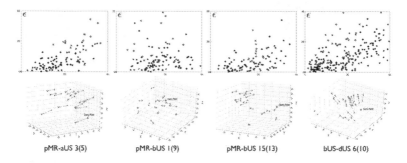

Fig. 5. Examples of category two landmark pairs. These landmarks have atypical $\hat{\gamma}(h)$'s, but their displacement vectors could be reasonable.

FLEs. In addition, we also identified 4 cluster cases and 11 isolated landmarks. All flagged data are summarized in Table 1. Figure 4 and Fig. 5 show the $\hat{\gamma}(h)$ of four different landmark pairs that were flagged with potential FLE's. Figure 6 provides two $\hat{\gamma}(h)$'s which were flagged with clusters or isolated landmarks.

Table 1. Indices of problematic landmark pairs, e.g., 1(9) means patient 1 and landmark pair No. 9.

		Certain	Unsure	Cluster	Isolated
RESECT	pMR-aUS	1(9), 2(10), 19(11) 2(8)	3(5), 4(3), 7(1, 4), 14(1),	n/a	18(14)
	pMR-bUS	1(9), 16(6)	1(13), 2(14), 3(1) 15(13), 25(15)	19	2(14), 19(1)
	bUS-aUS	1(7), 7(8), 12(11) 24(14)	15(3)	25	1(11), 18(12) 19(1)
	bUS-dUS	21(3), 27(11)	6(10), 7(22)	19	n/a
BITE	G1	3(4), 10(1)	n/a	12	2(3), 4(4) 9(6)
	G2	9(5)	12(1)	n/a	3(21)
	G4	n/a	1(6)	n/a	3(16)

Expert visual inspection was further performed for all flagged cases:

1. For "problematic" landmarks with possible localization errors, we sent the findings (mixed with good landmarks) to three experienced neuro-radiologists for validation and rating. They carefully examined the landmark coordinates in physical space using 3D Slicer [7] and assigned a score from [1(poor), 2(questionable), 3 (acceptable), 4 (good)]. Landmarks in Category 1 and category 2 received an average score of 1.5 and 2.4 respectively, which reinforced the effectiveness of the variogram. None of flagged landmarks were rated "good".

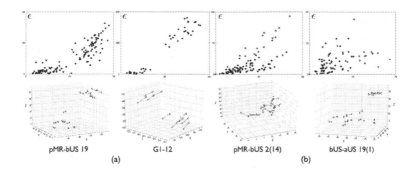

Fig. 6. Examples of (a) two flagged *clusters* and (b) two isolated landmarks.

2. For cluster and isolated cases, neuro-radiologists observed that landmarks were mainly located near the sulcus regions, and it would be difficult to add more corresponding landmarks to distribute the landmarks more evenly across the image (e.g. inside the resection cavity). In the context of image-guided neurosurgery, surgeons are interested in an accurate registration of the preoperative tumor boundary to the intraoperative coordinate space. Since there are no landmarks near the tumor boundary, it may be better to combine other evaluation criteria [24], or use weighted TRE in the registration of neurosurgical data [25, 29].

From this screening, we conclude that RESECT and BITE are both reliable datasets with a small number of landmarks that may have significant FLEs, and some cases where the landmark distribution is not ideal. Our findings do not detract from the general usefulness of these datasets, but they could benefit researchers or clinicians who intend to use them.

4   Discussion

Manual landmark annotation is primarily a subjective task, thus public datasets that are used by the registration community may have some non-negligible FLEs. In this work, we introduced using the variogram as an aid for visual inspection, but more importantly we want to raise the awareness of the importance of quality control over public datasets. After all, the quality of annotated landmarks is crucial not only to provide an unbiased evaluation of registration algorithms, but also to the clinical applicability of algorithms that are trained and tested using these landmarks. We suggest that:

1. Quality control, in the form of visual inspection by the dataset provider, or a third party, should be performed and documented;
2. The development process, strengths and weaknesses should be sufficiently detailed in the description of the dataset;
3. Dataset providers should provide a means to update their repository based on users' feedback, e.g., by adding or correcting annotations.

References

1. Bardosi, Z., Freysinger, W.: Estimating FLE distributions of manual fiducial localization in CT images. Int. J. Comput. Assist. Radiol. Surg. **11**, 1043–1049 (2016)
2. Beatriz Garcia, C., Solter, J., Bossa, Matias Husch, A.: On the composition and limitations of publicly availabble covid-19 x-ray imaging datasets. arXiv (2020)
3. Borovec, J.: BIRL: benchmark on image registration methods with landmark validation. arXiv (2020)
4. Borovec, J., Munoz-Barrutia, A.: ANHIR: automatic non-rigid histological image registration challenge. IEEE Trans. Med. Imaging **39**(10), 3042–3052 (2020)
5. Christensen, G.E., Geng, X., Kuhl, J.G., Bruss, J., Grabowski, T.J., Pirwani, I.A., Vannier, M.W., Allen, J.S., Damasio, H.: Introduction to the non-rigid image registration evaluation project (NIREP). In: Pluim, J.P.W., Likar, B., Gerritsen, F.A. (eds.) WBIR 2006. LNCS, vol. 4057, pp. 128–135. Springer, Heidelberg (2006). https://doi.org/10.1007/11784012_16
6. Cressie, N.: Statistics for Spatial Data. Wiley, New York (1991)
7. Fedorov, A., et al.: 3D slicer as an image computing platform for the quantitative imaging network. Mag. Resonan. Imaging **30**(9), 1323–1341 (2012)
8. Fitzpatrick, J.: The retrospective image registration evaluation project. InsightJournal (2007)
9. Fitzpatrick, J.: Fiducial registration error and target registration error are uncorrelated. In: Proceedings of SPIE Medical Imaging. p. 726102G. SPIE (2009)
10. Hellier, P., et al.: Retrospective evaluation of inter-subject brain registration. IEEE Trans. Med. Imaging **22**(9), 1120–1130 (2003)
11. Hering, A., Murphy, K., van Ginneken, B.: Learn2reg challenge: CT lung registration. In: MICCAI (2021)
12. Kabus, S., Klinder, T., Murphy, K., van Ginneken, B., Lorenz, C., Pluim, J.P.W.: Evaluation of 4D-CT lung registration. In: Yang, G.-Z., Hawkes, D., Rueckert, D., Noble, A., Taylor, C. (eds.) MICCAI 2009. LNCS, vol. 5761, pp. 747–754. Springer, Heidelberg (2009). https://doi.org/10.1007/978-3-642-04268-3_92
13. Klein, A., et al.: Evaluation of 14 nonlinear deformation algorithms applied to human brain MRI registration. Neuroimage **46**(3), 786–802 (2009)
14. Klein, A., et al.: Evaluation of volume-based and surface-based brain image registration methods. Neuroimage **51**(1), 214–220 (2010)
15. Luo, J., et al.: A Feature-driven active framework for ultrasound-based brain shift compensation. In: Frangi, A.F., Schnabel, J.A., Davatzikos, C., Alberola-López, C., Fichtinger, G. (eds.) MICCAI 2018. LNCS, vol. 11073, pp. 30–38. Springer, Cham (2018). https://doi.org/10.1007/978-3-030-00937-3_4
16. Luo, J., Frisken, S., Wang, D., Golby, A., Sugiyama, M., Wells III, W.: Are registration uncertainty and error monotonically associated? In: MICCAI 2020 (2020)
17. Machado, I., et al.: Deformable MRI-ultrasound registration using correlation-based attribute matching for brain shift correction: accuracy and generality in multi-site data. Neuroimage **202**(15), (2019)
18. Mercier, L., Del Maestro, R., Petrecca, K., Araujo, D., Haegelen, C., Collins, D.: Online database of clinical MR and ultrasound images of brain tumors. Med. Phys. **39**(6), 3253–3261 (2012)
19. Murphy, K., et al.: Evaluation of registration methods on thoracic CT: the empire10 challenge. IEEE Trans. Med. Imaging **30**(11), 1901–1920 (2011)
20. Oakden-Rayner, L.: Exploring large scale public medical image datasets. arXiv (2019)

21. Ou, Y., Akbari, H., Bilello, M., Da, X., Davatzikos, C.: Comparative evaluation of registration algorithms in different brain databases with varying difficulty. IEEE Trans. Med. Imaging **33**(10), 2039–2065 (2014)
22. Reinertsen, I., Collins, D., Drouin, S.: The essential role of open data and software for the future of ultrasound-based neuronavigation. Front. Oncol. **10** (2020)
23. Rohlfing, T.: Image similarity and tissue overlaps as surrogates for image registration accuracy: widely used but unreliable. IEEE Trans. Med. Imaging **31**(2), 153–16 (2012)
24. dos Santos, T., et al.: Pose-independent surface matching for intra-operative soft-tissue marker-less registration. Med. Image Anal. **18**(7), 1101–1114 (2014)
25. Shamir, R.R., Joskowicz, L., Shoshan, Y.: Fiducial optimization for minimal target registration error in image-guided neurosurgery. IEEE Trans. Med. Imaging **31**(3), 725–737 (2012)
26. Song, J.: Methods for evaluating image registration. Dissertation, University of Iowa (2017)
27. Sonka, M.: Handbook of medical imaging: medical image processing and analysis. In: SPIE (2000)
28. Sotiras, A., Davatzikos, C., Paragios, N.: Deformable medical image registration: A survey. IEEE Trans. Med. Imaging **32**(7), 1153–1190 (2013)
29. Thompson, S., Penney, G., Dasgupta, P., Hawkes, D.: Improved modelling of tool tracking errors by modelling dependent marker errors. IEEE Trans. Med. Imaging **32**(2), 165–177 (2013)
30. Wang, J., Zhang, M.: Deepflash: An efficient network for learning-based medical image registration. In: CVPR 2020, pp. 4444–4452. IEEE (2020)
31. West, J., Fitzpatrick, J., Wang, M., Woods, R.: Comparison and evaluation of retrospective intermodality brain image registration techniques. J. Comput. Assist. Tomogr. **21**(4), 554–566 (1997)
32. Xiao, Y., Fortin, M., Unsgard, G., Rivaz, H., Reinertsen, I.: Retrospective evaluation of cerebral tumors (resect): a clinical database of pre-operative MRI and intra-operative ultrasound in low-grade glioma surgeries. Med. Phys. **44**(7), 3875–3882 (2017)
33. Xiao, Y., Rivaz, H., Chabanas, M.: Evaluation of MRI to ultrasound registration methods for brain shift correction: the curious2018 challenge. IEEE Trans. Med. Imaging **39**(3), 777–786 (2020)
34. Xu, Z., et al.: Evaluation of six registration methods for the human abdomen on clinically acquired CT. IEEE Trans. Biomed. Eng. **63**(8), 1563–1572 (2016)
35. Yassa, M., Stark, C.E.: A quantitative evaluation of cross-participant registration techniques for MRI studies of the medial temporal lobe. Neuroimage **442**, 319–327 (2009)

Dual-Branch Squeeze-Fusion-Excitation Module for Cross-Modality Registration of Cardiac SPECT and CT

Xiongchao Chen[1]([✉]), Bo Zhou[1], Huidong Xie[1], Xueqi Guo[1], Jiazhen Zhang[2], Albert J. Sinusas[1,2,3], John A. Onofrey[1,2], and Chi Liu[1,2]

[1] Department of Biomedical Engineering, Yale University, New Haven, USA
{xiongchao.chen,chi.liu}@yale.edu
[2] Department of Radiology and Biomedical Imaging, Yale University,
New Haven, USA
[3] Department of Internal Medicine, Yale University, New Haven, USA

Abstract. Single-photon emission computed tomography (SPECT) is a widely applied imaging approach for diagnosis of coronary artery diseases. Attenuation maps (μ-maps) derived from computed tomography (CT) are utilized for attenuation correction (AC) to improve diagnostic accuracy of cardiac SPECT. However, SPECT and CT are obtained sequentially in clinical practice, which potentially induces misregistration between the two scans. Convolutional neural networks (CNN) are powerful tools for medical image registration. Previous CNN-based methods for cross-modality registration either directly concatenated two input modalities as an early feature fusion or extracted image features using two separate CNN modules for a late fusion. These methods do not fully extract or fuse the cross-modality information. Besides, deep-learning-based rigid registration of cardiac SPECT and CT-derived μ-maps has not been investigated before. In this paper, we propose a Dual-Branch Squeeze-Fusion-Excitation (DuSFE) module for the registration of cardiac SPECT and CT-derived μ-maps. DuSFE fuses the knowledge from multiple modalities to recalibrate both channel-wise and spatial features for each modality. DuSFE can be embedded at multiple convolutional layers to enable feature fusion at different spatial dimensions. Our studies using clinical data demonstrated that a network embedded with DuSFE generated substantial lower registration errors and therefore more accurate AC SPECT images than previous methods. Our source code is available at https://github.com/XiongchaoChen/DuSFE_CrossRegistration.

Keywords: Cardiac SPECT/CT · Cross-modality · Image registration · Attenuation correction

Supplementary Information The online version contains supplementary material available at https://doi.org/10.1007/978-3-031-16446-0_5.

1   Introduction

Myocardial perfusion imaging (MPI) using single-photon emission computed tomography (SPECT) is the most widely performed nuclear cardiology exam for diagnosis of ischemic heart diseases [5]. Photon attenuation within the patient's body is the major limitation that affects accurate diagnosis of cardiac SPECT [19]. In clinical practice, attenuation maps (μ-maps) derived from computed tomography (CT) are utilized for attenuation correction (AC) [22], which largely increases the diagnostic accuracy [17]. However, SPECT and CT scans are usually performed sequentially. Thus, improper patient positioning, voluntary movements, or mechanical misalignment of scanners could potentially induce the misregistration between SPECT and CT [8]. Previous studies showed that the misregistration can produce errors in the activity distribution of AC SPECT images [6]. Thus, cross-modality registration of SPECT/CT images is of vital importance for accurate clinical diagnosis of cardiac SPECT.

Cross-modality registration is quite challenging because the same structures in two modalities could present totally different intensity and texture patterns [1]. Traditional methods for cross-modality registration are based on either minimizing the absolute errors between image intensities within overlapping regions [7] or maximizing the mutual information (MI) between image volumes [15]. However, these metric-based methods typically ignore the image spatial information, and thus show poor performance in the registration of SPECT and CT-derived μ-maps, since some structures could be presented in the CT transmission scan but missing in the SPECT emission scan.

Deep learning has shown great potential in medical image registration [2]. Many methods using convolutional neural networks (CNN) were developed for cross-modality image registration. Sun et al. [21] proposed a DVNet to estimate the displacement vectors between CT and Ultrasound (US) images, in which image features were extracted by two separate CNN streams and channel-wise concatenated as a late fusion. Xu et al. [25] proposed a translation-based network for deformable registration of CT and magnetic resonance (MR) images, in which uni-modality registration of MR and CT-translated MR was combined with cross-modality registration of MR and CT. Guo et al. [9] developed a MSReg for rigid registration of transrectal ultrasound (TRUS) and MR images. The two modalities were first concatenated at the input layer as an early fusion, and then fed to a series of ResNetXt [24] for deep registration. Song et al. [20] adopted a non-local neural network [23] to recalibrate voxel weights of image features for rigid registration of TRUS and MR images.

However, the aforementioned deep learning methods do not fully extract or fuse the cross-modality information. Some methods directly concatenate the two input modalities as an early fusion [9,25]. Others first extract image features using two separate CNN streams and then concatenate the extracted features for a late fusion [20,21]. The extracted features can also be fused at different downsampling layers as recursive late fusion [14]. In addition, deep-learning-based rigid registration of cardiac SPECT and CT-derived μ-maps has not been investigated before. In this study, we propose a novel Dual-Branch

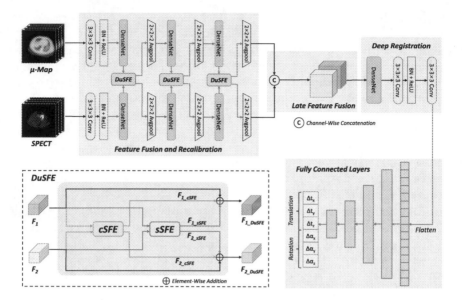

Fig. 1. Schematic of the proposed registration framework. The input μ-map and SPECT image are fed into two cross-connected CNN streams embedded with DuSFE for feature fusion. The extracted features are concatenated and input to a deep registration module followed by fully connected layers to estimate registration parameters.

Squeeze-Fusion-Excitation (DuSFE) attention module for feature fusion, recalibration, and registration of cardiac SPECT and CT-derived μ-maps, inspired by Squeeze-and-Excitation Networks (SENet) [10]. SENet was developed to recalibrate channel weights of feature maps, which was applied for image fusion [12], segmentation [18], and transformation [3,4]. In our study, the DuSFE module fuses the information of multiple modalities and then recalibrates both the channel-wise and spatial features of each modality in a dual-branch manner. DuSFE can be further embedded at different downsampling layers, enabling gradual feature fusion at different spatial dimensions. Our patient studies demonstrated that a network built with DuSFE generated significantly lower registration errors and more accurate AC SPECT images with a minimal increase in computational cost compared to previous methods.

2 Methods

2.1 Dataset and Preprocessing

The dataset of this study consisted of 450 anonymized clinical cardiac ^{99m}Tc-tetrofosmin SPECT MPI studies acquired on GE NM/CT 850c, a hybrid dual-head SPECT/8-slice CT scanner. The SPECT image with a matrix size of 64 $\times$ 64 $\times$ 64 and a voxel size of 6.8 $\times$ 6.8 $\times$ 6.8 mm^3 was reconstructed from 60-angle projections within photopeak window (126.5 to 154.5 keV) using ordered subset expectation maximization (OSEM, 10 subsets, 12 iterations) and then mean-normalized. The original voxel spacing of the CT images is $0.98 \times 0.98 \times 5\,mm^3$ with a matrix size of 512×512 in each slice. The CT values in Hounsfield unit were transformed into attenuation coefficients of μ-maps with the unit of cm^{-1}. The μ-maps were then cropped and interpolated into the same matrix and voxel size as SPECT images. The CT-derived μ-maps were all manually checked and registered with the SPECT images by technologists using vendor software. No data intensity augmentation was implemented in this study. The clinical characteristics of enrolled patients are listed in our supplementary materials.

In clinical practice of cardiac SPECT, the manual corrections are done only for rigid motions. Thus, we consider rigid motions in this study. A group of randomly generated transformation parameters (Δt_x, Δt_y, Δt_z, $\Delta \alpha_x$, $\Delta \alpha_y$, $\Delta \alpha_z$) were used to transform μ-maps to simulate misregistration. Ranges of translations (Δt_x, Δt_y, Δt_z) and rotations ($\Delta \alpha_x$, $\Delta \alpha_y$, $\Delta \alpha_z$) were limited to (8, 8, 4) voxels and (10, 10, 30) degrees with the interval of 0.01 voxels and $0.01°$. Wider ranges were assigned for Δt_x, Δt_y, and $\Delta \alpha_z$ since misregistration of SPECT and CT mainly exists within the transverse plane. Two groups of parameters were generated for each patient study. In total, 400, 100, and 400 cases were generated for training, validation, and testing.

2.2   Dual-Branch Squeeze-Fusion-Excitation Module

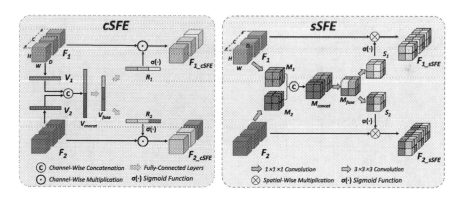

Fig. 2. Frameworks of cSFE and sSFE attention modules. The channel-wise or spatial features are encoded, fused, and applied back for recalibration in cSFE or sSFE.

The overview of our proposed registration network is presented in Fig. 1. The μ-map and SPECT image are input into two cross-connected CNN streams for feature fusion. Each CNN stream has a 3-layer downsampling structure. In each layer, two modalities are first fed into DenseNet [11] for feature extraction, and then jointly input to DuSFE for feature fusion and recalibration. The implementations of DenseNet are summarized in our supplementary materials.

The overview of our proposed DuSFE module is presented in the bottom dash box of Fig. 1. Two modalities are jointly input into two attention modules, channel-Squeeze-Fusion-Excitation (**cSFE**) for channel-wise recalibration and spatial-Squeeze-Fusion-Excitation (**sSFE**) for spatial recalibration. The frameworks of cSFE and sSFE attention modules are presented in Fig. 2.

In **cSFE**, two modalities F_1 and $F_2 \in \mathbb{R}^{H \times W \times D \times C}$ are squeezed into two vectors V_1 and $V_2 \in \mathbb{R}^C$ using global average pooling:

$$V_1(c) = \frac{1}{H \times W \times D} \sum_i^H \sum_j^W \sum_k^D F_1(i, j, k, c), \tag{1}$$

$$V_2(c) = \frac{1}{H \times W \times D} \sum_i^H \sum_j^W \sum_k^D F_2(i, j, k, c), \tag{2}$$

where c refers to the cth channel of F_1 and F_2. Then, V_1 and V_2 are channel-wise concatenated and fed into a fully connected layer with a weight of $w \in \mathbb{R}^{C \times 2C}$ and a bias of $b \in \mathbb{R}^C$ to produce a fused vector $V_{fuse} \in \mathbb{R}^C$ for feature fusion:

$$V_{fuse} = w[V_1, V_2] + b, \tag{3}$$

where $[\cdot]$ refers to the channel-wise concatenation operator. Next, V_{fuse} is input to two separate fully connected layers to generate two channel-wise recalibration weights R_1 and $R_2 \in \mathbb{R}^C$:

$$R_1 = w_1 V_{fuse} + b_1, R_2 = w_2 V_{fuse} + b_2, \tag{4}$$

where w_1 and $w_2 \in \mathbb{R}^{C \times C}$, b_1 and $b_2 \in \mathbb{R}^C$ are the weights and biases of the fully-connected layers. R_1 and R_2 are then applied back to the two input modalities using channel-wise multiplication, generating F_{1_cSFE} and F_{2_cSFE}:

$$F_{1\_cSFE} = \sigma(R_1) \odot F_1, F_{2\_cSFE} = \sigma(R_2) \odot F_2, \tag{5}$$

where $\sigma(\cdot)$ is sigmoid function and $\odot$ refers to the channel-wise multiplication.

In **sSFE**, F_1 and $F_2 \in \mathbb{R}^{H \times W \times D \times C}$ are squeezed using convolutional layers with kernels K_{in1} and $K_{in2} \in \mathbb{R}^{1 \times 1 \times 1 \times 1 \times C}$, generating two volumes M_1 and $M_2 \in \mathbb{R}^{H \times W \times D \times 1}$:

$$M_1 = K_{in1} * F_1, M_2 = K_{in2} * F_2, \tag{6}$$

where $*$ refers to the convolution operator. Then, M_1 and M_2 are channel-wise concatenated and fed into a convolutional layer with a kernel $K_{fuse} \in \mathbb{R}^{1 \times 1 \times 1 \times 1 \times 2}$ to produce a fused volume $M_{fuse} \in \mathbb{R}^{H \times W \times D \times 1}$:

$$M_{fuse} = K_{fuse} * [M_1, M_2]. \tag{7}$$

Next, M_{fuse} is input to two separate convolutional layers with kernels K_{out1} and $K_{out2} \in \mathbb{R}^{3 \times 3 \times 3 \times 1 \times 1}$ to generate spatial recalibration weights S_1 and S_2:

$$S_1 = K_{out1} * M_{fuse}, S_2 = K_{out2} * M_{fuse}. \tag{8}$$

S_1 and S_2 are then applied back to the two input modalities using spatial multiplication, generating F_{1_sSFE} and F_{2_sSFE}:

$$F_{1\_sSFE} = \sigma(S_1) \otimes F_1, F_{2\_sSFE} = \sigma(S_2) \otimes F_2, \tag{9}$$

where $\otimes$ refers to the spatial multiplication operator.

Finally, the channel-wise and spatial recalibrated feature maps are combined with the input features using element-wise addition:

$$F_{1\_DuSFE} = F_1 + F_{1\_cSFE} + F_{1\_sSFE}, \tag{10}$$

$$F_{2\_DuSFE} = F_2 + F_{2\_cSFE} + F_{2\_sSFE}. \tag{11}$$

With DuSFE, information from two modalities can be effectively fused to recalibrate the channel-wise and spatial features for each modality.

2.3 Deep Registration and Fully Connected Layers

As is shown in Fig. 1, image features of μ-map and SPECT recalibrated by DuSFE are then channel-wise concatenated for a late feature fusion. The fused features are input to a deep registration module to extract the spatial registration information. Fully connected layers are finally applied to the flattened volumes, estimating the rigid transformation parameters.

2.4 Implementation Details

In this study, we included a traditional method using mutual information [15], and recent deep learning methods DVNet [21], MSReg (one-stage) [9] and non-local attention [20] as benchmarks. The DuSFE modules in Fig. 1 were removed for ablation study, labeled as DenseNet. DenseNet, DenseNet with non-local attention added, and DenseNet with the proposed DuSFE were tested for comparison. All networks were trained for 300 epochs using Adam optimizers $(\beta_1 = 0.5, \beta_2 = 0.99)$ [13] with an initial learning rate of 5×10^{-5} and a decay rate of 0.99 per epoch. All the networks were supervised by $L1$ Loss between the predicted and ground-truth 6-digit transformation parameters. All the frameworks were built using PyTorch [16] and trained/tested on an NVIDIA Quadro RTX 8000 graphic card with a batch size of 4.

2.5 Quantitative Evaluations

The averaged registration errors of translation (ΔT) and rotation (ΔR) were calculated as:

$$\Delta T = \left(\left\| \Delta \hat{t}_x - \Delta t_x \right\|_1 + \left\| \Delta \hat{t}_y - \Delta t_y \right\|_1 + \left\| \Delta \hat{t}_z - \Delta t_z \right\|_1 \right) / 3, \tag{12}$$

$$\Delta R = \left(\left\| \Delta \hat{\alpha}_x - \Delta \alpha_x \right\|_1 + \left\| \Delta \hat{\alpha}_y - \Delta \alpha_y \right\|_1 + \left\| \Delta \hat{\alpha}_z - \Delta \alpha_z \right\|_1 \right) / 3, \tag{13}$$

where $(\Delta \hat{t}_x, \Delta \hat{t}_y, \Delta \hat{t}_z, \Delta \hat{\alpha}_x, \Delta \hat{\alpha}_y, \Delta \hat{\alpha}_z)$ and $(\Delta t_x, \Delta t_y, \Delta t_z, \Delta \alpha_x, \Delta \alpha_y, \Delta \alpha_z)$ are predicted and ground-truth parameters. Voxel-wise errors of the registered μ-maps and reconstructed AC SPECT images were quantified using normalized mean squared error (NMSE) and normalized mean absolute error (NMAE). Paired t-tests were applied for statistical evaluations.

Table 1. Registration errors of translation (mm) and rotation (degrees), number of network parameters, training time per batch, and testing time per case. The best results are marked in **bold**.

Methods	ΔT (mm)	ΔR (degrees)	#Parameter	Train	Test
Baseline (Motion)	22.78 ± 7.68	8.12 ± 3.17	–	–	–
Mutual Information [15]	7.96 ± 5.10	2.80 ± 2.08	–	–	3–5 s
DVNet [21]	4.35 ± 2.11	1.29 ± 0.79	5,440,764	0.48s	<0.05 s
MSReg [9]	3.94 ± 1.84	1.16 ± 0.78	11,820,998	0.88s	<0.05 s
DenseNet [11]	3.88 ± 1.77	1.01 ± 0.57	11,215,590	1.08s	<0.05 s
DenseNet+Non-Local Attention [20]	3.81 ± 1.63	0.70 ± 0.42	11,419,846	1.19s	<0.05 s
DenseNet+DuSFE (Proposed)	$\mathbf{3.33 \pm 1.63}$	$\mathbf{0.61 \pm 0.45}$	11,726,397	1.25s	<0.05 s

3   Results

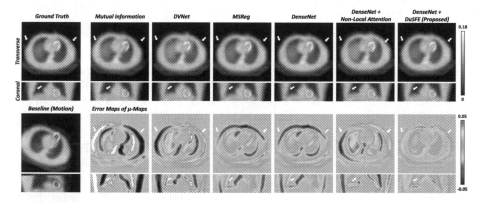

Fig. 3. Registered μ-maps (unit: cm^{-1}) with overlapped SPECT images using the generated transformation parameters.

As is shown in Table 1, all deep learning methods produced lower registration errors and shorter testing time than Mutual Information. Due to the shallow convolutional layers, DVNet output the lowest accuracy even though consumed fewer computational resources than other deep learning methods. DenseNet outperformed MSReg ($p[\Delta T] = 0.65$, $p[\Delta R] < 0.001$ with paired t-tests) since densely-connected layers can better extract input information. DenseNet+DuSFE significantly outperformed DenseNet ($p[\Delta T] < 0.001$, $p[\Delta R] < 0.001$) and DenseNet + Non-Local Attention ($p[\Delta T] < 0.001$, $p[\Delta R] < 0.001$). This demonstrated that our proposed DuSFE modules improved network performance and showed superior performance to the non-local attention module with nearly the same testing time and a minimal increase in computational cost.

Figure 3 shows sample registered μ-maps using the predicted registration parameters. Mutual Information showed the highest registration errors. DVNet

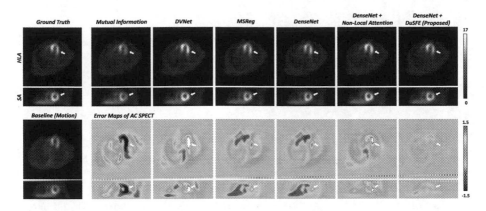

Fig. 4. Sample AC SPECT images reconstructed using the registered μ-maps. SPECT voxel values are the myocardial perfusion intensities after volume mean normalization.

produced the worst registrations among all deep learning methods. Our proposed DenseNet+DuSFE led to the best results with the lowest registration errors compared to other methods. Figure 4 shows sample AC SPECT images reconstructed using the registered μ-maps. Mutual Information showed the highest activity errors, and DVNet reconstructed the worst results among all deep learning methods. In contrast, our proposed DenseNet+DuSFE generated the most accurate AC SPECT image compared to other methods.

Table 2. Quantitative evaluations of registered μ-maps and reconstructed AC SPECT images in terms of NMSE and NMAE. The best results are marked in **bold**.

Methods	Registered μ-maps		Recon AC SPECT	
	NMSE(%)	NMAE(%)	NMSE(%)	NMAE(%)
Baseline (Motion)	35.81 ± 13.63	52.90 ± 14.23	23.34 ± 9.85	43.81 ± 10.85
Mutual Information [15]	8.59 ± 7.69	22.52 ± 10.54	3.67 ± 3.53	17.96 ± 8.44
DVNet [21]	2.94 ± 2.74	12.41 ± 6.12	1.21 ± 1.14	9.94 ± 4.82
MSReg [9]	2.46 ± 2.19	11.36 ± 5.35	0.99 ± 0.88	9.05 ± 4.13
DenseNet [11]	2.37 ± 2.10	11.14 ± 5.31	0.96 ± 0.84	8.89 ± 3.95
DenseNet+Non-Local Attention [20]	2.09 ± 1.79	10.55 ± 4.96	0.85 ± 0.70	8.43 ± 3.85
DenseNet+DuSFE (Proposed)	$\mathbf{1.79 \pm 1.65}$	$\mathbf{9.54 \pm 4.90}$	$\mathbf{0.75 \pm 0.70}$	$\mathbf{7.58 \pm 4.07}$

Table 2 evaluates the registered μ-maps and reconstructed AC SPECT images. Mutual Information output the highest errors. In comparison, our proposed DenseNet+DuSFE showed consistently the lowest errors in both μ-maps and SPECT images among all the methods. Compared to DenseNet+Non-Local Attention, DenseNet+DuSFE generated significantly lower errors in μ-maps ($p < 0.001$ for NMSE with paired t-tests) and AC SPECT ($p = 0.003$ for NMSE). It demonstrated that DuSFE modules enabled more accurate registration of

μ-maps and SPECT, which then improved the accuracy of AC SPECT images. Ablation studies investigating the contribution of each component of the DuSFE module are presented in our supplementary materials.

4   Conclusion

We propose a Dual-Branch Squeeze-Fusion-Excitation (DuSFE) module for the cross-modality registration of CT-derived μ-maps and cardiac SPECT images. This study is the first investigation of deep learning methods for the registration of cardiac SPECT/CT. DuSFE effectively fuses the knowledge from the two modalities and then recalibrates both the channel-wise and spatial features for each modality. DuSFE can be further embedded at different convolutional layers to enable gradual feature fusion at different spatial dimensions. In our experiments, a network embedded with DuSFE modules generated more consistent registration parameters with ground truth compared to other traditional and deep learning methods, which then enabled more accurate attenuation correction for cardiac SPECT.

References

1. Barbu, A., Ionasec, R.: Boosting cross-modality image registration. In: 2009 Joint Urban Remote Sensing Event, pp. 1–7. IEEE (2009)
2. Chen, X., Diaz-Pinto, A., Ravikumar, N., Frangi, A.F.: Deep learning in medical image registration. Prog. Biomed. Eng. **3**(1), 012003 (2021)
3. Chen, X., et al.: CT-free attenuation correction for dedicated cardiac SPECT using a 3D dual squeeze-and-excitation residual dense network. J. Nucl. Cardiol. 1–16 (2021)
4. Chen, X., et al.: Direct and indirect strategies of deep-learning-based attenuation correction for general purpose and dedicated cardiac SPECT. Eur. J. Nucl. Med. Mol. Imaging 1–15 (2022)
5. Danad, I., et al.: Comparison of coronary CT angiography, SPECT, PET, and hybrid imaging for diagnosis of ischemic heart disease determined by fractional flow reserve. JAMA Cardiol. **2**(10), 1100–1107 (2017)
6. Fricke, H., Fricke, E., Weise, R., Kammeier, A., Lindner, O., Burchert, W.: A method to remove artifacts in attenuation-corrected myocardial perfusion SPECT introduced by misalignment between emission scan and CT-derived attenuation maps. J. Nucl. Med. **45**(10), 1619–1625 (2004)
7. Gerlot-Chiron, P., Bizais, Y.: Registration of multimodality medical images using a region overlap criterion. CVGIP Graph. Models Image Process. **54**(5), 396–406 (1992)
8. Goetze, S., Wahl, R.L.: Prevalence of misregistration between SPECT and CT for attenuation-corrected myocardial perfusion SPECT. J. Nucl. Cardiol. **14**(2), 200–206 (2007)
9. Guo, H., Kruger, M., Xu, S., Wood, B.J., Yan, P.: Deep adaptive registration of multi-modal prostate images. Comput. Med. Imaging Graph. **84**, 101769 (2020)
10. Hu, J., Shen, L., Sun, G.: Squeeze-and-excitation networks. In: Proceedings of the IEEE Conference on Computer Vision and Pattern Recognition, pp. 7132–7141 (2018)

11. Huang, G., Liu, Z., Van Der Maaten, L., Weinberger, K.Q.: Densely connected convolutional networks. In: Proceedings of the IEEE Conference on Computer Vision and Pattern Recognition, pp. 4700–4708 (2017)
12. Joze, H.R.V., Shaban, A., Iuzzolino, M.L., Koishida, K.: MMTM: multimodal transfer module for CNN fusion. In: Proceedings of the IEEE/CVF Conference on Computer Vision and Pattern Recognition, pp. 13289–13299 (2020)
13. Kingma, D.P., Ba, J.: Adam: a method for stochastic optimization. arXiv preprint arXiv:1412.6980 (2014)
14. Liu, L., Aviles-Rivero, A.I., Schönlieb, C.B.: Contrastive registration for unsupervised medical image segmentation. arXiv preprint arXiv:2011.08894 (2020)
15. Maes, F., Collignon, A., Vandermeulen, D., Marchal, G., Suetens, P.: Multimodality image registration by maximization of mutual information. IEEE Trans. Med. Imaging **16**(2), 187–198 (1997)
16. Paszke, A., et al.: Pytorch: an imperative style, high-performance deep learning library. In: Advances in Neural Information Processing Systems, vol. 32 (2019)
17. Patchett, N., Pawar, S., Sverdlov, A., Miller, E.: Does improved technology in SPECT myocardial perfusion imaging reduce downstream costs? An observational study. Int. J. Radiol. Imaging Technol. **3**(1) (2017)
18. Roy, A.G., Navab, N., Wachinger, C.: Concurrent spatial and channel 'squeeze & excitation' in fully convolutional networks. In: Frangi, A.F., Schnabel, J.A., Davatzikos, C., Alberola-López, C., Fichtinger, G. (eds.) MICCAI 2018. LNCS, vol. 11070, pp. 421–429. Springer, Cham (2018). https://doi.org/10.1007/978-3-030-00928-1_48
19. Singh, B., Bateman, T.M., Case, J.A., Heller, G.: Attenuation artifact, attenuation correction, and the future of myocardial perfusion SPECT. J. Nucl. Cardiol. **14**(2), 153–164 (2007)
20. Song, X., et al.: Cross-modal attention for MRI and ultrasound volume registration. In: de Bruijne, M., et al. (eds.) MICCAI 2021. LNCS, vol. 12904, pp. 66–75. Springer, Cham (2021). https://doi.org/10.1007/978-3-030-87202-1_7
21. Sun, Y., Moelker, A., Niessen, W.J., van Walsum, T.: Towards robust CT-ultrasound registration using deep learning methods. In: Stoyanov, D., et al. (eds.) MLCN/DLF/IMIMIC -2018. LNCS, vol. 11038, pp. 43–51. Springer, Cham (2018). https://doi.org/10.1007/978-3-030-02628-8_5
22. Tavakoli, M., Naij, M.: Quantitative evaluation of the effect of attenuation correction in SPECT images with CT-derived attenuation. In: Medical Imaging 2019: Physics of Medical Imaging, vol. 10948, p. 109485U. International Society for Optics and Photonics (2019)
23. Wang, X., Girshick, R., Gupta, A., He, K.: Non-local neural networks. In: Proceedings of the IEEE Conference on Computer Vision and Pattern Recognition, pp. 7794–7803 (2018)
24. Xie, S., Girshick, R., Dollár, P., Tu, Z., He, K.: Aggregated residual transformations for deep neural networks. In: Proceedings of the IEEE Conference on Computer Vision and Pattern Recognition, pp. 1492–1500 (2017)
25. Xu, Z., et al.: Adversarial uni- and multi-modal stream networks for multimodal image registration. In: Martel, A.L., et al. (eds.) MICCAI 2020. LNCS, vol. 12263, pp. 222–232. Springer, Cham (2020). https://doi.org/10.1007/978-3-030-59716-0_22

Embedding Gradient-Based Optimization in Image Registration Networks

Huaqi Qiu[1]([✉]), Kerstin Hammernik[1,2], Chen Qin[1,3], Chen Chen[1],
and Daniel Rueckert[1,2]

[1] BioMedIA Group, Imperial College London, London, UK
huaqi.qiu15@imperial.ac.uk
[2] Klinikum rechts der Isar, Technical University of Munich, Munich, Germany
[3] Institute for Digital Communications, University of Edinburgh, Edinburgh, UK

Abstract. Deep learning (DL) image registration methods amortize the costly pair-wise iterative optimization by training deep neural networks to predict the optimal transformation in one fast forward-pass. In this work, we bridge the gap between traditional iterative energy optimization-based registration and network-based registration, and propose Gradient Descent Network for Image Registration (GraDIRN). Our proposed approach trains a DL network that embeds unrolled multi-resolution gradient-based energy optimization in its forward pass, which explicitly enforces image dissimilarity minimization in its update steps. Extensive evaluations were performed on registration tasks using 2D cardiac MR and 3D brain MR images. We demonstrate that our approach achieved state-of-the-art registration performance while using fewer learned parameters, with good data efficiency and domain robustness.

Keywords: Medical image registration · Deep learning · Unrolled optimization network

1 Introduction

Image registration aims to find the spatial transformation between corresponding anatomical or functional locations in different images. In medical imaging, image registration is one of the most fundamental tasks in image fusion, surgical intervention, motion analysis [3] and disease progression analysis [11]. Many traditional registration methods find the transformation for each pair of images by minimizing an energy function using iterative optimization [24], often over multiple resolutions. The energy function usually consists of an image dissimilarity term, which enforces the alignment between the images, and a regularization term which imposes constraints on the transformation such as smoothness and invertibility. However, traditional iterative optimization is computationally demanding, especially for 3D images and high-dimensional transformations.

Supplementary Information The online version contains supplementary material available at https://doi.org/10.1007/978-3-031-16446-0_6.

More recently, data-driven methods perform image-to-transformation mapping in one step using deep neural networks, which substantially speed up registration. Early *supervised* methods [23,28] rely on ground truth transformation (parameters) as supervision. To avoid dependency on ground truth transformation, *self-supervised* approaches [2,18,26] rely on dissimilarity metrics based on image intensities or semantic segmentation [2,10,16]. Recent advances extend the one-step approach of regressing the transformation by refining the transformation over multiple resolutions and/or multiple steps [9,17,18,22,29] analogous to traditional registration. However, these methods only enforce image dissimilarity minimization in the final training loss but not in the network forward pass steps.

Meanwhile, several methods in solving inverse problems such as image reconstruction and image de-noising [5,7,8,14] propose networks that unroll iterative optimization algorithms for a fixed number of iterations. These networks use learned regularization steps while explicitly enforcing data-consistency in their forward pass iterations and achieved state-of-the-art results. Inspired by these approaches, we propose a novel DL registration method which embeds an unrolled multi-resolution gradient descent in the registration network, as shown in Fig. 1. Concretely, the transformation update steps in our approach make use of adaptive image dissimilarity gradient to explicitly enforce image dissimilarity minimization, while using generalized regularization update steps learned from training data. Our main contributions in this work are as follows:

1. We introduce Gradient Descent Network for Image Registration (GraDIRN) which connects traditional iterative energy optimization and modern network-based registration by embedding an unrolled multi-resolution gradient descent in the registration network;
2. We extensively evaluate the efficacy of our proposed method which demonstrates state-of-the-art registration performance for both 2D intra-subject cardiac MR and 3D inter-subject brain MR registration tasks while being efficient in the number of learned parameters;
3. We perform further evaluations under data scarce and domain shift settings, and demonstrate that the proposed method can be trained effectively with limited data while being robust to domain shift.

Related Works. A few learning-based registration methods explored multi-step and multi-resolution iterative refinement of transformations [9,17,18,27,29] to improve registration accuracy and handling of large deformations. These approaches essentially learn to regress the transformation via multiple network predictions via the training loss, but explicit image alignment is not enforced in these multiple steps. Metric learning was proposed in [19], which uses a CNN to learn a constrained multi-Gaussian local smoothing regularization applied on vector momentum stationary velocity field. In contrast, our proposed network learns the gradient update steps of the optimization instead of applying the learned regularization on the transformation. Hence, our method can be formulated with any transformation model and trained with standard deep learning training methods and does not require customized optimizers. The variational registration network of [12] uses linearized brightness consistency in learning an auxiliary-variable optimization, which limits the use of arbitrary metrics and transformation models. In contrast, our proposed method uses gradient descent optimization, which is easier to extend to other image dissimilarity metrics and transformation models, especially through our implementation using auto-differentiation (see Sect. 2). In addition, unlike [12], we use multi-resolution optimization with parameter-efficient networks, achieving competitive registration performance without ad-hoc learning of initialization.

2 Method

Our proposed image registration framework can be encapsulated in a bi-level optimization view, which is illustrated in Fig. 1. The two levels of optimization are formulated as:

$$\min_{\theta} \mathbb{E}_{(I_m, I_f) \sim D}[\mathcal{L}(I_m, I_f, \phi^*(\theta))] \tag{1a}$$

$$\text{s.t. } \phi^*(\theta) \in \arg\min_{\phi} E(I_m, I_f, \phi). \tag{1b}$$

The lower-level optimization in Eq. (1b) finds the optimal transformation ϕ^* to align a given pair of moving image I_m and fixed image I_f by minimizing the energy functional E. We embed this optimization in the registration network by making the iterative steps that performs this optimization the forward pass of the network, which has trainable parameters θ (detailed in Sect. 2). Given the solution ϕ^* for each pair of images in the training dataset D, the higher-level optimization in Eq. (1a) finds the global optimal parameters for the network by minimizing the expectation of the loss function $\mathcal{L}(I_m, I_f, \phi^*(\theta))$ (detailed in Sect. 2).

Lower-Level Optimization (Forward Pass). To register a pair of images, the proposed network takes the image pair (I_m, I_f) as input and predicts the transformation ϕ^*, which is similar to existing registration networks (e.g. [2]). However, the structure of our network is designed to solve the lower-level optimization problem which is the energy minimization in Eq. (1b). The energy functional typically is of the form:

$$E(I_m, I_f, \phi) = \mathcal{D}(\mathcal{T}(I_m, \phi), I_f) + \alpha \mathcal{R}(\phi). \tag{2}$$

which contains an image dissimilarity $\mathcal{D}$ measured between the transformed moving image $\mathcal{T}(I_m, \phi)$ and the fixed image I_f, and a regularization term $\mathcal{R}$. The proposed network unrolls the energy functional minimization using a gradient descent-based optimization with fixed number of update steps. An update step to ϕ_t at step t given by:

$$\phi_{t+1} = \phi_t - \tau_t(\nabla\mathcal{D}(\mathcal{T}(I_m, \phi_t), I_f), +\nabla\mathcal{R}_{\theta_t}(\phi_t; I_m, I_f)), \tag{3}$$

where τ_t is the adaptive step sizes, $\nabla\mathcal{D}$ is the image dissimilarity gradient and $\nabla\mathcal{R}_{\theta_t}$ is the trainable generalized regularization gradient functional, w.r.t. to the transformation ϕ. This yields the network structure illustrated in Fig. 1 with details explained in the following sections.

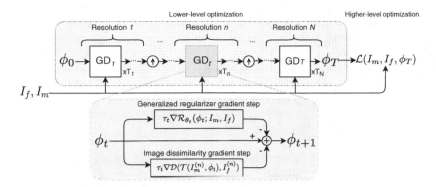

Fig. 1. The proposed method under the bi-level optimization view. The lower-level optimization, shown in the gray box, is a multi-resolution optimization using explicit image dissimilarity gradient steps and CNN-parameterized generalized regularizer steps. The blue block shows the inner structure of one gradient descent (GD) step. The higher-level optimization learns the parameters of the lower-level optimization by minimizing a loss function $\mathcal{L}$.

Image Dissimilarity Gradient. Instead of only enforcing image alignment in the loss function as most existing DL network-based methods, we explicitly enforce image dissimilarity minimization in our network forward pass. The image dissimilarity gradient w.r.t. the transformation, $\nabla\mathcal{D}$, is directly applied in each update step. The forward computation of this gradient needs to be differentiable to allow back-propagation. To implement this, we leverage the power of modern auto-differentiation engines [20] to create the forward computation graph of $\nabla\mathcal{D}$ automatically. This enables us to use arbitrary dissimilarity metrics such as sum of squared-difference (SSD) or normalized cross-correlation (NCC), as well as other transformation models.

Learned Regularizer Gradient. For the regularizer gradient steps, we take inspiration from previous works [5,8] and use a CNN to incorporate rich image information and learn more complex local regularization from training data. At each step t, the CNN takes the current solution ϕ_t and the image pair (I_m, I_f) as input, and outputs the gradient step corresponding to $\nabla\mathcal{R}_{\theta_t}$ in Eq. (3). We hypothesize that the use of explicit image dissimilarity gradient enables us to use more parameter-efficient networks in learning the *regularizer* steps and optimal registration. So we use a simple 5-layer CNN with 32 channels per layer, kernel size of 3 and LeakyReLU activation function. The formulation of our method is not limited to any specific network architecture.

Multi-resolution Optimization. The transformation is optimized over multiple resolutions to efficiently capture both local deformation and global deformation. We initialize ϕ_0 with identity transformation and update the transformation in a coarse-to-fine fashion. For resolution n, the transformation is updated T_n times then upsampled to a higher resolution. We simply use a dense displacement field as the transformation model thus use linear interpolation for upsampling to achieve continuous optimization between resolutions. The final solution is $\phi^* = \phi_T$ where $T = \sum_{n=1,2,...N} T_n$. We share the parameters of the CNNs within each resolution which, together with the adaptive step sizes, are the learnable parameters $\theta = \{\theta_t, \tau_t\}_{t=1,2,...T}$ that need to be determined by the high-level optimization.

Higher-Level Optimization (Training). The learnable parameters θ in the lower-level optimization are learned in the higher-level optimization. This is achieved by minimizing the expected loss $\mathcal{L}$ over a training dataset X:

$$\mathcal{L}(I_m, I_f, \phi^*(\theta)) = \mathcal{L}_{\mathcal{D}}(\mathcal{T}(I_m, \phi^*(\theta)), I_f) + \lambda \mathcal{L}_{\mathcal{R}}(\phi^*(\theta)). \tag{4}$$

given the solution $\phi^*(\theta)$ from the lower-level optimization. $\mathcal{L}_{\mathcal{D}}$ is a *self-supervised* loss using image dissimilarity, which is in the same mathematical form as the image dissimilarity term $\mathcal{D}$ in the energy function of the lower-level optimization for each training sample. The regularization loss we used is a standard diffusion penalty on the spatial variations of the transformation, namely $\mathcal{L}_{\mathcal{R}} = \frac{1}{|\Omega|} \sum_{\mathbf{x} \in \Omega} \|\nabla \phi(\mathbf{x})\|_2^2$, with $\mathbf{x}$ denoting a point in the spatial domain Ω. We use stochastic gradient-based optimization for the higher-level optimization using gradient of the loss function computed w.r.t. the learned parameters θ (not w.r.t. the transformation in Eq. (3)). Since the lower-level optimization is unrolled into the forward pass of the network, the higher-level optimization is simply a standard deep learning training without the need for customized optimizers.

3   Experiments

Tasks and Datasets. We extensively evaluate registration performance on: 1) 2D intra-subject cardiac MRI registration between the end-diastolic (ED) frame and end-systolic (ES) frame; 2) 3D inter-subject brain MRI registration. We use 220 cardiac cine-MR sequences from the publicly accessible UK Biobank (UKBB) study[1], with 100, 20 and 100 sequences used for training, validation and testing. We acquired semantic segmentation of the left ventricle cavity (LV), myocardium (Myo) and right ventricle cavity (RV) using a CNN-based segmentation model [1] for evaluation purposes. In addition, cardiac MRI of 150 subjects from the multi-vendor multi-center M&Ms dataset [4] were used to evaluate domain generalization, with 75 subjects from each MR scanner vendor. For the 3D brain MRI registration, we used T1-weighted MR images from the CamCAN open data inventory [25] which consist of structural brain MR scans of subjects aged between 18 and 90. The large structural variations in the dataset is challenging for inter-subject registration. We randomly select 200/10/100 scans for training/validation/testing. All scans are spatially aligned to a common MNI space via affine registration, skull-stripped using ROBEX, bias-field corrected using

---

[1] http://imaging.ukbiobank.ac.uk.

Table 1. Evaluation results on the UKBB and CamCAN dataset reported in mean (standard deviation). The number of learnable parameters in the models are indicated by "#params". The best results in each column are in bold, * marks results not significantly different with the best results (*p*-value > 0.001, one-sided Wilcoxon signed-rank test). Runtimes (CPU/GPU) are reported in seconds except 2D GPU in ms.

Dataset	Method	Dice↑	HD↓	$|J| < 0\%$ ↓	std(log($|J|$)) ↓	Runtime	#params
UKBB (2D)	Initial	0.500(0.058)	16.091(2.625)	n/a	n/a	n/a	n/a
	FFD	0.788(0.061)	10.970(3.006)	0.327(0.165)	1.093(0.317)	1.534/-	n/a
	VM	0.805(0.053)	10.243(2.725)	0.239(0.095)	0.976(0.208)	0.011/2.796	106K
	RC-VM	0.820(0.052)*	9.900(2.636)	0.212(0.079)	0.923(0.181)	0.101/59.502	954K
	GraDIRN	**0.821(0.052)**	**9.729(2.531)**	**0.188(0.076)**	**0.866(0.182)**	0.075/59.502	88.5K
CamCAN (3D)	Initial	0.621(0.043)	6.354(0.959)	n/a	n/a	n/a	n/a
	FFD	0.797(0.022)*	**5.113(0.934)**	0.084(0.060)	0.639(0.172)	16.435/-	n/a
	VM	0.780(0.026)	5.391(0.961)	0.060(0.050)	0.533(0.165)	0.858/0.003	320K
	RC-VM	0.794(0.022)	5.179(0.903)*	**0.047(0.041)**	**0.478(0.147)**	9.673/0.416	2883K
	GraDIRN	**0.799(0.022)**	5.147(0.857)*	0.056(0.050)	0.514(0.164)	4.589/0.220	269K

the N4 algorithm in SimpleITK. Segmentation of 138 cortical and sub-cortical structures was acquired using a multi-atlas segmentation tool MALPEM [15] for evaluation.

Evaluation Metrics. To comprehensively evaluate registration performances, we measure both the accuracy and the regularity of the transformation. In-lieu of ground truth transformation, we follow [2] and measure registration accuracy based on the agreement of anatomical structures between the registered images using Dice score and Hausdorff Distance (HD). To evaluate the regularity of the transformations, we calculate the determinant of the Jacobian of the transformation $|J| = |\nabla\phi|$, and measure local folding indicated by negative $|J|$ (reported in percentage denoted by $|J| < 0\%$) and spatial smoothness by std(log $|J|$).

Baselines and Implementation. We first compare the proposed method to a traditional iteratively multi-resolution registration method which uses B-spline free-form deformation (FFD) and an energy functional consisting of an image dissimilarity metric and Bending Energy regularization [21]. We use the implementation in Medical Image Registration ToolKit (MIRTK) with three resolution levels and the same image dissimilarity metric as our method. We also compare our proposed method to two deep learning based registration methods. One is the widely used VoxelMorph framework [2] (VM). The other is a recursive-cascaded method introduced in [29] (RC-VM) as a representative baseline for network-only (no explicit image matching) iterative DL registration, using VM as the base network for the cascade. We use 9 iterations ($T_N = 9$) in our method (GraDIRN) with 3 resolutions and 3 iterations per resolution ($T_n = 3$). The number of cascades on RC-VM is set to be the same. The DL baselines are trained using the same loss function as the ones used in the higher-level optimization of the proposed method.

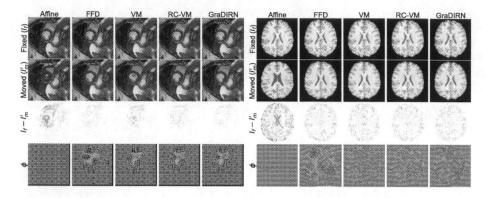

Fig. 2. Examples of cardiac MR and brain MR registration results. A mid-ventricle slice is shown for the cardiac registration results and an axial view is shown for the brain registration results. The first row shows the fixed image I_f (same for all methods), the second row shows the moving image transformed by the estimated transformation, the third row shows the relative intensity difference after registration, with the transformation shown in the final row.

All hyper-parameters are carefully tuned using the validation data set. Adam [13] optimizer is used for training, with $\beta_1 = 0.9$, $\beta_2 = 0.999$ and learning rate of 10^{-4}. Our code is available at: https://github.com/gradirn/gradirn.

Results and Discussion. Table 1 shows the results of quantitative evaluation of all the competing methods using NCC as the dissimilarity metric. On the 2D cardiac MR intra-subject registration task, the proposed method (GraDIRN) significantly outperforms FFD and VM, comparable with RC-VM on Dice score but better on HD. On the 3D brain MR registration task, the proposed method results in higher Dice than the learning-based baselines and comparable performance as FFD, which is computationally much slower. The learning-based iterative approach RC-VM significantly improves VM on both registration tasks but uses networks with 10× larger capacity. In contrast, our proposed method is able to match the performance of RC-VM with even less learned parameters than VM. Boxplots showing the Dice score for different anatomical structures can be found in the supplementary material. Visual examples of the registration results are shown in Fig. 2. We isolated and studied the effectiveness of the proposed use of the explicit dissimilarity gradient through ablation studies shown in Table 2. It can be seen that the recursive cascade mechanism and GraDIRN only with CNN updates perform inferior to GraDIRN with the dissimilarity gradient updates.

Table 2. Ablation study results (using SSD for image dissimilarity). † indicates no image dissimilarity gradient. RC-CNN[5] is a variant of RC-VM using the same 5-layer CNN in our GraDIRN as base network, where * indicate sharing every 3 cascades to match the number of parameters as GraDIRN.

Settings	Dice	HD	$|J| < 0\%$	$std(\log(|J|))$	#params
RC-CNN[5]	0.778 (0.054)	10.967 (2.721)	0.127 (0.064)	0.695 (0.191	265K
RC-CNN[5*]	0.774 (0.054)	11.075 (2.674)	0.129 (0.059)	0.704 (0.180)	88.5K
GraDIRN†	0.799 (0.052)	10.481 (2.738)	0.082 (0.050)	0.547 (0.182)	88.5K
GraDIRN	0.818 (0.053)	9.943 (2.766)	0.073 (0.041)	0.510 (0.163)	88.5K

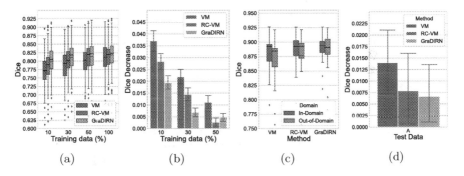

(a)   (b)   (c)   (d)

Fig. 3. *Data Efficiency:* Fig. 3a and 3b show the performance and performance decrease of competing methods trained with limited data; *Domain Robustness:* Fig. 3c and 3d show the performance and performance difference of models tested on M&Ms vendor A data but trained on vendor B (out-of-domain), compared to models trained on vendor A (in-domain).

Data Efficiency. We evaluate how the performance of competing method are affected when less training data is available. We trained all models with 10%, 30% and 50% of the original UK biobank training dataset, and tested on the original testing dataset. The results, shown in Fig. 3a and 3b, demonstrate that the proposed method can be more effectively trained with less data. With as little as 10% of the original training data, our method can still achieve superior accuracy over the non-learning FFD.

Domain Robustness. Learning-based registration methods are affected by domain shift between training and testing data but is rarely studied [6]. Therefore, we evaluate the *domain robustness* of the learning-based methods using cardiac MR data from different vendors in the M&Ms dataset [4]. Fig. 3c and 3d show the results of each model trained using the data from vendor B (Philips, in-domain) and tested on data from vendor A (Siemens, out-of-domain), which is a challenging cross-domain setting as reported in [4], compared to the same model trained using data from vendor A as reference. The proposed method shows better domain robustness, especially compared to VM, indicated by less Dice score drop and variation caused by domain shift.

4   Conclusion

In this paper, we present a novel learning-based registration network for deformable image registration which learns an unrolled multi-resolution gradient-based optimization with explicit image dissimilarity minimization embedded in the network forward pass. Extensive evaluations show that our approach obtains state-of-the-art registration performance while retaining parameter efficiency, data efficiency and domain robustness. By using gradient-based optimization and auto-differentiation, our framework can easily incorporate arbitrary differentiable image dissimilarity metrics and transformation models with existing forward-pass implementation.

Acknowledgments. This work was supported by the EPSRC Programme Grant EP/P001009/1.

References

1. Bai, W., et al.: Automated cardiovascular magnetic resonance image analysis with fully convolutional networks. J. Cardiovasc. Magn. Reson. **20**(1), 65 (2018)
2. Balakrishnan, G., Zhao, A., Sabuncu, M.R., Guttag, J.V., Dalca, A.V.: Voxelmorph: a learning framework for deformable medical image registration. IEEE Trans. Med. Imaging **38**(8), 1788–1800 (2019)
3. Bello, G.A., et al.: Deep learning cardiac motion analysis for human survival prediction. Nat. Mach. Intell. **1**(2), 95–104 (2019)
4. Campello, V.M., et al.: Multi-centre, multi-vendor and multi-disease cardiac segmentation: the M&MS challenge. IEEE Trans. Med. Imaging **40**(12), 3543–3554 (2021)
5. Chen, Y., Pock, T.: Trainable nonlinear reaction diffusion: a flexible framework for fast and effective image restoration. IEEE Trans. Pattern Anal. Mach. Intell. **39**(6), 1256–1272 (2017)
6. Ferrante, E., Oktay, O., Glocker, B., Milone, D.H.: On the adaptability of unsupervised CNN-based deformable image registration to unseen image domains. In: Shi, Y., Suk, H.-I., Liu, M. (eds.) MLMI 2018. LNCS, vol. 11046, pp. 294–302. Springer, Cham (2018). https://doi.org/10.1007/978-3-030-00919-9_34
7. Gilton, D., Ongie, G., Willett, R.: Neumann networks for linear inverse problems in imaging. IEEE Trans. Comput. Imaging **6**, 328–343 (2020)
8. Hammernik, K., et al.: Learning a variational network for reconstruction of accelerated MRI data. CoRR abs/1704.00447 (2017)
9. Hering, A., van Ginneken, B., Heldmann, S.: mlVIRNET: multilevel variational image registration network. In: Shen, D., et al. (eds.) MICCAI 2019. LNCS, vol. 11769, pp. 257–265. Springer, Cham (2019). https://doi.org/10.1007/978-3-030-32226-7_29
10. Hu, Y., et al.: Weakly-supervised convolutional neural networks for multimodal image registration. Med. Image Anal. **49**, 1–13 (2018)
11. Hua, X., et al.: Tensor-based morphometry as a neuroimaging biomarker for Alzheimer's disease: an MRI study of 676 ad, mci, and normal subjects. NeuroImage **43**(3), 458–469 (2008)

12. Jia, X., et al.: Learning a model-driven variational network for deformable image registration. IEEE Trans. Med. Imaging **41**(1), 199–212 (2021)
13. Kingma, D.P., Ba, J.: Adam: a method for stochastic optimization. In: ICLR (Poster) (2015)
14. Kobler, E., Klatzer, T., Hammernik, K., Pock, T.: Variational networks: connecting variational methods and deep learning. In: Roth, V., Vetter, T. (eds.) GCPR 2017. LNCS, vol. 10496, pp. 281–293. Springer, Cham (2017). https://doi.org/10.1007/978-3-319-66709-6_23
15. Ledig, C., et al.: Robust whole-brain segmentation: application to traumatic brain injury. Med. Image Anal. **21**(1), 40–58 (2015)
16. Lee, M.C.H., Oktay, O., Schuh, A., Schaap, M., Glocker, B.: Image-and-spatial transformer networks for structure-guided image registration. In: Shen, D., et al. (eds.) MICCAI 2019. LNCS, vol. 11765, pp. 337–345. Springer, Cham (2019). https://doi.org/10.1007/978-3-030-32245-8_38
17. Liu, R., Li, Z., Fan, X., Zhao, C., Huang, H., Luo, Z.: Learning deformable image registration from optimization: perspective, modules, bilevel training and beyond. IEEE Trans. Pattern Anal. Mach. Intell. (2021)
18. Mok, T.C.W., Chung, A.C.S.: Fast symmetric diffeomorphic image registration with convolutional neural networks. In: CVPR, pp. 4643–4652. Computer Vision Foundation/IEEE (2020)
19. Niethammer, M., Kwitt, R., Vialard, F.: Metric learning for image registration. In: CVPR, pp. 8463–8472. Computer Vision Foundation/IEEE (2019)
20. Paszke, A., et al.: Pytorch: an imperative style, high-performance deep learning library. In: NeurIPS, pp. 8024–8035 (2019)
21. Rueckert, D., Sonoda, L.I., Hayes, C., Hill, D.L.G., Leach, M.O., Hawkes, D.J.: Non-rigid registration using free-form deformations: application to breast MR images. IEEE Trans. Med. Imaging **18**(8), 712–721 (1999)
22. Sandkühler, R., Andermatt, S., Bauman, G., Nyilas, S., Jud, C., Cattin, P.C.: Recurrent registration neural networks for deformable image registration. In: NeurIPS, pp. 8755–8765 (2019)
23. Sokooti, H., de Vos, B., Berendsen, F., Lelieveldt, B.P.F., Išgum, I., Staring, M.: Nonrigid image registration using multi-scale 3D convolutional neural networks. In: Descoteaux, M., Maier-Hein, L., Franz, A., Jannin, P., Collins, D.L., Duchesne, S. (eds.) MICCAI 2017. LNCS, vol. 10433, pp. 232–239. Springer, Cham (2017). https://doi.org/10.1007/978-3-319-66182-7_27
24. Sotiras, A., Davatzikos, C., Paragios, N.: Deformable medical image registration: a survey. IEEE Trans. Med. Imaging **32**(7), 1153–1190 (2013)
25. Taylor, J.R., et al.: The Cambridge centre for ageing and neuroscience (Cam-CAN) data repository: structural and functional MRI, MEG, and cognitive data from a cross-sectional adult lifespan sample. Neuroimage **144**, 262–269 (2017)
26. de Vos, B.D., Berendsen, F.F., Viergever, M.A., Sokooti, H., Staring, M., Isgum, I.: A deep learning framework for unsupervised affine and deformable image registration. Med. Image Anal. **52**, 128–143 (2019)
27. Xu, J., Chen, E.Z., Chen, X., Chen, T., Sun, S.: Multi-scale neural ODEs for 3D medical image registration. In: de Bruijne, M., et al. (eds.) MICCAI 2021. LNCS, vol. 12904, pp. 213–223. Springer, Cham (2021). https://doi.org/10.1007/978-3-030-87202-1_21
28. Yang, X., Kwitt, R., Styner, M., Niethammer, M.: Quicksilver: fast predictive image registration - a deep learning approach. Neuroimage **158**, 378–396 (2017)
29. Zhao, S., Dong, Y., Chang, E.I., Xu, Y.: Recursive cascaded networks for unsupervised medical image registration. In: ICCV, pp. 10599–10609. IEEE (2019)

ContraReg: Contrastive Learning of Multi-modality Unsupervised Deformable Image Registration

Neel Dey[1]([✉]), Jo Schlemper[2], Seyed Sadegh Mohseni Salehi[2], Bo Zhou[3], Guido Gerig[1], and Michal Sofka[2]

[1] Department of Computer Science and Engineering, New York University, Brooklyn, NY, USA
neel.dey@nyu.edu
[2] Hyperfine Research, Guilford, CT, USA
[3] Department of Biomedical Engineering, Yale University, New Haven, CT, USA

Abstract. Establishing voxelwise semantic correspondence across distinct imaging modalities is a foundational yet formidable computer vision task. Current multi-modality registration techniques maximize hand-crafted inter-domain similarity functions, are limited in modeling nonlinear intensity-relationships and deformations, and may require significant re-engineering or underperform on new tasks, datasets, and domain pairs. This work presents ContraReg, an unsupervised contrastive representation learning approach to multi-modality deformable registration. By projecting learned multi-scale local patch features onto a jointly learned inter-domain embedding space, ContraReg obtains representations useful for non-rigid multi-modality alignment. Experimentally, ContraReg achieves accurate and robust results with smooth and invertible deformations across a series of baselines and ablations on a neonatal T1-T2 brain MRI registration task with all methods validated over a wide range of deformation regularization strengths.

1 Introduction

The spatial alignment (or *registration*) of images from sources capturing distinct anatomical characteristics enables well-informed biomedical decision-making via multi-modality information integration. For example, multi-modality registration of intra-operative to pre-operative imaging is crucial to various surgical procedures [13,24,33]. Consequently, several inter-domain image similarity functions have been developed to drive iterative or learning-based registration [11,14,38]. Yet, despite the decades-long development of multi-modality objectives, accurate deformable registration of images with highly nonlinear relationships between their appearance and shapes remains difficult.

Supplementary Information The online version contains supplementary material available at https://doi.org/10.1007/978-3-031-16446-0_7.

L. Wang et al. (Eds.): MICCAI 2022, LNCS 13436, pp. 66–77, 2022.
https://doi.org/10.1007/978-3-031-16446-0_7

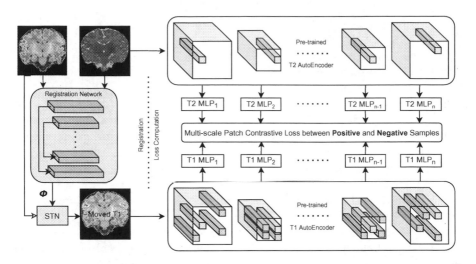

Fig. 1. ContraReg. Given displacements and a moved image from a multi-modality registration network (**left**), a contrastive loss is calculated on multi-scale patches extracted from modality-specific networks (**right**), such that corresponding locations have high mutual information. In practice, our implementation is bidirectional s.t. the inverse modality-pair loss is also computed.

Losses operating on intensity features (global and local 1D histograms [8, 34,38], local descriptors [14,37,39], edge-maps [11], among others) are typically hand-crafted and do not consistently generalize outside of the domain-pair they were originally proposed for and necessitate non-trivial domain expertise to tune towards optimal results. More recent multi-modality methods based on *learned* appearance similarity [28], simulation-driven semantic similarity [15], and image translation [29] have demonstrated strong registration performance but may only apply to supervised affine registration [28], require population-specific segmentation labels for optimal registration [15], or necessitate extensive and delicate GAN-based training frameworks [29].

To overcome these limitations, this work develops `ContraReg` (CR), an unsupervised representation learning framework for non-rigid multi-modality registration. CR requires that, once registered, corresponding positions and patches in the moved and fixed images have *high mutual information* in a jointly-learned multi-scale multi-modality embedding space. These characteristics are achieved via self-supervised contrastive training and only requires an unsupervised feature extractor (which can be pretrained or randomly-initialized and frozen). As a result, on the challenging task of neonatal inter-subject T1w-T2w diffeomorphic MRI registration, CR achieves higher anatomical overlap with comparable deformation characteristics to previous similarity metrics, validated over a wide range of regularization parameters. Finally, for experimental completeness, we then evaluate CR across a diversity of auxiliary losses and external negative sample selection and pretraining strategies.

2   Related Work

Hand-Crafted Similarity Losses. Mutual information and its variants [19,38] typically operate on image intensity histograms and may be limited in their ability to model complex non-rigid deformations. Conversely, local mutual information methods [8,34] are spatially-aware but may not have enough samples to build accurate patch intensity histograms. Other losses operating on intensity-derived local descriptors [14,39] or edges [11,37] learn domain-invariant features and have been successful in tasks such as body cavity MR-CT registration with relatively limited adoption in neuroimaging.

Simulation. Registration via translation approaches seek to simulate one modality from the other, such that the problem can be reduced to a mono-modality alignment [1,29,40]. While performant, recent methods can be susceptible to the hallucinatory or instability drawbacks of medical image translation leading to suboptimal alignment [20,31]. Recently, SynthMorph [15] simulates both deformations and synthetic appearances for neuroimages to train a general-purpose multi-modality network. `ContraReg` instead obtains highly accurate warps for a given dataset at the cost of dataset-specific training.

Learned Similarity Losses. Finally, several methods attempt to learn an inter-domain similarity metric via supervised learning with pre-aligned training images [9,18,28,36]. For example, CoMIR [28] uses supervised contrastive learning to learn affine registration between highly visually disparate modalities. In particular, `ContraReg` draws inspiration from PatchNCE [26], an image translation framework using contrastive losses on multi-scale patches. However, a straightforward extension of PatchNCE to registration is not possible and would lead to degenerate identity solutions to the PatchNCE loss as we require a warp between two distinct input images [17]. This work presents a different approach to incorporating multi-scale patches via *externally-trained* feature extractors which enables successful registration without degenerate solutions.

3   Methods

Figure 1 illustrates `ContraReg`. Architectural details are in the supplementary material.

Unsupervised Pre-training. To extract multi-scale n-dimensional features in an unsupervised manner, we first train modality-specific autoencoders A_1 and A_2 as domain-specific features can be beneficial to patchwise contrastive training [12]. Training is done on 128^3 crops with random flipping and brightness/contrast/saturation augmentation, using an $\mathcal{L}_1$ + Local NCC (window width = 7 voxels) reconstruction loss [2].

Registration Training. This work focuses on unsupervised learning of registration and multi-modality similarity. Given cross-modality volumes I_1 and I_2, a

VoxelMorph-style [5] U-Net with constant channel width (ch) predicts a stationary velocity field v, which when numerically integrated with ts time steps, yields an approximately diffeomorphic displacement ϕ. We focus on bidirectional registration and obtain the inverse warp via integrating $-v$. This network is trained with a $(1 - \lambda)\mathcal{L}_{sim} + \lambda\mathcal{L}_{reg}$ objective where $\mathcal{L}_{reg} = \|v\|_2^2$ is a regularizer controlling velocity (and indirectly displacement) field smoothness, $\mathcal{L}_{sim} = \frac{1}{2}(d_{12}(I_1\|I_2 \circ \phi) + d_{21}(I_2\|I_1 \circ \phi^{-1}))$ is a registration term s.t. $d_{12,\,21}$ measures inter-domain similarity, and λ is a hyperparameter.

Here, we define d_{12} and d_{21} is defined analogously. We first extract multi-scale spatial features $A_1^k(I_1)$ and $A_2^k(I_2 \circ \phi)$ using the autoencoders, where $k = 1, ..., L$ is the layer index and L is the number of layers. A perceptual registration loss [4] is inappropriate in this setting as these features correspond to different modality-specific spaces. Instead, we maximize a lower bound on mutual information between corresponding spatial locations in $A_1^k(I_1)$ and $A_2^k(I_2 \circ \phi)$ by minimizing a noise contrastive estimation loss [25]. As in [26], we project the channel-wise autoencoder features of size $\mathbb{R}^{N^k \times C^k}$ (where N^k is the number of spatial indices and C^k is the number of channels in layer k) onto a hyperspherical representation space to obtain features $F_1^k(A_1^k(I_1))$ and $F_2^k(A_2^k(I_2 \circ \phi))$ where $F_{1,2}$ are 3-layer 256-wide trainable ReLU-MLPs [3]. In this space, indices in correspondence $f_i^k = F_1^k((A_1^k(I_1))_i)$ and $f_i^{k+} = F_2^k((A_2^k(I_2 \circ \phi))_i)$, where $i = 1, ..., N^k$, are positive pairs. Similarly, f_i^k and $f_j^{k-} = F_2^k((A_2^k(I_2 \circ \phi))_j)$, where $j = 1, ..., N^k$ and $j \neq i$, are negative pairs.

For optimal contrastive learning, we sample a single positive pair and $ns \gg 1$ negative samples, and use the following loss with τ as a temperature hyperparameter:

$$d_{12}(I_1\|I_2 \circ \phi) = \sum_{k=1}^{L} \sum_{i=1}^{N^k} -\log\left(\frac{\exp(f_i^k \cdot f_i^{k+}/\tau)}{\exp(f_i^k \cdot f_i^{k+}/\tau) + \sum_{j=1, j\neq i}^{ns} \exp(f_i^k \cdot f_j^{k-}/\tau)} \right)$$

Notably, as medical images also acquire empty space outside of the body, random patch sampling will lead to the sampling of false positive and negative pairs (e.g., background voxels sampled as both positive and negative pairs). To this end, the masked CR (mCR) model samples voxel pairs only within the union of the binary foregrounds of I_1 and I_2 and resizes this mask to the layer-k specific resolution when sampling from $A_1^k(I_1)$ and $A_2^k(I_2 \circ \phi)$. We further investigate tolerance to false positive and negative training pairs and thus also train models without masking (denoted CR only).

Hypernetwork Optimization. Registration performance strongly depends on weighing λ correctly for a given dataset and $\mathcal{L}_{sim}$. Therefore, for fair comparison, the entire range of λ is evaluated for all benchmarked methods using hypernetworks [10] developed for registration [16, 23]. Specifically, the FiLM [27] based framework of [23] is used with a 4-layer 128-wide ReLU-MLP to generate a $\lambda \sim \mathcal{U}[0, 1]$-conditioned shared embedding, which is then linearly projected (with a weight decay of 10^{-5}) to each layer in the registration network to generate λ-conditioned scales and shifts for the network activations. At test time, we sample

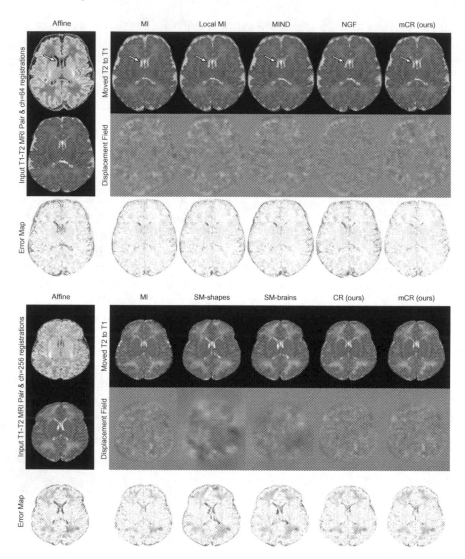

Fig. 2. T1w-T2w registration visualization between arbitrarily selected subjects for the (**top**) ch = 64 and (**bottom**) ch = 256 models. Error maps computed w.r.t. the T2w MRI of the target subject. Hypernetwork registration models are sampled with the same λ as Table 1.

17 registration networks for each method with dense λ sampling between $[0, 0.2)$ and sparse sampling between $[0.2, 1.0]$.

4   Experiments

Data. We compare registration methods by benchmarking on inter-subject multi-modality registration. We use pre-processed T1w and T2w MRI of newborns

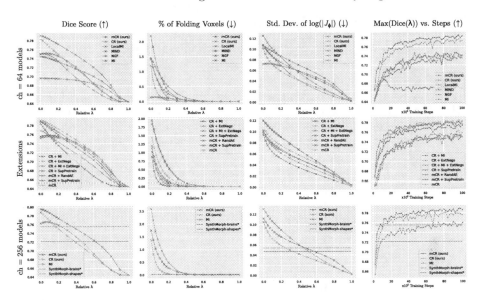

Fig. 3. Plots of registration accuracy vs. λ (**col. 1**), deformation qualities vs. λ (**cols. 2 & 3**), and accuracy vs. training steps (**col. 4**). Benchmarks are performed against commonly used multi-modality losses (**row 1**), extensions of the proposed techniques (**row 2**), and recent modality-pair agnostic methods (**row 3**). Across baseline losses, CR and mCR achieve the best tradeoff between accuracy and deformation characteristics (**row 1, cols. 1–3**). Further, using external losses and/or negatives reduces performance and supervised pretraining does not yield notable improvements (**row 2, cols. 1–3**). Compared to SynthMorph-brains [15], CR and mCR obtain higher accuracy (**row 3, col. 1**) in the $\lambda = 0.0 - 0.15$ and $0.0 - 0.3$ ranges, respectively, at the cost of more irregular warps (**row 3, cols. 2–3**). See Table 1 for an analysis of trading off accuracy for smoothness.

imaged at 29–45 weeks gestational age from dHCP [22], a challenging dataset due to rapid temporal development in morphology and appearance alongside inter-subject variability. We follow [7] for further preprocessing to obtain $160 \times 192 \times 160$ volumes at $0.6132 \times 0.6257 \times 0.6572\,\mathrm{mm}^3$ resolution and use $405/23/64$ images for training, validation, and testing.

Evaluation Methods. Registration evaluation is non-trivial due to competing objectives. Low smoothness regularization (λ) can allow for near-exact matching of appearance but with anatomically-implausible and highly irregular deformations. Conversely, high λ enables smooth deformations with suboptimal alignment. Therefore, we evaluate registration performance and robustness as a function of λ, via Dice and Dice30 (average of 30% of lowest dice scores) scores, respectively, calculated between the target and moved label maps of the input images (segmentations provided by dHCP [21]). To investigate deformation smoothness, we also evaluate the percentage of folding voxels and the standard deviation of the log Jacobian determinant of ϕ as a function of λ.

Benchmarked Methods. Using the same registration network with $ch = 64$ and $ts = 5$, we benchmark popular multi-modality metrics including Mutual Information (MI) (48 bins), local MI (48 bins, patch size = 9), MIND (distance = 2, patch size = 3), and normalized gradient fields, alongside the proposed mCR and CR models. We further compare against the general-purpose SynthMorph (SM)-shapes and brains models [15], by using their publicly released models and affine-aligning the images to their atlas. As SM uses $ch = 256$, we retrain the proposed registration models at that width. As we use public models, we cannot perform λ-conditioning and evaluation for SM. Further, as inter-subject dHCP registration can require large non-smooth deformations, we study whether a higher number of integration steps improves deformation characteristics (as in [35]) for the $ch = 256$ model, evaluating $ts = \{10, 16, 32\}$ with 32 as default.

To evaluate extensions of CR and mCR, we investigate whether combining them with a global loss (+ *MI*), incorporating more negative samples from an external randomly-selected subject (+ *ExtNegs*), or both (+ *MI* + *ExtNegs*) lead to improved results. We then evaluate the importance of feature extractor pretraining by using randomly-intialized *frozen* autoencoders instead as a worst-case feature extractor (+ *RandAE*). Finally, we evaluate whether contrastively pre-training the autoencoders and projection MLPs by using ground truth multi-modality image pairs alongside the reconstruction losses (+ *SupPretrain*) leads to improved results, with the following loss, where $I_{1,2}$ are from the same subject, $\lambda_{sp} = 0.1$, and $\hat{I}_{1,2}$ are the reconstructions,

$$\mathcal{L}_{A_1, A_2, F_1, F_2} = \lambda_{sp} d_{12}(I_1, I_2) + \sum_{i=1}^{2} (\|I_{Ti} - \hat{I_{Ti}}\|_1 + NCC(I_{Ti}, \hat{I_{Ti}})).$$

Implementation Details. All models were developed in TensorFlow 2.4 and were all trained for 10^5 iterations with Adam on a V100 GPU. For stability across all methods, we use a conservative learning rate of 5×10^{-5}. For the contrastive loss, we set $ns = 1024$ and $\tau = 0.007$. The autoencoder has 7 Conv-IN-LeakyReLU(0.2) blocks with 3 down/up sampling layers and 32-64-128-64-32-32-32-1 filters with its post-convolution features from the first 6 layers sampled for the contrastive loss. In practice, to avoid tuning the sampling strategy for λ as in [16], we add a rescaling constant $\alpha = 0.1$ to the objective function for CR and mCR with the form $\alpha(1 - \lambda)\mathcal{L}_{sim} + \lambda\mathcal{L}_{reg}$.

Results. Sample registration visualizations are provided in Fig. 2, performance scores versus λ are plotted in Fig. 3, and a study of trading-off registration accuracy for smoothness is tabulated in Table 1. We make the following experimental observations:

– *(m)CR achieves higher accuracy and converges faster than baseline losses.* Figure 3 (row 1) indicates that the proposed models achieve better Dice with comparable (mCR) or better (CR) folding and smoothness characteristics in comparison to baseline losses as a function of the 17 values of λ tested. Further, Table 1 reveals that if anatomical overlap is reduced to also achieve

Table 1. Trading off performance for invertibility. Registration accuracy (Dice), robustness (Dice30), and characteristics (% Folds, stddev. $\log|J_\varphi|$) for all benchmarked methods at values of λ that maintains the percentage of folding voxels at less than 0.5% of all voxels, as in [30], s.t. high performance is achieved alongside negligible singularities. This table is best interpreted in conjunction with Fig. 3, where results from all λ values are visualized. **A.** CR and mCR obtain improved accuracy and robustness ($A5$–6) with similar deformation characteristics to baseline losses ($A1$–4). **B.** At larger model sizes, mCR and CR still obtain higher registration accuracy and robustness ($B4$–5), albeit at the cost of more irregular deformations in comparison to SM ($B1$). **C.** Further adding external losses, negative samples, or both to CR harms performance ($C1$-3), supervised pretraining ($C4$–5) very marginally improves results over training from scratch ($A5\ 6$), and random feature extraction only slightly reduces Dice while smoothening displacements ($C6$). **D.** At a given λ, increasing integration steps yields marginal Dice and smoothness improvements.

Set	Width	Method	Opt. λ	Dice ($\uparrow$)	Dice30 ($\uparrow$)	% Folds ($\downarrow$)	sdlog$|J_\varphi|$ ($\downarrow$)
A	64	NGF [11]	0.0	0.696 ± 0.023	0.686	$\mathbf{0.141 \pm 0.043}$	**0.072**
	64	MI [38]	0.175	0.748 ± 0.021	0.739	0.461 ± 0.100	0.089
	64	LocalMI [8]	0.125	0.745 ± 0.023	0.737	0.402 ± 0.076	0.083
	64	MIND [14]	0.3	0.726 ± 0.023	0.716	0.258 ± 0.051	0.079
	64	CR (proposed)	0.05	0.776 ± 0.020	0.768	0.451 ± 0.074	0.083
	64	mCR (proposed)	0.125	$\mathbf{0.781 \pm 0.020}$	**0.774**	0.475 ± 0.070	0.084
B	256	SM-brains [15]	-	0.755 ± 0.020	0.749	0.023 ± 0.008	**0.048**
	256	SM-shapes [15]	-	0.721 ± 0.021	0.715	$\mathbf{0.017 \pm 0.011}$	0.056
	256	MI [38]	0.2	0.759 ± 0.021	0.750	0.487 ± 0.099	0.090
	256	CR (proposed)	0.075	0.774 ± 0.020	0.765	0.315 ± 0.0576	0.078
	256	mCR (proposed)	0.15	$\mathbf{0.780 \pm 0.021}$	**0.773**	0.416 ± 0.065	0.082
C	64	CR+MI	0.3	0.751 ± 0.021	0.742	$0.246 + 0.059$	0.080
	64	CR+ExtNegs	0.05	0.764 ± 0.020	0.756	0.489 ± 0.073	0.085
	64	CR+MI+ExtNegs	0.3	0.747 ± 0.021	0.739	0.214 ± 0.056	0.078
	64	CR+SupPretrain	0.025	0.778 ± 0.020	0.770	0.465 ± 0.075	0.084
	64	mCR+SupPretrain	0.075	0.778 ± 0.020	0.770	0.406 ± 0.067	0.081
	64	mCR+RandAE	0.1	0.778 ± 0.020	0.770	0.393 ± 0.070	0.80
D	256	CR (10 int. steps)	0.075	0.773 ± 0.021	0.764	0.341 ± 0.058	0.079
	256	CR (16 int. steps)	0.05	0.779 ± 0.020	0.772	0.462 ± 0.071	0.083
	256	CR (32 int. steps)	0.075	0.774 ± 0.020	0.765	0.315 ± 0.0576	0.078

negligible folding (defined as folds in 0.5% of all voxels [30]), CR and mCR still achieve the optimal tradeoff.

- *(m)CR achieves more accurate registration than label-trained methods at the cost of lower warp regularity.* While the public SM-brains model does not achieve the same Dice score as (m)CR, it achieves the third-highest performance behind (m)CR with substantially smoother deformations. We postulate that this effect stems from the intensity-invariant label-based training of SM-brains only looking at the semantics of the image, whereas our approach and other baselines are appearance based.

- *Masking consistently improves results.* Excluding false positive and false negative pairs from the training patches yields improved registration performance across all values of λ with acceptable increases in deformation irregularities vs. λ (Fig. 3 rows 1 & 3; cols 1–3). Importantly, contrastive training without foreground masks (CR) still outperforms other baseline losses and does so with smoother warps.
- *Pretraining has a marginal impact on (m)CR.* While still outperforming other baselines, using a *randomly-intialized & frozen* feature extractor achieves marginally lower dice with longer convergence times as compared to the full pretrained model.
- *Using external losses or negatives with (m)CR does not improve results.* Combining a global loss (MI) with CR does not improve results, which we speculate is due to the inputs already being globally affine-aligned. We also see a similar phenomenon to [26], where adding external negatives from other subjects lowers performance.
- *Self-supervision yields nearly the same performance as supervised pretraining.* Comparing rows A5–6 and C4–5 of Table 1 reveals that utilizing supervised pairs of aligned images for pretraining $A_{1,2}$ and $F_{1,2}$ yields very similar results, indicating that supervision is not required for optimal registration in this context.

5   Discussion

Limitations and Future Work. Some limitations exist in the presented material and will be addressed in subsequent work: (1) While we perform λ-conditioned hypernetwork registration to fairly compare benchmarked losses across all regularization strengths, hypernetworks may not exactly approximate all λ conditions. Further, hypernetworks were not trained for two of our baselines (SM-brains and shapes [15]) as we instead used their public models and we regularize for *velocity*-smoothness instead of *warp*-smoothness as in their work, both of which confound comparisons. (2) It is probable that combining our appearance-based approach with label-based simulation [15] would further improve results. (3) We did not explore other architectural configurations for the autoencoders and MLPs and it is plausible that there may be significant room for optimization. (4) We benchmarked the simulated inter-subject registration task and other use-cases such as pre-to-intra operative warping and preprocessing for multi-sensor fusion [6] may show different trends. (5) (m)CR currently requires ~15% more time per training iteration w.r.t. mutual information and can be optimized. (6) Unsupervised patch sampling may introduce false negative pairs in the contrastive loss and can be avoided with unsupervised *negative-free* patch representation learning methods [32].

Conclusions. This work presented ContraReg, a self-supervised contrastive representation learning approach to diffeomorphic non-rigid image registration. On the challenging task of inter-subject T1w-T2w registration with neonatal images showing high appearance and morphological variation, CR achieved high registration performance and robustness while maintaining desirable deformation qualities such as invertibility and smoothness. Finally, CR was validated across several baseline losses (including MI, MIND, NGF), training configurations, and frameworks, with results indicating that training supervision, losses, or external negative sampling strategies are not required.

Funding. N. Dey and G. Gerig were partially supported by NIH 1R01HD088 125-01A1. The dHCP data used in this study was funded by ERC Grant Agreement no. [319456].

References

1. Arar, M., Ginger, Y., Danon, D., Bermano, A.H., Cohen-Or, D.: Unsupervised multi-modal image registration via geometry preserving image-to-image translation. In: Proceedings of the IEEE/CVF Conference on Computer Vision and Pattern Recognition (2020)
2. Avants, B.B., Tustison, N.J., Song, G., Cook, P.A., et al.: A reproducible evaluation of ants similarity metric performance in brain image registration. Neuroimage **54**(3), 2033–2044 (2011)
3. Chen, T., Kornblith, S., Swersky, K., Norouzi, M., Hinton, G.: Big self-supervised models are strong semi-supervised learners. arXiv preprint arXiv:2006.10029 (2020)
4. Czolbe, S., Krause, O., Feragen, A.: Semantic similarity metrics for learned image registration. In: Proceedings of the Fourth Conference on Medical Imaging with Deep Learning (2021)
5. Dalca, A.V., Balakrishnan, G., Guttag, J., Sabuncu, M.R.: Unsupervised learning of probabilistic diffeomorphic registration for images and surfaces. Med. Image Anal. **57**, 226–236 (2019)
6. Dey, N., et al.: Multi-modal image fusion for multispectral super-resolution in microscopy. In: Medical Imaging 2019: Image Processing. vol. 10949, pp. 95–101. SPIE (2019)
7. Dey, N., Ren, M., Dalca, A.V., Gerig, G.: Generative adversarial registration for improved conditional deformable templates. In: Proceedings of the IEEE/CVF International Conference on Computer Vision (ICCV), pp. 3929–3941, October 2021
8. Guo, C.K.: Multi-modal image registration with unsupervised deep learning. Master's thesis, Massachusetts Institute of Technology (2019)
9. Gutierrez-Becker, B., Mateus, D., Peter, L., Navab, N.: Guiding multimodal registration with learned optimization updates. Med. Image Anal. **41**, 2–17 (2017)
10. Ha, D., Dai, A., Le, Q.V.: Hypernetworks. arXiv preprint arXiv:1609.09106 (2016)
11. Haber, E., Modersitzki, J.: Intensity gradient based registration and fusion of multi-modal images. In: Larsen, R., Nielsen, M., Sporring, J. (eds.) MICCAI 2006. LNCS, vol. 4191, pp. 726–733. Springer, Heidelberg (2006). https://doi.org/10.1007/11866763_89
12. Han, J., Shoeiby, M., Petersson, L., Armin, M.A.: Dual contrastive learning for unsupervised image-to-image translation. In: Proceedings of the IEEE/CVF Conference on Computer Vision and Pattern Recognition (CVPR) Workshops. pp. 746–755, June 2021

13. Hata, N., Dohi, T., Warfield, S., Wells, W., Kikinis, R., Jolesz, F.A.: Multimodality deformable registration of pre- and intraoperative images for MRI-guided brain surgery. In: Wells, W.M., Colchester, A., Delp, S. (eds.) MICCAI 1998. LNCS, vol. 1496, pp. 1067–1074. Springer, Heidelberg (1998). https://doi.org/10.1007/BFb0056296

14. Heinrich, M.P., Jenkinson, M., Bhushan, M., Matin, T., Gleeson, F.V., Brady, M., Schnabel, J.A.: Mind: Modality independent neighbourhood descriptor for multi-modal deformable registration. Med. Image Anal. **16**(7), 1423–1435 (2012)

15. Hoffmann, M., Billot, B., Greve, D.N., Iglesias, J.E., Fischl, B., Dalca, A.V.: Synthmorph: learning contrast-invariant registration without acquired images. IEEE Trans. Med. Imaging **41**(3), 543–558 (2021)

16. Hoopes, A., Hoffmann, M., Fischl, B., Guttag, J., Dalca, A.V.: HyperMorph: amortized hyperparameter learning for image registration. In: Feragen, A., Sommer, S., Schnabel, J., Nielsen, M. (eds.) IPMI 2021. LNCS, vol. 12729, pp. 3–17. Springer, Cham (2021). https://doi.org/10.1007/978-3-030-78191-0_1

17. Jing, L., Vincent, P., LeCun, Y., Tian, Y.: Understanding dimensional collapse in contrastive self-supervised learning. arXiv preprint arXiv:2110.09348 (2021)

18. Lee, D., Hofmann, M., Steinke, F., Altun, Y., Cahill, N.D., Scholkopf, B.: Learning similarity measure for multi-modal 3D image registration. In: 2009 IEEE Conference on Computer Vision and Pattern Recognition, pp. 186–193. IEEE (2009)

19. Loeckx, D., Slagmolen, P., Maes, F., Vandermeulen, D., Suetens, P.: Nonrigid image registration using conditional mutual information. Inf. Process. Med. Imaging. **20**, 725–737 (2009)

20. Lu, J., Öfverstedt, J., Lindblad, J., Sladoje, N.: Is image-to-image translation the panacea for multimodal image registration? A comparative study. arXiv preprint arXiv:2103.16262 (2021)

21. Makropoulos, A., Gousias, I.S., Ledig, C., Aljabar, P., et al.: Automatic whole brain MRI segmentation of the developing neonatal brain. IEEE Trans. Med. Imaging **33**(9), 1818–1831 (2014)

22. Makropoulos, A., et al.: The developing human connectome project: a minimal processing pipeline for neonatal cortical surface reconstruction. Neuroimage **173**, 88–112 (2018)

23. Mok, T.C.W., Chung, A.C.S.: Conditional deformable image registration with convolutional neural network. In: de Bruijne, M., et al. (eds.) MICCAI 2021. LNCS, vol. 12904, pp. 35–45. Springer, Cham (2021). https://doi.org/10.1007/978-3-030-87202-1_4

24. Nimsky, C., Ganslandt, O., Merhof, D., et al.: Intraoperative visualization of the pyramidal tract by diffusion-tensor-imaging-based fiber tracking. Neuroimage **30**, 1219–1229 (2006)

25. Oord, A.v.d., Li, Y., Vinyals, O.: Representation learning with contrastive predictive coding. arXiv preprint arXiv:1807.03748 (2018)

26. Park, T., Efros, A.A., Zhang, R., Zhu, J.-Y.: Contrastive learning for unpaired image-to-image translation. In: Vedaldi, A., Bischof, H., Brox, T., Frahm, J.-M. (eds.) ECCV 2020. LNCS, vol. 12354, pp. 319–345. Springer, Cham (2020). https://doi.org/10.1007/978-3-030-58545-7_19

27. Perez, E., Strub, F., de Vries, H., Dumoulin, V., Courville, A.C.: Film: visual reasoning with a general conditioning layer. In: AAAI (2018)

28. Pielawski, N., et al.: CoMIR: contrastive multimodal image representation for registration. In: 34th Conference on Advances in Neural Information Processing Systems (2020)

29. Qin, C., Shi, B., Liao, R., Mansi, T., Rueckert, D., Kamen, A.: Unsupervised deformable registration for multi-modal images via disentangled representations. In: Chung, A.C.S., Gee, J.C., Yushkevich, P.A., Bao, S. (eds.) IPMI 2019. LNCS, vol. 11492, pp. 249–261. Springer, Cham (2019). https://doi.org/10.1007/978-3-030-20351-1_19

30. Qiu, H., Qin, C., Schuh, A., et al.: Learning diffeomorphic and modality-invariant registration using b-splines. Proc. Mach. Learn. Res. **143**, 645–664 (2021)

31. Ren, M., Dey, N., Fishbaugh, J., Gerig, G.: Segmentation-renormalized deep feature modulation for unpaired image harmonization. IEEE Trans. Med. Imaging **40**(6), 1519–1530 (2021)

32. Ren, M., Dey, N., Styner, M.A., Botteron, K., Gerig, G.: Local spatiotemporal representation learning for longitudinally-consistent neuroimage analysis. arXiv preprint arXiv:2206.04281 (2022)

33. Risholm, P., Golby, A.J., Wells, W.: Multimodal image registration for preoperative planning and image-guided neurosurgical procedures. Neurosurg. Clinics **22**(2), 197–206 (2011)

34. Russakoff, D.B., Tomasi, C., Rohlfing, T., Maurer, C.R.: Image similarity using mutual information of regions. In: Pajdla, T., Matas, J. (eds.) ECCV 2004. LNCS, vol. 3023, pp. 596–607. Springer, Heidelberg (2004). https://doi.org/10.1007/978-3-540-24672-5_47

35. Schuh, A.: Computational models of the morphology of the developing neonatal human brain. Ph.D. thesis, Imperial College London (2018)

36. Simonovsky, M., Gutiérrez-Becker, B., Mateus, D., Navab, N., Komodakis, N.: A Deep metric for multimodal registration. In: Ourselin, S., Joskowicz, L., Sabuncu, M.R., Unal, G., Wells, W. (eds.) MICCAI 2016. LNCS, vol. 9902, pp. 10–18. Springer, Cham (2016). https://doi.org/10.1007/978-3-319-46726-9_2

37. Wachinger, C., Navab, N.: Entropy and laplacian images: Structural representations for multi-modal registration. Med. Image Anal. **16**(1), 1–17 (2012)

38. Wells, W.M., III., Viola, P., Atsumi, H., Nakajima, S., Kikinis, R.: Multi-modal volume registration by maximization of mutual information. Med. Image Anal. **1**(1), 35–51 (1996)

39. Woo, J., Stone, M., Prince, J.L.: Multimodal registration via mutual information incorporating geometric and spatial context. IEEE Trans. Image Process. **24**, 757–769 (2014)

40. Zhou, B., Augenfeld, Z., Chapiro, J., Zhou, S.K., Liu, C., Duncan, J.S.: Anatomy-guided multimodal registration by learning segmentation without ground truth: application to intraprocedural CBCT/MR liver segmentation and registration. Med. Image Anal. **74** (2021)

Swin-VoxelMorph: A Symmetric Unsupervised Learning Model for Deformable Medical Image Registration Using Swin Transformer

Yongpei Zhu[✉][iD] and Shi Lu

Graduate School at Shenzhen, Tsinghua University, Shenzhen 518055, China
zhuyp20@mails.tsinghua.edu.cn

Abstract. Deformable medical image registration is widely used in medical image processing with the invertible and one-to-one mapping between images. While state-of-the-art image registration methods are based on convolutional neural networks, few attempts have been made with Transformers which show impressive performance on computer vision tasks. Existing models neglect to employ attention mechanisms to handle the long-range cross-image relevance in embedding learning, limiting such approaches to identify the semantically meaningful correspondence of anatomical structures. These methods also ignore the topology preservation and invertibility of the transformation although they achieve fast image registration. In this paper, we propose a novel, symmetric unsupervised learning network Swin-VoxelMorph based on the Swin Transformer which minimizes the dissimilarity between images and estimates both forward and inverse transformations simultaneously. Specifically, we propose 3D Swin-UNet, which applies hierarchical Swin Transformer with shifted windows as the encoder to extract context features. And a symmetric Swin Transformer-based decoder with patch expanding layer is designed to perform the up-sampling operation to estimate the registration fields. Besides, our objective loss functions can guarantee substantial diffeomorphic properties of the predicted transformations. We verify our method on two datasets including ADNI and PPMI, and it achieves state-of-the-art registration accuracy while maintaining desirable diffeomorphic properties.

Keywords: Medical image registration · Swin transformer · Swin-VoxelMorph · Diffeomorphic registration fields

1 Introduction

Deformable image registration is crucial in a variety of medical imaging analysis, which is aimed to estimate the appropriate non-linear transformation to align

Supplementary Information The online version contains supplementary material available at https://doi.org/10.1007/978-3-031-16446-0_8.

a pair of images. The deformable registration produces the nonlinear voxel-wise mapping between images, which facilitates the atlas-based annotation, statistical shape analysis, and shape comparison of anatomical structures. To accomplish the task of deformable registration effectively, we need to infer the semantic correspondence of fine-grained structures. The volumetric images vary in shapes and scales, so it is a challenging problem to identify the real matching anatomical structures.

It is known that traditional deformable registration has high computational cost due to iterative optimization of large-scale parameters [13]. Several deep learning-based approaches are proposed to train convolutional neural networks (CNNs) that map input pairs to output deformation [6,15,16,19,21–23,25,27]. The CNN performs the end-to-end inference of the displacement or velocity fields from a pair of images, using regularization, such as the smoothness and the Jacobian determinant [5,6], for the invertible and the diffeomorphic transformations. Moreover, the symmetric registration infers a pair of diffeomorphic maps regarding the middle of the geodesic path [6]. However, on the one hand, although these methods achieve fast registration and comparable registration performance, the substantial diffeomorphic properties of the registration field are not guaranteed, including topology-preservation and the invertibility of the transformation. On the other hand, these methods conduct an inference directly from the CNN-based low-level local embedding without considering the global relevance of the image pair. Thus, the resultant alignment may suffer implausible voxel-wise mapping, where the prior affine transformation and landmark annotation are required to circumvent the trap of local minima. What's more, registration is the process of establishing such correspondence by comparing different parts of the moving to the fixed image. Unlike CNNs, one point is that the self-attention mechanisms in a Transformer have an unlimited size effective receptive field. A CNN has a narrow field of view: it performs convolution locally, and its field of view grows in proportion to the CNN's depth, the shallow layers have a relatively small receptive field, limiting the CNN's ability to associate the distant parts between two images [28]. The U-Net (or other multi-scale pyramid modules) was proposed to overcome this limitation by introducing down- and up-sampling operations. However, several problems remain: (1) The receptive fields of the first several layers are still restricted by the convolution kernel size, and the global information of an image can only be viewed at the deeper layers of the network. (2) As the convolutional layers deepen, the impact from far-away voxels decays quickly [29]. However, Transformer is capable of handling such issues and focusing on the parts that need deformation.

Recently, the transformer has been extended to computer vision tasks, such as object detection [14], image recognition [12], and segmentation [10,11]. The transformer facilitates the global embedding of images by the relevance modeling of image words. Attention was utilized in various image processing tasks by highlighting salient feature regions and suppressing irrelevant ones [9]. Liao et al. [8] adopted an attention-driven hierarchical strategy and a greedy supervised method in rigid CT registration. An auto-attention mechanism was introduced to multiple regions for reliable visual cues in the registration of X-ray and CT images [7]. However, such attention schemes solved the long-range dependencies of a single image or the rigid transformation, which can not effectively deal with the cross-image semantic correspondence and deformable registration.

To solve these difficulties, we propose a symmetric unsupervised learning network Swin-VoxelMorph which can minimize the dissimilarity between images and estimates both forward and inverse transformations simultaneously. On the one hand, the proposed method exploits the self-attention scheme to model the inter- and intra-image global contextual relevances explicitly. The transformer model conducts the relevance modeling and the feature enhancement on two kinds of image embedding for semantically meaningful correspondences of anatomical structures. The learnable embedding module is used to predict the registration fields, which takes the strength of both the low-level spatial features and the high-level contextual relevance-based enhancements. One difficulty in unsupervised deformable registration is to identify the semantic correspondence between anatomical structures. The proposed model addresses the cross-image and global relevance to improve the discriminative ability of image embedding for voxel-wise correspondence. To the best of our knowledge, we are the first to explicitly exploit Swin Transformer for deformable medical image registration. On the other hand, driven by [6], we also use several objective loss functions which can guarantee substantial diffeomorphic properties of the predicted transformations. We verify our method on two datasets including ADNI and PPMI, and obtain excellent improvement on magnetic resonance image (MRI) registration with higher average Dice scores and better diffeomorphic registration fields (lower non-positive Jacobian locations) compared with state-of-the-art methods. The contributions of this paper are two folds:

(1) We are the first to propose 3D Swin-UNet, a pure Transformer-based 3D U-shaped Encoder-Decoder network, to explicitly exploit Swin Transformer for deformable medical image registration. The learnable embedding module, taking the strength of both the low-level spatial features and the high-level contextual relevance-based enhancements, is used to predict the registration fields.
(2) Our objective functions including orientation and inverse consistency constraint can guarantee the topology-preservation and inverse consistency of the predicted transformations.

2   Method

2.1   Network Structures

Deformable image registration refers to the process of warping one (moving) image to align with another (fixed) image to maximize the similarity between the registered images. Figure 1 shows the overview of our proposed symmetric architecture Swin-VoxelMorph. Let $M, F \in \mathbb{R}^{H \times W \times D}$ be moving and fixed image volumes. The optimization problem aims to minimize the dissimilarity of the fixed image F and warped image $M(\phi)$ while maintaining a smooth displacement field ϕ. We take M, F as inputs, and compute ϕ based on parameter θ (the kernels of the convolutional layers) using the proposed transformer-based architecture 3D Swin-UNet which is shown in Fig. 2, where $\phi = Id + u$, u denotes a flow field of displacement vectors, and Id denotes the identity. We warp M to $M(\phi_{MF})$ and F to $F(\phi_{FM})$ using differentiable spatial transformation functions.

The deep neural network (g_θ) here is built from the Swin-UNet [10] and consists of a 3-level hierarchical encoder-decoder with skip connections, which concatenates M and F into a 2-channel 3D image as the input. The basic unit of 3D Swin-UNet is Swin Transformer block [4]. In the encoder, the medical images are split into non-overlapping patches with patch size of $4 \times 4 \times 4$ to transform the inputs into sequence embeddings. By such partition approach, the feature dimension of each patch becomes to $4 \times 4 \times 4 \times 2 = 128$. Furthermore, a linear embedding layer is applied to projected feature dimension into arbitrary dimension (represented as C). The transformed patch tokens will generate the hierarchical feature representations by passing through several Swin Transformer blocks and patch merging layers. Specifically, Swin Transformer block is responsible for feature representation learning and patch merging layer is responsible for down-sampling and increasing dimension. Inspired by 3D U-Net [3], we design a symmetric transformer-based decoder which is composed of Swin Transformer block and patch expanding layer. The extracted context features are fused with multi scale features from encoder via skip connections to complement the loss of spatial information caused by down-sampling. In contrast to patch merging layer, a patch expanding layer is specially designed to perform up-sampling. The patch expanding layer reshapes feature maps of adjacent dimensions into a large feature maps with 2× up-sampling of resolution. Finally, the last patch expanding layer is used to perform 4× up-sampling to restore the resolution of the feature maps to the input resolution ($D \times W \times H$), and then a linear projection layer is applied on these up-sampled features to estimate two registration fields ϕ_{MF} and ϕ_{FM}.

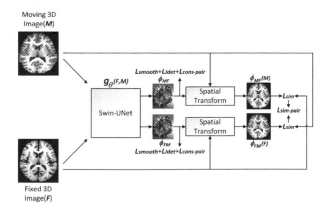

Fig. 1. Overview of our method Swin-VoxelMorph.

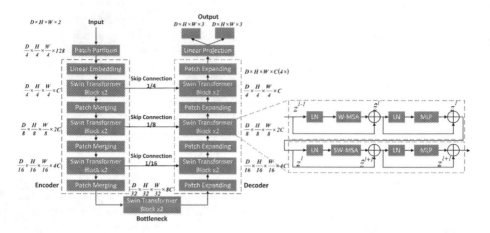

Fig. 2. The architecture of Swin-Unet with Swin transformer block, which is composed of encoder, bottleneck, decoder and skip connections. Here C = 96.

2.2   Loss Function

Similar to the existing CNN-based methods [19], the optimization problem for registration is typically described as:

$$\mathcal{L}(I_1, I_2, \boldsymbol{\phi}) = \mathcal{L}_{sim}(I_1, I_2(\boldsymbol{\phi})) + \mathcal{L}_{reg}(\boldsymbol{\phi}) \tag{1}$$

$I_2(\boldsymbol{\phi})$ is I_2 warped by $\boldsymbol{\phi}$. $\mathcal{L}_{sim}$ measures image similarity between $I_2(\boldsymbol{\phi})$ and I_1, $\mathcal{L}_{reg}$ imposes regularization on $\boldsymbol{\phi}$.

Here, we set $\mathcal{L}_{sim}$ to the mean squared voxelwise difference of $I_2(\boldsymbol{\phi})$ and I_1, namely $\mathcal{L}_{sim}(I_1, I_2(\boldsymbol{\phi})) = MSE(I_1, I_2(\boldsymbol{\phi})) = \frac{1}{|\Omega|} \sum_{p \in \Omega} [I_1(p) - I_2(\boldsymbol{\phi}(p))]^2$. Specifically, our proposed similarity loss function $\mathcal{L}_{sim-pair}$ consists of two symmetric loss terms, which measures the pairwise dissimilarity between the warped M to F and warped F to M:

$$\mathcal{L}_{sim-pair}(F, M, \boldsymbol{\phi}) = \mathcal{L}_{sim}(F, M(\boldsymbol{\phi}_{MF})) + \mathcal{L}_{sim}(M, F(\boldsymbol{\phi}_{FM})) \tag{2}$$

where $\boldsymbol{\phi}_{MF}$ and $\boldsymbol{\phi}_{FM}$ are differentiable and invertible in a bidirectional fashion.

Existing learning-based methods [21] often regularize the transformation $\boldsymbol{\phi}$ with a regularization loss function, such as a L2-norm on the spatial gradients of $\boldsymbol{\phi}$. Here, we define $\mathcal{L}_{smooth}(\boldsymbol{\phi})$ as follows:

$$\mathcal{L}_{smooth}(\boldsymbol{\phi}) = \sum_{p \in \Omega} (\| \nabla \boldsymbol{\phi}_{MF}(p) \|^2 + \| \nabla \boldsymbol{\phi}_{FM}(p) \|^2) \tag{3}$$

Local Orientation Consistency Constraint. Although the smoothness of the deformation field can be controlled by the weight of the regularizer, the global regularizer may greatly degrade the registration accuracy of the model, especially when a large weight is assigned for the regularizer. In addition, these regularizers are not sufficient to guarantee a topology-preservation transformation. To address this issue, we apply a selective Jacobian determinant regularization loss $\mathcal{L}_{Jdet}(\phi)$, which imposes a local orientation consistency constraint on the estimated ϕ and guarantees a topology-preservation transformation:

$$\mathcal{L}_{Jdet}(\phi) = \frac{1}{N} \sum_{p \in \Omega} (\sigma(-(\mid J(\phi_{MF})(p) \mid)) + \sigma(-(\mid J(\phi_{FM})(p) \mid))) \tag{4}$$

N denotes the total number of elements in $\mid J(\phi)(p) \mid$, $\sigma(\cdot) = ReLU(\cdot)$ represents an activation function and $\mid J(\phi)(p) \mid$ denotes the Jacobian determinant of deformation field ϕ at position p. The lower number of negative Jacobian determinant will lead to better diffeomorphic property of registration field [26].

Inverse Consistency Constraint. Here, we extend the objective function by adding an inverse consistency constraint $\mathcal{L}_{cons-pair}$ [1]. Inverse-consistent registration means the bidirectional deformations estimated between an image pair should share the same pathway. That is, the composition of forward and backward deformations should be identity or close to identity. Therefore, the loss $\mathcal{L}_{cons-pair}$ can be defined by:

$$\mathcal{L}_{cons-pair}(\phi) = \frac{1}{|\Omega|} \sum_{p \in \Omega} [(\phi_{MF} \circ \phi_{FM})(p) - \phi_0]^2 \tag{5}$$

During training, the composition results would be gradually approaching to identity, resulting smooth and invertible deformations. Therefore, the complete loss function is:

$$\mathcal{L}_{total} = \mathcal{L}_{sim-pair} + \lambda_1 \mathcal{L}_{smooth} + \lambda_2 \mathcal{L}_{Jdet} + \lambda_3 \mathcal{L}_{cons-pair} \tag{6}$$

where λ_1, λ_2 and λ_3 are the weights to balance the contributions of $\mathcal{L}_{smooth}$, $\mathcal{L}_{Jdet}$ and $\mathcal{L}_{cons-pair}$, respectively.

3 Experiments

3.1 Datasets, Preprocessing and Evaluation Criteria

Datasets and Preprocessing. We validate our method on two datasets, ADNI [18] and PPMI [24], including 1961 T1-weighted brain MRI scans. And we split the datasets into 1569, 196 and 196 (8:1:1) volumes for train, validation, and test sets respectively. Specifically, we register each scan to an atlas computed using external data [17]. We focus on atlas-based registration, each input volume pair consists of the atlas (F) and a random volume (M) from the dataset. Standard preprocessing steps for structural brain MRI are performed, including skull stripping, resampling and affine spatial normalization for each scan using FreeSurfer [17], and crop the resulting images to $160 \times 192 \times 224$. Segmentation maps including 29 anatomical structures are obtained using FreeSurfer for evaluation.

Table 1. Summary of results on test set: mean Dice scores over all anatomical structures and subjects (higher is better), mean runtime, and mean percentage of locations with non-positive Jacobian (lower is better). Standard deviations are presented in parentheses. The best results are in bold.

Method	Avg. Dice	GPU sec	CPU sec	% of $\mid J(\boldsymbol{\phi})(p) \mid \leq 0$
Affine only	0.583 (0.158)	0	0	0
ANTs SyN (CC)	0.748 (0.132)	-	9054 (2021)	0.144 (0.092)
VoxelMorph (MSE) [19]	0.754 (0.140)	0.54 (0.02)	141 (1.22)	0.188 (0.082)
VoxelMorph-diff [15,16]	0.753 (0.135)	0.44 (0.01)	51 (0.22)	6.2e–6 (7.3e–5)
DeepFLASH [25]	0.761 (0.115)	0.52 (0.01)	134 (1.13)	0.175 (0.125)
SYMNet [6]	0.763 (0.113)	**0.41 (0.03)**	**48 (0.14)**	4.5e–5 (3.7e–4)
Swin-VoxelMorph (ours)	**0.775 (0.128)**	0.43 (0.01)	52 (1.12)	**2.4e–6 (2.3e–5)**

Evaluation Criteria. We expect the regions in $M(\boldsymbol{\phi})$ and F corresponding to the same anatomical structure to overlap well, and quantify the volume overlap between structures using the Dice score. The Jacobian matrix $J(\boldsymbol{\phi})(p) = \nabla \boldsymbol{\phi}(p) \in \mathbb{R}^{3 \times 3}$ captures the local properties of $\boldsymbol{\phi}$. We compute the numbers of all non-background voxels for which $\mid J(\boldsymbol{\phi})(p) \mid \leq 0$, where $\boldsymbol{\phi}$ is not diffeomorphic.

Implementation. Our experiments are implemented by PyTorch [2] on NVIDIA GTX 2080Ti GPUs and adopt the Adam optimizer [20] with a learning rate of 10^{-4}. We set the epochs as 1500, batch size as 1, steps of per epoch as 100. We select the model that obtain the highest Dice on the validation set and get the best results with $\lambda_1 = 0.01, \lambda_2 = 1000, \lambda_3 = 10$ which were tuned by grid search.

3.2   Results

Registration Performance. Table 1 shows average Dice and percentage of voxels with non-positive Jacobian determinant over all subjects and structures for different methods. We can see that Swin-VoxelMorph achieves the overall best performance in terms of average Dice, while producing the best diffeomorphic registration fields (less non-positive Jacobian voxels), which implies that our resulting registration fields guarantee the desirable diffeomorphic properties. Figure 3 shows the examples of moved images with overlaid boundaries of ventricles (yellow), transformation fields, and Jacobian determinant of transformations estimated by different experiments. From the red box in the upper two rows of right panel, our method captures clearer details of moved images and performs better registration than other methods, it can handle various changes in shape of structures, such as ventricles and hippocampi. The transformation fields, and estimated Jacobian determinant corresponding to the top images are shown in the lower two rows of right panel. Note that the value of colorbar indicates how volume changes in Jacobian determinant, our method produces less non-positive Jacobian voxels, which gracefully guarantees the smoothness of transformation fields without artifacts. The boxplots in Fig. 4 illustrate the Dice

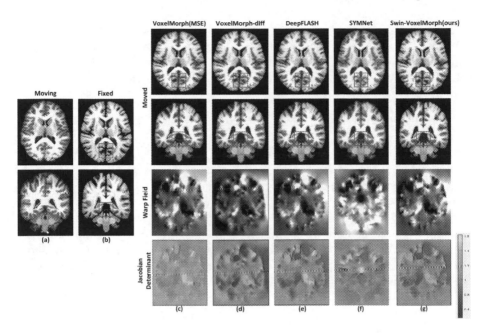

Fig. 3. Comparison of two example MR slices for different experiments. Left: (a) moving image, (b) atlas. Right: (c) (d) (e) (f) moved images, transformation fields and Jacobian determinant of transformations by VoxelMorph (MSE), VoxelMorph-diff, Deep-FLASH, SYMNet and Swin-VoxelMorph.

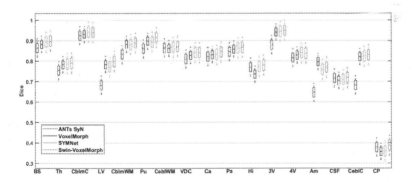

Fig. 4. Boxplots illustrating Dice scores of anatomical structures for ANTs SyN, VoxelMorph (MSE), SYMNet and Swin-VoxelMorph. Left and right brain hemispheres are combined into one structure for visualization. Brain stem (BS), thalamus (Th), cerebellum cortex (CblmC), lateral ventricle (LV), cerebellum white matter (CblmWM), putamen (Pu), cerebral white matter (CeblWM), ventral DC (VDC), caudate (Ca), pallidum (Pa), hippocampus (Hi), 3rd ventricle (3V), 4th ventricle (4V), amygdala (Am), CSF (CSF), cerebral cortex (CeblC), and choroid plexus (CP) are included.

score distribution of anatomical structures for ANTs SyN, VoxelMorph (MSE), SYMNet and our proposed method Swin-VoxelMorph. Swin-VoxelMorph performs better performance in most anatomical structures than other methods, such as Brain stem (BS), thalamus (Th), lateral ventricle (LV).

4   Conclusions

In conclusion, we propose a symmetric unsupervised learning network Swin-VoxelMorph that guarantees topology preservation and invertibility of the transformation. First, the proposed pure Transformer-based 3D U-shaped Encoder-Decoder network Swin-UNet explicitly exploit Swin Transformer to predict better registration fields for deformable medical image registration, which can provide more precise anatomical alignment. Second, our objective functions can enforce the inverse consistency of the predicted transformations. Results show that our method can outperform state-of-the-art methods in registration accuracy and the quality of diffeomorphic properties.

References

1. Shen, Z.Y., Han, X., Xu, Z.L., Niethammer, M.: Networks for joint affine and non-parametric image registration. In: Proceedings of the IEEE Conference on Computer Vision and Pattern Recognition, pp. 4224–4233 (2019)
2. Paszke, A. et al.: Automatic differentiation in pytorch. In: NIPS-W (2017)
3. Çiçek, Ö., Abdulkadir, A., Lienkamp, S.S., Brox, T., Ronneberger, O.: 3D U-Net: learning dense volumetric segmentation from sparse annotation. In: International Conference on Medical Image Computing and Computer-Assisted Intervention, pp. 424–432 (2016)
4. Liu, Z., et al.: Swin transformer: hierarchical vision transformer using shifted windows. arXiv preprint arXiv:2103.14030 (2021)
5. Zhang, J.: Inverse-consistent deep networks for unsupervised deformable image registration. arXiv preprint arXiv:1809.03443 (2018)
6. Mok, T.C.W., Chung, A.: Fast symmetric diffeomorphic image registration with convolutional neural networks. In: Proceedings of the IEEE/CVF Conference on Computer Vision and Pattern Recognition, pp. 4644–4653 (2020)
7. Miao, S., et al.: Dilated FCN for multi-agent 2D/3D medical image registration. In: Thirty-Second AAAI Conference on Artificial Intelligence (2018)
8. Liao, R., et al.: An artificial agent for robust image registration. In: Proceedings of the AAAI Conference on Artificial Intelligence, vol. 31 (2017)
9. Schlemper, J., et al.: Attention gated networks: learning to leverage salient regions in medical images. Med. Image Anal. **53**, 197–207 (2019)
10. Cao, H., et al.: Swin-UNet: UNet-like pure transformer for medical image segmentation. arXiv preprint arXiv:2105.05537 (2021)
11. Chen, J., et al.: TransuNet: transformers make strong encoders for medical image segmentation. arXiv preprint arXiv: 2102.04306 (2021)
12. Dosovitskiy, A., et al.: An image is worth 16 x 16 words: transformers for image recognition at scale. arXiv preprint arXiv:2010.11929 (2020)

13. Sotiras, A., Davatzikos, C., Paragios, N.: Deformable medical image registration: a survey. IEEE Trans. Med. Imaging **32**(7), 1153–1190 (2013)

14. Carion, N., Massa, F., Synnaeve, G., Usunier, N., Kirillov, A., Zagoruyko, S.: End-to-end object detection with transformers. arXiv preprint arXiv: 2005.12872 (2020)

15. Dalca, A.V., Balakrishnan, G., Guttag, J., Sabuncu, M.R.: Unsupervised learning for fast probabilistic diffeomorphic registration. In: Frangi, A.F., Schnabel, J.A., Davatzikos, C., Alberola-López, C., Fichtinger, G. (eds.) MICCAI 2018. LNCS, vol. 11070, pp. 729–738. Springer, Cham (2018). https://doi.org/10.1007/978-3-030-00928-1_82

16. Dalca, A.V., Balakrishnan, G., Guttag, J., Sabuncu, M.R.: Unsupervised learning of probabilistic diffeomorphic registration for images and surfaces. arXiv preprint arXiv: 1903.03545 (2019)

17. Fischl, B.: Freesurfer. Neuroimage **62**(2), 774–781 (2012)

18. Susanne, C., et al.: Ways toward an early diagnosis in Alzheimers disease: the Alzheimers disease neuroimaging Initiative (ADNI). Alzheimer's Dementia **1**(1), 55–66 (2005)

19. Balakrishnan, G., Zhao, A., Sabuncu, M.R., Guttag, J., Dalca, A.V.: An unsupervised learning model for deformable medical image registration. In: Proceedings of the IEEE Conference on Computer Vision and Pattern Recognition, pp. 9252–9260 (2018)

20. Diederik, P.K., Jimmy, B.: ADAM: a method for stochastic optimization. arXiv preprint arXiv:1412.6980 (2014)

21. Balakrishnan, G., Zhao, A., Sabuncu, M.R., Guttag, J., Dalca, A.V.: VoxelMorph: a learning framework for deformable medical image registration. IEEE Trans. Med. Imaging **99**, 1788–1800 (2019)

22. Sheikhjafari, A., Punithakumar, K.: Unsupervised deformable image registration with fully connected generative neural network. In: MIDL (2018)

23. Hou, B., Miolane, N., Khanal, B., Lee, M.: Deep pose estimation for image-based registration. In: MIDL (2018)

24. Marek, K., et al.: The Parkinson progression marker initiative (PPMI). Prog. Neurobiol. **95**(4), 629–635 (2011)

25. Wang, J., Zhang, M.M.: DeepFLASH: an efficient network for learning-based medical image registration. In: Proceedings of the IEEE Conference on Computer Vision and Pattern Recognition (CVPR) (2020)

26. Gu, D., et al.: Pair-wise and group-wise deformation consistency in deep registration network. In: Martel, A.L., et al. (eds.) MICCAI 2020. LNCS, vol. 12263, pp. 171–180. Springer, Cham (2020). https://doi.org/10.1007/978-3-030-59716-0_17

27. Vos, B.D., Berendsen, F.F., Viergever, M.A., Staring, M., Išgum, I.: End-to-end unsupervised deformable image registration with a convolutional neural network. In: Deep Learning in Medical Image Analysis and Multimodal Learning for Clinical Decision Support, pp. 204–212 (2017)

28. Luo, W.J., Li, Y.J., Urtasun, R., Zemel, R.: Understanding the effective receptive field in deep convolutional neural networks. In: Conference on Advances in Neural Information Processing Systems, vol. 29 (2016)

29. Li, S.H., Sui, X.C., Luo, X.D., Xu, X.X., Liu, Y., Goh, R.: Medical image segmentation using squeeze-and-expansion transformers. arXiv preprint arXiv:2105.09511 (2021)

Non-iterative Coarse-to-Fine Registration Based on Single-Pass Deep Cumulative Learning

Mingyuan Meng[1] (ID), Lei Bi[1(✉)] (ID), Dagan Feng[1,2] (ID), and Jinman Kim[1] (ID)

[1] School of Computer Science, The University of Sydney, Sydney, Australia
`lei.bi@sydney.edu.au`
[2] Med-X Research Institute, Shanghai Jiao Tong University, Shanghai, China

Abstract. Deformable image registration is a crucial step in medical image analysis for finding a non-linear spatial transformation between a pair of fixed and moving images. Deep registration methods based on Convolutional Neural Networks (CNNs) have been widely used as they can perform image registration in a fast and end-to-end manner. However, these methods usually have limited performance for image pairs with large deformations. Recently, iterative deep registration methods have been used to alleviate this limitation, where the transformations are iteratively learned in a coarse-to-fine manner. However, iterative methods inevitably prolong the registration runtime, and tend to learn separate image features for each iteration, which hinders the features from being leveraged to facilitate the registration at later iterations. In this study, we propose a Non-Iterative Coarse-to-finE registration Network (NICE-Net) for deformable image registration. In the NICE-Net, we propose: (i) a Single-pass Deep Cumulative Learning (SDCL) decoder that can cumulatively learn coarse-to-fine transformations within a single pass (iteration) of the network, and (ii) a Selectively-propagated Feature Learning (SFL) encoder that can learn common image features for the whole coarse-to-fine registration process and selectively propagate the features as needed. Extensive experiments on six public datasets of 3D brain Magnetic Resonance Imaging (MRI) show that our proposed NICE-Net can outperform state-of-the-art iterative deep registration methods while only requiring similar runtime to non-iterative methods.

Keywords: Image registration · Cumulative learning · Large deformations

1 Introduction

Deformable image registration is a fundamental requirement for a variety of clinical tasks such as tumor growth monitoring and organ atlas creation [1]. It aims to find a non-linear spatial transformation between a pair of fixed and moving images, which warps the moving image to align with the fixed image. Traditional registration methods address deformable registration as an iterative optimization problem. However, iterative

Supplementary Information The online version contains supplementary material available at https://doi.org/10.1007/978-3-031-16446-0_9.

L. Wang et al. (Eds.): MICCAI 2022, LNCS 13436, pp. 88–97, 2022.
https://doi.org/10.1007/978-3-031-16446-0_9

optimization is time-consuming, especially for high-resolution 3D images such as brain Magnetic Resonance Imaging (MRI) [2], which limits its clinical applications as fast registration is widely desired in clinical practice. Recently, deep registration methods based on Convolutional Neural Networks (CNNs) have been widely used to perform fast and end-to-end registration in a non-iterative manner [3]. However, non-iterative deep registration methods usually work well for image pairs with small deformations while having degraded performance for large deformations [4, 5].

Iterative deep registration methods have been proposed to alleviate this limitation and are regarded as the state-of-the-art [6–10], in which the registration is performed by iteratively warping the moving image in a coarse-to-fine manner. Iterative coarse-to-fine registration usually is implemented by using multiple cascaded networks [6–9]. The first network performs coarse registration at the beginning and each following network is used to refine the registration based on the warped image derived from its former network. For example, Zhao et al. [8] proposed a Recursive Cascaded Network (RCN), where multiple CNNs were cascaded and were trained end-to-end. Mok et al. [9] proposed a Laplacian pyramid Image Registration Network (LapIRN), in which multiple CNNs at different pyramid levels were cascaded. However, these methods rely on multiple networks to perform coarse-to-fine registration, which inevitably raises a huge requirement for GPU memory. Recently, Shu et al. [10] proposed to use a single network (ULAE-net) to perform iterative coarse-to-fine registration. At each iteration, the ULAE-net produces a transformation to warp the moving image, and then the warped image is fed into the ULAE-net again to perform finer registration at the next iteration. However, these iterative deep registration methods all have certain limitations: (i) iterative learning inevitably increases computational loads and prolongs the registration runtime, and (ii) iterative methods usually learn separate image features for each iteration, which hinders the features from being leveraged at later iterations and also adds extra computational loads due to repeated feature learning. Hu et al. [11] proposed a Dual-stream Pyramid Registration Network (Dual-PRNet), in which coarse-to-fine registration is performed in a non-iterative manner. The Dual-PRNet, through warping image feature maps, can produce coarse-to-fine transformations within one iteration. However, its registration accuracy is unable to match iterative deep registration methods. In addition, few coarse-to-fine registration methods impose constraints on the transformations to keep their invertibility. Mok et al. [9] attempted to impose diffeomorphic constraints on the transformations in the LapIRN. However, this dramatically degraded the registration accuracy.

In this study, we propose a Non-Iterative Coarse-to-finE registration Network (NICE-Net) for deformable image registration. Compared to the state-of-the-art iterative deep registration methods, our NICE-Net can perform more accurate registration with a single network in a single iteration. The technical contributions of our NICE-Net are in two folds: (i) we propose a Single-pass Deep Cumulative Learning (SDCL) decoder that can cumulatively learn coarse-to-fine transformations within a single (iteration) pass of the network, and (ii) we propose a Selectively-propagated Feature Learning (SFL) encoder that can learn common image features for the whole coarse-to-fine registration process and selectively propagate the features as needed. We also incorporated penalizing negative Jacobian determinants into the loss function in coarse-to-fine registration, which allows to keep the transformation invertibility with a marginal degradation on the registration accuracy. We performed comprehensive experiments on six public datasets of 3D brain MRI.

2 Method

Image registration aims to find a spatial transformation ϕ that warps a moving image I_m to a fixed image I_f, so that the warped image $I_m \circ \phi$ is spatially aligned with the fixed image I_f. In this study, the moving image I_m and fixed image I_f are two volumes defined in a 3D spatial domain $\Omega \subset \mathbb{R}^3$, and the ϕ is parameterized as a displacement field, following [4]. For coarse-to-fine registration settings, we define L as the number of registration steps. At the ith step ($i \in \{1, 2, \ldots, L\}$), a transformation ϕ_i is produced with the ϕ_1 as the coarsest transformation and the ϕ_L as the finest transformation. It should be noted that, for existing iterative methods [8–10], the L also is the number of the cascaded networks (or running iterations), as they implement each registration step with a separate network (or iteration). However, our NICE-Net can implement all L registration steps within one iteration. In addition, we create two image pyramids by downsampling the I_f and I_m with trilinear interpolation to obtain $I_f{}^i \in \{I_f{}^1, I_f{}^2, \ldots, I_f{}^L\}$ and $I_m{}^i \in \{I_m{}^1, I_m{}^2, \ldots, I_m{}^L\}$, where the $I_f{}^i$ and $I_m{}^i$ are the downsampled I_f and I_m by a factor of $0.5^{(L-i)}$ with $I_f{}^L = I_f$ and $I_m{}^L = I_m$.

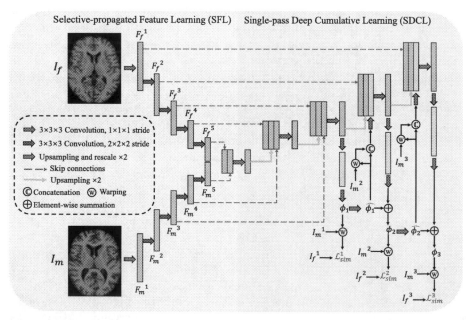

Fig. 1. Architecture of the NICE-Net. The registration step, L, is set as 3 for illustration.

The architecture of the proposed NICE-Net is illustrated in Fig. 1, which consists of a SFL encoder (detailed in Sect. 2.1) and a SDCL decoder (detailed in Sect. 2.2). The

SFL encoder extracts image features and selectively propagates the features to the SDCL decoder through skip connections. The SDCL decoder performs L-step coarse-to-fine registration.

2.1 Selectively-Propagated Feature Learning (SFL)

The SFL encoder is a dual-path encoder with selective feature propagation. Unlike the existing deep registration methods that usually learn coupled image features from the concatenated fixed/moving images [4, 5, 8, 9], the SFL encoder learns features from the I_f and I_m separately using two paths. This dual-path design can derive uncoupled features of I_f and I_m, which enables us to selectively propagate different features to perform different steps of coarse-to-fine registration. For example, the features of I_f should always be propagated, as the I_f is the registration target for all registration steps. However, the features of I_m are important for the first step but not necessary for later, because the later steps refine the transformation based on the intermediary warped image (derived from its former step) rather than based on the original I_m. This selective feature propagation allows the network to learn common image features for the whole coarse-to-fine registration process without the need for repeated feature learning for each registration step.

Specifically, the SFL encoder has two identical, weight-shared paths, P_f and P_m, which takes I_f and I_m as input, respectively. Each path consists of five successive $3 \times 3 \times 3$ convolutional layers, followed by LeakyReLU activation with parameter 0.2. Except for the first convolutional layer, each convolutional layer has a stride of 2 to reduce the resolution of feature maps. Through the SFL encoder, we can obtain two 5-level feature pyramids, $F_f{}^i \in \{F_f{}^1, F_f{}^2, \ldots, F_f{}^5\}$ and $F_m{}^i \in \{F_m{}^1, F_m{}^2, \ldots, F_m{}^5\}$, where the $F_f{}^i$ and $F_m{}^i$ are the output of the ith convolutional layer of P_f and P_m. For feature propagation, the $F_f{}^i \in \{F_f{}^1, F_f{}^2, \ldots, F_f{}^5\}$ and $F_m{}^i \in \{F_m{}^L, F_m{}^{L+1}, \ldots, F_m{}^5\}$ are propagated to the SDCL decoder through skip connections. As exemplified in Fig. 1, when $L = 3$, the $F_m{}^1$ and $F_m{}^2$ are not propagated to the SDCL decoder.

2.2 Single-Pass Deep Cumulative Learning (SDCL)

Cumulative learning is a cognitive process of cumulating knowledge for subsequent cognitive development [13]. By the name (single-pass deep cumulative learning), we aim to emphasize two characteristics of the SDCL decoder: (i) it can perform coarse-to-fine registration in a single pass (iteration) of the network, and (ii) the coarse-to-fine registration is performed as a cumulative learning process, where the knowledge (features and transformations) learned at former steps can be cumulated and facilitate later steps. This is different from the existing iterative methods as they usually learn separate features for each iteration, in which the knowledge learned at each step is collapsed into a warped image and is not cumulated for later steps.

Specifically, the SDCL decoder uses five successive $3 \times 3 \times 3$ convolutional layers to cumulate features. An upsampling layer is used after each convolutional layer, except for the last one, to increase the resolution of feature maps by a factor of 2. LeakyReLU activation with parameter 0.2 is used after each convolutional layer. These five convolutional layers can support up to 5-step coarse-to-fine registration. However, for L-step coarse-to-fine registration ($L < 5$), only the last L convolutional layers are used for the L registration steps, while the other $(5 - L)$ convolutional layers are only used to cumulate features. As exemplified in Fig. 1, when $L = 3$, the first two convolutional layers are used to cumulate features, and the first registration step is performed after the third convolutional layer to produces the ϕ_1. The ϕ_1 is upsampled by a factor of 2 to be $\widehat{\phi_1}$, and the $\widehat{\phi_1}$ is used to warp the $I_m{}^2$. Then, the warped image $I_m{}^2 \circ \widehat{\phi_1}$ and the $\widehat{\phi_1}$ are fed into a convolutional layer to be leveraged at the second registration step. The second registration step also produces a transformation based on the cumulated features, but this transformation needs to be voxel-wisely added to the $\widehat{\phi_1}$ to derive the ϕ_2. We repeat this process until the ϕ_L is derived. The ϕ_L is the final output of the NICE-Net, which can warp the I_m to align with the I_f.

2.3 Unsupervised Training

The proposed NICE-Net is end-to-end trained using an unsupervised loss $\mathcal{L}$ without ground-truth labels. The loss $\mathcal{L}$ is defined as $\mathcal{L} = \sum_{i=1}^{L} \frac{1}{2^{(L-i)}} \left(\mathcal{L}_{sim}^i + \sigma \mathcal{L}_{reg}^i \right)$, where the $\mathcal{L}_{sim}^i$ is a similarity term that penalizes the differences between the warped image $I_m{}^i \circ \phi_i$ and the fixed image $I_f{}^i$, the $\mathcal{L}_{reg}^i$ is a regularization term that penalizes unrealistic transformations ϕ_i, and the σ is a regularization parameter.

As the local normalized cross-correlation (NCC) has been reported as a successful similarity metric in many deformable registration methods [8–12], we use negative NCC with window size 9^3 as the $\mathcal{L}_{sim}^i$. The $\mathcal{L}_{reg}^i$ imposes L2 regularization on the ϕ_i to encourage its smoothness and also has a term $\mathcal{L}_{inv}^i$ to enhance its invertibility, which is defined as $\mathcal{L}_{reg}^i = \sum_{p \in O} \| \nabla \phi_i(p) \|^2 + \lambda \mathcal{L}_{inv}^i$ with the λ as a regularization parameter. As the ϕ_i is not invertible at the voxel p where the Jacobian determinant is negative ($|J\phi_i(p)| \leq 0$) [14], we adopt the regularization loss proposed by Kuang et al. [15] as the $\mathcal{L}_{inv}^i$ to explicitly penalize the negative Jacobian determinants of ϕ_i.

3   Experimental Setup

3.1   Datasets

We evaluated our NICE-Net with the task of inter-patient 3D brain MRI registration, and this task has been well benchmarked for registration with large deformations [8–11]. We used 2,760 T1–weighted brain MRI volumes for training, which were acquired from four public datasets: ADNI [16], ABIDE [17], ADHD [18], and IXI [19]. For validation and testing, we used two public datasets of brain MRI with manual segmentation: Mindboggle101 [20] and Buckner40 [21]. The Mindboggle101 dataset contains 101 MRI volumes. We randomly separate the dataset into 50 volumes for validation and 51 volumes for testing. The Buckner40 dataset consists of 40 MRI volumes and we used the dataset only for testing.

We performed brain extraction and intensity normalization for each MRI volume by FreeSurfer [21]. Then, each volume was affine-transformed and resampled to align with a MNI-152 brain template with 1mm isotropic voxels by FLIRT [22]. Finally, all volumes were cropped into $144 \times 192 \times 160$ voxels.

3.2 Implementation Details

We implemented the NICE-Net using Keras with a Tensorflow backend on an Intel Core i5-9400 CPU and a 12 GB Titan V GPU. We used an ADAM optimizer with a learning rate of 0.0001 and a batch size of 1 to train the network for 100,000 iterations. At each iteration, two volumes were randomly picked from the training set as the fixed and moving images. A total of 200 image pairs, randomly picked from the validation set, were used to monitor the training process and to optimize hyper-parameters. The σ is set as 1 to ensure that the $\mathcal{L}_{sim}$ and $\sigma\mathcal{L}_{reg}$ have close values, while the λ is set as 10^{-4} to ensure that the percentage of negative Jacobian determinants is no more than 0.05% (Table S1 in Supplementary Materials). We also trained a NICE-Net with $\lambda = 0$ to maximize the registration accuracy. Our code is available at https://github.com/MungoMeng/Registration-NICE-Net.

3.3 Comparison Methods

The proposed NICE-Net was compared to eight state-of-the-art registration methods, including two traditional methods, three non-iterative deep registration methods, and three iterative deep registration methods. The included traditional methods are SyN [23] and NiftyReg [24]. We ran them using cross-correlation as similarity measure with the parameters tuned on the validation set. The included non-iterative deep registration methods are Voxelmorph (VM) [4], Diffeomorphic Voxelmorph (DifVM) [5], and Dual-PRNet [11]. The included iterative deep registration methods are RCN [8], LapIRN [9], and ULAE-net [10]. For a fair comparison, we reimplemented all deep registration methods with Keras and used the same NCC loss as the similarity metric. We set $L = 3$ for the iterative deep registration methods (RCN, LapIRN, and ULAE-net), which makes them use out all the GPU memory (12 GB). Moreover, as the default VM and DifVM have fewer parameters than other methods, we increased their feature map channels to make them use out all the GPU memory as well.

3.4 Experimental Settings

We first compared the NICE-Net with the eight comparison methods for subject-to-subject registration. In this experiment, we set $L = 3$ for our NICE-Net, which is consistent with the RCN, LapIRN, and ULAE-net. Then, we performed an ablation study, where the NICE-Net with $\lambda = 0$ was evaluated with different $L \in \{1, 2, 3, 4, 5\}$. When $L = 1$, the NICE-Net only performs one-step registration, which means the SDCL decoder is not working and the SFL encoder has been degraded as a normal dual-path encoder without selective feature propagation.

A total of 200, 100 testing pairs were randomly picked from the Mindboggle101, Buckner40 testing sets for evaluation. The registration accuracy was evaluated by the Dice similarity coefficients (DSC) between fixed and warped segmentation masks. A two-sided $P < 0.05$ is considered to indicate a statistically significant difference. The transformation invertibility was evaluated by the percentage of negative Jacobian determinants (NJD). A lower NJD indicates a more invertible transformation.

4   Results and Discussion

The results of our NICE-Net and the comparison methods are shown in Table 1, and the qualitative comparison is shown in Fig. S1 in Supplementary Materials. Compared to the VM and DifVM, the iterative deep registration methods (RCN, LapIRN, and ULAE-net) achieved higher DSCs but had nearly double runtime as they performed iterative coarse-to-fine registration to handle large deformations. The Dual-PRNet also achieved higher DSCs than the VM and DifVM but cannot outperform the iterative deep registration methods. This suggests that the Dual-PRNet, although can realize non-iterative coarse-to-fine registration, is a non-optimal solution for large deformation registration. In the Dual-PRNet, the transformation produced at each registration step is based on the feature maps warped by its adjacent former step, while the knowledge learned at other former steps (except for the adjacent one) can hardly be leveraged. However, in our NICE-Net, coarse-to-fine registration is performed as a cumulative learning process, where the knowledge (features and transformations) learned at all coarser steps are cumulated and facilitate the registration at finer steps. Therefore, our NICE-Net ($\lambda = 0$) achieved significantly higher DSCs than all the comparison methods while only requiring similar runtime to the non-iterative methods. We noted that a recent study shows that the Dual-PRNet can be enhanced by computing local correlations between features or by joint learning with segmentation [25]. We anticipate that our NICE-Net can also benefit from these enhancements, and we will investigate its relative performance in our future study.

When $\lambda = 10^{-4}$, our NICE-Net achieved the lowest NJDs with a small degradation on DSCs. Compared to the NICE-Net ($\lambda = 10^{-4}$), the DifVM and LapIRN can achieve similar NJDs but had significantly lower DSCs; the ULAE-net can achieve similar DSCs but had much higher NJDs. These results demonstrate that our NICE-net can outperform the state-of-the-art iterative deep registration methods on all registration accuracy, registration speed, and transformation invertibility.

The results of the ablation study are shown in Table 2. The NICE-Net with $L = 1$ is regarded as the baseline, in which the SFL encoder and the SDCL decoder are not employed. The NICE-Net with $L > 1$ achieved higher DSCs than the baseline, which can be attributed to the use of our proposed SFL encoder and SDCL decoder. When the L varied from 2 to 5, the DSC improved with a slight increase in runtime, which suggests that, in our NICE-Net, increasing registration steps results in higher registration accuracy while only adding a negligible computational load. This also means, if we set L as 5, the NICE-Net can outperform the RCN, LapIRN, and ULAE-net by a larger margin while still keeping its advantage on registration speed. However, for the iterative deep registration methods, increasing L means they have to cascade more networks or run the network for more iterations, which inevitably requires more GPU memory and further prolongs their runtime. We illustrate the results of the NICE-Net with $L = 5$ in Fig. 2. We found that the NICE-Net can perform finer registration after each step, gradually making the moving image I_m closer to the fixed image I_f.

Table 1. Results of our NICE-Net and the comparison methods.

Methods	Mindboggle101		Buckner40		Runtime (second)	
	DSC	NJD	DSC	NJD	CPU	GPU
SyN	$0.548^{*,\ddagger}$	0.26%	$0.577^{*,\ddagger}$	0.25%	3793	/
NiftyReg	$0.567^{*,\ddagger}$	0.34%	$0.610^{*,\ddagger}$	0.30%	166	/
VM	$0.558^{*,\ddagger}$	2.53%	$0.592^{*,\ddagger}$	2.22%	3.85	0.395
DifVM	$0.531^{*,\ddagger}$	0.04%	$0.574^{*,\ddagger}$	0.02%	3.92	0.446
Dual-PRNet	$0.586^{*,\ddagger}$	2.23%	$0.618^{*,\ddagger}$	2.13%	4.47	0.467
RCN	$0.592^{*,\ddagger}$	3.95%	$0.630^{*,\ddagger}$	4.02%	6.75	0.692
LapIRN	$0.596^{*,\ddagger}$	0.04%	$0.625^{*,\ddagger}$	0.03%	6.52	0.624
ULAE-net	$0.610^{\ddagger}$	2.00%	$0.640^{\ddagger}$	1.94%	7.21	0.730
NICE-Net ($\lambda = 10^{-4}$)	0.608	**0.03%**	0.639	**0.02%**	4.17	0.423
NICE-Net ($\lambda = 0$)	**0.621**	2.01%	**0.649**	1.96%	4.17	0.427

Bold: the highest DSC and lowest NJD for each testing set are in bold.

*: $P < 0.05$, in comparison to the NICE-Net ($\lambda = 10^{-4}$).

‡: $P < 0.05$, in comparison to the NICE-Net ($\lambda = 0$).

Table 2. Results of our NICE-Net with different L.

NICE-Net with $L =$		1	2	3	4	5
Mindboggle101	DSC	0.565	0.601	0.621	0.624	**0.626**
	NJD	2.26%	2.08%	2.09%	2.08%	2.11%
Buckner40	DSC	0.599	0.629	0.649	0.652	**0.654**
	NJD	2.05%	1.98%	1.98%	1.95%	1.96%
Runtime	CPU	3.84	4.06	4.17	4.18	4.18
(second)	GPU	0.398	0.412	0.427	0.439	0.445

Bold: the highest DSC for each testing set is in bold, while the lowest NJD is not in bold as all methods achieved similar NJDs.

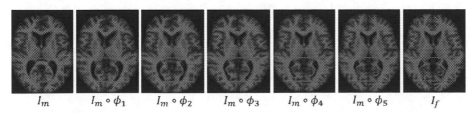

I_m $I_m \circ \phi_1$ $I_m \circ \phi_2$ $I_m \circ \phi_3$ $I_m \circ \phi_4$ $I_m \circ \phi_5$ I_f

Fig. 2. Registration results of the NICE-Net with $L = 5$. From life to right are the moving image, the images warped by 5 registration steps, and the fixed image.

5   Conclusion

We have outlined a Non-Iterative Coarse-to-finE registration Network (NICE-Net) for deformable image registration. Unlike the existing iterative deep registration methods, our NICE-Net can perform coarse-to-fine registration with a single network in a single iteration. The experimental results show that the proposed NICE-Net can outperform the state-of-the-art iterative deep registration methods on both registration accuracy and transformation invertibility while only requiring similar runtime to non-iterative registration methods.

Acknowledgement. This work was supported in part by Australian Research Council (ARC) grants (IC170100022 and DP200103748).

References

1. Haskins, G., Kruger, U., Yan, P.: Deep learning in medical image registration: a survey. Mach. Vis. Appl. **31**(1–2), 1–18 (2020). https://doi.org/10.1007/s00138-020-01060-x
2. Sotiras, A., Davatzikos, C., Paragios, N.: Deformable medical image registration: a survey. IEEE Trans. Med. Imaging. **32**(7), 1153–1190 (2013)
3. Xiao, H., et al.: A review of deep learning-based three-dimensional medical image registration methods. Quant. Imaging Med. Surg. **11**(12), 4895–4916 (2021)
4. Balakrishnan, G., Zhao, A., Sabuncu, M.R., Guttag, J., Dalca, A.V.: Voxelmorph: a learning framework for deformable medical image registration. IEEE Trans. Med. Imaging **38**(8), 1788–1800 (2019)
5. Dalca, A.V., Balakrishnan, G., Guttag, J., Sabuncu, M.R.: Unsupervised learning of probabilistic diffeomorphic registration for images and surfaces. Med. Image Anal. **57**, 226–236 (2019)
6. De Vos, B.D., Berendsen, F.F., Viergever, M.A., Sokooti, H., Staring, M., Išgum, I.: A deep learning framework for unsupervised affine and deformable image registration. Med. Image Anal. **52**, 128–143 (2019)
7. Hering, A., van Ginneken, B., Heldmann, S.: mlVIRNET: multilevel variational image registration network. In: Shen, D., et al. (eds.) Medical Image Computing and Computer Assisted Intervention – MICCAI 2019. Lecture Notes in Computer Science, vol. 11769, pp. 257–265. Springer, Cham (2019). https://doi.org/10.1007/978-3-030-32226-7_29
8. Zhao, S., et al.: Recursive cascaded networks for unsupervised medical image registration. In: Proceedings of the IEEE International Conference on Computer Vision, pp. 10600–10610 (2019)
9. Mok, T.C.W., Chung, A.C.S.: Large deformation diffeomorphic image registration with Laplacian pyramid networks. In: Martel, A.L., et al. (eds.) Medical Image Computing and Computer Assisted Intervention – MICCAI 2020. LNCS, vol. 12263, pp. 211–221. Springer, Cham (2020). https://doi.org/10.1007/978-3-030-59716-0_21
10. Shu, Y., Wang, H., Xiao, B., Bi, X., Li, W.: Medical image registration based on uncoupled learning and accumulative enhancement. In: deBruijne, M., et al. (eds.) Medical Image Computing and Computer Assisted Intervention – MICCAI 2021. LNCS, vol. 12904, pp. 3–13. Springer, Cham (2021). https://doi.org/10.1007/978-3-030-87202-1_1
11. Xiaojun, H., Kang, M., Huang, W., Scott, M.R., Wiest, R., Reyes, M.: Dual-stream pyramid registration network. In: Shen, D., et al. (eds.) Medical Image Computing and Computer Assisted Intervention – MICCAI 2019. LNCS, vol. 11765, pp. 382–390. Springer, Cham (2019). https://doi.org/10.1007/978-3-030-32245-8_43

12. Meng, M., Bi, L., Fulham, M., Feng, D.D., Kim, J.: Enhancing Medical Image Registration via Appearance Adjustment Networks. arXiv preprint arXiv:2103.05213 (2021)
13. Thórisson, K.R., Bieger, J., Li, X., Wang, P.: Cumulative learning. In: International Conference on Artificial General Intelligence, pp. 198–208. Springer, Cham (2019)
14. Ashburner, J.: A fast diffeomorphic image registration algorithm. Neuroimage **38**(1), 95–113 (2007)
15. Kuang, D., Schmah, T.: FAIM – a ConvNet method for unsupervised 3D medical image registration. In: Suk, H.-Il., Liu, M., Yan, P., Lian, C. (eds.) Machine Learning in Medical Imaging. LNCS, vol. 11861, pp. 646–654. Springer, Cham (2019). https://doi.org/10.1007/978-3-030-32692-0_74
16. Mueller, S.G., et al.: Ways toward an early diagnosis in Alzheimer's disease: the Alzheimer's Disease Neuroimaging Initiative (ADNI). Alzheimers Dement. **1**(1), 55–66 (2005)
17. Di Martino, A., et al.: The autism brain imaging data exchange: towards a large-scale evaluation of the intrinsic brain architecture in autism. Mol. Psych. **19**(6), 659–667 (2014)
18. Milham, M.P., Fair, D., Mennes, M., Mostofsky, S.H.: The ADHD-200 consortium: a model to advance the translational potential of neuroimaging in clinical neuroscience. Front. Syst. Neurosci. **6**, 62 (2012)
19. The Information eXtraction from Images (IXI) dataset. https://brain-development.org/ixi-dataset/. Accessed 19 Jan 2022
20. Klein, A., Tourville, J.: 101 labeled brain images and a consistent human cortical labeling protocol. Front. Neurosci. **6**, 171 (2012)
21. Fischl, B.: FreeSurfer. Neuroimage **62**(2), 774–781 (2012)
22. Jenkinson, M., Smith, S.M.: A global optimisation method for robust affine registration of brain images. Med. Image Anal. **5**(2), 143–156 (2001)
23. Avants, B.B., Epstein, C.L., Grossman, M., Gee, J.C.: Symmetric diffeomorphic image registration with cross-correlation: evaluating automated labeling of elderly and neurodegenerative brain. Med. Image Anal. **12**(1), 26–41 (2008)
24. Modat, M., et al.: Fast free-form deformation using graphics processing units. Comput. Methods Programs Biomed. **98**(3), 278–284 (2010)
25. Kang, M., Hu, X., Huang, W., Scott, M.R., Reyes, M.: Dual stream pyramid registration network. Med. Image Anal. **78**, 102374 (2022)

DSR: Direct Simultaneous Registration for Multiple 3D Images

Zhehua Mao[1], Liang Zhao[1(✉)], Shoudong Huang[1], Yiting Fan[2], and Alex P. W. Lee[3]

[1] Robotics Institute, Faculty of Engineering and Information Technology, University of Technology Sydney, Ultimo, NSW 2007, Australia
Liang.Zhao@uts.edu.au
[2] Department of Cardiology, Shanghai Chest Hospital, Shanghai Jiao Tong University, Shanghai, China
[3] Division of Cardiology, Department of Medicine and Therapeutics, Prince of Wales Hospital and Laboratory of Cardiac Imaging and 3D Printing, Li Ka Shing Institute of Health Science, Faculty of Medicine, The Chinese University of Hong Kong, Hong Kong, China

Abstract. This paper presents a novel algorithm named Direct Simultaneous Registration (DSR) that registers a collection of 3D images in a simultaneous fashion without specifying any reference image, feature extraction and matching, or information loss or reuse. The algorithm optimizes the global poses of local image frames by maximizing the similarity between a predefined panoramic image and local images. Although we formulate the problem as a Direct Bundle Adjustment (DBA) that jointly optimizes the poses of local frames and the intensities of the panoramic image, by investigating the independence of pose estimation from the panoramic image in the solving process, DSR is proposed to solve the poses only and proved to be able to obtain the same optimal poses as DBA. The proposed method is particularly suitable for the scenarios where distinct features are not available, such as Transesophageal Echocardiography (TEE) images. DSR is evaluated by comparing it with four widely used methods via simulated and in-vivo 3D TEE images. It is shown that the proposed method outperforms these four methods in terms of accuracy and requires much fewer computational resources than the state-of-the-art accumulated pairwise estimates (APE). Codes of DSR are available at https://github.com/ZH-Mao/DSR.

1 Introduction

Image registration is a fundamental task for many medical image analysis problems where valuable information conveyed by two or more images needs to be combined and examined [14,20]. In recent decades, mainstream medical imaging techniques, such as CT, MRI, and Ultrasound (US), have evolved from 2D to

---

Supplementary Information The online version contains supplementary material available at https://doi.org/10.1007/978-3-031-16446-0_10.

L. Wang et al. (Eds.): MICCAI 2022, LNCS 13436, pp. 98–107, 2022.
https://doi.org/10.1007/978-3-031-16446-0_10

3D, which proposes new challenges to medical image registration, such as feature extraction and high computational complexity [15]. Compared to feature-based methods [13], direct (intensity-based) methods [14,16] have occupied a dominant position in the field of medical image registration [7,18] because of their avoidance of feature extraction and high accuracy, especially when handling images that lack distinct features, such as 3D Transesophageal Echocardiography (3D TEE) images. Direct methods estimate the frame poses by maximizing the similarity between the images. Widely used similarity metrics include sum-of-squared differences (SSD), correlation ratio (CR), and mutual information (MI) [14].

Registration of a collection of images is much more complex than pairwise registration [20]. One solution to this problem is to deduce the global poses from the results of pairwise registration [2,11,16,21]. This strategy, although intuitive, is usually biased to the selected reference image and inevitably brings in accumulating errors. In comparison, a better strategy is to optimize the poses of all local frames simultaneously to avoid biases. In [9], a framework called congealing is proposed, which uses underlying entropic information of images for alignment. A large number of images are necessary for congealing because the estimation is done with the information at one location at a time [20]. And as [3] pointed out, employing entropy for congealing is problematic due to its poor optimization characteristics. Recently in [20], an accumulated pairwise estimates (APE) method is proposed for simultaneous registration. The method considers overlapping areas of images in the objective function multiple times, thus may have the information reuse issue and bring in extra complexity in the optimization.

In this paper, we propose a novel direct simultaneous registration (DSR) method which optimizes global poses of a collection of 3D images directly based on image intensity. The novelties of the paper include: 1) simultaneous registration is formulated as a direct bundle adjustment (DBA) problem, which redefines classical bundle adjustment (BA) [17] by jointly optimizing the poses of local frames and the intensities of the predefined panorama; 2) DBA uses intensity information directly instead of the extracted and matched feature points of the local 2D images in classical BA. Therefore, our method can deal with images lacking distinct features such as 3D TEE images; 3) importantly, we prove in DBA, the pose estimation is independent of the intensities of the panorama during the optimization process; 4) based on 3), we derive DSR that *only* solves the poses *without* solving the intensities of the panorama but obtaining the same poses as DBA. Simulated and in-vivo 3D TEE images are used to evaluate the proposed DSR method compared with pairwise [2], Lie normalization [21], sequential [11], and APE [20] methods. Running in a simultaneous fashion, DSR is an unbiased method that can employ all intensity information of images without information reuse, which is an elegant way to obtain the optimal poses of local frames with high accuracy.

2 Methodology

2.1 Direct Bundle Adjustment

Suppose there are m frames of 3D images taken from different viewpoints denoted as $\mathbf{I} = \{I_1, ..., I_i, ..., I_m\}$. Correspondingly, the rigid transformation for each frame is parameterized in Lie algebra space [6] with the pose parameters $\mathbf{x}_\xi = [\boldsymbol{\xi}_1^\top, ..., \boldsymbol{\xi}_i^\top, ..., \boldsymbol{\xi}_m^\top]^\top \in \mathbb{R}^{6m}$. Simultaneous registration is the process of estimating the optimal pose parameters of all local frames $\hat{\mathbf{x}}_\xi$ simultaneously in order to align all the images in one global coordinate frame.

Assume M is defined as a 3D panoramic image in the global frame. M consists of n voxels $\{\mathbf{p}_1, ..., \mathbf{p}_j, ..., \mathbf{p}_n\}$ where $\mathbf{p}_j \in \mathbb{R}^3$, which fuses all the local frame images. The intensity of voxel $\mathbf{p}_j$ in M is obtained from fusing different points' intensities in local images. Denote the intensity of $\mathbf{p}_j$ in M and $\mathbf{p}_j$'s corresponding point $\mathbf{p}_{ij}$ in local frame I_i as $M(\mathbf{p}_j)$ and $I_i(\mathbf{p}_{ij})$, respectively. The intensity difference between $M(\mathbf{p}_j)$ and $I_i(\mathbf{p}_{ij})$ is

$$e_{ij}(\boldsymbol{\xi}_i, M(\mathbf{p}_j)) = M(\mathbf{p}_j) - I_i(\omega(\boldsymbol{\xi}_i, \mathbf{p}_j)) = M(\mathbf{p}_j) - I_i(\mathbf{p}_{ij}), \qquad (1)$$

where $\mathbf{p}_{ij} = \omega(\boldsymbol{\xi}_i, \mathbf{p}_j) = T(\boldsymbol{\xi}_i)\mathbf{p}_j$ transforms $\mathbf{p}_j$ to $\mathbf{p}_{ij}$, and $T(\cdot) \in SE(3)$ maps the pose parameters $\boldsymbol{\xi}_i$ to a 3D Euclidean transformation. When calculating the intensity difference e_{ij} in (1), the intensity of $\mathbf{p}_{ij}$ in I_i is obtained using trilinear interpolation to reduce the error of the intensity difference computation.

Inspired by the conventional BA framework that considers both the 3D point positions and camera poses in the optimization [1,17], we propose the DBA framework that jointly optimizes the poses of local frames and the intensities of the panoramic image (instead of 3D point positions in BA). The overall state parameters considered in DBA are $\mathbf{x} = [\mathbf{x}_\xi^\top, \mathbf{x}_M^\top]^\top$, where $\mathbf{x}_M = [M(\mathbf{p}_1), ..., M(\mathbf{p}_j), ..., M(\mathbf{p}_n)]^\top$ are the intensities of voxels in M. Then, we seek to obtain the optimal solution $\hat{\mathbf{x}} = [\hat{\mathbf{x}}_\xi^\top, \hat{\mathbf{x}}_M^\top]^\top$ that minimizes the sum-of-squared intensity differences between the panoramic image and the local images, i.e.

$$\hat{\mathbf{x}} = \underset{\mathbf{x}_\xi, \mathbf{x}_M}{\arg\min} \sum_{j=1}^{n} \sum_{i=1}^{m} \sigma(\mathbf{p}_{ij})(e_{ij}(\boldsymbol{\xi}_i, M(\mathbf{p}_j)))^2, \qquad (2)$$

where $\sigma(\mathbf{p}_{ij}) = 1$ if the transformed point $\mathbf{p}_{ij}$ is within Image I_i, i.e. $\mathbf{p}_j$ is observed in I_i, otherwise $\sigma(\mathbf{p}_{ij}) = 0$. Such a formulation of DBA circumvents the process of feature extraction and matching in most BA problems. Additionally, since we take the intensities of the panoramic image into account, DBA can also obtain the optimal panoramic image besides the global poses of local frames.

Gauss-Newton (GN) method is commonly used to solve nonlinear least-squares (NLLS) problems like (2). The method obtains the solution by starting with parameters initialization and then updating the parameters using the step changes calculated from GN equation in each iteration until the algorithm converges. If we write the overall observed intensity differences as a concatenation vector $e(\mathbf{x}) = [..., e_{ij}, ...]^\top$, the objective function of (2) can be rewritten as $f(\mathbf{x}) = e(\mathbf{x})^\top e(\mathbf{x})$. And step changes $\Delta\mathbf{x}$ in each iteration can be calculated from the GN equation:

$$J(\mathbf{x})^\top J(\mathbf{x})\Delta\mathbf{x} = -J(\mathbf{x})^\top e(\mathbf{x}), \qquad (3)$$

where $J(\mathbf{x})$ is the Jacobian matrix of $e(\mathbf{x})$ w.r.t. $\mathbf{x}$.

Let $J_{ij}(\mathbf{x})$ denote one row of $J(\mathbf{x})$, which is the gradient of one intensity difference e_{ij} w.r.t. $\mathbf{x} = [\mathbf{x}_\xi^\top, \mathbf{x}_M^\top]^\top$. It is shown in (1) that e_{ij} is only dependent on $\boldsymbol{\xi}_i$ and $M(\mathbf{p}_j)$, thus only two blocks in $J_{ij}(\mathbf{x})$ are nonzero, i.e.

$$\frac{\partial e_{ij}(\boldsymbol{\xi}_i, M(\mathbf{p}_j))}{\partial \boldsymbol{\xi}_i} = -\frac{\partial I_i}{\partial \omega(\boldsymbol{\xi}_i, \mathbf{p}_j)} \frac{\partial \omega(\boldsymbol{\xi}_i, \mathbf{p}_j)}{\partial \boldsymbol{\xi}_i}, \text{ and } \frac{\partial e_{ij}(\boldsymbol{\xi}_i, M(\mathbf{p}_j))}{\partial (M(\mathbf{p}_j))} = 1,$$

which indicates $J_{ij}(\mathbf{x})$ is very sparse.

Although the optimal poses and panoramic image can be obtained simultaneously, DBA seems more difficult to solve than traditional multi-image registration problems since a much higher order state vector is involved. However, we can further prove that the pose optimization is actually independent of the panoramic image in the GN iterations (see Sect. 2.2), which means we do not need to solve the intensities of the panoramic image but can obtain exactly the same optimal poses as solving the complete DBA. This is also an important property that conventional BA frameworks do not have.

2.2   Simultaneous Registration Without Intensity Optimization

Theorem: *When solving (2) with GN iterations, the optimization of poses is independent of the intensities of the panoramic image.*

Proof: If we write Jacobian matrix of $e(\mathbf{x})$ w.r.t. $\mathbf{x}_\xi$ and $\mathbf{x}_M$ separately as $J(\mathbf{x}) = [J_\xi, J_M]$, then (3) can be rewritten as the following format:

$$\begin{bmatrix} H_{\xi\xi} & H_{\xi M} \\ H_{M\xi} & H_{MM} \end{bmatrix} \begin{bmatrix} \Delta \mathbf{x}_\xi \\ \Delta \mathbf{x}_M \end{bmatrix} = \begin{bmatrix} b_\xi \\ b_M \end{bmatrix}, \tag{4}$$

where $H_{\xi\xi} = J_\xi^\top J_\xi, H_{\xi M} = H_{M\xi}^\top = J_\xi^\top J_M, H_{MM} = J_M^\top J_M, b_\xi = -J_\xi^\top e(\mathbf{x})$, and $b_M = -J_M^\top e(\mathbf{x})$. Then, through Schur complement [23], the step changes of poses and intensities of voxels can be computed sequentially as:

$$\left(H_{\xi\xi} - H_{\xi M} H_{MM}^{-1} H_{\xi M}^\top\right) \Delta \mathbf{x}_\xi = (b_\xi - H_{\xi M} H_{MM}^{-1} b_M), \tag{5}$$

$$H_{MM} \Delta \mathbf{x}_M = b_M - H_{\xi M}^\top \Delta \mathbf{x}_\xi. \tag{6}$$

Suppose intensity differences $e(\mathbf{x})$ are decomposed into two components $e(\mathbf{x}) = \mathbf{A} - \mathbf{B}$, where $\mathbf{A} = [..., M(\mathbf{p}_j), ...]^\top$ and $\mathbf{B} = [..., I_i(\mathbf{p}_{ij}), ...]^\top$ represent observed intensities of the panoramic image and their corresponding intensities in local frames, respectively. The right side of (5) becomes:

$$b_\xi - H_{\xi M} H_{MM}^{-1} b_M = -J_\xi^\top (\mathbf{A} - \mathbf{B}) + J_\xi^\top J_M (J_M^\top J_M)^{-1} J_M^\top (\mathbf{A} - \mathbf{B})$$
$$= -J_\xi^\top (\mathbf{A} - J_M (J_M^\top J_M)^{-1} J_M^\top \mathbf{A}) - J_\xi^\top (J_M (J_M^\top J_M)^{-1} J_M^\top \mathbf{B} - \mathbf{B}). \tag{7}$$

It is shown from $J_{ij}(\mathbf{x})$ that there is one and only one nonzero element 1 in each row of J_M. The nonzero element means the voxel $\mathbf{p}_j$ is observed in the local frame i and corresponds to the intensity difference $e_{ij} = M(\mathbf{p}_j) - I_i(\mathbf{p}_{ij})$. Therefore, according to the observed status of the panoramic image in the local frames which is indicated by the structure of J_M, it can be easily deduced that $\mathbf{A} = J_M \mathbf{x}_M$. Substituting $\mathbf{A}$ to the first term on the right side of (7), we have:

$$-J_\xi^\top (J_M \mathbf{x}_M - J_M (J_M^\top J_M)^{-1} J_M^\top J_M \mathbf{x}_M) = \mathbf{0}. \tag{8}$$

Then, (5) becomes:

$$\left(H_{\xi\xi} - H_{\xi M} H_{MM}^{-1} H_{\xi M}^\top\right) \Delta \mathbf{x}_\xi = -J_\xi^\top (J_M H_{MM}^{-1} J_M^\top \mathbf{B} - \mathbf{B}), \tag{9}$$

which indicates that the step change $\Delta \mathbf{x}_\xi$ is independent of intensities $\mathbf{x}_M$ in every GN iteration. Therefore, obtaining the optimal poses is independent of the intensities of panoramic image M during the optimization process.   **Q.E.D.**

Although H_{MM} in (9) has a huge dimension due to the large number of intensities in M, H_{MM} is sparse and diagonal because of the sparse structure of J_M. The value of a diagonal element represents the number of times that the corresponding voxel of M has been observed in the local frames in the current iteration. So, the inverse of diagonal matrix H_{MM} can be easily computed by finding the inverse of each diagonal element, which makes solving (9) efficient.

Such an independent property of DBA is very attractive since it allows us to optimize the poses only using (9), which is equivalent to solving the complete DBA problem using (4). A 3D image typically contains millions of voxels but we only need six parameters to represent its pose. Therefore, the independence of optimizing poses to intensities can greatly help us reduce the dimension of the solution space. For distinction with DBA, we call this method DSR.

In addition, after $\hat{\mathbf{x}}_\xi$ is obtained, the NLLS problem in (2) becomes a linear least-squares problem. Therefore, if required, we can calculate the optimal panoramic image easily in only one step from the following closed-form formula:

$$\hat{\mathbf{x}}_M = -H_{MM}^{-1} J_M^\top \mathbf{B}. \tag{10}$$

The implementation process of DSR is summarized in Algorithm 1 in the supplementary materials.

3   Experiments and Results

Registration of US images is usually more challenging than other modalities like CT and MRI due to the relatively low signal-to-noise ratio. Additionally, registration of a collection of 3D TEE images is especially valuable to overcome the drawback of small field of view (FoV) of 3D TEE probes. Thus, in this section, 3D TEE images are used as examples to evaluate the proposed DSR algorithm compared with the pairwise [2], Lie normalization [21], sequential [11], and APE [20] methods. Both simulated and in-vivo experiments are performed.

3.1   Simulated Experiments

Five sequences of 3D images (in grayscale ranging from 0 to 255) are simulated by transforming a 3D TEE volume to a real 3D CT scan of the heart with different

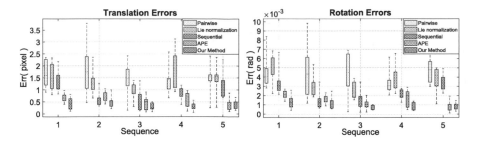

Fig. 1. Accuracy of DSR method compared to pairwise [2], Lie normalization [21], sequential [11], and APE [20] methods using 5 sequences of simulated 3D TEE images.

poses and cropping the corresponding image area. The FoV of the simulated TEE images is the same as the 3D TEE image to get similar imagery information as real TEE volumes. Each sequence contains 11 frames of 3D images. The magnitude of these transformations varies between $+/-$ 12 degrees for rotations and $+/-$ 15 pixels for translations, which are typical ranges of poses in our obtained in-vivo 3D TEE images. Multiplicative speckle noise [10] in the original US signal can be transformed into a kind of additive noise close to Gaussian distribution in the obtained US images after logarithmic compression [10,24]. Thus, Gaussian noise with a standard deviation of 25 is generated randomly and added to the intensities of these five sequences of images.

The accuracy of the proposed DSR method is evaluated by comparing it with pairwise, Lie normalization, sequential, and APE methods via simulated datasets. For fair comparisons, pairwise, sequential, and APE methods use the SSD as the similarity metric, GN method as optimization solver, and the initial pose parameters in each method are the same. Lie normalization optimizes poses obtained from pairwise methods and does not directly involve images [21]. Thus, we use the results from the pairwise registration as the input to Lie normalization. The mean absolute errors (MAE) of translation and Euler angles obtained from the proposed DSR and other four methods are compared in Fig. 1.

It is shown from Fig. 1 that MAE of the results obtained from DSR, sequential, and APE methods are much smaller than the pairwise and Lie normalization methods in most of the cases, which indicates the better accuracy of these three methods. Additionally, among DSR, sequential, and APE methods, the accuracy of DSR is within 0.5 pixels for translations in most of the cases and is within 1×10^{-3} rad for rotations in more than half cases. Although the accuracy of APE is the closest to DSR among four competing methods, it still has larger errors than DSR. The errors of APE are greater than 0.5 pixels for translations and greater than 1×10^{-3} rad for rotations in more than half of experiments. And the results show that the accuracy of both translations and rotations from the sequential method is lower than DSR and APE. Furthermore, it is seen from Fig. 1 that the distribution of errors from DSR is more concentrated than the others, which indicates it also has better robustness than the other four methods.

The above comparisons indicate that the proposed method has the highest accuracy, followed by APE. Both these two simultaneous registration methods are more accurate than the other three which are deduced from pairwise registration. In addition, compared with the proposed DSR method, one apparent drawback of APE is its much higher computational complexity. Since both DSR and APE use the sum-of-squared intensity differences as the objective function, the computational complexities for both methods are closely related to the number of intensity differences. Suppose there are m images, each image has h pixels, and every two images have around $\alpha\%$ overlapping area, the computational complexity of APE is around $\boldsymbol{O}(m(m-1)/2 \times \alpha\% \times h)$ [19] since APE considers all the combinations of images, while that of DSR is only $\boldsymbol{O}(m \times h)$. In the simulated experiments for each sequence, it is found that APE calculates around four times as many intensity differences as DSR and needs around 4–5 times longer time than DSR for each iteration. Theoretically, the more images involved, the higher the computational complexity of APE is, and the more time it takes than DSR.

3.2   In-Vivo Experiments

In the in-vivo experiments, forty-six 3D TEE images from six patients (Patient #1 to #6) are collected using an iE33 ultrasound system (Philips Medical Systems) equipped with an X7-2 real-time 3D transducer. ECG-gating technique [5] is used to assist capture ECG-gated 3D TEE images so that registration of these images can be considered as rigid. The number of images in each dataset varies from 6 to 11. Each 3D TEE image contains around six million voxels. Since the proposed DSR, sequential, and APE methods outperformed the other two methods in terms of accuracy, in this section, the proposed method is compared with the sequential and APE methods only. Pose parameters of three methods are initialized using the results from the pairwise method. It is found that such an initialization method is enough for DSR to converge to the correct results.

Analyzing the accuracy of a registration algorithm based on in-vivo datasets is complex because the ground-truth poses are usually not available. If images are aligned using the estimated poses, visually we can confirm that the stitching areas of the aligned images should be smooth and without misalignment if the poses are accurate. Therefore, to evaluate the accuracy of the proposed DSR method, pairwise images are aligned using the poses obtained by the sequential, APE, and DSR methods, respectively.

Similar to the results in our simulated experiments, aligned images obtained from DSR have the best quality, followed by APE and then the sequential method. In all the aligned images, there is no misalignment found from the proposed DSR in the experiments, while some apparent misalignment is found from the results of APE and sequential methods. Several examples are displayed in Fig. 2. Additionally, although APE can obtain results that are closer to those from the proposed method than the sequential method, it requires a much longer time for each iteration. In the experiments, APE usually needs around 2–5 times longer time than the proposed method for each iteration.

To further evaluate the accuracy of the proposed method, in-vivo 3D TEE images in each dataset are fused using (10) and the estimated poses from DSR. We manually select areas which contain sharp boundaries like the left atrium

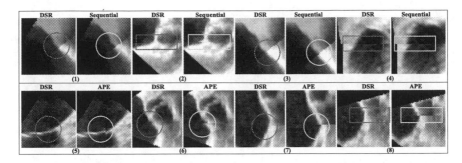

Fig. 2. Comparisons of the aligned images using poses from sequential, APE, and DSR.

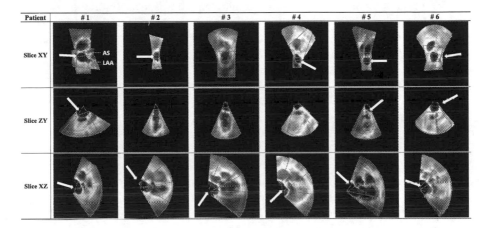

Fig. 3. Fused 3D TEE images using registration results from DSR for six in-vivo datasets. LA walls which have sharp structures in the images are indicated by white arrows in selected areas. Colored frames are the boundaries of two registered volumes. (Color figure online)

(LA) wall in the fused images for evaluation since generally, misalignment caused by poses with low accuracy can be easily found in these areas. The selected regions are shown in Fig. 3 with three orthogonal slices and two of the registered images in the fused images are highlighted in color boundaries. By observing the LA walls which are indicated by white arrows in Fig. 3, it is shown that the stitching areas have smooth transition and no misalignment is found in the images, which suggests good quality of alignments have been obtained by DSR.

The motivation for our current study is to enlarge the FoV of 3D TEE to assist transcatheter left atrial appendage (LAA) occlusion [4]. First, the enlarged FoV of 3D TEE allows the LAA to be observed completely (see Patient # 1 in Fig. 3) to facilitate device size selection for LAA occlusion [12]. Secondly, a complete structure of the left atrium in the enlarged 3D TEE image allows measuring the relative position and orientation of LAA w.r.t. atrial septum (AS) to facilitate the planning for LAA occlusion [4]. By counting the number of voxels, it is found that the FoV of the fused image is enlarged to 2.18, 2.10, 2.02, 2.01, 1.80, and 2.06 times as compared with the original single TEE volume of Patient # 1 to # 6, respectively.

4 Conclusion

Starting from the framework of direct bundle adjustment, a novel direct simultaneous registration algorithm for 3D images is proposed in the paper. The method can optimize the poses of a collection of local images simultaneously without any information loss or reuse. Results from the simulated and in-vivo experiments demonstrate that the proposed method outperforms the other four competing methods in terms of accuracy and is more efficient than the state-of-the-art APE method. From the results of simulated experiments, it is evident that our method improved the accuracy of registration by more than 50% compared to the other four methods for most cases. In-vivo experiments also show accurate structures and extended field of view of the fused images, indicating a good quality of registration and a significant potential clinical value of the proposed method.

The proposed method can be very useful in practice when real-time performance is not required, e.g. using the enlarged FoV of 3D TEE for surgical planning of LAA occlusion. Our current focus is more on accuracy than efficiency, thus we implemented DSR in MATLAB on CPU. Since the linear system (4) has a special sparse structure that is similar to other bundle adjustment problems, it is very promising for us to use techniques in [22] to achieve parallel implementation of DSR on GPU. Additionally, optimization techniques used in g2o [8] and parallax BA [25] could also help us achieve the fast implementation. Our future work will focus on the efficient implementation of DSR.

References

1. Alismail, H., Browning, B., Lucey, S.: Photometric bundle adjustment for vision-based SLAM. In: Lai, S.-H., Lepetit, V., Nishino, K., Sato, Y. (eds.) ACCV 2016. LNCS, vol. 10114, pp. 324–341. Springer, Cham (2017). https://doi.org/10.1007/978-3-319-54190-7_20
2. Carminati, M.C., et al.: Reconstruction of the descending thoracic aorta by multiview compounding of 3-d transesophageal echocardiographic aortic data sets for improved examination and quantification of atheroma burden. Ultrasound Med. Biol. **41**(5), 1263–1276 (2015)
3. Cox, M., Sridharan, S., Lucey, S., Cohn, J.: Least-squares congealing for large numbers of images. In: 2009 IEEE 12th International Conference on Computer Vision, pp. 1949–1956. IEEE (2009)
4. Fan, Y., et al.: Device sizing guided by echocardiography-based three-dimensional printing is associated with superior outcome after percutaneous left atrial appendage occlusion. J. Am. Soc. Echocardiogr. **32**(6), 708–719 (2019)
5. Fenster, A., Downey, D.B., Cardinal, H.N.: Three-dimensional ultrasound imaging. Phys. Med. Biol. **46**(5), R67 (2001)

6. Hall, B.C.: Lie Groups, Lie Algebras, and Representations. GTM, vol. 222. Springer, Cham (2015). https://doi.org/10.1007/978-3-319-13467-3
7. Hill, D.L., Batchelor, P.G., Holden, M., Hawkes, D.J.: Medical image registration. Phys. Med. Biol. **46**(3), R1 (2001)
8. Kümmerle, R., Grisetti, G., Strasdat, H., Konolige, K., Burgard, W.: g2o: a general framework for graph optimization. In: 2011 IEEE International Conference on Robotics and Automation, pp. 3607–3613. IEEE (2011)
9. Learned-Miller, E.G.: Data driven image models through continuous joint alignment. IEEE Trans. Pattern Anal. Mach. Intell. **28**(2), 236–250 (2005)
10. Loizou, C.P.: Comparative evaluation of despeckle filtering in ultrasound imaging of the carotid artery. IEEE Trans. Ultrason. Ferroelect. Freq. Control **52**(10), 1653–1669 (2005)
11. Mao, Z., Zhao, L., Huang, S., Fan, Y., Lee, A.P.W.: Direct 3d ultrasound fusion for transesophageal echocardiography. Comput. Biol. Med. **134**, 104502 (2021)
12. Morais, P., et al.: Semiautomatic estimation of device size for left atrial appendage occlusion in 3-d tee images. IEEE Trans. Ultrason. Ferroelect. Freq. Control **66**(5), 922–929 (2019)
13. Ni, D., et al.: Reconstruction of volumetric ultrasound panorama based on improved 3d sift. Comput. Med. Imaging Graph. **33**(7), 559–566 (2009)
14. Oliveira, F.P., Tavares, J.M.R.: Medical image registration: a review. Comput. Methods Biomech. Biomed. Eng. **17**(2), 73–93 (2014)
15. Schneider, R.J., et al.: Real-time image-based rigid registration of three-dimensional ultrasound. Med. Image Anal. **16**(2), 402–414 (2012)
16. Szeliski, R.: Image alignment and stitching a tutorial. Found. Trends ® Comput. Graph. Vision. **2**(1), 1–104 (2006)
17. Triggs, B., McLauchlan, P.F., Hartley, R.I., Fitzgibbon, A.W.: Bundle adjustment–a modern synthesis. In: Triggs, B., Zisserman, A., Szeliski, R. (eds.) IWVA 1999. LNCS, vol. 1883, pp. 298 372. Springer, Heidelberg (2000). https://doi.org/10. 1007/3-540-44480-7_21
18. Viergever, M.A., Maintz, J.A., Klein, S., Murphy, K., Staring, M., Pluim, J.P.: A survey of medical image registration - under review. Med. Image Anal. **33**, 140–144 (2016)
19. Wachinger, C., Navab, N.: Structural image representation for image registration. In: 2010 IEEE Computer Society Conference on Computer Vision and Pattern Recognition-Workshops, pp. 23–30. IEEE (2010)
20. Wachinger, C., Navab, N.: Simultaneous registration of multiple images: similarity metrics and efficient optimization. IEEE Trans. Pattern Anal. Mach. Intell. **35**(5), 1221–1233 (2012)
21. Wachinger, C., Wein, W., Navab, N.: Three-dimensional ultrasound mosaicing. In: Ayache, N., Ourselin, S., Maeder, A. (eds.) MICCAI 2007. LNCS, vol. 4792, pp. 327–335. Springer, Heidelberg (2007). https://doi.org/10.1007/978-3-540-75759-7_40
22. Wu, C., Agarwal, S., Curless, B., Seitz, S.M.: Multicore bundle adjustment. In: CVPR 2011, pp. 3057–3064. IEEE (2011)
23. Zhang, F.: The Schur complement and its applications, vol. 4. Springer, New York (2006). https://doi.org/10.1007/b105056
24. Zhang, J., Cheng, Y.: Despeckling Methods for Medical Ultrasound Images. Springer, Singapore (2020). https://doi.org/10.1007/978-981-15-0516-4
25. Zhao, L., Huang, S., Sun, Y., Yan, L., Dissanayake, G.: Parallaxba: bundle adjustment using parallax angle feature parametrization. Int. J. Robot. Res. **34**(4–5), 493–516 (2015)

Multi-modal Retinal Image Registration Using a Keypoint-Based Vessel Structure Aligning Network

Aline Sindel[1(✉)], Bettina Hohberger[2], Andreas Maier[1], and Vincent Christlein[1]

[1] Pattern Recognition Lab, FAU Erlangen-Nürnberg, Erlangen, Germany
aline.sindel@fau.de
[2] Department of Ophthalmology, Universitätsklinikum Erlangen, Erlangen, Germany

Abstract. In ophthalmological imaging, multiple imaging systems, such as color fundus, infrared, fluorescein angiography, optical coherence tomography (OCT) or OCT angiography, are often involved to make a diagnosis of retinal disease. Multi-modal retinal registration techniques can assist ophthalmologists by providing a pixel-based comparison of aligned vessel structures in images from different modalities or acquisition times. To this end, we propose an end-to-end trainable deep learning method for multi-modal retinal image registration. Our method extracts convolutional features from the vessel structure for keypoint detection and description and uses a graph neural network for feature matching. The keypoint detection and description network and graph neural network are jointly trained in a self-supervised manner using synthetic multi-modal image pairs and are guided by synthetically sampled ground truth homographies. Our method demonstrates higher registration accuracy as competing methods for our synthetic retinal dataset and generalizes well for our real macula dataset and a public fundus dataset.

Keywords: Multi-modal retinal image registration · Convolutional neural networks · Graph neural networks

1 Introduction

For the diagnosis of retinal disease, such as diabetic retinopathy, glaucoma, or age-related macular degeneration, and for the long-term monitoring of their progression, ophthalmological imaging is essential. Images are recorded over varying time periods using different multi-modal imaging systems, such as color fundus (CF), infrared (IR), fluorescein angiography (FA), or the more recent optical coherence tomography (OCT) and OCT angiography (OCTA). For the comparison and fusion of the information from different images by the ophthalmologists, multi-modal image registration is required to accurately align the vessel structures in the images.

Supplementary Information The online version contains supplementary material available at https://doi.org/10.1007/978-3-031-16446-0_11.

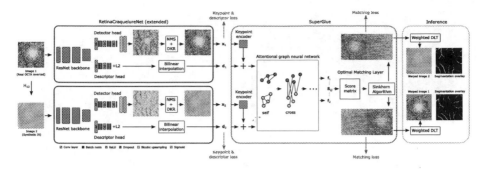

Fig. 1. Our keypoint-based vessel structure aligning network (KPVSA-Net) for multi-modal retinal registration uses a CNN to extract cross-modal features of the vessel structures in both images and a graph neural network for descriptor matching. Our method is end-to-end and self-supervisedly trained by using synthetically augmented image pairs. During inference, the homography is predicted based on the matches and scores using weighted direct linear transform (DLT).

Multi-modal retinal registration methods can be summarized into global methods to predict an affine transform or a homography and local methods that estimate a non-rigid displacement field. In this work, we concentrate on feature-based methods that apply keypoint detection, description, matching, and computation of the global transform. Classical methods estimate *e.g.* the partial intensity invariant feature descriptor (PIIFD) [5] and Harris corner detector. This was extended by [24] using speed up robust feature (SURF) detector, PIIFD, and robust point matching, called SURF-PIIFD-RPM. With the use of deep learning, some steps or even all steps are replaced by neural networks. The retinal method DeepSPA [12] uses a convolutional neural network (CNN) to classify patches of vessel junctions based on a step pattern representation. The keypoint detection and description network RetinaCraquelureNet [19] is trained on small multi-modal retinal image patches centered at vessel bifurcations and uses mutual nearest neighbor matching and random sample consensus (RANSAC) [7] for homography estimation. In GLAMpoints [22], homography guided self-supervised learning is applied to train a UNet [17] for keypoint detection combined with RootSIFT [1] descriptors for retinal image data. The weakly supervised method by Wang *et al.* [25] sequentially trains a vessel segmentation network using style transfer and the mean phase image as guidance, the self-supervised SuperPoint [6] network, and an outlier network using context normalization [26], which they adapt for the homography estimation task. End-to-end networks are often designed to directly compute the parameters of the transform. To predict affine and non-rigid transforms, there is for instance the image and spatial transformer networks (ISTN) for structure-guided image registration that learns a representation of the segmentation maps during training [13]. An approach [2] on spatial transformers and CycleGANs [28] for multi-modal image registration uses cross-modality translation between the modalities to employ a mono-modality metric.

In this paper, we propose an end-to-end deep learning method for multi-modal retinal image registration, named *Keypoint-based Vessel Structure*

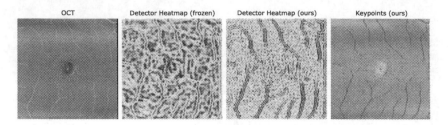

Fig. 2. Keypoint confidence heatmap (from low confidence blue to high confidence red) without (middle left) and with (middle right) our novel self-supervised keypoint and descriptor loss in combination with the differentiable keypoint refinement. The extracted keypoints (most right) of our multi-modal registration method are color-coded based on their confidence (red is high). (Color figure online)

Aligning Network (KPVSA-Net). We employ prior knowledge by extracting deep features of the vessel structure using the keypoint detection and description network RetinaCraquelureNet [19]. In contrast to vessel segmentation based methods, we extract the features directly from multi-modal images to learn distinctive cross-modal descriptors. We build an end-to-end network for feature extraction and matching by extending RetinaCraquelureNet and combining it with the graph neural network SuperGlue [18]. We jointly train both networks using a novel self-supervised keypoint and descriptor loss and a self-supervised matching loss guided by sampled homographies. We created a synthetically augmented dataset by training an image translation technique to generate synthetic retinal images. Our network incorporates and connects knowledge about the local and global position, visual appearance, and context between keypoints showing high registration accuracy.

2   Methods

2.1   Synthetic Augmentations for Multi-modal Retinal Images

Our proposed method is trained end-to-end in a self-supervised manner guided only by synthetically sampled ground truth homographies. To apply the self-supervised technique to multi-modal images, we make use of unpaired image-to-image translation using the cycle consistency [28]. For each modality combination, we train one CycleGAN [28] to augment the training dataset by generating synthetic images of the other modalities. To train our registration method, we sample random homographies on the fly to transform the second image. Afterwards, we crop both images at the same randomly selected position to a fixed patch size and recalculate the homographies based on the new corner points. We augment both patches independently with photometric augmentations such as color jittering, Gaussian blurring, sharpening, Gaussian random noise, and small random crops. Prior to warping, we jointly augment the full-size images with geometric transformations such as horizontal and vertical flipping, rotation, and elastic deformation by random noise.

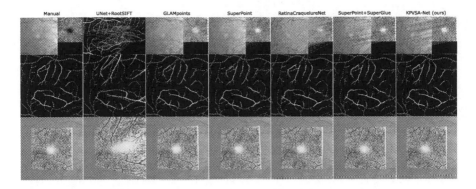

Fig. 3. Qualitative results for one IR-OCTA example.

2.2 Multi-modal Retinal Keypoint Detection and Description Network

We employ and extend the fully-convolutional RetinaCraquelureNet [19,20] for our end-to-end pipeline (see Fig. 1). The network architecture is composed of a ResNet [9] backbone and a keypoint detection and description head. The keypoint detection head has two output channels ("vessel", "background"), which we reduce to only one channel to directly predict the keypoint confidence score. We set the feature dimension of the description head to 256-D to reduce the parameters for end-to-end learning. We pretrain the network from scratch using multi-modal retinal image patches centered at supervised keypoint positions with a binary cross-entropy loss for keypoint detection and a cross-modal bidirectional quadruplet descriptor loss [19,20].

Then, we fit the network into our pipeline. In order to directly use the output of the detection head as keypoint confidence scores, we add a batch normalization layer after the last 1×1 convolutional layer and add a sigmoid activation after the bicubic upsampling layer. With these modifications the predictions of the detector are scaled to the range zero to one. Then, we apply non-maximum suppression (NMS) to the keypoint confidence heatmap and extract the top $N_{\max}$ keypoints from the NMS heatmap [19,20]. This step is non-differentiable, therefore we apply a differentiable subpixel keypoint refinement (DKR) that allows the gradients to flow back to the small regions around the keypoints. Inspired by recent works [11,14,15,27], we extract 5×5 patches from the confidence heatmap which are centered at the $N_{\max}$ keypoint positions and compute for each patch p the spatial softargmax of the normalized patch $(p - s_{\mathrm{NMS}})/t$, where s_{NMS} is the value of the NMS score map and t the temperature for the softmax. The refined keypoint positions are the sum of the initial coordinates and the soft subpixel coordinates. The corresponding descriptors are linearly interpolated at the refined keypoint coordinates [20].

Based on the idea of the bidirectional quadruplet descriptor loss ($\mathcal{L}_{\mathrm{Desc}}$) [20], we design a self-supervised keypoint and descriptor loss ($\mathcal{L}_{\mathrm{KD}}$) that is guided by ground truth homographies instead of labeled matching keypoint pairs as

Table 1. Quantitative evaluation for our synthetic retina test dataset. Models with *
are fine-tuned on our synthetic augmented dataset.

Metrics	Success rate for MHE (SR_{MHE}) [%] ↑						MHE ↓	Dice ↑
	$\epsilon = 1$	$\epsilon = 2$	$\epsilon = 3$	$\epsilon = 4$	$\epsilon = 5$	$\epsilon = 10$	Mean ± Std	Mean ± Std
Before Reg	0.0	0.0	0.0	0.0	0.0	0.0	78.10 ± 36.44	.083 ± .04
UNet+RootSIFT	7.6	20.1	27.1	32.4	35.8	42.2	368.93 ± 2739.36	.433 ± .34
GLAMpoints*	14.9	44.7	60.9	70.2	75.5	82.9	95.07 ± 812.65	.639 ± .25
SuperPoint*	11.0	33.3	55.6	67.7	76.6	90.7	8.61 ± 53.55	.709 ± .16
RCN (512-D)	13.7	43.1	57.8	65.4	69.0	73.2	107.70 ± 1055.37	.596 ± .31
(SP+SG)*	35.2	74.4	91.6	96.4	98.3	99.5	1.84 ± 4.48	.775 ± .11
(SP*+SG)*	39.9	79.5	92.9	97.4	**99.1**	**99.7**	1.49 ± 1.50	.781 ± .10
RCN-D*+SG*	47.4	88.2	95.1	97.0	98.2	99.0	1.46 ± 2.51	.783 ± .11
RCN-KD*+SG*	50.4	90.2	95.1	97.3	98.1	99.2	1.32 ± 1.55	.783 ± .11
RCN-DK*-D*+SG*	55.1	89.9	96.1	97.9	98.7	99.4	**1.29 ± 2.13**	.782 ± .11
KPVSA-Net	**74.2**	**94.9**	**98.1**	**98.6**	98.7	99.1	1.36 ± 6.45	**.789 ± .11**

in [20]. Within the detected keypoints in both images, positive keypoint pairs
are automatically determined based on mutual nearest neighbor matching of the
keypoint coordinates whose reprojection error is smaller than a threshold τ. For
the positive descriptor pairs (anchor $\mathbf{d}_a$ and positive counterpart $\mathbf{d}_p$), the closest
non-matching descriptors in both directions are selected analogously to [20]:

$$\mathcal{L}_{Desc}(\mathbf{d}_a, \mathbf{d}_p, \mathbf{d}_u, \mathbf{d}_v) = \max[0, m + D(\mathbf{d}_a, \mathbf{d}_p) - D(\mathbf{d}_a, \mathbf{d}_u)] \\ + \max[0, m + D(\mathbf{d}_p, \mathbf{d}_a) - D(\mathbf{d}_p, \mathbf{d}_v)], \tag{1}$$

where m is the margin, $D(x, y)$ the Euclidean distance, $\mathbf{d}_u$ the closest negative
to $\mathbf{d}_a$, and $\mathbf{d}_v$ is the closest negative to $\mathbf{d}_p$. However, since this self-supervised
descriptor loss formulation depends on the number of matchable keypoints in
the images with a coordinate distance smaller than τ, it could encourage the
reduction of the number of positive pairs N_p to minimize the loss. To account
for that and to refine the keypoint positions, we include a term into our loss
to also minimize the reprojection error of the coordinates of the positive pairs
(anchor $\mathbf{x}_a$, and warped coordinates of the positive counterpart $\hat{\mathbf{x}}_p$) which is
weighted by β. This leads to our self-supervised keypoint and descriptor loss:

$$\mathcal{L}_{KD}(\mathbf{d}_a, \mathbf{d}_p, \mathbf{d}_u, \mathbf{d}_v, \mathbf{x}_a, \hat{\mathbf{x}}_p) = \frac{1}{N_p} \sum_{i}^{N_p} \mathcal{L}_{Desc}(\mathbf{d}_{ai}, \mathbf{d}_{pi}, \mathbf{d}_{ui}, \mathbf{d}_{vi}) \\ + \frac{\beta}{N_p^2} \sum_{i}^{N_p} D(\mathbf{x}_{ai}, \hat{\mathbf{x}}_{pi}). \tag{2}$$

Table 2. Quantitative evaluation for the IR-OCT-OCTA dataset. Models with * are fine-tuned on our synthetic augmented dataset.

Metrics	IR-OCT		IR-OCTA		OCT-OCTA		All		All ME ↓	All MAE ↓	Dice ↑
	Success Rates (ME <= 7, MAE <= 10) [%] ↑								Mean ± Std	Mean ± Std	Mean ± Std
	ME	MAE	ME	MAE	ME	MAE	ME	MAE			
Before Reg	0.0	0.0	0.0	0.0	30.0	26.7	10.0	8.9	123.89 ± 79.25	128.59 ± 79.65	$.117 \pm .13$
Manual	100.0	100.0	100.0	100.0	100.0	100.0	100.0	100.0	1.95 ± 0.73	3.13 ± 1.12	$.481 \pm .09$
UNet+RootSIFT	13.3	6.7	13.3	8.3	73.3	65.0	33.3	26.7	210.09 ± 452.84	640.46 ± 2166.14	$.300 \pm .22$
GLAMpoints*	40.0	11.7	61.7	25.0	100.0	85.0	67.2	40.6	8.43 ± 9.62	20.53 ± 31.13	$.456 \pm .12$
SuperPoint*	35.0	16.7	26.7	21.7	100.0	93.3	53.9	43.9	89.98 ± 427.20	365.69 ± 2292.21	$.405 \pm .18$
RCN (512-D)	78.3	41.7	81.7	46.7	100.0	96.7	86.7	61.7	4.63 ± 2.41	10.53 ± 8.03	$.534 \pm .09$
(SP+SG)*	86.7	80.0	80.0	78.3	100.0	100.0	88.9	86.1	19.14 ± 111.81	66.99 ± 611.31	$.506 \pm .15$
(SP*+SG)*	100.0	90.0	93.3	88.3	100.0	100.0	97.8	92.8	3.85 ± 2.46	7.08 ± 5.64	$.533 \pm .10$
KPVSA-Net	96.7	**91.7**	**98.3**	**93.3**	100.0	100.0	**98.3**	**95.0**	$\mathbf{3.67 \pm 2.97}$	$\mathbf{6.88 \pm 8.45}$	$\mathbf{.542 \pm .10}$

2.3   Keypoint Matching Using a Graph Convolutional Neural Network

For keypoint matching, we incorporate the graph convolutional neural network SuperGlue [18] into our method which consists of three building blocks, see Fig. 1. The keypoint coordinates are encoded as high dimensional feature vectors using a multilayer perceptron, and a joint representation is computed for the descriptors and the encoded keypoints [18].

The attentional graph neural network (GNN) uses alternating self- and cross-attention layers to learn a more distinctive feature representation. The nodes of the graph are the keypoints' representations of both images. The self attention layers connect the keypoints within the same image, while the cross-attention layers connect a keypoint to all keypoints in the other image. Information is propagated along both the self- and cross-edges via messages. At each layer the keypoints' representations for each image are updated by aggregation of the messages using multi-head attention [23]. Lastly, a 1×1 convolutional layer is used to obtain the final descriptors [18].

The optimal matching layer is used to compute the partial soft assignment matrix $\mathbf{P}$, which assigns for each keypoint at most one single keypoint in the other image. Based on the score matrix of the similarity of the descriptors, $\mathbf{P}$ is iteratively solved using the differentiable Sinkhorn algorithm [21]. To account for unmatchable keypoints, a dustbin is added to the $N \times M$ score matrix [18]. The negative log-likelihood of $\mathbf{P}$ is minimized [18]:

$$\mathcal{L}_{SG}(\mathbf{P}, \mathcal{M}, \mathcal{I}, \mathcal{J}) = -\kappa \sum_{(i,j) \in \mathcal{M}} \log \mathbf{P}_{i,j} - \sum_{i \in \mathcal{I}} \log \mathbf{P}_{i,N+1} - \sum_{j \in \mathcal{J}} \log \mathbf{P}_{M+1,j}, \quad (3)$$

where κ is the weight for the positive matches $\mathcal{M}$, $\mathcal{I}$ denotes the unmatchable keypoints of image I_I, and $\mathcal{J}$ the unmatchable keypoints of image I_J which are all those whose reprojection errors are higher than τ. We compute the $\mathcal{L}_{SG}$ and the ground truth matches twice, once based on matching from image I_I to I_J and once vice versa, *i.e.* the matching loss is the sum of both.

3 Experiments

3.1 Multi-modal Retinal Datasets

For our IR-OCT-OCTA retinal dataset, provided by the Department of Oph-thalmology, FAU Erlangen-Nürnberg, the maculas of 46 controls were measured by Spectralis OCT II, Heidelberg Engineering up to three times a day result-ing in 134 images per modality and 402 images in total. The multi-modal image triplets consist of IR images (768×768) and en-face OCT and OCTA projections of the SVP layer (Par off) of the macula (both 512×512). We split the images for each modality into training: 89, validation: 15, and test set: 30. Secondly, we split the public color fundus (CF: $576 \times 720 \times 3$) and fluorescein angiography (FA: 576×720) dataset [4,8] that consists of 29 image pairs of controls and 30 pairs of patients with diabetic retinopathy into training: 35, validation: 10, and test set: 14. For our synthetic dataset, we generate 1119 multi-modal pairs of real and synthetic images for training, 205 for validation, and 386 for testing. Due to our self-supervised training, we do not need any annotations, hence we only annotated 6 control points per image for the test sets. OCT, OCTA, and FA images are inverted for our experiments to depict all vessels in dark.

3.2 Implementation and Experimental Details

KPVSA-Net is implemented in PyTorch and we use the Kornia framework [16] for data augmentation, homography estimation using weighted direct linear transform (DLT), and image warping. To initialize both networks, we pretrain our adapted version of RetinaCraquelureNet (RCN: 256-D) from scratch (back-bone + detection head: learning rate of $\eta = 1 \cdot 10^{-3}$, 100 epochs; complete network: $\eta = 1 \cdot 10^{-4}$, 25 epochs; for both: with early stopping and linear decay of η to 0 starting at 10) and use the SuperGlue weights of the Outdoor dataset. Then, we train KPVSA-Net end-to-end using Adam solver for 100 epochs with $\eta = 1 \cdot 10^{-4}$ for SuperGlue and $\eta = 1 \cdot 10^{-6}$ for the detector and descriptor heads of RCN (frozen ResNet backbone) and then decay η linearly to zero for the next 400 epochs with early stopping and a batch size of 8. The keypoint and descriptor loss and matching loss are equally weighted, $m = 1$, $\beta = 300$, $t = 0.1$, $\kappa = 0.45$, $\tau = 3$, training patch size of 384, $N_{max} = 512$ (synthetic dataset) or $N_{max} = 1024$ (real datasets), and matching score threshold of 0.2 for DLT.

For the comparison, we used the original configuration of RetinaCraque-lureNet (RCN: 512-D) [19] and we fine-tuned SuperPoint [6] (SP*) and GLAM-points [22] with our synthetic multi-modal dataset by extending the training code of [11,22]. Then, we jointly fine-tuned SuperGlue and the descriptors of the pretrained SuperPoint model (SP+SG)* for 100 epochs using our synthetic dataset and training strategy. Likewise, we jointly fine-tuned SuperGlue and the SP* model (SP*+SG)*. For the feature-based comparison methods, we use N_{max} of 2000 or 4000 (synthetic/real), mutual nearest neighbor matching and RANSAC [7] (reprojection error of 5) for homography estimation using OpenCV. For vessel segmentation and Dice score computation, we trained a UNet with

Table 3. Quantitative evaluation for the public CF-FA dataset. Models with * are fine-tuned on our synthetic augmented dataset.

Metrics	SR_{ME} [%] ↑		SR_{MAE} [%] ↑		ME ↓	MAE ↓	Dice ↑
	$\epsilon = 2$	$\epsilon = 3$	$\epsilon = 3$	$\epsilon = 5$	Mean ± Std	Mean ± Std	Mean ± Std
Before Reg	0.0	0.0	0.0	0.0	52.12 ± 42.26	61.07 ± 42.17	.122 ± .03
Manual	100.0	100.0	92.9	100.0	0.73 ± 0.34	1.24 ± 0.71	.606 ± .08
UNet+RootSIFT	64.3	85.7	71.4	85.7	2.93 ± 4.49	6.84 ± 14.20	.643 ± .14
GLAMpoints*	25.0	64.3	21.4	57.1	3.34 ± 2.36	6.42 ± 5.21	.567 ± .11
SuperPoint*	71.4	85.7	46.4	78.6	1.85 ± 0.72	3.41 ± 1.38	.636 ± .09
RCN (512-D)	71.4	**100.0**	64.3	89.3	1.70 ± 0.55	3.04 ± 1.37	.658 ± .09
(SP+SG)*	85.7	**100.0**	71.4	**100.0**	1.56 ± 0.51	2.58 ± 0.85	.648 ± .10
(SP*+SG)*	**92.9**	100.0	85.7	**100.0**	1.55 ± 0.46	2.53 ± 0.86	**.661** ± .09
KPVSA-Net	**92.9**	100.0	**92.9**	**100.0**	**1.50** ± 0.36	**2.47** ± 0.67	.659 ± .09

synthetically augmented multi-modal images using CycleGANs based on the CF images and manual segmentations of the HRF dataset [3,10]. The registration success rate for the real datasets is computed for the mean Euclidean error (ME) and maximum Euclidean error (MAE) of 6 manual target control points and warped source control points using the predicted homography and an error threshold ϵ. For the synthetic dataset, we compute the success rate of the mean homography error (MHE) [6] for different ϵ based on warping the corner points of the source image using the ground truth and the predicted homography.

3.3 Results

The quantitative results of the synthetic dataset are summarized in Table 1. Our KPVSA-Net shows the highest success rates for homography estimation for low error thresholds and in total the highest Dice score of the registered images. For error thresholds larger than 4, the two SuperPoint+SuperGlue variants show comparable results. All SuperGlue-based methods achieve higher scores than the feature-based methods that use RANSAC. The bottom rows of Table 1 show our ablation study. First, RCN (256-D) with training only the descriptor head, without keypoint refinement, and without our novel loss variant in combination with SuperGlue (RCN-D*+SG*) already shows an improvement of 7.5 % compared to (SP*+SG)* for $\epsilon <= 1$. Enabling the keypoint detector and descriptor to learn (RCN-KD*+SG*) improves further by 3 %, and using the differential keypoint refinement (DKR) (RCN-DK*-D*+SG*) achieves 5 % more, and finally our full method KPVSA-Net additionally achieves 19 % plus for $\epsilon <= 1$. The high accuracy for low error thresholds could be seen as the effect of the combination of our novel loss and DKR that pulls matching keypoints and descriptors closer together. The effect of both terms on the keypoint heatmap is visualized in Fig. 2. The left heatmap of the frozen detector highlights the vessel structures. Adding the single described steps only marginally change the visual appearance of the heatmap. Our final model has a refining effect on the heatmap (right) by thinning the high response area (red). Further, our loss also had a positive effect on SuperGlue by speeding up the convergence of both losses.

The evaluation results for our real IR-OCT-OCTA dataset is shown in Table 2 and for the public dataset in Table 3. For the single multi-modal domain pairs, the twice fine-tuned (SP*+SG)* model has a slightly higher success rate for IR-OCT, but our method is slightly better for IR-OCTA and OCT-OCTA and for the total dataset. Generally, the errors are a bit higher for the real dataset and the best Dice score (ours) only has 54.2 % instead of 78.9 % for the synthetic dataset, but good results are still achieved. Since there is no ground truth for the real dataset, some inaccuracies come from the manual control points and also due to small deformations in the vessels or motion artifacts. The registration task for the CF-FA dataset is less complex, resulting in smaller ME and MAE for all methods and relatively close results for RCN, (SP+SG)*, (SP*+SG)*, and our method. We also tested the conventional method SURF+PIIFD+RPM [24] using their Matlab implementation. Results are in the supplementary material, as it achieved bad results for CF-FA and failed for the IR-OCT-OCTA dataset.

A qualitative IR-OCTA registration result is shown in Fig. 3. RootSIFT applied to the vessel segmentation predicted by the UNet finds the least number of correct matches and does not predict an acceptable homography. GLAM-points detects more keypoints and matches than SuperPoint, but their registration results are comparable. The matches of RetinaCraquelureNet are concentrated on vessel structures resulting in a more precise registration. Super-Point+SuperGlue filters out most false matches, but only shows a small number of matches in total. Our KPVSA-Net, however, detects a larger number of strong matches and results in a sightly more accurate overlay of the segmented vessels.

4 Conclusion

Our method incorporates prior knowledge of the vessel structure into an end-to-end trainable pipeline for retinal image registration. Using a graph neural network for image matching, spatial and visual information is connected to form a more distinctive descriptor. In the evaluation, our method demonstrates high registration accuracy for our synthetic retinal dataset and generalizes well for our real clinical dataset and the public fundus dataset. As there are some small deformations of the vessels, which cannot be handled with a perspective transform, we will look into non-rigid approaches as a further step of investigation.

References

1. Arandjelović, R., Zisserman, A.: Three things everyone should know to improve object retrieval. In: Proceedings of IEEE CVPR 2012, pp. 2911–2918 (2012). https://doi.org/10.1109/CVPR.2012.6248018
2. Arar, M., Ginger, Y., Danon, D., Bermano, A.H., Cohen-Or, D.: Unsupervised multi-modal image registration via geometry preserving image-to-image translation. In: Proceedings of IEEE/CVF CVPR 2020 (2020). https://doi.org/10.1109/CVPR42600.2020.01342

3. Budai, A., Bock, R., Maier, A., Hornegger, J., Michelson, G.: Robust vessel segmentation in fundus images. Int. J. Biomed. Imaging (2013). https://doi.org/10.1155/2013/154860

4. CF-FA: Fundus fluorescein angiogram photographs & colour fundus images of diabetic patients. https://sites.google.com/site/hosseinrabbanikhorasgani/datasets-1/fundus-fluorescein-angiogram-photographs-colour-fundus-images-of-diabetic-patients. Accessed 01 Mar 2022

5. Chen, J., Tian, J., Lee, N., Zheng, J., Smith, R.T., Laine, A.F.: A partial intensity invariant feature descriptor for multimodal retinal image registration. IEEE Trans. Biomed. Eng. **57**(7), 1707–1718 (2010). https://doi.org/10.1109/TBME.2010.2042169

6. DeTone, D., Malisiewicz, T., Rabinovich, A.: SuperPoint: self-supervised interest point detection and description. In: Proceedings of IEEE CVPR Workshops 2018 (2018). https://doi.org/10.1109/CVPRW.2018.00060

7. Fischler, M.A., Bolles, R.C.: Random sample consensus: a paradigm for model fitting with applications to image analysis and automated cartography. Commun. ACM **24**(6), 381–395 (1981). https://doi.org/10.1145/358669.358692

8. Hajeb Mohammad Alipour, S., Rabbani, H., Akhlaghi, M.R.: Diabetic retinopathy grading by digital curvelet transform. Comput. Math. Methods Med. **2021**, 761901 (2012). https://doi.org/10.1155/2012/761901

9. He, K., Zhang, X., Ren, S., Sun, J.: Deep residual learning for image recognition. In: Proceedings of IEEE CVPR 2016, pp. 770–778 (2016). https://doi.org/10.1109/CVPR.2016.90

10. HRF: High-Resolution Fundus (HRF) Image Database. https://www5.cs.fau.de/research/data/fundus-images/. Accessed 01 Mar 2022

11. Jau, Y.Y., Zhu, R., Su, H., Chandraker, M.: Deep keypoint-based camera pose estimation with geometric constraints. In: Proceedings of IEEE IROS 2020, pp. 4950–4957 (2020). https://doi.org/10.1109/IROS45743.2020.9341229

12. Lee, J., Liu, P., Cheng, J., Fu, H.: A deep step pattern representation for multimodal retinal image registration. In: Proceedings of IEEE ICCV 2019, pp. 5076–5085 (2019). https://doi.org/10.1109/ICCV.2019.00518

13. Lee, M.C.H., Oktay, O., Schuh, A., Schaap, M., Glocker, B.: Image-and-spatial transformer networks for structure-guided image registration. In: Shen, D., et al. (eds.) MICCAI 2019. LNCS, vol. 11765, pp. 337–345. Springer, Cham (2019). https://doi.org/10.1007/978-3-030-32245-8_38

14. Nibali, A., He, Z., Morgan, S., Prendergast, L.: Numerical Coordinate Regression with Convolutional Neural Networks. arXiv:1801.07372 (2018)

15. Ono, Y., Trulls, E., Fua, P., Yi, K.M.: LF-Net: learning local features from images. In: Proceedings of NIPS 2018, vol. 31, pp. 6234–6244 (2018)

16. Riba, E., Mishkin, D., Ponsa, D., Rublee, E., Bradski, G.: Kornia: an open source differentiable computer vision library for PyTorch. In: Proceedings of IEEE WACV 2020 (2020). https://doi.org/10.1109/WACV45572.2020.9093363

17. Ronneberger, O., Fischer, P., Brox, T.: U-Net: convolutional networks for biomedical image segmentation. In: Navab, N., Hornegger, J., Wells, W.M., Frangi, A.F. (eds.) MICCAI 2015. LNCS, vol. 9351, pp. 234–241. Springer, Cham (2015). https://doi.org/10.1007/978-3-319-24574-4_28

18. Sarlin, P.E., DeTone, D., Malisiewicz, T., Rabinovich, A.: SuperGlue: learning feature matching with graph neural networks. In: Proceedings of IEEE/CVF CVPR 2020, pp. 4937–4946 (2020). https://doi.org/10.1109/CVPR42600.2020.00499

19. Sindel, A., et al.: A keypoint detection and description network based on the vessel structure for multi-modal retinal image registration. In: Bildverarbeitung für die Medizin 2022. I, pp. 57–62. Springer, Wiesbaden (2022). https://doi.org/10.1007/978-3-658-36932-3_12

20. Sindel, A., Maier, A., Christlein, V.: CraquelureNet: matching the crack structure in historical paintings for multi-modal image registration. In: Proceedings of IEEE ICIP 2021, pp. 994–998 (2021). https://doi.org/10.1109/ICIP42928.2021.9506071

21. Sinkhorn, R., Knopp, P.: Concerning nonnegative matrices and doubly stochastic matrices. Pac. J. Math. **21**(2), 343–348 (1967). https://doi.org/10.2140/pjm.1967.21.343

22. Truong, P., Apostolopoulos, S., Mosinska, A., Stucky, S., Ciller, C., Zanet, S.D.: GLAMpoints: greedily learned accurate match points. In: Proceedings of IEEE ICCV 2019, pp. 10732–10741 (2019). https://doi.org/10.1109/ICCV.2019.01083

23. Vaswani, A., et al.: Attention is all you need. In: Proceedings of NIPS 2017, vol. 30, pp. 5998–6008 (2017)

24. Wang, G., Wang, Z., Chen, Y., Zhao, W.: Robust point matching method for multimodal retinal image registration. Biomed. Signal Process. Control **19**, 68–76 (2015). https://doi.org/10.1016/j.bspc.2015.03.004

25. Wang, Y., et al.: Robust content-adaptive global registration for multimodal retinal images using weakly supervised deep-learning framework. IEEE Trans. Image Process. **30**, 3167–3178 (2021). https://doi.org/10.1109/TIP.2021.3058570

26. Yi, K.M., Trulls, E., Ono, Y., Lepetit, V., Salzmann, M., Fua, P.: Learning to find good correspondences. In: Proceedings of IEEE CVPR (2018). https://doi.org/10.1109/CVPR.2018.00282

27. Zhao, X., Wu, X., Miao, J., Chen, W., Chen, P.C.Y., Li, Z.: ALIKE: accurate and lightweight keypoint detection and descriptor extraction. IEEE Trans. Multimedia (2022). https://doi.org/10.1109/TMM.2022.3155927

28. Zhu, J.Y., Park, T., Isola, P., Efros, A.A.: Unpaired image-to-image translation using cycle-consistent adversarial networks. In: Proceedings of IEEE ICCV 2017, pp. 2242–2251 (2017). https://doi.org/10.1109/ICCV.2017.244

A Deep-Discrete Learning Framework for Spherical Surface Registration

Mohamed A. Suliman$^{(\boxtimes)}$, Logan Z. J. Williams, Abdulah Fawaz, and Emma C. Robinson

Department of Biomedical Engineering, School of Biomedical Engineering and Imaging Science, King's College London, London SE1 7EH, UK
{mohamed.suliman,logan.williams,abdulah.fawaz,emma.robinson}@kcl.ac.uk

Abstract. Cortical surface registration is a fundamental tool for neuroimaging analysis that has been shown to improve the alignment of functional regions relative to volumetric approaches. Classically, image registration is performed by optimizing a complex objective similarity function, leading to long run times. This contributes to a convention for aligning all data to a global average reference frame that poorly reflects the underlying cortical heterogeneity. In this paper, we propose a novel unsupervised learning-based framework that converts registration to a multilabel classification problem, where each point in a low-resolution control grid deforms to one of fixed, finite number of endpoints. This is learned using a spherical geometric deep learning architecture, in an end-to-end unsupervised way, with regularization imposed using a deep Conditional Random Field (CRF). Experiments show that our proposed framework performs competitively, in terms of similarity and areal distortion, relative to the most popular classical surface registration algorithms and generates smoother deformations than other learning-based surface registration methods, even in subjects with atypical cortical morphology. The code can be found in https://github.com/mohamedasuliman/DDR/.

Keywords: Deep learning · Unsupervised learning · Cortical surface registration · Conditional random fields

1 Introduction

The human cerebral cortex is highly convoluted structure, with complex patterns of functional organisation that vary considerably across individuals [1, 13]. Image registration is an important tool that supports comparison of brain images, through mapping of all data to a global average space. However, the degree of variation of cortical morphology and topography across individuals generates considerable uncertainty with regards to the optimal mapping between brains.

Supplementary Information The online version contains supplementary material available at https://doi.org/10.1007/978-3-031-16446-0_12.

Recently, cortical surface registration algorithms [11,22,23,27] have led to improvements in the precision with which it is possible to compare features on the cortical surface through learning mappings that regularize deformations with respect to displacements along with the cortical sheet. Increasingly, these methods support multimodal registration [22,23,28], allowing improved evaluation of cortical functional areas [5,13]. However, increasing evidence suggests that there is a limit to these improvements since cortical topographies vary in ways that break the diffeomorphic assumptions of classical registration algorithms [13].

To this end, learning-based registration algorithms [6,16] present an attractive framework for exploring these problems, on the grounds that they train fast, unsupervised deformation frameworks that can learn to adapt to sub-populations in the data [6]. Previous learning-based registration frameworks have predominately been generated for 2D or 3D Euclidean domains such as brain volumes [3,6–8], lung CT [12,15,16], and histology [4,20,24]. However, increasing efforts have been made to adapt convolutional networks to non-Euclidean domains [19,21,29], resulting in the development of tools for learning-based registration of surfaces and point clouds [2,26,28]. Most notably, the recent S3Reg framework [28] proposes the first learning-based registration framework for cortical surfaces, leveraging the Spherical U-Net algorithm [29] to learn multi-resolution hexagonal filters across regular subdivisions of an icosphere.

One limitation of the Spherical U-Net is that its hexagonal convolutions do not generate a rotationally equivariant solution since the lack of a global coordinate system on a sphere causes filter orientation to flip at the poles. When learning registrations for S3Reg, this generates distortions that must be corrected. To overcome this issue, S3Reg must learn three registration networks for three different spherical orientations. Following that, the learned warps across the networks are averaged while masking the discontinuities. Recent work showed that contrary to Spherical U-Net, MoNet convolutions (learned from a mixture of Gaussian kernels) could indeed be trained to be rotationally equivariant (as filters do not have fixed orientation) [9]. Therefore, we develop a new framework for spherical cortical registration based on MoNet, which also takes inspiration from deep-discrete registration frameworks [15,16] designed to learn larger deformations than deep regression frameworks. We hypothesize that this could improve the generalization of our framework to brains with atypical topographies.

Contributions. In this paper, we propose the first deep-discrete framework for cortical surface registration. We validate on the alignment of cortical folds and compare the proposed network against state-of-the-art classical [11,22,23, 27] and learning-based [28] methods. Specific focus is placed on evaluating the smoothness of the generated warps and the capacity of the network to generalize to atypical cortical morphologies.

2 Method

The proposed method combines ideas from the discrete frameworks of [16,22,23] to propose a Deep-Discrete spherical Registration (DDR) network for alignment of cortical surface features. The full DDR architecture consists of three networks that compose global rigid rotations and non-linear warps (learned in a coarse-to-fine fashion). The objective is to learn a spatial transformation $\boldsymbol{\Phi} : M \to F$, that aligns cortical features on a moving mesh (M) to those of a fixed mesh (F) by optimizing a dissimilarity metric $\mathcal{L}$ of the form:

$$\hat{\boldsymbol{\theta}} = \arg\min_{\theta} \mathcal{L}\left(\boldsymbol{\Phi_\theta}; F, M\right) + \Sigma\left(\boldsymbol{\Phi_\theta}\right), \qquad (1)$$

where $\boldsymbol{\theta}$ are transformation parameters that parametrize $\boldsymbol{\Phi}$, while $\Sigma\left(\cdot\right)$ is a regularization function that imposes smoothness on $\boldsymbol{\Phi}$.

Let $f\left(\cdot\right)$ represents our deep learning network architecture, with $\boldsymbol{\eta}$ being a set of learnable parameters; then, our deep learning image registration problem may be represented as

$$\boldsymbol{\theta} = f_\eta\left(F, M\right). \qquad (2)$$

In all cases, data is presented to the network as concatenated cortical metric maps of F and M, defined on a sphere S^2 that is parametrized by a sixth-order icosphere (that has 40962 vertices). The base architecture of each network is a MoNet U-Net.

2.1 Rotation Architecture

Registration is learned in 3 stages, with the first network learning global rotations. To obtain the rotation matrix between M and F, we use a MoNet U-Net to estimate the 12 parameters of the rotation matrix. With conventional rotation estimation methods, such as quaternions and Euler angles, being shown to be discontinuous in the real Euclidean spaces of four or fewer dimensions [31], we apply the continuous 6D representation formula of the 3D rotations estimation proposed in [31]. The network optimization is driven using an unsupervised mean-squared-error loss. The rotationally aligned subjects are then passed to the next registration stage.

2.2 Deep-Discrete Networks

Deformable registration is subsequently learned using two deep-discrete networks, which learn optimal displacements as a classification problem, regularized by a deep CRF. Let $\{\mathbf{c}_i\}_{i=1}^{N_c} \in G \subset S^2$ be a set of N_c control points, on the input image sphere, generated from a low-resolution icosphere (bottom left of Fig. 1), and let $\{\mathbf{l}_i\}_{i=1}^{N_l} \in S^2$ represent a set of label points, defined around each control point $\mathbf{c}_i$, from a high-order icosphere (bottom left of Fig. 1). Then, the objective of DDR is to learn to predict the optimal label (displacement) for each control point to ensure features of the fixed and moving mesh optimally overlap. Importantly unlike classical discrete frameworks [22,23], for which run-time is linked to the label dimensionality, DDR is far less constrained by the extent of the label space.

Figure 1 shows an overview of our proposed approach. The first part of the network takes M and F concatenated to a single input, then passes this through

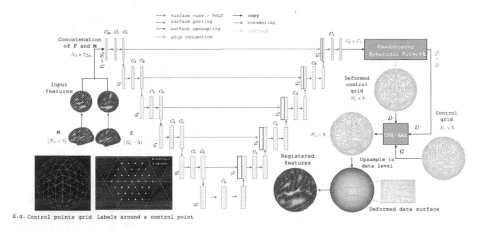

Fig. 1. DDR network architecture. The dimensions in red represent the input and the output dimensions at different levels on the network, while blue boxes represent features in the spherical space. N_d is the number of data vertices, N_c is the total number of control points, N_l is the number of labels around each control point, and f_{in} is the number of features in each subject. (Color figure online)

a U-Net followed by a feedforward spherical network (FSN) to output $Q = \text{Softmax}(U) \in \mathbb{R}^{N_c \times N_l}$: softmax probabilities for each label. The second part of the network is a CFR-RNN network, which imposes smoothness by encouraging neighboring control points to take similar labels.

Classifier Architecture. The surface U-Net implements a symmetric encoder-decoder architecture with six resolution stages i, each defined at a different icosphere order. The number of icosphere vertices V_i at each stage is related to the previous one through $V_{i+1} = (V_i + 6)/4$. MoNet convolutional filters [19] with a kernel size of 3, spherical polar pseudo-coordinates, and mean aggregation operators are applied to learn C_i features at each level. In our network, we set $C_{i+1} = 2C_i$ for all i. Each convolution is followed by a LeakyReLU activation with parameter 0.2. Downsampling and upsampling are performed using the hexagonal mean pooling and transpose convolution operations proposed by [29].

The learned features at the final stage of the decoder, which is of dimensionality of $N_d \times C_1$, are then passed to a feedforward spherical network that decompresses channel dimensions over r convolutional layers, each learning $\bar{C}_i$ features, to return an output of resolution $N_d \times N_l$ (a label prediction for each location in the input mesh); then regularized by downsampling label predictions U to the desired control point resolution of $N_c \times N_l$. Once optimal labels are determined from the softmax operation Q, we deform our control grid accordingly using the spherical coordinates of the labels, i.e., $\mathbf{l}_i$.

CRF-RNN Network: On its own, the classifier is of limited use since cortical registration is an ill-posed problem with many possible solutions. Therefore, smoothness is imposed through a CRF-RNN, adapted from [30], that optimizes the following CRF energy cost function:

$$E = \sum_i Q_{(\mathbf{c}_i, \mathbf{l}_i)} + \sum_{i \neq j} \varphi\left(\mathbf{l}_{\mathbf{c}_i}, \mathbf{l}_{\mathbf{c}_j}\right). \tag{3}$$

Here, $Q_{(\mathbf{c}_i, \mathbf{l}_i)}$ represents the cost (likelihood) of deforming $\mathbf{c}_i$ to $\mathbf{l}_i$ while

$$\varphi\left(\mathbf{l}_{\mathbf{c}_i}, \mathbf{l}_{\mathbf{c}_j}\right) = \mu\left(\mathbf{l}_i, \mathbf{l}_j\right) K_G\left(\mathbf{l}_{\mathbf{c}_i}, \mathbf{l}_{\mathbf{c}_j}\right), \tag{4}$$

measures the pairwise cost of deforming $\mathbf{c}_i$ and $\mathbf{c}_j$ to the label points $\mathbf{l}_i$ and $\mathbf{l}_j$, respectively. Moreover, μ is a learnable label compatibility function that captures correspondences between different pairs of label points (i.e., penalizing the assignment of different labels to different control points with similar properties), and K_G is a Gaussian kernel of the form [18,30]

$$K_G\left(\mathbf{l}_{\mathbf{c}_i}, \mathbf{l}_{\mathbf{c}_j}\right) = \omega\left(\mathbf{c}_i, \mathbf{c}_j\right) \exp\left(-\frac{1}{2\gamma^2}\left(\left(\mathbf{l}_{\mathbf{c}_i} - \mathbf{l}_{\mathbf{c}_j}\right) \Lambda \left(\mathbf{l}_{\mathbf{c}_i} - \mathbf{l}_{\mathbf{c}_j}\right)\right)\right), \tag{5}$$

with $\mathbf{l}_{\mathbf{c}_i}$ being the spatial location of the deformed $\mathbf{c}_i$, ω being learnable filter weights, Λ being symmetric, positive-definite, kernel characterization matrix, and γ being a kernel parameter. Energy (3) is optimized using the Recurrent Neural Network (RNN) implementation of [30], which is based on learning multiple iterations of a mean-field CRF.

Final Deformed Grid and the Loss Function: The updated deformed control grid from the CRF-RNN network is upsampled to the input data icosphere order using barycentric interpolation. Then, the moving image features are resampled to the deformed data grid and compared to those of the fixed image. Optimization is driven using an unsupervised loss function that is a sum of the mean-squared error (MSE) and the cross-correlation (CC). To allow for more user control over the balance between accurate alignment and smooth deformation, we add a diffusion regularization penalty on the spatial gradients of the $\boldsymbol{\Phi}$ in the form $\Sigma\left(\boldsymbol{\Phi}_\theta\right) = \lambda\left(|\nabla\boldsymbol{\Phi}_{\mathbf{x}}| + |\nabla\boldsymbol{\Phi}_{\mathbf{y}}| + |\nabla\boldsymbol{\Phi}_{\mathbf{z}}|\right)$. Here, we apply the hexagonal filter in [29] to compute ∇. Hence, our loss function takes the form

$$\frac{1}{N_d} \sum_{i=1}^{N_d} \left(\|F_{\mathbf{v}_i} - M_{\mathbf{v}_i}\|_2^2 - \frac{cov\left(F_{\mathbf{v}_i}, M_{\mathbf{v}_i}\right)}{\sigma_{F_{\mathbf{v}_i}} \sigma_{M_{\mathbf{v}_i}}}\right) + \lambda\left(|\nabla\boldsymbol{\Phi}_{\mathbf{x}}| + |\nabla\boldsymbol{\Phi}_{\mathbf{y}}| + |\nabla\boldsymbol{\Phi}_{\mathbf{z}}|\right), \tag{6}$$

where $F_{\mathbf{v}_i}$ and $M_{\mathbf{v}_i}$ denote the corresponding feature values at vertex i on the sphere, $cov\left(\cdot, \cdot\right)$ is the covariance operator, whereas σ is the standard deviation.

Coarse to Fine Registration: As with surface registration methods, we perform multi-stage registration in the form of coarse-to-fine using two DDR networks. The first network is trained to align image features using a coarse grid of control points. The deformed grid is then upsampled to the higher level using the hexagonal upsampling method and passed to the second network that uses a higher resolution control grid.

3   Experiments

To validate our proposed framework, we conduct a series of experiments that register individual cortical surfaces to an atlas. In each case, the proposed framework was compared against classical surface registration methods: FreeSurfer [11], Spherical Demons [27], and Multimodal Surface Matching (MSM) [22,23], as well as the learning-based method S3Reg [28].

Datasets and Preprocessing: Experiments were performed using cortical surface data collected as a part of the adult Human Connectome Project (HCP) [14] resampled to a regular icosphere of order 6 using barycentric interpolation. A total number of 1110 brain MRI scans were used in the experiments with 888-111-111 split for train-validation-test and batch sizes of 1 for all. For simplicity, registration was driven solely using sulcal depth as a feature, i.e., $C_{in} = 2$; however, we point out that the network can be straightforwardly adapted to accept multi-channel features.

Implementation and Training: MoNet filters are implemented using the PyTorch Geometric library [10], while optimization is performed using ADAM [17] with a learning rate of 10^{-3}. During the coarse registration stage, we use $N_c = 162$ vertices formed from an icosphere of order 2 with a 26.7 mm distance between adjacent points. $N_l = 600$ labels are generated from an icosphere of order 5 with 3.7 mm neighboring distances. Finally, we set $C_1 = 32, \gamma = 0.7, \lambda = 1.5, r = 1$, and $\bar{C}_1 = 600$. For the fine registration, a total of $N_c = 2542$ points, formed using the vertices of an icosphere of order 4 with 6.9 mm neighboring distances, are applied. $N_l = 1000$ label vertices are generated from an icosphere of order 8 with 0.4 mm neighboring distances. Finally, we let $C_1 = 2, \gamma = 0.2, \lambda = 0.6, r = 5$, and set $[\bar{C}_i]_{i=1}^5 = [8, 16, 64, 128, 1000]$. All networks are trained independently on 100 epochs, and we report the network performance with the best validation score.

Baseline Registration Methods: We validate against the official implementations of Spherical Demons (SD)[1], MSM Pair[2], MSM Strain[3], and the Spherical U-Net multi-stage registration algorithm (S3Reg)[4]. Freesurfer is run as part of the HCP Pipeline, so we obtain its result from there.

To achieve fair comparison across all methods, we ran parameter optimization and report performance across all runs. For SD, we run an additional 11 experiments by setting the number of smooth iterations to take [1, 5, 10] and the smoothing variance σ_x to be [1, 2, 6, 10]. For MSM Pair, we run 22 experiments modifying the regularization penalty $\lambda \in [0.0001, 0.2]$, while for MSM Strain, we run 22 experiments with $\lambda \in [0.0001, 0.9]$. For S3Reg, we ran 7 more

[1] https://github.com/ThomasYeoLab/CBIG
[2] Available through FSLv6.0.
[3] https://github.com/ecr05/MSM_HOCR
[4] https://github.com/zhaofenqiang/SphericalUNetPackage

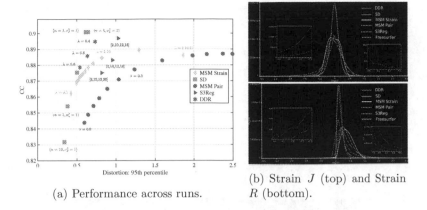

(a) Performance across runs.   (b) Strain J (top) and Strain R (bottom).

Fig. 2. a) Similarity performances of all methods vs. the 95th percentile of the areal distortion at multiple regularization levels. b) Histogram plots comparing methods distortions J and R across all test subjects for runs with CC ~ 0.88.

experiments by varying smoothness regularization at different registration levels to take the sets $[2, 5, 6, 8]$, $[2, 10, 12, 20]$, $[2, 10, 12, 14]$, $[2, 5, 12, 16]$, $[2, 10, 6, 8]$, $[2, 10, 12, 8]$, and $[2, 5, 6, 16]$; in each case training for 100 epochs and reporting the performance of the network with the best validation score. As FreeSurfer is not tunable by the user, we only report its results with default parameterization. Note that all these methods register two surfaces at 4 levels of icosphere subdivisions (coarse to fine), with S3Reg having an additional spherical transform network that ensures a diffeomorphic registration.

Evaluation Metrics: All methods are compared in terms of cross correlation (CC) similarity, areal strain (J), shape strain (R), and run time. Here $J = \lambda_1 \lambda_2$ and $R = \lambda_1 / \lambda_2$, where λ_1 and λ_2 represent the eigenvalues of the local deformation gradient F_{pqr} estimated from the deformation of each triangular face, defined by vertices: p, q, r. Note that $\log_2 J$ is equivalent to areal distortion while $\log_2 R$ is equivalent to shape distortion.

Results: Figure 2a plots the similarity performances of the different runs of all methods versus the 95th percentile of the absolute values of J. At each similarity level, DDR returns distortions within the range of the best classical methods (SD and MSM Strain) and reduced extremes of $|J|$ relative to that of S3Reg.

This trend is repeated across the full distributions of $|J|$ and $|R|$ for each comparable run. Figure 2b plots the full histogram distributions for $|J|$ and $|R|$ across all runs that return a CC value of approximately 0.88. Most of the areal distortions of SD and DDR at this CC level are around zero. However, S3Reg, MSM Pair, and Freesurfer all lead to extreme distortions across subjects, with an average of 150 vertices at each subject having $|J|$ above 2 in S3Reg compared to 0.567 for DDR.

Table 1 further reports summary statistics for these histogram distributions in terms of the mean, max, 95th, and 98th percentiles of $|J|$, the mean and the

Table 1. Distortions measures and average runtime for different methods obtained for CC ~ 0.88; top: classical methods, bottom: learning-based methods.

Methods	CC Similarity	Areal distortion				Shape distortion		Avg. time	
		Mean	Max	95%	98%	Mean	Max	CPU	GPU
Freesurfer	0.75	0.34	11.73	0.82	1.00	0.63	6.77	30 min	-
MSM Pair	0.877	0.41	9.17	1.24	1.76	0.62	9.05	13 min	-
MSM Strain	0.880	0.27	1.06	0.53	0.66	0.64	1.93	1 h	-
SD	0.875	0.18	2.00	0.50	0.65	0.24	1.98	1 min	-
S3Reg	0.875	0.266	22.22	0.82	1.16	0.51	21.65	8.8 s	8.0 s
DDR	0.878	**0.19**	**2.66**	**0.53**	**0.71**	**0.26**	**3.14**	**7.7 s**	**2.3 s**

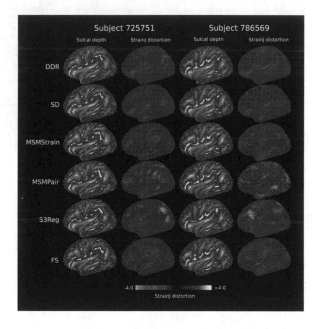

Fig. 3. Qualitative comparisons of sulcal depth alignment for 2 subjects. Results reflect distortion values presented in Fig. 2 and Table. 1. Columns 1 and 3 show registered sulcal depth maps; columns 2 and 4 reflect strain J across the surface. Cyan areas of the distortion maps highlight significant distortions.

max of $|R|$, and the mean CC, obtained across all runs. Again, DDR performs comparably to SD and MSM Strain, whereas S3Reg and MSM Pair provide the worst performance. These values reflect the best performance of S3Reg (in terms of distortion) across all runs. In terms of average run time, for a PC with NVIDIA Titan RTX 24 GB GPU and Intel Core i9-9820X 3.30 GHz CPU, DDR has the least GPU and CPU times across all methods. Figure 3 presents a qualitative comparison of the alignment quality for 2 subjects across all methods, together with the strain J metrics across the surface. Results show that DDR, SD, and

MSM Strain generate comparable alignment for reduced distortion relative to S3Reg and MSM Pair that produce alignments that result in peaks of high distortions. More results are provided in [25].

4   Conclusions

In this work, we propose the first deep-discrete registration (DDR) framework for cortical surface alignment that aligns two surfaces by deforming a set of control points on the surface into a finite set of possible deformations. Our results show that DDR outperforms other deep learning-based cortical surface registration frameworks (S3Reg) in terms of similarity and distortions measures and provides a competitive performance to state-of-the-art conventional surface registration methods. Future work will extend DDR to multimodal alignment with high dimensional feature sets and address topographical variation.

References

1. Amunts, K., Malikovic, A., Mohlberg, H., Schormann, T., Zilles, K.: Brodmann's areas 17 and 18 brought into stereotaxic space-where and how variable? Neuroimage **11**(1), 66–84 (2000)
2. Aoki, Y., Goforth, H., Srivatsan, R.A., Lucey, S.: Pointnetlk: robust & efficient point cloud registration using pointnet. In: Proceedings of the IEEE/CVF Conference on Computer Vision and Pattern Recognition, pp. 7163–7172 (2019)
3. Balakrishnan, G., Zhao, A., Sabuncu, M.R., Guttag, J., Dalca, A.V.: VoxelMorph: a learning framework for deformable medical image registration. IEEE Trans. Med. Imaging **38**(8), 1788–1800 (2019)
4. Borovec, J., et al.: ANHIR: automatic non-rigid histological image registration challenge. IEEE Trans. Med. Imaging **39**(10), 3042–3052 (2020)
5. Coalson, T.S., Van Essen, D.C., Glasser, M.F.: The impact of traditional neuroimaging methods on the spatial localization of cortical areas. Proc. Natl. Acad. Sci. **115**(27), E6356–E6365 (2018)
6. Dalca, A., Rakic, M., Guttag, J., Sabuncu, M.: Learning conditional deformable templates with convolutional networks. In: 33rd Advances in neural Information Processing Systems, vol. 32 (2019)
7. De Vos, B.D., Berendsen, F.F., Viergever, M.A., Sokooti, H., Staring, M., Išgum, I.: A deep learning framework for unsupervised affine and deformable image registration. Med. Image Anal. **52**, 128–143 (2019)
8. Fan, J., Cao, X., Xue, Z., Yap, P.-T., Shen, D.: Adversarial similarity network for evaluating image alignment in deep learning based registration. In: Frangi, A.F., Schnabel, J.A., Davatzikos, C., Alberola-López, C., Fichtinger, G. (eds.) MICCAI 2018. LNCS, vol. 11070, pp. 739–746. Springer, Cham (2018). https://doi.org/10.1007/978-3-030-00928-1_83
9. Fawaz, A., et al.: Benchmarking geometric deep learning for cortical segmentation and neurodevelopmental phenotype prediction. bioRxiv (2021)
10. Fey, M., Lenssen, J.E.: Fast graph representation learning with PyTorch geometric. In: ICLR Workshop on Representation Learning on Graphs and Manifolds (2019)

11. Fischl, B., Sereno, M.I., Tootell, R.B., Dale, A.M.: High-resolution intersubject averaging and a coordinate system for the cortical surface. Hum. Brain Mapp. **8**(4), 272–284 (1999)
12. Fu, Y., et al.: LungregNet: an unsupervised deformable image registration method for 4D-CT lung. Med. Phys. **47**(4), 1763–1774 (2020)
13. Glasser, M.E., et al.: A multi-modal parcellation of human cerebral cortex. Nature **536**(7615), 171–178 (2016)
14. Glasser, M.E., et al.: The minimal preprocessing pipelines for the human connectome project. Neuroimage **80**, 105–124 (2013)
15. Heinrich, M.P.: Closing the gap between deep and conventional image registration using probabilistic dense displacement networks. In: Shen, D., Liu, T., Peters, T.M., Staib, L.H., Essert, C., Zhou, S., Yap, P.-T., Khan, A. (eds.) MICCAI 2019. LNCS, vol. 11769, pp. 50–58. Springer, Cham (2019). https://doi.org/10.1007/978-3-030-32226-7_6
16. Heinrich, M.P., Hansen, L.: Highly accurate and memory efficient unsupervised learning-based discrete CT registration using 2.5d displacement search. In: Martel, M.P., et al. (eds.) MICCAI 2020. LNCS, vol. 12263, pp. 190–200. Springer, Cham (2020). https://doi.org/10.1007/978-3-030-59716-0_19
17. Kingma, D.P., Ba, J.: Adam: a method for stochastic optimization. arXiv preprint arXiv:1412.6980 (2014)
18. Krähenbühl, P., Koltun, V.: Efficient inference in fully connected CRFs with Gaussian edge potentials. In: Advances in neural Information Processing Systems, vol. 24 (2011)
19. Monti, F., Boscaini, D., Masci, J., Rodola, E., Svoboda, J., Bronstein, M.M.: Geometric deep learning on graphs and manifolds using mixture model CNNs. In: Proceedings of the IEEE Conference on Computer Vision and Pattern Recognition, pp. 5115–5124 (2017)
20. Pielawski, N., et al.: CoMIR: contrastive multimodal image representation for registration. Adv. Neural. Inf. Process. Syst. **33**, 18433–18444 (2020)
21. Qi, C.R., Su, H., Mo, K., Guibas, L.J.: Pointnet: deep learning on point sets for 3D classification and segmentation. In: Proceedings of the IEEE Conference on Computer Vision and Pattern Recognition, pp. 652–660 (2017)
22. Robinson, E.K., et al.: Multimodal surface matching with higher-order smoothness constraints. Neuroimage **167**, 453–465 (2018)
23. Robinson, E.K., et al.: MSM: a new flexible framework for multimodal surface matching. Neuroimage **100**, 414–426 (2014)
24. Shao, W., et al.: ProsRegNet: a deep learning framework for registration of MRI and histopathology images of the prostate. Med. Image Anal. **68** (2021)
25. Suliman, M.A., Williams, L.Z., Fawaz, A., Robinson, E.C.: A deep-discrete learning framework for spherical surface registration. arXiv preprint arXiv:2203.12999 (2022)
26. Wang, Y., Solomon, J.M.: Deep closest point: learning representations for point cloud registration. In: Proceedings of the IEEE/CVF International Conference on Computer Vision, pp. 3523–3532 (2019)
27. Yeo, B.T., Sabuncu, M.R., Vercauteren, T., Ayache, N., Fischl, B., Golland, P.: Spherical demons: fast diffeomorphic landmark-free surface registration. IEEE Trans. Med. Imaging **29**(3), 650–668 (2009)
28. Zhao, F., et al.: S3reg: superfast spherical surface registration based on deep learning. IEEE Trans. Med. Imaging **40**(8), 1964–1976 (2021)

29. Zhao, F., et al.: Spherical U-net on cortical surfaces: methods and applications. In: Chung, A.C.S., Gee, J.C., Yushkevich, P.A., Bao, S. (eds.) IPMI 2019. LNCS, vol. 11492, pp. 855–866. Springer, Cham (2019). https://doi.org/10.1007/978-3-030-20351-1_67
30. Zheng, S., et al.: Conditional random fields as recurrent neural networks. In: Proceedings of the IEEE International Conference on Computer Vision, pp. 1529–1537 (2015)
31. Zhou, Y., Barnes, C., Lu, J., Yang, J., Li, H.: On the continuity of rotation representations in neural networks. In: Proceedings of the IEEE/CVF Conference on Computer Vision and Pattern Recognition, pp. 5745–5753 (2019)

Privacy Preserving Image Registration

Riccardo Taiello[1,2,3]($\boxtimes$), Melek Önen[2], Olivier Humbert[3], and Marco Lorenzi[1,3]

[1] Epione Research Project, Inria, Sophia Antipolis, France
{riccardo.taiello,marco.lorenzi}@inria.fr
[2] EURECOM, Sophia Antipolis, France
melek.onen@eurecom.fr
[3] Université Côte d'Azur, Nice, France
olivier.humbert@univ-cotedazur.fr

Abstract. Image registration is a key task in medical imaging applications, allowing to represent medical images in a common spatial reference frame. Current literature on image registration is generally based on the assumption that images are usually accessible to the researcher, from which the spatial transformation is subsequently estimated. This common assumption may not be met in current practical applications, since the sensitive nature of medical images may ultimately require their analysis under privacy constraints, preventing to share the image content in clear form. In this work, we formulate the problem of image registration under a privacy preserving regime, where images are assumed to be confidential and cannot be disclosed in clear. We derive our privacy preserving image registration framework by extending classical registration paradigms to account for advanced cryptographic tools, such as secure multi-party computation and homomorphic encryption, that enable the execution of operations without leaking the underlying data. To overcome the problem of performance and scalability of cryptographic tools in high dimensions, we first propose to optimize the underlying image registration operations using gradient approximations. We further revisit the use of homomorphic encryption and use a packing method to allow the encryption and multiplication of large matrices more efficiently. We demonstrate our privacy preserving framework in linear and non-linear registration problems, evaluating its accuracy and scalability with respect to standard image registration. Our results show that privacy preserving image registration is feasible and can be adopted in sensitive medical imaging applications.

Keywords: Image registration · Privacy enhancing technologies · Trustworthiness

1 Introduction

Image Registration is a crucial task in medical imaging applications, allowing to spatially align imaging features between two or multiple scans. Image registration

---

Supplementary Information The online version contains supplementary material available at https://doi.org/10.1007/978-3-031-16446-0_13.

L. Wang et al. (Eds.): MICCAI 2022, LNCS 13436, pp. 130–140, 2022.
https://doi.org/10.1007/978-3-031-16446-0_13

is a key component of state-of-the-art methods for atlas-based segmentation [9, 31], morphological and functional analysis [3,11], multi-modal data integration [17], and longitudinal analysis [4,26].

Overall, typical registration paradigms are based on a given transformation model (e.g. affine or non-linear), a cost function and an associated optimization routine. A large number of image registration approaches have been proposed in the literature over the last decades, covering a variety of assumptions under-lying the spatial transformations, similarity metric, image dimensionality and optimization strategy [30].

Image registration is the workhorse of many real-life medical imaging software and applications, including public web-based services for automated segmentation and labeling of medical images. Using these services generally requires uploading and exchanging medical images over the Internet, to subsequently perform image registration with respect to one or multiple (potentially proprietary) atlases. There are also emerging data analysis paradigms, such as Federated Learning (FL) [22], where medical images can be jointly analysed in multi-centric scenarios to perform group analysis [14]. In these setting, the creation of registration-based image templates [3] is currently not possible without disclosing the image information. Due to the evolving juridical landscape on data protection, these applications of image registration are no longer compliant with regulations currently existing in many countries, such as the European General Data Protection Regulation (GDPR) [2], or the US Health Insurance Portability and Accountability Act (HIPAA) [1]. Medical imaging information falls within the realm of personal health data [20] and its sensitive nature should ultimately require the analysis under privacy preserving constraints, for instance by preventing to share the image content in clear form.

Advanced cryptographic tools enabling data processing without disclosing it in clear hold great potential in sensitive data analysis problems (e.g., [19]). Examples of such approaches are Secure-Multi-Party-Computation (MPC) [33] and Homomorphic Encryption (HE) [27]. While MPC allows multiple parties to jointly compute a common function over their private inputs and discover no more than the output of this function, HE enables computation on encrypted data without disclosing neither the input data nor the result of the computation.

This work presents a new methodological framework allowing image registration under privacy constraints. To this end, we reformulate the typical image registration problem to integrate cryptographic tools, namely MPC or FHE, thus preserving the privacy of the image data. Due to the well known scalability issues of privacy preserving techniques, we investigate strategies for the practical use of privacy preserving image registration (PPIR) through gradient approximations, array packing and matrix partitioning. In our experiments we evaluate the effectiveness of PPIR in linear and non-linear registration problems. Our results demonstrate the feasibility of PPIR, and pave the way to the application of image registration in sensitive medical imaging applications.

2   Problem Statement

Given images $I, J : \mathbb{R}^d \mapsto \mathbb{R}$, image registration aims at estimating the parameters $\mathbf{p}$ of a spatial transformation $\mathbf{W_p} \in \mathbb{R}^d \mapsto \mathbb{R}^d$, either linear or non-linear, maximizing the spatial overlap between J and the transformed image $I(\mathbf{W_p})$. For example, a typical cost function to optimize the registration problem is the sum of squared intensity differences (SSD) evaluated on the set of image coordinates:

$$\text{SSD}(I, J, \mathbf{p}) = \text{argmin}_\mathbf{p} \sum_\mathbf{x} \left[I(\mathbf{W_p}(\mathbf{x})) - J(\mathbf{x}) \right]^2 \tag{1}$$

Equation (1) can be typically optimized through gradient-based methods, where the parameters $\mathbf{p}$ are iteratively updated until convergence. In particular, under a Gauss-Newton optimization scheme, the parameters update of the spatial transformation can be computed through Eq. (2):

$$\mathbf{\Delta_p} = H^{-1} \cdot \sum_\mathbf{x} S(\mathbf{x}) \cdot (I(\mathbf{W_p}(\mathbf{x})) - J(\mathbf{x})), \tag{2}$$

where $S(\mathbf{x}) = \nabla I(\mathbf{x}) \frac{\partial \mathbf{W_p}(\mathbf{x})}{\partial \mathbf{p}}$ quantifies image and transformation gradients, and $H = \sum_\mathbf{x} \left(\nabla I(\mathbf{x}) \frac{\partial \mathbf{W_p}(\mathbf{x})}{\partial \mathbf{p}} \right)^T \left(\nabla I(\mathbf{x}) \frac{\partial \mathbf{W_p}(\mathbf{x})}{\partial \mathbf{p}} \right)$ is the second order term obtained from Eq. (1) through linearization [5,24].

The solution of this problem requires the joint availability of both images I and J, as well as of the gradients of I and of $\mathbf{W_p}$. In a privacy preserving setting, this information may not be available, and the computation of Eq. (2) is therefore impossible. We thus consider a scenario with two parties, $party_1$, and $party_2$, whereby $party_1$ owns image I and $party_2$ owns image J. The parties wish to collaboratively optimize the image registration problem without disclosing their respective images to each other. We assume that only $party_1$ has access to the transformation parameters $\mathbf{p}$, and that is also in charge of computing the update at each optimization step. In particular, to compute the registration update $\mathbf{\Delta p}$ of Eq. (2), the only operation requiring the joint availability of information from both parties is the term $R = \sum_\mathbf{x} S(\mathbf{x}) \cdot J(\mathbf{x})$, which can be computed as a matrix-vector multiplication on vectorized quantities, $R = S^T \cdot J$.

3   Methods

Before presenting PPIR in Sect. 3.2, we introduce in Sect. 3.1 the cryptographic tools underlying the proposed framework.

3.1   Secure Computation

Secure Multi-Party Computation. Introduced by Yao in [33], MPC is a cryptographic tool that allows multiple parties to jointly compute a common function over their private inputs (secrets) and discover no more than the output of this function. Among existing MPC protocols, additive secret sharing consists of first splitting every secret s into additive shares $\langle s \rangle_i$, such that $\sum_{i=1}^{n} \langle s \rangle_i = s$, where n is the number of collaborating parties. Each party i receives one share $\langle s \rangle_i$, and executes an arithmetic circuit in order to obtain the final output of the function. In this paper, we adopt the two-party computation protocol defined in SPDZ [12], whereby the actual function is mapped into an arithmetic circuit and all computations are performed within a finite ring with modulus Q. Additions consist of locally adding shares of secrets, while multiplications require interaction between parties. Following [12], SPDZ defines a dedicated MPCMUL operation to compute matrix-vector multiplication within a secure two-party protocol. **Homomorphic Encryption.** Initially introduced by Rivest et al. in [27], HE enables the execution of operations over encrypted data without disclosing neither the input data, nor the result of the computation. Hence, party 1 encrypts the input with her public key and sends this encryption to party 2. Party 2, in turn, evaluates a circuit over this encrypted input and sends the result, which still remains encrypted, back to party 1 which can finally decrypt the result. Among various HE schemes, CKKS [10] supports the execution of all operations over encrypted real values and is considered as a fully homomorphic encryption (FHE). With CKKS, an input vector is mapped to a polynomial and further encrypted with a public key in order to obtain a pair of polynomials $c = (c_0, c_1)$. The original function is further mapped into a set of operations that are supported by CKKS, which are executed over c. The performance and security of CKKS depends on multiple parameters including the degree of the polynomial N, which is usually sufficiently large (e.g. $N = 4096$, or $N = 8192$).

3.2   PPIR: Privacy Preserving Image Registration

In order to ensure the privacy of images I and J against $party_2$ and $party_1$ respectively, we propose to investigate the use of MPC and FHE to develop PPIR. Figure 1 illustrates how these two cryptographic tools are employed to ensure the privacy of the images during registration. As previously mentioned, the only operation that needs to be jointly executed by the parties in a privacy preserving manner is the matrix-vector multiplication: $R = S^T \cdot J$, where S^T is only known to $party_1$, and J to $party_2$.

When MPC is integrated (Fig. 1a), $party_1$ secretly shares the matrix S^T to obtain $(\langle S_1 \rangle, \langle S_2 \rangle)$, while $party_2$ secretly shares the image J to obtain $(\langle J_1 \rangle, \langle J_2 \rangle)$. Each party further receives its corresponding share, namely: $party_1$ holds $(\langle S_1 \rangle, \langle J_1 \rangle)$ and $party_2$ holds $(\langle S_2 \rangle, \langle J_2 \rangle)$. Parties further execute a circuit with the MPCMUL operations to compute the 2-party dot product between S^T and J. The parties further synchronize to let $party_1$ to obtain the product, and to finally calculate $\mathbf{\Delta p}$ (see Eq. (2)).

When using FHE (Fig. 1b), $party_2$ uses a FHE key k to encrypt J and obtain: $[\![J]\!] \leftarrow \text{ENC}(k, J)$. This encrypted image is sent to $party_1$, who computes the encrypted result $[\![R]\!]$ of the matrix-vector multiplication. In this framework, only the vector J is encrypted, and therefore $party_1$ executes scalar multiplications

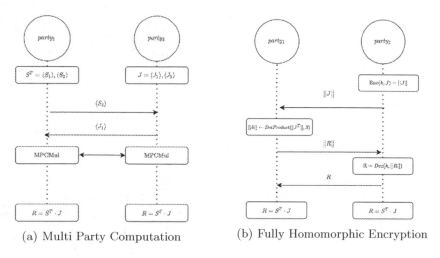

(a) Multi Party Computation   (b) Fully Homomorphic Encryption

Fig. 1. Proposed framework to compute the matrix-vector multiplication $S^T \cdot J$ relying on MPC and FHE.

and additions in the encrypted domain only (which are less costly than multiplications over two encrypted inputs). The encrypted result $[\![R]\!]$ is sent back to $party_2$, which can obtain the result through decryption: $R = \text{DEC}(k, [\![R]\!])$. Finally, $party_1$ receives R in clear form and can therefore compute $\mathbf{\Delta p}$.

Thanks to the privacy and security guarantees of these cryptographic tools, during the entire registration procedure the content of the image data S and I is never disclosed to the opposite party. Nevertheless, effectively optimizing Eq. (1) with MPC or FHE is particularly challenging, due to the computational bottleneck of these techniques when applied to large dimensional objects [7, 16], notably affecting computation time and communication bandwidth between parties. To tackle this issue, in what follows we introduce in the schemes of Fig. 1 computational strategies to effectively reduce the dimensionality of the image information through sampling, and to improve the scalability of the algebraic operations when using these cryptographic tools.

Gradient Sampling. The update of Eq. (2) is computed on the vectorized images, which are large-dimensional arrays representing all the image pixels (or voxels). Since the registration gradient is in general mostly driven by a fraction of the image content, e.g. image boundaries in case of the SSD metric, a reasonable approximation of Eq. (2) can be obtained by assessment on relevant image locations only. This idea has been introduced in medical image registration [21,29,32], and is here adopted to reduce the dimensionality of the arrays on which encryption is performed. In our works we test two different techniques: *(i)*: Uniformly Random Selection (URS), proposed by [21,32], in which a random subset of dimension $l \leq s$ of spatial coordinates is sampled at every iteration with uniform probabilities, $Pr(\mathbf{x}) = \frac{1}{s}$; and *(ii)*: Gradient Magnitude Sampling (GMS)

[29], consisting in sampling a subset of coordinates with probability proportional to the norm of the image gradient, $Pr(\mathbf{x}) \sim \|\nabla I(\mathbf{x})\|$.

Matrix Partitioning in FHE. In addition to gradient sampling, we propose a specific optimization dedicated to PPIR with FHE, in particular when the CKKS algorithm is adopted. CKKS allows packing multiple inputs into a single ciphertext to decrease the number of homomorphic operations. In order to optimize the matrix-vector multiplication, we propose to partition the image vector J into K sub-arrays of dimension D, and the matrix S^T into K submatrices of dimension $|\mathbf{p}| \times D$. Once all sub-arrays J_i are encrypted, we propose to iteratively apply the (DOTPRODUCT) proposed by [7] between each sub-matrix and corresponding sub-array; these intermediate results are then summed up to obtain the final result, namely: $[\![R]\!] = \sum_{i=0}^{K} \text{DOTPRODUCT}\left([\![J_i^T]\!], S_i\right) = S^T \cdot [\![J]\!]$.

4 Experimental Results

We demonstrate and assess PPIR in two examples based on linear and non-linear alignment of respectively positron emission tomography (PET) and anatomical magnetic resonance (MR) images.

Dataset. PET data consists of 18-Fluoro-Deoxy-Glucose (^{18}FDG) whole body Positron Emission Tomography (PET). The images here considered are a frontal view of the maximum intensity projection reconstruction, obtained by 2D projection of the voxels with highest intensity across views (1260×1090 pixels).

MR images are obtained from brain scans of the Alzheimer's Disease Neuroimaging Initiative [23]. Images underwent a standard processing pipeline to estimate grey matter density maps [3]. The subsequent registration experiments are performed on the extracted mid-coronal slice, of dimension 121×121 pixels.

Implementation. PET image alignment was performed by optimizing the transformation $\mathbf{W_p}$ of Eq. (1) with respect to affine registration parameters. The registration of brain grey matter density images was performed by non-linear registration based on a cubic spline model (one control point every five pixels along both dimensions). For both affine and non-linear cases, the registration was performed between two randomly selected patients' images.

Concerning the PPIR framework with the affine transformation, tests are carried for both MPC and FHE by considering the entire images, and by using gradient approximation techniques (Sect. 3). The sampling seed for gradient approximation is the same for each test. Due to the smaller dimension of the brain grey matter images, non-linear PPIR with cubic-splines is applied directly to the full data. For MPC we set as prime modulus $Q = 2^{32}$. For FHE, we define the polynomial degree modulus as $N = 4096$, and set the resizing parameter D to optimize the trade-off between runtime and bandwidth. Since D needs to be a divider of the image size, for PET image data we set $D = 128$, while for the grey matter images we set $D = 121$. The PPIR framework is implemented using two state-of-the-art libraries: PySyft [28] supporting SPDZ's two-party computation, and TenSeal [7] for CKKS. All the experiments are executed on a machine with an

Intel(R) Core(TM) i7-7800X CPU @ (3.50 GHz × 12) using 132 GB of RAM. For each registration configuration, the optimization is repeated 10 times, to account for the random generation of the MPC shares and FHE encryption keys. The code is released in a `GitHub` repository[1]. We used Weights & Biases [8] for experiment tracking, and the links of our tracked results are available in the `GitHub` repository.

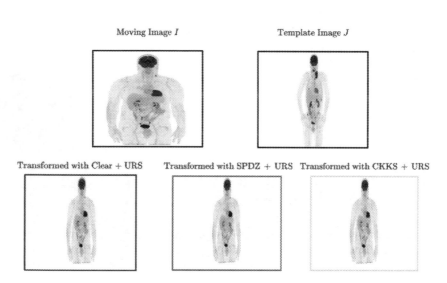

Fig. 2. Qualitative results for affine registration. The red frame is the transformed moving image using CLEAR +URS registration. Green and Yellow frames are the transformed images using respectively MPC+URS and FHE+URS PPIR. The yellow image is the transformed moving using PPIR with CKKS. (Color figure online)

The quality of PPIR is assessed by comparing the registration results with respect to the ones obtained with standard registration on clear images (CLEAR). The metrics considered are the image intensity difference at the optimum, the overall number of iterations required to converge, and the displacement root mean square difference (RMSE) between CLEAR and PPIR. We also evaluate the performance of PPIR in terms of average computation (running time) and communication (bandwidth) across iterations.

Results. Table 1 (Registration metrics) shows that affine PPIR through SPDZ leads to negligible differences with respect to CLEAR in terms of number of iterations, intensity and displacement. Registration with CKKS is instead not possible when considering the entire images, due to computational complexity, and is also associated to generally larger approximations when using URS and GMS. Nevertheless, Fig. 2 shows that neither MPC nor FHE do decrease the overall quality of the affine registered images. Additional registration results

---
[1] https://github.com/rtaiello/pp_image_registration.

Table 1. Affine registration test. Registration metrics are reported as mean and standard deviation. Efficiency metrics in terms of average across iterations. RMSE: root mean square error.

Affine registration metrics			
Solution	Intensity Error (SSD)	Num. Interation	Displacement RMSE CLEAR vs PPIR (mm)
CLEAR	4.34 ± 0.0	118 ± 0.0	-
SPDZ	4.34 ± 0.0	114.8 ± 4.0	1.81 ± 0.02
CKKS	✗	✗	✗
CLEAR + URS	4.38 ± 0.0	61 ± 0.0	-
SPDZ + URS	4.34 ± 0.0	60.4 ± 6.85	16.49 ± 3.74
CKKS $(D = 128)$ + URS	4.34 ± 0.10	61.80 ± 4.82	23.31 ± 2.72
CLEAR + GMS	4.34 ± 0.0	63 ± 0.0	-
SPDZ + GMS	4.34 ± 0.0	59.80 ± 6.20	6.21 ± 1.49
CKKS $(D = 128)$ + GMS	4.34 ± 0.05	60.4 ± 5.12	5.17 ± 1.40

Affine efficiency metrics				
Solution	Time $party_1$ (s)	Time $party_2$ (s)	Comm. $party_1$ (MB)	Comm. $party_2$ (MB)
CLEAR	0.0	0.0	-	-
SPDZ	0.13	0.13	1.54	1.54
CKKS	✗	✗	✗	✗
CLEAR + URS	0.0	0.0	-	-
SPDZ + URS	0.02	0.02	0.20	0.20
CKKS $(D = 128)$ + URS	2.55	0.02	0.06	0.01
CLEAR + GMS	0.0	0.0	-	-
SPDZ + GMS	0.02	0.02	0.20	0.20
CKKS $(D = 128)$ + GMS	2.51	0.02	0.06	0.01

Table 2. Non-linear registration test. Registration metrics are reported as mean and standard deviation. Efficiency metrics in terms of average across iterations. RMSE: root mean square error.

Cubic splines registration metrics			
Solution	Intensity Error (SSD)	Num. Interation	Displacement RMSE CLEAR vs PPIR (mm)
CLEAR	0.65 ± 0.0	413 ± 0.0	-
SPDZ	0.65 ± 0.0	345.70 ± 91.22	7.31 ± 1.86
CKKS	0.64 ± 0.0	224.7 ± 79.15	9.50 ± 4.34

Cubic splines efficiency metrics				
Solution	Time $party_1$ (s)	Time $party_2$ (s)	Comm. $party_1$ (MB)	Comm. $party_2$ (MB)
CLEAR	0.0	0.0	-	-
SPDZ	0.63	0.63	21.47	28.98
CKKS	3.41	0.00	0.06	0.01

are available in Appendix. Table 1 (Efficiency metrics) shows that SPDZ performed on the full images has highest computation time and communication bandwidth. These figures sensibly improve when using URS or GMS, by factors 10× and 20× for respectively time and bandwidth. Concerning CKKS, we note the uneven time and bandwidth requirements between clients, due to the asymmetry of encryption operations and communication protocol (Fig. 1). Finally, Table 2 reports the metrics for the non-linear registration test. Concerning registration accuracy, we draw similar conclusions to the affine case, where SPDZ leads to minimum differences with respect to CLEAR, while CKKS seems slightly inferior. SPDZ is associated to lower execution time and higher computation bandwidth, due to the larger number of parameters of the cubic splines, affecting the size of the matrix S. While CKKS has higher execution time, the demanded bandwidth is inferior to the one of SPDZ, since the encrypted template image is transmitted only once.

5   Conclusion

This work introduces privacy preserving image registration (PPIR), a novel framework to allow image registration when images are confidential and cannot be disclosed in clear. PPIR is developed with MPC and FHE and implements effective strategies to mitigate their known computational and communication overhead. PPIR is demonstrated and evaluated through a series of quantitative benchmarks in both linear and non-linear image registration problems. Our results highlight the existing trade-off between registration performance and efficiency of the different PPIR schemes.

Future extensions of this work will be devoted to the benchmarking of our framework in more general scenarios, involving 3D medical image data and multimodal registration problem. The application to multimodal data will require the extension of our framework to account for different similarity metrics, such as Mutual Information or Normalized Cross-Correlation [25,32]. Moreover, the effectiveness of sampling through URS and GMS motivates the adoption of sparse image registration frameworks, especially for non-linear registration [13,15]. Another relevant research direction concerns the development of PPIR in deep-learning based approaches [6,18].

Overall, this study shows that PPIR is feasible and can therefore be adopted in sensitive medical imaging applications.

References

1. Health Resources and Services Administration. Health insurance portability and accountability act, 1, U.S. Department of Labor, Employee Benefits Security Administration (1996)
2. Regulation (EU) 2016/679 of the European Parliament and of the Council of 27 April 2016 on the protection of natural persons with regard to the processing of personal data and on the free movement of such data, and repealing directive 95/46/EC (General Data Protection Regulation) (2016–05–04). European Union

3. Ashburner, J., Friston, K.J.: Voxel-based morphometry-the methods. Neuroimage **11**(6), 805–821 (2000)
4. Ashburner, J., Ridgway, G.R.: Symmetric diffeomorphic modeling of longitudinal structural MRI. Front. Neurosci. **6**, 197 (2013)
5. Baker, S., Matthews, I.: Lucas-Kanade 20 years on: a unifying framework. Int. J. Comput. Vision **56**(3), 221–255 (2004)
6. Balakrishnan, G., Zhao, A., Sabuncu, M.R., Guttag, J., Dalca, A.V.: VoxelMorph: a learning framework for deformable medical image registration. IEEE Trans. Med. Imaging **38**(8), 1788–1800 (2019)
7. Benaissa, A., Retiat, B., Cebere, B., Belfedhal, A.E.: TenSEAL: a library for encrypted tensor operations using homomorphic encryption. CoRR abs/2104.03152 (2021). https://arxiv.org/abs/2104.03152
8. Biewald, L.: Experiment tracking with weights and biases (2020). https://www.wandb.com/. software available from wandb.com
9. Cardoso, M.J., et al.: STEPs: similarity and truth estimation for propagated segmentations and its application to hippocampal segmentation and brain parcellation. Med. Image Anal. **17**(6), 671–684 (2013)
10. Cheon, J.H., Kim, A., Kim, M., Song, Y.: Homomorphic encryption for arithmetic of approximate numbers. In: Takagi, T., Peyrin, T. (eds.) ASIACRYPT 2017. LNCS, vol. 10624, pp. 409–437. Springer, Cham (2017). https://doi.org/10.1007/978-3-319-70694-8_15
11. Dale, A.M., Fischl, B., Sereno, M.I.: Cortical surface-based analysis: I. segmentation and surface reconstruction. Neuroimage. **9**(2), 179–194 (1999)
12. Damgard, I., Pastro, V., Smart, N., Zakarias, S.: Multiparty computation from somewhat homomorphic encryption. Cryptology, ePrint Archive, report 2011/535 (2011). https://ia.cr/2011/535
13. Fawzi, A., Frossard, P.: Image registration with sparse approximations in parametric dictionaries. SIAM J. Imaging Sci. **6**(4), 2370–2403 (2013)
14. Gazula, H., et al.: Decentralized multisite VBM analysis during adolescence shows structural changes linked to age, body mass index, and smoking: a COINSTAC analysis. Neuroinformatics **19**(4), 553–566 (2021)
15. Ha, I.Y., Wilms, M., Handels, H., Heinrich, M.P.: Model-based sparse-to-dense image registration for Realtime respiratory motion estimation in image-guided interventions. IEEE Trans. Biomed. Eng. **66**(2), 302–310 (2018)
16. Haralampieva, V., Rueckert, D., Passerat-Palmbach, J.: A systematic comparison of encrypted machine learning solutions for image classification. In: Proceedings of the 2020 Workshop on Privacy-preserving Machine Learning in Practice, pp. 55–59 (2020)
17. Heinrich, M.P., et al.: Non-local shape descriptor: a new similarity metric for deformable multi-modal registration. In: Fichtinger, G., Martel, A., Peters, T. (eds.) MICCAI 2011. LNCS, vol. 6892, pp. 541–548. Springer, Heidelberg (2011). https://doi.org/10.1007/978-3-642-23629-7_66
18. Krebs, J., Delingette, H., Mailhé, B., Ayache, N., Mansi, T.: Learning a probabilistic model for diffeomorphic registration. IEEE Trans. Med. Imaging **38**(9), 2165–2176 (2019)
19. Lauter, K.: Private AI: Machine Learning on Encrypted Data. Technical report (2021). eprint report https://eprint.iacr.org/2021/324.pdf
20. Lotan, E., et al.: Medical imaging and privacy in the era of artificial intelligence: myth, fallacy, and the future. J. Am. College Radiol. **17**(9), 1159–1162 (2020)

21. Mattes, D., Haynor, D.R., Vesselle, H., Lewellen, T.K., Eubank, W.: PET-CT image registration in the chest using free-form deformations. IEEE Trans. Med. Imaging **22**(1), 120–128 (2003)
22. McMahan, B., Moore, E., Ramage, D., Hampson, S., y Arcas, B.A.: Communication-efficient learning of deep networks from decentralized data. In: Artificial Intelligence and Statistics, pp. 1273–1282. PMLR (2017)
23. Mueller, S.G., et al.: The Alzheimer's disease neuroimaging initiative. Neuroimaging Clin. **15**(4), 869–877 (2005)
24. Pennec, X., Cachier, P., Ayache, N.: Understanding the "Demon's Algorithm": 3D non-rigid registration by gradient descent. In: Taylor, C., Colchester, A. (eds.) MICCAI 1999. LNCS, vol. 1679, pp. 597–605. Springer, Heidelberg (1999). https://doi.org/10.1007/10704282_64
25. Pilu, M.: A direct method for stereo correspondence based on singular value decomposition. In: Proceedings of IEEE Computer Society Conference on Computer Vision and Pattern Recognition, pp. 261–266. IEEE (1997)
26. Reuter, M., Rosas, H.D., Fischl, B.: Highly accurate inverse consistent registration: a robust approach. Neuroimage **53**(4), 1181–1196 (2010)
27. Rivest, R.L., Adleman, L., Dertouzos, M.L., et al.: On data banks and privacy homomorphisms. Found. Sec. Comput. **4**(11), 169–180 (1978)
28. Ryffel, T., et al.: A generic framework for privacy preserving deep learning. arXiv preprint arXiv:1811.04017 (2018)
29. Sabuncu, M.R., Ramadge, P.J.: Gradient based nonuniform subsampling for information-theoretic alignment methods. In: The 26th Annual International Conference of the IEEE Engineering in Medicine and Biology Society, vol. 1, pp. 1683–1686. IEEE (2004)
30. Schnabel, J.A., Heinrich, M.P., Papież, B.W., Brady, J.M.: Advances and challenges in deformable image registration: from image fusion to complex motion modelling. Med. Image Anal. **33**, 145–148 (2016)
31. Shattuck, D.W., Prasad, G., Mirza, M., Narr, K.L., Toga, A.W.: Online resource for validation of brain segmentation methods. NeuroImage **45**(2), 431–439 (2009)
32. Viola, P., Wells, W.M., III.: Alignment by maximization of mutual information. Int. J. Comput. Vision **24**(2), 137–154 (1997)
33. Yao, A.C.: Protocols for secure computations. In: 23rd Annual Symposium on Foundations of Computer Science (SFCS 1982), pp. 160–164. IEEE (1982)

Deformer: Towards Displacement Field Learning for Unsupervised Medical Image Registration

Jiashun Chen[1], Donghuan Lu[2], Yu Zhang[1(✉)], Dong Wei[2(✉)], Munan Ning[2], Xinyu Shi[1], Zhe Xu[3], and Yefeng Zheng[2]

[1] School of Computer Science and Engineering, Southeast University, Nanjing, China
zhang_yu@seu.edu.cn
[2] Tencent Healthcare Co., Jarvis Lab, Shenzhen, China
donwei@tencent.com
[3] Biomedical Engineering, The Chinese University of Hong Kong, Hong Kong, China

Abstract. Recently, deep-learning-based approaches have been widely studied for deformable image registration task. However, most efforts directly map the composite image representation to spatial transformation through the convolutional neural network, ignoring its limited ability to capture spatial correspondence. On the other hand, Transformer can better characterize the spatial relationship with attention mechanism, its long-range dependency may be harmful to the registration task, where voxels with too large distances are unlikely to be corresponding pairs. In this study, we propose a novel Deformer module along with a multi-scale framework for the deformable image registration task. The Deformer module is designed to facilitate the mapping from image representation to spatial transformation by formulating the displacement vector prediction as the weighted summation of several bases. With the multi-scale framework to predict the displacement fields in a coarse-to-fine manner, superior performance can be achieved compared with traditional and learning-based approaches. Comprehensive experiments on two public datasets are conducted to demonstrate the effectiveness of the proposed Deformer module as well as the multi-scale framework.

Keywords: Deformable image registration · Displacement bases · Multi-scale framework

1 Introduction

Deformable image registration (DIR), which aims to estimate a proper deformable field ϕ that can warp the moving image I_m to align with the fixed image I_f, is

---

J. Chen and D. Lu—Equal contribution and the work was done at Tencent Jarvis Lab.

Supplementary Information The online version contains supplementary material available at https://doi.org/10.1007/978-3-031-16446-0_14.

L. Wang et al. (Eds.): MICCAI 2022, LNCS 13436, pp. 141–151, 2022.
https://doi.org/10.1007/978-3-031-16446-0_14

an essential procedure in various medial image analysis tasks, such as surgical navigation [8], image reconstruction [18] and atlas construction [5]. Traditional registration approaches [1,27,28] align voxels with similar appearance through solving an optimization problem for each volume pair. Unfortunately, the computational intensive optimization limits their usage in practical clinical applications.

Recently, unsupervised deep-learning-based DIR approaches [2,12,29–31] have been widely studied for their computational efficiency. Many methods, such as VoxelMorph [2], Dual-PRNet [12] and FAIM [17], adopt the convolutional neural network (CNN) as their backbone because of its superior performance for various vision tasks [13,25]. However, CNN shows limited capability in capturing spatial relationship [24], which becomes a bottleneck for these methods. With the recent development of vision Transformer, some efforts have also been made to explore its effectiveness in DIR task [3]. Although its attention mechanism [24] is potentially more suitable to characterize spatial relationship, directly applying it for DIR task may lead to inferior performance due to its long-range dependency. Because of the fixed anatomical structure of medical scans, preserving tissue discontinuity [4] is essential for medical image registration task. Therefore, the corresponding voxel should only be found in a limited local range, which could be undermined by the long-range dependency.

To this end, we propose a Deformer module to explicitly exploit the intrinsic property of registration task for facilitating the mapping from image representation to spatial transformation. We make a simple yet critical formulation that the displacement between a pair of voxels can be considered as the weighted summation of several basic vectors (referred as displacement bases as well) with three elements, representing the x, y and z components, respectively. Leveraging attention mechanism's ability to capture spatial relationship from image representation, the proposed Deformer module adopts two separate branches to implement such a paradigm. The first branch learns the displacement bases, denoting the potential deformable directions, while the other one predicts the attention weight for each basis, representing the offset length along each direction. Thus, the voxel-wise displacement can be obtained via matrix product of the basis vectors and the attention weights. In addition, the multi-head strategy is applied to enable the Deformer module to extract latent information from different representation subspaces. Furthermore, a multi-scale framework, namely Deformer-based Multi-scale Registration (DMR) is customized to further boost the performance. Unlike previous methods, which either successively predict the displacement fields at different scales [1,21,28] or only exploit multi-scale feature maps through U-Net architecture [2,22], we propose to introduce the Deformer module along with an auxiliary loss at each scale to learn the displacement fields in a coarse-to-fine manner and automatically fuse them through the tailored refining network, such that the information at different scales can be fully exploited without intensive successive computation.

2   Method

Problem Setting. Given a pair of moving and fixed medical 3D scans (called images or volumes as well) $\{M, F\} \in \mathbb{R}^{D \times W \times H}$, the objective of image registration is to estimate a deformation field $\phi \in \mathbb{R}^{3 \times D \times W \times H}$ such that the warped moving scan $\mathcal{T}(M, \phi) \in \mathbb{R}^{D \times W \times H}$ can be aligned with the fixed scan F, where D denotes the depth, W the width, H the height and 3 for the 3D spatial dimension. Specifically, the ϕ can be represented as $Id + u$, where Id denotes identity transformation and u represents the displacement field. To be consistent with previous registration studies [2,3,15], a spatial transformation network [14] is adopted to map the moving image to the fixed image with the estimated displacement field.

Method Overview. As shown in Fig. 1, the proposed DMR framework consists of three main components, the multi-scale encoder to extract L ($L = 4$ in this study) pairs of feature maps $\{f_M^l, f_F^l\}_{l=1}^L$ from both the moving image M and the fixed image F, the proposed Deformer modules to exploit the interaction between M and F to deliver the displacement vector fields from coarse to fine, and the refining network to combine the latent information from different representation subspaces to enable high-resolution large-deformable registration. The detailed explanations of the Deformer module, the DMR network, as well as the loss function are stated in the following sections.

Deformer Module. To facilitate the mapping of the image representation to spatial relationship and increase the interpretability of the network, a Deformer module is designed to learn the displacement field. Based on the linear algebra theory, a displacement vector between two voxels can be formulated as the weighted summation of several basic vectors. For implementing this paradigm through network, the proposed Deformer module adopts attention mechanism with two separate branches, as displayed in Fig. 1b.

The first branch, i.e., the left branch in Fig. 1b, adopts a linear projection to convert every voxel-wise feature vector into N bases, each of which consists of three elements to represent the displacement values in three spatial directions, i.e., the x, y and z axes, respectively. In addition, we adopt the multi-head strategy [26] so that the information from different representation subspaces

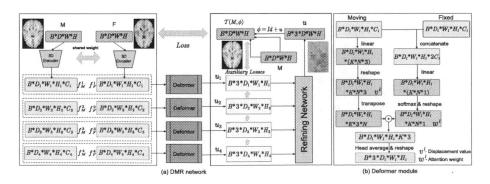

(a) DMR network   (b) Deformer module

Fig. 1. The proposed DMR framework (a) and Deformer module (b).

can be obtained, leading to $K \times N$ bases for each voxel, where K represents the number of heads in each Deformer module. Note that only the feature maps of the moving images f_M^l are employed in this branch, which is sufficient to extract the most representative displacement bases for denoting the most likely deformation directions as demonstrated by the ablation study. On the other hand, the second branch, i.e., the right branch in Fig. 1b, adopts the concatenated feature map $[f_M^l, f_F^l]$ from both the moving and fixed images to learn the attention weight for each displacement basis. The similarity between the moving image and the fixed image is measured by a linear layer followed by a softmax function to impose the non-linearity of the module. It is worth mentioning that both linear projections are performed on each pair of voxel-wise feature vectors independently, resulting in a small number of parameters comparing with standard CNN or Transformer block. Besides, the latent information of the nearby voxels has already been incorporated into the feature vector through the CNN-based encoder. Therefore, the similarity measurement is not limited to the voxels at the same location, and the field-of-view is expanded with the decreasing of the feature map resolution. Finally, the attention weights are multiplied to the displacement bases followed by a head-wise average to obtain the displacement field u^l at scale l. The overall process can be formulated as:

$$u^l = \frac{1}{K} \sum_{i=1}^{K} \sum_{j=1}^{N} w_{i,j}^l \times v_{i,j}^l, \quad l = 1, ..., L, \tag{1}$$

$$v_{i,j}^l = fc_1(f_M^l), \quad w_{i,j} = fc_2([f_M^l, f_F^l]), \tag{2}$$

where $v_{i,j}^l$ denotes the displacement basis, $w_{i,j}$ is the attention weight, $[\cdot]$ represents the concatenation operation, while fc_1 and fc_2 denote the mapping functions of two branches, respectively.

Network Architecture. In order to fully exploit the latent information at different representation subspaces without introducing the intensive computation of successive network, we propose a DMR framework to learn displacement fields at different scales via the proposed Deformer module along with auxiliary loss to provide additional guidance.

As shown in Fig. 1, we first adopt a multi-scale CNN encoder to extract the latent representations at different scales from both the moving and fixed images. Specifically, sharing a similar architecture as [2], the encoder is composed of L 3D convolution blocks, each of which consists of a convolutional layer with a stride of 2 and a kernel size of 4, and a batch normalization layer followed by a leaky rectified linear unit (LeakyReLU) with a negative slope of 0.2. Therefore, the encoder can extract a sequence of L pairs of intermediate feature maps $\{f_M^l, f_F^l\}_{l=1}^{L}$ with different scales through different convolution blocks. Note that both the moving and the fixed images are fed into the same encoder for feature extraction.

The refining network consists of repeated application of the fusion block followed by a convolution head to convert the last feature map to the final displacement field at the original resolution. Specifically, we denote the output feature map of fusion block l as g^l, then the displacement field u^l at scale l is converted to a feature map h^l with a fixed number of channels C via a convolution block. Subsequently, the feature map of the last fusion block g^{l+1} is upsampled by a bilinear interpolation and added to h^l followed by the concatenation of the latent representations f_M^l and f_F^l to provide image information, formulated as:

$$g^l = \begin{cases} h^l, & l = L \\ [2 \times upsample(g^{l+1}) + h^l, f_M^l, f_F^l], otherwise. \end{cases} \tag{3}$$

The final component of the fusion block is another convolution block, i.e., Conv3d reducer, for reducing the channel of output high-level latent representations to C. After three cascaded fusion blocks, a convolution head including three decoding blocks, each of which has two successive structures with a convolutional layer and a ReLU activation function, is applied to deliver the final displacement field. An upsample layer is introduced after the first decoding block to restore the original resolution. More details about the refining network can be found in the supplementary materials.

Loss Function. To validate the effectiveness of the proposed DMR framework and Deformer module, we adopt the most commonly used objective function [2] for a fair comparison, which is defined as:

$$\mathcal{L}(M, F, \phi) = \mathcal{L}_{sim}(\mathcal{T}(M, \phi), F) + \lambda \mathcal{L}_{reg}(\phi), \tag{4}$$

where λ is the regularization trade-off parameter, setting as 1 empirically. The first term $\mathcal{L}_{sim}(\mathcal{T}(M, \phi), F)$ measures the similarity between the warped moving images and the fixed scans using local normalized cross-correlation. The second term $\mathcal{L}_{reg}(\phi)$ is a regularization imposed on the displacement fields to penalize local spatial variation.

As stated above, we propose to impose penalty on the intermediate displacement field at each scale to provide direct guidance for each level of Deformer module as well as the feature extractor. It is worth mentioning that the intermediate displacement fields should be upsampled to the original scale to warp the moving image for the computation of objective function. The overall loss function can be written as:

$$\mathcal{L}_{total} = \mathcal{L}(M, F, \phi) + \sum_{l=1}^{L} \beta_l \mathcal{L}(M, F, \phi^l), \tag{5}$$

where β_l is the weight for the intermediate loss function at scale l.

3   Experiments and Discussion

Datasets. To validate the performance of the proposed approach, we conduct experiments on two publicly available datasets, i.e., the LONI Probabilistic Brain

Atlas (LPBA40) dataset [23] and the Neurite subset of the Open Access Series of Imaging Studies (Neurite-OASIS) dataset [19]. The LPBA40 dataset [23] contains 40 3D volumes of whole-brain Magnetic Resonance Imaging (MRI) scans from normal volunteers, which is divided into 29, 3 and 8 scans for training, validation and testing, respectively. Skull stripping and spatial normalization are performed on each scan, followed by padding and cropping to ensure the same size of $160 \times 192 \times 160$ voxels for each scan. Manual annotation of 56 structures are provided as the ground truth. The Neurite-OASIS dataset[1] is from the learn2reg 2021 challenge [11] and is a part of the OASIS Dataset Project [19], It contains 414 inter-patient 3D T1-weighted MRI brain scans from abnormal subjects with various stages of cognitive decline, which is split into 374, 20 and 20 scans for training, validation and testing, respectively. The scans are preprocessed by the challenge organizer, including skull stripping and spatial normalization via FreeSurfer and SAMSEG, and then cropped to $224 \times 192 \times 160$ voxels. The subcortical segmentation maps of the 35 anatomical structures are provided as the ground truth for evaluation.

Evaluation Criteria. In the experiments of both datasets, we use subject-to-subject registration for optimization, where each pair of volume is selected randomly from the training sets. For evaluation, 8 LPBA40 and 20 Neurite-OASIS scans are mapped to a standard atlas [1]. Following previous works [2,15], we adopt the commonly used average Dice score of the region-of-interest (ROI) masks between the warped images and fixed images as the main evaluation metric. To quantify the diffeomorphism and smoothness of the deformation fields, the average percentage of voxels with non-positive Jacobian determinant ($|J_\phi| \leq 0$) in the deformation fields, the standard deviation of the Jacobian determinant ($std(|J_\phi|)$) the number of parameters, GPU memory and average running time to register each pair of scans on Neurite-OASIS dataset are also provided as supplementary metrics.

Implementation Details. Our method is implemented with PyTorch 1.4 and optimized using Adam optimizer [16] with mini-batch stochastic gradient descent. The model is trained on 4 NVIDIA V100 GPUs for 2,000 epochs. The batch size is set as 4 pairs. The learning rate is set as 4×10^{-4} for the LPBA40 dataset, and 10^{-3} for the Neurite-OASIS dataset to reduce the time consumption as it contains more images with larger size compared to LPBA40. Similar to previous studies [2,21], no data augmentation is employed in our experiments. As for the Deformer modules, the head number K is 8 for all scales and the number N of displacement bases for each head is 64. In the refining network, C is set to 128. For optimization, we measure image similarity using local normalized cross-correlation with windows size of $9 \times 9 \times 9$ in all the loss functions. The regularization parameter λ is empirically set as 1.0 and the weights β_l are all set to 1. Our implementation is publicly available at https://github.com/CJSOrange/DMR-Deformer.

---

[1] https://learn2reg.grand-challenge.org/Datasets/.

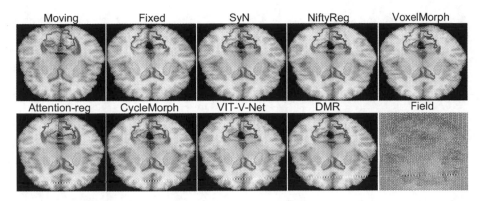

Fig. 2. Qualitative results with segmentation labels of the example axial MR slices from the moving, fixed and warped images from different methods. The color curves represent the boundaries of several structures, including caudate (pink/red), putamen (brown/green), and lingual gyrus (blue/purple). The last image in the second row is the visualization of the final displacement field of our method. (Color figure online)

Comparison Study. For a quantitative comparison, we first compare with five state-of-the-art methods. Two of them are traditional methods, i.e., SyN [1] and NiftyReg [20], two of them utilize convolution neural networks, including VoxelMorph [2] and CycleMorph [15], and the rest two approaches incorporate vision Transformer or attention mechanism into the network, i.e., VIT-V-Net [3] and Attention-reg [24]. The results of these approaches are obtained based on the official codes released by the authors. As shown in Table 1, the proposed approach achieves 68.4% in Dice on the LPBA40 dataset and 80.4% in Dice on Neurite-OASIS, which outperforms the second best methods by 1.5% and 1.6%, respectively. Our method only generates a small percentage of folding voxels (0.624% and 1.024%) on both datasets, indicating reasonable smooth deformation fields. Moreover, we can reduce last three metrics to 7.2M/46.7G/0.61s by using a single head with little performance degradation, as shown in Table 1 of the supplementary. Figure 2 illustrates the registration results of various methods for qualitative analysis. Similar to the quantitative comparison, the proposed DMR achieves the most appealing qualitative results with better alignment between the warped image and the anatomical structure boundaries. For comparing with other multiple cascaded networks on Neurite-OASIS, we add a weakly-supervised Dice loss. DMR achieves 84.2% Dice which is comparable to Learn2Reg winner LapIRN [21] (86.2% Dice), and is superior to DLIR [6] (82.9%) and mIVIRNET [10] (83.4%). For detailed evaluation of the Dice scores for individual anatomical structures and more visualization of segmentation results as well as the displacement fields, please refer to the supplementary materials.

Ablation Study. For ablation study, we first conduct experiments to verify the effectiveness of the proposed Deformer module along with the auxiliary losses.

Table 1. Comparison results of the proposed DMR framework and other state-of-the-art methods on LPBA40 [23] and Neurite-OASIS [19].

Method	LPBA40			Neurite-OASIS					
	Dice (%)	$|J_\phi| \leq 0$ (%)	std($|J_\phi|$)	Dice (%)	$|J_\phi| \leq 0$ (%)	std($|J_\phi|$)	Para(M)	Memo(G)	Time(s)
SyN [1]	66.5	0	0.126	78.0	0	0.124	-	-	1504
NiftyReg [20]	66.9	0.135	0.093	78.5	0.102	0.197	-	-	378
VoxelMorph [2]	64.2	0.961	0.379	78.1	1.236	0.463	0.573	34.9	0.56
CycleMorph [15]	65.0	0.437	0.216	78.8	0.854	0.377	0.784	42.8	0.58
VIT-V-Net [3]	61.3	1.307	0.481	78.2	2.045	0.902	31.6	60.5	0.85
Attention-reg [24]	62.7	0.808	0.342	77.5	1.435	0.501	0.883	56.4	0.78
DMR (Ours)	**68.4**	0.624	0.334	**80.4**	1.024	0.441	7.9	120.3	0.63

Specifically, we compare the Deformer module with four variants: 1) Deformer-A: feeding the concatenated feature maps to the left branch for displacement basis extraction, instead of using only the feature maps of the moving images; 2) Deformer-B: removing the left branch of the Deformer module, which is equivalent to fix the displacement bases as (0, 0, 1), (0, 1, 0) and (1, 0, 0); 3) CNN: replacing the Deformer module with a CNN block, i.e., 3D ResNet [9]; 4) Transformer: replacing the Deformer module with a vision Transformer block [7]. It is worth mentioning that with only two fully connected layers performed on voxel-wise feature vectors, the proposed Deformer module has fewer parameters compared with CNN or Transformer (7.98M vs. 12.35M and 132M). The results in Table 2 demonstrate that the proposed Deformer module can better characterize the spatial transformation from image representation and using the moving images alone is sufficient to find optimal displacement bases.

We further evaluate the impact of Deformer modules at different scales by gradually removing the Deformer modules from fine to coarse scales (1/2, 1/4, 1/8 and 1/16). Naturally, the auxiliary loss at the same scale is removed along with the Deformer module. As shown in Table 3, with the removing of Deformer modules, we can observe steadily degeneration of registration performance from 68.4% to 66.2% in Dice on the LPBA40 dataset, supporting the assumption that the multi-scale Deformer module and the corresponding auxiliary loss can effectively improve the registration ability of the network. The impact of more hyper-parameters can be found in the supplementary materials.

Table 2. Evaluation of different conversion modules on LPBA40 [23], including Deformer-A, Deformer-B, CNN and Transformer.

Method	Dice (%)	$|J_\phi| \leq 0$(%)	std($|J_\phi|$)
Deformer (Ours)	68.4	0.624	0.334
Deformer-A (Ours)	68.0	0.702	0.368
Deformer-B (Ours)	66.2	0.945	0.432
CNN [9]	66.7	0.896	0.426
Transformer [7]	66.3	1.003	0.455

Table 3. The impact of the number of Deformer modules on LPBA40 [23]. "✓" represents applying the Deformer module at this scale.

Scale				LPBA40		
1/2	1/4	1/8	1/16	Dice (%)	$|J_\phi| \leq 0$(%)	std($|J_\phi|$)
✓	✓	✓	✓	68.4	0.624	0.334
	✓	✓	✓	67.8	0.706	0.354
		✓	✓	67.1	0.751	0.368
			✓	66.7	0.813	0.382
				66.2	0.867	0.395

4   Conclusion

In this paper, we proposed a novel Deformer module along with a multi-scale framework for unsupervised deformable registration. The Deformer module was designed to formulate the prediction of displacement vector as the learning of most likely deformation directions and the offset length via attention mechanism. With the two fully connected layers applied on each pair of voxel-wise feature vectors independently, the Deformer module could better characterize the local spatial correlation with fewer parameters comparing with CNN or Transformer. Further, we showed that introducing the Deformer module along with auxiliary loss in a multi-scale manner to learn the displacement fields from coarse to fine could substantially boost the registration performance. Experiments on two publicly available datasets demonstrated that our strategy outperformed the traditional and learning-based benchmark methods.

Acknowledgements. This work was funded by the Scientific and Technical Innovation 2030-"New Generation Artificial Intelligence" (No. 2020AAA0104100), Key R&D Program of China (2018AAA0100104, 2018AAA0100100) and Natural Science Foundation of Jiangsu Province (BK20211164).

References

1. Avants, B.B., Epstein, C.L., Grossman, M., Gee, J.C.: Symmetric diffeomorphic image registration with cross-correlation: evaluating automated labeling of elderly and neurodegenerative brain. Med. Image Anal. **12**(1), 26–41 (2008)
2. Balakrishnan, G., Zhao, A., Sabuncu, M.R., Guttag, J., Dalca, A.V.: VoxelMorph: a learning framework for deformable medical image registration. IEEE Trans. Med. Imaging **38**(8), 1788–1800 (2019)
3. Chen, J., He, Y., Frey, E.C., Li, Y., Du, Y.: ViT-V-Net: vision transformer for unsupervised volumetric medical image registration. arXiv preprint arXiv:2104.06468 (2021)
4. Chen, X., Xia, Y., Ravikumar, N., Frangi, A.F.: A deep discontinuity-preserving image registration network. In: de Bruijne, M., et al. (eds.) MICCAI 2021. LNCS, vol. 12904, pp. 46–55. Springer, Cham (2021). https://doi.org/10.1007/978-3-030-87202-1_5
5. Dalca, A.V., Rakic, M., Guttag, J., Sabuncu, M.R.: Learning conditional deformable templates with convolutional networks. arXiv preprint arXiv:1908.02738 (2019)
6. De Vos, B.D., Berendsen, F.F., Viergever, M.A., Sokooti, H., Staring, M., Išgum, I.: A deep learning framework for unsupervised affine and deformable image registration. Med. Image Anal. **52**, 128–143 (2019)
7. Dosovitskiy, A., et al.: An image is worth 16x16 words: transformers for image recognition at scale. arXiv preprint arXiv:2010.11929 (2020)
8. Gou, S., Chen, L., Gu, Y., Huang, L., Huang, M., Zhuang, J.: Large-deformation image registration of CT-TEE for surgical navigation of congenital heart disease. Comput. Math. Methods Med. **2018** (2018)
9. Hara, K., Kataoka, H., Satoh, Y.: Can spatiotemporal 3D CNNs retrace the history of 2D CNNs and ImageNet? In: Proceedings of the IEEE Conference on Computer Vision and Pattern Recognition, pp. 6546–6555 (2018)

10. Hering, A., van Ginneken, B., Heldmann, S.: mlVIRNET: multilevel variational image registration network. In: Shen, D., et al. (eds.) MICCAI 2019. LNCS, vol. 11769, pp. 257–265. Springer, Cham (2019). https://doi.org/10.1007/978-3-030-32226-7_29

11. Hering, A., et al.: Learn2Reg: comprehensive multi-task medical image registration challenge, dataset and evaluation in the era of deep learning. arXiv preprint arXiv:2112.04489 (2021)

12. Hu, X., Kang, M., Huang, W., Scott, M.R., Wiest, R., Reyes, M.: Dual-stream pyramid registration network. In: Shen, D., et al. (eds.) MICCAI 2019. LNCS, vol. 11765, pp. 382–390. Springer, Cham (2019). https://doi.org/10.1007/978-3-030-32245-8_43

13. Huang, G., Liu, Z., Van Der Maaten, L., Weinberger, K.Q.: Densely connected convolutional networks. In: Proceedings of the IEEE Conference on Computer Vision and Pattern Recognition, pp. 4700–4708 (2017)

14. Jaderberg, M., Simonyan, K., Zisserman, A., et al.: Spatial transformer networks. In: Advances in Neural Information Processing Systems, vol. 28, pp. 2017–2025 (2015)

15. Kim, B., et al.: CycleMorph: cycle consistent unsupervised deformable image registration. Med. Image Anal. **71**, 102036 (2021)

16. Kingma, D.P., Ba, J.: Adam: a method for stochastic optimization. arXiv preprint arXiv:1412.6980 (2014)

17. Kuang, D., Schmah, T.: FAIM – a ConvNet method for unsupervised 3D medical image registration. In: Suk, H.-I., Liu, M., Yan, P., Lian, C. (eds.) MLMI 2019. LNCS, vol. 11861, pp. 646–654. Springer, Cham (2019). https://doi.org/10.1007/978-3-030-32692-0_74

18. Li, R., et al.: Real-time volumetric image reconstruction and 3D tumor localization based on a single X-ray projection image for lung cancer radiotherapy. Med. Phys. **37**(6Part1), 2822–2826 (2010)

19. Marcus, D.S., Wang, T.H., Parker, J., Csernansky, J.G., Morris, J.C., Buckner, R.L.: Open Access Series of Imaging Studies (OASIS): cross-sectional MRI data in young, middle aged, nondemented, and demented older adults. J. Cogn. Neurosci. **19**(9), 1498–1507 (2007)

20. Modat, M., et al.: Fast free-form deformation using graphics processing units. Comput. Methods Programs Biomed. **98**(3), 278–284 (2010)

21. Mok, T.C.W., Chung, A.C.S.: Large deformation diffeomorphic image registration with laplacian pyramid networks. In: Martel, A.L., et al. (eds.) MICCAI 2020. LNCS, vol. 12263, pp. 211–221. Springer, Cham (2020). https://doi.org/10.1007/978-3-030-59716-0_21

22. Rohé, M.-M., Datar, M., Heimann, T., Sermesant, M., Pennec, X.: SVF-Net: learning deformable image registration using shape matching. In: Descoteaux, M., Maier-Hein, L., Franz, A., Jannin, P., Collins, D.L., Duchesne, S. (eds.) MICCAI 2017. LNCS, vol. 10433, pp. 266–274. Springer, Cham (2017). https://doi.org/10.1007/978-3-319-66182-7_31

23. Shattuck, D.W., et al.: Construction of a 3D probabilistic atlas of human cortical structures. Neuroimage **39**(3), 1064–1080 (2008)

24. Song, X., et al.: Cross-modal attention for MRI and ultrasound volume registration. In: de Bruijne, M., et al. (eds.) MICCAI 2021. LNCS, vol. 12904, pp. 66–75. Springer, Cham (2021). https://doi.org/10.1007/978-3-030-87202-1_7

25. Tan, M., Le, Q.: EfficientNet: rethinking model scaling for convolutional neural networks. In: International Conference on Machine Learning, pp. 6105–6114. PMLR (2019)

26. Vaswani, A., et al.: Attention is all you need. In: Advances in Neural Information Processing Systems, pp. 5998–6008 (2017)

27. Vercauteren, T., Pennec, X., Perchant, A., Ayache, N.: Diffeomorphic demons: efficient non-parametric image registration. Neuroimage **45**(1), S61–S72 (2009)

28. Wang, H., et al.: Validation of an accelerated 'demons' algorithm for deformable image registration in radiation therapy. Phys. Med. Biol. **50**(12), 2887 (2005)

29. Xu, Z., et al.: Double-uncertainty guided spatial and temporal consistency regularization weighting for learning-based abdominal registration. arXiv preprint arXiv:2107.02433 (2021)

30. Xu, Z., Luo, J., Yan, J., Li, X., Jayender, J.: F3RNET: full-resolution residual registration network for deformable image registration. Int. J. Comput. Assist. Radiol. Surg. **16**(6), 923–932 (2021)

31. Xu, Z., et al.: Adversarial uni- and multi-modal stream networks for multimodal image registration. In: Martel, A.L., et al. (eds.) MICCAI 2020. LNCS, vol. 12263, pp. 222–232. Springer, Cham (2020). https://doi.org/10.1007/978-3-030-59716-0_22

End-to-End Multi-Slice-to-Volume Concurrent Registration and Multimodal Generation

Amaury Leroy[1,3,4]($\boxtimes$), Marvin Lerousseau[2], Théophraste Henry[4],
Alexandre Cafaro[1,3,4], Nikos Paragios[1], Vincent Grégoire[3], and Eric Deutsch[4]

[1] Therapanacea, Paris, France
a.leroy@therapanacea.eu
[2] CentraleSupélec, Paris-Saclay University, Gif-sur-Yvette, France
[3] Department of Radiation Oncology, Centre Léon Bérard, Lyon, France
[4] Gustave Roussy, Inserm 1030, Paris-Saclay University, Villejuif, France

Abstract. For interventional procedures, a real-time mapping between treatment guidance images and planning data is challenging yet essential for successful therapy implementation. Because of time and machine constraints, it involves imaging of different modalities, resolutions and dimensions, along with severe out-of-plane deformations to handle. In this paper, we introduce MSV-RegSyn-Net, a novel, scalable, deep learning-based framework for concurrent slice-to-volume registration and high-resolution modality transfer synthesis. It consists of an end-to-end pipeline made up of (i) a cycle generative adversarial network for multimodal image translation combined with (ii) a multi-slice-to-volume deformable registration network. The concurrent nature of our approach creates mutual benefit for both tasks: image translation is naturally eased by explicit handling of out-of-plane deformations while registration benefits from bringing multimodal signals into the same domain. Our model is fully unsupervised and does not require any ground-truth deformation or segmentation mask. It obtains superior qualitative and quantitative performance for multi-slice MR to 3D CT pelvic imaging compared to state-of-the-art traditional and learning-based methods on both tasks.

Keywords: Multimodal registration · 2D-3D · Image-to-Image translation · Generative adversarial network · Unsupervised learning

1 Introduction

Mapping 3D planning data into the 2D interventional frame of reference enables the overlay of each image's specific information and is thus crucial for successful treatment. Some popular clinical settings in this context of Slice-to-Volume registration [8] refer to ultrasound towards CT/MR (guided breast or prostate

Supplementary Information The online version contains supplementary material available at https://doi.org/10.1007/978-3-031-16446-0_15.

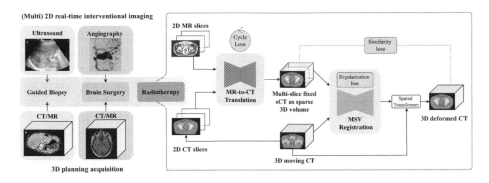

Fig. 1. Left: clinical applications where planning and interventional steps involve various images challenging to map. Right: overall architecture of our concurrent network for RT case. The CT volume acts as 3D for the registration task (2) while being sliced in 2D for MR-to-CT translation purpose (1). The monomodality setting induced by (1) benefits to (2), and the backpropagation path yields to a leverage from (2) to (1). Left image examples are from [17, 18]

biopsies), angiography to CT/MR for cardiac and brain surgeries, or 2D MR to CT for radiotherapy (RT). Matching radiology and digital pathology is another domain where the same challenges are to be addressed due to the partial correspondences between the recovered specimen and prior 3D imaging acquisition.

In this respect, one has to face three main challenges: (i) anatomical changes and tissue deformation, (ii) sparse, partial-view and low-quality data during treatment deployment due to acquisition time limitations, and (iii) constraints on the nature/modality of images that can be acquired. Early literature to solve them was mostly focusing on solving the registration problem, and the objective was to determine a mapping between the interventional data and the planning 3D images by covering mostly plane selection and in-plane deformations.

Traditional Deformable Image Registration (DIR) methods like SyN [1], Demons [23, 24] or Drop [9, 10] align two volumes through optimization of an energy function. Recently, learning-based methods have spread out due to impressive performance and the ability to infer transformation parameters for any input volume pair from a unique model, first in a supervised setting [3, 4, 16, 22], but more and more without labels [2, 25].

(Multi)-Slice-to-Volume (MSV) or (Multi-)2D-3D registration was initially addressed using conventional optimization methods [7] and deep learning was slowly introduced as an initialization step but an iterative classical refinement optimization was still needed for these hybrid approaches [5, 19, 21]. The difficult challenges compared to 3D registration are related to the lack of information and the multitude of degrees of freedom, explaining that very few studies have tackled fully one-shot learning-based approaches. Monomodal methods for image-guided interventions include [15] with X-ray images thanks to ground-truth deformations, and [12] with rigid registration on ultrasound images.

The initial objective of MSV registration was to bring planning information into the interventional setting through direct mapping between the two modalities. The same objective can be met through an image synthesis approach that learns to create the planning full 3D high-resolution modality from the partial interventional volumes. This field of research has taken advantage of the recent breakthroughs in image-to-image translation, which is a transfer learning task where an image is transformed to fit the domain of one another. Generative Adversarial Networks (GANs) are the cornerstone of such field, Pix2pix and CycleGANs derived frameworks for paired (and unpaired, respectively) images being predominant models to solve it [11,14,30].

In this paper, we propose a novel end-to-end learning framework for joint MSV registration and modality transfer synthesis. Our contributions are three-fold and include (i) combining a translation-based cycleGAN module and a registration network in an unsupervised end-to-end setting, (ii) solving the 2D-3D registration challenge in one shot without the need of iterative optimization, and (iii) leveraging registration outputs to improve generation task through pixel-wise supervision. To our knowledge, this is the first time a study attempts to take up all these challenges at once. Similar adversarial methods coupled with registration have emerged either as an intermediary step to generate synthetic images of the same modality as the source image and come back to a monomodal setting [27], or as a supervised end-to-end workflow where the discriminator tries to tell if images are aligned based on ground truth transformations [28]. In order to demonstrate the efficiency of the proposed approach, we consider the task of MSV registration for treatment adaptation and target volume tracking in the context of RT. We focus on pelvic prostate tumors given that this area is associated with severe anatomical changes between planning and treatment days. The methodology is applied to address 0,35T (TrueFisp sequence)/1,5T (T2) multi-slice MR to 3D CT mapping. We outperform state-of-the-art methods in each task and demonstrate the benefit of coupling them.

2   Methods

Without loss of generality, we consider that 3D volumes are CT scans and that multi-slice volumes are partial MR imaging (Fig. 1). Given such a pair from the same patient, our approach (i) generates multi-slice synthetic CT from MR (Subsect. 2.1), (ii) which is then forwarded into a registration network to warp the original CT (Subsect. 2.2).

2.1   Synthetic CT Generation from MR

We tackle synthetic CT (sCT) generation from a n-slice MR by performing n concurrent and independent 2D single-slice MR-to-CT translation. For a given slice x_i of a multi-slice MR x, a generator G_{CT} produces a single-slice synthetic CT $G_{CT}(x_i)$, which is forwarded into a discriminator D_{CT} along with a true CT slice randomly sampled from the associated volume. To ensure that $G_{CT}(x_i)$ is concordant with x_i on a pixel-basis, a second generator G_{MR} is asked to reconstruct x_i from $G_{CT}(x_i)$ by minimizing their L1 distance, denoted as L_{rec}.

As performed in CycleGAN [30], a second discriminator D_{MR} is added to the MR domain, along with an identity loss L_{Id} for robustness. Both generators and discriminators are trained in an adversarial fashion with a loss denoted L_{adv}. Detailed loss definitions for CT domain (symmetric for MR) are the following:

$$L_{adv}(ct) = E_{ct}[\log(D_{CT}(ct))] + E_{mr}[\log(1 - D_{CT} \circ G_{CT}(mr))] . \tag{1}$$

$$L_{rec}(ct) = E_{ct}[||G_{CT} \circ G_{MR}(ct) - ct||_1] , L_{Id}(ct) = E_{ct}[||G_{CT}(ct) - ct||_1] . \tag{2}$$

As proven successful by other works on medical image generation [27,29], our framework also takes advantage of the structure-consistency loss Modality Independent Neighbourhood Descriptor (MIND) [13] denoted as L_{MIND} which assesses structural similarity around each voxel x regardless of the intensity distribution.

$$L_{\text{MIND-CT}} = E_{mr \sim p(mr)} \left[\frac{1}{N} \sum_x ||\text{MIND}_x(G_{CT}(mr)) - \text{MIND}_x(mr)||_1 \right] , \tag{3}$$

where N is a hyper-parameter equal to image size times the size of the non-local region to consider, fixed at 9 in practice. The total loss of the system is:

$$L_{\text{trans}} = L_{\text{adv}} + \lambda_{\text{rec}} L_{\text{rec}} + \lambda_{\text{Id}} L_{\text{Id}} + \lambda_{\text{MIND}} L_{\text{MIND}}, \tag{4}$$

where λ_{rec}, λ_{Id}, λ_{MIND} are weights balancing each loss. We provide thorough details of the complete pipeline in supplementary Fig. 1.

2.2 Multi-Slice-to-Volume Registration

The goal of the MSV registration module is to map the (moving) patient 3D CT m onto the (fixed) previously generated multi-slice sCT f from the associated MR. The global pipeline, as well as implementation details, are detailed in supplementary Fig. 2. Since the input MR has originally a smaller number of slices than the corresponding CT, the first step consists in creating a volume f the size of the CT which is filled with the 2D sCT at their corresponding axial location within the MR, and zeros otherwise. The MSV registration module is formalized as a network that produces a 3D displacement field $R(f, m)$ for each moving voxel. This is done with a slightly different version of VoxelMorph [2], where f and m are forwarded in two specific encoders, yielding one latent representation per input. An element-wise subtraction operator then merges both latent vectors into a single encoded representation, similar to [6] that demonstrated the efficiency of this approach compared to the traditional concatenation operator. A decoder further processes the merged latent vector onto two decoding stages: one that outputs a simple affine transformation ϕ_{lin}, the second one outputting a deformable transformation ϕ_{def}. The final displacement field $R(f, m)$ is obtained by summing element-wise ϕ_{lin} and ϕ_{def}. Finally, a parameterless and differentiable spatial transformer applies $R(f, m)$ onto m with interpolation. This registration is fully unsupervised and does not require pre-registration. It is trained by maximizing the similarity between f and $R(f, m)(m)$.

Since f is sparse, a classical volumetric loss would not be suitable as it would induce noise within the gradient of pixels registered onto empty slices by imposing such pixels to be equal to 0. To circumvent this issue, we propose to mask the pixel-wise loss for empty slices as follows:

$$L_{sim}^{2D}(f, R(f, m)(m)) = \sum_{i : f_i \neq 0} \left\| f_i - R(f, m)(m)_i \right\|_2 . \tag{5}$$

Besides the mean squared error, the Normalized Cross-Correlation (NCC) loss could be used, and we show in our experiments that the performances of both are similar.

Because the loss is masked for CT slices within the original sparse sCT, there are additional degrees of freedom for the registration. To bypass this issue, we add a 3D regularization loss L_{regu} that penalizes large local variations of the displacement field by minimizing the mean squared error of the spatial gradient of $R(f, m)$ as proposed in [2].

Together, L_{sim} and L_{regu} help balance the final transformation between a precise, smooth and realistic mapping, while enforcing the continuity of inter-slice displacements with respect to the surrounding non-empty ones. The total registration loss can be formulated as

$$L_{reg}(f, m, R) = \lambda_{sim} L_{sim}^{2D}(f, R(f, m)(m)) + \lambda_{regu} L_{regu}^{3D}(R(f, m)) . \tag{6}$$

In total, the comprehensive loss of the global system, including both MR-to-CT generation and registration is $L_{total} = L_{\text{trans}} + L_{reg}$.

3   Experiments and Results

3.1   Dataset and Preprocessing

We assessed the performance of our pipeline to pelvis 3D CT and 2D MR imaging. More precisely, we extracted two private clinical datasets for patients undergoing RT. The first dataset refers to 451 pairs between the planning CT and the 0,35T TrueFISP sequences of treatment delivery. The second example involves 217 pairs between the planning CT and the 1,5T T2 sequences. Such a gap in texture resolution is an argument for the ability of our method to perform in many study cases. The ratio between the 3D planning CT and the multi-slice treatment MR in terms of slices was 10:1.

We preprocessed independently both datasets with normalization, resampling and cropping to get $256 \times 256 \times 96$ (x, y, z) volumes with an (x, y) resolution of $1\,\text{mm}^2$ and a z resolution of $3\,\text{mm}$. For each volume and modality, 8 anatomical structures were segmented by internal experts: anal canal, bladder, left/right femoral head, rectum, penile bulb, seminal vesicle and prostate - when applicable -. We split each dataset into three groups for training (60%), validation (20%) and testing (20%).

3.2   Implementation Details

We implemented our model on Python 3.9 with GPU-based Pytorch backend [20] on NVIDIA Geforce GTX 1080 and drew our code from CycleGAN and Voxelmorph source papers [2,30], with modifications explained above. More precisely, the architecture of discriminators is inspired by PatchGAN, with the addition of residual blocks between the contracting and expanding paths. They act as skip connections to ensure stability in image reconstruction. The two generator structures (respectively discriminators) are identical, the only difference being the input fed to them. As for the registration network, the classical UNet architecture with skip connections is used except that there are two independent encoding stages for each input, merged by subtraction. We pretrained the CT-MR translation task as an initialization step to avoid mode collapse when trying to feed improper sCT to the registration network. Then, for the concurrent approach, Adam optimizer was selected for gradient descent calculus, with $\beta_1 = 0.5, \beta_2 = 0.99$. A cyclical learning rate with triangular schedule up to 2×10^{-4} was set, and we chose the value of weights $\lambda_{rec} = \lambda_{Id} = 10$, $\lambda_{MIND} = \lambda_{sim} = 5$, and $\lambda_{regu} = 0.1$ to have balanced leverage between each component. We also tried to add affine regularization into the form of identity matrix similarity, but it was counterproductive for volumes where a strong linear transform is of mandatory for global mapping. Finally, we trained for 800 epochs with a batch size of 2 patients for registration, corresponding to sub-batches of 20 2D images for MR-to-CT translation due to the inter-slice ratio.

3.3   Baseline Methods

We benchmarked our method for both tasks against state-of-the-art algorithms. For modality transfer synthesis, we compared our performance with a Cycle-GAN framework in 2D, with and without MIND loss. For the registration task, we considered the traditional SyN algorithm with mutual information similarity measure available in ANTs software, considering the set of 2D sCT slices as a stacked volume with a 3D-3D setting [1]. We ran affine and deformable registration on CPU as baselines. We also implemented Voxelmorph method on multimodal raw images with MIND [13] and SSIM [26] similarity measures and changed the loss computation to fit with the 2D-3D setting. All parameters were optimized to give the best results. Finally, we performed ablative studies on our own approach. We tried (i) a fully affine registration by blocking the deformable block of the network, (ii) the whole pipeline without MIND loss on generation block, and (iii) the pipeline split into two independent training.

3.4   Results for MR-to-CT Translation

A sample of generated sCT from corresponding MR is shown in bottom Fig. 2, taken from the test set of the 1.5 T2 cohort (see more in the supplementary Fig. 3). Qualitatively, the end-to-end model yields to more realistic CT-like images with a finer reconstruction of edges and tissue texture. We also computed quantitative structure-based metrics summed up in Table 1. SSIM assesses the structural degradation of a reconstructed image, while FID measures the distance between distributions of generated and original sets as latent vectors. Formulas for these two metrics are explained in the supplementary material. They advocate for a better MT-to-CT translation on both datasets with the end-to-end pipeline, the CycleGAN alone having the worst performance. It is worth noticing the crucial contribution of MIND loss to the translation network, as the independent approach with MIND outperforms the concurrent one without MIND. Hence, we can reasonably affirm that both the concurrent registration part and the MIND loss help the generation by giving feedback on reconstruction error through backpropagation.

Table 1. Quantitative results of our pipeline and baseline methods proving the benefit of concurrent approach and MIND integration. Higher SSIM and lower FID are better.

Method	0.35T TrueFISP → 3D CT		1.5T T2 → 3D CT	
	SSIM	FID	SSIM	FID
CycleGAN	0.751 ± 0.03	132.5	0.763 ± 0.02	124.4
CycleGAN + MIND	0.768 ± 0.08	112.1	0.769 ± 0.02	116.8
Ours (no MIND)	0.763 ± 0.01	112.9	0.768 ± 0.04	119.1
Ours	**0.789 ± 0.06**	**89.8**	**0.795 ± 0.05**	**80.4**

3.5   Results for Multi-Slice-to-Volume Registration

To assess the performance of the registration task, we apply the inferred transformation to segmentation labels, which are never used for training (Fig. 2). For quantitative results, we computed the Dice score and the Hausdorff Distance between fixed and deformed masks. Average performance is presented in Table 2, while organ-specific measurements are detailed in supplementary Fig. 4. Our end-to-end method reaches the best performance among all other baseline approaches. Both NCC and MSE losses have similar behaviors. SyN algorithm gives poorer results than VoxelMorph framework, the latter being also satisfying and more precise with MIND loss. It proves the benefit of handling multimodality through image-to-image translation instead of a direct multimodal similarity measure. The associated runtime is slightly longer, but remain in an acceptable range compared to non-learning-based methods which are orders of magnitude slower. Indeed, the average runtime per images pair - not reported in Table 2 for clarity sake - is 319 s for SyN method that only supports CPU computation, 1.24 s for Voxelmorph on GPU, and 1.98 s for our method on GPU.

From the ablation studies, three conclusions emerge: (i) the deformable block is essential since it allows to handle out-of-plane deformations, (ii) the MIND loss from the generation network again helps the mapping thanks to better-defined textures, and (iii) the concurrent approach outperforms the independent

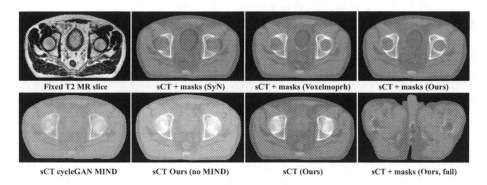

Fig. 2. Visual results for our method. Top: SyN, and to a lesser degree Voxelmorph, yield to worse registration results between warped CT (red) and fixed sCT (yellow). Bottom: MR-to-CT results, proving better realism and texture consistency for our method. Bottom right: a special case when our method fails, usually for little organs that are present on one slice only and thus provide limited signal. (Color figure online)

training. It is also important to note that we have a significant difference in performance depending on the organ considered (supplementary Fig. 4) due to partial presence on the multi-slice volume for small ones, explaining some failures as displayed in bottom right Fig. 2. Overall, our model performs well on both tasks for two datasets with different MR sequences and resolutions, which proves its robustness and versatility.

Table 2. Mean (Standard Deviation) registration performance in terms of Dice Score (%) and Hausdorff Distance (*mm*). Row split is by method (baselines/ablative studies/proposed method)

Method	0.35T TrueFISP → 3D CT		1.5T T2 → 3D CT	
	Dice	Hausdorff	Dice	Hausdorff
SyN (ANTs) affine	69.9 ± 1.7	12.05 ± 0.09	68.7 ± 0.9	13.49 ± 0.10
SyN deformable	75.2 ± 1.2	9.72 ± 0.13	76.1 ± 1.1	9.19 ± 0.11
VoxelMorph (SSIM)	81.2 ± 1.6	7.96 ± 0.10	80.9 ± 0.9	7.91 ± 0.08
VoxelMorph (MIND)	81.5 ± 1.5	7.82 ± 0.07	81.3 ± 1.5	7.88 ± 0.14
Ours (affine)	70.5 ± 1.2	11.22 ± 0.09	69.4 ± 0.8	11.94 ± 0.14
Ours (no MIND)	79.8 ± 1.1	8.86 ± 0.08	80.8 ± 1.2	7.88 ± 0.06
Ours (no end-to-end)	81.2 ± 1.2	8.01 ± 0.08	81.4 ± 0.9	7.62 ± 0.12
Ours (NCC)	**84.6 ± 0.9**	**7.25 ± 0.05**	85.3 ± 1.4	**6.24 ± 0.09**
Ours (MSE)	**83.8 ± 1.2**	**7.48 ± 0.13**	**86.1 ± 1.0**	**5.84 ± 0.15**

4   Conclusion

In this work, we proposed MSV-RegSyn-Net, a novel unsupervised concurrent framework for MSV mapping and modality transfer synthesis. In addition to leveraging both tasks in an end-to-end pipeline, we prove on two clinical datasets the mutual benefit triggered by the joint architecture, leading to better performance than state-of-the-art methods. The computational time, around 2 s, is also in line with them, but should still be improved in order to allow real-time mapping during interventional procedure. Nevertheless, the model is versatile as we built a methodological concept applicable to images from various modalities and quality, but also different slice spacing, thickness or orientation. We chose a slice ratio of 10:1 to test the approach on extreme cases where the problem is formulated with few slices, and even if it is not tested yet, we have good reasons to think it would yield to enhanced performance with an increased number of slices as it constrains the deformation field and gives more information. This constitutes future investigation for proper generalization proof, as well as a unique Slice-to-Volume challenge as for ultrasound imaging, or changing the field of view coverage between both modalities. More importantly, future works include an ambitious study between histological images and 3D CT in H&N cancer. The aim would be to register them on the CT volume to extract relevant biological features of the environment and better understand tumor cellular heterogeneity at the diagnosis stage, but also to be able to generate synthetic histology towards a non-invasive virtual biopsy.

References

1. Avants, B.B., Epstein, C.L., Grossman, M., Gee, J.C.: Symmetric diffeomorphic image registration with cross-correlation: evaluating automated labeling of elderly and neurodegenerative brain. Med. Image Anal. **12**(1), 26–41 (2008). https://doi.org/10.1016/j.media.2007.06.004
2. Balakrishnan, G., Zhao, A., Sabuncu, M.R., Guttag, J., Dalca, A.V.: VoxelMorph: a learning framework for deformable medical image registration. IEEE Trans. Med. Imaging **38**(8), 1788–1800 (2019). https://doi.org/10.1109/TMI.2019.2897538. http://arxiv.org/abs/1809.05231, arXiv:1809.05231
3. Cao, X., Yang, J., Wang, L., Xue, Z., Wang, Q., Shen, D.: Deep Learning based Inter-Modality Image Registration Supervised by Intra-Modality Similarity. arXiv:1804.10735, April 2018. http://arxiv.org/abs/1804.10735
4. Cao, X., et al.: Deformable image registration based on similarity-steered CNN regression. In: Descoteaux, M., Maier-Hein, L., Franz, A., Jannin, P., Collins, D.L., Duchesne, S. (eds.) MICCAI 2017. LNCS, vol. 10433, pp. 300–308. Springer, Cham (2017). https://doi.org/10.1007/978-3-319-66182-7_35
5. Esteban, J., Grimm, M., Unberath, M., Zahnd, G., Navab, N.: Towards fully automatic X-Ray to CT registration. In: Shen, D., et al. (eds.) MICCAI 2019. LNCS, vol. 11769, pp. 631–639. Springer, Cham (2019). https://doi.org/10.1007/978-3-030-32226-7_70
6. Estienne, T., et al.: Deep learning-based concurrent brain registration and tumor segmentation. Front. Comput. Neurosci. **14** (2020). https://www.frontiersin.org/article/10.3389/fncom.2020.00017

7. Ferrante, E., Paragios, N.: Non-rigid 2D-3D medical image registration using Markov random fields. In: Mori, K., Sakuma, I., Sato, Y., Barillot, C., Navab, N. (eds.) MICCAI 2013. LNCS, vol. 8151, pp. 163–170. Springer, Heidelberg (2013). https://doi.org/10.1007/978-3-642-40760-4_21

8. Ferrante, E., Paragios, N.: Slice-to-volume medical image registration: a survey. Med. Image Anal. **39**, 101–123 (2017). https://doi.org/10.1016/j.media.2017.04.010. https://www.sciencedirect.com/science/article/pii/S1361841517300701

9. Glocker, B., Komodakis, N., Tziritas, G., Navab, N., Paragios, N.: Dense image registration through MRFs and efficient linear programming. Med. Image Anal. **12**(6), 731–741 (2008). https://doi.org/10.1016/j.media.2008.03.006. https://www.sciencedirect.com/science/article/pii/S1361841508000297

10. Glocker, B., Sotiras, A., Komodakis, N., Paragios, N.: Deformable medical image registration: setting the state of the art with discrete methods. Annu. Rev. Biomed. Eng. **13**, 219–244 (2011). https://doi.org/10.1146/annurev-bioeng-071910-124649

11. Goodfellow, I.J., et al.: Generative Adversarial Networks. arXiv:1406.2661, June 2014. http://arxiv.org/abs/1406.2661

12. Guo, H., Xu, X., Xu, S., Wood, B.J., Yan, P.: End-to-end ultrasound frame to volume registration. In: de Bruijne, M., et al. (eds.) MICCAI 2021. LNCS, vol. 12904, pp. 56–65. Springer, Cham (2021). https://doi.org/10.1007/978-3-030-87202-1_6

13. Heinrich, M.P., et al.: MIND: modality independent neighbourhood descriptor for multi-modal deformable registration. Med. Image Anal. **16**(7), 1423–1435 (2012). https://doi.org/10.1016/j.media.2012.05.008. https://www.sciencedirect.com/science/article/pii/S1361841512000643

14. Isola, P., Zhu, J.Y., Zhou, T., Efros, A.A.: Image-to-Image Translation with Conditional Adversarial Networks. arXiv:1611.07004, November 2018. http://arxiv.org/abs/1611.07004

15. Jaganathan, S., Wang, J., Borsdorf, A., Shetty, K., Maier, A.: Deep Iterative 2D/3D Registration. arXiv:2107.10004, vol. 12904, pp. 383–392 (2021). https://doi.org/10.1007/978-3-030-87202-1_37. http://arxiv.org/abs/2107.10004

16. Krebs, J., et al.: Robust non-rigid registration through agent-based action learning. In: Descoteaux, M., Maier-Hein, L., Franz, A., Jannin, P., Collins, D.L., Duchesne, S. (eds.) MICCAI 2017. LNCS, vol. 10433, pp. 344–352. Springer, Cham (2017). https://doi.org/10.1007/978-3-319-66182-7_40

17. MacDonald, M.E., Dolati, P., Mitha, A.P., Eesa, M., Wong, J.H., Frayne, R.: Hemodynamic alterations measured with phase-contrast MRI in a giant cerebral aneurysm treated with a flow-diverting stent. Radiol. Case Rep. **10**(2), 1109 (2015). https://doi.org/10.2484/rcr.v10i2.1109. https://www.sciencedirect.com/science/article/pii/S1930043316300334

18. McWilliams, J.P., Lee, E.W., Yamamoto, S., Loh, C.T., Kee, S.T.: Image-guided tumor ablation: emerging technologies and future directions. Semin. Interv. Radiol. **27**(3), 302–313 (2010). https://doi.org/10.1055/s-0030-1261789. https://www.ncbi.nlm.nih.gov/pmc/articles/PMC3324186/

19. Miao, S., Wang, Z.J., Liao, R.: Real-time 2D/3D Registration via CNN Regression. arXiv:1507.07505, April 2016. http://arxiv.org/abs/1507.07505

20. Paszke, A., et al.: PyTorch: an imperative style, high-performance deep learning library. In: Advances in Neural Information Processing Systems, vol. 32. Curran Associates, Inc. (2019). https://proceedings.neurips.cc/paper/2019/hash/bdbca288fee7f92f2bfa9f7012727740-Abstract.html

21. Pei, Y., et al.: Non-rigid craniofacial 2D-3D registration using CNN-based regression. In: Cardoso, M.J., et al. (eds.) DLMIA/ML-CDS -2017. LNCS, vol. 10553, pp. 117–125. Springer, Cham (2017). https://doi.org/10.1007/978-3-319-67558-9_14

22. Sokooti, H., de Vos, B., Berendsen, F., Lelieveldt, B.P.F., Išgum, I., Staring, M.: Nonrigid image registration using multi-scale 3D convolutional neural networks. In: Descoteaux, M., Maier-Hein, L., Franz, A., Jannin, P., Collins, D.L., Duchesne, S. (eds.) MICCAI 2017. LNCS, vol. 10433, pp. 232–239. Springer, Cham (2017). https://doi.org/10.1007/978-3-319-66182-7_27

23. Thirion, J.P.: Non-rigid matching using demons. In: Proceedings CVPR IEEE Computer Society Conference on Computer Vision and Pattern Recognition, pp. 245–251, June 1996. https://doi.org/10.1109/CVPR.1996.517081. ISSN 1063-6919

24. Thirion, J.P.: Image matching as a diffusion process: an analogy with Maxwell's demons. Med. Image Anal. 2(3), 243–260 (1998). https://doi.org/10.1016/S1361-8415(98)80022-4. https://www.sciencedirect.com/science/article/pii/S1361841598800224

25. de Vos, B.D., Berendsen, F.F., Viergever, M.A., Staring, M., Išgum, I.: End-to-End Unsupervised Deformable Image Registration with a Convolutional Neural Network. arXiv:1704.06065, vol. 10553, pp. 204–212 (2017). https://doi.org/10.1007/978-3-319-67558-9_24. http://arxiv.org/abs/1704.06065

26. Wang, Z., Bovik, A., Sheikh, H., Simoncelli, E.: Image quality assessment: from error visibility to structural similarity. IEEE Trans. Image Process. 13(4), 600–612 (2004). https://doi.org/10.1109/TIP.2003.819861

27. Xu, Z., et al.: Adversarial Uni- and Multi-modal Stream Networks for Multi-modal Image Registration. arXiv:2007.02790, September 2020. http://arxiv.org/abs/2007.02790

28. Yan, P., Xu, S., Rastinehad, A.R., Wood, B.J.: Adversarial Image Registration with Application for MR and TRUS Image Fusion. arXiv:1804.11024, October 2018. http://arxiv.org/abs/1804.11024

29. Yang, H., et al.: Unpaired Brain MR-to-CT Synthesis using a Structure-Constrained CycleGAN. arXiv:1809.04536, September 2018. http://arxiv.org/abs/1809.04536

30. Zhu, J.Y., Park, T., Isola, P., Efros, A.A.: Unpaired Image-to-Image Translation using Cycle-Consistent Adversarial Networks. arXiv:1703.10593, August 2020. http://arxiv.org/abs/1703.10593

Fast Spherical Mapping of Cortical Surface Meshes Using Deep Unsupervised Learning

Fenqiang Zhao, Zhengwang Wu, Li Wang, Weili Lin, and Gang Li[✉]

Department of Radiology and BRIC, University of North Carolina at Chapel Hill,
Chapel Hill, NC, USA
gang_li@med.unc.edu

Abstract. Spherical mapping of cortical surface meshes provides a more convenient and accurate space for cortical surface registration and analysis and thus has been widely adopted in neuroimaging field. Conventional approaches typically first inflate and project the original cortical surface mesh onto a sphere to generate an initial spherical mesh which contains large distortions. Then they iteratively reshape the spherical mesh to minimize the metric (distance), area or angle distortions. However, these methods suffer from two major issues: 1) the iterative optimization process is computationally expensive, making them not suitable for large-scale data processing; 2) when metric distortion cannot be further minimized, either area or angle distortion is minimized at the expense of the other, which is not flexible to generate application-specific meshes based on both of them. To address these issues, for the first time, we propose a deep learning-based algorithm to learn the mapping between the original cortical surface and spherical surface meshes. Specifically, we take advantage of the Spherical U-Net model to learn the spherical diffeomorphic deformation field for minimizing the distortions between the icosahedron-reparameterized original surface and spherical surface meshes. The end-to-end unsupervised learning scheme is very flexible to incorporate various optimization objectives. We further integrate it into a coarse-to-fine multi-resolution framework for better correcting fine-scaled distortions. We have validated our method on 800+ cortical surfaces, demonstrating reduced distortions than FreeSurfer (the most popularly used tool), while speeding up the process from 20 min to 5 s.

1 Introduction

In neuroimaging studies, cortical surface-based analysis is known to have special advantages over volumetric analysis of the structure and function of the highly convoluted cerebral cortex [5], e.g., better visualization of folded cortical regions, more accurate spatial normalization of the cortex and precise measurements of cortical properties [16]. To do surface-based analysis, a fundamental and critical process is spherical mapping of cortical surface meshes [5]. By taking advantage

© The Author(s), under exclusive license to Springer Nature Switzerland AG 2022
L. Wang et al. (Eds.): MICCAI 2022, LNCS 13436, pp. 163–173, 2022.
https://doi.org/10.1007/978-3-031-16446-0_16

of the spherical topology of the cortical surfaces, it maps the highly folded cortical surface onto a sphere with minimum distortion to reduce the errors and complexity of downstream procedures (like registration and parcellation [6]) and thus enable accurate inter-subject comparison and longitudinal analysis. Therefore, it has been widely adopted in neuroimage analysis tools, e.g., FreeSurfer [4], CARET [3], and HCP pipeline [8], as a routine use to visualize and analyze brain cortical surfaces in the spherical domain [17].

Typical spherical mapping processes can be divided into two steps: generation of an initial spherical mesh and distortion correction of the initial spherical mesh, as shown in Fig. 1. For the first step, a widely used method is to iteratively smooth and inflate the brain surface mesh until the projected spherical mesh has no mesh self-intersections [3,5], or with an additional unfolding step if having self-intersections [5]. Another type of method, e.g., the Laplace-Beltrami operator [1] and its faster version [2], circle packing [11], harmonic energy minimization [9], and Least Squares Conformal Mapping (LSCM) [13], uses conformal mapping to generate an initial angle-preserving spherical map, but not attempt to minimize area distortion. Therefore, the initial spherical meshes generally still have large distortions to be corrected. Then the second step aims to optimize the spherical mesh by minimizing one or more of the three standard distortion metrics, i.e., metric distortion (aka distance distortion), angle distortion, and area distortion [18], to which the optimal solutions are isometric, conformal, and equiareal mappings, respectively [7]. The ideal mapping is no doubt the isometric mapping, which can conserve both area and angle information from the original cortical surface mesh and thus measuring relative areas and locations on the sphere is essentially the same as doing so on the original surface. Therefore, FreeSurfer [5] and CARET [3] choose to directly minimize metric distortion by solving a large-scale nonlinear optimization problem. However,due to the highly folded nature of the cortex and prohibitive cost for computing global distances, it is impossible to obtain an ideal isometric spherical map. Typically, a quasi-isometric map is obtained with either angle or area distortion optimized at the expense of the other [7]. For the initial discrete quasi-conformal maps [1,9,11,13], area and metric distortions are usually further minimized while keeping the angle distortion as minimal as possible. Tosun et al. [22] build on the Laplace-Beltrami operator [1] and add a Mobius transformation to further minimize the area distortion. Nie et al. [19] add a spring energy to the LSCM model [13] to reduce the metric and area distortion while maintaining the conformal map. Alternatively, the error functional to be minimized can also account for both area and angle distortion [15], or area and length distortions [21], or area and secondarily local metric distortions [24]. However, there is no consensus on which metric most influences the accuracy of spherical mapping and which mapping is most close to isometry. Therefore, a flexible spherical mapping method with adjustable weights of different distortion measurements for different applications is critically desired.

Another limitation of previous methods is that they solve the complex distortion optimization problem iteratively and independently for each pair of the original and spherical surface, which is very time-consuming. Although some conformal mapping techniques is fast, such as LSCM [13,19] and eigenfunctions of the Laplace-Beltrami operator used in FastSurfer [10], they only produce the initial quasi-conformal maps, which have large area distortions and need to be further optimized. According to [12], metric properties are preserved best using FreeSurfer [5], which means it generates the closest isometric spherical mapping results and thus becomes the most popular and widely used tool in current neuroimaging studies. However, it takes about 20 min on average even using the latest CPUs. When processing large-scale neuroimage data, the increased computation time is becoming the major barrier for downstream analysis.

These drawbacks of available spherical mapping methods and current success of deep learning in learning effective representations for spherical data [26] and triangle meshes [14] inspire us to develop the first deep learning-based spherical mapping algorithm that is fast enough to handle large-scale neuroimage data, while not decreasing the accuracy compared to the state-of-the-art FreeSurfer [5]. To this end, we take advantage of the Spherical U-Net model [30] to learn the deformation field for minimizing the distortions between the icosahedron-reparameterized original cortical surface and its corresponding spherical meshes. It requires no supervised information such as ground truth deformation field or spherical mesh obtained via conventional tools or simulations for training, thus we construct an end-to-end network which enables flexible weights between different distortion metrics. We further integrate the Spherical U-Net models into a coarse-to-fine multi-resolution learning framework to better learn fine-scaled deformations and achieve more robust results and lower distortions. Most importantly, our proposed method is extremely fast, taking only 5 s to achieve comparable accuracy with FreeSurfer and 11 s with finer resolution to achieve better performance, compared with 20 min in FreeSurfer.

2   Method

2.1   Overall Design and Conception

As shown in Fig. 1, our method starts with an initial spherical mesh generated by the surface inflation and projection (IAP) strategy in FreeSurfer [5] due to its popularity. Then we can fairly compare our method with the state-of-the-art spherical mesh optimization algorithm in FreeSurfer. Let R^0 be the original cortical surface mesh and S^0 be the initial spherical mesh, both with N_v vertices $\{v_n\}_{n=1}^{N_v}$ and N_T faces $\{T_{n,ijk}\}_{n=1}^{N_T}$ where ijk denotes the vertices in n-th triangle. The aim of spherical mesh optimization is to find a spherical deformation field ϕ that can minimize the distortions J between R^0 and $S^0 \circ \phi$:

$$\hat{\phi} = \arg\min_{\phi} J(R^0, S^0 \circ \phi), \tag{1}$$

Since directly learning effective representations for arbitrary cortical surface meshes with different vertex number and triangular connectivity using graph-based CNNs is difficult and inconvenient [26], we take advantage of the regular

grid structure of icosahedron discretized sphere [26] and propose to reparameterize the surface meshes using it. Of note, distortions of surface spherical mapping
is independent of surface parameterizations [7], so the minimization of distortions on the original mesh R^0 and S^0 is equivalent to that on icosahedron-
reparameterized meshes R^{0*} and S^{0*}, i.e.,

$$\arg \min_{\phi} J(R^0, S^0 \circ \phi) \Leftrightarrow \arg \min_{\phi} J(R^{0*}, S^{0*} \circ \phi) \tag{2}$$

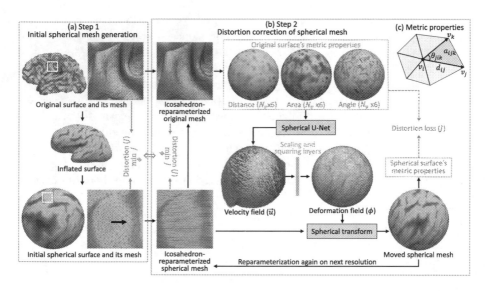

Fig. 1. An overview of our method. The Spherical U-Net takes the icosahedron-
reparameterized original surface's metric properties ($N_v \times 18$) as input and predicts
the deformation field ϕ to minimize the distortions between the original and spherical
meshes. The surface maps of metric properties are color-coded by the average distance,
area, and angle, respectively. Other surfaces are color-coded by average convexity, which
is for display purposes only and not used in the model.

To solve this optimization problem, we employ the popular and powerful
Spherical U-Net model [26] on icosahedron discretized spheres. It extends convolution, pooling, and other operations to the sphere using the 1-ring kernel on
the icosahedron and constructs the network by replacing all operations in the
standard U-Net [20] with spherical operation counterparts. It has shown impressive performance in learning effective features with high efficiency for cortical
surface parcellation [26,27,30], registration [25,27], data harmonization [29] and
atlas construction [28]. Here we leverage it to learn high-level geometric features
from the original surface mesh to predict the diffeomorphic deformation field for
moving each vertex on the spherical mesh to its optimal position on the sphere,
where each vertex has the same metric properties with its matching vertex on

the original surface mesh. In this way, the relative position of each vertex and triangle face on the sphere is the same as that on original surface mesh, which is the ideal solution, isometric mapping, for spherical mapping of cortical surfaces.

Therefore, as shown in Fig. 1(c), we first explicitly compute the metric properties of original meshes after reparameterization, and then feed them into the model instead of implicitly learning them from $\{v_n\}_{n=1}^{N_v}$, i.e., $d_{ij} = ||v_i - v_j||$, $a_{ijk} = \frac{1}{2}||(v_j - v_i) \times (v_k - v_i)||$, $\theta_{jik} = \arccos \frac{(v_j - v_i)(v_k - v_i)}{||v_j - v_i|| ||v_k - v_i||}$, representing the distance, area, and angle metrics, respectively. Aggregating from the local 1-ring neighborhood, we can form the metric property matrix $I(N_v \times 18)$. Then Spherical U-Net takes it as an 18-channel input and output the stationary velocity field u. The diffeomorphic deformation field is obtained through the exponential mapping $\phi = exp(u)$ and numerically through the scaling and squaring layers [25], thus preserving the topology of the mesh with no self-intersections. Finally, warping the initial spherical mesh S^0 by predicted deformation field ϕ^0 using Spherical Transform layer [25] yields optimized spherical mesh: $S^1 = S^0 \circ \phi^0$.

2.2 Coarse-to-Fine Multi-resolution Framework

The initial spherical mesh generally has large nonuniform distortions, making it difficult to learn small deformations for correcting fine-scaled distortions. Therefore, we propose to optimize the meshes on multiple resolutions in a coarse-to-fine manner. After obtaining the first optimized spherical mesh S^1, we reparameterize it again using an icosahedron with higher resolution, resulting in new spherical mesh S^{1*} and original mesh R^{1*}. Then we train a new Spherical U-Net with higher input resolution to minimize the residual distortions $J(R^{1*}, S^{1*})$, represented as:

$$\phi^t = \arg\min_{\phi} J(R^{t*}, S^{t*} \circ \phi), \ S^{t+1} = S^t \circ \phi^t \qquad (3)$$

with progressively increased resolution. The final optimal $\hat{\phi}$ is obtained by combining all the deformation fields: $\hat{\phi} = \phi^0 \circ \phi^1 \circ \cdots \circ \phi^t$ until the final S^{t+1} arriving at an acceptable level of distortion. A graphic illustration of this process we specifically performed in this paper can be found in Fig. 2.

2.3 Loss Functions

We follow [12,13,19,24] to define the metric and area distortions as local relative differences, and angle distortion after market share normalization [12]:

$$J_d(R, S) = \min_{e \in \mathbb{R}^+} \frac{1}{N_v} \sum_{i=1}^{N_v} \left(\frac{1}{6} \sum_{j \in \mathcal{N}(i)} \frac{|e \cdot d_{ij}^S - d_{ij}^R|}{d_{ij}^R}\right), \qquad (4)$$

$$J_a(R, S) = \min_{e \in \mathbb{R}^+} \frac{1}{N_v} \sum_{i=1}^{N_v} \left(\frac{1}{6} \sum_{jk \in \mathcal{N}(i) \ and \ ijk \in \{T_{n,ijk}\}} \frac{|e \cdot a_{ijk}^S - a_{ijk}^R|}{a_{ijk}^R}\right) \qquad (5)$$

$$J_\theta(R, S) = \frac{1}{N_v} \sum_{i=1}^{N_v} \left(\frac{1}{6} \sum_{jk \in \mathcal{N}(i) \ and \ ijk \in \{T_{n,ijk}\}} |\theta_{jik}^{S'} - \theta_{jik}^{R'}|\right) \qquad (6)$$

where R and S denote metrics computed on original and spherical meshes, respectively, $\mathcal{N}(i)$ is the 1-ring neighborhood vertices of v_i, $'$ means that all angles are normalized using the so-called market share of angles at each vertex [12].

To smooth the deformation field ϕ, we use the same operator ∇_s as in [25] on the spherical surface to approximate the spherical deformation's gradients and accordingly penalize it as: $J_s = 1/N_v \sum_{i=1}^{N_v} ||\nabla_s Q_{v_i}(\boldsymbol{u})||$, where $Q_{v_i}(\boldsymbol{u})$ represents the local 1-ring velocity field of vertex v_i. Then the total loss function is:

$$J(R^*, S^* \circ \phi) = \lambda_d J_d + \lambda_a J_a + \lambda_\theta J_\theta + \lambda_s J_s \tag{7}$$

Consequently, it will drive the network to learn the deformation field that moves each vertex on the spherical mesh to its optimal position on the sphere, where the original surface's metric properties can be perfectly recovered and preserved on the spherical mesh, fulfilling the mission of isometric spherical mapping.

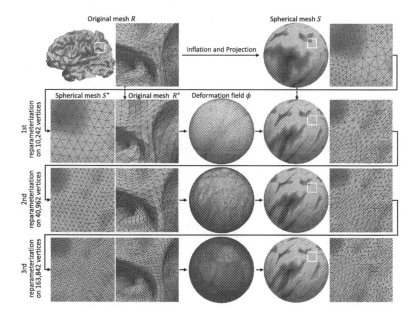

Fig. 2. Our coarse-to-fine multi-resolution optimization process.

3   Experiments and Results

3.1   Experimental Setting

We used an infant dataset with 864 cortical surfaces, which were reconstructed via iBEAT V2.0 Cloud (http://www.ibeat.cloud/) [17,23]. All surfaces were inflated and projected onto the sphere with no self-intersections using FreeSurfer (v7.1.1) [4], and "average convexity" feature at each vertex is also obtained during this process, which is for display purposes only in this paper and not used in the method. Then we used FreeSurfer's spherical mapping algorithm with default parameter setting to obtain the baseline results for comparison. We also adopted the quasi-conformally mapping method in FastSurfer [10] for comparison using its publicly available code with default parameters.

We implemented our method using PyTorch framework based on the public Spherical U-Net's code. In experiments, we found training 3 Spherical U-Net models at 3 resolutions, i.e., 5-, 6-, and 7-th with 10,242, 40,962, and 163,842 vertices respectively, is sufficient to achieve good results, because a sphere with 163,842 vertices is enough to preserve detailed geometric information of the original cortical surface (as shown in Fig. 2). All surfaces were randomly split into the training, validation, and testing sets with the proportion of 6:1:3. We used Adam optimizer with a fixed learning rate 1e–4 for training all the models. λ_d and λ_s during training are 1.0 and 10.0, respectively; λ_a is 1.0, 1.0, and 2.0 at the 3 resolutions. Since metric distortion already contains the area and angle information, to reduce the model complexity and ease the burden of fine-tuning multiple hyper-parameters, we only fine-tuned λ_d and λ_a and set $\lambda_\theta = 0$ in this preliminary study. Another model was trained with $\lambda_a = 0.5$ at each resolution to investigate the influences of smaller area weight. We run all the experiments on a PC with an NVIDIA RTX2080 Ti GPU and an Intel Core i7-9700K CPU.

To quantitatively compare all methods, a little different from the vertex-wise distortions in Eqs. 4, 5 and 6, we calculate the edge-wise, triangle-wise, and angle-wise distortions between the original surface mesh R and the corresponding spherical mesh S without reparameterization, which directly reflects the distortion from surface reconstruction results. All three standard distortion metrics are reported in case that one metric is optimized at the cost of the other. All results are reported based on the hold-out test set.

Table 1. Average distortions of different spherical mapping methods. * indicates significant difference (p-value < 0.05) compared to FreeSurfer.

	Metric dist. (%)	Area dist. (%)	Angle dist. (°)	Run time
IAP	39.37 ± 1.30	73.19 ± 2.13	11.57 ± 0.23	7.2 ± 3.7 (s)
FastSurfer [10]	47.95 ± 4.33	80.34 ± 5.70	13.45 ± 1.32	3.4 ± 0.8 (s)
FreeSurfer [5]	19.97 ± 0.94	10.11 ± 4.19	17.60 ± 1.21	20.7 ± 10.2 (min)
FLASH [2]	41.84 ± 5.88	74.71 ± 8.36	$\mathbf{1.34 \pm 0.21}$	1.5 ± 0.2 (s)
Ours (2 resolutions)	$21.19 \pm 1.40^*$	$10.93 \pm 1.46^*$	$16.07 \pm 0.55^*$	4.8 ± 0.7 (s)
Ours (3 resolutions)	$\mathbf{19.40 \pm 1.03^*}$	$\mathbf{9.41 \pm 1.34^*}$	$16.59 \pm 0.63^*$	11.3 ± 1.8 (s)
Ours ($\lambda_a = 0.5$)	20.05 ± 0.92	$15.35 \pm 2.46^*$	$14.16 \pm 0.57^*$	11.3 ± 1.8 (s)

3.2   Results

Quantitative Analysis. As shown in Table 1, our method achieves comparable accuracy with FreeSurfer using only 2 resolutions, but runs extremely faster than FreeSurfer, taking only 5 s to process a cortical surface, while using FreeSurfer to process all the 864 surfaces with a single PC needs about 2 weeks (20 min/surface), which seriously hinders the downstream data analysis. With one more resolution on the 163,842 vertices sphere, our method outperforms FreeSurfer in all three distortion metrics. This indicates our method did find a more optimal solution (closer to isometric mapping) than FreeSurfer by learning effective cortical geometric representations at high levels of abstraction from the whole dataset. The IAP, FLASH [2], and FastSurfer [10] have smaller angle distortions than ours, but their metric distortions are too large to be employed for subsequent surface registration and parcellation algorithms, thus the resulting meshes need to be further optimized before being practically used in neuroimaging analysis.

Comparing the models trained with smaller λ_a, we can find that when the metric distortion cannot be further minimized, either angle distortion or area distortion is optimized at the expense of the other, which validates the relationships of the three standard distortions [7]. While there are many other energy functions and evaluation metrics used in previous works [5,15,19,21,22], our method is very flexible to incorporate those objective functions and provides a convenient way to explore the best possible isometric mapping using different combinations of distortion metrics, and thus can generate application-specific mapping results.

Note that all the run times are reported based on CPU for fair comparison, although our method is a little faster on GPU by speeding up the inference process of Spherical U-Net. However, the most time-consuming process, i.e., spherical mesh reparameterization, which takes up most of the time, is still relatively slow on both CPU and GPU [25]. Also note that our method use the IAP strategy to generate the initial spherical mesh and average convexity map, which takes an extra ∼7 sec. Nevertheless, it is still much faster than FreeSurfer.

Qualitative Analysis. Figure 3 shows our method achieves smaller and smaller distortions when resolution increases, validating the capability of Spherical U-Net learning increasingly finer deformations to progressively recover the original mesh's detailed metric properties using the coarse-to-fine multi-resolution framework. Besides, our method provides more homogeneous distribution of metric distortion across the whole cortex than FreeSurfer, while IAP and FastSurfer retain large metric distortions and the resulting average convexity maps are extremely misshaped and will inevitably have bad influences on subsequent analysis.

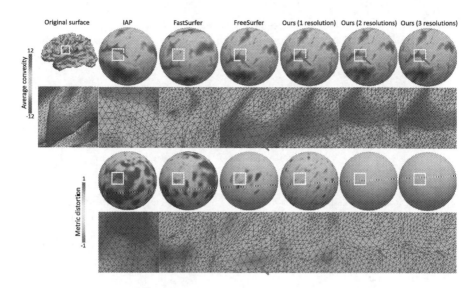

Fig. 3. Spherical mapping results of a randomly selected surface color-coded by average convexity and metric distortion maps.

4   Conclusion

In this paper, we propose the first deep learning-based algorithm for spherical mapping of cortical surface meshes. Our method takes advantage of Spherical U-Net and icosahedron-reparameterized sphere structure to effectively and efficiently learn the diffeomorphic deformation field for correcting distortions on the spherical mesh. It requires no ground truth and enables flexible weights between different distortion metrics. Further combining it with a coarse-to-fine multi-resolution framework yields state-of-the-art results, closer to isometric mapping than other methods. Most importantly, our method is extremely (200+ times) faster than the most popular and widely used tool FreeSurfer. More than 800 cortical surfaces were successfully processed by our method, demonstrating its high practical usefulness in large-scale neuroimaging analysis.

Acknowledgements. This work was supported in part by the National Institutes of Health (NIH) under Grants MH116225, MH117943, MH123202, and AG075582.

References

1. Angenent, S., Haker, S., Tannenbaum, A., Kikinis, R.: On the Laplace-Beltrami operator and brain surface flattening. IEEE Trans. Med. Imaging **18**(8), 700–711 (1999)
2. Choi, P.T., Lam, K.C., Lui, L.M.: Flash: Fast landmark aligned spherical harmonic parameterization for genus-0 closed brain surfaces. SIAM J. Imag. Sci. **8**(1), 67–94 (2015)

3. Drury, H.A., Van Essen, D.C., Anderson, C.H., Lee, C.W., Coogan, T.A., Lewis, J.W.: Computerized mappings of the cerebral cortex: a multiresolution flattening method and a surface-based coordinate system. J. Cogn. Neurosci. **8**(1), 1–28 (1996)
4. Fischl, B.: Freesurfer. Neuroimage **62**(2), 774–781 (2012)
5. Fischl, B., Sereno, M.I., Dale, A.M.: Cortical surface-based analysis: Ii: inflation, flattening, and a surface-based coordinate system. Neuroimage **9**(2), 195–207 (1999)
6. Fischl, B., Sereno, M.I., Tootell, R.B., Dale, A.M.: High-resolution intersubject averaging and a coordinate system for the cortical surface. Hum. Brain Mapp. **8**(4), 272–284 (1999)
7. Floater, M.S., Hormann, K.: Surface parameterization: a tutorial and survey. In: Advances in Multiresolution for Geometric Modelling, pp. 157–186 (2005)
8. Glasser, M.F., et al.: The minimal preprocessing pipelines for the human connectome project. Neuroimage **80**, 105–124 (2013)
9. Gu, X., Wang, Y., Chan, T.F., Thompson, P.M., Yau, S.T.: Genus zero surface conformal mapping and its application to brain surface mapping. IEEE Trans. Med. Imaging **23**(8), 949–958 (2004)
10. Henschel, L., Conjeti, S., Estrada, S., Diers, K., Fischl, B., Reuter, M.: FastSurfer-a fast and accurate deep learning based neuroimaging pipeline. Neuroimage **219**, 117012 (2020)
11. Hurdal, M.K., Stephenson, K.: Cortical cartography using the discrete conformal approach of circle packings. Neuroimage **23**, S119–S128 (2004)
12. Ju, L., Hurdal, M.K., Stern, J., Rehm, K., Schaper, K., Rottenberg, D.: Quantitative evaluation of three cortical surface flattening methods. Neuroimage **28**(4), 869–880 (2005)
13. Ju, L., Stern, J., Rehm, K., Schaper, K., Hurdal, M., Rottenberg, D.: Cortical surface flattening using least square conformal mapping with minimal metric distortion. In: 2004 2nd IEEE International Symposium on Biomedical Imaging: Nano to Macro (IEEE Cat No. 04EX821), pp. 77–80. IEEE (2004)
14. Kipf, T.N., Welling, M.: Semi-supervised classification with graph convolutional networks. arXiv preprint arXiv:1609.02907 (2016)
15. Kruggel, F.: Robust parametrization of brain surface meshes. Med. Image Anal. **12**(3), 291–299 (2008)
16. Li, G., Nie, J., Wang, L., Shi, F., Gilmore, J.H., Lin, W., Shen, D.: Measuring the dynamic longitudinal cortex development in infants by reconstruction of temporally consistent cortical surfaces. Neuroimage **90**, 266–279 (2014)
17. Li, G., et al.: Computational neuroanatomy of baby brains: A review. Neuroimage **185**, 906–925 (2019)
18. Liseikin, V.D.: Grid Generation Methods, vol. 1. Springer Dordrecht (1999). https://doi.org/10.1007/978-90-481-2912-6
19. Nie, J., et al.: Least-square conformal brain mapping with spring energy. Comput. Med. Imaging Graph. **31**(8), 656–664 (2007)
20. Ronneberger, O., Fischer, P., Brox, T.: U-Net: convolutional networks for biomedical image segmentation. In: Navab, N., Hornegger, J., Wells, W.M., Frangi, A.F. (eds.) MICCAI 2015. LNCS, vol. 9351, pp. 234–241. Springer, Cham (2015). https://doi.org/10.1007/978-3-319-24574-4_28
21. Shen, L., Makedon, F.: Spherical parameterization for 3d surface analysis in volumetric images. In: International Conference on Information Technology: Coding and Computing, 2004. Proceedings. ITCC 2004. vol. 1, pp. 643–649. IEEE (2004)

22. Tosun, D., Rettmann, M.E., Prince, J.L.: Mapping techniques for aligning sulci across multiple brains. Med. Image Anal. **8**(3), 295–309 (2004)

23. Wang, L., et al.: Volume-based analysis of 6-month-old infant brain mri for autism biomarker identification and early diagnosis. In: Frangi, A.F., Schnabel, J.A., Davatzikos, C., Alberola-López, C., Fichtinger, G. (eds.) MICCAI 2018. LNCS, vol. 11072, pp. 411–419. Springer, Cham (2018). https://doi.org/10.1007/978-3-030-00931-1_47

24. Yotter, R.A., Thompson, P.M., Gaser, C.: Algorithms to improve the reparameterization of spherical mappings of brain surface meshes. J. Neuroimaging **21**(2), e134–e147 (2011)

25. Zhao, F., et al.: S3reg: superfast spherical surface registration based on deep learning. IEEE Trans. Med. Imaging **40**, 1964–1976 (2021)

26. hao, F., et al.: Spherical deformable u-net: Application to cortical surface parcellation and development prediction. IEEE Trans. Med. Imaging **40**(4), 1217–1228 (2021)

27. Zhao, F., Wu, Z., Wang, L., Lin, W., Xia, S., Li, G.: A Deep network for joint registration and parcellation of cortical surfaces. In: de Bruijne, M., Cattin, P.C., Cotin, S., Padoy, N., Speidel, S., Zheng, Y., Essert, C. (eds.) MICCAI 2021. LNCS, vol. 12904, pp. 171–181. Springer, Cham (2021). https://doi.org/10.1007/978-3-030-87202-1_17

28. Zhao, F., Wu, Z., Wang, L., Lin, W., Xia, S., Li, G.: Learning 4D infant cortical surface atlas with unsupervised spherical networks. In: de Bruijne, M., Cattin, P.C., Cotin, S., Padoy, N., Speidel, S., Zheng, Y., Essert, C. (eds.) MICCAI 2021. LNCS, vol. 12902, pp. 262–272. Springer, Cham (2021). https://doi.org/10.1007/978-3-030-87196-3_25

29. Zhao, F., et al.: Harmonization of infant cortical thickness using surface-to-surface cycle-consistent adversarial networks. In: Shen, D., et al. (eds.) MICCAI 2019. LNCS, vol. 11767, pp. 475–483. Springer, Cham (2019). https://doi.org/10.1007/978-3-030-32251-9_52

30. Zhao, F., et al.: Spherical U-net on cortical surfaces: methods and applications. In: Chung, A.C.S., Gee, J.C., Yushkevich, P.A., Bao, S. (eds.) IPMI 2019. LNCS, vol. 11492, pp. 855–866. Springer, Cham (2019). https://doi.org/10.1007/978-3-030-20351-1_67

Learning-Based US-MR Liver Image Registration with Spatial Priors

Qi Zeng[1]([✉]), Shahed Mohammed[1], Emily H. T. Pang[2], Caitlin Schneider[1], Mohammad Honarvar[1], Julio Lobo[1], Changhong Hu[3], James Jago[3], Gary Ng[3], Robert Rohling[1,4], and Septimiu E. Salcudean[1]

[1] Department of Electrical and Computer Engineering,
The University of British Columbia, Vancouver, BC, Canada
qizeng@ece.ubc.ca
[2] Vancouver General Hospital, Vancouver, BC, Canada
[3] Philips Healthcare, Bothell, WA, USA
[4] Department of Mechanical Engineering, The University of British Columbia,
Vancouver, BC, Canada

Abstract. Registration of multi-modality images is necessary for the assessment of liver disease. In this work, we present an image registration workflow which is designed to achieve reliable alignment for subject-specific magnetic resonance (MR) and intercostal 3D ultrasound (US) images of the liver. Spatial priors modeled from the right rib segmentation are utilized to generate the initial alignment between the MR and US scans without the need of any additional tracking information. For rigid alignment, tissue segmentation models are extracted from the MR and US data with a learning-based approach to apply surface point cloud registration. Local alignment accuracy is further improved via the LC2 image similarity metric-based non-rigid registration technique. This workflow was validated with *in vivo* liver image data for 18 subjects. The best average TRE of rigid and non-rigid registration obtained with our dataset was at 6.27 ± 2.82 mm and 3.63 ± 1.87 mm, respectively.

Keywords: US-MR image registration · Deep learning

1 Introduction

Non-alcoholic fatty liver disease (NAFLD) refers to a broad spectrum of diseases, with prevalence of 20–30% throughout the world; imaging plays an important part in its assessment, and the gold standard is provided by MR imaging [19]. Quantitative US is emerging as an alternative to MRI, but before it can replace MR - as badly needed for population screening - the two modalities need to be compared. The need for this comparison provided the motivation for our study. Ultrasound (US) to magnetic resonance (MR) image registration has always been an active research topic driven by the applications in computer aided intervention. As US and MR imaging examine different tissue physical properties, it is challenging to develop a generic approach for image alignment.

© The Author(s), under exclusive license to Springer Nature Switzerland AG 2022
L. Wang et al. (Eds.): MICCAI 2022, LNCS 13436, pp. 174–184, 2022.
https://doi.org/10.1007/978-3-031-16446-0_17

In the existing literature, techniques based on classic image similarity metrics such as NCC [1,28] and MI [14] often under-perform for US-MR data [15]. Later works focused on the development of US-MR specific metrics. The correlation ratio (CR) proposed in [23] quantifies the functional correlation between overlapping imaging volumes. Combined with a cubic B-splines free-form deformation (FFD) model, CR has shown improved performance in brain surgical data [16,22]. Competing methods proposed in [5,26] analyze the linear fitting of the feature space constructed by the image intensity and gradient profile. The idea of quantifying image similarity via a modality-independent image descriptor has also been investigated in [8]. Variants of these methods were all top ranked in the CuRIOUS2018 challenge [29] and represent the current state of the art. Despite their success for brain surgical data, the performance of these methods has not been validated and compared with benchmark liver US-MR datasets.

Model based approaches can also provide options when common features presented in the overlapping US-MR volume can be extracted. As suggested in [20], the hepatic vascular trees in the liver could be modeled for image alignment. This idea has been used to automatically generate vascular models via learning-based methods for the rigid and non-rigid registration of US and MR/CT images as in [24] and [25]. When the US imaging FOV is sufficiently large, the diaphragm surface could also be used as a good feature for rigid image alignment [10].

Learning-based image registration methods that employ end-to-end weakly-supervised and un-supervised learning frameworks based on deep fully convolutional neural networks (FCN) have been proposed and validated in mono-modality image registration tasks [2,4]. To improve the performance for large deformations, strategies such as introducing multi-scale Laplacian Pyramids in the network design and adapting graphical models for deformation field estimation, have also been attempted [7,17]. For cross-modality image registration, Hu *et al.* validated an FCN-based weakly-supervised method named Label-reg for prostate US-MR data, with promising performance [9]. However, from recent image registration competitions, such as CuRIOUS2018 and Learn2Reg, we note that early techniques still outperform learning-based methods.

All aforementioned techniques require a good initial alignment of the image pairs. The current practice is to use a tracked US imaging setup for US data collection where manual initialization and calibration are often required. While learning-based methods do not provide yet an end-to-end registration solution, they perform robustly in feature detection in different imaging modalities. If the common tissue structures could be reliably extracted from the US-MR image pairs, achieving a good initial alignment with the matching structures should be feasible with the aid of some prior knowledge of the data. Based on this observation, we developed a learning assisted US-MR registration workflow for liver image data. The novelty of our approach is that we automatically estimate the initial US-MR alignment by using the modeled right intercostal spaces from MR images as spatial priors for US transducer placements, without the need of using any US tracking hardware. Because it mimics the way sonographers search for acoustic windows while performing intercostal liver scans, such an approach

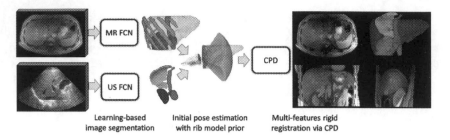

Fig. 1. Registration workflow overview

can ensure that the matching US-MR liver tissue features are roughly in-line to provide a good initial condition for further alignment optimization. Tissue structures extracted by a learning method from the US-MR image pairs are then used to refine the alignment. We validate this method with a *in vivo* dataset of 18 subjects, and the results show that accurate image volume alignment could be achieved with good robustness.

2   Methods

The registration workflow proposed in this work is graphically summarized in Fig. 1. For a given US-MR 3D image pair, we start with FCN-based image segmentation. We trained a dedicated FCN for each of the two imaging modalities to segment shared features, which include the liver (diaphragm in US), the inferior vena cava (IVC), the gallbladder and the right kidney. In addition, the MR FCN is also trained to label the right rib bones. These segmentations are then converted into surface point clouds. While performing intercostal US liver scans, the transducer should be placed in a laterally situated intercostal space and the image plane should be parallel to the ribs for a maximized imaging FOV. Given such spatial prior of the transducer position, we developed a simple approach to estimate the possible poses of the US probe by modeling the subject-specific intercostal space from the MR rib bone segmentation. We then select a subset of possible guesses of the US probe poses as the initial alignment, where the transformations of the US volumes are computed and applied. To refine the rigid alignment, we use the Coherent Point Drift (CPD) algorithm [18] to complete the multi-feature surface point cloud registration. After the rigid alignment is finalized, the Linear Correlation of Linear Combination (LC2) image similarity metric based non-rigid registration [5,26] is also applied to further improve the local alignment accuracy.

Data and Material: Our US data were collected with an EPIQ 7G system with an X6-1 xMATRIX array transducer (Philips Healthcare, Bothell, WA). Free-hand 3D B-mode imaging volumes of the liver were collected with a FOV of 90° lateral × 60° elevational × 16 cm depth and a spatial resolution at

$0.468 \times 0.323 \times 0.673$ mm^3. From 26 subjects, a total of 165 imaging volumes were collected. Image features include the diaphragm, inferior vena cava (IVC), gallbladder and right kidney. These were manually segmented by an experienced research assistant. The results were edited by an experienced radiologist. Our MR dataset consisted of 67 liver abdominal multi-echo fast field echo scans (mFFE) collected with two different scanners, an Achieva 3T and an Elition 3T (Philips Inc., Best, Netherlands). The image resolution is $2.679 \times 2.679 \times 5$ mm^3, and the average intensity map for multi-echos is used. Image labels were prepared similarly to the ultrasound data, with additions of the right rib cage and the full liver tissue volume. These labeled US and mFFE data were used for the training and validation of our learning-based image segmentation. In these datasets, we have 18 subjects, including 13 healthy volunteers and 5 patients, who completed both US-MR imaging exams. These 18 cases with subject-specific US Bmode - mFFE data pairs were used to validate our image registration workflow. For these subjects, we also have the enhanced T1 high-resolution isotropic volume excitation scans (eTHRIVE) performed with a resolution at $0.938 \times 0.938 \times 3$ mm^3. As eTRHIVE data have better soft tissue contrast, they were used to perform the final non-rigid registration in the workflow.

FCN-Based Image Segmentation: As the imaging FOV of the US and MR data are different and not aligned initially, we trained two FCNs to segment the B-mode and the mFFE image volumes separately. The network structure was based on the Dense-Vnet [6]. US and MR image volumes inputs were resized and re-sampled to [128, 128, 64] and [112, 112, 48] with the resolution at $2 \times 2 \times 2$ mm^3 and $2.679 \times 2.679 \times 2.679$ mm^3, respectively. Both the US and MR Dense-Vnets shared the following settings. The number of dense block and filter kernels at the three down-sampled resolutions were [4, 8, 16] and [12, 24, 24], respectively. All dense blocks has a fixed dilation ratio of [5, 5, 5] and a drop off rate of $p = 0.25$. The softmax predictor of the US network outputs five classes: including diaphragm, IVC, gallbladder, right kidney and background. The MR network had one additional class for the right rib bones. We also switched to segmenting the entire liver volume for the MR data in contrast to segmenting the diaphragm for US data. The average Intersection-Over-Union (IoU) was used as the loss metric, where all classes shared an equal weight, i.e. $Loss = 1 - \overline{IoU}$. We trained the networks using the Adam optimizer with a fixed learning rate of $l = 1e^{-4}$ and a batch size of 10 for 1000 epochs. Random elastic deformation with a max amplitude of 2 voxels were applied to image inputs for data argumentation. The surface model maker from [12] was used to generate surface point clouds from the network outputs.

Initial Alignment: Our approach for estimating the initial alignment between B-mode and mFFE data pairs was based on the spatial priors obtained from the subject-specific right intercostal space modeling. First, we computed the rib bone centerlines with a simple iterative method as follows. From a single MR axial slice with rib disc cross-section labels, we used the Fuzzy C-mean clustering

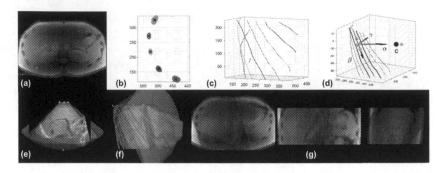

Fig. 2. Initial alignment estimation: (a)-(c) rib centerline estimation; (d) US probe initial pose estimated in the MR volume along an intercostal space midline; (e) fiducial template in the US volume; and (f)-(g) 3D model and slice views of the initial alignment.

algorithm [3] to estimate the rib bone disc centres as shown in Fig. 2 (a)-(b). A two stages clustering operation was utilized to address the issue of unknown cluster number. In the first iteration, we assumed the maximum number of rib disc centers presented in a single slice was $N_{\text{rib-max}} \leq 7$ and we applied the clustering algorithm. Then the redundant clusters were identified by examining the pairwise disc centers distance with a threshold of ($\leq 1\,\text{cm}$) and merged. The second iteration used the updated cluster number to estimate the correct disc centres. As rib disc centres were found for all the 2D slices, the centerline lists were then generated via nearest neighbor search and dynamic tree expansion in 3D, see Fig. 2(c). The intercostal space midlines were then computed for all neighbouring rib pairs representing the possible US probe positions. Figure 2(d) shows an example where the centerline for ribs 7–10 are in blue, and the intercostal space midlines are in red.

To estimate the orientation of the US probe, we assumed the axial centerline of the B-mode imaging volume was aligned to the center of the MR mFFE image volume denoted as C. Then, for a selected probe position P along a intercostal midline S, we computed three direction vectors representing the Euler axes of the probe pose in the following order: 1. $\boldsymbol{\alpha}$ as the B-mode volume centerline direction along $\boldsymbol{PC}$; 2. $\boldsymbol{\beta}$ as the projection of the tangent vector $\hat{S}$ at P to the normal plane of $\boldsymbol{\alpha}$; and 3. $\boldsymbol{\gamma}$ as the normal vector of the plane defined by $\boldsymbol{\alpha}$ and $\boldsymbol{\beta}$. With the estimated initial pose, a 6 points fiducial template was mirrored in both of the US B-mode and MR mFFE volumes based on the spatial dimension of the US scan as shown in Fig. 2(d)-(e). The coordinates of these fiducial markers were used to solve the rigid transformation $T_{initial}$ via Singular Value Decomposition (SVD). Figure 2(f)-(g) shows an example of the resulting initial alignment.

Rigid and Non-rigid Registration: We use a two stage approach for multi-feature rigid registration using the CPD algorithm. First, we group the surface point clouds of the matching IVC, gallbladder and kidney segmentation models for the initial rigid alignment optimization. In the second stage, the point clouds of the diaphragm surface model from the US B-mode volume and the full liver surface model from the MR mFFE volume were added for the final rigid alignment optimization. At each optimization stage, the parameters we optimized included the rotation parameters r and the translation parameters $t \in R^3$, while the scaling factor s was locked at 1. For CPD hyper-parameter tuning, grid search was applied to obtain the best point cloud outlier ratio setting at $\omega = 0.01$. Then for a given initial transducer pose, we have the optimized rigid transformation computed as $T_{\mathrm{rigid}} = T_{\mathrm{stage\ 2}} \cdot T_{\mathrm{stage\ 1}} \cdot T_{\mathrm{initial}}$. This workflow was repeated with six randomly selected initial alignment poses between ribs 7–10 for each B-mode - mFFE image pairs. The averaged transformation $\bar{T}_{\mathrm{rigid}}$ was utilized to finalize the rigid alignment, so that the spatial bias could be avoided.

For non-rigid registration, a Free-Form Deformation (FFD) model driven by the LC2 metric optimization was used to further refine the local alignment accuracy. FFD was deployed in the US volume with a $3 \times 3 \times 3$ control grid. The input patch size of the LC2 metric was at $3 \times 3 \times 3$, and the alignment optimization was completed with the BOBYQA algorithm [21]. In our experiments, rigid registration was performed with the 18 cases of subject-specific B-mode - mFFE images pairs where segmentations were extracted, followed by the non-rigid registration performed for both of the B-mode - mFFE and B-mode - eTHRIVE pairs. Our mFFE and eTRHIVE volumes data were pre-aligned using a NCC based affine registration with the average TRE < 3 mm, thus no additional rigid registration was performed for the B-mode - eTHRIVE data pairs.

3   Results and Discussion

Our learning-based image segmentaion was evaluated with the performance metrics standardized by the CHAOS challenge [11]. All four performance metrics

Table 1. Learning-based image segmentation results

MR mFFE:	DICE (%)	RAVD (%)	ASSD (mm)	MSSD (mm)
Liver	92.2 ± 1.5	6.0 ± 4.2	2.5 ± 0.5	26.1 ± 11.4
Rib	68.9 ± 6.1	14.4 ± 11.4	1.9 ± 0.7	32.8 ± 9.6
IVC	74.0 ± 9.5	20.6 ± 17.1	2.0 ± 0.8	12.6 ± 5.4
Gallbladder	73.9 ± 10.7	27.3 ± 17.1	2.0 ± 0.8	11.8 ± 6.2
Kidney	91.4 ± 2.7	7.1 ± 5.8	1.4 ± 0.6	11.2 ± 11.4
mFFE Avg.	80.1 ± 6.1	15.1 ± 11.1	2.0 ± 0.7	18.9 ± 8.8
US B-mode:	DICE (%)	AVD (%)	ASSD (mm)	MSSD (mm)
Diaphragm	83.2 ± 4.4	7.8 ± 7.6	1.4 ± 0.5	16.9 ± 8.9
IVC	85.9 ± 4.3	7.0 ± 6.2	1.2 ± 0.3	10.6 ± 8.6
Gallbladder	90.0 ± 2.5	6.9 ± 6.1	0.9 ± 0.2	6.3 ± 3.1
Kidney	90.7 ± 2.5	6.1 ± 5.7	1.5 ± 0.3	9.6 ± 4.2
B-mode Avg.	87.5 ± 0.3	6.9 ± 6.4	1.3 ± 0.3	10.8 ± 6.2

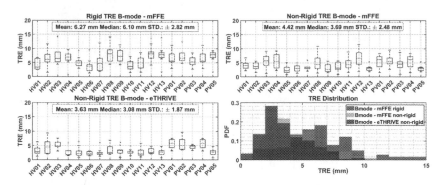

Fig. 3. Registration results: the first three bar plots show the case-by-case TRE distribution in different registration settings, and bottom right compares the overall TRE distribution over all 18 cases.

were included, namely Dice Coefficient, Relative Absolute Volume Difference (RAVD), Average Symmetric Surface Distance (ASSD), and Maximum Symmetric Surface distance (MSSD). Results for both of the US Bmode and MR mFFE data are summarized in Table 1, where the metrics reported are the averaged results from a five-fold cross-validation performed with all cases in our US B-mode and MR mFFE data pool. The training and validation cases ratio were at 80% and 20%, respectively. For the 18 cases of subject-specific US and MR data, their segmentation results were stored for later image registration validation, only when they were serving as the left out cases during the cross-validation.

In both of the US B-mode and MR mFFE multi-class segmentation tasks the trained Desen-Vnet showed promising performance. For the mFFE data, the worse performance was observed for the rib class with a relatively low average Dice score at 69% and a large MSSD at 32.8 mm. This is mainly due to the extremely unbalanced class label, where the rib voxels only populate around 1–2% of an axial slice of the mFFE volume. To validate that our rib models computed from the segmentation are sufficiently accurate as the reference of initial US-MR alignment, we compared the centerline generated from our method with the ground truth generated with the MVTK package [13] using the manual label map. The average RMSE and 95% Hausdorff distance across all cases were at 2.15 ± 1.96 mm and 10.32 ± 5.06 mm, respectively.

For registration performance evaluation, 10–15 landmarks pairs were hand picked by a radiologist for all 18 cases. To ensure the results reflected the alignment accuracy of the liver internal tissue in matching imaging volumes, all selected landmarks were positioned at the vascular branching points along the main hepatic vasculature. Quantitative results are graphically presented in Fig. 3. Among all 18 cases, the average target registration error (TRE) reported by rigid registration was 6.27 ± 2.82 mm, and the average TRE in each individual case was all below 10 mm, which was well under the viable clinical threshold. With the aligned B-mode - mFFE data, LC2 non-rigid registration further reduced the average TRE to 4.42 ± 2.48 mm. An even better improvement was achieved

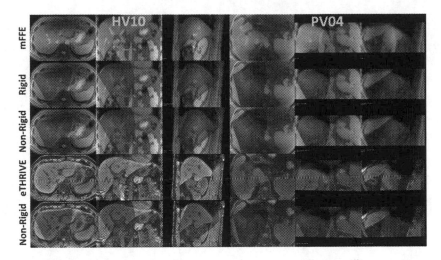

Fig. 4. Sample registration results: healthy volunteer #10 (HV10) (left) and patient #04 (PV04) (right); B-mode images are presented as overlays in red. (Color figure online)

with the B-mode - eTHRIVE image pairs where the lowest average TRE was reported as 3.63 ± 1.87 mm. As eTRHIVE data have a higher spatial resolution and better soft tissue contrast, such improvement for the image similarity metric based method is to be expected. The bottom right of Fig. 3 presents the overall PDF distribution of the TRE from all cases, where the improvement of alignment accuracy obtained from non-rigid registration could be better visualized.

Some image data samples are graphically presented in Fig. 4. The healthy volunteer example on the left showcases an ideal condition, where images from different modalities all provided a high contrast. It is clear that the rigid alignment provided by our method achieves an accurate overlap for hepatic vasculature trees, which ensures that the later non-rigid registration has a good initial condition for further refinement of local alignment. In the more challenging case shown on the right, the patient had a high body to mass index (BMI) > 35, and suffered from a chronic liver condition, causing the low image quality found in both mFFE and T1 data. Rib shadow also reduced the available acoustic window of the 3D B-mode volume. As the key features including IVC, gallbladder, and diaphragm could be extracted, our approach still achieved good results.

Note that the registration accuracy obtained in our rigid alignment step was already comparable to what was recently reported by a non-rigid hepatic vessels tree matching technique as in [24]. In this early technique, manual segmentation of the vessels trees on the MR data was required to perform image alignment. In contrast, we used automatic segmentation. Also, as the earlier technique only applied non-rigid alignment optimization to the segmented vessel trees, a relatively higher average TRE was obtained as 7.1 ± 3.7 mm. Our rigid alignment step had already outperformed this. With the aid of non-rigid registration, we could further reduce the average TRE by nearly 50%.

In this work, Dense-Vnet image segmentation was implemented with Tensor-flow 2.6 and trained with a NVIDIA RTX 3090 GPU. The average training time was ~6 h, and average image inference time is ~0.8 s. The rigid registration work-flow was implemented in MATLAB. Rib space modeling and CPD optimization could be completed within <90 s in each case. For LC2 non-rigid registration, the Imfusion suite was utilized [27].

4   Conclusion

In this work, we presented a novel US-MR liver image registration workflow. With the aid of spatial priors from the modeled the intercostal space, an initial alignment between the 3D freehand US scans and the MR imaging volumes could be achieved without the need of additional tracking information. Tissue feature models from both the US and MR data were segmented with learning-based methods for point cloud rigid registration. The LC2 based non-rigid method was also applied to refine the local alignment. *In vivo* validation with 18 cases showed promising results. Further investigation of the advanced rigid multi-object point cloud registration and learning-based non-rigid registration techniques will be targeted for the future work. A comparison to the conventional US-MR image registration workflow with tracked US imaging hardware is also warranted in a later study to better validate the performance gain of the proposed method.

Acknowledgment. This project is funded by Natural Sciences and Engineering Research Council of Canada (NSERC). We deeply appreciate the support from the Charles A. Laszlo Chair in Biomedical Engineering held by Prof. Salcudean.

References

1. Avants, B., Epstein, C., Grossman, M., Gee, J.: Symmetric diffeomorphic image registration with cross-correlation: evaluating automated labeling of elderly and neurodegenerative brain. Med. Image Anal. **12**, 26–41 (2008)
2. Balakrishnan, G., Zhao, A., Sabuncu, M.R., Guttag, J., Dalca, A.V.: VoxelMorph: a learning framework for deformable medical image registration. IEEE Trans. Med. Imaging **38**(8), 1788–1800 (2019)
3. Bezdek, J.C.: Pattern Recognition with Fuzzy Objective Function Algorithms. Plenum Press, New York (1981)
4. de Vos, B.D., Berendsen, F.F., Viergever, M.A., Sokooti, H., Staring, M., Išgum, I.: A deep learning framework for unsupervised affine and deformable image registration. Med. Image Anal. **52**, 128–143 (2019)
5. Fuerst, B., Wein, W., Müller, M., Navab, N.: Automatic ultrasound-MRI registration for neurosurgery using the 2D and 3D LC2 metric. Med. Image Anal. **18**(8), 1312–1319 (2014)
6. Gibson, E., Giganti, F., Hu, Y.: Automatic multi-organ segmentation on abdominal CT with dense V-networks. IEEE Trans. Med. Imaging **37**(8), 1822–1834 (2018)

7. Heinrich, M.P.: Closing the gap between deep and conventional image registration using probabilistic dense displacement networks. In: Shen, D., et al. (eds.) MICCAI 2019. LNCS, vol. 11769, pp. 50–58. Springer, Cham (2019). https://doi.org/10.1007/978-3-030-32226-7_6

8. Heinrich, M.P., Jenkinson, M., Bhushan, M., et al.: Mind: modality independent neighbourhood descriptor for multi-modal deformable registration. Med. Image Anal. **16**(7), 1423–1435 (2012)

9. Hu, Y., et al.: Weakly-supervised convolutional neural networks for multimodal image registration. Med. Image Anal. **49**, 1–13 (2018)

10. Kadoury, S., et al.: A model-based registration approach of preoperative MRI with 3d ultrasound of the liver for interventional guidance procedures. In: 2012 9th IEEE International Symposium on Biomedical Imaging (ISBI), pp. 952–955 (2012)

11. Kavur, A.E., et al.: CHAOS challenge - combined (CT-MR) healthy abdominal organ segmentation. Med. Image Anal. **69**, 101950 (2021)

12. Lorensen, W.E., Cline, H.E.: Marching cubes: a high resolution 3d surface construction algorithm. In: Proceedings of the 14th Annual Conference on Computer Graphics and Interactive Techniques, pp. 163–169 (1987)

13. Luca, A., David, S., Simone, M., Richard, I.: The vascular modeling toolkit. http://www.vmtk.org/

14. Maes, F., Vandermeulen, D., Suetens, P.: Medical image registration using mutual information. Proc. IEEE **91**(10), 1699–1722 (2003)

15. Maintz, J., Viergever, M.A.: A survey of medical image registration. Med. Image Anal. **2**(1), 1–36 (1998)

16. Masoumi, N., Xiao, Y., Rivaz, H.: Arena: inter-modality affine registration using evolutionary strategy. Int. J. Comput. Assist. Radiol. Surg. **14**, 441–450 (2019)

17. Mok, T.C.W., Chung, A.C.S.: Large deformation diffeomorphic image registration with Laplacian pyramid networks. In: Martel, A.L., et al. (eds.) MICCAI 2020. LNCS, vol. 12263, pp. 211–221. Springer, Cham (2020). https://doi.org/10.1007/978-3-030-59716-0_21

18. Myronenko, A., Song, X.: Point set registration: coherent point drift. IEEE Trans. Pattern Anal. Mach. Intell. **32**(12), 2262–2275 (2010)

19. Nguyen, D., Talwalkar, J.A.: Noninvasive assessment of liver fibrosis. Hepatology **53**(6), 2107–2110 (2011)

20. Porter, B., et al.: Three-dimensional registration and fusion of ultrasound and MRI using major vessels as fiducial markers. IEEE Trans. Med. Imaging **20**(4), 354–359 (2001)

21. Powell, M.J.: The BOBYQA algorithm for bound constrained optimization without derivatives, vol. 2. Cambridge NA report NA2009/06, University of Cambridge, Cambridge (2009)

22. Rivaz, H., Chen, S.J.S., Collins, D.L.: Automatic deformable MR-Ultrasound registration for image-guided neurosurgery. IEEE Trans. Med. Imaging **34**(2), 366–380 (2015)

23. Roche, A., Malandain, G., Pennec, X., Ayache, N.: Multimodal Image Registration by Maximization of the Correlation Ratio. Ph.D. thesis, INRIA (1998)

24. Thomson, B.R., et al.: MR-to-US registration using multiclass segmentation of hepatic vasculature with a reduced 3D U-Net. In: Martel, A.L., et al. (eds.) MICCAI 2020. LNCS, vol. 12263, pp. 275–284. Springer, Cham (2020). https://doi.org/10.1007/978-3-030-59716-0_27

25. Wei, W., Xu, H., Alpers, J., et al.: Fast registration for liver motion compensation in ultrasound-guided navigation. In: 2019 IEEE 16th International Symposium on Biomedical Imaging (ISBI 2019), pp. 1132–1136 (2019)

26. Wein, W., Brunke, S., Kamen, A., Callstrom, M., Navab, N.: Automatic CT-ultrasound registration for diagnostic imaging and image-guided intervention. Med. Image Anal. **12**(5), 577–585 (2008)
27. Wein, W.: Imfusion. https://www.imfusion.com
28. Woods, R., Mazziotta, J., Cherry, S.R.: MRI-PET registration with automated algorithm. J. Comput. Assist. Tomogr. **17**, 536–546 (1993)
29. Xiao, Y., Rivaz, H., Chabanas, M., et al.: Evaluation of MRI to ultrasound registration methods for brain shift correction: the CuRIOUS2018 challenge. IEEE Trans. Med. Imaging **39**(3), 777–786 (2020)

Unsupervised Deep Non-rigid Alignment by Low-Rank Loss and Multi-input Attention

Takanori Asanomi[1](✉), Kazuya Nishimura[1], Heon Song[1], Junya Hayashida[1], Hiroyuki Sekiguchi[2], Takayuki Yagi[2], Imari Sato[3], and Ryoma Bise[1,3]

[1] Kyushu University, Fukuoka, Japan
{takanori.asanomi,bise}@human.ait.kyushu-u.ac.jp
[2] Luxonus, Kawasaki, Japan
[3] National Institute of Informatics, Tokyo, Japan

Abstract. We propose a deep low-rank alignment network that can simultaneously perform non-rigid alignment and noise decomposition for multiple images despite severe noise and sparse corruptions. To address this challenging task, we introduce a low-rank loss in deep learning under the assumption that a set of well-aligned, well-denoised images should be linearly correlated, and thus, that a matrix consisting of the images should be low-rank. This allows us to remove the noise and corruption from input images in a self-supervised learning manner (*i.e.*, without requiring supervised data). In addition, we introduce multi-input attention modules into Siamese U-nets in order to aggregate the corruption information from the set of images. To the best of our knowledge, this is the first attempt to introduce a low-rank loss for deep learning-based non-rigid alignment. Experiments using both synthetic data and real medical image data demonstrate the effectiveness of the proposed method. The code will be publicly available in https://github.com/asanomitakanori/Unsupervised-Deep-Non-Rigid-Alignment-by-Low-Rank-Loss-and-Multi-Input-Attention.

1 Introduction

Many imaging technologies, such as photoacoustic (PA) imaging [12], require multiple scans to capture entire portions of the human body because a one-shot image captures only a local area, whereas successively scanned images overlap with previous images. In multi-scan imaging, a shot image often contains severe noise and sparse corruption over the foreground object (*e.g.*, thin blood vessels), as shown in Fig. 1. To reduce such noise, image averaging has often been used, where it is assumed that the target objects do not move during the scan. However, a patient tends to move during the scan, which degrades the image quality. For example, in Fig. 1, the vessels in the red box have very low contrast in the image with motion, whereas they are clearly observed in the image without motion. Accordingly, it is essential to accurately align shot images.

© The Author(s), under exclusive license to Springer Nature Switzerland AG 2022
L. Wang et al. (Eds.): MICCAI 2022, LNCS 13436, pp. 185–195, 2022.
https://doi.org/10.1007/978-3-031-16446-0_18

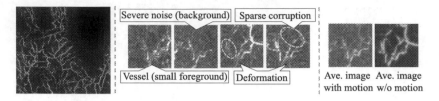

Fig. 1. Left: Example of reconstructed wide-view image of a hand in photoacoustic imaging. **Middle:** Multi-scan images at red dotted box contain severe noise and sparse corruption. Yellow ellipses and green curves indicate examples of sparse corruption and deformation, respectively. **Right:** Image averaging results from multi-scanning with and without motion. Body motion degrades quality of averaged image. (Color figure online)

To align shot images, non-rigid registration (alignment) is useful. It estimates a deformable transformation that transforms a source image (a moving object) into a target image (a fixed object). Current methods [1,2,13,20,24,25] train registration networks by minimizing the similarity of the transformed target and the source image with a regularization term, for which these losses can be computed in a self-supervised manner. Those methods use MSE and cross-correlation as similarity measures, according to the assumption that the target images have high quality; that is, the images should not contain severe noise or corruption, such as reconstructed MRI images. In contrast to the previous works, we aim to align shot images that will be used to reconstruct the final image in multi-scan imaging, and the assumption rarely occurs in multi-scan imaging.

Low-rank optimization-based alignment methods [3,16,26] have the potential to address the alignment of such challenging data, by introducing well-studied techniques for sparse and low-rank optimization (*e.g.*, robust PCA [4]) into alignment methods. However, optimization-based methods always require an optimization process for test data, which becomes computationally expensive when registering many images or large images. In addition, current low-rank-based methods assume a parallel translation or affine transform and are thus not suitable for non-rigid deformation. Jia *et al.* proposed a low-rank representation method for registration. The motivation of this paper is representing features of a single image by low-rank projection, *i.e.*, the low-rank was not used to align the set of images.

In this paper, we propose a deep learning-based low-rank non-rigid alignment method for noisy, corrupted images. Given a set of noisy shot images that were captured at the same position, the proposed method aligns the images while decomposing their noise. Inspired by the low-rank optimization-based methods [3,16], we introduce a low-rank loss in a deep learning framework. To the best of our knowledge, this is the first attempt to introduce a low-rank loss for deep learning-based alignment of objects with non-rigid deformation. Note that low-rank losses have not been widely used in deep learning applications, although low-rank regularization has been used for network compression [10,27].

In addition, we introduce a multi-attention module to complement the sparse corruption. For error complementation, it is important to aggregate the

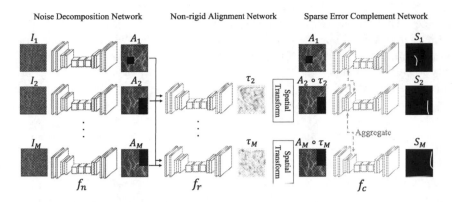

Fig. 2. Overview of proposed method, which consists of three subnetworks f_n, f_r, f_c.

information from a set of shot images. For example in Fig. 1, let us consider the vessel images that contain corruption in different locations: we can see vessels on the right side in third image from the left, but we cannot see them at the same place (yellow ellipse) in the fourth image. To identify such corruption, we need to check a set of input images. To aggregate the information from multiple images, we introduce a self-attention technique [23] that has been used in transformers and in many tasks, such as classification [7], detection [5] and segmentation [9,17]. In vision tasks, current methods that use self-attention focus on aggregating wide-range contexts and spatial dependencies in a single input image. In contrast, our multi-input attention modules in Siamese U-nets interchange the features of multiple images extracted by each U-net and aggregate them to identify uncommon components (*i.e.*, corruption). Another advantage of multi-input attention is that it does not depend on the order of the inputs, whereas a simple 3D convolution layer does depend on the order.

Our network can be trained in a self-supervised manner (requiring no manual annotation) so that it simultaneously aligns multiple input images while decomposing the noise and sparse error components by using the proposed low-rank loss. Thanks to introducing the low-rank optimization into deep learning, the runtime of our method was much faster than the optimization-based methods. Our experiments on both synthetic data and real photoacoustic imaging demonstrate the effectiveness of the proposed method.

2   Deep Non-rigid Alignment Using Low-Rank Loss

Figure 2 shows an overview of the proposed method. Given M images $\boldsymbol{I}_1, ..., \boldsymbol{I}_M (\boldsymbol{I}_i \in \mathbb{R}^{w \times h})$ of the same object, which contain severe dense noise as well as corrupted, misaligned foregrounds, we can train a network in a self-supervised manner so that it can align the images by decomposing them into a low-rank foreground (aligned object), dense background (severe noise), and sparse error components (corruption). To address this problem, we designed an entire network that consists of three subnetworks: 1) noise decomposition network f_n that decomposes an input image I_i into a corrupted foreground component $A_i \in \mathbb{R}^{w \times h}$ and noise components $B_i \in \mathbb{R}^{w \times h}$, such that $I_i = A_i + B_i$; 2) non-rigid deformation network f_r that estimates a displacement vector field τ_i to specify the vector offset from A_i to A_1 for each pixel, where $A_i \circ \tau_i$ denotes a warped image using τ_i; and 3) sparse error complement network f_c that estimates a sparse error component S_i, which represents a corrupted area in the aligned foreground.

The aligned images $\{L_i = A_i \circ \tau_i + S_i \in \mathbb{R}^{w \times h}\}_{i=1}^{M}$ should be linearly correlated. More precisely, let us denote an aligned and decomposed image matrix as $\mathbf{L} = [\text{vec}(L_1)|...|\text{vec}(L_M)]^T \in \mathbb{R}^{M \times N}$, $\mathbf{L}$ should be approximately low-rank, in which $\text{vec}(\cdot)$ denotes the vectorize operator, and $N = wh$. Accordingly, we introduce a low-rank loss function to train the entire network for simultaneous decomposition and non-rigid alignment. Hereafter, we denote the input, denoised, noise, and sparse error matrixes as $\mathbf{I}$, $\mathbf{A}$, $\mathbf{B}$, $\mathbf{S}$, respectively, in the same manner as with $\mathbf{L}$. Note also that $\mathbf{A} \circ \tau$ indicates that the transformation τ_i is applied to each individual row A_i.

Noise Decomposition Network: Given $I_1, ..., I_M$ that were captured in the same place but contain different noise patterns and corruption, the network f_n is trained to decompose an input image I_i into a corrupted foreground A_i and dense noise B_i, wherein Siamese networks are applied to every i-th image. This network estimates only the foreground components in $\mathbf{A}$, while the noise component $\mathbf{B}$ can be computed as $\mathbf{B} = \mathbf{I} - \mathbf{A}$. We use the U-net architecture [18] for this network. We assume that an input image contains the foreground region of the same object together with random noise, whose properties are consistent among the individual images (*e.g.*, Gaussian noise with the same mean and variance in each image, but with different noise patterns).

Let us consider the case when the input images are aligned. The distribution of the average intensity of the noise components at the same position $(\overline{B \circ \tau(p)} = \frac{1}{M} \sum_i B_i \circ \tau_i(p))$ can be approximated by a Gaussian distribution with a constant mean and small variance in accordance with the central limit theorem and the law of large numbers [3], where p is a position coordinate in an image. We use this property for regularization to extract the noise components during training, as follows:

$$\text{loss}_{noise} = \|\mathbf{a}(\mathbf{B} \circ \tau) - \mathbf{b}\|^2, \quad \mathbf{B} = \mathbf{I} - \mathbf{A}, \tag{1}$$

where $\mathbf{a}$ denotes a $1 \times M$ vector whose elements are all $\frac{1}{M}$. The dot product of $\mathbf{a}$ and an $M \times 1$ vector gives the average of the vector's elements; thus, $\mathbf{a}(\mathbf{B} \circ \tau)$ gives a $1 \times N$ mean vector, where each element is $\overline{B \circ \tau(p)}$. $\mathbf{b}$ denotes a $1 \times N$ vector whose elements are all a constant value b that indicates the mean of the Gaussian. We automatically set b to the median value in the input image, because we assume that the foreground region is sparse than the background. As a result, the term $\|\mathbf{a}(\mathbf{B} \circ \tau) - \mathbf{b}\|^2$ penalizes the loss function when the mean of the aligned backgrounds at the same positions deviates from b. In other words, if a noise component contains foreground signals, it penalizes the loss because the statistical properties of the foreground signals are different from those of the noise.

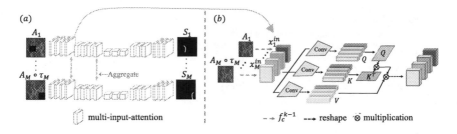

Fig. 3. (a) Network architecture of multi-input attention U-net f_c. Multi-input attention modules (green block) are inserted in U-net architecture. (b) Overview of multi-input attention module. (Color figure online)

Non-rigid Deformation Network: Given a set of paired images $\{A_1, A_i\}_{i=2}^M$ (target and source) that were estimated by f_n, the non-rigid deformation network f_r estimates the displacement vector field τ_i, which indicates the vector offset from the source A_i to target A_1 for each pixel. The displacement field τ_i stored in a 2-ch $w \times h$ image, for which each pixel p, $\tau_i(p)$ is a displacement $(\Delta x, \Delta y)$ so that $A_1(p)$ and $A_i \circ \tau_i(p)$ have similar intensity.

For the backbone of this network, we use VoxelMorph [2], which has a U-net architecture and takes a single input formed by concatenating the source and target images into a 2-channel 2D image. This network can be trained in an unsupervised way. The original VoxelMorph learns optimal network parameters by minimizing the deformation loss as: $\text{loss}_{def} = \lambda_{mse} \sum_i \|A_i \circ \tau_i - A_1\|^2 + \lambda_{sm} \sum_i |\nabla \tau_i|_1 + \lambda_r \sum_i |\tau_i|_1$. Here, the first term represents the differences (*e.g.*, MSE) between $A_i \circ \tau_i$ and A_1, the second term indicates regularization that ensures smoothness of the spatial gradients of the displacement, and the third term represents regularization that avoids large displacement. In our case, because the foreground regions are sparse, we used the l1 norm.

The main difference from VoxelMorph is that we use a low-rank loss $\text{loss}_{low} = \|A \circ \tau + S\|_*$, where $\| \cdot \|_*$ denotes the nuclear norm. This loss measures the similarity between the source and target images, because a warped source image $A_i \circ \tau_i + S_i$ should be linearly correlated with the target image $A_1 + S_1$.

This low-rank loss is calculated by simultaneously considering images in a batch; that is, given a set of paired images $\{A_i, A_1\}_{i=2}^M$, the Siamese networks estimate a set of displacement fields $\{\tau_k\}_{i=2}^M$, which is denoted by τ. Note that the low-rank loss is used for training all three networks. Recently, differentiated singular value decomposition (SVD) [21] was proposed, and deep learning libraries, such as PyTorch now provide backpropagation of SVD. This enables us to update the network weights by using the proposed loss function.

Sparse Error Complement Network: Given $\{A_i \circ \tau_i\}_{k=1}^M$, the network f_c estimates the sparse error components S_i of each image. This can be considered a task of finding common (foreground) and sparse uncommon (sparse error) components, because the corruption is sparse and its locations vary across the images in a batch. Our multi-input attention in M Siamese U-nets (called multi-input attention U-nets) aggregates a set of input images in order to interchange the features extracted from the Siamese U-nets as shown in Fig. 3.

We denote the i-th input feature for the multi-input attention module in the j-th layer as $\boldsymbol{x}_i^{in} = f_c^{(j-1)}(\boldsymbol{A}_i \circ \boldsymbol{\tau}_i)$, which is an output from the module's previous layer $f_c^{(j-1)}$, as shown in Fig. 3(b). In the multi-input attention module, $\boldsymbol{x}_i^{in}$ is converted into a query ($\boldsymbol{q}_i$), key ($\boldsymbol{k}_i$), and value ($\boldsymbol{v}_i$) by convolution, and the matrix is then flattened into a vector with dimension C. We denote the matrices consisting of sets of queries, keys, and values of the input images as $\mathbf{Q} = [\boldsymbol{q}_1|...|\boldsymbol{q}_M]^T \in \mathbb{R}^{M \times C}$, $\mathbf{K} = [\boldsymbol{k}_1|...|\boldsymbol{k}_M]^T \in \mathbb{R}^{M \times C}$, and $\mathbf{V} = [\boldsymbol{v}_1|...|\boldsymbol{v}_M]^T \in \mathbb{R}^{M \times C}$, respectively. The multi-input attention output is then defined as follows:

$$\boldsymbol{x}_i^{out} = \boldsymbol{x}_i^{in} + \text{Attention}(\mathbf{Q}, \mathbf{K}, \mathbf{V})_i, \tag{2}$$

$$\text{Attention}(\mathbf{Q}, \mathbf{K}, \mathbf{V}) = \text{reshape}(\text{softmax}(\mathbf{Q}\mathbf{K}^\top)\mathbf{V}), \tag{3}$$

where reshape($\cdot$) reshapes an input vector to a matrix with the same shape as $\boldsymbol{x}_i^{in}$, Attention$(\mathbf{Q}, \mathbf{K}, \mathbf{V})_i$ denotes the reshaped vector of the i-th attention matrix, and softmax($\cdot$) represents the softmax operator to each row vector individually. Here, in the multi-input attention module, the information extracted by the Siamese networks from all the input images is interchanged and aggregated. It can be expected that important information for sparse decomposition will be extracted. To train this network, we use the low-rank loss, loss_{low}, with the sparse loss, $\text{loss}_{sp} = |\mathbf{S}|_1$. This formulation is often used for robust-PCA.

The total loss function of the proposed method is as follows:

$$\text{loss} = \lambda_l \text{loss}_{low} + \lambda_{sp} \text{loss}_{sp} + \lambda_n \text{loss}_{noise} + \text{loss}_{def}, \tag{4}$$

where the λ are the weights of each loss. Our method can train the whole network end-to-end, and the low-rank loss is used for training all the subnetworks.

3   Experiments

Our main target is registration of multiple shot images that are intermediate data in multi-scan imaging, which have sparse foreground regions over dense noisy background with corruption. This is a different condition from the MRI images, and there are no public dataset for such condition. We thus used two synthetic data for quantitative evaluation and one real data for qualitative evaluation.

Experimental Setup: We implemented our method by using PyTorch [15]. We trained all the networks in an end-to-end manner with the ADAM optimizer [11] on an NVIDIA GeForce 3090 GPU, Intel(R) Core(TM) i9-10980XE CPU @ 3.00 GHz. The mini-batch size was 8, and the learning rate was 3e−3. After early stopping using validation data, we used the weights that gave the best validation performance. All the codes will be publicly available.

Quantitative Evaluation: To evaluate our method, we used two datasets: 1) the vessel dataset [6], which contains blood vessel images and segmented masks; and

Table 1. Average dice scores and runtime (sec).

Method	Medical		Simulation	
	Dice	Time	Dice	Time
RASL [16]	0.554	2.598	0.549	1.947
LAFB [3]	0.589	0.865	0.607	0.653
VMorph [2]	0.536	0.034	0.579	0.035
RCN [28]	0.572	0.400	0.656	0.307
ULAE [19]	0.563	0.143	0.544	0.089
CDIR [14]	0.592	0.073	0.537	0.104
Ours	**0.611**	0.116	**0.683**	0.147

Table 2. Ablation study results for averages over all two datasets. **MA** denotes multi-input attention.

Method	f_n	f_c	MA	Dice
VMorph [2]				0.551
Ours	✓			0.614
Ours	✓	✓		0.640
Ours	✓	✓	✓	**0.647**

2) simulated photoacoustic (PA) images, in which vessel regions were captured by acoustic sensors and PA images were reconstructed by K-wave [22].

In our method, multiple images are simultaneously fed into our Siamese networks as a mini-batch and then aligned with decomposing the noise and sparse corruption. We thus generated a batch of eight images from one sample by applying non-rigid deformation and adding noise and corruption. The non-rigid deformation was applied via a b-spline transformation [8] with random displacement ($[-6.4, 6.4]$ pixels). The corruption was added to the deformed images by replacing randomly selected 6×6 regions with 0. Then, we added noise (mean of 0.2, a standard deviation of 0.4) to all pixels.

We compared our method with the following methods: (1) RASL [16] and (2) LAFB [3], which require low-rank optimization for testing; and (3) Voxel-Morph (VMorph) [2], (4) RCN [28], (5) ULAE [19], (6) CDIR [14], which are state-of-the-art unsupervised deep-learning-based methods. Because an advantage of CDIR is the ease of tuning hyper-parameters in inference, we used various parameters (0.1, 1, 4, 8) for CDIR, and we show the best results.

We evaluated the methods by comparing the overlap of the foreground regions between the source and deformed target images (the Dice score for the foreground region). Dice has often been used in major registration papers (*e.g.*,VoxelMorph [2]) as the performance metric without using the ground truth of the displacement fields. Dice is correlated to the similarity of displacement fields. If the warped source is very similar to the target by displacing noise regions to foreground regions, Dice takes a small value. If foreground regions are properly transformed, Dice becomes high.

In Table 1, our method outperformed the other methods in terms of the Dice score. The other methods had difficulty handling the non-rigid deformation. Moreover, because the deep-learning-based methods can not have a denoise function, our method performed better than those methods.

We also compared the average runtimes for inference. For fair comparison, we used a CPU for all the methods. The deep-learning-based methods (as well as our method) were much faster (5–20 times) than the optimization-based methods, because they required optimization during inference.

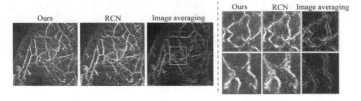

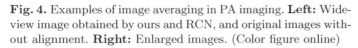

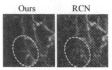

Fig. 4. Examples of image averaging in PA imaging. **Left:** Wideview image obtained by ours and RCN, and original images without alignment. **Right:** Enlarged images. (Color figure online)

Fig. 5. Example of complementation for corruption; Signals in yellow circle was complemented by ours. (Color figure online)

Even though some of the comparison methods have a large amount of the network parameters, such as RCN (three times ours), our method was better than these methods. In real multi-scan imaging, thousands of images must be aligned to construct a wide-view image (as described in the next section), and it is thus important to reduce the runtime.

In addition, Table 2 lists the results of an ablation study. Each module improved the performance further. In particular, the complement network f_c using multi-attention improved the performance from 0.614 to 0.647, and the proposed method using all the modules thus achieved the best performance. We also performed a non-parametric multiple comparison test. In the results, our method was significantly better than all the methods with $p < 0.01$.

Qualitative Evaluation Using Real PA Images: We next demonstrate the effectiveness of our method in an application of photoacoustic (PA) [12] imaging, which is a promising new technology for early clinical diagnosis of cancer, tumor angiogenesis, and many other diseases. The evaluation was qualitative, because severe noise and corruption made it difficult to establish a ground-truth for the foreground mask from each shot image. In real PA devices, an image averaging technique is often used to reduce noise. Image averaging is effective as long as the sample is static; however, when body motion occurs during a scan, the image quality deteriorates significantly.

In this example, hands were scanned with a PA imaging system that scans local areas multiple times. During these scan, the hand was shaken slowly to introduce body motion. The total number of shot images was 2048. Each successively scanned image overlapped 90% of the previously scanned image, and the total scanning time was about 2 min. We used different data from different patients for training and testing. To construct the entire image, we applied our method to align multiple images in the same local area, and the estimated low-rank images were stitched into the entire image.

Figure 4 shows the example wide-view images of the registration results for our method, RCN [28] (the best method besides ours), and image averaging without alignment. The small images on the right in Fig. 4 are enlarged images of the red and blue boxes in the wide-view images. In the results without alignment, the vessels seemed blurry and duplicated because of the body motion. As for RCN, the alignment succeeded in some regions but still exhibited noise. Moreover, even when RCN was successful, it aligned not only the vessels but also noise, and the image averaging was thus meaningless. In contrast, for our results, the vessels were obviously clearer than in the RCN and the original images, and severe noise was reduced. Accordingly, we confirmed that the proposed method significantly improved the image quality in PA imaging. During multi-scan, the relative position from objects to the light source was shifted, and thus corruptions often occur as shown in Fig. 1. Figure 5 shows the example of complementation. The result of RCN has a corrupted region (yellow circle). In contrast, our method succeeded to complement the corruption.

4   Conclusion

This paper proposed a deep non-rigid alignment method that can simultaneously perform non-rigid alignment, noise decomposition and sparse error complementation. To address this challenging problem, we introduced the low-rank loss and multi-input attention modules. The low-rank loss enables noise removal during foreground image alignment, and the multi-input attention module enables aggregation of the information from multiple input images to estimate corrupted regions. In experiments, our method outperformed baseline methods, and it demonstrated its effectiveness in real medical imaging. We expect that this trainable low-rank framework will contribute to many applications.

Acknowledgment. This work was supported by AMED under Grant Number JP20he2302002 and JSPS KAKENHI Grant Numbers JP20H04211.

References

1. Balakrishnan, G., Zhao, A., Sabuncu, M.R., Guttag, J., Dalca, A.V.: An unsupervised learning model for deformable medical image registration. In: CVPR, pp. 9252–9260 (2018)
2. Balakrishnan, G., Zhao, A., Sabuncu, M.R., Guttag, J., Dalca, A.V.: VoxelMorph: a learning framework for deformable medical image registration. IEEE Trans. Med. Imaging **38**(8), 1788–1800 (2019)
3. Bise, R., Zheng, Y., Sato, I., Toi, M.: Vascular registration in photoacoustic imaging by low-rank alignment via foreground, background and complement decomposition. In: Ourselin, S., Joskowicz, L., Sabuncu, M.R., Unal, G., Wells, W. (eds.) MICCAI 2016. LNCS, vol. 9902, pp. 326–334. Springer, Cham (2016). https://doi.org/10.1007/978-3-319-46726-9_38
4. Candès, E.J., Li, X., Ma, Y., Wright, J.: Robust principal component analysis? J. ACM **58**(3), 1–37 (2011)
5. Carion, N., Massa, F., Synnaeve, G., Usunier, N., Kirillov, A., Zagoruyko, S.: End-to-end object detection with transformers. In: Vedaldi, A., Bischof, H., Brox, T., Frahm, J.-M. (eds.) ECCV 2020. LNCS, vol. 12346, pp. 213–229. Springer, Cham (2020). https://doi.org/10.1007/978-3-030-58452-8_13

6. Ding, L., Bawany, M., Kuriyan, A., Ramchandran, R., Wykoff, C., Sharma, G.: Recovery-fa19: Ultra-widefield fluorescein angiography vessel detection dataset. In: IEEE Dataport (2019)
7. Dosovitskiy, A., et al.: An image is worth 16x16 words: transformers for image recognition at scale. In: ICLR (2021). https://openreview.net/forum?id=YicbFdNTTy
8. Eppenhof, K.A., Pluim, J.P.: Pulmonary CT registration through supervised learning with convolutional neural networks. IEEE Trans. Med. Imaging **38**(5), 1097–1105 (2018)
9. Gao, Y., Zhou, M., Metaxas, D.: UTnet: a hybrid transformer architecture for medical image segmentation. arXiv preprint arXiv:2107.00781 (2021)
10. Idelbayev, Y., Carreira-Perpinán, M.A.: Low-rank compression of neural nets: learning the rank of each layer. In: CVPR, pp. 8049–8059 (2020)
11. Kingma, D.P., Ba, J.: Adam: a method for stochastic optimization. arXiv preprint arXiv:1412.6980 (2014)
12. Li, C., Wang, L.V.: Photoacoustic tomography and sensing in biomedicine. Phys. Med. Biol. **54**(19), R59 (2009)
13. Li, H., Fan, Y.: Non-rigid image registration using fully convolutional networks with deep self-supervision. arXiv preprint arXiv:1709.00799 (2017)
14. Mok, T.C.W., Chung, A.C.S.: Conditional deformable image registration with convolutional neural network. In: de Bruijne, M., et al. (eds.) MICCAI 2021. LNCS, vol. 12904, pp. 35–45. Springer, Cham (2021). https://doi.org/10.1007/978-3-030-87202-1_4
15. Paszke, A., et al.: Pytorch: an imperative style, high-performance deep learning library. In: NeurIPS, pp. 8026–8037 (2019)
16. Peng, Y., Ganesh, A., Wright, J., Xu, W., Ma, Y.: RASL: robust alignment by sparse and low-rank decomposition for linearly correlated images. IEEE Trans. Pattern Anal. Mach. Intell. **34**(11), 2233–2246 (2012)
17. Petit, O., Thome, N., Rambour, C., Soler, L.: U-net transformer: self and cross attention for medical image segmentation. arXiv preprint arXiv:2103.06104 (2021)
18. Ronneberger, O., Fischer, P., Brox, T.: U-net: convolutional networks for biomedical image segmentation. In: Navab, N., Hornegger, J., Wells, W.M., Frangi, A.F. (eds.) MICCAI 2015. LNCS, vol. 9351, pp. 234–241. Springer, Cham (2015). https://doi.org/10.1007/978-3-319-24574-4_28
19. Shu, Y., Wang, H., Xiao, B., Bi, X., Li, W.: Medical image registration based on uncoupled learning and accumulative enhancement. In: de Bruijne, M., et al. (eds.) MICCAI 2021. LNCS, vol. 12904, pp. 3–13. Springer, Cham (2021). https://doi.org/10.1007/978-3-030-87202-1_1
20. Sotiras, A., Davatzikos, C., Paragios, N.: Deformable medical image registration: a survey. IEEE Trans. Med. Imaging **32**(7), 1153–1190 (2013)
21. Townsend, J.: Differentiating the singular value decomposition. Technical report (2016). https://j-towns.github.io/papers/svd-derivative.pdf
22. Treeby, B.E., Cox, B.T.: k-Wave: MATLAB toolbox for the simulation and reconstruction of photoacoustic wave fields. J. Biomed. Optics **15**(2), 1–12 (2010)
23. Vaswani, A.,et al.: Attention is all you need. arXiv preprint arXiv:1706.03762 (2017)
24. de Vos, B.D., Berendsen, F.F., Viergever, M.A., Sokooti, H., Staring, M., Išgum, I.: A deep learning framework for unsupervised affine and deformable image registration. Med. Image Anal. **52**, 128–143 (2019)

25. de Vos, B.D., Berendsen, F.F., Viergever, M.A., Staring, M., Išgum, I.: End-to-end unsupervised deformable image registration with a convolutional neural network. In: Cardoso, M.J., et al. (eds.) DLMIA/ML-CDS -2017. LNCS, vol. 10553, pp. 204–212. Springer, Cham (2017). https://doi.org/10.1007/978-3-319-67558-9_24

26. Wu, Y., Shen, B., Ling, H.: Online robust image alignment via iterative convex optimization. In: 2012 IEEE Conference on Computer Vision and Pattern Recognition, pp. 1808–1814. IEEE (2012)

27. Yu, X., Liu, T., Wang, X., Tao, D.: On compressing deep models by low rank and sparse decomposition. In: CVPR, pp. 7370–7379 (2017)

28. Zhao, S., et al.: Recursive cascaded networks for unsupervised medical image registration. In: ICCV, pp. 10600–10610 (2019)

Transformer Lesion Tracker

Wen Tang[1], Han Kang[1], Haoyue Zhang[1,2], Pengxin Yu[1], Corey W. Arnold[2], and Rongguo Zhang[1(✉)]

[1] InferVision Medical Technology Co., Ltd., Beijing, China
zrongguo@infervision.com
[2] Computational Diagnostic Lab, UCLA, Los Angeles, USA

Abstract. Evaluating lesion progression and treatment response via longitudinal lesion tracking plays a critical role in clinical practice. Automated approaches for this task are motivated by prohibitive labor costs and time consumption when lesion matching is done manually. Previous methods typically lack the integration of local and global information. In this work, we propose a transformer-based approach, termed Transformer Lesion Tracker (TLT). Specifically, we design a Cross Attention-based Transformer (CAT) to capture and combine both global and local information to enhance feature extraction. We also develop a Registration-based Anatomical Attention Module (RAAM) to introduce anatomical information to CAT so that it can focus on useful feature knowledge. A Sparse Selection Strategy (SSS) is presented for selecting features and reducing memory footprint in Transformer training. In addition, we use a global regression to further improve model performance. We conduct experiments on a public dataset to show the superiority of our method and find that our model performance has improved the average Euclidean center error by at least 14.3% (6 mm vs. 7 mm) compared with the state-of-the-art (SOTA). Code is available at https://github.com/TangWen920812/TLT.

Keywords: Transformer · Cross attention · Registration

1 Introduction

The ability to accurately locate the location of follow-up lesions and subsequent quantitative assessment, referred to as "lesion tracking," is crucial to a variety of medical applications, in particular, cancer management. In practice, physicians need to spend significant time and effort to precisely match the same lesion across different time points. Thus, its investigation into a fully automated method of lesion tracking or lesion matching is highly desirable. However, compared with a large number of studies on lesion segmentation and detection [19,22], there are very few studies on lesion tracking [4,11]. In the field of natural images, there is a similar problem called target tracking or object tracking, for which several deep

Supplementary Information The online version contains supplementary material available at https://doi.org/10.1007/978-3-031-16446-0_19.

learning-based methods have been proposed [3,12,23]. One of the simplest and most straightforward ideas is to apply these existing methods to lesion tracking tasks. However, lesion tracking is different from the aforementioned visual tracking in a number of aspects: (1) Medical imaging data are mostly in 3D format. (2) The lesion size varies at different time points, such as increasing, shrinking, or stabilizing. (3) The appearance of the lesion may change during the follow-up examination while its anatomical location remains unchanged. Thus, an effective lesion tracker should account for the differences in the lesion itself and be able to use anatomical information effectively. However, existing registration-based trackers [18,21] are not robust for small-sized lesions or heavily deformed lesions due to lack of sensitivity to local details, and Siamese networks [9,12] overlook the information around the lesion. Cai et al. [4] first provided an open-source dataset for lesion tracking and designed Deep Lesion Tracker (DLT), which combines the advantages of both strategies and obtained a baseline on this dataset. Although a large kernel size is extracted in cross correlation layers of DLT to encode the global image context, it is still susceptible to the inductive bias in convolution, leading to deviation in the aggregation of information around the lesion.

In this work, we leverage Transformer architecture, inspired by TransT [7], to replace existing cross correlation, and propose a novel Transformer Lesion Tracking framework (named TLT) using 3D features. To achieve our model, we design a Cross Attention-based Transformer (CAT) to capture global information. To better focus on useful features, we also introduce anatomical priors via the proposed Registration-based Anatomical Attention Module (RAAM) into CAT. Meanwhile, considering the memory cost in training process, we present a Sparse Selection Strategy (SSS) to extract the local effective information from the whole template image as input for CAT. In addition, we use a global regression as output to reduce the effect of insufficient multi-scale information and accelerate convergence. The experimental results show that the proposed method achieves better performance on the open-source dataset compared with the state-of-the-art methods.

2   Related Work

Registration-Based Trackers. The anatomy presented in a patient's medical images at different time points should be similar in the absence of surgery or similar treatment. Thus, lesion tracker should follow a spatial consistency that the tissue or the structure around a lesion, and the organ in which the lesion is located will not change significantly. Under this assumption, existing registration methods, such as Voxelmorph [1], provide solutions for lesion tracking. Since registration algorithms [10,15] focus on alignment or optimization on global structures, registration-based lesion trackers achieve decent performance for large-sized lesions or relatively stable lesions [18,21]. Still, due to the lack of sensitivity of registration algorithms to image details, these registration-based methods obtain reduced performance when dealing with small-sized lesions or heavily deformed lesions. In this study, we treat image registration as an auxiliary operation, thereby improving model training efficiency as well as performance. Specifically, we select the mask registered via an affine registration method [15] as the prior attention and introduce it into the Transformer. The subsequent ablation experiment results demonstrate the effectiveness of this operation.

Siamese Networks. In recent years, Siamese-based methods have been popular in the field of visual object tracking. SiamFC [2], and its variants such as SiamRPN [13] and SiamRPN++ [12], are among the representative works. Subsequently, existing studies have demonstrated that lesion tracking could also be done using Siamese-based methods. Gomariz et al. [9] and Liu et al. [14] applied 2D Siamese networks for lesion tracking in ultrasound sequences. Whereas Rafael-Palou et al. [17] performed 3D Siamese networks to track lung nodules on CT series. Cai et al. [4] followed SiamRPN++ to use 3D Siamese networks to conduct universal lesion tracking in whole body CT images. These Siamese-based methods mainly consist of two parts: a backbone network for feature extraction and a correlation module to calculate the similarity between the template patch and the searching sub-region. However, such module is susceptible to the inductive bias of convolution operation and fails to fully utilize the global context, leading to local optimum in the optimization process. Thus, we introduce an attention-based Transformer architecture to focus on the key object in the global feature space, while replacing the correlation part.

Transformer-Based Tracking. In recent years, Transformer architecture [24] has taken over recurrent neural networks in natural language processing [8,20], and has also had an impact on the status of convolutional neural networks in computer vision [6,16]. More recently, Chen et al. [7] proposed a target tracking method on natural images with Transformer architecture instead of the cross correlation layers and achieved SOTA results. However, several issues remain to be addressed when applying Transformer to lesion tracking on 3D medical images. Specifically, to reduce memory cost and acquire features of different sized lesion adaptively, we design a sparse selection strategy to extract irregular patches from template feature maps as input to Transformer. To introduce prior anatomical structure information to Transformer, we create a registration-based attention guidance for auxiliary model training.

3   Method

Problem Description. Same as object tracking [2], lesion tracking aims to find its corresponding position in the searching image I_s when given a lesion in the template image I_t. Similar to [4], we simplify this task: given a lesion l in I_t with its known center c_t and radius r_t, we seek a mapping function $\mathcal{F}$ to predict the center c_s of l in I_s.

Overview. In this lesion tracking task, we define the baseline CT scan as the template image $I_t \in \mathbb{R}^{D_{t0} \times H_{t0} \times W_{t0}}$, and a corresponding follow-up CT scan as the searching image $I_s \in \mathbb{R}^{D_{s0} \times H_{s0} \times W_{s0}}$. D_{t0}, H_{t0} and W_{t0} represent the depth, height and width of the template image, respectively. And D_{s0}, H_{s0} and W_{s0} are similarly defined for searching image. The proposed lesion tracking network (TLT) mainly consists of three components, as shown in Fig. 1. The feature extractor stacks 3D convolution and downsampling layers to efficiently represent the input volumes. The proposed sparse selection strategy is used for memory reducing and efficient feature acquisition. Then, the cross attention-based Transformer (CAT) is used to fuse the features of the searching and the selected template. In the CAT, a mask gained from the registration-based anatomical attention module (RAAM) is inserted to enhance fused features. Finally, the center predictor is responsible for getting the result from the output of Transformer.

3.1 Feature Extractor and Sparse Selection Strategy

In the proposed network, a modified 3D ResNet18 with shared weights is employed as the feature extractor. Compared with the original one, we remove the last stage of ResNet18, and take outputs of the fourth stage as final outputs. We also adjust the stride of the first convolutional layer from $2 \times 2 \times 2$ to $1 \times 1 \times 1$ to obtain a larger feature resolution. Considering the parameter redundancy and overfitting in 3D networks, the number of feature channels in each stage is reduced by half or more (see Fig. 1). Putting I_t and I_s through the learnable feature extractor respectively, their own image features $F_{t,ori} \in \mathbb{R}^{C \times D_t \times H_t \times W_t}$, $F_{s,ori} \in \mathbb{R}^{C \times D_s \times H_s \times W_s}$ are obtained for subsequent processes, where $D_t, H_t, W_t = \frac{D_{t0}}{8}, \frac{H_{t0}}{8}, \frac{W_{t0}}{8}$, $D_s, H_s, W_s = \frac{D_{s0}}{8}, \frac{H_{s0}}{8}, \frac{W_{s0}}{8}$, $C = 192$.

As shown in Fig. 1(a), template-based feature mining via the proposed sparse selection strategy (SSS) precede the CTA to select features and to reduce memory cost. This is feasible because the location of the lesion in the template input I_t is known, and we believe the features $F_{t,ori}$ to have already incorporated local contextual information. The following are the details of the SSS flow. Given a lesion in the template image, we first generate a three-dimensional Gaussian map G based on the known center and radius of the lesion, which is formulated by:

$$G(c,r) = exp(-\frac{\sum_{i \in (x,y,z)}(i - c^i)^2}{\sum_{i \in (x,y,z)}(2r^i)^2}) \tag{1}$$

Specifically, for the lesion l in I_t with its center c_t and radius r_t, the generated Gaussian map G_t is $G_t(c_t, r_t)$. Next, we resize G_t to the size of $F_{t,ori}$ by trilinear interpolation, and obtain the resized Gaussian map $\widetilde{G}_t$. Selecting a threshold Tr and using $\widetilde{G}_t$ as a reference mask, we extract valid features $F_{t,sparse}$ from the $F_{t,ori}$ as an input of the Transformer: $F_{t,sparse} = F_{t,ori}(x,y,z|\widetilde{G}_t(x,y,z) > Tr)$

3.2 Cross Attention-Based Transformer

Unlike the similarity-based correlation module used in the previous Siamese-based networks, we design a Cross Attention-based Transformer (CAT) to combine global and local context. Queries Q, keys K and values V are encoded from same source in Transformer [24]. But in CAT, to grab global context and blend multiple features of different sizes, we adopt cross-attention (CA), in which K, V

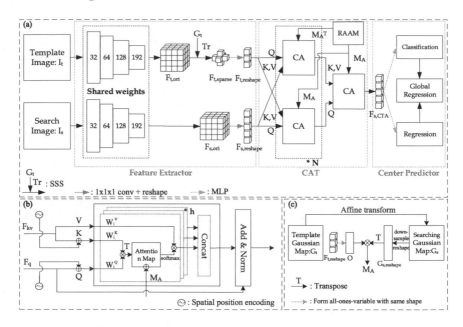

Fig. 1. (a) Overall structure of the proposed network. (b) Cross attention in CAT. (c) Structure of RAAM

are stemmed from the same input while Q from another. In TLT, we put a CA on each of the template and searching path respectively (see Fig 1(a)). In CA of the template line, K and V are encoded from the reshaped $F_{s,ori}$: $F_{s,reshape} \in \mathbb{R}^{D_s H_s W_s \times C}$ and Q is encoded from the reshaped $F_{t,sparse}$: $F_{t,reshape} \in \mathbb{R}^{L \times C}$, $L = \text{len}(F_{t,sparse})$. While in CA of the searching line, K, V and Q have the opposite origins to those in the template one. In short, as shown in Fig. 1(b), Q is encoded from the features which need enhancement (F_q), and K, V are encoded from the other (F_{kv}). We apply CA on each lines for $N(N = 3)$ times, and use another CA on searching line to obtain the final output features: $F_{s,\text{CTA}}$.

We further create a novel structure called Registration-based Anatomical Attention Module (RAAM) to calculate an anatomical information mask M_A, whose transpose is taken as M_A^T (see Fig. 1(c)). As described above, the anatomical information is needed for lesion tracking. Thus, we create a matrix to provide the anatomical information for each of template and searching side. For template side, we assume all the voxels in $F_{t,reshape}$ are of the same importance, and we build a matrix $O \in \mathbb{R}^{L \times 1}$, in which all elements are 1. For searching side, we first use an affine registration method [15] to roughly align I_t and I_s by solving: $\mathcal{T}_{\text{Aff}} = \arg\min||\mathcal{T}_{\text{Aff}}(I_t) - I_s||_1$. We choose to use an affine registration method instead a non-rigid one because the non-rigid registration is slow and provides restriction to the attention that limit the model's ability to learn for local variation and details. Then, we can obtain a registration-based Gaussian map $G_s = \mathcal{T}_{\text{Aff}}(G_t)$. Afterwards, we downsample G_s to the size of $F_{s,ori}$ and reshape it to $G_{s,reshape} \in \mathbb{R}^{D_s H_s W_s \times 1}$, which is defined as the matrix of searching side. Finally, M_A can be calculated by the following formula:

$$M_A = O \otimes G_{s,reshape}^{\mathrm{T}} \tag{2}$$

where $\otimes$ is matrix multiplication operation, and $M_A \in \mathbb{R}^{L \times D_s H_s W_s}$. So the attention we use in CAT at each head (see Fig. 1(b)) can be define as following:

$$\text{Attention}_i(Q, K, V) = \text{softmax}(\frac{(QW_i^Q)(KW_i^K)^{\mathrm{T}}}{\sqrt{d_k}} + M_A)(VW_i^V), \tag{3}$$

where W_i^Q, W_i^K, W_i^V are parameter matrices, d_k is the dimension of key, $i \in \{1, ..., h\}$ is the index of head and h is the number of heads in multiple head attention.

3.3   Center Predictor and Training Loss

Similar to the head of detection networks, our center predictor consists of a classification branch and a regression branch, where each branch is a multilayer perceptron (MLP). The classification head is to classify if a voxel from the output is inside of a lesion, and the regression head is to regress the exact center position. In detail, after inputting the features $F_{s,\text{CTA}}$, the predictor outputs the classification results $\hat{Y} \in \mathbb{R}^{1 \times D_s H_s W_s}$ and center coordinates $\hat{C} \in \mathbb{R}^{3 \times D_s H_s W_s}$. During training, we define the ground truth as a Gaussian map generated by Eq. 1 with the target center c_s and the corresponding radius r_s. We downsample it to obtain the Gaussian label G_L which matches the size of $\hat{Y}$, and obtain label $Y = \frac{G_L - min(G_L)}{max(G_L) - min(G_L)}$. L1 loss is used as the regression loss, which is formulated as:

$$L_r = ||\hat{c} - c_s||_1, \ \hat{c} = \sum \text{softmax}(\hat{Y}) * \hat{C} \tag{4}$$

where $\hat{c}$ is the final output of the center predictor, which we define as global regression. Meanwhile, a focal loss [4] is used as the classification loss for auxiliary training:

$$L_c = \sum_i \begin{cases} (1 - \hat{y}_i)^\alpha \log(\hat{y}_i) & \text{if } y_i = 1 \\ (1 - y_i)^\beta (\hat{y}_i)^\alpha \log(1 - \hat{y}_i) & \text{otherwise} \end{cases} \tag{5}$$

where y_i and $\hat{y}_i$ are the i-th elements in Y and $\hat{Y}$, respectively, and $\alpha = \beta = 2$.

4   Experiments and Experimental Results

4.1   Dataset and Experiment Setup

Dataset. We validate our method on a public dataset, DLS [4], which consists of CT image pairs inherited from DeepLesion [27]. There are 3008, 403 and 480 lesion pairs for training, validation, and testing in this dataset, respectively.

Table 1. Lesion tracking comparison on Deep Lesion Tracking testing dataset. * represents the p value of paired t-test is smaller than 0.05.

Method	CPM@ 10 mm	CPM@ Radius	MED_X (mm)	MED_Y (mm)	MED_Z (mm)	MED (mm)
Affine [15]	48.33	65.21	4.1 ± 5.0	5.4 ± 5.6	7.1 ± 8.3	11.2 ± 9.9
VoxelMorph [1]	49.90	65.59	4.6 ± 6.7	5.2 ± 7.9	6.6 ± 6.2	10.9 ± 10.9
LENS-LesioGraph [25, 28]	63.85	80.42	$\mathbf{2.6 \pm 4.6}$	2.7 ± 4.5	6.0 ± 8.6	8.0 ± 10.1
VULD-LesionGraph [5, 28]	64.69	76.56	3.5 ± 5.2	4.1 ± 5.8	6.1 ± 8.8	9.3 ± 10.9
VULD-LesaNet [5, 26]	65.00	77.81	3.5 ± 5.3	4.0 ± 5.7	6.0 ± 8.7	9.1 ± 10.8
SiamRPN++ [12]	68.85	80.31	3.8 ± 4.8	3.8 ± 4.8	4.8 ± 7.5	8.3 ± 9.2
LENS-LesaNet [25, 26]	70.00	84.58	2.7 ± 4.8	$\mathbf{2.6 \pm 4.7}$	5.7 ± 8.6	7.8 ± 10.3
DEEDS [10]	71.88	85.52	2.8 ± 3.7	3.1 ± 4.1	5.0 ± 6.8	7.4 ± 8.1
DLT-Mix [4]	78.65	88.75	3.1 ± 4.4	3.1 ± 4.5	4.2 ± 7.6	7.1 ± 9.2
DLT [4]	78.85	86.88	3.5 ± 5.6	2.9 ± 4.9	4.0 ± 6.1	7.0 ± 8.9
TransT [7]	79.59	88.99	3.4 ± 5.9	5.4 ± 6.1	1.8 ± 2.2	7.6 ± 7.9
TLT	$\mathbf{87.37^*}$	$\mathbf{95.32^*}$	3.0 ± 6.2	3.7 ± 5.2	$\mathbf{1.7 \pm 2.1}$	$\mathbf{6.0 \pm 7.7^*}$

Since the ground truth lesion center of all lesions in this dataset and the corresponding radius are defined, we could mutually track within a lesion pair. Therefore, a total of 906 and 960 directed lesion pairs are used for evaluation in validation and testing sets, respectively.

Evaluation Metrics. The center point matching (CPM) accuracy is selected to evaluate the performance of lesion matching. As defined in [4], a match will be counted correct when the Euclidean distance between ground truth and predicted centers is smaller than a threshold (@10 mm: $\min(10\,\text{mm}, r_s)$, @Radius: r_s). The mean Euclidean distance (MED) in mm $+/-$ standard deviation between ground truth and predicted centers, and its projections in each direction (denoted as MED_X, MED_Y and MED_Z, respectively) [4] are also used for model evaluation.

Implementation Details. The proposed method is implemented using PyTorch (v1.5.1). The network is optimized by Adam with initial learning rate of 0.0001 and trained for 300 epochs. The batch size is 4 and the number of parameters of the model is 5.98M. All CT volumes have been resampled to the isotropic resolution of 1 mm before feeding into the network. This training setting is used in all deep learning-based methods selected for comparison. For the affine registration method [15] and DEEDS [10], following the setting of [4] and [10], all CT volumes are resampled to an isotropic resolution of 2 mm.

4.2 Experimental Results and Discussion

Model Comparison. We took TransT [7] as baseline, and selected DLT and other state-of-the-art approaches in [4] for comparison. Table 1 shows the quantitative results of these methods. Our method yields a CPM@10 mm of 87.37, a CPM@*Radius* of 95.32, and a MED of 6.0 ± 7.7, which outperforms all the

Table 2. Ablation study on each module and different thresholds. * represents the p value of paired t-test is smaller than 0.05.

SSS	RAAM	Global Regressor	CPM@ 10 mm	MED (mm)	Threshold	CPM@10 mm	MED(mm)
					0.9	83.57	6.80 ± 8.12
					0.8	83.99	6.65 ± 7.99
			79.59	7.58 ± 7.91	0.7	**87.37***	**5.98 ± 7.68***
✓			84.78	6.76 ± 7.86	0.6	86.70	6.26 ± 7.88
✓	✓		86.58	6.30 ± 7.79	0.5	86.37	6.20 ± 7.83
✓	✓	✓	**87.37***	**5.98 ± 7.68***	0.4	85.01	6.39 ± 7.98

compared methods in terms of both CPM and MED metrics. A paired t-test is used on CPM@10 mm, CPM@$Radius$ and MED to perform statistical tests. Moreover, we observe that transformer-based methods, TransT and our TLT, both achieving large improvements in terms of MED$_Z$ compared with methods that use convolution to compute similarity. This may be because the Transformer focuses more on the information in the z-axis direction, which is also consistent with physician cognition.

Ablation Study. To evaluate the effectiveness of various configurations in our proposed method, we conduct ablation experiments from two aspects: module setting and threshold setting. A paired t-test is also used for statistical tests. Table 2 shows the experimental results. The results show that accuracy drops with each module change, which validates the competence of our proposed method. Meanwhile, it is observed that the threshold of 0.7 is much better than that of other thresholds. Therefore, we choose 0.7 as the thresholds Tr in our TLT.

Discussion. As we observe, in ablation study, the SSS module leads to the biggest improvement. To verify this, we also perform ablation study with only one single module removed, as shown in Table 1 in supplementary materials. This happens when there are many small lesions in the dataset, such as lung nodules. If these small lesions are cropped on the original image, due to downsampling, the feature map will become very small, and in the last several downsampling processes will always become one voxel, which could lead to a decline in performance. The SSS solves this problem by selecting voxels on the last feature map. Even if only one voxel on the feature map is selected, this voxel can still obtain more surrounding information in the networks than without SSS. Meanwhile, based on our observations, we found that when the registration method failed, sometimes our model would fail as well. This is because we use registration to feed anatomical information to the transformer, and anatomical information helps the transformer accelerate convergence, which forms a dependency. In addition, when there are similar lesions in similar locations, such as two solid nodules at the edge of the right upper lung, and only a few layers difference in the z-axis direction, the model will also be confused.

5   Conclusion

This paper presents a novel Transformer-based framework for lesion tracking by leveraging both the anatomical prior and the cross image relevance. We further introduce a global regression to integrate multi-scale information while using sparse selection strategy to reduce memory consumption. TLT achieves the state-of-the-art performance on DLT dataset, significantly exceeding previous methods in lesion tacking accuracy. Future work includes multi-institutional validation and reader studies to examine the efficiency improvement for physicians in clinical setting.

Acknowledgment. This work was funded by Science and Technology Innovation 2030-New Generation Artificial Intelligence Major Project (2021ZD0111104).

References

1. Balakrishnan, G., Zhao, A., Sabuncu, M.R., Guttag, J., Dalca, A.V.: An unsupervised learning model for deformable medical image registration. In: Proceedings of the IEEE Conference on Computer Vision and Pattern Recognition, pp. 9252–9260 (2018)
2. Bertinetto, L., Valmadre, J., Henriques, J.F., Vedaldi, A., Torr, P.H.S.: Fully-convolutional Siamese networks for object tracking. In: Hua, G., Jégou, H. (eds.) ECCV 2016. LNCS, vol. 9914, pp. 850–865. Springer, Cham (2016). https://doi.org/10.1007/978-3-319-48881-3_56
3. Bolme, D.S., Beveridge, J.R., Draper, B.A., Lui, Y.M.: Visual object tracking using adaptive correlation filters. In: 2010 IEEE Computer Society Conference on Computer Vision And Pattern Recognition, pp. 2544–2550. IEEE (2010)
4. Cai, J., et al.: Deep lesion tracker: monitoring lesions in 4d longitudinal imaging studies. In: Proceedings of the IEEE/CVF Conference on Computer Vision and Pattern Recognition, pp. 15159–15169 (2021)
5. Cai, J., et al.: Deep volumetric universal lesion detection using light-weight pseudo 3D convolution and surface point regression. In: Martel, A.L., et al. (eds.) MICCAI 2020. LNCS, vol. 12264, pp. 3–13. Springer, Cham (2020). https://doi.org/10.1007/978-3-030-59719-1_1
6. Carion, N., Massa, F., Synnaeve, G., Usunier, N., Kirillov, A., Zagoruyko, S.: End-to-end object detection with transformers. In: Vedaldi, A., Bischof, H., Brox, T., Frahm, J.-M. (eds.) ECCV 2020. LNCS, vol. 12346, pp. 213–229. Springer, Cham (2020). https://doi.org/10.1007/978-3-030-58452-8_13
7. Chen, X., Yan, B., Zhu, J., Wang, D., Yang, X., Lu, H.: Transformer tracking. In: Proceedings of the IEEE/CVF Conference on Computer Vision and Pattern Recognition, pp. 8126–8135 (2021)
8. Devlin, J., Chang, M.W., Lee, K., Toutanova, K.: BERT: pre-training of deep bidirectional transformers for language understanding. arXiv preprint arXiv:1810.04805 (2018)
9. Gomariz, A., Li, W., Ozkan, E., Tanner, C., Goksel, O.: Siamese networks with location prior for landmark tracking in liver ultrasound sequences. In: 2019 IEEE 16th International Symposium on Biomedical Imaging (ISBI 2019), pp. 1757–1760. IEEE (2019)

10. Heinrich, M.P., Jenkinson, M., Brady, M., Schnabel, J.A.: MRF-based deformable registration and ventilation estimation of lung CT. IEEE Trans. Med. Imaging **32**(7), 1239–1248 (2013)
11. Hering, A., et al.: Whole-body soft-tissue lesion tracking and segmentation in longitudinal CT imaging studies. In: Medical Imaging with Deep Learning, pp. 312–326. PMLR (2021)
12. Li, B., et al.: Evolution of Siamese visual tracking with very deep networks. In: Proceedings of the IEEE Conference on Computer Vision and Pattern Recognition, Long Beach, CA, USA, pp. 16–20 (2019)
13. Li, B., Yan, J., Wu, W., Zhu, Z., Hu, X.: High performance visual tracking with Siamese region proposal network. In: Proceedings of the IEEE Conference on Computer Vision and Pattern Recognition, pp. 8971–8980 (2018)
14. Liu, F., Liu, D., Tian, J., Xie, X., Yang, X., Wang, K.: Cascaded one-shot deformable convolutional neural networks: developing a deep learning model for respiratory motion estimation in ultrasound sequences. Med. Image Anal. **65**, 101793 (2020)
15. Marstal, K., Berendsen, F., Staring, M., Klein, S.: Simpleelastix: a user-friendly, multi-lingual library for medical image registration. In: Proceedings of the IEEE Conference on Computer Vision and Pattern Recognition Workshops, pp. 134–142 (2016)
16. Parmar, N., et al.: Image transformer. In: International Conference on Machine Learning, pp. 4055–4064. PMLR (2018)
17. Rafael-Palou, X., et al.: Re-identification and growth detection of pulmonary nodules without image registration using 3d Siamese neural networks. Med. Image Anal. **67**, 101823 (2021)
18. Raju, A., et al.: Co-heterogeneous and adaptive segmentation from multi-source and multi-phase CT imaging data: a study on pathological liver and lesion segmentation. In: Vedaldi, A., Bischof, H., Brox, T., Frahm, J.-M. (eds.) ECCV 2020. LNCS, vol. 12368, pp. 448–465. Springer, Cham (2020). https://doi.org/10.1007/978-3-030-58592-1_27
19. Shao, Q., Gong, L., Ma, K., Liu, H., Zheng, Y.: Attentive CT lesion detection using deep pyramid inference with multi-scale booster. In: Shen, D., et al. (eds.) MICCAI 2019. LNCS, vol. 11769, pp. 301–309. Springer, Cham (2019). https://doi.org/10.1007/978-3-030-32226-7_34
20. Synnaeve, G., et al.: End-to-end ASR: from supervised to semi-supervised learning with modern architectures. arXiv preprint arXiv:1911.08460 (2019)
21. Tan, M., et al.: A new approach to evaluate drug treatment response of ovarian cancer patients based on deformable image registration. IEEE Trans. Med. Imaging **35**(1), 316–325 (2015)
22. Tang, W., et al.: M-SEAM-NAM: multi-instance self-supervised equivalent attention mechanism with neighborhood affinity module for double weakly supervised segmentation of COVID-19. In: de Bruijne, M., et al. (eds.) MICCAI 2021. LNCS, vol. 12907, pp. 262–272. Springer, Cham (2021). https://doi.org/10.1007/978-3-030-87234-2_25
23. Teed, Z., Deng, J.: RAFT: recurrent all-pairs field transforms for optical flow. In: Vedaldi, A., Bischof, H., Brox, T., Frahm, J.-M. (eds.) ECCV 2020. LNCS, vol. 12347, pp. 402–419. Springer, Cham (2020). https://doi.org/10.1007/978-3-030-58536-5_24
24. Vaswani, A., et al.: Attention is all you need. Adv. Neural Inf. Process. Syst. **30**, 1–7 (2017)

25. Yan, K., et al.: Learning from multiple datasets with heterogeneous and partial labels for universal lesion detection in CT. IEEE Trans. Med. Imaging **40**(10), 2759–2770 (2020)
26. Yan, K., Peng, Y., Sandfort, V., Bagheri, M., Lu, Z., Summers, R.M.: Holistic and comprehensive annotation of clinically significant findings on diverse CT images: learning from radiology reports and label ontology. In: Proceedings of the IEEE/CVF Conference on Computer Vision and Pattern Recognition, pp. 8523–8532 (2019)
27. Yan, K., Wang, X., Lu, L., Summers, R.M.: DeepLesion: automated mining of large-scale lesion annotations and universal lesion detection with deep learning. J. Med. Imaging **5**(3), 036501 (2018)
28. Yan, K., et al.: Deep lesion graphs in the wild: relationship learning and organization of significant radiology image findings in a diverse large-scale lesion database. In: Proceedings of the IEEE Conference on Computer Vision and Pattern Recognition, pp. 9261–9270 (2018)

LiftReg: Limited Angle 2D/3D Deformable Registration

Lin Tian[1]([⊠]), Yueh Z. Lee[2], Raúl San José Estépar[3], and Marc Niethammer[1]

[1] Department of Computer Science, University of North Carolina at Chapel Hill, Chapel Hill, USA
lintian@cs.unc.edu
[2] Department of Radiology, University of North Carolina at Chapel Hill, Chapel Hill, USA
[3] Harvard Medical School, Boston, USA

Abstract. We propose LiftReg, a 2D/3D deformable registration approach. LiftReg is a deep registration framework which is trained using sets of digitally reconstructed radiographs (DRR) and computed tomography (CT) image pairs. By using simulated training data, LiftReg can use a high-quality CT-CT image similarity measure, which helps the network to learn a high-quality deformation space. To further improve registration quality and to address the inherent depth ambiguities of very limited angle acquisitions, we propose to use features extracted from the backprojected 2D images and a statistical deformation model. We test our approach on the DirLab lung registration dataset and show that it outperforms an existing learning-based pairwise registration approach.

Keywords: Registration · Lung · Limited angle · Deep learning

1 Introduction

The goal of 2D/3D medical image registration is to estimate a spatial transformation between a patient's 3D image volume and one or multiple 2D images under patient deformation. It is widely used in radiation therapy and for image-guided interventional procedures to obtain patient motion, e.g., to compute dose accumulation for multi-fraction radiotherapy, or device locations [5]. In such applications, Computed Tomography (CT) is a commonly used 3D imaging modality and radiographs are generally adopted to obtain 2D projection images because of their comparatively low radiation dose and fast acquisition speed [8]. In practice, only a limited number of radiographs can be acquired, typically within a limited angle range, resulting in a lack of spatial information in the projection direction and in consequence in spatial ambiguities. Large non-rigid motions (e.g., between lung inspiration/expiration) make registration in this setting particularly challenging.

Supplementary Information The online version contains supplementary material available at https://doi.org/10.1007/978-3-031-16446-0_20.

L. Wang et al. (Eds.): MICCAI 2022, LNCS 13436, pp. 207–216, 2022.
https://doi.org/10.1007/978-3-031-16446-0_20

The conventional approach for 2D/3D deformable image registration (DIR) is to numerically solve an optimization problem to determine the transformation parameters which best explain the deformation between a CT image and a corresponding set of 2D radiographs [2,11,16,19]. Image similarity is assessed between the 2D radiographs and the respective simulated CT projections, i.e., the digitally reconstructed radiographs (DRR) [14]. However, given very limited angle radiograph acquisitions, assessing image similarity in such a way is susceptible to spatial ambiguity due to the lack of spatial information in the projection direction.

Compared to the optimization-based 2D/3D DIR methods, current learning-based approaches replace optimization by prediction at test-time and and can therefore significantly reduce registration runtime [3,7,10,17]. Zhang [17] proposes 2D3D-regnet which uses a U-Net as the backbone network and directly predicts deformation vector fields (DVF) given a CT image and a set of radiographs. Evaluation is on a lung dataset [18] with small deformations (mean landmark distances of 6.5 mm) and results in a mean target registration error (mTRE) of 4.3 mm after registration for a scanning angle of 30°. This work computes the similarity loss in 2D space, thus it faces the aforementioned spatial ambiguity issues. Other work [7,10] leverages prior information during training to restrict deformations to a reasonable transformation space. Specifically, this stream of work proposes building a parametric deformation subspace with respect to an atlas image via principal component analysis (PCA) computed from a prior cohort of data from which deformation fields are extracted. Though greatly reducing the complexity of the problem, the spatial ambiguity issue of the 2D similarity measure is still not addressed. Foote et al. [3] build a subject-specific deformation subspace and train a subject-specific network with the ground truth coefficients computed from 3D image pairs of the same subject. While this approach does not suffer from the spatial ambiguity issue, the approach assumes that training data and test data come from the same patient and multiple 3D images of the same patient are available during training. Thus, the approach is not directly applicable to finding deformations between one CT image and a set of radiographs.

The critical question for 2D/3D DIR is then: what kind of information can we leverage to address the spatial ambiguity? One advantage of deep learning is that extra information can assist the learning without changing the problem setting during inference. Thus, leveraging precise 3D information in the loss function during training is expected to reduce spatial ambiguity while retaining generalizability at test time when 3D image pairs are not available. However, this information has not been used for the current existing methods. In addition, how much spatial information the features extracted from 2D images can convey also plays an important role. Compared to the 2D features adopted in [3,7,10], our network can extract 3D spatial information from a multi-channel backprojected volume. Moreover, we can further reduce the complexity brought by the spatial ambiguity and large freedom of transformation model via prior knowledge of the motion as used in the previously discussed atlas registration approaches.

We propose LiftReg for 2D/3D registration. Our contributions include:

1) We propose Lift3D, a module to backproject 2D images to 3D. We experimentally show that Lift3D helps improve 2D/3D registration performance.

2) We propose LiftReg, a pairwise 2D/3D learning based DIR framework which leverages the precise spatial information in DRR-CT pairs via a *3D* CT-CT similarity loss and by using a statistical deformation model for image motion.
3) We demonstrate that LiftReg outperforms an existing learning based 2D/3D pairwise DIR method [17] on the public DirLab lung dataset with a limited scanning angle of 30° for both coarse and fine structures (e.g. lung vessels).

2   Problem Formulation

Let the two images $I_s : \Omega_s \to \mathbb{R}$ and $I_t : \Omega_t \to \mathbb{R}$ defined in 3 dimensional space $\Omega \subset \mathbb{R}^3$ represent the source and target images and $\mathbf{P}_t = \{P_i | i = 1...N, P_i : \mathbb{R}^2 \to \mathbb{R}\}$ be the set of 2D projections of I_t. Our goal is to find the spatial mapping $\varphi : \Omega_s \to \Omega_t$ which makes the warped source image $I_s \circ \varphi^{-1}$ consistent with the projections $\mathbf{P}_t$. One non-parametric model for φ^{-1} is the deformation vector field (DVF), $u(x) : \Omega_t \to \mathbb{R}^3$, which captures the displacement between corresponding points in the target and source domains: $\varphi^{-1}(x) = x + u(x)$.

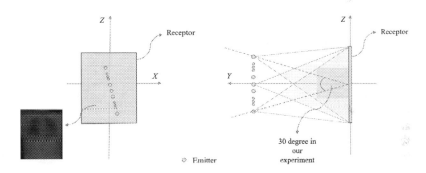

Fig. 1. $\mathbf{P}_t$ acquisition geometry [13]. Left: geometry in top-down view. Emitters are evenly distributed along a line which is not necessarily aligned with the axis of the receptor. Right: side view of the geometry where the patient is in between the emitters and the receptor. The emitters are activated consecutively to acquire $\mathbf{P}_t$.

The projections $\mathbf{P}_t$ can be acquired based on different geometries: e.g., parallel beam, fan beam and cone beam geometries [6]. In this work, we follow the stationary chest tomosynthesis (s-DCT) imaging geometry in [13] where several emitters are evenly placed along a line parallel to the receptor covering a limited angle. The receptor stays stationary while the emitters are activated consecutively to obtain the individual projections. Figure 1 shows the s-DCT geometry.

3   Method

3.1   PCA-Based Deformation Vector Field Subspace

Our first goal is to obtain a PCA-based 3D deformation model. To this end, we compute the gold standard DVFs, $u(x)$, of the training dataset of 3D CT image pairs (I_s, I_t) via an in-house trained 3D/3D deep registration network. Note that other deep registration networks could be used to obtain the gold standard DVFs. The in-house 3D/3D deep registration network is used only to obtain registrations fast. We use singular value decomposition on the displacement fields to obtain the eigenvectors $E = \{e_i | e_i \in \mathbb{R}^s, s = D \times H \times W \times 3, i = 1...N_e\}$ which explain 99% of the displacement field variance which form our parametric DVF subspace.

In contrast to atlas and group-wise registration [3,7,10] where the transformation model is defined in a common atlas space, in our case the transformation model DVF, $u(x)$, is defined in the target domain, Ω_t, which is different for each image pair (I_s, I_t). Hence, the deformation space needs to account for deformations within and across patients. To alleviate this issue we only focus on the deformation driven by the region of interest (ROI), namely the lung region. Specifically, we train the 3D/3D deep registration network guided by a similarity loss computed on the ROI only. Thus, it focuses the deformation prediction inside the lung. In addition, the images are processed so that the ROI is centered in the image volume. With the constructed subspace, the transformation model can be expressed as

$$\varphi^{-1}(x) = x + \bar{u} + \sum_{i=1}^{N_e} \alpha_i e_i \,, \tag{1}$$

where α_i are the basis coefficients, and $\bar{u}$ indicates the mean DVF.

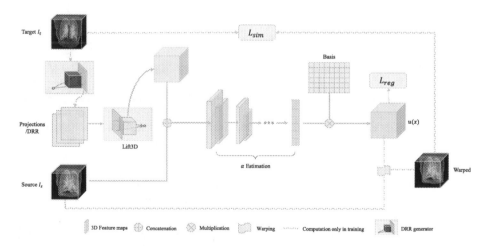

Fig. 2. Network structure for LiftReg. The network contains three modules: Lift3D, α estimation, and a warping module. Lift3D backprojects the 2D images to 3D space. α estimation contains several convolutional blocks and fully connect layers to predict the coefficients of the DVF subspace. The warping module warps the source image I_s based on the predicted $\varphi^{-1}(x)$. The computation graph for training is denoted as an orange dotted line. Learnable modules are shown in green. The 3D feature maps are drawn as 2D feature maps for simplicity. (Color figure online)

3.2 Network Structure

We use a convolutional neural network (CNN) $\mathcal{F}_\theta$ to predict the basis coefficients $\{\alpha_i\}$ given a 3D source image and a set of target projections $(I_s, \mathbf{P}_t)$: $\{\alpha_i\} = \mathcal{F}_\theta(I_s, \mathbf{P}_t)$. The network $\mathcal{F}_\theta$ contains three major modules: Lift3D, α estimation, and a warping module. The network first backprojects $\mathbf{P}_t$ to 3D space based on the associated geometry in which the $\mathbf{P}_t$ are acquired. The α estimation module takes as input the lifted 3D image and I_s to predict the $\{\alpha_i\}$. The corresponding transformation φ^{-1} is computed via Eq. (1). Figure 2 shows an overview of $\mathcal{F}_\theta$. Next, we introduce each module in detail.

Lift3D. Since the radiographs $\mathbf{P}_t$ are in 2D space, it is difficult to extract 3D information using a 2D feature extractor. Hence, we lift the 2D images to 3D image space. Specifically, we backproject the 2D images based on their associated emitter positions. For each pixel in P_i, there is a backprojection ray associated to its emitter position. We assign the intensity of the pixel in P_i to all the voxels along the ray. Thus, we obtain a set of 3D volumes $\{I_t^i | i = 0...N\}$. We then concatenate this set of 3D images into one N channel 3D volume of size of $D \times W \times H$. This approach has two benefits: (1) geometry information is now explicitly contained in the input to the network; (2) the visual differences across N lifted 3D volumes can provide visual 3D features for the following network modules. For practical purposes, we implement Lift3D using the following discretization approach. We transform the voxel position x in 3D to its corresponding pixel position in P_i and assign the interpolated intensity in P_i to x. Given the emitter positions $\{c_i = (c_i^0, c_i^1, c_i^2) | i = 0...N, c_i \in \mathbb{R}^3\}$, we construct the transformation matrix T to transform a 3D coordinate to a 2D homogeneous coordinate in the projection space, which is similar to the intrinsic matrix used in a pinhole camera model. Given T, we can compute the intensity at position $x \in \Omega_t$ as

$$I_t(x) = P_i(Tx), T = \begin{bmatrix} c_i^1 & 0 & c_i^0 \\ 0 & c_i^1 & c_i^2 \\ 0 & 0 & 1 \end{bmatrix} \tag{2}$$

where c_i^j is the jth component of emitter position c_i.

α **Estimation.** This module predicts the coefficients $\{\alpha_i\}$ given I_s and the lifted 3D volumes $\{I_t^i | i = 0, ...N\}$. We first concatenate $\{I_t^i | i = 0, ...N\}$ and I_s along the channel dimension. We then pass the concatenated multi-channel 3D volume to multiple layers of convolution blocks where each block contains one convolutional layer, one activation layer and a pooling layer. Lastly, we flatten out the feature maps and apply three fully connect layers to predict the $\{\alpha_i\}$. The detailed structure is described in the supplementary.

Warping Module. After obtaining $\{\alpha_i\}$, we compute the DVF via Eq. (1) and apply the transformation to I_s using a spatial transformer [4].

3.3 Network Training

Current learning-based 2D/3D DIR methods train their models using a CT/DRR dataset and 2D projection losses. They do not use the 3D volume associated with the DRRs. Instead, we use it to obtain precise 3D information available during training, but not needed at test time, to help network training.

We use two loss terms: a 3D similarity loss and a regularizer on the deformation field. The overall loss is

$$\mathcal{L} = \mathcal{L}_{sim} + \lambda\mathcal{L}_{reg}, \tag{3}$$

where $\lambda > 0$. We use Normalized Cross-correlation (NCC) as the similarity measure. To help the network focus on information within the lung ROI, we mask the lung region based on the pre-computed segmentation maps S_s and S_t (for I_s and I_t respectively) before computing the similarity loss. Specifically, the similarity loss is defined as

$$\mathcal{L}_{sim}(I_s, I_t, S_s, S_t) = 1 - NCC(I_t \odot S_t, (I_s \odot S_s) \circ \varphi^{-1}), \tag{4}$$

where $\odot$ denotes element-wise multiplication.

We use a diffusion regularizer [9] to encourage smooth displacement fields u:

$$\mathcal{L}_{reg}(u) = \frac{1}{|\Omega|} \sum ||Du||_F^2, \tag{5}$$

where $|\Omega|$ is the total volume of the domain and D denotes the Jacobian and $||\cdot||_F^2$ denotes the squared Frobenius norm.

4   Experiments

4.1   Data Preparation

We use COPDGene and DirLab for training and evaluation respectively.

COPDGene. The COPDGene dataset [12] collects inspiratory and expiratory chest CT scans for 10,000 patients using multi-detector CT scanners on full inspiration (200 mAs) and at the end of normal expiration (50 mAs). We use a subset of 120 inhale/exhale CT image pairs of the COPDGene dataset with given segmentation masks. We resample the CT images to isotropic spacing of 2.2 mm and crop or pad evenly along each dimension to obtain an $160 \times 160 \times 160$ volume with the lung ROI approximately in the center. We compute the associated DRRs via the DRR generator proposed in [16] with the pre-defined geometry as described in Sect. 2. The DRRs are computed based on the entire CT image containing the ROI and the surrounding tissues. The resulting DRRs have a size of 200×200. After processing, the training dataset contains 120 sets of $(I_s, I_t, \mathbf{P}_t)$, among which 100 pairs are used for training and 20 pairs are used for validation.

DirLab. The DirLab dataset [1] contains 10 pairs of inspiration-expiration lung CT images. Each CT image comes with 300 anatomical landmarks that are manually identified and registered by an expert in thoracic imaging. We applied the same processing to DirLab as for COPDGene and obtain 10 pairs of $(I_s, \mathbf{P}_t)$. The segmentation maps of all scans are computed automatically[1]. Of note, during evaluation, the 3D volume I_t is not used.

---

[1] https://hub.docker.com/r/acilbwh/chestimagingplatform.

4.2 Evaluation Metrics

We use the following two evaluation metrics for all our experiments.

Mean Target Registration Error (mTRE). This metric computes the mean distance of corresponding landmarks between the warped and the target image. The reported mTRE in our experiments are the mean mTRE of all 10 pairs of DirLab in millimeters. The landmarks are annotated inside the lung based on the lung vessel structure [1]. This metric is used to evaluate the spatial accuracy of the registration method for fine structures (e.g. lung vessels).

DICE. The Dice's coefficient measures how much overlap exists between two sets. We compute it between the warped segmentation mask and the target segmentation mask to measure how similar the ROI shapes are after registration.

4.3 Validation of the DVF Subspace

We compute the gold standard DVFs for the COPDGene dataset via an in-house trained CNN for 3D/3D deformable registration. We construct the subspace by applying PCA to the gold standard DVFs of our COPDGene-train dataset. We form the basis for the deformation space using the eigenvectors which cover 99% of the data variance. This results in $N_e = 56$ basis vectors for the DVF subspace. We project the original DVF into this subspace. Then we compare the mTRE, DICE and $\%|J|_{<0}$ between the original DVF and the reconstructed DVF. $\%|J|_{<0}$ denotes the percentage of voxels having negative Jacobian determinant of φ^{-1}, i.e. exhibiting folding which represents an unrealistic deformation. Table 1 shows the results. Though the DICE scores decrease significantly, the landmark error only worsens by 2 mm. This is within acceptable range considering the before-registration mTRE is 23.36 mm. The mTRE and DICE score of the reconstructed DVF can be regarded as an upper-bond of the DVF subspace.

Table 1. Validation of the DVF subspace. This table shows mTRE, DICE and $\%|J|_{<0}$ on the original DVF and using the reconstructed DVF from the built subspace.

	Original DVF			Reconstructed DVF		
	mTRE[mm]↓	DICE[%]↑	$\%|J|_{<0}$↓	mTRE[mm]↓	DICE[%]↑	$\%|J|_{<0}$↓
COPDGene-train	-	98.72	0.046	-	96.46	0.020
COPDGene-val	-	98.85	0.047	-	90.90	0.011
DirLab	3.24/23.36	98.82	0.038	5.34/23.36	91.88	0.007

4.4 Pairwise 2D/3D Deformable Image Registration

We conduct an ablation study on the Lift3D module and compare our LiftReg method with other existing approaches for pairwise 2D/3D DIR [16,17].

Ablation Study. To study how the Lift3D module affects the result, we train a network which concatenates the 2D images $\mathbf{P}_t$ and repeats them along the depth direction so that we obtain a 3D volume of size $200 \times 160 \times 200$. Then we resample it to the same size as I_s and concatenate it with I_s. The rest of the network including α estimation and loss are the same. We denote this network structure as LiftReg-noLift3D. Table 2 shows the results of LiftReg and LiftReg-noLift3D. The landmark error and DICE score of the segmentation masks are improved from 13.89 mm to 12.74 mm and from 83.69% to 85.70% respectively by adding the Lift3D module. This demonstrates that Lift3D provides better spatial information than concatenation.

Comparison with Existing Methods. We compare with an optimization-based method [16] which utilizes large deformation diffeomorphic metric mapping (LDDMM) as the transformation model and optimizes over it using the 2D similarity measure. We use the official public code from this work and run it on the DirLab dataset. We also compare to 2D3D-regnet which uses a UNet as the backbone to predict a DVF given $(I_s, \mathbf{P}_t)$. Since the implementation of 2D3D-regnet is not published, we implement it in PyTorch and adapt it to use the s-DCT geometry. To conduct a fair comparison, we train 2D3D-regnet and LiftReg on COPDGene-train and pick the best model based on the validation score of COPDGene-val. We use the NCC similarity loss as the validation score.

Table 2 shows that LiftReg improves the DICE score from 73.55% to 85.70% and reduces the mTRE for landmarks inside the lung from 23.36 mm to 12.74 mm. LiftReg outperforms the approach in [16] and 2D3D-regnet on both metrics. Compared to the learning-based method 2D3D-regnet, LiftReg shows a stronger improvement for mTRE than DICE. One possible explanation could be that the 2D similarity loss contains enough information to guide the learning of the coarse structure such as the boundary of the lung. Hence, while the 3D similarity measure does not results in a significant performance boost for the registration of the lung mask it improve the alignment of fine structures (e.g. lung vessels).

Table 2. Evaluation on DirLab. Metrics on DirLab for LiftReg and existing methods. X, Y, Z represent the mean absolute landmark error along each axis depicted in Fig. 1. From the perspective of CT image orientation, X is the left-right, Y is anterior-posterior, and Z is the superior-inferior direction.

Method	mTRE[mm] ↓	X[mm] ↓	Y[mm] ↓	Z[mm] ↓	DICE[%]↑
Before registration	23.36 ± 6.00	3.97 ± 1.16	15.37 ± 7.48	13.72 ± 5.22	73.55 ± 8.36
Tian et al. [16]	17.39 ± 4.46	3.79 ± 1.09	12.72 ± 5.12	8.57 ± 2.94	83.11 ± 5.61
2D3D-regnet	16.94 ± 4.39	3.58 ± 0.96	9.63 ± 4.76	10.71 ± 3.98	84.58 ± 6.04
LiftReg-noLift3D	13.89 ± 3.63	3.51 ± 1.16	7.978 ± 3.66	8.39 ± 3.67	83.69 ± 3.62
LiftReg	$\mathbf{12.74 \pm 3.10}$	$\mathbf{3.43 \pm 1.10}$	$\mathbf{7.63 \pm 2.93}$	$\mathbf{7.43 \pm 2.15}$	$\mathbf{85.70 \pm 3.30}$

5   Conclusion

We proposed LiftReg which predicts the basis coefficients of a constructed DVF subspace given a 3D volume and a set of 2D projection images. We demonstrated that LiftReg with statistical deformation model, 3D similarity loss, and Lift3D module outperforms existing pairwise 2D/3D DIR methods in a dataset containing large deformations. A limitation of our method is that it assumes the DRRs are equivalent to real radiographs. This might not be true if we consider scattering effects, beam hardening, and veiling glare [15]. Interesting future work would be to combine image translation with DRR generation to improve the realism of DRRs with respect to real radiographs; to add support for dynamic geometry where the emitter number N and emitter positions can vary; and to explore more advanced statistical deformation models.

Acknowledgement. Thanks to Peirong Liu (UNC), Dr. Rong Yuan (Peking University), and Boqi Chen (UNC) for providing valuable suggestions on during the writing of the manuscript. The research reported in this publication was supported by the National Institutes of Health (NIH) under award numbers NIH 1 R01 HL149877 and NIH 1 R01 EB028283. The content is solely the responsibility of the authors and does not necessarily represent the official views of the NIH.

References

1. Castillo, R., et al.: A reference dataset for deformable image registration spatial accuracy evaluation using the copdgene study archive. Phys. Med. Biol. **58**(9), 2861 (2013)
2. Flach, B., Brehm, M., Sawall, S., Kachelrieß, M.: Deformable 3D–2D registration for CT and its application to low dose tomographic fluoroscopy. Phys. Med. Biol. **59**(24), 7865 (2014)
3. Foote, M.D., Zimmerman, B.E., Sawant, A., Joshi, S.C.: Real-time 2D-3D deformable registration with deep learning and application to lung radiotherapy targeting. In: Chung, A.C.S., Gee, J.C., Yushkevich, P.A., Bao, S. (eds.) IPMI 2019. LNCS, vol. 11492, pp. 265–276. Springer, Cham (2019). https://doi.org/10.1007/978-3-030-20351-1_20
4. Jaderberg, M., Simonyan, K., Zisserman, A., et al.: Spatial transformer networks. In: Advances in Neural Information Processing Systems, vol. 28, pp. 2017–2025 (2015)
5. Jaffray, D., Kupelian, P., Djemil, T., Macklis, R.M.: Review of image-guided radiation therapy. Expert Rev. Anticancer Ther. **7**(1), 89–103 (2007)
6. Kalender, W.A.: X-ray computed tomography. Phys. Med. Biol. **51**(13), R29 (2006)
7. Li, P., Pei, Y., Guo, Y., Ma, G., Xu, T., Zha, H.: Non-rigid 2D–3D registration using convolutional autoencoders. In: 2020 IEEE 17th International Symposium on Biomedical Imaging (ISBI), pp. 700–704. IEEE (2020)
8. Markelj, P., Tomaževič, D., Likar, B., Pernuš, F.: A review of 3D/2D registration methods for image-guided interventions. Med. Image Anal. **16**(3), 642–661 (2012)
9. Modersitzki, J.: Numerical Methods for Image Registration. OUP, Oxford (2003)
10. Pei, Y., et al.: Non-rigid craniofacial 2D-3D registration using CNN-based regression. In: Cardoso, M.J., et al. (eds.) DLMIA/ML-CDS -2017. LNCS, vol. 10553, pp. 117–125. Springer, Cham (2017). https://doi.org/10.1007/978-3-319-67558-9_14
11. Prümmer, M., Hornegger, J., Pfister, M., Dörfler, A.: Multi-modal 2D–3D non-rigid registration. In: Medical Imaging 2006: Image Processing, vol. 6144, p. 61440X. International Society for Optics and Photonics (2006)

12. Regan, E.A., et al.: Genetic epidemiology of COPD (COPDGene) study design. COPD J. Chronic Obstr. Pulm. Dis. **7**(1), 32–43 (2011)
13. Shan, J., et al.: Stationary chest tomosynthesis using a carbon nanotube x-ray source array: a feasibility study. Phys. Med. Biol. **60**, 81–100 (2015). https://doi.org/10.1088/0031-9155/60/1/81
14. Sherouse, G.W., Novins, K., Chaney, E.L.: Computation of digitally reconstructed radiographs for use in radiotherapy treatment design. Int. J. Radiat. Oncol. Biol. Phys. **18**(3), 651–658 (1990)
15. Staub, D., Murphy, M.J.: A digitally reconstructed radiograph algorithm calculated from first principles. Med. Phys. **40**(1), 011902 (2013)
16. Tian, L., et al.: Fluid registration between lung CT and stationary chest tomosynthesis images. In: Martel, A.L., et al. (eds.) MICCAI 2020. LNCS, vol. 12263, pp. 307–317. Springer, Cham (2020). https://doi.org/10.1007/978-3-030-59716-0_30
17. Zhang, Y.: An unsupervised 2D–3D deformable registration network (2D3D-RegNet) for cone-beam CT estimation. Phys. Med. Biol. **66**(7), 074001 (2021)
18. Zhang, Y., Tehrani, J.N., Wang, J.: A biomechanical modeling guided CBCT estimation technique. IEEE Trans. Med. Imaging **36**(2), 641–652 (2016)
19. Zikic, D., Groher, M., Khamene, A., Navab, N.: Deformable registration of 3D vessel structures to a single projection image. In: Medical Imaging 2008: Image Processing, vol. 6914, p. 691412. International Society for Optics and Photonics (2008)

XMorpher: Full Transformer for Deformable Medical Image Registration via Cross Attention

Jiacheng Shi[1], Yuting He[1], Youyong Kong[1,2,3], Jean-Louis Coatrieux[2,3], Huazhong Shu[1,2,3], Guanyu Yang[1,2,3(✉)], and Shuo Li[4]

[1] LIST, Key Laboratory of Computer Network and Information Integration, (Southeast University), Ministry of Education, Nanjing, China
yang.list@seu.edu.cn

[2] Jiangsu Provincial Joint International Research Laboratory of Medical Information Processing, Nanjing, China

[3] Centre de Recherche en Information Biomédicale Sino-Français (CRIBs), Rennes, France

[4] Department of Medical Biophysics, University of Western Ontario, London, ON, Canada

Abstract. An effective backbone network is important to deep learning-based Deformable Medical Image Registration (DMIR), because it extracts and matches the features between two images to discover the mutual correspondence for fine registration. However, the existing deep networks focus on single image situation and are limited in registration task which is performed on paired images. Therefore, we advance a novel backbone network, XMorpher, for the effective corresponding feature representation in DMIR. **1)** It proposes a novel full transformer architecture including dual parallel feature extraction networks which exchange information through cross attention, thus discovering multi-level semantic correspondence while extracting respective features gradually for final effective registration. **2)** It advances the Cross Attention Transformer (CAT) blocks to establish the attention mechanism between images which is able to find the correspondence automatically and prompts the features to fuse efficiently in the network. **3)** It constrains the attention computation between base windows and searching windows with different sizes, and thus focuses on the local transformation of deformable registration and enhances the computing efficiency at the same time. Without any bells and whistles, our XMorpher gives Voxelmorph 2.8% improvement on DSC, demonstrating its effective representation of the features from the paired images in DMIR. We believe that our XMorpher has great application potential in more paired medical images. Our XMorpher is open on https://github.com/Solemoon/XMorpher

1 Introduction

A powerful backbone network is important to deep learning (DL)-based Deformable Medical Image Registration (DMIR) [1,5,15]. The backbone network

L. Wang et al. (Eds.): MICCAI 2022, LNCS 13436, pp. 217–226, 2022.
https://doi.org/10.1007/978-3-031-16446-0_21

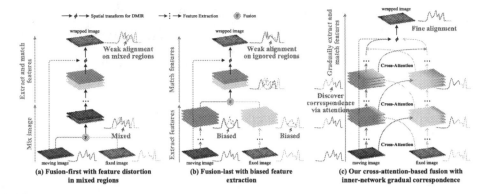

Fig. 1. The limitations of existing methods and our superiority. (a) Fusion-first with feature distortion in mixed regions making inaccurate representation for corresponding features. (b) Fusion-last with biased feature extraction losing correspondence of ignored features. (c) Our cross-attention-based fusion with inner-network gradual correspondence for fine alignment of different level features.

is able to extract the features of moving and fixed images in DMIR and then match the features to obtain correspondences from moving images to fixed images, thus contributing to a fine registration with these effective correspondences. The moving images are transformed into the same coordinate system as the fixed images after registration, which makes it convenient and efficient to compare different images for doctors, thus greatly promoting the efficiency of diagnosis and reducing the cost of disease.

Although existing deep networks [13,16] have strong performance in single image feature representation, these Single Image Networks (SINs) are still limited in feature extraction and match of a pair of images in DMIR: **1)** *Fusion-first with feature distortion in mixed regions.* As shown in Fig. 1(a), some DMIR methods [1,2,19] fuse the moving and fixed images to simulate the single-image input condition, and the fusion is sent to a SIN for moving-fixed features. But these methods mix the feature extraction and feature matching processes together, leading to the feature distortion and weak alignment in the mixed regions, thus making the networks unable to identify one-to-one correspondences between the image pairs. The inefficient capacity of feature representation finally contributes to the absence of critical structures and poor registering details. **2)** *Fusion-last with biased feature extraction.* As shown in Fig.1(b), these networks [11] send moving and fixed images to dual SINs respectively and fuse features from different networks at the end. But these networks separate the feature extraction and feature matching processes absolutely, leading to final match of two biased features from different SINs, thus making the networks ignore the different levels (such as multiscale) of the features in some regions. The unicity of feature representation limits the correspondence of different information between images and leads to poor registration finally.

The attention mechanism of transformer [7] provides the potential application in registration because of its outstanding capacity of catching relevance in images, but existing researches of transformer [3,10,12,21] only focus on single image scenarios and lack related design for moving-fixed correspondence between two images in DMIR. These transformers utilize the self-attention function to obtain an output with the weight information which points out the areas needing to be focused in one image. This mechanism digs out the relationships of internal basic elements and extracts the most task-related features, and thus transformer has a good performance in single-image tasks and is potential in DMIR. **However**, current transformers [4,20] for DMIR still take the same attention mechanism as single-image tasks which focus on the relevance in one image but ignore the correspondences between image pairs. The competence of capturing correspondences between moving and fixed images restrains transformers to find effective registering features for fine registration.

In this paper, we proposed a novel transformer, X-shape Morpher (XMorpher) for dual images input in DMIR, it advances Cross Attention to the transformer architecture for efficient and multi-level semantic feature fusion, thus effectively improving the performance of registration. In short, the contributions of our work are summarized as follows: **1)** We proposed a novel full transformer backbone network for DMIR. As shown in Fig. 1(c), it includes dual parallel feature extraction sub-networks whose respective features are fused and matched in the form of cross attention. Through the progressive and commutative network, the features from different images are fused and matched gradually through the cross-attention-based fusion modules, thus achieving effective feature representation of moving-fixed correspondences and gaining fine-grained multi-level semantic information for fine registration. **2)** We present a new attention mechanism, Cross Attention Transformer (CAT) block, for sufficient communication between a pair of features from moving and fixed images. CAT block utilizes the attention mechanism to compute the mutual relevance, thus learning the correspondences between two images and promoting the features to match automatically in the network. **3)** We constrain the feature matching process in windows based on the local transformation of DMIR, which narrows the searching range between moving and fixed images, thus increase the computation efficiency and reduce the interference from similar structure if matching in a large space. This window-based feature communication greatly improve the accuracy and efficiency of registration.

2 Methodology

As is shown in Fig. 2, XMorpher is based on DL-based registration networks [2,19], and it is used to extract and match moving and fixed features in registration for effective representation of input image pairs. The final representation generates the DVF ϕ and obtain the fine wrapped image w through spatial transform [9]. Our XMorpher includes: **1)** A X-shape transformer architecture with dual parallel U-shape feature extraction sub-networks which keeps exchanging information through cross-attention-based feature fusion modules. **2)** CAT blocks for feature fusion between two features tokens from different sub-networks. **3)** Multi-size window partition in CAT for precise local-wise correspondences.

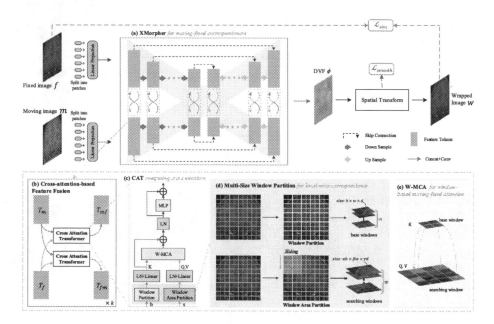

Fig. 2. Overall architecture of our XMorpher. (a) It includes dual U-shape networks which exchange features through our cross-attention-based feature fusion. (b) The feature fusion module is composed of two CAT blocks sharing parameters for mutual correspondences. (c) The detailed construction of our CAT block which fuses two input features into one with attention information. (d) Our two different methods of window partition to generate base and searching windows. (e) We compute the cross attention between base and searching windows through W-MCA.

2.1 XMorpher for Efficient and Multi-level Semantic Feature Representation in Registration

I. X-Shape Architecture with Parallel Communicating Feature Extraction Networks. As shown in Fig. 2(a), we utilize dual U-shape networks to extract the features of moving and fixed images respectively and the two networks communicate through feature fusion modules, thus forming a X-shape network, so we name it as XMorpher. The two parallel networks follow the structure of Unet [13] with encoding and decoding parts, but we replace the convolutions with our CAT blocks which play important role in the attention-wise feature fusion modules (Fig. 2(b)) between the two networks. Through the parallel communicating networks, our XMorpher exchange cross-image information vertically and keeps refining features horizontally. So the final output features have strong ability of representing the correspondences between moving and fixed images.

II. Cross-attention-Based Feature Fusion Module. As shown in Fig. 2(b), the corresponding features T_m and T_f coming from the parallel sub-networks obtain their mutual attention through two CAT blocks by exchanging the order of inputs. Then the two outputs with the other's attention return to the original pipelines and prepare for next deeper communication. There are k times of communication in total in a feature fusion module for sufficient mutual information. Through the attention-wise feature fusion modules between two networks, features from different networks with different semantic information communicate frequently, thus our XMorpher keeping learning multi-level semantic features for final fine registration.

2.2 Cross Attention Transformer Block for Corresponding Atention

CAT block aims to compute new feature tokens with corresponding relevance from input feature b to feature s through the attention mechanism. As shown in Fig. 2(c), b and s are respectively partitioned in different ways (described in Sect. 2.3) into two sets of windows, base window set S_{ba} and searching window set S_{se}, for next window-based attention calculation. S_{ba} and S_{se} have the same size n and different window sizes. Each base window in S_{ba} is projected to the query set $query$ and each searching window is projected to knowledge set key and $value$ through linear layer. Then our Window-based Muti-head Cross Attention (W-MCA) compute the cross attention between two windows and the attention is added to the base window so that each base window gets the corresponding weighed information from searching window. Finally, the new output sct is sent to a 2-layer MLP [18] with GELU non-linearity to enhance learning ability. A LayerNorm (LN) layer is applied before each W-MCA and each MLP module to guarantee validity of each layer.

2.3 Multi-size Window Partitions for Local-Wise Correspondence

I. Window Partition (WP) and Window Area Partition (WAP). Since the deformable image registration focuses on local displacement of voxel and there is no large span correspondence between moving and fixed images, we proposed the window-based cross attention mechanism which utilizes multi-size window partitions to limit attention computation in windows. Multi-size window partitions include two different methods, WP and WAP, to divide the input feature tokens b and s into windows of different sizes. As shown in Fig. 2(d), WP partition feature tokens directly into base window set S_{ba} with size of $n \times h \times w \times d$ and WAP enlarges the window size with the magnifications α, β and γ. So the base and searing window size are calculated as:

$$h_{ba}, w_{ba}, d_{ba} = h, w, d$$
$$h_{se}, w_{se}, d_{se} = \alpha \cdot h, \beta \cdot w, \gamma \cdot d \tag{1}$$

where h_{ba}, w_{ba}, d_{ba} are the size of base windows and h_{se}, w_{se}, d_{se} are the size of searching windows. To obtain the same amount of two window sets, WAP takes advantage of a sliding window and the stride is set as the base window size, and thus S_{se} has size of $n \times \alpha \cdot h \times \beta \cdot w \times \gamma \cdot d$. Through the corresponding windows with different sizes, CAT blocks compute the cross attention between two feature tokens efficiently and avoid large-span searches for precise correspondence.

II. Window-Based Muti-head Cross Attention (W-MCA). We proposed W-MCA to compute the cross attention between acquired base windows and searching windows to find the mutual correspondences. W-MCA is a function mapping a query and a set of key-value pairs to an output, where the query comes from the base windows, keys and values come from the searching windows. The output is computed as a weighted sum of the values, where the weight assigned to each value is computed by a compatibility function of the query with the corresponding key. W-MCA adopts multi-head attention [18] for ample representation subspaces. W-MCA computes the dot products of query and keys and applies a softmax function to obtain the weights on the values. So our cross attention is computed as:

$$W - MCA\left(Q_{ba}, K_{se}, V_{se}\right) = softmax\left(\frac{Q_{ba}K_{se}^{T}}{\sqrt{d}}\right)V_{se} \qquad (2)$$

where Q_{ba}, K_{se}, V_{se} are the *query, key* and *value* matrices. $Q_{ba} \in \mathbb{R}^{n \times s \times c}$ is the linear projection of S_{ba} and $K_{se}, V_{se} \in \mathbb{R}^{n \times \mu \cdot s \times c}$ are linear projections of S_{se}, $s = h \times w \times d$ and $\mu = \alpha \cdot \beta \cdot \gamma$, and c is the dimension of each feature token.

3   Experiment

3.1   Experiment Protocol

We perform effective experiments to evaluate our XMorpher's superiority both in unsupervised and semi-supervised strategies. **1)** *Dataset.* We validate the performance of our XMorpher on the whole heart registration tasks on the CT dataset from MM-WHS 2017 Challenge [22] which has 20 labeled images and 40 unlabeled images and ASOCA [6] which has 60 unlabeled images. We use all the unlabeled images (100 images) and 5 labeled images to compose 500 labeled-unlabeled image pairs and 9900 unlabeled-unlabeled image pairs as the training set for unsupervised and semi-supervised experiments. The remaining 15 of the labeled images compose 210 image pairs as testing set. All images were preprocessed to the same spatial coordinates through affine transformation [17]. **2)** *Implementation.* We apply our XMorpher as backbone in two registration frameworks: unsupervised Voxelmorph [1] (VM-XMorpher) and semi-supervised PC-Reg [8] (PC-XMorpher). Furthermore, the hyperparameters of XMorpher is set as $h = w = d = 2$ and $\alpha = \beta = \gamma = 3$. The proposed framework is implemented with PyTorch on NVIDIA GeForce RTX 3090 GPUs with 24 GB memory. **3)** *Comparison settings.* We set up a set of comparative experiments to prove the advancement of our XMorpher. Controlled experiments include BSpline [14], Voxelmorph [1], PC-Reg [8], Transmorph [4]. **4)** *Evaluation metrics.* We use the mean dice similarity coefficients (DSC) of all labels to evaluate the performance of registration and the Jacobian matrix ($|J(\psi)| \leqslant 0$ (%)) to evaluate the rationality of registration fields.

Table 1. The proposed XMorphers achieve the state-of-the-art performance on DSC both under unsupervised and semi-supervised strategies, as well as have top-ranked performance on Jacobian matrix ($|J_\phi| \leq 0$ (%)).

Method	Un-/Semi-	Backbone	DSC	$|J_\phi| \leq 0$ (%)
Affine initialization	-	-	69.2 ± 7.2	-
BSpline [14]	Unsup	-	80.9 ± 7.6	5.25 ± 3.27
Voxelmorph [1]		CNN	80.2 ± 5.5	4.02 ± 0.82
Transmorph [4]		CNN+Transformer	81.1 ± 5.2	3.46 ± 0.75
Our no-cross XMorpher		Full Transformer	81.5 ± 5.4	**0.94 ± 0.26**
Our VM-XMorpher		Full Transformer	**83.0 ± 4.7**	3.15 ± 0.79
PC-Reg[8]	Semi	CNN	86.0 ± 2.5	0.36 ±, 0.20
Our PC-XMorpher		Full Transformer	**86.9 ± 2.4**	**0.32 ± 0.18**

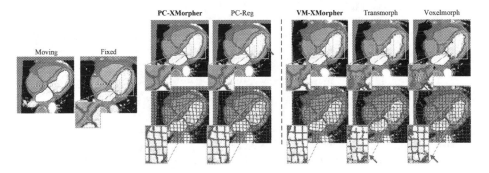

Fig. 3. The visual results of Voxelmorph, Transmorph, PC-Reg and ours. XMorphers have obvious visual advantages both in unsupervised and semi-supervised strategies.

3.2   Results and Analysis

Quantitative Comparison. Our VM-XMorpher achieves the highest DSC score of 83.0% and has the top-ranked performance on Jacobian matrix at the same time (Table 1), which shows that it not only has a strong registration effect, but also has a strong maintenance of the image structure. VM-XMorpher is 2.8% higher on DSC and 0.87% lower on Jacobian matrix than Voxelmorph [1], illustrating that XMorpher represents the correspondence effectively and thus results in refined details and strong topology preservation compared with fusion-first networks. VM-XMorpher still has an obvious improvement in contrast to Transmorph [4] which combines the CNN and transformer, evaluating that cross attention mechanism has an superiority over the existing transformers and full transformer is good at focus on the cross-image correspondence. Furthermore, PC-Reg has achieved considerable performance on registration while our PC-XMorpher is still 0.9% higher on DSC and has better performance on Jacobian matrix. These results prove the superiority of our XMorpher under different training strategies.

Visual Superiority. Figure 3 shows one case of the visual results of our XMorpher and other compared experiments in different training strategies.

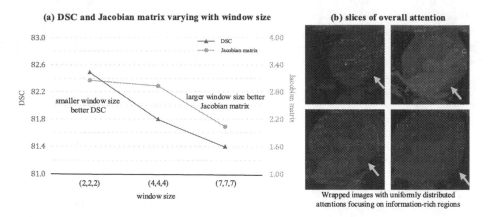

Fig. 4. (a) The DSC and Jacobian matrix of XMorpher have inverse variation with the window size. (b)The uniformly distributed window attentions indicate that XMorpher effectively find the keys in every windows and the keys correspond to the heart region.

Our PC-XMorpher has better details compared with PC-reg such as the more smooth boundaries. Furthermore, our XMorpher has obvious visual superiority under unsupervised experiments.VM-XMorpher still has much better ability of boundary recognition than other methods and stronger resolution of the neighbouring regions while other models (Voxelmorph, Transmorph) have the obvious mixture of two borders. Furthermore, the deformation grids of VM-XMorpher is also smooth compared with other methods which have many cracks in the grids.

Ablation Study. Through the ablation experiments, we demonstrated the effect of CAT blocks and the influence of the window size. **a)** Ablation for CAT blocks. We designed no-cross XMorpher whose input is the concatenation of moving and fixed images. Its transformer blocks computes the internal attention of the concatenation and the other components are same as XMorpher. Our VM-XMorpher has 1.5% increase on DSC demonstrating that the effective correspondence representation enhances the interaction between the two images in DMIR but brings the risk of less smooth deformation at the same time. But our VM-XMorpher still has better performance on Jacobian matrix than other models. **b)** Ablation for window size. Figure 4(a) demonstrates that the larger windows has better performance on the Jacobian matrix because the more structure information of the images will be extracted in a wider horizon, but the smaller windows result in a better DSC owing to finer searching space.

Analysis of Visual Cross Attention. The uniformly distributed visual attention (Fig. 4(b)) illustrates that the window-based attention mechanism disperses the correspondence into windows and takes advantage of these uniform mappings of small regions for a fine registration. Furthermore, the high-attention regions with ample information correspond to the heart region, demonstrating the powerful image comprehensive ability of our XMorpher.

4   Conclusion

We propose a full transformer network XMorpher which effectively represents multi-level correspondence between moving and fixed images. Furthermore, we use window-based CAT blocks to extract and match the features in the network efficiently to obtain final cross-image correspondences for fine registration. The compared experiments have prove that XMorpher has outstanding performance in DMIR with different training strategies and we believe that it has great application prospect in diagnosis and treatment. We also want to use our XMorpher on MindSpore[1], which is a new deep learning computing framework.

Acknowledgment. This work was supported in part by the National Natural Science Foundation under grants (62171125, 61828101), CAAI-Huawei MindSpore Open Fund, CANN (Compute Architecture for Neural Networks), Ascend AI Processor, and Big Data Computing Center of Southeast University.

References

1. Balakrishnan, G., Zhao, A., Sabuncu, M.R., Guttag, J., Dalca, A.V.: An unsupervised learning model for deformable medical image registration. In: Proceedings of the IEEE Conference on Computer Vision and Pattern Recognition, pp. 9252–9260 (2018)
2. Balakrishnan, G., Zhao, A., Sabuncu, M.R., Guttag, J., Dalca, A.V.: Voxelmorph: a learning framework for deformable medical image registration. IEEE Trans. Med. Imaging **38**(8), 1788–1800 (2019)
3. Chen, J., et al.: TransUNet: transformers make strong encoders for medical image segmentation. arXiv preprint arXiv:2102.04306 (2021)
4. Chen, J., Du, Y., He, Y., Segars, W.P., Li, Y., Frey, E.C.: Transmorph: transformer for unsupervised medical image registration. arXiv preprint arXiv:2111.10480 (2021)
5. De Vos, B.D., Berendsen, F.F., Viergever, M.A., Sokooti, H., Staring, M., Išgum, I.: A deep learning framework for unsupervised affine and deformable image registration. Med. Image Anal. **52**, 128–143 (2019)
6. Gharleghi, R., Samarasinghe, D.G., Sowmya, P.A., Beier, D.S.: Automated segmentation of coronary arteries, March 2020. https://doi.org/10.5281/zenodo.3819799, https://doi.org/10.5281/zenodo.3819799
7. Han, K., et al.: A survey on vision transformer. IEEE In: Transactions on Pattern Analysis and Machine Intelligence (2022)
8. He, Y., et al.: Few-shot learning for deformable medical image registration with perception-correspondence decoupling and reverse teaching. IEEE J. Biomed. Health Inform. **26**, 1177–1187 (2021)
9. He, Y., Li, T., Yang, G., Kong, Y., Chen, Y., Shu, H., Coatrieux, J.-L., Dillenseger, J.-L., Li, S.: Deep complementary joint model for complex scene registration and few-shot segmentation on medical images. In: Vedaldi, A., Bischof, H., Brox, T., Frahm, J.-M. (eds.) ECCV 2020. LNCS, vol. 12363, pp. 770–786. Springer, Cham (2020). https://doi.org/10.1007/978-3-030-58523-5_45

---

[1] https://www.mindspore.cn/.

10. Khan, S., Naseer, M., Hayat, M., Zamir, S.W., Khan, F.S., Shah, M.: Transformers in vision: a survey. ACM Comput. Surv. (CSUR) (2021)
11. Klein, S., Staring, M., Murphy, K., Viergever, M.A., Pluim, J.P.: Elastix: a toolbox for intensity-based medical image registration. IEEE Trans. Med. Imag. **29**(1), 196–205 (2009)
12. Liu, Z., et al.: Swin transformer: hierarchical vision transformer using shifted windows. In: Proceedings of the IEEE/CVF International Conference on Computer Vision, pp. 10012–10022 (2021)
13. Ronneberger, O., Fischer, P., Brox, T.: U-Net: convolutional networks for biomedical image segmentation. In: Navab, N., Hornegger, J., Wells, W.M., Frangi, A.F. (eds.) MICCAI 2015. LNCS, vol. 9351, pp. 234–241. Springer, Cham (2015). https://doi.org/10.1007/978-3-319-24574-4_28
14. Rueckert, D., Sonoda, L.I., Hayes, C., Hill, D.L., Leach, M.O., Hawkes, D.J.: Nonrigid registration using free-form deformations: application to breast MR images. IEEE Trans. Med. Imaging **18**(8), 712–721 (1999)
15. Sotiras, A., Davatzikos, C., Paragios, N.: Deformable medical image registration: A survey. IEEE Trans. Med. Imaging **32**(7), 1153–1190 (2013)
16. Tajbakhsh, N., Shin, J.Y., Gurudu, S.R., Hurst, R.T., Kendall, C.B., Gotway, M.B., Liang, J.: Convolutional neural networks for medical image analysis: Full training or fine tuning? IEEE Trans. Med. Imaging **35**(5), 1299–1312 (2016)
17. Tustison, N., et al.: Large-scale evaluation of ants and freesurfer cortical thickness measurements. Neuroimage **99**, 166–179 (2014)
18. Vaswani, A., et al.: Attention is all you need. In: Advances in Neural Information Processing Systems, vol. 30 (2017)
19. Vos, B.D.d., Berendsen, F.F., Viergever, M.A., Staring, M., Išgum, I.: End-to-end unsupervised deformable image registration with a convolutional neural network. In: Deep Learning In Medical Image Analysis and Multimodal Learning for Clinical Decision Support, pp. 204–212. Springer, Cham (2017). https://doi.org/10.1007/978-3-319-67558-9
20. Zhang, Y., Pei, Y., Zha, H.: Learning dual transformer network for diffeomorphic registration. In: de Bruijne, M., et al. (eds.) MICCAI 2021. LNCS, vol. 12904, pp. 129–138. Springer, Cham (2021). https://doi.org/10.1007/978-3-030-87202-1_13
21. Zheng, S., et al.: Rethinking semantic segmentation from a sequence-to-sequence perspective with transformers. In: Proceedings of the IEEE/CVF Conference on Computer Vision and Pattern Recognition, pp. 6881–6890 (2021)
22. Zhuang, X., Shen, J.: Multi-scale patch and multi-modality atlases for whole heart segmentation of MRI. Med. Image Anal. **31**, 77–87 (2016)

Weakly-Supervised Biomechanically-Constrained CT/MRI Registration of the Spine

Bailiang Jian[1,2(✉)], Mohammad Farid Azampour[1,8], Francesca De Benetti[1,2], Johannes Oberreuter[2,3], Christina Bukas[2,4], Alexandra S. Gersing[5,6], Sarah C. Foreman[5,6], Anna-Sophia Dietrich[5,6], Jon Rischewski[5,6], Jan S. Kirschke[5,6], Nassir Navab[1,7], and Thomas Wendler[1,2]

[1] Chair for Computer Aided Medical Procedures and Augmented Reality, Technische Universität München, Garching, Germany
{bailiang.jian,wendler}@tum.de
[2] ScintHealth GmbH, Munich, Germany
[3] Reply SpA, Munich, Germany
[4] Helmholtz AI, Helmholtz Zentrum München, Munich, Germany
[5] Department of Radiology, Technische Universität München, Munich, Germany
[6] Department of Neuroradiology, Technische Universität München, Munich, Germany
[7] Computer Aided Medical Procedures Lab, Laboratory for Computational Sensing+Robotics, Johns Hopkins University, Baltimore, MD, USA
[8] Department of Electrical Engineering, Sharif University of Technology, Tehran, Iran

Abstract. Computed Tomography (CT) and Magnetic Resonance Imaging (MRI) are two of the most informative modalities in spinal diagnostics and treatment planning. CT is useful when analysing bony structures, while MRI gives information about the soft tissue. Thus, fusing the information of both modalities can be very beneficial. Registration is the first step for this fusion. While the soft tissues around the vertebra are deformable, each vertebral body is constrained to move rigidly. We propose a weakly-supervised deep learning framework that preserves the rigidity and the volume of each vertebra while maximizing the accuracy of the registration. To achieve this goal, we introduce anatomy-aware losses for training the network. We specifically design these losses to depend only on the CT label maps since automatic vertebra segmentation in CT gives more accurate results contrary to MRI. We evaluate our method on an in-house dataset of 167 patients. Our results show that adding the anatomy-aware losses increases the plausibility of the inferred transformation while keeping the accuracy untouched.

Keywords: CT/MRI registration · Deep learning image registration · Biomechanical constraints · Spine

Supplementary Information The online version contains supplementary material available at https://doi.org/10.1007/978-3-031-16446-0_22.

1   Introduction

CT and MRI images are the most used imaging modalities for understanding the pathologies of the spine and defining the therapeutic approach. Experts need both modalities for proper diagnosis in complex clinical situations as each modality provides different information [10]. CT has higher contrast in bony structures [16,24], whereas MRI can be used to detect lesions and tumors of the spinal cord, the intervertebral discs, and the inner anatomy of the vertebral bodies [21]. As a result, registering spinal images from different modalities benefits various clinical contexts, ranging from improved diagnosis and proper treatment planning to personalized therapeutic decisions.

A major problem when registering articulated rigid structures is their relative motion and the soft tissue deformations due to patient movement. Indeed, rigid registration cannot address the problem of the varying curvature of patients' spine during different imaging sessions, as well as a global deformable registration ignores the difference between soft tissues and bony structures.

Few works have addressed the problem of rigid structures in conventional deformable registration. [12] and [3] defined a way to interpolate the deformations of rigid objects based on euclidean distance transform. [6] defined groups of springs between vertebrae and penalized the change in length of them. In addition, [11] penalized the inter-voxel distance change in rigid bodies. [18] proposed penalizing deviations of the Jacobian determinant of the deformation from unity to preserve the volume of lesions in breast MRI registration. [23] introduced the latter as one of the rigidity penalties in deformable registration, while proposing to use the orthonormality of a rigid transform as a rigidity penalty in registering digital subtraction angiography images. However, these approaches are based on time-consuming conventional iterative optimization methods, and their performance highly depends on the initialization and parameter settings. In more recent years, convolutional neural networks were used to do deep learning-based image registration (DLIR) [8]. Their main advantage is that they enable inferring a plausible transformation in a single iteration, using a model trained optimizing only image similarity and deformation smoothness [2,4,14]. A biomechanically-constrained method for DLIR of MRI-CT images of the prostate, proposed by [5], consists of training on finite element modeling-generated motion fields. However, it required the segmentation of the prostate in both modalities to establish the surface point cloud correspondence. This segmentation is non-trivial for the spine in MRI.

Another hurdle for unsupervised DLIR methods is the selection of the similarity metric for multi-modal image registration. For registration of MRI-CT of the pelvis, [15] introduced a new metric for unsupervised training of a deep network called self-correlation descriptor. [13] reduced the problem of MRI-CT registration of images of the neck to a mono-modal one by training a neural network to synthesize CT images from MRI. None of the above consider the rigidity of bony structures and the constraints that they impose on the deformation field. As a result, those methods are not suitable for spinal image fusion.

Our work introduces a weakly-supervised anatomy-aware method for registering spinal MR-CT images. We acknowledge that vertebrae segmentation is not a trivial task for MRI, thus we only rely on label maps from CT for training. Further, we devise losses and metrics to deal with the biomechanical constraints imposed by bony structures. Our main contributions (MC) are:

1. Proposal of a framework for rigidity-preserving MRI/CT deformable registration of the spine taking rigidly aligned CT/MRI images as input
2. Introduction of the rigid dice (RD) loss and rigid field (RF) loss for rigidity-preservation
3. Adaptation of rigidity penalties used in conventional registration of spine to DLIR (orthonormal condition (OC), properness condition (PC))
4. Extensive evaluation and ablation study of different losses on an in-house dataset with 167 patients
5. Analysis of target clinical application for each penalty using different metrics

2   Method

Architecture. Let $\mathcal{F} : \Omega_f \to \mathbb{R}$ denote the fixed image, and $\mathcal{M} : \Omega_m \to \mathbb{R}$ denote the moving image, where $\Omega_f \in \mathbb{R}^3$ and $\Omega_m \in \mathbb{R}^3$ represent the coordinate space of $\mathcal{F}$ and $\mathcal{M}$. Our training loss consists of three terms. Firstly, the network learns to establish spatial correspondence between fixed and moving images by computing a dense deformation field (DDF) $\phi : \Omega_f \to \Omega_m$ through an intensity-based image similarity loss $\mathcal{L}_{\text{sim}}$. Second, a smootheness regularizer $\mathcal{L}_{\text{smooth}}$ ensures the output DDF is plausible and realistic. Lastly, we define rigidity penalties $\mathcal{L}_{\text{rigid}}$ between the moving label and the warped label, or on the deformation vectors inside the rigid bodies, to guarantee each of them is transformed rigidly. Overall, the network is trained by minimizing the following loss function:

$$\mathcal{L} = \mathcal{L}_{\text{sim}}(\mathcal{F}, \mathcal{M} \circ \phi) + \lambda_{\text{smooth}}\mathcal{L}_{\text{smooth}}(\mathbf{v}) + \lambda_{\text{rigid}} \sum_{i}^{N} \mathcal{L}_{\text{rigid}}(s_{\mathcal{M}}^i, s_{\mathcal{M}}^i \circ \phi, \phi) \quad (1)$$

where $\mathcal{M} \circ \phi : \Omega_f \to \mathbb{R}$ represents the warped moving image, $s_{\mathcal{M}}^i : \Omega_m \to \{0, 1\}$ is the binary segmentation label of the ith rigid body in the moving image, N is the number of rigid bodies, i.e., the vertebrae, and $\mathbf{v}$ is the stationary velocity field (SVF) parameterizing the DDF ϕ. The smoothness regularizer is computed as the $l2$-norm of the diffusion on the spatial gradient of the SVF $\mathbf{v}$.

We adopt the diffeomorphic version of VoxelMorph (VXM) [2] as our baseline network. It comprises a 3D UNet [19] and two convolutional layers with 32 filters each to output the SVF $\mathbf{v}$. The UNet consists of an encoder with convolution filter channels $[32, 32, 64, 64]$ and a decoder with channels $[64, 64, 64, 64]$. To guarantee the invertibility and topology preservation, the predicted deformations are parameterized using the SVF under the Log-Euclidean framework. $\mathbf{v}$ is integrated using the *scaling and squaring* method [1] with $T = 7$ time steps to obtain the diffeomorphic DDF ϕ [2]. The code is publicly available.[1].

---

[1] https://github.com/BailiangJ/spine-ct-mr-registration.

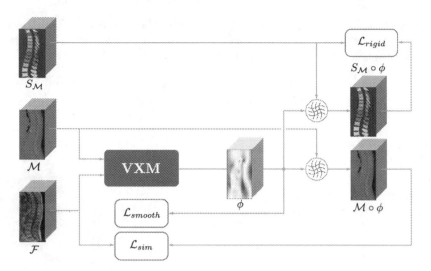

Fig. 1. An overview of the architecture: A VXM network takes as input a CT as moving image $\mathcal{M}$, its label map $\mathcal{S_M}$, and an MRI as fixed image $\mathcal{F}$. The output is a DDF ϕ. Three losses are applied on the warped CT ($\mathcal{L}_{\text{sim}}$), the warped label map ($\mathcal{L}_{\text{rigid}}$), and the DDF itself ($\mathcal{L}_{\text{smooth}}$).

Rigid Dice Loss. To penalize structural changes on rigid parts, i.e. the vertebrae, we use a RD loss. Let ϕ be the inferred deformation, then for each vertebra in the moving image (v_i) with binary segmentation label $s_{\mathcal{M}}^i$, we calculate the closest rigid transform ($T_{\text{rigid}}^{i,\phi}$) by solving the equation:

$$T_{\text{rigid}}^{i,\phi} = \underset{T_{\text{rigid}}}{\text{argmin}} \left(s_{\mathcal{M}}^i \circ T_{\text{rigid}} - s_{\mathcal{M}}^i \circ \phi \right)^2. \tag{2}$$

Then the RD loss for each vertebra can be defined as:

$$\mathcal{L}_{\text{rigid dice}}^i = 1 - 2 * \frac{\left| (s_{\mathcal{M}}^i \circ T_{\text{rigid}}^{i,\phi}) \cap (s_{\mathcal{M}}^i \circ \phi) \right|}{\left| s_{\mathcal{M}}^i \circ T_{\text{rigid}}^{i,\phi} \right| + \left| s_{\mathcal{M}}^i \circ \phi \right|} \tag{3}$$

Rigid Field Loss. To enforce a rigid transformation for each rigid body, we evaluate if the deformation field within the rigid body is close to a rigid deformation using the RF loss. Let $P_i = \{\mathbf{p}_j\}_{j=1,...,n}, \mathbf{p}_j \in s_{\mathcal{M}}^i$ be a set of randomly selected points from ith vertebra (v_i) in the moving image and $Q_i = \{\mathbf{q}_j\}_{j=1,...,n}, \mathbf{q}_j \in s_{\mathcal{M}}^i \circ \phi$ the set of corresponding points to P_i in the warped image. Using P_i and Q_i, we can compute the average rigid transform for v_i (ϕ_{rigid}^i) by solving a least squares problem with singular value decomposition (SVD) [22]. Then, by minimizing the distance between the predicted deformation vectors and the average rigid transform vectors inside each vertebra, the network learns to move it rigidly (see also Supplementary Material (SM)).

$$\mathcal{L}^i_{\text{rigid field}} = \sum_{\mathbf{z} \in s^i_{\mathcal{M}} \circ \phi, \mathbf{z} \in \mathbb{R}^3} (\phi^i_{\text{rigid}}(\mathbf{z}) - \phi(\mathbf{z}))^2 / \left| s^i_{\mathcal{M}} \circ \phi \right| \qquad (4)$$

Properness Condition. We adapt the penalty of the determinant of the Jacobian proposed by [18] to the DLIR scenario and call it PC as proposed by [23]. To implement it, first, we compute the ideal rotation matrix R of every voxel $\mathbf{z} \in \Omega_{\mathcal{F}}$ from the Jacobian of the DDF ϕ: $R(\mathbf{z}) = J_\phi(\mathbf{z})$. Then, we constrain the rotation matrices $R(\mathbf{z})$ of voxels inside each vertebra to have a proper unity determinant by minimizing the $l2$-distance between the Jacobian determinant and constant one:

$$\mathcal{L}_{\text{pc}} = \frac{1}{N} \sum_i^N \frac{1}{\left| s^i_{\mathcal{M}} \circ \phi \right|} \sum_{\mathbf{z} \in s^i_{\mathcal{M}} \circ \phi, \mathbf{z} \in \mathbb{R}^3} \left\| \det J_\phi(\mathbf{z}) - 1 \right\|_2^2 \qquad (5)$$

Orthonormal Condition. We include the OC proposed by [23], by computing the inner product of the Jacobian of the DDF J_ϕ and by penalizing the deviation of it from an identity matrix using the matrix norm. By forcing the rotation $R(\mathbf{z})$ of every voxel $\mathbf{z}$ inside each vertebra to be orthonormal, the rigidity is preserved:

$$\mathcal{L}_{\text{oc}} = \frac{1}{N} \sum_i^N \frac{1}{\left| s^i_{\mathcal{M}} \circ \phi \right|} \sum_{\mathbf{z} \in s^i_{\mathcal{M}} \circ \phi, \mathbf{z} \in \mathbb{R}^3} \left\| J_\phi(\mathbf{z})^T J_\phi(\mathbf{z}) - I \right\|_{\text{fro}}^2 \qquad (6)$$

3   Experiments

Dataset. We use an in-house dataset of 167 patients. The spatial resolution of the CTs ranges from $(0.2, 0.2, 0.4)$ mm to $(1.5, 1.5, 5)$ mm, while the T1-weighted MRIs have voxel spacing from $(0.3, 0.3, 2.7)$ mm to $(1, 1, 5)$ mm. The dataset has different fields of views and covers different part of spines, which in total, results in images of 1280 vertebrae. We split our dataset into training, validation and test sets with 117, 25 and 25 patients in each set, respectively. During training and inference, all images are resampled to 1 mm isotropic spacing, and the intensities are normalized to $[0, 1]$. Vertebra detection and segmentation on CT images is done automatically using the framework of [20]. For MRI, an expert annotated the central point of each vertebra, and manually segmented the validation and test set. The vertebral central points of both modalities are used to rigidly register each image pair. The ground truth segmentation labels are used for measuring the registration accuracy in terms of Dice score (DSC).

Hyperparameter Tuning of Image-Similarity and Smoothness. We investigated three different image similarity losses: normalized mutual information (NMI) [25], normalized gradient fields [7,17], and a modality-independent neighbourhood descriptor (MIND)-based [9] loss. MIND achieved the highest validation DSC. The hyperparameter λ_{smooth} was optimized with respect to the

MIND-based similarity loss based on the validation set. Considering both the registration accuracy (given by the DSC) and the validity of the inferred transformation (given by the standard deviation of the logarithm of the Jacobian determinant, $\mathrm{SD}\log|J_\phi|$), we find 0.1 to have the best validation performance so $\lambda_{\mathrm{smooth}}$ is fixed to 0.1 for the rest of the experiments see SM.

Ablation Studies. To measure the effect of each loss we employed for rigidity, we perform an ablation study for each of them. First, we train our network without any rigidity penalties ($\lambda_{\mathrm{rigid}} = 0$) for 500 epochs to get our baseline model. Then, starting from the milestone at 400 epochs, we add each of the rigidity penalties and train for another 100 epochs. We also compare our method with one conventional approach [23] (denoted as *Staring*), which takes NMI with OC and PC as loss function and iteratively optimizes for each pair of data.

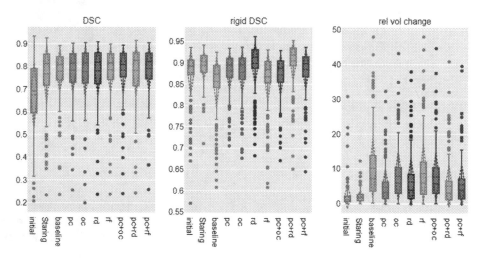

Fig. 2. Boxplots depicting the DSC, rigid DSC and relative volume change $\%\Delta\mathrm{vol}$ of initial dataset, conventional method, baseline and each loss setting.

Results. Table 1 gives a detailed summary of our experiments (see SM for weights setting). The baseline method performs better than the conventional *Staring* method, with 1.5% improvement in DSC and 100× faster speed (243s vs max. 4s). However, it cannot guarantee the rigidity of the vertebrae and their volume drastically changes during registration. Our proposed anatomy-aware losses alleviate this issue. Specifically, $\mathcal{L}_{\mathrm{pc}}$ contributes significantly to the volume preservation, with only 4.8% loss per vertebra and $\mathcal{L}_{\mathrm{oc}}$ results in sharper borders (see sagittal view in Fig. 3). The $\mathcal{L}_{\mathrm{rigid\ dice}}$, $\mathcal{L}_{\mathrm{rigid\ field}}$ and $\mathcal{L}_{\mathrm{oc}}$ attain higher rigid DSC than the baseline method, among which the RD loss achieves the highest level of rigidity, with 5.7% improvement over the baseline, and helps maintaining the details in the process area (see axial view in Fig. 3). The combinations of PC and other penalties reduce the volume loss while maintaining

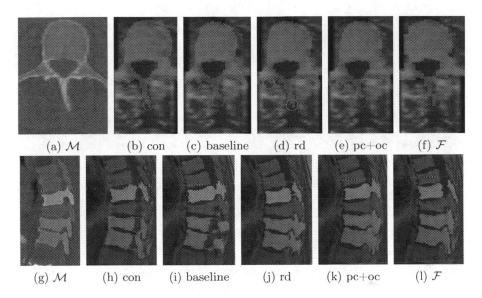

(a) $\mathcal{M}$	(b) con	(c) baseline	(d) rd	(e) pc+oc	(f) $\mathcal{F}$

| (g) $\mathcal{M}$ | (h) con | (i) baseline | (j) rd | (k) pc+oc | (l) $\mathcal{F}$ |

Fig. 3. Example axial (top) and sagittal (bottom) slices of moving image (CT) and fixed image (MRI) overlaid by warped label from conventional, baseline, and other methods with different rigidity penalties.

the rigidity of the vertebrae, and yielding plausible and smooth DDF. Figure 2 shows the boxplots of our experiments. The outliers are the cases where the boundary vertebrae are incomplete in CT/MRI images. With comparable registration accuracy, the proposed anatomy-aware losses significantly preserve the volume and rigid properties of the vertebrae. Qualitative results of the different methods are displayed in Fig. 3, where the red circles are showing regions of incorrect warped labels, while the greens outline correct ones. As shown in the axial slices, the incomplete transverse processes in MR images limit our method from getting high rigid DSC, since the network cannot predict missing parts. Figure 4 shows the quiver plots of the DDF. The displacement vectors inside each vertebra have uniform value in method with OC loss, while for the baseline, the magnitude of the displacements inside vertebra is not consistent (the colors vary). It indicates that with rigidity penalties, our method constrains the vertebra's deformation to be rigid.

PC During Inference. To validate PC's effectiveness in volume preservation, we compare its performance with the direct volume loss, which tries to penalize the volume change before and after the registration directly. We also compute PC as a metric (lower is better), during inference (see SM). With a similar %Δvol, the direct volume loss gets a higher PC than training with PC in the test set. It indicates that PC preserves the volume in a more realistic way, without any contraction or expansion in compensation. Moreover, training with OC can also decrease PC, which implies that enforcing the orthonormality of the transforma-

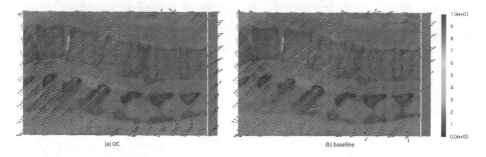

(a) OC   (b) baseline

Fig. 4. Quiver plots of DDF on a sagittal slices of fixed image (MRI) from (a) OC and (b) baseline. The arrows show the direction of the displacement vectors, and the color represents the magnitude. (Color figure online)

Table 1. Quantitative summary of the test set results given as averages (SD). DSC indicates the mean Dice score over all vertebrae. Rigid DSC computes the DSC between the warped label $s^i_\mathcal{M} \circ \phi$ and the rigidly transformed label $s^i_\mathcal{M} \circ T^i_{\text{rigid}}$, and OC estimates the orthonormality of deformations inside the vertebrae, both are to measure the level of rigidity kept during registration. $\%\Delta$vol represents the relative volume change of each vertebra between source label $s^i_\mathcal{M}$ and warped label $s^i_\mathcal{M} \circ \phi$. To assess the plausibility of the inferred transformation, $|J_\phi|_{\leq 0}$ indicates the number of folding voxels in the DDF, SD log$|J_\phi|$ measures the smoothness of the DDF.

Method	DSC ↑	Rigid DSC ↑	OC ↓	%Δvol ↓	$|J_\phi|_{\leq 0}$ ↓	SD log$|J_\phi|$ ↓
Initial	0.67(0.15)	0.88(0.05)	-	4.16(3.95)	-	-
Staring	0.77(0.13)	0.89(0.03)	**0.03(0.02)**	2.02(1.65)	0	**0.04(0.01)**
Baseline	0.78(0.10)	0.86(0.06)	1.00(1.11)	10.21(8.91)	0.04(0.20)	0.13(0.05)
pc	0.78(0.10)	0.88(0.04)	0.51(0.61)	**4.80(5.08)**	1.60(7.84)	0.12(0.05)
oc	0.78(0.11)	0.88(0.05)	0.31(0.39)	7.90(7.09)	0.12(0.59)	0.13(0.05)
rd	0.78(0.12)	0.90(0.05)	0.94(1.39)	6.32(6.77)	0.64(3.14)	0.13(0.05)
rf	0.79(0.10)	0.87(0.06)	0.98(1.22)	8.74(8.59)	0.08(0.39)	0.13(0.05)
pc+oc	0.78(0.10)	0.87(0.05)	0.41(0.45)	7.73(7.08)	0	0.12(0.05)
pc+rd	0.78(0.11)	**0.90(0.05)**	0.84(1.41)	5.12(6.13)	18.30(63.20)	0.13(0.06)
pc+rf	**0.79(0.10)**	0.89(0.05)	0.82(1.21)	5.51(5.94)	2.40(11.80)	0.13(0.06)

tion also contributes to unity determinant. Furthermore, the RD loss also results in a low PC, which indicates that it not only focuses on the edges of vertebrae to preserve the shape, but also reduces expansion/contraction inside the vertebrae, thus indeed enforces rigid deformation.

4   Conclusion and Discussion

We presented a framework for rigidity- and volume- preserving deformable registration of spinal CT/MRI. Compared to previous supervised DLIR methods, our approach only requires the moving label (MC 1). We define two novel rigidity penalties (RD and RF) to constrain the movement of the vertebrae (MC 2), and include PC and OC in the DLIR scenario (MC 3). Compared to conventional methods, our algorithm achieves higher accuracy and is significantly faster. Moreover, we present evidences to select different loss functions based on the clinical application by a detailed evaluation of their performance, as they have different benefits (MC 3). $\mathcal{L}_{pc}$ is helpful in bone cement estimation in vertebroplasty or kyphoplasty, in which the volume of vertebrae in the warped CT should be preserved [3]. When the CT and MRI need to be flawlessly fused, i.e., the image shapes should match perfectly, like in surgical planning, the preferred losses are $\mathcal{L}_{oc}$ or $\mathcal{L}_{rigid\ dice}$. If the smoothness/feasibility of the transformation plays a more important role, e.g., in differential diagnostics, the $\mathcal{L}_{rigid\ field}$ is a suitable choice.

Acknowledgements. This work was partially supported by the Bavarian State Ministry of Economics in the frame of the BayVFP Funding Line Digitalization - Information and Communication Technology, grant DIK0127/01 ("DigiBiop").

References

1. Arsigny, V., Commowick, O., Pennec, X., Ayache, N.: A log-euclidean framework for statistics on diffeomorphisms. In: Larsen, R., Nielsen, M., Sporring, J. (eds.) MICCAI 2006. LNCS, vol. 4190, pp. 924–931. Springer, Heidelberg (2006). https://doi.org/10.1007/11866565_113

2. Balakrishnan, G., Zhao, A., Sabuncu, M.R., Guttag, J., Dalca, A.V.: A log-Euclidean framework for statistics on diffeomorphisms. IEEE Trans. Med. Imaging **38**(8), 1788–1800 (2019)

3. Bukas, C., et al.: Patient-specific virtual spine straightening and vertebra inpainting: an automatic framework for osteoplasty planning. In: de Bruijne, M., Cattin, P.C., Cotin, S., Padoy, N., Speidel, S., Zheng, Y., Essert, C. (eds.) MICCAI 2021. LNCS, vol. 12904, pp. 529–539. Springer, Cham (2021). https://doi.org/10.1007/978-3-030-87202-1_51

4. De Vos, B.D., Berendsen, F.F., Viergever, M.A., Sokooti, H., Staring, M., Išgum, I.: A deep learning framework for unsupervised affine and deformable image registration. Med. Image Anal. **52**, 128–143, (2019)

5. Fu, Y., et al.: Deformable MR-CBCT prostate registration using biomechanically constrained deep learning networks. Med. Phys. **48**(1), 253–263 (2021)

6. Gill, S., et al.: Biomechanically constrained groupwise ultrasound to CT registration of the lumbar spine. Med. Image Anal. **16**(3), 662–674 (2012)

7. Haber, E., Modersitzki, J.: Intensity gradient based registration and fusion of multi-modal images. In: Larsen, R., Nielsen, M., Sporring, J. (eds.) MICCAI 2006. LNCS, vol. 4191, pp. 726–733. Springer, Heidelberg (2006). https://doi.org/10.1007/11866763_89

8. Haskins, G., Kruger, U., Yan, P.: Deep learning in medical image registration: a survey. Mach. Vis. Appl. **31**(1), 1–18 (2020)

9. Heinrich, M.P., Jenkinson, M., Papież, B.W., Brady, S.M., Schnabel, J.A.: Towards realtime multimodal fusion for image-guided interventions using self-similarities. In: Mori, K., Sakuma, I., Sato, Y., Barillot, C., Navab, N. (eds.) MICCAI 2013. LNCS, vol. 8149, pp. 187–194. Springer, Heidelberg (2013). https://doi.org/10.1007/978-3-642-40811-3_24

10. Kim, G.U., Chang, M.C., Kim, T.U., Lee, G.W.: Diagnostic modality in spine disease: a review. Asian Spine Journal 14(6), 910 (2020)

11. Kim, J., Matuszak, M.M., Saitou, K., Balter, J.M.: Distance-preserving rigidity penalty on deformable image registration of multiple skeletal components in the neck. Med. Phys. 40(12), (2013)

12. Little, J.A., Hill, D.L., Hawkes, D.J.: Deformations incorporating rigid structures. Comput. Vis. Image Underst. 66(2), 223–232 (1997)

13. McKenzie, E.M., Santhanam, A., Ruan, D., O'Connor, D., Cao, M., Sheng, K.: Multimodality image registration in the head-and-neck using a deep learning-derived synthetic ct as a bridge. Med. Phys. 47(3), 1094–1104 (2020)

14. Mok, Tony C. W.., Chung, Albert C. S..: Conditional deformable image registration with convolutional neural network. In: de Bruijne, M., et al. (eds.) MICCAI 2021. LNCS, vol. 12904, pp. 35–45. Springer, Cham (2021). https://doi.org/10.1007/978-3-030-87202-1_4

15. Momin, S., et al.: CT-MRI pelvic deformable registration via deep learning. In: Medical Imaging 2021: Image-Guided Procedures, Robotic Interventions, and Modeling. vol. 11598, p. 1159818. International Society for Optics and Photonics (2021)

16. Parizel, P., et al.: Trauma of the spine and spinal cord: imaging strategies. Eur. Spine J. 19(1), 8–17 (2010)

17. Pluim, J.P.W., Maintz, J.B.A., Viergever, M.A.: Image registration by maximization of combined mutual information and gradient information. In: Delp, S.L., DiGoia, A.M., Jaramaz, B. (eds.) MICCAI 2000. LNCS, vol. 1935, pp. 452–461. Springer, Heidelberg (2000). https://doi.org/10.1007/978-3-540-40899-4_46

18. Rohlfing, T., Maurer, C.R., Bluemke, D.A., Jacobs, M.A.: Volume-preserving non-rigid registration of MR breast images using free-form deformation with an incompressibility constraint. IEEE Trans. Med. Imaging 22(6), 730–741 (2003)

19. Ronneberger, O., Fischer, P., Brox, T.: U-Net: convolutional networks for biomedical image segmentation. In: Navab, N., Hornegger, J., Wells, W.M., Frangi, A.F. (eds.) MICCAI 2015. LNCS, vol. 9351, pp. 234–241. Springer, Cham (2015). https://doi.org/10.1007/978-3-319-24574-4_28

20. Sekuboyina, A., Rempfler, M., Kukačka, J., Tetteh, G., Valentinitsch, A., Kirschke, J.S., Menze, B.H.: Btrfly Net: vertebrae labelling with energy-based adversarial learning of local spine prior. In: Frangi, A.F., Schnabel, J.A., Davatzikos, C., Alberola-López, C., Fichtinger, G. (eds.) MICCAI 2018. LNCS, vol. 11073, pp. 649–657. Springer, Cham (2018). https://doi.org/10.1007/978-3-030-00937-3_74

21. Shah, L.M., Salzman, K.L.: Imaging of spinal metastatic disease. Int. J. Surg. Oncol. 2011 (2011)

22. Sorkine-Hornung, O., Rabinovich, M.: Least-squares rigid motion using svd (2017)

23. Staring, M., Klein, S., Pluim, J.P.: A rigidity penalty term for nonrigid registration. Med. Phys. 34(11), 4098–4108 (2007)

24. Tins, B.: Technical aspects of ct imaging of the spine. Insights Imaging 1(5), 349–359 (2010)

25. Wells, W.M., III., Viola, P., Atsumi, H., Nakajima, S., Kikinis, R.: Multi-modal volume registration by maximization of mutual information. Med. Image Anal. 1(1), 35–51 (1996)

Collaborative Quantization Embeddings for Intra-subject Prostate MR Image Registration

Ziyi Shen[1]([✉]), Qianye Yang[1], Yuming Shen[2], Francesco Giganti[3],
Vasilis Stavrinides[1], Richard Fan[4], Caroline Moore[1], Mirabela Rusu[4],
Geoffrey Sonn[4], Philip Torr[2], Dean Barratt[1], and Yipeng Hu[1]

[1] University College London, London, UK
joanshen0508@gmail.com
[2] University of Oxford, Oxford, UK
[3] University College London Hospital NHS Foundation Trust, London, UK
[4] Stanford University, Stanford, CA 94305, USA

Abstract. Image registration is useful for quantifying morphological changes in longitudinal MR images from prostate cancer patients. This paper describes a development in improving the learning-based registration algorithms, for this challenging clinical application often with highly variable yet limited training data. First, we report that the latent space can be clustered into a much lower dimensional space than that commonly found as bottleneck features at the deep layer of a trained registration network. Based on this observation, we propose a hierarchical quantization method, discretizing the learned feature vectors using a jointly-trained dictionary with a constrained size, in order to improve the generalisation of the registration networks. Furthermore, a novel collaborative dictionary is independently optimised to incorporate additional prior information, such as the segmentation of the gland or other regions of interest, in the latent quantized space. Based on 216 real clinical images from 86 prostate cancer patients, we show the efficacy of both the designed components. Improved registration accuracy was obtained with statistical significance, in terms of both Dice on gland and target registration error on corresponding landmarks, the latter of which achieved 5.46 mm, an improvement of 28.7% from the baseline without quantization. Experimental results also show that the difference in performance was indeed minimised between training and testing data.

Keywords: Registration · Quantization · Prostate cancer

1 Introduction

Whilst the diagnostic value in multiparametric MR imaging for prostate cancer, before or after biopsy for histopathology examination, has been identified [14,18],

Supplementary Information The online version contains supplementary material available at https://doi.org/10.1007/978-3-031-16446-0_23.

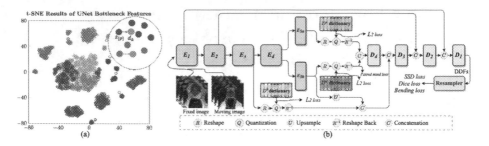

Fig. 1. Demonstration of the proposed prostate registration framework. (a) The t-SNE [10] visualization of the encoder outputs of a U-Net-like prostate registration network. (b) The network structure of HiCo-Net.

attention has been quickly turned to using this non-invasive imaging technique to monitor the disease at its early stage. Many have speculated that the temporal changes in morphology and intensity pattern in prostate gland can indicate the progression of the cancer [7]. Establishing spatial correspondence between two or more images, medical image registration has been proposed for aligning MR images from prostate cancer patients acquired at different time points. The estimated intra-subject spatial transformation, representing corresponding spatial locations between prostate glands, is an important quantitative tool to track the radiological evolution of prostate glands [24]. Aligning anatomical structures in lower pelvic region has been recognised to be challenging using 'classical' iterative algorithms [27], perhaps due to the highly patient-specific imaging characteristics in organs, such as prostate glands being having distinct patient-specific intensity patterns on T2-weighted MR images. Recent development has focused on learning-based algorithms for their effective and efficient inference [1,5,6,12,21,22]. Empirically, only a few 'types' of MR image features are reliably useful for establishing correspondence, such as volume, shape, anatomical and pathological structures, within or around the prostate gland and potential cancerous regions [24]. In addition, prostate capsules and different types of pathology are known to be highly variable and specific to individual patients [19,28]. Therefore, features are more likely to be 'easy-to-learn' to the distinct inter-subject differences.

We argue that these two above intuitions may warrant a compact feature adequately containing intra-subject correspondence for this application, although a deep network may still be required to learn such a representation [8]. However, deep models are over-parametrized [13], where the hidden representation may still carry information that is not related the task. With limited MR training data in a real clinical application, this redundancy and over-parametrization degrade the learned features' ability to generalize, leading to overfitting.

To illustrate this redundancy, we visualize the t-SNE [10] results of the deep features for registering prostate MR images in Fig. 1 (a). Given an N-sample prostate image set, we extract the bottleneck features of all samples, producing N feature maps with a size of $W \times H \times T \times C$. Here, $W \times H \times T$ refers to the shape of the output feature, while C is the channel number. Each C-dimensional vector represents a super-pixel in the encoded feature. We visualize the t-SNE result of all super-pixels in the set. It is shown in Fig. 1 (a) that the features are scattered into a limited numbers of groups. In other words, one can roughly represent the whole feature space using a smaller number of latent topics, consistent with the above discussion in limited corresponding structures and inter-subject variability.

This observation opens the door to compress the features with deep vector quantization (VQ) [15,16,20]. We refer to the anatomical knowledge of prostate, whose appearance varies from subjects, and propose to represent the neural features with a small set of vocabulary vectors, where useful anatomical and pathological structures are preserved. This ideology has been proved effective with limited training samples [4], which is indeed the case our task.

In this paper, the aforementioned motivation drives us to a VQ-based prostate registration solution. Specifically, we apply VQ to the middle of a registration U-Net [17] to make effective use of the feature space. The dictionary of a vector quantizer is usually data-driven. To efficiently improve the anatomical and pathological awareness of the model, we introduce another quantizer in parallel to the randomly initialized one, of which the dictionary preserves the specific local features of prostate interior. This is done by abstracting knowledge from a deep prostate segmentation network. The combination of the data-driven and the pre-defined quantizers is termed **collaborative quantization**. In addition, we explore the multi-scale structure of prostate MR images to fit both the global and local patterns of a moving image to the fixed one, which suggests a **hierarchical quantization** structure similar to [16]. Therefore, we name our model as Hierarchically & Collaboratively Quantized Network (HiCo-Net).

Our contributions can be summarised as follows: (1) We propose a feature quantization framework as regularization to alleviate the gap between training and test data for registration (2) We introduce a collaborative quantizer that encodes structure features of the gland boundary to better represent lesions and landmarks. (3) Our experiments show that the proposed HiCo-Netsuccessfully relieves the overfitting problem in weakly-supervised longitudinal prostate image registration, and outperforms the state-of-the-art.

2   Method

We consider a pairwise MR image registration problem. Let $\mathcal{X} = \{\mathbf{x}_i\}_{i=1}^n$ be the collection of images pairs of prostate, where $\mathbf{x}_i = (\mathbf{x}_i^s, \mathbf{x}_i^t)$ denotes a pair, with n being the number of image pairs. $\mathbf{x}_i^s$ and $\mathbf{x}_i^t$ respectively refers to the moving image and the fixed one. Each image pair comes with a pair of prostate gland anatomical segmentation maps $(\mathbf{m}_i^s, \mathbf{m}_i^t)$ for weakly-supervised training. For each $\mathbf{x}_i$, the goal is to predict a dense displacement field (DDF) $\mathbf{u}_i$ to establish voxel-level correspondence.

2.1   Preliminary: Deep Vector Quantization

VQ [20] quantizes an arbitrary representation tensor using a fixed number of values defined by a dictionary $\mathcal{D} = \{\mathbf{d}_i\}_{i=1}^{K}$, $\mathbf{d}_i \in \mathbb{R}^C$, where K is the dictionary size and C is the dimensionality of each code. Specifically, an output of an encoder $E(\mathbf{x}) \in \mathbb{R}^{H \times W \times T \times C}$ is obtained by passing an MR image pair $\mathbf{x}$ through a CNN. We are going to quantize each C-dimensional vector of $E(\mathbf{x})$. For simplicity, the rest of this paper denotes a voxel super-position in a raster scan order with a coordinate $p = 1 \cdots HWT$, i.e., $E(\mathbf{x})_{[p]} \in \mathbb{R}^C$. Hence, a vector quantization operator $Q(\cdot)$ can be defined as follows:

$$\mathbf{z}_{[p]} = Q\left(E(\mathbf{x})_{[p]}; \mathcal{D}\right) = \mathbf{d}_k, \text{ where } k = \underset{i}{\operatorname{argmin}} \|E(\mathbf{x})_{[p]} - \mathbf{d}_i\|. \tag{1}$$

Then, $\mathbf{z}$ replaces $E(\mathbf{x})$ and is forwarded to the rest of the network. The encoder receives the gradients from top of the quantizer through the straight-through estimator [2], i.e., $\partial \mathbf{z}/\partial E := \mathbb{I}$. VQ incorporates two additional loss terms to enforce the output of the encoder to be similar to the quantized results:

$$\mathcal{L}_{\mathrm{Q}}(E(\mathbf{x}), \mathcal{D}) = \sum_p \left\|\mathrm{sg}\left(E(\mathbf{x})_{[p]}\right) - \mathbf{z}_{[p]}\right\|_2^2 + \beta \left\|E(\mathbf{x})_{[p]} - \mathrm{sg}\left(\mathbf{z}_{[p]}\right)\right\|_2^2, \tag{2}$$

where $\mathrm{sg}(\cdot)$ is the stop-gradient operator and $\beta = 0.25$ is the hyperparameter.

2.2   Model Overview

Figure 1 (b) depicts the schematic of HiCo-Net. It generally undergoes a U-Net-like structure with an encoder $E(\cdot)$ and a decoder $D(\cdot)$. An image pair $\mathbf{x} = (\mathbf{x}^s, \mathbf{x}^t)$ is firstly concatenated together and then rendered to the encoder, while the decoder produces $\mathbf{u}$, the desired DDF. We particularly denote the output of each residual block as $E_1(\mathbf{x}), E_2(\mathbf{x}) \cdots$. Notably, $E_4(\mathbf{x})$ is rendered to two parallel convolutional layers, $E_{5a}(\mathbf{x})$ and $E_{5b}(\mathbf{x})$, that are followed be two quantizers. We respectively term them the collaborative quantizer (Sect. 2.5) and the vanilla one (Sect. 2.3). The skip connection between $E_3(\mathbf{x})$ and the decoder is quantized as well. Since it also mixes multi-scale information from $E_{5b}(\mathbf{x})$ afterwards, we name it the hierarchical quantizer (Sect. 2.4). The intuition behind this design is given in their respective sections as follows. The DDF output then contributes to the conventional weakly-supervised prostate registration losses with a resampler.

2.3   Vanilla Quantization

We first introduce a vanilla quantizer that quantizes the output of $E_{5b}(\mathbf{x})$. It behaves identical to the original VQ operation [20]. Shown in Fig. 1(b), its dictionary $\mathcal{D}^v$ is randomly initialized and is updated by back-propagation during training. In this way, the global information, a relatively fixed structure of the MR prostate images, is regularized for better generalization to test data. We denote the quantization loss for the vanilla quantizer as $\mathcal{L}_{\mathrm{V}}(\mathbf{x}) = \mathcal{L}_{\mathrm{Q}}(E_{5b}(\mathbf{x}), \mathcal{D}^v)$.

2.4 Hierarchical Quantization

Image features of a deep network often carry local information, which can benefit from multi-scale modelling for positional alignment. A hierarchical representation quantizer has been proved to be effective to perceiving this [16].

To implement this, we employ a hierarchical quantizer to quantize the output of $E_3(\mathbf{x})$, of which the dictionary is denoted as $\mathcal{D}^h$. The quantized result is added by the output of $E_4(\mathbf{x})$. Since the voxel sizes of them mismatch, one needs to firstly upsample $E_4(\mathbf{x})$, as is shown in Fig. 1(b). $\mathcal{D}^h$ is randomly initialized. The hierarchical quantizer introduces a quantization loss as $\mathcal{L}_H(\mathbf{x}) = \mathcal{L}_Q(E_3(\mathbf{x}), \mathcal{D}^h)$.

2.5 Collaborative Quantization

As is discussed in Sect. 1, the awareness of prostate contour is of key importance to this prostate registration task. This inspires us to transfer knowledge to our model from a deep segmentation network, without requiring segmentation during inference. VQ allows us to conveniently initialize the dictionary values according to the segmentation network's output as prior knowledge. In particular, we first train a U-Net-based segmentation network on the training dataset, and then extract an $H \times W \times T \times C$ tensor for each image with its encoder. Each C-dimensional vector of all images' features is treated as an instance for K-means clustering. We cache the values of K cluster centers produced by K-means, and use them to initialize the dictionary of the collaborative quantizer, i.e., $\mathcal{D}^c$. An analogy of this procedure is provided in the supplemental.

The collaborative quantizer takes input from $E_{5a}(\mathbf{x})$ as a compensation to the fully-data-driven vanilla quantizer by concatenating their outputs afterwards. We similarly define its quantization loss as $\mathcal{L}_C(\mathbf{x}) = \mathcal{L}_Q(E_{5a}(\mathbf{x}), \mathcal{D}^c)$.

2.6 Training

Quantization Loss. The training objective of HiCo-Net is a combination of the quantization losses and the conventional weakly-supervised registration ones. We first define the overall quantization loss of an image pair $\mathbf{x}$:

$$\mathcal{L}_{\text{Quant}}(\mathbf{x}) = \mathcal{L}_V(\mathbf{x}) + \mathcal{L}_C(\mathbf{x}) + \mathcal{L}_H(\mathbf{x}). \tag{3}$$

The three quantization terms above can have equal weights as they are mutually independent, and are imposed to different stages of the registration network.

SSD Loss. The Sum-of-Square Differences (SSD) loss [1] measures the similarity between the translated image and the fixed one. One needs to firstly resample $\mathbf{x}^s$ using the DDF $\mathbf{u}$ and then compute

$$\mathcal{L}_{\text{SSD}}(\mathbf{x}) = \left\| \mathbf{u} \otimes \mathbf{x}^s - \mathbf{x}^t \right\|_2^2, \tag{4}$$

where $\otimes$ refers to the resampling operation.

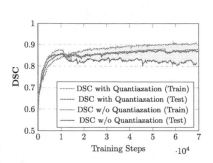

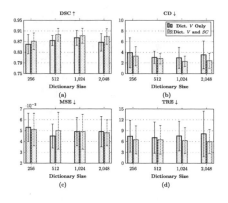

Fig. 2. Illustration of how $\mathcal{D}^c$ is initialized before training.

Fig. 3. Demonstration ablation study of dictionary size.

Dice Loss. This loss has shown effectiveness in aligning organ shapes and positions [23], and is applied to the masks:

$$\mathcal{L}_{\text{Dice}}(\mathbf{x}) = -\operatorname{Dice}\left(\mathbf{u} \otimes \mathbf{m}^{\text{s}},\ \mathbf{m}^{\text{t}}\right). \tag{5}$$

Bending Regularization. We use this regularization term $\mathcal{L}_{\text{Bend}}(\mathbf{u})$ [26] to penalise the non-smoothness of the generated DDF.

Overall Training Objective. By defining the losses above, we can simply compose a linear combination of them as the final loss of HiCo-Net as follows:

$$\mathcal{L}_{\text{All}}(\mathbf{x}) = \lambda_Q \mathcal{L}_{\text{Quant}}(\mathbf{x}) + \lambda_S \mathcal{L}_{\text{SSD}}(\mathbf{x}) + \lambda_D \mathcal{L}_{\text{Dice}}(\mathbf{x}) + \lambda_B \mathcal{L}_{\text{bend}}(\mathbf{u}), \tag{6}$$

where $\lambda_Q = 1$, $\lambda_S = 1$, $\lambda_D = 1$ and $\lambda_B = 50$ are hyperparameters. Our models are trained with stochastic gradient descent algorithms.

3   Experiment

3.1   Experimental Settings

Implementation. We use a basic U-Net equipped with skip connections between encoder and decoder. Our encoder consists of 4 residual blocks, a total of 12 convolutional layers. In addition, we add 2 convolutional layers to expand heads for the subsequent hierarchical and collaborative quantization operators as shown in Fig. 1(b). The channel size of the hierarchical dictionary $\mathcal{D}^h$ is 128. The vanilla dictionary $\mathcal{D}^v$ and collaborative one $\mathcal{D}^c$ both have a feature channel number of 256. We by default set the vocabulary size of $\mathcal{D}^h$ and $\mathcal{D}^v$ to 1024, while fixing the size of $\mathcal{D}^c$ one to 512. As per the initialization of $\mathcal{D}^c$, we use a U-Net as our segmentation network, which is utilized to collect features for K-means clustering. Note that the segmentation network is not involved in our registration training. We set training batch size to 4, and use the Adam optimizer with

Table 1. Ablation study of hierarchical and collaborative quantization.

$\mathcal{D}^{\mathrm{v}}$	$\mathcal{D}^{\mathrm{h}}$	$\mathcal{D}^{\mathrm{c}}$	DSC	CD	MSE	TRE
w/o registration			0.700 ± 0.097	12.63 ± 5.810	0.051 ± 0.014	13.72 ± 5.833
			0.859 ± 0.038	4.187 ± 2.050	0.049 ± 0.013	7.657 ± 4.212
✓			0.884 ± 0.028	2.958 ± 1.967	0.049 ± 0.013	7.529 ± 4.109
✓	✓		0.887 ± 0.264	2.644 ± 1.469	0.048 ± 0.014	6.158 ± 3.539
✓		✓w/o pretrain	0.865 ± 0.027	3.011 ± 1.635	0.050 ± 0.015	7.551 ± 4.435
✓		✓	0.892 ± 0.028	2.308 ± 0.967	0.049 ± 0.016	6.248 ± 3.577
✓	✓	✓	0.881 ± 0.025	3.091 ± 1.557	0.043 ± 0.013	5.457 ± 3.489

a learning rate of 10^{-4}. The network is trained for 1000 epochs at most, taking three days on an NVIDIA Tesla V100 GPU. The network architecture and code are available at https://github.com/joanshen0508/HiCo-Net.

Dataset. The utilized dataset consists of 216 longitudinal prostate T2-weighted MR images from 86 patients, acquired from University College London Hospitals NHS Foundation. It is divided into three folds, containing 70, 6, and 10 patients for training, validation, and test. Each patient has 2-4 images, with an average interval between consecutive visits of 18.1 and a standard deviation of 10.3 months. Before training, we resample the data to $0.7 \times 0.7 \times 0.7 \,\mathrm{mm}^3$ and normalize the intensity to $[0, 1]$. To train the proposed prostate registration model, we also crop the dataset and generate the dataset with the size of $128 \times 128 \times 102$. On the test set, 141 anatomical and pathological landmarks are manually identified on moving and fixed images, including patient-specific fluid-filled cysts, calcification and centroids of zonal boundaries.

Evaluation Metrics. We adopt the conventional weakly-supervised registration metrics including Dice Similarity Coefficient (DSC) and Centroid Distance (CD) between the prostate glands. The Mean-Squared Error (MSE) between the fixed image and wrapped moving image is as well reported. Registration should support downstream clinical image analysis task. To demonstrate the effectiveness of our method, we further report the Target Registration Error(TRE), which calculates the difference of landmarks between fixed image and predicted result.

3.2 Ablation Study

The Effect of Feature Quantization. We first build a registration model without quantization similar to [24] and compare it with a variant of HiCo-Net that only involves the vanilla quantizer. As shown in Fig. 2, our quantized version effectively narrows the accuracy gap between training and test, observing no overfitting problem. We also report the performance of HiCo-Net with different combinations of the three quantizers in Table 1. Compared with the unquantized baseline, the TRE is reduced from 7.657 ± 4.212 mm to 6.248 ± 3.577 mm (`p_value` $= 0.0001$ under paired t-test) when applying the

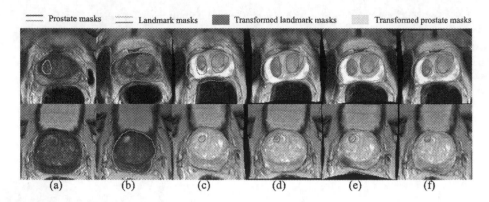

Fig. 4. Effect of proposed method. (a) moving image. **(b)** fixed image. **(c)** w/o quantization. **(d)** w/ $\mathcal{D}^v$. **(e)** w/ $\mathcal{D}^v$ and $\mathcal{D}^h$. **(f)** w/ $\mathcal{D}^v, \mathcal{D}^h$ and $\mathcal{D}^c$.

Table 2. Comparison with the-state-of-the-arts prostate registration methods.

Method	DSC	CD	MSE	TRE	Run-time
NiftyReg [11]	0.270 ± 0.304	22.869 ± 11.761	0.041 ± 0.019	21.147 ± 15.841	45.76
VoxelMorph [1]	0.763 ± 0.081	8.842 ± 3.156	0.053 ± 0.015	8.833 ± 5.147	0.69
DeepTag [25]	0.822 ± 0.083	7.594 ± 2.905	0.052 ± 0.013	7.458 ± 4.815	1.95
Contrastive [9]	0.856 ± 0.117	4.973 ± 2.407	0.054 ± 0.018	8.2166 ± 4.407	0.31
Basic U-Net	0.859 ± 0.038	4.187 ± 2.050	0.049 ± 0.013	7.657 ± 4.212	0.62
VAE-like	0.865 ± 0.029	3.623 ± 2.189	0.045 ± 0.019	7.626 ± 3.948	0.72
HiCo-Net	0.881 ± 0.025	3.091 ± 1.557	0.043 ± 0.013	5.457 ± 3.489	0.68

vanilla and collaborative quantization, and it further decreases to 5.457 ± 3.489 mm (`p_value` < 0.0001) when employing all the three quantizers.

Hierarchical and Collaborative Quantization. The hierarchical quatization scheme mixes the global and local information, and obtains the best results in Table 1. We also consider randomly initializing the values of $\mathcal{D}^c$. Its gain against the single-quantizer baseline is marginal, but once initialized by segmentation feature vectors, the collaborative embedding improves the spatial alignment to focus on the local semantic discrepancy, and obtains a better registration performance. We provide qualitative comparison results in Fig. 4. The proposed method performs well on aligning local patterns to the fixed image. We evaluate the dictionary size of $\mathcal{D}^v$ and $\mathcal{D}^c$, shown in Fig. 3, which suggests a dictionary size of 512 and 1024 for $\mathcal{D}^v$ and $\mathcal{D}^c$ respectively is the best option.

Inter-subject Extension. To explore quantization for further generic application, we also validate the proposed method on inter-subject prostate MR data [3]. We notice that the performance increases with quantization (DSC: $0.80 \pm 0.11 \rightarrow 0.86 \pm 0.04$, CD: $4.17 \pm 2.43 \rightarrow 2.12 \pm 1.33$, MSE: $0.04 \pm 0.02 \rightarrow 0.03 \pm 0.02$). This task is challenging as the presence of prostate varies from different identities.

3.3   Comparison with Existing Methods

We compare HiCo-Net with a non-optimised iterative method [11] and some well-known deep registration methods [1, 9, 25]. To further validate the encoder-decoder structure, a common U-net and a VAE framework are implemented for prostate registration. As shown in Table 2, the proposed method obtains competitive results in all metrics. Remarkably, the number of negative Jacobian determinants of our method is 0.0 ± 0.0. The consuming time is also reported. In addition, our collaborative quantization algorithm is free from additional sub-network embedding, avoiding large memory consumption.

4   Conclusion

In this paper, we proposed a collaborative quantization framework for prostate MR image registration, which was named HiCo-Net. We introduced a hierarchical quantizer that jointly regularizes the global and local latent information to benefit the displacement prediction. In addition, we designed a collaborative dictionary that was equipped with helpful anatomical structure knowledge to perceive the local semantic discrepancy. The experiments showed that this method performed favorably against state-of-the-art registration methods and bypassed the overfitting problem for our dataset with a moderate size. Representing and quantizing inter-subject cues for registration can be our future work.

Acknowledgements. This work was supported by the International Alliance for Cancer Early Detection, an alliance between Cancer Research UK [C28070/A30912; C73666/A31378], Canary Center at Stanford University, the University of Cambridge, OHSU Knight Cancer Institute, University College London and the University of Manchester. This work was also supported by the Wellcome/EPSRC Centre for Interventional and Surgical Sciences [203145Z/16/Z].

References

1. Balakrishnan, G., Zhao, A., Sabuncu, M.R., Guttag, J., Dalca, A.V.: VoxelMorph: a learning framework for deformable medical image registration. IEEE Trans. Med. Imaging **38**(8), 1788–1800 (2019)
2. Bengio, Y., Léonard, N., Courville, A.: Estimating or propagating gradients through stochastic neurons for conditional computation. arXiv preprint arXiv:1308.3432 (2013)
3. Bloch, N., et al.: NCI-ISBI 2013 challenge: automated segmentation of prostate structures. Cancer Imaging Arch. **370**(6), 5 (2015)
4. Chen, K., Lee, C.G.: Incremental few-shot learning via vector quantization in deep embedded space. In: ICLR (2021)
5. Chen, X., Meng, Y., Zhao, Y., Williams, R., Vallabhaneni, S.R., Zheng, Y.: Learning unsupervised parameter-specific affine transformation for medical images registration. In: de Bruijne, M., Cattin, P.C., Cotin, S., Padoy, N., Speidel, S., Zheng, Y., Essert, C. (eds.) MICCAI 2021. LNCS, vol. 12904, pp. 24–34. Springer, Cham (2021). https://doi.org/10.1007/978-3-030-87202-1_3

6. Kim, B., Kim, D.H., Park, S.H., Kim, J., Lee, J.G., Ye, J.C.: CycleMorph: cycle consistent unsupervised deformable image registration. Med. Image Anal. **71** (2021)

7. Kim, C.K., Park, B.K., Lee, H.M., Kim, S.S., Kim, E.: MRI techniques for prediction of local tumor progression after high-intensity focused ultrasonic ablation of prostate cancer. Am. J. Roentgenol. **190**(5), 1180–1186 (2008)

8. Liu, F., et al.: SAME: deformable image registration based on self-supervised anatomical embeddings. In: de Bruijne, M., et al. (eds.) MICCAI 2021. LNCS, vol. 12904, pp. 87–97. Springer, Cham (2021). https://doi.org/10.1007/978-3-030-87202-1_9

9. Liu, L., Aviles-Rivero, A.I., Schönlieb, C.B.: Contrastive registration for unsupervised medical image segmentation. arXiv preprint arXiv:2011.08894 (2020)

10. Maaten, L.v.d., Hinton, G.: Visualizing data using t-SNE. Journal of Mach. Learn. Res. **9**(Nov), 2579–2605 (2008)

11. Modat, M., et al.: Fast free-form deformation using graphics processing units. Comput. Methods Programs Biomed. **98**(3), 278–284 (2010)

12. Mok, T.C.W., Chung, A.C.S.: Large deformation diffeomorphic image registration with laplacian pyramid networks. In: Martel, A.L., Martel, A.L., et al. (eds.) MICCAI 2020. LNCS, vol. 12263, pp. 211–221. Springer, Cham (2020). https://doi.org/10.1007/978-3-030-59716-0_21

13. Molchanov, D., Ashukha, A., Vetrov, D.: Variational dropout sparsifies deep neural networks. In: ICML, pp. 2498–2507. PMLR (2017)

14. Moore, C.M., et al.: Reporting magnetic resonance imaging in men on active surveillance for prostate cancer: the precise recommendations-a report of a european school of oncology task force. Eur. Urol. **71**(4), 648–655 (2017)

15. Peng, J., Liu, D., Xu, S., Li, H.: Generating diverse structure for image inpainting with hierarchical VQ-VAE. In: CVPR. pp. 10775–10784 (2021)

16. Razavi, A., Van den Oord, A., Vinyals, O.: Generating diverse high-fidelity images with VQ-VAE-2. In: Advances in Neural Information Processing Systems, vol. 32 (2019)

17. Ronneberger, O., Fischer, P., Brox, T.: U-Net: convolutional networks for biomedical image segmentation. In: Navab, N., Hornegger, J., Wells, W.M., Frangi, A.F. (eds.) MICCAI 2015. LNCS, vol. 9351, pp. 234–241. Springer, Cham (2015). https://doi.org/10.1007/978-3-319-24574-4_28

18. Schoots, I.G., Petrides, N., Giganti, F., Bokhorst, L.P., Rannikko, A., Klotz, L., Villers, A., Hugosson, J., Moore, C.M.: Magnetic resonance imaging in active surveillance of prostate cancer: a systematic review. Eur. Urol. **67**(4), 627–636 (2015)

19. Song, X., et al.: Cross-modal attention for mri and ultrasound volume registration. In: de Bruijne, M., et al. (eds.) MICCAI 2021. LNCS, vol. 12904, pp. 66–75. Springer, Cham (2021). https://doi.org/10.1007/978-3-030-87202-1_7

20. Van Den Oord, A., Vinyals, O., et al.: Neural discrete representation learning. In: Conference on Advances in Neural Information Processing Systems, vol. 30 (2017)

21. Wang, J., Zhang, M.: DeepFlash: an efficient network for learning-based medical image registration. In: CVPR, pp. 4444–4452 (2020)

22. Xu, J., Chen, E.Z., Chen, X., Chen, T., Sun, S.: Multi-scale neural odes for 3d medical image registration. In: de Bruijne, M., et al. (eds.) MICCAI 2021. LNCS, vol. 12904, pp. 213–223. Springer, Cham (2021). https://doi.org/10.1007/978-3-030-87202-1_21

23. Xu, Zhenlin, Niethammer, Marc: DeepAtlas: joint semi-supervised learning of image registration and segmentation. In: Shen, D., et al. (eds.) MICCAI 2019. LNCS, vol. 11765, pp. 420–429. Springer, Cham (2019). https://doi.org/10.1007/978-3-030-32245-8_47

24. Yang, Q., Fu, Y., Giganti, F., Ghavami, N., Chen, Q., Noble, J.A., Vercauteren, T., Barratt, D., Hu, Y.: Longitudinal image registration with temporal-order and subject-specificity discrimination. In: MICCAI. pp. 243–252. Springer (2020)

25. Ye, M., Kanski, M., Yang, D., Chang, Q., Yan, Z., Huang, Q., Axel, L., Metaxas, D.: Deeptag: An unsupervised deep learning method for motion tracking on cardiac tagging magnetic resonance images. In: CVPR. pp. 7261–7271 (June 2021)

26. Zeng, Q., et al.: Label-driven magnetic resonance imaging (MRI)-transrectal ultrasound (TRUS) registration using weakly supervised learning for MRI-guided prostate radiotherapy. Phys. Med. Biol. **65**(13) (2020)

27. Zhang, M., et al.: Frequency diffeomorphisms for efficient image registration. In: Niethammer, M., et al. (eds.) IPMI 2017. LNCS, vol. 10265, pp. 559–570. Springer, Cham (2017). https://doi.org/10.1007/978-3-319-59050-9_44

28. Zhang, Yungeng, Pei, Yuru, Zha, Hongbin: Learning Dual transformer network for diffeomorphic registration. In: de Bruijne, M., et al. (eds.) MICCAI 2021. LNCS, vol. 12904, pp. 129–138. Springer, Cham (2021). https://doi.org/10.1007/978-3-030-87202-1_13

Mesh-Based 3D Motion Tracking in Cardiac MRI Using Deep Learning

Qingjie Meng[1]($\boxtimes$), Wenjia Bai[1,2,3], Tianrui Liu[4], Declan P. O'Regan[5], and Daniel Rueckert[1,6]

[1] BioMedIA, Department of Computing, Imperial College London, London, UK
q.meng16@imperial.ac.uk

[2] Data Science Institute, Imperial College London, London, UK

[3] Department of Brain Sciences, Imperial College London, London, UK

[4] National University of Defense Technology, Changsha, China

[5] MRC London Institute of Medical Sciences, Imperial College London, London, UK

[6] Klinikum Rechts der Isar, Technical University Munich, Munich, Germany

Abstract. 3D motion estimation from cine cardiac magnetic resonance (CMR) images is important for the assessment of cardiac function and diagnosis of cardiovascular diseases. Most of the previous methods focus on estimating pixel-/voxel-wise motion fields in the full image space, which ignore the fact that motion estimation is mainly relevant and useful within the object of interest, *e.g.*, the heart. In this work, we model the heart as a 3D geometric mesh and propose a novel deep learning-based method that can estimate 3D motion of the heart mesh from 2D short- and long-axis CMR images. By developing a differentiable mesh-to-image rasterizer, the method is able to leverage the anatomical shape information from 2D multi-view CMR images for 3D motion estimation. The differentiability of the rasterizer enables us to train the method end-to-end. One advantage of the proposed method is that by tracking the motion of each vertex, it is able to keep the vertex correspondence of 3D meshes between time frames, which is important for quantitative assessment of the cardiac function on the mesh. We evaluate the proposed method on CMR images acquired from the UK Biobank study. Experimental results show that the proposed method quantitatively and qualitatively outperforms both conventional and learning-based cardiac motion tracking methods.

Keywords: Mesh · Differentiable rasterizer · Multi-view images

1 Introduction

Estimating left ventricular (LV) myocardial motion is important for the detection of LV dysfunction and the diagnosis of myocardial diseases [7,20]. Most of

Supplementary Information The online version contains supplementary material available at https://doi.org/10.1007/978-3-031-16446-0_24.

recent cardiac motion tracking approaches utilize cine cardiac magnetic resonance (CMR) images to estimate a dense motion field which represents pixel-/voxel-wise deformation across the entire image, *e.g.*, [2,4,13,20–22,32,33]. However, it remains challenging to use this type of motion estimation for certain clinical applications where the heart and its motion needs to be represented on a 3D geometric mesh with known vertex correspondence across time frames, *e.g.*, pathological cardiac remodeling [14] and motion-based characterization of LV phenotypes [15]. Transforming image space pixel-/voxel-wise deformation to mesh space vertex deformation has several limitations. In specific, a pixel-wise motion field only considers the motion of the heart within a single view plane and does not provide complete 3D motion information. Using post-processing steps to convert pixel-/voxel-wise motion fields to 3D mesh displacements can compromise motion estimation accuracy due to interpolation operation and the lack of through-plane motion.

In this work, we propose an end-to-end trainable network for estimating the 3D motion of the myocardial mesh from cine CMR images. Our method integrates short-axis (SAX) and long-axis (LAX) view images, which enables estimating both in-plane and through-plane mesh motion. In the proposed method, the intensity information of the input multi-view images are utilized to directly estimate a 3D mesh displacement. The estimated mesh displacement explicitly models the 3D motion of each vertex from the end-diastolic (ED) frame to the t-th frame, and thus is able to maintain vertex correspondence between time frames. A differentiable mesh-to-image rasterizer is introduced during training to generate 2D soft segmentations from the mesh, which allows leveraging 2D multi-view anatomical shape information for 3D mesh displacement estimation. During inference, our model generates a sequence of meshes, which shows the myocardial motion across the cardiac cycle. Extracting different anatomical view planes from the meshes can further generate 2D myocardial segmentations.

The main contributions of this paper are summarized as follows: (1) We address the problem of 3D cardiac motion tracking on the geometric mesh. The proposed method learns vertex-wise displacements of the 3D myocardial mesh directly from 2D SAX and LAX cine CMR images via an end-to-end trainable network. (2) We introduce a differentiable mesh-to-image rasterizer to leverage 2D anatomical shape information from different anatomical views for 3D motion estimation. (3) The proposed method is able to perform joint cardiac motion estimation and segmentation across the cardiac cycle.

Related Work. Many cardiac motion estimation methods use conventional and deep learning-based image registration to estimate pixel-/voxel-wise motion fields [8,16,21,25,27,30,33,34]. For example, a free form deformation (FFD) method that proposed by Rueckert et al. [25] for non-rigid image registration has been used for cardiac motion estimation in many recent works, *e.g.*, [2,4,20,26,28]. Vercauteren et al. [30] introduced a non-parametric diffeomorphic image registration method which has been used for cardiac motion tracking [22]. In recent years, deep learning-based image registration methods have also been applied to cardiac motion estimation: Qin et al. [21] proposed a joint deep learning network for simultaneous cardiac segmentation and motion estimation. In particular, the U-Net architecture [24] has been widely used for learning-based image registration [3,31] and further for cardiac motion estimation [27,34]. Compared to image registration-based cardiac motion estimation, several other methods focus on anatomical motion estimation in mesh space. They explore mesh matching or mesh registration to estimate displacements for each vertex of the mesh. For example, Papademetris et al. [17] proposed a method that uses biomechanical modeling and shape-tracking approach to estimate the motion of myocardial mesh. Abdelkhalek et al. [1] built a framework to compute mesh displacements via point clouds alignment. These mesh motion estimation approaches compute mesh displacements only from dynamic shape information, without considering intensity information from images. In contrast to the existing deep learning-based cardiac motion estimation methods, our method combines image information with the myocardial mesh which contains the epi- and endocardial surfaces of the heart. We estimate 3D mesh displacements by using the intensity information of 2D images from multiple anatomical views.

2   Method

Our goal is to estimate 3D mesh displacements of the LV myocardium from 2D SAX and LAX CMR images. Our task is formulated as follows: Let $\{I_0^{sa}, I_0^{2ch}, I_0^{4ch}\}$ be the 2D SAX, 2CH and 4CH view images of the ED frame and $\{I_t^{sa}, I_t^{2ch}, I_t^{4ch}\}$ be the multi-view images of the t-th frame. $0 \leqslant t \leqslant T - 1$ and T is the number of frames in the cardiac cycle. We want to estimate a 3D mesh displacement $\Delta V_t \in \mathbb{R}^{N \times 3}$ for the input ED frame mesh ($\{V_0, F\}$) by using these ED and t-th frame multi-view images. Here, $V_0 \in \mathbb{R}^{N \times 3}$ and F refer to the vertices and faces of the input ED frame mesh, respectively. N is the number of vertices and ΔV_t represents the motion of vertices from ED frame to the t-th frame.

The schematic architecture of the proposed method is shown in Fig. 1. For model training, the proposed method can be separated into three components: First, a mesh displacement estimation module learns the motion of a myocardial mesh from intensity images. Second, a mesh prediction module evolves the input ED frame mesh to the t-th frame mesh based on the learned mesh displacement. Finally, a differentiable mesh-to-image rasterizer is used to produce soft segmentations by extracting 2D planes (in the SAX and LAX orientations) from the predicted t-th frame mesh. This enables using 2D anatomical shape information to supervise 3D mesh displacement estimation.

2.1   Mesh Displacement Estimation

In this module, we estimate a mesh displacement ΔV_t from the input images via predicting an intermediate voxel-wise 3D motion field. In specific, a hybrid network composed of 2D CNNs and 3D CNNs learns a voxel-wise 3D motion field Φ_t from the input SAX and LAX view images. The 2D CNNs learn and combine the 2D features of multi-view images. The 3D CNNs with a encoder-decoder architecture predict Φ_t by further learning 3D representations from the combined 2D features. Φ_t has the same size to the input SAX stacks and represents the

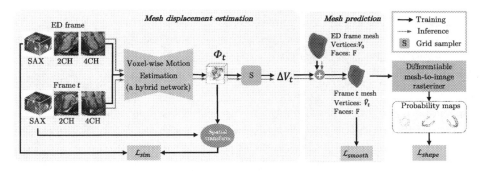

Fig. 1. An overview of the proposed method. Mesh displacement estimation module takes multi-view images as input and learns mesh displacement ΔV_t. By updating the myocardial mesh of the ED frame with ΔV_t, mesh prediction module predicts the mesh of the t-th frame. During training, a differential mesh-to-image rasterizer is built to extract different anatomical view planes from the t-th frame mesh, which generates 2D soft segmentations (probability maps) and thus enables leveraging 2D shape information for 3D mesh displacement estimation.

motion of image voxels from the ED frame to the t-th frame. Subsequently, a grid sampler is utilized to generate ΔV_t from the obtained Φ_t. In detail, for each vertex of the input ED frame mesh, its displacement is sampled from Φ_t by using bi-linear interpolation at the coordinates of this vertex.

Overall, ΔV_t is estimated from the input multi-view images by

$$\Delta V_t = S(H(I_0^k, I_t^k), V_0), \quad k = \{sa, 2ch, 4ch\}. \tag{1}$$

Here, $H(\cdot, \cdot)$ is the hybrid network, $S(\cdot, \cdot)$ is the grid sampler and $\Phi_t = H(I_0^k, I_t^k)$.

As ground truth mesh displacement is usually unavailable, ΔV_t can not be directly evaluated. Instead, we evaluate Φ_t in a self supervision manner. We transform the SAX stack of the t-th frame (I_t^{sa}) to the ED frame using Φ_t via a spatial transformer [11]. By minimizing the image similarity loss in Eq. 2, Φ_t is encouraged to reflect the motion of the myocardium.

$$\mathcal{L}_{sim} = \|I_0^{sa} - I_t^{sa} \circ \Phi_t\|^2 \tag{2}$$

2.2 Mesh Prediction

With the estimated ΔV_t, the myocardial mesh of the ED frame ($\{V_0, F\}$) can be deformed to the t-th frame ($\{\hat{V}_t, F\}$) by

$$\hat{V}_t = V_0 + \Delta V_t. \tag{3}$$

A Laplacian smoothing loss[1] $\mathcal{L}_{smooth}$ is used to evaluate the smoothness of the predicted t-th frame mesh. The Laplacian of $\hat{v}_t^i$ is defined by $L(\hat{v}_t^i)$,

$$L(\hat{v}_t^i) = \frac{1}{|\mathcal{N}_i|} \sum_{j \in \mathcal{N}_i} (\hat{v}_t^i - \hat{v}_t^j) \tag{4}$$

---

[1] Implemented by pytorch3d.loss.mesh_laplacian_smoothing().

Here, $\mathcal{N}_i$ is the set of adjacent vertices to $\hat{v}_t^i$ and $\{\hat{v}_t^i, \hat{v}_t^j\} \in \hat{V}_t$.

2.3 Differentiable Mesh-to-Image Rasterizer

Because of the low through-plane resolution in SAX stacks, the image similarity loss ($\mathcal{L}_{sim}$) on its own is not sufficient to guarantee a 3D motion estimation, especially in the longitudinal direction. To address this problem, we propose a differentiable mesh-to-image rasterizer to extract 2D soft segmentations from the 3D mesh and thus enables 2D anatomical shape information from multiple views to supervise 3D mesh displacement estimation. These 2D soft segmentations are probability maps which contain the probability of the mesh intersecting the different view planes. The closer a vertex to a plane, the higher probability the vertex lies in the plane. The probability map enables the differentiability of the rasterization and further supports the end-to-end training of the proposed method. The input of the differentiable rasterizer is the mesh $\{\hat{V}_t, F\}$ and the outputs are 2D probability maps on SAX, 2CH and 4CH view planes ($\{P_t^{sa}, P_t^{2ch}, P_t^{4ch}\}$). In detail, the coordinates of $\hat{v}_t^i$ ($\hat{v}_t^i \in \hat{V}_t, i = [0, 1, ..., N]$) are first transformed to the image space of different anatomical planes using the information about the relative position in the DICOM header. Then, the probability of each vertex being on a specific view plane is computed by:

$$p_t^{ik} = e^{-\tau d_{ik}^2}, \quad d_{ik} = |z^{ik} - z^k|, \quad k = \{sa, 2ch, 4ch\} \tag{5}$$

Here p_t^{ik} refers to the probability of $\hat{v}_t^i$ belonging to the plane k, and τ is the hyper-parameter which controls the sharpness the exponential function. d_{ik} is the distance between $\hat{v}_t^i$ and the plane k, with (x^{ik}, y^{ik}, z^{ik}) is the transformed coordinates of $\hat{v}_t^i$ and z^k is the slice corresponding to the plane k. The vertices satisfying $|z^{ik} - z^k| < 1$ are selected as the intersection of $\{\hat{V}_t, F\}$ and plane k, and their probability values form the probability map P_t^k.

The obtained probability maps are compared to 2D ground truth binary segmentations $\{B_t^{sa}, B_t^{2ch}, B_t^{4ch}\}$ (only contain anatomy boundary) by a shape loss $\mathcal{L}_{shape}$. We utilize a Weighted Hausdorff Distance[2](WHD$(\cdot, \cdot)$) [23] to measure the distance between these anatomy boundaries,

$$\mathcal{L}_{shape} = \sum\nolimits_{k=\{sa, 2ch, 4ch\}} \text{WHD}(P_t^k, B_t^k). \tag{6}$$

2.4 Optimization

Our model is an end-to-end trainable framework and the overall objective is a linear combination of three loss terms,

$$\mathcal{L} = \mathcal{L}_{shape} + \lambda \mathcal{L}_{sim} + \beta \mathcal{L}_{smooth}, \tag{7}$$

where λ and β are hyper-parameters chosen experimentally depending on the dataset. We use the Adam optimizer (learning rate $= 10^{-4}$) to update the network parameters. Our model is implemented by Pytorch and is trained on a NVIDIA RTX A5000 GPU with 24 GB of memory.

---

[2] Implemented by https://github.com/javiribera/locating-objects-without-bboxes.

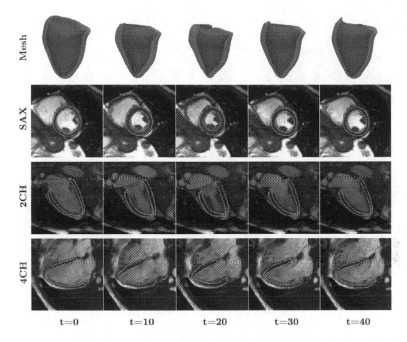

Fig. 2. Examples of motion tracking results. The ED frame mesh is deformed to the t-th frame using the mesh displacements generated by the proposed method. 2D segmentation on SAX, 2CH and 4CH view planes (Row 2–4) are generated by extracting the corresponding planes from the predicted t-th frame mesh. Red contours are predicted segmentation while green contours are ground truth. (Color figure online)

3   Experiments and Results

Experiments were performed on randomly selected 530 subjects from the UK Biobank study [19]. Each subject contains SAX, 2CH and 4CH view cine CMR sequences and each sequence contains 50 frames. SAX view images were resampled by linear interpolation from a spacing of $\sim 1.8 \times 1.8 \times 10$ mm to a spacing of $1.25 \times 1.25 \times 2$ mm while 2CH and 4CH view images were resampled from $\sim 1.8 \times 1.8$ mm to 1.25×1.25 mm. Based on the center of the intersecting line between the middle slice of the SAX stack and the LAX view images, the SAX, 2CH and 4CH view images are cropped to cover the whole LV in the center. The binary segmentations used in Eq. 6 were obtained via an automated tool provided in [9], followed by manual quality control. The myocardial meshes of the ED frame and the ES frame are reconstructed from the binary segmentations using marching cube algorithm. Each mesh contain $\sim 20k$ vertices. We split the dataset into 400/50/80 for train/validation/test and train the proposed model for 300 epochs. The hyper-parameters in Eq. 7 are selected as $\lambda = 300, \beta = 200$ and τ in Eq. 5 is set to 3. The detailed architecture of the hybrid network (Sect. 2.1) and motion tracking videos are presented in the supplementary material.

Table 1. Comparison of other cardiac motion tracking methods. The results are reported as "mean (standard deviation)". ↑ indicates the higher value the better while ↓ indicates the lower value the better. Best results in bold.

Methods	Anatomical views	Mean surface distance ↓	HD (mm) ↓			BoundF (%) ↑		
			SAX	2CH	4CH	SAX	2CH	4CH
FFD [25]	SAX	3.02(0.86)	21.31(4.66)	15.17(4.52)	15.95(4.84)	62.15(7.48)	77.60(6.97)	77.79(7.13)
dDemons [30]	SAX	3.20(0.90)	**20.32(5.03)**	15.01(3.48)	15.72(3.41)	63.67(6.92)	77.38(5.99)	80.29(5.83)
3D-UNet [6]	SAX	3.35(0.88)	20.45(5.15)	14.44(2.99)	14.83(3.57)	60.64(7.74)	74.63(6.01)	76.06(6.08)
Ours	SAX. 2CH, 4CH	**1.98(0.44)**	20.76(4.82)	**7.44(4.04)**	**8.62(4.49)**	**71.49(8.82)**	**87.21(6.97)**	**84.24(6.84)**

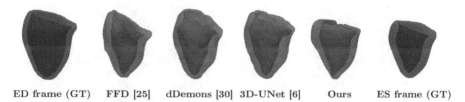

ED frame (GT)   FFD [25]   dDemons [30]   3D-UNet [6]   Ours   ES frame (GT)

Fig. 3. Motion estimation using baseline methods and the proposed method. Green meshes are ground truth (GT) meshes of the ED and ES frames. Red meshes are the predicted ES frame meshes based on different methods. (Color figure online)

Mesh Motion Tracking Performance. The proposed method is utilized to estimate mesh displacements in the full cardiac cycle. For each test subject, with the obtained $\{\Delta V_t | t = [0, 49]\}$, the myocardial mesh of the ED frame ($t = 0$) is deformed to the t-th frame. Red meshes in Fig. 2 shows that the estimated mesh displacement ΔV_t enables 3D myocardial motion tracking on meshes. In addition, we extracted SAX/2CH/4CH view planes from the predicted t-th frame mesh and generated the predicted 2D segmentations on different view planes. Figure 2 shows the effectiveness of ΔV_t by comparing the predicted and the ground truth 2D myocardial segmentations (only contain anatomy boundaries).

Comparison Study. We compared the proposed method with three state-of-the-art cardiac motion tracking approaches, including a B-spline free form deformation (FFD) algorithm[3] [25], a diffeomorphic Demons (dDemons) algorithm[4] [30] and 3D-UNet[5] [6]. We quantitatively evaluated the performance using the following metrics: Mean surface distance, Hausdorff distance (HD) and Boundary F-score (BoundF). Here, surface distance evaluates the distance between the predicted and the ground truth ES frame meshes. The Hausdorff distance and Boundary F-score compare the predicted and the ground truth 2D myocardial segmentations on SAX, 2CH and 4CH view planes. The Hausdorff distance quantifies the contour distance while Boundary F-score evaluates contour alignment accuracy as described in [5,10,18]. For fair comparison, we

---

[3] Implemented by using the MIRTK toolkit: http://mirtk.github.io/.

[4] https://github.com/InsightSoftwareConsortium/SimpleITK-Notebooks/Python/66.

[5] https://github.com/wolny/pytorch-3dunet.

Table 2. Mesh displacement estimation with **different anatomical views**.

Anatomical views	HD (mm) ↓		
	SAX	2CH	4CH
SAX	21.09(4.56)	9.29(4.80)	12.12(5.51)
SAX+2CH	**20.35(5.41)**	9.99(4.36)	11.98(4.14)
SAX+2CH+ 4CH	20.76(4.82)	**7.44(4.04)**	**8.62(4.49)**

Table 3. Mesh displacement estimation with **different losses**.

Loss	HD (mm) ↓		
	SAX	2CH	4CH
$\mathcal{L}_{shape}$	**20.21(5.12)**	13.31(2.77)	14.36(4.24)
$\mathcal{L}_{shape} + \mathcal{L}_{smooth}$	20.73(4.73)	12.19(3.09)	14.05(3.26)
$\mathcal{L}_{shape} + \mathcal{L}_{smooth} + \mathcal{L}_{sim}$	20.76(4.82)	**7.44(4.04)**	**8.62(4.49)**

evaluated several sets of hyper-parameter values for all methods and selected hyper-parameters that achieve the best Hausdorff distance on the validation set. Table 1 shows the quantitative comparison results and Fig. 3 further shows the qualitatively results. From Table 1, we observe that the proposed method outperforms all baseline methods, demonstrating the effectiveness of the proposed method for estimating mesh displacements. In addition, the proposed method achieves the best performance regarding to 2CH and 4CH view segmentations in Table 1 and obtains the ES frame mesh which is most similar to the ground truth ES frame mesh in Fig. 3. These results illustrate that in contrast to all baseline methods which only show motion within SAX plane, the proposed method is able to estimate through-plane motion along the longitudinal direction. Finally, we compared the average inference time of different methods. The FFD [25] is 16 s and the dDemons [30] is 28 s (both are only available on CPUs) while the 3D-UNet [6] is 1.1 s and our method is 1.0 s (both are on GPUs).

Ablation Study. For the proposed method, we explore the effects of using different anatomical views and loss combinations. Table 2 shows that adding the images and shape information of LAX views improves the performance. This might be because LAX views can introduce high-resolution through-plane information for 3D motion estimation. Table 3 shows that proposed method performs best, which illustrates the importance of each loss component.

Discussion. An alternative to our method would be to estimate mesh displacement directly from input images via fully connected networks (FCNs) without voxel-wise 3D motion estimation. However, using FCNs to estimate displacement of $\sim 20K$ vertices needs large GPU memory, which may not always be available. More importantly, voxel-wise 3D motion estimation is able to explicitly connect the anatomical motion in image space to mesh space. $\mathcal{L}_{smooth}$ is introduced as an overall regularization term to directly constrain the smoothness of the deformed mesh. The regularization loss for the voxel-wise 3D motion field could be added. But the extra loss may increase the complexity of model training. In contrast to the commonly used 3D-to-2D projection which obtains a silhouette by utilizing camera parameters, e.g., [12,29], our differentiable mesh-to-image rasterizer focuses on slicing a 3D mesh to 2D soft segmentations. Weighted Hausdorff Distance is one example to compute $\mathcal{L}_{shape}$, as it can evaluate the distance between soft-labeled and hard-labeled point sets. Other boundary similarity measurements may also be applied to this loss component in our task. In the evaluation, we quantitatively evaluated the performance on the ES frame. This is because ground truth meshes are only available at the ED and ES frames in our current dataset. We choose hyper-parameters using grid search (*i.e.*, $\lambda = [100, 300, 500]$, $\beta = [100, 200, 300]$ and $\tau = [2, 3]$) and we select the hyper-parameters with the best performance on the validation data.

4   Conclusion

In this paper, we propose a image-based mesh motion estimation network for 3D myocardial motion tracking. The proposed method is an end-to-end trainable network which estimates 3D mesh displacements from the intensity information of 2D SAX and LAX view CMR images. Experimental results demonstrate the effectiveness of the proposed method compared with other competing methods. For future work, we will apply our method to clinical association studies.

Acknowledgment. This research has been conducted using the UK Biobank Resource under application number 40616. This work is supported by the British Heart Foundation (RG/19/6/34387, RE/18/4/34215); Medical Research Council (MC-A658-5QEB0); National Institute for Health Research (NIHR) Imperial College Biomedical Research Centre. W. Bai was supported by EPSRC DeepGeM Grant (EP/W01842X/1).

References

1. Abdelkhalek, M., Aguib, H., Moustafa, M., Elkhodary, K.: Enhanced 3D myocardial strain estimation from multi-view 2D CMR imaging. arXiv preprint arXiv:2009.12466 (2020)
2. Bai, W., et al.: A population-based phenome-wide association study of cardiac and aortic structure and function. Nat. Med. **26**, 1654–1662 (2020)
3. Balakrishnan, G., Zhao, A., Sabuncu, M.R., Guttag, J.V., Dalca, A.V.: Voxelmorph: a learning framework for deformable medical image registration. IEEE Trans. Med. Imaging **38**(8), 1788–1800 (2019)
4. Bello, G., et al.: Deep learning cardiac motion analysis for human survival prediction. Nat. Mach. Intell. **1**, 95–104 (2019)
5. Cheng, D., Liao, R., Fidler, S., Urtasun, R.: Darnet: deep active ray network for building segmentation. In: CVPR, pp. 7423–7431 (2019)
6. Çiçek, Ö., Abdulkadir, A., Lienkamp, S.S., Brox, T., Ronneberger, O.: 3D U-Net: learning dense volumetric segmentation from sparse annotation. In: Ourselin, S., Joskowicz, L., Sabuncu, M.R., Unal, G., Wells, W. (eds.) MICCAI 2016. LNCS, vol. 9901, pp. 424–432. Springer, Cham (2016). https://doi.org/10.1007/978-3-319-46723-8_49
7. Claus, P., Omar, A.M.S., Pedrizzetti, G., Sengupta, P.P., Nagel, E.: Tissue tracking technology for assessing cardiac mechanics: principles, normal values, and clinical applications. JACC Cardiovasc. Imaging **8**(12), 1444–1460 (2015)

8. Craene, M.D., et al.: Temporal diffeomorphic free-form deformation: application to motion and strain estimation from 3D echocardiography. Med. Image Anal. **16**(2), 427–450 (2012)

9. Duan, J., et al.: Automatic 3D bi-ventricular segmentation of cardiac images by a shape-refined multi- task deep learning approach. IEEE Trans. Med. Imaging **38**(9), 2151–2164 (2019)

10. Gur, S., Shaharabany, T., Wolf, L.: End to end trainable active contours via differentiable rendering. In: ICLR (2020)

11. Jaderberg, M., Simonyan, K., Zisserman, A., Kavukcuoglu, K.: Spatial transformer networks. In: NeurIPS (2015)

12. Kato, H., Ushiku, Y., Harada, T.: Neural 3D mesh renderer. In: CVPR (2018)

13. Loecher, M., Perotti, L.E., Ennis, D.B.: Using synthetic data generation to train a cardiac motion tag tracking neural network. Med. Image Anal. **74**, 102223 (2021)

14. Mansi, T., et al.: A statistical model for quantification and prediction of cardiac remodelling: application to Tetralogy of Fallot. IEEE Trans. Med. Imaging **30**(9), 1605–1616 (2011)

15. de Marvao, A., et al.: Precursors of the hypertensive heart phenotype develop in normotensive adults: a high resolution 3D MRI study. JACC Cardiovasc. Imaging (2015)

16. McLeod, K., Prakosa, A., Mansi, T., Sermesant, M., Pennec, X.: An incompressible log-domain demons algorithm for tracking heart tissue. In: Camara, O., Konukoglu, E., Pop, M., Rhode, K., Sermesant, M., Young, A. (eds.) STACOM 2011. LNCS, vol. 7085, pp. 55–67. Springer, Heidelberg (2012). https://doi.org/10.1007/978-3-642-28326-0_6

17. Papademetris, X., Sinusas, A.J., Dione, D.P., Duncan, J.S.: Estimation of 3D left ventricular deformation from echocardiography. Med. Image Anal. **5**(1), 17–28 (2001)

18. Perazzi, F., Pont-Tuset, J., McWilliams, B., Van Gool, L., Gross, M., Sorkine-Hornung, A.: A benchmark dataset and evaluation methodology for video object segmentation. In: CVPR (2016)

19. Petersen, S., et al.: UK Biobank's cardiovascular magnetic resonance protocol. J. Cardiovasc. Magn. Reson. **18**, 1–7 (2015)

20. Puyol-Antón, E., et al.: Regional multi-view learning for cardiac motion analysis: application to identification of dilated cardiomyopathy patients. IEEE Trans. Biomed. Eng. **66**(4), 956–966 (2019)

21. Qin, C., et al.: Joint learning of motion estimation and segmentation for cardiac MR image sequences. In: Frangi, A.F., Schnabel, J.A., Davatzikos, C., Alberola-López, C., Fichtinger, G. (eds.) MICCAI 2018. LNCS, vol. 11071, pp. 472–480. Springer, Cham (2018). https://doi.org/10.1007/978-3-030-00934-2_53

22. Qin, C., Wang, S., Chen, C., Qiu, H., Bai, W., Rueckert, D.: Biomechanics-informed neural networks for myocardial motion tracking in MRI. In: Martel, A.L., et al. (eds.) MICCAI 2020. LNCS, vol. 12263, pp. 296–306. Springer, Cham (2020). https://doi.org/10.1007/978-3-030-59716-0_29

23. Ribera, J., Guera, D., Chen, Y., Delp, E.J.: Locating objects without bounding boxes. In: CVPR, pp. 6472–6482 (2019)

24. Ronneberger, O., Fischer, P., Brox, T.: U-Net: convolutional networks for biomedical image segmentation. In: Navab, N., Hornegger, J., Wells, W.M., Frangi, A.F. (eds.) MICCAI 2015. LNCS, vol. 9351, pp. 234–241. Springer, Cham (2015). https://doi.org/10.1007/978-3-319-24574-4_28

25. Rueckert, D., Sonoda, L., Hayes, C., Hill, D., Leach, M., Hawkes, D.: Nonrigid registration using free-form deformations: application to breast MR images. IEEE Trans. Med. Imaging **18**(8), 712–721 (1999)

26. Shi, W., et al.: A comprehensive cardiac motion estimation framework using both untagged and 3-D tagged MR images based on nonrigid registration. IEEE Trans. Med. Imaging **31**, 1263–1275 (2012)

27. Ta, K., Ahn, S.S., Stendahl, J.C., Sinusas, A.J., Duncan, J.S.: A semi-supervised joint network for simultaneous left ventricular motion tracking and segmentation in 4D echocardiography. In: Martel, A.L., et al. (eds.) MICCAI 2020. LNCS, vol. 12266, pp. 468–477. Springer, Cham (2020). https://doi.org/10.1007/978-3-030-59725-2_45

28. Tobon-Gomez, C., et al.: Benchmarking framework for myocardial tracking and deformation algorithms: an open access database. Med. Image Anal. **17**(6), 632–648 (2013)

29. Tung, H.Y.F., Tung, H.W., Yumer, E., Fragkiadaki, K.: Self-supervised learning of motion capture. In: NeurIPS (2017)

30. Vercauteren, T., Pennec, X., Perchant, A., Ayache, N.: Non-parametric diffeomorphic image registration with the demons algorithm. In: Ayache, N., Ourselin, S., Maeder, A. (eds.) MICCAI 2007. LNCS, vol. 4792, pp. 319–326. Springer, Heidelberg (2007). https://doi.org/10.1007/978-3-540-75759-7_39

31. Xu, Z., et al.: Adversarial uni- and multi-modal stream networks for multimodal image registration. In: Martel, A.L., et al. (eds.) MICCAI 2020. LNCS, vol. 12263, pp. 222–232. Springer, Cham (2020). https://doi.org/10.1007/978-3-030-59716-0_22

32. Ye, M., et al.: Deeptag: an unsupervised deep learning method for motion tracking on cardiac tagging magnetic resonance images. In: CVPR (2021)

33. Yu, H., et al.: FOAL: fast online adaptive learning for cardiac motion estimation. In: CVPR (2020)

34. Zheng, Q., Delingette, H., Ayache, N.: Explainable cardiac pathology classification on cine MRI with motion characterization by semi-supervised learning of apparent flow. Med. Image Anal. **56**, 80–95 (2019)

Data-Driven Multi-modal Partial Medical Image Preregistration by Template Space Patch Mapping

Ding Xia[1]([✉]), Xi Yang[2], Oliver van Kaick[3], Taichi Kin[1], and Takeo Igarashi[1]

[1] The University of Tokyo, 7 Chome-3-1 Hong, Bunkyo City, Tokyo 113-8654, Japan
xia-ding1995@g.ecc.u-tokyo.ac.jp
[2] Jilin University, No. 2699, Qianjin Street, Changchun 130012, Jilin, China
[3] Carleton University, 1125 Colonel, Ottawa K1S 5B6, Canada

Abstract. Image registration is an essential part of Medical Image Analysis. Traditional local search methods (e.g., Mean Square Errors (MSE) and Normalized Mutual Information (NMI)) achieve accurate registration but require good initialization. However, finding a good initialization is difficult in partial image matching. Recent deep learning methods such as images-to-transformation directly solve the registration problem but need images of mostly same sizes and already roughly aligned. This work presents a learning-based method to provide good initialization for partial image registration. A light and efficient network learns the mapping from a small patch of an image to a position in the template space for each modality. After computing such mapping for a set of patches, we compute a rigid transformation matrix that maps the patches to the corresponding target positions. We tested our method to register a 3DRA image of a partial brain to a CT image of a whole brain. The result shows that MSE registration with our initialization significantly outperformed baselines including naive initialization and recent deep learning methods without template. You can access our source code in https://github.com/ApisXia/PartialMedPreregistration.

Keywords: Multi-modal · Partial image · Preregistration · Patch mapping

1 Introduction

Multi-modal medical image registration (fusion or alignment) merges information from various medical imaging devices, helping surgeons obtain a holistic view of the target organ. The target of our work is medical imaging of the human brain by registering two types of modalities: three-dimensional rotational angiography (3DRA) [5,6,16], which provides detailed information of the 3D vasculature

Supplementary Information The online version contains supplementary material available at https://doi.org/10.1007/978-3-031-16446-0_25.

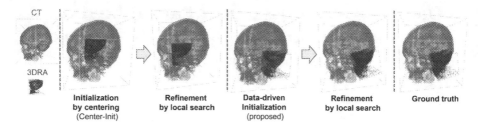

Fig. 1. Overview and demonstration of our proposed initialization method and center-initialization methods.

of patients, and CT angiography [9,13], which provides additional information about surrounding bone and soft tissue. We assume that the target organ is identical (same patient, same time), so the images can be aligned with a rigid transformation. This paper explicitly targets partial image registration, where one of the images (3DRA) only partially covers the target organ (brain), which is common and critical because only the part containing the lesion area of the brain is often scanned in medical practice due to radiation exposure concerns.

Popular multi-modal registration methods use Mean Square Errors (MSE) or Normalized Mutual Information (NMI) [15,21], which are essentially a local search. Thus, they require good initialization. A naive but still popular initialization approach in practice is to align the center of the two input images [7,20]. However, this heuristic does not work well for partial image registration where the image centers are far apart.

Closely related to our problem, a few recent works have introduced deep learning supervised models to learn a transformation for rigid registration of multi-modal medical images. Zheng et al. [24,25] proposed a model based on lightweight CNNs to hierarchically regress the 6Dof pose parameters of 2D X-ray images. Yan et al. [22] proposed the adversarial image registration network (AIR-net) based on the GAN framework with simultaneously trained CNNs for transformation parameter estimation and registration quality evaluation. Sloan et al. [18] align MR T1- and T2-weighted images using a variety of neural networks which incorporate user knowledge of the task. Yao et al. [23] proposed a hierarchical registration framework that combines the conventional method and regression CNNs for image-guided radiotherapy (IGRT). Bashiri et al. [1] propose a transformation method to obtain accurate alignment of multi-modal images in both cases, with full and partial overlap, by manifold learning. Moreover, Guo et al. [4] introduced a coarse-to-fine multi-stage registration (MSReg) framework, which consists of N consecutive networks for registration of multi-modal prostate images. Liao et al. [10] introduced a Point-Of-Interest Network, which directly computes 2D/3D registration by establishing point-to-point correspondence between multiple views of digitally reconstructed radiographs (DRRs) and X-ray images. Song et al. [19] develop a self-attention mechanism specifically for cross-modal image registration.

The aforementioned deep learning methods assume that the two images cover the same region (whole brain) and are mostly aligned already [4,19,22,25].

Moreover, most of them require that the inputs of different modalities have the same sizes. Thus, these methods do not work well for partial image registration without proper initialization and preprocessing. If registration fails, then manual initialization is necessary. A popular method is to specify a few landmarks on image slices manually, but the process is tedious and requires expertise. Our work aims to eliminate or minimize the need for such manual initialization.

Our paper introduces a template-space patch mapping (TSPM) method providing reliable initialization for local-search registration in rigid multi-modal partial image registration. Instead of matching two images directly, we register the two images to a common template space using a pre-trained neural network. We use patch-based mapping to handle images of diverse sizes and a RANSAC-based fitting algorithm to remove outliers. The network is trained with manually registered images. We then run traditional local search registration on the given initialization to obtain the final registration result. We tested our method on the dataset of 93 pairs of 3DRA (partial, moving image) and CT (fixed images) volumes. The results show that registration with our learning-based initialization achieves registration error 4.453 mm, which significantly outperforms registration with naive initialization by centering (Fig. 1).

2   Method

Figure 2 describes the overall workflow of our method. The 3DRA volume is considered the moving image in this image registration application, and the CT volume is the fixed image. Compared to the pipeline of traditional registration methods, we replace the common initialization methods, like center-initialization, with our novel deep-learning-based initialization method, TSPM. Then we use the output of our method as initialization for precise alignment (refinement) using traditional local search. Our method prioritizes robustness on the global scale rather than precision on the local scale because it is more critical to reliably return a roughly correct alignment than seek local precision sacrificing global alignment.

2.1   Template-Space Patch Mapping (TSPM)

The proposed Template-Space Patch Mapping method takes the 3DRA volume as input and provides the predicted position in the template space as output, as shown in the circled part of Fig. 2. The method comprises two parts: prediction of patch locations in the template space and rough transformation calculation based on these predictions.

As for the template space, we randomly picked a case from a collection of registered images to define the template. In practice, different templates will not affect the performance of our method, but we still recommend choosing templates with typical skull shapes. The CT volume of this case is scaled to fit a 128 px cubic space with its center aligned to the center of the space. The rest space in the cubic space is filled with the background density of the template CT volume.

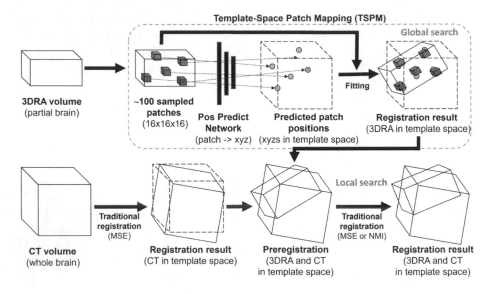

Fig. 2. The proposed workflow.

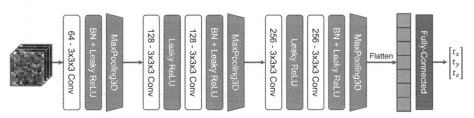

Fig. 3. Overview of the position prediction network structure.

Next, we randomly sample a fixed number (100 in our implementation) of small image patches ($16 \times 16 \times 16$ px) from the moving image. We discard image patches with more than 40% background regions and re-sample patches until we have enough qualified patches. Then, we feed each image patch to a pre-trained position prediction network and obtain its target position $\theta = \{t_x, t_y, t_z\}$ in a shared template space as output, without considering the rotation of patches. The network consists of five layers of 3D convolution and two layers of fully-connected networks (Fig. 3).

Last, we compute the rigid transformation matrix that moves the patches to the corresponding target positions as closely as possible. We use the method described in Sect. 3.3 of [12], which first computes an affine transformation by least-squares fitting and then extracts a rigid transformation by polar decomposition. In order to improve the robustness of the predicted rigid transformation matrix, we also apply RANSAC [3] to filter outliers because some patches have insignificant features and fail in template location prediction. We randomly select six data points from the patch set in our pipeline and calculate the best-fitting transformation. Other settings in RANSAC is error threshold (10) and minimum pick number (20). We count inliers whose distance between the predicted patch positions and transformation results is less than a threshold (10 mm). We repeat the process at least 2,000 iterations and return the rigid transformation matrix $\boldsymbol{A}_{mov}$ with the most number of inlier points (we continue iterations until we get more than 30 inliers).

2.2 Pipeline Execution

As we have the output of our proposed method as initialization, we use Air-Lab [17] to do alignment and refinement with traditional local search methods (MSE and NMI). Because the original version of AirLab is incapable of processing partial volumes, we modified the code as needed.

The corresponding fixed volume is preprocessed like that of the template case first. Next, we register it to the template space using a traditional local search method and get the rigid transformation matrix $\boldsymbol{A}_{fix}$. Now we have moving and fixed volume in the same template space. The relative rigid transformation $\boldsymbol{A}^*$ from the moving volume to the fixed volume can be simply obtained as $\boldsymbol{A}^* = \boldsymbol{A}_{fix}^{-1}\boldsymbol{A}_{mov}$. We then apply traditional local search registration to precisely register the moving image to the fixed image. Since the two images are already mostly aligned, these local search methods quickly and reliably find a precise alignment.

3 Experiments

Data and Preprocessing. The dataset we used for experiments contains 93 pairs of 3DRA and CT images. All of them were collected and registered by medical professionals using existing tools. 3DRA images are partial, which is common in daily medical image collection. We categorize the 3DRA images into four categories according to their largest spacing: tiny (<70 mm, $\times14$), small (70–110 mm, $\times16$), medium (110–135 mm, $\times13$), and large (>135 mm, $\times50$). Different brain regions are covered with similar probabilities. The Cerebellum is more frequently collected, while the Front lobe is less often.

Surgeons created the ground-truth registered dataset with Amira [20] by these steps: 1) Manually initialize a rough relative position and rotation between 3DRA and CT images; 2) Crop down CT to the size of 3DRA due to the automatic workflow of NMI in Amira requires the input of 2 modalities has the same sizes; 3) Manually verify the results.

For the training of our position prediction network, we randomly sampled 150 small patches for each case as we describe in Sect. 2. The density of input 3DRA patches is confined in $[-500, 3000]$ and scaled to $[-0.5, 0.5]$. The output of the network is a position (xyz) in the canonical space (using $[0, 1]$ to represent actual $[0, 128]$ template space). We adopt the L1 loss as the loss function because compared to the L2 loss, L1 is less sensitive to outliers.

Implementation. Our proposed method and the other baseline methods are implemented with PyTorch 1.9 [14] and deployed on the same machine, equipped with an Nvidia Titan RTX GPU and an Intel Core (i9-9960X) CPU. The implementation of the traditional registration in our pipeline is based on AirLab [17]. For initializing the model, we adopt Adam optimizer [8] with a fixed learning rate of 0.001. We strictly divide trainset and testset and run 5-fold cross-validation taking 1/5 of the data as test data and 4/5 as training data, and train all the methods from scratch (1000 epochs for our initialization model). The training/testing stage only uses patches from corresponding cases.

Measurements. As suggested by professional neurosurgeons, we define anchor error as the average distance between the predicted positions of predefined anchor points and their ground truth positions. In our experiments, the anchor points are taken from a $5 \times 5 \times 5$ mesh grid filling each 3DRA volume, with a total of 125 points. We did not exclude background points. We set a threshold of 4 mm for the registration success as experts suggested. The same threshold is used in the literature [21]. Errors below this threshold are acceptable, and the result will be sent to later processing in the clinical practice. Professional neurosurgeons will rerun registration with manual initialization if the error is more prominent than this threshold.

Baseline Methods. To evaluate the performance of the proposed model, we compared our model with two initialization methods and two deep-learning-based methods. As for the initialization method, the first is naive center initialization (Center-Init). We aligned the center of moving and fixed images, but we did not change orientation. The second is a variant of our method without image patches (w/o Patches). We directly map the entire moving image to the template space by using a network that computes a rigid transformation (translation and rotation) for an image. In the refinement stage, we also tested two different metrics (NMI, MSE).

For deep-learning-based models, we chose two recent models as baseline: Attention-Reg [19] (AttenReg) and Multi-modal SDAE [2] (SDAE+DNN). Attention-Reg is an end-to-end rigid registration method with two entire images as input. We modified the input size to $96 \times 96 \times 96$ for our dataset. The 3DRA image is put in the center of cubic space to meet the input constraints of the model and the space is filled with background values. Multi-modal SDAE is an end-to-end model learning whether patches from different modalities match. We could not access the open-sourced code of this paper, so we implemented our version and modified it to satisfy the requirement of our dataset. We adopt the code [11] for the pre-train stage and construct the DNN with similar five layers (2048-1024-256-128-2) from the paper. We trained all models directly using the given training images (4/5 of the dataset) without any data augmentation as in our proposed method.

Results. The summary of the results with a 4 mm anchor error threshold is given in Table 1. We combined and analyzed the results of five folds. Compared to Center-Init, our proposed method provides better performance, demonstrating

Table 1. Summary statistics with 4 mm anchor error threshold.

Methods	MSE					NMI		w/o Refinement	
	Cent.	w/o P.	Prop.	Atten.	SDAE.	Cent.	Prop.	Atten.	SDAE.
Success	60	66	**83**	75	3	58	**71**	1	0
Failure	33	27	**10**	18	90	35	**22**	92	93
Success ratio	65%	71%	**89%**	81%	3%	62%	**76%**	1%	0%

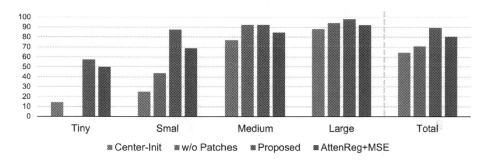

Fig. 4. Success ratio in each image size.

that proper initialization is critical for iterative registration methods. For w/o Patches, it is harder for the model to predict a rough registration with incomplete images. As for Attention-Reg, if we directly apply this for registration, the success ratio is only 1% (w/o refinement). We believe the additional preprocessing process for dataset affects the accuracy of the model. If we regarded it as another pre-registration method and apply refinement, it achieves the second-best performance, which means it could roughly register partial images but lacks accuracy without the refinement stage. Multi-modal SDAE has an unexpectedly bad result (122.967 mm in anchor error), which we believe is due to two reasons. Firstly, the fully-connected work used in this paper may not handle this problem well. Secondly, ranking the similarities of patch pairs does not guarantee we can find the correct pairs.

Figure 4 shows success ratio for 4 different image sizes. We compared four methods with MSE as the similarity metric in the refinement stage. Attention-Reg is considered as a pre-registration method in this figure. With Medium and Large 3DRA images, the performance of the four methods is close (all of them are over 78%), which implies that for 3DRA images containing large parts of brains, it does not matter what kind of initialization you choose, but other factors, like the design of models or data collection, do matter. Besides, Center-Init works poorly when the image size is small, as expected. Because center-initialization always aligns the center of 3DRA and CT images, when it comes to small and partial 3DRA images, the actual positions are far away from the initial positions. The performance of w/o Patches and Attention-Reg is not as good as the proposed method for small images. Meanwhile, these models need to predict more parameters (3 for translation, 3 for rotation) than ours (3 for positions),

Table 2. Detailed statistics of the measured errors.

Methods	Anchor error (mm)			Parameters	Time (s)
	Mean	CI 95 (%)	Median		
Center-Init	12.512	8.737–16.286	1.017	0	16.580
w/o Patches	13.708	8.720–18.696	1.017	13,344,390	19.773
Proposed	**4.453**	**1.398–7.508**	**0.894**	3,846,531	28.583
Attention-Reg [19]	8.074	4.476–11.673	0.988	1,838,601	21.202
Prop. w/o Refinement	14.512	13.006–16.018	13.648		24.180
Prop. w/o RANSAC	13.303	6.771–19.834	1.020		20.427

making it harder to train. When the size of 3DRA images is tiny, the Center-Init and w/o Patches method will predict the position with a significant error. Our method works robustly even when image size is tiny compared to other methods. The overall success ratios are better than others. Nevertheless, when the size of 3DRA images decreases, our proposed method exhibits an increasing number of failures with large prediction errors showing that it is inherently difficult.

Table 2 shows the detailed statistics of 4 methods and two variants of the proposed model. Similar to Table 1, our proposed method has the least error. The proposed method without refinement also has decent performance. Moreover, the RANSAC is critical for our proposed method because it can filter wrong predictions and improve the robustness of our pipeline. We also have a relatively small parameter size, which allows our model to run on CPU-only devices. Besides, in the training stage, compared to Attention-Reg, which requires 3 GPU (around 40 GB GPU memory) for batch size 8, the proposed method only requires 1 GPU (around 3.6 GB GPU memory) with batch size 64, which enables surgeons to quickly and easily train the models they need. The last column explains the execution time for completing the entire pipeline (Input: Unregistered DICOM format file; Output: Registered DICOM format file).

Discussion. Our method is a supervised learning method. Thus, we need a sufficient amount of training data for each modality. We believe it is not a problem in practice because we expect medical institutions to have a large set of annotated ground truths through long-term clinical accumulation. However, training data can be a bottleneck if one wants to apply the proposed method to other organs or modalities without existing training data. Specifically, patch sampling could be a problem. If image volumes are small and the patch size is large, we could not have enough samples. While with small patch sizes, samples might not have enough information for registration. We picked the patch size by trading off the patch number and prediction accuracy.

We tested our method as initialization for rigid registration. Similarly, our method can be helpful for initialization for deformable registration as well. Our method can also be trivially extended to allow deformation for fitting image patches to the target positions in the template space.

Our current implementation is rudimentary as an initial exploration, and there are many venues to improve the performance further. One possibility is to apply data augmentation. We currently do not apply any data augmentation, but various data augmentation methods such as random rotation could improve performance. Another option is to evaluate the confidence of patch position prediction. Replacing MSE with a more sophisticated DL-based local search would further enhance the final results.

4   Conclusion

This paper introduced a novel learning-based initialization method for partial image registration. By comparing the proposed network with traditional methods and other learning-based methods, we demonstrate the efficiency and accuracy of the proposed Template-Space Patch Mapping method. We also analyzed the success ratio for different image sizes. Our proposed method has clear advantages in cases with small image sizes. We hope to try our method on other medical applications in the future and help surgeons to alleviate their workloads.

Acknowledgement. This research was supported by AMED under Grant Number JP18he1602001, Japan and JST CREST under Grant Number JPMJCR17A1, Japan.

References

1. Bashiri, F.S., Baghaie, A., Rostami, R., Yu, Z., D'Souza, R.M.: Multi-modal medical image registration with full or partial data: a manifold learning approach. J. Imaging **5**(1), 5 (2019)
2. Cheng, X., Zhang, L., Zheng, Y.: Deep similarity learning for multimodal medical images. Comput. Methods Biomech. Biomed. Eng. Imaging Vis. **6**(3), 248–252 (2018)
3. Fischler, M.A., Bolles, R.C.: Random sample consensus: a paradigm for model fitting with applications to image analysis and automated cartography. Commun. ACM **24**(6), 381–395 (1981)
4. Guo, H., Kruger, M., Xu, S., Wood, B.J., Yan, P.: Deep adaptive registration of multi-modal prostate images. Comput. Med. Imaging Graph. **84**, 101769 (2020)
5. Heautot, J., et al.: Analysis of cerebrovascular diseases by a new 3-dimensional computerised x-ray angiography system. Neuroradiology **40**(4), 203–209 (1998)
6. Hochmuth, A., Spetzger, U., Schumacher, M.: Comparison of three-dimensional rotational angiography with digital subtraction angiography in the assessment of ruptured cerebral aneurysms. Am. J. Neuroradiol. **23**(7), 1199–1205 (2002)
7. Kin, T., et al.: A new strategic neurosurgical planning tool for brainstem cavernous malformations using interactive computer graphics with multimodal fusion images. J. Neurosurg. **117**(1), 78–88 (2012)
8. Kingma, D.P., Ba, J.: Adam: a method for stochastic optimization. arXiv preprint arXiv:1412.6980 (2014)
9. Kumamaru, K.K., Hoppel, B.E., Mather, R.T., Rybicki, F.J.: CT angiography: current technology and clinical use. Radiol. Clin. **48**(2), 213–235 (2010)

10. Liao, H., Lin, W.A., Zhang, J., Zhang, J., Luo, J., Zhou, S.K.: Multiview 2D/3D rigid registration via a point-of-interest network for tracking and triangulation. In: Proceedings of the IEEE/CVF Conference on Computer Vision and Pattern Recognition, pp. 12638–12647 (2019)
11. Lukiyanov, V.: Pytorch implementation of SDAE (stacked denoising autoencoder) (2018). https://github.com/vlukiyanov/pt-sdae
12. Müller, M., Heidelberger, B., Teschner, M., Gross, M.: Meshless deformations based on shape matching. ACM Trans. Graph. (TOG) **24**(3), 471–478 (2005)
13. Napel, S., et al.: Ct angiography with spiral CT and maximum intensity projection. Radiology **185**(2), 607–610 (1992)
14. Paszke, A., et al.: Pytorch: an imperative style, high-performance deep learning library. In: Advances in Neural Information Processing Systems, vol. 32 (2019)
15. Pluim, J., Maintz, J., Viergever, M.: Mutual-information-based registration of medical images: a survey. IEEE Trans. Med. Imaging **22**(8), 986–1004 (2003). https://doi.org/10.1109/TMI.2003.815867
16. Raabe, A., Beck, J., Rohde, S., Berkefeld, J., Seifert, V.: Three-dimensional rotational angiography guidance for aneurysm surgery. J. Neurosurg. **105**(3), 406–411 (2006)
17. Sandkühler, R., Jud, C., Andermatt, S., Cattin, P.C.: Airlab: autograd image registration laboratory. arXiv preprint arXiv:1806.09907 (2018)
18. Sloan, J.M., Goatman, K.A., Siebert, J.P.: Learning rigid image registration - utilizing convolutional neural networks for medical image registration. In: Proceedings of the 11th International Joint Conference on Biomedical Engineering Systems and Technologies - BIOIMAGING, pp. 89–99. INSTICC, SciTePress (2018). https://doi.org/10.5220/0006543700890099
19. Song, X., et al.: Cross-modal attention for MRI and ultrasound volume registration. In: de Bruijne, M., et al. (eds.) MICCAI 2021. LNCS, vol. 12904, pp. 66–75. Springer, Cham (2021). https://doi.org/10.1007/978-3-030-87202-1_7
20. Stalling, D., Westerhoff, M., Hege, H.C., et al.: Amira: a highly interactive system for visual data analysis. In: The Visualization Handbook, vol. 38, pp. 749–67 (2005)
21. Studholme, C., Hill, D., Hawkes, D.: An overlap invariant entropy measure of 3D medical image alignment. Pattern Recognit. **32**(1), 71–86 (1999)
22. Yan, P., Xu, S., Rastinehad, A.R., Wood, B.J.: Adversarial image registration with application for MR and TRUS image fusion. In: Shi, Y., Suk, H.-I., Liu, M. (eds.) MLMI 2018. LNCS, vol. 11046, pp. 197–204. Springer, Cham (2018). https://doi.org/10.1007/978-3-030-00919-9_23
23. Yao, Z., et al.: A supervised network for fast image-guided radiotherapy (IGRT) registration. J. Med. Syst. **43**(7), 1–8 (2019)
24. Zheng, J., Miao, S., Liao, R.: Learning CNNs with pairwise domain adaption for real-time 6DoF ultrasound transducer detection and tracking from X-Ray images. In: Descoteaux, M., Maier-Hein, L., Franz, A., Jannin, P., Collins, D.L., Duchesne, S. (eds.) MICCAI 2017. LNCS, vol. 10434, pp. 646–654. Springer, Cham (2017). https://doi.org/10.1007/978-3-319-66185-8_73
25. Zheng, J., Miao, S., Wang, Z.J., Liao, R.: Pairwise domain adaptation module for CNN-based 2-D/3-D registration. J. Med. Imaging **5**(2), 021204 (2018)

Global Multi-modal 2D/3D Registration via Local Descriptors Learning

Viktoria Markova[1,2(✉)], Matteo Ronchetti[1], Wolfgang Wein[1], Oliver Zettinig[1], and Raphael Prevost[1]

[1] ImFusion GmbH, Munich, Germany
[2] Technical University of Munich, Munich, Germany
v.markova@tum.de

Abstract. Multi-modal registration is a required step for many image-guided procedures, especially ultrasound-guided interventions that require anatomical context. While a number of such registration algorithms are already available, they all require a good initialization to succeed due to the challenging appearance of ultrasound images and the arbitrary coordinate system they are acquired in. In this paper, we present a novel approach to solve the problem of registration of an ultrasound sweep to a pre-operative image. We learn dense keypoint descriptors from which we then estimate the registration. We show that our method overcomes the challenges inherent to registration tasks with freehand ultrasound sweeps, namely, the multi-modality and multidimensionality of the data in addition to lack of precise ground truth and low amounts of training examples. We derive a registration method that is fast, generic, fully automatic, does not require any initialization and can naturally generate visualizations aiding interpretability and explainability. Our approach is evaluated on a clinical dataset of paired MR volumes and ultrasound sequences.

Keywords: Ultrasound · Magnetic resonance · Image registration · Feature learning · Deep learning

1 Introduction

Multi-modal registration, the overlaying of data acquired from different modalities, is an important task in the medical computing domain. A common application is procedure planning and subsequent intervention for diagnostic or treatment. Prostate biopsies, for example, are planned on Magnetic Resonance (MR) images, which may visualize cancerous regions, but executed under ultrasound (US) guidance [14]. Another example is image-guided surgery, which is the standard of care in intracranial neurosurgery [7] and is also performed for the abdominal section [13].

V. Markova and M. Ronchetti—The two authors contributed equally to this paper.

© The Author(s), under exclusive license to Springer Nature Switzerland AG 2022
L. Wang et al. (Eds.): MICCAI 2022, LNCS 13436, pp. 269–279, 2022.
https://doi.org/10.1007/978-3-031-16446-0_26

There exist well-performing local optimization methods for multi-modal registration [28], however, they require a good starting pose initialization. In the clinical practise, this is often realized by asking the clinician to select landmarks on both images and confirm a correct registration. This takes time and an active participation of highly trained personal. In addition, the approach is not applicable for automatic batch processing in wide studies.

In this work, we tackle the registration initialization of US and MRI, in particular of abdominal images. Ultrasound is inexpensive, fast and flexible, but poses multiple challenges: it is quite noisy, contains artifacts and deforms the tissue during acquisition. Moreover, an ultrasound frame has a restricted field of view in an arbitrary orientation contrary to MR or Computed Tomography (CT) images. Additionally, the abdominal area is particularly challenging as the organs and tissues are deformable and highly influenced both by the pressure required for US acquisition and respiration of the patient.

Until recently, prior works either use manually selected correspondences or a starting pose [3], a reference tracker or tool that moves the image in the correct vicinity [3,5,29]. Another viable automated (but application-specific) approach is registration from segmentation [12,25].

Correspondences between points are essential tool for tackling many computer vision problems such as visual localization [1] simultaneous localization and mapping [24] and structure-from-motion [24]. In recent years learned keypoint detectors and descriptors [2,11,22,23] have been successfully applied to computer vision problems involving natural images, replacing hand-crafted approaches such as SIFT [9] and ORB [18]. Keypoint correspondences can be processed to compute robust solutions [6], filtered to enforce constraints [21] and can provide enough information to estimate non-rigid transformations [15,19]. Furthermore the visual and intuitive nature of point-to-point correspondences provides interpretability and explainability. Despite all these advantages, to the best of our knowledge, these approaches have been applied the medical domain only to a limited extend. In [27] Wang et al. use keypoints learned by random forests to register mono-modal brain images. Another paper [4] shows promising registration results from learned keypoints, with the downsides of it being specific to the modalities of X-ray to CT and requiring manual labeling annotation.

In this paper, we propose a method to discover, extract and match keypoints from ultrasound and MR images. Our contributions consist in adapting the chosen network method to the multi-modal and cross-dimensional setting (as the ultrasound frames are 2D and the MR image is 3D) while handling imprecise ground-truth. In order to not consider the ultrasound fan geometry but rather the structural features, we further augment the ultrasound data by cropping it in a random polygon shape.

The method's advantages include its genericity, as it is applicable across modalities and different data dimensions. It is completely independent of the initial pose. The method can be easily extended to a deformable one. It is explainable as one can visualize the computed similarities and diagnose for potential problems and biases in the data or training setup.

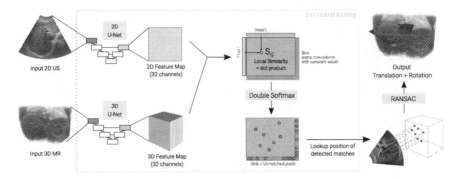

Fig. 1. Overview of the proposed method. The images are fed to two separate feature extraction networks outputting dense feature maps, which are combined in a matching module, all end-to-end trainable. The matches are extracted via a confidence threshold and processed with RANSAC to retrieve the pose.

2   Approach

Our registration method, summarized in Fig. 1, is based on detection and matching of local features across modalities. The training is done end-to-end using pose as the only supervision, therefore, it does not require the tedious definition and annotation of specific anatomical landmarks. After extraction of the matches, we classically deploy RANSAC [6] to estimate the pose.

2.1   Challenges of Local Feature Extraction for Medical Images

Our method is based on the LoFTR algorithm proposed in [23]. There are however a number of key differences between the problem at hand and the original paper (for tracking of 2D natural images), which requires us to generalize and adapt the method in several ways.

Multi-modality and Multi-dimensionality. Different modalities exhibit different visual appearances and also emphasize different structures. We overcome this issue by jointly training two distinct networks (a 2D model for US and a 3D one for MR) to produce cross-modality descriptors.

Inaccuracy of Ground Truth. This comes from different sources: MRI and US taken at different times, respiration, deformation caused by probe pressure. Ground truth registration is generally unreliable to create perfect correspondences. As learning a detector on inaccurate correspondences would hardly produce repeatable detections, we use a detector-free architecture that distributes keypoints uniformly on a grid at $\frac{1}{8}$ resolution. Furthermore, we propose a softer loss that, by taking into consideration the spatial proximity of target keypoints, does not over-penalize matches that do not exactly align with the ground truth.

Scarcity of Data and Similarity of Motion. The scarce availability of training data makes it harder to train deep models while avoiding overfitting. In particular, if the dataset contains sweeps with similar frame geometry and motion, the network might consider the borders of the fan-shaped frame as important spatial clues and take less into consideration the content of the ultrasound frame itself. We mitigate this issue with data augmentation and design a random masking scheme (PolyCrop) that prevents the overfitting to the field of view.

Moreover, based on early experiments and due to the dataset size, we decided not to use the Transformer and Coarse-to-Fine modules of LoFTR.

2.2   Detector-Free Local Feature Networks

We use Convolutional Neural Networks (CNN) to extract local features from the US frame and the MR volume. The architecture of both networks is very similar to a U-Net [17] without the last upsampling layers, and makes use of residual blocks [8], leaky ReLUs [10] non-linearities and instance normalization layers [26]. The output of both models is a uniform grid of 32-dimensional descriptors at $\frac{1}{8}$ the input resolution. We indicate the local US and MR features produced by these models with $\mathbf{f}^{\mathrm{US}}$ and $\mathbf{f}^{\mathrm{MR}}$ respectively. A single index $i \in \Omega_{\mathrm{US}}$ (resp. $j \in \Omega_{\mathrm{MR}}$) is used to identify a position on the descriptors grid.

Differentiable Matching. In order to train the networks end-to-end, the matching too needs to be differentiable. Similarly to [20,23], we define the similarity between two descriptors as their dot product, which allows the networks to encode the quality of a keypoint in the norm of its descriptor. We thus store the similarity scores in a $|\Omega_{\mathrm{US}}| \times |\Omega_{\mathrm{MR}}|$ matrix:

$$\mathbf{S}_{i,j} = \begin{cases} \langle \mathbf{f}_i^{\mathrm{US}}, \mathbf{f}_j^{\mathrm{MR}} \rangle & \text{if } i \leq |\Omega_{\mathrm{US}}| \text{ and } j \leq |\Omega_{\mathrm{MR}}| \\ \alpha & \text{otherwise} \end{cases} \tag{1}$$

Both the last row and the last column of $\mathbf{S}$ are filled with a learned value α which represents a sink for all keypoints that are not matched at all in the other image. We use the dual-softmax operator [16] to convert the score matrix $\mathbf{S}$ into a soft assignment matrix $\mathbf{A}$. Formally, the score of a match (i, j) is defined as:

$$\mathbf{A}_{i,j} = \mathrm{Softmax}_j(\mathbf{S}_{i,\cdot}) \cdot \mathrm{Softmax}_i(\mathbf{S}_{\cdot,j}). \tag{2}$$

Loss Function. Ground truth matches are defined by computing soft assignments from the US grid to the MR one. For every cell i of the US grid, we compute the position of its center p_i and apply the ground truth deformable registration to obtain the corresponding position on the MR q_i. We then denote as $m(i)$ the cell corresponding to q_i, i.e. the matching cell of i. Our loss is the negative log-likelihood of the ground truth soft matches w:

$$\mathcal{L} = -\frac{\sum_{i,j} w(i,j) \log(\mathbf{A}_{i,j})}{\sum_{i,j} w(i,j)} \tag{3}$$

$$\text{where } w(i,j) = \begin{cases} \exp(-\beta\|j - m(i)\|) & \text{if } i \leq |\Omega_{\text{US}}| \text{ and } j \leq |\Omega_{\text{MR}}| \\ 1 & \text{otherwise} \end{cases} \tag{4}$$

2.3 Multiple Frames

If the ultrasound is acquired with the help of an external tracking system, this can be naturally exploited by the method. The tracking provides relative pose of the frames to each other, which can be used to take into account matches from multiple frames for the final pose estimation with RANSAC [6].

3 Experiments

3.1 Datasets

The dataset consists of 16 patients who have each a T1-weighted MR image taken and a number of ultrasound sweeps with a curvilinear probe before surgery. No special sonographic protocol has been enforced during the acquisition, the operator simply acquired one or two sweeps to maximize tumor and liver gland visibility. The ground truth pose has been obtained by manually registering every sweep to its pre-operative MR image by a domain expert. We generate correspondences using deformable registration and evaluate on rigid pose estimation. Our dataset contains 30 sweeps with 3957 frames. We train four-fold cross-validation and show ablation studies.

We resample both MR and ultrasound images to have uniform spacing of 1.25 mm. Sweeps with transversal orientation appear three times more often than intracoastal ones, we therefore sample more frequently the intracostals to balance the dataset. Gaussian noise augmentation and random cropping are used to mitigate over-fitting.

Finally, we introduce a novel augmentation to the ultrasound frames that we call "PolyCrop" for random convex polygon cropping. Ultrasound frames taken with a curvilinear probe have an intrinsic shape (fan geometry) that cannot cover a whole rectangular image, therefore black pixels are added around the ultrasound data to obtain a rectangular image. This process creates strong edges that are consistent across images. The trained model can use these edges as spatial clues. For example to infer that a certain part of the image is in the top left of the ultrasound frame. This would prevent the model from generalizing to different sweep motions. Our PolyCrop augmentation, randomizes the location of these edges rendering them not informative. A random convex polygon is generated and applied as mask on the frame. All pixels outside of it are turned black.

3.2   Baselines and Main Results

Our baseline for comparison is the method proposed in [12], which is based global registration of segmentation maps. We make use of the proprietary implementation available in the ImFusion Suite 2.36.3 software, which segments liver, diaphragm and vena cava.

We report the results on the pose error with mean, standard deviation and median (in degrees for the rotation part, mm for the translational part). Additionally, we comment on the statistical significance of the results.

Our registration method is evaluated both as-is ("Initialization"), and as an initialization for a local multi-modal registration algorithm ("After Registration"). This algorithm, which optimizes the pose of the US volume together with the deformation of the MR, has been shown to achieve good results [28] but requires a close initialization. While this local registration is not part of our work, it is relevant to study whether our pose initialization falls into the capture range of such an algorithm. For those experiments, we used the implementation provided in the same software. Table 1 shows the comparison between the proposed method and the baseline. Our approach is evaluated both using a single US frame (no tracking required) and using the entire sweep. Even on single frames, our method significantly outperforms the baseline. The superiority is statistically significant as shown by the Wilcoxon signed-rank test. The p-values for all four reported metrics are $\leq 10^{-5}$ for the multi-frame variant (as this is better comparable to the baseline method).

The last two rows of the table quantify the progress towards the ultimate goal of fully automatic multi-modal registration. The threshold of the fifth row is chosen in accordance with the reported capture range of the local optimization algorithm [28]. Our method favors relatively well with 45% with tracking and 32% without. The percentages grow significantly with the broader threshold depicted in the row below. The distribution of pose errors is depicted in Fig. 2 using a violin plot. It can be noticed that, while the majority of cases are registered with good results, a few failure cases exist.

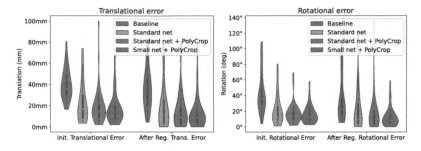

Fig. 2. Violin plots of the distributions of translational (left) and rotational (right) errors split across methods. Black rectangles are boxplots, white dots are medians.

Table 1. Comparison between pose prediction error between the proposed method, both with tracking (multiple frames) and without (single frame) and the baseline.

	Baseline	Proposed	
	All frames	All frames	Single frame
Init. Rot. (deg)	$44.0 \pm 26.2(35.5)$	$16.2 \pm 11.9(12.4)$	$21.3 \pm 16.3(18.4)$
Init. Trans. (mm)	$40.5 \pm 14.8(14.4)$	$16.7 + 13.8(13.8)$	$21.5 \pm 16.9(17.8)$
After Reg. Rot. (deg)	$34.6 \pm 29.0(22.3)$	$12.7 \pm 12.9(8.2)$	$17.5 \pm 18.4(13.1)$
After Reg. Trans. (mm)	$35.5 \pm 19.6(32.5)$	$12.7 \pm 15.9(9.1)$	$17.4 \pm 18.0(10.9)$
After R. $< 10°$ & < 10 mm	6.7%	45.2%	32.3%
After R. $< 15°$ & < 20 mm	10.0%	74.2%	49.5%

3.3   Ablation Studies

We quantify the effects of Polycrop augmentation and network size through ablation studies with results summarized in Table 2. For easier interpretation, the fifth and sixth rows show the percentage of high-error and well-initialized cases. The error distributions are also depicted in Fig. 2 with violin plots.

The column "Polycrop + standard net" (Table 2) contains the results with the PolyCrop augmentation described in Sect. 3.1. We observe an improvement in the pose initialization compared to "No poly + standard net". Both the median in translation and rotation error in the initial pose drop by more than 3° and millimeters respectively. These improvements, naturally, carry over to the end pose after the local optimization.

We experiment with a smaller version of our networks and compare "Polycrop + standard net" with "Polycrop + smaller net". A size reduction in the network leads to faster training and inference, as well as, smaller memory requirements. The smaller model achieves better results on all the metrics except on the median error after registration refinement. A possible cause of this improvement is that the smaller model, being less subject to over-fitting, produces a lower number of high-error cases while being slightly worse in the majority of cases. This can be observed in Fig. 2 by noticing the shorter tails of the distribution.

Table 2. Ablation studies results. Comparison between pose prediction errors. The tracking is utilized and matches from multiple frames used for the pose estimation.

Method	No polycrop	Polycrop	Polycrop
Metric	+ standard net	+ standard net	+ smaller net
Init. Rotation (deg)	$22.4 \pm 19.5(12.0)$	$18.0 \pm 14.3(14.7)$	$16.2 \pm 11.9(12.4)$
Init. Trans. (mm)	$23.1 \pm 19.6(16.7)$	$19.9 \pm 20.0(14.2)$	$16.7 \pm 13.8(13.8)$
After Reg. Rotation (deg)	$21.0 \pm 26.0(10.2)$	$15.7 \pm 25.7(6.5)$	$12.7 \pm 12.9(8.2)$
After Reg. Trans. (mm)	$19.5 \pm 22.7(10.4)$	$15.3 \pm 20.1(8.8)$	$12.7 \pm 15.9(9.1)$
Init. $> 50°$ or >50 mm	12.9%	6.7%	3.2%
Init. $< 25°$ & <25 mm	58.1%	73.3%	80.6%

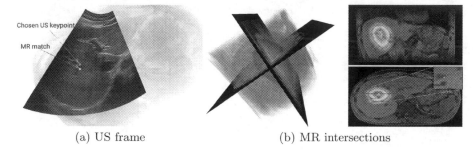

(a) US frame　　　　　　　　　　(b) MR intersections

Fig. 3. Similarity visualization. On the left (a), the US frame with the chosen keypoint, it's corresponding match on the MR. The MR and US are registered with the ground truth, thus if the method were perfect, the two points would be at the same position. On the right (b) two intersections of the MR and their visualization. (Color figure online)

3.4 Similarity Visualization

Our method can be inspected and its results visualized and interpreted. Figure 3 depicts, as a heatmap, a row of the similarity matrix $\mathbf{S}$ (defined in Eq. 1) i.e. the similarity between each MR voxel and the selected point in the US frame (green dot). The matched MR keypoint (maximum of the heatmap) is shown as a yellow dot. The shape of the heatmap can be used to identify the main direction of uncertainty, in this example its elongation across the axis of motion implies the presence of tubular features.

4　Conclusions

We proposed a new approach for multi-modal image registration. Our method, based on learned keypoint descriptors, is fast, fully-automatic, interpretable and can be generalized to other modalities. Our approach adapts and generalizes one of the latest advances from the computer vision community to overcome challenges inherent to multi-modal and multi-dimensional medical images.

On challenging abdominal US + MR data, our method can fully automatically pre-align the data in >80% of all attempts for tracked 3D freehand sweeps. In addition, a single US frame successfully registers in about half of the attempts; this can yield significant workflow improvements for interventions where time is of the essence, and hence the ultrasound registration step is required to be brief and simple. We, therefore, believe that the proposed method can become an important ingredient in image-guided surgery systems that require intra-operative registration, as well as easier to use diagnostic fusion systems.

This study focused on rigid pose estimation. A natural extension of this work would be to use the learned correspondences to estimate a dense deformation field. The single frame performance of our algorithm suggests an application in ultrasound SLAM, where the sweep motion needs to be reconstructed. Capture range of image based registration methods might be improved by using the dense local descriptors produced by our networks to define a distance metric between images. Finally, it should be possible to improve on our results by tuning the network architecture and collecting a larger dataset or incorporating other supervisory signals, such as segmentation, into the training loss.

References

1. Brachmann, E., Rother, C.: Visual camera re-localization from RGB and RGB-D images using DSAC. IEEE Trans. Pattern Anal. Mach. Intell. **44**(9), 5847–5865 (2021)
2. DeTone, D., Malisiewicz, T., Rabinovich, A.: SuperPoint: self-supervised interest point detection and description. In: CVPR (2018)
3. D'Onofrio, M., Belcù, A., Gaitini, D., Corréas, J.M., Brady, A., Clevert, D.: European society of radiology (ESR): abdominal applications of ultrasound fusion imaging technique: liver, kidney, and pancreas. Insights Imaging **10**(1), 6 (2019)
4. Esteban, J., Grimm, M., Unberath, M., Zahnd, G., Navab, N.: Towards fully automatic X-Ray to CT registration. In: Shen, D., et al. (eds.) MICCAI 2019. LNCS, vol. 11769, pp. 631–639. Springer, Cham (2019). https://doi.org/10.1007/978-3-030-32226-7_70
5. Favazza, C.P., et al.: Development of a robust MRI fiducial system for automated fusion of MR-US abdominal images. J. Appl. Clin. Med. Phys. **19**(4), 261–270 (2018)
6. Fischler, M., Bolles, R.: Random sample consensus: a paradigm for model fitting with applications to image analysis and automated cartography. Commun. ACM **24**(6), 381–395 (1981)
7. Galloway, R.L., Herrell, S.D., Miga, M.I.: Image-guided abdominal surgery and therapy delivery. J. Healthc. Eng. **3**(2), 203–228 (2012)
8. He, K., Zhang, X., Ren, S., Sun, J.: Deep residual learning for image recognition. In: Proceedings of the IEEE Conference on Computer Vision and Pattern Recognition, pp. 770–778 (2016)
9. Lowe, D.G.: Distinctive image features from scale-invariant keypoints. Int. J. Comput. Vision **60**(2), 91–110 (2004)
10. Maas, A.L., Hannun, A.Y., Ng, A.Y.: Rectifier nonlinearities improve neural network acoustic models. In: Proceedings of ICML, vol. 30, p. 3. Citeseer (2013)

11. Mishchuk, A., Mishkin, D., Radenovic, F., Matas, J.: Working hard to know your neighbor's margins: local descriptor learning loss. In: Advances in Neural Information Processing Systems, vol. 30 (2017)
12. Müller, M., et al.: Deriving anatomical context from 4D ultrasound. In: 4th biannual Eurographics Workshop on Visual Computing for Biology and Medicine (2014)
13. Najmaei, N., Mostafavi, K., Shahbazi, S., Azizian, M.: Image-guided techniques in renal and hepatic interventions. Int. J. Med. Robot. Comput. Assist. Surg. **9**(4), 379–395 (2013)
14. Nassiri, N., et al.: Step-by-step: fusion-guided prostate biopsy in the diagnosis and surveillance of prostate cancer. Int. Braz. J. Urol. Off. J. Braz. Soc. Urol. **45**(6), 1277–1278 (2019)
15. Ou, Y., Sotiras, A., Paragios, N., Davatzikos, C.: Dramms: deformable registration via attribute matching and mutual-saliency weighting. Med. Image Anal. **15**(4), 622–639 (2011). Special section on IPMI 2009
16. Rocco, I., Cimpoi, M., Arandjelović, R., Torii, A., Pajdla, T., Sivic, J.: Neighbourhood consensus networks. In: Advances in Neural Information Processing Systems, vol. 31 (2018)
17. Ronneberger, O., Fischer, P., Brox, T.: U-Net: convolutional networks for biomedical image segmentation. In: Navab, N., Hornegger, J., Wells, W.M., Frangi, A.F. (eds.) MICCAI 2015. LNCS, vol. 9351, pp. 234–241. Springer, Cham (2015). https://doi.org/10.1007/978-3-319-24574-4_28
18. Rublee, E., Rabaud, V., Konolige, K., Bradski, G.: Orb: an efficient alternative to sift or surf. In: 2011 International Conference on Computer Vision, pp. 2564–2571 (2011)
19. Rühaak, J., et al.: Estimation of large motion in lung CT by integrating regularized keypoint correspondences into dense deformable registration. IEEE Trans. Med. Imaging **36**(8), 1746–1757 (2017)
20. Sarlin, P.E., DeTone, D., Malisiewicz, T., Rabinovich, A.: SuperGlue: learning feature matching with graph neural networks. In: CVPR (2020)
21. Shi, J., Yang, H., Carlone, L.: Robin: a graph-theoretic approach to reject outliers in robust estimation using invariants. In: 2021 IEEE International Conference on Robotics and Automation (ICRA), pp. 13820–13827 (2021)
22. Song, Y., Cai, L., Li, J., Tian, Y., Li, M.: SEKD: self-evolving keypoint detection and description. In: CVPR (2020)
23. Sun, J., Shen, Z., Wang, Y., Bao, H., Zhou, X.: LoFTR: detector-free local feature matching with transformers. In: CVPR (2021)
24. Tang, J., et al.: Self-supervised 3D keypoint learning for ego-motion estimation. CoRL (2020)
25. Thomson, B.R., et al.: MR-to-US registration using multiclass segmentation of hepatic vasculature with a reduced 3D U-Net. In: Martel, A.L., et al. (eds.) MICCAI 2020. LNCS, vol. 12263, pp. 275–284. Springer, Cham (2020). https://doi.org/10.1007/978-3-030-59716-0_27
26. Ulyanov, D., Vedaldi, A., Lempitsky, V.: Instance normalization: the missing ingredient for fast stylization. arXiv preprint arXiv:1607.08022 (2016)
27. Wang, J., Liu, Y., Noble, J.H., Dawant, B.M.: Automatic selection of landmarks in T1-weighted head MRI with regression forests for image registration initialization. J. Med. Imaging **4**(4), 044005 (2017)

28. Wein, W., Ladikos, A., Fuerst, B., Shah, A., Sharma, K., Navab, N.: Global registration of ultrasound to MRI using the LC^2 metric for enabling neurosurgical guidance. In: Mori, K., Sakuma, I., Sato, Y., Barillot, C., Navab, N. (eds.) MICCAI 2013. LNCS, vol. 8149, pp. 34–41. Springer, Heidelberg (2013). https://doi.org/10.1007/978-3-642-40811-3_5

29. Xiao, Y., et al.: Evaluation of MRI to ultrasound registration methods for brain shift correction: the curious2018 challenge. IEEE Trans. Med. Imaging **39**(3), 777–786 (2020)

Adapting the Mean Teacher
for Keypoint-Based Lung Registration
Under Geometric Domain Shifts

Alexander Bigalke$^{(\boxtimes)}$ ⓘ, Lasse Hansen ⓘ, and Mattias P. Heinrich ⓘ

Institute of Medical Informatics, University of Lübeck, Lübeck, Germany
{alexander.bigalke,l.hansen,mattias.heinrich}@uni-luebeck.de

Abstract. Recent deep learning-based methods for medical image registration achieve results that are competitive with conventional optimization algorithms at reduced run times. However, deep neural networks
generally require plenty of labeled training data and are vulnerable to
domain shifts between training and test data. While typical intensity
shifts can be mitigated by keypoint-based registration, these methods
still suffer from geometric domain shifts, for instance, due to different fields of view. As a remedy, in this work, we present a novel approach to geometric domain adaptation for image registration, adapting a
model from a labeled source to an unlabeled target domain. We build on
a keypoint-based registration model, combining graph convolutions for
geometric feature learning with loopy belief optimization, and propose to
reduce the domain shift through self-ensembling. To this end, we embed
the model into the Mean Teacher paradigm. We extend the Mean Teacher
to this context by 1) adapting the stochastic augmentation scheme and
2) combining learned feature extraction with differentiable optimization. This enables us to guide the learning process in the unlabeled target domain by enforcing consistent predictions of the learning student
and the temporally averaged teacher model. We evaluate the method
for exhale-to-inhale lung CT registration under two challenging adaptation scenarios (DIR-Lab 4D CT to COPD, COPD to Learn2Reg). Our
method consistently improves on the baseline model by 50%/47% while
even matching the accuracy of models trained on target data. Source code
is available at https://github.com/multimodallearning/registration-da-
mean-teacher.

Keywords: Registration · Geometric domain adaptation · Mean
teacher

1 Introduction

Image registration is a fundamental task in medical image analysis, for instance
required for multi-modal data fusion or patient monitoring over time. For a
long time, the state of the art for image registration was dominated by conventional optimization methods [19], whose high accuracy comes at the cost of

© The Author(s), under exclusive license to Springer Nature Switzerland AG 2022
L. Wang et al. (Eds.): MICCAI 2022, LNCS 13436, pp. 280–290, 2022.
https://doi.org/10.1007/978-3-031-16446-0_27

high run times. In recent years, learning-based methods—driven by deep neural networks—achieved competitive performances [9]. These methods substantially reduce inference times, but they involve two other significant drawbacks. First, high performance is strongly dependent on the availability of labeled training data, which are costly to collect. Second, deep neural networks often generalize poorly to shifted domains. Once trained in a labeled source domain, the models are likely to suffer a performance drop when deployed on data from a shifted target domain. While shifts in intensity distributions—typical for medical imaging—can be mitigated by keypoint-based registration [8], such methods still suffer from geometric domain shifts, for instance, due to varying fields of view under different imaging protocols. Fine-tuning or re-training on data from the shifted domain could alleviate the performance drop but is often impractical due to high labeling costs. Alternatively, domain adaptation [24] is a promising technique to adapt a model from a labeled source to an unlabeled target domain. While extensively explored for medical classification and segmentation tasks [7], domain adaptation for image registration has rarely been studied in the literature [13,14] and will be the focus of this work.

Existing works on domain adaptive registration rely on two different concepts. Mahapatra et al. [14] increase the invariance of a generative registration model to the type of input images by encoding the images to the latent space of an autoencoder. In a different approach, Kruse et al. [13] adapt the concept of maximum classifier discrepancy [17] to multi-modal registration. However, this requires the quantization of displacement fields and the use of a classification architecture instead of state-of-the-art registration models. Generally, domain adaptive registration is challenging because concepts established for other tasks are often unsuitable for registration. The mainstream approach of domain-invariant feature learning through adversarial learning [5,23] or reconstruction [1,6], for instance, was primarily used in classification tasks. In consequence, the methods focus on the alignment of global feature vectors. This is insufficient for registration, which highly depends on the identification of local correspondences. Alternatively, Tsai et al. [22] proposed domain adaptation in the output space, where the distributions of predictions in source and target domain are aligned through adversarial learning. This concept was successfully applied to semantic segmentation [22] and human pose estimation [25]. However, the raw displacement fields output by registration models are less structured than segmentation masks or human poses such that aligning their distributions might be ineffective. Instead of distribution matching, self-ensembling [4] addresses the domain shift by imposing consistency constraints in the output space. The method is based on the framework of the Mean Teacher [21], comprising a learning student model and a so-called teacher model, which represents a temporal ensemble with its weights corresponding to the exponential moving average (EMA) of the student model. Supervision on unlabeled target data is then provided by enforcing consistent predictions of student and teacher model. Beyond classification [4], this concept has successfully been adapted to diverse tasks, including medical image segmentation [16,26] and clinical human pose estimation [20].

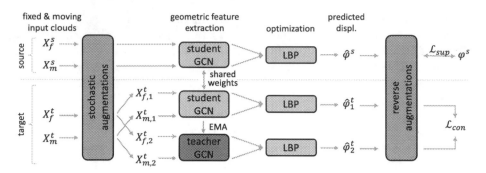

Fig. 1. Overview of our proposed self-ensembling framework for domain adaptive keypoint-based image registration.

Contributions. In this work, we extend the concept of self-ensembling to geometric domain adaptation for image registration, embedding a keypoint-based registration model into the Mean Teacher paradigm (see Fig. 1). Our framework is built upon the keypoint-based method by Hansen et al. [8], which aligns two point clouds (extracted from the input scan pair) by combining a Graph Convolutional Network (GCN) for learned geometric feature extraction with loopy belief propagation (LBP) for alignment. To incorporate the method into the Mean Teacher framework, we present two crucial modifications of the standard Mean Teacher. First, we adapt the stochastic augmentation scheme to the specific characteristics of the registration task by incorporating inverse geometric transformations. Second, we present the first Mean Teacher that combines learned feature extraction (GCN) with differentiable optimization (LBP). Notably, the differentiability of LBP enables us to impose the consistency constraint between student and teacher model on the final predicted displacement fields after LBP. That way, the adaptation of the GCN can benefit from the regularizing effect of LBP. Overall, our method offers a simple and robust adaptation procedure. It involves only few hyper-parameters and does not rely on intricate adversarial optimization as previous works. We experimentally evaluate our method for exhale-to-inhale lung CT registration, considering two different geometric domain shifts (varying field of view and breathing type). Results demonstrate substantial improvements compared to the baseline model and even competitive performance with fully-supervised models.

2   Methods

2.1   Problem Statement

Given fixed and moving input scans $F, M \in \mathbb{R}^{H \times W \times D}$, the goal of registration is to predict a displacement field φ that spatially aligns M to F within a given region of interest. We address this task in the classical domain adaptation setting, where training data comprises a labeled source dataset $\mathcal{S}$ and an unlabeled target dataset $\mathcal{T}$. $\mathcal{S}$ consists of triplets $(\boldsymbol{F}^s, \boldsymbol{M}^s, \boldsymbol{\varphi}^s)$ of scan pairs $(\boldsymbol{F}^s, \boldsymbol{M}^s)$ with corresponding ground truth displacement fields $\boldsymbol{\varphi}^s$. $\mathcal{T}$ contains scan pairs $(\boldsymbol{F}^t, \boldsymbol{M}^t)$ without any ground truth. Given the training data, we aim to learn a function f with parameters $\boldsymbol{\theta}$ that predicts displacement fields $\hat{\boldsymbol{\varphi}} = f(\boldsymbol{F}, \boldsymbol{M}; \boldsymbol{\theta})$ and achieves the best possible performance on the target domain. In the following, we first introduce our baseline model f for standard supervised learning on source data (Sect. 2.2) and subsequently present our self-ensembling framework for domain adaptation (Sect. 2.3).

2.2   Baseline Model

Most learning-based methods perform registration based on intensities in dense voxel space. Instead, we formulate registration as the pure geometric alignment of two point clouds $\boldsymbol{X}_f \in \mathbb{R}^{N_f \times 3}$, $\boldsymbol{X}_m \in \mathbb{R}^{N_m \times 3}$, representing distinct keypoints of the input scans. The underlying motivation is that this reduces the vulnerability to intensity shifts between source and target domain, enabling us to focus on remaining geometric shifts. The general efficacy of learning-based registration of point clouds in a fully-supervised setting has previously been demonstrated by the authors of [8]. We adopt their model as our baseline and briefly summarize its major components.

First, fixed and moving point clouds $\boldsymbol{X}_f$ and $\boldsymbol{X}_m$ are extracted from the input scans using the Foerstner algorithm and non-maximum suppression [10]. Second, a GCN g extracts point-wise geometric features $g(\boldsymbol{X}_f; \boldsymbol{\theta}_g)$, $g(\boldsymbol{X}_m; \boldsymbol{\theta}_g)$ from the raw coordinates of both clouds. The GCN is based on the edge convolution from [24], operating on the knn-graph of the clouds to account for neighborhood relations. Third, the extracted features are used to guide the inference of final displacement vectors with LBP. Specifically, correspondence probabilities between fixed keypoints and candidate sets from the moving cloud are computed via LBP by jointly minimizing a data cost and a regularization cost. While the latter enforces smoothness of the predicted displacement field, the data cost is defined as the distance between geometric features and induces high correspondence probabilities between points with similar features. Thus, effective feature extraction with the GCN is crucial for the assignment of accurate correspondences. Finally, displacement vectors are inferred by integrating the probabilities over the corresponding displacements between fixed and candidate points, allowing for more accurate displacement vectors than hard assignments. We formally summarize the combination of GCN and LBP as

$$\hat{\boldsymbol{\varphi}} = LBP(g(\boldsymbol{X}_f; \boldsymbol{\theta}_g), g(\boldsymbol{X}_m; \boldsymbol{\theta}_g)) =: f(\boldsymbol{X}_f, \boldsymbol{X}_m; \boldsymbol{\theta}), \quad \hat{\boldsymbol{\varphi}} \in \mathbb{R}^{N_f \times 3} \quad (1)$$

and refer the reader to [8] for more details. As such, f is fully differentiable, enabling end-to-end learning of parameters $\boldsymbol{\theta}$ by minimizing the supervised loss

$$\mathcal{L}_{sup} = \|\hat{\boldsymbol{\varphi}} - \boldsymbol{\varphi}\|_1 \quad (2)$$

2.3   Domain-Adaptive Registration with the Mean Teacher

To adapt the baseline model to a shifted target domain, we propose a novel self-ensembling framework, embedding the model into the Mean Teacher paradigm [4,21]. An overview of the method is shown in Fig. 1. The framework extends the baseline model, and now includes two GCNs for feature extraction, namely a student GCN with weights $\boldsymbol{\theta}$ and a teacher GCN with weights $\boldsymbol{\theta'}$. The student network is optimized via gradient descent, whereas the weights of the teacher are the exponential moving average of the student's weights, updated as

$$\boldsymbol{\theta}'_i = \alpha\boldsymbol{\theta}'_{i-1} + (1-\alpha)\boldsymbol{\theta}_i \tag{3}$$

at iteration i with the momentum α. The student is optimized by minimizing the joint loss function

$$\mathcal{L}(\boldsymbol{\theta};\boldsymbol{\theta}',\mathcal{S},\mathcal{T}) = \mathcal{L}_{sup}(\boldsymbol{\theta};\mathcal{S}) + \lambda(t)\mathcal{L}_{con}(\boldsymbol{\theta};\boldsymbol{\theta}',\mathcal{T}) \tag{4}$$

composed of the supervised loss $\mathcal{L}_{sup}$ (cf. Eq. 2) on labeled source data and a consistency loss $\mathcal{L}_{con}$ on unlabeled target data, weighted by a time-dependent factor $\lambda(t)$. The consistency loss penalizes different predictions by student and teacher model. Implementing $\mathcal{L}_{con}$ for the given registration problem requires two subtle but decisive adaptations of the standard Mean Teacher for classification.

First, the standard Mean Teacher imposes the consistency constraint at the output of the learning network, which usually coincides with the final prediction. In our case, however, the output of the learning GCN is an intermediate representation, and we observed that applying consistency constraints at this level hampers the learning process. Instead, we propose to align predicted displacement vectors after LBP. That way, the adaptation process can benefit from the regularizing effect of LBP.

Second, an important component of the Mean Teacher is the application of different stochastic augmentations to the input of teacher and student streams. Unlike classification, however, registration requires the augmentation of pairs of inputs instead of single inputs. Moreover, the associated displacement fields in the output space are not invariant to the input transformation (as is the case for classification), but they are transformed together with the input. For $\mathcal{L}_{con}$ to be meaningful, transformations applied at the input level need to be reversed at the output level such that predictions in teacher and student streams are aligned. To ensure reversibility at the output level, we sample one transformation for each stream and apply it to both fixed and moving cloud, yielding two augmented pairs $(\boldsymbol{X}^t_{f,1},\boldsymbol{X}^t_{m,1}),(\boldsymbol{X}^t_{f,2},\boldsymbol{X}^t_{m,2})$. In practice, we transform point clouds by random rotation, translation and scaling. The reverse transformation of the displacement vectors is then given by inverse scaling and rotation (displacement vectors are invariant to the synchronous translation of both inputs). Denoting reverse augmentations as $\text{aug}^{-1}(.)$, we formalize the consistency loss as

$$\mathcal{L}_{con} = \left\|\text{aug}_1^{-1}(f(\boldsymbol{X}^t_{f,1},\boldsymbol{X}^t_{m,1};\boldsymbol{\theta})) - \text{aug}_2^{-1}(f(\boldsymbol{X}^t_{f,2},\boldsymbol{X}^t_{m,2};\boldsymbol{\theta}'))\right\|_1 \tag{5}$$

At early epochs, the weights of the teacher model are still close to the random initialization, inducing noisy gradients from $\mathcal{L}_{con}$. Therefore, the weighting factor

$\lambda(t) = \lambda_0 \cdot \exp(-5(1 - \min(t/T, 1)^2))$ depends on the current epoch t and steadily increases from 0 to λ_0 during the first T epochs, as suggested by [21].

3 Experiments

3.1 Experimental Setup

Datasets and Pre-processing. We evaluate our method for exhale-to-inhale lung CT registration under two adaptation scenarios using three public datasets. First, we consider the DIR-Lab COPD dataset [2] as source and the Learn2Reg (L2R) Task 2 dataset [12] as target domain. The domain shift consists in exhale scans from the target domain exhibiting a cropped field of view such that upper and lower parts of the lungs are partially cut off. Our training data comprise 10 labeled scan pairs from COPD and 12 unlabeled pairs from the train/val split of L2R. Evaluation is performed on the official test split of L2R (10 scan pairs). Second, we perform adaptation from the DIR-Lab 4D CT dataset [3] as the source to the COPD dataset as the target domain. While scans from 4D CT were acquired from patients with shallow resting breathing, scan pairs from COPD show actively forced full inhalation and exhalation. Thus, the domain gap consists in the breathing type, yielding deformations with different characteristics. Here, evaluation is performed via 5-fold cross-validation on the 10 scans from COPD. For each fold, training data include the 10 labeled scan pairs from 4D CT and 8 unlabeled scan pairs from COPD, and we evaluate the trained model on the remaining 2 scan pairs from COPD. In both adaptation scenarios, labels for source data are available in the form of landmark correspondences. To supervise predicted displacement vectors for the keypoints in the fixed cloud, we interpolate displacements of the landmarks to the entire volume and grid-sample at the keypoint locations. Scans from all domains are pre-processed in an identical way. We resample inhale scans to $1.75 \times 1.25 \times 1.75$ mm and exhale scans to $1.75 \times 1.00 \times 1.25$ mm to compensate for a different volume scaling during inspiration and expiration. Subsequently, we crop fixed-size regions of interest with $192 \times 192 \times 208$ vx around the centre of automatically generated lung masks.

Implementation Details. We implement our framework in PyTorch and optimize parameters of the student GCN with the Adam optimizer. Batches are composed of 4 source and 4 target samples. Training is performed for 100 epochs with a constant learning rate of 0.01. Hyper-parameters of the baseline model (GCN architecture and LBP parameters) are adopted from [8]. Hyper-parameters of the self-ensembling framework are determined via cross-validation on the training samples from Learn2Reg and set to $\lambda_0 = 1$, $\alpha = 0.98$, and $T = 20$ epochs. Stochastic augmentations include random rotations around all axes by angles from $[-10°, 10°]$, random scaling by a global factor from $[0.9, 1.1]$, and random translation by a vector from $[-0.1, 0.1]^3$.

Table 1. Results for both adaptation scenarios, reported as TRE in mm.

Method	COPD →L2R	4D CT →COPD
Initial	10.24	11.99
VM++ source	4.34	3.55
VM++ target	3.09	2.46
Source-only	4.96	4.02
Target-only	2.61	2.26
Ours	2.64	2.01
Ours + Adam	2.38	1.93

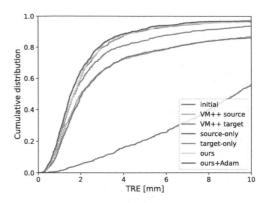

Fig. 2. Cumulative target registration errors for adaptation from COPD to L2R.

Baseline Methods. 1) As a lower bound (*source-only*), we train the baseline model on source data without any adaptation techniques. 2) As an upper bound (*target-only*), we train the baseline model on labeled training data from the target domain. 3) As an alternative domain adaptation technique, we experimented with DANN [5]. Specifically, we used max pooling to condense geometric features into a global feature vector and aligned the source and target distributions of these global features by adversarial learning. As expected, this approach turned out to be unsuitable for registration and lead to divergence. 4) As an intensity-based baseline method, we use the recent Voxelmorph++ (*VM++*) [11], which combines an extension of Voxelmorph with instance optimization through Adam. We train the model once on source and once on target data.

Metrics. We interpolate predicted displacement vectors at sparse keypoints to the entire volume and report the mean target registration error (TRE) at available landmark correspondences. We also inspected the regularity of the interpolated deformation fields. However, due to the regularizing effect of LBP, all methods predict smooth deformation fields (percentages of folding voxels $|J_\varphi|_{<0} < 10^{-4}$) such that a quantitative comparison does not provide additional insights.

3.2 Results

Quantitative results of our experiments are shown in Table 1 and reveal consistent findings under both adaptation scenarios. First, both our source-only model and the VM++ source model perform substantially worse than their respective counterparts trained on target data, increasing the TRE by 40 to 90%. This demonstrates that both considered domain shifts pose severe problems for intensity- and keypoint-based methods and need to be addressed by effective adaptation methods. Second, and most importantly, our proposed method effectively adapts the baseline model to the target domain. Specifically, it achieves

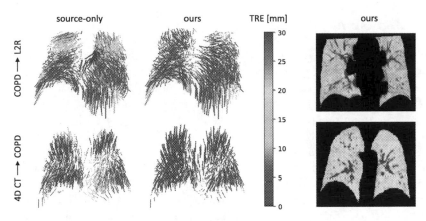

Fig. 3. Qualitative results for one sample case from each adaptation scenario. The first two columns show predicted displacement vectors by the source-only model and by our model. The linewidth is proportional to the distance of displacements, and colors encode the TRE (clamped to 30 mm). The last column shows overlaid CT slices after registration by our method. Inhale and exhale scans are shown in orange and blue shades, respectively, adding up to grayscale in case of alignment. (Color figure online)

mean TREs of 2.64 mm and 2.01 mm, respectively, thus improving on the source-only model by 47%/50% while matching or even surpassing the performance of the target-only model. This demonstrates that our self-ensembling framework effectively leverages unlabeled target data to close the domain gap. Third, we investigate how far we can push the accuracy of our method by fine-tuning the displacement fields with MIND-based instance optimization with Adam [18]. This further reduces the TRE to 2.38 mm and 1.93 mm. A detailed comparison of all discussed methods for COPD→L2R is shown in Fig. 2. Finally, it is notable that our method compares favorably to the state-of-the-art LapIRN [15], the winner of the recent Learn2Reg challenge, which is slightly superior on the L2R test set (TRE = 1.98 mm) but clearly inferior to our method on COPD (TRE = 3.83 mm).

Qualitative results are presented in Fig. 3. The first two columns visualize the effect of the studied domain gaps. For COPD→L2R, errors of the source-only model primarily occur in the superior part of the lung, which is partially outside the scanning region in exhale scans of the target domain while fully visible on source data. For 4DCT→COPD, the source-only model mainly fails in the anterior region of the lung, which is strongly deformed by full inspiration-expiration (target domain) but relatively static during shallow breathing (source domain). Our method substantially reduces these errors, highlighting the efficient adaptation to the target domain. Finally, the CT overlays (last column) show the largely accurate alignment of inner lung structures by our method.

4   Conclusion

In this work, we addressed geometric domain adaptation in the context of image registration and proposed a novel self-ensembling framework. Specifically, we embedded a keypoint-based registration model into the Mean Teacher paradigm and thus guided the learning process in the target domain by consistency-based supervision. In our experiments for exhale-to-inhale registration of lung CT scans, we demonstrated that our method successfully reduced the domain gap under two challenging adaptation settings, including different breathing types and imaging protocols. Specifically, it surpassed the baseline model by 50%/47% and even matched the performance of a supervised model trained on labeled target data. These results indicate great potential of the Mean Teacher framework for medical image registration, demonstrating its capability to improve feature learning in the absence of labels. While our use case of keypoint-based registration under geometric shifts is rather specific, our method is flexible and can easily be adapted to diverse scenarios, including domain adaptation under intensity shifts with classical 3D CNNs and semi-supervised learning. However, experimental evaluation under these settings is needed and will be the subject of future work.

Acknowledgement. We gratefully acknowledge the financial support by the Federal Ministry for Economic Affairs and Climate Action of Germany (FKZ: 01MK20012B) and by the Federal Ministry for Education and Research of Germany (FKZ: 01KL2008).

References

1. Bousmalis, K., Trigeorgis, G., Silberman, N., Krishnan, D., Erhan, D.: Domain separation networks. Adv. Neural. Inf. Process. Syst. **29**, 343–351 (2016)
2. Castillo, R., et al.: A reference dataset for deformable image registration spatial accuracy evaluation using the copdgene study archive. Physics in Medicine & Biology **58**(9), 2861 (2013)
3. Castillo, R., et al.: A framework for evaluation of deformable image registration spatial accuracy using large landmark point sets. Phys. Med. Biol. **54**(7), 1849 (2009)
4. French, G., Mackiewicz, M., Fisher, M.: Self-ensembling for visual domain adaptation. In: International Conference on Learning Representations (2018)
5. Ganin, Y., Lempitsky, V.: Unsupervised domain adaptation by backpropagation. In: International Conference on Machine Learning. pp. 1180–1189. PMLR (2015)
6. Ghifary, M., Kleijn, W.B., Zhang, M., Balduzzi, D., Li, W.: Deep reconstruction-classification networks for unsupervised domain adaptation. In: Leibe, B., Matas, J., Sebe, N., Welling, M. (eds.) ECCV 2016. LNCS, vol. 9908, pp. 597–613. Springer, Cham (2016). https://doi.org/10.1007/978-3-319-46493-0_36
7. Guan, H., Liu, M.: Domain adaptation for medical image analysis: a survey. IEEE Trans. Biomed. Eng. **69**, 1173–1185 (2021)
8. Hansen, L., Heinrich, M.P.: Deep learning based geometric registration for medical images: how accurate can we get without visual features? In: Feragen, A., Sommer, S., Schnabel, J., Nielsen, M. (eds.) IPMI 2021. LNCS, vol. 12729, pp. 18–30. Springer, Cham (2021). https://doi.org/10.1007/978-3-030-78191-0_2

9. Haskins, G., Kruger, U., Yan, P.: Deep learning in medical image registration: a survey. Mach. Vision Appl. **31**, 1–18 (2020). https://doi.org/10.1007/s00138-020-01060-x

10. Heinrich, M.P., Handels, H., Simpson, I.J.A.: Estimating large lung motion in COPD patients by symmetric regularised correspondence fields. In: Navab, N., Hornegger, J., Wells, W.M., Frangi, A.F. (eds.) MICCAI 2015. LNCS, vol. 9350, pp. 338–345. Springer, Cham (2015). https://doi.org/10.1007/978-3-319-24571-3_41

11. Heinrich, M.P., Hansen, L.: Voxelmorph++ going beyond the cranial vault with keypoint supervision and multi-channel instance optimisation. arXiv preprint arXiv:2203.00046 (2022)

12. Hering, A., Murphy, K., van Ginneken, B.: Learn2reg challenge: CT lung registration - training data, May 2020. https://doi.org/10.5281/zenodo.3835682, https://doi.org/10.5281/zenodo.3835682

13. Kruse, C.N., Hansen, L., Heinrich, M.P.: Multi-modal unsupervised domain adaptation for deformable registration based on maximum classifier discrepancy. In: Bildverarbeitung für die Medizin 2021. I, pp. 192–197. Springer, Wiesbaden (2021). https://doi.org/10.1007/978-3-658-33198-6_47

14. Mahapatra, D., Ge, Z.: Training data independent image registration using generative adversarial networks and domain adaptation. Pattern Recogn. **100** (2020)

15. Mok, T.C.W., Chung, A.C.S.: Conditional deformable image registration with convolutional neural network. In: de Bruijne, M., et al. (eds.) MICCAI 2021. LNCS, vol. 12904, pp. 35–45. Springer, Cham (2021). https://doi.org/10.1007/978-3-030-87202-1_4

16. Perone, C.S., Ballester, P., Barros, R.C., Cohen-Adad, J.: Unsupervised domain adaptation for medical imaging segmentation with self-ensembling. Neuroimage **194**, 1–11 (2019)

17. Saito, K., Watanabe, K., Ushiku, Y., Harada, T.: Maximum classifier discrepancy for unsupervised domain adaptation. In: Proceedings of the IEEE Conference on Computer Vision and Pattern Recognition, pp. 3723–3732 (2018)

18. Siebert, H., Hansen, L., Heinrich, M.P.: Fast 3D registration with accurate optimisation and little learning for learn2reg 2021. arXiv preprint arXiv:2112.03053 (2021)

19. Sotiras, A., Davatzikos, C., Paragios, N.: Deformable medical image registration: a survey. IEEE Trans. Med. Imaging **32**(7), 1153–1190 (2013)

20. Srivastav, V., Gangi, A., Padoy, N.: Unsupervised domain adaptation for clinician pose estimation and instance segmentation in the or. arXiv preprint arXiv:2108.11801 (2021)

21. Tarvainen, A., Valpola, H.: Mean teachers are better role models: Weight-averaged consistency targets improve semi-supervised deep learning results. In: Conference on Advances in Neural Information Processing Systems, vol. 30 (2017)

22. Tsai, Y.H., Hung, W.C., Schulter, S., Sohn, K., Yang, M.H., Chandraker, M.: Learning to adapt structured output space for semantic segmentation. In: Proceedings of the IEEE conference on computer vision and pattern recognition, pp. 7472–7481 (2018)

23. Tzeng, E., Hoffman, J., Saenko, K., Darrell, T.: Adversarial discriminative domain adaptation. In: Proceedings of the IEEE Conference on Computer Vision and Pattern Recognition, pp. 7167–7176 (2017)

24. Wang, M., Deng, W.: Deep visual domain adaptation: a survey. Neurocomputing **312**, 135–153 (2018)

25. Yang, W., Ouyang, W., Wang, X., Ren, J., Li, H., Wang, X.: 3D human pose estimation in the wild by adversarial learning. In: Proceedings of the IEEE Conference on Computer Vision and Pattern Recognition, pp. 5255–5264 (2018)

26. Yu, L., Wang, S., Li, X., Fu, C.-W., Heng, P.-A.: Uncertainty-aware self-ensembling model for semi-supervised 3D left atrium segmentation. In: Shen, D., et al. (eds.) MICCAI 2019. LNCS, vol. 11765, pp. 605–613. Springer, Cham (2019). https://doi.org/10.1007/978-3-030-32245-8_67

DisQ: Disentangling Quantitative MRI Mapping of the Heart

Changchun Yang[1], Yidong Zhao[1], Lu Huang[2], Liming Xia[2], and Qian Tao[1(✉)]

[1] Department of Imaging Physics, Delft University of Technology,
Delft, The Netherlands
q.tao@tudelft.nl

[2] Tongji Medical College, Huazhong University of Science and Technology,
Wuhan, China

Abstract. Quantitative MRI (qMRI) of the heart has become an important clinical tool for examining myocardial tissue properties. Because heart is a moving object, it is usually imaged with electrocardiogram and respiratory gating during acquisition, to "freeze" its motion. In reality, gating is more-often-than-not imperfect given the heart rate variability and nonideal breath-hold. qMRI of the heart, consequently, is characteristic of varying image contrast as well as residual motion, the latter compromising the quality of quantitative mapping. Motion correction is an important step prior to parametric mapping, however, a long-standing difficulty for registering the dynamic sequence is that the contrast across frames varies wildly: depending on the acquisition scheme some frames can have extremely poor contrast, which fails both traditional optimization-based and modern learning-based registration methods. In this work, we propose a novel framework named *DisQ*, which Disentangles Quantitative mapping sequences into the latent space of *contrast* and *anatomy*, fully unsupervised. The disentangled latent spaces serve for the purpose of generating a series of images with identical contrast, which enables easy and accurate registration of all frames. We applied our DisQ method to the modified Look-Locker inversion recovery (MOLLI) sequence, and demonstrated improved performance of T_1 mapping. In addition, we showed the possibility of generating a dynamic series of baseline images with exactly the same shape, *strictly* registered and perfectly "frozen". Our proposed DisQ methodology readily extends to other types of cardiac qMRI such as T_2 mapping and perfusion.

Keywords: Quantitative magnetic resonance imaging · T_1 mapping · Unsupervised disentangled representation · Motion correction

1 Introduction

Quantitative magnetic resonance imaging (qMRI) has become an important clinical tool for noninvasive evaluation of tissue integrity [23]. In qMRI, quantitative information of tissue is derived from a dynamic sequence of baseline images

© The Author(s), under exclusive license to Springer Nature Switzerland AG 2022
L. Wang et al. (Eds.): MICCAI 2022, LNCS 13436, pp. 291–300, 2022.
https://doi.org/10.1007/978-3-031-16446-0_28

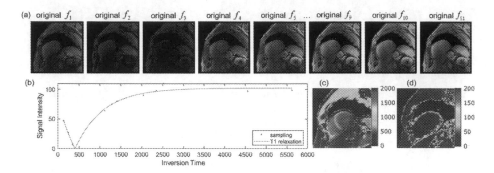

Fig. 1. (a) An example of MOLLI T_1 mapping sequence with 11 baseline images (denoted by f). (b) The 3-parameter signal model for T_1 fitting. (c) The computed T_1 map. Colorbar in the range of 0–2000 ms. (d) The corresponding standard deviation (SD) error map of T_1 mapping with colorbar 0–200 ms.

acquired with modulated MR imaging parameters. Based on the underlying physics, quantification of tissue properties is obtained by fitting a parametric signal model, under the assumption that the series of baseline images are aligned anatomically. However, this assumption is often violated in cardiac qMRI where the object is constantly moving. Even with careful electrocardiogram and respiratory gating, the baseline images often contain residual motion, which compromises the quality of quantitative mapping and undermines the value of qMRI.

Quantification of myocardial T_1 relaxation time is among the most important applications of qMRI in current radiology practice [6]. A widely used MRI sequence is the modified Look-Locker inversion (MOLLI) recovery [13], normally with 11 baseline images, governed by the following 3-parameter function:

$$s\left(t_{\mathrm{inv}}\right) = A - B \cdot \exp\left(-\frac{t_{\mathrm{inv}}}{T_1^*}\right) \tag{1}$$

where s is the signal intensity at t_{inv}, the inversion time during acquisition (11 in total), and A, B and T_1^* are the three parameters. The true T_1 is calculated as $T_1 = (\frac{B}{A} - 1) \cdot T_1^*$. Figure 1 illustrates an example of MOLLI T_1 baseline images (a) and parametric mapping (b-d). In this example, we can appreciate the dynamic change in baseline images and poor myocardium-blood contrast in some of them, e.g. the 3rd image in (a), as well as the residual motion in (b).

To realize accurate quantitative mapping, motion correction by image registration is an important step prior to parametric mapping. Popular registration methods include traditional optimization-based methods and modern learning-based methods. Xue *et al.* [22] proposed to use synthetic image estimation for myocardial motion correction, iteratively improved mapping accuracy. PCA-based method was proposed at [7, 21] for groupwise registration. Learning-based methods explode [1, 16, 17] with the potential of deep learning, can be divided into two categories: supervised [18] and unsupervised (VoxelMorph [1]).

A fundamental difficulty for registering the dynamic sequence is that the contrast across frames varies wildly: depending on acquisition scheme some frames can have extremely poor contrast (e.g. near the signal nulling point), which can fail both traditional optimization-based and modern learning-based registration methods. In this work, we propose a novel solution to this problem by first addressing the issue of contrast, inspired by the recent success of unsupervised disentangled representation learning in computer vision [4,9,12] and medical imaging [5,14,17,24]. Our rationale is as follows: according to the underlying physics, an MR image can be modeled as an function of anatomical tissue property and acquisition parameters. Therefore, when appropriately formulated, cardiac qMRI images can be disentangled to their *anatomical representation* and *contrast representation*. With such disentanglement, we may unify baseline images either in terms of contrast (for easy image registration), or anatomy (for direct quantitative mapping).

For the problem to be well-posed, existing methods for anatomy and shape disentanglement in medical imaging normally requires the dataset to share at least one common factor, i.e. multiple contrast of the same anatomy, or same contrast of different anatomy. As such, most work focused on brain MRI as the same anatomy requirement can be easily satisfied. However, for a moving object, cardiac qMRI is characteristic of varying image contrast as well as residual motion. In this work, we propose a framework named "Disentangling Quantitative MRI" (DisQ) to decompose the dynamic cardiac images under the condition of simultaneous anatomy and contrast change. We validated the method on MOLLI T_1 mapping, the most popular qMRI application of heart, but the methodology can be extended to other quantitative sequences. Our contributions include:

- This is among the first work to address cardiac qMRI analysis from an anatomy-contrast disentanglement perspective;
- We propose a novel network architecture and a number effective bootstrapping strategies, dedicate to cardiac qMRI (characteristic of simultaneous contrast and anatomy change), evaluate on the clinical T_1 mapping data;
- We demonstrate the possibility of generating *strictly* registered baseline images for cardiac qMRI, beyond any existing registration methods.

2   Methodology

2.1   Overall Framework: Disentangling Latent Spaces

A schematic plot of our proposed method is shown in Fig. 2. Let $f_t^s \in F_T^S$ denote the input baseline MOLLI image of t-th inversion time of the s-th subject. As shown in Fig. 2(a), we aim to decompose an image pair $\{f_i^s, f_j^s\}$ of the same subject to their anatomical representations $\{a_i^s = E^A(f_i^s), a_j^s = E^A(f_j^s)\}$ by an anatomical encoder E^A and separate contrast representations $\{c_i^s = E^C(f_i^s), c_j^s = E^C(f_j^s)\}$ by a contrast encoder E^C. The generator G then reconstructs the images from their anatomical and contrast representations. As in prior work [3,14], we optimize the *self-reconstruction* and *cross-reconstruction* losses to learn the disentangled latent spaces. With a pair $\{a_i^s, c_j^s\}$ derived from

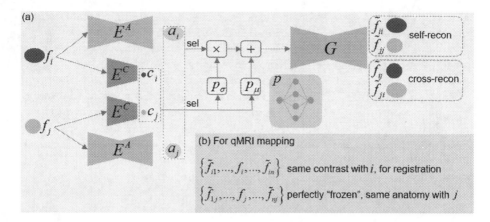

Fig. 2. (a) DisQ: the overview of network architecture to disentangle anatomy and contrast of paired baseline images f_i and f_j. The a and c decomposed from each image will be selected one at a time for reconstruction. See text for Projector p and architecture details. (b) Two ways DisQ can potentially be used in analyzing cardiac qMRI: (1) unify the contrast for motion correction, (2) unify the anatomy for direct quantitative mapping.

images of any two baseline images, G can synthesize an image $\tilde{f}_{ji}^s$, which should be similar to the image f_j^s with contrast c_j^s.

$$L_{\text{self}-\text{recon}} = \frac{1}{ST}\sum_{s=1}^{S}\sum_{i=1}^{T}\mathbb{E}_{f_i^s \sim F_T^S}\left\|\tilde{f}_{ii}^s - f_i^s\right\|_1, \tag{2}$$

$$L_{\text{cross}-\text{recon}} = \frac{1}{ST(T-1)}\sum_{s=1}^{S}\sum_{i=1}^{T}\sum_{j=1,j\neq i}^{T}\mathbb{E}_{f_i^s,f_j^s \sim F_T^S}\left\|\tilde{f}_{ji}^s - f_j^s\right\|_1, \tag{3}$$

where $\tilde{f}_{ji}^s = G(E^C(f_j^s), E^A(f_i^s))$. Under this generic framework, we present further technical novelties that enable disentanglement of cardiac qMRI.

2.2   Bootstrapping Disentangled Representations

Anatomy Encoder. Our shared anatomical encoder E^A is built from the basic architecture of the U-Net [20], to extract anatomical information a. It is desirable that the extracted a is limited in capacity (with minimal information on contrast), but at the same time captures the anatomy. We therefore design a to be a one-hot encoded multi-channel map through a straight-through Gumbel-softmax (STGS) layer [5,24]. Consequently, the generator G cannot reconstruct images without extra information of contrast since the one-hot encoding strictly restricts the capacity of a.

For the same subject, the learned multi-channel anatomical representations a_i^s, a_j^s should share similarity, but are not exactly identical due to the residual motion of the heart. Instead of enforcing identity of anatomy, we consider the the two anatomies similar, as two weak augmentations of the true "frozen" shape of the subject. We formulate this into an anatomical similarity loss to encourage loosely similar a between the two learned anatomy representations:

$$L_{\text{anatomy}} = 1 - \frac{\langle a_i^s, a_j^s \rangle}{\|a_i^s\|_2 \cdot \|a_j^s\|_2}. \tag{4}$$

which promotes the two anatomy representation a_i^s and a_j^s to be as close as possible, while allowing minor deviations (residual motion). We will present ablation study to validate this loss.

Contrast Encoder. The second latent space is the contrast representations c capturing the contrast information in different baseline images. Given that the underlying T_1 relaxation function (Eq. 1) is simple, the latent space of contrast should be intrinsically low-dimensional. We encode the contrast information into a low-dimensional vector by a shared encoder E^C. We employ an information bottleneck loss [2,19] here to limit the information capacity of c and avoid informative leakage:

$$L_{\text{contrast}} = \left\| \|c\|_2^2 - C \right\|_1, \tag{5}$$

where C is the bottleneck capacity controlling the amount of information in the latent contrast representation. The choice of C will be presented in section Implementation.

Projector. The input for DisQ is two qMRI frames $\{f_i^s, f_j^s\}$ of the same subject, but with different acquisition parameters (in the case of MOLLI at different t_{inv}). Feeding them into the DisQ network, we can obtain $\{a_i^s, a_j^s\}$ and $\{c_i^s, c_j^s\}$ respectively, to represent their anatomies and contrasts. Consequently, by combining a and c in pairs, we can generate four synthetic images. Two of them are self-reconstruction, with c broadcasted to the same height and width as a. A code z is obtained after the broadcasted c being concatenated with the selected a in the channel dimension, and is sent to the generator G for reconstruction. The other two are cross-reconstruction, where we adopt a different concatenated mechanism. As one-hot encoding of STGS tends to have high variance with this gradient estimator, we proposed to reduce the variance of STGS inspired by Rao-Blackwellization [15]. We thereby introduce bias here to counteract the variance of STGS, which is realized by a projector p, expressed by:

$$z_{ji}^s = p_\sigma(c_j^s) \cdot a_i^s + p_\mu(c_j^s), \tag{6}$$

where p_σ and p_μ are two fully connected layers constructing the projector p.

Overall Loss. Our overall loss function is defined as $L_{\text{overall}} = \lambda_1 L_{\text{recon}} + \lambda_2 L_{\text{per}} + \lambda_3 L_{\text{anatomy}} + \lambda_4 L_{\text{contrast}}$, where L_{recon} sums up $L_{\text{self-recon}}$ (Eq. 2) and $L_{\text{cross-recon}}$ (Eq. 3), L_{per} is the perceptual loss introduced in [8]: $\|\text{VGG}(\tilde{f}) - \text{VGG}(f)\|_1$, where f is the original image, $\tilde{f}$ is the reconstructed image.

3   Experiments

3.1   Dataset

In total 102 MOLLI T_1 acquisitions were included in this study. The images were acquired by a 3.0T Ingenia MR-scanner (Philips Healthcare,Best, The Nether-lands), in three short-axis slices: apical, mid, and basal. Both native and post-contrast T_1 mapping were performed using the same 3-3-5 scheme provided by the manufacturer. Each data has a dimension of $256 \times 256 \times 3 \times 11$. We randomly split the dataset into 80 for training, 11 for validation, and 11 for testing. The myocardium of left ventricle were manually annotated as the region of interest.

3.2   Implementation

Training. The four hyperparameters for our objective function L_{overall} were set to $\lambda_1 = 2, \lambda_2 = 0.03, \lambda_3 = 0.02, \lambda_4 = 10^{-8}$. The hyperparameter C in Eq. 5 was increased per epoch: $1000 \times e^{0.002i}$. The channel numbers of a and c in DisQ were set to 3 and 2, and our model was trained for 300 epochs by the Adam optimizer with learning rate of 3×10^{-4}. During training, we randomly selected two baseline images from the same MOLLI sequence, but at two different inversion time. Our codes are released at https://github.com/Changchun-Yang/DisQ.

Evaluation. For every MOLLI data, we choose the t-th baseline image f_t as the reference, then all other frames $i \in \{1...T\}, i \neq t$ along with f_t are fed into the DisQ to get all the reconstructed results. We then generate two new sequence of images with reference to f_t: $\{\tilde{f}_{t1}, ..., f_t, ..., \tilde{f}_{tT}\}$, and $\{\tilde{f}_{1t}, ..., f_t, ..., \tilde{f}_{Tt}\}$. The first sequence share the same contrast with f_t, but retains the anatomy of the original baseline images. This sequence of images (with the same contrast) is then used for residual motion correction. The derived deformation field is then applied to the original baseline image series for a motion-corrected MOLLI. The second sequence keeps the original contrast of baseline images while sharing the same anatomy, hence with cardiac motion perfectly "frozen". This sequence of generated images can be directly used for T1 mapping. Quantitative metrics include the value and standard deviation (SD) error of the T_1 map as in [10]. The unsupervised registration network is adopted from the baseline VoxelMorph [1]. We set t as 5 in our experiments, but our results were not sensitive to its choice.

Comparative and Ablation Study. We evaluated the proposed bootstrap-ping strategies by comparative and ablation studies. In particular, we performed ablation study for the proposed anatomy loss L_{anatomy} and projector p. As a base-line, we implemented the same network architecture, by substituting L_{anatomy} with the common MAE loss, and removing the projector p. This baseline is denoted as **Dis**. The proposed anatomy loss and projector were then integrated in this baseline model one by one to create ablation models. All models in com-parison however carried the contrast loss L_{contrast}, which is important for rea-sonable disentanglement of contrast. In addition, the T_1 mapping results of the originally acquired data (with residual motion) was denoted as **Org**. The T_1 mapping results after VoxelMorph registration is denoted as **Morph**. We further implemented the PCA-based groupwise registration [7,21] using the traditional *elastix* toolbox [11] as another method in comparison, denoted as **Groupwise**.

3.3   Results

Quantitative Analysis. We first present and analyze our quantitative results. As shown in Table 1, we calculated the mean and standard deviation (std) of SD error within the myocardium region for all listed methods. We see that the accuracy of fitting is the lower on the uncorrected original MOLLI data, while the mapping results of learning-based **Morph** and optimization-based **Groupwise** were both significantly improved compared with **Org**. When using the disentanglement framework **Dis**, the T1 mapping based on the generated dataset of **Dis** achieved the worst results. This implies sub-optimal disentanglement, i.e., information leakage between a and c in **Dis**. The results improved when adding $L_{anatomy}$ and p. Specifically, the former improved mean and the latter std. This confirms that $L_{anatomy}$ guarantees anatomy disentanglement in presence of residual motion, and that the proposed projector p is efficient in reducing variance. Our **DisQ** achieved further improved results in both mean and std. The mean SD error of ours was still slightly higher than **Groupwise**, however latter demanded lengthy optimization.

Table 1. The mean and standard deviation of fitting quantitative T_1 maps. (Unit: ms)

Method	Org	Morph	Dis	Dis+$L_{anatomy}$	Dis+p	Dis + $L_{anatomy}$+ p (Our DisQ)	Groupwise
Mean	47.9	39.1	57.9	41.2	43.8	**36.6**	**32.2**
Standard deviation	24.6	22.5	26.3	25.9	21.3	**19.9**	21.0

Qualitative Analysis. We select 11 baseline images of one subject from our test MOLLI sequence, and original 11 frames are shown in Fig. 1(a). Then we show the generated cross-reconstructed data using DisQ in Fig. 3, which is unified through two strategies, either in terms of contrast (for easy image registration, Fig. 3(a)), or anatomy (for direct quantitative mapping, Fig. 3(b)). They share the contrast or anatomy from the selected inversion time respectively. We also show the quantitative native and post-contrast T_1 maps and their SD in Fig. 4, it can be seen that compared with **DisQ**, the SD of **Org** is very obvious at the motion boundary, and **Morph** is affected by drastic changes in contrast and may locally produce large errors.

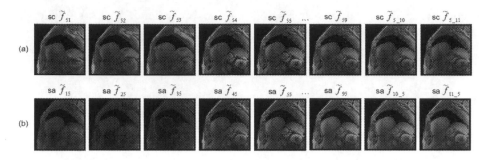

Fig. 3. Utilizing DisQ to analyze cardiac qMRI: (a) all images have the same contrast (*sc*, from the 5th frame), respective anatomies, (b) all images share the same anatomy (*sa*, also from the 5th frame), while preserving their respective contrasts. $\tilde{f}_{ij}$ represents contrast from frame i, anatomy from j.

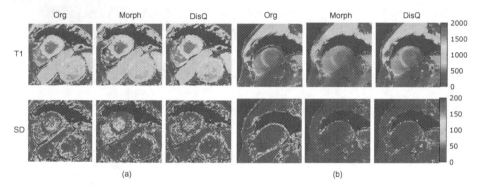

Fig. 4. The resulting quantitative T_1 maps and corresponding SD error maps of (a) native and (b) post-contrast MOLLI sequences. Colorbar in the unit of ms. (Color figure online)

Computational Time. The training time for our disentanglement architecture is ~10 h on one 3090Ti GPU, and ~300 ms for inference on a pair of cross reconstructed images. For the registration network, we use the original Voxelmorph, and training time is ~6 h and evaluation time is ~400 ms for pairwise registration. For Groupwise registration by Elastix toolbox, the inference time is ~9000 s. In comparison, our pipeline only takes ~7 s for disentangling and registering of one MOLLI sequence.

4   Conclusion

In this work, we propose a novel image disentanglement framework DisQ (Disentangling Quantitative MRI) to discompose cardiac qMRI images into their *anatomical representation* and *contrast representation* in the latent space. This is among the first work to address cardiac qMRI analysis from an anatomy-contrast disentanglement perspective, with effective bootstrapping strategies proposed to tackle simultaneous changes of contrast and anatomy in cardiac qMRI. We applied DisQ to analyze the clinical MOLLI sequences (both native and post-contrast), and demonstrated improved precision for the final cardiac T1 map. Our proposed DisQ methodology is generic, which readily extends to other types of cardiac qMRI such as T_2 mapping and perfusion. Future work is warranted to investigate its generalizability to other qMRI sequences with different underlying physics.

Acknowledgement. The authors gratefully acknowledge TU Delft AI Initiative for financial support.

References

1. Balakrishnan, G., Zhao, A., Sabuncu, M.R., Guttag, J., Dalca, A.V.: VoxelMorph: a learning framework for deformable medical image registration. IEEE Trans. Med. Imaging **38**(8), 1788–1800 (2019)
2. Burgess, C.P., et al.: Understanding disentangling in β-VAE. arXiv preprint arXiv:1804.03599 (2018)
3. Chartsias, A., et al.: Disentangle, align and fuse for multimodal and semi-supervised image segmentation. IEEE Trans. Med. Imaging **40**(3), 781–792 (2020)
4. Denton, E.L., et al.: Unsupervised learning of disentangled representations from video. Adv. Neural Inf. Process. Syst. **30** (2017)
5. Dewey, B.E., et al.: A disentangled latent space for cross-site MRI harmonization. In: Martel, A.L., et al. (eds.) MICCAI 2020, Part VII. LNCS, vol. 12267, pp. 720–729. Springer, Cham (2020). https://doi.org/10.1007/978-3-030-59728-3_70
6. Haaf, P., Garg, P., Messroghli, D.R., Broadbent, D.A., Greenwood, J.P., Plein, S.: Cardiac T1 mapping and extracellular volume (ECV) in clinical practice: a comprehensive review. J. Cardiovasc. Magn. Reson. **18**(1), 1–12 (2017)
7. Huizinga, W., et al.: PCA-based groupwise image registration for quantitative MRI. Med. Image Anal. **29**, 65–78 (2016)
8. Johnson, J., Alahi, A., Fei-Fei, L.: Perceptual losses for real-time style transfer and super-resolution. In: Leibe, B., Matas, J., Sebe, N., Welling, M. (eds.) ECCV 2016, Part II. LNCS, vol. 9906, pp. 694–711. Springer, Cham (2016). https://doi.org/10.1007/978-3-319-46475-6_43
9. Karras, T., Laine, S., Aila, T.: A style-based generator architecture for generative adversarial networks. In: Proceedings of the IEEE/CVF Conference on Computer Vision and Pattern Recognition, pp. 4401–4410 (2019)
10. Kellman, P., Hansen, M.S.: T1-mapping in the heart: accuracy and precision. J. Cardiovasc. Magn. Reson. **16**(1), 1–20 (2014). https://doi.org/10.1186/1532-429X-16-2
11. Klein, S., Staring, M., Murphy, K., Viergever, M.A., Pluim, J.P.: Elastix: a toolbox for intensity-based medical image registration. IEEE Trans. Med. Imaging **29**(1), 196–205 (2009)
12. Locatello, F., et al.: Challenging common assumptions in the unsupervised learning of disentangled representations. In: International Conference on Machine Learning, pp. 4114–4124. PMLR (2019)

13. Messroghli, D.R., Radjenovic, A., Kozerke, S., Higgins, D.M., Sivananthan, M.U., Ridgway, J.P.: Modified look-locker inversion recovery (MOLLI) for high-resolution T1 mapping of the heart. Magn. Reason. Med. Off. J. Int. Soc. Magn. Reason. Med. **52**(1), 141–146 (2004)

14. Ouyang, J., Adeli, E., Pohl, K.M., Zhao, Q., Zaharchuk, G.: Representation disentanglement for multi-modal brain MRI analysis. In: Feragen, A., Sommer, S., Schnabel, J., Nielsen, M. (eds.) IPMI 2021. LNCS, vol. 12729, pp. 321–333. Springer, Cham (2021). https://doi.org/10.1007/978-3-030-78191-0_25

15. Paulus, M.B., Maddison, C.J., Krause, A.: Rao-blackwellizing the straight-through gumbel-softmax gradient estimator. arXiv preprint arXiv:2010.04838 (2020)

16. Qin, C., et al.: Joint learning of motion estimation and segmentation for cardiac MR image sequences. In: Frangi, A.F., Schnabel, J.A., Davatzikos, C., Alberola-López, C., Fichtinger, G. (eds.) MICCAI 2018, Part II. LNCS, vol. 11071, pp. 472–480. Springer, Cham (2018). https://doi.org/10.1007/978-3-030-00934-2_53

17. Qin, C., Shi, B., Liao, R., Mansi, T., Rueckert, D., Kamen, A.: Unsupervised deformable registration for multi-modal images via disentangled representations. In: Chung, A.C.S., Gee, J.C., Yushkevich, P.A., Bao, S. (eds.) IPMI 2019. LNCS, vol. 11492, pp. 249–261. Springer, Cham (2019). https://doi.org/10.1007/978-3-030-20351-1_19

18. Qiu, H., Qin, C., Le Folgoc, L., Hou, B., Schlemper, J., Rueckert, D.: Deep learning for cardiac motion estimation: supervised vs. unsupervised training. In: Pop, M., et al. (eds.) STACOM 2019. LNCS, vol. 12009, pp. 186–194. Springer, Cham (2020). https://doi.org/10.1007/978-3-030-39074-7_20

19. Ren, X., Yang, T., Wang, Y., Zeng, W.: Rethinking content and style: exploring bias for unsupervised disentanglement. In: Proceedings of the IEEE/CVF International Conference on Computer Vision, pp. 1823–1832 (2021)

20. Ronneberger, O., Fischer, P., Brox, T.: U-Net: convolutional networks for biomedical image segmentation. In: Navab, N., Hornegger, J., Wells, W.M., Frangi, A.F. (eds.) MICCAI 2015, Part III. LNCS, vol. 9351, pp. 234–241. Springer, Cham (2015). https://doi.org/10.1007/978-3-319-24574-4_28

21. Tao, Q., van der Tol, P., Berendsen, F.F., Paiman, E.H., Lamb, H.J., van der Geest, R.J.: Robust motion correction for myocardial t1 and extracellular volume mapping by principle component analysis-based groupwise image registration. J. Magn. Reson. Imaging **47**(5), 1397–1405 (2018)

22. Xue, H., et al.: Motion correction for myocardial t1 mapping using image registration with synthetic image estimation. Magn. Reson. Med. **67**(6), 1644–1655 (2012)

23. van Zijl, P., et al.: Quantitative assessment of blood flow, blood volume and blood oxygenation effects in functional magnetic resonance imaging. Nat. Med. **4**(2), 159–167 (1998)

24. Zuo, L., et al.: Unsupervised MR harmonization by learning disentangled representations using information bottleneck theory. NeuroImage **243**, 118569 (2021)

Learning Iterative Optimisation for Deformable Image Registration of Lung CT with Recurrent Convolutional Networks

Fenja Falta$^{(\boxtimes)}$, Lasse Hansen, and Mattias P. Heinrich

Institute of Medical Informatics, University of Luebeck, Lübeck, Germany
`fenja.falta@student.uni-luebeck.de`

Abstract. Deep learning-based methods for deformable image registration have continually been increasing in accuracy. However, conventional methods using optimisation remain ubiquitous, as they often outperform deep learning-based methods regarding accuracy on test data. Recent learning-based methods for lung registration tasks prevalently employ instance optimisation on test data to achieve state-of-the-art performance. We propose a fully deep learning-based approach, that aims to emulate the structure of gradient-based optimisation as used in conventional registration and thus learns how to optimise. Our architecture consists of recurrent updates on a convolutional network with deep supervision. It uses a dynamic sampling of the cost function, hidden states to imitate information flow during optimisation and incremental displacements for multiple iterations. Our code is publicly available at https://github.com/multimodallearning/Learn2Optimise/.

Keywords: Image registration · Optimisation · Convolutional network

1 Introduction

Deformable image registration is an immanent part of medical imaging processing. With the advances in machine learning over the last years, deformable image registration based on deep learning has become more and more prevalent and image registration algorithms can generally be divided into approaches based on conventional optimisation, deep learning-based approaches and those that combine both. Intra-patient lung registration is one of multiple common medical registration tasks with clinical applications such as regional COPD analysis or nodule tracking. As the Learn2Reg 2021 challenge [10] has shown, methods that rely solely on deep learning do not yet achieve state-of-the-art performance in regards to intra-patient lung registration. The best four submissions to the challenge were either completely conventional optimisation-based or employed instance optimisation after application of a deep learning model. Deep learning based submissions to the Learn2Reg challenge aimed to predict the displacement based on fixed and

L. Wang et al. (Eds.): MICCAI 2022, LNCS 13436, pp. 301–309, 2022.
https://doi.org/10.1007/978-3-031-16446-0_29

moving image features directly through feedforward networks. We propose a *learn to optimise* (L2O) network with a different approach to deformable image registration by employing a recurrent network to emulate instance optimisation.

1.1 Related Work

Neural networks, especially recurrent ones, have been previously used to mimic and improve upon the procedure of optimisation.

Andrychowicz et al. [1] discretly parameterised an optimiser and based on that employed a recurrent network to learn an optimiser function. Previous works have emulated optimisation specifically for image registration: Teed and Deng [23] introduced the architecture RAFT, which uses a recurrent network to iteratively update a displacement field by sampling from a (hypothetical) dense correlation volume. They achieved state-of-the-art performance on KITTI and demonstrated that their network was highly efficient and able to generalise well. Liu et al. [14] used a recurrent multi-scale network to solve a differomorphic registration task with geometric constraints. While the spatial transformer loss [11] is widely employed for unsupervised (metric-based) learning of feedforward registration networks [6] its gradients may provide limited guidance for complex registration tasks and thus explain some of the limitations of DL-based methods in lung registration. [12] aims at improving the gradient estimation through linearised multi-sampling, but do not employ a trainable optimiser.

Recurrent networks have also been succesfully applied to further medical image registration tasks: Lu et al. [15] used recurrent networks to incorporate the temporal aspect of 4DCT data. Sandkühler et al. [20] calculated a sequence of local displacements with a recurrent network, which they then compose to obtain final global displacement. Sun et al. [22] used recurrent reinforcement learning to achieve robustness in multimodal brain image registration. These methods are different to our work, in that they either directly rely on multiple frames of an input sequence, are limited to 2D data or realise a cascade of multiple feedforward networks that do not resemble gradient based optimisation of a cost function.

1.2 Adam Optimisation

In image registration we aim to compute a displacement field φ that minimises an objective function $f(\varphi)$ that usually consists of a distance metric of a warped moving image $M \circ \varphi$ and a fixed image F along with a regularisation for φ.

In iterative optimisation, the displacement field gets updated with every iteration. In conventional first-order gradient descent, the update is dependent on the gradient of f. For high-dimensional optimisation problems like image registration, it may be more beneficial to approximate the gradient ∇f with a transformation that comprises a smaller number of control points, i.e. a free-form deformation. Stochastic gradient descent can be used to speed up convergence by adding a factor of randomness through sampling [21].

In Adam optimisation [13], the update rule is extended by including estimates of first and second momentum of the gradients, and determining each update from the gradient of the current sample as well as the previous update. Each update is thus dependent on all previous updates.

1.3 Our Contribution

We propose a novel recurrent framework using an iterative dynamic cost sampling step and a trainable optimiser that is specifically aimed at mimicking Adam optimisation but can substantially reduce the required number of iterations. The sampled features themselves are identical to the minimal information required to estimate gradients of the dissimilarity between an image pair used in one iteration of conventional displacements optimisation. Specifically, image features are only provided to the network indirectly in the form of displacement costs. We further provide the network with hidden state features to provide the network with necessary information to calculate gradient momentum like Adam optimisation does. Based on this information the optimiser network is enabled to learn larger gradient steps (leap frogging) based on deep (multi-step) supervision with keypoint correspondences that also promotes nearly equal-sized optimisation steps of the displacement field with each iteration.

2 Methods

2.1 Pre-registration

In order to evaluate our method as an alternative to instance optimisation we first employ a recent feedforward (non-recurrent) learning based deformable registration called VoxelMorph++ (VM++) [8]. For VM++, VoxelMorph [2] is adapted to the lung registration task by training it with automatically extracted keypoint correspondences from an accurate but long-running conventional registration algorithm (corrField [7]). The network is intended to be fine-tuned with instance optimisation.

2.2 Extraction of Optimisation Inputs

We extract a total of 45 optimisation inputs for each image voxel/control point. Three of those channels are made up of the current predicted displacements φ^t. For the first iteration they are initialised either with the displacement field obtained by VoxelMorph++ or an identity transform. For each voxel eight displacements coordinates are computed using a fixed grid of subpixel offsets, resulting in 24 feature channels. For each sampled coordinate a dissimilarity cost (i.e. 8 features in total) is calculated and also fed into the network. To determine the cost term, MIND features [9] of the moving image are sampled at the displacement coordinates and for each voxel and displacement the dissimilarity to the fixed image, i.e. the sum of squared distance to the fixed features, is calculated. Displacements and coordinates can be used to approximate the gradients for an iterative gradient descent, which follows e.g. [18]. The remaining 10 feature channels are hidden states that are propagated through all iterations. Through

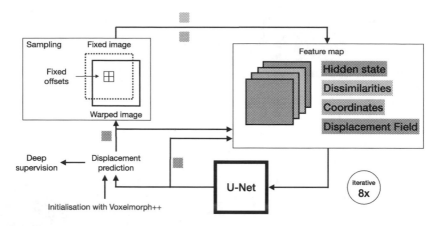

Fig. 1. Schematic depiction of our *learn to optimise* network. The feature map used in our recurrent network consists of four types of features. **Displacement Field**: Last predicted displacement. **Coordinates**: For every voxel, a fixed number of possible displacements is sampled. **Dissimilarities**: Displacement cost for each of the sampled displacements. **Hidden states**: Part of the U-Net output that is not supervised.

these, the model is able to save information about previous update steps and incorporate them similar to how Adam uses momenta. All features get updated with each recurrent application of the network. That means the coordinates and dissimilarity costs dynamically change across recurrent states and mimic the iterative fashion of conventional registration.

2.3 Optimiser Network

The feature map is fed into a U-Net [19] architecture with roughly 1 million trainable parameters. The network output comprises 13 feature channels, three forming the predicted displacements, while the remaining ten represent the hidden states of the network. During training, we apply eight recurrent iterations of the network, for which we employ deep keypoint supervision. We weight the loss linearly stronger with each iteration, to support the network in getting increasingly closer to the optimal value with each iteration, aiming at a behaviour similar to gradient descent. All weights are shared across iterations, which means the number of iterations does not have to be fixed and can be varied at inference time. A schematic illustration of our method is depicted in Fig. 1.

2.4 Comparison to Feed-Forward Nets and Adam Optimisation

Our method differs from networks that aim to directly predict a displacement field based on the input of two images. Foremost, the moving and fixed image features themselves are not directly given as input to the network. Instead, the network is only provided with similarity costs and displacement coordinates. Moreover, the employed U-Net architecture has a small capacity with few parameters, which forces the model to generalise more strongly.

The method, however, also differs from Adam optimisation in some important aspects. Since the hidden states are not supervised, the model does not necessarily make direct use of first and second momentum but could learn more useful nonlinear relations between previous updates, current coordinates, dissimilarity costs and the desired displacement update (during training). Additionally, while Adam optimisation solely has information about the current image it is optimising, our model can make use of further information over the image population, e.g. keypoint positions across multiple patients, through training.

3   Experiments and Results

Table 1. Mean target registration errors in mm of our and comparison methods on the 4DCT and COPD datasets.

	Initial	LapIRN		VM++	Adam		L2O (ours)	
		w/o Adam	w. Adam		w/o Pre-Reg	w. Pre-Reg	w/o Pre-Reg	w. Pre-Reg
4DCT	6.33	2.06	1.60	4.40	2.38	1.33	2.01	1.69
COPD	11.99	3.96	3.83	5.30	7.52	2.18	4.13	2.24

We train our network on the public EMPIRE10 (selected cases), DIR-Lab COPD and DIR-Lab 4DCT datasets [3–5,17], which contain a total of 28 pairs of ex and inspiratory lung CT scans. Experiments were conducted in a 5-fold cross-validation. We evaluate our method on the public COPD and 4DCT datasets. Each registration pair is annotated with 300 manual corresponding landmarks, that are used to assess the registration accuracy. We compare our learning based L2O approach with continuous Adam based optimisation in two settings: 1) on the original inhale and exhale scans and 2) as instance optimisation step for image pairs, that are pre-registered using the widely used Voxelmorph framework (in the afore described VM++ variant). LapIRN [16] as winner of the recent Learn2Reg challenge [10] was chosen as a comparison method with the deep learning-based state-of-the-art. It was evaluated with and without subsequent instance optimisation using Adam. Our proposed optimisation framework itself is analysed in different ablation studies, investigating the effect of different number of optimisation iterations and the use of deep supervision.

Implementation Details: All experiments were conducted on an Nvidia RTX A4000 using PyTorch 1.10. The 850 employed epochs of training for our L2O framework need 8.2 h per fold and 7 GB GPU memory. Hyperparameters were optimised on a single training fold and kept fixed for all further experiments.

General Results: Quantitative results of our and comparison methods can be found in Table 1. Our learned optimisation model reduces the TRE from 6.33 mm to 1.69 mm and from 11.99 mm to 2.24 mm for the 4DCT and COPD datasets, respectively, whereas VM++ alone, which is used as pre registration

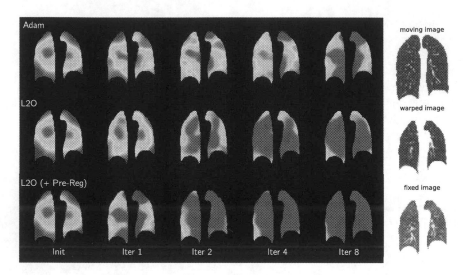

Fig. 2. Left: Residual target registration error (TRE) for Adam and our proposed L2O approach (with and without pre-registration) after 1,2,4 and 8 iterations on case #5 of the COPD dataset. Warm and cold colors correspond to high and low errors, respectively. Right: Moving, warped and fixed image (masked around the lung) of the same case for L2O with pre-registration.

in our experiments, only achieves TREs of 4.40 mm and 5.30 mm. Our method clearly outperforms Adam in settings without pre-registration, while yielding lower accuracy on the 4DCT dataset with pre-registration, where Adam reaches a target registration error of 1.33 mm and achieving on par results for the COPD dataset with pre-registration (2.18 mm vs 2.24 mm). However, the log-Jacobian determinants of displacement fields yield mean standard deviations of 0.04 for Adam and 0.02 for L2O as well as significant lower number of foldings for L2O, indicating that our optimisation approach produces smoother and less complex deformations. In addition, results reported for L2O are already achieved after 8 optimisation steps, whereas Adam needed at least 50 iterations for convergence. The comparison with the state-of-the-art (LapIRN + Adam) is also favourable. While the accuracy is roughly comparable for the 4DCT dataset, the TRE is almost two times better for the COPD dataset (3.83 mm versus 2.24 mm). A visual comparison of individual optimisation steps of Adam and L2O in Fig. 2 provides further insights. The spatial residual error of the target registration is shown after 1, 2, 4 and 8 iterations. The iterative improvement is clearly visible in both methods. However, Adam gets stuck in local minima at the lung surfaces. The faster convergence of L2O is also evident. The biggest improvements can already been seen in the first 2 iterations. When starting from a pre-registered scan pair, the improvement of the registration errors is in particular evident in the boundary regions.

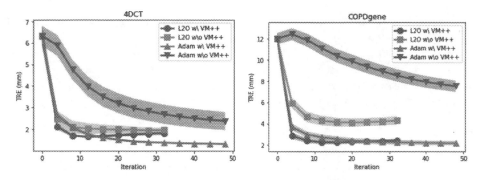

Fig. 3. Comparison of target registration error (TRE) between Adam and our L2O approach depending on the number of iterations. We present results with and without pre registration (using VM++).

Ablation Studies: Figure 3 shows target registration errors in the course of the individual optimisation steps. L2O shows the fastest convergence in all settings and is only outperformed by Adam after 16 and 24 iterations on the 4DCT and COPD dataset with pre-registration, respectively. It should be noted that the number of iterations where only altered during inference and it is thus likely that the results for L2O can be further improved when more optimisation steps are considered during training (which then of course may come at the cost of longer training times). Finally, deep supervision seems to be of great importance for learning a meaningful optimisation at each iteration. Omitting deep supervision increases the TRE by 0.5 mm and 1 mm for 4DCT and COPD, respectively.

4   Discussion

We proposed a framework that learns gradient-based optimisation steps for deformable image registration using a recurrent deep learning network. The structure of our model as well as the evaluation results indicate that our model emulates an optimisation rather than directly estimating a displacement field for given input images.

The network uses less iterations than Adam optimisation, indicating it does not only approximate first-order gradients and imitate gradient descent, but rather learns how to optimise using all available information and overcomes this limitation of gradient descent algorithms.

Since registration error slightly increases at inference time after using a large number of iterations, we hypothesise that our model learns typical properties of all given image pairs that are in relation to optimal alignment, i.e. the distance of landmarks in the training images, and optimises its internal parameters so that these properties are matched after executing the set number of iterations. This means in contrast to conventional optimisation it makes use of the population-wide information that is provided during training. Additionally, our model is less dependent on an accurate pre-registration, which demonstrates that it is also more robust with respect to local minima.

In conclusion, even though our model does not yet always surpass Adam instance optimisation, it combines advantages of deep learning and gradient descent algorithms and yields promising results when it comes to compensating disadvantages of conventional optimisation.

References

1. Andrychowicz, M., et al.: Learning to learn by gradient descent by gradient descent. Adv. Neural Inf. Process. Syst. **29**, 1–9 (2016)
2. Balakrishnan, G., Zhao, A., Sabuncu, M.R., Guttag, J., Dalca, A.V.: VoxelMorph: a learning framework for deformable medical image registration. IEEE Trans. Med. Imaging **38**(8), 1788–1800 (2019)
3. Castillo, E., Castillo, R., Martinez, J., Shenoy, M., Guerrero, T.: Four-dimensional deformable image registration using trajectory modeling. Phys. Med. Biol. **55**(1), 305 (2009)
4. Castillo, R., et al.: A reference dataset for deformable image registration spatial accuracy evaluation using the COPDgene study archive. Phys. Med. Biol. **58**(9), 2861 (2013)
5. Castillo, R., et al.: A framework for evaluation of deformable image registration spatial accuracy using large landmark point sets. Phys. Med. Biol. **54**(7), 1849 (2009)
6. De Vos, B.D., Berendsen, F.F., Viergever, M.A., Sokooti, H., Staring, M., Išgum, I.: A deep learning framework for unsupervised affine and deformable image registration. Med. Image Anal. **52**, 128–143 (2019)
7. Heinrich, M.P., Handels, H., Simpson, I.J.A.: Estimating large lung motion in COPD patients by symmetric regularised correspondence fields. In: Navab, N., Hornegger, J., Wells, W.M., Frangi, A.F. (eds.) MICCAI 2015. LNCS, vol. 9350, pp. 338–345. Springer, Cham (2015). https://doi.org/10.1007/978-3-319-24571-3_41
8. Heinrich, M.P., Hansen, L.: Voxelmorph++ going beyond the cranial vault with keypoint supervision and multi-channel instance optimisation. In: 10th International Workshop on Biomedical Image Registration (2022)
9. Heinrich, M.P., et al.: MIND: modality independent neighbourhood descriptor for multi-modal deformable registration. Med. Image Anal. **16**(7), 1423–1435 (2012)
10. Hering, A., et al.: Learn2Reg: comprehensive multi-task medical image registration challenge, dataset and evaluation in the era of deep learning. arXiv preprint arXiv:2112.04489 (2021)
11. Jaderberg, M., et al.: Spatial transformer networks. Adv. Neural Inf. Process. Syst. **28**, 1–9 (2015)
12. Jiang, W., Sun, W., Tagliasacchi, A., Trulls, E., Yi, K.M.: Linearized multi-sampling for differentiable image transformation. In: Proceedings of the IEEE/CVF International Conference on Computer Vision, pp. 2988–2997 (2019)
13. Kingma, D.P., Ba, J.: Adam: a method for stochastic optimization. In: ICLR (2015)
14. Liu, R., Li, Z., Fan, X., Zhao, C., Huang, H., Luo, Z.: Learning deformable image registration from optimization: perspective, modules, bilevel training and beyond. IEEE Trans. Pattern Anal. Mach. Intell. (2021)
15. Lu, J., Jin, R., Song, E., Ma, G., Wang, M.: Lung-CRNet: a convolutional recurrent neural network for lung 4DCT image registration. Med. Phys. **48**(12), 7900–7912 (2021)

16. Mok, T.C.W., Chung, A.C.S.: Large deformation diffeomorphic image registration with Laplacian pyramid networks. In: Martel, A.L., et al. (eds.) MICCAI 2020. LNCS, vol. 12263, pp. 211–221. Springer, Cham (2020). https://doi.org/10.1007/978-3-030-59716-0_21

17. Murphy, K., et al.: Evaluation of registration methods on thoracic CT: the empire10 challenge. IEEE Trans. Med. Imaging 30(11), 1901–1920 (2011)

18. Papenberg, N., Bruhn, A., Brox, T., Didas, S., Weickert, J.: Highly accurate optic flow computation with theoretically justified warping. Int. J. Comput. Vision 67(2), 141–158 (2006)

19. Ronneberger, O., Fischer, P., Brox, T.: U-Net: convolutional networks for biomedical image segmentation. In: Navab, N., Hornegger, J., Wells, W.M., Frangi, A.F. (eds.) MICCAI 2015. LNCS, vol. 9351, pp. 234–241. Springer, Cham (2015). https://doi.org/10.1007/978-3-319-24574-4_28

20. Sandkühler, R., Andermatt, S., Bauman, G., Nyilas, S., Jud, C., Cattin, P.C.: Recurrent registration neural networks for deformable image registration. Adv. Neural Inf. Process. Syst. 32, 1–11 (2019)

21. Sandkühler, R., Jud, C., Andermatt, S., Cattin, P.C.: AirLab: autograd image registration laboratory. arXiv preprint arXiv:1806.09907 (2018)

22. Sun, S., et al.: Robust multimodal image registration using deep recurrent reinforcement learning. In: Jawahar, C.V., Li, H., Mori, G., Schindler, K. (eds.) ACCV 2018. LNCS, vol. 11362, pp. 511–526. Springer, Cham (2019). https://doi.org/10.1007/978-3-030-20890-5_33

23. Teed, Z., Deng, J.: RAFT: recurrent all-pairs field transforms for optical flow. In: Vedaldi, A., Bischof, H., Brox, T., Frahm, J.-M. (eds.) ECCV 2020. LNCS, vol. 12347, pp. 402–419. Springer, Cham (2020). https://doi.org/10.1007/978-3-030-58536-5_24

Electron Microscope Image Registration Using Laplacian Sharpening Transformer U-Net

Kunzi Xie$^{(\boxtimes)}$, Yixing Yang, Maurice Pagnucco, and Yang Song

School of Computer Science and Engineering, University of New South Wales,
Sydney, Australia
{kunzi.xie,yang.song1}@unsw.edu.au

Abstract. Image registration is an essential task in electron microscope (EM) image analysis, which aims to accurately warp the moving image to align with the fixed image, to reduce the spatial deformations across serial slices resulted during image acquisition. Existing learning-based registration approaches are primarily based on Convolution Neural Networks (CNNs). However, for the requirements of EM image registration, CNN-based methods lack the capability of learning global and long-term semantic information. In this work, we propose a new framework, Cascaded LST-UNet, which integrates a sharpening skip-connection layer with the Swin Transformer based U-Net structure in a cascaded manner for unsupervised EM image registration. Our experimental results on a public dataset show that our method consistently outperforms the baseline approaches.

Keywords: Image registration · Swin transformer · Deep learning · Electron microscopy

1 Introduction

Image registration plays a vital role in serial-section Electron Microscope (EM) image analysis. In the process of EM image acquisition, acquired images are prone to nonlinear deformations such as tissue contraction, compression and expansion. As a 3D image stack in a serial section, such deformations of individual slices can lead to further artifacts and significantly affect structural continuity across slices. Image registration is thus an important step to reduce deformation artifacts across slices to aid downstream analysis tasks. Figure 1 shows examples of paired EM slices, and it is easy to notice that there are many misaligned regions that may mislead the subsequent analysis.

Traditional EM registration methods use regularization to solve challenging deformation problems. For example, bUwarpJ [1] and Elastic [9] apply iterative optimisation for registration. However, these methods are slow and the registration results are usually unsatisfactory. With the development of deep-learning based methods for medical image analysis, Convolutional Neural Networks (CNNs) have been introduced for image registration. Lv et al. [11] proposed

L. Wang et al. (Eds.): MICCAI 2022, LNCS 13436, pp. 310–319, 2022.
https://doi.org/10.1007/978-3-031-16446-0_30

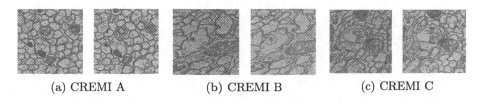

(a) CREMI A   (b) CREMI B   (c) CREMI C

Fig. 1. Examples are three pairs of fixed (left) and moving (right) images in CREMI A, B and C datasets. The fixed images are one of the slices, while the moving images are an elastic transformation of an adjacent slice of the fixed ones. Red circles highlight some of the deformations.

a CNN-based image registration method to obtain motion-free abdominal images throughout the respiratory cycle in magnetic resonance imaging (MRI). DirNet [16] combines a Spatial Transformer Network (STN) with a CNN which aims to learn similarity metrics between fixed and moving images for MRI registration. VoxelMorph [2] first adopted a U-Net [14] like structure to obtain the deformable fields which are combined with a STN to produce end-to-end registration results on MRI. Moreover, many methods based on VoxelMorph are developed to improve medical image alignment. For instance, an improved symmetric VoxelMorph [12] method was proposed to maximize the similarity between paired images within the space of diffeomorphic maps, which achieved a significant improvement on MRI registration. CycleMorph [8] designed an implicit regularization to preserve topology during the deformation to improve registration performance on medical images.

The ssEMnet method [18] first studied the problem of image registration on EM data, which combines a CNN-based auto-encoder and STN for image registration. Weakly supervised learning [13] was incorporated to improve the registration between images with sudden and significant structural changes on EM images. Furthermore, an approach [17] aimed to reduce the negative effect of section thickness on image registration was also developed, which improved the registration results significantly. Even though deep learning-based image registration methods have shown promising results on EM images, they still suffer loss of global information since EM images have an extensive observation range and high resolution. In other words, EM images contain many spatially continuous structures with fine details, which makes CNN-based models' intrinsic locality a critical bottleneck for EM image registration. Moreover, most existing CNN-based models [5] can only successfully handle small displacements and are thus not suitable for complex EM images. Also, deep learning methods can benefit from the cascade mechanism for medical image registration. The general architecture of recursive cascaded networks [20] enables learning deep cascades for deformable image registration. The study [19] presents a cascaded feature warping network for estimated coarse-to-fine registration.

In this work, we develop a novel image registration method which is specifically designed for serial-section EM images. To leverage the power of deep learning, we design a Cascaded Laplacian-sharpening Swin Transformer U-Net

(LST-UNet), which is a Swin-UNet [4] like structure with Laplacian sharpening skip-connection layers. LST-UNet is designed to obtain sufficient global features which are essential for EM image registration because serial EM data suffers from many significant deformation regions scattered across the tissue section. Our approach concatenates fixed images and moving images as input of LST-UNet to obtain displacement fields. Then, STN [7] module is used to obtain the moved image based on the displacement field and moving image. In our model, the Swin-UNet baseline can exploit global information and the sharpening skip-connection layer is designed to solve the problem of blurred feature maps caused by the concatenation of low-level and high-level semantic features. Also, to improve continuous registration, we introduce a cascaded architecture, where each cascade of LST-UNet learns to perform a progressive deformation for the current warped image. Our method is unsupervised as it does not require the expected registration output as the ground truth. Experiments are conducted on three sub-dataset of the CREMI dataset[1]. The results demonstrate the advantage of our method over CNN-based approaches.

2   Methods

As shown in Fig. 2, the registration flow is a Cascaded LST-UNet, with each cascading block consisting of an LST-UNet and an STN module. LST-UNet takes the fixed and moving images as input and generates a displacement field; then, based on the displacement field, the STN module [7] is applied to produce the moved image. The second cascade takes the moved image as the moving image and conducts another round of registration to obtain the final transformed image. Following the experimental setup in [21], the initial moving image is generated during the training process by elastic transformation of an original image slice, and the original image of its adjacent slice is the fixed image. Such a setup is used because the EM images in CREMI are pre-registered, and hence we need to generate deformed images to simulate the original, unregistered images. Note that the cascaded LST-UNets are trained sequentially; in other words, the training is not end-to-end and each cascade is trained separately.

2.1   Displacement Field Generation

In the image registration task, displacement fields are used to warp moving images to obtain the registered image. Previous studies have shown that segmentation models such as U-Net can be applied to generate the displacement fields [2,21]. However, deformations in EM images are usually more extensive with global variations. For example, as shown in Fig. 1, there are many deformed neural regions across serial slices and each image is filled with diverse structures of nerves and neuroses. Therefore, long-range information is critical for EM image registration, whereas the standard U-Net structure is not able to capture global information comprehensively.

---

[1] https://cremi.org.

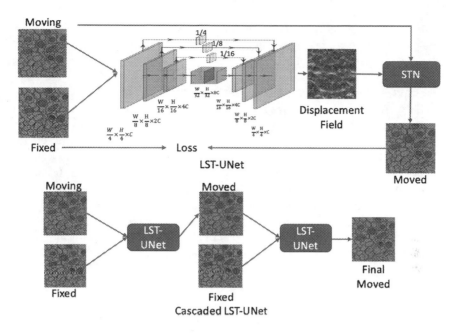

Fig. 2. Overview of Cascaded LST-UNet.

To tackle this issue, we propose to use the Transformer-based Swin-UNet [4] to replace U-Net for displacement field generation. To be more specific, Swin-UNet is a U-Net like Transformer model for medical image segmentation and it builds the encoder, bottleneck and decoder layers with Swin Transformer (ST) blocks [10] rather than convolutional layers. Each ST block contains a LayerNorm (LN) layer, multi-head self-attention module, residual connection and 2-layer multi-layer perceptrons (MLP) with a GELU non-linear layer. Then, the window-based multi-head self-attention (W-MSA) module and shifted window-based multi-head self-attention (SW-MSA) module are added in the two successive ST blocks, respectively.

The main advantage of Swin-UNet is that it effectively captures long-range semantic information with the Transformer modules. In addition, it utilizes the U-Net structure for medical image segmentation, and hence can be adapted directly in place of U-Net for displacement field generation in image registration frameworks.

2.2   Feature Enhancement

While the Swin-UNet model can be used to generate displacement fields, based on our experiments, we find that it may cause blurred feature maps during the skip-connection between the low-level and high-level semantic information interaction. The skip connections aim to alleviate the loss of spatial information caused by down-sampling in Swin-UNet. However, the mismatch problem is generated during the fusion as the encoder features are low-level, but the decoder features are high-level. Thus, the fusion of different features will lead to blurred feature maps during the connections.

To address this issue, inspired by [22], we propose to use a Laplacian Sharpening Skip-Connection to insert a Laplacian filter into the skip-connections of Swin-UNet. A Laplacian filter is a classic edge enhancing filter and is usually used for image sharpening since it preserves and emphasizes the high-frequency components which represent fine-grained image details by sharpening changes in image intensity. In our model, the encoder features are processed by the Laplacian filter before being concatenated with the decoder features. It can help balance the semantic gap caused by U-Net skip-connection processing between the encoder and decoder and also help sharpen the details in feature maps during the feature extraction. Therefore, we use the Laplacian filter as the kernel in the convolution layers for skip connections in Swin-UNet. The resultant network is thus called LST-UNet, *i.e.*, Laplacian-sharpening Swin Transformer U-Net.

2.3   Cascaded Registration

After obtaining the displacement filed from our LST-UNet, an STN module [7] is used for registration. STN is an effective and widely-used model for medical image registration, which leverages a spatial transformation layer to enable traditional neural networks to perform 2D image alignment in an unsupervised way. The final aim for image registration is to minimize differences between registered and fixed images. STN computes a pixel location of the displacement field in a moving image for each pixel. Because image values are only defined at integer locations, STN linearly interpolates the values at eight neighbouring pixels. Benefiting from its differentiable properties, we can back-propagate errors during optimisation.

Furthermore, in traditional registration methods, images are usually transformed through an iterative process to optimize the objective function. This idea has been adopted in deep learning-based registration via a cascaded mechanism [20], in which the deformation fields are processed through deep neural networks recursively. In our problem, to further boost the power of our LST-UNet, we design a cascaded framework and the moved images are processed recursively through two cascades of LST-UNet. In each cascade, the model takes the moving image and fixed image as input and the output would be the moving image for the next stage or the final transformed image.

2.4   Loss Function

For the loss function, we use a two-term loss function:

$$\mathcal{L}(F, M, \phi) = \mathcal{L}_{sim}(F, M(\phi)) + \lambda \mathcal{L}_{smooth} \tag{1}$$

where F, M and ϕ represent the fixed image, moving image and the displacement field, respectively. The first term $\mathcal{L}_{sim}$ penalizes the dissimilarity between the moved and fixed images; the second term $\mathcal{L}_{smooth}$ penalizes local variations in ϕ; and λ is the regularisation parameter. More specifically, $\mathcal{L}_{sim}$ is constructed by combining the Pearson's correlation coefficient (PCC) [15] and the structural similarity index (SSIM) [3]. While PCC is robust to noise, it is also found to be less sensitive to blurry images. SSIM will measure detailed structures in the images but also highlight noise and artifacts. Therefore, the proposed loss function combines SSIM and PCC with equal weights to achieve a balance:

$$
\begin{aligned}
\mathcal{L}_{sim}(F, M(\phi)) = \tfrac{1}{2}\big\{&\big(1 - PCC(F, M(\phi))\big) \\
&+\big(1 - SSIM(F, M(\phi))\big)\big\}
\end{aligned}
\tag{2}
$$

$\mathcal{L}_{smooth}$ follows the standard formulation using a diffusion regularization on its spatial gradients:

$$
\mathcal{L}_{smooth}(\phi) = \|\triangledown\phi\|_2^2
\tag{3}
$$

3 Experiments and Results

3.1 Dataset and Evaluation

Our experimental study was conducted on the Circuit Reconstruction from Electron Microscopy Images (CREMI) dataset[2], which contains whole-brain *serial* EM image sets of Drosophila. This dataset has been commonly used in EM image registration studies [6,17,18], and a portion of this dataset has been manually annotated with neuron segmentation labels. We conduct quantitative evaluation on CREMI A, CREMI B and CREMI C, where each set consists of 125 images (slices) and each image is of size 1250×1250 pixels. For each set, we randomly select 100 serial EM images as the training data and the rest 25 images as the testing set. CREMI B and CREMI C contain more challenges because their tissues have more irregular shapes and significant variations in sizes, whereas CREMI A is quite homogeneous in size and shape.

We implemented the models using Pytorch and the training was conducted on NVIDIA Tesla P100 GPUs. We used the SGD optimizer with a learning rate of 0.0001 for CREMI A and C, and 0.000001 for CREMI B. The training process includes 20 epochs and each epoch trains a batch set of 8 slices. The parameter λ is set to 0.01 which performs the best in our experiments. All original images are first resized to 896×896 pixels and cropped into non-overlapping patches. Both fixed and moving images are then of size 448×448 pixels.

Following [21], we first conduct experiments on *paired* EM images. Here, *paired* images use one of the *serial* EM images as the fixed image, and an elastic transformation of its adjacent image as the moving image. In addition, we conduct experiments on *serial* EM images, based on each consecutive image pair from front to back of the whole image stack. For quantitative evaluation, we compute the Dice coefficient between the segmentation mask of the fixed image and the registered segmentation mask of the moving image. The latter is obtained by deforming the moving image's segmentation mask using the generated displacement field with the STN module.

---

[2] https://cremi.org.

3.2   Results

In Table 1, the results present the Dice scores of different registration methods using paired and serial images for CREMI A, B and C. ssEMnet [18] combines an autoencoder with a STN module for serial EM image registration. VoxelMorph as the popular image registration method is compared in our experiment, too. The third model is an U-Net based approach [21], which was proposed for EM image registration and evaluated by the 3D method on the same CREMI dataset. In addition, as our Laplacian-sharpening skip-connection method is inspired by Sharp U-Net [22], which enhances the power of classic U-Net in medical segmentation, we include the Sharp U-Net model in the experiments. We also include Swin-UNet [4] in place of our LST-UNet for comparison. It can be easily seen that our LST-UNet outperforms all other methods. This is because LST-UNet not only achieves good capability in capturing global and long-range semantic information by leveraging the Transformer mechanism but also reduces the obscurity of the blurred feature maps by using the Laplacian skip-connections. With these techniques, our models can achieve higher registration performance on EM images. Generally, LST-UNet and Cascaded LST-UNet achieve the best two Dice scores, and Cascaded LST-UNet provides the best performance on CREMI A and B but not CREMI C. This is because for some images in CREMI C, one cascade of LST-UNet have converged enough while the second cascade of LST-UNet could cause an over-registration problem and reduce performance. The average time required for registering a pair of image slices is about 27 s. The baseline method [21] requires about 10 s on average for paired image registration. Our method is slower than the baseline since our method uses the cascaded mechanism which causes the longer time consumption.

Table 1. Dice results of image registration.

Model	Paired	Serial	Paired	Serial	Paired	Serial
	CREMI A		CREMI B		CREMI C	
ssEMnet [18]	0.8249	0.9013	0.8234	0.9091	0.8310	0.9201
VoxelMorph [2]	0.8374	0.9076	0.8316	0.9218	0.8332	0.9215
U-Net based [21]	0.8339	0.9156	0.8337	0.9295	0.8347	0.9149
Sharp U-Net [22]	0.8492	0.9213	0.8354	0.9475	0.8459	0.9392
Swin-UNet [4]	0.8610	0.9324	0.8522	0.9547	0.8597	0.9458
LST-UNet	0.8680	0.9478	0.8687	0.9625	**0.8753**	**0.9507**
Cascaded LST-UNet	**0.8787**	**0.9550**	**0.8723**	**0.9670**	0.8746	0.9500

We also visualize the registration results in Fig. 3, which shows the fixed image, moving image and registration results using the U-Net based method [21] and our Cascaded LST-UNet. It can be seen that our result can better align with the fixed image. Compared to the U-Net based method, in the example from CREMI A, we can see that our results contain sharper and more visually distinguishable structural details in the red area compared to the U-Net based method. Moreover, in the green area, the U-Net based method result is blurry and very different from the fixed image, but our method works better on this continuous structure with fewer artifacts. In the example from CREMI C, the registration results show a similar pattern although the performance is not as good as that on the CREMI A example.

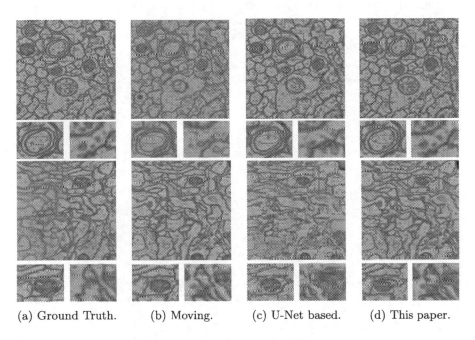

(a) Ground Truth.   (b) Moving.   (c) U-Net based.   (d) This paper.

Fig. 3. Visualization of registration results on CREMI A (top two rows) and CREMI C (bottom two rows) compared to U-Net based method [21].

4   Conclusion

In this paper, we propose a Cascaded LST-UNet model for EM image registration. We leverage the power of a Transformer for EM image registration by adopting the Swin-Unet with Laplacian sharpening for feature extraction and global semantic information interactive learning. Experimental results on a public serial EM image dataset demonstrate that our Cascaded LST-UNet framework outperforms the baseline models. In our future work, we will explore how to combine our framework with intrinsic locality learning to further improve registration performance. Also, we will extend our approach to other types of 3D medical image registration problems.

References

1. Arganda-Carreras, I., Sorzano, C.O., Kybic, J., Ortiz-de Solorzano, C.: bUnwarpJ: consistent and elastic registration in ImageJ, methods and applications. In: Second ImageJ User and Developer Conference, vol. 12 (2008)
2. Balakrishnan, G., Zhao, A., Sabuncu, M.R., Guttag, J., Dalca, A.V.: VoxelMorph: a learning framework for deformable medial image registration. IEEE Trans. Med. Imaging **38**(8), 1788–1800 (2019)
3. Brunet, D., Vrscay, E.R., Wang, Z.: On the mathematical properties of the structural similarity index. IEEE Trans. Image Process. **21**(4), 1488–1499 (2011)
4. Cao, H., et al.: Swin-UNet: UNet-like pure transformer for medical image segmentation. arXiv:2105.05537 (2021)
5. Dalca, A.V., Balakrishnan, G., Guttag, J., Sabuncu, M.R.: Unsupervised learning for fast probabilistic diffeomorphic registration. In: Frangi, A.F., Schnabel, J.A., Davatzikos, C., Alberola-López, C., Fichtinger, G. (eds.) MICCAI 2018, Part I. LNCS, vol. 11070, pp. 729–738. Springer, Cham (2018). https://doi.org/10.1007/978-3-030-00928-1_82
6. Fu, D., Kuduvalli, G.: A fast, accurate, and automatic 2D–3D image registration for image-guided cranial radiosurgery. Med. Phys. **35**(5), 2180–2194 (2008)
7. Jaderberg, M., Simonyan, K., Zisserman, A., Kavukcuoglu, K.: Spatial Transformer Networks. In: Neural Information Processing Systems (2015)
8. Kim, B., Kim, D.H., Park, S.H., Kim, J., Lee, J.G., Ye, J.: CycleMorph: cycle consistent unsupervised deformable image registration. Med. Image Anal. **71**, 102036 (2021)
9. Klein, S., Staring, M., Murphy, K., Viergever, M.A., Pluim, J.P.: Elastix: a toolbox for intensity-based medical image registration. IEEE Trans. Med. Imaging **29**(1), 196–205 (2009)
10. Liu, Z., et al.: Swin Transformer: Hierarchical vision transformer using shifted windows. arXiv preprint arXiv:2103.14030 (2021)
11. Lv, J., Yang, M., Zhang, J., Wang, X.: Respiratory motion correction for free-breathing 3D abdominal MRI using CNN-based image registration: a feasibility study. Brit. J. Radiol. **91**, 20170788 (2018)
12. Mok, T.C., Chung, A.: Fast symmetric diffeomorphic image registration with convolutional neural networks. In: IEEE/CVF Conference on Computer Vision and Pattern Recognition (CVPR), pp. 4644–4653 (2020)
13. Nguyen-Duc, T., Yoo, I., Thomas, L., Kuan, A., Lee, W., Jeong, W.: Weakly supervised learning in deformable EM image registration using slice interpolation. In: International Symposium on Biomedical Imaging (ISBI), pp. 670–673 (2019)
14. Ronneberger, O., Fischer, P., Brox, T.: U-Net: convolutional networks for biomedical image segmentation. In: Navab, N., Hornegger, J., Wells, W.M., Frangi, A.F. (eds.) MICCAI 2015, Part III. LNCS, vol. 9351, pp. 234–241. Springer, Cham (2015). https://doi.org/10.1007/978-3-319-24574-4_28
15. Sedgwick, P.: Pearson's correlation coefficient. BMJ **345**, e4483–e4483 (2012)
16. de Vos, B.D., Berendsen, F.F., Viergever, M.A., Staring, M., Išgum, I.: End-to-end unsupervised deformable image registration with a convolutional neural network. In: Cardoso, M.J., et al. (eds.) DLMIA/ML-CDS -2017. LNCS, vol. 10553, pp. 204–212. Springer, Cham (2017). https://doi.org/10.1007/978-3-319-67558-9_24
17. Xin, T., Chen, B., Chen, X., Han, H.: UTR: unsupervised learning of thickness-insensitive representations for electron microscope image. In: IEEE International Conference on Image Processing (ICIP), pp. 155–159 (2021)

18. Yoo, I., Hildebrand, D.G.C., Tobin, W.F., Lee, W.-C.A., Jeong, W.-K.: ssEMnet: serial-section electron microscopy image registration using a spatial transformer network with learned features. In: Cardoso, M.J., et al. (eds.) DLMIA/ML-CDS -2017. LNCS, vol. 10553, pp. 249–257. Springer, Cham (2017). https://doi.org/10.1007/978-3-319-67558-9_29

19. Zhang, L., Zhou, L., Li, R., Wang, X., Han, B., Liao, H.: Cascaded feature warping network for unsupervised medical image registration. In: International Symposium on Biomedical Imaging (ISBI), pp. 913–916 (2021)

20. Zhao, S., Dong, Y., Chang, E.I., Xu, Y., et al.: Recursive cascaded networks for unsupervised medical image registration. In: International Conference on Computer Vision (ICCV), pp. 10600–10610 (2019)

21. Zhou, S., et al.: Fast and accurate electron microscopy image registration with 3D convolution. In: Shen, D., et al. (eds.) MICCAI 2019, Part I. LNCS, vol. 11764, pp. 478–486. Springer, Cham (2019). https://doi.org/10.1007/978-3-030-32239-7_53

22. Zunair, H., Hamza, A.B.: Sharp U-Net: Depthwise convolutional network for biomedical image segmentation. Comput. Biol. Med. **136**, 104699 (2021)

Image Reconstruction

Undersampled MRI Reconstruction with Side Information-Guided Normalisation

Xinwen Liu[1]([✉])[iD], Jing Wang[2], Cheng Peng[3], Shekhar S. Chandra[1], Feng Liu[1], and S. Kevin Zhou[4,5]

[1] School of Information Technology and Electrical Engineering, The University of Queensland, Brisbane, Australia
xinwen.liu@uq.net.au
[2] The Commonwealth Scientific and Industrial Research Organisation, Canberra, Australia
[3] Johns Hopkins University, Baltimore, USA
[4] Center for Medical Imaging, Robotics, Analytic Computing and Learning (MIRACLE), School of Biomedical Engineering and Suzhou Institute for Advanced Research, University of Science and Technology of China, Suzhou, China
[5] Key Laboratory of Intelligent Information Processing of Chinese Academy of Sciences (CAS), Institute of Computing Technology, CAS, Beijing, China

Abstract. Magnetic resonance (MR) images exhibit various contrasts and appearances based on factors such as different acquisition protocols, views, manufacturers, scanning parameters, etc. This generally accessible appearance-related side information affects deep learning-based undersampled magnetic resonance imaging (MRI) reconstruction frameworks, but has been overlooked in the majority of current works. In this paper, we investigate the use of such side information as normalisation parameters in a convolutional neural network (CNN) to improve undersampled MRI reconstruction. Specifically, a **S**ide **I**nformation-**G**uided **N**ormalisation (SIGN) module, containing only few layers, is proposed to efficiently encode the side information and output the normalisation parameters. We examine the effectiveness of such a module on two popular reconstruction architectures, D5C5 and OUCR. The experimental results on both brain and knee images under various acceleration rates demonstrate that the proposed method improves on its corresponding baseline architectures with a significant margin.

Keywords: Deep learning · Undersampled MRI reconstruction

Supplementary Information The online version contains supplementary material available at https://doi.org/10.1007/978-3-031-16446-0_31.

1   Introduction

Magnetic resonance imaging (MRI) is a non-invasive imaging modality that produces high contrast in vivo imaging of soft-tissue with non-ionizing radiation. However, due to hardware constraints, MRI suffers from a long scanning time, which impedes its application to real-time imaging. Undersampling the measurements is a common approach that accelerates the imaging process, but can result in blurriness and artifacts that are not suitable for diagnosis purposes.

Deep learning (DL) has been widely studied to reconstruct the high-quality images from the undersampled measurements [2,7,14,20,32]. Initially, convolutional neural networks (CNN) have been employed [10,24,26] to directly map the undersampled images or measurements to fully-sampled ones. Later, imaging model has been integrated into the learning pipeline, and model-based learning has achieved the state-of-the-art performance [1,9,13,18,19,21–23,26,27,30]. More recently, transformers have been integrated into the CNN-based networks for MRI undersampled reconstruction [4,6,16,29]. These networks can reconstruct MR images with a high fidelity.

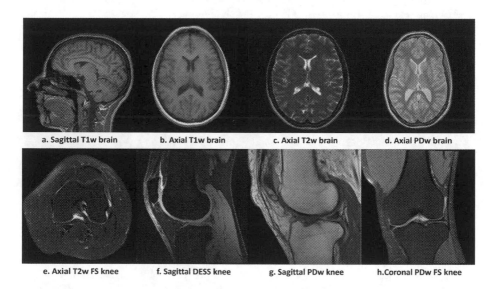

a. Sagittal T1w brain   b. Axial T1w brain   c. Axial T2w brain   d. Axial PDw brain

e. Axial T2w FS knee   f. Sagittal DESS knee   g. Sagittal PDw knee   h.Coronal PDw FS knee

Fig. 1. MR images of various views, anatomies and acquisition protocols acquired on different machines. a and d are from IXI database; b, c, e, g and h are from fastMRI database [15,28]; and f is from SKM-TEA database [3].

MR images present various appearances based on different acquisition protocols, imaging views, scanning parameters, manufacturers, etc. Figure 1 shows examples of MR images with diverse appearances. When comparing b, c and d, we can observe that for axial brain images, varying acquisition protocols results in differences in brightness, contrast and saturation. This image style variations with acquisition protocols can also be observed by comparing f and g. In addition, due to the hardware differences, images acquired on different machines with divergent scanning parameters present variant noise levels and resolutions. The same subject with different views also shows dissimilar structures. All these differences during acquisitions result in different image styles, which can affect the performance of undersampled reconstruction algorithms [8,17,25,31].

Based on such an observation and inspired by recent works on style-related normalisation [5,11,12,17], we propose a **S**ide **I**nformation-**G**uided **N**ormalisation (SIGN) module that can be inserted in CNN-based reconstruction networks to obtain higher quality reconstructed image. Specifically, the SIGN module is a sub-network that contains a few linear, normalisation, and non-linear layers. We leverage the side information, which is commonly accessible, and encode it in the SIGN module. SIGN's outputs are used to normalise the feature maps generated by the reconstruction backbone. In this study, we inserted the SIGN modules into the popular D5C5 [21] and OUCR [7] backbones. The experiments on brain and knee images under $4\times$ and $6\times$ acceleration show that these networks can obtain significantly better performances by including SIGN modules.

2   Methods

2.1   Problem Formulation

Reconstructing an image $\mathbf{x} \in \mathbb{C}^N$ from undersampled measurement $\mathbf{y} \in \mathbb{C}^M$ ($M \ll N$) with side information is formulated as an inverse problem [21,32]:

$$\min_{\mathbf{x}} \quad \mathcal{R}(\mathbf{x}, \mathbf{s}) + \lambda \|\mathbf{y} - \mathbf{F}_u \mathbf{x}\|_2^2, \tag{1}$$

where $\mathbf{s} = [\mathbf{s}_e, \mathbf{s}_c]$ represents the side information encoded as input vectors to the model, $\mathcal{R}$ is the regularisation term on $\mathbf{x}$ and $\mathbf{s}$, $\lambda \in \mathbb{R}$ denotes the balancing coefficient between $\mathcal{R}$ and data consistency (DC) term, $\mathbf{F}_u \in \mathbb{C}^{M \times N}$ is an undersampled Fourier encoding matrix. In model-based learning, Eq. (1) is incorporated in the network architecture with $\mathcal{R}$ approximated by the convolution and linear layers.

We divide the side information into two types: categorical variables $\mathbf{s}_e = (s_e^1, s_e^2, ..., s_e^{n_1})$ and continuous variables $\mathbf{s}_c = (s_c^1, s_c^2, ..., s_c^{n_2})$ based on the specific piece of information. For attributes such as views, acquisition protocols and manufacturers, they are in distinct groups with a finite number of categories. We use embedding vectors to represent each of these categorical variables. The scanning parameters, such as repetition time (TR), echo time (TR) and flip angles, are continuous variables, which are stacked as vectors. Formally, for each categorical variable $s_e^i, i = 1, 2, ..., n_1$, we can obtain the embedded vector $\mathbf{V}_e^i$ as:

$$\mathbf{V}_e^i = Embedding(s_e^i). \tag{2}$$

For the continuous variables $\mathbf{s}_c$, we have:

$$\mathbf{V}_c = \mathbf{W}\mathbf{s}_c + \mathbf{b}, \tag{3}$$

where $\mathbf{V}_c$ is the representation of continuous information, and $\mathbf{W}$ and $\mathbf{b}$ are parameters of the linear mapping layer.

2.2   Side Information-Guided Normalisation (SIGN) Module

To integrate the side information into a network and interact with the main reconstruction network, we propose a Side Information-Guided Normalisation (SIGN) module. Figure 2 shows the architecture of the proposed SIGN module, which contains linear layers, non-linear activation function (ReLU) and layer normalisation (LN). The inputs to the SIGN module are the side information and the outputs are the parameters to be fed into the reconstruction backbone.

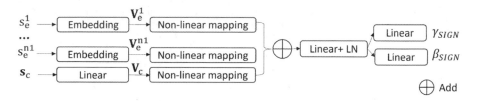

Fig. 2. The architecture of Side Information-Guided Normalisation (SIGN) module. The inputs are the side information, and the outputs are the parameters to interact with the reconstruction backbone.

First, the side information $\mathbf{s}$ is encoded into vectors $\{\mathbf{V}_e^i\}$ and $\mathbf{V}_c$. Then, these vectors are passed through the non-linear mapping blocks in parallel. Each of these blocks comprise a fully-connected layer, LN, and ReLU. The latent individual side information features are merged together by element-wise additive operation. At the end, the merged features are fed into another fully-connected layers to further model relationships among each piece of side information. The output parameters γ_{SIGN} and β_{SIGN} are sent into the reconstruction backbone.

Motivated by [5,11,12,17], the changes of contrasts and texture distributions in images can be mainly described by the mean and variance of feature maps in a deep CNN. Thus, we propagate the encoded side information to control the mean and standard deviation of each feature map in the reconstruction backbone. Note before applying the affine parameters on each layer, we normalize the feature maps per instance to a zero mean and a unit standard deviation. Since different layers have different feature distributions, the SIGN module is not shared cross layers. Formally, for layer l with feature map h_l in the reconstruction backbone:

$$\text{SIGN}(h_l) = \gamma_{SIGN}^l \left(\frac{h_l - \mu(h_l)}{\sigma(h_l)} \right) + \beta_{SIGN}^l, \tag{4}$$

where γ_{SIGN}^l and β_{SIGN}^l are the outputs of the SIGN module, and $\mu(h_l)$ and $\sigma(h_l)$ are the mean and standard deviation of the feature map, respectively, computed across spatial dimensions $(H \times W)$ independently for each channel.

2.3   Reconstruction with D5C5 and OUCR Backbones

D5C5 [21] and OUCR [7] are high performance backbones for undersampled MRI reconstruction. D5C5 is a deep cascaded network that contains five interleaved CNN blocks and data consistency (DC) layers. In each of the CNN block, there are five convolutional layers with ReLU activation function and a residual connection at the end. As shown in Fig. 3, we insert the SIGN modules into the CNN blocks after each of the convolutional layers, except the last one.

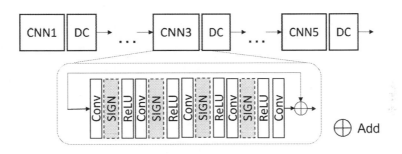

Fig. 3. The D5C5 reconstruction architecture with the SIGN modules inserted after convolution layers.

OUCR is a convolutional recurrent neural network (CRNN) that contains the over complete CRNN (OC-CRNN), the under complete CRNN (UC-CRNN) and a refine module, as shown in Fig. 4. The encoder in UC-CRNN uses maxpooling to reduce the feature map size before being fed into the residual block and the decoder which upsamples the feature map to the original size. The OC-CRNN enlarges the feature map size in the encoder with the upsampling operations. The enlarged feature maps are fed into the residual block and the decoder where the feature maps is down-sampled to the original size. Both OC-CNN and UC-CNN contain an ordinary residual block of convolutions with a skip connection. At the end of the network, a refine block with stacked convolutional layers and ReLU activation functions refine and output the reconstructed results. More details of OUCR can be found in [7]. The SIGN modules are inserted after each convolutional layer, except the last convolutional layers in the decoder and refine module, which are used to reserve varied feature maps. The numbers of hidden nodes in the fully-connected layers of SIGN modules are assigned to be the same as the number of feature maps in the corresponding layers, except the one in the linear layer after add operation, which is double of the feature map numbers.

The networks are trained with a mean-absolute-error loss. First, we pretrain the backbone and SIGN modules together. To better optimise the networks, we fix the parameters of the convolutional layers, and only fine-tune the parameters of the linear layers in SIGN modules.

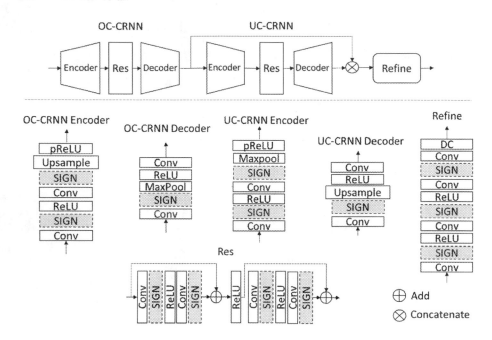

Fig. 4. The OUCR reconstruction architecture with the SIGN model inserted after convolution layers.

3   Experiments and Results

3.1   Datasets and Network Configuration

We evaluate the proposed method on both brain and knee datasets. The brain dataset contains DICOM images from the NYU fastMRI[1] database [15, 28] and IXI database[2]. The side information in the brain dataset include contrast (T1-weighted, T2-weighted, proton-density-weighted, and magnetic resonance angiogram), views (axial and sagittal), source (Siemens, Philip and GE), and scanning parameters (repetition time, echo time and flip angle). The knee dataset is comprised of DICOM images from the NYU fastMRI database and SKM-TEA database [3]. The side information in the knee dataset contains contrast (T2-weighted fat saturated, proton-density-weighted, proton-density-weighted fat saturated, and double echo steady state) and views (axial, sagittal and coronal) and scanning parameters (repetition time, echo time and flip angle). It is noted that for IXI database, the scanning parameters are unknown, so we code it as zeros, and the images are indistinguishable from the manufacturers, so we code it as unknown source. In total, there are 10,534 brain slices from 437 volumes and 11,406 knee slices from 246 volumes. For each dataset, 80% of the

---

[1] fastmri.med.nyu.edu.

[2] https://brain-development.org/ixi-dataset/.

volumes are randomly extracted for training, 10% for validation, and 10% for testing.

For this experiment, all the data are emulated single-coil magnitude-only images. We crop and resize the images into 320×320 and retrospectively undersampled the Cartesian k-space with 1D Gaussian sampling pattern. The evaluation is conducted under acceleration rates of $4\times$ and $6\times$ using structural similarity index (SSIM) and peak signal-to-noise ratio (PSNR) as performance metrics. We calculate and report the mean value of the metrics for reconstructed test images.

The experiments are carried out on NVIDIA SXM-2 Tesla V100 Accelerator Units. The networks are implemented on Pytorch and trained using the Adam optimizer with a weight decay to prevent over-fitting.

3.2   Results

The quantitative comparison of the proposed method and baseline models is shown in Table 1. The first row shows the metrics of the undersampled images reconstructed directly from the zero-filled k-space. D5C5 (row 2) and OUCR (row 4) both improve the PSNR and SSIM over the undersampled images, with OUCR outperforming D5C5 on all cases, which is consistent with [7]. Comparing D5C5 and D5C5+SIGN, the proposed design improves PSNR by about 2–2.5 dB on brain images, and 1.5 dB on knee images. The improvements are also observed on SSIM, with about 1.5% and 2% on brain and knee images, respectively. For the experiments on OUCR backbone, the performances of OUCR+SIGN are consistently better than those of OUCR. Overall, the experiments show that the simple and effective design of SIGN improves the baseline model with a considerable margin. OUCR+SIGN performs slightly lower than D5C5+SIGN. The reason could be due to the complexity of OUCR. Different from D5C5 which has a unified straightforward architecture, OUCR has recurrent designs, multiple residual connections, and varying sizes of feature maps [7]. More careful consideration in inserting SIGN module has the potential to improve the results but is out of the scope of this paper.

Figure 5 shows the examples of reconstructed brain images under $4\times$ acceleration with different methods. The first column is the fully-sampled images and the second column represents the undersampled images, which are blurry and full of artifacts. As shown in the third column, D5C5 can reconstruct the images. In the forth column, D5C5+SIGN further improves the images with more detailed information preserved, as pointed by the arrows. Similar trend can also be observed by comparing the fifth column (OUCR) and the sixth column (OUCR+SIGN). OUCR with the SIGN inserted in the network recovers the images with higher visual fidelity.

Table 1. Quantitative comparison on the reconstruction of brain and knee images under acceleration rates of 4× and 6×.

	4×				6×			
	PSNR (dB)		SSIM (%)		PSNR (dB)		SSIM (%)	
	Brain	Knee	Brain	Knee	Brain	Knee	Brain	Knee
Undersampled	29.92	30.04	79.27	79.16	22.03	24.63	60.02	66.49
D5C5	39.29	35.34	96.89	90.69	36.03	33.23	94.62	87.51
D5C5+SIGN	**41.70**	**37.18**	**97.93**	**93.02**	**38.16**	**34.66**	**96.39**	**89.75**
OUCR	40.29	36.48	97.44	92.29	36.93	34.16	95.58	89.17
OUCR+SIGN	**41.64**	**37.06**	**97.94**	92.93	37.96	34.47	96.27	89.51

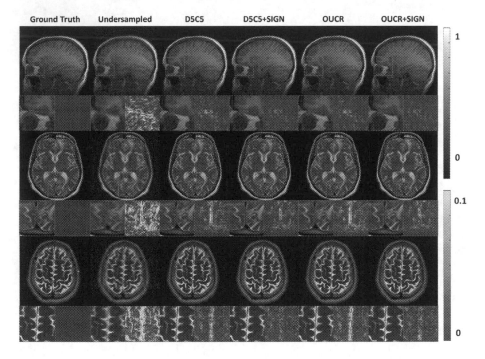

Fig. 5. The reconstructed brain images under 4× acceleration with different methods.

3.3   Further Analysis

This section further investigates the effectiveness of the proposed SIGN module. As an example, we test the D5C5+SIGN model in recovering 4× accelerated brain images. In the first experiment, we set the side information of each image with a random label. The results show that the PSNR drops from 41.70 dB to 40.93 dB. Then, we evaluate the reconstruction with wrong side information. For example, for the image with axial view, we assign it to be the sagittal view. The performance drops by approximately 1 dB.

In addition, the importance of each side information is evaluated by masking out one or more branch of the side information in SIGN. When only using the contrast information, the performance goes down to 41.39 dB. With view information alone, PSNR is 40.94 dB. If both contrast and view information are used, PSNR becomes 41.42 dB. More comparison and results can be found in the supplementary material (Tables S1-2). Overall, reconstructing images with wrong or missing side information leads to a worse performance.

4 Conclusion

In this paper, we propose to utilise the side information as normalisation parameters to improve the undersampled MRI reconstruction. Experimental results demonstrate the proposed approach can improve the baseline models significantly on both brain and knee images under 4× and 6× acceleration. While the current design is based on the popular D5C5 and OUCR architectures, the proposed framework is extendable to other network architectures. The current study is based on the single-coil magnitude-only images for proof-of-concept. In the future, we will adapt the network to multi-coil complex-valued datasets.

References

1. Aggarwal, H.K., Mani, M.P., Jacob, M.: MoDL: model-based deep learning architecture for inverse problems. IEEE Trans. Med. Imaging **38**(2), 394–405 (2018)
2. Chandra, S.S., Bran Lorenzana, M., Liu, X., Liu, S., Bollmann, S., Crozier, S.: Deep learning in magnetic resonance image reconstruction. J. Med. Imaging Radiat. Oncol. **65**(5), 564–577 (2021)
3. Desai, A.D., Schmidt, A.M., Rubin, E.B., Sandino, C.M., Black, M.S., Mazzoli, V., et al.: SKM-TEA: a dataset for accelerated mri reconstruction with dense image labels for quantitative clinical evaluation. In: Thirty-Fifth Conference on Neural Information Processing Systems Datasets and Benchmarks Track (Round 2) (2021)
4. Feng, C.-M., Yan, Y., Fu, H., Chen, L., Xu, Y.: Task transformer network for joint mri reconstruction and super-resolution. In: de Bruijne, M., et al. (eds.) MICCAI 2021. LNCS, vol. 12906, pp. 307–317. Springer, Cham (2021). https://doi.org/10.1007/978-3-030-87231-1_30
5. Gu, J., Ye, J.C.: AdaIN-based tunable cyclegan for efficient unsupervised low-dose CT denoising. IEEE Trans. Comput.l Imaging **7**, 73–85 (2021)
6. Guo, P., Mei, Y., Zhou, J., Jiang, S., Patel, V.M.: Reconformer: ACcelerated MRI reconstruction using recurrent transformer. arXiv preprint arXiv:2201.09376 (2022)
7. Guo, P., Valanarasu, J.M.J., Wang, P., Zhou, J., Jiang, S., Patel, V.M.: Over-and-under complete convolutional rnn for mri reconstruction. In: de Bruijne, M., et al. (eds.) MICCAI 2021. LNCS, vol. 12906, pp. 13–23. Springer, Cham (2021). https://doi.org/10.1007/978-3-030-87231-1_2
8. Guo, P., Wang, P., Zhou, J., Jiang, S., Patel, V.M.: Multi-institutional collaborations for improving deep learning-based magnetic resonance image reconstruction using federated learning. In: Proceedings of the IEEE/CVF Conference on Computer Vision and Pattern Recognition, pp. 2423–2432 (2021)

9. Hammernik, K., et al.: Learning a variational network for reconstruction of accelerated MRI data. Magn. Reson. Med. **79**(6), 3055–3071 (2018)
10. Han, Y., Sunwoo, L., Ye, J.C.: k-space deep learning for accelerated MRI. IEEE Trans. Med. Imaging **39**(2), 377–386 (2019)
11. Huang, X., Belongie, S.: Arbitrary style transfer in real-time with adaptive instance normalization. In: Proceedings of the IEEE International Conference on Computer Vision, pp. 1501–1510 (2017)
12. Khan, S., Huh, J., Ye, J.C.: Switchable and tunable deep beamformer using adaptive instance normalization for medical ultrasound. IEEE Trans. Med. Imaging **41**, 266–278 (2021)
13. Knoll, F., Hammernik, K., Kobler, E., Pock, T., Recht, M.P., Sodickson, D.K.: Assessment of the generalization of learned image reconstruction and the potential for transfer learning. Magn. Reson. Med. **81**(1), 116–128 (2019)
14. Knoll, F., et al.: Advancing machine learning for MR image reconstruction with an open competition: Overview of the 2019 fast MRI challenge. Magn. Reson. Med. **84**(6), 3054–3070 (2020)
15. Knoll, F., Zbontar, J., Sriram, A., Muckley, M.J., Bruno, M., Defazio, A., et al.: fastMRI: a publicly available raw k-space and DICOM dataset of knee images for accelerated MR image reconstruction using machine learning. Radiology: Artif. Intell. **2**(1), e190007 (2020)
16. Korkmaz, Y., Dar, S.U., Yurt, M., Özbey, M., Cukur, T.: Unsupervised MRI reconstruction via zero-shot learned adversarial transformers. IEEE Trans. Med. Imaging **41**, 1747–1763 (2022)
17. Liu, X., Wang, J., Liu, F., Zhou, S.K.: Universal undersampled MRI reconstruction. In: de Bruijne, M., et al. (eds.) MICCAI 2021. LNCS, vol. 12906, pp. 211–221. Springer, Cham (2021). https://doi.org/10.1007/978-3-030-87231-1_21
18. Liu, X., Wang, J., Sun, H., Chandra, S.S., Crozier, S., Liu, F.: On the regularization of feature fusion and mapping for fast MR multi-contrast imaging via iterative networks. Magn. Reson. Imaging **77**, 159–168 (2021)
19. Qin, C., Schlemper, J., Caballero, J., Price, A.N., Hajnal, J.V., Rueckert, D.: Convolutional recurrent neural networks for dynamic MR image reconstruction. IEEE Trans. Med. Imaging **38**(1), 280–290 (2018)
20. Recht, M.P., et al.: Using deep learning to accelerate knee MRI at 3T: results of an interchangeability study. Am. J. Roentgenol. **215**(6), 1421–1429 (2020)
21. Schlemper, J., Caballero, J., Hajnal, J.V., Price, A.N., Rueckert, D.: A deep cascade of convolutional neural networks for dynamic MR image reconstruction. IEEE Trans. Med. Imaging **37**(2), 491–503 (2017)
22. Sriram, A., et al.: End-to-end variational networks for accelerated MRI reconstruction. In: Martel, A.L., et al. (eds.) MICCAI 2020. LNCS, vol. 12262, pp. 64–73. Springer, Cham (2020). https://doi.org/10.1007/978-3-030-59713-9_7
23. Sriram, A., Zbontar, J., Murrell, T., Zitnick, C.L., Defazio, A., Sodickson, D.K.: GrappaNet: combining parallel imaging with deep learning for multi-coil MRI reconstruction. In: Proceedings of the IEEE/CVF Conference on Computer Vision and Pattern Recognition, pp. 14315–14322 (2020)
24. Wang, S., Su, Z., Ying, L., Peng, X., Zhu, S., Liang, F., Feng, D., Liang, D.: Accelerating magnetic resonance imaging via deep learning. In: 2016 IEEE 13th International Symposium on Biomedical Imaging, pp. 514–517. IEEE (2016)
25. Wei, K., Aviles-Rivero, A., Liang, J., Fu, Y., Schönlieb, C.B., Huang, H.: Tuning-free plug-and-play proximal algorithm for inverse imaging problems. In: International Conference on Machine Learning, pp. 10158–10169. PMLR (2020)

26. Yang, G., Yu, S., Dong, H., Slabaugh, G., Dragotti, P.L., Ye, X., et al.: DAGAN: Deep de-aliasing generative adversarial networks for fast compressed sensing MRI reconstruction. IEEE Trans. Med. Imaging **37**(6), 1310–1321 (2017)

27. Yang, Y., Sun, J., Li, H., Xu, Z.: Deep ADMM-Net for compressive sensing MRI. In: Proceedings of the 30th International Conference on Neural Information Processing Systems, pp. 10–18 (2016)

28. Zbontar, J., Knoll, F., Sriram, A., Murrell, T., Huang, Z., Muckley, M.J., et al.: fastMRI: an open dataset and benchmarks for accelerated MRI. arXiv preprint arXiv:1811.08839 (2018)

29. Zhou, B., Schlemper, J., Dey, N., Salehi, S.S.M., Liu, C., Duncan, J.S., Sofka, M.: Dsformer: a dual-domain self-supervised transformer for accelerated multi-contrast mri reconstruction. arXiv preprint arXiv:2201.10776 (2022)

30. Zhou, B., Zhou, S.K.: DuDoRNet: learning a dual-domain recurrent network for fast MRI reconstruction with deep T1 prior. In: Proceedings of the IEEE/CVF Conference on Computer Vision and Pattern Recognition, pp. 4273–4282 (2020)

31. Zhou, S.K., et al.: A review of deep learning in medical imaging: Imaging traits, technology trends, case studies with progress highlights, and future promises. In: Proceedings of the IEEE (2021)

32. Zhou, S.K., Rueckert, D., Fichtinger, G.: Handbook of Medical Image Computing and Computer Assisted Intervention. Academic Press, London (2019)

Noise2SR: Learning to Denoise from Super-Resolved Single Noisy Fluorescence Image

Xuanyu Tian[1], Qing Wu[1], Hongjiang Wei[2], and Yuyao Zhang[1,3](✉)

[1] School of Information Science and Technology, ShanghaiTech University, Shanghai, China
zhangyy8@shanghaitech.edu.cn
[2] School of Biomedical Engineering, Shanghai Jiao Tong University, Shanghai, China
[3] Shanghai Engineering Research Center of Intelligent Vision and Imaging, ShanghaiTech University, Shanghai, China

Abstract. Fluorescence microscopy is a key driver to promote discoveries of biomedical research. However, with the limitation of microscope hardware and characteristics of the observed samples, the fluorescence microscopy images are susceptible to noise. Recently, a few self-supervised deep learning (DL) denoising methods have been proposed. However, the training efficiency and denoising performance of existing methods are relatively low in real scene noise removal. To address this issue, this paper proposed self-supervised image denoising method Noise2SR (N2SR) to train a simple and effective image denoising model based on single noisy observation. Our Noise2SR denoising model is designed for training with paired noisy images of different dimensions. Benefiting from this training strategy, Noise2SR is more efficiently self-supervised and able to restore more image details from a single noisy observation. Experimental results of simulated noise and real microscopy noise removal show that Noise2SR outperforms two blind-spot based self-supervised deep learning image denoising methods. We envision that Noise2SR has the potential to improve more other kind of scientific imaging quality.

Keywords: Image denoising · Self-supervised learning · Fluorescence microscopy image

1 Introduction

Fluorescence Microscopy is indispensable technique to boost the biomedical research in observing the spatial-temporal qualities of cells and tissues [13]. It is susceptible to the influence of noise since the power of photons captured by a microscopic detector are typically weak. A direct way to promote the

Supplementary Information The online version contains supplementary material available at https://doi.org/10.1007/978-3-031-16446-0_32.

signal-to-noise ratio (SNR) of microscopy images is to increase the exposure time or excitation dosage. However, dynamic or real time imaging (e.g. analyzing neural activity) requires high frame rate [14,21,23], which limits the exposure time. While the high excitation dosage can be detrimental for sample health, and even causing inevitable damage [7,10]. These contradictions can be alleviated via improvement of microscopy hardware, however, there are physical limits that are not easy to overcome. Therefore, it is of great importance to denoise and improve the quality of fluorescence microscopy images.

Conventional image denoising methods [3,4] require additional assumptions on noise distribution and clean image prior, which are typically general and does not leverage information of specific content of the noisy image. In recent years, a bunch of deep learning (DL) methods based on Convolution Neural Networks (CNN) have been proposed for image denoising and the performance outperformed conventional methods [16,24]. Some Deep learning methods have been adopted by microscopists [2,17,18]. Weigert et al. presented the content-aware image restoration (CARE) framework in the context of fluorescence microscopy data [22] and achieved superior performance. However, their method requires pairs of low-SNR and High-SNR images for supervised learning. High-SNR images are difficult or even unavailable in fluorescence microscopy which poses an obstacle for conventional supervised learning denoising methods. Lehtinen et al. introduced Noise2Noise (N2N) [12] denoising method, proposed that based on multiple noisy observations of identical image content, the requirement of clean or high-SNR image can be overcome in certain conditions. N2N can be trained with two independent noisy images of same scene and yield results close to supervised denoising learning. Unfortunately, in many scenarios of Microscopy imaging, even the acquisition of two noisy images is still difficult. Subsequently, single image self-supervised image denoising methods such as Noise2Void(N2V) [8] and Noise2Self (N2S) [1] have been proposed. The blind-spot network takes an image masking the center pixel as input and the value of center pixel is used as training target. But these training strategies are not efficient enough since only few pixels can contribute to the loss function [9]. And the denoising performance of self-supervised methods is relatively low in real scene noise removal.

Inspired by the recent single-image denoising works [1,6,8], we propose an effective self-supervised image denoising method Noise2SR (N2SR). Benefiting from the superior performance of recent image SR algorithm, our method is able to build up larger blind regions for training the denoising network, thus further improving single-image denoising performance. Our approach consists of a sub-sampler module that generates sub-sampled noisy images from the original one; and an image SR module that improves the sub-sampled noisy image resolution to that of the original one. Therefore, the resolution improved sub-sampled noisy image and the rest of the original image make up the noisy image pair for self-supervised denoising network training. The training loss function is designed without any regularization term and to tackle the size difference issue between the paired images. After model training, the original noisy image goes through the denoising SR network cascading with a down-sampling operation to generate the final denoised image. To evaluate the performance of proposed Noise2SR, we conduct extensive experiments on publicly available Fluorescence Microscopy Denoising (FMD) dataset [25] for synthetic noise and real Poisson-Gaussian noise removal. The experimental results indicate that Noise2SR outperformances blind-spot network based self-supervised image denoising methods (N2V & N2S), and preserves more original image details from the corrupted images.

2   Proposed Method

2.1   Problem Formulation

Noise2Noise (N2N) is a deep-learning-based denoising model that is trained on two independent noisy observations $\{\mathbf{y}_1, \mathbf{y}_2\}$ of the same object $\mathbf{x}$, where $\mathbf{y}_1 = \mathbf{x}+\mathbf{n}_1$, $\mathbf{y}_2 = \mathbf{x}+\mathbf{n}_2$, and the noises $\mathbf{n}_1$ and $\mathbf{n}_2$ are i.i.d. N2N attempts to minimize the loss term of θ:

$$\arg\min_{\theta} \mathbb{E}_{\mathbf{y}_1,\mathbf{y}_2} \|f_\theta(\mathbf{y}_1) - \mathbf{y}_2\|_2^2 \tag{1}$$

where f_θ is the denoising network parameterized by θ. N2N proves that when the expectation of noisy images $\mathbf{y}_1, \mathbf{y}_2$ is equal to the clean image $\mathbf{x}$, minimizing the loss term of Eq. 1 can converge to the same solution of supervised training. **Paired Noisy Images with Different Resolution.** Pipeline of the proposed method is demonstrated in Fig. 1. N2N training requires at least two independent noisy observations of a same object which limits its application scenario. Thus, we propose a sub-sampler module (Sect. 2.2) to extract sub-sample image $\mathbf{y}_J$ from the noisy image $\mathbf{y}$. Our Noise2SR model is trained with paired noisy images with different resolution to learn image denoising. With different dimensions of $\mathbf{y}_J$ and $\mathbf{y}$, the model can not learn an identity mapping. Thus an additional image SR module with up-sampling scale 2 is composed into the denoising network f_θ. Specifically, the Noise2SR network takes sub-sample image $\mathbf{y}_J$ as input and the complement part $\mathbf{y}_{J^c}$ in image $\mathbf{y}$ as labeling for training (Sect. 2.3). We thus extend the loss function term Eq. 1 to $\arg\min_\theta \mathbb{E}_{\mathbf{x},\mathbf{y}} \|f_\theta(\mathbf{y}_J)_{J^c} - \mathbf{y}_{J^c}\|_2^2$, where J^c is the complement region of the sub-sampler region J in the noisy image $\mathbf{y}$.

Theorem 1. *Let* $\mathbf{y} = \mathbf{x} + \mathbf{n}$ *be an image corrupted by zero-mean noise with variance* $\sigma_{\mathbf{n}}^2$. $\mathbf{y}_J$ *is subset of the noisy image* $\mathbf{y}$ *and* $\mathbf{y}_{J^c}$ *is the complement of* $\mathbf{y}_J$. *Suppose the noise* $\mathbf{n}$ *is independent to clean image* $\mathbf{x}$ *and the noise* $\mathbf{n}$ *is pixel-wise independent. Then it holds that*

$$\mathbb{E}_{\mathbf{x},\mathbf{y}} \|f_\theta(\mathbf{y}_J)_{J^c} - \mathbf{y}_{J^c}\|_2^2 = \mathbb{E}_{\mathbf{x},\mathbf{y}} \|f_\theta(\mathbf{y}_J)_{J^c} - \mathbf{x}_{J^c}\|_2^2 + \sigma_{\mathbf{n}}^2 \tag{2}$$

Theorem 1 states that the optimizing $\arg\min_\theta \mathbb{E}_{\mathbf{x},\mathbf{y}} \|f_\theta(\mathbf{y}_J)_{J^c} - \mathbf{y}_{J^c}\|_2^2$ yields the same solution as the supervised training (The proof is given in the supplementary material). On the basis of this conclusion, we propose a self-supervised denoising method Noise2SR.

2.2   Sub-sampler Module

The goal of sub-sampler module is to generate the sub-sampled image $\mathbf{y}_J$ and complement image $\mathbf{y}_{J^c}$ from the noisy input image $\mathbf{y}$. Figure 2 illustrates the

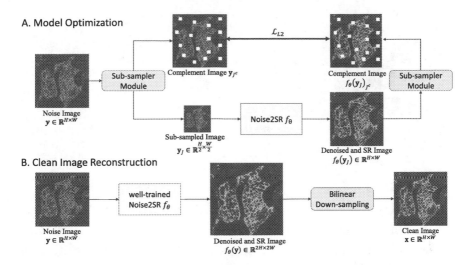

Fig. 1. Overview of our proposed Noise2SR model. **A. Model Optimization**: N2SR takes sub-sampled noise image $\mathbf{y}_J$ derived from sub-sampler module as input to generate the denoised and SR image $f_\theta(\mathbf{y}_J)$. Then, N2SR can be optimized by minimizing the loss computed between the complement image $\mathbf{y}_{J^c}$ and $f_\theta(\mathbf{y}_J)_{J^c}$. **B. Clean Image Reconstruction**: The well-trained N2SR takes the whole noise image $\mathbf{y}$ as input and the clean image $\mathbf{x}$ can be generated from the denoised and SR image $f_\theta(\mathbf{y})$ with down-sampling operation.

workflow of the sub-sampler module for a noisy input example of 4×4. The details of sub-sampler are described below:

1. The image $y \in \mathbb{R}^{H \times W}$ is divided into a number of $\lfloor H/2 \times W/2 \rfloor$ cells with each cell of size 2×2.
2. The (i, j)-th pixel of sub-sampled image $\mathbf{y}_J \in \mathbb{R}^{\lfloor H/2 \times W/2 \rfloor}$ is randomly selected from the i-th row and j-th column cell.
3. The complement image $\mathbf{y}_{J^c}$ masks the selected pixels from $\mathbf{y}$ which can be expressed as $\mathbf{y}_{J^c} = \mathbf{m}_J \odot y$, where $\mathbf{m}_J$ is binary mask and $\odot$ is Hadamard product.

2.3   Model Optimization

The pipeline of model optimization is shown in the Fig. 1 **A**. The sub-sampled noisy image $\mathbf{y}_J \in \mathbb{R}^{H/2 \times W/2}$ and the complement image $\mathbf{y}_{J^c} \in \mathbb{R}^{H \times W}$ (positions of white spots are filled with zeros) are firstly extracted from the original noisy input image $\mathbf{y} \in \mathbb{R}^{H \times W}$ through the sub-sampler module. Then, the SR denoising network is optimized by minimizing the prediction error $\mathcal{L}_{L2}$ between the complement image $\mathbf{y}_{J^c}$ and the output of N2SR-net $f_\theta(\mathbf{y}_J)_{J^c}$. The loss function $\mathcal{L}_{L2}$ is denoted as below:

$$\mathcal{L}_{L2} = \frac{1}{m} \sum_{i=1}^{m} (f_\theta(\mathbf{y}_J)_{J^c} - \mathbf{y}_{J^c})^2 \tag{3}$$

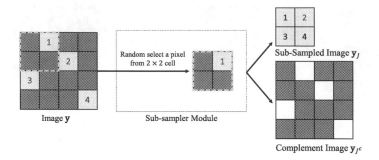

Fig. 2. Workflow of the sub-sampler module for a noise input image example of 4×4.

where m is the mini-batch size during each training iteration.

Network Architecture. Following the previous works [1,8,12], we employ U-Net [20] as the backbone network of our proposed N2SR model. To generate the denoised SR image with same dimensions as the original noisy image **y** from the noisy input sub-sampled image $\mathbf{y}_J$, we propose a simple SR module including a transposed convolutional layer of $2\times$ factor [5] and two convolutional layers of 1×1 kernel size after the U-Net. Specially, we set the output channel of U-Net as 256 allowing the network to propagate context information to the transpose convolution layer. The transpose convolutional layer is used to implement the upsampling operation and the last two convolutional layers are used to generate the denoised SR result.

2.4   Clean Image Reconstruction

The pipeline of clean image reconstruction using well-trained N2SR model is shown in Fig. 1.**B**, which is presented into two steps: (i). We first feed the noise input image $\mathbf{y} \in \mathbb{R}^{H \times W}$ into the N2SR network to generate the denoised and super-resolution result $f_\theta(\mathbf{y}) \in \mathbb{R}^{2H \times 2W}$; (ii). We then apply bilinear down-sampling operator on image $f_\theta(\mathbf{y})$ to get the desired clean image $\mathbf{x} \in \mathbb{R}^{H \times W}$ with same dimensions as the input noisy image **y**. In supplementary material, we provide the comparisons of the denoised and super-resolution results by our model and other denoising methods combined with interpolation methods.

3   Experiment

3.1   Setup

Datasets. We evaluate the proposed Noise2SR on both simulated noise and real noise removal experiments using the Fluorescence Microscopy Denoising (FMD) dataset [25]. In FMD dataset, each sample is scanned 50 times to generate 50 noisy observations. The averaging image of the 50 images is then used as high-SNR reference image. In **simulated noise evaluation** experiment, we add simulated additive Gaussian noise ($\sigma = 15$), Poisson noise ($\lambda = 20$) and Poisson-Gaussian noise

($\sigma = 5, \lambda = 15$) in the averaging high-SNR images respectively, and the averaging images are considered as denoising ground truth (GT) in this case. For each simulated noise dataset, we generate two independent noisy images for 180 samples and split them into three parts: 270 images in training set, 54 images for validation set and 36 images for test set. In the **real scene noise evaluation** experiment, we use the confocal and two-photon microscopy data with noise level 1 (raw noisy image without any processing) in FMD dataset, which consisting 9000 images in 9 imaging configurations (combination of microscopy modalities and biological samples). For each imaging configuration, we randomly selected one noisy image from #1 to #18 FOV and split them into training and validation set. The test set consists of 3 images respectively selected from #19 and #20 FOV in each imaging configuration. Thus, there are 54 images in the test set.

Baseline & Metrics. We employ one classic unsupervised denoiser BM3D [11,15] and three deep learning denoisers including Noise2Noise (N2N) [12], Noise2Void (N2V) [8] and Noise2Self (N2S) [1] as baselines. *Note that N2N is trained on independent noisy image pairs while N2V, N2S and the proposed N2SR are trained on a single noisy image.* The three deep learning models are implemented by PyTorch framework [19] and the network structure is U-Net following the same structure as Noise2Noise [12]. Considering the constraint of GPU Memory and training efficiency, we randomly crop 128×128 image patches from the original images of size 512×512 for every training iteration. We evaluate the performance of denoising results quantitatively using two metrics: Peak Signal-to-Noise (PSNR) and Structural Similarity Index Measure (SSIM).

3.2 Results

Validation Study on the Simulated Noise Experiment Dataset. In Table 1, we show the quantitative results of all methods on the test set of the simulation noise data. To sum up, N2N achieves the best performance and our self-supervised N2SR obtains suboptimal results in most cases. Figure 3 demonstrates the qualitative evaluation results of all the compared methods. Compared with self-supervised N2V, N2S and even N2N, our N2SR preserves more image details, and the detail textures are quite consistent with that in the GT

Table 1. Performance of simulated noise experiment with all compared method denoising results (PSNR (dB)/SSIM) on the test set. The best and second performance are highlighted in red and blue, respectively.

Noise Type	Methods				
	BM3D	N2V	N2S	N2SR (Ours)	N2N
Gaussian ($\sigma = 15$)	34.15/0.8572	34.56/0.8871	34.99/0.8938	35.27/0.8936	35.42/0.9002
Poisson ($\lambda = 20$)	31.32/0.8601	33.27/0.8801	33.45/0.8812	33.50/0.8827	33.62/0.8873
mix Poisson ($\lambda = 15$) & Gaussian ($\sigma = 5$)	28.01/0.8271	31.69/0.8512	31.43/0.8461	31.80/0.8523	32.56/0.8633

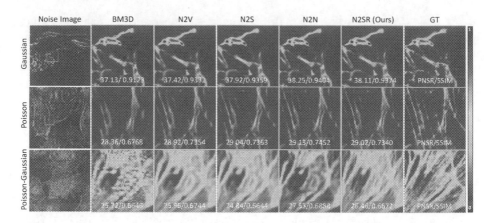

Fig. 3. Qualitative result of simulated noise experiment with all the compared methods on confocal microscopy data of zebrafish embryo cells with additive Gaussian noise ($\sigma = 15$) and BPAE(F-actin) data with Poisson ($\lambda = 20$) and Poisson-Gaussian ($\sigma = 5, \lambda = 15$) noise.

images. When there is only Gaussian noise added, all DL methods perform similar and stable. While under additive Poisson and mixed Gaussian-Poisson noise, the advantages of the proposed N2SR are more prominent in both qualitative and quantitative assessments. Theoretically, the microscopy imaging system is affected by mixed Gaussian-Poisson background noise. Based on the simulation data results we envision N2SR is more efficient than other single-image denoising methods to reduce real scene microscopy image noise.

Performance on the Real Scene Experiment Dataset. In Table 2, we demonstrate the quantitative comparison of all the compared methods on the test set of real scene experiment dataset. The high-SNR reference image is considered as ground truth for computing the evaluation metrics. Overall, our N2SR

Table 2. Quantitative results (PSNR (dB)/SSIM) of all compared method on the test set of the FMD dataset with noise level 1 (raw).

Microscopy	Samples	Methods				
		BM3D	N2V	N2S	N2SR(Ours)	N2N
Confocal	BPAE (Nuclei)	34.63/0.9683	39.04/0.9784	39.42/0.9800	39.69/0.9822	39.67/0.9828
	BPAE(F-actin)	32.97/0.8956	33.43/0.8917	34.02/0.9082	34.45/0.9114	34.44/0.9150
	BPAE (Mito)	31.16/0.9301	32.27/0.9303	33.06/0.9405	33.47/0.9443	33.61/0.9484
	Zebrafish	29.09/0.8732	33.97/0.9098	34.06/0.9108	34.14/0.9131	34.14/0.9167
	Mouse Brain	33.07/0.9457	37.11/0.9603	37.40/0.9612	37.49/0.9651	37.74/0.9652
Two-Photon	BPAE (Nuclei)	29.12/0.9120	32.91/0.9202	32.92/0.9216	33.17/0.9334	33.23/0.9328
	BPAE (F-actin)	27.98/0.7653	28.36/0.7678	28.48/0.7833	28.66/0.7916	28.93/0.7970
	BPAE (Mito)	29.79/0.8596	31.42/0.8622	31.33/0.8660	31.72/0.8754	31.89/0.8817
	Mouse Brain	31.38/0.9088	33.69/0.9046	33.82/0.9059	34.25/0.9194	34.27/0.9185

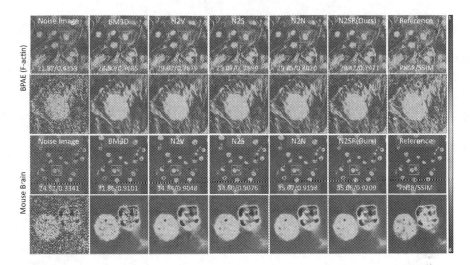

Fig. 4. Qualitative results of all the compared methods on two-photon microscopy data (BPAE (F-actin) and Mouse Brain).

significantly outperforms the other two self-supervised N2V and N2S networks and the traditional denoiser BM3D. Moreover, compared with N2N, N2SR achieves a comparable performance. Figure 4 illustrates the Qualitative results of all the compared methods on two representative test samples (BPAE (F-actin), #19 FOV, and Mouse Brain, #19 FOV). On the BPAE (F-actin) test sample, our N2SR preserves the sharpest image details which are very similar to those in the reference image. On the test sample Mouse Brain, we observe that only our N2SR and N2N produce clean image background while well maintaining clear foreground tissues and sharp tissue boundaries. In contrast, N2V and N2S cannot completely remove background noise; N2V even produced fuzzy artifacts on the tissue boundary. As the microscopy imaging system produces mixed Gaussian-Poisson background noise, the well-behaved real scenes denoised result is consistent with what we found in the simulation experiment.

4   Conclusion

In this paper, we propose Noise2SR, a self-supervised denoising method for single noisy fluorescence image denoising task. Our method does not require multiple noisy observations and external noise distribution assumptions. We propose a sub-sampler and an SR module in the denoising network, assuring that Noise2SR can be trained with constructed paired noisy images with different image dimensions. Our method builds up a larger blind region for training the denoising network compared with other existing blind-spot networks, thus further improving the training efficiency and single-image denoising task performance. The qualitative and quantitative results from simulated noise and real Poisson-Gaussian noise removal of FMD dataset show that out Noise2SR outperforms a conventional denoiser BM3D and two blind-spot based self-supervised image denoising methods and achieves comparable performance to Noise2Noise.

Acknowledgements. This study is supported by the National Natural Science Foundation of China (No. 62071299, 61901256, 91949120).

References

1. Batson, J., Royer, L.: Noise2Self: blind denoising by self-supervision. In: International Conference on Machine Learning, pp. 524–533. PMLR (2019)
2. Beier, T., et al.: Multicut brings automated neurite segmentation closer to human performance. Nat. Methods **14**(2), 101–102 (2017)
3. Buades, A., Coll, B., Morel, J.M.: A non-local algorithm for image denoising. In: 2005 IEEE Computer Society Conference on Computer Vision and Pattern Recognition (CVPR 2005), vol. 2, pp. 60–65. IEEE (2005)
4. Dabov, K., Foi, A., Katkovnik, V., Egiazarian, K.: Image denoising by sparse 3-D transform-domain collaborative filtering. IEEE Trans. Image Process. **16**(8), 2080–2095 (2007)
5. Dumoulin, V., Visin, F.: A guide to convolution arithmetic for deep learning. ArXiv e-prints, March 2016
6. Huang, T., Li, S., Jia, X., Lu, H., Liu, J.: Neighbor2neighbor: self-supervised denoising from single noisy images. In: Proceedings of the IEEE/CVF Conference on Computer Vision and Pattern Recognition (CVPR), pp. 14781–14790, June 2021
7. Icha, J., Weber, M., Waters, J.C., Norden, C.: Phototoxicity in live fluorescence microscopy, and how to avoid it. BioEssays **39**(8), 1700003 (2017)
8. Krull, A., Buchholz, T.O., Jug, F.: Noise2Void-learning denoising from single noisy images. In: Proceedings of the IEEE/CVF Conference on Computer Vision and Pattern Recognition, pp. 2129–2137 (2019)
9. Laine, S., Karras, T., Lehtinen, J., Aila, T.: High-quality self-supervised deep image denoising. Adv. Neural Inf. Process. Syst. **32** (2019)
10. Laissue, P.P., Alghamdi, R.A., Tomancak, P., Reynaud, E.G., Shroff, H.: Assessing phototoxicity in live fluorescence imaging. Nat. Methods **14**(7), 657–661 (2017)
11. Lebrun, M.: An analysis and implementation of the BM3D image denoising method. Image Process. On Line **2012**, 175–213 (2012)
12. Lehtinen, J., et al.: Noise2noise: Learning image restoration without clean data. In: International Conference on Machine Learning, pp. 2965–2974. PMLR (2018)
13. Lichtman, J.W., Conchello, J.A.: Fluorescence microscopy. Nat. Methods **2**(12), 910–919 (2005)
14. Lu, R., et al.: Video-rate volumetric functional imaging of the brain at synaptic resolution. Nat. Neurosci. **20**(4), 620–628 (2017)
15. Mäkinen, Y., Azzari, L., Foi, A.: Collaborative filtering of correlated noise: exact transform-domain variance for improved shrinkage and patch matching. IEEE Trans. Image Process. **29**, 8339–8354 (2020)
16. Mao, X., Shen, C., Yang, Y.B.: Image restoration using very deep convolutional encoder-decoder networks with symmetric skip connections. Adv. Neural Inf. Process. Syst. **29** (2016)

17. Nehme, E., Weiss, L.E., Michaeli, T., Shechtman, Y.: Deep-STOM: super-resolution single-molecule microscopy by deep learning. Optica **5**(4), 458–464 (2018)
18. Ouyang, W., Aristov, A., Lelek, M., Hao, X., Zimmer, C.: Deep learning massively accelerates super-resolution localization microscopy. Nat. Biotechnol. **36**(5), 460–468 (2018)
19. Paszke, A., et al.: PyTorch: an imperative style, high-performance deep learning library. Adv. Neural Inf. Process. Syst. **32** (2019)
20. Ronneberger, O., Fischer, P., Brox, T.: U-Net: convolutional networks for biomedical image segmentation. In: Navab, N., Hornegger, J., Wells, W.M., Frangi, A.F. (eds.) MICCAI 2015, Part III. LNCS, vol. 9351, pp. 234–241. Springer, Cham (2015). https://doi.org/10.1007/978-3-319-24574-4_28
21. Skylaki, S., Hilsenbeck, O., Schroeder, T.: Challenges in long-term imaging and quantification of single-cell dynamics. Nat. Biotechnol. **34**(11), 1137–1144 (2016)
22. Weigert, M., et al.: Content-aware image restoration: pushing the limits of fluorescence microscopy. Nat. Methods **15**(12), 1090–1097 (2018)
23. Weisenburger, S., et al.: Volumetric Ca2+ imaging in the mouse brain using hybrid multiplexed sculpted light microscopy. Cell **177**(4), 1050–1066 (2019)
24. Zhang, K., Zuo, W., Chen, Y., Meng, D., Zhang, L.: Beyond a gaussian denoiser: residual learning of deep CNN for image denoising. IEEE Trans. Image Process. **26**(7), 3142–3155 (2017)
25. Zhang, Y., et al.: A Poisson-Gaussian denoising dataset with real fluorescence microscopy images. In: Proceedings of the IEEE/CVF Conference on Computer Vision and Pattern Recognition, pp. 11710–11718 (2019)

RPLHR-CT Dataset and Transformer Baseline for Volumetric Super-Resolution from CT Scans

Pengxin Yu[1], Haoyue Zhang[1,2], Han Kang[1], Wen Tang[1], Corey W. Arnold[2], and Rongguo Zhang[1(✉)]

[1] Infervision Medical Technology Co., Ltd., Beijing, China
zrongguo@infervision.com
[2] Computational Diagnostics Lab, UCLA, Los Angeles, USA

Abstract. In clinical practice, anisotropic volumetric medical images with low through-plane resolution are commonly used due to short acquisition time and lower storage cost. Nevertheless, the coarse resolution may lead to difficulties in medical diagnosis by either physicians or computer-aided diagnosis algorithms. Deep learning-based volumetric super-resolution (SR) methods are feasible ways to improve resolution, with convolutional neural networks (CNN) at their core. Despite recent progress, these methods are limited by inherent properties of convolution operators, which ignore content relevance and cannot effectively model long-range dependencies. In addition, most of the existing methods use pseudo-paired volumes for training and evaluation, where pseudo low-resolution (LR) volumes are generated by a simple degradation of their high-resolution (HR) counterparts. However, the domain gap between pseudo- and real-LR volumes leads to the poor performance of these methods in practice. In this paper, we build the first public real-paired dataset RPLHR-CT as a benchmark for volumetric SR, and provide baseline results by re-implementing four state-of-the-art CNN-based methods. Considering the inherent shortcoming of CNN, we also propose a transformer volumetric super-resolution network (TVSRN) based on attention mechanisms, dispensing with convolutions entirely. This is the first research to use a pure transformer for CT volumetric SR. The experimental results show that TVSRN significantly outperforms all baselines on both PSNR and SSIM. Moreover, the TVSRN method achieves a better trade-off between the image quality, the number of parameters, and the running time. Data and code are available at https://github.com/smilenaxx/RPLHR-CT.

Keywords: Volumetric super-resolution · CT · Deep learning · Transformer

Pengxin Yu and Haoyue Zhang contribute equally to this work.

The original version of the chapter has been revised. A footnote has been added to confirm that both authors contributed equally to the contribution. A correction to this chapter can be found at https://doi.org/10.1007/978-3-031-16446-0_76

Supplementary Information The online version contains supplementary material available at https://doi.org/10.1007/978-3-031-16446-0_33.

L. Wang et al. (Eds.): MICCAI 2022, LNCS 13436, pp. 344–353, 2022.
https://doi.org/10.1007/978-3-031-16446-0_33

1   Introduction

Volumetric medical imaging, such as computed tomography (CT) and magnetic resonance imaging (MRI), is an important tool in diagnostic radiology. Although high-resolution volumetric medical imaging provides more anatomical and functional details that benefit diagnosis [3,22,24], long acquisition time and high storage cost limit the wide application in clinical practice. As a result, it is routine to acquire anisotropic volumes in practice, which have high in-plane resolution and low through-plane resolution. However, the disparity in resolution can lead to several challenges: (1) the inability to display sagittal or coronal views with adequate detail [10]; (2) the insufficiency of spatial resolution to observe the details of lesions [24] and; (3) the challenge to the robustness of 3D medical image processing algorithms [8,16]. A feasible solution is to use super-resolution (SR) algorithms [26] to upsample anisotropic volumes along the depth dimension, in order to restore high resolution (HR) from low resolution (LR). This approach is referred to as "volumetric SR."

CNN-based algorithms have achieved outstanding performance in SR for natural images [20] and these techniques have been introduced for volumetric SR [1,4,6,12,13,15,17,18,23,25]. Though significant advances have been made, CNN-based algorithms remain limited by the inherent weaknesses of convolution operators. On the one hand, using the same convolution kernel to restore various regions may neglect the content relevance. Liu et al. [13] take this into consideration and propose a multi-stream architecture based on lung segmentation to recover different regions separately, but this is hard to be a one-size-fits-all solution. On the other hand, the non-local content similarity of images has been used as an effective prior in image restoration [27]. Unfortunately, the local processing principle of the convolution operator makes algorithms difficult to effectively model long-range dependence. Recently, transformer networks have shown good performance in several visual problems of natural image [5,14], including SR [2,11]. Self-attention mechanism is the key to the success of transformer. Compared to CNN-based algorithms, transformer can model long-range dependence in the input domain and perform dynamic weight aggregation of features to obtain input-specific feature representation enhancement [9]. These results prompted us to explore a transformer-based SR method.

Another impediment to the application of volumetric SR methods is data. Most relevant studies use HR volume as ground truth and degrade it to construct paired pseudo-LR volumes with which to train and evaluate methods [4,15,17, 18,23,25]. For instance, Peng et al. [17] perform sparse sampling on the depth dimension of thin CT to obtain pseudo thick CT. Zhao et al. [25] simulate pseudo-LR MRI by applying an ideal low-pass filter to the isotropic T2-weighted MRI followed by an anti-ringing Fermi filter. However, the performance will be affected when test on the real-LR volume [1] because of the domain gap between pseudo- and real-LR volume. To avoid it, some studies collect real-paired LR-HR volumes [1,6,12,13,16]. For example, Liu et al. [13] collect 880 real pairs of chest CTs and construct a progressive upsampling model to reconstruct 1 mm CT from 5 mm CT. In the field of MRI, a large data set containing 1,611 real pairs of T1-weighted MRIs have been used to develop the proposed SCSRN method [12]. However, a benchmark to objectively evaluate various volumetric SR methods is still lacking.

To address this deficiency, the first goal of this work is to curate a medium-sized dataset, named Real-Paired Low- and High-Resolution CT (RPLHR-CT), for volumetric SR. RPLHR-CT contains real-paired thin-CTs (slice thickness 1 mm) and thick-CTs (slice thickness 5 mm) of 250 patients. To the best of our knowledge, RPLHR-CT is the first benchmark for volumetric SR, which enables method comparison. The other goal of our work is to explore the potential of transformer for volumetric SR. Specifically, we propose a novel Transformer Volumetric Super-Resolution Network (TVSRN). TVSRN is designed as an asymmetric encoder-decoder architecture with transformer layer, without any convolution operations. TVSRN is the first pure transformer used for CT volumetric SR. We re-implement and benchmark state-of-the-art CNN-based volumetric SR algorithms developed for CT and show that our TVSRN outperforms existing algorithms significantly. Additionally, TVSRN achieves a better trade-off between image quality, the number of parameters, and running time.

2   Dataset and Methodology

2.1   RPLHR-CT Dataset

Dataset Description. The RPLHR-CT dataset is composed of 250 paired chest CTs from patients. All data have been anonymized to ensure privacy. Philips machines were used to perform CT scans and the raw data were then reconstructed to thin CT (1 mm) and thick CT (5 mm) images. Thus, recovering thin CT (HR volume) from thick CT (LR volume) for this dataset is a volumetric SR task with an upsampling factor of 5 in the depth dimension. The CT scans are saved in NIFTI (.nii) format with volume sizes of $L \times 512 \times 512$, where 512×512 is the size of CT slices, and L is the number of CT slices, ranging from 191 to 396 for thin CT and 39 to 80 for thick CT. The thin CT and the corresponding thick CT have the same in-plane resolution, ranging in $[0.604, 0.795]$, and are aligned according to spatial location.

Dataset split and Evaluation Metric. We randomly split the RPLHR-CT dataset into 100 train, 50 validation and 100 test CT pairs. For evaluation, we quantitatively assess the performance of all methods in terms of peak signal to noise ratio (PSNR) and structural similarity (SSIM) [21]. Significance is tested by one-sided Wilcoxon signed-rank test.

Dataset Analysis. To analysis the difference between the thin CT and thick CT, we group slices in thin CT and thick CT into three categories of slice-pairs according to their spatial relationship, as shown on the left side of Fig. 1. We use PSNR and SSIM to access the changes in the similarity of three slice-pairs in train, validation and test CT pairs. As shown on the right side of Fig. 1, the results indicate that the similarity of slice-pairs at the same spatial location in thin CT and thick CT, namely **Match**, is the highest, while the similarity decreases significantly as the spatial distance becomes larger.

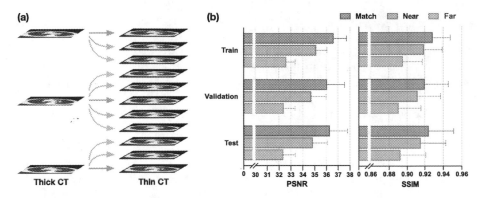

Fig. 1. (a) Three categories of slice-pairs according to their spatial relationship in thin CT and thick CT. Match: same position, shown in blue; Near: 1 mm apart, shown in red; Far: 2 mm apart, show in green. (b) The degree of similarity between the three slice-pairs on the three datasets. (Color figure online)

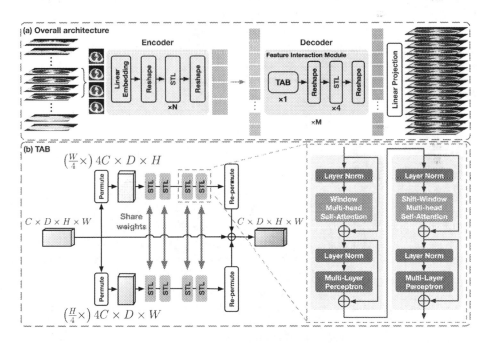

Fig. 2. (a) Illustration of the proposed Transformer Volumetric Super-Resolution Network architecture. (b) Details of TAB. The purple dashed box represents two consecutive swin transformer layers. The batch dimension is indicated in parentheses. (Color figure online)

2.2   Network Architecture

Inspired by MAE [7], we treat volumetric SR as a task to recover the masked regions from the visible regions, where the visible regions refer to the slices in the LR volume and the masked regions refer to the slices in the corresponding HR volume. As illustrated in Fig. 2, we also design our TVSRN with an asymmetric encoder-decoder architecture, but with several targeted modifications. First, in TVSRN, the encoder and the decoder are equally important, and to better model the relationship between the visible regions and the masked regions, the decoder uses a larger amount of parameters than the encoder. Second, instead of the standard transformer layer [5], we use the swin transformer layer (STL) [14], which is less computationally intensive and more suitable for high resolution image, as the basic component of TVSRN. Third, we propose Through-plane Attention Blocks to exploit the spatial positional relationship of volumetric data to achieve better performance.

Encoder is used to map the LR volume to a latent representation. The consecutive slices from LR volumes are denoted as the input $X_e^{in} \in \mathbb{R}^{1 \times D \times H \times W}$ of *encoder*, where D, H and W are the depth, height and width, and the channel is 1. X_e^{in} is firstly fed into the *Linear Embedding*, whose number of feature channel is C, to extract shallow features and output $F_s \in \mathbb{R}^{C \times D \times H \times W}$. Then, F_s is reshaped to $F_0 \in \mathbb{R}^{CD \times H \times W}$. We stack N STLs to extract deep features from F_0 as:

$$F_i = H_i^{STL}(F_{i-1}), \quad i = 1, 2, ..., N \qquad (1)$$

where $H_i^{STL}(\cdot)$ denotes the i-th STL. Finally, F_N is reshaped to 3D output $X_e^{out} \in \mathbb{R}^{C \times D \times H \times W}$.

Decoder is used to recovery the HR volume from the latent representation. As shown in Fig. 2(a), mask tokens are introduced after the *encoder*, and the full set of X_e^{out} and mask tokens is input to the *decoder* as $X_d^{in} \in \mathbb{R}^{C \times D' \times H \times W}$, where D' is the depth of ground truth. The mask tokens are learned vector that indicates the missing slices in the LR volumes compared to the HR counterpart. *Decoder* stack M Feature Interaction Modules (FIMs), which consists of one Through-plane Attention Block (TAB), four STLs and two reshape operations. The reshape operations are used to reshape the input feature map into the size expected by the next block. The output of the *decoder* is X_d^{out} with the same size as X_d^{in}. Note that the design of asymmetric *decoder* can easily be adapted to other upsampling rates by changing the number of mask tokens.

The details of TAB are illustrated in Fig. 2(b). TAB is the first block in each FIM. There are two parallel branches in TAB that perform self-attention on the input from coronal and sagittal views, respectively. In both views, the depth dimension will become an axis of the STL's window, so the relative position relationship between slices will be incorporated into the calculation. The parameter weights of the corresponding STL on the two parallel branches are shared. Given the input feature z_{in} of TAB, the output is computed as:

$$z_0^{sag} = P^{sag}(z_{in}), \ z_0^{cor} = P^{cor}(z_{in})$$
$$z_j^{sag} = H_j^{STL}(z_{j-1}^{sag}), \ z_j^{cor} = H_j^{STL}(z_{j-1}^{cor}), \ j = 1, 2, 3, 4$$
$$z_{out} = z_{in} + P_{re}^{sag}(z_4^{sag}) + P_{re}^{cor}(z_4^{cor}) \tag{2}$$

where $P^{sag}(\cdot)$ and $P^{cor}(\cdot)$ are permutation operations that transform the input to sagittal and coronal view, respectively. $P_{re}^{sag}(\cdot)$ and $P_{re}^{cor}(\cdot)$ denote re-permutation operations that reshape the input back to original size. In addition, TAB contains residual connection, which allow the aggregation of different levels of features.

Reconstruction Target. The X_d^{out} is fed into the *Linear Projection* to obtain the pixel-wise prediction $\hat{Y} \in \mathbb{R}^{D' \times H \times W}$. The L_1 pixel loss is formulated as:

$$L_{pixel} = \frac{1}{D' \times H \times W} \sum_{k,i,j} |\hat{Y}_{k,i,j} - Y_{k,i,j}| \tag{3}$$

where Y is the ground truth HR volume.

Architecture Hyper-parameters. For each STL, the patch size is 1×1 and the window sizes of x-axis, y-axis and z-axis are set to 8, 8 and 4. For *Linear Embedding*, the channel number C is 8. The number of STLs in encoder and FIMs in decoder is set to $N = 4$ and $M = 1$, respectively.

3   Experiments and Results

Implementation Details. We normalize the intensity of the CT images from $[-1024, 2048]$ to $[0, 1]$. During training, $4 \times 256 \times 256$ cubes from thick CTs are used as input and the corresponding $16 \times 256 \times 256$ cubes from thin CTs are used as ground truth, in where $16 = (4 - 1) \times 5 + 1$. During inference, we feed cubes from thick CTs to the model in a sliding window manner, in which the overlap of depth dimension is 1 and the rest is 0. If the depth of untested cubes is less than 4, we feed the last 4 slices into the model. For multiple predictions on the same coordinate, we take the average as the final value. TVSRN is trained with Adam optimizer. The learning rate is 0.0001 and the batch size is 1. For the comparison methods, we follow descriptions provided in the original papers to re-implement the models, as none have public code available. Settings not detailed in the original paper will remain consistent with our work. Data augmentation include random cropping and horizontal flipping. The framework is implemented in PyTorch, and trained on NVIDIA A6000 GPUs.

3.1   Results and Analysis

Figure 3(a) summarizes the quantitative comparisons of our method and other state-of-the-art CT volumetric SR methods: ResVox [6], MPU-Net [13], SAINT [17] and DA-VSR [18]. For ResVox, the noise reduction part is removed. For MPU-Net, we do not use the multi-stream architecture due to the lack of

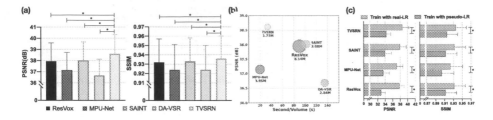

Fig. 3. (a) Quantitative comparisons of our TVSRN and other state-of-the-art methods. ∗ indicates $p < 0.001$. (b) PSNR vs. processing time of each volume with number of parameters shown in circle size. (c) quantitative results of pseudo images experiment.

available lung masks. TVSRN achieves PSNR of 38.609 ± 1.721 and SSIM of 0.936 ± 0.024, outperforms others significantly ($p < 0.001$). Moreover, as shown in Fig. 3(b), compared to other methods, TVSRN achieves a better trade-off in terms of the PSNR (optimal), the number of parameters (optimal), and the running time (suboptimal). We also perform the comparison on an external test set, where TVSRN also achieved the best performance. Detailed numerical results on the internal test set and external test set are presented in the supplementary material. In addition, a sample-by-sample performance scatterplot is given in the supplementary material.

We visualize the axial, coronal and sagittal views of HR CT volume obtained by different methods. It is clear in Fig. 4 that TVSRN has the richest details and the least amount of structural artifacts remaining in different views.

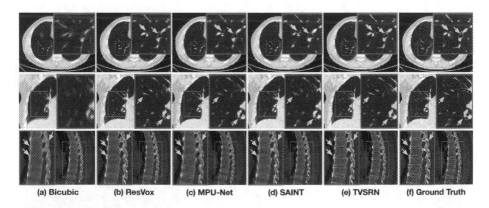

(a) Bicubic   (b) ResVox   (c) MPU-Net   (d) SAINT   (e) TVSRN   (f) Ground Truth

Fig. 4. Visual comparisons of different methods against TVSRN. The first and second rows show the axial view and coronal view respectively, displayed as lung window. The third row is sagittal view, displayed as bone window. Yellow arrows point to areas of marked difference. (Color figure online)

3.2 Domain Gap Analysis

We conduct a pseudo images experiment to illustrate the effect of the domain gap. Specifically, we degrade the training data to obtain pseudo-LR volumes, and use these data to train several different methods. All settings are the same as those in the previous section, except for the training data. For testing, real-LR volumes in the internal test set are used as input to calculate the PSNR and SSIM. As shown in Fig. 3(c), the results show that both PSNR and SSIM of various methods are significantly decreased to varying degrees ($p < 0.001$). Please refer to the supplemental material for more details of degradation.

3.3   Ablation Study

The ablation study is used to verify the contribution of each component in TVSRN on performance. The full TVSRN is compared to:

- TVSRN$_{ViT}^{Encoder}$. A standard transformer-based method based on [5]. We map each patch of size $1 \times 16 \times 16$ to token with length of 512 and set the number of transformer layers to eight. Instead of asymmetric *decoder*, it uses subpixel conversion [19] to perform upsampling.
- TVSRN^{Encoder}. Only the *encoder* of TVSRN was used. N is increasd to eight and C is increased to 32. The upsampling method is subpixel convert.
- TVSRN$^{w/o\,TAB}$. TAB is not used in TVSRN, that is, the relative position relationship among slices is ignored in the network.

Table 1. Results of ablation study for TVSRN in terms of PSNR and SSIM. The best results are **bolded**, and the second best results are <u>underlined</u>. * denotes statistically significant ($p < 0.001$) against above method with one-sided Wilcoxon signed-rank test.

Designs	Param	PSNR($\uparrow$)	SSIM($\uparrow$)
TVSRN$_{ViT}^{Encoder}$	17.15M	35.537 ± 1.353	0.918 ± 0.026
TVSRN^{Encoder}	1.58M	$38.364 \pm 1.675^*$	$0.934 \pm 0.024^*$
TVSRN$^{w/o\,TAB}$	1.56M	<u>$38.497 \pm 1.700^*$</u>	<u>$0.935 \pm 0.024^*$</u>
TVSRN	1.73M	$\mathbf{38.609 \pm 1.721^*}$	$\mathbf{0.936 \pm 0.024^*}$

Model performance is summarized in Table 1. Notable observations include: 1) among all designs, TVSRN$_{ViT}^{Encoder}$ has the most parameters but the worst performance, which indicates that it is not feasible to simply apply the transformer to the volumetric SR; 2) replacing standard transformer layer with STL can greatly reduce the number of parameters and improve the performance by a large margin (up to 2.827 dB); 3) asymmetric decoder can improve performance slightly without changing the number of parameters; 4) improvements can be seen from TVSRN$^{w/o\,TAB}$ to TVSRN, indicating the effectiveness of modeling the relative position relationship among slices. A sample-by-sample performance scatterplots in supplemental material is used to further illustrate the effectiveness of individual components.

4   Conclusion

A persistent problem with volumetric SR is the lack of real-paired data for training and evaluation, which makes it challenging generalize algorithms to real-world datasets for practical applications. In this paper, we presented the RPLHR-CT Dataset, which is the first open real-paired dataset for volumetric SR, and provided baseline results by re-implementing four state-of-the-art SR methods. We also proposed a convolution-free transformer-based network, which significantly outperformed existing CNN-based methods and has the least number of parameters and the second shortest running time. In the future, we will enlarge the RPLHR-CT Dataset and investigate new volumetric SR training strategies, such as semi-supervised learning or using unpaired real data.

Acknowledgment. This work was funded by the National Key Research and Development Project (2021YFC2500703).

References

1. Bae, W., Lee, S., Park, G., Park, H., Jung, K.H.: Residual CNN-based image super-resolution for CT slice thickness reduction using paired CT scans: preliminary validation study (2018)
2. Chen, H., et al.: Pre-trained image processing transformer. In: Proceedings of the IEEE/CVF Conference on Computer Vision and Pattern Recognition, pp. 12299–12310 (2021)
3. Chen, M., et al.: Diagnostic performance for erosion detection in sacroiliac joints on MR T1-weighted images: comparison between different slice thicknesses. Eur. J. Radiol. **133**, 109352 (2020)
4. Chen, Y., Shi, F., Christodoulou, A.G., Xie, Y., Zhou, Z., Li, D.: Efficient and accurate MRI super-resolution using a generative adversarial network and 3D multi-level densely connected network. In: Frangi, A.F., Schnabel, J.A., Davatzikos, C., Alberola-López, C., Fichtinger, G. (eds.) MICCAI 2018. LNCS, vol. 11070, pp. 91–99. Springer, Cham (2018). https://doi.org/10.1007/978-3-030-00928-1_11
5. Dosovitskiy, A., et al.: An image is worth 16x16 words: transformers for image recognition at scale. In: International Conference on Learning Representations (2020)
6. Ge, R., Yang, G., Xu, C., Chen, Y., Luo, L., Li, S.: Stereo-correlation and noise-distribution aware ResVoxGAN for dense slices reconstruction and noise reduction in thick low-dose CT. In: Shen, D., et al. (eds.) MICCAI 2019. LNCS, vol. 11769, pp. 328–338. Springer, Cham (2019). https://doi.org/10.1007/978-3-030-32226-7_37
7. He, K., Chen, X., Xie, S., Li, Y., Dollár, P., Girshick, R.: Masked autoencoders are scalable vision learners. arXiv preprint arXiv:2111.06377 (2021)
8. Isensee, F., Jaeger, P.F., Kohl, S.A., Petersen, J., Maier-Hein, K.H.: nnU-Net: a self-configuring method for deep learning-based biomedical image segmentation. Nat. Methods **18**(2), 203–211 (2021)
9. Khan, S., Naseer, M., Hayat, M., Zamir, S.W., Khan, F.S., Shah, M.: Transformers in vision: a survey. arXiv preprint arXiv:2101.01169 (2021)
10. Kodama, F., Fultz, P.J., Wandtke, J.C.: Comparing thin-section and thick-section CT of pericardial sinuses and recesses. Am. J. Roentgenol. **181**(4), 1101–1108 (2003)

11. Liang, J., Cao, J., Sun, G., Zhang, K., Van Gool, L., Timofte, R.: SwinIR: image restoration using swin transformer. In: Proceedings of the IEEE/CVF International Conference on Computer Vision, pp. 1833–1844 (2021)
12. Liu, G., et al.: Recycling diagnostic MRI for empowering brain morphometric research-critical & practical assessment on learning-based image super-resolution. Neuroimage **245**, 118687 (2021)
13. Liu, Q., Zhou, Z., Liu, F., Fang, X., Yu, Y., Wang, Y.: Multi-stream progressive up-sampling network for dense CT image reconstruction. In: Martel, A.L., et al. (eds.) MICCAI 2020. LNCS, vol. 12266, pp. 518–528. Springer, Cham (2020). https://doi.org/10.1007/978-3-030-59725-2_50
14. Liu, Z., et al.: Swin transformer: hierarchical vision transformer using shifted windows. arXiv preprint arXiv:2103.14030 (2021)
15. Lu, Z., Li, Z., Wang, J., Shi, J., Shen, D.: Two-stage self-supervised cycle-consistency network for reconstruction of thin-slice MR images. In: de Bruijne, M., et al. (eds.) MICCAI 2021. LNCS, vol. 12906, pp. 3–12. Springer, Cham (2021). https://doi.org/10.1007/978-3-030-87231-1_1
16. Park, S., et al.: Computer-aided detection of subsolid nodules at chest CT: improved performance with deep learning-based CT section thickness reduction. Radiology **299**(1), 211–219 (2021)
17. Peng, C., Lin, W.A., Liao, H., Chellappa, R., Zhou, S.K.: Saint: spatially aware interpolation network for medical slice synthesis. In: Proceedings of the IEEE/CVF Conference on Computer Vision and Pattern Recognition, pp. 7750–7759 (2020)
18. Peng, C., Zhou, S.K., Chellappa, R.: DA-VSR: domain adaptable volumetric super-resolution for medical images. In: de Bruijne, M., et al. (eds.) MICCAI 2021. LNCS, vol. 12906, pp. 75–85. Springer, Cham (2021). https://doi.org/10.1007/978-3-030-87231-1_8
19. Shi, W., et al.: Real-time single image and video super-resolution using an efficient sub-pixel convolutional neural network. In: Proceedings of the IEEE Conference on Computer Vision and Pattern Recognition, pp. 1874–1883 (2016)
20. Wang, Z., Chen, J., Hoi, S.C.: Deep learning for image super-resolution: a survey. IEEE Trans. Pattern Anal. Mach. Intell. **43**(10), 3365–3387 (2020)
21. Wang, Z., Bovik, A.C., Sheikh, H.R., Simoncelli, E.P.: Image quality assessment: from error visibility to structural similarity. IEEE Trans. Image Process. **13**(4), 600–612 (2004)
22. Xu, F., et al.: Diagnostic performance of diffusion-weighted imaging for differentiating malignant from benign intraductal papillary mucinous neoplasms of the pancreas: a systematic review and meta-analysis. Front. Oncol. **11**, 2550 (2021)
23. Xuan, K., et al.: Reducing magnetic resonance image spacing by learning without ground-truth. Pattern Recognit. **120**, 108103 (2021)
24. Yang, J., et al.: *AlignShift*: bridging the gap of imaging thickness in 3D anisotropic volumes. In: Martel, A.L., et al. (eds.) MICCAI 2020. LNCS, vol. 12264, pp. 562–572. Springer, Cham (2020). https://doi.org/10.1007/978-3-030-59719-1_55
25. Zhao, C., Dewey, B.E., Pham, D.L., Calabresi, P.A., Reich, D.S., Prince, J.L.: Smore: a self-supervised anti-aliasing and super-resolution algorithm for MRI using deep learning. IEEE Trans. Med. Imaging **40**(3), 805–817 (2020)
26. Zhou, S.K., et al.: A review of deep learning in medical imaging: imaging traits, technology trends, case studies with progress highlights, and future promises. Proc. IEEE **109**(5), 820–838 (2021)
27. Zhou, S., Zhang, J., Zuo, W., Loy, C.C.: Cross-scale internal graph neural network for image super-resolution. arXiv preprint arXiv:2006.16673 (2020)

A Learnable Variational Model for Joint Multimodal MRI Reconstruction and Synthesis

Wanyu Bian[1], Qingchao Zhang[1], Xiaojing Ye[2], and Yunmei Chen[1(✉)]

[1] University of Florida, Gainesville, FL 32611, USA
{wanyu.bian,qingchaozhang,yun}@ufl.edu
[2] Georgia State University, Atlanta, GA 30302, USA
xye@gsu.edu

Abstract. Generating multi-contrasts/modal MRI of the same anatomy enriches diagnostic information but is limited in practice due to excessive data acquisition time. In this paper, we propose a novel deep-learning model for joint reconstruction and synthesis of multi-modal MRI using incomplete k-space data of several source modalities as inputs. The output of our model includes reconstructed images of the source modalities and high-quality image synthesized in the target modality. Our proposed model is formulated as a variational problem that leverages several learnable modality-specific feature extractors and a multimodal synthesis module. We propose a learnable optimization algorithm to solve this model, which induces a multi-phase network whose parameters can be trained using multi-modal MRI data. Moreover, a bilevel-optimization framework is employed for robust parameter training. We demonstrate the effectiveness of our approach using extensive numerical experiments.

Keywords: MRI reconstruction · Multimodal MRI synthesis · Deep neural network · Bilevel-optimization

1 Introduction

Magnetic resonance imaging (MRI) is a prominent leading-edge medical imaging technology which provides diverse image contrasts under the same anatomy. Multiple different contrast images are generated by varying the acquisition parameters, e.g. T1-weighted (T1), T2-weighted (T2) and Fluid Attenuated Inverseion Recovery (FLAIR). They have similar anatomical structure but highlight different soft tissue which enriches the diagnostic information for clinical applications and research studies comparing to single modality [10]. A major limitation of

This work was supported in part by National Science Foundation under grants DMS-1925263, DMS-2152960, and DMS-2152961.

Supplementary Information The online version contains supplementary material available at https://doi.org/10.1007/978-3-031-16446-0_34.

MRI is its relatively long data acquisition time during MRI scans. It does not only cause patient discomfort, but also makes MR images prone to motion artifacts which degrade the diagnostic accessibility. A mainstream routine to reduce the MRI acquisition time is to reconstruct partially undersampled k-space acquisitions, another approach is to synthesize target modality MR image from fully-sampled acquisitions of source modality images [7,24].

Compressed sensing MRI (CS-MRI) reconstruction is a predominant approach for accelerating MR acquisitions, which solves an inverse problem formulated as a variational model. In recent decades, deep learning based models have leveraged large datasets and further explored the potential improvement of reconstruction performance. Most of the deep learning based reconstruction methods employ end-to-end deep networks [11,19,23]. To overcome the weakness of the end-to-end black-box networks, several learnable optimization algorithms (LOAs) have been developed attracted much attention, which possess of a more interpretable network architecture. LOA-based reconstruction methods unfold the iterative optimization algorithm into a multi-phase network in which the regularization and image transformation are learned to improve the network performance [1,2,4,15], e.g. ADMM-Net [20], ISTA-Net$^+$ [25] and PD-Net [5].

Multimodal MR image synthesis in recent years has emerged using various deep learning frameworks, where a main stream is to start with source modalities from the image domain and synthesize the images of the target modalities [6,18,22]. For instance, GAN-based methods are mostly end-to-end from images to images with encoder-decoder architectures in their generator networks. MM-GAN [17] channel-wisely concatenates all the available modalities with a zero image for missing modality and imputes the missing input incorporating curriculum learning for GAN. Multimodal MR (MM) [12], MMGradAdv [3] and Hi-Net [26] exploit the correlations between multimodal data and apply robust feature fusion method to form a unified latent representation. A rarely explored approach [7] starts from undersampled k-space data of the source modalities to generate target modality images. This paper further explored this approach and the major differences from [7] to ours are: (i) In [7] it requires that the target modality is heavily undersampled and the source modality is lightly undersampled, while our method does not require any of the k-space information of target modality nor the source modality to be lightly undersampled which is much less limitations in real-world applications; (ii) Instead of learning the mapping from image to image, we learn the mapping from the features of source images to the target image since features provide more direct information to synthesize images of a new modality and (iii) We formulate the joint reconstruction and synthesis problem in a variational model and propose a convergent algorithm as the architecture of the deep neural network so that the network is interpretable and convergent.

In order to synthesize target modality by using partially scanned k-space data from source modalities in stead of fully scanned data that used in the state-of-the-art multimodal synthesis, in this paper, we propose to jointly reconstruct undersampled multiple source modality MR images and synthesize the target modality image. Our contributions are summarized as follows: (1) We propose a novel LOA for joint multimodal MRI reconstruction and synthesis with theoretical analysis guarantee; (2) The parameters and hyper-parameters of the network induced by our LOA are learned using a bilevel optimization algorithm robust parameter training; (3) Extensive experimental results demonstrate the efficiency of the proposed method and high quality of the reconstructed/synthesized images.

We demonstrate that our proposed joint synthesis-reconstruction network can further improve image reconstruction quality over existing sole reconstruction networks using the same partial k-space measurements. This improvement is due to the additional image feature information provided by the synthesis functionality of our network, which is trained by comprehensive image data of all relevant modalities together. Moreover, the synthesized images can serve as additional references to radiologists when the corresponding k-space data cannot be acquired in practice.

2   Proposed Method

2.1   Model

In this section, we provide the details of the proposed model for joint MRI reconstruction and synthesis. Given the partial k-space data $\{\mathbf{f}_1, \mathbf{f}_2\}$ of the source modalities (e.g. T1 and T2), our goal is to reconstruct the corresponding images $\{\mathbf{x}_1, \mathbf{x}_2\}$ *and* synthesize the image $\mathbf{x}_3$ of the missing modality (e.g. FLAIR) without its k-space data. To this end, we propose to learn three modality-specific feature extraction operators $\{h_{w_i}\}_{i=1}^3$, one for each of these three modalities. Then, we design regularizers of these images by combining these learned operators and a robust sparse feature selection operator (we use $(2,1)$-norm in this work). To synthesize the image $\mathbf{x}_3$ using $\mathbf{x}_1$ and $\mathbf{x}_2$, we employ another feature-fusion operator g_θ which learns the mapping from the features $h_{w_1}(\mathbf{x}_1)$ and $h_{w_2}(\mathbf{x}_2)$ to the image $\mathbf{x}_3$. Our proposed model reads as

$$\min_{\mathbf{x}_1, \mathbf{x}_2, \mathbf{x}_3} \Psi_{\Theta, \gamma}(\mathbf{x}_1, \mathbf{x}_2, \mathbf{x}_3) := \tfrac{1}{2} \sum_{i=1}^{2} \|P_i F \mathbf{x}_i - \mathbf{f}_i\|_2^2 + \tfrac{1}{3} \sum_{i=1}^{3} \|h_{w_i}(\mathbf{x}_i)\|_{2,1} \tag{1}$$
$$+ \tfrac{\gamma}{2} \|g_\theta([h_{w_1}(\mathbf{x}_1), h_{w_2}(\mathbf{x}_2)]) - \mathbf{x}_3\|_2^2,$$

where the first term in (1) is the data fidelity for the source modalities that ensures consistency between the reconstructed images $\{\mathbf{x}_1, \mathbf{x}_2\}$ and the sensed partial k-space data $\{\mathbf{f}_1, \mathbf{f}_2\}$. Here, F stands for the discrete Fourier transform and P_i is the binary matrix representing the k-space mask when acquiring data for $\mathbf{x}_i$. In (1), h_{w_i} represents the modality-specific feature extraction operator which maps the input $\mathbf{x}_i \in \mathbb{C}^n$ to a high-dimensional feature tensor $h_{w_i}(\mathbf{x}_i) \in \mathbb{C}^{m \times d}$, where m is the spatial dimension and d is the channel number of the feature tensor. The second term is the regularization of all modalities $\{\mathbf{x}_1, \mathbf{x}_2, \mathbf{x}_3\}$ to enhance sparsity of the their feature tensors, where $\|h_{w_i}(\mathbf{x}_i)\|_{2,1} = \sum_{j=1}^{m} \|h_{w_i,j}(\mathbf{x}_i)\|$. Here each $h_{w_i,j} \in \mathbb{R}^d$ can be viewed as a feature vector at spatial location j. The last term in (1) is to synthesize $\mathbf{x}_3$ by learning a mapping $g_\theta : \mathbb{C}^{m \times 2d} \to \mathbb{C}^n$ that maps the concatenated features of $\mathbf{x}_1$

and $\mathbf{x}_2$ (i.e. $[h_{w_1}(\mathbf{x}_1), h_{w_2}(\mathbf{x}_2)]$) to $\mathbf{x}_3$, and $[\cdot, \cdot]$ represents the concatenation of the arguments. Here g_θ maps features of x_1 and x_2 to the target image so that more useful information can be used to generate the target image comparing to the mappings from source images to the target image.

In our implementation, we parameterize the modality-specific feature extraction operator h_{w_i} and the synthesis mapping g_θ as vanilla CNNs with l and l' layers respectively, both of which use the smoothed rectified linear unit [4] as activation. For notation simplicity, we let Θ in (1) denote the collection of all parameters in the convolution operators of the function Ψ, i.e. $\Theta = \{w_1, w_2, w_3, \theta\}$.

The weight γ is a hyper-parameter which plays a critical role in balancing the reconstruction part (first two terms in (1)) and the image synthesis part (last term in (1)) of the model (1), and hence has significant impact to the final image reconstruction and synthesis quality. To address this important issue, we propose to use a bi-level hyper-parameter tuning framework to learn γ by minimizing the reconstruction loss on both validation and training data sets. Details of this hyper-parameter tuning will be provided in Sect. 2.3.

2.2   Efficient Learnable Optimization Algorithm

In this section, we present a novel and efficient learnable optimization algorithm (LOA) for solving the nonconvex nonsmooth minimization problem (1). (Comprehensive convergence analysis of this algorithm is provided in Supplementary Material.) Then we design a DNN whose architecture exactly follows this algorithm, and the parameters of the DNN can be learned from data. In this way, the DNN inherits all the convergence properties of the LOA.

Since the second sum in the minimization problem (1) is nonsmooth due to the $l_{2,1}$-norm, we first approximate these nonsmooth terms using their smooth surrogates $\|h_{w_i}(\mathbf{x}_i)\|_{\varepsilon_{2,1}} = \sum_{j=1}^m \left(\sqrt{\|\overline{h_{w_i,j}(\mathbf{x}_i)}\|^2 + \varepsilon^2} - \varepsilon \right)$, where $\varepsilon > 0$ is the parameter representing the smoothing level. Thus, for every fixed ε, we obtain a smooth surrogate function $\Psi_{\Theta,\gamma}^\varepsilon$ of the nonsmooth objective $\Psi_{\Theta,\gamma}$, and we can apply a gradient descent step to update our approximation to the solution of (1). In our algorithm, the smoothing level ε is automatically reduced and tends to 0, such that the surrogate approaches the original nonsmooth regularizers in (1). More precisely, let $\mathbf{X} = \{\mathbf{x}_1, \mathbf{x}_2, \mathbf{x}_3\}$ for notation simplicity, then we solve the problem $\min_{\mathbf{X}} \Psi_{\Theta,\gamma}(\mathbf{X})$ with initial $\mathbf{X}^{(0)}$ using Algorithm 1 (the initial $\mathbf{X}^{(0)}$ is obtained from a pre-trained initial network, which is illustrated in detail in Sect. 3.1). At Line 3 of Algorithm 1, we compute a gradient descent update with step size obtained by line search while the smoothing parameter $\varepsilon_t > 0$ is fixed. In Line 4, the algorithm updates ε_t based on a reduction criterion. The reduction of ε_t ensures that the specified subsequence (the subsequence who met the ε_t reduction criterion) must have an accumulation point that is a Clarke stationary point [4] of the optimization problem (1), as given in Theorem 1, whose proof is provided in Supplementary Materials. We create a multi-phase network whose architecture exactly follows Algorithm 1 with a prescribed phase number $\hat{T}$, where each phase of the network performs one iteration of the algorithm.

Algorithm 1: Learnable Descent Algorithm

1: **Input:** $\mathbf{X}^{(0)}$, $0 < \eta < 1$, and ε_0, $a, \sigma > 0$, $t = 0$. Max T, tolerance $\epsilon_{\text{tol}} > 0$.
2: **for** $t = 0, 1, 2, \ldots, T - 1$ **do**
3:     $\mathbf{X}^{(t+1)} = \mathbf{X}^{(t)} - \alpha_t \nabla \Psi_{\Theta,\gamma}^{\varepsilon_t}(\mathbf{X}^{(t)})$, where the step size α_t is obtained through
        line search s.t. $\Psi_{\Theta,\gamma}^{\varepsilon_t}(\mathbf{X}^{(t+1)}) - \Psi_{\Theta,\gamma}^{\varepsilon_t}(\mathbf{X}^{(t)}) \leq -\frac{1}{a}\|\mathbf{X}^{(t+1)} - \mathbf{X}^{(t)}\|^2$ holds.
4:     **if** $\|\nabla \Psi_{\Theta,\gamma}^{\varepsilon_t}(\mathbf{X}^{(t+1)})\| < \sigma\eta\varepsilon_t$, set $\varepsilon_{t+1} = \eta\varepsilon_t$; **otherwise**, set $\varepsilon_{t+1} = \varepsilon_t$.
5:     **if** $\sigma\varepsilon_t < \epsilon_{\text{tol}}$, **terminate** and go to Line 6,
6: **end for** and **output** $\mathbf{X}^{(t)}$.

Theorem 1. *Suppose that $\{\mathbf{X}^{(t)}\}$ is the sequence generated by Algorithm 1 with any initial $\mathbf{X}^{(0)}$, $\epsilon_{\text{tol}} = 0$ and $T = \infty$. Let $\{\mathbf{X}^{(t_l+1)}\}$ be the subsequence that satisfies the reduction criterion in step 4 of Algorithm 1. Then $\{\mathbf{X}^{(t_l+1)}\}$ has at least one accumulation point, and every accumulation point of $\{\mathbf{X}^{(t_l+1)}\}$ is a Clarke stationary point of $\min_{\mathbf{X}} \Psi_{\Theta,\gamma}(\mathbf{X})$.*

2.3   Bilevel Optimization Algorithm for Network Training

Suppose that we randomly sample $\mathcal{M}_{tr}$ data pairs $\{\mathcal{D}_i^{tr}\}_{i=1}^{\mathcal{M}_{tr}}$ for training and $\mathcal{M}_{val}$ data pairs $\{\mathcal{D}_i^{val}\}_{i=1}^{\mathcal{M}_{val}}$ for validation, where each $\mathcal{D}_i^{tr}$ (or $\mathcal{D}_i^{val}$) is composed of data pair $\{(\mathbf{f}_1^i, \mathbf{f}_2^i), \mathbf{X}^{*i}\}$, $\mathbf{f}_1^i, \mathbf{f}_2^i$ denote the given partial k-space data, and $\mathbf{X}^{*i} = \{\mathbf{x}_1^{*i}, \mathbf{x}_2^{*i}, \mathbf{x}_3^{*i}\}$ denotes the corresponding reference images.

To find the optimal value of the important hyper-parameter γ for the synthesis term in (1), we employ a bilevel optimization framework which solves for Θ on training set for any given γ in the lower-level problem and tunes the optimal hyper-parameter γ on validation set in the upper-level problem. More precisely, our bilevel optimization framework reads as:

$$\min_{\gamma} \quad \sum_{i=1}^{\mathcal{M}_{val}} \ell(\Theta(\gamma), \gamma; \mathcal{D}_i^{val}) \quad \text{s.t.} \quad \Theta(\gamma) = \arg\min_{\Theta} \sum_{i=1}^{\mathcal{M}_{tr}} \ell(\Theta, \gamma; \mathcal{D}_i^{tr}), \quad (2)$$

where $\quad \ell(\Theta, \gamma; \mathcal{D}_i) := \frac{\mu}{2}\|g_\theta([h_{w_1}(\mathbf{x}_1^{*i}), h_{w_2}(\mathbf{x}_2^{*i})]) - \mathbf{x}_3^{*i}\|_2^2$

$$+ \sum_{j=1}^{3}\left(\frac{1}{2}\|\mathbf{x}_j^{(\hat{T})}(\Theta, \gamma; \mathcal{D}_i) - \mathbf{x}_j^{*i}\|_2^2 + (1 - SSIM(\mathbf{x}_j^{(\hat{T})}(\Theta, \gamma; \mathcal{D}_i), \mathbf{x}_j^{*i}))\right),$$

$$(3)$$

and the $\mathbf{x}_j^{(\hat{T})}(\cdot)$ denotes the output of the $\hat{T}$-phase network for the jth modality. The first term of the loss function ℓ in (3) presses g_θ to accurately synthesize $\mathbf{x}_3$. The second term is to minimize the difference between the network output and the ground truth in the least square sense. The third term is to promote high structural similarity index [21] of the reconstructed/synthesized images. In (2), the lower-level optimization learns the network parameters Θ with any fixed coefficient γ on the training set, and the upper-level tunes the hyper-parameter γ on the validation set, which mitigates the challenging overfitting issue.

The bi-level optimization problem (2) is very difficult to solve. In this work, we employ the penalty method proposed in [13] to solve this problem. For notation simplicity, we denote $\mathcal{L}(\Theta, \gamma; \mathcal{D}) := \sum_{i=1}^{\mathcal{M}} \ell(\Theta, \gamma; \mathcal{D}_i)$ then rewrite (2) as

$$\min_{\gamma} \mathcal{L}(\Theta(\gamma), \gamma; \mathcal{D}^{val}) \quad \text{s.t.} \quad \Theta(\gamma) = \arg\min_{\Theta} \mathcal{L}(\Theta, \gamma; \mathcal{D}^{tr}). \tag{4}$$

Following [13], we relax the lower-level optimization problem to its first-order necessary condition:

$$\min_{\gamma} \mathcal{L}(\Theta(\gamma), \gamma; \mathcal{D}^{val}) \quad \text{s.t.} \quad \nabla_{\Theta}\mathcal{L}(\Theta(\gamma), \gamma; \mathcal{D}^{tr}) = 0. \tag{5}$$

Furthermore, we impose a quadratic penalty on the constraint and further relax the above problem as

$$\min_{\Theta,\gamma} \left\{ \widetilde{\mathcal{L}}(\Theta, \gamma; \mathcal{D}^{tr}, \mathcal{D}^{val}) := \mathcal{L}(\Theta, \gamma; \mathcal{D}^{val}) + \frac{\lambda}{2}\|\nabla_{\Theta}\mathcal{L}(\Theta, \gamma; \mathcal{D}^{tr})\|^2 \right\}. \tag{6}$$

Due to the large volume of the datasets, it is not possible to solve (6) in full-batch. Here we train the parameters using the mini-batch stochastic alternating direction method summarized in Algorithm 2.

Algorithm 2: Mini-batch alternating direction penalty algorithm

---

1: **Input** $\mathcal{D}^{tr}$, $\mathcal{D}^{val}$, $\delta_{tol} > 0$, **Initialize** Θ, γ, δ, $\lambda > 0$ and $\nu_{\delta} \in (0,1)$, $\nu_{\lambda} > 1$.
2: **while** $\delta > \delta_{tol}$ **do**
3:      Sample training and validation batch $\mathcal{B}^{tr} \subset \mathcal{D}^{tr}$, $\mathcal{B}^{val} \subset \mathcal{D}^{val}$.
4:      **while** $\|\nabla_{\Theta}\widetilde{\mathcal{L}}(\Theta, \gamma; \mathcal{B}^{tr}, \mathcal{B}^{val})\|^2 + \|\nabla_{\gamma}\widetilde{\mathcal{L}}(\Theta, \gamma; \mathcal{B}^{tr}, \mathcal{B}^{val})\|^2 > \delta$ **do**
5:          **for** $k = 1, 2, \ldots, K$ (inner loop) **do**
6:              $\Theta \leftarrow \Theta - \rho_{\Theta}^{(k)} \nabla_{\Theta}\widetilde{\mathcal{L}}(\Theta, \gamma; \mathcal{B}^{tr}, \mathcal{B}^{val})$
7:          **end for**
8:          $\gamma \leftarrow \gamma - \rho_{\gamma} \nabla_{\gamma}\widetilde{\mathcal{L}}(\Theta, \gamma; \mathcal{B}^{tr}, \mathcal{B}^{val})$
9:      **end while** and **update** $\delta \leftarrow \nu_{\delta}\delta$, $\lambda \leftarrow \nu_{\lambda}\lambda$.
10: **end while** and **output:** Θ, γ.

---

3 Experiments

3.1 Initialization Networks

The initials $\{\mathbf{x}_1^{(0)}, \mathbf{x}_2^{(0)}, \mathbf{x}_3^{(0)}\}$ are obtained through the Initialization Networks (INIT-Nets) shown in Fig. 1, where the **k-space interpolation block** interpolates the missing components of the undersampled k-space data then fed into the **initial reconstruction block** in the image domain after inverse Fourier transform. All blocks are designed in residual structure [8]. To train the INIT-Nets, we minimize the difference between its outputs and the ground truth with loss $L^I(\mathbf{x}_j^{(0)}, \mathbf{x}_j^*) = \|\mathbf{x}_j^{(0)} - \mathbf{x}_j^*\|_1$, $j = 1, 2, 3$. The INIT-Nets only produce initial approximate images with limited accuracy, so we fed them into the Joint Reconstruction and Synthesis Network (JRS-Net) illustrated in Sect. 2.2 to obtain the final results. INIT-Nets are pre-trained whose parameters are fixed during training the JRS-Net.

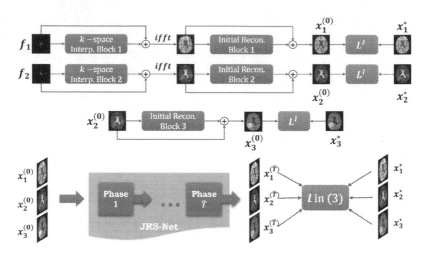

Fig. 1. The overall architecture of the proposed network for joint multimodal MRI reconstruction and synthesis: INIT-Nets (up and middle), JRS-Net (bottom).

3.2 Experiment Setup

The datasets are from BRATS 2018 challenge [14] which were scanned from four modalities T1, T2, Flair and T1-weighted contrast-enhanced (T1CE) and we picked high-grade gliomas (HGG) set which consists 210 patients. We applied Fourier transform to the images and undersampled the k-space using a radial mask of sampling ratio 40% to obtain partial k-space data for training. We randomly took the center 10 slices from 6 patients as test set with cropped size 160×180 and split the rest of HGG dataset into training and validation sets with 1020 images separately. We compared with four state-of-the-art multimodal MR synthesis methods: Multimodal MR (MM) [3], MM-GAN [17], MMGradAdv [12] and Hi-Net [26]. The hyper-parameter selection for our algorithm is provided in Supplementary Material. Three metrics are used for evaluation: peak signal-to-noise ratio (PSNR) [9], structural similarity (SSIM) [21], and normalized mean squared error (NMSE) [16].

3.3 Experimental Results and Evaluation

We take four synthesis directions T1 + T2 → FLAIR, T1 + FLAIR → T2, T2 + FLAIR → T1 and T1 + T2 → T1CE. Table 1 reports the quantitative result, which indicates that the proposed method outperforms MM and GAN-based methods (MM-GAN, MMGradAdv, Hi-Net). The average PSNR of our method improves 0.67 dB comparing to the baseline Hi-Net, SSIM improves about 0.01, and NMSE reduces about 0.01. We also conduct the pure-synthesis experiment (T1 + T2 → FLAIR) by inputting fully-scanned source data, where the model (1) minimizes w.r.t. $\mathbf{x}_3$ only and excludes the data-fidelity terms. This result is in Table 1 where the PSNR value is 1.16 dB higher than baseline method Hi-Net. Table 2 shows that the joint reconstruction and synthesis improves PSNR

Table 1. Quantitative comparison of the synthesis results.

	Methods	PSNR	SSIM	NMSE
T1 + T2 → FLAIR	MM [3]	22.89 ± 1.48	0.6671 ± 0.0586	0.0693 ± 0.0494
	MM-GAN [17]	23.35 ± 1.03	0.7084 ± 0.0370	0.0620 ± 0.0426
	MMGradAdv [12]	24.03 ± 1.40	0.7586 ± 0.0326	0.0583 ± 0.0380
	Hi-Net [26]	25.03 ± 1.38	0.8499 ± 0.0300	0.0254 ± 0.0097
	Proposed	**26.19 ± 1.34**	**0.8677 ± 0.0307**	**0.0205 ± 0.0087**
$\mathbf{f}_{T1} + \mathbf{f}_{T2}$ → FLAIR	Proposed	**25.74 ± 1.25**	**0.8597 ± 0.0315**	**0.0215 ± 0.0085**
T1 + FLAIR → T2	MM [3]	23.89 ± 1.61	0.6895 ± 0.0511	0.0494 ± 0.0185
	MM-GAN [17]	24.15 ± 0.90	0.7217 ± 0.0432	0.0431 ± 0.0114
	MMGradAdv [12]	25.06 ± 1.49	0.7597 ± 0.0486	0.0406 ± 0.0165
	Hi-Net [26]	25.95 ± 1.50	0.8552 ± 0.0410	0.0229 ± 0.0070
$\mathbf{f}_{T1} + \mathbf{f}_{FLAIR}$ → T2	Proposed	**26.52 ± 1.57**	**0.8610 ± 0.0438**	**0.0207 ± 0.0072**
T2 + FLAIR → T1	MM [3]	23.53 ± 2.18	0.7825 ± 0.0470	0.0301 ± 0.0149
	MM-GAN [17]	23.63 ± 2.31	0.7908 ± 0.0421	0.0293 ± 0.0119
	MMGradAdv [12]	24.73 ± 2.23	0.8065 ± 0.0423	0.0252 ± 0.0118
	Hi-Net [26]	25.64 ± 1.59	0.8729 ± 0.0349	0.0130 ± 0.0097
$\mathbf{f}_{T2} + \mathbf{f}_{FLAIR}$ → T1	Proposed	**26.31 ± 1.80**	**0.9085 ± 0.0311**	**0.0112 ± 0.0113**
T1 + T2 → T1CE	MM [3]	23.37 ± 1.56	0.7272 ± 0.0574	0.0312 ± 0.0138
	MM-GAN [17]	23.68 ± 0.97	0.7577 ± 0.0637	0.0302 ± 0.0133
	MMGradAdv [12]	24.23 ± 1.90	0.7887 ± 0.0519	0.0273 ± 0.0136
	Hi-Net [26]	25.21 ± 1.20	0.8650 ± 0.0328	0.0180 ± 0.0134
$\mathbf{f}_{T1} + \mathbf{f}_{T2}$ → T1CE	Proposed	**25.91 + 1.21**	**0.8726 ⊥ 0.0340**	**0.0167 ± 0.0133**

Table 2. Quantitative comparison of the reconstructed T1 and T2 images without and with joint synthesis of FLAIR images.

Modality	FLAIR involved?	PSNR	SSIM	NMSE
T1	No	37.00 ± 0.74	0.9605 ± 0.0047	0.0008 ± 0.0002
	Yes	37.49 ± 0.83	0.9628 ± 0.0074	0.0007 ± 0.0002
T2	No	37.24 ± 1.22	0.9678 ± 0.0028	0.0027 ± 0.0010
	Yes	37.67 ± 1.34	0.9663 ± 0.0043	0.0024 ± 0.0009

by 0.46 dB comparing to purely reconstructing T1 and T2 without synthesizing FLAIR. We think this is because that the synthesis operator g_θ also leverages data $\mathbf{x}_3$ to assist shaping the feature maps of $\mathbf{x}_1$ and $\mathbf{x}_2$, which improves the reconstruction quality of the latter images.

Figure 2 displays the synthetic MRI results on different source and target modality images. The proposed synthetic images preserve more details and distinct edges of the tissue boundary (indicated by the magnified red windows and green arrows) and the synthetic images are more alike the ground truth images comparing to other referenced methods.

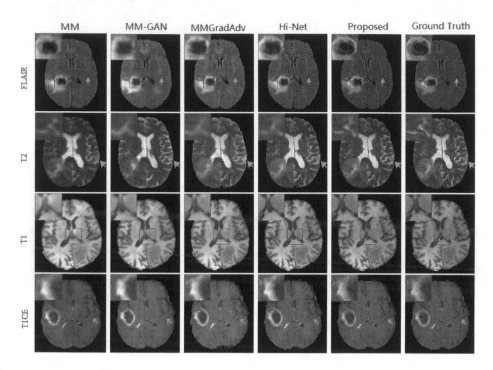

Fig. 2. Qualitative comparison between the state-of-the-art multimodal synthesis methods and proposed method. From first row to last row: T1 + T2 → FLAIR, T1 + FLAIR → T2, T2 + FLAIR → T1 and T1 + T2 → T1CE.

4   Conclusion

We propose a novel deep model that simultaneously reconstructs the source modality images from the partially scanned k-space MR data and synthesizes the target modality image without any k-space information by iterating an LOA with convergence guaranteed. The network is trained by a bilevel-optimization training algorithm that uses training and validation sets to further improve the performance. Extensive experiments on brain MR data with different modalities validate the magnificent performance of the proposed model.

References

1. Bian, W., Chen, Y., Ye, X.: An optimal control framework for joint-channel parallel MRI reconstruction without coil sensitivities. Magn. Reson. Imaging **89**, 1–11 (2022)
2. Bian, W., Chen, Y., Ye, X., Zhang, Q.: An optimization-based meta-learning model for MRI reconstruction with diverse dataset. J. Imaging **7**(11), 231 (2021)
3. Chartsias, A., Joyce, T., Giuffrida, M.V., Tsaftaris, S.A.: Multimodal MR synthesis via modality-invariant latent representation. IEEE Trans. Med. imaging **37**(3), 803–814 (2017)

4. Chen, Y., Liu, H., Ye, X., Zhang, Q.: Learnable descent algorithm for nonsmooth nonconvex image reconstruction. SIAM J. Imaging Sci. **14**(4), 1532–1564 (2021)
5. Cheng, J., Wang, H., Ying, L., Liang, D.: Model learning: primal dual networks for fast MR imaging. In: Shen, D., et al. (eds.) MICCAI 2019, Part III. LNCS, vol. 11766, pp. 21–29. Springer, Cham (2019). https://doi.org/10.1007/978-3-030-32248-9_3
6. Dar, S.U., Yurt, M., Karacan, L., Erdem, A., Erdem, E., Çukur, T.: Image synthesis in multi-contrast MRI with conditional generative adversarial networks. IEEE Trans. Med. Imaging **38**(10), 2375–2388 (2019)
7. Dar, S.U., Yurt, M., Shahdloo, M., Ildız, M.E., Tınaz, B., Çukur, T.: Prior-guided image reconstruction for accelerated multi-contrast MRI via generative adversarial networks. IEEE J. Sel. Top. Signal Process. **14**(6), 1072–1087 (2020)
8. He, K., Zhang, X., Ren, S., Sun, J.: Deep residual learning for image recognition. In: Proceedings of the IEEE Conference on Computer Vision and Pattern Recognition, pp. 770–778 (2016)
9. Hore, A., Ziou, D.: Image quality metrics: PSNR vs. SSIM. In: 2010 20th International Conference on Pattern Recognition, pp. 2366–2369. IEEE (2010)
10. Iglesias, J.E., Konukoglu, E., Zikic, D., Glocker, B., Van Leemput, K., Fischl, B.: Is synthesizing MRI contrast useful for inter-modality analysis? In: Mori, K., Sakuma, I., Sato, Y., Barillot, C., Navab, N. (eds.) MICCAI 2013, Part I. LNCS, vol. 8149, pp. 631–638. Springer, Heidelberg (2013). https://doi.org/10.1007/978-3-642-40811-3_79
11. Lee, D., Yoo, J., Tak, S., Ye, J.C.: Deep residual learning for accelerated MRI using magnitude and phase networks. IEEE Trans. Biomed. Eng. **65**(9), 1985–1995 (2018)
12. Liu, X., Yu, A., Wei, X., Pan, Z., Tang, J.: Multimodal MR image synthesis using gradient prior and adversarial learning. IEEE J. Sel. Top. Signal Process. **14**(6), 1176–1188 (2020)
13. Mehra, A., Hamm, J.: Penalty method for inversion-free deep bilevel optimization. arXiv preprint arXiv:1911.03432 (2019)
14. Menze, B.H., et al.: The multimodal brain tumor image segmentation benchmark (brats). IEEE Trans. Med. Imaging **34**(10), 1993–2024 (2014)
15. Monga, V., Li, Y., Eldar, Y.C.: Algorithm unrolling: interpretable, efficient deep learning for signal and image processing. IEEE Signal Process. Mag. **38**(2), 18–44 (2021)
16. Poli, A., Cirillo, M.: On the use of the normalized mean square error in evaluating dispersion model performance. Atmos. Environ. Part A Gen. Top. **27**, 2427–2434 (1993)
17. Sharma, A., Hamarneh, G.: Missing MRI pulse sequence synthesis using multimodal generative adversarial network. IEEE Trans. Med. Imaging **39**(4), 1170–1183 (2019)
18. Sohail, M., Riaz, M.N., Wu, J., Long, C., Li, S.: Unpaired multi-contrast MR image synthesis using generative adversarial networks. In: Burgos, N., Gooya, A., Svoboda, D. (eds.) SASHIMI 2019. LNCS, vol. 11827, pp. 22–31. Springer, Cham (2019). https://doi.org/10.1007/978-3-030-32778-1_3
19. Sriram, A., et al.: End-to-end variational networks for accelerated MRI reconstruction. In: Martel, A.L., et al. (eds.) MICCAI 2020, Part II. LNCS, vol. 12262, pp. 64–73. Springer, Cham (2020). https://doi.org/10.1007/978-3-030-59713-9_7
20. Sun, J., Li, H., Xu, Z., et al.: Deep ADMM-net for compressive sensing MRI. Adv. Neural Inf. Process. Syst. **29** (2016)

21. Wang, Z., et al.: Image quality assessment: from error visibility to structural similarity. IEEE Trans. Image Process. **13**(4), 600–612 (2004)
22. Welander, P., Karlsson, S., Eklund, A.: Generative adversarial networks for image-to-image translation on multi-contrast MR images-a comparison of CycleGAN and unit. arXiv preprint arXiv:1806.07777 (2018)
23. Yang, G., et al.: DAGAN: deep de-aliasing generative adversarial networks for fast compressed sensing MRI reconstruction. IEEE Trans. Med. imaging **37**(6), 1310–1321 (2017)
24. Yang, Y., Wang, N., Yang, H., Sun, J., Xu, Z.: Model-driven deep attention network for ultra-fast compressive sensing MRI guided by cross-contrast MR image. In: Martel, A.L., et al. (eds.) MICCAI 2020, Part II. LNCS, vol. 12262, pp. 188–198. Springer, Cham (2020). https://doi.org/10.1007/978-3-030-59713-9_19
25. Zhang, J., Ghanem, B.: ISTA-Net: interpretable optimization-inspired deep network for image compressive sensing. In: Proceedings of the IEEE Conference on Computer Vision and Pattern Recognition, pp. 1828–1837 (2018)
26. Zhou, T., Fu, H., Chen, G., Shen, J., Shao, L.: Hi-Net: hybrid-fusion network for multi-modal MR image synthesis. IEEE Trans. Med. Imaging **39**(9), 2772–2781 (2020)

Autofocusing+: Noise-Resilient Motion Correction in Magnetic Resonance Imaging

Ekaterina Kuzmina[1], Artem Razumov[1], Oleg Y. Rogov[1], Elfar Adalsteinsson[2], Jacob White[2], and Dmitry V. Dylov[1($\boxtimes$)]

[1] Skolkovo Institute of Science and Technology, Moscow, Russia
d.dylov@skoltech.ru
[2] Massachusetts Institute of Technology, Cambridge, MA, USA

Abstract. Image corruption by motion artifacts is an ingrained problem in Magnetic Resonance Imaging (MRI). In this work, we propose a neural network-based regularization term to enhance *Autofocusing*, a classic optimization-based method to remove rigid motion artifacts.

The method takes the best of both worlds: the optimization-based routine iteratively executes the blind demotion and deep learning-based prior penalizes for unrealistic restorations and speeds up the convergence. We validate the method on three models of motion trajectories, using synthetic and real noisy data. The method proves resilient to noise and anatomic structure variation, outperforming the state-of-the-art motion correction methods.

Keywords: Motion artifacts · Motion correction · Autofocusing · MRI

1 Introduction

Magnetic Resonance Imaging (MRI) non-invasively measures precise anatomical and functional patterns within the human body. During the scan, it is nearly impossible for the patients to remain still in the scanner, with the movement of several millimeters or more being typical even for a healthy adult [7]. Despite delivering superb detail and accelerating the acquisition, powerful MRI machines are invariably prone to motion artifacts. This stems from the voxels of the modern sensors, such as those in the high-resolution 7-Tesla scanners, so small that even a miniature patient movement results in severe voxel displacements [10].

Generally, motion artifacts degrade the scan's quality, manifesting themselves as ghosting or blurring in the image [35]. The nature of these artifacts is convoluted, with many possible causing factors, ranging from the motion of an inner organ to that of the scanned body part, to the specifics of the k-space trajectory

---

E. Kuzmina and A. Razumov—Equal contribution.

Supplementary Information The online version contains supplementary material available at https://doi.org/10.1007/978-3-031-16446-0_35.

in the signal acquisition protocol, to the patient's trembling, *etc.* The periodic movements, such as cardiac motion and arterial pulsation, introduce distinctive well-defined patterns, whereas an arbitrary motion of the patient leads to a uniform image blur [8,37].

Motion artifacts lessen the overall diagnostic value of MRI data and may lead to misinterpretation when confused with pathology. The effect of motion alone, *e.g.*, is estimated to introduce a 4% error into the measurement of the gray matter in the brain [24]. That is especially crucial on the low signal-to-noise ratio (SNR) scans in the presence of noise or when the pathology is smaller than the voxel size of the scanner. Compensating for the motion artifacts is referred to as *motion correction*, or *demotion*, and is one of the most important tasks in the medical vision.

The demotion methods can be broadly classified into *prospective* (during the scan, *e.g.*, [20]) and *retrospective* (after the scan, e.g., [21]). In the latter category, 'Autofocusing' [2] optimization algorithm became classic, allowing the motion parameters to be found *iteratively* with respect to a chosen quality metric and assuming the image corruption model is known. Any motion model, however, is hardly universal, given the omni-directional and non-uniform movements make the selection of a proper metric problematic [18]. Perception-based metrics could alleviate the challenge [5,11,31]; however, MRI-specific standards for visual evaluation of motion artifacts do not exist [30].

Another powerful optimization-based Autofocusing method to remove motion artifacts is GradMC [16], the latest version of which compensates for *non-rigid* physiological motions by distilling local *rigid* motion of separate patches of the image. Instrumental in some cases, the method fails to handle sufficiently large movements and is computationally complex. In the presence of certain noise levels or when an object's structure varies abruptly GradMC underperforms and can introduce new artefacts.

With the advent of deep learning, the optimization methods were somewhat substituted by the convolutional neural networks (CNNs) [1,9,14], improving convergence of the non-convex motion parameter optimization procedure and/or increasing the reconstruction quality. A plethora of CNN-based *deblurring* methods, such as popular DnCNN [39], have then been implemented [30,31], without taking the physical nature of the MRI artifacts into account. Same applies to a generative adversarial network (GAN) approach MedGAN [14], entailing extra adversarial loss functions and the associated long training routine.

In the majority of works on MRI motion correction, the corrupted data are either private [14,31] or generated by a model [1,5,30]. Herein, we also resort to the latter and employ a physics-based model to introduce the rigid motion artifacts. We propose to enhance the widely used Autofocusing algorithm by a CNN-extracted prior knowledge about k-space specific motion corruption model, adding to the popular algorithm the new attributes of stability to anatomic structure variation and resilience to noise. Figure 1 summarizes the proposed method.

2   Methods

Motion Artifact Model. We restrict the modeling to the problem of rigid body movements. The corrupted image $\hat{X}_{\theta,\alpha}$ can be obtained via sequential affine

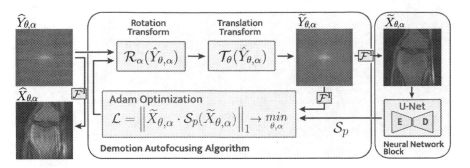

Fig. 1. Autofocusing+: proposed motion correction method. The classic Autofocusing output $\widetilde{Y}_{\theta,\alpha}$ (left) is iteratively regularized with U-Net output image (*i.e.*, the prior) $\mathcal{S}_p(\widetilde{Y}_{\theta,\alpha})$ (right). The L1-minimization of the regularized output updates the motion parameters θ and α.

transforms of the clean image X: rotation $\mathcal{R}_\alpha(\cdot)$ and translation $\mathcal{T}_\theta(\cdot)$, characterized in the k-space domain by the trajectory parameters α and θ, respectively [2]). Denoting $Y = \mathcal{F}(X)$ as the Fourier transform,

$$\hat{X}_{\theta,\alpha} = \mathcal{F}^{-1}(\mathcal{R}_\alpha(\mathcal{T}_\theta(Y))) \,. \tag{1}$$

In practice, the k-space rotation[1] is performed by multiplying each column of the coordinate grid G by a rotation matrix:

$$G_\alpha = \begin{bmatrix} \cos\alpha & \sin\alpha \\ -\sin\alpha & \cos\alpha \end{bmatrix} \cdot G \,, \tag{2}$$

which destroys the uniformity of the equispaced periodic frequencies and requires methods, such as Non-Uniform Fourier Transform (GPU-based NUFFT) [6], to place the frequency components on a new uniform grid correctly:

$$\mathcal{R}_\alpha(Y) = \mathrm{NUFFT}(Y, G_\alpha) \,. \tag{3}$$

Likewise, the translation operation[2] can be formalized as:

$$\mathcal{T}_\theta(Y) = |Y| \exp(-j2\pi\angle Y + \theta) \,, \tag{4}$$

where θ is the shift parameter, $\angle Y$ and $|Y|$ are the angle and the magnitude of the complex values of Y. The motion artifacts, generated by Eqs. (3) and (4), have to be reversible $(\mathcal{T}_\theta^{-1}(\mathcal{T}_\theta(X)) = X, \mathcal{R}_\alpha^{-1}(\mathcal{R}_\alpha(X)) = X)$ and commutative $(\mathcal{T}_\theta(\mathcal{R}_\alpha(X)) = \mathcal{R}_\alpha(\mathcal{T}_\theta(X)))$. The motion vectors, set by various configurations of harmonic trajectories and parametrized by α and θ, along with the modified k-space and the resulting artifacts are shown in Fig. 2.

---

[1] Fourier Rotation Theorem [15] allows for the equal rotation in the Image space.

[2] Fourier Shift Theorem [15] connects the pixel shifts to a phase change in k-space.

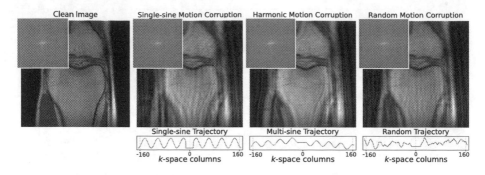

Fig. 2. MR image corrupted with different motion artifact trajectories in k-space (insets show the corresponding spectra). Second raw: corresponding motion vectors. The movement trajectories considered: *single-sine*, *multi-sine* (or *harmonic*), and *random* (random contribution of multiple waves to the overall trajectory).

Autofocusing+ Algorithm. The optimization task of finding motion trajectories can be formulated as *a blind demotion*, because the amplitude and the motion trajectory are unknown:

$$\underset{\theta,\alpha}{\operatorname{argmin}} \left\| \hat{X}_{\theta,\alpha} \right\|_1 . \tag{5}$$

For the optimization routine (ref. Algorithm 1), previously conjugate gradient and LBFGS were used, but because of the computational complexity of our method, we apply basic Adam gradient descent [12] to iteratively update the motion vectors *w.r.t.* the image quality metric.

Inspired by previous studies [17,36], L1-norm was used as the image quality measure $\mathcal{L}_{AF}$. The L1-norm choice is rational because the motion artifacts blur sharp edges in the image and, therefore, decrease the image sparsity by 'redistributing' intensity values between the neighboring pixels[3]. Besides L1, other metrics could prove useful in certain scenarios, *e.g.*, the entropy (as in GradMC). We refer to [18] for the evaluation of 24 different autofocusing metrics. Below, the Adam-based Autofocusing algorithm is referred to as 'baseline Autofocusing' or just 'Autofocusing'.

U-Net as an Additional Prior. Our idea is to use a CNN alongside the image quality metric in the optimization procedure to improve the image restoration quality via an additional image prior [13,29]. Naturally, a simple U-Net [25] architecture was considered for such a regularization task.

Importantly, in the proposed pipeline (See Fig. 1), the CNN is the part of the minimized function, the parameters of which are also trainable. That is, we propose to use CNN as a part of loss and then learn the parameters of this loss

---

[3] Our experimentation confirmed that L1-norm is a superior choice, outperforming the other metrics used with Autofocusing algorithms [18] (not shown).

Algorithm 1. Autofocusing+ Optimization

---

input $\hat{Y}_{\theta,\alpha} \in \mathbb{C}^{n \times n}$ // k-space corrupted by motion with parameters θ, α
output $\hat{Y}_{\theta,\alpha} \in \mathbb{C}^{n \times n}$ // Refined k-space
  for train epoch **do**
    for optimization step **do**
      Compute image quality metric $\mathcal{L}_{AF} = \left\| \hat{X}_{\theta,\alpha} \cdot \mathcal{S}_p(\hat{X}_{\theta,\alpha}) \right\|_1$
      Calculate gradients for Autofocusing parameters θ, α
      Update Autofocusing parameters θ, α with *Adam Gradient Descent*
    end for
    Compute loss between target and refined image $\mathcal{L}_{NN}(\hat{X}_{\theta,\alpha}, X)$
    Calculate gradients for Neural Network parameters p
    Update Neural Network parameters p with *Adam Gradient Descent*
  end for

---

in the Autofocusing algorithm. As such, given the refined image $\hat{X}_{\theta,\alpha}$ and the output of the network $\mathcal{S}_p(\hat{X}_{\theta,\alpha})$, the optimization problem can be re-written as

$$\theta(p), \alpha(p) = \underset{\theta,\alpha}{\mathrm{argmin}} \left\| \hat{X}_{\theta,\alpha} \cdot \mathcal{S}_p(\hat{X}_{\theta,\alpha}) \right\|_1 , \tag{6}$$

where $\mathcal{S}_p(\cdot)$ and p are the CNN inference output and its weights, respectively. For consistency between various extents of corruption by the motion, a sigmoid is applied to the final layer of the network to scale all its values from 0 to 1. Thus, the output of the network scales the corrupted image prior to the L1-norm.

Basic U-Net architecture with the blocks consisting of Instance Norm and Leaky ReLu is then trained as follows:

$$p = \underset{p}{\mathrm{argmin}} \left\| X - \mathcal{R}_{\alpha(p)}^{-1} \left(\mathcal{T}_{\theta(p)}^{-1}(\hat{X}_{\theta,\alpha}) \right) \right\|_1 , \tag{7}$$

introducing new hyperparameters: the number of autofocusing steps in Algorithm 1 and the learning rate. Figures 3, 4, 5 showcase the algorithm's performance.

3 Experiments

Data. `fastMRI` dataset with the raw k-space data was used [38]. To train and evaluate the model, the 20% of central proton density weighted single-coil knee slices, acquired at 3T and 1T, were selected, comprising 150 scans for training, 100 scans for validation, and 53 scans for testing. Magnitude-only images were cropped to the size of 320×320 pixels and then corrupted with the motion artifact model described in Sect. 2. Motion vectors were selected randomly from the reported ranges at each training step.

Metrics. The reconstructed images are compared using four metrics: PSNR, SSIM [33], MS-SSIM [34], and VIF (Visual Information Fidelity [11,27]).

Implementation Details. To train U-Net inside the algorithm, Adam optimizer was used with $\beta_1 = 0.900$, $\beta_2 = 0.999$, and the learning rate $lr = 5 \times 10^{-5}$.

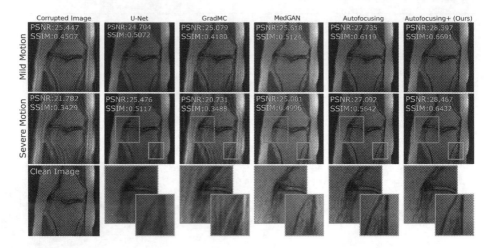

Fig. 3. Comparison of different demotion methods for mild (first row) and severe (second row) corruption with harmonic trajectories for the data from low-SNR MRI machine (1T, real noise). The brightness was adjusted for viewer's convenience.

The gradients are accumulated at each iteration of Autofocusing algorithm, with the total number of steps set to 30 for training and 80 for validation, and with the rate of updating the motion parameters $lr = 3\times10^{-4}$. When the Autofocusing optimization ends, L1-loss between the ground truth and the refined image is taken and the error is backpropagated to optimize the weights of U-Net. Thus, the dependence on parameters θ, α, and the weights p, implicit in Eqs. (7) and (6), is examined. On average, it takes 160 epochs to converge. No augmentation was required.

The upper bound for the motion vector was set to $2°$ rotations and 5 pixel translations, and the corruption model dismissed the central 8% of the k-space, ensuring the low frequencies, responsible for the content, are preserved [16]. Random motion vector was generated from the Gaussian distribution and then smoothed with Savitzky-Golay filter [26] with the kernel size of 20.

The source code is available at https://github.com/cviaai/AF-PLUS/.

4   Results

The comparison between the state-of-the-art (SOTA) optimization- and deep learning-based algorithms is shown in Fig. 3 and Fig. S2 for mild and severe motion corruptions. The validation of our method (trained only with mild harmonic motion trajectories) was performed with all three types of motion trajectories shown in Fig. 2. A full comparison of the trajectories is presented in Fig. 4, suggesting that the technique is functional for each of them, even the random one. We refer to Supplementary material for all four quality metrics and each motion trajectory (Table S2), while presenting only selected metrics herein for brevity, with the focus on the harmonic corruption as the most realistic [14].

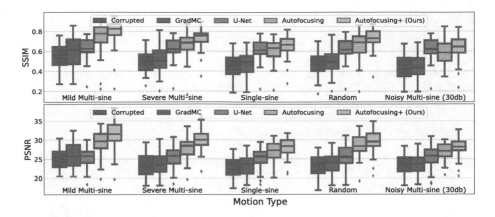

Fig. 4. Motion correction via different methods (mild corruption, 3T, synthetic noise). Autofocusing+ statistically outperforms SOTA models (max p-value $< 10^{-5}$).

Resilience to Noise. The motion correction methods have to be resilient to noise (*e.g.*, electronic [4]) and abrupt fluctuations in the detail of an anatomic structure (*e.g.*, when the ligaments of the joint appear next to the motion arti-fact). These cases are thoroughly studied in Fig. 5, where either classic opti-mization or deep learning methods sometimes fail to function. On the opposite, Autofocusing+ is consistent and robust on all images, showing resilience to the strongest noise levels (90 dB). In the synthetic noise experiments, the noise is modeled as Gaussian distribution $\mathcal{N}(\mu, \sigma^2)$ added to the signal in k-space: $Y' = Y + \mathcal{N}(\mu, \sigma^2)$ [19], where Y' is a noise-corrupted spectrum, μ is the mean, and σ is the standard deviation of the noise.

We also validated our algorithm on a real-noise data subset, a part of `fastMRI` acquired at 1T, where the SNR and the contrast are visually sub-optimal (the factual noise level is unknown). Although all methods fluctuate more severely than in the case of synthetic noise, the t-test confirms that our algorithm still outperforms the second best method (classic Autofocusing) with statistical sig-nificance (max p-value < 0.0047).

5   Discussion

As can be seen in Figs. 4 and 5, Autofocusing+ always outperforms the SOTA models for all four metrics, all noise levels, and all motion trajectories. This affirms that the addition of neural network helps to regularize the optimization problem and improves the performance of the baseline Autofocusing method. Even visually (Fig. 5(C)), Autofocusing+ succeeds in the cases where the classic optimization alone fails to refine the detail and even introduces new artifacts. We observe that such new artifacts correspond to abrupt variation of pixel intensity in the anatomic detail, where the structure 'couples' with the motion artifacts. The use of the neural network, however, extracts *prior knowledge* for the image

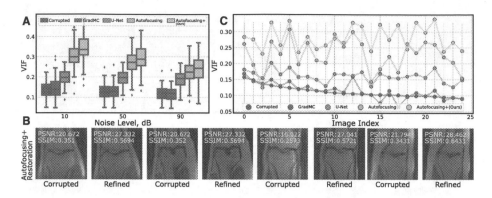

Fig. 5. Demotion results for harmonic motion corruption and real noise (1T scans). **A.** Performance for different noise levels (max p-value < 0.0047). **B.** Example of real noisy images restored by Autofocusing+. **C.** Performance of all methods on 25 random images in the real-noise dataset. In some cases, classic Autofocusing fails to restore the image (*e.g.*, image #2, #14, and #17), whereas Autofocusing+ handles the demotion.

quality measure and eliminates the issue, making the reconstruction stable and the image well-refined.

The evaluation of the reconstructed knee images for *mild* motion harmonic trajectories in Fig. 3 and Fig. S1 reveals only subtle differences in the performance of various methods. However, the *severe* corruption makes the classical optimization-based approaches inapt for removing the artifacts, whereas Autofocusing+ refines image detail, making the fine structure acceptable visually and leaving the uniform regions intact. According to Fig. 5, Autofocusing+ is also efficient in the demotion task in the presence of noise, being functional both for high levels of added noise and for real low-SNR noisy MRI scans.

It can also be noticed that a simple deblurring with a stand-alone U-Net yields approximately the same consistent output for different noise levels and the strengths of motion corruption (Table S2 in Supplementary material), learning to 'smooth out' the motion artefact patterns instead of fixing them [23,29]. This results in an irreversible loss of the fine tissue structure, making the use of optimization-based demotion methods more justified and preferred in practice.

Hence, our method takes the best of both worlds: the optimization-based routine iteratively performs the blind demotion with interpretable measure of the image detail and the deep learning-based prior helps to penalize for unrealistic restorations. The latter is especially useful in practice as it helps prevent the emergence of new artifacts, sometimes induced by neural networks, such as GANs, in MRI reconstructions [3,32]. To showcase that, we also compared our method to MedGAN [32], one of the SOTA deep learning approaches. MedGAN also alleviated the mild (PSNR: 25.90 ± 2.5, SSIM 0.613 ± 0.1) and the severe (PSNR: 23.14 ± 2.7, SSIM 0.610 ± 0.1) harmonic corruptions. Visually, medGAN images look better than U-Net, however, there is some fine blur in the texture and some new details (see Fig. 3), typically attributed to such generative models. On the contrary, Autofocusing+ takes the physical nature of the motion into account and cannot 'draw' the new features.

Limitations. Having focused on synthetic motion models above, we also report that Autofocusing+ successfully worked on one real motion-corrupted scan from [16], resembling the outcome of our simulated models. Once any real k-space motion-corrupted datasets become available, additional validation will follow.

Similarly to other synthetic motion works [5,16,22], a Cartesian sampling with 2D in-plane motions in the phase encoding direction was assumed. Elastic movements (*e.g.*, compression and stretching in the soft tissues [8]) were beyond the scope of our work and should be revisited, following, *e.g.*, [37].

Stemming from the baseline Autofocusing, and similarly to other optimization-based methods, there is room to improve *the inference time* of Autofocusing+ which takes 7–9 min to process a batch of 10 images. Parallel computing and the pertinent efficient acceleration of the gradients and the Fourier transforms [28] should work well and will be the subject of future work. Likewise, the study of different neural network architectures should be conducted.

Conclusion. In this work, we presented Autofocusing+, a new deep learning-based regularization method to enhance the classic optimization algorithm for compensating the corruption caused by the subject's motion. The blind demotion routine uses the regularizer as an image prior penalizing for unrealistic restorations and improving the reconstruction quality. We validated the method on three models of motion trajectories, proving resilience to noise and anatomic structure variation, and outperforming the SOTA motion correction algorithms.

References

1. Al-masni, M.A., et al.: Stacked U-Nets with self-assisted priors towards robust correction of rigid motion artifact in brain MRI. arXiv preprint arXiv:2111.06401 (2021)
2. Atkinson, D., Hill, D.L., Stoyle, P.N., Summers, P.E., Keevil, S.F.: Automatic correction of motion artifacts in magnetic resonance images using an entropy focus criterion. IEEE Trans. Med. Imaging **16**, 903–910 (1997)
3. Belov, A., Stadelmann, J., Kastryulin, S., Dylov, D.V.: Towards ultrafast MRI via extreme k-space undersampling and superresolution. In: de Bruijne, M., et al. (eds.) MICCAI 2021. LNCS, vol. 12906, pp. 254–264. Springer, Cham (2021). https://doi.org/10.1007/978-3-030-87231-1_25
4. Brown, R.W., Cheng, Y.C.N., Haacke, E.M., Thompson, M.R., Venkatesan, R.: Magnetic Resonance Imaging: Physical Principles and Sequence Design. Wiley, Hoboken (2014)
5. Duffy, B.A., et al.: Retrospective motion artifact correction of structural MRI images using deep learning improves the quality of cortical surface reconstructions. NeuroImage **230**, 117756 (2021)
6. Fessler, J.A., Sutton, B.P.: Nonuniform fast fourier transforms using min-max interpolation. IEEE Trans. Signal Process. **51**, 560–574 (2003)

7. Friston, K.J., Williams, S., Howard, R., Frackowiak, R.S., Turner, R.: Movement-related effects in fMRI time-series. Magn. Reson. Med. **35**, 346–355 (1996)
8. Godenschweger, F., et al.: Motion correction in MRI of the brain. Phys. Med. Biol. **61**(5), R32 (2016)
9. Haskell, M.W., et al.: Network accelerated motion estimation and reduction (NAMER): convolutional neural network guided retrospective motion correction using a separable motion model. Magn. Reson. Med. **82**, 1452–1461 (2019)
10. Havsteen, I., Ohlhues, A., Madsen, K.H., Nybing, J.D., Christensen, H., Christensen, A.: Are movement artifacts in magnetic resonance imaging a real problem?-A narrative review. Front. Neurol. **8**, 232 (2017)
11. Kastryulin, S., Zakirov, J., Pezzotti, N., Dylov, D.V.: Image quality assessment for magnetic resonance imaging (2022). https://arxiv.org/abs/2203.07809
12. Kingma, D.P., Ba, J.L.: Adam: a method for stochastic optimization (2015)
13. Kingma, D.P., Welling, M.: Auto-encoding variational bayes. arXiv preprint arXiv:1312.6114 (2013)
14. Küstner, T., Armanious, K., Yang, J., Yang, B., Schick, F., Gatidis, S.: Retrospective correction of motion-affected MR images using deep learning frameworks. Magn. Reson. Med. **82**(4), 1527–1540 (2019)
15. Larkin, K.G., Oldfield, M.A., Klemm, H.: Fast fourier method for the accurate rotation of sampled images. Opt. Commun. **139**(1–3), 99–106 (1997)
16. Loktyushin, A., Nickisch, H., Pohmann, R., Schölkopf, B.: Blind multirigid retrospective motion correction of MR images. Magn. Reson. Med. **73**, 1457–1468 (2015)
17. Lustig, M., Donoho, D.L., Santos, J.M., Pauly, J.M.: Compressed sensing MRI. IEEE Signal Process. Mag. **25**(2), 72–82 (2008)
18. McGee, K.P., Manduca, A., Felmlee, J.P., Riederer, S.J., Ehman, R.L.: Image metric-based correction (autocorrection) of motion effects: analysis of image metrics. JMRI **11**, 174–181 (2000)
19. Mohan, J., Krishnaveni, V., Guo, Y.: A survey on the magnetic resonance image denoising methods. Biomed. Signal Process. Control **9**, 56–69 (2014)
20. Nehrke, K., Börnert, P.: Prospective correction of affine motion for arbitrary MR sequences on a clinical scanner. Magn. Reson. Med. **54**, 1130–1138 (2005)
21. Nielles-Vallespin, S., et al.: In vivo diffusion tensor MRI of the human heart: reproducibility of breath-hold and navigator-based approaches. Magn. Reson. Med. **70**(2), 454–465 (2013)
22. Oksuz, I., et al.: Deep learning using K-space based data augmentation for automated cardiac MR motion artefact detection. In: Frangi, A.F., Schnabel, J.A., Davatzikos, C., Alberola-López, C., Fichtinger, G. (eds.) MICCAI 2018. LNCS, vol. 11070, pp. 250–258. Springer, Cham (2018). https://doi.org/10.1007/978-3-030-00928-1_29
23. Pronina, V., Kokkinos, F., Dylov, D.V., Lefkimmiatis, S.: Microscopy image restoration with deep Wiener-Kolmogorov filters. In: Vedaldi, A., Bischof, H., Brox, T., Frahm, J.-M. (eds.) ECCV 2020. LNCS, vol. 12365, pp. 185–201. Springer, Cham (2020). https://doi.org/10.1007/978-3-030-58565-5_12
24. Reuter, M., et al.: Head motion during MRI acquisition reduces gray matter volume and thickness estimates. NeuroImage **107**, 107–115 (2015)
25. Ronneberger, O., Fischer, P., Brox, T.: U-Net: convolutional networks for biomedical image segmentation. In: Navab, N., Hornegger, J., Wells, W.M., Frangi, A.F. (eds.) MICCAI 2015. LNCS, vol. 9351, pp. 234–241. Springer, Cham (2015). https://doi.org/10.1007/978-3-319-24574-4_28

26. Savitzky, A., Golay, M.J.: Smoothing and differentiation of data by simplified least squares procedures. Anal. Chem. **36**, 1627–1639 (1964)
27. Sheikh, H.R., Bovik, A.C.: Image information and visual quality. IEEE Trans. Image Process. **15**, 430–444 (2006)
28. Shipitsin, V., Bespalov, I., Dylov, D.V.: Global adaptive filtering layer for computer vision. arXiv preprint arXiv:2010.01177 (2020)
29. Siddique, N., Paheding, S., Elkin, C.P., Devabhaktuni, V.: U-net and its variants for medical image segmentation: a review of theory and applications. IEEE Access **9**, 82031–82057 (2021)
30. Sommer, K., et al.: Correction of motion artifacts using a multiscale fully convolutional neural network. Am. J. Neuroradiol. **41**, 416–423 (2020)
31. Tamada, D., Kromrey, M.L., Ichikawa, S., Onishi, H., Motosugi, U.: Motion artifact reduction using a convolutional neural network for dynamic contrast enhanced MR imaging of the liver. Magn. Reson. Med. Sci. **19**, 64 (2020)
32. Upadhyay, U., Chen, Y., Hepp, T., Gatidis, S., Akata, Z.: Uncertainty-guided progressive GANs for medical image translation. In: de Bruijne, M., et al. (eds.) MICCAI 2021. LNCS, vol. 12903, pp. 614–624. Springer, Cham (2021). https://doi.org/10.1007/978-3-030-87199-4_58
33. Wang, Z., Bovik, A.C., Sheikh, H.R., Simoncelli, E.P.: Image quality assessment: from error visibility to structural similarity. IEEE Trans. Image Process. **13**, 600–612 (2004)
34. Wang, Z., Simoncelli, E.P., Bovik, A.C.: Multiscale structural similarity for image quality assessment. In: The Thrity-Seventh Asilomar Conference on Signals, Systems & Computers, 2003, vol. 2, pp. 1398–1402. IEEE (2003)
35. Wood, M.L., Henkelman, R.M.: MR image artifacts from periodic motion. Med. Phys. **12**, 143–151 (1985)
36. Yang, Z., Zhang, C., Xie, L.: Sparse MRI for motion correction (2013)
37. Zaitsev, M., Maclaren, J., Herbst, M.: Motion artifacts in MRI: a complex problem with many partial solutions (2015)
38. Zbontar, J., et al.: fastMRI: an open dataset and benchmarks for accelerated MRI. arXiv preprint arXiv:1811.08839 (2018)
39. Zhang, K., Zuo, W., Chen, Y., Meng, D., Zhang, L.: Beyond a Gaussian denoiser: residual learning of deep CNN for image denoising. IEEE Trans. Image Process. **26**(7), 3142–3155 (2017)

Tagged-MRI Sequence to Audio Synthesis via Self Residual Attention Guided Heterogeneous Translator

Xiaofeng Liu[1]([✉]), Fangxu Xing[1], Jerry L. Prince[2], Jiachen Zhuo[3], Maureen Stone[3], Georges El Fakhri[1], and Jonghye Woo[1]

[1] Massachusetts General Hospital and Harvard Medical School, Boston, MA, USA
xliu61@mgh.harvard.edu
[2] Johns Hopkins University, Baltimore, MD, USA
[3] University of Maryland, Baltimore, MD, USA

Abstract. Understanding the underlying relationship between tongue and oropharyngeal muscle deformation seen in tagged-MRI and intelligible speech plays an important role in advancing speech motor control theories and treatment of speech related-disorders. Because of their heterogeneous representations, however, direct mapping between the two modalities—i.e., two-dimensional (mid-sagittal slice) plus time tagged-MRI sequence and its corresponding one-dimensional waveform—is not straightforward. Instead, we resort to two-dimensional spectrograms as an intermediate representation, which contains both pitch and resonance, from which to develop an end-to-end deep learning framework to translate from a sequence of tagged-MRI to its corresponding audio waveform with limited dataset size. Our framework is based on a novel fully convolutional asymmetry translator with guidance of a self residual attention strategy to specifically exploit the moving muscular structures during speech. In addition, we leverage a pairwise correlation of the samples with the same utterances with a latent space representation disentanglement strategy. Furthermore, we incorporate an adversarial training approach with generative adversarial networks to offer improved realism on our generated spectrograms. Our experimental results, carried out with a total of 63 tagged-MRI sequences alongside speech acoustics, showed that our framework enabled the generation of clear audio waveforms from a sequence of tagged-MRI, surpassing competing methods. Thus, our framework provides the great potential to help better understand the relationship between the two modalities.

1 Introduction

To facilitate our understanding of speech motor control in healthy and disease populations, associating dynamic imaging data with speech audio waveforms is an essential step in identifying the underlying relationship between tongue and oropharyngeal muscle deformation and its corresponding acoustic information [19,20,31]. Naturally, audio data recorded during scanning sessions need to be

© The Author(s), under exclusive license to Springer Nature Switzerland AG 2022
L. Wang et al. (Eds.): MICCAI 2022, LNCS 13436, pp. 376–386, 2022.
https://doi.org/10.1007/978-3-031-16446-0_36

strictly paired and temporally synced with the dynamic tagged-MRI data to maintain their underlying relationship. However, when examining such paired data, we often face the following difficulties: 1) recorded audio data may be lost or non-existent from previously established tagged-MRI protocols; 2) audio waveforms may be heavily corrupted from scanner noise or poorly controlled noise-reduction protocols; and 3) time-stamps between tagged-MRI and its audio recording do not match and cannot be easily reconstructed without heavy manual intervention. All of these situations prevent pairing of the two data sources and cause missing, partial, or incomplete audio data. Therefore, recovering audio from imaging data itself becomes a necessary topic to be explored.

Heterogeneous data representations between the low-frame rate image sequence (i.e., two-dimensional (mid-sagittal slice) plus time (2D+t) tagged-MRI sequence) and high-frequency one-dimensional (1D) audio waveform make their translation a challenging task [4,18,21,22,29]. Besides, cross-modality speech models often lose pitch information [1,5]. In contrast, a two-dimensional (2D) mel spectrogram converted from its 1D audio waveform represents the energy distribution of audio signals over the frequency domain along the time axis, which contains both pitch and resonance information of audio signals [1,5,8,9]. Then, mel spectrograms can be converted back into audio waveforms [7]. Accordingly, in this work, we opt to use the 2D mel spectrograms as an intermediate means to bridge the gap between tagged-MRI sequences and audio waveforms. This strategy has been applied to cine-MRI to spectrogram synthesis [19].

As a related development in lip reading, early works have focused on using convolutional neural networks (CNN) and linear predictive coding analysis or line spectrum pairs decomposition [5,23] to achieve the goal. These methods, however, failed to maintain the frequency and periodicity of waveforms. To alleviate this, Lip2AudSpec [1] adopted a recurrent neural network (RNN) for the temporal modeling of CNN features, followed by applying fully connected layers to carry out the synthesis of spectrograms from 2D+t videos. However, it is challenging to train RNNs in general [24,28], thereby likely yielding a suboptimal solution, especially when the network is trained on a limited number of datasets [27]. In addition, the fully connected layers employed in Lip2AudSpec cannot capture spatial and temporal correlations [12], and demand massive to-be-trained parameters [6]. Furthermore, image sequences for audio analysis have a large amount of regions that are redundant or irrelevant for voice generation.

To sidestep these issues, we propose a self residual attention-guided heterogeneous translator to achieve an efficient tagged-MRI sequence to spectrogram synthesis. Specifically, we use an end-to-end asymmetric fully convolutional encoder-decoder translator as our backbone. Without the use of RNN and fully connected layers, our network has 10× fewer network parameters than Lip2AudSpec [1]. To explicitly exploit the movements of the tongue and vocal cords, the residual of adjacent frames are processed via a self-learned attention network to render the attention masks to guide the information extraction process. With our framework, we are able to largely eliminate the redundant regions in the tagged-MRI sequence, which allows us to bypass an additional delineation effort. Furthermore, an additional optimization constraint in latent space is imposed following

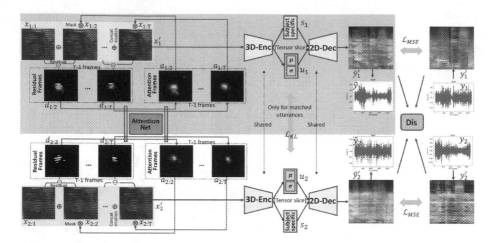

Fig. 1. Illustration of our self residual attention guided heterogeneous translator with latent space disentanglement and adversarial training. Only the gray masked modules are used at the testing stage.

a prior knowledge that part of the feature representation of the same utterance (e.g., "ageese" or "asouk" in this work) are similar to each other. To facilitate the disentanglement of utterance-specific and subject-specific factors in our fully convolutional network, we adopt a tensor slice operation with an information bottleneck to achieve the separation. For pairs with the same utterance, we explicitly enforce their utterance content part as close as possible using the Kullback-Leibler (KL) divergence. Then, the decoder takes into account both the utterance content and the style of the articulation for the spectrogram synthesis. In addition, a generative adversarial network (GAN) loss [26] is added on to yield improved realism on the synthesized spectrograms.

The main contributions of this work can be summarized as follows:

- To our knowledge, this is the first attempt at translating tagged-MRI sequences to audio waveforms.
- We propose a novel self residual attention guided heterogeneous translator to achieve efficient tagged-MRI-to-spectrogram synthesis.
- The utterance and subject factors disentanglement and adversarial training are further explored to improve synthesis performance.

Both quantitative and qualitative evaluation results using a total of 63 participants demonstrate superior performance in synthesis over comparison methods.

2   Methodology

Given a set of training pairs $\{x_i, y_i\}_{i=1}^{N}$ with a sequence of tagged-MRI $x_i \in \mathbb{R}^{H_x \times W_x \times T_x}$ and its corresponding quasi-synchronous audio spectrogram

$y_i \in \mathbb{R}^{1 \times L}$, we target to learn a parameterized heterogeneous translator $\mathcal{F}$: $x_i \rightarrow \tilde{y}'_i$ to generate a spectrogram $\tilde{y}'_i \in \mathbb{R}^{H_s \times W_s}$ from x_i, with the aim to resemble the spectrogram y'_i of y_i. We denote the height, width and frames of x_i as H_x, W_x, and T_x, respectively. In addition, L is the length of the waveform y_i, and $H_s \times W_s$ indicates the size of the spectrogram. In this work, all of the audio waveforms are converted into mel spectrograms with $\mathcal{M} : y_i \rightarrow y'^1_i$ as an intermediate means to facilitate the translation. The mel-scale results from the non-linear transformations of a Hz-scale, thereby emphasizing the human voice frequency (e.g., 40 to 1000 Hz) and suppressing the high-frequency instrument noise.

2.1   Asymmetric Fully-CNN Translator with Self Residual Attention

In order to achieve the heterogeneous translation, we propose a novel self residual attention guided fully CNN translator with a pairwise disentanglement scheme, as shown in Fig. 1. We note that the generation of temporal sequences usually relies on RNNs, which can be challenging to train [24,28]. In addition, connecting CNNs with RNNs using the fully connected layers is likely to lose the relative spatial and temporal information [12]. Considering the inherent discrepancy between x_i and y'_i, we equip our f with an asymmetric encoder-decoder structure. Since the input sequence of tagged-MRI x_i usually has a fixed number of MR images, e.g., $T = 26$, we use the 3D-CNN encoder [13] for fast encoding. Notably, each 3D convolutional layer yields the same dimension in the temporal direction, where the dimension is reduced by half after each 3D MaxPooling operation to adaptively summarize the temporal information. For the decoder, we adopt a 2D-CNN with deconvolutional layers to synthesis $\tilde{y}'_i$. With the training pair $\{x_i, y_i\}$, the reconstruction loss can be a crucial supervision signal. We empirically adopt the mean square error (MSE) loss as:

$$\mathcal{L}_{rec} = ||\tilde{y}'_i - y'_i||^2_2 = ||\mathcal{F}(x_i) - \mathcal{M}(y_i)||^2_2. \tag{1}$$

Compared with conventional video analysis, tagged-MRI sequences contain highly redundant and irrelevant information for audio synthesis, since voice generation only involves a small region of interest, including the tongue and vocal cords. To specifically explore the moving muscular structures from tagged-MRI sequences, we explicitly emphasize the moving muscular structures related to speech production with an attention strategy. In particular, we denote the t-th time frame in each x_i as $x_{i:t}$, $t \in \{1, \cdots, T\}$, and calculate the difference between two adjacent frames $d_{i:t} = |x_{i:t} - x_{i:t-1}|$ for $t \in \{2, \cdots, T\}$ as the residual frames to indicate the moving regions. Then, each residual frame $d_{i:t} \in \mathbb{R}^{H_x \times W_x}$ is processed with a self-trained attention network $\mathcal{A}$ to yield the fine-grained corresponding attention mask $a_{i:t} \in \mathbb{R}^{H_x \times W_x}$ for $t \in \{2, \cdots, T\}$. Then, the obtained attention mask $a_{i:t}$ is multiplied by the original tagged-MRI frame $x_{i:t}$ to generate the attentive frame $x'_{i:t} = a_{i:t} \otimes x_{i:t}$, which allows the network to filter the

---

[1] Link: The librosa for audio to mel-spectrogram.

redundant static parts out. We adopt a conventional 2D encoder-decoder structure as $\mathcal{A}$, which is jointly optimized with $\mathcal{F}$, by minimizing $\mathcal{L}_{rec}$. Therefore, $\mathcal{A}$ is encouraged to adaptively learn to keep the essential information to guarantee synthesis performance, following a self-training fashion. Of note, we do not need an additional attention label to guide the training.

2.2 Pair-Wise Disentanglement Training

To exploit prior knowledge of the utterance content similarity in the latent space, an additional constraint is imposed in the latent space. We first disentangle the latent feature as an utterance-specific factor u_i and a subject-specific factor s_i. Then, similar to deep metric learning [16], the recorded x_i, speaking the same utterance, is encouraged to have similar latent representations as u_i. Empirically, although a multi-branch network can be used to split two parts, it could be inefficient for a fully-CNN framework. Instead, therefore, we propose to differentiate the specific channels in the feature representation from the tensor slice operation [12][2].

For a pair of inputs $\{x_1, x_2\}$ with the same utterance, we explicitly enforce their $\{u_1, u_2\}$ to approximate each other. We opt to measure and minimize their discrepancy using the KL divergence with the reparameterization trick. In practice, we leverage the Gaussian prior and choose a few channels for the feature to denote the mean μ_i and variance σ_i, where μ_i has the same size as σ_i. We then make use of the reparametrization trick $u_i = \mu_i + \sigma_i \odot \epsilon_i$ to represent u_i with μ_i and σ_i, where $\epsilon \in \mathcal{N}(0, I)$ [17]. The detailed KL divergence between u_1 and u_2 is given by:

$$\mathcal{L}_{KL} = -\frac{1}{2} \sum_{m=1}^{M} [1 + \log\frac{\sigma_{1m}^2}{\sigma_{2m}^2} - \frac{\sigma_{1m}^2}{\sigma_{2m}^2} - \frac{(\mu_{1m} - \mu_{2m})^2}{\sigma_{2m}^2}], \qquad (2)$$

where M represents the number of channels of the mean or variance ($M = 14$ in our implementation). $\mathcal{L}_{KL}$ is only applied to the same utterance pairs.

In parallel, s_i is encouraged to inherit the subject-specific factors with an implicit complementary constraint [11,15]. By enforcing the information bottleneck, i.e., compact or low-dimensional latent feature [11], s_i has to incorporate all the necessary complementary content (e.g., subject-specific style of the articulation) other than u_i to achieve accurate reconstruction. Therefore, the generative task in the decoder is essentially taking s_i conditioned on u_i, which models an utterance-conditioned spectrogram distribution, following a divide-and-conquer strategy [2,14].

2.3 Adversarial Loss and Overall Training Protocol

To further improve quality in our generated spectrograms, we leverage a GAN module. The discriminator $\mathcal{D}$ takes as input both the real mel spectrogram

---

[2] Link: Slicing the tensor in PyTorch.

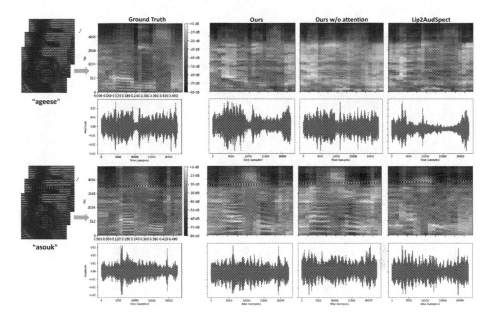

Fig. 2. Comparisons of our framework with Lip2AudSpect and ablation studies of the attention strategy. The audio files are attached in supplementary materials.

$y'_i = \mathcal{M}(y_i)$ the generated mel spectrogram $\tilde{y}'_i$, followed by identifying which is generated or real. The binary cross-entropy loss of the discriminator can be expressed as:

$$\mathcal{L}_{\mathcal{D}} = \mathbb{E}_{y'_i}\{\log(\mathcal{D}(y'_i))\} + \mathbb{E}_{\tilde{y}'_i}\{\log(1 - \mathcal{D}(\tilde{y}'_i))\}. \tag{3}$$

In contrast, the translator attempts to confuse the discriminator, by yielding realistic spectrograms [17]. Notably, the translator does not involve real spectrograms in $\log(\mathcal{D}(y'_i))$ [26]. Therefore, the translator can be trained, by optimizing the following objective:

$$\mathcal{L}_{\mathcal{F}:\mathcal{D}} = \mathbb{E}_{\tilde{y}'_i}\{-\log(1 - \mathcal{D}(\tilde{y}'_i))\}. \tag{4}$$

In summary, we jointly optimize the following objectives for the translator, attention network, and discriminator:

$$\min_{\mathcal{F}} \mathcal{L}_{rec} + \beta\mathcal{L}_{KL} + \lambda\mathcal{L}_{\mathcal{F}:\mathcal{D}}; \quad \min_{\mathcal{A}} \mathcal{L}_{rec}; \quad \min_{\mathcal{D}} \mathcal{L}_{\mathcal{D}}, \tag{5}$$

where β and λ represent the weighting parameters. Of note, $\beta = 0$ for the pairs with the different utterances.

In testing, the translator $\mathcal{F}$ is used to make inference, as shown in Fig. 1; in addition, the pairwise inputs and the discriminator are not used. Thus, the pairwise framework and additional adversarial training do not affect the inference speed in implementation. Of note, it is straightforward to convert the spectrograms into waveforms, once we obtain the spectrograms[3].

---

[3] Link: The librosa library for reversing mel-spectrogram to audio.

Table 1. Numerical comparisons in testing with leave-one-out evaluation. The best results are **bold**.

Methods	Corr2D for spectrogram ↑	PESQ for waveform ↑
Lip2AudSpect [1]	0.665 ± 0.014	1.235 ± 0.021
Ours	$\mathbf{0.813} \pm 0.010$	$\mathbf{1.620} \pm 0.017$
Ours w/o Attention	0.781 ± 0.012	1.517 ± 0.025
Ours w/o Pair-wise Disentangle	0.798 ± 0.010	1.545 ± 0.019
Ours w/o GAN	0.808 ± 0.012	1.586 ± 0.023

3   Experiments and Results

To demonstrate the effectiveness of our framework, a total of 63 pairs of tagged-MRI sequences and audio waveforms were acquired, while a total of 43 participants performed a speech word "asouk," and a total of 20 participants performed a speech word "ageese," following a periodic metronome-like sound. A Siemens 3.0T TIM Trio system was used to acquire our data for which we used a 12-channel head coil and a 4-channel neck coil using a segmented gradient echo sequence [10,30]. Imaging parameters are as follows: the field of view was 240 mm × 240 mm on the mid-sagittal slice with a resolution of 1.87 mm × 1.87 mm. Each tagged-MRI sequence had 26 time frames, which was then resized to 128 × 128. The corresponding audio waveforms had their length varying from 21,832 to 24,175. To augment the datasets, we utilized a sliding window alongside the audio to crop a section with 21,000 time points, generating 100× audio data. Then, we used the Librosa library to convert all of the audio waveforms into mel spectrograms with the size of 64 × 64. In our evaluation, leave-one-out evaluation is used in a subject-independent manner.

In practice, our encoder took five 3D convolutional layers, followed by the tensor slice and a decoder with four 2D deconvolutional layers. The rectified linear unit (ReLU) was used as an activation unit, while the sigmoid function was utilized to normalize the final output of each pixel. The attention network used a 2D encoder and decoder structure with four convolutional and four symmetric deconcolutional layers, which is followed by the 1 × 1 convolution with sigmoid unit. We used three convolutional layers and two fully connected layers with a sigmoid output as our discriminator. We separate the latent representation with 128 channels into three parts, i.e., 14 channels for both the mean and variance of the utterance-specific factors, and the remaining 100 channels for the subject-specific factors. Due to space limitations, we provide the detailed network structure in supplementary.

We implemented our framework using PyTorch and trained it on an NVIDIA V100 GPU, which took about 4.5 h. In testing, the inference took only 0.5 s. The learning rate was set at $lr_{\mathcal{F}} = 10^{-3}$, $lr_{\mathcal{A}} = 10^{-3}$, and $lr_{\mathcal{D}} = 10^{-4}$ and the

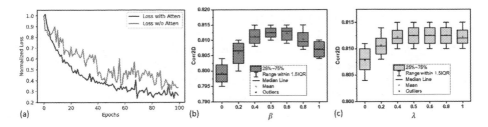

Fig. 3. (a) Comparison of normalized loss using our framework with or without the self residual attention strategy. Sensitivity analysis of β (b) and λ (c).

momentum was set at 0.5. To balance the involved optimization objectives, we used $\beta = 0.5$ or 0 for the same or different utterance pairs, and set $\lambda = 0.5$.

Figure 2 shows the qualitative results of our framework with and without the attention strategy and a comparison method. For comparison, we reimplemented Lip2AudSpect [1] suitable to process tagged MRI data. We can see that our generated spectrogram and the recovered corresponding audio waveforms align better with the ground truth than the Lip2AudSpect, which uses a relatively sophisticated CNN-RNN-fully connected structure. We note that the 3D CNN used in Lip2AudSpect has a temporal window size of 5, which can only extract the local temporal correlation. Thus, Lip2AudSpect relies on RNN for long-term temporal modeling, which renders a difficulty in training on a limited number of datasets. To show the effectiveness of our self-attention strategy, we also provide the ablation study in Fig. 2, showing our superior performance over the comparison methods.

For quantitative evaluation, we followed [1] to adopt 2D Pearson's correlation coefficient (Corr2D) to measure the spectrogram synthesis quality in the frequency domain [3]. In addition, the standard Perceptual Evaluation of Speech Quality (PESQ) was used to measure the quality of generated waveforms in the time domain [25]. The numerical comparisons among our framework, its ablation studies, and Lip2AudSpect [1] are provided in Table 1. The standard deviation was reported by three random trials. Our framework outperformed Lip2AudSpect [1] consistently. In addition, the synthesis performance was improved by the attention strategy, by a large margin. Furthermore, the performances of the pair-wise disentanglement and GAN loss were demonstrated as the ablation studies, showing their effectiveness in our overall network design to yield accurate synthesis results.

In Fig. 3(a), we show that our proposed self residual attention strategy achieves a stable loss decrease, via the information extraction module, without being distracted by the redundant surrounding areas. As shown in Figs. 3(b) and 3(c), the performance is relatively stable for $\beta \in [0.4, 0.6]$ to impose pair-wise disentanglement. In addition, the GAN loss was effective for $\lambda \in [0.4, 0.8]$.

4   Discussion and Conclusion

In this work, we proposed a novel framework to synthesize spectrograms from tagged-MRI sequences. The audio waveforms can also be obtained from the synthesized spectrograms. In particular, we proposed an efficient fully convolutional asymmetry translator with help of a self residual attention strategy to specifically focus on the moving muscular structures for speech production. Additionally, we used a pairwise correlation of the samples with the same utterances with a latent space representation disentanglement scheme. Furthermore, we incorporated an adversarial training approach with GAN to yield improved results on our generated spectrograms. Our experimental results showed that our framework was able to successfully synthesize spectrograms (and clear waveforms) from tagged-MRI sequences, outperforming the Lipreading based method. Therefore, our framework offered the potential to help clinicians improve treatment strategies for patients with speech-related disorders. In future work, we will investigate the use of full three-dimensional plus time tagged-MRI sequences as well as tracking information from tagged-MRI to achieve spectrogram synthesis.

Acknowledgements. This work is supported by NIH R01DC014717, R01DC018511, and R01CA133015.

References

1. Akbari, H., Arora, H., Cao, L., Mesgarani, N.: Lip2audspec: speech reconstruction from silent lip movements video. In: ICASSP, pp. 2516–2520. IEEE (2018)
2. Che, T., et al.: Deep verifier networks: verification of deep discriminative models with deep generative models. In: AAAI (2021)
3. Chi, T., Ru, P., Shamma, S.A.: Multiresolution spectrotemporal analysis of complex sounds. J. Acoust. Soc. Am. **118**(2), 887–906 (2005)
4. Chung, J.S., Zisserman, A.: Lip reading in the wild. In: Lai, S.-H., Lepetit, V., Nishino, K., Sato, Y. (eds.) ACCV 2016. LNCS, vol. 10112, pp. 87–103. Springer, Cham (2017). https://doi.org/10.1007/978-3-319-54184-6_6
5. Ephrat, A., Peleg, S.: Vid2speech: speech reconstruction from silent video. In: ICASSP, pp. 5095–5099. IEEE (2017)
6. Goodfellow, I., Bengio, Y., Courville, A.: Deep Learning (adaptive Computation And Machine Learning Series). MIT Press, Cambridge (2017)
7. Griffin, D., Lim, J.: Signal estimation from modified short-time Fourier transform. IEEE Trans. Acoust. Speech Signal Process. **32**(2), 236–243 (1984)
8. He, G., Liu, X., Fan, F., You, J.: Classification-aware semi-supervised domain adaptation. In: Proceedings of the IEEE/CVF Conference on Computer Vision and Pattern Recognition Workshops, pp. 964–965 (2020)
9. He, G., Liu, X., Fan, F., You, J.: Image2audio: facilitating semi-supervised audio emotion recognition with facial expression image. In: Proceedings of the IEEE/CVF Conference on Computer Vision and Pattern Recognition Workshops, pp. 912–913 (2020)
10. Lee, J., Woo, J., Xing, F., Murano, E.Z., Stone, M., Prince, J.L.: Semi-automatic segmentation of the tongue for 3D motion analysis with dynamic MRI. In: ISBI, pp. 1465–1468. IEEE (2013)

11. Liu, X., Chao, Y., You, J.J., Kuo, C.C.J., Vijayakumar, B.: Mutual information regularized feature-level Frankenstein for discriminative recognition. In: IEEE TPAMI (2021)

12. Liu, X., Che, T., Lu, Y., Yang, C., Li, S., You, J.: AUTO3D: novel view synthesis through unsupervisely learned variational viewpoint and global 3D representation. In: Vedaldi, A., Bischof, H., Brox, T., Frahm, J.-M. (eds.) ECCV 2020. LNCS, vol. 12354, pp. 52–71. Springer, Cham (2020). https://doi.org/10.1007/978-3-030-58545-7_4

13. Liu, X., Guo, Z., You, J., Kumar, B.V.: Dependency-aware attention control for image set-based face recognition. IEEE Trans. Inf. Forensic. Secur. **15**, 1501–1512 (2019)

14. Liu, X., et al.: Domain generalization under conditional and label shifts via variational Bayesian inference. In: IJCAI (2021)

15. Liu, X., Li, S., Kong, L., Xie, W., Jia, P., You, J., Kumar, B.: Feature-level Frankenstein: Eliminating variations for discriminative recognition. In: CVPR, pp. 637–646 (2019)

16. Liu, X., Vijaya Kumar, B., You, J., Jia, P.: Adaptive deep metric learning for identity-aware facial expression recognition. In: CVPR, pp. 20–29 (2017)

17. Liu, X., et al.: Dual-cycle constrained bijective VAE-GAN for tagged-to-cine magnetic resonance image synthesis. In: ISBI, pp. 1448–1452. IEEE (2021)

18. Liu, X., Xing, F., Prince, J.L., Stone, M., El Fakhri, G., Woo, J.: Structure-aware unsupervised tagged-to-cine MRI synthesis with self disentanglement. In: Medical Imaging 2022: Image Processing, vol. 12032, pp. 470–476. SPIE (2022)

19. Liu, X., et al.: CMRI2spec: Cine MRI sequence to spectrogram synthesis via a pairwise heterogeneous translator. In: ICASSP 2022–2022 IEEE International Conference on Acoustics, Speech and Signal Processing (ICASSP), pp. 1481–1485. IEEE (2022)

20. Liu, X., et al.: Tagged-MRI to audio synthesis with a pairwise heterogeneous deep translator. J. Acoust. Soc. Am. **151**(4), A133–A133 (2022)

21. Liu, X., et al.: Generative self-training for cross-domain unsupervised tagged-to-cine MRI synthesis. In: de Bruijne, M., et al. (eds.) MICCAI 2021. LNCS, vol. 12903, pp. 138–148. Springer, Cham (2021). https://doi.org/10.1007/978-3-030-87199-4_13

22. Liu, X., et al.: Symmetric-constrained irregular structure inpainting for brain MRI registration with tumor pathology. In: Crimi, A., Bakas, S. (eds.) BrainLes 2020. LNCS, vol. 12658, pp. 80–91. Springer, Cham (2021). https://doi.org/10.1007/978-3-030-72084-1_8

23. Michelsanti, D., et al.: An overview of deep-learning-based audio-visual speech enhancement and separation. IEEE/ACM Trans. Audio Speech Lang. Process. **29**, 1368–1396 (2021)

24. Pascanu, R., Mikolov, T., Bengio, Y.: On the difficulty of training recurrent neural networks. In: ICML, pp. 1310–1318. PMLR (2013)

25. Recommendation, I.T.: Perceptual evaluation of speech quality PESQ): an objective method for end-to-end speech quality assessment of narrow-band telephone networks and speech codecs. Rec. ITU-T P. 862 (2001)

26. Salimans, T., Goodfellow, I., Zaremba, W., Cheung, V., Radford, A., Chen, X.: Improved techniques for training gans. NIPS **29**, 2234–2242 (2016)

27. Wang, J., et al.: Automated interpretation of congenital heart disease from multiview echocardiograms. Med. Image Anal. **69**, 101942 (2021)

28. Xie, W., Liang, L., Lu, Y., Luo, H., Liu, X.: Deep 3D-CNN for depression diagnosis with facial video recording of self-rating depression scale questionnaire. In: JBHI (2021)

29. Xing, F., Liu, X., Kuo, J., Fakhri, G., Woo, J.: Brain MR atlas construction using symmetric deep neural inpainting. IEEE J. Biomed. Health Inform. **26**, 3185–3196 (2022)

30. Xing, F., et al.: 3D tongue motion from tagged and cine MR images. In: Mori, K., Sakuma, I., Sato, Y., Barillot, C., Navab, N. (eds.) MICCAI 2013. LNCS, vol. 8151, pp. 41–48. Springer, Heidelberg (2013). https://doi.org/10.1007/978-3-642-40760-4_6

31. Yu, Y., Shandiz, A.H., Tóth, L.: Reconstructing speech from real-time articulatory MRI using neural vocoders. In: 2021 29th European Signal Processing Conference (EUSIPCO), pp. 945–949. IEEE (2021)

Only-Train-Once MR Fingerprinting for Magnetization Transfer Contrast Quantification

Beomgu Kang[1] , Hye-Young Heo[2] , and HyunWook Park[1]([✉])

[1] School of Electrical Engineering, Korea Advanced Institute of Science and Technology, Daejeon, Republic of Korea
{almona,hwpark}@kaist.ac.kr
[2] Division of MR Research, Department of Radiology, Johns Hopkins University, Baltimore, MD, USA
hheo1@jhmi.edu

Abstract. Magnetization transfer contrast magnetic resonance fingerprinting (MTC-MRF) is a novel quantitative imaging technique that simultaneously measures several tissue parameters of semisolid macromolecule and free bulk water. In this study, we propose an Only-Train-Once MR fingerprinting (OTOM) framework that estimates the free bulk water and MTC tissue parameters from MR fingerprints regardless of MRF schedule, thereby avoiding time-consuming process such as generation of training dataset and network training according to each MRF schedule. A recurrent neural network is designed to cope with two types of variants of MRF schedules: 1) various lengths and 2) various patterns. Experiments on digital phantoms and *in vivo* data demonstrate that our approach can achieve accurate quantification for the water and MTC parameters with multiple MRF schedules. Moreover, the proposed method is in excellent agreement with the conventional deep learning and fitting methods. The flexible OTOM framework could be an efficient tissue quantification tool for various MRF protocols.

Keywords: Deep learning · MR fingerprinting · Magnetization transfer contrast · Recurrent neural network · Transfer learning

1 Introduction

Magnetization transfer contrast (MTC) imaging is a MRI technique that provides information about semisolid macromolecular protons, based on the transfer of their magnetization to surrounding free bulk water [5,20,24]. Since the macromolecules are not directly detectable in MRI, due to the extremely short T_2, the continuous saturation of solute protons with radiofrequency (RF) irradiation and the subsequent transfer of proton allow us to assess the macromolecular protons indirectly from the reduced water signal. In traditional MTC experiments, magnetization transfer ratio (MTR), the ratio between two images acquired with and

© The Author(s), under exclusive license to Springer Nature Switzerland AG 2022
L. Wang et al. (Eds.): MICCAI 2022, LNCS 13436, pp. 387–396, 2022.
https://doi.org/10.1007/978-3-031-16446-0_37

without RF saturation, has been widely used in the clinic [2,18]. Nonetheless, the qualitative nature of MTR metric, including its high dependency on scan parameters and tissue relaxation effects, limits its clinical usefulness.

To address this issue, magnetic resonance fingerprinting (MRF) technique was introduced in MTC imaging as a promising and time efficient technique that simultaneously quantified multiple tissue parameters [6,10,16]. In MRF acquisition, time-varying signal evolution is achieved by intentionally varying imaging parameters for each scan. The acquired evolution is the distinguishing characteristics for a set of tissue parameters, so called a fingerprint. Then, the acquired fingerprints of a voxel are mapped with a pre-calculated dictionary. However, dictionary matching based techniques suffer from an exhaustive search and the dictionary discretization issue. Recent studies in deep learning based MRF techniques have showed their powerful ability to map a MR fingerprint space to a tissue parameter space, greatly accelerating the reconstruction and improving the quantification accuracy [1,11,13,17].

However, the deep neural networks were constrained to a single MRF schedule corresponding to the training dataset. If the MRF schedule is changed, the deep neural network has to be trained with new training dataset that was generated with the new MRF schedule. This process is very time consuming and inefficient. Therefore, the utility of MRF techniques would benefit greatly from the development of streamlined deep learning frameworks or even only-train-once methods for various MRF sequences. Recently, to streamline the deep learning process, dataset generation was accelerated using a parallel execution of large-scale MR signal simulations with exact MR physics models on graphics processing units (GPUs) [21,22]. To further accelerate the simulations, deep neural networks have been proposed as surrogate physics models for computing MR signals [4,15,23]. Although the simulation-accelerated approach can largely reduce the time

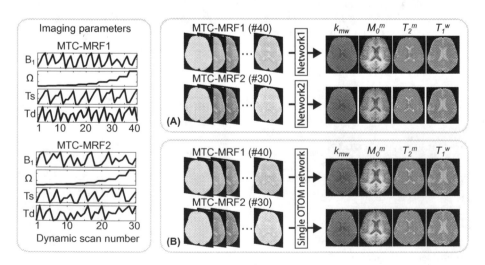

Fig. 1. (A) The original deep learning MRF framework. (B) The proposed framework.

complexity of MR signal models, re-training of the deep neural network remains to be a challenge.

In this study, we propose an Only-Train-Once MR fingerprinting (OTOM) framework that maps a MR fingerprint space and a scan parameter space into a tissue parameter space. The proposed method can be applied to any MRF schedules unlike the previous deep learning based studies dedicated to only a single fixed MRF schedule (Fig. 1).

2   Methods

2.1   Signal Model: Transient-State MTC-MRF

A two pool exchange model, including the free bulk water pool (w) and the semisolid macromolecule pool (m), is used to simulate the MTC-MRF signal in the presence of proton exchange and RF irradiation. The magnetization of each pool can be described with the modified Bloch-McConnell equations. By solving the coupled differential equation, the transient-state MTC-MRF signal evolution ($S_{MTC-MRF}$) can be described using the following signal equation [8,19]:

$$S_{MTC-MRF}(T_1^w, T_1^m, T_2^w, T_2^m, k_{mw}, M_0^m; B_1, \Omega, Ts, Td)$$
$$= \left[M_0^w \left(1 - e^{-Td/T_1^w} \right) - M_{ss}^w \right] e^{-\lambda Ts} + M_{ss}^w$$

where T_1^i and T_2^i are the longitudinal and transverse relaxation times of a pool i, respectively; k_{ij} is the proton exchange rate from a pool i to a pool j; M_0^i is the equilibrium magnetization of a pool i; M_{ss}^w is the steady-state longitudinal magnetization of the free bulk water; B_1 is the RF saturation power; Ω is the frequency offset of the RF saturation; Ts is the saturation time; Td is the relaxation delay time.

Deep learning was incorporated with the analytical solution of the MTC-MRF signal model to understand complex relation among the fingerprint space ($S_{MTC-MRF}$), the scan parameter space (B_1, Ω, Ts, and Td) and the tissue parameter space (k_{mw}, M_0^m, T_2^m and T_1^w).

2.2   Proposed Model

Recurrent Neural Network (RNN). The RNN architecture was designed to quantify the free bulk water and semisolid MTC parameters from given MTC fingerprints and the corresponding scan parameters. As shown in Fig. 2A, the architecture of the proposed quantification network consists of bi-directional LSTM (Long short-term memory) [3] and a single fully connected layer (Dense in Fig. 2A). The bi-LSTM (bi-directional LSTM) processes an input sequence in two ways: moving forward from the start to the end of the sequence, and moving backward from the end to the start of the sequence. LSTM extracts features from each time point of the input sequence and accumulates the features in the form of a hidden state. Forward and backward hidden states at the end are

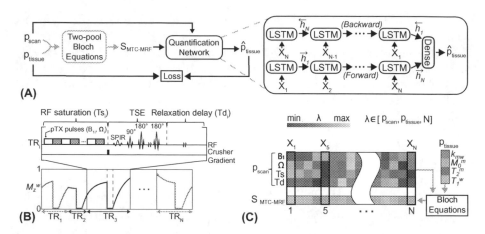

Fig. 2. An overview of the OTOM framework. (A) A recurrent neural network for the water and MTC quantification. (B) The evolution of the longitudinal magnetization of water according to the turbo spin-echo (TSE)-based MTC-MRF schedule. (C) The length (N), scan parameters (p_{scan}), and tissue parameters (p_{tissue}) are randomly sampled within the pre-defined range and used to generate MRF signal through Bloch equations.

concatenated and fed to the dense layer to estimate the four tissue parameters (p_{tissue}) of k_{mw}, M_0^m, T_2^m, and T_1^w, as follows:

$$\overrightarrow{h}_i = R\left(X_i, \overrightarrow{h}_{i-1}; \theta\right) \tag{1}$$

$$\overleftarrow{h}_i = R\left(X_i, \overleftarrow{h}_{i+1}; \theta\right) \tag{2}$$

$$\widehat{p}_{tissue} = f\left(\overrightarrow{h}_N, \overleftarrow{h}_1\right) \tag{3}$$

$$X_i = [S_{MTC-MRF}, B_1, \Omega, Ts, Td]_i, \ i = 1, \cdots, N \tag{4}$$

where X_i is the input vector of ith time point; $\overrightarrow{h}_i$ and $\overleftarrow{h}_i$ are the forward and backward hidden states, respectively, at i^{th} time point; θ represents the parameters of the LSTM; R denotes the LSTM network; f is the dense layer followed by rectified linear units (ReLU); and N is the number of dynamic scans of the MRF sequence. The LSTM consists of three layers with 512 hidden units. The RNN architecture was trained by minimizing the absolute difference between the label parameter p_{tissue} and the estimated parameter $\widehat{p}_{tissue}$, as follows:

$$L_\theta = |p_{tissue} - \widehat{p}_{tissue}| \tag{5}$$

The RNN network was implemented using Pytorch 1.8.1 on an NVIDIA TITAN RTX GPU (Santa Clara, CA). The adaptive moment estimation (ADAM) optimizer [14] was used with the initial learning rate of 10^{-3} and a batch size of 256. The learning rate was scheduled to be decreased by a factor of 0.1 for every 5 epochs. The training data was randomly divided into two parts: 90% for training and 10% for validation. The validation loss was used for model selection and early stopping.

Dataset Generation. The analytical solution of Bloch-McConnell equations (Eq. (1)) was used to generate MTC-MRF signal ($S_{MTC-MRF}$) for given tissue parameters and scan parameters. To train the RNN model that successfully processes random MRF schedules, two variants of MRF schedules with respect to the length and the pattern were considered (Fig. 2C). For scan parameters $p_{scan}=[B_1, \Omega, \text{Ts}, \text{Td}]$,

1) The length of MRF (N) was randomly selected within the range of 10 to 40.
2) The MRF schedule s $= [p_{scan,1}, p_{scan,2}, \ldots, p_{scan,N}]$ was randomly sampled, where every scan parameter was constrained to the pre-defined range: 8–50 ppm for frequency offsets (Ω); 0.5–2.0 µT for RF saturation power (B_1); 0.4–2.0 s for RF saturation time (Ts); and 3.5–5.0 s for relaxation delay time (Td).

For tissue parameters $p_{scan} = [k_{mw}, M_0^m, T_2^m, T_1^w]$, each parameter was randomly sampled. The ranges of tissue parameters were: 5–100 Hz for k_{mw}; 2–17% for M_0^m; 1–100 µs for T_2^m; and 0.2–3.0 s for T_1^w. To generate the training dataset, 80 million combinations of scan and tissue parameters were chosen as explained. Finally, white Gaussian noise (SNR = 46 dB) was added to the simulated MTC-MRF signals. The Gaussian noise level was determined from the estimated SNR of the acquired *in vivo* images.

Transfer Learning (TL). To gauge how the OTOM is well optimized for each schedule, TL was used. The OTOM is a baseline container model that can processes any given MRF schedule. Therefore, TL to a specific MRF schedule was available to further optimize the network. For the training dataset, ten million sets of tissue parameters were randomly sampled with the target MRF sequence. The OTOM-T (OTOM-Transfer) network was trained for 3 epochs with the adaptive moment estimation (ADAM) optimizer. The learning rate was scheduled to be decreased by a factor of 0.1 for every 2 epochs and the initial rate was 10^{-4} with a batch size of 256.

3 Experiments

3.1 Digital Phantom Study: Bloch Simulation

The performance of the OTOM framework was validated with the Bloch-McConnell equation-based simulation (Fig. 3). Four digital phantoms were constructed to have five uniformly sampled constant values for a single parameter while the other parameters were randomly sampled within the pre-defined ranges. Five uniformly sampled values for each phantom were: 5, 25, 50, 75, 100 Hz for k_{mw}, 2, 6, 10, 14, and 17 % for M_0^m, 1, 25, 50, 75, and 100 µs for T_2^m, and 0.2, 0.9, 1.6, 2.3, and 3.0 s for T_1^w. The quantification accuracy was evaluated

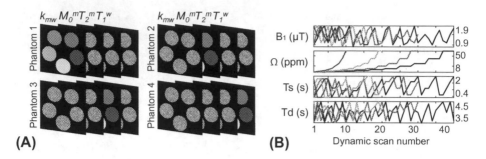

Fig. 3. Bloch-McConnell equation-based digital phantom study. (A) Ground truths for four digital phantoms (B) Four pseudo-random (PR) schedules with different numbers of dynamic scans (N = 10, 20, 30, and 40) were used to simulate MTC-MRF images.

Table 1. Quantitative evaluation of mean absolute error (MAE) from OTOM, FCNN and Bloch fitting methods for Bloch-McConnell equation-based digital phantoms.

Schedule with length	Method	MAE			
		k_{mw} (Hz)	M_0^m (%)	T_2^m (μs)	T_1^w (ms)
PR#40	OTOM	10.29	0.581	1.501	21.70
	FCNN	**10.09**	**0.547**	**1.385**	**20.75**
	Bloch fitting	12.07	0.735	2.437	24.06
PR#30	OTOM	11.19	0.658	1.708	23.23
	FCNN	**11.18**	**0.644**	**1.638**	**22.89**
	Bloch fitting	13.10	0.842	2.728	26.74
PR#20	OTOM	11.84	0.783	2.044	31.81
	FCNN	**11.78**	**0.778**	**1.971**	**31.50**
	Bloch fitting	13.70	1.037	3.725	43.53
PR#10	OTOM	**13.91**	0.980	2.713	42.37
	FCNN	13.94	**0.973**	**2.689**	**42.10**
	Bloch fitting	16.10	1.325	4.896	61.85

using pseudo-random (PR) schedules with various numbers of dynamic scans (N = 10, 20, 30, and 40) by calculating mean absolute errors (MAE). Reconstruction results of the OTOM method were compared with those of the Bloch fitting [6] and FCNN-based deep learning approach [13]. For the FCNN method, four different FCNN networks were respectively trained for the corresponding four PR schedules. The PR schedules were generated by minimizing the information redundancy between multiple dynamic scans [12].

3.2 In Vivo Experiments

Six healthy volunteers (M/F: 2/4; age: 36.2 ± 3.7 years) were scanned on a Philips Achieva 3T MRI system with the approval of the institutional review

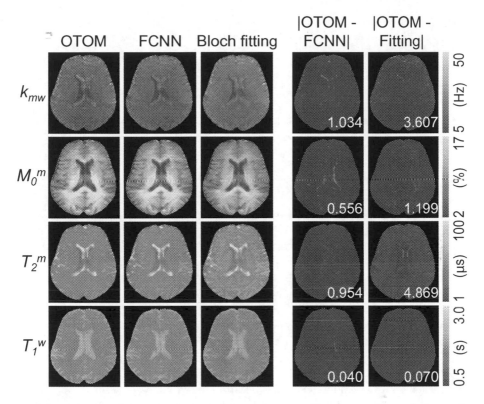

Fig. 4. Representative MTC parameters and water T_1 map estimated using the OTOM, FCNN, and Bloch fitting methods. Difference images of the estimated maps with OTOM versus FCNN and fitting methods. The mean difference value of each map is shown in the insert (white).

board at Johns Hopkins university, and written informed consent was obtained prior to the MRI experiments. The 3D MTC-MRF images were acquired from a fat-suppressed (spectral pre-saturation with inversion recovery) multi-shot TSE pulse sequence. All image scans were obtained with 4× compressed sensing (CS) accelerations in the two phase-encoding directions (ky-kz) [9]. The imaging parameters were: TE = 6 ms; FOV = $212 \times 186 \times 60\,\text{mm}^3$, spatial resolution = $1.8 \times 1.8 \times 4\,\text{mm}^3$, slice-selective 120° refocusing pulses, turbo factor = 104, and slice oversampling factor = 1.4. The two-channel time-interleaved parallel RF transmission (pTX) technique was used to achieve continuous RF saturation of 100% duty-cycle by distributing the saturation burden into two amplifiers [7]. Forty dynamic scans were acquired with various RF saturation powers (B_1), frequency offsets (Ω), RF saturation times (Ts), and relaxation delay times (Td) according to the PR schedule. To normalize the MTC-MRF images, an additional unsaturated image (S_0) was acquired.

Table 2. Quantitative evaluation of OTOM-T (OTOM-Transfer) and FCNN methods with PR #40 schedule on Bloch-McConnell equation-based digital phantoms.

Method	MAE				Data preparation and training
	k_{mw} (Hz)	M_0^m (%)	T_2^m (μs)	T_1^w (ms)	
OTOM (Baseline)	10.29	0.581	1.501	21.70	-
OTOM-T	**10.06**	**0.545**	**1.343**	**19.79**	170 (min)
FCNN	10.09	0.547	1.385	20.75	370 (min)

3.3   Results and Discussion

As shown in Table 1, the OTOM and FCNN methods showed considerably similar quantification error. The OTOM framework successfully decoded fingerprints into tissue parameters irrespective of their MRF schedules. Moreover, both OTOM and FCNN methods showed a high degree of the reconstruction accuracy for every tissue parameter compared to the Bloch fitting approach. Moreover, both deep learning methods take advantage of low computational complexity for tissue parameter quantification due to their simple feed-forward deployments in test phase (110 s for OTOM and 6 s for FCNN with an image matrix of $256 \times 256 \times 9 \times 40$). In comparison, the Bloch fitting method suffers from the high computational cost for the tissue parameter mapping (one hour with an image matrix of $256 \times 256 \times 9 \times 40$). However, the FCNN approach is constrained to a specific MRF schedule and thus a time-consuming re-training process of neural networks is required for other MRF schedules, thereby limiting its clinical utility. On the contrary, the proposed OTOM can immediately cope with various MRF sequences.

Figure 4 shows the excellent agreement between the estimated *in vivo* maps from the OTOM method and those from the FCNN method (p < 0.05 for all parameters; correlation coefficients of 0.89, 0.98, 0.99, and 0.96, respectively for k_{mw}, M_0^m, T_2^m and T_1^w). The estimated parameter maps from the fitting method were also in excellent agreement with those from the OTOM method (0.81, 0.99, 0.94, and 0.99, respectively for k_{mw}, M_0^m, T_2^m and T_1^w).

In addition, the OTOM-T network, achieved by transfer learning of the trained OTOM network to a certain MRF schedule, showed higher accuracy than the OTOM and FCNN methods (Table 2). Note that the same dataset was used to train the OTOM-T and FCNN. However, the performance gain from the use of transfer learning is small: the normalized root mean square errors (nRMSE) difference between OTOM and OTOM-T were 0.26, 0.42, 0.21, and 0.02% for k_{mw}, M_0^m, T_2^m and T_1^w. This refers that the OTOM network is well optimized for various schedules.

4   Conclusion

We proposed an Only-Train-Once MR fingerprinting (OTOM) framework to estimate the free bulk water and MTC parameters from MR fingerprints regardless of the MRF sequence. Unlike the previous deep learning studies, the proposed method was trained with numerous patterns and lengths of MRF sequence, allowing us to plug any MRF sequence rather than a fixed MRF sequence. The flexible OTOM framework could be an efficient tissue quantification tool for various MRF protocols.

Acknowledgement. This work was supported by the Korea Medical Device Development Fund grant funded by the Korea government (the Ministry of Science and ICT, the Ministry of Trade, Industry and Energy, the Ministry of Health and Welfare, the Ministry of Food and Drug Safety) (Project Number: 1711138003, KMDF-RnD KMDF_PR_20200901_0041-2021-02), and by grants from the National Institutes of Health (R01EB029974 and R01NS112242).

References

1. Cohen, O., Zhu, B., Rosen, M.S.: MR fingerprinting deep reconstruction network (drone). Magn. Resonan. Med. **80**(3), 885–894 (2018). https://doi.org/10.1002/mrm.27198

2. Filippi, M., Rocca, M.A., Martino, G., Horsfield, M.A., Comi, G.: Magnetization transfer changes in the normal appearing white matter precede the appearance of enhancing lesions in patients with multiple sclerosis. Ann. Neurol. **43**(6), 809–814 (1998). https://doi.org/10.1002/ana.410430616

3. Graves, A., Schmidhuber, J.: Framewise phoneme classification with bidirectional LSTM and other neural network architectures. Neural Netw. **18**(5–6), 602–10 (2005). https://doi.org/10.1016/j.neunet.2005.06.042

4. Hamilton, J.I., Seiberlich, N.: Machine learning for rapid magnetic resonance fingerprinting tissue property quantification. Proc. IEEE Inst. Electr. Electron. Eng. **108**(1), 69–85 (2020). https://doi.org/10.1109/JPROC.2019.2936998

5. Henkelman, R.M., Huang, X., Xiang, Q.S., Stanisz, G.J., Swanson, S.D., Bronskill, M.J.: Quantitative interpretation of magnetization transfer. Magn. Reson. Med. **29**(6), 759–66 (1993). https://doi.org/10.1002/mrm.1910290607

6. Heo, H.Y., et al.: Quantifying amide proton exchange rate and concentration in chemical exchange saturation transfer imaging of the human brain. Neuroimage **189**, 202–213 (2019). https://doi.org/10.1016/j.neuroimage.2019.01.034

7. Heo, H.Y., et al.: Prospective acceleration of parallel RF transmission-based 3d chemical exchange saturation transfer imaging with compressed sensing. Magn. Reson. Med. **82**(5), 1812–1821 (2019). https://doi.org/10.1002/mrm.27875

8. Heo, H.Y., Zhang, Y., Lee, D.H., Hong, X., Zhou, J.: Quantitative assessment of amide proton transfer (apt) and nuclear overhauser enhancement (NOE) imaging with extrapolated semi-solid magnetization transfer reference (EMR) signals: application to a rat glioma model at 4.7 tesla. Magn. Reson. Med. **75**(1), 137–49 (2016). https://doi.org/10.1002/mrm.25581

9. Heo, H.Y., Zhang, Y., Lee, D.H., Jiang, S., Zhao, X., Zhou, J.: Accelerating chemical exchange saturation transfer (CEST) MRI by combining compressed sensing and sensitivity encoding techniques. Magn. Reson. Med. **77**(2), 779–786 (2017). https://doi.org/10.1002/mrm.26141

10. Hilbert, T., et al.: Magnetization transfer in magnetic resonance fingerprinting. Magn. Reson. Med. **84**(1), 128–141 (2020). https://doi.org/10.1002/mrm.28096

11. Kang, B., Kim, B., Schar, M., Park, H., Heo, H.Y.: Unsupervised learning for magnetization transfer contrast MR fingerprinting: application to CEST and nuclear overhauser enhancement imaging. Magn. Reson. Med. **85**(4), 2040–2054 (2021). https://doi.org/10.1002/mrm.28573

12. Kang, B., Kim, B., Park, H., Heo, H.Y.: Learning-based optimization of acquisition schedule for magnetization transfer contrast MR fingerprinting. NMR Biomed. **35**(5), e4662 (2022). https://doi.org/10.1002/nbm.4662

13. Kim, B., Schar, M., Park, H., Heo, H.Y.: A deep learning approach for magnetization transfer contrast MR fingerprinting and chemical exchange saturation transfer imaging. Neuroimage **221**, 117165 (2020). https://doi.org/10.1016/j.neuroimage.2020.117165

14. Kingma, D.P., Ba, J.: Adam: a method for stochastic optimization (2017)

15. Liu, H., van der Heide, O., van den Berg, C.A.T., Sbrizzi, A.: Fast and accurate modeling of transient-state, gradient-spoiled sequences by recurrent neural networks. NMR Biomed. **34**(7), e4527 (2021). https://doi.org/10.1002/nbm.4527

16. Ma, D., et al.: Magnetic resonance fingerprinting. Nature **495**(7440), 187–92 (2013). https://doi.org/10.1038/nature11971

17. Perlman, O., Farrar, C.T., Heo, H.Y.: MR fingerprinting for semisolid magnetization transfer and chemical exchange saturation transfer quantification. NMR Biomed. e4710. https://doi.org/10.1002/nbm.4710

18. Perrin, J., et al.: Sex differences in the growth of white matter during adolescence. NeuroImage **45**(4), 1055–1066 (2009). https://doi.org/10.1016/j.neuroimage.2009.01.023

19. Quesson, B., Thiaudiere, E., Delalande, C., Chateil, J.F., Moonen, C.T., Canioni, P.: Magnetization transfer imaging of rat brain under non-steady-state conditions. contrast prediction using a binary spin-bath model and a super-lorentzian lineshape. J. Magn. Reson. **130**(2), 321–8 (1998). https://doi.org/10.1006/jmre.1997.1326

20. Sled, J.G.: Modelling and interpretation of magnetization transfer imaging in the brain. Neuroimage **182**, 128–135 (2018). https://doi.org/10.1016/j.neuroimage.2017.11.065

21. Wang, D., Ostenson, J., Smith, D.S.: SNAPMRF: GPU-accelerated magnetic resonance fingerprinting dictionary generation and matching using extended phase graphs. Magn. Reson. Imaging **66**, 248–256 (2020). https://doi.org/10.1016/j.mri.2019.11.015

22. Xanthis, C.G., Aletras, A.H.: COREMRI: a high-performance, publicly available MR simulation platform on the cloud. PLoS ONE **14**(5), e0216594 (2019). https://doi.org/10.1371/journal.pone.0216594

23. Yang, M., Jiang, Y., Ma, D., Mehta, B.B., Griswold, M.A.: Game of learning BLOCH equation simulations for MR fingerprinting. arXiv preprint arXiv:2004.02270 (2020)

24. van Zijl, P.C.M., Lam, W.W., Xu, J., Knutsson, L., Stanisz, G.J.: Magnetization transfer contrast and chemical exchange saturation transfer MRI features and analysis of the field-dependent saturation spectrum. Neuroimage **168**, 222–241 (2018). https://doi.org/10.1016/j.neuroimage.2017.04.045

AutoGAN-Synthesizer: Neural Architecture Search for Cross-Modality MRI Synthesis

Xiaobin Hu[1,2,3(✉)], Ruolin Shen[1], Donghao Luo[3], Ying Tai[3], Chengjie Wang[3], and Bjoern H. Menze[1,2]

[1] Department of Computer Science, Technical University of Munich, Munich, Germany
xiaobin.hu@tum.de
[2] Department of Quantitative Biomedicine, University of Zurich, Zürich, Switzerland
[3] Tencent Youtu Lab, Shanghai, China

Abstract. Considering the difficulty to obtain complete multi-modality MRI scans in some real-world data acquisition situations, synthesizing MRI data is a highly relevant and important topic to complement diagnosis information in clinical practice. In this study, we present a novel MRI synthesizer, called *AutoGAN-Synthesizer*, which automatically discovers generative networks for cross-modality MRI synthesis. Our AutoGAN-Synthesizer adopts gradient-based search strategies to explore the generator architecture by determining how to fuse multi-resolution features and utilizes GAN-based perceptual searching losses to handle the trade-off between model complexity and performance. Our AutoGAN-Synthesizer can search for a remarkable and light-weight architecture with **6.31** *Mb* parameters only occupying *12* GPU hours. Moreover, to incorporate richer prior knowledge for MRI synthesis, we derive K-space features containing the low- and high-spatial frequency information and incorporate such features into our model. To our best knowledge, this is the first work to explore AutoML for cross-modality MRI synthesis, and our approach is also capable of tailoring networks given either different multiple modalities or just a single modality as input. Extensive experiments show that our AutoGAN-Synthesizer outperforms the state-of-the-art MRI synthesis methods both quantitatively and qualitatively. The code are available at https://github.com/HUuxiaobin/AutoGAN-Synthesizer.

Keywords: Cross-modality MRI synthesis · Generative adversarial networks · Neural architecture search

---

X. Hu and R. Shen—Equal contribution.

Supplementary Information The online version contains supplementary material available at https://doi.org/10.1007/978-3-031-16446-0_38.

L. Wang et al. (Eds.): MICCAI 2022, LNCS 13436, pp. 397–409, 2022.
https://doi.org/10.1007/978-3-031-16446-0_38

1   Introduction

Magnetic Resonance Imaging (MRI) has currently become prominent in neurology with the use of high-field scanners, given that MRI contrasting agent is less likely to cause an allergic reaction compared with X-ray or CT scan using iodine-based substances [24]. However, due to modality corruption, incorrect machine settings, allergies to specific contrast agents, and limited available time [7], it is often not guaranteed to obtain a complete set of MRI sequences to provide rich information for clinical diagnosis and therapy. In this regard, the development of cross-modality or cross-protocol MRI synthesis techniques is important to homogenize and "repair" such real-world data collections via efficient data infilling and re-synthesis, and make them accessible for algorithms that require complete data sets as input [2,10,23,30].

Recently a large number of algorithms for medical image synthesis have been proposed with the rapid growth of deep learning techniques [6,11,27,37]. Among them, generative adversarial networks (GANs) with the advantage of recovering an unprecedented level of image realism [15] have achieved significant advancement for medical image synthesis. For example, Ea-GANs [32] incorporated edge information and focused on the textural details of image content structure for cross-modality MRI synthesis. SA-GANS [33] added a sample-adaptive path additionally to learn the relationship of each sample with its neighboring training samples. MM-GAN [5] and mustGAN [34] were designed to deal with multi-modal MRI synthesis with structures capable of fusing latent representations of each input modality. However, these state-of-art methods [5,7,10,13,32–34,36,38] fixed the network architecture for various input modality combinations (e.g., T1, T1-weighted, Flair, T1+Flair, etc.) and ignored the mapping uniqueness between each source domain and target domain pair, and therefore could not reach the optimal solution for all situations using the same network structure.

Inspired by the great potential of neural architecture search (NAS) in computer vision field [8,17–19,25,31,35,40], we explore NAS to automatically find an optimal network with fewer computation costs and parameters for different input modalities. Searching for a dedicated MRI synthesizer is essentially promising because the problem nature of using one network for many synthesis tasks caters to the NAS principle of construing one search architecture for multi-jobs. However, how to search the architecture of generative networks according to the different input modalities given to the synthesizer is still unexplored so far. In this paper, we aim to adaptively optimize and construct the neural architecture that is capable of understanding how to extract and merge features according to different input modalities. Specifically, we adopt a GAN-based structure as the backbone of NAS, where the generator of the GAN is searched by gradient-based NAS from the multi-scale module-based search space. Our main contributions of the AutoGAN-Synthesizer are as follows: (1). Aiming at the recovery of realistic texture while constraining model complexity, we propose a GAN-based perceptual searching loss that jointly incorporates the content loss and model complexity. (2). To incorporate richer priors for MRI synthesis, we exploit MRI *K-space* knowledge containing low-frequency (e.g., contrast and brightness) and

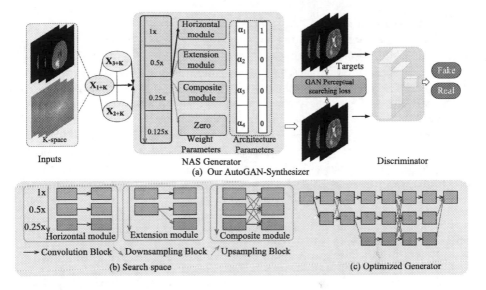

Fig. 1. (a). Overall architecture of our proposed AutoGAN-Synthesizer. The AutoGAN-Synthesizer contains two parts: 1) A NAS-based generator to adaptively build up an architecture based on input modalities (X_{1+k}, X_{2+k} or X_{3+k}). X_{i+k} represents the input with i modalities and the corresponding K-space features (denoted as k). 2) A discriminator to distinguish between the synthesis and real modality. (b). Generator search space consisting of three modules to capture and fuse the detailed information and the global features from different multi-scale branches: horizontal module, extension module and the composite module. (c). An example of an optimized generator including the three proposed modules.

high-frequency information (e.g., edges and content details), to guide the NAS network to extract and merge features. (3). Considering that the low- and high-resolution of multi-scale networks can capture the global structure and local details respectively, we use a novel multi-scale module-based search space which is specifically designed for multi-resolution fusion. The module-based searching setting is also capable of reducing search time while maintaining the performance. (4). Finally, our searching strategy can produce a light-weight network with **6.31** *Mb* parameters from module-based search space only taking *12* GPU hours and achieve state-of-the-art performance. From our knowledge, this is the first work to explore AutoML for cross-modality MRI synthesis tasks.

2   Proposed Method

Motivation: Most recent-used networks for MRI synthesis usually adopt an encoder-decoder structure [7,14,32,38], which recovers the high-resolution features mainly based on the low-resolution representation received from successive convolutional blocks in the encoder. This latent representation contains only high-level features and loses lots of detailed information, leading the recovered images neither semantically strong nor spatially precise. Inspired by the fact that the low- and high-resolution branches of multi-scale networks are capable of capturing global structure and preserving the local details respectively [8,22,28], we design a generator based on a multi-scale structure including three modules: *horizontal module* connects different resolution input in parallel without any fusion, *extension module* adds a downsampling block to extend a lower-resolution scale and *composite module* fuses cross-resolution representations to exchange information. An overview of our AutoGAN-Synthesizer is shown in Fig. 1. Specifically, the framework contains an adaptive generator constructed by neural architecture search according to input modalities and a typical discriminator to distinguish between predictions and ground truths.

2.1 NAS-Based Generator Search

Generator Search Space: There exists an open question on how to extract or fuse the features of modalities in a multi-scale generator. To solve this question, we propose three different modules (Fig. 1(b)) to give guidelines for extracting and merging multi-resolution features: namely *horizontal module, extension module* and *composite module*. These three modules behave differently to mimic the coarse-to-fine framework and exploit multiple possibilities of multi-scale fusion. Specifically, the horizontal module horizontally connects features via convolution block without feature fusion among multi-scales. As shown in Fig. 1(b), the feature resolution at the same scale keeps identical but is reduced by 0.5 when the scale goes deeper. The extension module extends a lower-resolution scale via a down-sampling block. This connection helps to exploit the high-level priors extracted at the low-resolution scale and simultaneously remain the unchanged resolution at the high-resolution scale. The composite module merges multi-resolution features by skip connection, stride convolution and up-sampling block, which can be summarized as:

$$F_g = \sum \mathcal{M}_{r \to g}(F_r) \tag{1}$$

where r is the resolution of the input feature maps while g is the resolution of the output features. F_r represents the input feature maps with resolution r and F_g denotes the output feature maps with resolution g after combing all the features from other resolution scales. $\mathcal{M}_{r \to g}(\cdot)$ is the mapping function defined as follows:

$$\mathcal{M}_{r \to g}(F_r) = \begin{cases} F_r & r == g \\ Upsampled\ F_r & r < g \\ Downsampled\ F_r & r > g \end{cases} \tag{2}$$

Compared with the common fusion scheme [5,26], that only fuses high-resolution features with the upsampled low-resolution features unidirectionally, this module aggregates the feature fusion via a bidirectional way among multi-resolution representations. Thus, this powerful multi-resolution fusion scheme catches more spatial information extracted from all resolution scales and therefore is semantically stronger.

The combination of three modules constructs a superior neural architecture which gives guidance on how to extract and merge the features catering to the requirements of different input modalities. An example of an optimized generator could be found in Fig. 1(c). The input modalities are imported into a super-network with two fixed horizontal modules, S modules selected from horizontal, extension, and composite modules candidates, and a final composite module followed by a 1×1 convolutional layer. During the searching process, the progressive structure can gradually add the multi-resolution modules and endow the output with multi-resolution knowledge.

2.2 GAN-Based Perceptual Loss Function

In order to recover a realistic and faithful image, we add both the perceptual and pixel-level loss into our generator loss function:

$$\mathcal{L}_{Generator} = \mathcal{L}_{content} + \lambda_{adv}\mathcal{L}_{adv} + \lambda_{complexity}\mathcal{L}_{complexity}, \tag{3}$$

where $\mathcal{L}_{content}$ is the content loss consisting of pixel-level loss (mean square loss) and texture-level loss (perceptual loss) between the ground-truth and reconstructed images. $\mathcal{L}_{adv}$ is the adversarial loss based on binary cross-entropy formulation to make the reconstructed image closer to the ground-truths. $\mathcal{L}_{complexity}$ is the loss term for calculating the model complexity (e.g., FLOPS, consuming time, and model size).

2.3 K-space Learning

K-space is the spatial frequency representation of MRI images. Due to the long scan time acquiring MRI images, several MRI reconstruction methods based on under-sampled K-space learning are proposed for fast MRI [1,9,14]. Inspired by this, we embed K-space learning into our pipeline to introduce frequency priors of MRI images, which is defined as follows:

$$\hat{x}(k) = \mathcal{F}[x]\{k\} = \int_{R^2} e^{-jk \cdot r} x(r) \, dr, \tag{4}$$

where $k \in \mathbb{R}^2$ represents the spatial frequency and $j^2 = -1$. $x(r)$ is the pixel intensity in real space while $\hat{x}(k)$ is the calculated intensity in frequency domain. K-space is computed according to the input modalities and is used as the input together with the MRI images in real space.

2.4 Implementation Details

Searching Setting: For each different input modality, we search for a new architecture to give guidance on how to extract and fuse the multi-modality features. First, we train the warm-up stage (ten epochs) to get desirable weights of convolution layers and then train a searching stage with 200 epochs for optimizing the structure of architecture. For updating the parametric model, we adopt the standard SGD optimizer with the momentum of 0.9 and the learning rate decays from 0.025 to 0.001 by cosine annealing strategy [20]. Besides, to optimize the architecture parameters, Adam optimizer [16] is used with a learning rate of 0.0005. The batch size is 16 by randomly cropping and padding image size 240×240. Overall, the whole searching process consumes 12 h.

Training Setting: After finding an architecture, we train this for 500 epochs with batch size 16 and image size 240×240. The Adam optimizer with the learning rate of 0.0005 is adopted. All training experiments are implemented in Pytorch with a Tesla V100.

3   Experimental Results

3.1   Experimental Settings

We evaluate the performance of AutoGAN-Synthesizer on one-to-one and multiple-to-one cross-modality MRI synthesis tasks using two public brain MRI datasets: BRATS2018 and IXI. BRATS2018 dataset [3,4,21] collects multimodality MR image sets from patients with brain tumors including four different modalities: native (T1), T1-weighted and contrast-enhanced (T1ce), T2-weighted (T2), and T2 Fluid Attenuated Inversion Recovery (FLAIR), where each scan has the size of $240 \times 240 \times 155$. In this paper, we conduct one-to-one and multi-to-one synthesis tasks on BRATS2018 dataset to show the effectiveness of our method. Following [7], we randomly select 50 low grade glioma (LGG) from total 75 LGG patients as the training set while another unseen 15 patients are selected as the test. Following [7,32,34], we also use the public IXI dataset[1] to verify the model generalization. IXI dataset collected multi-modality MR images from healthy subjects at three different hospitals. It is randomly divided into training (25 patients), validation (5 patients), and test patients (10 patients). For each subject, after removing some cases with major artifacts, approximately 100 axial cross sections that contained brain tissue are manually selected.

Evaluation Metrics: Following studies [32,33], three metrics are used to evaluate the quantitative performance: normalized root mean-squared error (NRMSE), peak signal-to-noise ratio (PSNR) and structural similarity (SSIM) [29].

---

[1] https://brain-development.org/ixi-dataset/.

Table 1. Quantitative results of Flair-T2 (BRATS2018 dataset) and T1-T2 (IXI dataset) MRI cross-modality synthesis tasks.

Methods	Flair-T2 (BRATS2018 dataset)			T1-T2 (IXI dataset)			Model size
	PSNR	SSIM	NRMSE	PSNR	SSIM	NRMSE	Params(M)
CycleGAN [39]	20.70 ± 2.37	0.83 ± 0.05	0.45 ± 0.14	23.03 ± 1.01	0.74 ± 0.05	0.48 ± 0.05	11.38
Pix2pix [12]	24.64 ± 3.97	0.88 ± 0.04	0.34 ± 0.19	25.70 ± 1.61	0.84 ± 0.05	0.32 ± 0.06	54.41
pGAN [7]	25.20 ± 4.34	0.89 ± 0.04	0.34 ± 0.22	26.62 ± 1.72	0.85 ± 0.05	0.29 ± 0.06	11.36
cGAN [7]	23.67 ± 3.99	0.87 ± 0.04	0.35 ± 0.16	23.77 ± 1.80	0.77 ± 0.05	0.31 ± 0.06	11.37
Hi-Net [38]	24.46 ± 3.56	0.87 ± 0.04	0.32 ± 0.15	25.63 ± 1.50	0.83 ± 0.05	0.33 ± 0.06	**3.87**
Ours	$\mathbf{25.54 \pm 3.91}$	$\mathbf{0.90 \pm 0.03}$	$\mathbf{0.30 \pm 0.17}$	$\mathbf{27.37 \pm 1.81}$	$\mathbf{0.86 \pm 0.04}$	$\mathbf{0.29 \pm 0.05}$	6.30

3.2   Comparisons with State-of-the-Art Methods

To verify the performance of our AutoGAN-Synthesizer, we compare it with five recent state-of-the-art methods: CycleGAN [39], Pix2pix [12], pGAN and cGAN [7], and Hi-Net [38]. To ensure a fair comparison with state-of-the-art methods, we train all networks on the same dataset by the open-source implementations as well as the recommended hyper-parameters from authors.

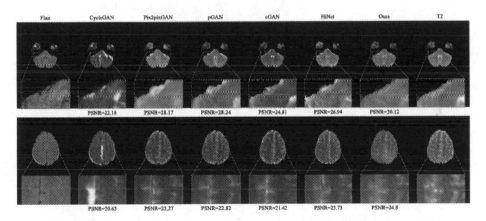

Fig. 2. Qualitative results of FLAIR →T2 synthesis experiments on glioma patients in BRATS2018 dataset. Compared with other state-of-art results, our synthetic images recover favorable tissue contrast, tumor, and anatomy knowledge which have great potential in clinical diagnoses and treatments.

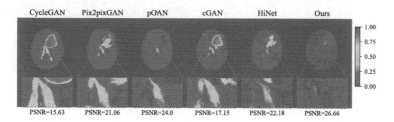

Fig. 3. Visual performance of synthetic T2 modality difference maps compared with other state-of-art methods on BRATS2018 dataset.

One-to-One Cross-Modality MRI Synthesis Tasks: We focus on synthesizing T2 contrasts that are complementary to T1 contrasts, and offer better information for investigating fluid-filled structures within tissue. The experimental results for one-to-one synthesis tasks are listed in Table 1. For FLAIR-T2 cross-modality synthesis task, Table 1 shows that our AutoGAN achieves better performance than other cutting-edge methods on three metrics. Figures 2 and 3 show the qualitative comparison between our proposed AutoGAN and other five state-of-art methods on BRATS2018 dataset. The difference maps are generated based on the pixel intensity and visualized in the type of heat maps. It can be seen that our synthetic images have clearer details in the zoomed rectangles, and also preserve favorable tissue contrast, tumor, and anatomy knowledge which have great potentials in clinical diagnoses and treatments. Overall, our methods could reach higher fidelity with the target images and our method can search for satisfactory synthesis networks which are better than manually designed architectures. The superiority of AutoGAN is mainly attributed to our module-based search space, which can well exploit the information fusion between the low- and high-resolution features. As shown in Table 1, the quantitative results on the IXI dataset also imply that our AutoGAN achieve better generalization than other methods.

Model Complexity: It can be seen from Table 1 that our AutoGAN achieves SOTA performance only using very light-weight network architecture with 6.30 Mb parameters, which is nearly half of the other manually-designed networks (around 11 Mb) [7,39].

Multiple-to-One Cross-Modality MRI Synthesis Tasks. To verify the effectiveness of our method on multiple-to-one tasks, we conduct experiments with different combinations of input modalities on BRATS2018 dataset in Fig. 4(b). Compared with Hi-Net that is specifically designed for two modalities input, our AutoGAN demonstrates considerable improvements, with PSNR rising from 24.95 dB (Hi-Net) to 27.12 dB (ours) in the task of FLAIR+T1→T2. Figure 4(b) also verifies that our method can fuse multiple input modalities and provide a promising performance. In addition, it illustrates that more input modality knowledge can also boost the synthesis performance. Figure 4(a) shows qualitative results of different multiple modalities input tested on the searched

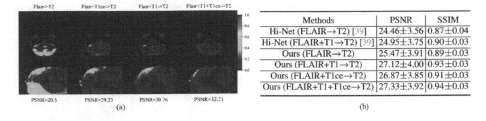

Methods	PSNR	SSIM
Hi-Net (FLAIR→T2) [39]	24.46±3.56	0.87±0.04
Hi-Net (FLAIR+T1→T2) [39]	24.95±3.75	0.90±0.03
Ours (FLAIR→T2)	25.47±3.91	0.89±0.03
Ours (FLAIR+T1→T2)	27.12±4.00	0.93±0.03
Ours (FLAIR+T1ce→T2)	26.87±3.85	0.91±0.03
Ours (FLAIR+T1+T1ce→T2)	27.33±3.92	0.94±0.03

Fig. 4. Multiple-to-one MRI cross modality synthesis tasks on BRATS2018 dataset: (a). Qualitative comparison of difference maps. (b). Quantitative results.

models by our AutoGAN. The results of FLAIR+T1+T1ce→T2 task are much better than the other three configurations in visualization, which is consistent with the observation from quantitative evaluation. It also verifies that different modalities contains partly complementary knowledge, which can boost the synthesis performance.

3.3 Ablation Study

Study of Each Component: We conduct an ablation study to demonstrate the effectiveness of each component, *i.e.*, the perceptual and adversarial part of our loss function, and the MRI K-space learning strategy. In Fig. 5(a), we list all results of different configurations on these three components in FLAIR →T2 synthesis tasks on BRATS2018 dataset. It indicates that the perceptual and adversarial loss can further improve quantitative performance. After adding the perceptual and adversarial loss, our algorithm can rehabilitate highly-realistic images with better structure similarity and peak signal-to-noise ratio. Furthermore, MRI K-space features embedded in the network can introduce additional information and therefore can also boost performance improvement. Figure 6 shows the qualitative results of the ablation study. We find that adding each component successively can obtain better synthetic images. In Fig. 6, the FLAIR image has poor quality and therefore is challenging to synthesize a reasonable T2 image. However, with the help of perceptual loss, adversarial loss, and K-space learning, the results are further improved and the missing part is gradually compensated.

Effectiveness of Our Search Strategy: To verify the effectiveness of our search strategy in AutoGAN, we compare our search strategy with random policy by randomly sampling 20 models from our search spaces. From Fig. 5(b), compared with random policy, our AutoGAN can search superior networks with less model size but better performance. More specifically, the networks from random policy have a wide range of model sizes from 6 Mb to around 12.5 Mb. But the search strategy of our AutoGAN is capable of constraining the model size of network within a much smaller interval by greatly reducing both the

Configurations			Performance
Perceptual	Adversarial	K-space	PSNR/SSIM
×	×	×	25.23/0.87
✓	×	×	25.29/0.89
×	✓	×	25.37/0.90
✓	✓	×	25.47/0.89
×	✓	✓	25.49/0.90
✓	×	✓	25.35/0.89
✓	✓	✓	**25.54/0.90**

(a)

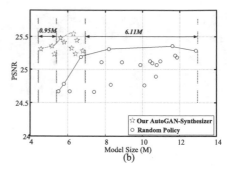

(b)

Fig. 5. (a). Ablation study of our GAN-based loss and MRI K-space features on BRATS2018 dataset (FLAIR →T2). (b). Comparison of our search strategy with random policy. Our AutoGAN can search light-weight networks with better performance.

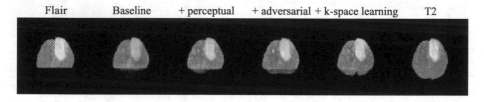

Fig. 6. Visualization results of our ablation study, showing the effectiveness of three components in our pipeline: *i.e.,* perceptual loss, adversarial loss and K-space learning. The version of baseline represents the network without three components, +*perceptual* means the baseline with only perceptual loss, +*adversarial* denotes baseline with perceptual and adversarial loss and +*Kspace* represents our complete method with perceptual, adversarial loss and K-space learning.

lower-bound and the upper-bound of the model sizes without sacrificing the performance. This superiority makes it easier to deploy AI models in a variety of resource-constrained clinical scenarios.

4   Conclusion

We propose AutoGAN-Synthesizer to automatically design a generative network knowing how to extract and fuse features according to different input modalities for cross-modality MRI synthesis. A novel GAN-based perceptual searching loss incorporating specialized MRI K-space features is proposed to rehabilitate a highly-realistic image and to balance the trade-off between model complexity and performance. The proposed method outperforms other manually state-of-art synthesis algorithms and restores faithful tumor and anatomy information.

References

1. Aggarwal, H.K., Mani, M.P., Jacob, M.: Multi-shot sensitivity-encoded diffusion MRI using model-based deep learning (MODL-MUSSELS). In: ISBI, pp. 1541–1544. IEEE (2019)
2. Armanious, K., et al.: MedGAN: medical image translation using GANs. Comput. Med. Imaging Graph. **79**, 101684 (2020)
3. Bakas, S., et al.: Advancing the cancer genome atlas glioma MRI collections with expert segmentation labels and radiomic features. Sci. Data **4**, 170117 (2017)
4. Bakas, S., et al.: Identifying the best machine learning algorithms for brain tumor segmentation, progression assessment, and overall survival prediction in the brats challenge. arXiv preprint arXiv:1811.02629 (2018)
5. Chartsias, A., Joyce, T., Giuffrida, M.V., Tsaftaris, S.A.: Multimodal MR synthesis via modality-invariant latent representation. IEEE Trans. Med. Imaging **37**(3), 803–814 (2017)
6. Costa, P., et al.: End-to-end adversarial retinal image synthesis. IEEE Trans. Med. Imaging **37**(3), 781–791 (2017)
7. Dar, S.U., Yurt, M., Karacan, L., Erdem, A., Erdem, E., Çukur, T.: Image synthesis in multi-contrast MRI with conditional generative adversarial networks. IEEE Trans. Med. Imaging **38**(10), 2375–2388 (2019)
8. Gou, Y., Li, B., Liu, Z., Yang, S., Peng, X.: Clearer: multi-scale neural architecture search for image restoration. NeurIPS. **33**, 17129–17140 (2020)
9. Han, Y., Sunwoo, L., Ye, J.C.: k-space deep learning for accelerated MRI. IEEE Trans. Med. Imaging **39**(2), 377–386 (2019)
10. Hu, X.: Multi-texture GAN: exploring the multi-scale texture translation for brain MR images. arXiv preprint arXiv:2102.07225 (2021)
11. Huang, Y., Shao, L., Frangi, A.F.: Simultaneous super-resolution and cross-modality synthesis of 3d medical images using weakly-supervised joint convolutional sparse coding. In: CVPR, pp. 6070–6079 (2017)
12. Isola, P., Zhu, J.Y., Zhou, T., Efros, A.A.: Image-to-image translation with conditional adversarial networks. In: CVPR, pp. 1125–1134 (2017)
13. Joyce, T., Chartsias, A., Tsaftaris, S.A.: Robust multi-modal MR image synthesis. In: Descoteaux, M., et al. (eds.) MICCAI 2017. LNCS, vol. 10435, pp. 347–355. Springer, Cham (2017). https://doi.org/10.1007/978-3-319-66179-7_40
14. Jun, Y., Shin, H., Eo, T., Hwang, D.: Joint deep model-based MR image and coil sensitivity reconstruction network (Joint-ICNet) for fast MRI. In: CVPR, pp. 5270–5279 (2021)
15. Karras, T., Aila, T., Laine, S., Lehtinen, J.: Progressive growing of GANs for improved quality, stability, and variation. In: International Conference on Learning Representations (2018)
16. Kingma, D.P., Ba, J.: Adam: a method for stochastic optimization. arXiv preprint arXiv:1412.6980 (2014)
17. Liu, C., et al.: Progressive neural architecture search. In: Ferrari, V., Hebert, M., Sminchisescu, C., Weiss, Y. (eds.) ECCV 2018. LNCS, vol. 11205, pp. 19–35. Springer, Cham (2018). https://doi.org/10.1007/978-3-030-01246-5_2
18. Liu, H., Simonyan, K., Yang, Y.: Darts: Differentiable architecture search. In: ICLR (2018)

19. Liu, Z., Wang, H., Zhang, S., Wang, G., Qi, J.: NAS-SCAM: neural architecture search-based spatial and channel joint attention module for nuclei semantic segmentation and classification. In: Martel, A.L., et al. (eds.) MICCAI 2020. LNCS, vol. 12261, pp. 263–272. Springer, Cham (2020). https://doi.org/10.1007/978-3-030-59710-8_26

20. Loshchilov, I., Hutter, F.: SGDR: stochastic gradient descent with warm restarts. arXiv preprint arXiv:1608.03983 (2016)

21. Menze, B.H., et al.: The multimodal brain tumor image segmentation benchmark (brats). IEEE Trans. Med. Imaging 34(10), 1993–2024 (2014)

22. Nah, S., Hyun Kim, T., Mu Lee, K.: Deep multi-scale convolutional neural network for dynamic scene deblurring. In: CVPR, pp. 3883–3891 (2017)

23. Nie, D., et al.: Medical image synthesis with deep convolutional adversarial networks. IEEE Trans. Biomed. Eng. 65(12), 2720–2730 (2018)

24. Qianye, Y., Li, N., Zhao, Z., Xingyu, F., Eric, I., Chang, C., Xu, Y.: MRI cross-modality image-to-image translation. Sci. Rep. 10(1), 1–8 (2020)

25. Real, E., Aggarwal, A., Huang, Y., Le, Q.V.: Regularized evolution for image classifier architecture search. In: AAAI, vol. 33, pp. 4780–4789 (2019)

26. Ronneberger, O., Fischer, P., Brox, T.: U-net: convolutional networks for biomedical image segmentation. In: Navab, N., Hornegger, J., Wells, W.M., Frangi, A.F. (eds.) MICCAI 2015. LNCS, vol. 9351, pp. 234–241. Springer, Cham (2015). https://doi.org/10.1007/978-3-319-24574-4_28

27. Sharma, A., Hamarneh, G.: Missing MRI pulse sequence synthesis using multimodal generative adversarial network. IEEE Trans. Med. Imaging 39(4), 1170–1183 (2019)

28. Wang, J., et al.: Deep high-resolution representation learning for visual recognition. IEEE Trans. Pattern Anal. Mach. Intell. 43, 3349–3364 (2020)

29. Wang, Z., Bovik, A.C., Sheikh, H.R., Simoncelli, E.P.: Image quality assessment: from error visibility to structural similarity. IEEE Trans. Image Process. 13(4), 600–612 (2004)

30. Welander, P., Karlsson, S., Eklund, A.: Generative adversarial networks for image-to-image translation on multi-contrast MR images-a comparison of cyclegan and unit. arXiv preprint arXiv:1806.07777 (2018)

31. Yan, X., Jiang, W., Shi, Y., Zhuo, C.: MS-NAS: multi-scale neural architecture search for medical image segmentation. In: Martel, A.L., et al. (eds.) MICCAI 2020. LNCS, vol. 12261, pp. 388–397. Springer, Cham (2020). https://doi.org/10.1007/978-3-030-59710-8_38

32. Yu, B., Zhou, L., Wang, L., Shi, Y., Fripp, J., Bourgeat, P.: EA-GANs: edge-aware generative adversarial networks for cross-modality MR image synthesis. IEEE Trans. Med. Imaging 38(7), 1750–1762 (2019)

33. Yu, B., Zhou, L., Wang, L., Shi, Y., Fripp, J., Bourgeat, P.: Sample-adaptive GANs: linking global and local mappings for cross-modality MR image synthesis. IEEE Trans. Med. Imaging 39(7), 2339–2350 (2020)

34. Yurt, M., Dar, S.U., Erdem, A., Erdem, E., Oguz, K.K., Çukur, T.: mustGAN: multi-stream generative adversarial networks for MR image synthesis. Med. Image Anal. 70, 101944 (2021)

35. Zhang, H., Li, Y., Chen, H., Shen, C.: Memory-efficient hierarchical neural architecture search for image denoising. In: CVPR, pp. 3657–3666 (2020)

36. Zhang, R., Pfister, T., Li, J.: Harmonic unpaired image-to-image translation. arXiv preprint arXiv:1902.09727 (2019)

37. Zhang, Y., Li, K., Li, K., Fu, Y.: MR image super-resolution with squeeze and excitation reasoning attention network. In: CVPR, pp. 13425–13434 (2021)

38. Zhou, T., Fu, H., Chen, G., Shen, J., Shao, L.: Hi-net: hybrid-fusion network for multi-modal MR image synthesis. IEEE Trans. Med. Imaging **39**(9), 2772–2781 (2020)
39. Zhu, J.Y., Park, T., Isola, P., Efros, A.A.: Unpaired image-to-image translation using cycle-consistent adversarial networks. In: ICCV, pp. 2223–2232 (2017)
40. Zhu, Z., Liu, C., Yang, D., Yuille, A., Xu, D.: V-NAS: neural architecture search for volumetric medical image segmentation. In: 3DV, pp. 240–248. IEEE (2019)

Multi-scale Super-Resolution Magnetic Resonance Spectroscopic Imaging with Adjustable Sharpness

Siyuan Dong[1]([envelope]), Gilbert Hangel[2], Wolfgang Bogner[2], Georg Widhalm[3], Karl Rössler[3], Siegfried Trattnig[2], Chenyu You[1], Robin de Graaf[4], John A. Onofrey[4], and James S. Duncan[1,4]

[1] Electrical Engineering, Yale University, New Haven, CT, USA
s.dong@yale.edu
[2] Biomedical Imaging and Image-Guided Therapy, Highfield MR Center, Medical University of Vienna, Vienna, Austria
[3] Neurosurgery, Medical University of Vienna, Vienna, Austria
[4] Radiology and Biomedical Imaging, Yale University, New Haven, CT, USA

Abstract. Magnetic Resonance Spectroscopic Imaging (MRSI) is a valuable tool for studying metabolic activities in the human body, but the current applications are limited to low spatial resolutions. The existing deep learning-based MRSI super-resolution methods require training a separate network for each upscaling factor, which is time-consuming and memory inefficient. We tackle this multi-scale super-resolution problem using a Filter Scaling strategy that modulates the convolution filters based on the upscaling factor, such that a single network can be used for various upscaling factors. Observing that each metabolite has distinct spatial characteristics, we also modulate the network based on the specific metabolite. Furthermore, our network is conditioned on the weight of adversarial loss so that the perceptual sharpness of the super-resolved metabolic maps can be adjusted within a single network. We incorporate these network conditionings using a novel Multi-Conditional Module. The experiments were carried out on a ^{1}H-MRSI dataset from 15 high-grade glioma patients. Results indicate that the proposed network achieves the best performance among several multi-scale super-resolution methods and can provide super-resolved metabolic maps with adjustable sharpness. Our code is available at https://github.com/dsy199610/Multiscale-SR-MRSI-adjustable-sharpness.

Keywords: Brain MRSI · Super-resolution · Network conditioning

1 Introduction

Magnetic Resonance Spectroscopic Imaging (MRSI) is a non-invasive imaging technique that can provide spatial maps of metabolites in the tissue of interest. MRSI has become an invaluable tool in studying neurological diseases, cancer

L. Wang et al. (Eds.): MICCAI 2022, LNCS 13436, pp. 410–420, 2022.
https://doi.org/10.1007/978-3-031-16446-0_39

and diabetes [5]. Although hardware and acceleration techniques have continuously evolved [2], MRSI is limited to its coarse spatial resolutions due to the low concentration of metabolites. Therefore, a post-processing approach to increase the spatial resolution would greatly benefit MRSI applications.

Most of the traditional post-processing methods for super-resolution MRSI rely on model-based regularization using anatomical MRI [18,19,22], which often results in slow and unrealistic reconstructions. With the advances in deep learning-based image super-resolution techniques [30], a few data-driven methods have been proposed for super-resolving MRSI metabolic maps and achieved promising results [9,17]. These methods train neural networks to upscale a low resolution metabolic map to a higher resolution map under a fixed upscaling factor, for which we call single-scale super-resolution methods. However, the required upscaling factor depends on the MRSI application and is usually unknown before training the network. Training a separate network for each possible upscaling factor is time-consuming and requires large memory for storing network parameters. Additionally, due to the limited amount of in vivo MRSI data, the training dataset typically contains multiple metabolites, but the existing method treats all metabolites equivalently and does not consider the distinct spatial characteristics of each metabolite [9]. Furthermore, the adversarial loss is incorporated to improve the perceptual quality of the super-resolved metabolic maps [9]. It is well-known that more heavily weighted adversarial loss generates sharper images with more high-frequency details, whereas the risk of introducing artifacts (artificial features that make images look more realistic) also increases [7,20,30]. The current method requires training a separate network for each weight [9] to tune the trade-off between image sharpness and image fidelity, which is again sub-optimal in terms of training time and memory.

To tackle these limitations, we propose a unified MRSI super-resolution network built upon a novel Multi-Conditional Module (MCM) that can be conditioned on multiple hyperparameters: upscaling factor, type of metabolite and weight of adversarial loss. The proposed module efficiently integrates multiple functionalities into a single network, reducing the total training time and network size. This makes our method unique from previous works that only consider the upscaling factor [28,29]. Our network is able to (1) achieve comparable performance as the networks trained under a single-scale setting, (2) learn the super-resolution process based on the specific metabolite, and (3) provide multiple levels of sharpness for each super-resolved metabolic map.

2   Methods

Previous literature indicates that multi-parametric MRI contains meaningful spatial priors for super-resolution MRSI [9,17,18,22]. Hence, we provide our network with T1-weighted (T1) and fluid-attenuated inversion recovery (FLAIR) MRI in addition to the low resolution MRSI metabolic map as the input. We adopt the Multi-encoder UNet as the overall architecture (Fig. 1(a)) because it has been demonstrated to perform better than the single-encoder structure when processing information from multi-modal images [6,9]. Our main innovation is incorporating multiple conditions into the network through a specialized MCM block (Fig. 1(b)), which is detailed in the following sections.

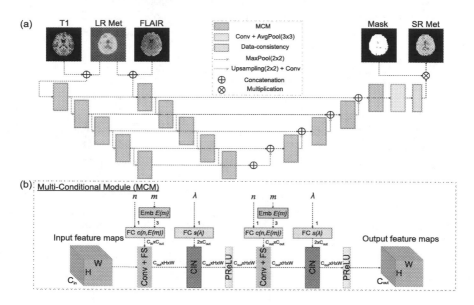

Fig. 1. Proposed network for multi-scale super-resolution MRSI with adjustable sharpness. (a) The overall architecture is a Multi-encoder UNet [6], which is appended with a Data-consistency module to guarantee that the corresponding k-space components of output images are consistent with experimental measurements [26]. We masked out the pixels in the network output that do not have valid ground truth due to quality-filtering. LR/SR Met: low-resolution/super-resolution metabolic maps. (b) The architecture of MCM. n, m and λ represent input resolution, type of metabolite and weight of adversarial loss. C, H and W are feature maps' channel number, height and width. The embedding layer $E(m)$ learns a transformation matrix that maps each metabolite name m to a vector of length 3. This vector is concatenated with the input resolution n and fed into the fully-connected (FC) layers c(n, E(m)). Conv+FS: Convolution layer with Filter Scaling, Emb: embedding layer, CIN: Conditional Instance Normalization [15], PReLU: Parametric ReLU [13].

2.1 Multi-scale Super-Resolution

Given that $L \in \mathbb{R}^{n \times n}$ is the low resolution metabolic map (we assume equal height and width n), the aim is to reconstruct a super-resolved map $S \in \mathbb{R}^{N \times N}$ using a neural network F:

$$S = F(L, \mathrm{T1}, \mathrm{FLAIR}) \tag{1}$$

such that S is close to the high resolution ground truth $I \in \mathbb{R}^{N \times N}$. In real practices, the experimentally acquired metabolic map may have different matrix sizes depending on the acquisition protocol, i.e. n is unknown. Assuming that the target matrix size N is fixed, the upscaling factor $\frac{N}{n}$ is unknown before seeing the test data. To avoid training a separate single-scale network for each n, one straightforward approach is to train a network with a dataset mixed with all possible n. However, the network needs to learn a fixed set of parameters to compromise between different n, which could result in sub-optimal performance. One recently proposed blind super-resolution technique modulates the feature map statistics (mean and standard deviation) after the convolution layers under the guidance of degradation [16]. However, based on our experiments, only modulating the feature map statistics cannot fully exploit the modulation potential. Another work proposed to use auxiliary Hypernetworks [11] to predict the parameters of the main network under the guidance of upscaling factor [14]. While predicting all network parameters with Hypernetworks have great modulation capability, the amount of network parameters is significantly increased [23].

To this end, we propose to use Filter Scaling [1,32] to modulate the network parameters without significantly increasing the network size. Specifically, for a convolution layer with C_{in} input channels and C_{out} output channels, the convolution filters $f \subset \mathbb{R}^{C_{in} \times C_{out} \times k \times k}$ ($k = 3$) are scaled based on n:

$$f' = c(n) * f \qquad (2)$$

where f' is the scaled convolution filters. The function $c(n) \in \mathbb{R}^{C_{in} \times C_{out}}$ is implemented as fully-connected layers that output a scaling factor for each $k \times k$ filter. This Filter Scaling strategy mostly retains the modulation capability of Hypernetworks but avoids generating all convolution filters, which requires the output dimension of $c(n)$ to be $C_{in} \times C_{out} \times k \times k$.

2.2   Metabolite-Awareness

The main challenge of developing data-driven methods for enhancing MRSI is the lack of abundant in vivo data. For data augmentation, the existing method uses a dataset consisting of metabolic maps derived from multiple metabolites [9]. However, different metabolites have distinct spatial characteristics, so the super-resolution process should not be identical. Based on this observation, we propose a metabolite-specific modulation of the network parameters. We use the same Filter Scaling strategy as in Eq. 2 but with an additional input $E(m)$:

$$f' = c(n, E(m)) * f \qquad (3)$$

where m is the types of metabolite, such as glutamate (Glu) or glycine (Gly), and E is a trainable embedding layer that converts words to numerical vectors.

2.3   Adjustable Sharpness

Our loss function consists of pixelwise loss, structural loss and adversarial loss [9]. The pixelwise loss penalizes the pixelwise difference between the network output

S and the ground truth I using L1 norm, i.e. $L_{pixel} = \frac{1}{N^2}\sum_{i,j}^{N,N} |S_{i,j} - I_{i,j}|$. The structural loss maximizes a structurally-motivated image quality metric Multiscale Structural Similarity (MS-SSIM) [31,34], i.e. $L_{structural} = 1 - \text{MS-SSIM}(S, I)$. The adversarial loss [30] uses a discriminator (a 4-layer CNN followed by FC layers, trained alternatively with the generator) to minimize the perceptual difference between S and I, which was implemented as a Wasserstein GAN [10]. The overall loss is a weighted sum of the three components:

$$Loss = (1 - \alpha)L_{pixel} + \alpha L_{structural} + \lambda L_{adversarial} \qquad (4)$$

where $\alpha \in [0,1]$ and $\lambda \geq 0$ are the hyperparameters. To be more specific, λ controls a trade-off between image fidelity and image sharpness.

We propose to condition our network on λ such that this trade-off can be tuned within a single network. Inspired by a recent work on hyperparameter tuning [23], we use Conditional Instance Normalization [15] to modulate the feature map statistics based on λ:

$$y = s_{1:C}(\lambda)(\frac{x - \mu(x)}{\sigma(x)}) + s_{C+1:2C}(\lambda) \qquad (5)$$

where $\mu(x) \in \mathbb{R}^C$ and $\sigma(x) \in \mathbb{R}^C$ are the channel-wise mean and standard deviation of the feature map x with channel number C. $s(\lambda) \in \mathbb{R}^{2C}$ is fully-connected layers that provide modulated channel-wise standard deviation in the first half of the output $s_{1:C}(\lambda)$ and modulated mean in the second half of the output $s_{C+1:2C}(\lambda)$. In this way, λ controls the sharpness of the final output by modulating the feature maps after each convolution layer.

3   Experiments and Results

3.1   Data Acquisition and Preprocessing

Due to the low concentration of metabolites, acquiring high resolution MRSI with acceptable SNR is always a challenge. We collected a unique 3D brain MRSI dataset from 15 high-grade glioma patients, with high resolution and high SNR [12]. ^{1}H-MRSI, T1 and FLAIR were acquired with a Siemens Magnetom 7T whole-body-MRI scanner. Informed consent and IRB approval were obtained. The MRSI sequences were acquired in 15 min, with an acquisition delay of 1.3 ms and a repetition time of 450 ms. The measurement matrix is $64 \times 64 \times 39$, corresponding to $3.4 \times 3.4 \times 3.4 \, \text{mm}^3$ nominal resolution. The 3D metabolic maps were quantified from the voxel spectra using LCModel v6.3-1 [24]. The spectra with insufficient quality (SNR < 2.5 or FWHM > 0.15 ppm) or close to the skull are rejected in a quality-filtering step. MRI images were skull-stripped and co-registered via FSL v5.0 [27].

From each 3D MRSI scan, we selected 11–18 axial slices that have sufficient voxels inside the brain, resulting in 2D metabolic maps of 64×64. These maps were regarded as the high resolution ground truth ($N = 64$). The corresponding low resolution maps were obtained by truncating $n \times n$ components at the center of k-space. We focus on 7 metabolites, namely total choline (tCho), total creatine (tCr), N-acetyl-aspartate (NAA), Gly, glutamine (Gln), Glu and inositol (Ins). The selected metabolites are important markers for the detection and characterization of tumors, stroke, multiple sclerosis and other disorders [5].

3.2   Implementation Details

The channel numbers for MCM are $8, 16, 32, 64, 128$ at each feature level. The numbers of fully-connected layers and latent feature sizes for $c(n)$, $c(n, E(m))$, $s(\lambda)$ are 5, 7, 5 and 32, 64, 64, respectively. Due to the limited number of patients, we adopted 5-fold cross-validation, and we used 9 patients for training, 3 for validation and 3 for testing in each fold. Therefore, the evaluations were performed on all 15 patients, which we believe makes our results reliable. The average numbers of metabolic maps used for training, validation and testing are 890, 297 and 297, respectively. The training data was substantially augmented using random flipping, rotation and shifting during training. n is uniformly sampled from the even integers between 16 and 32, and λ is uniformly sampled between 0 and 0.1. α is set to 0.84 as recommended in previous literature [34]. All networks were trained with Adam optimizer [21], batch size of 8, initial learning rate of 0.0001 and 100 epochs. Experiments were implemented in PyTorch v1.1.0 on NVIDIA GTX 1080 and V100 GPUs, with a maximum memory usage of $\sim$2.3 GB.

3.3   Results and Discussion

We first compare our Filter Scaling strategy with several other multi-scale super-resolution methods. In this part, the trainings were performed without the adversarial loss ($\lambda = 0$), because adversarial training lacks a deterministic objective function, which makes it hard to reliably compare the learning capabilities of different networks [25]. The second part demonstrates the functionality of adjustable sharpness, for which the adversarial loss was included in the training.

Multi-scale Super-Resolution and Metabolite-Awareness. To set a gold standard for the multi-scale super-resolution methods, we first trained 9 separate Multi-encoder UNet for $n = 16, 18, 20, 22, 24, 26, 28, 30, 32$ in a single-scale setting (denoted as Single-scale). As the baseline multi-scale super-resolution method, a Multi-encoder UNet was trained with n randomly sampled from those 9 values but without any conditioning (denoted as Unconditioned). We also implemented the AMLayer that only modulates the features maps [16] and the Hypernetworks that predict all network parameters [14], both conditioned on n. To ensure fairness, we set the same layer numbers and latent sizes for the Hypernetworks as for $c(n)$. Finally, we implemented two versions of our method, one uses Filter Scaling conditioned on n (Eq. 2, denoted as Filter Scaling), and the other uses Filter Scaling conditioned on both n and m (Eq. 3, denoted as Filter Scaling with Met). We performed the Wilcoxon signed-rank test on PSNR and SSIM for each pair of methods. As shown in Table 1, Filter Scaling achieves the same levels of PSNR and SSIM compared to the Single-scale networks (insignificant differences, p-value > 0.05), whereas the other methods perform worse (significant differences, p-value < 0.05). Note that Filter Scaling requires much fewer network parameters than HyperNetworks due to the smaller output dimension of fully-connected layers $c(n)$. With the incorporation of metabolite-specific modulation, Filter Scaling with Met achieves even higher metrics and performs the best among all the methods (significant differences, p-value < 0.05).

Table 1. Quantitative evaluations for different multi-scale super-resolution methods in terms of peak signal-to-noise ratio (PSNR), structural similarity index (SSIM), total training time (shown in GPU hours) and the total number of network parameters (shown in millions). PSNR and SSIM are presented in mean $\pm$ standard deviation calculated over all 5-fold cross validation and 9 values of n.

Method	PSNR	SSIM	Train time	Params
Single-scale	30.81 ± 2.90	0.9473 ± 0.0237	14.4 h	8.7M
Unconditioned	30.65 ± 2.82	0.9458 ± 0.0244	1.6 h	1.0M
AMLayer [16]	30.70 ± 2.86	0.9462 ± 0.0242	1.9 h	1.5M
Hypernetworks [14]	30.78 ± 2.88	0.9471 ± 0.0240	1.7 h	26M
Filter Scaling (ours)	30.81 ± 2.91	0.9474 ± 0.0238	1.7 h	3.9M
Filter Scaling with Met (ours)	$\mathbf{30.86 \pm 2.92}$	$\mathbf{0.9477 \pm 0.0240}$	1.8 h	6.9M

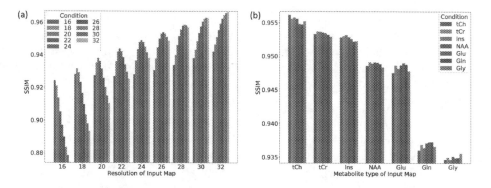

Fig. 2. Performance of our method under different combinations of network inputs (horizontal axis) and network conditions (color bars). (a) Study of the resolution. The plot shows the average SSIM computed over 5-fold cross-validation and all metabolites. (b) Study of the metabolite type. The plot shows the average SSIM computed over 5-fold cross-validation and all 9 values of n. (Color figure online)

To justify that our network learns the super-resolution process according to the conditions, we studied different combinations of input metabolic maps and conditions. The performance (measured using SSIM) is maximized when the resolution given in the condition matches with the input map's resolution (Fig. 2(a)), meaning that conditioning on n helps the network to super-resolve the input map at the desired extent. Figure 2(b) shows that the performance is maximized when the metabolite given in the condition matches with the metabolite of the input map (except only one failure case for NAA). This indicates that metabolite-specific modulation helps the network to super-resolve the input map based on each metabolite's distinct spatial characteristics.

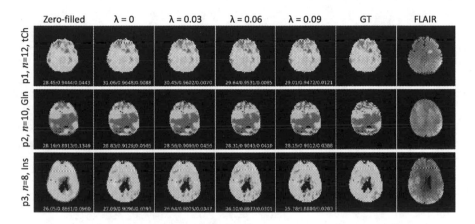

Fig. 3. Sharpness adjustability. From left to right are the standard k-space zero-filling, our method at $\lambda = 0, 0.03, 0.06, 0.09$, ground truth (GT) and the FLAIR anatomical reference. From top to bottom are the super-resolution results of different metabolites tCh, Gln and Ins, each at a different input resolution ($n = 12, 10, 8$) and from a different patient (p1, p2, p3). The numbers below each image are PSNR/SSIM/LPIPS.

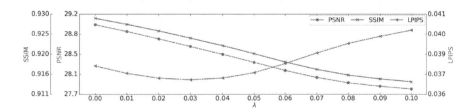

Fig. 4. Quantitative evaluations of different λ. The curves show mean scores of PSNR, SSIM and LPIPS, calculated over 5-fold cross validation and 9 values of n.

Adjustable Sharpness. Figure 3 shows a visualization of the super-resolved maps given by our network conditioning at $\lambda = 0, 0.03, 0.06, 0.09$, as well as the standard k-space zero-filling method. The results indicate that conditioning at

$\lambda = 0$ may generate metabolic maps that are blurry compared to the ground truth. Conditioning the network on greater levels of λ can increase the image sharpness, especially at some high-frequency features. For example, in the last row of Fig. 3, the Ins hotspot at the tumor is blurred at $\lambda = 0$. Using larger λ gives better contrast at the tumor, which can be useful for better tumor detection in clinical studies. Besides, we report the quantitative analysis of the trade-off between image fidelity and image sharpness in Fig. 4. The image fidelity metrics, such as PSNR and SSIM, are inevitably degraded by the adversarial loss when a larger λ is used and are therefore not sufficient to measure the improvement in perceptual quality. To measure the perceptual improvement quantitatively, we report the Learned Perceptual Image Patch Similarity (LPIPS), which was demonstrated to correlate well with human perceptual judgment [33]. The network achieves the best average LPIPS at around $\lambda = 0.03$ (lower is better), meaning that the output maps are perceptually the most proximal to the ground truth at this level. Using $\lambda > 0.03$ results in worsened LPIPS, which means the images are at a high risk of being overly sharpened. Therefore, we recommend tuning the network between $\lambda = 0$ and 0.03, depending on how much image fidelity and image sharpness are pursued.

4   Conclusion

This work presents a novel MCM to incorporate multiple conditions into a MRSI super-resolution network, which avoids training a separate network for each combination of hyperparameters. The network uses a Filter Scaling strategy to incorporate the upscaling factor and the type of metabolite into the learning process, outperforming several other multi-scale super-resolution methods. Moreover, our network is conditioned on the weight of adversarial loss, which provides sharpness adjustability. The method could potentially be applied clinically for faster data acquisition and more accurate diagnosis. For further validation, we can compare our results with tumor segmentation maps or histopathology to see if our method can help to better identify molecular markers for tumors. Future works will also extend the method to other MRSI applications, including mappings of other nuclei, e.g. ^{2}H [4,8], or other organs, e.g. liver [3].

Acknowledgements. This work was supported by the NIH grant R01EB025840, R01CA206180 and R01NS035193.

References

1. Alharbi, Y., Smith, N., Wonka, P.: Latent filter scaling for multimodal unsupervised image-to-image translation. In: Proceedings of the IEEE/CVF Conference on Computer Vision and Pattern Recognition, pp. 1458–1466 (2019)
2. Bogner, W., Otazo, R., Henning, A.: Accelerated MR spectroscopic imaging-a review of current and emerging techniques. NMR Biomed. **34**(5), e4314 (2021)
3. Coman, D., et al.: Extracellular PH mapping of liver cancer on a clinical 3T MRI scanner. Magn. Reson. Med. **83**(5), 1553–1564 (2020)

4. De Feyter, H.M., et al.: Deuterium metabolic imaging (DMI) for MRI-based 3D mapping of metabolism in vivo. Sci. Adv. **4**(8), eaat7314 (2018)
5. De Graaf, R.A.: In Vivo NMR Spectroscopy: Principles and Techniques. Wiley, New York (2019)
6. Dolz, J., Ben Ayed, I., Desrosiers, C.: Dense multi-path U-Net for Ischemic stroke lesion segmentation in multiple image modalities. In: Crimi, A., Bakas, S., Kuijf, H., Keyvan, F., Reyes, M., van Walsum, T. (eds.) BrainLes 2018. LNCS, vol. 11383, pp. 271–282. Springer, Cham (2019). https://doi.org/10.1007/978-3-030-11723-8_27
7. Dong, S., et al.: Invertible sharpening network for MRI reconstruction enhancement. arXiv preprint arXiv:2206.02838 (2022)
8. Dong, S., De Feyter, H.M., Thomas, M.A., de Graaf, R.A., Duncan, J.S.: A deep learning method for sensitivity enhancement in deuterium metabolic imaging (DMI). In: Proceedings of the 28th Annual Meeting of ISMRM, No. 0391 (2020)
9. Dong, S., et al.: High-resolution magnetic resonance spectroscopic imaging using a multi-encoder attention u-net with structural and adversarial loss. In: 2021 43rd Annual International Conference of the IEEE Engineering in Medicine & Biology Society (EMBC), pp. 2891–2895. IEEE (2021)
10. Gulrajani, I., Ahmed, F., Arjovsky, M., Dumoulin, V., Courville, A.: Improved training of Wasserstein GANs. arXiv preprint arXiv:1704.00028 (2017)
11. Ha, D., Dai, A., Le, Q.V.: Hypernetworks. arXiv preprint arXiv:1609.09106 (2016)
12. Hangel, G., et al.: High-resolution metabolic imaging of high-grade gliomas using 7T-CRT-FID-MRSI. NeuroImage Clin. **28**, 102433 (2020)
13. He, K., Zhang, X., Ren, S., Sun, J.: Delving deep into rectifiers: surpassing human-level performance on ImageNet classification. In: Proceedings of the IEEE International Conference on Computer Vision, pp. 1026–1034 (2015)
14. Hu, X., Mu, H., Zhang, X., Wang, Z., Tan, T., Sun, J.: Meta-SR: a magnification-arbitrary network for super-resolution. In: Proceedings of the IEEE/CVF Conference on Computer Vision and Pattern Recognition, pp. 1575–1584 (2019)
15. Huang, X., Belongie, S.: Arbitrary style transfer in real-time with adaptive instance normalization. In: Proceedings of the IEEE International Conference on Computer Vision, pp. 1501–1510 (2017)
16. Hui, Z., Li, J., Wang, X., Gao, X.: Learning the non-differentiable optimization for blind super-resolution. In: Proceedings of the IEEE/CVF Conference on Computer Vision and Pattern Recognition, pp. 2093–2102 (2021)
17. Iqbal, Z., Nguyen, D., Hangel, G., Motyka, S., Bogner, W., Jiang, S.: Super-resolution 1H magnetic resonance spectroscopic imaging utilizing deep learning. Front. Oncol. **9**, 1010 (2019)
18. Jain, S., et al.: Patch-based super-resolution of MR spectroscopic images: application to multiple sclerosis. Front. Neurosci. **11**, 13 (2017)
19. Kasten, J., Klauser, A., Lazeyras, F., Van De Ville, D.: Magnetic resonance spectroscopic imaging at superresolution: overview and perspectives. J. Magn. Reson. **263**, 193–208 (2016)
20. Kim, D.W., Chung, J.R., Kim, J., Lee, D.Y., Jeong, S.Y., Jung, S.W.: Constrained adversarial loss for generative adversarial network-based faithful image restoration. ETRI J. **41**(4), 415–425 (2019)
21. Kingma, D.P., Ba, J.: Adam: a method for stochastic optimization. arXiv preprint arXiv:1412.6980 (2014)
22. Lam, F., Liang, Z.P.: A subspace approach to high-resolution spectroscopic imaging. Magn. Reson. Med. **71**(4), 1349–1357 (2014)

23. Mok, T.C.W., Chung, A.C.S.: Conditional deformable image registration with convolutional neural network. In: de Bruijne, M., et al. (eds.) MICCAI 2021. LNCS, vol. 12904, pp. 35–45. Springer, Cham (2021). https://doi.org/10.1007/978-3-030-87202-1_4

24. Provencher, S.W.: LCmodel & LCMgui user's manual. LCModel version, vol. 6(3) (2014)

25. Salimans, T., Goodfellow, I., Zaremba, W., Cheung, V., Radford, A., Chen, X.: Improved techniques for training GANs. Adv. Neural. Inf. Process. Syst. **29**, 2234–2242 (2016)

26. Schlemper, J., Caballero, J., Hajnal, J.V., Price, A.N., Rueckert, D.: A deep cascade of convolutional neural networks for dynamic MR image reconstruction. IEEE Trans. Med. Imaging **37**(2), 491–503 (2017)

27. Smith, S.M., et al.: Advances in functional and structural MR image analysis and implementation as FSL. Neuroimage **23**, S208–S219 (2004)

28. Tan, C., Zhu, J., Lio', P.: Arbitrary scale super-resolution for brain MRI images. In: Maglogiannis, I., Iliadis, L., Pimenidis, E. (eds.) AIAI 2020. IAICT, vol. 583, pp. 165–176. Springer, Cham (2020). https://doi.org/10.1007/978-3-030-49161-1_15

29. Wang, L., Wang, Y., Lin, Z., Yang, J., An, W., Guo, Y.: Learning a single network for scale-arbitrary super-resolution. In: Proceedings of the IEEE/CVF International Conference on Computer Vision, pp. 4801–4810 (2021)

30. Wang, Z., Chen, J., Hoi, S.C.: Deep learning for image super-resolution: a survey. IEEE Trans. Pattern Anal. Mach. Intell. **43**(10), 3365–3387 (2020)

31. Wang, Z., Simoncelli, E.P., Bovik, A.C.: Multiscale structural similarity for image quality assessment. In: The Thirty-Seventh Asilomar Conference on Signals, Systems & Computers, 2003, vol. 2, pp. 1398–1402. IEEE (2003)

32. Yang, H., Sun, J., Yang, L., Xu, Z.: A unified Hyper-GAN model for unpaired multi-contrast MR image translation. In: de Bruijne, M., et al. (eds.) MICCAI 2021. LNCS, vol. 12903, pp. 127–137. Springer, Cham (2021). https://doi.org/10.1007/978-3-030-87199-4_12

33. Zhang, R., Isola, P., Efros, A.A., Shechtman, E., Wang, O.: The unreasonable effectiveness of deep features as a perceptual metric. In: Proceedings of the IEEE Conference on Computer Vision and Pattern Recognition, pp. 586–595 (2018)

34. Zhao, H., Gallo, O., Frosio, I., Kautz, J.: Loss functions for image restoration with neural networks. IEEE Trans. Comput. Imaging **3**(1), 47–57 (2016)

Progressive Subsampling for Oversampled Data - Application to Quantitative MRI

Stefano B. Blumberg[1(✉)], Hongxiang Lin[1,3], Francesco Grussu[1,2], Yukun Zhou[1], Matteo Figini[1], and Daniel C. Alexander[1]

[1] University College London (UCL), London, UK
hxlin@zhejianglab.edu.cn, stefano.blumberg.17@ucl.ac.uk
[2] Vall d'Hebron Barcelona Hospital, Barcelona, Spain
[3] Zhejiang Lab, Hangzhou, China

Abstract. We present PROSUB: PROgressive SUBsampling, a deep learning based, automated methodology that subsamples an oversampled data set (e.g. channels of multi-channeled 3D images) with minimal loss of information. We build upon a state-of-the-art dual-network approach that won the MICCAI MUlti-DIffusion (MUDI) quantitative MRI (qMRI) measurement sampling-reconstruction challenge, but suffers from deep learning training instability, by subsampling with a hard decision boundary. PROSUB uses the paradigm of recursive feature elimination (RFE) and progressively subsamples measurements during deep learning training, improving optimization stability. PROSUB also integrates a neural architecture search (NAS) paradigm, allowing the network architecture hyperparameters to respond to the subsampling process. We show PROSUB outperforms the winner of the MUDI MICCAI challenge, producing large improvements >18% MSE on the MUDI challenge sub-tasks and qualitative improvements on downstream processes useful for clinical applications. We also show the benefits of incorporating NAS and analyze the effect of PROSUB's components. As our method generalizes beyond MRI measurement selection-reconstruction, to problems that subsample and reconstruct multi-channeled data, our code is [7].

Keywords: Magnetic Resonance Imaging (MRI) Protocol Design · Recursive feature elimination · Neural architecture search

1 Introduction

Multi-modal medical imaging gives unprecedented insight into the microstructural composition of living tissues, and provides non-invasive biomarkers that hold promise in several clinical contexts. In particular, quantitative MRI fits a

Supplementary Information The online version contains supplementary material available at https://doi.org/10.1007/978-3-031-16446-0_40.

model in each pixel of a multi-channel acquisition consisting of multiple images each with unique contrast obtained by varying multiple MRI acquisition parameters, see e.g. [22]. This provides pixel-wise estimates of biophysical tissue properties [16]. In spite of this potential, comprehensively sampling high-dimensional acquisition spaces leads to prohibitively long acquisition times, which is a key barrier to more widespread adoption of qMRI in clinical use.

The MUlti-DIffusion (MUDI) MRI challenge [1,30] addressed this by providing data covering a densely-sampled MRI acquisition space (3D brain images with 1344 channels). The task was to reconstruct the full set of measurements from participant-chosen measurements from a small subsample, i.e. to obtain economical, but maximally informative acquisition protocols for any model that the full data set supports. That involves two sub-tasks: selecting the most informative measurements, and reconstructing the full data set from them. The challenge winner was SARDU-Net [17,18,30] with a dual-network strategy, that respectively subsamples the measurements, then reconstructs the full dataset from the subsampled data. However, SARDU-Net selects different sets of measurements with a hard decision boundary on each training batch, altering the second network's input across different batches. This can cause instability, see supplementary materials and [8,25] show similar issues produce training instability. Furthermore, the popularity of paradigms such as recursive feature elimination (RFE), suggests that subsampling all of the measurements required immediately, is suboptimal. These two issues may lead to substandard performance.

We propose PROSUB, a novel automated methodology that selects then reconstructs measurements from oversampled data. Unlike classical approaches to experiment design [4], we approach the MUDI challenge in a new model-independent way. PROSUB builds upon the SARDU-Net by (i) using a form of RFE which progressively removes measurements across successive RFE steps and (ii) learning an average measurement score across RFE steps, which chooses the measurements to remove or preserve. This enhances the stability of our optimization procedure. Within each RFE step, PROSUB (iii) progressively subsamples the required measurements during deep learning training, building upon [8,25], that improves training stability. Also, PROSUB (iv) incorporates a generic neural architecture search (NAS) paradigm in concurrence to the RFE - so the architectures may respond to the measurement subsampling process.

Our implementation [7] is based on AutoKeras [24], KerasTuner [29]. PROSUB outperforms the SARDU-Net and SARDU-Net with AutoKeras NAS by $> 18\%$ MSE on the publicly available MUDI challenge data [2,30]. We show qualitative improvements on downstream processes: $T2^*$, FA, T1, Tractography useful in clinical applications [5,10,14,20,27]. We examine the effect of how PROSUB's components, including NAS, improve performance. We release the code [7] as PROSUB is not limited to subsampling MRI data for microstructure imaging.

2   Related Work and Preliminaries

Problem Setting. Suppose we have an oversampled dataset $\mathbf{x} = \{\mathbf{x}_1, ..., \mathbf{x}_n\} \in \mathbb{R}^{n \times N}$ where each sample has N measurements $\mathbf{x}_i \in \mathbb{R}^N$. The aim is to subsample

$M < N$ measurements $\widetilde{\mathbf{x}} = \{\widetilde{\mathbf{x}}_1, ..., \widetilde{\mathbf{x}}_n\} \in \mathbb{R}^{n \times M}$, $\widetilde{\mathbf{x}}_i \in \mathbb{R}^M$, with the same M elements of each $\mathbf{x}_i$ in each $\widetilde{\mathbf{x}}_i$. We aim to lose as little information as possible when choosing $\widetilde{\mathbf{x}}$, thereby enabling the best recovery of the full data set $\mathbf{x}$. We therefore have two interconnected problems i) choosing which measurements to subsample, ii) reconstructing the original measurements from the subsampled measurements. We achieve this by (i) constructing a binary mask m containing M ones and $N - M$ zeros so $\widetilde{\mathbf{x}} = m \cdot \mathbf{x}$, (ii) with a neural network $\mathcal{R}$.

SARDU-Net and Dual-Network Approaches. The SARDU-Net [17,18,30], which is used for model-free quantitative MRI protocol design and won the MUDI challenge [30], has two stacked neural networks, trained in unison. The first network learns weight w from $\mathbf{x}$. $N - M$ smallest values of w are clamped to 0 and the first network subsamples and selects the measurements, by outputting $\mathbf{x} \cdot w$. The second network then predicts the original data from $\mathbf{x} \cdot w$. Related dual-network approaches include [11], which processed large point clouds, differing from our problem, as we do not assume our data has a spatial structure. We build upon the SARDU-Net and we use it as a baseline in our experiments.

Recursive Feature Elimination (RFE.) One of the most common paradigms for feature selection is RFE, which has a long history in machine learning [3,34]. Recursively over steps $t = 1, ..., T$, RFE prunes the least important features based on some task-specific importance score, successively analyzing less and less features over successive steps. We use a form of RFE in PROSUB.

Neural Architecture Search (NAS). Selecting neural network architecture hyperparameters e.g. number of layers and hidden units, is a task data-dependent problem, where the most common strategies are random search [6] or grid search [26]. NAS approaches, see e.g. [12], outperform classical approaches with respect to time required to obtain high-performing models and can broadly be seen as a subfield of Automated Machine Learning (AutoML) [21]. PROSUB uses a generic NAS paradigm which optimizes network architectures over successive steps $t = 1, ..., T$ in an outer loop. In an inner loop, with fixed architecture (and fixed t), we perform standard deep learning training across epochs $e - 1, ..., E$, caching network training and validation performance r_t^e after each epoch. At the end of step t, the previous losses $\{r_j^i : i \leq E, j \leq t\}$ are used to update the network architectures for step $t + 1$. Our implementation is based on AutoKeras [24], with KerasTuner [29], which has good documentation and functionality.

3   Methods

We address the interdependency of the sampling-reconstruction problem with a dual-network strategy in Sect. 3.1, illustrated in Fig. 1. In Sect. 3.2 we progressively construct our mask m, used to subsample the measurements. PROSUB has an outer loop: steps $t = 1, ..., T$ where we simultaneously perform NAS and RFE, choosing the measurements to remove via a score, averaged across the steps, whilst simultaneously updating the network architecture hyperparameters.

For fixed t, we perform deep learning training as an inner loop across epochs $e = 1, ..., E$, where we learn the aforementioned score and also progressively subsample the measurements. We summarize PROSUB in algorithm 1.

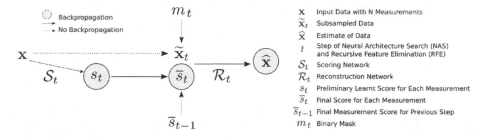

Fig. 1. The computational graph of PROSUB.

3.1   Scoring-Reconstruction Networks

Inspired by [11,17], we use two neural networks $\mathcal{S}_t, \mathcal{R}_t$, trained in unison, to address the interdependency of our two interconnected problems.

Scoring Network. The first network $\mathcal{S}_t$ learns a preliminary score with a sigmoid activation in its last layer, to weight each measurement:

$$s_t = \mathcal{S}_t(\mathbf{x}) \quad s_t \in (0, 2)^{n \times N}. \tag{1}$$

Mask. As described in Sect. 2, we use an array $m_t \in [0,1]^N$ as a mask

$$\widetilde{\mathbf{x}}_t = m_t \cdot \mathbf{x} \tag{2}$$

to subsample the measurements. We describe in Sect. 3.2, how we progressively and manually set m_t to have $N - M$ entries with 0.

Average Measurement Score. To score each measurement in step t, we use an exponential moving average, commonly used in time-series analysis (e.g. [19]), across the scores of previous steps $\overline{s}_1, ..., \overline{s}_{t-1}$ and s_t, to obtain a better estimate of the score and reduce the effect of the current learnt score σ_t, if network performance is poor. With moving average coefficient hyperparameter α_t we calculate

$$\overline{s}_t = \alpha_t \cdot s_t + (1 - \alpha_t) \cdot \overline{s}_{t-1} \tag{3}$$

and we use $\alpha_t = \frac{T-t}{T-1}$. The averaged score $\overline{s}_t$ is used to weight the subsampled measurements and to construct the mask (described in Sect. 3.2).

Reconstruction Network. The second network $\mathcal{R}_t$ takes the weighted subsampled measurements to estimate $\mathbf{x}$ with $\widehat{\mathbf{x}}$, then passed through $Loss$ (we use MSE)

$$L = Loss(\widehat{\mathbf{x}}, \mathbf{x}), \quad \widehat{\mathbf{x}} = \mathcal{R}_t(\widetilde{\mathbf{x}}_t \cdot \overline{s}_t) \tag{4}$$

and the gradients from L are then backpropagated through $\mathcal{R}_t, \mathcal{S}_t$.

Algorithm 1. PROSUB: PROgressive SUBsampling for Oversampled Data

Data and Task: $\mathbf{x} = \{\mathbf{x}_1, ..., \mathbf{x}_n\}$, $\mathbf{x}_i \in \mathbb{R}^N$, $M < N$

Training and NAS: $1 \leq E_d \leq E$, $1 < T_1 < T$, $NAS \leftarrow AutoKeras$

Scoring and RFE: $\alpha_t \leftarrow \frac{T-t}{T-1}$, $D_t \leftarrow \approx \frac{N-M}{T-T_1+1}$

Initialize: $m_1 \leftarrow [1]^N$, $\bar{s}_0 \leftarrow [0]^N$

```
 1: for t ← 1, ..., T₁, ..., T do                              ▷ RFE and NAS steps
 2:     if 1 ≤ t < T₁ then
 3:         D = ∅                                    ▷ No measurements to subsample
 4:     else if T₁ ≤ t ≤ T then                              ▷ Subsampling stage
 5:         D = argmin{s̄ₜ₋₁[j] : mₜ[j] = 1}      ▷ Measurements to subsample Eq. 5
            ⱼ₌₁,...,Dₜ
 6:     end if
 7:     for e ← 1, ..., E_d, ..., E  do                  ▷ Training and validation epoch
 8:         mₜᵉ ← max{mₜ − (e−E_d)𝕀ₑ≥E_d/E_d · 𝕀ᵢ∈D(i), 0}         ▷ Compute mask Eq. 6
 9:         sₜ = 𝒮(x),  x̃ₜ = mₜᵉ · xₜ                  ▷ Forward pass Eq. 1,2
10:         s̄ₜ = αₜ · sₜ + (1 − αₜ) · s̄ₜ₋₁          ▷ Average measurement score Eq. 3
11:         rₜᵉ ← L(x̂, x),  L = L(x̂, x),  x̂ = ℛₜ(x̃ · s̄ₜ) ▷ Forward/backward pass Eq.4
12:     end for
13:     Use NAS, {rⱼⁱ : i ≤ E, j ≤ t}, to calculate ℛₜ₊₁, 𝒮ₜ₊₁    ▷ Update architectures
14:     mₜ₊₁ ← mₜᴱ, cache s̄ₜ
15: end for
16: return mₜ, s̄ₜ, ℛₜ – use as described in Sect. 2
```

3.2   Constructing the Mask to Subsample the Measurements

We construct a mask m_t^c, used to subsample the measurements in Sect. 2 and Eq. 2. We progressively set $N - M$ entries of m_t^e to zero across NAS and RFE outer loop $t = 1, ..., T$ and deep learning inner loop $e = 1, ..., E$. We refer to Algorithm 1 for clarity.

Outer Loop: Choosing the Measurements to Remove. Following standard practise in RFE e.g. [3,34], we remove the measurements recursively, in our case, across steps $t = 1, ..., T$ in algorithm-line 1. We split the RFE in two stages, by choosing a dividing step, hyperparameter $1 < T_1 < T$.

In the first stage $t = 1, ..., T_1$ the optimization procedure learns scores $\bar{s}_t$ and optimizes the network architectures via NAS. In algorithm-line 3, we choose no measurements to subsample ($D = \emptyset$) thus the mask $m_t^e = m_t$ is fixed in algorithm-line 8.

In the second stage $t = T_1, ..., T$, we perform standard RFE. We first choose a hyperparameter $D_t \in \mathbb{N}$ – the number of measurements to subsample in step t. In this paper, we remove the same number of measurements per step, so $D_t \approx \frac{N-M}{T-T_1+1}$. In algorithm-line 5 we then choose the measurements to remove in RFE step t, which correspond to those with the lowest scores in the previous step

$$D = \underset{j=1,...,D_t}{\arg\min}\{\bar{s}_{t-1}[j] : m_t[j] = 1\}, \quad m_t \in \{0,1\}^N \tag{5}$$

where here m_t indicates whether the measurement has been removed in previous steps $< t$. Our rationale is since the subsampled measurements are weighted by the score, used as inputs to the reconstruction network in Eq. 4, setting lowest-scored values to 0 may have small effect on the performance (in Eq. 4).

Inner Loop: Progressively Subsampling the Measurements by Altering the Mask During Training. Given D – computed in the outer loop algorithm-line 5 we progressively, manually, alter the mask m_t^e in the inner loop of deep learning training algorithm-line 7, i.e. gradually setting the value of these measurements to 0 in $\widetilde{\mathbf{x}}_t$. We are inspired by [8,25] which used a similar approach to improve training stability. We alter m_t^e across chosen epochs $e = E_d, ..., 2 \cdot E_d - 1 \leq E$ for hyperparameter $E_d < \frac{E}{2}$, used in algorithm-line 8, for indicator function $\mathbb{I}$:

$$m_t^e = \max\left\{m_t - \frac{(e - E_d)\mathbb{I}_{e \geq E_d}}{E_d} \cdot \mathbb{I}_{i \in D}(i), 0\right\}. \tag{6}$$

4   Experiments and Results

MUDI Dataset and Task. Data of images from 5 subjects are from the MUDI challenge [1,30], publicly available at [2]. Data features a variety of diffusion and relaxometry (i.e. T1 and T2*) contrasts, and were acquired with the ZEBRA MRI technique [22]. The total acquisition time for these oversampled data sets was ≈ 1 h, corresponding to the acquisition of $N = 1344$ measurements in this dense parameter space, resulting in 5, 3D brain images with 1344 channels (here unique diffusion- T2* and T1- weighting contrasts), with $n \approx 558K$ brain voxels. Detailed information is in [22,30]. We used the same task as the MICCAI MUDI challenge [30], where the participants were asked to find the most informative subsets of size $M = 500, 250, 100, 50$ out of N, while also estimating the fully-sampled signals from each of these subsets, and the evaluation is MRI signal prediction MSE. The winner of the original challenge [1,30] was the aforementioned SARDU-Net [17,30]. In this paper, we also consider smaller subsets $M = 40, 30, 20, 10$.

Experimental Settings. We did five-fold cross validation using two separate subjects for validation and testing. We compare PROSUB and PROSUB w/o NAS with four baselines: i) SARDU-Net-v1: winner of the MUDI challenge [17,30]; ii) SARDU-Net-v2: latest official implementation of (i) [15,18]; iii) SARDU-Net-v2-BOF: five runs of (ii) with different initializations, choosing the best model from the validation set; iv) SARDU-Net-v2-NAS: integrating (ii) with AutoKeras NAS. To reduce total computational time with NAS techniques, we performed all of the tasks in succession. We first use algorithm 1 with $T_1, T, M = 4, 8, 500$, then take the final model, as initialization for Algorithm 1 with $T_1, T, M = 1, 5, 250$, performing this recursively for $M = 100, 50, 40, 30, 20, 10$, using the best model for each different M. Consequently, SARDU-Net-v2-BOF and the NAS techniques in Table 1 are trained for approximately the same number of epochs. We performed a brief search for

NAS hyperparameters. We examined the effect of PROSUB's components and present all hyperparameters in the supplementary materials.

Table 1. Whole brain Mean-Squared-Error between $N = 1344$ reconstructed measurements and N ground-truth measurements, on leave-one-out cross validation on five MUlti-DIffusion (MUDI) challenge subjects. The SARDU-Net won the MUDI challenge.

		MUDI challenge subsamples M for $N = 1344$			
		500	250	100	50
SARDU-Net-v1 [17,30]	Baseline	1.45 ± 0.14	1.72 ± 0.15	4.73 ± 0.57	5.15 ± 0.63
SARDU-Net-v2 [15,18]	Baseline	0.88 ± 0.10	0.89 ± 0.01	1.36 ± 0.14	1.66 ± 0.10
SARDU-Net-v2-BOF [15,18]	Baseline	0.83 ± 0.10	0.86 ± 0.10	1.30 ± 0.12	1.67 ± 0.12
SARDU-Net-v2-NAS	Baseline	0.82 ± 0.13	0.99 ± 0.12	1.34 ± 0.26	1.76 ± 0.24
PROSUB w/o NAS	Ours	0.66 ± 0.08	0.67 ± 0.09	$\mathbf{0.88 \pm 0.07}$	1.54 ± 0.11
PROSUB	Ours	$\mathbf{0.49 \pm 0.07}$	$\mathbf{0.61 \pm 0.11}$	0.89 ± 0.11	$\mathbf{1.35 \pm 0.11}$
		M = 40	30	20	10
SARDU-Net-v1 [17,30]	Baseline	6.10 ± 0.79	21.0 ± 6.07	19.8 ± 9.26	22.8 ± 6.57
SARDU-Net-v2 [15,18]	Baseline	1.95 ± 0.12	2.27 ± 0.20	3.01 ± 0.45	4.41 ± 1.39
SARDU-Net-v2-BOF [15,18]	Baseline	1.86 ± 0.18	2.15 ± 0.23	2.61 ± 0.24	$3.74 + 0.66$
SARDU-Net-v2-NAS	Baseline	2.23 ± 0.22	6.00 ± 7.14	2.82 ± 0.41	4.27 ± 1.66
PROSUB w/o NAS	Ours	1.81 ± 0.18	2.18 ± 0.17	2.72 ± 0.34	3.91 ± 0.22
PROSUB	Ours	$\mathbf{1.53 \pm 0.05}$	$\mathbf{1.87 \pm 0.19}$	$\mathbf{2.50 \pm 0.40}$	$\mathbf{3.48 \pm 0.55}$

Main Results. We present quantitative results in Table 1 and note PROSUB's large improvements >18% MSE over all four baselines on the MUDI challenge sub-tasks. Using the Wilcoxon one-sided signed-rank test, a non-parametric statistical test comparing paired brain samples, our methods improvements have p-values of 7.14E−08, 9.29E−07, 3.20E−06, 9.29E−07 over the four respective baselines with Bonferroni correction, thus are statistically significant. We provide qualitative comparisons on a random test subject in Fig. 2 on downstream processes (T2*,FA,T1,Tractography), useful in clinical applications [5,10,14,20,27].

Discussion. Without explicitly optimizing PROSUB's network architecture and training hyperparameters (fixing PROSUB's hyperparameters to the SARDU-Net hyperparameters at $M = 500$), the PROSUB still outperforms all SARDU-Net baselines for MUDI Challenge M. Concerning NAS, we note the SARDU-Net-v2-NAS generally underperforms the SARDU-Net w/o NAS. Examining network performance during NAS (e.g. supplementary materials), this is due to SARDU-Net performance being unstable due to its hard measurement selection, thus its performance is vulnerable to changes in architecture. Passing poor results to the NAS then reduces the effectiveness of the NAS in identifying high-performing architectures for small M. In contrast, PROSUB's progressive subsampling allows the NAS to identify better architectures than the SARDU-Net-v2-NAS. PROSUB also outperforms the PROSUB w/o NAS i.e. the NAS

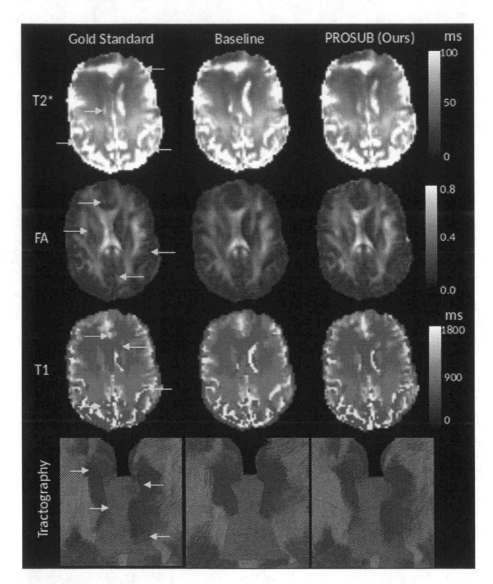

Fig. 2. Qualitative comparison of downstream processes with useful clinical applications [5,10,14,20,27], of reconstructed $N = 1344$ measurements from chosen $M = 50$ samples, on a random test subject. PROSUB results are visually closer to the gold standard than the baseline. As MUDI data provides combined diffusion and relaxometry information, to evaluate the practical impact of the different reconstructions we estimated T1, T2* values and DTI parameters with a dictionary-based approach in [13]. We show whole-brain probabilistic tractography examining reconstructed fibre tracts, colors correspond to direction, on multi-shell/tissue constrained spherical deconvolution via iFOD2 in [23]. Quantative improvements are, Baseline - Ours MSE, e.g. FA: 0.006 - 0.004, on NODDI parametric maps [33]: 0.022 - 0.007 FICVF, 0.023 - 0.005 FISO, 0.020 - 0.013 ODI.

is able to identify better performing architectures than the architecture chosen by the SARDU-Net for $M = 500$. In the supplementary materials, we analyze the effect of PROSUB's components, note removing any of the three non-NAS contributions worsens performance; we also show increasing network capacity in the PROSUB does not necessarily improve performance; we also list the architectures chosen by the NAS for SARDU-Net-v2-NAS and PROSUB.

5   Future Work

In future work, we could add an additional cost function to address the cost of obtaining specific combination of measurements from sets of MRI acquisition parameters; and develop a novel NAS algorithm to account for the concurrence of the subsampling process and architecture optimization. Our approach extends to many other quantitative MRI applicationse.g. [4,9,16], other imaging problems e.g. [31], and wider feature selection/experiment design problems e.g. [28,32].

Acknowledgements. We thank: Tristan Clark and the HPC team (James O'Connor, Edward Martin); MUDI Organizers (Marco Pizzolato, Jana Hutter, Fan Zhang); Amy Chapman, Luca Franceschi, Marcela Konanova and Shinichi Tamura; NVIDIA for donating the GPU for winning 2019 MUDI. Funding details SB: EPRSC and Microsoft scholarship, EPSRC grants M020533 R006032 R014019, NIHR UCLH Biomedical Research Centre, HL: Research Initiation Project of Zhejiang Lab (No. 2021ND0PI02), FG: Fellowships Programme Beatriu de Pinós (2020 BP 00117), Secretary of Universities and Research (Government of Catalonia).

References

1. MUlti-dimensional DIffusion (MUDI) MRI challenge 2019. https://web.archive.org/web/20200209111131/http://cmic.cs.ucl.ac.uk/cdmri
2. MUlti-dimensional DIffusion (MUDI) MRI challenge 2019 data. https://www.developingbrain.co.uk/data/
3. Scikit-learn recursive feature elimination. https://scikit-learn.org/stable/modules/generated/sklearn.feature_selection.RFE.html
4. Alexander, D.C.: A general framework for experiment design in diffusion MRI and its application in measuring direct tissue-microstructure features. Magn. Reson. Med. **60**(2), 439–448 (2008)
5. Andica, C., et al.: MR biomarkers of degenerative brain disorders derived from diffusion imaging. J. Magn. Reson. Imaging **52**(6), 1620–1636 (2020)
6. Bergstra, J., Bengio, Y.: Random search for hyper-parameter optimization. J. Mach. Learn. Res. **13**, 281–305 (2012)
7. Blumberg, S.B.: PROSUB code. https://github.com/sbb-gh/PROSUB
8. Blumberg, S.B., et al.: Multi-stage prediction networks for data harmonization. In: Shen, D., et al. (eds.) MICCAI 2019. LNCS, vol. 11767, pp. 411–419. Springer, Cham (2019). https://doi.org/10.1007/978-3-030-32251-9_45
9. Brihuega-Moreno, O., Heese, F.P., Hall, L.D.: Optimization of diffusion measurements using Cramer-Rao lower bound theory and its application to articular cartilage. Magn. Reson. Med. **50**, 1069–1076 (2003)

10. Deoni, S.C.L.: Quantitative relaxometry of the brain. Topics Magn. Reson. Imaging **21**(2), 101–113 (2010)
11. Dovrat, O., Lang, I., Avidan, S.: Learning to sample. In: Computer Vision and Pattern Recognition (CVPR) (2019)
12. Elsken, T., Metzen, J.H., Hutter, F.: Neural architecture search: a survey. J. Mach. Learn. Res. **20**, 1–21 (2019)
13. Garyfallidis, E., et al.: DIPY, a library for the analysis of diffusion MRI data. Front. Neuroinform. **8**, 8 (2014)
14. Granziera, C., et al.: Quantitative magnetic resonance imaging towards clinical application in multiple sclerosis. Brain **144**(5), 1296–1311 (2021)
15. Grussu, F.: SARDU-Net code. https://github.com/fragrussu/sardunet
16. Grussu, F., et al.: Multi-parametric quantitative in vivo spinal cord MRI with unified signal readout and image denoising. NeuroImage **217**, 116884 (2020)
17. Grussu, F., et al.: SARDU-Net: a new method for model-free, data-driven experiment design in quantitative MRI. In: International Society for Magnetic Resonance in Medicine (ISMRM) (2020)
18. Grussu, F., et al.: Feasibility of data-driven, model-free quantitative MRI protocol design: Application to brain and prostate diffusion-relaxation imaging. Front. Phys. **9**, 615 (2021)
19. Hamilton, J.D.: Time Series Analysis. Princeton University Press, Princeton (1994)
20. Henderson, F., Abdullah, K.G., Verma, R., Brem, S.: Tractography and the connectome in neurosurgical treatment of gliomas: the premise, the progress, and the potential. Neurosurg. Focus **48**(2), E6 (2020)
21. Hutter, F., Kotthoff, L., Vanschoren, J. (eds.): Automated Machine Learning. TSSCML, Springer, Cham (2019). https://doi.org/10.1007/978-3-030-05318-5
22. Hutter, J., et al.: Integrated and efficient diffusion-relaxometry using ZEBRA. Sci. Rep. **8**(1), 1–13 (2018)
23. Jeurissen, B., Tournier, J.D., Dhollander, T., Connelly, A., Sijbers, J.: Multi-tissue constrained spherical deconvolution for improved analysis of multi-shell diffusion MRI data. NeuroImage **103**, 411–426 (2014)
24. Jin, H., Song, Q., Hu, X.: Auto-keras: An efficient neural architecture search system. In: International Conference on Knowledge Discovery & Data Mining (KDD) (2019)
25. Karras, T., Aila, T., Laine, S., Lehtinen, J.: Progressive growing of GANs for improved quality, stability, and variation. In: International Conference on Learning Representations (ICLR) (2018)
26. Larochelle, H., Erhan, D., Courville, A., Bergstra, J., Bengio, Y.: An empirical evaluation of deep architectures on problems with many factors of variation. In: International conference on Machine learning (ICML) (2007)
27. Lehéricy, S., Roze, E., Goizet, Mochel, F.: MRI of neurodegeneration with brain iron accumulation. Curr. Opin. Neurol. **33**(4), 462–473 (2020)
28. Marinescu, R.V., et al.: TADPOLE challenge: accurate Alzheimer's disease prediction through crowdsourced forecasting of future data. In: Rekik, I., Adeli, E., Park, S.H. (eds.) PRIME 2019. LNCS, vol. 11843, pp. 1–10. Springer, Cham (2019). https://doi.org/10.1007/978-3-030-32281-6_1
29. O'Malley, T., et al.: KerasTuner (2019)
30. Pizzolato, M., et al.: Acquiring and predicting MUltidimensional DIffusion (MUDI) data: an open challenge. In: Bonet-Carne, E., Hutter, J., Palombo, M., Pizzolato, M., Sepehrband, F., Zhang, F. (eds.) Computational Diffusion MRI. MV, pp. 195–208. Springer, Cham (2020). https://doi.org/10.1007/978-3-030-52893-5_17

31. Prevost, R., Buckley, D.L., Alexander, D.C.: Optimization of the DCE-CT protocol using active imaging. In: 2010 IEEE International Symposium on Biomedical Imaging (ISBI): From Nano to Macro, pp. 776–779 (2010)
32. van der Putten, P., van Somere, M.: CoIL challenge 2000: The insurance company case. Technical report, Institute of Advanced Computer Science (2000)
33. Zhang, H., Schneider, T., Wheeler-Kingshott, C.A., Alexander, D.C.: NODDI: practical in vivo neurite orientation dispersion and density imaging of the human brain. NeuroImage **61**(4), 1000–1016 (2012)
34. Zheng, A., Casari, A.: Feature Engineering for Machine Learning: Principles and Techniques for Data Scientists. O'Reilly, Sebastopol (2018)

Deep-Learning Based T_1 and T_2 Quantification from Undersampled Magnetic Resonance Fingerprinting Data to Track Tracer Kinetics in Small Laboratory Animals

Yuning Gu[1], Yongsheng Pan[1], Zhenghan Fang[2], Jingyang Zhang[1], Peng Xue[1], Mianxin Liu[1], Yuran Zhu[3], Lei Ma[1], Charlie Androjna[4], Xin Yu[3(✉)], and Dinggang Shen[1,5(✉)]

[1] Department of Biomedical Engineering, ShanghaiTech University, Shanghai, China
dgshen@shanghaitech.edu.cn
[2] Department of Biomedical Engineering, Johns Hopkins University, Baltimore, MD, USA
[3] Department of Biomedical Engineering, Case Western Reserve University, Cleveland, OH, USA
xin.yu@case.edu
[4] Cleveland Clinic Pre-Clinical Magnetic Resonance Imaging Center, Cleveland Clinic Foundation, Cleveland, OH, USA
[5] Shanghai United Imaging Intelligence Co., Ltd., 200230 Shanghai, China

Abstract. In human MRI studies, magnetic resonance fingerprinting (MRF) allows simultaneous T_1 and T_2 mapping in 10 s using 48-fold undersampled data. However, when "reverse translated" to preclinical research involving small laboratory animals, the undersampling capacity of the MRF method decreases to 8 fold because of the low SNR associated with high spatial resolution. In this study, we aim to develop a deep-learning based method to reliably quantify T_1 and T_2 in the mouse brain from highly undersampled MRF data, and to demonstrate its efficacy in tracking T_1 and T_2 variations induced by MR tracers. The proposed method employs U-Net as the backbone for spatially constrained T_1 and T_2 mapping. Several strategies to improve the robustness of mapping results are evaluated, including feature extraction with sliding window averaging, implementing physics-guided training objectives, and implementing data-consistency constraint to iteratively refine the inferred maps by a cascade of U-Nets. The quantification network is trained using mouse-brain MRF datasets acquired before and after Manganese (Mn^{2+}) enhancement. Experimental results show that robust T_1 and T_2 mapping can be achieved from MRF data acquired in 30 s (4-fold further acceleration), by using a simple combination of sliding window averaging for feature extraction and U-Net for parametric quantification. Meanwhile, the T_1 variations induced by Mn^{2+} in mouse brain are faithfully detected. Code is available at https://github.com/guyn-idealab/Mouse-MRF-DL/.

Keywords: Deep learning · MR fingerprinting · Contrast-enhanced MRI

L. Wang et al. (Eds.): MICCAI 2022, LNCS 13436, pp. 432–441, 2022.
https://doi.org/10.1007/978-3-031-16446-0_41

1 Introduction

Magnetic resonance fingerprinting (MRF) is a quantitative MRI technique that allows simultaneous T_1 and T_2 quantification with unprecedented efficiency [1]. MRF employs variable acquisition parameters (e.g., flip angles), to generate signal evolution (i.e., fingerprint) that is uniquely dependent on the T_1 and T_2 relaxation properties of a tissue. Because the variable acquisition parameters prevent the signal from reaching steady-state, increasing the number of acquired image frames can always add new information and thus enhance the accuracy of parameter estimation [1].

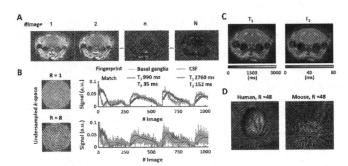

Fig. 1. Schematics of classic MRF method. **A.** MRF image series with temporally-varying T_1 and T_2 weighting. **B.** Representative fingerprints and matched templates in the basal ganglia (green) and CSF (red), from MRF data with undersampling rates (R) of 1 (top row, fully sampled) and 8 (bottom row). **C.** T_1 and T_2 maps derived from matched templates. **D.** Images reconstructed from human and mouse MRF data with R of 48.

The classic MRF framework acquires 1000–2000 image frames in 10–20 s for robust T_1 and T_2 mapping, with the quantification performed by template matching method (Fig. 1A-C) [1]. The method prepares a dictionary of theoretical signal templates, which is simulated according to MR physics for a full-range of discretized T_1–T_2 pairs. The quantified T_1 and T_2 values in each pixel can therefore be derived from the template that best matches the acquired MRF signal. In human 2D MRF scans, the template matching method allows accurate T_1 and T_2 mapping using ~1000 image frames reconstructed from 48-fold undersampled MRF data [1, 2].

Deep-learning methods are gaining in MRI field owing to their outstanding versatility and performance [3–6]. When applied to MRF, these methods significantly improve the efficiency of T_1 and T_2 mapping, i.e., maintaining the quantification accuracy while using less amount of MRF data. The first-generation method train multi-layer perceptron (MLP) to learn the mapping from simulated MRF signal templates to the T_1 and T_2 values [7]. Although MLP methods accommodates a wide range of T_1 and T_2 distribution, they require complementary methods, such as compressed-sensing reconstruction, to suppress the reconstruction noise (e.g., aliasing) in the highly undersampled MRF datasets. Later, convolutional neural networks (CNNs), such as U-Net [8], have been employed to learn the end-to-end mapping from aliased MRF images to the artifact-free T_1 and T_2 maps [9–12]. The CNNs show strong capability of exploiting spatial correlation among neighboring pixels, hence featuring higher robustness to reconstruction noises (e.g., aliasing) in MRF images. Further, CNN framework can also incorporate the physics constraint to guide parametric quantification. For example, [12] imposes data-consistency constraint to iteratively refine the maps inferred by CNN. These methods allow T_1 and T_2 mapping from <500 image frames, enabling 2- to 4-fold further accelerated MRF acquisition.

Encouraged by the success of MRF on the clinical side, efforts have also been devoted to "reverse translating" MRF method to facilitate preclinical research, especially in tracking the kinetics of MR tracers (e.g., Mn^{2+}) [13, 14]. The MR tracers have been widely used in preclinical studies for non-invasive evaluation of tissue perfusion [15] and functionality [16], and visualization of drug delivery pathway [17]. The simultaneous T_1 and T_2 mapping enabled by MRF provides a unique opportunity for tracking two MR tracers in a single scan, enabling efficient capture of multiple tissue properties [14].

However, the MRF images are of significantly lower quality in small laboratory animals than in humans (Fig. 1D), due to factors including reduced SNR from smaller voxels and lack of parallel imaging capability. The classic template matching method enabled merely 8-fold undersampling in mice, yielding ~2-min acquisition time for one slice [13, 14]. Further acceleration of 2D MRF method is desired to track tracer dynamics in mice either with higher temporal resolution, or with full organ coverage.

Therefore, in this study, we aim at exploiting deep-learning based methods for T_1 and T_2 mapping from highly undersampled MRF data in small laboratory animals, and evaluating its efficacy in tracking tracer distribution. The contributions of this study are: 1) With a U-Net structure implemented as the backbone to perform spatially constrained T_1 and T_2 mapping, which is a common practice in previous works, we further employ three strategies to improve its tolerance to reconstruction noises. Firstly, efficient feature extraction from aliased images may allow better awareness of the U-Net to detailed structural information. We compare the feature extraction strategy using MLP and sliding window averaging [18]. Secondly, in the supervised training of the U-Net, we implement a physics-based objective to ensure that fingerprints simulated from inferred parametric maps can match the reconstruction. Finally, the simulated fingerprints undergo data-consistency correction, and is sent to a cascade of U-Nets to iteratively refine the inferred T_1 and T_2 maps. 2) We evaluate proposed method using *in vivo* MRF data acquired from mouse brain in a manganese (Mn^{2+}) enhanced MRI study. After training the networks with both baseline and post-contrast MRF datasets, we show that the proposed method *not only* allows 4-fold further accelerated data acquisition over the classic MRF method, *but also* can faithfully detect the large T_1 variations related to Mn^{2+} accumulation in mouse brain.

2 Method

The T_1 and T_2 quantification from MRF data with N_t image frames can be considered as solving the following optimization problem:

$$\underset{T_1(x),T_2(x)}{\arg\min} \sum_{n=1}^{N_t} \|\mathbf{y}_R(\mathbf{k}_R(n), n) - \mathbf{U}(n) \circ NUFFT(\mathbf{I}(x, n|T_1(x), T_2(x)))\|_2^2. \quad (1)$$

where $\mathbf{y}_R \in \mathbb{C}^{\frac{N_k}{R} \times N_t}$ is the k-space data with an undersampling rate of R, acquired at $\frac{N_k}{R}$ k-space locations denoted by $\mathbf{k}_R$. With $R = 1$, the k-space is fully sampled by N_k points $\mathbf{k}$. $\mathbf{I} \in \mathbb{C}^{N_x \times N_t}$ represents the spatial-domain image frames consisting of N_x pixels at spatial locations $\mathbf{x}$. For MRF, $\mathbf{I}$ is an aggregation of the individual fingerprint determined by the underlying T$_1$ and T$_2$ values in each pixel. After applying non-uniform fast Fourier transform (NUFFT) [19] and undersampling masks U (Fig. 2B) to the image series $\mathbf{I}$, the resultant k-space data should match the acquired k-space data $\mathbf{y}_R$.

2.1 Parametric Quantification by Template Matching Algorithm

The classic MRF method addresses Eq. (1) using template matching algorithm. Inverse NUFFT (INUFFT) is first performed on the undersampled k-space data $\mathbf{y}_R$ to reconstruct aliased images $\mathbf{I}_R$. To quantify T$_1$ and T$_2$ values from $\mathbf{I}_R$, the template matching algorithm pre-calculates a dictionary of signal templates $\mathbf{D} \in \mathbb{C}^{N_{entry} \times N_t}$ for discretized T$_1$–T$_2$ pairs $(\mathbf{T}_{1,\mathbf{d}}, \mathbf{T}_{2,\mathbf{d}})$, with $N_{entry} = N_{T_1} \times N_{T_2}$ covering N_{T_1} T$_1$ values and N_{T_2} T$_2$ values. The templates are simulated by solving Bloch equation [1], $\mathbf{D}(i, n) = f(\mathbf{T}_{1,\mathbf{d}}(i), \mathbf{T}_{2,\mathbf{d}}(i), n | \mathbf{P}_{ACQ}(n)) \in \mathbb{C}^{1 \times N_t}$, where $i = 1, \ldots, N_{entry}$, $n = [1, ..., N_t]$, and $\mathbf{P}_{ACQ}$ denotes acquisition parameters. For acquired fingerprint $\mathbf{I}_R(x_j, n) \in \mathbb{C}^{1 \times N_t}$ at spatial location x_j, the template $\mathbf{D}(\hat{i}, n)$ producing the highest L2-normalized inner product with $\mathbf{I}_R(x_j, n)$ will be selected as the matched template, with

$$\hat{i} = \underset{l}{\mathrm{argmax}} \left\| \left(\frac{\mathbf{I}_R(x_j, n)}{\|\mathbf{I}_R(x_j, n)\|_2^1} \right) \cdot \left(\frac{\mathbf{D}(i,n)}{\|\mathbf{D}(i,n)\|_2^1} \right)^H \right\|_2^2. \tag{2}$$

From the matched template $\mathbf{D}(\hat{i}, n)$, we can retrieve the estimated $\mathbf{T}_{1,\mathbf{d}}(\hat{i})$ and $\mathbf{T}_{2,\mathbf{d}}(\hat{i})$ for the spatial location x_j. Hence T$_1$ and T$_2$ maps can be derived after traversing all x_js.

2.2 Deep-Learning Method for Parametric Quantification

We propose a deep-learning framework as an improved quantification method to enable further accelerated MRF acquisition from mouse brain using both fewer spiral arms and fewer image frames. The schematics of the quantification framework is shown in Fig. 2A. Its backbone uses cascade U-Nets combined with data-consistency constraint to iteratively refine the estimated the T$_1$ and T$_2$ maps.

Sliding Window Averaging. Instead of directly sending the reconstruction $\mathbf{I}^{in}$ to the U-Net, [9, 10] show that extraction of temporal features can improve the quantification results. These studies employ MLPs to perform feature extraction. However, since there is no ground-truth for "useful" features that may help T$_1$ and T$_2$ quantification, training these networks might require large amount of training data. Here we propose to implement a simple sliding window averaging [18] operation for feature extraction. This strategy combines k-space data sampled by complementary spiral arms across multiple time frames, significantly mitigating aliasing artifacts while maintaining temporal information in the resultant images denoted by $\mathbf{I}^{win}$ (Fig. 2B). In this study, we applied sliding-window averaging with a fixed window size of 48 image frames and a fixed stride of 16 frames, leading to total of $N_{win} = (N_t - 48)/16$ images.

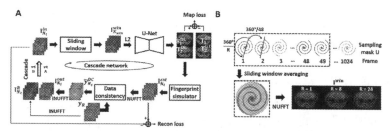

Fig. 2. Schematics of proposed deep-learning method for T_1 and T_2 quantification. **A.** The cascade network for T_1 and T_2 quantification. $\mathbf{I}$, images; $\mathbf{y}$, k-space data; N_t and N_{win}, number of image frames before and after sliding window averaging; T_i^{GT} and T_i^{DL}, ground-truth and inferred T_1 and T_2 maps. Dashed hollow arrow represents data flow to the next cascade. **B.** Choice of sampling masks with undersampling rate R and effects of sliding window averaging.

U-Net Architecture. The parametric quantification module uses the same U-Net architecture as in [9] to learn the mapping from L2-normalized (see Eq. (2)) image series $\mathbf{I}^{win}$ to T_1 and T_2 maps. The real and imaginary components of $\mathbf{I}^{win}$ are concatenated and passed to the U-Net. The U-Net consists of 3 down-sampling layers (maximal pooling 2×2) followed by 3 up-sampling layers (transpose convolution 2×2), extracting local to global spatial features at 3 scales. Skip connection is used to guide the up-sampling process with high-resolution features extracted in down-sampling layers [8].

Fingerprint Simulator. A fingerprint simulation network [12, 20] is implemented to simulate images $\tilde{\mathbf{I}}^{est}$ from the estimated T_1 and T_2 maps. The simulator employs a four-layer MLP, and is pre-trained for full-range discretized T_1–T_2 pairs under the supervision of signal templates simulated by solving the Bloch equation (Sect. 2.1). In the quantification framework, parameters of the simulation network are fixed. The simulated signal templates will be rescaled back according to input images $\mathbf{I}^{in}$ to derive $\tilde{\mathbf{I}}^{est}$, with the scaling factor being proton density [1].

Data-consistency Correction. The simulated images $\tilde{\mathbf{I}}^{est}$ undergo data-consistency correction [21] according to the acquired k-space data $\mathbf{y}_R$.

$$\mathbf{y}_{DC}(\mathbf{k}, n) = \begin{cases} NUFFT\left(\tilde{\mathbf{I}}(\mathbf{x}, n)\right), & for\ k \notin \mathbf{k}_R(n), \\ \frac{1}{1+\alpha}NUFFT\left(\tilde{\mathbf{I}}(\mathbf{x}, n)\right) + \frac{\alpha}{1+\alpha}\mathbf{y}_R(\mathbf{k}_R(n), n), & for\ k \in \mathbf{k}_R(n), \end{cases} \quad (3)$$

with $\mathbf{y}_{DC} \in \mathbb{C}^{N_k \times N_t}$ being the corrected k-space data, and α being a trainable scaler to modify $\mathbf{y}_{DC}$ according to the confidence in acquired k-space data $\mathbf{y}_R$. The images sent to the downstream quantification network becomes $\mathbf{I}^{out}(\mathbf{x}, n) = INUFFT(\mathbf{y}_{DC}(\mathbf{k}, n))$.

Training Objectives. Supervised learning is performed using the ground-truth T$_1$ and T$_2$ maps generated by template matching from fully sampled 2D MRF data (Sect. 2.1). The loss function aims to minimize the mean absolute percentage error (MAPE) between inferred T$_1^{DL}(x)$, T$_2^{DL}(x)$ and the ground truth T$_1^{GT}(x)$, T$_2^{GT}(x)$,

$$loss_{map} = \frac{1}{N_x}\left(\sum_{j=1}^{N_x}\left|\frac{T_1^{DL}(x_j)-T_1^{GT}(x_j)}{T_1^{GT}(x_j)}\right| + \sum_{j=1}^{N_x}\left|\frac{T_2^{DL}(x_j)-T_2^{GT}(x_j)}{T_2^{GT}(x_j)}\right|\right) \quad (4)$$

Meanwhile, the differences between $\tilde{\mathbf{I}}^{est}$ and the input reconstruction $\mathbf{I}^{in}$ should be minimized to ensure that the mapping process obeys the law of MR physics.

$$loss_{physics} = \frac{\sum_{n=1}^{N_t}\sum_{j=1}^{N_x}\left|\tilde{\mathbf{I}}^{est}(x_j,n)-\mathbf{I}^{in}(x_j,n)\right|}{N_tN_x} \quad (5)$$

The network parameters in the quantification module will therefore be updated by minimizing the combined loss function $loss_{map} + \lambda \cdot loss_{physics}$.

3 Experiments

3.1 Dataset and Experimental Setting

Animal Protocol. All animal protocols were approved by the Institutional Animal Care and Use Committee of the Cleveland Clinic Foundation. The MRI studies were performed on a horizontal 7T Bruker Biospec scanner (Bruker Biospin, Billerica, MA, USA) using a 35-mm quadrature birdcage coil. We conducted manganese-enhanced MRI (MEMRI) study on 4- to 6-month-old C57BL/6 mice (N = 15). Mn^{2+} was administered via intraperitoneal injection of bicine-buffered MnCl$_2$ (60 mg/kg) solution (pH = 7.4) [22]. Each mouse underwent 4 injections performed every two weeks. MR experiments were performed before and 24-h post each Mn-injection. To summarize, we have 8 datasets from each mouse, and 120 datasets in total.

MRF Acquisition. The MRF sequence uses sinusoidally varied flip angles designed in [1] and acquires one image every 10 ms (TR = 10 ms), yielding 1024 images in 10 s. A 9-s delay was inserted between two acquisitions. Therefore, each acquisition took 19-s scan time. A spiral trajectory [23] was designed for imaging field-of-view of 2×2 cm^2 and matrix size of 128×128. It fully samples the corresponding k-space by 48 arms, yielding fully-sampled 2D MRF data in 16 min by 48 acquisitions.

Network Training. In each fold of cross validation, 96 MRF datasets from 12 mice were used to train the cascade U-Nets, and 24 MRF datasets from the remaining 3 mice were used for testing. The training set were augmented by 2 fold using left-right flipping of the reconstructed images and maps. To train the cascade network, the network parameters of the first U-Net were first optimized by the training objectives proposed in Sect. 2.2. The derived network parameters were then used as the initial parameters in training the network with two cascade U-Nets, and so on and so forth until the T$_1$ and T$_2$ estimation converges. In this study, cascade with depth 1 and 2 were evaluated. All networks were implemented in PyTorch and trained using a NIVIDIA 3080 GPU. The training process used ADAM optimizer with a learning rate of 1e−4, a batch size of 1, and 500 epochs. The weight λ for the physics loss (5) was chosen empirically to be 0.1 for the best mapping results.

Further, the fingerprint simulation network took paired T_1 and T_2 maps as the input, and generated 2048 image frames composed of real and imaginary components of MRF signals. It uses four 1×1 convolutional layers with 256, 512, 1024, and 2048 kernels. The fingerprint simulator was pre-trained using MRF signal templates covering 128 T_1 values ranging from 100 to 4270 ms, and 128 T_2 values ranging from 5 to 400 ms.

3.2   Results and Discussion

The T_1 and T_2 mapping results were first evaluated for MRF data acquired with 1024 image frames and a undersample rate R of 24 (i.e., 2 spiral arms). Representative T_1 and T_2 maps are shown in Fig. 3, while quantitative metrics including MAPE, PSNR $= 20 \cdot log_{10} \dfrac{\max(T_i^{GT})}{\sqrt{\frac{1}{N_x} \sum \|T_i^{NN} - T_i^{GT}\|^2}}$, and structural similarity [24] are listed in Table 1.

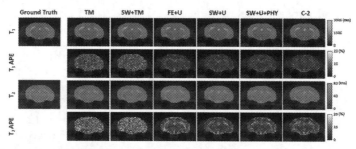

Fig. 3. Representative T_1, T_2, and their absolute percentage error (APE) maps from MRF data acquired with 1024 images and an undersampling rate of 24 (R = 24). The following methods are evaluated: TM, template matching; SW + TM, sliding window and template matching; FE + U, feature extraction and U-Net; SW + U, sliding window and U-Net; SW + U + PHY, sliding window and U-Net trained by both mapping and physics loss; C-2, two cascades of SW + U + PHY with data-consistency correction applied in between.

Efficacy of Sliding Window Averaging. Previously, principal feature maps were first extracted along the temporal dimension by principal component analysis or deep learning method [9, 10], to facilitate down-stream parametric quantification. Our results showed that the sliding window averaging (SW + U) module outperformed the feature extraction network proposed in [9] (FE + U). Considering the limited amount of training data and lower image quality in mice, training a network for feature extraction may not be optimal. In contrast, the sliding window averaging allows coarse recovery of spatial and temporal information without creating additional trainable parameters, which might help the U-Net to more efficiently learn the spatial-temporal features.

Table 1. Comparison of T$_1$ and T$_2$ mapping results using 1024 image frames with R = 24.

	T1			T2		
	MAPE (%)	PSNR (dB)	SSIM	MAPE (%)	PSNR (dB)	SSIM
TM	6.3 ± 0.2	30.8 ± 1.3	0.92 ± 0.02	10.1 ± 0.5	36.1 ± 1.0	0.95 ± 0.01
SW + TM	6.6 ± 0.2	30.4 ± 1.2	0.92 ± 0.02	10.6 ± 0.6	35.6 ± 1.0	0.95 ± 0.01
FE + U	3.7 ± 0.2	36.4 ± 1.5	0.96 ± 0.01	6.5 ± 0.4	34.7 ± 2.8	0.91 ± 0.06
SW + U	**3.4 ± 0.2**	**37.3 ± 1.3**	**0.97 ± 0.01**	**5.4 ± 0.3**	37.8 ± 1.9	0.96 ± 0.02
SW + U + PHY	3.5 ± 0.2	37.3 ± 1.2	0.97 ± 0.01	5.5 ± 0.3	37.9 ± 1.7	0.96 ± 0.02
C-2	3.5 ± 0.2	37.2 ± 1.2	0.97 ± 0.01	5.5 ± 0.3	**38.1 ± 1.9**	**0.97 ± 0.02**

Efficacy of Physics-guided Training Objectives. Compared to training the network by minimizing only the mapping error (SW + U), simultaneously minimizing the differences between the images simulated using physics model from inferred maps and the input images (SW + U + PHY) led to minor changes in the resultant T$_1$ and T$_2$ maps. The results suggested that the mapping method learned by the U-Net could be already in compliance with the physics model. However, the trained model still cannot be generalized to T$_1$ or T$_2$ values far beyond the training set. For example, the U-Net trained by pre-contrast datasets cannot correctly quantify T$_1$ in the post-contrast datasets.

Table 2. Comparison of deep-learning based T$_1$ and T$_2$ mapping from different number of image frames and an undersampling rate of 24 (R = 24). The results of template matching using 8-fold undersampled data (R = 8) are listed at the bottom for comparison.

R	N_t	T1			T2		
		MAPE (%)	PSNR (dB)	SSIM	MAPE (%)	PSNR (dB)	SSIM
24	512	3.6 ± 0.2	36.9 ± 1.3	0.97 ± 0.01	7.4 ± 0.4	34.9 ± 1.4	0.93 ± 0.03
	768	3.5 ± 0.2	37.0 ± 1.2	0.97 ± 0.01	5.8 ± 0.3	37.3 ± 1.7	0.96 ± 0.02
	1024	**3.4 ± 0.2**	**37.3 ± 1.3**	**0.97 ± 0.01**	**5.4 ± 0.3**	37.8 ± 1.9	0.96 ± 0.02
8	1024	3.5 ± 0.1	36.8 ± 1.4	0.97 ± 0.01	5.6 ± 0.2	**39.2 ± 0.8**	**0.98 ± 0.00**

Efficacy of Cascade Network. Applying two cascades of the quantification modules (C-2) led to marginal differences against the one-round output. Since the mouse brain has much simpler structure compared to human brain, estimation in the majority of brain tissue turned out to be good enough in the first iteration. However, the estimation error of CSF and surrounding pixels remained high as they can be overwhelmed by brain pixels in the training objective functions.

Minimal Number of Image Frames. We expected the deep-learning method to have comparable performance to the template matching results using 1024 images and an

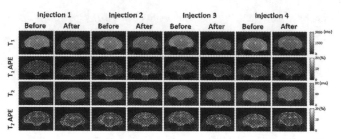

Fig. 4. T_1, T_2, and absolute percentage error (APE) maps before and after Mn^{2+} injection using deep learning method. MRF data was acquired with 768 images and 24-fold undersampling.

undersampling rate of 8. As listed in Table 2 and shown in Fig. 4, the method was accurate for MRF acquisition with 768 images and an undersampling rate of 24. However, with 512 images, significant errors were found in T_2 estimation of the CSF pixels.

4 Conclusions

We develop a deep-learning method for accurate T_1 and T_2 quantification in the mouse brain from **4-fold further accelerated** MRF acquisition as compared to the baseline method. The method is capable of tracking the T_1 variations induced by Mn^{2+}, making it a promising candidate to simultaneously track two MR tracers (e.g., Mn^{2+} as T_1 tracer and Dy^{3+} as T_2 tracer) in future work. However, the T_2 estimation of CSF and surrounding pixels remains challenging. Augmenting the training data using simulated MRF data and assigning focal loss may help improve the T_2 quantification in CSF.

Acknowledgements. This work is supported in part by National Science Foundation of China (grant number 62131015), and Science and Technology Commission of Shanghai Municipality (STCSM) (grant number 21010502600).

References

1. Ma, D., et al.: Magnetic resonance fingerprinting. Nature **495**, 187–192 (2013)
2. Jiang, Y., et al.: MR fingerprinting using fast imaging with steady state precession (FISP) with spiral readout. Magn. Reson. Med. **74**, 1621–1631 (2015)
3. Xiang, L., et al.: Deep embedding convolutional neural network for synthesizing CT image from T1-weighted MR image. Med. Image Anal. **47**, 31–44 (2018)
4. Nie, D., et al.: 3-D fully convolutional networks for multimodal isointense infant brain image segmentation. IEEE Trans. Cybern. **49**(3), 1123–1136 (2019)
5. Pan, Y., Liu, M., Lian, C., Zhou, T., Xia, Y., Shen, D.: Synthesizing missing PET from MRI with cycle-consistent generative adversarial networks for Alzheimer's disease diagnosis. In: Frangi, A.F., Schnabel, J.A., Davatzikos, C., Alberola-López, C., Fichtinger, G. (eds.) Medical Image Computing and Computer Assisted Intervention – MICCAI 2018. Lecture Notes in Computer Science, vol. 11072, pp. 455–463. Springer, Cham (2018). https://doi.org/10.1007/978-3-030-00931-1_52

6. Zhang, J., Gu, R., Wang, G., Gu, L.: Comprehensive importance-based selective regularization for continual segmentation across multiple sites. In: de Bruijne, M., et al. (eds.) Medical Image Computing and Computer Assisted Intervention – MICCAI 2021. LNCS, vol. 12901, pp. 389–399. Springer, Cham (2021). https://doi.org/10.1007/978-3-030-87193-2_37

7. Song, P., et al.: HYDRA: hybrid deep magnetic resonance fingerprinting. Med. Phys. **46**, 4951–4969 (2019)

8. Ronneberger, O., Fischer, P., Brox, T.: U-Net: convolutional networks for biomedical image segmentation. In: Navab, N., Hornegger, J., Wells, W.M., Frangi, A.F. (eds.) Medical Image Computing and Computer-Assisted Intervention — MICCAI 2015. LNCS, vol. 9351, pp. 234–241. Springer, Cham (2015). https://doi.org/10.1007/978-3-319-24574-4_28

9. Fang, Z., et al.: Deep learning for fast and spatially constrained tissue quantification from highly accelerated data in magnetic resonance fingerprinting. IEEE Trans. Med. Imaging **38**, 2364–2374 (2019)

10. Chen, Y., et al.: High-resolution 3D MR Fingerprinting using parallel imaging and deep learning. Neuroimage **206**, 1–28 (2020)

11. Balsiger, F., et al.: Spatially regularized parametric map reconstruction for fast magnetic resonance fingerprinting. Med. Image Anal. **64**, 101741 (2020)

12. Chen, D., Davies, M.E., Golbabaee, M.: Compressive MR fingerprinting reconstruction with neural proximal gradient iterations. In: Martel, A.L., et al. (eds.) Medical Image Computing and Computer Assisted Intervention – MICCAI 2020. LNCS, vol. 12262, pp. 13–22. Springer, Cham (2020). https://doi.org/10.1007/978-3-030-59713-9_2

13. Gu, Y., et al.: Fast magnetic resonance fingerprinting for dynamic contrast-enhanced studies in mice. Magn. Reason. Med. **80**, 2681–2690 (2018)

14. Anderson, C.E., et al.: Dynamic, simultaneous concentration mapping of multiple MRI contrast agents with dual contrast - magnetic resonance fingerprinting. Sci. Rep. **9**, 1–11 (2019)

15. Shiroishi, M.S., et al.: Principles of T2*-weighted dynamic susceptibility contrast MRI technique in brain tumor imaging. J. Magn. Reason. Imaging **41**, 296–313 (2015)

16. Dedeurwaerdere, S., et al.: Manganese-enhanced MRI reflects seizure outcome in a model for mesial temporal lobe epilepsy. Neuroimage **68**, 30–38 (2013)

17. Hu, H., et al.: Dysprosium-modified tobacco mosaic virus nanoparticles for ultra-high-field magnetic resonance and near-infrared fluorescence imaging of prostate cancer. ACS Nano **11**, 9249–9258 (2017)

18. Cao, X., et al.: Robust sliding-window reconstruction for accelerating the acquisition of MR fingerprinting. Magn. Reason. Med. **78**, 1579–1588 (2017)

19. Fessler, J.A., Sutton, B.P.: Nonuniform fast fourier transforms using min-max interpolation. IEEE Trans. Signal Process. **51**, 560–574 (2003)

20. Hamilton, J.I.: Machine learning for rapid magnetic resonance fingerprinting tissue property quantification. Proc IEEE **108**, 69–85 (2020)

21. Eo, T., et al.: KIKI-net: cross-domain convolutional neural networks for reconstructing undersampled magnetic resonance images. Magn. Reason. Med. **80**, 2188–2201 (2018)

22. Malheiros, J.M., et al.: Manganese-enhanced magnetic resonance imaging detects mossy fiber sprouting in the pilocarpine model of epilepsy. Epilepsia **53**, 1225–1232 (2012)

23. Pipe, J.G., et al.: Spiral trajectory design: a flexible numerical algorithm and base analytical equations. Magn. Reason. Med. **71**, 278–285 (2014)

24. Wang, Z., et al.: Image quality assessment: from error visibility to structural similarity. IEEE Trans. Image Process. **13**, 600–612 (2004)

NAF: Neural Attenuation Fields for Sparse-View CBCT Reconstruction

Ruyi Zha[✉], Yanhao Zhang, and Hongdong Li

Australian National University, Canberra, Australia
ruyi.zha@anu.edu.au

Abstract. This paper proposes a novel and fast self-supervised solution for sparse-view CBCT reconstruction (Cone Beam Computed Tomography) that requires no external training data. Specifically, the desired attenuation coefficients are represented as a continuous function of 3D spatial coordinates, parameterized by a fully-connected deep neural network. We synthesize projections discretely and train the network by minimizing the error between real and synthesized projections. A learning-based encoder entailing hash coding is adopted to help the network capture high-frequency details. This encoder outperforms the commonly used frequency-domain encoder in terms of having higher performance and efficiency, because it exploits the smoothness and sparsity of human organs. Experiments have been conducted on both human organ and phantom datasets. The proposed method achieves state-of-the-art accuracy and spends reasonably short computation time.

Keywords: CBCT · Sparse view · Implicit neural representation

1 Introduction

Cone Beam Computed Tomography (CBCT) is an emerging medical imaging technique to examine the internal structure of a subject noninvasively. A CBCT scanner emits cone-shaped X-ray beams and captures 2D projections at equal angular intervals. Compared with the conventional Fan Beam CT (FBCT), CBCT enjoys the benefits of high spatial resolution and fast scanning speed [19]. Recent years have witnessed the blossoming of low dose CT, which delivers a significantly lower radiation dose during the scanning process. There are two ways to reduce the dose: decreasing source intensity or projection views [8]. This paper focuses on the latter, *i.e.*, sparse-view CBCT reconstruction.

Sparse-view CBCT reconstruction aims to retrieve a volumetric attenuation coefficient field from dozens of projections. It is a challenging task in two respects. First, insufficient views lead to notable artifacts. As a comparison, the traditional CBCT obtains hundreds of images. The inputs of sparse-view CBCT are $10\times$

Supplementary Information The online version contains supplementary material available at https://doi.org/10.1007/978-3-031-16446-0_42.

fewer. Second, the spatial and computational complexity of CBCT reconstruction is much higher than that of FBCT reconstruction due to the dimensional increase of inputs. CBCT relies on 2D projections to build a 3D model, while FBCT simplifies the process by stacking 2D slides restored from 1D projections (but in the sacrifice of time and dose).

Existing CBCT approaches can be divided into three categories: analytical, iterative and learning-based methods. Analytical methods estimate attenuation coefficients by solving the Radon transform and its inverse. A typical example is the FDK algorithm [7]. It produces good results in an ideal scenario but copes poorly with ill-posed problems such as sparse views. The second family, iterative methods, formulates reconstruction as a minimization process. These approaches utilize an optimization framework combined with regularization modules. While iterative methods perform well in ill-posed problems [2,20], they require substantial computation time and memory. Recently, learning-based methods have become popular with the rise of AI. They use deep neural networks to 1) predict and extrapolate projections [3,22,24,28], 2) regress attenuation coefficients with similar data [11,27], and 3) make optimization process differentiable [1,6,10]. Most of these methods [3,11,22,27] need extensive datasets for network training. Moreover, they rely on neural networks to remember what a CT looks like. Therefore it is difficult to apply a trained model of one application to another. While there are self-supervised methods [1,28], they operate under FBCT settings considering network capacity and memory consumption. Their performance and efficiency drop when applied to the CBCT scenario.

Apart from the aforementioned work designated for CT reconstruction, efforts have been made to deal with other ill-posed problems, such as 3D reconstruction in the computer vision field. Similar to CT reconstruction, 3D reconstruction uses RGB images to estimate 3D shapes, which are usually represented as discrete point clouds or meshes. Recent studies propose [13,16] Implicit Neural Representation (INR) as an alternative to those discrete representations. INR parameterizes a bounded scene as a neural network that maps spatial coordinates to metrics such as occupancy and color. With the help of position encoder [14,21], INR is capable to learn high-frequency details.

This paper proposes Neural Attenuation Fields (NAF), a fast self-supervised solution for sparse-view CBCT reconstruction. Here we use 'self-supervised' to highlight that NAF requires no external CT scans but the X-ray projections of the interested object. Inspired by 3D reconstruction work [13,16], we parameterize the attenuation coefficient field as an INR and imitates the X-ray attenuation process with a self-supervised network pipeline. Specifically, we train a Multi-Layer Perceptron (MLP), whose input is an encoded spatial coordinate (x, y, z) and whose output is the attenuation coefficient μ at that location. Instead of using a common frequency-domain encoding, we adopt hash encoding [14], a learning-based position encoder, to help the network quickly learn high-frequency details. Projections are synthesized by predicting the attenuation coefficients of sampled points along ray trajectories and attenuating incident beams accordingly. The network is optimized with gradient descent by minimizing the error between real and synthesized projections. We demonstrate that NAF quantitatively and qualitatively outperforms existing solutions on both human organ and phantom datasets. While most INR approaches take hours for training, our method can reconstruct a detailed CT model within 10–40 minutes, which is comparable to iterative methods.

In summary, the main contributions of this work are:

- We propose a novel and fast self-supervised method for sparse-view CBCT reconstruction. Neither external datasets nor structural prior is needed except projections of a subject.
- The proposed method achieves state-of-the-art accuracy and spends relatively short computation time. The performance and efficiency of our method make it feasible for clinical CT applications.
- The code will be publicly available for investigation purposes.

2 Method

2.1 Pipeline

The pipeline of NAF is shown in Fig. 1. During a CBCT scanning, an X-ray source rotates around the object and emits cone-shaped X-ray beams. A 2D panel detects X-ray projections at equal angular intervals. NAF then uses the scanner geometry to imitate the attenuation process discretely. It learns CT shapes by comparing real and synthesized projections. After the model optimization, the final CT image is generated by querying corresponding voxels.

NAF consists of four modules: ray sampling, position encoding, attenuation coefficient prediction, and projection synthesis. First, we uniformly sample points

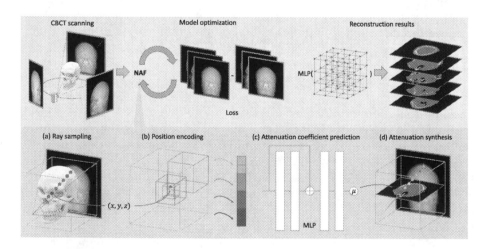

Fig. 1. NAF pipeline. Gray block: The CBCT scanner captures X-ray projections from different views. Blue block: NAF simulates projections. Orange block: NAF is optimized by comparing real and synthesized projections. Green block: NAF generates a CT model by querying corresponding voxels. (Color figure online)

along X-ray paths based on the scanner geometry. A position encoder network then encodes their spatial coordinates to extract valuable features. After that, an MLP network consumes the encoded information and predicts attenuation coefficients. The last step of NAF is to synthesize projections by attenuating incident X-rays according to the predicted attenuation coefficients on their paths.

2.2 Neural Attenuation Fields

Ray Sampling. Each pixel value of a projection image results from an X-ray passing through a cubical space and getting attenuated by the media inside. We sample N points at the parts where rays intersect the cube. A stratified sampling method [13] is adopted, where we divide a ray into N evenly spaced bins and uniformly sample one point at each bin. Setting N greater than the desired CT size ensures that at least one sample is assigned to every grid cell that an X-ray traverses. The coordinates of sampled points are then sent to the position encoding module.

Position Encoding. A simple MLP can theoretically approximate any function [9]. Recent studies [18,21], however, reveal that a neural network prefers to learn low-frequency details due to "spectral bias". To this end, a position encoder is introduced to map 3D spatial coordinates to a higher dimensional space.

A common choice is the *frequency encoder* proposed by Mildenhall *et al.* [13]. It decomposes a spatial coordinate $\mathbf{p} \in \mathbb{R}^3$ into L sets of sinusoidal components at different frequencies. While frequency encoder eases the difficulty of training networks, it is considered quite cumbersome. In medical imaging practise [26,28], the size of encoder output is set to 256 or greater. The following network must be wider and deeper to cope with the inflated inputs. As a result, it takes hours to train millions of network parameters, which is not acceptable for fast CT reconstruction.

Frequency-domain encoding is a dense encoder because it utilizes the entire frequency spectrum. However, dense encoding is redundant for CBCT reconstruction for two main reasons. First, a human body usually consists of several homogeneous media, such as muscles and bones. Attenuation coefficients remain approximately uniform inside one medium but vary between different media. High-frequency features are not necessary unless for points near edges. Second, natural objects favor smoothness. Many organs have simple shapes, such as spindle (muscle) or cylinder (bone). Their smooth surfaces can be easily learned with low-dimensional features.

To exploit the aforementioned characteristics of the scanned objects, we use the *hash encoder* [14], a learning-based sparse encoding solution. The equation of hash encoder $\mathcal{M}_{\mathcal{H}}$ is:

$$\mathcal{M}_{\mathcal{H}}(\mathbf{p}; \boldsymbol{\Theta}) = [\mathcal{I}(\mathbf{H}_1), \cdots, \mathcal{I}(\mathbf{H}_L)]^T, \quad \mathbf{H} = \{\mathbf{c} | h(\mathbf{c}) = (\bigoplus c_j \pi_j) \bmod T\}. \quad (1)$$

Hash encoder describes a bounded space by L multiresolution voxel grids. A trainable feature lookup table $\boldsymbol{\Theta}$ with size T is assigned to each voxel grid. At each resolution level, we 1) detect neighbouring corners **c** (cubes with different colors in Fig. 1(b)) of the queried point **p**, 2) look up their corresponding features **H** in a hash function fashion h [23], and 3) generate a feature vector with linear interpolation $\mathcal{I}$. The output of a hash encoder is the concatenation of feature vectors at all resolution levels. More details of hash function and its symbols can be found in [14].

Compared with frequency encoder, hash encoder produces much smaller outputs (32 in our setting) with competitive feature quality for two reasons. On the one hand, the many-to-one property of hash function conforms to the sparsity nature of human organs. On the other hand, a trainable encoder can learn to focus on relevant details and select suitable frequency spectrum [14]. Thanks to hash encoder, the subsequent network is more compact.

Attenuation Coefficient Prediction. We represent the bounded field with a simple MLP $\boldsymbol{\Phi}$, which takes the encoded spatial coordinates as inputs and outputs the attenuation coefficients μ at that position. As illustrated in Fig. 1(c), the network is composed of 4 fully-connected layers. The first three layers are 32-channel wide and have ReLU activation functions in between, while the last layer has one neuron followed by a sigmoid activation. A skip connection is included to concatenate the network input to the second layer's activation. By contrast, Zang *et al.* [28] use a 6-layer 256-channel MLP to learn features from a frequency encoder. Our network is 10× smaller.

Attenuation Synthesis. According to Beer's Law, the intensity of an X-ray traversing matter is reduced by the exponential integration of attenuation coefficients on its path. We numerically synthesize the attenuation process with:

$$I = I_0 \exp(-\sum_{i=1}^{N} \mu_i \delta_i), \tag{2}$$

where I_0 is the initial intensity and $\delta_i = \|\mathbf{p}_{i+1} - \mathbf{p}_i\|$ is the distance between adjacent points.

2.3 Model Optimization and Output

NAF is updated by minimizing the L2 loss between real and synthesized projections. The loss function $\mathcal{L}$ is defined as:

$$\mathcal{L}(\boldsymbol{\Theta}, \boldsymbol{\Phi}) = \sum_{r \in \mathbf{B}} \|I_r(\mathbf{r}) - I_s(\mathbf{r})\|^2, \tag{3}$$

where $\mathbf{B}$ is a ray batch, and I_r and I_s are real and synthesized projections for ray $\mathbf{r}$ respectively. We update both hash encoder $\boldsymbol{\Theta}$ and attenuation coefficient network $\boldsymbol{\Phi}$ during the training process.

The final output is formulated as a discrete 3D matrix. We build a voxel grid with the desired size and pass the voxel coordinates to the trained MLP to predict the corresponding attenuation coefficients. A CT model thus is restored.

3   Experiments

3.1   Experimental Settings

Data. We conduct experiments on five datasets containing human organ and phantom data. Details are listed in Table 1.

Human Organ: We evaluate our method using public datasets of human organ CTs [4,12], including chest, jaw, foot and abdomen. The chest data are from LIDC-IDRI dataset [4], and the rest are from Open Scientific Visualization Datasets [12]. Since these datasets only provide volumetric CT scans, we generate projections by a tomographic toolbox TIGRE [5]. In TIGRE [5], we capture 50 projections with 3% noise in the range of 180°. We train our model with these projections and evaluate its performance with the raw volumetric CT data.

Phantom: We collect a phantom dataset by scanning a silicon aortic phantom with GE C-arm Medical System. This system captures 582 500 × 500 fluoroscopy projections with position primary angle from −103° to 93° and position secondary angle of 0°. A 512 × 512 × 510 CT image is also generated with inbuilt algorithms as the ground truth. We only use 50 projections for experiments.

Baselines. We compare our approach with four baseline techniques. **FDK** [7] is firstly chosen as a representative of analytical methods. The second method **SART** [2] is a robust iterative reconstruction algorithm. **ASD-POCS** [20] is another iterative method with a total-variation regularizer. We implement a CBCT variant of IntraTomo [28], named **IntraTomo3D**, as an example of frequency-encoding deep learning methods.

Implementation Details. Our proposed method is implemented in PyTorch [17]. We use Adam optimizer with a learning rate that starts at 1×10^{-3} and steps down to 1×10^{-4}. The batch size is 2048 rays at each iteration. The sampling quantity of each ray depends on the size of CT data. For example, we sample 192 points along each ray for the 128 × 128 × 128 chest CT. We use the same hyper-parameter setting for hash encoder as [14]. More details of hyper-parameters can be found in the supplementary material. All experiments are conducted on a single RTX 3090 GPU. We evaluate five methods quantitatively in terms of peak signal-to-noise ratio (PNSR) and structural similarity (SSIM) [25]. PSNR (dB) statistically assesses the artifact suppression performance, while SSIM measures the perceptual difference between two signals. Higher PNSR/SSIM values represent the accurate reconstruction and vice versa.

Table 1. Details of CT datasets used in the experiments.

Dataset name	CT dimension	Scanning method	Scanning range	Number of projections	Detector resolution
Chest [4]	128 × 128 × 128	TIGRE [5]	0°–180°	50	256 × 256
Jaw [12]	256 × 256 × 256	TIGRE [5]	0°–180°	50	512 × 512
Foot [12]	256 × 256 × 256	TIGRE [5]	0°–180°	50	512 × 512
Abdomen [12]	512 × 512 × 463	TIGRE [5]	0°–180°	50	1024 × 1024
Aorta	512 × 512 × 510	GE C-arm	−103°–93°	50 (582)	500 × 500

3.2   Results

Performance. Our method produces quantitatively best results in both human organ and phantom datasets as listed in Table 2. Both PSNR and SSIM values are significantly higher than other methods. For example, the PSNR value of our method in the abdomen dataset is 3.07 dB higher than that of the second-best method **SART**.

We also provide visualization results of different methods in Fig. 2. **FDK** restores low-quality models with notable artifacts, as analytical methods demand large amounts of projections.

Table 2. PSNR/SSIM measurements of five methods on five datasets.

	Chest	Jaw	Foot	Abdomen	Aorta
FDK [7]	22.89/.78	28.59/.78	23.92/.58	22.39/.59	12.11/.21
SART [2]	32.12/.95	32.67/.93	30.13/.93	31.38/.92	27.31/.77
ASD-POCS [20]	29.78/.92	32.78/.93	28.67/.89	30.34/.91	27.30/.76
IntraTomo3D [28]	31.94/.95	31.95/.91	31.43/.91	30.43/.90	29.38/.82
NAF (Ours)	**33.05/.96**	**34.14/.94**	**31.63/.94**	**34.45/.95**	**30.34/.88**

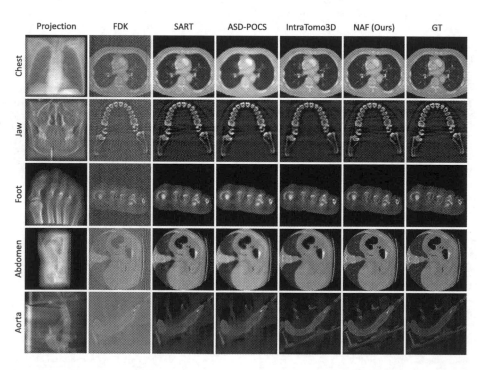

Fig. 2. Qualitative results of five methods. From left to right: examples of X-ray projections, slices of 3D CT models reconstructed by five methods, and the ground truth CT slices.

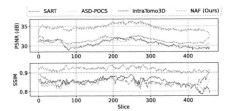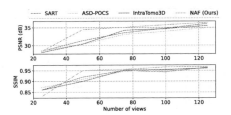

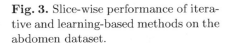

Fig. 3. Slice-wise performance of iterative and learning-based methods on the abdomen dataset.

Fig. 4. Performance under different number of views on the abdomen dataset.

Iterative method **SART** suppresses noise in the sacrifice of losing certain details. The reconstruction results of **ASD-POCS** are heavily smeared because total-variation regularization encourages removing high-frequency details, including unwanted noise and expected tiny structures. **IntraTomo3D** produces clean results. However, edges between media are slightly blurred, which shows that the frequency encoder fails to teach the network to focus on edges. With the help of hash encoding, results of the proposed **NAF** have the most details, clearest edges and fewest artifacts. Figure 3 indicates that **NAF** outperforms other methods in all slices of the reconstructed CT volume.

Figure 4 shows the performance of iterative methods and learning-based methods under different number of views. It is clear that the performance increases with the rise of input views. Our methods achieves better results than others under most circumstances.

Time. We record the running time of iterative and learning-based methods as shown in Fig. 5. All methods use CUDA [15] to accelerate the computation process. Overall, the methods spend less time on datasets with small projections (chest, jaw and foot) and increasingly more time on big datasets (abdomen and aorta). **IntraTomo3D** requires more than one hour to train the network. Benefiting from the compact network design, **NAF** spends similar running time to iterative methods and is $3\times$ faster than the frequency-encoding deep learning method **IntraTomo3D**.

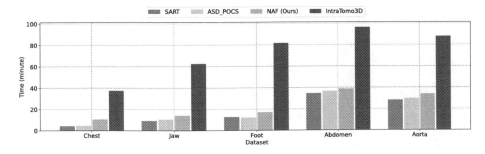

Fig. 5. Running time that iterative and learn-based methods take to converge to stable results.

4   Conclusion

This paper proposes NAF, a fast self-supervised learning-based solution for sparse-view CBCT reconstruction. Our method trains a fully-connected deep neural network that consumes a 3D spatial coordinate and outputs the attenuation coefficient at that location. NAF synthesizes projections by attenuating incident X-rays based on the predicted attenuation coefficients. The network is updated by minimizing the projection error. We show that frequency encoding is not computationally efficient for tomographic reconstruction tasks. As an alternative, a learning-based encoder entitled hash encoding is adopted to extract valuable features. Experimental results on human organ and phantom datasets indicate that the proposed method achieves significantly better results than other baselines and spends reasonably short computation time.

References

1. Adler, J., Öktem, O.: Learned primal-dual reconstruction. IEEE Trans. Med. Imaging **37**(6), 1322–1332 (2018)
2. Andersen, A.H., Kak, A.C.: Simultaneous algebraic reconstruction technique (SART): a superior implementation of the art algorithm. Ultrason. Imaging **6**(1), 81–94 (1984)
3. Anirudh, R., Kim, H., Thiagarajan, J.J., Mohan, K.A., Champley, K., Bremer, T.: Lose the views: limited angle CT reconstruction via implicit sinogram completion. In: Proceedings of the IEEE Conference on Computer Vision and Pattern Recognition, pp. 6343–6352 (2018)
4. Armato III, S.G., et al.: The Lung Image Database Consortium (LIDC) and Image Database Resource Initiative (IDRI): a completed reference database of lung nodules on CT scans. Med. Phys. **38**(2), 915–931 (2011)
5. Biguri, A., Dosanjh, M., Hancock, S., Soleimani, M.: TIGRE: a MATLAB-GPU toolbox for CBCT image reconstruction. Biomed. Phys. Eng. Express **2**(5), 055010 (2016)
6. Chen, H., et al.: Learned experts' assessment-based reconstruction network ("learn") for sparse-data CT, arXiv preprint arXiv:1707.09636 (2017)
7. Feldkamp, L.A., Davis, L.C., Kress, J.W.: Practical cone-beam algorithm. Josa a **1**(6), 612–619 (1984)
8. Gao, Y., et al.: Low-dose x-ray computed tomography image reconstruction with a combined low-mas and sparse-view protocol. Opt. Express **22**(12), 15190–15210 (2014)
9. Hornik, K., Stinchcombe, M., White, H.: Multilayer feedforward networks are universal approximators. Neural Netw. **2**(5), 359–366 (1989)
10. Kang, E., Chang, W., Yoo, J., Ye, J.C.: Deep convolutional framelet denosing for low-dose CT via wavelet residual network. IEEE Trans. Med. Imaging **37**(6), 1358–1369 (2018)
11. Kasten, Y., Doktofsky, D., Kovler, I.: End-To-end convolutional neural network for 3D reconstruction of knee bones from Bi-planar X-ray images. In: Deeba, F., Johnson, P., Würfl, T., Ye, J.C. (eds.) MLMIR 2020. LNCS, vol. 12450, pp. 123–133. Springer, Cham (2020). https://doi.org/10.1007/978-3-030-61598-7_12

12. Klacansky, P.: Open scientific visualization datasets (2022). http://klacansky.com/open-scivis-datasets/

13. Mildenhall, B., Srinivasan, P.P., Tancik, M., Barron, J.T., Ramamoorthi, R., Ng, R.: NeRF: representing scenes as neural radiance fields for view synthesis. In: Vedaldi, A., Bischof, H., Brox, T., Frahm, J.-M. (eds.) ECCV 2020, Part I. LNCS, vol. 12346, pp. 405–421. Springer, Cham (2020). https://doi.org/10.1007/978-3-030-58452-8_24

14. Müller, T., Evans, A., Schied, C., Keller, A.: Instant neural graphics primitives with a multiresolution hash encoding. arXiv:2201.05989, January 2022

15. NVIDIA, Vingelmann, P., Fitzek, F.H.: Cuda, release: 10.2.89 (2020). http://developer.nvidia.com/cuda-toolkit

16. Park, J.J., Florence, P., Straub, J., Newcombe, R., Lovegrove, S.: DeepSDF: learning continuous signed distance functions for shape representation. In: Proceedings of the IEEE/CVF Conference on Computer Vision and Pattern Recognition, pp. 165–174 (2019)

17. Paszke, A., et al.: Pytorch: An imperative style, high-performance deep learning library. In: Wallach, H., Larochelle, H., Beygelzimer, A., d'Alché-Buc, F., Fox, E., Garnett, R. (eds.) Advances in Neural Information Processing Systems, vol. 32, pp. 8024–8035. Curran Associates, Inc. (2019). http://papers.neurips.cc/paper/9015-pytorch-an-imperative-style-high-performance-deep-learning-library.pdf

18. Rahaman, N., et al.: On the spectral bias of neural networks. In: International Conference on Machine Learning, pp. 5301–5310. PMLR (2019)

19. Scarfe, W.C., Farman, A.G., Sukovic, P., et al.: Clinical applications of cone-beam computed tomography in dental practice. J. Can. Dent. Assoc. **72**(1), 75 (2006)

20. Sidky, E.Y., Pan, X.: Image reconstruction in circular cone-beam computed tomography by constrained, total-variation minimization. Phys. Med. Biol. **53**(17), 4777 (2008)

21. Tancik, M., et al.: Fourier features let networks learn high frequency functions in low dimensional domains. Adv. Neural Inf. Process. Syst. **33**, 7537–7547 (2020)

22. Tang, C., et al.: Projection super-resolution based on convolutional neural network for computed tomography. In: 15th International Meeting on Fully Three-Dimensional Image Reconstruction in Radiology and Nuclear Medicine, vol. 11072, p. 1107233. International Society for Optics and Photonics (2019)

23. Teschner, M., Heidelberger, B., Müller, M., Pomerantes, D., Gross, M.H.: Optimized spatial hashing for collision detection of deformable objects. In: VMV, vol. 3, pp. 47–54 (2003)

24. Wang, C., et al.: Improving generalizability in limited-angle Ct reconstruction with sinogram extrapolation. In: de Bruijne, M., et al. (eds.) MICCAI 2021, Part VI. LNCS, vol. 12906, pp. 86–96. Springer, Cham (2021). https://doi.org/10.1007/978-3-030-87231-1_9

25. Wang, Z., Bovik, A.C., Sheikh, H.R., Simoncelli, E.P.: Image quality assessment: from error visibility to structural similarity. IEEE Trans. Image Process. **13**(4), 600–612 (2004)

26. Wu, Q., et al.: IREM: high-resolution magnetic resonance image reconstruction via implicit neural representation. In: de Bruijne, M., et al. (eds.) MICCAI 2021, Part VI. LNCS, vol. 12906, pp. 65–74. Springer, Cham (2021). https://doi.org/10.1007/978-3-030-87231-1_7

27. Ying, X., Guo, H., Ma, K., Wu, J., Weng, Z., Zheng, Y.: X2CT-GAN: reconstructing CT from biplanar x-rays with generative adversarial networks. In: Proceedings of the IEEE/CVF Conference on Computer Vision and Pattern Recognition, pp. 10619–10628 (2019)
28. Zang, G., Idoughi, R., Li, R., Wonka, P., Heidrich, W.: IntraTomo: self-supervised learning-based tomography via sinogram synthesis and prediction. In: Proceedings of the IEEE/CVF International Conference on Computer Vision, pp. 1960–1970 (2021)

UASSR: Unsupervised Arbitrary Scale Super-Resolution Reconstruction of Single Anisotropic 3D Images via Disentangled Representation Learning

Jiale Wang, Runze Wang, Rong Tao, and Guoyan Zheng[✉]

Institute of Medical Robotics, School of Biomedical Engineering, Shanghai Jiao Tong University, No. 800, Dongchuan Road, Shanghai 200240, China
guoyan.zheng@sjtu.edu.cn

Abstract. Deep learning-based single image super resolution (SISR) algorithms have great potential to recover high-resolution (HR) images from low-resolution (LR) inputs. However, most studies require paired LR and HR images for a supervised training, which are difficult to organize in clinical applications. In this paper, we propose an unsupervised arbitrary scale super-resolution reconstruction (UASSR) method based on disentangled representation learning, eliminating the requirement of paired images for training. Applying our method to applications of generating HR images with high inter-plane resolution from LR images with low inter-plane resolution. At the inference stage, we design a strategy to fuse multiple reconstructed HR images from different views to achieve better super-resolution (SR) result. We conduct experiments on one publicly available dataset including 507 MR volumes of the knee joint and an in-house dataset containing 130 CT volumes of the lower spine. Results from our comprehensive experiments demonstrate superior performance of UASSR over other state-of-the-art methods. A reference implementation of our method can be found at: https://github.com/jialewang1/UASSR.

Keywords: Unsupervised image super-resolution · Arbitrary scale · Disentangled representation learning · Magnetic resonance imaging · Computed tomography

---

This study was partially supported by the Natural Science Foundation of China via project U20A20199, by Shanghai Municipal S&T Commission via Project 20511105205, and by the key program of the medical engineering interdisciplinary research fund of Shanghai Jiao Tong University via project YG2019ZDA22 and YG2019ZDB09.

Supplementary Information The online version contains supplementary material available at https://doi.org/10.1007/978-3-031-16446-0_43.

L. Wang et al. (Eds.): MICCAI 2022, LNCS 13436, pp. 453–462, 2022.
https://doi.org/10.1007/978-3-031-16446-0_43

1   Introduction

Magnetic resonance (MR) images and computed tomography (CT) are widely used in clinics. However, the images obtained are anisotropic due to the limitation of scan time and hardware capacity in clinical practice [8]. In order to speed up scanning in clinical routine, only a few two-dimensional (2D) slices are acquired even though the interested anatomical structures are in three-dimensional (3D). The acquired medical images have high in-plane resolution but low inter-plane resolution, i.e., large spacing between slices. Such anisotropic images will lead to poor visual experience and have a great impact on medical image analysis algorithms, including diagnosis and segmentation. Therefore, we investigate the problem of reducing the slice spacing [16] via super-resolution reconstruction. We term the 3D image with large slice spacing as low-resolution (LR) image and the image with small slice spacing as high-resolution (HR) image. We aim to reconstruct HR image from LR input, which is an ill-posed inverse problem and has a great challenge.

Deep learning-based single image super resolution (SISR) algorithms have shown great potential to recover HR images from LR inputs. Dong et al. [4] proposed the SRCNN method, which applied convolutional neural networks (CNN) to image super resolution and achieved better result than traditional interpolation and regularization-based methods. Kim et al. [10] proposed the VDSR method, which applied global residuals to learn high-frequency partial residuals between HR and LR images. Leding et al. [11] introduced SRGAN, which used generative adversarial network (GAN) [6] to solve the SR problem. They argued for that $L1$ and $L2$ loss usually led to the loss of the high frequency details and over-smoothing of the recovered images. SRGAN used both perceptual loss and adversarial loss to improve the realism of the recovered images. Benefited from the well-designed network structures, all these models have been adopted to 3D medical image successfully [2,3,13]. Despite significant progress, however, there are still space for further improvement. First, most algorithms tend to use a fixed up-sampling scale, which is insufficient for real clinical applications. As most models can only learn a fixed mapping relationship between LR and HR images, they require a large number of networks to be trained to perform arbitrary scale super-resolution, leading to much larger computational complexity and longer time. Second, most networks require a large amount of paired LR and HR training images for training, which are unrealistic in clinical practice.

In this paper, we consider the SR problem as image translation from LR domain to HR domain. We propose an unsupervised arbitrary scale super-resolution reconstruction (UASSR) method. UASSR is an end-to-end disentangled cycle-consistent adversarial network including two auto-encoders for reconstruction and two discriminators for adversarial learning. The auto-encoders are realized by two encoders and two generators. The encoders disentangle each image into a content space and a resolution space. We assume that the content space represents the image content and structure, which is domain-invariant while the resolution space represents the image resolution, which is domain-specific. The generators ensemble the content space and the resolution space to translate an image from source domain to target domain. Our contributions can be summarized as follows:

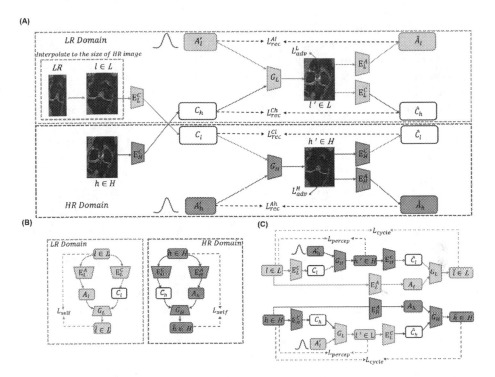

Fig. 1. The network architecture of UASSR, which consists of (A) disentangled resolution translation, (B) self reconstruction and (C) cross-cycle reconstruction. Specially, the input l and h are unpaired LR and HR images. Different colors show different domains, i.e., yellow represents the LR domain, green represents the HR domain and white shows the shared content space. (Color figure online)

- We propose a novel UASSR network, which translate arbitrary scale LR images to HR images via disentangled cycle-consistent adversarial network. UASSR eliminates the requirement of paired LR and HR images for training.
- In order to reconstruct HR images from anisotropic 3D images, we design a strategy to fuse information from different views to achieve better reconstruction accuracy.
- We conduct experiments on one publicly available dataset including 507 3D MR volumes of the knee joint and an in-house dataset containing 130 3D CT volumes of the lower spine to evaluate the performance of UASSR.

2 Methodology

2.1 The UASSR Architecture

For a LR image with arbitrary down-sampling scales, we first interpolate it into the same size as the HR image as shown in Fig. 1-(A). We regard such an interpolated image as an image in the LR domain. The SR problem is then treated as image translation from the LR domain to the HR domain [7,12]. Let $\mathcal{L}$ and $\mathcal{H}$ represent the LR and HR domains, respectively. Our method learns a nonlinear mapping between these two domains using unpaired LR and HR images. Concretely, we first embed arbitrary scale images onto a shared content space $\mathcal{C}$ and a resolution specific space $\mathcal{A}$. We employ two auto-encoders to learn disentangled resolution translation between the LR and HR domains and two discriminators with one for each domain to do adversarial learning. Such embeddings then allow us to achieve SR via image translation as presented below.

Resolution Translation. We use the auto-encoders to realize resolution translation. As shown in Fig. 1-(A), the auto-encoders consist of two content encoders $\{E_{\mathcal{L}}^{\mathcal{C}}, E_{\mathcal{H}}^{\mathcal{C}}\}$, two resolution encoders $\{E_{\mathcal{L}}^{\mathcal{A}}, E_{\mathcal{H}}^{\mathcal{A}}\}$, and two generators $\{G_{\mathcal{L}}, G_{\mathcal{H}}\}$. The encoders in both domains respectively encode an input image to a domain-invariant content space $\mathcal{C}$ and a domain-specific resolution space $\mathcal{A}$. And the generation networks respectively combine the content space and resolution space code to generate the translated images. For example, to translate the LR image $l \in \mathcal{L}$ to HR image $h \in \mathcal{H}$. We first randomly sample from the prior distribution $p(\mathcal{A}_h') \sim \mathcal{N}(0, \mathbf{I})$ to get the resolution space code $\mathcal{A}_h'$, which is empirically set as a 8-bit vector. We then combine the resolution space code $\mathcal{A}_h'$ and the content of the LR image $\mathcal{C}_l = E_{\mathcal{L}}^{\mathcal{C}}(l)$ to generate the translated HR image $h' \in \mathcal{H}$ through the generator $G_{\mathcal{H}}$. Similarly, we can get the translated LR image $l' \in \mathcal{L}$ through the generator $G_{\mathcal{L}}(\mathcal{C}_h, \mathcal{A}_l')$, where $\mathcal{C}_h = E_{\mathcal{H}}^{\mathcal{C}}(h)$; $\mathcal{A}_l'$ is also sampled from the prior distribution $p(\mathcal{A}_l') \sim \mathcal{N}(0, \mathbf{I})$. At testing stage, we only need the $G_{\mathcal{H}}(E_{\mathcal{L}}^{\mathcal{C}}(l), \mathcal{A}_h')$ to reconstruct HR images from LR images.

Disentangled Representation Learning. UASSR is trained for self reconstruction and cross-cycle reconstruction. As shown in Fig. 1-(B), when the content and resolution code are from the same image, we can use the self reconstruction loss L_{self} to regularize training. As shown in Fig. 1-(C), when the content and resolution code are from different images, we can use the cross-cycle consistency loss L_{cycle} to regularize the training. We define the self-reconstruction loss and the cross-reconstruction loss as follows:

$$L_{\text{self}} = \left\| G_{\mathcal{L}}\left(E_{\mathcal{L}}^{\mathcal{C}}(l), E_{\mathcal{L}}^{\mathcal{A}}(l)\right) - l \right\|_1 + \left\| G_{\mathcal{H}}\left(E_{\mathcal{H}}^{\mathcal{C}}(h), E_{\mathcal{H}}^{\mathcal{A}}(h)\right) - h \right\|_1 \quad (1)$$

$$L_{\text{cycle}} = \| G_{\mathcal{L}}(E_{\mathcal{H}}^{\mathcal{C}}(h'), E_{\mathcal{L}}^{\mathcal{A}}(l)) - l \|_1 + \| G_{\mathcal{H}}(E_{\mathcal{L}}^{\mathcal{C}}(l'), E_{\mathcal{H}}^{\mathcal{A}}(h)) - h \|_1 \quad (2)$$

where $l' = G_{\mathcal{L}}(E_{\mathcal{H}}^{\mathcal{C}}(h), \mathcal{A}_l')$, $h' = G_{\mathcal{H}}(E_{\mathcal{L}}^{\mathcal{C}}(l), \mathcal{A}_h')$.

Adversarial Learning. As shown in Fig. 1-(A), we use Generative adversarial Network(GAN) [6] to learn the translation between LR and HR image domains better. A GAN typically contains a generation network and a discrimination network. We use the discriminator $D_{\mathcal{L}}$ to judge whether the image is from LR image domain, and the discriminator $D_{\mathcal{H}}$ to judge whether the image is from HR image domain. The auto-encoders try to generate the image of target domain to fool the discriminators so that the distribution of the translated image can match the target image domain. The minmax game is trained by:

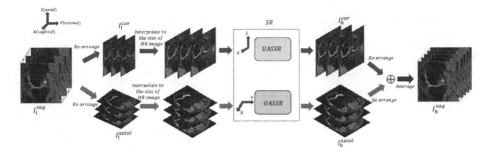

Fig. 2. Illustration of the strategy for super-resolution reconstruction of anisotropic 3D images with arbitrary slice spacings. I_l^{sag} represents an anisotropic 3D image with voxel spacing (V_x^l, V_y^l, V_z^l). I_l^{cor} and I_l^{axial} are separately the stacked 2D LR slices with pixel spacing (V_x^l, V_z^l) and (V_x^l, V_y^l). I_h^{cor} and I_h^{axial} are separately the stacked 2D HR slices with pixel spacing (V_x^h, V_z^h) and (V_x^h, V_y^h). I_h^{sag} represents the reconstructed 3D HR image with voxel spacing (V_x^h, V_y^h, V_z^h)

$$L_{adv}^{\mathcal{L}} = \mathbb{E}_{l \sim P_{\mathcal{L}}(l)} \left[\log D_{\mathcal{L}}(l) \right] + \mathbb{E}_{h \sim P_{\mathcal{H}}(h)} \left[\log(1 - D_{\mathcal{L}}(l^{'})) \right] \tag{3}$$

$$L_{adv}^{\mathcal{H}} = \mathbb{E}_{h \sim P_{\mathcal{H}}(h)} \left[\log D_{\mathcal{H}}(h) \right] + \mathbb{E}_{l \sim P_{\mathcal{L}}(l)} \left[\log(1 - D_{\mathcal{H}}(h^{'})) \right] \tag{4}$$

Structure Invariant Learning. In order to preserve the image content and overall spatial structure in the cross-cycle translation processes $\mathcal{T}_{l \to h^{'} \to \hat{i}} : \mathcal{L} \to \mathcal{H} \to \mathcal{L}$ and $\mathcal{T}_{h \to l^{'} \to \hat{h}} : \mathcal{H} \to \mathcal{L} \to \mathcal{H}$, as shown in Fig. 1-(C), we use pretrained vgg16 network ϕ to extract high-level features to compute the perceptual loss [9]:

$$L_{percep} = \frac{1}{CHW} \left\| \phi(h^{'}) - \phi(l) \right\|_2^2 + \frac{1}{CHW} \left\| \phi(l^{'}) - \phi(h) \right\|_2^2 \tag{5}$$

where C, H, W respectively represents the channel, the height and the width of the extracted features.

Joint Optimization. As shown in Fig. 1-(A), latent reconstruction loss $L_{latent} = L_{rec}^{\mathcal{C}_l} + L_{rec}^{\mathcal{C}_h} + L_{rec}^{\mathcal{A}_l} + L_{rec}^{\mathcal{A}_h}$ is used to preserve the invertible mapping between the image and the latent space. In details, we have:

$$L_{latent} = \| \hat{\mathcal{C}}_l - \mathcal{C}_l \|_1 + \| \hat{\mathcal{C}}_h - \mathcal{C}_h \|_1 + \| \hat{\mathcal{A}}_l - \mathcal{A}_l^{'} \|_1 + \| \hat{\mathcal{A}}_h - \mathcal{A}_h^{'} \|_1 \tag{6}$$

where $\hat{\mathcal{C}}_l = E_{\mathcal{H}}^{\mathcal{C}}((G_{\mathcal{H}}(\mathcal{C}_l, \mathcal{A}_h^{'}))$, $\hat{\mathcal{C}}_h = E_{\mathcal{L}}^{\mathcal{C}}((G_{\mathcal{L}}(\mathcal{C}_h, \mathcal{A}_l^{'}))$, $\hat{\mathcal{A}}_l = E_{\mathcal{L}}^{\mathcal{A}}(G_{\mathcal{L}}(\mathcal{C}_h, \mathcal{A}_l^{'}))$, $\hat{\mathcal{A}}_h = E_{\mathcal{H}}^{\mathcal{A}}(G_{\mathcal{H}}(\mathcal{C}_l, \mathcal{A}_h^{'}))$.

Then the overall loss is:

$$L_{total} = \left(L_{adv}^{\mathcal{L}} + L_{adv}^{\mathcal{H}} \right) + \lambda_1(L_{self} + L_{cycle}) + \lambda_2 L_{latent} + \lambda_3 L_{percep} \tag{7}$$

where λ_1, λ_2, and λ_3 are parameters controlling the relative weights of different losses.

2.2 Super-Resolution Reconstruction from Anisotropic 3D Images with Arbitrary Slice Spacings

After training, UASSR can generate a HR image from a LR image. We further design a strategy to fuse multiple reconstructed HR images from different views at the inference stage to achieve better SR result. Concretely, let $I_h(x, y, z)$ denote a 3D HR image with voxel spacing (V_x^h, V_y^h, V_z^h) and $I_l(x, y, z)$ denotes a 3D LR image with voxel spacing (V_x^l, V_y^l, V_z^l). We assume that $(V_x^l = K*V_x^h, V_y^l = V_y^h, V_z^l = V_z^h)$ where K is the up-sampling scale from LR to HR. As shown in Fig. 2, I_l^{sag} represents the 3D LR image, which is acquired by sagittal plane. We re-arrange it to get the stacked 2D coronal slices I_l^{cor} and axial slices I_l^{axial}. Then, we interpolate them to have the same size as I_h^{cor} and I_h^{axial}, which are taken as the input to UASSR to get respectively stacked 2D HR image I_h^{cor} and I_h^{axial}. Finally, we re-arrange the HR output I_h^{cor}, I_h^{axial} and average them to get the final 3D HR reconstruction I_h^{sag}.

3 Experiments

3.1 Experimental Setup

Datasets. We evaluate the proposed UASSR on a publicly available OAI-ZIB [1] dataset including 507 3D MR volumes of the knee joint and an in-house dataset containing 130 3D CT volumes of the lower spine. The OAI-ZIB dataset is a large public knee MR image dataset with manual segmentation. These HR images were acquired by sagittal plane and the voxel spacing is $0.7 \times 0.36 \times 0.36$ mm^3. We downsample along the sagittal axis by scale factors $K = \{2, 4, 8\}$ to generate LR images with the voxel spacing $(0.7 \times K) \times 0.36 \times 0.36$ mm^3. We also collected an in-house dataset of spine CT scans with manual segmentation. The HR voxel spacing is $0.3 \times 0.3 \times 1.0$ mm^3. We downsample alone the saggital axis by scale factors $K = \{2, 4, 8\}$ to generate the LR images with the voxel spacing $(0.3 \times K) \times 0.3 \times 1.0$ mm^3.

Implementation Details. To train UASSR, each sample of training data is unpaired LR and HR images. As shown in Fig. 1-(A), the LR image is first interpolated to the size of HR image before being fed to UASSR for training. All images are normalized to the range between -1.0 and 1.0. Optimization is performed using Adam with a batch size of 1. The initial learning rate is set to 0.0001 and decreased by a factor of 5 every 2 epochs. Model is trained for 10 epochs. We empirically set $\lambda_1 = 10$, $\lambda_2 = \lambda_3 = 1$.

3.2 Experimental Results

We compare UASSR with the state-of-the-art (SOTA) methods including both supervised SR methods such as ArSSR [15], RDN [19], ResCNN [5] and unsupervised SR methods such as SMORE [20], CycleGan [17]. Two widely used metrics as used in previous studies [5,14,15], peak signal-to-nosie ratio (PSNR) and structural similarity index (SSIM), are used to measure the performance of different methods. In addition, we also use a deep-learning-based perceptual similarity measure LPIPS as introduced in [18] and Dice similarity coefficient to evaluate the segmentation accuracy of the reconstructed HR images for quantitative evaluation. On both datasets, we conducted a two-fold cross-validation study.

Table 1. Mean of results on both datasets when UASSR was compared with other SOTA methods.

Dataset		Knee							Spine			
Scale	Method	PSNR↑	SSIM↑	LPIPS↓	Dice↑				PSNR↑	SSIM↑	LPIPS↓	Dice↑
					FB	FC	TB	TC				
2×	ArSSR [15]	38.77	0.92	0.23	98.4	88.6	98.3	84.6	34.35	0.96	0.04	94.3
	RDN [19]	38.98	0.93	0.24	98.4	88.8	98.5	84.7	38.95	0.97	0.05	95.1
	ResCNN [5]	37.47	0.92	0.24	98.4	88.8	98.5	84.7	40.29	0.98	0.05	95.3
	SMORE [20]	38.41	0.90	0.15	98.0	84.3	98.0	82.3	**46.8**	**0.99**	**0.01**	95.4
	CycleGan [17]	38.17	0.89	0.13	98.3	88.4	98.4	84.1	41.32	0.98	0.02	95.3
	UASSR (Ours)	**40.54**	**0.94**	**0.09**	**98.6**	89.2	**98.6**	**85.2**	45.94	**0.99**	**0.01**	**95.5**
4×	ArSSR [15]	35.94	0.85	0.51	96.6	84.7	97.2	79.5	27.86	0.79	0.17	91.3
	RDN [19]	35.87	0.86	0.47	97.0	87.2	97.6	81.8	32.28	0.91	0.15	93.3
	ResCNN [5]	35.61	0.86	0.47	96.2	87.3	97.4	82.3	33.00	0.95	0.14	93.9
	SMORE [20]	**38.24**	**0.89**	0.36	97.5	86.2	97.9	82.2	37.99	0.98	0.05	95.0
	CycleGan [17]	33.43	0.76	0.28	95.2	76.6	95.2	67.2	36.97	0.97	0.02	94.9
	UASSR (Ours)	37.30	0.87	**0.15**	**98.0**	**87.8**	**98.2**	**84.0**	**42.92**	**0.99**	**0.01**	**95.5**
8×	ArSSR [15]	34.69	0.82	0.60	92.8	77.5	93.7	68.7	25.03	0.85	0.22	84.8
	RDN [19]	33.69	0.80	0.64	69.8	64.5	76.2	47.6	25.98	0.81	0.25	76.5
	ResCNN [5]	33.79	0.81	0.57	73.1	77.5	82.4	64.5	26.52	0.87	0.24	79.9
	SMORE [20]	**35.87**	**0.84**	0.53	86.0	65.4	88.0	58.8	29.53	0.92	0.13	93.4
	CycleGan [17]	32.73	0.72	0.51	77.6	52.7	80.3	27.5	22.66	0.79	0.13	86.0
	UASSR (Ours)	35.64	0.83	**0.24**	**96.9**	**84.8**	**97.4**	**79.9**	**33.43**	**0.96**	**0.03**	**94.7**
Segmentation on GT		-	-	-	98.6	89.2	98.6	85.4	-	-	-	96.0

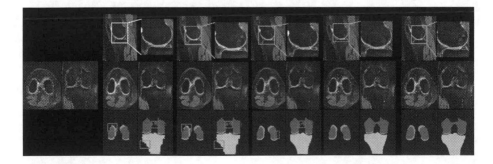

Fig. 3. Visual comparison of different methods on the knee joint dataset when the upsampling scale is $K = 4$. The first row presents the interpolated sagittal slices and the zoomed results. The second and the third rows respectively show the super resolution and the segmentation results of the coronal and axial view.

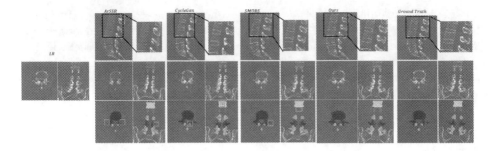

Fig. 4. Visual comparison of different methods on the lower spine dataset where the up-sampling scale is $K = 8$. The row layout is same as Fig. 3

Table 2. Ablation study on the knee joint dataset

Scale	Method	PSNR↑	SSIM↑	LPIPS↓	Dice↑			
					FB	FC	TB	TC
2×	Coronal	39.78	0.92	0.10	98.5	88.9	98.5	85.1
	Axial	38.99	0.91	0.12	98.4	88.8	98.4	84.9
	With fusion	**40.54**	**0.94**	**0.09**	**98.6**	**89.2**	**98.6**	**85.2**
4×	Coronal	36.33	0.84	0.18	97.8	87.5	98.1	83.7
	Axial	35.98	0.83	0.19	97.8	87.2	97.9	82.9
	With fusion	**37.30**	**0.87**	**0.15**	**98.0**	**87.8**	**98.2**	**84.0**
8×	Coronal	34.46	0.78	0.29	96.1	83.7	97.0	**80.1**
	Axial	34.11	0.77	0.29	95.9	82.3	96.5	75.4
	With fusion	**35.64**	**0.83**	**0.24**	**96.9**	**84.8**	**97.4**	79.9

Main Study. Table 1 shows the mean of evaluation results with arbitrary up-sampling scales $K = \{2, 4, 8\}$ for each method on both datasets. Paired t-test shows that p-values for all evaluation metrics achieved by ours and the second-best method are all smaller than $1e - 4$, demonstrating a statistically significant improvement of our method over other SOTA methods. Furthermore, other SOTA methods require to train one model for each scale while our method can evaluate arbitrary scales by training one model. Additionally, our method achieves the best performance on both visual perception and segmentation evaluation even when compared with supervised SR methods. On the knee joint dataset, we evaluated Dice similarity coefficients for the femoral bone (FB), the femoral cartilage (FC), the tibia bone (TB), and the tibial cartilage (TC). On the lower spine dataset, we compute the mean Dice value of vertebral segmentation for vertebra L1–L5. Figure 3 shows the 4× super-resolution results when evaluated on the knee joint dataset. Figure 4 shows the 8× super-resolution results when evaluated on the lower spine dataset, where we only show the qualitative results of the top-4 methods. Both qualitative and quantitative results demonstrated that UASSR achieved better results than other SOTA methods.

Ablation Study. We also conduct an ablation study to evaluate the effectiveness of the fusion strategy. Table 2 shows the result of the ablation study on the knee joint dataset. For each resolution, the first two rows show the results without fusion while the third row presents the results with fusion. From the result, it can be seen that the result of multi-view fusion is better than the result of single-view.

4   Conclusion

In summary, we proposed an unsupervised arbitrary scale super-resolution reconstruction (UASSR) method based on disentangled representation learning, eliminating the requirement of paired images for training. Applying our method to applications of generating HR images with high inter-plane resolution from LR images with low inter-plane resolution. At the inference stage, we designed a strategy to fuse multiple reconstructed HR images from different views to achieve better SR result. We conducted experiments on one publicly available dataset including 507 3D MR volumes of the knee joint and an in-house dataset containing 130 3D CT volumes of the lower spine. Results from our comprehensive experiments demonstrated superior performance of UASSR over other state-of-the-art methods.

References

1. Ambellan, F., Tack, A., Ehlke, M., Zachow, S.: Automated segmentation of knee bone and cartilage combining statistical shape knowledge and convolutional neural networks: data from the osteoarthritis initiative. Med. Image Anal. **52**, 109–118 (2019)
2. Chen, Y., Shi, F., Christodoulou, A.G., Xie, Y., Zhou, Z., Li, D.: Efficient and accurate MRI super-resolution using a generative adversarial network and 3D multi-level densely connected network. In: Frangi, A.F., Schnabel, J.A., Davatzikos, C., Alberola-López, C., Fichtinger, G. (eds.) MICCAI 2018. LNCS, vol. 11070, pp. 91–99. Springer, Cham (2018). https://doi.org/10.1007/978-3-030-00928-1_11
3. Chen, Y., Xie, Y., Zhou, Z., Shi, F., Christodoulou, A.G., Li, D.: Brain MRI super resolution using 3D deep densely connected neural networks. In: 2018 IEEE 15th International Symposium on Biomedical Imaging (ISBI 2018), pp. 739–742. IEEE (2018)
4. Dong, C., Loy, C.C., He, K., Tang, X.: Learning a deep convolutional network for image super-resolution. In: Fleet, D., Pajdla, T., Schiele, B., Tuytelaars, T. (eds.) ECCV 2014. LNCS, vol. 8692, pp. 184–199. Springer, Cham (2014). https://doi.org/10.1007/978-3-319-10593-2_13
5. Du, J., et al.: Super-resolution reconstruction of single anisotropic 3D MR images using residual convolutional neural network. Neurocomputing **392**, 209–220 (2020)
6. Goodfellow, I., et al.: Generative adversarial nets. In: Advances in Neural Information Processing Systems, vol. 27 (2014)
7. Huang, X., Liu, M.Y., Belongie, S., Kautz, J.: Multimodal unsupervised image-to-image translation. In: Proceedings of the European Conference on Computer Vision (ECCV), pp. 172–189 (2018)

8. Jia, Y., Gholipour, A., He, Z., Warfield, S.K.: A new sparse representation framework for reconstruction of an isotropic high spatial resolution MR volume from orthogonal anisotropic resolution scans. IEEE Trans. Med. Imaging **36**(5), 1182–1193 (2017)
9. Johnson, J., Alahi, A., Fei-Fei, L.: Perceptual losses for real-time style transfer and super-resolution. In: Leibe, B., Matas, J., Sebe, N., Welling, M. (eds.) ECCV 2016. LNCS, vol. 9906, pp. 694–711. Springer, Cham (2016). https://doi.org/10.1007/978-3-319-46475-6_43
10. Kim, J., Lee, J.K., Lee, K.M.: Accurate image super-resolution using very deep convolutional networks. In: Proceedings of the IEEE Conference on Computer Vision and Pattern Recognition, pp. 1646–1654 (2016)
11. Ledig, C., et al.: Photo-realistic single image super-resolution using a generative adversarial network. In: Proceedings of the IEEE Conference on Computer Vision and Pattern Recognition, pp. 4681–4690 (2017)
12. Lee, H.Y., Tseng, H.Y., Huang, J.B., Singh, M., Yang, M.H.: Diverse image-to-image translation via disentangled representations. In: Proceedings of the European Conference on Computer Vision (ECCV) (2018)
13. Pham, C.H., Ducournau, A., Fablet, R., Rousseau, F.: Brain MRI super-resolution using deep 3D convolutional networks. In: 2017 IEEE 14th International Symposium on Biomedical Imaging (ISBI 2017), pp. 197–200. IEEE (2017)
14. Wang, Z., Bovik, A.C., Sheikh, H.R., Simoncelli, E.P.: Image quality assessment: from error visibility to structural similarity. IEEE Trans. Image Process. **13**(4), 600–612 (2004)
15. Wu, Q., et al.: An arbitrary scale super-resolution approach for 3-dimensional magnetic resonance image using implicit neural representation. arXiv preprint arXiv:2110.14476 (2021)
16. Xuan, K., et al.: Reducing magnetic resonance image spacing by learning without ground-truth. Pattern Recogn. **120**, 108103 (2021)
17. You, C., et al.: CT super-resolution GAN constrained by the identical, residual, and cycle learning ensemble (GAN-circle). IEEE Trans. Med. Imaging **39**(1), 188–203 (2019)
18. Zhang, R., Isola, P., Efros, A.A., Shechtman, E., Wang, O.: The unreasonable effectiveness of deep features as a perceptual metric. In: Proceedings of the IEEE Conference on Computer Vision and Pattern Recognition, pp. 586–595 (2018)
19. Zhang, Y., Tian, Y., Kong, Y., Zhong, B., Fu, Y.: Residual dense network for image super-resolution. In: Proceedings of the IEEE Conference on Computer Vision and Pattern Recognition, pp. 2472–2481 (2018)
20. Zhao, C., Dewey, B.E., Pham, D.L., Calabresi, P.A., Reich, D.S., Prince, J.L.: Smore: a self-supervised anti-aliasing and super-resolution algorithm for MRI using deep learning. IEEE Trans. Med. Imaging **40**(3), 805–817 (2020)

WavTrans: Synergizing Wavelet and Cross-Attention Transformer for Multi-contrast MRI Super-Resolution

Guangyuan Li[1], Jun Lyu[1(✉)], Chengyan Wang[2], Qi Dou[3], and Jing Qin[4]

[1] School of Computer and Control Engineering, Yantai University, Yantai, China
ljdream0710@pku.edu.cn
[2] Human Phenome Institute, Fudan University, Shanghai, China
[3] Department of Computer Science and Engineering, The Chinese University of Hong Kong, Shatin, Hong Kong
[4] Centre for Smart Health, School of Nursing, The Hong Kong Polytechnic University, Kowloon, Hong Kong

Abstract. Current multi-contrast MRI super-resolution (SR) methods often harness convolutional neural networks (CNNs) for feature extraction and fusion. However, existing models have some shortcomings that prohibit them from producing more satisfactory results. First, during the feature extraction, some high-frequency details in the images are lost, resulting in blurring boundaries in the reconstructed images, which may impede the following diagnosis and treatment. Second, the perceptual field of the convolution kernel is limited, making the networks difficult to capture long-range/non-local features. Third, most of these models are solely driven by training data, neglecting prior knowledge about the correlations among different contrasts, which, once well leveraged, will effectively enhance the performance with limited training data. In this paper, we propose a novel model to synergize wavelet transforms with a new cross-attention transformer to comprehensively tackle these challenges; we call it *WavTrans*. Specifically, we harness one-level wavelet transformation to obtain the detail and approximation coefficients in the reference contrast MR images (*Ref*). While the approximation coefficients are applied to compress the low-frequency global information, the detail coefficients are utilized to represent the high-frequency local structure and texture information. Then, we propose a new residual cross-attention swin transformer to extract and fuse extracted features to establish long-distance dependencies between features and maximize the restoration of high-frequency information in *Tar*. In addition, a multi-residual fusion module is designed to fuse the high-frequency information in the upsampled *Tar* and the original *Ref* to ensure the restoration of detailed information. Extensive experiments demonstrate that *WavTrans* outperforms the SOTA methods by a considerable margin with upsampling factors of 2-fold and 4-fold. Code will be available at https://github.com/XAIMI-Lab/WavTrans.

Keywords: Multi-contrast SR reconstruction · Wavelet domains · Cross-attention swin transformer

© The Author(s), under exclusive license to Springer Nature Switzerland AG 2022
L. Wang et al. (Eds.): MICCAI 2022, LNCS 13436, pp. 463–473, 2022.
https://doi.org/10.1007/978-3-031-16446-0_44

1   Introduction

Magnetic resonance imaging (MRI) is a widely used image modality in clinical diagnosis, as it can provide clear body tissue structures, particularly soft tissues, without causing ionising radiation. However, prolonged MRI acquisition in a claustrophobic environment may cause patient discomfort and produce motion artifacts [9]. Straightforward shortening of imaging time may lead to low resolution with low signal-to-noise ratio. In the end, accelerating MRI acquisition speed while acquiring high-resolution (HR) images has become one of the hot spots in medical imaging computing. Super-resolution (SR) technology employs back-end enhancement to improve MR image quality without upgrading hardware facilities [6], which reconstructs the low-resolution (LR) images into HR images to achieve accelerated MRI acquisition. Traditional SR methods based on hand-crafted features [2,4,18,21] present poor performance with high upsampling factors (UFs). Recent years, some deep learning (DL) based MRI SR reconstruction methods [15,16,19] have been proposed to overcome the shortcomings of traditional approaches and achieved better SR results.

While these DL-based methods have achieved remarkable improvements, most of them only conduct the SR reconstruction using single contrast MR images, neglecting other contrast information that could provide complementary information for better reconstruction. MRI can obtain multi-contrast images with the same anatomy by setting different scan parameters, and they can provide complementary information to each other. For example, in clinical diagnosis, the repetition time and echo time of T1-weighted images (T1) are shorter than T2-weighted images (T2), while the imaging process of the proton density weighted images (PD) is faster than fat-suppressed proton density weighted images (FS-PD). In this regard, T1 and PD can be used as reference (Ref) images to guide LR target (Tar) images T2 and FS-PD in SR reconstruction [23]. Some multi-contrast SR reconstruction methods [5,14,20,26,27] have been proposed and yielded better performance than single-contrast SR methods. However, these multi-contrast methods still have the following shortcomings. 1) MR images will lose some high-frequency detailed information during feature extraction, resulting in blurred images, particularly at the boundaries, after multi-contrast feature fusion. 2) The limited perceptual field of convolution operation fails to capture long-range dependencies to better restore the anatomical structures in the resultant SR MR images. 3) More importantly, most of these models are solely driven by training data, neglecting prior knowledge about the correlations among different contrasts, which, once well leveraged, will effectively enhance the performance with limited training data.

We present a novel model that introduces wavelet transforms into a cross-attention transformer to comprehensively address these shortcomings; we call the proposed model *WavTrans*. Specifically, we employ one-level wavelet transformation [1] on the *Ref* images to obtain both the approximation and the detail coefficients. While the approximation coefficients are applied to compress the low-frequency global information, the detail coefficients are utilized to represent the high-frequency local structure and texture information. We propose to perform the feature extraction based on the detail coefficients to guide Tar for upsampling restore, ensuring that the high-frequency detail information is well preserved and hence the quality of the reconstructed Tar can be improved. Then, we develop a new residual cross-attention swin transformer, which is inspired by recently proposed transformers euipped with attention mechanisms [3,12], to establish long-distance dependencies among feature maps, and then better capture remote/non-local information. In addition, a multi-residual fusion module is designed to fuse the high-frequency information in the upsampled Tar and the original Ref to restore detailed information in SR images. We extensively evaluate the proposed model on the famous fastMRI [25] dataset and an in-house dataset. Experimental results demonstrate that our method outperforms state-of-the-art methods by a considerable margin with UFs of both 2-fold and 4-fold.

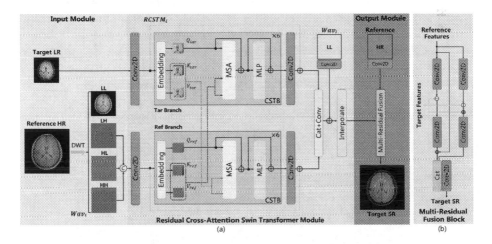

Fig. 1. (a) The network architecture of our proposed method, $Wav_i, (i = [1, 2, \cdots])$ denotes the approximation and detail coefficients, $RCSTM_i, (i = [1, 2, \cdots])$ denotes residual cross-attention swin transformer module. Note that the network architecture shown in the figure is for UF of 2-fold, $i.e.$, $i = 1$. When UF of 4-fold, the number of Wav and $RCSTM$ is 2, $i.e.$, $i = 2$. MSA: multi-head self-attention. MLP: multi-layer perceptron. CSTB: cross-attention swin transformer block. (b) The architecture of multi-residual fusion module.

2   Methodology

2.1   Overall Architecture

As shown in Fig. 1(a), discrete wavelet transformation (DWT) is used for Ref HR to obtain details and approximate coefficients [24]. The detail coefficients are used to guide Tar for upsampling restore; approximate coefficients are used for low-frequency global information supplementation and further DWT operations. Specifically, first, the features in Tar LR and detail coefficients are initially extracted using 3×3 Conv2D (stride of 1). Second, the residual cross-attention swin transformer module (RCSTM) is used to extract and fuse depth features. Then, the output of RCSTM is concatenated to obtain the fused Tar features. Next, the fused Tar features are supplemented with low-frequency global information using the approximation coefficients, and an interpolate operation with upsampling as 2-fold is performed. Finally, the next-scale upsampling RCSTM or multi-residual fusion is performed, and more specific details of each module are presented in the following sections.

Wavelet Transform. Wavelet transform is a convenient and effective tool for multi-resolution representation. In our study, the simplest wavelet, Haar wavelet [1] is employed [7,17]. DWT decomposes the Ref images into approximate and detail coefficients through a series of filtering and downsampling operations. The approximation LL captures the low-frequency global information in Ref to complement global topological information in Tar and the DWT decomposition at the next scale. The detail coefficients vertical detail (LH), horizontal detail (HL), diagonal detail (HH) capture the high-frequency local information in Ref, which are used to guide Tar upsampling restore to maximize the retention of detail information.

Residual Cross-Attention Swin Transformer. To better use the detail coefficients for Tar features, we design the RCSTM as a multi-branch, as shown in Fig. 1(a), including Tar branch and Ref branch. In our experiments, the RCSTM consists of L (we set $L = 6$) cross-attention swin transformer blocks (CSTB) and a 3×3 Conv2D. RCSTM can be expressed as follows:

$$F_{out} = Conv\left(CSTB\left(F_L\right)\right) + F_{in}, \tag{1}$$

where F_L denotes the output of the last CSTB layer, F_{in} represents the input features. This design has been demonstrated to have two advantages [10]: 1) the 3×3 convolution using spatially invariant filters can enhance the translational equivalence of the swin transformer; 2) residual connections can aggregate features at different levels and improve network performance.

CSTB is one of the critical parts of our method, which is upon on the swin transformer. It models the bidirectional correspondences between grids of Tar and Ref and performs a dual feature aggregation. As shown in Fig. 1(a), the Tar/Ref features are reshaped with size $\frac{HW}{N^2} \times N^2 \times C$ into non-overlapping local windows of size $N \times N$ with the number $\frac{HW}{N^2}$ (we set $N = 8$). Next, local attention is calculated separately for each window. Specifically, a local window feature $\mathcal{F}$, the query (Q), key (K), and value (V) is denoted as:

$$Q = \mathcal{F}P_Q, K = \mathcal{F}P_K, V = \mathcal{F}P_V, \tag{2}$$

where P_Q, P_K, and P_V denote the projection matrix shared between different windows. The key to cross-attention is exchanging and fusing Q, K, and V

between different contrast features. As shown in Fig. 1(a), the key and value in the Tar branch are used in the Ref branch; similarly, the key and value in the Ref branch are used in the Tar branch, as follows:

$$Attention\,(Q_t, K_r, V_r) = softmax\left(Q_t K_r/\sqrt{d} + B\right) V_r, \tag{3}$$

$$Attention\,(Q_r, K_t, V_t) = softmax\left(Q_r K_t/\sqrt{d} + B\right) V_t, \tag{4}$$

where $\{Q_t, K_t, V_t\}$ and $\{Q_r, K_r, V_r\}$ denote Q, K, and V in Tar and Ref branches, respectively; B denotes the learnable relative positional encoding; d is the dimension of K. Note that we set the number of MSA is 6. Finally, we use a multi-layer perceptron [22] for further feature transformation.

Multi-Residual Fusion. Since DWT cannot obtain detail coefficients at the same scale as the original Ref HR, we designed the multi-residual fusion (MRF) block to address it. MRF extracts high-frequency information from the original Ref and the upsampled Tar and fuses them, ensuring that the upsampled Tar can maximum restore the edge contour details. As shown in Fig. 1(b), the first residual is the Ref high-frequency feature refinement residual (purple line); the second residual is the Tar residual (brown line). Specifically, the first residual is used to refine the high-frequency details in the Ref as follows:

$$\hat{\mathcal{F}}_{ref} = conv\,(conv\,(\mathcal{F}_{ref}) - \mathcal{F}_{tar}) + \mathcal{F}_{ref}, \tag{5}$$

where $conv$ means a 3×3 Conv2D with a stride of 1, $\mathcal{F}_{ref}$ denotes the features in the original Ref HR, $\mathcal{F}_{tar}$ represents the upsampled Tar features, and $\hat{\mathcal{F}}_{ref}$ means the Ref features with high-frequency detail information. Similarly, the second residual is used to refine the high-frequency details in the Tar features:

$$\hat{\mathcal{F}}_{tar} = conv\,((\mathcal{F}_{tar} - conv\,(\mathcal{F}_{ref})) + \mathcal{F}_{tar}). \tag{6}$$

Finally, $\hat{\mathcal{F}}_{ref}$ and $\hat{\mathcal{F}}_{tar}$ are concatenated, and through a convolution layer to get the final output Tar SR.

2.2 Objective Function

K-space Data Consistency Loss. We set a fidelity term loss $\mathcal{L}_{dc}$ in the objective function to complement the missing frequency domain information in the Tar SR images. Specifically, the I_{SR} and I_{HR} are transformed into the frequency domain via Fourier transform to obtain K_{SR} and K_{HR}. Using the undersampling mask M to judge the sampling in K_{SR}, the sampled coefficients are replaced with the coefficients in K_{HR}, and the unsampled coefficients remain unchanged, as:

$$\boldsymbol{K}_{DC}[m, n] = \begin{cases} \boldsymbol{K}_{SR}[m, n] & (m, n) \notin M \\ \frac{\boldsymbol{K}_{SR}[m,n] + \lambda \boldsymbol{K}_{HR}[m,n]}{1+\lambda} & (m, n) \in M, \end{cases} \tag{7}$$

where $\lambda \geq 0$ is the noise level, here λ is set to infinity, $[m, n]$ is the matrix indexing operation. Mean squared error is used to calculate the error between $\boldsymbol{K}_{DC}$ and $\boldsymbol{K}_{HR}$, as:

$$\mathcal{L}_{dc} = \mathbb{E}_{(\boldsymbol{K}_{DC}, \boldsymbol{K}_{HR})} \|\boldsymbol{K}_{DC} - \boldsymbol{K}_{HR}\|_2. \tag{8}$$

Image Reconstruction Loss. We use L1-pixel loss to calculate the pixel difference between the Tar SR images and the original Tar images, named as $\mathcal{L}_{img}$:

$$\mathcal{L}_{img} = \mathbb{E}_{(\boldsymbol{I}_{SR}, \boldsymbol{I}_{HR})} \|\boldsymbol{I}_{SR} - \boldsymbol{I}_{HR}\|_1, \tag{9}$$

where $\boldsymbol{I}_{SR}$ is the reconstructed Tar SR images, and $\boldsymbol{I}_{HR}$ is the original Tar HR images. Therefore, the full objective of our method is defined as:

$$\mathcal{L}_{full} = \alpha\mathcal{L}_{dc} + \beta\mathcal{L}_{img}, \tag{10}$$

where α and β weight the trade-off between the $\mathcal{L}_{dc}$ and $\mathcal{L}_{img}$.

3   Experiments

Datasets and Baselines. Our experiments use in-house datasets brain and public dataset fastMRI [25] knee, respectively. We filter out 513 and 125 pairs of T1 and T2-FLAIR full k-space sampling data for training and validation/test from 30 healthy subjects for the in-house brain dataset (acquisition parameters are TE(T1): 2.3 ms, TE(T2): 120 ms). For fastMRI dataset, we filter out 320 and 80 pairs knee MR images of PD and FS-PD volumes for training and validation/test. We unify the two datasets into 256×256 complex-valued images by cropping on k-space, used as the label during training. We adopt a commonly used downsampling treatment, which is implemented in the frequency domain [14,15]. Specifically, we first converted the original images of size 256×256 into the k-space. Then, the down-sampling is implemented along the phase-encoding direction with only central low-frequency region are retained. For instance, the central 50% and 25% data are kept for the down-sampling factors of 2 and 4, respectively. Finally, we used the inverse Fourier transform to convert the modified data back into the images domain to produce LR images. We compare our method with a single-contrast SR methods EDSR [11] and three state-of-the-art multi-contrast methods, MCSR [14], MINet [5], and MASA [13].

Experimental Setup. We implement our method in PyTorch with NVIDIA Tesla V100 GPUs (4×16 GB) workstations. The Adam [8] optimizer is adopted during training, with the learning rate of 1e−4, batch size of 2, and epochs of 200. The parameters α and β are set to 0.0001 and 1, respectively. The upsampling factors are set to 2-fold and 4-fold, respectively. All the compared approaches are retrained using their defaulting parameter sets.

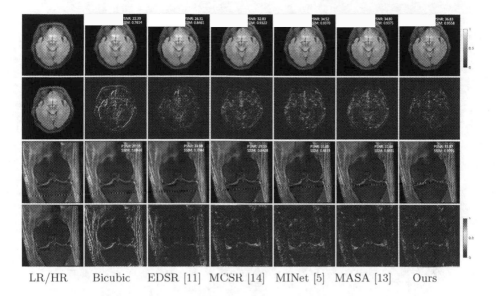

LR/HR   Bicubic   EDSR [11]   MCSR [14]   MINet [5]   MASA [13]   Ours

Fig. 2. Qualitative results of different SR reconstruction methods on the brain and knee datasets with the UF of 4-fold. Except for the first column, the first/third row is the SR reconstructed images obtained by different methods, and the second/fourth row is the corresponding error maps.

Qualitative Visualization Results. The SR reconstructed images and error maps of each method under the brain and knee datasets with the UF of 4-fold are shown in Fig. 2. The more prominent the texture in the error map, the worse the reconstruction. As can be observed, the image quality of the single-contrast SR method is lower than the multi-contrast method. Among the multi-contrast SR reconstruction methods, our method reconstructs the SR image with a minor error, has sharper texture details, and eliminates the sense of edge blurring. The results demonstrate that our method enables Tar images maximum use and fusion of high-frequency detail information in Ref HR images.

Quantitative Metrics Results. Table 1 reports the quantitative metrics scores with in-house and fastMRI datasets under 2-fold and 4-fold upsampling. As can be seen, our method has the best quantitative metrics results compared to other comparison methods, which shows that our approach has better SR reconstruction performance. Even though upsampling 4-fold is challenging, our method can still reconstruct SR images with high accuracy, which is due to our approach can provide sufficient detail information for the Tar images and restore the maximum high-frequency details in the images.

Table 1. Quantitative results (mean and standard deviation) on in-house and fastMRI datasets with different UFs, PSNR:dB, SSIM, and RMSE (10^{-2}). Red numbers indicate the method with the best results.

Methods		Bicubic	EDSR [11]	MCSR [14]	MINet [5]	MASA [13]	Ours
Parameters		-	1.518M	3.396M	6.898M	4.027M	2.102M
Flops		-	16.275G	103.81G	866.933G	180.134G	162.889G
Inference time		-	7.17 s	9.14 s	10.23 s	9.77 s	10.98 s
UF	Metrics	in-house Brain					
2×	PSNR	28.18(1.97)	34.15(1.78)	39.39(1.57)	40.53(1.60)	41.37(1.49)	43.01(1.69)
	SSIM	0.85(0.03)	0.94(0.01)	0.96(0.01)	0.97(0.01)	0.97(0.01)	0.98(0.01)
	RMSE	2.21(0.97)	1.58(1.14)	1.04(0.75)	1.01(0.72)	0.71(0.57)	0.57(0.34)
4×	PSNR	22.30(2.36)	26.07(2.13)	32.25(1.83)	34.29(1.10)	34.55(1.02)	35.97(0.87)
	SSIM	0.74(0.02)	0.83(0.02)	0.93(0.01)	0.94(0.02)	0.95(0.02)	0.96(0.01)
	RMSE	8.08(2.43)	6.67(2.32)	4.81(1.37)	3.17(1.68)	2.74(1.54)	1.84(1.13)
UF	Metrics	fastMRI [25] Knee					
2×	PSNR	23.97(2.37)	29.50(2.58)	34.25(1.29)	35.36(1.24)	35.82(1.13)	37.24(0.90)
	SSIM	0.79(0.03)	0.85(0.03)	0.93(0.02)	0.94(0.01)	0.94(0.02)	0.95(0.01)
	RMSE	4.11(0.90)	3.50(1.10)	2.19(1.02)	1.78(0.63)	1.50(0.49)	1.26(0.44)
4×	PSNR	19.75(2.37)	24.14(1.62)	28.13(1.25)	30.91(1.38)	31.23(1.14)	33.05(0.97)
	SSIM	0.64(0.03)	0.69(0.03)	0.82(0.03)	0.86(0.02)	0.86(0.03)	0.90(0.01)
	RMSE	7.16(2.19)	6.12(2.06)	3.31(1.10)	2.86(1.03)	2.41(0.87)	1.66(0.77)

Table 2. Ablation study on different variant network under in-house brain dataset with UF = 4-fold, PSNR: dB, SSIM, and RMSE (10^{-2}). Red numbers indicate the method with the best results.

Variant	Modules				Metrics		
	DC	Wavelet	RCSTM	MRF	PSNR	SSIM	RMSE
w/o DC	×	✓	✓	✓	29.45(1.55)	0.87(0.02)	5.17(2.37)
w/o Wav	✓	×	✓	✓	32.14(1.52)	0.93(0.01)	3.63(1.91)
w/o RCSTM	✓	✓	×	✓	32.31(1.60)	0.93(0.01)	3.21(1.61)
w/o MRF	✓	✓	✓	×	35.12(1.10)	0.95(0.01)	2.34(1.26)
Full Version	✓	✓	✓	✓	35.97(0.87)	0.96(0.01)	1.84(1.13)

Ablation Study. To verify the contribution of each module in the network, we designed three variant networks to perform the ablation study. 1) w/o DC, which is our model without using k-space data consistency loss. 2) w/o Wav, which is our model without using wavelets to extract the detail coefficients in the Ref images. 3) w/o RCSTM, which is our model without using the residual cross-attention swin transformer and uses the general swin transformer instead. 4) w/o MRF, which is our model without using the multi-residual fusion module and uses a simple concatenate instead of it. We summarize the 4× enlargement results on in-house brain dataset in Table 2. As can be seen, w/o DC shows that k-space data consistency loss can effectively restore the frequency domain information in MR images. w/o Wav performs the worst, which is consistent with our conclusion that the detail coefficients can effectively restore the high-frequency detail information in Tar images and improve the image quality. Since w/o RCSTM does not use RCSTM to fuse Tar with the detail coefficients effectively, the results of w/o RCSTM are not optimal. Furthermore, from the w/o MRF and full version results, we observe that the MRF module can further improve the quality of the images, which is due to its ability to fuse the high-frequency information in the Tar and original Ref images.

4   Conclusion

We have proposed a joint wavelet and residual cross-attention swin transformer network for multi-contrast SR reconstruction to effectively restore the Tar images detail information with guidance from Ref images. Specifically, we use DWT to get the Ref images detail and approximation coefficients. The detail coefficients are used for feature extraction and fusion with the Tar images through the RCSTM; the approximation coefficients are used to supplement the low-frequency global information for the Tar images. In addition, MRF is used to fuse the high-frequency detail information in the upsampled Tar and the original Ref. The results demonstrate that our method outperformed the state-of-the-art multi-contrast SR reconstruction methods. This study provides a potential direction for further research into the processing between multi-contrast images for MRI super-resolution.

Acknowledgements. This work was supported in part by National Natural Science Foundation of China under Grant 61902338 and 62001120, the Shanghai Sailing Program (No. 20YF1402400), a grant of Hong Kong Research Grants Council under General Research Fund (no. 15205919).

References

1. Akansu, A.N., Haddad, R.A., Haddad, P.A., Haddad, P.R.: Multiresolution Signal Decomposition: Transforms, Subbands, and Wavelets. Academic Press, Cambridge (2001)
2. Bhatia, K.K., Price, A.N., Shi, W., Hajnal, J.V., Rueckert, D.: Super-resolution reconstruction of cardiac MRI using coupled dictionary learning. In: 2014 IEEE 11th International Symposium on Biomedical Imaging (ISBI), pp. 947–950. IEEE (2014)
3. Chen, C.F.R., Fan, Q., Panda, R.: Crossvit: cross-attention multi-scale vision transformer for image classification. In: Proceedings of the IEEE/CVF International Conference on Computer Vision, pp. 357–366 (2021)
4. Dong, C., Loy, C.C., He, K., Tang, X.: Image super-resolution using deep convolutional networks. IEEE Trans. Pattern Anal. Mach. Intell. **38**(2), 295–307 (2015)
5. Feng, C.-M., Fu, H., Yuan, S., Xu, Y.: Multi-contrast MRI super-resolution via a multi-stage integration network. In: de Bruijne, M., et al. (eds.) MICCAI 2021. LNCS, vol. 12906, pp. 140–149. Springer, Cham (2021). https://doi.org/10.1007/978-3-030-87231-1_14

6. Feng, C.-M., Yan, Y., Fu, H., Chen, L., Xu, Y.: Task transformer network for joint MRI reconstruction and super-resolution. In: de Bruijne, M., et al. (eds.) MICCAI 2021. LNCS, vol. 12906, pp. 307–317. Springer, Cham (2021). https://doi.org/10.1007/978-3-030-87231-1_30

7. Huang, H., He, R., Sun, Z., Tan, T.: Wavelet-SRNet: a wavelet-based CNN for multi-scale face super resolution. In: Proceedings of the IEEE International Conference on Computer Vision, pp. 1689–1697 (2017)

8. Kingma, D.P., Ba, J.: Adam: a method for stochastic optimization. arXiv preprint arXiv:1412.6980 (2014)

9. Li, G., Lv, J., Tong, X., Wang, C., Yang, G.: High-resolution pelvic MRI reconstruction using a generative adversarial network with attention and cyclic loss. IEEE Access **9**, 105951–105964 (2021)

10. Liang, J., Cao, J., Sun, G., Zhang, K., Van Gool, L., Timofte, R.: SwinIR: image restoration using swin transformer. In: Proceedings of the IEEE/CVF International Conference on Computer Vision, pp. 1833–1844 (2021)

11. Lim, B., Son, S., Kim, H., Nah, S., Mu Lee, K.: Enhanced deep residual networks for single image super-resolution. In: Proceedings of the IEEE Conference on Computer Vision and Pattern Recognition Workshops, pp. 136–144 (2017)

12. Lin, W., et al.: CAT: cross-attention transformer for one-shot object detection. arXiv preprint arXiv:2104.14984 (2021)

13. Lu, L., Li, W., Tao, X., Lu, J., Jia, J.: MASA-SR: matching acceleration and spatial adaptation for reference-based image super-resolution. In: Proceedings of the IEEE/CVF Conference on Computer Vision and Pattern Recognition, pp. 6368–6377 (2021)

14. Lyu, Q., et al.: Multi-contrast super-resolution MRI through a progressive network. IEEE Trans. Med. Imaging **39**(9), 2738–2749 (2020)

15. Lyu, Q., Shan, H., Wang, G.: MRI super-resolution with ensemble learning and complementary priors. IEEE Trans. Comput. Imaging **6**, 615–624 (2020)

16. Qiu, D., Zhang, S., Liu, Y., Zhu, J., Zheng, L.: Super-resolution reconstruction of knee magnetic resonance imaging based on deep learning. Comput. Methods Programs Biomed. **187**, 105059 (2020)

17. Qu, L., Zhang, Y., Wang, S., Yap, P.T., Shen, D.: Synthesized 7T MRI from 3T MRI via deep learning in spatial and wavelet domains. Med. Image Anal. **62**, 101663 (2020)

18. Shi, F., Cheng, J., Wang, L., Yap, P.T., Shen, D.: LRTV: MR image super-resolution with low-rank and total variation regularizations. IEEE Trans. Med. Imaging **34**(12), 2459–2466 (2015)

19. Steeden, J.A., et al.: Rapid whole-heart CMR with single volume super-resolution. J. Cardiovasc. Magn. Reson. **22**(1), 1–13 (2020)

20. Stimpel, B., Syben, C., Schirrmacher, F., Hoelter, P., Dörfler, A., Maier, A.: Multimodal super-resolution with deep guided filtering. In: Bildverarbeitung für die Medizin 2019. I, pp. 110–115. Springer, Wiesbaden (2019). https://doi.org/10.1007/978-3-658-25326-4_25

21. Tourbier, S., Bresson, X., Hagmann, P., Thiran, J.P., Meuli, R., Cuadra, M.B.: An efficient total variation algorithm for super-resolution in fetal brain MRI with adaptive regularization. Neuroimage **118**, 584–597 (2015)

22. Vaswani, A., et al.: Attention is all you need. In: Advances in Neural Information Processing Systems, pp. 5998–6008 (2017)

23. Xiang, L., et al.: Deep-learning-based multi-modal fusion for fast MR reconstruction. IEEE Trans. Biomed. Eng. **66**(7), 2105–2114 (2018)

24. You, S., et al.: Fine perceptive GANs for brain MR image super-resolution in wavelet domain. IEEE Trans. Neural Netw. Learn. Syst. (2022)
25. Zbontar, J., et al.: fastMRI: an open dataset and benchmarks for accelerated MRI. arXiv preprint arXiv:1811.08839 (2018)
26. Zeng, K., Zheng, H., Cai, C., Yang, Y., Zhang, K., Chen, Z.: Simultaneous single- and multi-contrast super-resolution for brain MRI images based on a convolutional neural network. Comput. Biol. Med. **99**, 133–141 (2018)
27. Zheng, H., et al.: Multi-contrast brain MRI image super-resolution with gradient-guided edge enhancement. IEEE Access **6**, 57856–57867 (2018)

DuDoCAF: Dual-Domain Cross-Attention Fusion with Recurrent Transformer for Fast Multi-contrast MR Imaging

Jun Lyu[1], Bin Sui[1], Chengyan Wang[2(✉)], Yapeng Tian[3], Qi Dou[4],
and Jing Qin[5]

[1] School of Computer and Control Engineering, Yantai University, Yantai, China
[2] Human Phenome Institute, Fudan University, Shanghai, China
wangcy@fudan.edu.cn
[3] University of Rochester, Rochester, USA
[4] Department of Computer Science and Engineering, The Chinese University of Hong Kong, Shatin, Hong Kong
[5] Centre for Smart Health, School of Nursing, The Hong Kong Polytechnic University, Kowloon, Hong Kong

Abstract. Multi-contrast magnetic resonance imaging (MC-MRI) has been widely used for the diagnosis and characterization of tumors and lesions, as multi-contrast MR images are capable of providing complementary information for more comprehensive diagnosis and evaluation. However, it usually suffers from long scanning time to acquire multi-contrast MR images; in addition, long scanning time may lead to motion artifacts, degrading the image quality. Recently, many studies have proposed to employ the fully-sampled image of one contrast with short acquisition time to guide the reconstruction of the other contrast with long acquisition time so as to speed up the scanning. However, these studies still have two shortcomings. First, they simply concatenate the features of the two contrast images together without digging and leveraging the inherent and deep correlation between them. Second, as aliasing artifacts are complicated and non-local, sole image domain reconstruction with local dependencies is far from enough to eliminate these artifacts and achieve faithful reconstruction results. We present a novel **Du**al-**Do**main **C**ross-**A**ttention **F**usion (DuDoCAF) scheme with recurrent transformer to comprehensively address these shortcomings. Specifically, the proposed CAF scheme enables deep and effective fusion of features extracted from two modalities. The dual-domain recurrent learning allows our model to restore signals in both k-space and image domains, and hence more comprehensively remove the artifacts. In addition, we tame recurrent transformers to capture long-range dependencies from the fused feature maps to further enhance reconstruction performance. Extensive experiments on public fastMRI and clinical brain datasets demonstrate that the proposed DuDoCAF outperforms the state-of-the-

Supplementary Information The online version contains supplementary material available at https://doi.org/10.1007/978-3-031-16446-0_45.

art methods under different under-sampling patterns and acceleration rates.

Keywords: MRI reconstruction · Cross-attention fusion · Recurrent transformer · Dual-domain reconstruction

1 Introduction

Magnetic resonance imaging (MRI) is widely used in clinical practice, as it is non-invasive and capable of providing superior soft tissue contrast. Multi-contrast (MC) MR images are obtained from different pulse sequences, which form the image intensity changes between different tissues [11,14]. For example, in brain examination, the T1 weighted images (T1WIs) are used for observing the morphological information, while the fluid attenuated inversion recovery (FLAIR) images are used to detect the edema and inflammation [12]. Similarly, in knee imaging, proton density weighted images (PDWIs) provide the knee structure information while fat-suppressed proton density weighted images (FS-PDWIs) can suppress fat signals and highlight cartilage ligaments [2]. Unfortunately, MR imaging is inherently time-consuming as data are acquired sequentially in k-space. The total scanning time for a typical clinical protocol is about 15–20 min. To this end, reconstructing high-quality MC images from limited acquired measurements to reduce scanning time is highly demanded in practice.

Recently, several studies [3–5,11,15,17,20,21] demonstrated that it is a promising way to employ a fully-sampled reference image of one contrast with short acquisition time, such as T1WI and PDWI, to reconstruct the under-sampled target image of the other contrast with longer scanning time, such as FLAIR and FS-PDWI. A key concern of this reconstruction task is that how to fuse the two or more MC images so that their complementary information can be sufficiently leveraged. Early studies either simply stack the MC images in the input layer [15,17] or extract MC features in different branches separately and then stack information in deeper layers, which ignore the inherent and rich correlations among different contrasts. Later, generative adversarial network (GAN) based models, such as rsGAN [3] and Y-net [4], have been developed for synergistic recovery of under-sampled multi-contrast acquisitions. Some multi-scale integration networks [5,11] have also been proposed to extract multi-scale information among the contrasts and incorporate data consistency units for MRI acceleration. Although certain improvement has been made, these algorithms still lack of effective mechanisms to sufficiently harness the correlations between MC images. In addition, the long-range dependencies in the fused features are not well modeled for more faithful reconstruction.

Recently, many transformer based models [7,10] have been introduced to capture global interactions between contexts for fast MRI reconstruction. Feng et al. [7] proposed a task transformer for multi-task learning, which allows to transfer shared structure representation to the task specific branch for MRI reconstruction and super-resolution. Korkmaz et al. [10] introduced zero-shot

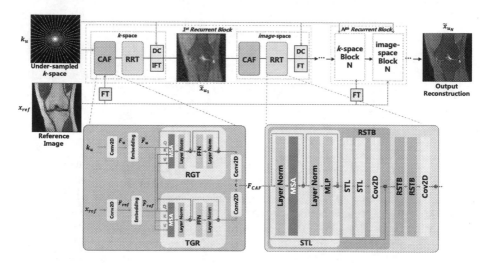

Fig. 1. The architecture of our proposed Dual-Domain Cross-Attention Fusion based Recurrent Transformer (DuDoCAF) for fast multi-contrast MR Imaging.

learned adversarial transformers for unsupervised reconstruction in accelerated MRI. However, these methods focus on restoring images in mono-space and do not exploit any k-space information, which is essential for our task. As each signal in the k-space is estimated from all the values in image domain via Fourier transform, only using constrains in sole image-space cannot effectively reconstruct high-quality aliasing-free images. In this regard, a dual domain recurrent network (DuDoRNet) [21] is proposed to accelerate MR imaging, which demonstrates the advantages of cross domain learning. Inspired by this work, we propose a novel MC MR reconstruction method via cross domain learning.

To address above-mentioned limitations, we propose a novel dual-domain cross-attention fusion mechanism (DuDoCAF) with recurrent transformer for fast multi-contrast MR Imaging. Unlike existing models that merely concatenate the features of MC MR images, the proposed CAF mechanism is able to deeply and effectively fuse the features extracted from these two contrast images in a bidirectional way so that complementary information of two contrasts can be sufficiently harnessed. We further tame the residual-reconstruction transformer to model the long-range dependencies based on the fused feature maps in both domains to counteract aliasing artifacts and faithfully reconstruct the target images. In addition, the recurrent dual-domain learning makes the reconstruction results more interpretable, which is important in clinical practice. Extensive experiments on two representative datasets demonstrate that our proposed method gains remarkable margins over several state-of-the-art methods under different sampling patterns and acceleration factors.

2   Methods

2.1   Network Architecture

The network architecture of the proposed model is illustrated in Fig. 1. We denote the complex-valued fully-sampled k-space as k. The corresponding image x reconstructed from k can be obtained by $x = \mathcal{F}^{-1}k$, where $\mathcal{F}^{-1}$ is the inverse Fourier Transform (IFT). To accelerate MR imaging, we employ binary mask M to define the under-sampling trajectory, e.g. cartesian, radial, and spiral. Thus, the under-sampled k-space can be defined as $k_u = Mk$, and correspondingly, $x_u = \mathcal{F}^{-1}Mk$. Given the under-sampled k-space data k_u of the target modality (e.g., FLAIR and FS-PDWI), and the fully-sampled image x_{ref} of the reference modality (e.g., T1WI and PDWI), we aim to reconstruct the MR image $\tilde{x}_{u_N}$ from k_u, where N is the number of recurrent blocks in the proposed model. As shown in Fig. 1, the proposed model is mainly composed of three modules: 1) the cross-attention fusion (CAF) module, which is employed to deeply and effectively fuse information of different modalities, 2) the residual-reconstruction transformer (RRT), which is harnessed to more faithfully reconstruct the target modality in both domains by capturing more long-range dependencies in the fused k-space and image, 3) the recurrent restoration blocks with data consistency (DC) layer in both k-space and image-space. We spell out their mechanisms as follows.

2.2   Cross-Attention Fusion

In order to ensure that the reference image can effectively guide the target image reconstruction, we need to fuse the two different contrast images. Inspired by [1,13,18], we designed the cross-attention fusion module to establish a bidirectional correspondence between the reference and target images and perform dual feature aggregation.

First, to extract shallow features of under-sampled target $k_u \in \mathbb{R}^{H \times W \times 2}$ and the reference $k_{ref} \in \mathbb{R}^{H \times W \times 2}$, we employ a 3×3 convolutional layer conv to obtain an initial representation $\mathbf{F}_u = \text{Conv}(k_u)$, $\mathbf{F}_{ref} = \text{Conv}(k_{ref}) \in \mathbb{R}^{H \times W \times C}$. Then, the features are reshaped into non-overlapping local windows of size $N \times N$ with the number $\frac{H \times W}{N^2}$. We obtain $\hat{\mathbf{F}}_u, \hat{\mathbf{F}}_{ref} \in \mathbb{R}^{d \times C}$ after the embedding operation, where $d = \frac{H \times W}{N^2} N^2$. The CAF block consists of two sub-modules: reference guide target (RGT) and target guide reference (TGR), and its mechanism can be formulated as:

$$\mathbf{F}_{CAF} = \text{concat}(\text{conv}(\text{RGT}(\hat{\mathbf{F}}_u, \hat{\mathbf{F}}_{ref}), \text{conv}(\text{TGR}(\hat{\mathbf{F}}_u, \hat{\mathbf{F}}_{ref}))), \quad (1)$$

where $\mathbf{F}_{CAF}$ indicates the fused feature of the two contrast images, which will be fed into the following RRT module. The operator concat means the channel-wise concatenation operator.

Then, the attention mechanism jointly learns the $W_Q^{ref}, W_K^{ref}, W_V^{ref}$ and W_Q^u, W_K^u, W_V^u, which are the query (Q), key (K), and value (V) weight matrices for reference and target images, respectively. Here, all weight metrics have the same dimensions $d \times d$. Take the RGT for example, the attention is calculated by encoding target as queries and taking reference as keys and values:

$$Q_u = \hat{\mathbf{F}}_u W_Q^{ref}, K_{ref} = \hat{\mathbf{F}}_{ref} W_K^{ref}, V_{ref} = \hat{\mathbf{F}}_{ref} W_V^{ref},$$

$$\text{Attention} = \text{softmax}\left(\frac{Q_u \cdot K_{ref}^T}{\sqrt{d}}\right) V_{ref}. \tag{2}$$

The TGR is similar to RGT, except that the reference is encoded to queries and target is used as keys and values and thus form a cross-attention mechanism. As described in [16], the attention can be learned over multiple heads in parallel. If the attention is split into H heads, the dimension of the output of each head is $d_{head} = \frac{d}{H}$. Then, the multi-head self-attention (MSA) mechanism is implemented to extract information from different representation subspaces:

$$\text{MultiHeadAttn} = \text{concat}\left(\text{head}_1, \cdots, \text{head}_H\right) W^O,$$

$$\text{head}_i = \text{Attention}\left(QW_i^Q, KW_i^K, VW_i^V\right), \tag{3}$$

where $W_i^Q \in \mathbb{R}^{d \times d_{head}}$, $W_i^K \in \mathbb{R}^{d \times d_{head}}$, $W_i^V \in \mathbb{R}^{d \times d_{head}}$ and $W^O \in \mathbb{R}^{d \times d}$ are weights to be learned. Next, the output is sent to a feed-forward Network (FFN) block consisted of two linear transformation with ReLU activation, defined as:

$$\text{FFN}(x) = \max\left(0, xW_1 + b_1\right) W_2 + b_2, \tag{4}$$

where W_1, W_2 and b_1, b_2 are the weight matrices and biases vectors, respectively. The LayerNorm (LN) layer is added before both MSA and FFN, and the residual connection is employed for both parts.

2.3   Residual Reconstruction Transformer

The long-range dependencies embedded in the fused feature maps obtained from the CAF are essential for efficient and robust image reconstruction, as it is depending on these dependencies that we reconstruct the target image based on under-sampled signals. To effectively capture these long-range dependencies, we develop the RRT module, which consists of three residual swin transformer block (RSTB) and a convolutional layer. It can be formulated as:

$$F_i = H_{RSTB_i}\left(F_{i-1}\right), i = 1, 2, 3,$$

$$F_{RRT} = H_{conv}\left(F_i\right), \tag{5}$$

where $F_0 = F_{CAF}$. Each RSTB contains a patch embedding operator, three cascaded swin transformer layers (STL) [11], a patch unembedding operator, a convolution, and a residual connection between the input and output of RSTB. It can be expressed as:

$$F_{i,0} = H_{Emb_i}\left(F_{i-1}\right)$$

$$F_{i,j} = H_{STL_{i,j}}\left(F_{i,j-1}\right), \quad j = 1, 2, 3 \tag{6}$$

$$F_i = H_{CONV_i}\left(H_{Unemb_i}\left(F_{i,j}\right) + F_{i-1}\right)$$

where $H_{Emb_i}(\cdot)$ is the patch embedding from $F_{i-1} \in \mathbb{R}^{H \times W \times C}$ to $F_{i,0} \in \mathbb{R}^{HW \times C}$, and $H_{Unemb\ i}(\cdot)$ is the patch unembedding from $F_{i,j} \in \mathbb{R}^{HW \times C}$ to $\mathbb{R}^{H \times W \times C}$. The whole process of the STL can be expressed as:

$$
\begin{aligned}
F' &= H_{(S)W-MSA}\left(H_{LN}(F)\right) + F \\
F'' &= H_{MLP}\left(H_{LN}(F')\right) + F'
\end{aligned}
\tag{7}
$$

where F and F'' are the input and output of the STL. $H_{MLP}(\cdot)$ and $H_{LN}(\cdot)$ denote the multilayer perceptron and the layer normalization layer. Windows multi-head self-attention (W-MSA) and shifted windows multi-head self-attention (SW-MSA) $H_{(S)W-MSA}(\cdot)$ are alternatively applied in consecutive STLs.

2.4 Dual-Domain Recurrent Learning

Each recurrent block of DuDoCAF contains a k-space block, an image reconstruction block, and two interleaved data consistency (DC) layers. In i-th restoration block of image domain, the optimization can be expressed as minimizing the following model:

$$
\arg\min_{\theta_{img}}(\|M\mathcal{F}\mathcal{H}_{img}(x_{u_i}, x_{ref}; \theta_{img}) - k_u\|_2^2 + \lambda \|x_f - \mathcal{H}_{img}(x_{u_i}, x_{ref}; \theta_{img})\|_2^2),
\tag{8}
$$

where $\mathcal{H}_{img}$ is the image restoration network with parameters θ_{img}, the input of the network is x_{u_i} which comes from the $(i-1)$-th k-space reconstruction block and x_{ref} is the fully-sampled reference image. The first term is the data consistency constraint that ensures the consistency of the reconstruction image in k-space and the second term is a regularization term models the relationship between the reconstructed image $\tilde{x}$ and the fully-sampled image x_f. Similarly, the k-space reconstruction optimization can be formulated as:

$$
\arg\min_{\theta_k}(\|M\mathcal{H}_k(k_{u_i}, k_{ref}; \theta_k) - k_u\|_2^2 + \lambda \|k_f - \mathcal{H}_k(k_{u_i}, k_{ref}; \theta_k)\|_2^2),
\tag{9}
$$

where $\mathcal{H}_k$ is the k-space reconstruction network with parameters θ_k. Therefore, the final loss for DuDoCAF is $\mathcal{L} = \sum_{i=1}^{N}(\mathcal{L}_{img_i} + \mathcal{L}_{k_i})$, in which N represents the number of recurrent blocks.

3 Experiments

Datasets and Implementation. We evaluate our proposed method on two raw MRI datasets: **1)** Clinical brain MRI dataset, which was collected using a 3T Philips Ingenia MRI system (Philips Healthcare, Best, the Netherlands) scanner, including T1W and FLAIR imaging. The dataset consists of 36 healthy subjects and 5 patients. We randomly selected 616 images for training and 250 images (150 from healthy subject and 100 from patients) for testing. **2)** Public fastMRI [9] dataset with paired multi-contrast DICOM images. Following [6,19], we filtered out 240 pairs of PDWI and FS-PDWI knee images, 400 for training and the rest 80 images for testing. Both datasets are real k-space data and the matrix size are 256×256. The under-sampling masks include $8\times$ random, $10\times$ radial and $10\times$ spiral pattern.

Experiments were carried out on a system equipped with GPUs of NVIDIA Tesla V100 (4 cores, each with 32 GB memory). The Adam optimizer [8] is used for the training. The model used a batch size of 2 and learning rate of 10^{-4} for 200 epochs. We set $N = 3$ recurrent groups in our network. For fair comparison, the competing methods all use their default parameter settings. Code will be available at https://github.com/XAIMI-Lab/DuDoCAF.

Comparison with State-of-the-Arts. On both datasets, we have compared our approach with four recent state-of-the-art methods including: YNet [4], UF-T2 [17], MINet [5] and DuDoRNet [21]. The calculated FLOPs (G) and Parameters (M) of all mentioned models are listed in the supplementary material. Figure 2 shows that knee images reconstructed using YNet and UF-T2 still have aliasing artifacts that are obvious at the edge and in the vessel area. The MINet, DuDoRNet and Ours greatly improved the ZF image quality by recovering sharpness and adding more structural details to the ZF images. However, the yellow arrow shows that, as for fine vessel information, Ours has better reconstruction performance. The reconstructed brain images are shown in supplementary material.

Table 1. Quantitative results on two datasets with different under-sampling masks, in terms of SSIM and PSNR. The best and second-best results are marked in red and blue, respectively.

Dataset	Methods	Random (8×)		Radial (10×)		Spiral (10×)	
		PSNR	SSIM	PSNR	SSIM	PSNR	SSIM
fastMRI	Y-net	24.96 ± 1.77	0.79 ± 0.01	25.58 ± 1.62	0.81 ± 0.04	25.13 ± 1.51	0.78 ± 0.04
	UF-T2	24.99 ± 1.88	0.79 ± 0.01	25.81 ± 1.55	0.81 ± 0.04	25.80 ± 1.63	0.79 ± 0.04
	MINet	25.32 ± 2.03	0.81 ± 0.01	26.19 ± 1.94	0.82 ± 0.03	26.11 ± 2.28	0.81 ± 0.03
	DuDoRNet	26.14 ± 1.72	0.83 ± 0.01	28.01 ± 1.52	0.86 ± 0.03	26.76 ± 1.91	0.83 ± 0.04
	Ours	27.45 ± 1.52	0.86 ± 0.01	28.91 ± 1.32	0.88 ± 0.03	28.90 ± 1.59	0.87 ± 0.03
Brain	Y-net	33.91 ± 2.71	0.92 ± 0.02	35.20 ± 2.49	0.31 ± 0.03	33.41 ± 3.90	0.95 ± 0.03
	UF-T2	34.02 ± 2.62	0.93 ± 0.02	35.97 ± 2.57	0.95 ± 0.02	33.95 ± 3.95	0.95 ± 0.03
	MINet	36.32 ± 2.77	0.95 ± 0.03	36.65 ± 3.62	0.96 ± 0.03	34.23 ± 3.12	0.96 ± 0.04
	DuDoRNet	38.28 ± 2.84	0.96 ± 0.02	39.85 ± 3.36	0.97 ± 0.02	38.41 ± 4.27	0.97 ± 0.03
	Ours	39.41 ± 2.46	0.96 ± 0.01	41.31 ± 3.22	0.98 ± 0.01	39.82 ± 4.46	0.98 ± 0.02

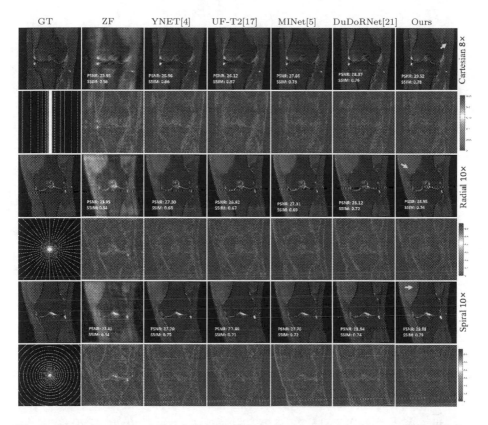

Fig. 2. Reconstruction results from different under-sampling trajectory. The sampling pattern mask and difference images are shown on the second, fourth, and sixth row.

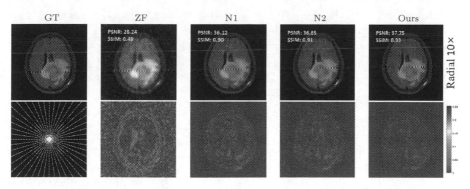

Fig. 3. Visual comparison of DuDoCAF results from each recurrent block using radial sampling (10×).

Figure 3 shows the intermediate results of DuDoCAF with 10× radial under-sampling. We can observe the gradual improvement of the reconstruction quality from iteration block N1 to N3. Table 1 shows the mean ± std PSNR and SSIM values on two datasets with different under-sampling masks. As can be seen, the DuDoCAF yields the best results on all experiments. This indicates that our model is able to effectively fuse multi-contrast images which boosts the reconstruction performance. It is worth noting that YNet and UF-T2 reconstructions are far less than MINet results, which indicates that it is optimal to learn the interaction between two different contrast images step by step. More importantly, the DuDoRNet shows the second-best results demonstrates the powerful reconstruction ability of dual-domain learning.

Table 2. Ablative study on different settings of DuDoCAF under 8× acceleration on knee dataset. The best and second-best result are marked in red and blue, respectively.

Methods	CAF	DD	RP	Random(8×)		Radial (10×)		Spiral (10×)	
				PSNR	SSIM	PSNR	SSIM	PSNR	SSIM
Baseline			✓	25.88 ± 2.01	0.81 ± 0.04	26.91 ± 1.67	0.85 ± 0.05	26.40 ± 1.81	0.84 ± 0.06
w/o CAF		✓	✓	26.42 ± 1.94	0.83 ± 0.05	27.18 ± 1.89	0.85 ± 0.04	26.98 ± 1.73	0.85 ± 0.04
w/o DD	✓		✓	26.79 ± 2.02	0.83 ± 0.04	27.95 ± 1.66	0.86 ± 0.04	27.45 ± 1.78	0.84 ± 0.04
Ours	✓	✓	✓	27.45 ± 1.52	0.86 ± 0.03	28.91 ± 1.32	0.88 ± 0.03	28.90 ± 1.59	0.87 ± 0.03

Ablation Study. Two key components are estimated, including: dual-domain (DD) learning and Cross-Attention Fusion (CAF) with reference image prior (RP) passing to the network. As shown in Table 2, (A) Baseline represents the network only consists of Residual Reconstruction Transformer block in the k-space domain. (B) w/o CAF adds DD learning to the Baseline network. (C) w/o DD adds the CAF block to the Baseline architecture. (D) Ours indicates combination of Baseline, DD and CAF module. This indicates that learning from both k-space and image domain is really important even when adopting the cross-attention fusion strategy. Besides, the reconstruction results of w/o CAF are worse than those w/o DD, which clarifies the importance of fusing two contrast image features and exploiting the deep correlation between them.

4   Conclusion

We proposed a novel dual-domain cross-attention fusion mechanism (DuDoCAF) with recurrent transformer for fast multi-contrast MR Imaging. Firstly, the CAF module is able to better fuse the features of the fully-sampled reference images and under-sampled target images. Besides, the residual-reconstruction transformer helps the network to extract more informative features of the image for the target-contrast image restoration. Furthermore, the adopt dual-domain recurrent learning strategy is helpful to obtain better reconstructed images and reduce artifacts. Extensive experimental results show that, under different sampling patterns and acceleration factors, our proposed method significantly outperforms other state-of-the-art methods. In the future, we will extend the DuDoCAF from single-coil to a multi-coil reconstruction.

Acknowledgements. This work was supported in part by National Natural Science Foundation of China under Grant 61902338 and 62001120, the Shanghai Sailing Program (No. 20YF1402400), The Hong Kong Polytechnic University under Project of Strategic Importance (no. 1-ZE2Q).

References

1. Chen, C.F.R., Fan, Q., Panda, R.: CrossViT: cross-attention multi-scale vision transformer for image classification. In: Proceedings of the IEEE/CVF International Conference on Computer Vision, pp. 357–366 (2021)
2. Chen, W., et al.: Accuracy of 3-T MRI using susceptibility-weighted imaging to detect meniscal tears of the knee. Knee Surg. Sports Traumatol. Arthrosc. **23**(1), 198–204 (2015)
3. Dar, S.U., Yurt, M., Shahdloo, M., Ildız, M.E., Tınaz, B., Çukur, T.: Prior-guided image reconstruction for accelerated multi-contrast MRI via generative adversarial networks. IEEE J. Sel. Top. Signal Process. **14**(6), 1072–1087 (2020)
4. Do, W.J., Seo, S., Han, Y., Ye, J.C., Choi, S.H., Park, S.H.: Reconstruction of multicontrast MR images through deep learning. Med. Phys. **47**(3), 983–997 (2020)
5. Feng, C.-M., Fu, H., Yuan, S., Xu, Y.: Multi-contrast MRI super-resolution via a multi-stage integration network. In: de Bruijne, M., et al. (eds.) MICCAI 2021. LNCS, vol. 12906, pp. 140–149. Springer, Cham (2021). https://doi.org/10.1007/978-3-030-87231-1_14
6. Feng, C.M., Yan, Y., Chen, G., Fu, H., Xu, Y., Shao, L.: Accelerated multi-modal MR imaging with transformers. arXiv preprint arXiv:2106.14248 (2021)
7. Feng, C.-M., Yan, Y., Fu, H., Chen, L., Xu, Y.: Task transformer network for joint MRI reconstruction and super-resolution. In: de Bruijne, M., et al. (eds.) MICCAI 2021. LNCS, vol. 12906, pp. 307–317. Springer, Cham (2021). https://doi.org/10.1007/978-3-030-87231-1_30
8. Kingma, D.P., Ba, J.: Adam: a method for stochastic optimization. In: ICLR (Poster) (2015)
9. Knoll, F., et al.: fastMRI: a publicly available raw k-space and DICOM dataset of knee images for accelerated MR image reconstruction using machine learning. Radiol. Artif. Intell. **2**(1), e190007 (2020)
10. Korkmaz, Y., Dar, S.U., Yurt, M., Özbey, M., Cukur, T.: Unsupervised MRI reconstruction via zero-shot learned adversarial transformers. IEEE Trans. Med. Imaging (2022)
11. Liu, X., Wang, J., Sun, H., Chandra, S.S., Crozier, S., Liu, F.: On the regularization of feature fusion and mapping for fast MR multi-contrast imaging via iterative networks. Magn. Reson. Imaging **77**, 159–168 (2021)
12. Menze, B.H., et al.: The multimodal brain tumor image segmentation benchmark (BRATS). IEEE Trans. Med. Imaging **34**(10), 1993–2024 (2014)
13. Sachan, T., Pinnaparaju, N., Gupta, M., Varma, V.: SCATE: shared cross attention transformer encoders for multimodal fake news detection. In: Proceedings of the 2021 IEEE/ACM International Conference on Advances in Social Networks Analysis and Mining, pp. 399–406 (2021)

14. Sun, H., et al.: Extracting more for less: multi-echo MP2RAGE for simultaneous T1-weighted imaging, T1 mapping, mapping, SWI, and QSM from a single acquisition. Magn. Reson. Med. **83**(4), 1178–1191 (2020)

15. Sun, L., Fan, Z., Fu, X., Huang, Y., Ding, X., Paisley, J.: A deep information sharing network for multi-contrast compressed sensing MRI reconstruction. IEEE Trans. Image Process. **28**(12), 6141–6153 (2019)

16. Vaswani, A., et al.: Attention is all you need. In: Advances in Neural Information Processing Systems, vol. 30 (2017)

17. Xiang, L., et al.: Deep-learning-based multi-modal fusion for fast MR reconstruction. IEEE Trans. Biomed. Eng. **66**(7), 2105–2114 (2018)

18. Xu, Y., Zhao, H., Zhang, Z.: Topicaware multi-turn dialogue modeling. In: The Thirty-Fifth AAAI Conference on Artificial Intelligence (AAAI 2021) (2021)

19. Xuan, K., Sun, S., Xue, Z., Wang, Q., Liao, S.: Learning MRI k-space subsampling pattern using progressive weight pruning. In: Martel, A.L., et al. (eds.) MICCAI 2020. LNCS, vol. 12262, pp. 178–187. Springer, Cham (2020). https://doi.org/10.1007/978-3-030-59713-9_18

20. Yang, Y., Wang, N., Yang, H., Sun, J., Xu, Z.: Model-driven deep attention network for ultra-fast compressive sensing MRI guided by cross-contrast MR image. In: Martel, A.L., et al. (eds.) MICCAI 2020. LNCS, vol. 12262, pp. 188–198. Springer, Cham (2020). https://doi.org/10.1007/978-3-030-59713-9_19

21. Zhou, B., Zhou, S.K.: DuDoRNet: learning a dual-domain recurrent network for fast MRI reconstruction with deep T1 prior. In: Proceedings of the IEEE/CVF Conference on Computer Vision and Pattern Recognition, pp. 4273–4282 (2020)

Weakly Supervised MR-TRUS Image Synthesis for Brachytherapy of Prostate Cancer

Yunkui Pang[1], Xu Chen[2], Yunzhi Huang[3], Pew-Thian Yap[1], and Jun Lian[1(✉)]

[1] University of North Carolina, Chapel Hill, NC 27599, USA
jun_lian@med.unc.edu
[2] College of Computer Science and Technology, Huaqiao University,
Xiamen 361021, China
[3] School of Automation, Nanjing University of Information Science and Technology,
Nanjing 210044, China

Abstract. Prostate magnetic resonance imaging (MRI) offers accurate details of structures and tumors for prostate cancer brachytherapy. However, it is unsuitable for routine treatment since MR images differ significantly from trans-rectal ultrasound (TRUS) images conventionally used for radioactive seed implants in brachytherapy. TRUS imaging is fast, convenient, and widely available in the operation room but is known for its low soft-tissue contrast and tumor visualization capability in the prostate area. Conventionally, practitioners usually rely on prostate segmentation to fuse the two imaging modalities with non-rigid registration. However, prostate delineation is often not available on diagnostic MR images. Besides, the high non-linear intensity relationship between two imaging modalities poses a challenge to non-rigid registration. Hence, we propose a method to generate a TRUS-styled image from a prostate MR image to replace the role of the TRUS image in radiation therapy dose pre-planning. We propose a structural constraint to handle non-linear projections of anatomical structures between MR and TRUS images. We further include an adversarial mechanism to enforce the model to preserve anatomical features in an MR image (such as prostate boundary and dominant intraprostatic lesion (DIL)) while synthesizing the TRUS-styled counterpart image. The proposed method is compared with other state-of-art methods with real TRUS images as the reference. The results demonstrate that the TRUS images synthesized by our method can be used for brachytherapy treatment planning for prostate cancer.

Keywords: MR · TRUS · Synthesize · Weakly supervised

Supplementary Information The online version contains supplementary material available at https://doi.org/10.1007/978-3-031-16446-0_46.

1   Introduction

Permanent low dose rate (LDR) brachytherapy is a highly effective internal radiation treatment for low- and intermediate-risk prostate cancer [16,18]. Transrectal ultrasound (TRUS) is the standard of care imaging modality for treatment planning and radioactive seed implant in prostate LDR brachytherapy. However, TRUS images are usually of low quality, hindering the accurate segmentation of normal structures and lesions. On the other hand, magnetic resonance imaging (MRI) has superior soft-tissue contrast and is the preferred imaging method for the diagnosis of prostate cancer. However, MRI is unavailable in most operative rooms. TRUS requires an ultrasound transducer probe inserted into the rectum, whereas MRI uses either an external magnet coil or an endorectal coil. The unique imaging mechanisms of TRUS and MRI cause significant differences in image appearance and organ deformation between the two imaging modalities. These factors pose significant challenges to the registration of TRUS and MRI images.

With the introduction of deep learning methods, especially GAN [6] and U-Net [19], cross-modality image synthesis has become a helpful solution to improve image quality in clinic. However, it is usually impractical to collect sufficient paired data needed for supervised training of these models due to high expenses and limited hospital imaging capacity. Unsupervised learning [5] or semi-supervised learning [3] provides a practical solution to this limitation by requiring only unpaired data. For example, Yang et al. [21] synthesizes brain and abdomen CT from MRI with an unsupervised approach.

The synthesis between MR and US images is rarely reported in the literature. Onofrey et al. [17] introduced a method based on principal component analysis (PCA) and dictionary learning to derive US-like prostate images from MR images. However, the synthesized images fail to preserve most of the anatomical structures in the original MR images. Jiao et al. [9] proposed an unsupervised method based on CycleGAN to synthesize fetal brain MR from US images. To our knowledge, this is the only work that uses deep learning to synthesize MR from US images. However, our empirical evaluation indicates that the method falls short in generating images that meet our clinical requirements for prostate case. In this work, we propose a novel weakly supervised learning strategy based on DCLGAN [7] to generate TRUS-like images from MR images for LDR prostate brachytherapy planning and treatment. The synthesized TRUS image preserves anatomical structures in the corresponding MR image. This allows physicians to perform dose planning directly on the synthesized TRUS image, reducing unnecessary operation room time spent on waiting for completing treatment planning when the patient is under anesthesia. The synthesized image can also be easily fused with real-time treatment TRUS images for guiding seeds implant.

2   Methods

Here, we introduce a novel approach to synthesizing high-quality US images from MR images. Based on [20], we take an weakly-supervised learning approach

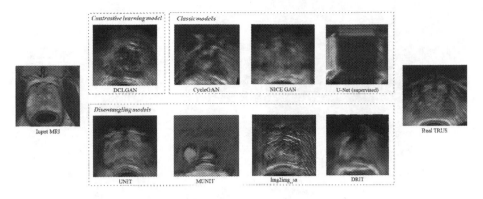

Fig. 1. Comparison of different models performed on one sample of the validation set. The leftmost image is the MR image input to the models. The rightmost image is the corresponding target TRUS image. DCLGAN based on contrastive learning performs the best. Some disentangling models perform better than classic models. But not all disentangling models perform well. One explanation for the poor performance is that the models fail to disentangle the representation of appearance and structure when there is a large gap between two modalities.

with content disentanglement using unpaired data. To test which model is most suitable for this task, we select the DCLGAN [7] using contrastive learning, together with some existing models with disentanglement (UNIT [13], MUNIT [8], img2img_sa [10], DRIT [12]) and classic models (CycleGAN [22], NICE GAN [4], U-Net (supervised) [19]). The results shown in Fig. 1 indicate that the image synthesized by DCLGAN is most similar to the appearance of the US image, with a more visible prostate contour. Therefore, we choose DCLGAN as our base model.

2.1 Network Architecture

Our model consists of two main generators (G and H). During inference, G takes an MR image as input and outputs the corresponding US-styled image. During training, G learns MR-TRUS synthesis via a GAN loss and additional constraints. H generates MR from TRUS for cycle consistency constraint. The overall model structure is shown in Fig. 2. Although DCLGAN produces images with style closest to US images, some important details such as prostate contour and sub-structures inside the prostate are not correctly synthesized. Therefore, we add extra modules to constrain the synthesis procedure. The appearance discriminator constrains the model to generate the style of the target modality. The structure discriminator reinforces the model's ability to disentangle anatomical structures from the input image. The appearance discriminator performs well in practice, while the structure discriminator needs additional modules for further performance improvement. Therefore, we design anatomy-aware constraints to ensure the synthesized TRUS image is consistent with the anatomical structures of the MR image.

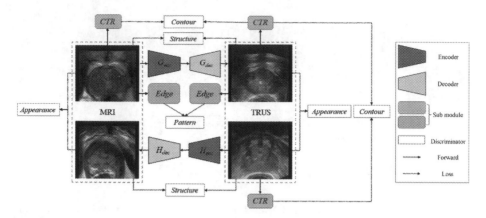

Fig. 2. The overall architecture of the proposed method. We focus to improve the generation ability of generator G (G_{enc} and G_{dec}). Generator H (H_{enc} and H_{dec}) are only used for cycle consistency purpose. The CTR module applies the prostate shape constraint on the generator G. An $Edge$ module is proposed to improve the quality of structural details synthesized within the prostate.

2.2   Prostate Segmentation

The CTR module shown in Fig. 2 is designed to constrain the shape of the synthesized prostate to be consistent with that in the real MR image. Figure 3(a) presents the details of the module. The $Contour$ discriminator is used to improve the shape similarity between synthesized contours. Since the manually annotated prostate label is often unavailable in diagnostic MR images in standard practice (MR is primarily used for cancer diagnosis and staging), we designed two strategies to train the segmentation module based on the availability of ground truth labels of the input image.

Supervised Prostate Segmentation on TRUS Image. TRUS is usually the imaging modality of choice for prostate cancer LDR brachytherapy treatment planning. The prostate contours and surrounding organs-at-risk are manually delineated at the beginning of clinical procedures. These contours are indispensable for subsequent radiation dose optimization and evaluation. Based on previous clinical cases, we design a supervised network to generate the prostate contour on the TRUS image (Fig. 3(a)). We treat it as a binary classification problem, with 0 representing background and 1 representing prostate. The loss function (BCE Loss in Fig. 3(a)) is

$$L_{\text{ctr\_sup}} = -(y \cdot \log(p) + (1 - y) \cdot \log(1 - p)), \tag{1}$$

where y is the ground truth class label and p is the predicted class.

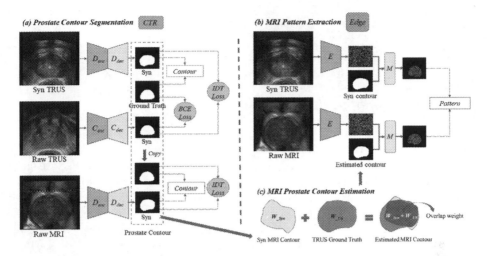

Fig. 3. Submodules for anatomical constraints. Part (a) corresponds to the *CTR* module in Fig. 2. Part (b) presents details of the *Edge* module in Fig. 2. Part (c) displays a method we employ to derive a more reasonable MR prostate contour based on the synthesized contour produced by part (a) and the TRUS ground truth.

Weakly Supervised Prostate Segmentation on MR Image. The prostate is usually not delineated on diagnostic MR images in the standard clinical workflow, posing a challenge in model training for automated prostate segmentation. Hence, we propose a weakly supervised method to address this problem. After rigid registration, the prostates on MR and TRUS images are partially overlapped (average Dice Similarity Coefficients (DSC) for real MR and real TRUS prostate contours on the test set is 77.15%). Therefore, the prostate label in the TRUS image can be utilized to guide the segmentation of the prostate on the MR image. Empirically, our method achieves a DSC of 70.13% between the synthesized and real MR prostate contours on the test data. We use a discriminator (*Contour* in Fig. 3(a)) to distinguish between the synthesized contour and prostate contour on the TRUS image. The loss function for the discriminator is

$$L_{\text{D\_mr}} = L_{\text{D\_syn}} = E_x[\log D(x)] + E_z[\log(1 - D(G(z)))] \tag{2}$$

where $L_{\text{D\_mr}}$ is the segmentation loss of the MR image and $L_{\text{D\_syn}}$ is segmentation loss of the synthesized TRUS image. x denotes the real contour and z is the synthesized contour. Additionally, an overlap loss is employed to measure the position and size of the synthesized contour. The overlap loss (IDT Loss in Fig. 3(a)) is

$$L_{\text{op\_mr}} = L_{\text{op\_syn}} = \frac{1}{N} \sum (|x - z|) \tag{3}$$

where N is the total number of pixels in the image. x and z are the real and synthesized contours, respectively. As for the segmentation of synthesized TRUS images, the network and the loss functions are the same. The two losses are weighted when training the model:

$$L_{\text{ctr\_mr}} = \lambda_{\text{D\_mr}} \cdot L_{\text{D\_mr}} + \lambda_{\text{op\_mr}} \cdot L_{\text{op\_mr}},$$
$$L_{\text{ctr\_syn}} = \lambda_{\text{D\_syn}} \cdot L_{\text{D\_syn}} + \lambda_{\text{op\_syn}} \cdot L_{\text{op\_syn}}. \tag{4}$$

2.3   MR Image Pattern Extraction

The segmentation of the small structures inside the prostate, such as the urethra and DIL, is critical for treating tumors and sparing organs at risk. These structures are visible on the MR image but have poor contrast on the TRUS image. We devise a module called *Edge* (Fig. 2, Fig. 3(b) and (c)) to help the model capture anatomical structures on MR images and transfer them onto US-style images. We first use the Sobel filter [11] to extract edges E from the MR and synthesized TRUS images. Next, we apply softmax on contours generated by the models introduced in Sect. 2.2 to produce mask M for use in masking operation

$$E_{\text{mask}} = E \cdot M, \ M[i,j] \in \{0,1\}, \forall i,j \in [1,n] \tag{5}$$

Since the intensity of the MR prostate varies largely even after intensity normalization, the Sobel filter might introduce some background noise to the edges representing anatomical structures. Therefore, we use a discriminator instead of a supervised method as one of the constraints to train the generator G in Fig. 2. The training objective is an adversarial loss:

$$L_{\text{edge}} = E_x[\log D(x)] + E_z[\log(1 - D(G(z)))] \tag{6}$$

To improve the accuracy of the segmentation of the prostate on MR image, we add weight to the synthesized MR contour ($W_{\text{\_syn}} \in (0,1)$) and TRUS ground truth contour ($W_{\text{\_trus}} = 1 - W_{\text{\_syn}}$) to preserve important contour details while diminishing the influence of unrelated tissues. In practice, $W_{\text{\_trus}} > W_{\text{\_syn}}$ produces better result. The contour estimation reinforces edges in the central portion while weakening periphery edges with a lower confidence level.

2.4   Joint Optimization Objective

In this section, we introduce the training objective for the two main generators G and H in Fig. 2. For generator H, the loss function is

$$L_H = \lambda_1 \cdot L_{\text{syn}}(H(y), x) + \lambda_2 \cdot L_{\text{nce}}(H(y), y) + \lambda_3 \cdot L_{\text{idt}}(H(y), x) \tag{7}$$

x and y are the input MR and TRUS images respectively. The adversarial loss L_{syn} optimizes the appearance of synthesized MR and real MR image. The Noise Contrastive Estimation (NCE) loss [14] constrains the consistency of the structure information between synthesized MR and TRUS image. The L_{idt} is an L1 loss, constraining the style similarity. As for generator G, the loss function is

$$L_G = \lambda_1 \cdot L_{\text{syn}}(G(x), y) + \lambda_2 \cdot L_{\text{nce}}(G(x), x) + \lambda_3 \cdot L_{\text{idt}}(G(x), y)$$
$$+ \lambda_4 \cdot L_{\text{idt}}(D_{\text{ae}}(x), y\_ctr) + \lambda_5 \cdot L_{\text{idt}}(D_{\text{ae}}(x), D(G(x))) + \lambda_6 \cdot L_{\text{edge}} \tag{8}$$

y_ctr is the input prostate contour of the TRUS image. The purpose of the first three losses is similar to generator H. The fourth and fifth losses are L1 losses proposed to restrict the shape of the synthesized prostate contour. $D_{ae}(x)$ is the autoencoder D described in Sect. 2.2 and Fig. 3. The final loss L_{edge} is discussed in Sect. 2.3. The details about network implementation, parameter selection and training settings are described in the Appendix.

3 Experiments

3.1 Dataset Preparation

We collected TRUS data from 48 patients' intra-operative images used for treatment planning in UNC hospital. We collected a total of 69 MR images from UNC hospital, NCI-ISBI 2013 [2] and I2CVB [1] dataset. All images were resampled to a voxel spacing of $0.3 \times 0.3 \times 1\,mm^3$. We used rigid body registration to align images from two domains and cropped each image to a size of $224 \times 224 \times 36$. Among the TRUS and MR images, we had eight paired data. We partitioned two of them into the validation set and six into the testing set. The rest unpaired data were divided into the training set.

Table 1. Quantitative results. (a) *PSNR (MR)*: Peak Signal-to-Noise Ratio between real MR and synthesized TRUS. (b) *SSIM (MR)*: Structural Similarity between real MR and synthesized TRUS. (c) *PSNR (TRUS)*: Peak Signal-to-Noise Ratio between real TRUS and synthesized TRUS. (d) *DSC*: Dice Similarity Coefficients between deformed MR prostate contour and TRUS prostate contour.

Method	PSNR (MR)	SSIM (MR)	PSNR (TRUS)	DSC
U-Net (supervised) [19]	19.473 ± 1.10	0.682 ± 0.02	11.569 ± 0.29	0.216 ± 0.15
Fetal Brain model [9]	16.730 ± 0.85	0.763 ± 0.01	9.494 ± 0.52	0.311 ± 0.30
CycleGAN [22]	21.961 ± 0.73	0.817 ± 0.02	15.834 ± 1.61	0.737 ± 0.12
DCLGAN [7]	24.508 ± 1.19	0.776 ± 0.03	15.821 ± 0.12	0.736 ± 0.16
Ours (w/o CTR)	25.316 ± 0.86	0.890 ± 0.02	16.460 ± 1.96	0.738 ± 0.30
Ours (w/o Edge)	25.419 ± 1.06	0.827 ± 0.02	16.322 ± 1.41	0.819 ± 0.13
Ours	$\mathbf{26.671} \pm 0.43$	$\mathbf{0.901} \pm 0.02$	$\mathbf{17.268} \pm 1.71$	$\mathbf{0.881} \pm 0.12$

3.2 Experiment Design and Results

We compared our model with U-Net and some unsupervised models like Cycle GAN and DCLGAN. We implemented the model published by Jiao et al. [9], which is the latest work relevant to our project. We used the following metrics for performance evaluation: (i) **PSNR (MR)** (Peak Signal-to-Noise Ratio) between real MR and synthesized images to measure the quality of synthesized images compared with real MR images. (ii) **SSIM (MR)** (Structural Similarity) between real MR and synthesized images to evaluate the quality of anatomical

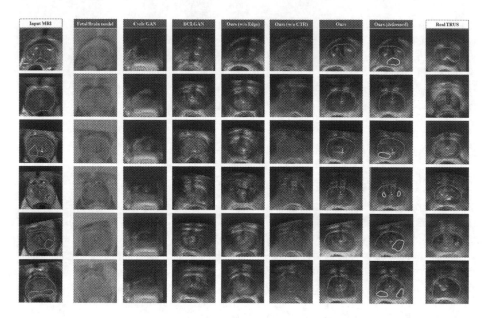

Fig. 4. Qualitative results. The green contours on input MR image are dominant intraprostatic lesions (DIL) labeled by physicians. The yellow contours (in the column of *Ours (deformed)*) are the DILs transformed from the original MR images after deformable registration. The red contours mark the prostates in the images. (Color figure online)

structures presented in synthesized TRUS images. (iii) **PSNR (TRUS)** between real TRUS and synthesized images to compare the quality of synthesized images with real TRUS images. (iv) **DSC** (Dice Similarity Coefficients) between the deformed MR prostate contour and the TRUS prostate contour. We employ DSC as a metric following the intuition that synthesized images with high quality and TRUS-like appearance will improve the registration accuracy compared with low-quality or cross-modality images. To derive the deformed contour on MR images, we first non-linearly register the synthesized TRUS to a real TRUS image. Then we apply the displacement field to the prostate contour on MR. We use NiftyReg [15] to perform the deformable registration.

Table 1 shows the comparison results. Our method performs the best on all the metrics. We also performed an ablation study by either removing the prostate segmentation module (w/o CTR) or the MR pattern extraction module (w/o Edge). It shows that the MR pattern extraction module has a larger impact on SSIM, consistent with our hypothesis that the module fosters the representation learning of anatomical structure. The prostate segmentation module affects more on DSC score, which indicates the module assists in synthesizing more vivid prostate contrast to support high precision deformation. The fetal brain model proposed by Jiao et al. [9] does not perform well, mainly because the model proposed is designed to synthesize US image from MR image (opposite to our task). The average DSC between the MR and TRUS prostate contour is 0.631 after applying the deformation field produced by deformable registration between original MR and TRUS image. The low DSC indicates the gap between the original MR and TRUS image. The qualitative results displayed in Fig. 4 demonstrate that our model narrows the gap, with the average DSC 0.881. And the prostate and DIL are more evident and more consistent with MR input images than those produced by other models.

4   Conclusion

This paper proposes a method that synthesizes TRUS images from unpaired MR images. To our knowledge, this is the first weakly supervised deep learning method to accomplish this task. We exert anatomy constraints with weakly supervised modules to emphasize the structure content of the synthesized TRUS image. The experiments demonstrate that our method improves the quality of synthesized TRUS image and makes it possible for the brachytherapy treatment for prostate cancer. For the next step, an unsupervised approach for MR to TRUS image synthesis might be a promising direction for further exploration.

Acknowledgements. This work was supported in part by NIH grant CA206100. Yunzhi Huang was in part supported by the National Natural Science Foundation of China under Grant No. 62101365 and the startup foundation of Nanjing University of Information Science and Technology.

References

1. Lemaître, G., Martí, R., Freixenet, J., Vilanova, J.C., Walker, P.M., Meriaudeau, F.: Computer-aided detection and diagnosis for prostate cancer based on mono and multi-parametric MRI: a review. Comput. Biol. Med. **60**, 8–31 (2015). https://doi.org/10.1016/j.compbiomed.2015.02.009. https://www.sciencedirect.com/science/article/pii/S001048251500058X
2. Bloch, N., Madabhushi, A., Huisman, H., et al.: NCI-ISBI 2013 challenge: automated segmentation of prostate structures (2015)
3. Chapelle, O., Schölkopf, B., Zien, A.: Semi-Supervised Learning (Adaptive Computation and Machine Learning). The MIT Press, Cambridge (2006)
4. Chen, R., Huang, W., Huang, B., Sun, F., Fang, B.: Reusing discriminators for encoding: towards unsupervised image-to-image translation (2020)
5. Ghahramani, Z.: Unsupervised learning. In: Bousquet, O., von Luxburg, U., Rätsch, G. (eds.) ML -2003. LNCS (LNAI), vol. 3176, pp. 72–112. Springer, Heidelberg (2004). https://doi.org/10.1007/978-3-540-28650-9_5
6. Goodfellow, I.J., et al.: Generative adversarial networks (2014)
7. Han, J., Shoeiby, M., Petersson, L., Armin, M.A.: Dual contrastive learning for unsupervised image-to-image translation. In: Proceedings of the IEEE/CVF Conference on Computer Vision and Pattern Recognition Workshops (2021)
8. Huang, X., Liu, M.Y., Belongie, S., Kautz, J.: Multimodal unsupervised image-to-image translation. In: ECCV (2018)

9. Jiao, J., Namburete, A.I.L., Papageorghiou, A.T., Noble, J.A.: Self-supervised ultrasound to MRI fetal brain image synthesis (2020)

10. Kang, T., Lee, K.H.: Unsupervised image-to-image translation with self-attention networks. In: 2020 IEEE International Conference on Big Data and Smart Computing (BigComp), February 2020. https://doi.org/10.1109/bigcomp48618.2020.00-92

11. Kanopoulos, N., Vasanthavada, N., Baker, R.L.: Design of an image edge detection filter using the Sobel operator. IEEE J. Solid-State Circuits **23**(2), 358–367 (1988)

12. Lee, H.Y., Tseng, H.Y., Huang, J.B., Singh, M.K., Yang, M.H.: Diverse image-to-image translation via disentangled representations. In: European Conference on Computer Vision (2018)

13. Liu, M.Y., Breuel, T., Kautz, J.: Unsupervised image-to-image translation networks (2018)

14. Ma, Z., Collins, M.: Noise contrastive estimation and negative sampling for conditional models: consistency and statistical efficiency (2018). https://doi.org/10.48550/ARXIV.1809.01812. https://arxiv.org/abs/1809.01812

15. Modat, M., et al.: Fast free-form deformation using graphics processing units. Comput. Methods Programs Biomed. **98**, 278–84 (2009). https://doi.org/10.1016/j.cmpb.2009.09.002

16. Morris, W., et al.: Population-based study of biochemical and survival outcomes after permanent 125I brachytherapy for low- and intermediate-risk prostate cancer. Urology **73**(4), 860–865 (2009). https://doi.org/10.1016/j.urology.2008.07.064

17. Onofrey, J.A., Oksuz, I., Sarkar, S., Venkataraman, R., Staib, L.H., Papademetris, X.: MRI-TRUS image synthesis with application to image-guided prostate intervention. In: Tsaftaris, S.A., Gooya, A., Frangi, A.F., Prince, J.L. (eds.) SASHIMI 2016. LNCS, vol. 9968, pp. 157–166. Springer, Cham (2016). https://doi.org/10.1007/978-3-319-46630-9_16

18. Prada, P., et al.: Long-term outcomes in patients younger than 60 years of age treated with brachytherapy for prostate cancer. Strahlentherapie und Onkologie **194**, 311–317 (2018). https://doi.org/10.1007/s00066-017-1238-2

19. Ronneberger, O., Fischer, P., Brox, T.: U-net: convolutional networks for biomedical image segmentation (2015)

20. Xie, G., Wang, J., Huang, Y., Zheng, Y., Zheng, F., Jin, Y.: A survey of cross-modality brain image synthesis (2022)

21. Yang, H., et al.: Unsupervised MR-to-CT synthesis using structure-constrained CycleGAN. IEEE Trans. Med. Imaging **39**(12), 4249–4261 (2020). https://doi.org/10.1109/TMI.2020.3015379

22. Zhu, J.Y., Park, .T., Isola, P., Efros, A.A.: Unpaired image-to-image translation using cycle-consistent adversarial networks (2020)

Domain-Adaptive 3D Medical Image Synthesis: An Efficient Unsupervised Approach

Qingqiao Hu[1], Hongwei Li[2,3], and Jianguo Zhang[1(✉)]

[1] Research Institute of Trustworthy Autonomous System,
Department of Computer Science and Engineering, Southern University of Science and Technology, Shenzhen, China
zhangjg@sustech.edu.cn
[2] Department of Computer Science, Technical University of Munich,
Munich, Germany
hongwei.li@tum.de
[3] Department of Quantitative Biomedicine, University of Zurich, Zürich, Switzerland

Abstract. Medical image synthesis has attracted increasing attention because it could generate missing image data, improve diagnosis, and benefits many downstream tasks. However, so far the developed synthesis model is not adaptive to unseen data distribution that presents domain shift, limiting its applicability in clinical routine. This work focuses on exploring domain adaptation (DA) of *3D* image-to-image synthesis models. First, we highlight the technical difference in DA between classification, segmentation, and synthesis models. Second, we present a novel efficient adaptation approach based on a 2D variational autoencoder which approximates 3D distributions. Third, we present empirical studies on the effect of the amount of adaptation data and the key hyperparameters. Our results show that the proposed approach can significantly improve the synthesis accuracy on unseen domains in a 3D setting. The code is publicly available at https://github.com/WinstonHuTiger/2D_VAE_UDA_for_3D_sythesis.

1 Introduction

Medical image synthesis is drawing increasing attention in medical imaging, because it could generate missing image data, improving diagnosis and benefits many downstream tasks such as image segmentation [3,5,16]. For example, missing modality is a common issue in multi-modal neuroimaging, e.g., due to motion in the acquisition process [2]. However, existing synthesis frameworks

---

Q. Hu and H. Li—Equal contributions to this work.

Supplementary Information The online version contains supplementary material available at https://doi.org/10.1007/978-3-031-16446-0_47.

are mostly developed and evaluated on single-domain data (e.g., images from the same scanner), with limited consideration of model robustness when testing on unseen image domains which might be collected from another imaging scanner or acquisition protocols. Hence, domain adaptation is crucial for the real-world deployment in clinical routine. In particular, unsupervised domain adaptation (UDA) is more practical as it does not require additional expensive supervision to fine-tune the pre-trained model.

It should be noted that UDA of classification [1,11,17] and segmentation [4,9,10,12,15] models are well explored in recent years. For image segmentation models, the problem formulation is as follows. Given two different *input domains* (i.e., source and target) with data X and its distribution $P(X)$, $\mathcal{D}_s = \{X_s, P(X_s)\}$, $\mathcal{D}_t = \{X_t, P(X_t)\}$ and a shared *output* space $\mathcal{Y} = \{Y\}$, a predictive model $f(\cdot)$ which approximates $P(Y|X)$ trained on the source domain $\mathcal{D}_s$ is likely to degrade on the target domain $\mathcal{D}_t$ which presents a domain shift. Among existing works, one of the key ideas is to match the *input space* for both domains in the feature space so that the mapping can be invariant to the inputs. It could be achieved by adversarial training [17] or prior matching [14].

As shown in Fig. 1, in both classification and segmentation tasks, the output label spaces in source and target domain are shared. For example, a segmentation model segments the same anatomical structure in both domains. However, in a synthesis model, the *output* spaces from source domain Y_s and target domain Y_t are most likely different, for example, the outputs images Y_s and Y_t could be from different scanners. In the UDA scenario, we only have access to the input of target domain X_s, thus matching the synthetic output $\hat{Y}_t$ to its real distribution is challenging as there is no observations of the outputs. Importantly, aligning X_t and X_s does not guarantee that the output would be close to Y_t but Y_s. Thus, most existing works in classification and segmentation could not be directly applied to synthesis model. Generally, we expect the generated output of the target domain $\hat{Y}_t$ to match a *reasonable* distribution of the target domain. In this work, we present the problem setting, upper bound and propose an efficient approach to perform UDA in a 3D setting.

Why 3D-UDA Is Necessary and Challenging? Previous work focusing on 2D or patch-based adaptation [4,8]. Although these works show promising results, they are limited to 2D or patch domains which is insufficient for many applications such as neuroimaging data which requires domain adaptation in a 3D fashion. The 3D image-to-image synthesis model dealing with full-volume imaging data is heavy-weight compared to patch-based method. However, extending existing work from 2D to 3D is non-trivial. In addition to model complexity, another challenge is that the number of 3D volumetric samples is very limited while 2D slices are more accessible.

Contributions. Our contribution is threefold: (1) We introduce unsupervised domain adaptation for 3D medical image synthesis and present the technical difference with existing setup in image classification and segmentation. (2) We

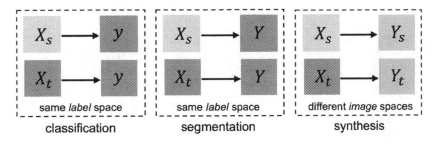

Fig. 1. Summary of the main differences in domain adaptation between image classification, segmentation, and synthesis tasks. The output spaces with the same colors indicate the output spaces have the same distribution. For example, a segmentation model segments the same anatomical structure in both domains.

propose an efficient 2D variational-autoencoder approach to perform UDA in a 3D manner. (3) We present empirical studies on the effects of the amount of data needed for adaptation and the effect of key hyper-parameters. Our results show that the proposed method can significantly improve the synthesis accuracy on unseen domains.

2 Methodology

Problem Definition. The objective is to adapt an volume-to-volume mapping $\Phi_s: X_s \rightarrow Y_s$ which is trained on a source domain to a target domain, so that when testing on input data X_t, the output could match the target distribution: Let $\mathcal{S}$ and $\mathcal{T}$ denote the source domain and the target domain, respectively. We observe N samples $S = \{(x_s^k, y_s^k)\}_{k=1}^{N}$ from $\mathcal{S}$, and M samples $T = \{x_t^j\}_{j=1}^{M}$ from $\mathcal{T}$. Notably, the samples from the target domain do not contain any output data.

Supervised Domain Adaptation. When there is some target data $\{X_t, P(X_t)\}$ available, one could use them to fine-tune the established mapping M and transfer the knowledge from source to target. When increasing the amount of data for tuning, the upper bound could be setup for *unsupervised* domain adaptation in which only the input data from the target domain can be accessible.

Unsupervised Domain Adaptation. In this setting, X_t is available while Y_t is not accessible. Since the goal of a synthesis model is to generate *reasonable* output. One straightforward approach is to match the 3D prior distributions of $\hat{Y}_t$ and Y_s. Although Y_s and Y_t are expected to be different, they largely share the underlying distribution, e.g., images from different scanners may present varied contrasts but share the same space of anatomical structure. However, directly modeling 3D distribution with limited data is challenging. As an alternative, we explore to model the 3D distribution with a 2D spatial variational autoencoder (s-VAE) which is effective and computationally efficient.

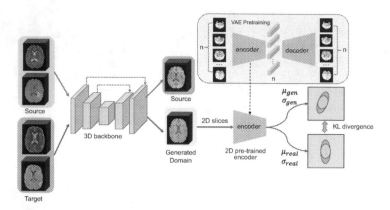

Fig. 2. The main framework of our proposed 3D-UDA method for cross-modality MR image synthesis. In the source domain (green), the 3D backbone is trained supervisedly with aligned image data, translating FLAIR and T2 to T1. A spatial 2D variational autoencoder is first trained in the source domain using T1 modality. The dimension of its latent space is n. Then, in the adaptation stage, we compute the KL-divergence between the prior distribution of the generated volume and the target 3D distribution learned by a 2D variational autoencoder. (Color figure online)

2D s-VAE for Modeling 3D Distribution. To encode 3D distribution in the 2D VAE's latent space, we proposed to train the VAE in a volumetric way, i.e., instead of training the 2D VAE with slices from different brain volumes, we take shuffled 2D slices from *a whole 3D volume* as the input. Thus, the batch size corresponds to the number of slices in the volume. We nickname such a form of VAE as spatial VAE (s-VAE). Doing this ensures that the 2D s-VAE learns the correlation between 2D slices. Since each latent code comes from a specific slice of a whole 3D brain volume, n latent codes with a certain sequence together can express the 3D distribution, while a standard 3D VAEs encode the distribution in their channel dimension. 2D s-VAE can reduce learnable parameters compared to 3D VAEs. The training of s-VAE is formulated as:

$$\mathcal{L}_{VAE} = D_{KL}(N(0,I)||N(\mu_{\hat{Y}_s}, \sigma_{\hat{Y}_s})) + ||Y_s - \hat{Y}_s||_2 \qquad (1)$$

Backbone 3D ConvNets for Image Synthesis. One basic component is a 3D ConvNets backbone for image synthesis. With the N paired samples from the source domain, supervised learning was conducted to establish a mapping Φ_s from the input image space X_s to the output space Y_s, optimized with an L1 norm loss: $\mathcal{L}_{syn} = \sum_{i=1}^{N} ||x_s^i - x_t^i||_1$.

3D UDA with 2D s-VAE. Once the 3D distribution of the output in source domain $P(Y_s)$ is learned by 2D s-VAE, we could match it with the posterior distribution $P(\hat{Y}_t)$ given the generated output $\hat{Y}_t$. Kullback-Leibler (KL) divergence is employed to match $P(\hat{Y}_t)$ and $P(Y_s)$, which can be formulated as

$$\mathcal{L}_{ada} = D_{KL}(P(Y_s)||P(\hat{Y}_t)) = \sum P(Y_s)log(\frac{P(Y_s)}{P(\hat{Y}_t)}) \tag{2}$$

However, just optimizing the KL divergence can be problematic since the mapping from input to output might suffer from catastrophic forgetting. Consequently, we perform supervised training on the source domain while adapting it to target domain with KL divergence. The whole UDA pipeline is shown in Fig. 2.

3   Experiments

Datasets and Preprocessing. We use the multi-center *BraTS* 2019 dataset [13] to perform cross-modality image-to-image synthesis and investigate domain adaptation. Specifically, we generate T1 images from the combination of FLAIR and T2 images. To create source and target domains for *UDA*, we split it into two subsets based on the IDs of medical centers. The first subset contains 146 paired multi-modal MR images from *CBICA* while the second subset consists of 239 paired MR images from *TCIA*. In the supervised image-to-image synthesis training process and domain adaptation process, input volumes loaded as gray scaled image are first cropped from (155, 240, 240) to (144, 192, 192) to save memory cost. Then three data argumentation methods are applied to the cropped volumes, including random rotation, random flip and adjusting contrast and brightness. The contrast level and brightness level are chosen from a uniform distribution (0.3, 1.5].

In our setting, there are two domain adaptation tasks: CBICA → TCIA; TCIA → CBICA. Specifically, in the first task, the image synthesis model is trained in a supervised manner using CBICA and then the model is adapted to TCIA subset. The second task is the reverse of the adaptation direction.

In the supervised training, all data from the source domain are used; in the unsupervised domain adaptation stage, we utilize 100 input volumes (FLAIR and T2) from the target domain without any output volumes (T1). The rest of volumes from the target domain are then evaluating the performance of all methods. The details of composition of datasets are summarized in Table 1.

Table 1. The composition of datasets for the settings of three scenarios in two domain adaptation tasks. (Adapt. = Adaptation)

Methods	CBICA → TCIA			TCIA → CBICA		
	Source	Target		Source	Target	
		Adapt. set	Test set		Adapt. set	Test set
Without DA	146	0	139	146	0	46
UDA	146	100	139	239	100	46
Supervised DA	0	[40, 100]	139	0	[40, 100]	46

Configuration of the Training Schedule. We use a 3D pix2pix model [7] as the pipeline to perform cross-modality synthesis. The generator of the pix2pix model has a large 9 × 9 × 9 receptive field and it has only four down-sampling stage to reduce computation complexity. FLAIR and T2 volumes are concatenated into a two-channel input. For the two domains, we train the 2D s-VAE model individually using T1 volumes from each of the source domain. A single volume is re-scaled from (240, 240, 155) dimension to 256 slices with dimension (256, 256). 2D s-VAE is trained for 300 epoch and the KL divergence loss weight is set to be 0.001. For the synthesis model, we first train the model using source dataset in a supervised way. Then, in the UDA process, we train the model for five epochs. In the first iteration of the UDA process, we perform supervised training on the source domain with previous hyper-parameters; in the second iteration, we fine-tune the 3D backbone with the pre-trained 2D s-VAE model. All models are trained on RTX 3090 with Pytorch 1.10.2. Due to page limit, details of the backbone synthesis architecture, 2D VAE and 3D VAE are shown in the Appendix.

Evaluation Protocol. We use structural similarity index (SSIM) [19] and peak signal-to-noise ratio (PSNR) to evaluate the image quality of the synthesized images. We further use a pre-trained nnUnet [6] on the *BraTS* 2020 dataset [13] to segment the generated images from different methods and report Dice scores. All the test images are not involved in the UDA process.

Table 2. Comparison of our methods with the lower bound, upper bound, two baselines, supervised method without domain shift and real images (only on Dice). The p-values for: a) ours vs. lower bound, and b) ours vs. 3D-VAE are all smaller than 0.0001, indicating our method outperforms the two methods significantly. We only report the mean of Dice score due to page limit.

Methods	CBICA →TCIA			TCIA → CBICA		
	SSIM	PSNR	Dice	SSIM	PSNR	Dice
Without DA (lower bound)	0.837 (± 0.030)	19.999 (± 2.150)	0.793	0.837 (± 0.027)	18.976 (± 3.685)	0.871
Without DA+augmentation	0.845 (± 0.028)	21.525 (± 2.204)	0.774	0.833 (± 0.029)	19.101 (± 3.646)	0.874
3D VAE UDA	0.844 (± 0.026)	21.183 (± 2.252)	0.772	0.832 (± 0.029)	19.278 (± 3.611)	0.874
2D s-VAE UDA (Ours)	**0.853** (± 0.024)	**22.217** (± 2.253)	0.773	**0.846** (± 0.024)	**19.591** (± 3.429)	0.874
Supervised DA ($n = 10$)	0.844 (± 0.024)	24.969 (± 2.634)	0.763	0.851 (± 0.014)	22.509 (± 2.062)	0.864
Supervised DA ($n = 40$)	0.869 (± 0.026)	24.933 (± 2.828)	0.790	0.852 (± 0.017)	23.811 (± 2.365)	0.866
Supervised DA ($n = 100$)	0.869 (± 0.026)	24.619 (± 2.953)	0.799	0.865 (± 0.017)	23.877 (± 2.611)	0.870
Upper bound	0.911 (± 0.0263)	25.519 (± 3.630)	0.820	0.896 (± 0.020)	24.656 (± 2.907)	0.867
Real Images	-	-	0.904	-	-	0.936

4   Results

4.1   Comparison of Methods

We first present the lower bound of the synthesis model without DA on the target domain. Then we present our proposed 2D s-VAE method. We also present the upper bound of a supervised DA. Quantitative results are summarized in Table 2. Moreover, we study the impact of the amount of volumes used in the UDA process and the impact of different batch sizes in 2D VAE reconstruction results, showed in Fig. 4.

Lower-Bound and Upper-Bound. The lower-bound of the UDA is pre-training on source domain and directly testing on the target domain. Notably basic data argumentation like random rotation rotation, random flipping are used to prevent models from over-fitting. As we can observe from row 1 of Table 2, it achieves the worst performance among all the methods. Given available paired data from the target domain, one could tune the pre-trained model (same as transfer learning) to adapt the model to the target domain. One could observe that increasing data from target domain for supervision improves the performance, from the three rows ('Supervised DA') in Table 2. The upper bound is defined by training and evaluating the method directly on the target domain. The last second row in Table 2 shows the results of five-fold cross validation on the target domain.

Heuristic Data Argumentation. Heuristic data argumentation could potentially improve the generalizability [20]. We perform contrast and brightness-related data augmentation considering that one of the most important domain shift is the image contrast between different scanners. We observe that it brings slight improvement in adaptation by comparing row 1 and row 2 in Table 2.

3D VAE *vs.* 2D s-VAE. As another baseline to be compared with our proposed efficient 2D s-VAE approach, we trained 3D VAEs using the volumetric data from the source domains. One could observe that the 3D VAE performs comparably with the heuristic data argumentation approach. This is partly because there are limited data to train the 3D VAE for learning a proper underlying distribution.

Our proposed 2D s-VAE method outperforms both data augmentation and the 3D VAE method on both SSIM and PSNR in two tasks. 3D VAE encoder is more computationally expensive, since the encoder of 3D VAE has 5.17M learnable parameters while 2D s-VAE only has 1.73M ones. Although there is still a visible performance gap between all the UDA methods and the upper bound, our 2D s-VAE method provides an effective and efficient solution when the output modality from the target domain is not accessible.

4.2 Analysis of Parameters

Impact of Batch Size on 2D s-VAE: In 2D s-VAE training process and the UDA process, slices of a whole brain MRI sequence serve as the input. To show the impact of batch size on 2D s-VAE, we explore the batch size of values, 32, 64, 128 and 256. To understand how much the VAE models the 3D distribution and visualize the results from the learned prior, we follow [18] to build a Guassian model of 2D slices, which models the correlation of 2D slices in the latent space

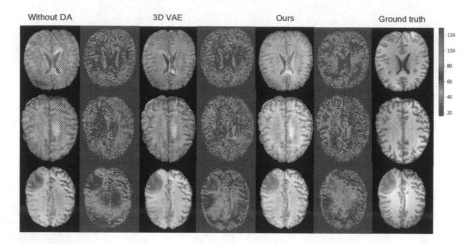

Fig. 3. Results on example slices achieved by different methods: (a) Without domain adaptation (DA), (b) 3D VAE, and (c) our 2D s-VAE. The difference map (in heatmap) is computed by subtracting the ground truth slice and the synthesized slice. We observe that our approach achieves best perceptual quality.

for sampling infinite number of 2D slices. As we show in Fig. 4(b), when batch size is 32, almost nothing can be sampled from the learned distribution; when batch size is 64, only noise can be sampled; when batch size is 128 (at this point half of the brain slices are used in a batch), brain shape can be visualized in the samples; when batch size is 256, brain structures are clear in the samples.

Impact of the Amount of Volumes: As we show in Fig. 4(b), we study the impact of amount of volumes used for the UDA process. We observe that for both CBICA → TCIA and TCIA → CBICA tasks, when the number of volumes is less than 70, the performance increases. However, when the number exceeds 70,

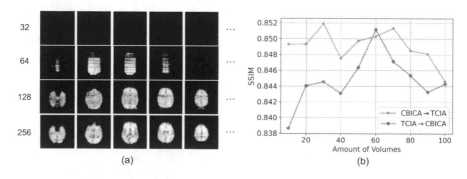

Fig. 4. (a): the reconstruction results influenced by different batch sizes. Larger batch size could better capture the 3D distribution. (b): the effect of the amount of volumes used for UDA from the target domain.

the performance starts to decrease. That is because the first continuing training batch in the UDA process contributes more to the results rather than the second batch. Although the first batch regulates the whole UDA process, it might hurt the performance in some degree.

5   Discussion

In this work, for the first time, we explore domain adaptation for medical image-to-image synthesis models. We first explain the difference between the domain adaptation of synthesis, classification and segmentation models. Then we introduce our efficient unsupervised domain adaptation method using 2D s-VAE when the target domain is not accessible. Finally, we show the effectiveness of our 2D s-VAE method and study some factors that influence the performance of our framework. In our approach, we translate the whole volume from one domain to another instead of using a patch-based method. Although whole-volume approaches are able to capture the full spatial information, it suffers from limited training data issues. As we have shown in Fig. 3, even after domain adaptation, we observed that the domain gap is challenging to overcome. Recent disentangled learning that could separate domain-specific and shared features effectively might improve the current results. Contrastive learning could be explored to better capture the representation of the source or target domains more effectively. Given the above limitations, we still wish our approach provides a new perspective for robust medical image synthesis for future research.

Acknowledgement. This work is supported in part by National Key Research and Development Program of China (No.: 2021YFF1200800) and Shenzhen Science, Technology and Innovation Commission Basic Research Project (No. JCYJ20180507181527806). H. L. was supported by Forschungskredit (No. FK-21-125) from UZH.

References

1. Ahn, E., Kumar, A., Fulham, M., Feng, D., Kim, J.: Unsupervised domain adaptation to classify medical images using zero-bias convolutional auto-encoders and context-based feature augmentation. IEEE Trans. Med. Imaging **39**(7), 2385–2394 (2020)
2. Conte, G.M., et al.: Generative adversarial networks to synthesize missing T1 and FLAIR MRI sequences for use in a multisequence brain tumor segmentation model. Radiology **300**(1), E319 (2021)
3. Conte, G.M., et al.: Generative adversarial networks to synthesize missing T1 and flair MRI sequences for use in a multisequence brain tumor segmentation model. Radiology **299**(2), 313–323 (2021)
4. Dou, Q., Ouyang, C., Chen, C., Chen, H., Heng, P.A.: Unsupervised cross-modality domain adaptation of convnets for biomedical image segmentations with adversarial loss. In: Proceedings of the 27th International Joint Conference on Artificial Intelligence, pp. 691–697 (2018)

5. Finck, T., et al.: Deep-learning generated synthetic double inversion recovery images improve multiple sclerosis lesion detection. Investig. Radiol. **55**(5), 318–323 (2020)
6. Isensee, F., Jaeger, P.F., Kohl, S.A., Petersen, J., Maier-Hein, K.H.: NNU-net: a self-configuring method for deep learning-based biomedical image segmentation. Nat. Methods **18**(2), 203–211 (2021)
7. Isola, P., Zhu, J.Y., Zhou, T., Efros, A.A.: Image-to-image translation with conditional adversarial networks. In: 2017 IEEE Conference on Computer Vision and Pattern Recognition (CVPR), pp. 5967–5976 (2017)
8. Kamnitsas, K., et al.: Unsupervised domain adaptation in brain lesion segmentation with adversarial networks. In: Niethammer, M., et al. (eds.) IPMI 2017. LNCS, vol. 10265, pp. 597–609. Springer, Cham (2017). https://doi.org/10.1007/978-3-319-59050-9_47
9. Kamnitsas, K., et al.: Unsupervised domain adaptation in brain lesion segmentation with adversarial networks. In: Niethammer, M., et al. (eds.) IPMI 2017. LNCS, vol. 10265, pp. 597–609. Springer, Cham (2017). https://doi.org/10.1007/978-3-319-59050-9_47
10. Karani, N., Erdil, E., Chaitanya, K., Konukoglu, E.: Test-time adaptable neural networks for robust medical image segmentation. Med. Image Anal. **68**, 101907 (2021)
11. Lenga, M., Schulz, H., Saalbach, A.: Continual learning for domain adaptation in chest x-ray classification. In: Medical Imaging with Deep Learning, pp. 413–423. PMLR (2020)
12. Liu, L., Zhang, Z., Li, S., Ma, K., Zheng, Y.: S-CUDA: self-cleansing unsupervised domain adaptation for medical image segmentation. Med. Image Anal. **74**, 102214 (2021)
13. Menze, B.H., et al.: The multimodal brain tumor image segmentation benchmark (brats). IEEE Trans. Med. Imaging **34**(10), 1993–2024 (2014)
14. Ouyang, C., Kamnitsas, K., Biffi, C., Duan, J., Rueckert, D.: Data efficient unsupervised domain adaptation for cross-modality image segmentation. In: Shen, D., et al. (eds.) MICCAI 2019. LNCS, vol. 11765, pp. 669–677. Springer, Cham (2019). https://doi.org/10.1007/978-3-030-32245-8_74
15. Perone, C.S., Ballester, P., Barros, R.C., Cohen-Adad, J.: Unsupervised domain adaptation for medical imaging segmentation with self-ensembling. NeuroImage **194**, 1–11 (2019)
16. Thomas, M.F., et al.: Improving automated glioma segmentation in routine clinical use through artificial intelligence-based replacement of missing sequences with synthetic magnetic resonance imaging scans. Investig. Radiol. **57**(3), 187–193 (2022)
17. Tzeng, E., Hoffman, J., Saenko, K., Darrell, T.: Adversarial discriminative domain adaptation. In: Proceedings of the IEEE Conference on Computer Vision and Pattern Recognition, pp. 7167–7176 (2017)
18. Volokitin, A., et al.: Modelling the distribution of 3D brain MRI using a 2D slice VAE. In: Martel, A.L., et al. (eds.) MICCAI 2020. LNCS, vol. 12267, pp. 657–666. Springer, Cham (2020). https://doi.org/10.1007/978-3-030-59728-3_64
19. Wang, Z., Bovik, A., Sheikh, H., Simoncelli, E.: Image quality assessment: from error visibility to structural similarity. IEEE Trans. Image Process. **13**(4), 600–612 (2004)
20. Zhang, L., et al.: Generalizing deep learning for medical image segmentation to unseen domains via deep stacked transformation. IEEE Trans. Med. Imaging **39**(7), 2531–2540 (2020)

What Can We Learn About a Generated Image Corrupting Its Latent Representation?

Agnieszka Tomczak[1,2](✉), Aarushi Gupta[3], Slobodan Ilic[1,2], Nassir Navab[1,4], and Shadi Albarqouni[1,5]

[1] Faculty of Informatics, Technical University of Munich, Munich, Germany
a.tomczak@tum.de
[2] Siemens AG, Munich, Germany
[3] Indian Institute of Technology Delhi, Helmholtz, New Delhi, India
[4] Clinic for Diagnostic and Interventional Radiology, University Hospital Bonn, Bonn, Germany
[5] Helmholtz AI, Helmholz Zentrum Munich, Munich, Germany

Abstract. Generative adversarial networks (GANs) offer an effective solution to the image-to-image translation problem, thereby allowing for new possibilities in medical imaging. They can translate images from one imaging modality to another at a low cost. For unpaired datasets, they rely mostly on cycle loss. Despite its effectiveness in learning the underlying data distribution, it can lead to a discrepancy between input and output data. The purpose of this work is to investigate the hypothesis that we can predict image quality based on its latent representation in the GANs bottleneck. We achieve this by corrupting the latent representation with noise and generating multiple outputs. The degree of differences between them is interpreted as the strength of the representation: the more robust the latent representation, the fewer changes in the output image the corruption causes. Our results demonstrate that our proposed method has the ability to i) predict uncertain parts of synthesized images, and ii) identify samples that may not be reliable for downstream tasks, e.g., liver segmentation task.

Keywords: GANs · Image synthesis · Uncertainty · Image quality

1 Introduction

Generative Adversarial Networks (GANs) [8] are state-of-the-art methods for image-to-image translation problems. It has been found that GANs are a promising technique for generating images of one modality based on another. Creating such images in a clinical setting could be highly effective, but only if the

Supplementary Information The online version contains supplementary material available at https://doi.org/10.1007/978-3-031-16446-0_48.

L. Wang et al. (Eds.): MICCAI 2022, LNCS 13436, pp. 505–515, 2022.
https://doi.org/10.1007/978-3-031-16446-0_48

images retain anatomical details and serve the downstream task. As Cohen et al. [5] described, GANs based on cycle consistency can "hallucinate" features (for example tumors) causing potentially wrong diagnoses. A clinically useful example of modality translation would be generating Computer Tomography (CT) images from Magnetic Resonance Imaging (MRI) scans, and vice versa. This problem has already been investigated multiple times [3,4,6,7,20,23] as an image-to-image translation task with multiple approaches: some of them focusing on shape consistency to preserve anatomical features [6,7,11,21,23], others proposing a multimodal approach to deal with the scalability issues [12,16,19]. Nevertheless, the main challenge remains: how to determine when a generative adversarial network can be trusted? The issue has a considerable impact on the medical field, where generated images with fabricated features have no clinical value. Recently, Upadhyay et al. [18] tackled this problem by predicting not only the output images but also the corresponding aleatoric uncertainty and then using it to guide the GAN to improve the final output. Their method requires changes in the optimization process (additional loss terms) and network architecture (additional output). They showed that for paired datasets it results in improved image quality, but did not clearly address the point that in medical imaging the visual quality of images does not always transfer to the performance on a downstream task. Our goal was to examine this problem from a different perspective and test the hypothesis: the more robust the image representation, the better the quality of the generated output and the end result. To this end, we present a noise injection technique that allows generating multiple outputs, thus quantifying the differences between these outputs and providing a confidence score that can be used to determine the uncertain parts of the generated image, the quality of the generated sample, and to some extent their impact on a downstream task.

2   Methodology

We design a method to test the assumption that the stronger the latent representation the better the quality of a generated image. In order to check the validity of this statement, we corrupt the latent representation of an image with noise drawn from normal distribution and see how it influences the generated output image. In other terms, given an image $x \in X$, domain $y \in Y$ and a Generative Adversarial Network G, we assume a hidden representation $h = E(x)$ with dimensions n, m, l, where E stands for the encoding part of G, and D for the decoding part. We denote the generated image as $\hat{x}$. Next, we construct k corrupted representation latent codes $\hat{h}$, adding to h noise vector η:

$$\eta_{1,...,k} \sim \mathcal{N}(0, \alpha\sigma^2_{h_{1,...,l}}) \tag{1}$$

where $\sigma^2_{h_{1,...,l}}$ is channel-wise standard deviation of input representation h. We can control the noise level with factor α. Before we add the noise vector, we eliminate the background noise with operation bin by masking it with zeros for all the channels where the output pixels are equal to zero, so do not contain any information.

$$bin(h) = h[\hat{x} > 0]$$

$$\hat{h}_{1,...,k} = h_1 + bin(h_1)\eta_1, ..., h_k + bin(h_k)\eta_k \tag{2}$$

Having now multiple representations for a single input image we can pass them to decoder D and generate multiple outputs:

$$\hat{x}_{1,...,k} = D(\hat{h}_1), ..., D(\hat{h}_k) \tag{3}$$

We use the multiple outputs to quantify the uncertainty connected with the representation of a given image. We calculate two scores: the variance (the average of the squared deviations from the mean) γ of our k generated images

$$\gamma = Var(\hat{x_1}, .., \hat{x_k}) \tag{4}$$

and the Mutual Information (MI) between the multiple outputs and our primary output $\hat{x}$ produced without noise injection.

$$MI(X;Y) = \sum_{y \in Y} \sum_{x \in X} p(x,y) log(\frac{p(x,y)}{p(x)p(y)})$$

$$\delta = \frac{1}{k} \sum_{0}^{k} MI(\hat{x}, (\hat{x}_i)) \tag{5}$$

We interpret the γ and δ as the measures of the representation quality. The variance γ can be considered as an uncertainty score - the higher the variance of generated outputs with the corrupt representations, the more uncertain the encoder is about produced representation. On the other hand, the MI δ score can be interpreted as a confidence score, quantifying how much information is preserved between the original output $\hat{x}$ and the outputs produced from corrupted representations $\hat{x_1}, ..., \hat{x_k}$. We calculate the MI based on a joint (2D) histogram, with number of bins equal to $\lfloor \sqrt{n/5} \rfloor$, where n is a number of pixels per image as proposed by [2].

3   Experiments and Results

We conducted a number of experiments using state-of-the-art architectures with the goal of demonstrating the effectiveness of our proposed method and confirming our hypothesis that the stronger the latent representation, the better and more reliable the image quality. Our proposed method was evaluated on two publicly available datasets, namely CHAOS [14] and LiTS [1] datasets.

3.1   Network Architectures and Implementation Details

TarGAN. As our main baseline we use TarGAN [3] network which uses a shape-consistency loss to preserve the shape of the liver. We trained the model for

100 epochs. We kept all the parameters unchanged with respect to the official implementation provided by the authors of TarGAN. We use PyTorch 1.10 to implement all the models and experiments. During inference, we constructed $k = 10$ corrupted representation with noise level $\alpha = 3$ and used them for evaluation of our method.

UP-GAN. We adapted the UP-GAN network from [18] to run on unpaired dataset as shown in [17]. UP-GAN uses an uncertainty guided loss along the standard cycle loss during training. The uncertainty loss defined for UP-GAN was used in every component of cycleGAN - identity loss and cycle loss for training of both generators. We kept the learning rate at 10^{-4} for T1 to T2 transfer and at 10^{-3} for CT to T1 and T2 transfer. We tuned the hyperparameters in the following manner: 0.5 for each of the discriminator losses, while the generators had a factor 1 with their cycle losses, 0.01 with the uncertainty cycle loss and factors of 0.1 and 0.0015 with identity losses. We trained all the three models for 100 epochs.

Datasets. We use data of each modality (CT, T1 and T2) from 20 different patients provided by the publicly available CHAOS19 dataset [14]. We randomly selected 50% of the dataset to be the training set and used the rest for testing. We followed [3] in setting liver as the target area, as the CT scans only have liver annotations. Besides, we used LiTS [1] dataset to evaluate our method on the pathological samples. The dataset contains CT scans of patients with liver tumors and corresponding segmentation masks. All images were resized to the size of 256×256.

Evaluation Metrics. We use FID [10] score to evaluate the quality of generated images and DICE score to evaluate segmentation results. We calculate the FID score using features extracted with Model Genesis [24].

3.2   Can We Use the Noise Injections to Identify Uncertain Parts of a Synthesized Image?

First, we conduct a sanity check experiment by blacking out a random 50×50 pixel patch from the input images (perturbed input) and measuring the proposed uncertainty and confidence scores on the corresponding synthesized images. Table 1 report the mean, median and variance of both uncertainty score (γ in Eq. 4) and confidence score (δ in Eq. 5) on both the original and perturbed images. One could observe that perturbed input has large variance and low confidence compared to the original input. This has been nicely visualized in Fig. 1 where the confidence scores of the perturbed corrupted images are much lower than the corresponding ones for the original images. This demonstrates the effectiveness of our proposed method in detecting uncertain synthesized images, e.g., perturbed images. The results suggest the possibility of finding a potential confidence threshold to eliminate uncertain synthesized images. Surprisingly, the model was able to nicely synthesize perturbed images hallucinating and replacing

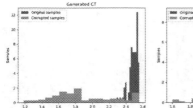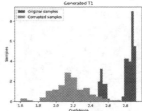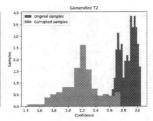

Fig. 1. Histograms of confidence values for original images and images corrupted by blacking out 50×50 pixel square. We can see significant drop of confidence for the corrupted inputs in all of the target modalities.

Table 1. The variance of multiple outputs with corrupted representation increases as we introduce a black patch on the input.

Variance (γ)		
Source $\rightarrow$ Target	Original input	Perturbed input
CT $\rightarrow$ T2	0.0176 (0.0176) $\pm$ 0.0018	0.0197 (0.0195) $\pm$ 0.0024
T2 $\rightarrow$ CT	0.0155 (0.0155) $\pm$ 0.0006	0.0199 (0.0195) $\pm$ 0.0031
T1 $\rightarrow$ T2	0.0022 (0.0022) $\pm$ 0.0003	0.0031 (0.0028) $\pm$ 0.0010
T2 $\rightarrow$ T1	0.0045 (0.0044) $\pm$ 0.0007	0.0104 (0.0115) $\pm$ 0.0048
T1 $\rightarrow$ CT	0.0179 (0.0183) $\pm$ 0.0015	0.0185 (0.0185) $\pm$ 0.0027
CT $\rightarrow$ T1	0.0567 (0.0573) $\pm$ 0.0034	0.0676 (0.0670) $\pm$ 0.0072
Confidence (δ)		
Source $\rightarrow$ Target	Original input	Perturbed input
CT $\rightarrow$ T2	2.2608 (2.2737) $\pm$ 0.0515	1.9398 (1.9529) $\pm$ 0.0939
T2 $\rightarrow$ CT	2.7330 (2.7410) $\pm$ 0.0348	2.2738 (2.1684) $\pm$ 0.3819
T1 $\rightarrow$ T2	2.0281 (2.0019) $\pm$ 0.0700	1.8230 (1.8364) $\pm$ 0.1736
T2 $\rightarrow$ T1	2.2648 (2.2573) $\pm$ 0.0360	1.9289 (1.8636) $\pm$ 0.2300
T1 $\rightarrow$ CT	2.7736 (2.7971) $\pm$ 0.0592	2.1120 (2.0829) $\pm$ 0.3806
CT $\rightarrow$ T1	2.1806 (2.1818) $\pm$ 0.0517	1.7222 (1.6939) $\pm$ 0.1122

the masked regions with reasonable healthy tissues. Nevertheless, our heatmaps were able to capture such uncertainty as shown in Fig. 2.

To validate our proposed method in more realistic clinical setting, we run the inference on the LiTS dataset, which consists of CT scans with tumors present. While one would expect to see high uncertainty for input images with tumors, since the model was trained on healthy data, we only observed this for the translation from CT to T1 and only for small tumors (*cf.* first two columns in Fig. 3). This was not the case for bigger tumors (third column) and for CT to T2 translation (last two columns). It seems that the network was confidently preserving big tumors with T1 target modality and all of the pathologies with T2 target modality, while small lesions in translation from CT to T1 - the ones

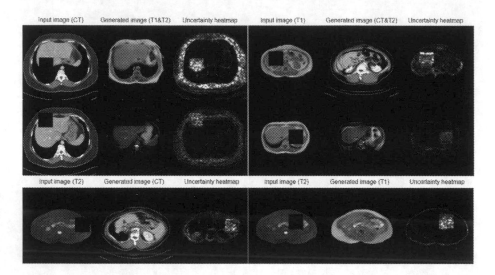

Fig. 2. Samples generated using input with randomly blacked out 50×50 pixel patch. We can see on uncertainty heat maps the lack of confidence when generating this part of the images. It is not reflected in the output image.

Table 2. Slightly corrupting the latent representation in GANs bottleneck leads to improved image quality. The lower the FID score, the better.

Image quality [FID]				
Source → Target	TarGAN	TarGAN ($\alpha = 0.5$)	TarGAN ($\alpha = 0.8$)	TarGAN ($\alpha = 1.0$)
T1 → CT	0.0649	**0.0612**	0.0616	0.0441
T2 → CT	**0.1475**	0.1496	0.1704	0.1787
CT → T1	0.0651	**0.0508**	0.0584	0.0563
T2 → T1	0.1200	**0.1135**	0.1278	0.1450
CT → T2	**0.0469**	0.0471	0.0601	0.0647
T1 → T2	0.0604	**0.0545**	0.0583	0.0668

that were not generated and probably filtered out as artifacts - caused spike in the uncertainty value.

3.3 Can We Use the Noise Injections to Improve the Quality of a Synthesized Image?

Our next experiment involved injecting noise into the training process. We investigated whether it would result in better image quality and a more robust representation. According to Table 2, injecting a small amount of noise ($\alpha = 0.5$) into half of the synthesized samples, during the training process, improved the final image quality. Nevertheless, it did not seem to translate to the end task: segmentation accuracy did not improve. We found out that introducing excess noise ($\alpha > 0.5$) or corrupting the majority of samples during training can cause confusion in the model, leading to deteriorated performance.

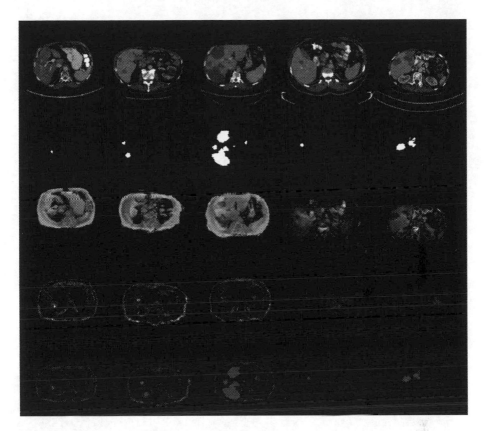

Fig. 3. CT slides from LiTS dataset containing tumor pathologies. From top to bottom, we show the input CT slice, corresponding tumor segmentation map, generated T1 or T2 images, the uncertainty heat map and the overlay of segmentation mask and uncertainty map.

3.4 Can We Correlate Our Confidence Score with the Quality of Downstream Task, E.g., Segmentation, on the Synthesized Image?

To address this question, we train three U-Net [15] networks to perform liver segmentation on three imaging modalities, namely CT, T1 and T2, and then run the inference on both the same imaging modality and the transferred synthesized ones and report the results in Table 3. On the diagonal we present the scores for the original modality which range from 0.95 for CT to 0.82 for T1, which are slightly different from the ones reported in [3] due to the fact of using a standard 2D U-Net and no enrichment technique [9]. Nevertheless, the segmentation results are acceptable for the CT to T1, CT to T2 and T1 to CT transferred images. However, the performance deteriorates for images where T2 scans are the source modality. This is reflected in the correlation scores as well (*cf.* Table 3 and Table 4). There is a correlation around and higher than 0.5 for

Table 3. Segmentation results on original input images (diagonal) and images transferred with TarGAN.

Segmentation quality [DICE]			
from\to	CT	T1	T2
CT	0.9506 (0.9711) ± 0.1003	0.6806 (0.7315) ± 0.2225	0.7302 (0.7529) ± 0.1692
T1	0.6900 (0.8546) ± 0.3735	0.8276 (0.9578) ± 0.3134	0.5272 (0.6671) ± 0.4059
T2	0.4085 (0.5321) ± 0.3652	0.5088 (0.5302) ± 0.3662	0.8349 (0.9537) ± 0.2777

Table 4. The FID scores and the absolute value of a correlation between the confidence score and DICE coefficient for our method and UP-GAN [18].

	Noise injections		UP-GAN [18]	
Source → Target	FID	Correlation	FID	Correlation
CT → T1	0.0651	0.5423	0.2022	0.0029
T1 → CT	0.0649	0.5441	0.1619	0.2188
CT → T2	0.0469	0.4946	0.1557	0.2540
T2 → CT	0.1475	0.2536	0.6540	0.0010
T1 → T2	0.0604	0.0546	0.1396	0.1021
T2 → T1	0.1200	0.3105	0.1656	0.0827

translations where the segmentor worked as well. This suggests that our method can be used most efficiently in cases where the images are generated well enough for the downstream task network to also perform well. If the generated images are of so low quality, that the segmentor fails completely (DICE < 0.5) the confidence value does not correlate with the DICE score.

3.5 How Does the Noise Injection Method Compare to Other Uncertainty Estimation Techniques?

We compare our method to the existing way of estimating aleatoric uncertainty, described in UP-GAN [18]. The quality of generated images is measured with FID scores and the correlation between the DICE coefficient and the mean of the estimated aleatoric uncertainty values as defined in [17]. It is not surprising that the FID scores are slightly lower than those of a TarGAN considering the absence of a shape-optimizing loss term. Furthermore, the aleatoric uncertainty does not correlate well with the DICE score, indicating that even though the aleatoric uncertainty might be useful in improving image quality as demonstrated in the paper, it does not translate directly into the downstream task of segmentation and cannot be used to indicate unsuitable samples. Among the differences between our method and [18], we emphasize that ours only affects the inference stage and can be used with basically any architecture, while the UP-GAN involves significant differences in the architecture (extra outputs of the network) and the optimization process (extra loss terms requiring parameter tuning).

4   Conclusion

In this work, we investigated the hypothesis that a robust latent representation results in a higher quality of a generated image and higher performance on a downstream task. We showed that there are indicators that the quality of latent representation corresponds to the final quality of a generated image. If the downstream task network performs well, it is possible to correlate it with the latent representation's quality. Additionally, we discovered that small noise injections during the training phase lead to more robust representation and slightly higher image quality. However, this does not necessarily lead to better segmentation results. We compared the noise injections to the aleatoric uncertainty estimation method as proposed by [17]. Although our approach has a smaller impact on the image quality itself, it is more indicative of performance on downstream tasks. Our method is easier to incorporate as it does not require changes in the model's architecture or the optimization process. The future work includes extending this method using adversarial attack techniques such as [13,22], investigating how it influences different end tasks, for example classification, and validating the method in more real-life scenarios.

References

1. Bilic, P., et al.: The liver tumor segmentation benchmark (LiTS), January 2019
2. Cellucci, C.J., Albano, A.M., Rapp, P.E.: Statistical validation of mutual information calculations: comparison of alternative numerical algorithms. Phys. Rev. E **71**, 066208, June 2005. https://doi.org/10.1103/PhysRevE.71.066208
3. Chen, J., Wei, J., Li, R.: TarGAN: target-aware generative adversarial networks for multi-modality medical image translation. In: de Bruijne, M., et al. (eds.) MICCAI 2021. LNCS, vol. 12906, pp. 24–33. Springer, Cham (2021). https://doi.org/10.1007/978-3-030-87231-1_3
4. Chen, S., Qin, A., Zhou, D., Yan, D.: Technical note: U-Net-generated synthetic CT images for magnetic resonance imaging-only prostate intensity-modulated radiation therapy treatment planning. Med. Phys. **45**, 5659–5665 (2018)
5. Cohen, J.P., Luck, M., Honari, S.: Distribution matching losses can hallucinate features in medical image translation. In: Frangi, A.F., Schnabel, J.A., Davatzikos, C., Alberola-López, C., Fichtinger, G. (eds.) MICCAI 2018. LNCS, vol. 11070, pp. 529–536. Springer, Cham (2018). https://doi.org/10.1007/978-3-030-00928-1_60
6. Emami, H., Dong, M., Nejad-Davarani, S., Glide-Hurst, C.: SA-GAN: structure-aware generative adversarial network for shape-preserving synthetic CT generation. In: International Conference on Medical Image Computing and Computer-Assisted Intervention (MICCAI) (2021)
7. Ge, Y., et al.: Unpaired MR to CT synthesis with explicit structural constrained adversarial learning. In: 2019 IEEE 16th International Symposium on Biomedical Imaging (ISBI 2019), pp. 1096–1099. IEEE (2019)

8. Goodfellow, I.J., et al.: Generative adversarial networks. In: Advances in Neural Information Processing Systems (NIPS) (2014)
9. Gupta, L., Klinkhammer, B., Boor, P., Merhof, D., Gadermayr, M.: GAN-based image enrichment in digital pathology boosts segmentation accuracy, pp. 631–639, October 2019. https://doi.org/10.1007/978-3-030-32239-7_70
10. Heusel, M., Ramsauer, H., Unterthiner, T., Nessler, B., Hochreiter, S.: GANs trained by a two time-scale update rule converge to a local Nash equilibrium. In: Proceedings of the 31st International Conference on Neural Information Processing Systems, pp. 6629–6640, NIPS 2017. Curran Associates Inc., Red Hook, NY, USA (2017)
11. Horvath, I., et al.: METGAN: generative tumour inpainting and modality synthesis in light sheet microscopy. In: Proceedings of the IEEE/CVF Winter Conference on Applications of Computer Vision, pp. 227–237 (2022)
12. Huang, P., et al.: CoCa-GAN: common-feature-learning-based context-aware generative adversarial network for glioma grading, pp. 155–163, October 2019. https://doi.org/10.1007/978-3-030-32248-9_18
13. Ilyas, A., Santurkar, S., Tsipras, D., Engstrom, L., Tran, B., Madry, A.: Adversarial examples are not bugs, they are features. arXiv preprint arXiv:1905.02175 (2019)
14. Kavur, A.E., et al.: CHAOS challenge - combined (CT-MR) healthy abdominal organ segmentation. Med. Image Anal. **69**, 101950 (2021). https://doi.org/10.1016/j.media.2020.101950, http://www.sciencedirect.com/science/article/pii/S1361841520303145
15. Ronneberger, O., Fischer, P., Brox, T.: U-Net: convolutional networks for biomedical image segmentation. In: Navab, N., Hornegger, J., Wells, W.M., Frangi, A.F. (eds.) MICCAI 2015. LNCS, vol. 9351, pp. 234–241. Springer, Cham (2015). https://doi.org/10.1007/978-3-319-24574-4_28
16. Shen, L., et al.: Multi-domain image completion for random missing input data. IEEE Trans. Med. Imaging **40**(4), 1113–1122 (2021). https://doi.org/10.1109/TMI.2020.3046444
17. Upadhyay, U., Chen, Y., Akata, Z.: Robustness via uncertainty-aware cycle consistency (2021)
18. Upadhyay, U., Chen, Y., Hepp, T., Gatidis, S., Akata, Z.: Uncertainty-guided progressive GANs for medical image translation. In: de Bruijne, M., et al. (eds.) MICCAI 2021. LNCS, vol. 12903, pp. 614–624. Springer, Cham (2021). https://doi.org/10.1007/978-3-030-87199-4_58
19. Xin, B., Hu, Y., Zheng, Y., Liao, H.: Multi-modality generative adversarial networks with tumor consistency loss for brain MR image synthesis. In: The IEEE International Symposium on Biomedical Imaging (ISBI) (2020)
20. Yang, J., Dvornek, N.C., Zhang, F., Chapiro, J., Lin, M.D., Duncan, J.S.: Unsupervised domain adaptation via disentangled representations: application to cross-modality liver segmentation. In: Shen, D., et al. (eds.) MICCAI 2019. LNCS, vol. 11765, pp. 255–263. Springer, Cham (2019). https://doi.org/10.1007/978-3-030-32245-8_29
21. Yu, B., Zhou, L., Wang, L., Shi, Y., Fripp, J., Bourgeat, P.: EA-GANs: edge-aware generative adversarial networks for cross-modality MR image synthesis. IEEE Trans. Med. Imaging **38**(7), 1750–1762 (2019). https://doi.org/10.1109/TMI.2019.2895894
22. Zhang, J., Chao, H., Kalra, M.K., Wang, G., Yan, P.: Overlooked trustworthiness of explainability in medical AI. medRxiv (2021). https://doi.org/10.1101/2021.12.23.21268289, https://www.medrxiv.org/content/early/2021/12/24/2021.12.23.21268289

23. Zhang, Z., Yang, L., Zheng, Y.: Translating and segmenting multimodal medical volumes with cycle- and shape-consistency generative adversarial network, pp. 9242–9251, June 2018. https://doi.org/10.1109/CVPR.2018.00963

24. Zhou, Z., et al.: Models genesis: generic autodidactic models for 3D medical image analysis. In: Shen, D., et al. (eds.) MICCAI 2019. LNCS, vol. 11767, pp. 384–393. Springer, Cham (2019). https://doi.org/10.1007/978-3-030-32251-9_42

3D CVT-GAN: A 3D Convolutional Vision Transformer-GAN for PET Reconstruction

Pinxian Zeng[1], Luping Zhou[2], Chen Zu[3], Xinyi Zeng[1], Zhengyang Jiao[1], Xi Wu[4], Jiliu Zhou[1,4], Dinggang Shen[5,6(✉)], and Yan Wang[1(✉)]

[1] School of Computer Science, Sichuan University, Chengdu, China
wangyanscu@hotmail.com
[2] School of Electrical and Information Engineering, University of Sydney, Camperdown, Australia
[3] Department of Risk Controlling Research, JD.COM, Beijing, China
[4] School of Computer Science, Chengdu University of Information Technology, Chengdu, China
[5] School of Biomedical Engineering, ShanghaiTech University, Shanghai, China
dinggang.shen@gmail.com
[6] Department of Research and Development, Shanghai United Imaging Intelligence Co., Ltd., Shanghai, China

Abstract. To obtain high-quality positron emission tomography (PET) scans while reducing potential radiation hazards brought to patients, various generative adversarial network (GAN)-based methods have been developed to reconstruct high-quality standard-dose PET (SPET) images from low-dose PET (LPET) images. However, due to the intrinsic locality of convolution operator, these methods have failed to explore global contexts of the entire 3D PET image. In this paper, we propose a novel 3D convolutional vision transformer GAN framework, named 3D CVT-GAN, for SPET reconstruction using LPET images. Specifically, we innovatively design a generator with a hierarchical structure that uses multiple 3D CVT blocks as the encoder for feature extraction and also multiple 3D transposed CVT (TCVT) blocks as the decoder for SPET restoration, capturing both local spatial features and global contexts from different network layers. Different from the vanilla 2D vision transformer that uses linear embedding and projection, our 3D CVT and TCVT blocks employ 3D convolutional embedding and projection instead, allowing the model to overcome semantic ambiguity problem caused by the attention mechanism and further preserve spatial details. In addition, residual learning and a patch-based discriminator embedded with 3D CVT blocks are added inside and after the generator, facilitating the training process while mining more discriminative feature representations. Validation on the clinical PET dataset shows that our proposed 3D CVT-GAN outperforms the state-of-the-art methods qualitatively and quantitatively with minimal parameters.

Keywords: Generative adversarial network (GAN) · Vision transformer · Positron emission tomography (PET) · PET reconstruction

© The Author(s), under exclusive license to Springer Nature Switzerland AG 2022
L. Wang et al. (Eds.): MICCAI 2022, LNCS 13436, pp. 516–526, 2022.
https://doi.org/10.1007/978-3-031-16446-0_49

1 Introduction

As one of the most advanced medical imaging technologies, positron emission tomography (PET) is widely employed in disease diagnosis and prevention [1–3]. In clinics, standard-dose PET imaging is preferred by physicians for its higher quality and more diagnostic information, however, the high radiation of the radioactive tracers during PET scanning is harmful to human body [4]. Faced with this dilemma, it is quite necessary to seek a win-win solution that can both obtain clinically acceptable high-quality PET images and reduce the radiation risk of patients.

Thanks to the development of deep learning, many studies based on convolutional neural networks (CNN) have been published in the research field of medical image analysis [4–18]. Particularly, inspired by the excellent performance of generative adversarial network (GAN) in preserving high-frequency texture information in images, Wang *et al.* first introduced the adversarial learning to PET image reconstruction task and proposed a 3D conditional GAN (3D-cGAN) model [7]. Furthermore, they proposed an auto-context locality adaptive GAN model based on both PET and MRI modalities to further boost the quality of reconstructed PET image [4]. Luo *et al.* proposed a rectification based adversarial network with spectrum constraint for PET reconstruction [15]. However, owing to the locality of the convolution operation, the aforementioned CNN-based methods show limitations in capturing long-range dependencies. Specific to the SPET reconstruction which is a dense voxel-wise prediction task, both local spatial details and global contexts are essential in extracting discriminative features.

Recently, vision transformer [19] and its variants [20, 21] have received widespread attention due to their superiority in capturing global semantic information by learning long-range dependencies. Yet, since the transformer-based methods completely abandon convolution in favor of global attention operation, it is computation-intensive to directly apply them to the voxel-wise medical image prediction task [22, 23]. To address this issue, numerous works on medical image processing [22–28] have combined the merits of CNN and transformer to preserve both local spatial details and global contexts with fewer parameters. Particularly, Luo *et al.* [23] first proposed a 3D Transformer-GAN model for high-quality SPET reconstruction. However, most of these works simply employ the transformer as an intermediate bottleneck module, without any direct interaction with the convolution, which may result in semantic ambiguity, as the transformer is generally not good at capturing low-level contextual information in the shallow layers of the network due to the intrinsic shortcomings of the attention mechanism [29].

Motivated to address the above limitations, in this paper, we further explore to combine the CNN and transformer in a more effective manner for SPET reconstruction. Inspired by the convolutional vision transformer [29], we propose a novel 3D convolutional vision transformer GAN model with an elaborate hierarchical structure, named 3D CVT-GAN, aiming to acquire clinically acceptable SPET images while reducing the radiation exposure to patients. Our 3D CVT-GAN embeds 3D convolution operation into two crucial parts of the transformer, i.e., embedding and projection, reaching a win-win situation of capturing global contexts and local spatial information while saving parameters. The contributions of our proposed method can be described as follows.

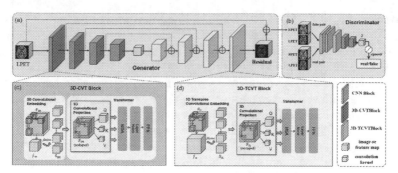

Fig. 1. Overview of the proposed 3D CVT-GAN

(1) Our method further explores the combination of CNN and Transformer in a 3D manner. Concretely, for the voxel-wise SPET reconstruction task, we replace the 2D linear embedding and linear projection in vanilla visual transformer with 3D convolutional embedding and projection, forming 3D convolutional vision transformer (CVT) block for encoding the input image. In this manner, our model is capable of tackling semantic ambiguity problem caused by the attention mechanism of transformer and further preserving local spatial details. Also, blessed with the smart integration of CNN and transformer, our model outperforms the state-of-the-art method Transformer-GAN with about only 1/5 parameters.

(2) Different from previous methods that simply use interpolation or transpose convolution for up-sampling, we also introduce the transformer in the decoding stage and design a TCVT block. The TCVT block utilizes transposed convolution to implement up-sampling when performing feature embedding, and applies transformer to model global contextual information for better learning high-level features, thereby further improving the quality of the reconstructed image.

(3) In order to learn more discriminative knowledge from image patches of the input image, we introduce a patch-based discriminator embedded with 3D CVT blocks to determine whether the input image is real or not. Moreover, residual learning is also integrated into our model, allowing the generator only needs to learn the difference between LPET and SPET, which facilitates the training and convergence of networks.

2   Methodology

Figure 1 displays the overview of our 3D CVT-GAN structure which consists of a hierarchical generator and a patch-based discriminator. The generator takes the LPET image as input, and respectively employs four 3D CVT blocks for down-sampling and four 3D TCVT blocks for up-sampling, to predict the residual between the LPET and SPET. The output residual is further added to the input LPET image, producing the estimated PET image (denoted as EPET) as the final output of the generator. Finally, the discriminator takes the real/fake PET image pair (i.e., the LPET image and corresponding real/fake target SPET image) as inputs, attempting to distinguish the fake image pair from the real ones.

2.1 Generator

3D CVT Block: As shown in Fig. 1(c), the 3D CVT block contains a 3D convolutional embedding and a transformer layer incorporated with 3D convolutional projection, learning both the local spatial details and global contexts at the layer level. For the 3D convolutional embedding in the m-th 3D CVT block ($m = 1, 2, 3, 4$), it takes the output of the previous block $e_{m-1} \in R^{C_{m-1} \times H_{m-1} \times W_{m-1} \times D_{m-1}}$ as input and produces a token sequence s_m. Note that, e_0 is the original LPET images, C is channel dimensions, H and W are the height and width of e, and D is the corresponding depth. Specifically, we first adopt a 3D convolutional operation to down-sample the e_{m-1} and obtain a new feature map $f_m \in R^{C_m \times H_m \times W_m \times D_m}$. The channel dimensions C_m of f_m is set to 64 for the first block and progressively doubled in the following blocks (i.e., $C_1 = 64, C_2 = 128$), and the kernel size k is set as 3, padding p as 1, and stride s as 2. The feature map f_m is further flattened and normalized by layer-normalization (LN), producing the token sequence $s_m \in R^{C_m \times (H_m \times W_m \times D_m)}$ with $H_m \times W_m \times D_m$ lengths and C_m dimensions. In this manner, the sequence length is reduced while the feature dimension of tokens is expanded, enabling the tokens to represent increasingly complex visual patterns. Additionally, since the convolution itself has encoded the positional information of tokens, our 3D convolutional embedding does not require any positional encoding, thus simplifying the architecture design of the model while maintaining its performance.

For the transformer layer, we first reshape the token sequence s_m into the same 3D shape as the previous f_m. Then, a 3D convolutional projection, which includes a depth-wise separable convolution [30] and a flattening operation, is employed to project the s_m into query $Q \in R^{C_m \times (H_m \times W_m \times D_m)}$, key $K \in R^{C_m \times \left(\frac{H_m}{2} \times \frac{W_m}{2} \times \frac{D_m}{2} \right)}$ and value $V \in R^{C_m \times \left(\frac{H_m}{2} \times \frac{W_m}{2} \times \frac{D_m}{2} \right)}$. Compared with the linear projection, our 3D convolutional projection allows the model to further capture local spatial details and reduce semantic ambiguity caused by the attention mechanism. In addition, by performing convolutional projection of K and V with the stride of 2, the number of tokens for K and V participated in the subsequent attention operation is lowered by 8-fold, which greatly reduces the computation cost. The above process can be formulated as:

$$Q \in R^{C_m \times (H_m \times W_m \times D_m)} = Flatten(conv3D(reshape(s_m), stride = 1)), \quad (1)$$

$$K, V \in R^{C_m \times \left(\frac{H_m}{2} \times \frac{W_m}{2} \times \frac{D_m}{2} \right)} = Flatten(conv3D(reshape(s_m), stride = 2)). \quad (2)$$

Like the original transformer, Q, K, V are then fed into a multi-head self-attention (MSA) sub-layer for modeling global contexts, which can be expressed as:

$$MSA(Q, K, V) = Concat(head_1, ..., head_h), \quad (3)$$

$$head_i = Attn\left(QW_i^Q, KW_i^K, VW_i^V\right) = Softmax\left(\frac{\left(QW_i^Q\right) \times \left(KW_i^K\right)^T}{\sqrt{d_k}} \right) \cdot VW_i^V, \quad (4)$$

where W_i^Q, W_i^K and W_i^V represents the linear layers that project Q, K, V to the latent space of the i-th head. Finally, through the layer-normalization (LN) and a feed-forward network (FFN), we can get the output of the m-th block e_m.

After the above operations, in each 3D CVT block, local spatial details can be effectively preserved by the convolutional embedding and projection, and the global contexts can be well captured by the attention mechanism in the transformer.

3D TCVT Block: As illustrated in Fig. 1(d), the architecture of the 3D TCVT block is similar to that of the 3D CVT block, the only difference between them lies in that the TCVT blocks utilize 3D transposed convolutional embedding for up-sampling, whereas the CVT blocks adopt 3D convolutional embedding for down-sampling. For the n-th 3D TCVT block ($n = 1, 2, 3, 4$), it takes $z_{n-1} \in R^{C_{n-1} \times H_{n-1} \times W_{n-1} \times D_{n-1}}$ as input and outputs $d_n \in R^{C_n \times H_n \times W_n \times D_n}$. To make full use of the complementary information from the hierarchical feature extracted by the encoder, z_n is obtained by adding the output d_{n-1} of the previous TCVT block and the output e_{4-n+1} of the corresponding CVT block (i.e., $z_n = d_{n-1} + e_{4-n+1}$, $n > 1$). Note that, the first TCVT block directly uses the output e_4 of the last CVT block as input. Specifically, the transposed convolution is applied to up-sample the input z_n, deriving feature map $f_n \in R^{C_n \times H_n \times W_n \times D_n}$ with channel dimensions C decreased and the height H, width W, and depth D doubled. Then, the token map is reshaped into a token sequence with the size of $C_n \times (H_n \times W_n \times D_n)$ to be further processed by the transformer layer like the 3D CVT block. By embedding transposed convolution into the transformer layer, the network can effectively fuse features extracted by shallow and deep layers, accomplishing up-sampling while encouraging less information loss.

Algorithm 1

   Parameters: The number of the 3D CVT blocks N_e and 3D TCVT blocks N_d.
   Initialize: $m = 1, n = 1, N_e = 4, N_d = 4$
   Input: *LPET* with the size of $64 \times 64 \times 64$
   $e_0 = LPET$
   While $m \leq N_e$: //*Encoding by 3D CVT block*
      $s_m = \text{ConvEmbed}(e_{m-1})$ // *3D Convolutional Embedding*
      $Q, K, V = \text{ConvProj}(s_m)$ // *Generate Q, K, V by 3D Convolutional Projection*
      $s_m = s_m + \text{MSA}(Q, K, V)$ // *Multi-head Self Attention*
      $e_m = s_m + \text{FFN}(\text{LN}(s_m))$ // *Feed-Forward Network*
      $m = m + 1$
   While $n \leq N_d$: //*Decoding*
      If $n == 1$:   // *For the 1ˢᵗ 3D TCVT block*
         $s_n = \text{TransConvEmbed}(e_{N_e})$ // *3D Transposed Convolutional Embedding*
      Else: // *For other 3D TCVT blocks*
         $z_n = d_{n-1} + e_{4-n+1}$ // *Residual Connection*
         $s_n = \text{TransConvEmbed}(z_n)$ // *3D Transposed Convolutional Embedding*
      $Q, K, V = \text{ConvProj}(s_n)$
      $s_n = s_n + \text{MSA}(Q, K, V)$
      $d_n = s_n + \text{FFN}(\text{LN}(s_n))$
      $n = n + 1$
   End while
   $EPET = LPET + d_{N_d}$
   Output: the reconstructed PET image *EPET*

The output of the last 3D TCVT block d_4. is the residual between LPET and SPET, which is further added to the input LPET to form the final output EPET of the generator. For a better understanding, we describe the procedure for the generator in Algorithm 1.

2.2 Discriminator

The patch-based discriminator shown in Fig. 1(b) takes a real/fake PET image pair (i.e., the LPET image and its corresponding real/fake SPET image) as input, aiming to determine whether the input image pair is real or fake. There are three CNN blocks for shallow feature extraction and two 3D CVT blocks used to learn deep representations. Specifically, each CNN block includes a $3 \times 3 \times 3$ convolution layer, a Batch Normalization layer, and a Leaky-ReLU activation function, while the 3D CVT block is the same as that in the generator. Then a sigmoid activation function is employed in the last 3D CVT block, generating the array Z with the size of $4 \times 4 \times 4$. The elemen Z_{ijk} in Z represents the probability that the patch at position $[i, j, k]$ of the input pair is real.

2.3 Objective Function

The objective function for our 3D CVT-GAN model contains two parts: the voxel-wise estimation error loss and adversarial loss, where the former is used to ensure that the appearance of the estimated PET is close to that of the real one, while the latter tends to narrow the gap between the data distribution of the estimated and real images.

In the paper, we apply the L1 loss as voxel-wise estimation error loss to minimize the distance between real SPET image y and the estimated images $G(x)$ reconstructed from LPET image x and to encourage less blurring, which is expressed in Eq. (5):

$$L1(G) = E_{x,y}\big[||y - G(x)||\big] \tag{5}$$

For the adversarial loss, the classic binary cross-entropy loss is employed. As each value in the output array of the discriminator D indicates the probability that the corresponding 3D patch is real, the total adversarial loss is obtained by averaging the binary cross-entropy loss between the output of D and the corresponding label (the label of a real SPET is constructed as an array of ones, while the estimated PET as an array of zeros). The whole training process is like a two-player min-max game between D and G, the generator G aims to minimize the adversarial loss, while the discriminator D tries to maximize adversarial loss. The adversarial loss can be defined as:

$$\min_{G} \max_{D} V(G, D) = E_{x,y}\big[logD(x, y)\big] + E_x\big[log(1 - D(x, G(x)))\big] \tag{6}$$

Overall, the final objective function is the weighted sum of the L1 loss and the adversarial loss, as formulated in Eq. (7):

$$V_{total} = \min_{G} \max_{D} V(G, D) + \lambda L1(G), \tag{7}$$

the weighting coefficient λ is empirically set to 100.

2.4   Details of Implementation

Our model is implemented by PyTorch framework and trained on NVIDIA GeForce RTX 3080 GPU with 10 GB memory. The generator G and the discriminator D are trained alternatively according to the standard process of GAN. The whole network is trained for 100 epochs with a batch size of 4, using Adam optimizer for network optimization. And the learning rates for G and D are both set to 2×10^{-4} for the first 50 epochs and decay linearly to 0 for the remaining 50 epochs. Only the well-trained G is utilized to reconstruct high-quality SPET images in the validation stage.

3   Experiments and Results

Datasets. Our proposed 3D CVT-GAN model is trained and validated on a clinical brain dataset. This dataset contains PET brain images collected from 16 subjects, including 8 normal control (NC) subjects and 8 mild cognitive impairment (MCI) subjects. For each subject, a standard dose of ^{18}F-Flurodeoxyglucose ([^{18}F] FDG) (averaging 203 MBq) was administered. All the PET scans were acquired on a Siemens Biograph mMR PET-MR system and the SPET and LPET images were obtained consecutively based on the standard imaging protocols. Specifically, the SPET images were obtained in a 12-min period within one hour of tracer injection, and the LPET scans were acquired in a subsequent 3-min short period to simulate the acquisition at a quarter of the standard dose of radioactive trace. The size of the obtained PET images is $128 \times 128 \times 128$. To mitigate the possibility of over-fitting caused by limited samples, we slice the entire PET image into overlapped patches with a stride of 8, thus obtaining 729 patches with the size of $64 \times 64 \times 64$. From each PET image, which provides sufficient training and validation samples. Also, we apply the "leave-one-out cross-validation (LOOCV)" strategy, i.e., we repeat the training-validation process for 16 times while each time one subject is for validation and the remaining 15 subjects are for training. By averaging the results obtained from the 16 training-validations, the performance of our model can be measured with more fairness and less bias.

Table 1. Quantitative comparison with four state-of-the-art SPET reconstruction methods in terms of PSNR, SSIM, and NMSE.

Method	NC subjects			MCI subjects			Params	GFLOPs
	PSNR	SSIM	NMSE	PSNR	SSIM	NMSE		
3D U-NET [31]	23.744	0.981	0.0245	24.165	0.982	0.0256	24M	40.50
Auto-Context [5]	23.867	-	0.0235	24.435	-	0.0264	41M	-
3D-cGAN [7]	24.024	-	0.0231	24.617	-	0.0256	127M	70.38
Transformer-GAN [23]	24.818	0.986	0.0212	25.249	0.987	0.0231	76M	**20.78**
3D CVT-GAN (ours)	**24.893**	**0.987**	**0.0182**	**25.275**	**0.987**	**0.0208**	**16M**	23.80

Comparative Experiments. We compare the proposed 3D CVT-GAN method with four state-of-the-art SPET reconstruction methods: (1) 3D U-NET [31], (2) Auto-Context [5], (3) 3D-cGAN [7], and (4) Transformer-GAN [23]. And the peak signal-to-noise (PSNR), structural similarity index (SSIM), and normalized mean squared error (NMSE) are used as quantitative evaluation metrics. Among them, PSNR indicates estimation accuracy in terms of the logarithmic decibel scale, while SSIM and NMSE represent the structural similarity and voxel-wise intensity differences between the real and estimated images, respectively.

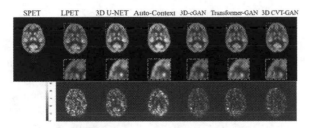

Fig. 2. Visual comparison of the reconstruction methods.

The comparison results are given in Table 1, from which we can see that our method outperforms the compared reconstruction methods in all three metrics, demonstrating the superiority of our method. Particularly, compared with the current state-of-the-art approach Transformer-GAN, in terms of PSNR and NMSE, our proposed 3D CVT-GAN method boosts the performance by 0.075 dB and 0.03 for NC subjects, and by 0.026 dB and 0.023 for MCI subjects. Moreover, since we use convolutional embedding and convolutional projection at the layer level without adding additional positional encoding, our model also has minimal parameters of 16 M, which further proves the advantages of our method. The visualization results of our method and the compared approaches are displayed in Fig. 2, where the first row shows the real SPET, LPET, and reconstructed images by different methods from left to right, and the second row presents the corresponding error maps of the reconstructed images and the real image. The darker color of the error map indicates the smaller error. As observed, compared with other state-of-the-art methods, the result obtained by our 3D CVT-GAN is closest to the real SPET image with the smallest error. Besides, the paired t-test is conducted on the results of our model and the second-best performer (Transformer-GAN) in Table 1. We achieve the p-values (PSNR/SSIM/NMSE) of 0.006/0.047/0.021 for NC, and 0.036/0.005/0.045 for MCI, which are consistently less than 0.05, showing our improvement is statistically significant.

Evaluation on Clinical Diagnosis. To evaluate the clinical application of the reconstructed SPET images, we further conduct an NC/MCI diagnosis experiment as the down-stream task. In this experiment, we cut the 3D image into 2D slices of 128×128 to form the dataset. Specifically, we first employ the target SPET images to train a simple multi-layer CNN classification network to judge whether the image is from an NC subject or MCI subject. Then, the PET images reconstructed by different methods are used for testing. The classification results in Fig. 3 reveal that the PET images reconstructed by our method are the closest to real SPET images, showing the great potential of our method for aiding clinical diagnosis.

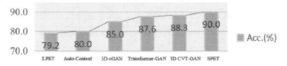

Fig. 3. Results of clinical NC/MCI diagnosis.

Ablation Study. To study the contributions of key components of the proposed 3D CVT-GAN model, we conduct ablation experiments through (1) replacing the 3D CVT and 3D TCVT blocks with simple convolution layers and transposed convolution layers, respectively, and removing the patch-based discriminator (denoted as Baseline), (2) introducing patch-based discriminator to the Baseline model (as Model-1), (3) add 3D CVT blocks to Model-1 (as Model-2), (4) replacing proposed convolution embedding and projection with linear layers (as Model-3), and (5) using the proposed model (i.e., adding TCVT block to Model-2). According to the results given in Table 2, it can be observed that the performance of the model progressively improves as we add patch-based discriminator, 3D CVT blocks, and 3D TCVT blocks to the Baseline. Moreover, when we replace the convolutional embedding and projection with linear layers, the performance largely decreases as the model fails to learn local spatial details.

Table 2. Quantitative comparison with models constructed in the ablation study in terms of PSNR, SSIM, and NMSE.

Model	NC subjects			MCI subjects		
	PSNR	SSIM	NMSE	PSNR	SSIM	NMSE
Baseline	23.744	0.981	0.0245	24.165	0.982	0.0256
Model-1	24.118	0.982	0.0237	24.570	0.982	0.0247
Model-2	24.434	0.982	0.0221	24.786	0.983	0.0238
Model-3	24.352	0.981	0.0232	24.477	0.983	0.0253
Proposed	**24.893**	**0.987**	**0.0182**	**25.275**	**0.987**	**0.0208**

4   Conclusion

In this paper, we innovatively proposed a 3D convolutional vision transformer-GAN model, named 3D CVT-GAN, to reconstruct high-quality SPET images from LPET images. Aiming to combine the advantages of CNN and transformer, we designed the transposed convolutional/convolutional embedding as well as the convolutional projection in 3D CVT and 3D TCVT blocks to achieve a win-win situation of obtaining local spatial details and global contexts while saving parameters. Additionally, we also adopted a patch-based discriminator incorporated with 3D CVT block, imposing attention on different image patches while learning more discriminative representations. Besides, residual learning is further introduced to facilitate network training. Experiments on a real human brain PET dataset have shown that our method outperforms the current state-of-the-art methods in both qualitative and quantitative measures.

Acknowledgement. This work is supported by National Natural Science Foundation of China (NFSC 62071314).

References

1. Feng, Q., Liu, H.: Rethinking PET image reconstruction: ultra-low-dose, sinogram and deep learning. In: Martel, A.L., et al. (eds.) MICCAI 2020. LNCS, vol. 12267, pp. 783–792. Springer, Cham (2020). https://doi.org/10.1007/978-3-030-59728-3_76
2. Wang, Y., Ma, G., An, L., et al.: Semi-supervised tripled dictionary learning for standard-dose PET image prediction using low-dose PET and multimodal MRI. IEEE Trans. Biomed. Eng. **64**(3), 569–579 (2016)
3. Kim, K., Wu, D., Gong, K., et al.: Penalized PET reconstruction using deep learning prior and local linear fitting. IEEE Trans. Med. Imaging **37**(6), 1478–1487 (2018)
4. Wang, Y., Zhou, L., Yu, B., et al.: 3D auto-context-based locality adaptive multi-modality GANs for PET synthesis. IEEE Trans. Med. Imaging **38**(6), 1328–1339 (2018)
5. Xiang, L., Qiao, Y., Nie, D., et al.: Deep auto-context convolutional neural networks for standard-dose PET image estimation from low-dose PET/MRI. Neurocomputing **267**, 406–416 (2017)
6. Spuhler, K., Serrano-Sosa, M., Cattell, R., et al.: Full-count PET recovery from low-count image using a dilated convolutional neural network. Med. Phys. **47**(10), 4928–4938 (2020)
7. Wang, Y., Yu, B., Wang, L., et al.: 3D conditional generative adversarial networks for high-quality PET image estimation at low dose. Neuroimage **174**, 550–562 (2018)
8. Gong, K., Guan, J., Kim, K., et al.: Iterative PET image reconstruction using convolutional neural network representation. IEEE Trans. Med. Imaging **38**(3), 675–685 (2018)
9. Zhan, B., Xiao, J., Cao, C., et al.: Multi-constraint generative adversarial network for dose prediction in radiotherapy. Med. Image Anal. **77**, 102339 (2022)
10. Häggström, I., Schmidtlein, C.R., et al.: DeepPET: a deep encoder-decoder network for directly solving the PET image reconstruction inverse problem. Med. Image Anal. **54**, 253–262 (2019)
11. Hu, L., Li, J., Peng, X., et al.: Semi-supervised NPC segmentation with uncertainty and attention guided consistency. Knowl.-Based Syst. **239**, 108021 (2022)
12. Mehranian, A., Reader, A.J.: Model-based deep learning PET image reconstruction using forward-backward splitting expectation-maximization. IEEE Trans. Radiat. Plasma Med. Sci. **5**(1), 54–64 (2020)
13. Tang, P., Yang, P., et al.: Unified medical image segmentation by learning from uncertainty in an end-to-end manner. Knowl. Based Syst. **241**, 108215 (2022)
14. Zhou, L., Schaefferkoetter, J.D., et al.: Supervised learning with cyclegan for low-dose FDG PET image denoising. Med. Image Anal. **65**, 101770 (2020)
15. Luo, Y., Zhou, L., Zhan, B., et al.: Adaptive rectification based adversarial network with spectrum constraint for high-quality PET image synthesis. Med. Image Anal. **77**, 102335 (2022)

16. Wang, K., Zhan, B., Zu, C., et al.: Semi-supervised medical image segmentation via a tripled-uncertainty guided mean teacher model with contrastive learning. Med. Image Anal. **79**, 102447 (2022)
17. Nie, D., Wang, L., Adeli, E., et al.: 3D fully convolutional networks for multimodal isointense infant brain image segmentation. IEEE Trans. Cybern. **49**(3), 1123–1136 (2018)
18. Shi, Y., Zu, C., Hong, M., et al.: ASMFS: Adaptive-similarity-based multi-modality feature selection for classification of Alzheimer's disease. Pattern Recogn. **126**, 108566 (2022)
19. Dosovitskiy, A., Beyer, L., Kolesnikov, A., et al.: An image is worth 16 x 16 words: Transformers for image recognition at scale. In: Proceedings of the IEEE/CVF International Conference on Computer Vision. IEEE, Venice (2020)
20. Hugo T., Matthieu C., et al.: Training data-efficient image transformers & distillation through attention. In: Proceedings of the 38th International Conference on Machine Learning, pp. 10347–10357. PMLR, Vienna (2021)
21. Wang, W., Xie, E., Li, X., et al.: Pyramid vision transformer: a versatile backbone for dense prediction without convolutions. In: Proceedings of the IEEE/CVF International Conference on Computer Vision, pp. 568–578. IEEE, Montreal (2021)
22. Zhang, Z., Yu, L., Liang, X., Zhao, W., Xing, L.: TransCT: dual-path transformer for low dose computed tomography. In: de Bruijne, M., et al. (eds.) MICCAI 2021. LNCS, vol. 12906, pp. 55–64. Springer, Cham (2021). https://doi.org/10.1007/978-3-030-87231-1_6
23. Luo, Y., et al.: 3D transformer-GAN for high-quality PET reconstruction. In: de Bruijne, M., et al. (eds.) MICCAI 2021. LNCS, vol. 12906, pp. 276–285. Springer, Cham (2021). https://doi.org/10.1007/978-3-030-87231-1_27
24. Wang, W., Chen, C., Ding, M., Yu, H., Zha, S., Li, J.: TransBTS: multimodal brain tumor segmentation using transformer. In: de Bruijne, M., et al. (eds.) MICCAI 2021. LNCS, vol. 12901, pp. 109–119. Springer, Cham (2021). https://doi.org/10.1007/978-3-030-87193-2_11
25. Zhang, Y., Liu, H., Hu, Q.: Transfuse: fusing transformers and CNNs for medical image segmentation. In: de Bruijne, M., Cattin, P.C., Cotin, S., Padoy, N., Speidel, S., Zheng, Y., Essert, C. (eds.) MICCAI 2021. LNCS, vol. 12901, pp. 14–24. Springer, Cham (2021). https://doi.org/10.1007/978-3-030-87193-2_2
26. Chen, J., Lu, Y., Yu, Q., et al.: TransuNet: transformers make strong encoders for medical image segmentation. arXiv preprint arXiv:2102.04306 (2021)
27. Gao, Y., Zhou, M., Metaxas, D.N.: UTNet: a hybrid transformer architecture for medical image segmentation. In: International Conference on Medical Image Computing and Computer-Assisted Intervention, pp. 61–71. Springer, Cham (2021)
28. Luthra, A., Sulakhe, H., Mittal, T., et al.: Eformer: edge enhancement based transformer for medical image denoising. In: Proceedings of the IEEE/CVF International Conference on Computer Vision, 2021 (2021)
29. Wu, H., Xiao, B., Codella, N., et al.: CVT: introducing convolutions to vision transformers. In: Proceedings of the IEEE/CVF International Conference on Computer Vision, pp. 22–31 (2021)
30. Ye, R., Liu, F., Zhang, L.: 3D depthwise convolution: reducing model parameters in 3D vision tasks. In: Meurs, M., Rudzicz, F. (eds.) Canadian AI 2019. LNCS (LNAI), vol. 11489, pp. 186–199. Springer, Cham (2019). https://doi.org/10.1007/978-3-030-18305-9_15
31. Çiçek, Ö., Abdulkadir, A., Lienkamp, S.S., Brox, T., Ronneberger, O.: 3D U-Net: learning dense volumetric segmentation from sparse annotation. In: Ourselin, S., Joskowicz, L., Sabuncu, M.R., Unal, G., Wells, W. (eds.) MICCAI 2016. LNCS, vol. 9901, pp. 424–432. Springer, Cham (2016). https://doi.org/10.1007/978-3-319-46723-8_49
32. Vaswani, A., Shazeer, N., Parmar, N., et al.: Attention is all you need. In: Advances in Neural Information Processing Systems, p. 30 (2017)

Classification-Aided High-Quality PET Image Synthesis via Bidirectional Contrastive GAN with Shared Information Maximization

Yuchen Fei[1], Chen Zu[2], Zhengyang Jiao[1], Xi Wu[3], Jiliu Zhou[1,3],
Dinggang Shen[4,5(✉)], and Yan Wang[1(✉)]

[1] School of Computer Science, Sichuan University, Chengdu, China
wangyanscu@hotmail.com
[2] Department of Risk Controlling Research, JD.COM, Chengdu, China
[3] School of Computer Science, Chengdu University of Information Technology, Chengdu, China
[4] School of Biomedical Engineering, ShanghaiTech University, Chengdu, China
dinggang.shen@gmail.com
[5] Department of Research and Development, Shanghai United Imaging Intelligence Co., Ltd.,
Shanghai, China

Abstract. Positron emission tomography (PET) is a pervasively adopted nuclear imaging technique, however, its inherent tracer radiation inevitably causes potential health hazards to patients. To obtain high-quality PET image while reducing radiation exposure, this paper proposes an algorithm for high-quality standard-dose PET (SPET) synthesis from low-dose PET (LPET) image. Specifically, considering that LPET images and SPET images come from the same subjects, we argue that there is abundant shared content and structural information between LPET and SPET domains, which is helpful for improving synthesis performance. To this end, we innovatively propose a bi-directional contrastive generative adversarial network (BiC-GAN), containing a master network and an auxiliary network. Both networks implement intra-domain reconstruction and inter-domain synthesis tasks, aiming to extract shared information from LPET and SPET domains, respectively. Meanwhile, the contrastive learning strategy is also introduced to two networks for enhancing feature representation capability and acquiring more domain-independent information. To maximize the shared information extracted from two domains, we further design a domain alignment module to constrain the consistency of the shared information extracted from the two domains. On the other hand, since synthesized PET images can be used to assist disease diagnosis, such as mild cognitive impairment (MCI) identification, the MCI classification task is incorporated into PET image synthesis to further improve clinical applicability of the synthesized PET image through direct feedback from the classification task. Evaluated on a Real Human Brain dataset, our proposed method is demonstrated to achieve state-of-the-art performance quantitatively and qualitatively.

Keywords: Positron emission tomography (PET) · Contrastive learning · Shared information · Generative adversarial network (GAN) · Image synthesis

L. Wang et al. (Eds.): MICCAI 2022, LNCS 13436, pp. 527–537, 2022.
https://doi.org/10.1007/978-3-031-16446-0_50

1 Introduction

Positron emission tomography (PET) is a pervasively exploited nuclear imaging technique that can provide crucial information for early disease diagnosis and treatment [1, 2]. In clinic, a standard-dose radioactive tracer is usually needed to acquire PET images of diagnostic quality. However, the inherent tracer radiation inevitably induces an increased risk of cancer and raises potential health hazards [3], while reducing dose may involve more noise and artifacts during imaging, resulting in suboptimal image quality. Accordingly, obtaining diagnostic-quality PET image at low dose is of great research significance.

In the past decades, numerous machine learning based methods have been developed to obtain the high-quality standard-dose PET (SPET) from the low-dose PET (LPET) [4–6]. Although these traditional algorithms have gained promising results, they are all based on manually-extracted features and have shown limitation in offering complex latent information. Recently, deep learning methods represented by convolutional neural network (CNN) and generative adversarial network (GAN) have been widely applied in medical image analysis and achieved remarkable success [7–17]. For instance, Wang *et al.* [12] first proposed a 3D GAN model for PET image synthesis, and they further [15] put forward a 3D locality-adaptive GANs with an auto-context strategy for SPET prediction. Lei *et al.* [16] proposed a cycle-consistent GAN framework for whole-body PET estimation. These existing approaches always translate LPET to SPET directly and only consider pixel-level differences between the real and synthesized SPET images. However, since the LPET images and the SPET images are from the same subjects, the above simple paradigm ignores the shared semantic content and structure information between LPET and SPET domains, which may lead to the distortion of the image content during the translation process [18]. In light of this, how to preserve the shared information between LPET and SPET domains for boosting the PET synthesis performance is a key issue to be addressed in this paper.

On the other hand, the synthesized PET images are expected to provide crucial clinical information for the diagnosis of cognitive impairment. Yet, current methods focus more on improving image quality and do not take into account the applications of the synthetic images in analytical and diagnostic tasks. Therefore, how to effectively improve the clinical applicability of synthetic PET images in diagnosis is another key issue that needs to be addressed in this paper.

In this paper, motivated to address the aforementioned key issues in current PET synthesis methods, we propose a novel end-to-end classification-aided bidirectional contrastive GAN (BiC-GAN for short) framework for high-quality SPET images synthesis from corresponding LPET images. Specifically, the proposed model mainly consists of two similar GAN-based networks, i.e., a master network and an auxiliary network, each realizing both inter-domain synthesis and intra-domain reconstruction tasks to extract the shared content and structure information between the LPET and SPET domains. Moreover, a domain alignment module is employed to maximize the shared information extracted from the two domains. Then, considering that contrastive learning (CL) has superior performance in learning robust image representation [19–23], we also introduce the CL strategy into the encoding stage, enabling more domain-independent content information to be extracted. Additionally, to enforce the clinical availability of synthe-sized SPET, the proposed model incorporates the mild cognitive impairment (MCI) classification task into PET image synthesis, so that the classification results could be fed back to the image synthesis task for improving the quality of the synthesized images for the target classification task.

2 Methodology

The architecture of the proposed BiC-GAN is illustrated in Fig. 1, which mainly consists of a master network and an auxiliary network, receiving LPET and SPET as input, respectively, to fully exploit the shared information between LPET and SPET domains through intra-domain reconstruction and inter-domain synthesis tasks. Both networks are equipped with a contrastive learning module to enhance their feature extraction capability and explore more domain-independent content information. Moreover, we further design a domain alignment module to align the features extracted from the LPET and SPET domains, thus maximizing the shared information from the two domains. In addition, a discriminator network is introduced to ensure distribution consistency between the real and synthesized images. Finally, in the master network, we further incorporate an MCI classifier designed to distinguish whether the synthetic images are from normal control (NC) subjects or subjects diagnosed with MCI, allowing the model to synthesize PET images of high diagnostic quality. The detailed architecture of our model will be described as follows.

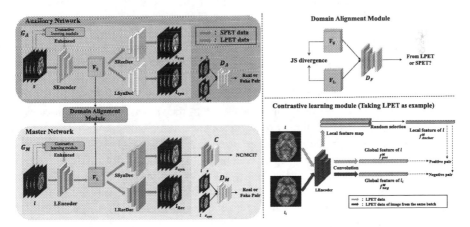

Fig. 1. Overall architecture of the proposed framework.

2.1 Master Network

Generator. The generator G_M of the master network takes LPET l as input and out-puts the reconstructed LPET l_{rec} and synthesized SPET s_{syn} images through a shared encoder *LEncoder* and two specific decoders, i.e., an intra-domain reconstruction decoder *LRecDec* and an inter-domain synthesis decoder *SSynDec*, respectively, making the shared encoder can fully excavate the shared information between LPET and SPET domains. Concretely, the encoder contains seven down-sampling blocks structured as 3×3 Convolution-BatchNorm-LeakyRelu-Maxpool, except for the last block which removes the Maxpool layer. Through the shared encoder, the size of input image l is reduced from 256×256 to 2×2, while the channel dimension is increased to 512. Both decoders have the same structure, each containing seven up-sampling blocks with Deconvolution-Convolution-BatchNorm-Relu structure for gradually restoring the features extracted by the shared encoder to target images. The 2×2 deconvolution with stride 2 is applied as an up-sampling operator. Following [24], we only use the skip connections in the synthesis task and drop them in the reconstruction task to prevent the intra-domain reconstruction decoder copying the features directly from the encoder instead of learning the mapping between them. The L1 loss is adopted to ensure that l_{rec} and s_{syn} are close to their corresponding ground truth, i.e., l and s, and to encourage less blurring, as formulated in Eq. (1):

$$L_1(G_M) = \alpha_1 \|s - s_{syn}\|_1 + \alpha_2 \|l - l_{rec}\|_1 \tag{1}$$

where α_1 and α_2 are hyperparameters to balance synthesis and reconstruction losses.

Discriminator. The discriminator D_M of the master network receives a pair of images, including the input LPET l and the corresponding real/synthesized SPET s/s_{syn}, aiming to distinguish the synthesized image pair from the real one. Specifically, the discriminator is designed with reference to pix2pix [25], whose structure is Conv-LeakyReLU-Conv-BatchNorm-LeakyReLU-Conv-Sigmoid. To enforce the distributions of the synthesized and real images to be consistent to fool the discriminator, we calculate an adversarial loss as follows:

$$L_{GAN}(G_M, D_M) = E_{l,s}\left[(D_M(l, s) - 1)^2\right] + E_s\left[D_M(l, s_{syn})^2\right] \tag{2}$$

Contrastive Learning Module. As illustrated in Fig. 1, a contrastive learning module is introduced to enhance the representation ability of the shared encoder. The core idea of contrastive learning is to pull positive samples towards anchor samples while pushing negative samples away in the embedding space. To achieve this, we should construct reasonable anchor, positive, and negative samples first. Specifically, taking the master network for example, we first obtain a local feature with the size of $512 \times 2 \times 2$ from the sixth down-sampling block of the shared encoder, then randomly select a vector of the local feature in the spatial dimension as the anchor sample $f_{anchor}^M \in R^{512 \times 1 \times 1}$. Meanwhile, the local feature will be further processed by a 3×3 convolution kernel and a max-pooling layer to produce a global feature. Since the global feature comes from the same image as the local feature, it can be regarded as a positive sample $f_{pos}^M \in R^{512 \times 1 \times 1}$. As for the global features extracted from other images in a batch, we treat them as negative features $\{f_{neg}^M\}$ with the same size as the anchor sample. Thus, we can calculate the contrastive loss as follows:

$$L_{CL}\left(f_{anchor}^M, f_{pos}^M, f_{neg}^M\right) = -\log \frac{exp\left(f_{anchor}^M \cdot f_{pos}^M\right)}{exp\left(f_{anchor}^M \cdot f_{pos}^M\right) + \sum_1^{B-1} exp\left(f_{anchor}^M \cdot f_{neg}^M\right)} \tag{3}$$

where "·" denotes dot product, B is the batch size. With contrastive learning, the shared encoder can be enhanced to extract more domain-independent content information.

MCI Classification. Taking the clinical reliability of the synthesized image into account, we further incorporate an MCI classifier (Cls) into the master network and use the feedback from classification results to improve the diagnostic quality of the synthesized images. The structure of the classifier is designed as binary classification CNN. Specifically, the synthesized SPET image s_{syn} with the size of 128×128 is first passed into three convolutional blocks with a kernel size of 3×3, stride of 1, and padding of 1, to halve the feature map size and increase the number of channels. Subsequently, the obtained feature maps are fed into three linear layers, followed by a sigmoid function to classify whether the synthesized image is from MCI patient. The closer the classification result is to 0, the more likely the image is to be from a patient with MCI. The BCE loss is adopted as classification loss, and $c_{s_{syn}}$, c_S represent class labels of s_{syn} and s.

$$L_{Classify}\left(c_{s_{syn}}, c_S\right) = -\left[c_S * log c_{s_{syn}} + (1 - c_S) * log\left(1 - c_{s_{syn}}\right)\right] \qquad (4)$$

2.2 Auxiliary Network

Unlike the master network which aims to extract shared information from the LPET domain, the auxiliary network is intended to extract the shared information from the SPET domain. By constraining the consistency of the shared information extracted by the two networks, the inter-domain shared information can be maximized, thus helping the master network to further improve the synthesis performance. The structure of the auxiliary network is identical to that of the master network. We use the same losses as the master network to constrain the auxiliary network, which is calculated as follows.

$$L_{Auxiliary} = L_{GAN}(G_A, D_A) + \beta_1 L_1(G_A) + \beta_2 L_{CL}\left(f_{anchor}^A, f_{pos}^A, f_{neg}^A\right) \qquad (5)$$

where f_{anchor}^A, f_{pos}^A and f_{neg}^A are the local feature and corresponding positive/negative features in auxiliary network, β_1 and β_2 are hyperparameters to balance the loss terms. $L_{GAN}(G_A, D_A)$, $L_1(G_A)$ and $L_{CL}\left(f_{anchor}^A, f_{pos}^A, f_{neg}^A\right)$ are calculated in the same manner as the corresponding loss in the master network detailed above.

2.3 Domain Alignment Module

In order to maximize the shared information between the LPET and SPET domains. We innovatively design a domain alignment (DA) module to align the features, F_L and F_S, extracted by master network and auxiliary network from LPET and SPET domains, respectively. Specifically, we introduce a feature discriminator D_F using features F_L and F_S as input to determine whether the input feature is extracted from SPET or LPET domain. Through adversarial learning, the features from the two domains are encouraged to be consistent, thus enabling the maximization of inter-domain shared information. The architecture of D_F is constructed as Convolution-LeakyReLU-Convolution-BatchNorm-LeakyReLU-Convolution, with a sigmoid activation function to produce the final output.

Moreover, considering the JS divergence could minimize the distribution differences of data, we further employ it to narrow the gap between the distributions of F_L and F_S to achieve domain alignment. The specific calculation of JS divergence and domain alignment adversarial loss are defined as:

$$JS(F_L, F_S) = \frac{1}{2} \sum F_L log \frac{F_L + \varepsilon}{\frac{F_L + F_S}{2} + \varepsilon} + \frac{1}{2} \sum F_S log \frac{F_S + \varepsilon}{\frac{F_S + F_L}{2} + \varepsilon} \qquad (6)$$

$$L_{GAN}(F_L, F_S) = E_{F_L}\left[(D_F(F_L) - 1)^2\right] + E_l\left[D_F(F_S)^2\right] \qquad (7)$$

The positive constant ε in Eq. (6) is introduced to avoid the null denominator and set as le-8 in our experiments. Based on all the above, the overall loss function of master network is shown as below:

$$L_{Master} = \lambda_1 L_{GAN}(G_M, D_M) + L_1(G_M) + \lambda_2 L_{CL}\left(f_{anchor}^M, f_{pos}^M, f_{pos}^M\right)$$
$$+ \lambda_3 L_{Classify}\left(c_{S_{syn}}, c_S\right) + \lambda_4 JS(F_L, F_S) + \lambda_5 L_{GAN}(F_L, F_S) \qquad (8)$$

2.4 Implementation Details

The proposed BiC-GAN model is trained alternatively as the original GAN. Specifically, we first fix the G_M, G_A and C to train the D_M, D_A and D_F, and then fix the D_M, D_A and D_F to train the G_M, G_A and C. All experiments are conducted on the PyTorch framework with the NVIDIA GeForce GTX 1080Ti with 11 GB memory. And the whole training process lasts for 300 epochs, utilizing Adam optimizer with batch size 4. In the first 100 epochs, the learning rates for both generator and discriminator networks are fixed as 0.0002, then linearly decay to 0 in the next 200 epochs. And the classifier learning rate is fixed to 0.0002 in all 300 epochs.

Based on our parameter selection studies, α_1 and α_2 in Eq. (1) are set to 300 and 30 to boost the performance of the synthesis task, while the ratio of the two is set as 1:1 for better maximization of shared information in the auxiliary network. To balance the loss terms, β_1 and β_2 are set as 100 and 1, λ_1, λ_2, λ_3, λ_4 and λ_5 are respectively set as 3, 3, 0.1, 0.01, and 1. In the test stage, only G_M is required to synthesize the SPET image.

3 Experiments and Results

We evaluate the proposed method on a Real Human Brain dataset, which contains paired LPET and SPET images collected from 16 subjects, including 8 normal control (NC) subjects and 8 mild cognitive impairment (MCI) subjects. To prevent the over-fitting problem caused by the limited samples, we split each 3D scan with the size of $128 \times 128 \times 128$ into 128 2D slices of size 128×128 and select 60 slices whose pixels are not all black as samples, thus extending the number of samples from 16 to 960. For quantitative comparison, three standard metrics are employed to study the performance of these methods, including peak signalo-noise ratio (PSNR), structural similarity index (SSIM), and normalized root-mean-square error (NRMSE). Note that, following AR-GAN [28], we compute these metrics on the entire 3D image including zero and non-zero pixels.

3.1 Ablation Studies

To verify the contributions of key components in the proposed BiC-GAN model, we break them up and reassemble them based on the GAN. Concretely, our experiment settings include: (1) the GAN network (i.e., *LEncoder* + *SSynDec* + *D_M*); (2) the BiC-GAN without contrastive learning and classifier (denoted as BiC-GAN w/o CL&Cls), (3) the BiC-GAN without contrastive learning (denoted as BiC-GAN w/o CL), and (4) the proposed BiC-GAN model. The qualitative results are presented in Fig. 2, from where we can clearly see that the synthesized images by the proposed method (4) are more analogous to the ground truth and preserve more content details with respect to the previous variant for both NC and MCI subjects, especially the regions indicated by the red boxes. The quantitative results are given in Table 1, it can be found that our proposed method progressively boosts the SPET image synthesis performance with the incorporation of each key component. Specifically, compared with the GAN model, our proposed method boosts the PSNR by 1.438dB for NC subjects and by 1.957dB for MCI subjects, respectively. Furthermore, we also calculate the classification accuracy using LPET images and synthetic SPET images separately. On the classification model pre-trained by target images, the classification accuracy using only LPET images is 76.7%, while our synthetic SPET images achieve a higher accuracy of 86.7%.

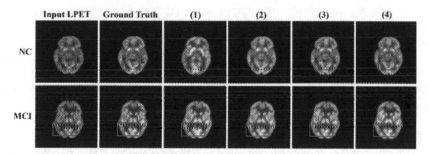

Fig. 2. Qualitative comparison of the proposed method with three variant models.

Table 1. Quantitative comparison of the proposed method with three variant models.

Method	NC subjects			MCI subjects		
	PSNR	SSIM	NRMSE	PSNR	SSIM	NRMSE
(1) GAN	26.819	0.893	0.187	26.307	0.883	0.194
(2) BiC-GAN w/o CL&Cls	28.064	0.897	0.167	27.946	0.889	0.173
(3) BiC-GAN w/o CL	28.161	0.893	0.166	28.146	0.890	0.170
(4) **Proposed**	**28.257**	**0.898**	**0.165**	**28.264**	**0.890**	**0.168**

3.2   Comparison with Existing State-of-the-Art Methods

To demonstrate the superiority of our proposed BiC-GAN method, we compare our method with four state-of-the-art image synthesis methods, including Stack GAN [12], GDL-GAN [26], Ea-GAN [27], and AR-GAN [28]. The quantitative results are reported in Table 2. As observed, the proposed method significantly outperforms the first three methods with comparable PSNR with the latest PET synthesis method AR-GAN. For NC subjects, our method enhances the synthesized image quality by 0.993dB PSNR, 0.006 SSIM, and 0.013 NRMSE in comparison with GDL-GAN. For MCI subjects, our method achieves the best overall performance with PSNR 28.264dB, SSIM 0.899, and NRMSE 0.168. Moreover, we have performed paired t-test to check whether the improvements are statistically significant. In most cases, the results show that the p-values are smaller than 0.05. Note that, although our BiC-GAN has minor improvement over AR-GAN, our BiC-GAN is lighter in model complexity. Concretely, our method contains 33M parameters while the AR-GAN has 8M parameters more. In terms of computational effort, our method costs 4.56 GFLOPs while the AR-GAN requires 7.57 GFLOPs.

We also present the qualitative comparison results in Fig. 3, where the first and second rows display the real SPET (ground truth) and synthesized images by five methods for NC and MCI subjects, respectively. We can find that the Ea-GAN method obtains the worst synthesis results with the most blurred structure, the GDL-GAN enriches the edge information of the generated image but its output still obviously differs from the ground truth. And the synthesized PET images of the proposed method for both NC and MCI subjects are most analogous to the ground truth, presenting sharper textures and more details compared with other generated results, especially the regions marked by the red boxes. In general, both qualitative and quantitative results demonstrate the superiority of our method in comparison with other advanced image synthesis methods.

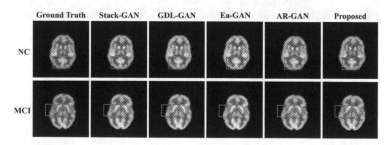

Fig. 3.   Visual comparison of the proposed method with four state-of-the-art approaches.

Table 2. Quantitative comparison of the proposed method with four state-of-the-art approaches. (*: T-test is conducted on proposed method and the comparison methods.)

Method	NC subjects			MCI subjects		
	PSNR	SSIM	NRMSE	PSNR	SSIM	NRMSE
Stack-GAN [15]	27.101*	0.891*	0.181*	26.769*	0.884*	0.194*
GDL-GAN [26]	27.264*	0.893	0.178*	27.081*	0.886	0.186*
Ea-GAN [27]	26.834*	0.891*	0.189*	26.385*	0.882*	0.202*
AR-GAN [28]	**28.396**	0.896	0.166	28.106*	**0.891**	**0.166**
Proposed	28.257	**0.898**	**0.165**	**28.264**	0.890	0.168

4 Conclusion

In this work, we presented a classification-aided bi-directional contrastive GAN for high-quality PET image synthesis from corresponding LPET image. Considering the shared content and structure information between LPET and SPET domains is helpful for improving synthesis performance, we innovatively designed a master network and an auxiliary network to extract shared information from LPET and SPET domains, respectively. And the contrastive learning strategy was introduced to boost the image representation capability, thus acquiring more domain-independent information. To maximize the shared information extracted from the two domains, we further applied a domain alignment module to constrain the consistency of the shared information extracted by the master and auxiliary networks. Moreover, an MCI classification task was incorporated in the master network to further improve the clinical applicability of the synthesized PET image through direct feedback from the classification task. Extensive experiments conducted on Real Human Brain dataset had demonstrated that our method achieves state-of-the-art performance by both qualitative and quantitative results. Considering the existence of extensive unpaired SPET images in clinics, in our future work, we will extend our method with semi-supervised learning for superior performance.

Acknowledgement. This work is supported by National Natural Science Foundation of China (NFSC 62071314).

References

1. Johnson, K.A., Schultz, A., Betensky, R.A., et al.: Tau positron emission tomographic imaging in aging and early Alzheimer disease. Ann. Neurol. **79**(1), 110–119 (2016)
2. Daerr, S., Brendel, M., Zach, C., et al.: Evaluation of early-phase [18 F]-florbetaben PET acquisition in clinical routine cases. NeuroImage Clin. **14**, 77–86 (2017)
3. Huang, B., Law, M.W.M., Khong, P.L.: Whole-body PET/CT scanning: estimation of radiation dose and cancer risk. Med. Phys. **251**(1), 166–174 (2009)
4. Wang, Y., Zhang, P., Ma, G., et al.: Predicting standard-dose PET image from low-dose PET and multimodal MR images using mapping-based sparse representation. Phys. Med. Biol. **61**(2), 791–812 (2016)

5. Kang, J., Gao, Y., Shi, F., et al.: Prediction of standard-dose brain PET image by using MRI and low-dose brain [18F] FDG PET images. Med. Phys. **42**(9), 5301–5309 (2015)
6. Wang, Y., Ma, G., An, L., et al.: Semi-supervised tripled dictionary learning for standard-dose PET image prediction using low-dose PET and multimodal MRI. IEEE Trans. Biomed. Eng. **64**(3), 569–579 (2016)
7. Zhan, B., Xiao, J., Cao, C., et al.: Multi-constraint generative adversarial network for dose prediction in radiotherapy. Med. Image Anal. **77**, 102339 (2022)
8. Xiang, L., Wang, Q., Nie, D., et al.: Deep embedding convolutional neural network for synthesizing CT image from T1-Weighted MR image. Med. Image Anal. **47**, 31–44 (2018)
9. Tang, P., Yang, P., et al.: Unified medical image segmentation by learning from uncertainty in an end-to-end manner. Knowl.-Based Syst. **241**, 108215 (2022)
10. Shi, Y., Zu, C., Hong, M., et al.: ASMFS: adaptive-similarity-based multi-modality feature selection for classification of Alzheimer's disease. Pattern Recogn. **126**, 108566 (2022)
11. Hu, L., Li, J., Peng, X., et al.: Semi-supervised NPC segmentation with uncertainty and attention guided consistency. Knowl.-Based Syst. **239**, 108021 (2022)
12. Wang, Y., Yu, B., Wang, L., et al.: 3D conditional generative adversarial networks for high-quality PET image estimation at low dose. Neuroimage **174**, 550–562 (2018)
13. Li, H., Peng, X., Zeng, J., et al.: Explainable attention guided adversarial deep network for 3D radiotherapy dose distribution prediction. Knowl.-Based Syst. **241**, 108324 (2022)
14. Bi, L., Kim, J., Kumar, A., Feng, D., Fulham, M.: Synthesis of positron emission tomography (PET) images via multi-channel generative adversarial networks (GANs). In: Cardoso, M.J. (ed.) CMMI/SWITCH/RAMBO-2017. LNCS, vol. 10555, pp. 43–51. Springer, Cham (2017). https://doi.org/10.1007/978-3-319-67564-0_5
15. Wang, Y., Zhou, L., Yu, B., et al.: 3D auto-context-based locality adaptive multi-modality GANs for PET synthesis. IEEE Trans. Med. Imaging **38**(6), 1328–1339 (2019)
16. Lei, Y., Dong, X., Wang, T., et al.: Whole-body PET estimation from low count statistics using cycle-consistent generative adversarial networks. Phys. Med. Biol. **64**(21), 215017 (2019)
17. Luo, Y., et al.: 3D transformer-GAN for high-quality PET reconstruction. In: de Bruijne, M., et al. (eds.) MICCAI 2021. LNCS, vol. 12906, pp. 276–285. Springer, Cham (2021). https://doi.org/10.1007/978-3-030-87231-1_27
18. Xie, X., Chen, J., Li, Y., Shen, L., Ma, K., Zheng, Y.: MI\$^2\$GAN: generative adversarial network for medical image domain adaptation using mutual information constraint. In: Martel, A.L., Abolmaesumi, P., Stoyanov, D., Mateus, D., Zuluaga, M.A., Zhou, S.K., Racoceanu, D., Joskowicz, L. (eds.) MICCAI 2020. LNCS, vol. 12262, pp. 516–525. Springer, Cham (2020). https://doi.org/10.1007/978-3-030-59713-9_50
19. Wang, K., Zhan, B., Zu, C., et al.: Semi-supervised medical image segmentation via a tripled-uncertainty guided mean teacher model with contrastive learning. Med. Image Anal. **79**, 102447 (2022)
20. Hadsell, R., Chopra, S., LeCun, Y.: Dimensionality reduction by learning an invariant mapping. In: IEEE Computer Society Conference on Computer Vision and Pattern Recognition, New York, pp. 1735–1742. IEEE (2006)
21. Xie, E., Ding, J., Wang, W., et al.: DetCo: unsupervised contrastive learning for object detection. In: Proceedings of the IEEE/CVF International Conference on Computer Vision, pp. 8392–8401. IEEE (2021)
22. He, K., Fan, H., Wu, Y., et al: Momentum contrast for unsupervised visual representation learning. In: Proceedings of the IEEE/CVF Conference on Computer Vision and Pattern Recognition, pp. 9726–9735. IEEE (2020)
23. Zeng, J., Xie, P.: Contrastive self-supervised learning for graph classification. In: Proceedings of the AAAI Conference on Artificial Intelligence, vol. 35, no. 12, pp. 10824–10832. AAAI (2021)

24. Chen, S., Bortsova, G., García-Uceda Juárez, A., van Tulder, G., de Bruijne, M.: Multi-task attention-based semi-supervised learning for medical image segmentation. In: Shen, D., et al. (eds.) MICCAI 2019. LNCS, vol. 11766, pp. 457–465. Springer, Cham (2019). https://doi.org/10.1007/978-3-030-32248-9_51

25. Isola, P., Zhu, J.Y., Zhou, T., et al.: Image-to-image translation with conditional adversarial networks. In: IEEE Computer Society Conference on Computer Vision and Pattern Recognition, Honolulu, pp. 1125–1134. IEEE (2017)

26. Nie, D., Trullo, R., Lian, J., et al.: Medical image synthesis with deep convolutional adversarial networks. IEEE Trans. Biomed. Eng. **65**(12), 2720–2730 (2018)

27. Yu, B., Zhou, L., Wang, L., et al.: Ea-gans: edge-aware generative adversarial networks for cross-modality mr image synthesis. IEEE Trans. Med. Imaging **38**(7), 1750–1762 (2019)

28. Luo, Y., Zhou, L., Zhan, B., et al.: Adaptive rectification based adversarial network with spectrum constraint for high-quality PET image synthesis. Med. Image Anal. **77**, 102335 (2021)

Swin Deformable Attention U-Net Transformer (SDAUT) for Explainable Fast MRI

Jiahao Huang[1,2], Xiaodan Xing[1], Zhifan Gao[3], and Guang Yang[1,2(✉)]

[1] National Heart and Lung Institute, Imperial College London, London, UK
g.yang@imperial.ac.uk
[2] Cardiovascular Research Centre, Royal Brompton Hospital, London, UK
[3] School of Biomedical Engineering, Sun Yat-sen University, Guangzhou, China

Abstract. Fast MRI aims to reconstruct a high fidelity image from partially observed measurements. Exuberant development in fast MRI using deep learning has been witnessed recently. Meanwhile, novel deep learning paradigms, e.g., Transformer based models, are fast-growing in natural language processing and promptly developed for computer vision and medical image analysis due to their prominent performance. Nevertheless, due to the complexity of the Transformer, the application of fast MRI may not be straightforward. The main obstacle is the computational cost of the self-attention layer, which is the core part of the Transformer, can be expensive for high resolution MRI inputs. In this study, we propose a new Transformer architecture for solving fast MRI that coupled Shifted Windows Transformer with U-Net to reduce the network complexity. We incorporate deformable attention to construe the explainability of our reconstruction model. We empirically demonstrate that our method achieves consistently superior performance on the fast MRI task. Besides, compared to state-of-the-art Transformer models, our method has fewer network parameters while revealing explainability. The code is publicly available at https://github.com/ayanglab/SDAUT.

Keywords: Fast MRI · Transformer · XAI

1 Introduction

Although magnetic resonance imaging (MRI) is widely utilised in clinical practice, it has been restricted by the prolonged scanning time. Fast MRI has relied heavily on image reconstruction from undersampled k-space data, e.g., using parallel imaging, simultaneous multi-slice, and compressed sensing (CS) [3]. However, these conventional methods were suffered from limited acceleration factors or slow nonlinear optimisation. Deep learning has recently proven enormous

Supplementary Information The online version contains supplementary material available at https://doi.org/10.1007/978-3-031-16446-0_51.

success in a variety of research domains, as well as shown the capability to sub-stantially accelerate MRI reconstruction with fewer measurements.

With its superior reconstruction quality and processing speed, convolutional neural networks (CNNs) based fast MRI methods [23,26,27] enabled enhanced latent feature extraction by the deep hierarchical structure, and were successfully developed for a wide range of MRI sequences and clinical applications [4,14,19].

Recently, taking advantage of sequence-to-sequence and deeper architectures, Transformers [22] showed superiority in computer vision tasks [2,6,16], mainly ascribed to their larger receptive fields and long-range dependency [16,18] com-pared to their CNN counterparts. Transformer based methods were then swiftly developed in medical image analysis, e.g., for segmentation [7], cross-modality synthesis [20], and reconstruction [13] with superior performance obtained.

However, the dense attention design, e.g., in Vision Transformer (ViT) [6], was quite unfriendly to tasks working on high-resolution image inputs, e.g., MRI super-resolution and reconstruction, leading to excessive memory and compu-tational costs. Moreover, visual elements tend to have a substantial variance in scale, and features could be influenced by the redundant attention [15]. Attempts using sparse attention, e.g., Shifted Windows (Swin) Transformer [15] signifi-cantly alleviated the memory and computational costs that could better fit the MRI reconstruction scenario [10–12]. Nevertheless, the selection of windows in Swin Transformer was data agnostic, which limited the capability of modelling long-range relationships and turned Swin Transformer into an *attention-style CNN*. On the other hand, most existing deep learning based MRI reconstruction methods, including CNN and Transformer, are still black-boxes [25] that are intricate for interpretation by the end-users.

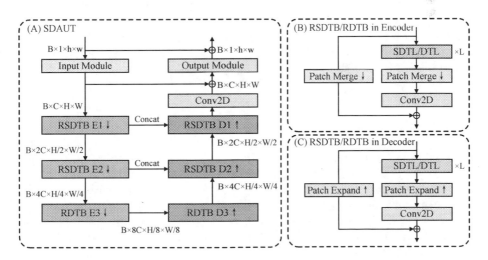

Fig. 1. (A) Structure of our Swin Deformable Attention U-Net Transformer (SDAUT); (B) Structure of residual (Swin) deformable Transformer Block (RSDTB/RDTB) in the encoder path; (C) The structure of RSDTB/RDTB in the decoder path.

Inspired by the deformable convolution networks [5], Xia et al. [24] proposed a ViT with deformable attention, namely DAT, in which the key and value were selected in a data-dependent way. DAT demonstrated advantages on classification and detection tasks; however, the dense attention design aggravated the memory and computational costs, making it difficult to be utilised in high-resolution MRI reconstruction.

In this work, we propose a Swin Deformable Attention U-Net Transformer (SDAUT) to combine dense and sparse deformable attention in different stages of a U-Net based Transformer. Sparse deformable attention is developed for shallow and high-resolution feature maps to preserve image details while reducing computational costs. Besides, dense deformable attention is leveraged for deep and low-resolution feature maps to exploit global information. This can also achieve long-range dependency at lower memory and computational costs. Furthermore, the utilisation of deformable attention can improve the reconstruction quality and enhance the explainability. We hypothesise that (1) the deformable attention Transformer can strengthen the performance of fast MRI with limited growth of computational cost; (2) the incorporation of U-Net architecture with both dense and sparse attention can reduce the number of network parameters significantly but improve the model performance; and (3) more importantly, our model is competent to achieve fast MRI while providing explainability.

2   Methods

2.1   U-Net Based Transformer

Our proposed SDAUT adopted an end-to-end U-Net [17] architecture, of which the input and output are undersampled zero-filled MRI images x_u and reconstructed MR images $\hat{x}_u$, respectively. The SDAUT is composed of three modules (Fig. 1): the input module (IM), the U-Net based Transformer module (UTM), and the output module (OM), which can be expressed as $F_{\mathrm{IM}} = \mathrm{H_{IM}}(x_u)$, $F_{\mathrm{UTM}} = \mathrm{H_{UTM}}(F_{\mathrm{IM}})$, and $F_{\mathrm{OM}} = \mathrm{H_{OM}}(F_{\mathrm{UTM}} + F_{\mathrm{IM}})$.

Input Module and Output Module. The input module is a 2D convolutional layer (Conv2D) with the stride of the patch size s, which turns pixels in an area of $s \times s$ into a patch and maps the shallow inputs $x_u \in \mathbb{R}^{1 \times h \times w}$ to deep feature representations $F_{\mathrm{IM}} \in \mathbb{R}^{C \times H \times W}$ ($H = h/s$ and $W = w/s$).

The output module is composed of a pixel shuffle Conv2D with the scale of the patch size s and a Conv2D. This module recovers the pixels from patches and maps the deep feature representations $(F_{\mathrm{IM}} + F_{\mathrm{UTM}}) \in \mathbb{R}^{C \times H \times W}$ to shallow output images $F_{\mathrm{OM}} \in \mathbb{R}^{1 \times h \times w}$. A residual connection from the input of the IM to the output of the OM turns the network into a refinement function $\hat{x}_u = F_{\mathrm{OM}} + x_u$ to stable the training and accelerate the converge process.

U-Net Based Transformer Module. Our novel UTM comprises six cascaded residual Transformer blocks (Fig. 1), where two downsampling residual Swin deformable Transformer blocks (RSDTBs) and one downsampling residual deformable Transformer block (RDTB) are cascaded in the encoder path, and one upsampling RDTB and two upsampling RSDTBs are in the symmetric decoder path. Between the downsampling and upsampling Transformer blocks with the same scale, skip connection and concatenation are utilised to pass the information in the encoder path directly to the decoder path, for better feature preservation in different stages. Three cascaded downsampling Transformer blocks can be expressed as $F_{E1} = H_{E1}(F_{IM})$, $F_{E1} = H_{E2}(F_{E1})$ and $F_{E3} = H_{E3}(F_{E2})$. Three cascaded upsampling Transformer blocks can be expressed as $F_{D3} = H_{D3}(F_{E3})$, $F_{D2} = H_{D2}(\text{Concat}(F_{D3}, F_{E2}))$ and $F_{D1} = H_{D1}(\text{Concat}(F_{D2}, F_{E1}))$. The final Conv2D can be expressed as $F_{UTM} = H_{CONV}(F_{D1})$.

Residual Swin Deformable Transformer Block. As Fig. 1(B) and (C) shown, an RSDTB consists of L cascaded Swin deformable Transformer layers (SDTLs) at the beginning and a Conv2D at the end. A residual connection is applied to connect the input and output of the RSDTB.

For the downsampling RSDTBs in the encoder path, two patch merging layers [15] are placed behind the SDTLs and in the shortcut connection to reduce the patch number (patch resolution) and increase the channel number (depth). For the upsampling RSDTBs in the decoder path, the patch merging layers are replaced by patch expending layers [1] to enlarge the patch number (patch resolution) and reduce the channel number (depth). The RSDTB can be expressed as $F_{i,j} = H_{SDTL_{i,j}}(F_{i,j-1})$ $(j = 1, 2, ..., L)$, and $F_i = H_{CONV_i}(H_{S_i}(F_{i,j})) + H_{S_i}(F_{i,0})$. In the encoder, $i \in \{E1, E2, E3\}$ and H_{S_i} denotes the patch merging layer. In the decoder, $i \in \{D3, D2, D1\}$ and H_{S_i} denotes the patch expending layer.

Swin Deformable Transformer Layer. The Swin deformable Transformer layer adopts a standard Transformer layer structure, which can be expressed as $F'_{i,j} = H_{SDMSA}(H_{LN}(F_{i,j-1})) + F_{i,j-1}$ and $F_{i,j} = H_{MLP}(H_{LN}(F'_{i,j})) + F'_{i,j}$. H_{SDMSA} denotes the Swin deformable multi-head self-attention, which is discussed in the next section. H_{LN} and H_{MLP} denote the Layer normalisation layer and multi-layer perceptron respectively.

2.2 Shifted Windows Deformable Attention

We propose a novel Swin deformable multi-head self-attention (SDMSA). Compared to deformable multi-head self-attention (DMSA) in DAT [24], spatial constraints are applied in SDMSA (Fig. 2). For an input feature map X, it is first split into N_w windows spatially, and then divided into N_h heads along the channels, which can be expressed as follows

$$X = (X^1, ..., X^w, ..., X^{N_w}), \quad X^w = \text{Concat}(X_1^w, ...X_h^w, ..., X_{N_h}^w), \quad (1)$$

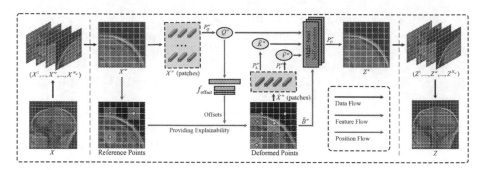

Fig. 2. The structure of Swin deformable Transformer layer, which also provides model explainability. The subscript of the heads $(1, ..., h, ..., N_h)$ is omitted for a clear illustration.

where $N_w = HW/W_s^2$ is the number of windows, and N_h is the number of heads. For an input feature map $X_h^w \in \mathbb{R}^{C/N_h \times W_s \times W_s}$, a set of uniform grid points $p \in \mathbb{R}^{W_s/r \times W_s/r \times 2}$ are generated as the reference points with a downsampling factor r. A two-layer CNN $f_{\text{offset}}(\cdot)$ with GeLU layer is trained to learn the offsets Δp of every reference point p. A bilinear interpolation function $\Phi(\cdot; \cdot)$ is utilised to sample the input feature map X_h^w according to the deformed points $p + \Delta p$, and generate the sampled feature map $\tilde{X}_h^w \in \mathbb{R}^{C/N_h \times W_s/r \times W_s/r}$. Details of $f_{\text{offset}}(\cdot)$ and $\Phi(\cdot; \cdot)$ can be found in [24].

The deformable attention for the wth window h^{th} head feature map X_h^w can be expressed as follows

$$Q_h^w = X_h^w P_{Q_h}{}^w, \quad \tilde{K}_h^w = \tilde{X}_h^w P_{K_h}{}^w, \quad \tilde{V}_h^w = \tilde{X}_h^w P_{V_h}{}^w, \tag{2}$$

$$\text{with} \quad \Delta p = a \tanh(f_{\text{offset}}(p)), \quad \tilde{X}_h^w = \Phi(X_h^w; p + \Delta p), \tag{3}$$

$$Z_h^w = \text{Attention}(Q_h^w, \tilde{K}_h^w, \tilde{V}_h^w) = \text{SoftMax}\left(Q_h^w \tilde{K}_h^{w^T}/\sqrt{d} + \tilde{B}_h^w\right) \tilde{V}_h^w, \tag{4}$$

where $P_{Q_h}{}^w$ and $P_{K_h}{}^w$ and $P_{V_h}{}^w$ are the projection matrices (Conv2Ds were used in practice) for query Q_h^w, key $\tilde{K}_h^w$, and value $\tilde{V}_h^w$. Besides, $\tilde{B}_h^w$ is the relative position bias, $d = C/N_h$ is the dimension of each head, and $a \tanh(\cdot)$ is used to avoid the overly-large offsets.

The attention outputs Z_h^w of different heads are concatenated with a projection $P_O{}^w$. Then the output Z^w of different windows are combined to generate the output Z of SDMSA, which can be expressed as follows

$$Z^w = \text{Concat}(Z_1^w, ...Z_h^w, ..., Z_{N_h}^w)P_O{}^w, \quad Z = (Z^1, ..., Z^w, ..., Z^{N_w}). \tag{5}$$

2.3 Loss Function

A content loss is applied to train our SDAUT, which is composed of a pixel-wise Charbonnier loss $\mathcal{L}_{\text{pixel}}$, a frequency Charbonnier loss $\mathcal{L}_{\text{freq}}$ and a perceptual VGG l_1 loss $\mathcal{L}_{\text{VGG}}$ between reconstructed MR images $\hat{x}_u$ and ground truth MR images x that totals $\mathcal{L}_{\text{Total}}(\theta) = \alpha \mathcal{L}_{\text{pixel}}(\theta) + \beta \mathcal{L}_{\text{freq}}(\theta) + \gamma \mathcal{L}_{\text{VGG}}(\theta)$.

3   Experimental Settings and Results

3.1   Implementation Details and Evaluation Methods

We used the Calgary Campinas dataset [21] to train and test our methods. In total, 67 cases of 12-channel T1-weight 3D acquisitions were included in our study and randomly divided into training (40 cases), validation (7 cases) and independent testing (20 cases) in a ratio of 6:1:3 approximately. For each case, 100 2D sagittal-view slices near the centre were used. Root sum squared was applied to convert multi-channel data into single channel data.

Our proposed methods (except 'KKDDKK-O-1' and 'KKDDKK-NO-1') were trained for 100,000 steps with a batch size of 8, on two NVIDIA RTX 3090 GPUs with 24 GB GPU RAM. The proposed methods with setting of 'KKDDKK-O-1' or 'KKDDKK-NO-1' were trained for 100,000 steps with a batch size of 2, on two NVIDIA Quadro RTX GPUs with 48 GB GPU RAM. The setting naming rule is explained in Ablation Studies. For the network parameter, the layer number L, downsampling factor r and window size W_s were set to 6, 1 and 8. The channel number and head number of different blocks were set to $[90, 180, 360, 720, 360, 180]$ and $[6, 12, 24, 24, 24, 12]$. The initial learning rate was set to 2×10^{-4} and decayed every 10,000 steps by 0.5 from the $50,000^{\text{th}}$ step. α, β and γ in the total loss function were set to 15, 0.1 and 0.0025, respectively.

Our proposed SDAUT was compared with other fast MRI methods, e.g., DAGAN [26], nPIDD-GAN [9], Swin-UNet [1] and SwinMR [11] using Gaussian 1D 30% and radial 10% mask.

Peak Signal-to-Noise Ratio (PSNR), Structural Similarity Index Measure (SSIM), and Fréchet Inception Distance (FID) [8] were used as evaluation metrics. Multiply Accumulate Operations (MACs) were applied to estimate the computational complexity for an input size of $1 \times 256 \times 256$.

Table 1. Quantitative comparison results using a Gaussian 1D 30% and radial 10% mask. (SDAUT$_x$: SDAUT-KKDDKK-O-x; MACs of the generator without the discriminator in the GAN based model; †: $p < 0.05$ by paired t-Test compared with our proposed SDAUT$_1$; std: standard deviation.)

Method	MACs (G)	Gaussian 1D 30%			Radial 10%		
		SSIM $_{\text{mean (std)}}$	PSNR $_{\text{mean (std)}}$	FID	SSIM $_{\text{mean (std)}}$	PSNR $_{\text{mean (std)}}$	FID
ZF	-	$0.883\ (0.012)^{\dagger}$	$27.81\ (0.82)^{\dagger}$	156.38	$0.706\ (0.022)^{\dagger}$	$23.53\ (0.82)^{\dagger}$	319.45
DAGAN	33.97*	$0.924\ (0.010)^{\dagger}$	$30.41\ (0.82)^{\dagger}$	56.04	$0.822\ (0.024)^{\dagger}$	$25.95\ (0.85)^{\dagger}$	132.58
nPIDD-GAN	56.44*	$0.943\ (0.009)^{\dagger}$	$31.81\ (0.92)^{\dagger}$	26.15	$0.864\ (0.023)^{\dagger}$	$27.17\ (0.97)^{\dagger}$	82.86
SwinUNet	11.52	$0.951\ (0.008)^{\dagger}$	$32.52\ (0.98)^{\dagger}$	31.16	$0.844\ (0.027)^{\dagger}$	$26.41\ (0.97)^{\dagger}$	71.19
SwinMR	800.73	$0.955\ (0.009)^{\dagger}$	$33.05\ (1.09)^{\dagger}$	21.03	$0.876\ (0.022)^{\dagger}$	$27.86\ (1.02)^{\dagger}$	59.01
SDAUT$_2$	57.91	$0.956\ (0.009)^{\dagger}$	$33.00\ (1.12)^{\dagger}$	22.54	$0.867\ (0.025)^{\dagger}$	$27.52\ (1.05)^{\dagger}$	62.92
SDAUT$_1$	293.02	**0.963 (0.007)**	**33.92 (1.11)**	**20.45**	**0.885 (0.025)**	**28.28 (1.14)**	**55.12**

3.2   Comparison Studies

Table 1 shows the quantitative results of the comparison using a Gaussian 1D 30% and radial 10% mask. Results demonstrate that our proposed method outperforms other CNN based fast MRI methods, and achieves similar results compared to SwinMR but with significantly lower computation complexity.

3.3   Ablation Studies

We set four groups of ablation studies to investigate the influence of different block settings and utilisation of the deformable attention. We used 'K' and 'D' to denote the RSDTB and RDTB in the U-Net architecture respectively, '-O' and '-NO' to denote with and without deformation (Offset vs. Non-Offset), and '-x' to denote the patch size. For example, 'KKDDKK-O-1' denotes the model variant with a patch size of 1, containing 2 RSDTBs ('KK') and 1 RDTB ('D') in the encoder path, and 1 RDTB ('D') and 2 RSDTBs ('KK') in the decoder path that combines the dense and sparse attention with deformable attention ('-O'). 'KKKKKK-NO-2' denotes the model variant with a patch size of 2, containing 6 RSDTBs ('KKKKKK') without deformable attention ('-NO'), where only sparse attention is applied.

Figure 3 shows that a smaller patch size (with a larger patch resolution) yields better performance (SSIM, PSNR and FID), but entails a larger computational cost (MACs). The utilisation of deformable attention ('-O') improves the reconstruction quality with small computation complexity growth (MACs). For the comparison of block settings in the network, compared to the model only using sparse attention ('K'), the model using both dense ('D') and sparse attention ('K') achieves better performance (SSIM and PSNR), though at the sacrifice of slightly larger computational cost (MACs), especially with lower patch size. The quantitative results table of ablation studies is in the Supplementary.

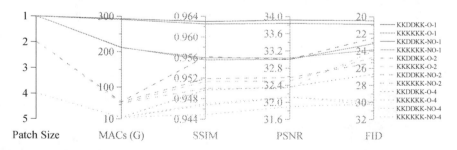

Fig. 3. Results of our ablation studies. 'K' and 'D' denote the RSDTB and RDTB in the U-Net architecture, respectively. '-O' and '-NO' represent with and without deformation (Offset vs. Non-Offset). It is of note that our best performed model variant 'KKDDKK-O-1' achieved better SSIM, PSNR and FID, but with relatively higher MACs.

4   Discussion and Conclusion

In this work, we have proposed a novel Swin Deformable Attention U-Net Transformer, i.e., SDAUT, for explainable fast MRI. Our experimental studies have proven our hypotheses:

(1) Deformable attention can strengthen the MRI reconstruction with only limited growth of computational cost. The MACs growth of using deformable attention has been no more than 1%.

(2) The incorporation of U-Net architecture can reduce the number of network parameters dramatically and enhance the model performance. Compared to SwinMR, which applies the Swin Transformer backbone with the same number of blocks and Transformer layers, our $SDAUT_2$ has achieved comparable performances with only 6.63% computational complexity and our $SDAUT_1$ has achieved better performance using 36.59% computational complexity (Table 1).

The combination of dense and sparse attention has gained superior model performance. This is because models with only sparse attention could encounter limitations of global dependency, and models applying only dense attention could increase the computational cost, yielding training difficulties. Figure 3 has shown that models using both dense and sparse attention ('KKDDKK') outperform models using only sparse attention ('KKKKKK'). However, the 'KKDDKK' model setting is more suitable when the patch resolution is not large (e.g., patch size 2 or 4). For smaller patch size of 1, the MACs have been increased by 37.98% (212.37G MACs for 'KKKKKK-O-1' vs. 293.02G MACs for 'KKDDKK-O-1'), which have lifted a much heavier computing burden.

(3) Our SDAUT has been competent to achieve fast MRI while unveiling model explainability (see Fig. 2). Figure 4(A)–(F) shows the deformed points, deformation fields and corresponding error maps between undersampled zero-

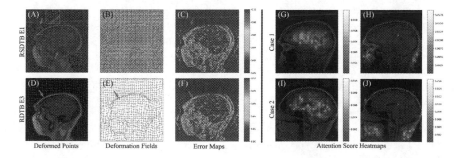

Fig. 4. (A)(D) Deformed points in RSDTB E1 (Encoder 1st block) and RDTB E3; (B)(E) Deformation fields in RSDTB E1 and RDTB E3; (C)(F) Error maps between the undersampled zero-filled MR images and the corresponding ground truth MR images; (G)–(J) Attention score heatmaps for a given query (green star) in RDTB E3. (Color figure online)

filled MR images x_u and corresponding ground truth x (more examples in the Supplementary). We can observe that the deformation field has shown clear differences in information-rich areas (e.g., brain tissue boundaries) and areas with more artefacts (e.g., remnant aliasing on both left and right sides of the head), deciphering higher uncertainties of the reconstruction. Deformable points have been trained to *recognise* and move to the border of the brain, reducing extraneous attention, and therefore improving the model performance.

Figure 4(G)–(J) shows the attention score heatmaps for a given query (green star) from different heads in RDTB E3 (more examples in the Supplementary). We can observe that different heads have *paid their attention* to different structures (features) in the MRI data, e.g., Fig. 4(G)(I) for the brain tissues and Fig. 4(H)(J) for the vertical high-contrast area (front mouth and back neck regions). Results have also shown that attention score maps show that a fixed head always focuses on specific structures in MSA, revealing how the multi-head mechanism works. Transformer can comprehend different features from the input, and perform attention operations for multiple features using its multi-heads mechanism, which has similar behaviours compared to kernels for different channels in the CNN based models.

Acknowledgement. This study was supported in part by the ERC IMI (101005122), the H2020 (952172), the MRC (MC/PC/21013), the Royal Society (IEC\ NSFC\211235), the NVIDIA Academic Hardware Grant Program, the SABER project supported by Boehringer Ingelheim Ltd, and the UKRI Future Leaders Fellowship (MR/V023799/1).

References

1. Cao, H., Wang, Y., Chen, J., Jiang, D., Zhang, X., Tian, Q., Wang, M.: Swin-Unet: Unet-like pure transformer for medical image segmentation. arXiv e-prints. arXiv:2105.05537, May 2021
2. Carion, N., Massa, F., Synnaeve, G., Usunier, N., Kirillov, A., Zagoruyko, S.: End-to-end object detection with transformers. In: Vedaldi, A., Bischof, H., Brox, T., Frahm, J.-M. (eds.) ECCV 2020. LNCS, vol. 12346, pp. 213–229. Springer, Cham (2020). https://doi.org/10.1007/978-3-030-58452-8_13
3. Chen, Y., et al.: AI-based reconstruction for fast MRI-a systematic review and meta-analysis. Proc. IEEE **110**(2), 224–245 (2022)
4. Cheng, J., et al.: Learning data consistency and its application to dynamic MR imaging. IEEE Trans. Med. Imaging **40**(11), 3140–3153 (2021)
5. Dai, J., et al.: Deformable convolutional networks. In: Proceedings of the IEEE International Conference on Computer Vision (ICCV), October 2017
6. Dosovitskiy, A., et al.: An image is worth 16×16 words: Transformers for image recognition at scale. arXiv e-prints. arXiv:2010.11929, October 2020
7. Hatamizadeh, A., et al.: UNETR: transformers for 3D medical image segmentation. In: Proceedings of the IEEE/CVF Winter Conference on Applications of Computer Vision (WACV), pp. 574–584, January 2022

8. Heusel, M., Ramsauer, H., Unterthiner, T., Nessler, B., Hochreiter, S.: GANs trained by a two time-scale update rule converge to a local Nash equilibrium. Adv. Neural Inf. Process. Syst. **30**, 1–9 (2017)

9. Huang, J., et al.: Edge-enhanced dual discriminator generative adversarial network for fast MRI with parallel imaging using multi-view information. Appl. Intell. (2021). https://doi.org/10.1007/s10489-021-03092-w

10. Huang, J., et al.: Data and physics driven learning models for fast MRI - fundamentals and methodologies from CNN, GAN to attention and transformers. arXiv e-prints. arXiv:2204.01706, April 2022

11. Huang, J., et al.: Swin transformer for fast MRI. Neurocomputing **493**, 281–304 (2022)

12. Huang, J., Wu, Y., Wu, H., Yang, G.: Fast MRI reconstruction: how powerful transformers are? arXiv e-prints. arXiv:2201.09400, January 2022

13. Korkmaz, Y., Yurt, M., Dar, S.U.H., Özbey, M., Cukur, T.: Deep MRI reconstruction with generative vision transformers. In: Haq, N., Johnson, P., Maier, A., Würfl, T., Yoo, J. (eds.) MLMIR 2021. LNCS, vol. 12964, pp. 54–64. Springer, Cham (2021). https://doi.org/10.1007/978-3-030-88552-6_6

14. Li, G., Lv, J., Tong, X., Wang, C., Yang, G.: High-resolution pelvic MRI reconstruction using a generative adversarial network with attention and cyclic loss. IEEE Access **9**, 105951–105964 (2021)

15. Liu, Z., et al.: Swin transformer: hierarchical vision transformer using shifted windows. In: Proceedings of the IEEE/CVF International Conference on Computer Vision (ICCV), pp. 10012–10022, October 2021

16. Parmar, N., et al.: Image transformer. In: International Conference on Machine Learning, pp. 4055–4064. PMLR (2018)

17. Ronneberger, O., Fischer, P., Brox, T.: U-net: convolutional networks for biomedical image segmentation. In: Navab, N., Hornegger, J., Wells, W.M., Frangi, A.F. (eds.) MICCAI 2015. LNCS, vol. 9351, pp. 234–241. Springer, Cham (2015). https://doi.org/10.1007/978-3-319-24574-4_28

18. Salimans, T., Karpathy, A., Chen, X., Kingma, D.P.: PixelCNN++: improving the PixelCNN with discretized logistic mixture likelihood and other modifications. arXiv e-prints. arXiv:1701.05517, January 2017

19. Schlemper, J., et al.: Stochastic deep compressive sensing for the reconstruction of diffusion tensor cardiac MRI. In: Frangi, A.F., Schnabel, J.A., Davatzikos, C., Alberola-López, C., Fichtinger, G. (eds.) MICCAI 2018. LNCS, vol. 11070, pp. 295–303. Springer, Cham (2018). https://doi.org/10.1007/978-3-030-00928-1_34

20. Shin, H.C., et al.: GANBERT: Generative adversarial networks with bidirectional encoder representations from transformers for MRI to PET synthesis. arXiv e-prints. arXiv:2008.04393, August 2020

21. Souza, R., et al.: An open, multi-vendor, multi-field-strength brain MR dataset and analysis of publicly available skull stripping methods agreement. NeuroImage **170**, 482–494 (2018)

22. Vaswani, A., et al.: Attention is all you need. In: Advances in Neural Information Processing Systems, vol. 30. Curran Associates, Inc. (2017)

23. Wang, S., et al.: Accelerating magnetic resonance imaging via deep learning. In: 2016 IEEE 13th International Symposium on Biomedical Imaging (ISBI), pp. 514–517. IEEE (2016)

24. Xia, Z., Pan, X., Song, S., Erran Li, L., Huang, G.: Vision transformer with deformable attention. arXiv e-prints. arXiv:2201.00520, January 2022

25. Yang, G., Ye, Q., Xia, J.: Unbox the black-box for the medical explainable AI via multi-modal and multi-centre data fusion: a mini-review, two showcases and beyond. Information Fusion **77**, 29–52 (2022)
26. Yang, G., et al.: DAGAN: deep de-aliasing generative adversarial networks for fast compressed sensing MRI reconstruction. IEEE Trans. Med. Imaging **37**, 1310–1321 (2018)
27. Yuan, Z., et al.: SARA-GAN: self-attention and relative average discriminator based generative adversarial networks for fast compressed sensing MRI reconstruction. Front. Neuroinform. **14**, 58 (2020)

Low-Dose CT Reconstruction via Dual-Domain Learning and Controllable Modulation

Xinchen Ye[1,2], Zheng Sun[1], Rui Xu[1,2(✉)], Zhihui Wang[1,2], and Haojie Li[1,2]

[1] DUT-RU International School of Information Science Engineering, Dalian
University of Technology, Dalian, China
xurui@dlut.edu.cn
[2] DUT-RU Co-research Center of Advanced ICT for Active Life, Dalian, China

Abstract. Existing CNN-based low-dose CT reconstruction methods
focus on restoring the degraded CT images by processing on the image
domain or the raw data (sinogram) domain independently, or leveraging
both domains by connecting them through some simple domain transform operators or matrices. However, both domains and their mutual
benefits are not fully exploited, which impedes the performance to go
step further. In addition, considering the subjective perceptual quality of
the restored image, it is more necessary for doctors to adaptively control
the denoising level for different regions or organs according to diagnosis
convenience, which cannot be done using existing deterministic networks.
To tackle these difficulties, this paper breaks away the shackles of general
paradigms and proposes a novel low-dose CT reconstruction framework
via dual-domain learning and controllable modulation. Specifically, we
propose a dual-domain base network to fully address the mutual dependencies between the image domain and sinogram domain. Upon this, we
integrate a controllable modulation module to adjust the latent features
of the base network, which allows to finely-grained control the reconstruction by considering the trade-off between artifacts reduction and
detail preservation to assist doctors in diagnosis. Experiments results on
Mayo clinic dataset and Osaka dataset demonstrate that our method
achieves superior performance.

Keywords: Low-dose CT · Reconstruction · Dual-domain ·
Controllable

1 Introduction

Computed tomography (CT) [3] is a popular diagnose assistant imagery method,
which is widely used in biology [13], medicine [18], airport security [1] and so

---

This work was supported by National Natural Science Foundation of China (NSFC)
under Grant 61772106, Grant 61702078 and Grant 61720106005, and by the Fundamental Research Funds for the Central Universities of China.

L. Wang et al. (Eds.): MICCAI 2022, LNCS 13436, pp. 549–559, 2022.
https://doi.org/10.1007/978-3-031-16446-0_52

on. Despite overwhelming evidence proving the contribution of CT in auxiliary diagnosis, its high radiation raises concerns about the risk of cancer or genetic damage. Thus, low-dose CT emerges with low radiation risk. However, the reduction of radiation dose brings negative impact on the imaging quality, e.g., noise or strip-type artifacts, leading to the decrease of diagnostic performance. Thus, effective processing techniques are urgently needed to yield high-quality CT images from their low-dose counterparts to solve the ill-posed inverse reconstruction problem and assist doctors in diagnosis and treatment.

Recently, most CNN-based methods do not rely on the projection data (sinogram), and can be directly applied on DICOM formatted low-dose CT images, which allows an easy integration into the current CNN workflow. e.g. RED-CNN [4], WGAN-VGG [19], MAP-NN [14], Q-AE [5], TransCT [22]. The main difficulty of post-processing methods comes from the non-stationary nature of the mottle noise and streak-like artifacts, which are caused by the back-projection process that projects sinogram into image domain. These artifacts are difficult to be removed because they often have strong magnitudes and do not obey any specific distribution models in the image domain. Therefore, some dual-domain low-dose CT reconstruction methods have been proposed to focus on the necessity of integrating the sinogram domain into the CNN-based methods. e.g. LPD [2], DP-ResNet [21]. Some of them process the sinogram data firstly and then re-project the processed sinogram data into CT image domain through a domain transform operation such as filtered back-projection (FBP) [9] or a transform operator module, and finally restore the CT images in the image domain. Others interact between two domains with hand-designed matrix which is used to simulate the projection process according to some prior knowledge and optimize the results iteratively.

However, existing dual-domain methods just process each domain independently, or connect both domains with some pre-defined domain transform operations or hand-designed prior matrix, which cannot fully exploit the mutual dependencies between both domains and may introduce unnecessary artifacts by the simple hand-designed ways of domain transformation. Besides, caused by mismatched resolution between the heterogeneous sinogram data and CT image, it is a challenge to implement adequate interaction between two domains and exploit their mutual benefits well. For example, the method proposed in LPD [2], where there is no information interaction between both domains, may cause a mismatch problem. The method proposed by TransCT [22] is to divide low-dose CT into high-frequency and low-frequency images through Gaussian filtering, and then use them as two branches for reconstruction and fusion, respectively. TransCT [22] does not actually use the information of sinogram domain, but only the information of image domain. Other methods such as LPD [2]and DP-ResNet [21] have proved that the two-domain method is better than the single-domain method. Therefore, we are motivated to propose a novel dual-domain framework to address the mutual dependencies through iteratively interlacing both domains with learnable convolution modules rather than any hand-designed prior matrix or operators.

In addition, existing methods use deterministic or fixed networks, which may require many noise-specific networks that need to be trained independently to deal with CT images with various noise levels. Furthermore, these methods usually aim to pursue high reconstruction accuracy in terms of the objective metrics, i.e., PSNR or SSIM. However, image quality assessment from personal opinion is relatively subjective, and high PSNR or SSIM values are not always consistent with high visual quality. As an important diagnose-assistant tool, CT images should pay more attention to the needs of doctors' diagnosis and should ensure rational de-noising level while protecting the texture of organs. This motivates us to design an interactive and controllable network for low-dose CT reconstruction, thus doctors can flexibly choose the results of corresponding denoising levels for different CT images or any specific organ and region according to their needs, so as to make the diagnosis more accurate.

In this paper, we propose a novel low-dose CT reconstruction method via dual-domain learning and controllable modulation to effectively reconstruct the low-dose CT images. As shown in Fig. 1, the framework consists of three branches, i.e., main branch, controller branch and fusion branch. The main branch is composed of several dual-domain blocks (DDB). Each DDB is composed of an PI block that transforms the features of sinogram domain into CT image features, and an PS block that takes image features as input and outputs sinogram features. Adaptive pooling layers [12] are used to realize the transformation and feature integration between both domains. Dense connections between DDBs are used to make the inputs from both domains pass through each stage of feature extraction and encourage the feature reuse. Thus, through iteratively projecting CT image features into sinogram domain and then back-projecting to image domain via learnable convolutions, the image details can be gradually preserved and simultaneously removing the noise. The controller branch takes a given adjustment parameter and a low-dose CT image as input, then the generated specialized features that characterize a desired denoising level are modulated on the features of DDB through fusion branch in a multi-scale fashion, enabling a richer depth representation. Experiments results on Mayo clinic dataset and Osaka dataset demonstrate that our method achieves superior performance in comparison with the other state-of-the-art methods, and can finely-grained control the reconstruction results according to the pre-defined adjustment hyper-parameter. Our contributions are summarized as follows:

1) An end-to-end deep controllable dual-domain network to realize highly accurate and dynamically adjusted low-dose CT reconstruction.
2) A dual-domain base network to fully exploit the mutual dependencies between heterogeneous data, benefiting the final reconstruction performance.
3) A controllable modulation module to realize the fine-grained control of low-dose CT reconstruction with arbitrary denoising level in one united model.

2   Method

Figure 1 outlines the whole architecture of our proposed framework. Let $I_L \in \mathbb{R}^{w \times h}$, $S_L \in \mathbb{R}^{w_l \times h_l}$ and α be the low-dose CT image, low-dose sinogram and the controller parameter as inputs, respectively. The goal is to predict the corresponding high-quality CT image $I_H \in \mathbb{R}^{w \times h}$. The framework can be divided into three branches, i.e., main branch (MB), controller branch (CB), and fusion branch (FB). MB can be regarded as our backbone and contains N stacked dual-domain blocks, while CB and FB include the same number of blocks as that of MB.

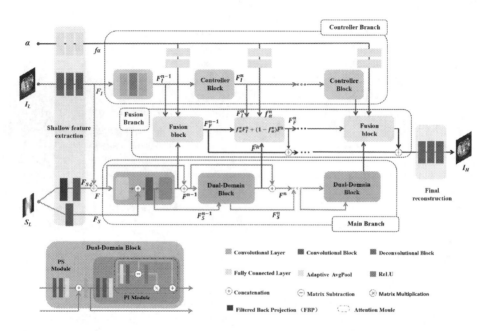

Fig. 1. Network architecture. Different colored rectangles are used to represent different branches and different operations in each branch. (Color figure online)

First, the shallow features $\{F_I, F_{S-I}\}, F_S, f_\alpha$ are extracted from I_L, S_L and α, respectively. The image features $\{F_I, F_{S-I}\}$ contains two groups that are extracted from I_L and S_L respectively, i.e., one directly obtained from I_L and the other transformed from sinogram features through the filtered back projection operation (FBP) operator on S_L:

$$F_I = ConvB^3(I_L), F_{S-I} = ConvB(\mathcal{FBP}(S_L)) \tag{1}$$

where $ConvB^3(\cdot)$ denotes consecutive three convolutional blocks $ConvB(\cdot)$, and each contains stacked batch normalization (BN) [8], 3×3 convolution and PReLU activation [7]. $\{F_I, F_{S-I}\}$ are then concatenated as the initial image features F.

Next, both image feature F and sinogram feature F_S are sent into MB, and the parameter feature f_α learned from fully connected layers together with F_I are fed into CB to obtain the controller features that are used to adjust the reconstruction results. Then, FB modulates the controller features onto the features of MB in a multi-scale fashion, and then output the final fused features F_F through concatenating all the features $\{F_F^n, n \in N\}$ from different fusion blocks. Finally, the high-quality CT image I_H is reconstructed from the fused features F_F through three convolutional blocks.

2.1 Main Branch (MB)

To realize the interaction between the image features F and the sinogram features F_S, we design our MB with N stacked dual-domain blocks (DDBs). As shown in the Fig. 1, each DDB is composed of an PS module and an PI module, connected by a convolution layer to adjust the channel dimension of features after concatenation.

PS takes image features as input and outputs sinogram features through two convolutional blocks and an adaptive pooling layer [12][1] that changes the size of the image features $\mathbb{R}^{w \times h}$ to meet that of sinogram $\mathbb{R}^{w_l \times h_l}$. We then concatenate the output of PS with the sinogram features of previous block F_S^{n-1}, and obtain the new sinogram features of current block F_S^n with a convolution layer:

$$F_S^n = Conv(Concat(PS^n(F^{n-1}), F_S^{n-1})), F_S^0 = F_S \qquad (2)$$

where n indicates current n-th DDB. $PS^n(\cdot)$ is the PS module in n-th DDB.

Next, PI first uses two convolutional blocks and an adaptive pooling layer to transform the features of sinogram domain F_S^n into CT image features. Then, we design a self-attention module to highlight and strengthen the useful structure and edge information of image features, which can preserve the image details and simultaneously remove the noise. Inspired by the feedback mechanism [20] that transmits features under a high-to-low-to-high resolution change process to highlight more effective image features, we use a pair operations of adaptive pooling layer and deconvolutional block[2] to compress the feature resolution to half of the original size $\mathbb{R}^{w/2 \times h/2}$ and unzip it to the original size $\mathbb{R}^{w \times h}$. Then, through the subtraction between the unzipped feature and the original feature, and the following activation from ReLU, we obtain the attention map, which is used to highlight the useful information of image features. The final CT image features of block n can be written as:

$$F^n = Concat(PI^n(F_S^{n-1}), F^{n-1})), F^0 = F \qquad (3)$$

where $PI^n(\cdot)$ denotes the n-th PI module.

Note that the interactions between different DDBs are exploited to make the inputs from both domains pass through each stage of feature extraction and encourage the feature reuse. Different from the work [2] that uses the FBP operator several times within their network, we only use it once at the beginning of the network. Through iteratively projecting CT image features into sinogram

---

[1] The adaptive pooling operation can reshape features with any size to a desired one.

[2] It contains stacked BN, deconvolution layer and PReLU activation.

domain and then back-projecting to image domain via learnable convolutions, the image details can be gradually preserved and simultaneously avoid the introduction of mottle noise and streak-like artifacts caused by FBP.

2.2 Controller Branch (CB) and Fusion Branch (FB)

The CB aims to generate a series of image features $\{F_I^n, n \in N\}$ from the shallow low-dose CT feature F_I through N controller blocks, and the adjustment features $\{F_\alpha^n, n \in N\}$ from f_α through two fully connected layers for each block. Each controller block is composed of two convolutional layers with an ReLU in the middle. These two groups of features can be further used to adaptively modulate on the features of dual-domain blocks in main branch through the fusion blocks, controlling the final reconstruction results. Upon this, we introduced a controller parameter α to adaptively modulate the features of CB onto those of MB. For a given fusion block n in FB, the fusion feature F_F^n can be expressed as the following formula:

$$F_F^n = f_\alpha^n \circ F_I^n + (1 - f_\alpha^n) \circ \widehat{F_I^n} \tag{4}$$

where $\widehat{F_I^n}$ denotes the intermediate feature of F_I^n before concatenation in the DDB. f_α^n can be regarded as a single-channel probabilistic weight map to balance the fusion between features of both branches. $\circ$ is element-wise multiplication.

2.3 Controllable Learning Strategy

We utilize a two-stage learning strategy with different loss functions to separately deal with the training of main branch and controller branch, thus to making the reconstruction results controllable.

On the first stage, we set $\alpha = 0$ and train the main branch only with dual-domain losses L_d:

$$L_d = ||I_H - I_F||_1 + \gamma_1||S_H - S_F||_1 \tag{5}$$

where γ_1 is a weight parameter. It respectively supervises the output of high-quality CT image I_H and sinogram S_H with full-dose groundtruths I_F and S_F. Note that, we pass the last sinogram feature F_S^N through a convolution layer to side-output the high-quality sinogram data S_H.

On the second stage, we set $\alpha = 1$ and freeze the parameters of main branch, and independently train the controller branch together with the fusion branch. We hope that by fully using the features of controller branch, the network inclines to generate the results with better subjective perception towards human vision, rather than simply approaching to the ground-truth. Inspired by recent perception-based image restoration methods [11,15], we design a perceptual loss [10] L_c^{per} to realize the perceptual reconstruction. Specifically, we use the pre-trained VGG network as a feature extractor, and measure the image difference on feature domain:

$$L_c^{per} = \sum_i ||VGG_i(I_H) - VGG_i(I_F)||_1 \tag{6}$$

Table 1. Objective comparisons on Osaka dataset.

Method	Domain	MGGO	HCM	NOD	EMP	RGGO	CON
FBP	Image	17.55/0.32	17.42/0.33	17.84/0.32	17.59/0.32	17.86/0.31	17.68/0.32
WGAN-VGG (TMI'18)	Image	21.45/0.43	21.08/0.42	22.13/0.47	22.02/0.48	22.71/0.52	21.92/0.47
MAP-NN (Nature'19)	Image	22.83/0.47	22.97/0.48	23.94/0.52	23.54/0.52	24.34/0.55	23.77/0.52
DP-ResNet (TMI'19)	Dual	25.33/0.52	25.82/0.52	26.59/0.55	26.85/0.57	**27.72**/0.62	**26.81**/0.57
Q-AE (TMI'20)	Image	21.79/0.42	21.34/0.43	22.79/0.47	22.66/0.49	23.25/0.51	22.26/0.51
Ours	Dual	**25.34/0.53**	**25.93/0.63**	**27.00/0.60**	**27.15/0.60**	27.58/**0.63**	26.60/**0.58**

$VGG_i(\cdot)$ denote the i-th layer of VGG network. We also introduce WGAN loss [6] L_c^{gan} to distinguish the image difference under a global adversarial fashion: Thus, the controller loss L_c for the second stage can be written as:

$$L_c = L_c^{per} + \gamma_2 L_c^{gan} \tag{7}$$

γ_2 is a weight parameter. In test phase, through the adjustment of input α, the desired CT image can be reconstructed considering the tradeoff between reconstruction accuracy and subjective perception.

As for our dual-domain branch, we have 6 DDBlocks and each DDB mainly contains four convolutional blocks with some adaptive poolings and a simple attention operator, which is a relatively small backbone and running faster than state-of-the arts. Once adding the controllable modulation part, the inference time may increase somewhat.

3 Experiments

In our experiments, the network was optimized by using Adam optimizer with momentum set to 0.9, $\beta_1 = 0.9$, $\beta_2 = 0.99$, and $\epsilon = 10^{-8}$. The initial learning rate is set to 10^{-5} and multiplied by 0.5 for every 50 epochs. All experiments are conducted using PyTorch and trained on one NVIDIA TITAN RTX.

It should be noted that our purpose is to provide doctors with superior CT images to help the diagnoses, but objective indicators such as PSNR [17] and SSIM [16] may not represent the truly-wanted CT images. Therefore, in the performance comparison and ablation study, we will simultaneously show the objective performance and the subjective visualization of the proposed method to demonstrate our effectiveness against other state-of-the-art methods.

Mayo Dataset. We use real clinical dataset authorized from the "2016 NIH-AAPM-Mayo Clinic Low Dose CT Grand Challenge" by Mayo Clinic for training and testing our proposed network. The dataset contains ten patients, in which each has different hundreds of full-dose CT images and paired quarter-dose CT images simulated by noise insertion. Through the official splitting, CT images from 9 patients are used to train and those of the rest are used to test.

Osaka Dataset. All CT volumes are captured by a GE Discovery CT750 HD CT scanner at Osaka university hospital. All the CT volumes from 129 patients contain 6 diffuse lung diseases, i.e., consolidation (CON), honeycombing (HCM), nodular opacity (NOD), emphysema (EMP), multi-focal ground-glass opacity (M-GGO), reticular ground-glass opacity (R-GGO). 6 patients with total 3030 pairs of low-dose images and their corresponding full-dose CT images are used to train. For the testing stage, we use about 600 CT images for each disease sampled from the remaining patients to evaluate the performance.

Performance Comparison. We compared with WGAN-VGG [19], MAP-NN [14], DP-ResNet [21] and Q-AE [5], from which DP-ResNet is a dual-domain based method while the rest are image-based methods. The qualitative comparison on Mayo and Osaka datasets are shown in Table 1 and Table 2. For Osaka, our method outperforms the state-of-the-art level for most of the categories of lung diseases (10 of 12 numbers are the best), which demonstrates our effectiveness. Similar conclusion can be obtained on Mayo dataset. As shown in Fig. 2, WGN-VGG presents obvious severe artifacts while MAP-NN contains over-smoothing phenomena. Although Q-AE achieves similar performance to our method in Mayo datasets, it lags behind other methods in Osaka datasets, presenting high noise-level. Compared with DP-ResNet, our method is closer to full-dose CT images in reconstruction details and subjective feelings, which can help doctors make better diagnosis.

Table 2. Objective comparisons on the clinic Mayo dataset.

Methods	Data domain	PSNR	SSIM
FBP	Image	29.2489	0.8759
WGAN-VGG (TMI'18)	Image	32.8646	0.8953
MAP-NN (Nature'19)	Image	33.1765	0.9122
DP-ResNet (TMI'19)	Dual	33.2207	0.9120
Q-AE (TMI'20)	Image	32.9275	0.9080
Ours	Dual	**33.4166**	**0.9155**

Ablation Study. 1) Controllability Analysis of Each Branch. As shown in Fig. 3, during the increase of α from 0 to 1, the focus of network reconstruction gradually changes from denoising to detail preservation. When $\alpha = 0$ (only MB working), the edge of the tissue reconstructed through the network is relatively blurred but showing the powerful denoising ability. When $\alpha = 1$ (only CB working), the contour of the honeycomb structure is clear, but the strip artifacts formed by noise of low-dose CT are also retained. When $\alpha = 0.6$ (fusing both branches), the structure of the honeycomb can still be distinguished, and the strip artifacts are largely denoised. Although the PSNR value is not the highest, but a slight noise in an image does not interfere with a diagnosis, and sharper honeycomb structure can help a lot. Thus, the result at $\alpha = 0.6$ can be finally chosen for the case of HCM lung disease to facilitate the diagnosis. 2) Image Domain vs. Dual

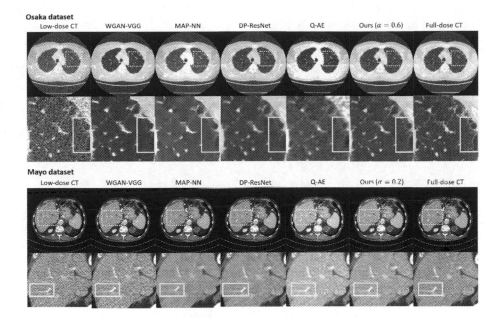

Fig. 2. Reconstruction results of HCM test sample of Osaka dataset (top) and test sample of Mayo dataset (bottom). The regions in the red boxes represent the lesion area in Osaka and liver area in Mayo. (Color figure online)

Domain. For fairly comparison, we only replace the low-dose sinogram input with low-dose CT image without decreasing the network capacity and we revise the adaptive pooling layer to meet the feature interaction in the DDB. As shown in Table 3, the case without sinogram domain "Ours w/o sinogram" is inferior to our final configuration, which demonstrates the effectiveness of integrating both domain to improve the reconstruction performance. 3) Number of DDB Blocks. We give the results that use 4,6,8 DDB blocks in the main branch. Finally, we

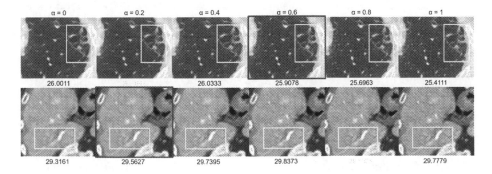

Fig. 3. Different α values of output images and their PSNR values from Osaka HCM dataset. The red boxes represent the lesion area in Osaka. (Color figure online)

choose to use 6 DDB blocks to build our main branch as backbone considering the tradeoff between accuracy and complexity.

Table 3. Ablation study on different configurations on Osaka dataset.

Case	PSNR	SSIM
Ours w/o Sinogram	25.3120	0.5223
Ours	**26.6038**	**0.5987**
DDB-4 Blocks	24.9797	0.5310
DDB-6 Blocks (Ours)	26.5397	0.5836
DDB-8 Blocks	**26.6038**	**0.5987**

4   Conclusion

In the paper, we propose a controllable dual-domain network to deal with the low-dose CT reconstruction. Experimental results demonstrate that our method has clinical value while simultaneously achieves the state-of-the-art performance.

References

1. American national standard for evaluating the image quality of x-ray computed tomography (ct)security-screening systems. ANSI N42.45-2011, pp. 1–58 (2011). https://doi.org/10.1109/IEEESTD.2011.5783279
2. Adler, J., Oktem, O.: Learned primal-dual reconstruction. IEEE Trans. Med. Imaging **37**, 1322–1332 (2017)
3. Brenner, D.J., Hall, E.J.: Computed tomography an increasing source of radiation exposure. N. Engl. J. Med. **357**(22), 2277–2284 (2007)
4. Chen, H., et al.: Low-dose CT with a residual encoder-decoder convolutional neural network. IEEE Trans. Med. Imaging **36**(12), 2524–2535 (2017). https://doi.org/10.1109/TMI.2017.2715284
5. Fan, F., et al.: Quadratic autoencoder (Q-AE) for low-dose CT denoising. IEEE Trans. Med. Imaging **39**(6), 2035–2050 (2020). https://doi.org/10.1109/TMI.2019.2963248
6. Gulrajani, I., Ahmed, F., Arjovsky, M., Dumoulin, V., Courville, A.: Improved Training of Wasserstein GANs. arXiv e-prints arXiv:1704.00028, March 2017
7. He, K., Zhang, X., Ren, S., Sun, J.: Delving deep into rectifiers: surpassing human-level performance on imagenet classification, pp. 1026–1034 (2015). https://doi.org/10.1109/ICCV.2015.123
8. Ioffe, S., Szegedy, C.: Batch normalization: accelerating deep network training by reducing internal covariate shift. In: Bach, F., Blei, D. (eds.) Proceedings of the 32nd International Conference on Machine Learning. Proceedings of Machine Learning Research, PMLR, Lille, France, 07–09 July 2015, vol. 37, pp. 448–456 (2015). http://proceedings.mlr.press/v37/ioffe15.html

9. Kak, A.: Digital Image Processing Techniques, pp. 111–169. Academic Press, Orlando (1984)

10. Ledig, C., et al.: Photo-realistic single image super-resolution using a generative adversarial network, pp. 105–114 (2017). https://doi.org/10.1109/CVPR.2017.19

11. Luo, Y.Y., Lu, H.G., Jia, N.: Super-resolution algorithm of satellite cloud image based on WGAN-GP. In: 2019 International Conference on Meteorology Observations (ICMO) (2019)

12. Mcfee, B., Salamon, J., Bello, J.P.: Adaptive pooling operators for weakly labeled sound event detection. IEEE/ACM Trans. Audio Speech Lang. Process. $26(11)$, 2180–2193 (2018)

13. Pluim, J., Fitzpatrick, J.: Image registration. IEEE Trans. Med. Imaging $22(11)$, 1341–1343 (2003). https://doi.org/10.1109/TMI.2003.819272

14. Shan, H., et al.: Competitive performance of a modularized deep neural network compared to commercial algorithms for low-dose CT image reconstruction. Nat. Mach. Intell. $1(6)$, 269 (2019)

15. Sun, W., Liu, B.D.: ESinGAN: enhanced single-image GAN using pixel attention mechanism for image super-resolution. In: 2020 15th IEEE International Conference on Signal Processing (ICSP) (2020)

16. Wang, Z., Bovik, A., Sheikh, H., Simoncelli, E.: Image quality assessment: from error visibility to structural similarity. IEEE Trans. Image Process. $13(4)$, 600–612 (2004). https://doi.org/10.1109/TIP.2003.819861

17. Wang, Z., Bovik, A.C.: Mean squared error: love it or leave it? A new look at signal fidelity measures. IEEE Signal Process. Mag. $26(1)$, 98–117 (2009). https://doi.org/10.1109/MSP.2008.930649

18. Whitmarsh, T., Humbert, L., De Craene, M., Del Rio Barquero, L.M., Frangi, A.F.: Reconstructing the 3D shape and bone mineral density distribution of the proximal femur from dual-energy x-ray absorptiometry. IEEE Trans. Med. Imaging $30(12)$, 2101–2114 (2011). https://doi.org/10.1109/TMI.2011.2163074

19. Yang, Q., et al.: Low-dose CT image denoising using a generative adversarial network with Wasserstein distance and perceptual loss. IEEE Trans. Med. Imaging $37(6)$, 1348–1357 (2018). https://doi.org/10.1109/TMI.2018.2827462

20. Ye, X., Sun, B., Wang, Z., Yang, J., Li, B.: PMBANet: progressive multi-branch aggregation network for scene depth super-resolution. IEEE Trans. Image Process. 29, 7427–7442 (2020)

21. Yin, X., et al.: Domain progressive 3D residual convolution network to improve low-dose CT imaging. IEEE Trans. Med. Imaging $38(12)$, 2903–2913 (2019). https://doi.org/10.1109/TMI.2019.2917258

22. Zhang, Z., Yu, L., Liang, X., Zhao, W., Xing, L.: TransCT: dual-path transformer for low dose computed tomography. In: de Bruijne, M., et al. (eds.) MICCAI 2021. LNCS, vol. 12906, pp. 55–64. Springer, Cham (2021). https://doi.org/10.1007/978-3-030-87231-1_6

Graph-Based Compression of Incomplete 3D Photoacoustic Data

Weihang Liao[1,4]($\boxtimes$), Yinqiang Zheng[2], Hiroki Kajita[3], Kazuo Kishi[3], and Imari Sato[1,2,4]

[1] Tokyo Institute of Technology, Tokyo, Japan
liao.w.ac@m.titech.ac.jp
[2] The University of Tokyo, Tokyo, Japan
[3] Keio University, Tokyo, Japan
[4] National Institute of Informatics, Tokyo, Japan

Abstract. Photoacoustic imaging (PAI) is a newly emerging bimodal imaging technology based on the photoacoustic effect; specifically, it uses sound waves caused by light absorption in a material to obtain 3D structure data noninvasively. PAI has attracted attention as a promising measurement technology for comprehensive clinical application and medical diagnosis. Because it requires exhaustively scanning an entire object and recording ultrasonic waves from various locations, it encounters two problems: a long imaging time and a huge data size. To reduce the imaging time, a common solution is to apply compressive sensing (CS) theory. CS can effectively accelerate the imaging process by reducing the number of measurements, but the data size is still large, and efficient compression of such incomplete data remains a problem. In this paper, we present the first attempt at direct compression of incomplete 3D PA observations, which simultaneously reduces the data acquisition time and alleviates the data size issue. Specifically, we first use a graph model to represent the incomplete observations. Then, we propose three coding modes and a reliability-aware rate-distortion optimization (RDO) to adaptively compress the data into sparse coefficients. Finally, we obtain a coded bit stream through entropy coding. We demonstrate the effectiveness of our proposed framework through both objective evaluation and subjective visual checking of real medical PA data captured from patients.

Keywords: Photoacoustic · Compression · Graph signal processing

1 Introduction

With the increasing demand for earlier and faster detection of diseases, the use of medical imaging has risen sharply, and it has become an essential tool in clinical practice. In recent decades, photoacoustic imaging (PAI) [25] has emerged as a

Supplementary Information The online version contains supplementary material available at https://doi.org/10.1007/978-3-031-16446-0_53.

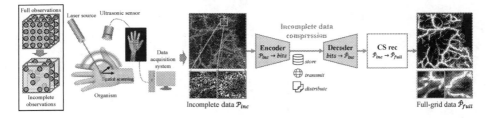

Fig. 1. Proposed workflow. We accelerate data acquisition by reducing the number of observations, and then we directly compress the incomplete data without solving a CS problem. The full-grid data is only reconstructed on the decoder side.

hybrid 3D imaging technology that combines light and ultrasound modalities. Based on the PA effect [3], PAI uses laser pulses to irradiate an imaging target and an ultrasonic sensor to detect the resulting sound waves and thus form images. As PAI offers both high optical contrast and good penetration capability [26], it is a favorable alternative to x-ray exposure for noninvasive visualization and analysis of the interior of the body [27,30]. Previous studies have shown that PAI is promising for use in comprehensive clinical application [2].

To reconstruct a 3D image of interior structure, PAI must record ultrasonic waves from various locations in the imaged target, which entails a long data acquisition time and significantly large data volume. This makes it difficult for PAI to capture dynamic targets, and it poses severe challenges for data storage and transmission. What is more, the long acquisition process poses burden on patients, as they need to keep still in scanning posture. Hence, this paper presents the first attempt to address both problems simultaneously. To reduce the data acquisition time, many previous studies have applied compressive sensing (CS) theory [4,8]. The basic idea is that, under certain conditions, it is possible to reconstruct complete PA data from a limited number of incomplete observations, thereby accelerating the data acquisition [1,10,11,16,19]. These incomplete observations intuitively have a smaller data size than the complete PA data. This naturally raises a question: can we directly compress incomplete observations after data acquisition without solving a CS problem, as shown in Fig. 1? If this is feasible, we can simultaneously accelerate the data acquisition process and alleviate the data size issue.

Compared with a traditional image/video compression task, the above question is much more complicated, which is mainly due to four factors. First, all popular image compression standards (e.g., JPEG [24], JPEG-2000 [6]) and video compression standards (e.g., AVC [29], HEVC [22]) are based on a regular pixel grid. In contrast, incomplete observations after random measurement are irregularly distributed and thus difficult to encode with conventional schemes. Second, it is important to capture the inter-voxel correlation in 3D space, as medical data contains abundant structural information. Although there have been studies on CS-based compression frameworks for 2D natural images [7,31], they treated incomplete measurements as a dimensionally reduced vector. That approach would lead to a loss of 3D structural information if we simply extended it to our problem. Instead, we need a tool that can capture the 3D inter-voxel correlation of incomplete data. Third, the learning-based methods [9,12] are difficult to perform on our problem, as PA is a relatively new technology and there is currently no large-scale dataset available. Last, PA data has a special feature in that different observations are not equally reliable. That is, different data regions have dissimilar reliabilities, depending on the amount of absorbed light energy [15]. Hence, we need a tailored rate-quality control scheme to adaptively handle observations with different reliability levels.

In this paper, we propose a graph-based coding framework to compress incomplete 3D PA observations. Graph signal processing (GSP) is an emerging technique [18,21], and graph-based coding has now been studied for nearly a decade [5,14,23,32]. Because GSP was originally designed for irregularly structured data in contexts such as social networks and wireless sensor networks [21], it provides a smart way to compress irregularly distributed, incomplete data that is difficult to handle with a traditional compression framework. By leveraging GSP, we designed a compression framework with the following characteristics: (i) We interpret incomplete observations as a graph that consists of a set of vertices representing data samples and a set of edges connecting the vertices. The weights of the edges reflect data similarities and capture the inherent correlation in 3D space. (ii) We propose three different coding modes and a reliability-aware rate-distortion optimization (RDO) technique, in order to adaptively compress PA observations with different reliability levels. (iii) We propose an adaptive quantization scheme based on the eigenvalues of a graph Laplacian matrix, and following application of that scheme, we perform entropy coding to obtain a coded bit stream. It is worth noting that, the proposed framework has the potential to improve patient experience, as it helps to reduce measurement points, resulting in a shortened scanning process.

In summary, the following are the main contributions of our work:

1. We developed a practical compression system that can handle incomplete 3D PA observations. We can thus simultaneously reduce the data acquisition time and alleviate the data storage issue.
2. To the best of our knowledge, we are the first to incorporate GSP into the problem of incomplete PA compression and design a multi-mode hybrid coding framework.
3. With the cooperation of medical doctors, we evaluated the proposed framework both objectively and subjectively on a real patient dataset.

2   Incomplete PA Data Compression

2.1   Overall Framework

The flow of our proposed method for incomplete PA compression is shown in Fig. 2. Consider an instance of incomplete 3D PA data $\mathcal{P}_{inc} \in \mathbb{R}^{W \times H \times D}$, where (W, H, D) denotes the width, height, and depth resolution of the regular 3D

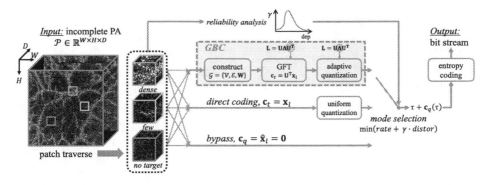

Fig. 2. Framework for incomplete data coding. We directly compress incomplete observations, and we implement three coding modes and reliability-aware RDO to adaptively handle various signal distributions in PA data.

grid. We assume that $\mathcal{P}_{inc}$ is randomly sampled with ratio K during the imaging process; that is, it only contains $W * H * D * K = M$ available elements, while other parts are null. We further assume that the sampling locations are known in advance, because that step is likely implemented by the imaging instrumentation hardware. We split $\mathcal{P}_{inc}$ into several small, non-overlapping patches $\mathcal{X}_l \in \mathbb{R}^{n \times n \times n}$, where $n < min\{W, H, D\}$, and $\sum_l \mathcal{X}_l = \mathcal{P}_{inc}$. A patch $\mathcal{X}_l$ contains m_l available elements, such that $m < n^3$ and $\sum_l m_l = M$. We then handle the data patch by patch.

As medical data tends to be sparse, the portion of meaningful information in $\mathcal{P}_{inc}$ is limited. In fact, many patches contain very few valid targets or even nothing but meaningless random noise, as shown in the dotted-line box in Fig. 2. Thus, we implement three different coding modes to adapt to different regions: a graph-based coding mode, a direct coding mode, and a bypass mode. For each patch, we first test all three coding modes and then apply reliability-aware rate-distortion optimization (RDO) to select the optimal mode. The details of the graph-based coding mode and the mode selection are described in Sects. 2.2 and 2.3, respectively.

2.2 Graph-Based Coding

We first discuss how we construct a graph for a patch, before introducing the graph Fourier transform (GFT) [20,21] and adaptive quantization. The graph-based coding scheme is shown in the gray box in Fig. 2.

For a PA patch $\mathcal{X}_l$, we construct a graph $\mathcal{G} = \{\mathcal{V}, \mathcal{E}, \mathbf{W}\}$. Here, $\mathcal{V}$ is the vertex set, which corresponds to all available elements in the current patch, and $|\mathcal{V}| = m_l$. $\mathcal{E}$ is the edge set, which is specified by triads $(v_i, v_j, \omega_{i,j})$ in which $v_i, v_j \in \mathcal{V}$ are a connected vertex pair, and $\omega_{i,j} \in [0, 1]$ is an edge weight that reflects their similarity. A larger (smaller) $\omega_{i,j}$ means that v_i and v_j are expected to be more similar (dissimilar). We obtain the graph by traversing each present voxel and connecting it with other present voxels in the two-hop neighborhood, i.e., $v_{x,y,d}$ connects with $v_{x\pm2}$, $v_{y\pm2}$, and $v_{d\pm2}$, if they exist. Finally, $\mathbf{W}$ is the adjacency matrix, which is an $m_l \times m_l$ symmetric matrix in which the (i,j)-th element $W_{i,j}$ is an edge weight $\omega_{i,j}$ if v_i, v_j are connected. Denoting the Euclidean distance between vertices v_i and v_j as $dist(i,j)$, we calculate the edge weight as follows:

$$\omega_{i,j} = \exp\left(-\frac{dist(i,j)^2}{\sigma^2}\right),\tag{1}$$

with the assumption that elements that are closer in distance are more likely to have similar intensities [5]. σ is the penalty factor for edge weight, which is set to 1 by default in our experiment.

Given the constructed graph $\mathcal{G} = \{\mathcal{V}, \mathcal{E}, \mathbf{W}\}$, we define the degree matrix $\mathbf{D}$ as an $m_l \times m_l$ diagonal matrix, in which a diagonal element $D_{i,i} = \sum_j W_{i,j}$, and we define the graph Laplacian matrix of $\mathcal{G}$ as $\mathbf{L} = \mathbf{D} - \mathbf{W}$. We then apply the eigen-decomposition $\mathbf{L} = \mathbf{U}\boldsymbol{\Lambda}\mathbf{U}^\top$, where $\boldsymbol{\Lambda}$ is a diagonal matrix with the eigenvalues of $\mathbf{L}$ along its diagonal, and $\mathbf{U}$ contains the eigenvectors of $\mathbf{L}$ as columns. Then, $\mathbf{U}^\top$ is the GFT, which can be used to decompose the signal into its frequency components as follows:

$$\mathbf{c}_t = \mathbf{U}^\top\mathbf{x}_l,\tag{2}$$

where the $\mathbf{c}_t \in \mathbb{R}^{m_l}$ are the transformed coefficients, and $\mathbf{x}_l$ is a vectorized form of the patch $\mathcal{X}_l$. Notice that the graph $\mathcal{G}$ and the transform $\mathbf{U}^\top$ are constructed in 3D space, which allows us to fully explore the inter-voxel correlation. As a result, we obtain better decomposed coefficients and higher compression performance than by directly applying a 1D transform (like a discrete cosine transform, DCT) to $\mathbf{x}_l$.

After transformation, we perform quantization to discard tiny coefficients that are close to zero. Conventional image compression frameworks like JPEG include a predefined quantization matrix that contains a different quantization step for each frequency component. However, that fixed quantization strategy is not suitable for a GFT, as we have a different transform basis for each patch. It is thus difficult to define a quantization step that works for all cases. Instead, we propose an adaptive quantization scheme based on the eigenvalues of $\mathbf{L}$. By analogy to the classical Fourier transform, the graph Laplacian eigenvalues provide a similar notion of frequency [21]. Intuitively, we want to discard more energy from high-frequency components, which tend to contain more noise and less usable information. Hence, we implement the adaptive quantization as follows:

$$\mathbf{c}_q = \text{sgn}(\mathbf{c}_t) \cdot \lfloor Q(\lambda_{max}\mathbf{I} - \boldsymbol{\Lambda})|\mathbf{c}_t|\rfloor.\tag{3}$$

Here, the $\mathbf{c}_q \in \mathbb{Z}^{m_l}$ are the quantized coefficients, Q is a scaling factor, λ_{max} is the maximum eigenvalue of $\mathbf{L}$, and $\mathbf{I}$ is the identity matrix. In addition, $\text{sgn}(\cdot)$ denotes the signum function, and $\lfloor\cdot\rfloor$ denotes the floor function. Through the proposed adaptive quantization, low-frequency components (i.e., those with small eigenvalues) are multiplied by a large scaling factor and thus preserve more information, while high-frequency components (those with large eigenvalues) are more easily quantized to 0.

2.3 Coding Mode Selection

The *graph-based coding mode* performs well for patches that contain dense information, because of the strong inter-element correlation. However, a GFT will lead to poor coding performance for those few targets and no target patches, as the correlation between noise is very weak or even nonexistent. Hence, we propose two alternative coding modes: (1) a *direct coding mode*, which skips the transformation process and directly performs quantization via $\mathbf{c}_q = \text{sgn}(\mathbf{x}_l) \cdot \lfloor Q|\mathbf{x}_l| \rfloor$; and (2) a *bypass mode*, which skips both the transformation and quantization and instead sets the coefficients $\mathbf{c}_q$ to be 0.

Next, we describe the reliability-aware rate-distortion optimization (RDO) to select the optimal coding mode for each data patch. For a given patch $\mathcal{X}_l$, we first try all three coding modes and then calculate the coding cost as follows:

$$cost(\tau) = \frac{\|\mathbf{c}_q(\tau)\|_1}{m_l} + \frac{Q \cdot \gamma}{10} \|\hat{\mathbf{x}}_l(\tau) - \mathbf{x}_l\|_2, \quad \tau = \{1, 2, 3\}. \tag{4}$$

In the first term, we use the $l-1$ norm of the quantized coefficients to approximate the bit consumption. In the second term, we measure the fidelity loss by calculating the mean square error between the original and reconstructed data; here, γ is a data-reliability-related weight for RDO. As shown in [15], PA data has a special feature in that signals from different regions have dissimilar reliabilities, depending on the absorbed light energy. As light propagates inside the material, the energy inevitably decreases because of scattering and attenuation. As a result, deeper regions of the imaging target absorb less light energy and thus have a weaker signal intensity and a lower signal-to-noise ratio (SNR). Intuitively, we want to perform finer compression for reliable data patches to maintain higher data fidelity, while performing slightly coarser compression for less reliable patches to reduce the bit rate consumption. Accordingly, we set the weight γ via the depth reliability analysis proposed in [15], which enables us to apply RDO that is adaptive to different data reliabilities.

After selecting the optimal coding mode, we record the mode indicator τ and the corresponding quantized coefficients $\mathbf{c}_q(\tau)$, and we send them to an entropy encoder to get the final bit stream. In our framework, we apply Huffman entropy coding for simplicity. On the decoder side, after entropy decoding to recover the coefficients and indicators, we choose the corresponding decoding mode for each patch accordingly. Next, we use compressive sensing [8] to reconstruct the full-grid data $\hat{\mathcal{P}}_{full}$ from the decoded data $\hat{\mathcal{P}}_{inc}$, as shown in Fig. 1. We solve this problem via the default basis-pursuit algorithm.

3 Experiment

3.1 Experimental Setting

We tested the proposed framework on real medical PA data that was captured from patients by the PAI-05 system [17]. The entire dataset is provided at high

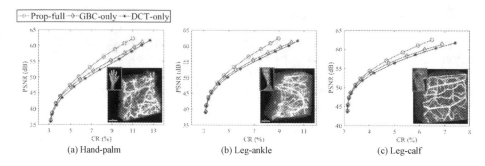

Fig. 3. PSNR rate-distortion curves ($K = 0.5$, results for other K and SSIM curves are in the supplementary material).

resolution for large human body parts, include the hand and leg. For this experiment, we cropped five local areas from both the whole hand and leg. The current device is able to captured complete, full-grid data. Thus, we artificially performed random sampling to obtain simulated incomplete observations, which we used as input to our compression framework. The complete dataset visualizations are given in the supplementary material.

For the sample ratios, patch size, and quantization scaling factors, we tested values of $K = \{0.3, 0.5, 0.7\}$, $n = 8$, and $Q = \{5, 10, 20, 30, 50, 70, 100, 150, 200, 250, 300\}$, respectively. The other parameters were fixed by definition. We designed three comparison methods for this configuration, as described below:

1. *Prop-full*: We implemented the entire proposed compression framework, including all three coding modes and reliability-aware RDO.
2. *GBC-only*: We only implemented the graph-based coding mode, without the other two modes and RDO mode selection.
3. *DCT-only*: We tested a standard DCT as a baseline. Specifically, we directly applied the DCT to $\mathbf{x}_l$ in Eq. (2), followed by a uniform quantization.

3.2   Objective Evaluation

We objectively evaluated the coding performance via two factors: the compression ratio (CR) and distortion. The CR is the ratio of the number of bits in the coded bit stream to the raw data size. For the distortion metrics, we chose the peak signal-to-noise ratio (PSNR) and the structural similarity (SSIM) [28], which are the most widely used. Figure 3 shows a portion of the experimental results. They indicate that the *Prop-full* method consistently achieved better performance than the comparison methods on different data. That is, with the same parameter setting, we could obtain a lower CR while maintaining a higher reconstruction quality. The performance improvement with our method was especially obvious for large-Q cases (the top-right regions of the RD curves). This is important for medical applications, which have very high fidelity requirements.

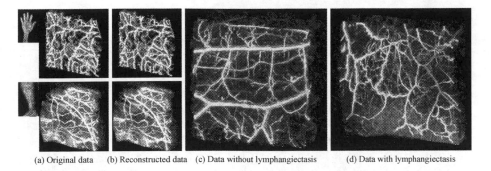

(a) Original data   (b) Reconstructed data   (c) Data without lymphangiectasis   (d) Data with lymphangiectasis

Fig. 4. Example data visualizations: images for (a, b) visual difference checking, and (c, d) lymph-blood vessel visualization combining two wavelength information for medical diagnosis, with lymph vessels marked in blue and blood vessels marked in yellow. (Color figure online)

In addition, we found that the performance advantage of our method became more obvious when the sampling ratio K was lower. This is because, when K was lower, the available pixel values were less smooth, making it difficult for the DCT to obtain sparse coefficients. Since the graph captured the correlation on an irregular grid, our method still maintained good compression performance for lower K. This demonstrates that our method has a significant advantage in applications that require high-speed imaging and thus allow very limited sampling rates. The complete experimental results with all the parameter comparisons are given in the supplementary material.

3.3 Subjective Assessment

In addition to the objective performance evaluation, we conducted a subjective test in which we invited four medical doctors to assess the visual quality subjectively. We showed the doctors the original data and the reconstructed data ($K = 0.5$, $Q = 100$) simultaneously, and we asked them two questions: (i) could they distinguish visual differences between the two data instances; and (ii) if yes, would the differences affect their interpretation of the data? Three of the doctors did not detect any visual differences; the other said that he could distinguish visual differences, but they would not have affected his interpretation and diagnosis. The data instances used for this comparison are shown in Figs. 4(a–b).

We further validated the effectiveness of our method in a real medical diagnostic task. As introduced in [13], a pair of PA data instances with different incident light wavelengths can be used to visualize lymph vessels and blood vessels differently, which can assist in the diagnosis and localization of lymphangiectasis. We thus selected two data instances, one with ill lymph vessels and the other without. We processed them both with our method ($K = 0.5$, $Q = 100$) and generated colorful visualizations like those shown in Fig. 4(c–d). Then, we asked a doctor to examine all the visualizations (healthy-original, healthy-ours, ill-original, ill-ours) separately. The doctor made the correct diagnosis on all the visualizations, which confirmed the validity of our proposed method.

4   Conclusion

This paper presented the first attempt to investigate the problem of directly compressing incomplete 3D PA observations. We proposed a graph-based coding scheme, in which we first construct a graph model to capture the inherent data correlation between incomplete observations. Then, we apply a GFT and adaptive quantization to compress the data into sparse coefficients. Finally, we encode the data into bit streams through Huffman coding. In addition, because of the special features of PA data, we proposed two other coding modes to cope with differences in the pixel distributions in different regions. We then combined reliability analysis and RDO to select the optimal coding mode for each patch. We experimentally verified our framework on real medical PA data from patients. The results for objective evaluation, subjective assessment, and real medical diagnosis by doctors showed that our method achieves satisfactory performance. Admittedly, our framework introduces some computational overhead. But, at the cost of offline calculation after data acquisition, the scanning process will be shortened, which is likely to improve patient experience.

Acknowledgement. This research was supported by AMED under Grant Number JP19he2302002, and partially supported by the ImPACT Program of the Council for Science, Technology and Innovation (Cabinet Office, Government of Japan).

References

1. Arridge, S., et al.: Accelerated high-resolution photoacoustic tomography via compressed sensing. arXiv preprint arXiv:1605.00133 (2016)
2. Attia, A.B.E., et al.: A review of clinical photoacoustic imaging: current and future trends. Photoacoustics **16**, 100144 (2019)
3. Bell, A.G.: Upon the production and reproduction of sound by light. J. Soc. Telegr. Eng. **9**(34), 404–426 (1880)
4. Candès, E.J., Wakin, M.B.: An introduction to compressive sampling. IEEE Signal Process. Mag. **25**(2), 21–30 (2008)
5. Chao, Y.H., Cheung, G., Ortega, A.: Pre-demosaic light field image compression using graph lifting transform. In: 2017 IEEE International Conference on Image Processing (ICIP), pp. 3240–3244. IEEE (2017)
6. Christopoulos, C., Skodras, A., Ebrahimi, T.: The JPEG2000 still image coding system: an overview. IEEE Trans. Consum. Electron. **46**(4), 1103–1127 (2000)
7. Cui, W., Jiang, F., Gao, X., Zhang, S., Zhao, D.: An efficient deep quantized compressed sensing coding framework of natural images. In: Proceedings of the 26th ACM International Conference on Multimedia, pp. 1777–1785 (2018)
8. Donoho, D.L.: Compressed sensing. IEEE Trans. Inf. Theory **52**(4), 1289–1306 (2006)
9. Guo, P., Li, D., Li, X.: Deep oct image compression with convolutional neural networks. Biomed. Opt. Express **11**(7), 3543–3554 (2020)

10. Guo, Z., Li, C., Song, L., Wang, L.V.: Compressed sensing in photoacoustic tomography in vivo. J. Biomed. Opt. **15**(2), 021311 (2010)
11. Haltmeier, M., Berer, T., Moon, S., Burgholzer, P.: Compressed sensing and sparsity in photoacoustic tomography. J. Opt. **18**(11), 114004 (2016)
12. Hu, Z., Lu, G., Xu, D.: FVC: a new framework towards deep video compression in feature space. In: Proceedings of the IEEE/CVF Conference on Computer Vision and Pattern Recognition, pp. 1502–1511 (2021)
13. Kajita, H., Kishi, K.: High-resolution imaging of lymphatic vessels with photoacoustic lymphangiography. Radiology **292**(1), 35–35 (2019)
14. Liao, W., Cheung, G., Muramatsu, S., Yasuda, H., Hayasaka, K.: Graph learning & fast transform coding of 3D river data. In: 2018 Asia-Pacific Signal and Information Processing Association Annual Summit and Conference (APSIPA ASC), pp. 1313–1317. IEEE (2018)
15. Liao, W., Subpa-asa, A., Zheng, Y., Sato, I.: 4D hyperspectral photoacoustic data restoration with reliability analysis. In: Proceedings of the IEEE/CVF Conference on Computer Vision and Pattern Recognition, pp. 4598–4607 (2021)
16. Liu, X., Peng, D., Guo, W., Ma, X., Yang, X., Tian, J.: Compressed sensing photoacoustic imaging based on fast alternating direction algorithm. Int. J. Biomed. Imaging **2012** (2012)
17. Nagae, K., et al.: Real-time 3D photoacoustic visualization system with a wide field of view for imaging human limbs. F1000Research **7** (2018)
18. Ortega, A., Frossard, P., Kovačević, J., Moura, J.M., Vandergheynst, P.: Graph signal processing: overview, challenges, and applications. Proc. IEEE **106**(5), 808–828 (2018)
19. Provost, J., Lesage, F.: The application of compressed sensing for photo-acoustic tomography. IEEE Trans. Med. Imaging **28**(4), 585–594 (2008)
20. Sandryhaila, A., Moura, J.M.: Big data analysis with signal processing on graphs: representation and processing of massive data sets with irregular structure. IEEE Signal Process. Mag. **31**(5), 80–90 (2014)
21. Shuman, D.I., Narang, S.K., Frossard, P., Ortega, A., Vandergheynst, P.: The emerging field of signal processing on graphs: extending high-dimensional data analysis to networks and other irregular domains. IEEE Signal Process. Mag. **30**(3), 83–98 (2013)
22. Sullivan, G.J., Ohm, J.R., Han, W.J., Wiegand, T.: Overview of the high efficiency video coding (HEVC) standard. IEEE Trans. Circuits Syst. Video Technol. **22**(12), 1649–1668 (2012)
23. Thanou, D., Chou, P.A., Frossard, P.: Graph-based compression of dynamic 3D point cloud sequences. IEEE Trans. Image Process. **25**(4), 1765–1778 (2016)
24. Wallace, G.K.: The JPEG still picture compression standard. IEEE Trans. Consum. Electron. **38**(1), xviii–xxxiv (1992)
25. Wang, L.V.: Tutorial on photoacoustic microscopy and computed tomography. IEEE J. Sel. Top. Quantum Electron. **14**(1), 171–179 (2008)
26. Wang, L.V., Hu, S.: Photoacoustic tomography: in vivo imaging from organelles to organs. Science **335**(6075), 1458–1462 (2012)
27. Wang, L.V., Yao, J.: A practical guide to photoacoustic tomography in the life sciences. Nat. Methods **13**(8), 627 (2016)
28. Wang, Z., Bovik, A.C., Sheikh, H.R., Simoncelli, E.P.: Image quality assessment: from error visibility to structural similarity. IEEE Trans. Image Process. **13**(4), 600–612 (2004)

29. Wiegand, T., Sullivan, G.J., Bjontegaard, G., Luthra, A.: Overview of the H. 264/AVC video coding standard. IEEE Trans. Circuits Syst. Video Technol. **13**(7), 560–576 (2003)
30. Xu, M., Wang, L.V.: Photoacoustic imaging in biomedicine. Rev. Sci. Instrum. **77**(4), 041101 (2006)
31. Yuan, X., Haimi-Cohen, R.: Image compression based on compressive sensing: end-to-end comparison with jpeg. IEEE Trans. Multimedia **22**(11), 2889–2904 (2020)
32. Zeng, J., Cheung, G., Chao, Y.H., Blanes, I., Serra-Sagristà, J., Ortega, A.: Hyperspectral image coding using graph wavelets. In: 2017 IEEE International Conference on Image Processing (ICIP), pp. 1672–1676. IEEE (2017)

DS³-Net: Difficulty-Perceived Common-to-T1ce Semi-supervised Multimodal MRI Synthesis Network

Ziqi Huang[1], Li Lin[1,2], Pujin Cheng[1], Kai Pan[1], and Xiaoying Tang[1(✉)]

[1] Department of Electrical and Electronic Engineering,
Southern University of Science and Technology, Shenzhen, China
tangxy@sustech.edu.cn
[2] Department of Electrical and Electronic Engineering,
The University of Hong Kong, Hong Kong SAR, China

Abstract. Contrast-enhanced T1 (T1ce) is one of the most essential magnetic resonance imaging (MRI) modalities for diagnosing and analyzing brain tumors, especially gliomas. In clinical practice, common MRI modalities such as T1, T2, and fluid attenuation inversion recovery are relatively easy to access while T1ce is more challenging considering the additional cost and potential risk of allergies to the contrast agent. Therefore, it is of great clinical necessity to develop a method to synthesize T1ce from other common modalities. Current paired image translation methods typically have the issue of requiring a large amount of paired data and do not focus on specific regions of interest, e.g., the tumor region, in the synthesization process. To address these issues, we propose a Difficulty-perceived common-to-T1ce Semi-Supervised multimodal MRI Synthesis network (DS³-Net), involving both paired and unpaired data together with dual-level knowledge distillation. DS³-Net predicts a difficulty map to progressively promote the synthesis task. Specifically, a pixelwise constraint and a patchwise contrastive constraint are guided by the predicted difficulty map. Through extensive experiments on the publicly-available BraTS2020 dataset, DS³-Net outperforms its supervised counterpart in each respect. Furthermore, with only 5% paired data, the proposed DS³-Net achieves competitive performance with state-of-the-art image translation methods utilizing 100% paired data, delivering an average SSIM of 0.8947 and an average PSNR of 23.60. The source code is available at https://github.com/Huangziqi777/DS-3_Net.

Keywords: Multimodal MRI synthesis · Difficulty-perceived guidance · Semi-supervised learning · Contrastive learning

---

Supplementary Information The online version contains supplementary material available at https://doi.org/10.1007/978-3-031-16446-0_54.

1   Introduction

Magnetic resonance imaging (MRI) is a non-radioactive clinical imaging method that is widely used in gliomas diagnosis [10,14]. In clinical practice, there are some relatively easy-to-obtain MRI modalities such as T1, T2 and fluid attenuation inversion recovery (FLAIR), since they can be simultaneously acquired in a single routine MRI scanning process by adjusting specific parameters. Contrarily, there are some difficult-to-obtain MRI modalities such as contrast-enhanced T1 (T1ce), since they require external intervention (e.g., injection of a contrast agent) exerted to the patient of interest. Compared with common MRI modalities, T1ce can clearly distinguish the parenchymal part of brain tumor, which is of great guiding significance for the diagnosis of tumor-related diseases. However, the contrast agent is usually radioactive and some patients are allergic to it, and there is also an increase in the scanning cost. As such, paired MRI data of common and T1ce modalities are very scarce but indispensable in clinical practice, especially in tumor diagnosis. In such context, there has been great interest in research topics related to missing modality [22,25,28,29].

Deep learning (DL) has been widely employed in image synthesis tasks. For natural images, Pix2pix [11] achieves good performance on paired image translation, while CycleGAN [31] and CUTGAN [19] perform well on unpaired image translation. For medical images, pGAN [4] incorporates a content-preserving perceptual loss into Pix2pix and applies it to translation across 2D brain MRI. MedGAN [1] takes into account image style transformation while maintaining content consistency, which performs well on the PET-versus-CT conversion task. MM-GAN [21] randomly drops out several input modalities and makes use of selective discriminators for the loss calculation, synthesizing high-quality images under a missing-modality setting. However, these existing DL methods rely heavily on a large number of annotated or paired images in the training phase for supervision. Recently, semi-supervised learning which can fully exploit unlabeled data gains increasing interest, especially in the medical image analysis realm which severely suffers from scarce data [3,9,30].

Synthesizing MRI containing brain tumor is a very challenging task. Conventional image synthesis frameworks [13,26] for synthesizing glioma-contained MRI, especially for synthesizing T1ce and FLAIR, are usually unsatisfactory, mainly because of the following reasons: 1) Huge domain gaps exist across different glioma-contained MRI modalities, manifesting in the intensity distribution. 2) A large amount of paired data are required for well training a pixel-level image reconstruction network, which contradicts the real-life clinical situation of scarce paired data. 3) The image pattern of the glioma region varies significantly from those of other brain structures, which makes it difficult to be synthesized even if other brain structures can be well reconstructed.

In this work, we propose a novel framework for synthesizing the difficult-to-obtain MRI modality T1ce, employing semi-supervised learning with limited paired data and a larger number of unpaired data. Our main contributions are four-fold: 1) To the best of our knowledge, this is the first semi-supervised framework applied to multimodal MRI synthesis for gliomas. 2) In light of the

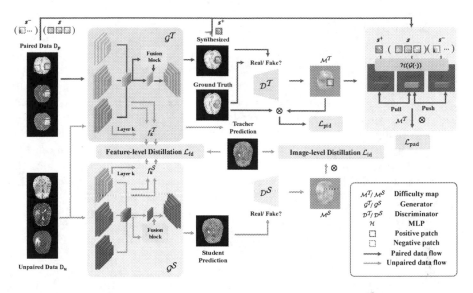

Fig. 1. Flowchart of our proposed DS³-Net. For simplicity, the GAN losses for the teacher network and the student network, and the patchwise difficulty-perceived contrastive loss which is similar between the teacher network and the student network, are not included in this figure.

teacher-student network, we make full use of unpaired multimodal MRI data through maintaining consistency in spaces of both high and low dimensions. 3) We innovatively estimate a difficulty-perceived map and adopt it to dynamically weigh both pixelwise and patchwise constraints according to the difficulty of model learning, and thus the model can assign the difficult-to-learn parts (such as the glioma region) more attention. 4) Extensive comparison experiments are conducted, both quantitatively and qualitatively.

2   Methodology

Let $D_p = \left\{ \left(x_i^{\mathcal{T}}, y_i^{\mathcal{T}} \right) \right\}_{i=1}^N$ denote the paired image dataset including the common MRI modalities $x_i^{\mathcal{T}} = \left\{ \left({}_1 x_i^{\mathcal{T}}, {}_2 x_i^{\mathcal{T}}, ...{}_n x_i^{\mathcal{T}} \right) \right\}_{n=1}^C$, where C is set as three including T1, T2 and FLAIR and y_i is the target modality which is T1ce in our case. Let $D_u = \left\{ \left(x_i^{\mathcal{S}} \right) \right\}_{i=1}^M$ denote the unpaired image dataset, with no corresponding T1ce. Note that the sample size of the unpaired dataset M is much larger than that of the paired datset N, with no patient-level overlap.

Our proposed Difficulty-perceived common-to-T1ce Semi-Supervised multimodal MRI Synthesis network (DS³-Net) is demonstrated in Fig. 1, including a teacher model for learning expertise knowledge from paired data and a student model for imitating the teacher's decision. The student model has the same architecture as the teacher model and the two models are encouraged to output consistent predictions.

2.1 Difficulty-Perceived Attention Map

One of the main challenges in conducting image synthesis to brain MRI containing glioma is that different regions have different synthesizing difficulties. For instance, normal brain tissues have relatively more straightforward intensity mapping relationships, while brain tumor regions often suffer from diverse patterns between common MRI and T1ce. Introducing an attention map to assess the synthesizing difficulty for each region is a feasible solution [16]. Therefore, we intuitively utilize a predicted map $\mathcal{M}$ from the discriminator to dynamically guide the synthesis process, as the well-generated regions can easily fool the discriminator while the poorly-generated regions can not. In our case, the discriminator is a 70×70 PatchGAN [12], leading to patch-level difficulty scores. Specifically, the difficulty map $\mathcal{M}^{\mathcal{T}}$ from the teacher model is defined as

$$\mathcal{M}^{\mathcal{T}} = \begin{cases} \left\| 1 - \mathcal{D}_{\mathcal{T}} \left(\mathcal{G}_{\mathcal{T}} \left(x_i^{\mathcal{T}} \right) \right) \right\|, & x_i^{\mathcal{T}} > 0 \\ 0.2, & x_i^{\mathcal{T}} = 0. \end{cases} \tag{1}$$

$\mathcal{D}_{\mathcal{T}}$ and $\mathcal{G}_{\mathcal{T}}$ respectively refer to the teacher network's discriminator and generator. For background pixels without any brain tissue, we set a small constant 0.2 to ensure that their synthesis results are normal.

2.2 Difficulty-Perceived Pixelwise and Patchwise Constraints

To fully utilize the multimodal information, we use three encoders each of which has nine ResNet blocks. We also employ fusion block modified from the SE module [8] by replacing sigmoid with softmax to better fuse the three common modalities before being inputted to the decoder.

L1 loss is adopted to provide a pixelwise constraint between the real T1ce $y_i^{\mathcal{T}}$ and the synthesized T1ce $\mathcal{G}_{\mathcal{T}}(x_i^{\mathcal{T}})$. We use the difficulty map $\mathcal{M}^{\mathcal{T}}$ to guide the L1 loss by assigning each pixel a difficulty score, allowing the poorly synthesized regions to gain more attention. Specifically, we introduce a pixelwise difficulty-perceived L1 loss $\mathcal{L}_{pid}^{\mathcal{T}}$ for the teacher network

$$\mathcal{L}_{pid}^{\mathcal{T}} = \mathcal{M}^{\mathcal{T}} \circ \left\| y_i^{\mathcal{T}} - \mathcal{G}_{\mathcal{T}}(x_i^{\mathcal{T}}) \right\|_1. \tag{2}$$

For the purpose of maintaining the same semantic information at the same location in a single sample, we use patchwise contrastive learning to constrain the parameters of different hidden layers. Specifically, we construct a positive pair $\left(z_l^s, z_l^{s+} \right)$ and a negative pair $\left(z_l^s, z_l^{s-} \right)$, where $z_l^s = \mathcal{H}_{(l)}(\mathcal{G}_{\mathcal{T}(l)}(x_i^s))$ refers to features extracted from patch s of the input x_i at the lth layer of the teacher network's generator $\mathcal{G}_{\mathcal{T}}$. Next, we map the selected features into a high-dimension space by an additional MLP $\mathcal{H}_{(l)}$. Similarly, $z_l^{s+} = \mathcal{H}_{(l)}(\mathcal{G}_{\mathcal{T}(l)}(\hat{y}_i^s))$ refers to features from the synthesized T1ce $\hat{y}_i$ at patch s, regarded as the positive sample, and z_l^{s-} represents features from patches different from s. We then pull the positive pair together and push the negative pair away via the InfoNCE loss [18]. The difficulty map $\mathcal{M}^{\mathcal{T}}$ is down-sampled to match the resolution of each hidden layer l^{th}, defined as $m_l^{\mathcal{T}}$, and is multiplied with each patch's features to re-distribute the patchwise importance. To be specific, the patchwise difficulty-perceived contrastive loss $\mathcal{L}_{pad}^{\mathcal{T}}$ is calculated as

$$\mathcal{L}_{pad}^{\mathcal{T}} = -\sum_{l \in L} m_l^{\mathcal{T}} \circ \log \left[\frac{\exp\left(z_l^s \cdot z_l^{s+}/\tau\right)}{\exp\left(z_l^s \cdot z_l^{s+}/\tau\right) + \sum \exp\left(z_l^s \cdot z_l^{s-}/\tau\right)\right)} \right], \quad (3)$$

where $L = \{0, 4, 8, 12, 16\}$ are the selected hidden layers and the temperature τ for the InfoNCE loss is empirically set as 0.07.

Furthermore, an LSGAN loss [17] is adopted, encouraging the synthesized distribution to be close to the real one. In summary, the total loss function $\mathcal{L}^{\mathcal{T}}$ of the teacher network is

$$\mathcal{L}^{\mathcal{T}} = \lambda_{pid}\mathcal{L}_{pid}^{\mathcal{T}} + \lambda_{pad}\mathcal{L}_{pad}^{\mathcal{T}} + \lambda_{GAN}\mathcal{L}_{GAN}^{\mathcal{T}}, \quad (4)$$

where λ_{pid}, λ_{pad} and λ_{GAN} are empirically set as 100, 1, 1.

2.3   Difficulty-Perceived Dual-Level Distillation

We feed the unpaired dataset D_u into the student network $\mathcal{N}_{\mathcal{S}}$ which is initialized with pre-trained weights from the teacher network. For semi-supervised learning, knowledge distillation [5,30] between the teacher and student models is one of the most common procedures to expand the dataset and perform parameter regularization. In our DS³-Net pipeline, both feature-level and image-level distillations are performed to ensure the consistency of the two models in both high-dimension and low-dimension spaces.

To be specific, we first input $x_i^{\mathcal{S}} \subset D_u$ into both $\mathcal{N}_{\mathcal{S}}$ and $\mathcal{N}_{\mathcal{T}}$ to obtain a coarse prediction $\mathcal{G}_{\mathcal{S}}(x_i^{\mathcal{S}})$ and a fine prediction $\mathcal{G}_{\mathcal{T}}(x_i^{\mathcal{S}})$. Given that the paired ground truth for x_i^s is not available, we treat the fine decision $\hat{q}_i^{\mathcal{T}}$ as the pseudo ground truth for the student network, and then conduct image-level distillation through an L1 loss function.

We expect the student model to imitate the teacher model in terms of representation at the high-dimension space to better handle the unpaired samples. Therefore, when one sample goes through the two networks, we extract the kth layer's features $f_k^{\mathcal{T}}$ and $f_k^{\mathcal{S}}$, and then perform feature-level distillation between the two networks by minimizing the feature discrepancy.

Apparently, the student discriminator $\mathcal{D}_{\mathcal{S}}$ can also produce a difficulty map $\mathcal{M}^{\mathcal{S}}$ for each unpaired sample and we employ the same difficulty guided strategy towards the distillation process. We thus have the image-level distillation loss

$$\mathcal{L}_{id}^{\mathcal{S}} = \mathcal{M}^{\mathcal{S}} \circ \left\| \mathcal{G}_{\mathcal{T}}(x_i^{\mathcal{S}}) - \mathcal{G}_{\mathcal{S}}(x_i^{\mathcal{S}}) \right\|_1, \quad (5)$$

and the feature-level distillation loss

$$\mathcal{L}_{fd}^{\mathcal{S}} = \frac{1}{K} \sum_{k \in L_{distill}} m_k^{\mathcal{S}} \circ \left\| f_k^{\mathcal{T}} - f_k^{\mathcal{S}} \right\|_1, \quad (6)$$

where $L_{distill} = \{4, 8, 12, 16, 21\}$, K denotes the number of the selected layers, and m_k^S represents the difficulty map down-sampled to the same size as that of the feature map of the kth layer.

Similar to the teacher model, the student model also has an LSGAN loss $\mathcal{L}_{GAN}^S$ and a patchwise difficulty-perceived contrastive loss $\mathcal{L}_{pad}^S$. Collectively, the loss function $\mathcal{L}^S$ for the student network is defined as

$$\mathcal{L}^S = \lambda_{id}\mathcal{L}_{id}^S + \lambda_{fd}\mathcal{L}_{fd}^S + \lambda_{pad}\mathcal{L}_{pad}^S + \lambda_{GAN}\mathcal{L}_{GAN}^S. \tag{7}$$

Here we empirically set λ_{id}, λ_{fd}, λ_{pad} and λ_{GAN} as 100, 1, 1 and 1.

3   Experiments and Results

3.1   Dataset

BraTS2020 [2] (https://www.med.upenn.edu/cbica/brats2020/) is a large publicly-available dataset, consisting in total 369 paired MRI data of T1, T2, FLAIR, and T1ce from gliomas patients. We divide each 3D image into 2D slices at the axial view. Each 2D slice is center-cropped to 224×224. We divide the entire dataset into training, validation, and test sets according to a ratio of 7:1:2 at the patient level, and use slices that contain tumor during the training phase. Since the tumor core (TC) containing the enhancing tumor (ET) is the key region to distinguish T1ce from other modalities while it usually constitutes only a small portion of the whole tumor, we adjust the proportion to be 1:1 for the numbers of slices with and without TC.

3.2   Training Strategy

At the first training stage, the paired dataset are utilized to pre-activate the teacher network, and we take the weights of the 5th epoch before convergence as the initialization weights for the next stage of training to prevent overfitting. Specifically, each difficulty map score is set to be the constant 1 in the first stage which ensures a stable output from the initial network. In the second stage, we start with the difficulty maps delivered by the discriminators and train the two networks together by optimizing the final loss function $\mathcal{L} = \mathcal{L}^T + (1 - \frac{t}{T})\mathcal{L}^S$, where $t \in [0, T)$ represents the current epoch counting and T is the total number of the training epochs. All methods are implemented with Pytorch using NVIDIA RTX 3090 GPUs. AdamW [15] is chosen to be the optimizer and the batch size is set as 6 with equivalent numbers of paired and unpaired samples. The learning rates in the first stage for the generator $\mathcal{G}^T$, the MLP $\{\mathcal{H}_{(l)}|l \in \mathcal{L}\}$ and the discriminator $\mathcal{D}^T$ are respectively set as 0.0006, 0.0006 and 0.0003, and these values are attenuated to a fifth of the original numbers in the second training phase. For the student network training, we have the same learning rate setting as that for the initial teacher network and train for a total of 100 epochs. All of the learning rate settings follow the linear decay strategy.

3.3 Results

In the training phase, we consider a few percentages (e.g., 5%, 10% and 50%) of the full training set as our paired dataset and the rest as the unpaired dataset. To better evaluate our method, we compare DS³-Net with several state-of-the-art (SOTA) methods including two for natural images (Pix2pix [11] and CUTGAN [19]) and two for medical images (pGAN [4] and MedGAN [1]).

The structure similarity index measure (SSIM), peak signal-to-noise ratio (PSNR) [6] and mean squared error (MSE) are employed to evaluate the effectiveness of DS³-Net. Besides, because T1ce plays a crucial role in identifying ET and TC [7,24,27], we perform tumor segmentation using the synthesized T1ce together with the three common modalities and use the Dice scores [23] of ET and TC to assess the quality of the synthesized T1ce. The entire test set is divided into five folds, four of which are used for training the segmentation network and one for testing. UNet [20] is employed as our segmentation network. During the testing phase, we use the student network to deliver the prediction. All comparison results are listed in Table 1.

Table 1. Quantitative evaluations for DS³-Net with different percentages of paired data. Bold metric represents the best performance.

Paired percentage	Method	Image quality			Segmentation quality		Params.
		SSIM↑	PSNR↑	MSE↓	ET Dice↑	TC Dice↑	
0%	CUTGAN [19]	0.7982	17.63	0.020	33.9%	56.1%	11M
5%	DS³-Net (paired only)	0.8691	21.97	**0.008**	39.5%	63.7%	-
	Pix2pix [11]	0.8691	23.44	0.008	38.7%	59.4%	-
	DS³-Net	**0.8947**	**23.60**	0.009	**43.3%**	**66.0%**	-
10%	DS³-Net (paired only)	0.8763	23.01	**0.007**	43.6%	65.3%	-
	Pix2pix [11]	0.8845	22.85	0.010	38.8%	60.7%	-
	DS³-Net	**0.8943**	**23.90**	0.008	**43.6%**	**66.9%**	-
50%	DS³-Net (paired only)	**0.8895**	23.73	0.006	44.1%	67.9%	-
	Pix2pix [11]	0.8883	23.53	0.005	39.3%	62.1%	-
	DS³-Net	0.8893	**23.79**	**0.005**	44.9%	**68.1%**	-
100%	pGAN [4]	0.8846	23.56	0.010	36.7%	61.8%	11M
	MedGAN [1]	0.8900	24.34	0.011	37.8%	58.3%	11M
	Pix2pix [11]	**0.9007**	**25.02**	**0.004**	41.7%	65.0%	11M
	DS³-Net	0.8959	24.26	0.005	**47.8%**	**67.2%**	33M

We observe that the semi-supervised training strategy can effectively improve the synthesized T1ce's quality and the segmentation performance of ET and TC compared to the vanilla supervised method (namely DS³-Net (paired only)), as demonstrated in Table 1. Apparently, DS³-Net achieves competitive performance with full-data training methods, even with only 5% paired data for training, especially in segmenting ET and TC. To qualitatively illustrate the performance,

Table 2. Ablation studies for each component of DS³-Net.

Component	SSIM↑	PSNR↑	MSE↓
DS³-Net w.o. $\mathcal{M}_T/\mathcal{M}_S$	0.8884	21.38	0.012
DS³-Net w.o. $\mathcal{L}_{fd}$	0.8883	21.33	0.012
DS³-Net w.o. $\mathcal{L}_{id}$	0.7424	13.43	0.063
DS³-Net teacher network $\mathcal{N}_T$	0.8715	20.67	0.013
DS³-Net student network $\mathcal{N}_S$	**0.8947**	**23.60**	**0.009**

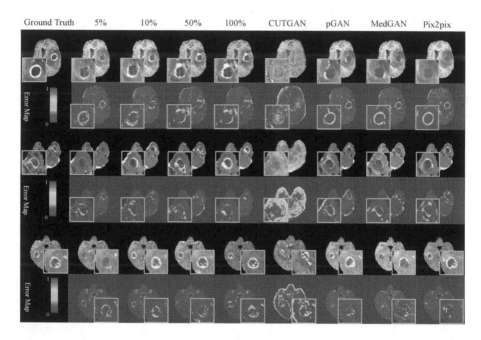

Fig. 2. Visualization of synthesized T1ce and the corresponding error maps from different methods. Each percentage represents DS³-Net trained with different paired percentage.

we display visualizations of the synthesized T1ce from different methods in Fig. 2. It can be easily observed that DS³-Net performs well in synthesizing tumor regions and achieves competitive performance with other SOTA methods trained with 100% paired data. Error maps are also presented in Fig. 2, revealing that the erroneous regions mainly focus around the tumor, but our proposed DS³-Net can effectively alleviate this dilemma to some extent (also see Fig. A1 of the appendix). Additionally, by zooming the tumor regions for visualization, DS³-Net is found to deliver T1ce with a clearer boundary for ET compared with other SOTA methods.

Ablation studies are conducted with 5% paired data training, to assess each component's importance in the proposed DS³-Net. As shown in Table 2, removing any of the proposed components deteriorates the synthesization performance in terms of all evaluation metrics. In addition, it can be found that without $\mathcal{L}_{id}$, DS³-Net suffers dramatic degradation, revealing that image-level distillation is an indispensable component in our framework. Since the student network inputs more data and receives reliable guidance from the teacher network, the image quality is effectively improved compared with that from the teacher network.

4 Conclusion

In this work, we propose a novel difficulty-perceived semi-supervised multimodal MRI synthesis pipeline to generate the difficult-to-obtain modality T1ce from three common easy-to-obtain MRI modalities including T1, T2, and FLAIR. Difficulty-perceived maps are adopted to guide the synthesization process of important regions, and dual-level distillation enables the model to train a well-performing network with limited paired data. Extensive experiments are conducted on a large publicly-available dataset, and the effectiveness of DS³-Net is successfully identified.

Acknowledgement. This study was supported by the National Natural Science Foundation of China (62071210); the Shenzhen Science and Technology Program (RCYX20210609103056042); the Shenzhen Basic Research Program (JCYJ202009251 53847004, JCYJ20190809120205578).

References

1. Armanious, K., et al.: MedGAN: medical image translation using GANs. Comput. Med. Imaging Graph. **79**, 101684 (2020)
2. Bakas, S., et al.: Advancing the cancer genome atlas glioma MRI collections with expert segmentation labels and radiomic features. Sci. Data **4**(1), 1–13 (2017)
3. Chen, X., Yuan, Y., Zeng, G., Wang, J.: Semi-supervised semantic segmentation with cross pseudo supervision. In: Proceedings of the IEEE/CVF Conference on Computer Vision and Pattern Recognition, pp. 2613–2622. (2021)
4. Dar, S.U., Yurt, M., Karacan, L., Erdem, A., Erdem, E., Çukur, T.: Image synthesis in multi-contrast MRI with conditional generative adversarial networks. IEEE Trans. Med. Imaging **38**(10), 2375–2388 (2019)
5. Hinton, G., Vinyals. O., Dean. J.: Distilling the knowledge in a neural network. arXiv e-prints (2015). arXiv:1503.02531
6. Hore, A., Ziou, D.: Image quality metrics: PSNR vs. SSIM. In: 2010 20th International Conference on Pattern Recognition, pp. 2366–2369 (2010)
7. Huang, Z., Lin, L., Cheng, P., Peng, L., Tang, X.: Multi-modal brain tumor segmentation via missing modality synthesis and modality-level attention fusion. In: 2022 26th International Conference on Pattern Recognition. (Under review) (2022)
8. Hu, J., Shen, L., Sun, G.: Squeeze-and-excitation networks. In: Proceedings of the IEEE/CVF conference on Computer Vision and Pattern Recognition, pp. 7132–7141 (2018)

9. Ibrahim, M.S., Vahdat, A., Ranjbar, M., Macready, W.G.: Semi-supervised semantic image segmentation with self-correcting networks. In: Proceedings of the IEEE/CVF Conference on Computer Vision and Pattern Recognition, pp. 12715–12725 (2020)

10. Işın, A., Direkoğlu, C., Şah, M.: Review of MRI-based brain tumor image segmentation using deep learning methods. Procedia Comput. Sci. **102**, 317–324 (2016)

11. Isola, P., Zhu, J.Y., Zhou, T., Efros, A.A.: Image-to-image translation with conditional adversarial networks. In: Proceedings of the IEEE/CVF Conference on Computer Vision and Pattern Recognition, pp. 1125–1134 (2017)

12. Li, C., Wand, M.: Precomputed real-time texture synthesis with Markovian generative adversarial networks. In: Leibe, B., Matas, J., Sebe, N., Welling, M. (eds.) ECCV 2016. LNCS, vol. 9907, pp. 702–716. Springer, Cham (2016). https://doi.org/10.1007/978-3-319-46487-9_43

13. Li, H., et al.: DiamondGAN: unified multi-modal generative adversarial networks for MRI sequences synthesis. In: Shen, D., et al. (eds.) MICCAI 2019. LNCS, vol. 11767, pp. 795–803. Springer, Cham (2019). https://doi.org/10.1007/978-3-030-32251-9_87

14. Liu, S., et al.: Multimodal neuroimaging computing: a review of the applications in neuropsychiatric disorders. Brain Inform. **2**(3), 167–180 (2015). https://doi.org/10.1007/s40708-015-0019-x

15. Loshchilov, I., Hutter, F.: Fixing Weight decay regularization in Adam. arXiv e-prints (2017). arxiv:1711.05101

16. Ma, B., et al.: MRI image synthesis with dual discriminator adversarial learning and difficulty-aware attention mechanism for hippocampal subfields segmentation. Comput. Med. Imaging Graph. **86**, 101800 (2020)

17. Mao, X., Li, Q., Xie, H., Lau, R.Y., Wang, Z., Paul Smolley, S.: Least squares generative adversarial networks. In Proceedings of the IEEE International Conference on Computer Vision, pp. 2794–2802 (2017)

18. Van den Oord, A., Li, Y., Vinyals, O.: Representation learning with contrastive predictive coding. arXiv e-prints (2018). arXiv:1807.03748

19. Park, T., Efros, A.A., Zhang, R., Zhu, J.-Y.: Contrastive learning for unpaired image-to-image translation. In: Vedaldi, A., Bischof, H., Brox, T., Frahm, J.-M. (eds.) ECCV 2020. LNCS, vol. 12354, pp. 319–345. Springer, Cham (2020). https://doi.org/10.1007/978-3-030-58545-7_19

20. Ronneberger, O., Fischer, P., Brox, T.: U-net: convolutional networks for biomedical image segmentation. In: Navab, N., Hornegger, J., Wells, W.M., Frangi, A.F. (eds.) MICCAI 2015. LNCS, vol. 9351, pp. 234–241. Springer, Cham (2015). https://doi.org/10.1007/978-3-319-24574-4_28

21. Sharma, A., Hamarneh, G.: Missing MRI pulse sequence synthesis using multimodal generative adversarial network. IEEE Trans. Med. Imaging **39**(4), 1170–1183 (2019)

22. Shen, Y., Gao, M.: Brain tumor segmentation on MRI with missing modalities. In: Chung, A.C.S., Gee, J.C., Yushkevich, P.A., Bao, S. (eds.) IPMI 2019. LNCS, vol. 11492, pp. 417–428. Springer, Cham (2019). https://doi.org/10.1007/978-3-030-20351-1_32

23. Taha, A.A., Hanbury, A.: Metrics for evaluating 3D medical image segmentation: analysis, selection, and tool. BMC Med. Imaging **15**(1), 1–28 (2015)

24. Wu, J., Tang, X.: Brain segmentation based on multi-atlas and diffeomorphism guided 3D fully convolutional network ensembles. Pattern Recogn. **115**, 107904 (2021)

25. Yang, J., et al.: Fast t2w/flair MRI acquisition by optimal sampling of information complementary to pre-acquired t1w MRI, arXiv e-prints (2021). arXiv:2111.06400

26. Yurt, M., Dar, S.U., Erdem, A., Erdem, E., Oguz, K.K., Çukur, T.: mustGAN: multi-stream generative adversarial networks for MR image synthesis. Med. Image Anal. **70**, 101944 (2021)

27. Zhang, Y., Wu, J., Liu, Y., Chen, Y., Wu, E.X., Tang, X.: Mi-UNet: multi-inputs UNet incorporating brain parcellation for stroke lesion segmentation from t1-weighted magnetic resonance images. IEEE J. Biomed. Health Inform. **25**(2), 526–535 (2021)

28. Zhou, T., Canu, S., Vera, P., Ruan, S.: Brain tumor segmentation with missing modalities via latent multi-source correlation representation. In: Martel, A.L., et al. (eds.) MICCAI 2020. LNCS, vol. 12264, pp. 533–541. Springer, Cham (2020). https://doi.org/10.1007/978-3-030-59719-1_52

29. Zhou, T., Canu, S., Vera, P., Ruan, S.: Latent correlation representation learning for brain tumor segmentation with missing MRI modalities. IEEE Trans. Image Process. **30**, 4263–4274 (2021)

30. Zhou, Y., Chen, H., Lin, H., Heng, P.-A.: Deep semi-supervised knowledge distillation for overlapping cervical cell instance segmentation. In: Martel, A.L., et al. (eds.) MICCAI 2020. LNCS, vol. 12261, pp. 521–531. Springer, Cham (2020). https://doi.org/10.1007/978-3-030-59710-8_51

31. Zhu, J.Y., Park, T., Isola, P., Efros, A.A.: Unpaired image-to-image translation using cycle-consistent adversarial networks. In: Proceedings of the IEEE International Conference on Computer Vision, pp. 2223–2232 (2017)

Invertible Sharpening Network for MRI Reconstruction Enhancement

Siyuan Dong[1], Eric Z. Chen[2], Lin Zhao[3], Xiao Chen[2], Yikang Liu[2], Terrence Chen[2], and Shanhui Sun[2(✉)]

[1] Electrical Engineering, Yale University, New Haven, CT, USA
s.dong@yale.edu
[2] United Imaging Intelligence, Cambridge, MA, USA
shanhui.sun@uii-ai.com
[3] Computer Science, University of Georgia, Athens, GA, USA

Abstract. High-quality MRI reconstruction plays a critical role in clinical applications. Deep learning-based methods have achieved promising results on MRI reconstruction. However, most state-of-the-art methods were designed to optimize the evaluation metrics commonly used for natural images, such as PSNR and SSIM, whereas the visual quality is not primarily pursued. Compared to the fully-sampled images, the reconstructed images are often blurry, where high-frequency features might not be sharp enough for confident clinical diagnosis. To this end, we propose an invertible sharpening network (InvSharpNet) to improve the visual quality of MRI reconstructions. During training, unlike the traditional methods that learn to map the input data to the ground truth, InvSharpNet adapts a backward training strategy that learns a blurring transform from the ground truth (fully-sampled image) to the input data (blurry reconstruction). During inference, the learned blurring transform can be inverted to a sharpening transform leveraging the network's invertibility. The experiments on various MRI datasets demonstrate that InvSharpNet can improve reconstruction sharpness with few artifacts. The results were also evaluated by radiologists, indicating better visual quality and diagnostic confidence of our proposed method.

Keywords: MRI Recon · Sharpness enhancement · Invertible networks

1 Introduction

Due to the hardware limitations, the Magnetic Resonance Imaging (MRI) acquisition time is inherently long. Taking fewer measurements (under-sampling) can accelerate the acquisition but can lead to aliasing artifacts and loss of

---

S. Dong—This work was done during the internship at United Imaging Intelligence.

Supplementary Information The online version contains supplementary material available at https://doi.org/10.1007/978-3-031-16446-0_55.

L. Wang et al. (Eds.): MICCAI 2022, LNCS 13436, pp. 582–592, 2022.
https://doi.org/10.1007/978-3-031-16446-0_55

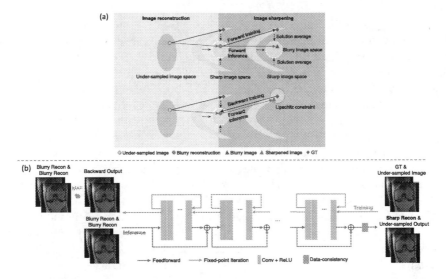

Fig. 1. (a) Difference between traditional methods and our method for sharpening MRI reconstruction. The MRI reconstructions are often blurry compared to the ground truth due to the solution average. The traditional forward training does not fundamentally overcome this problem and still leads to a blurry image. Our backward training utilizes a INN that learns a mapping function with Lipschitz constraints such that the predictions in the inference are close to the input in training (i.e., ground truth). (b) Architecture of InvSharpNet. During training, ground truth (GT) and the under-sampled image are passed through InvSharpNet in the inverse direction, where the fixed-point iteration algorithm is used to invert the residual blocks [2]. The backward loss (Eq. 2) is imposed between the backward output and two duplicates of the blurry reconstruction (Blurry Recon). During inference, the Blurry Recon is passed through the network in the forward direction to obtain a sharpened reconstruction (Sharp Recon).

high-frequency information. MRI reconstruction aims to recover clinically interpretable images from the under-sampled images. Recently, deep learning-based methods have achieved state-of-the-art performances in solving MRI reconstruction problems [4,5,8,9,14,18,22]. These methods usually train neural networks to learn a mapping from under-sampled images to fully-sampled images.

However, it is observed that those deep learning approaches cannot produce images as sharp as those fully-sampled images. MRI reconstruction from under-sampled data is an ill-posed problem since it is a one-to-many problem (one under-sampled image corresponds to multiple possible fully-sampled images). Most deep learning-based methods fulfill the reconstruction task utilizing loss functions derived from metrics such as peak signal-to-noise ratio (PSNR) and structural similarity (SSIM) [6,9,14]. To get a better PSNR, the mean-squared-error (MSE) and mean-absolute-error (MAE) losses are often used. However, as discussed in [11,13,20], training with MSE or MAE results in an image that is a pixelwise average or median of all possible solutions during network inference. This leads to an over-smoothing effect on the areas that are supposed to be rich in high-frequency details, and therefore the reconstructed images have suboptimal visual quality and might result in low diagnostic confidence. One way to improve the perceptual quality is adding a structural loss, which is usually achieved through maximizing SSIM [15, 21, 22]. However, it is still not sufficient to reach a comparable level of sharpness as the ground truth. Currently, the most popular method to improve image visual quality is adding an adversarial loss [12, 19, 25], which showed improved image visual quality compared to the methods based on only MAE and SSIM. However, it is well-known that training with adversarial loss may introduce artificial features due to the generative nature of adversarial networks. Artifacts in medical images may lead to incorrect medical diagnosis [1], which makes the adversarial loss less reliable to be implemented clinically.

We propose a new learning framework by converting the traditional one-to-many problem to a one-to-one problem, differentiating it from previous works that propose new loss functions but still in a conventional learning fashion. We observe that given a fixed under-sampling mask, one fully-sampled image corresponds to one under-sampled image; given a fixed reconstruction network, one under-sampled image corresponds to one blurry reconstruction. In another observation, invertible neural networks (INN) such as [2, 7] guarantee learning a bidirectional one-to-one mapping. These observations inspire us to learn an invertible one-to-one mapping between a fully sampled image and a reconstructed image. We propose an invertible sharpening network (InvSharpNet) that can enhance the visual quality of reconstructed images through a backward training strategy from sharp fully-sampled images to blurry reconstructed images. To the best of our knowledge, we are the first to propose to learn an inverse mapping from ground truth to input data, which converts a one-to-many problem into a one-to-one problem and overcomes the blurry issue. Experimental results demonstrate that the backward training strategy can improve the sharpness of the images and generate fewer artifacts compared to the adversarial loss. Radiologists' evaluations also justify that our method gives a better visual quality and higher diagnostic confidence than compared methods.

2   Methods

2.1   Problem Formulation

Let $K \in \mathbb{C}^{H \times W}$ denote the fully-sampled k-space measurement with dimension of $H \times W$, and the corresponding fully-sampled image I is obtained from inverse Fourier transform $I = \mathcal{F}^{-1}(K)$. To accelerate data acquisition, it is often to take only a portion of the k-space measurements, which is equivalent to applying an under-sampling binary mask M on K. The corresponding under-sampled image is $Y = \mathcal{F}^{-1}(MK)$. The goal of MRI reconstruction is to find a mapping $R = \mathcal{R}(Y)$ such that R is as close to I as possible. The deep learning-based MRI reconstruction methods train neural networks to approximate the reconstruction mapping $\mathcal{R}$ [15, 21, 22]. This work aims to enhance the reconstructions R by training a sharpening network $\mathcal{S}$ such that $R_{sharp} = \mathcal{S}(R)$, where R_{sharp} better approximates the ground truth I in terms of the visual sharpness.

2.2   Backward Training

Figure 1(a) shows a conceptual difference between traditional forward training and our proposed backward training for sharpening MRI reconstructions. The sharp image space contains images that are visually comparable to the fully-sampled images in terms of sharpness. MRI reconstruction networks are trained to map an under-sampled image to the ground truth, which is located in the sharp image space. However, training with a pixelwise loss (MAE or MSE) maps the under-sampled image to the blurry image space due to the solution average problem.

The traditional method to improve the blurry reconstruction is training a refinement network in the forward direction that maps the reconstruction to the ground truth [16,19]. One way to achieve this is training the refinement network with a weighted sum of MAE and structural loss based on Multiscale SSIM (MSSIM) [24] between the network output and ground truth [15]:

$$\mathcal{L}_{forward} = (1 - \alpha)||\mathcal{S}(R) - I||_1 + \alpha(1 - \mathrm{MSSIM}(\mathcal{S}(R), I)) \qquad (1)$$

However, this forward training cannot overcome the solution average issue and the output image still resides in the blurry image space (Fig. 1(a)). Therefore, the refinement with forward training does not improve the visual quality.

We propose an InvSharpNet that adopts backward training to learn an image blurring transform. Specifically, the ground truth image is fed into the output side of InvSharpNet and then inversely passed through the network to obtain an image at the input side, leveraging the network's invertibility. The MAE between this backward output and the blurry reconstruction is minimized:

$$\mathcal{L}_{backward} = ||\mathcal{S}^{-1}(I, Y) - R||_1 \qquad (2)$$

The under-sampled image Y is also provided as the input to provide information about under-sampling mask (see Sect. 2.3). As shown in Fig. 1(a), the backward training learns a blurring transform from the ground truth to the blurry reconstruction. At inference, InvSharpNet is used in the forward direction such that the blurry reconstruction is regarded as the network's input. InvSharpNet is designed based on iResNet [2] which imposes Lipschitz constraint on the network layers. The Lipschitz constraint guarantees that a small difference in network's input will not result in a large difference in network's output, meaning that the output in inference is close to the input in training. Therefore, InvSharpNet can obtain a sharpened image close to the ground truth in the sharp image space.

2.3   Network Architecture

Our InvSharpNet, shown in Fig. 1(b), contains 12 convolution blocks, and each has 5 convolution layers with 128 channels in each intermediate layer.

Lipschitz Constraint. The Lipschitz constant of each convolution layer should be less than 1 to achieve full invertibility, and the inverse is computed via a fixed-point iteration algorithm [2]. Given the output of each convolution block, the input is computed by iteratively looping through the block. A small Lipschitz constant, e.g. $c = 0.5$, requires fewer iterations to guarantee full invertibility but significantly inhibits the network's learning capability [2]. A large Lipschitz constant, e.g. $c = 0.9$, retains greater learning capability but requires more iterations to compute the inverse. One more iteration is equivalent to a 1-fold increase in network size. Therefore, a large c could significantly increase the memory usage and training time. We choose $c = 0.7$ and 2 iterations to balance the trade-off between learning capability and training time (see Sect. 3.2).

Conditioning on Under-Sampling Mask. In order to learn a mapping from the ground truth to a specific reconstruction that depends on the under-sampling mask, we let InvSharpNet condition on the corresponding mask. This can be achieved by concatenating the ground truth with the under-sampled image as the input during training, since the under-sampled image is generated with the under-sampling mask M and thus contains the mask information. As INN requires the same dimensionality on input and output, the network outputs two images, and we train both of them to approach the blurry reconstruction using Eq. 2. During inference, two duplicates of the reconstruction are input to the network in the forward direction. The output corresponding to the ground truth during training is taken as the sharpened reconstruction.

Data Fidelity. A DC layer is appended at the network's output in the forward (inference) direction to make the prediction consistent with measurements [5].

3   Experiments

We demonstrate the sharpening performance of InvSharpNet based on reconstructions from two models: PC-RNN [22], which ranked among the best-performed methods in 2019 fastMRI challenge [9], and U-Net [17]. We name these two reconstruction models as recon model 1 and 2, respectively.

We first implemented a refinement network that only uses the forward training (Eq. 1) with α set to 0.84 as suggested in [15]. We also implemented the conditional Wasserstein GAN (cWGAN) [12,16,19] by training with a weighted sum of forward and adversarial loss:

$$\mathcal{L}_{cWGAN} = \mathcal{L}_{forward} + \gamma \mathcal{L}_{adv} \tag{3}$$

where γ controls the trade-off between evaluation metrics and visual quality. $\gamma = 0.01$ and $\gamma = 0.02$ were tested to observe the difference. After that, we implemented two versions of InvSharpNet: one uses the backward training proposed in Eq. 2 and the other one uses a bidirectional training

$$\mathcal{L}_{bi} = \mathcal{L}_{forward} + \beta \mathcal{L}_{backward} \tag{4}$$

with β set to 2. The bidirectional training can be regarded as a compromise between evaluation metrics and visual quality. We used the same network architecture, illustrated in Fig. 1(b), for all methods. Trainings were performed with 50k iterations, batch size of 8 and a learning rate of 0.001 with Adam optimizer. Experiments were implemented in PyTorch on NVIDIA Tesla V100 GPUs.

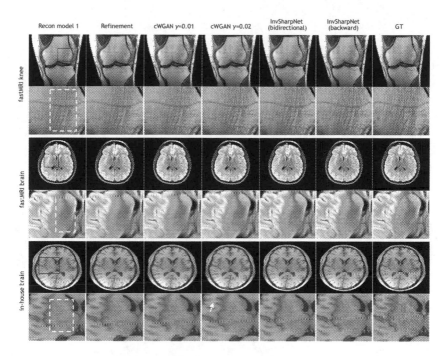

Fig. 2. Qualitative comparisons. The red boxes indicate the zoom-in areas and the yellow dashed boxes show regions where sharpness difference can be observed. The yellow arrow is an example of artifacts introduced by cWGAN. GT = Ground Truth. (Color figure online)

3.1 Datasets

fastMRI Knee Dataset. [10] includes 34,742 2D images from 973 subjects for training and 7,135 images from 199 subjects for evaluation, including modalities of proton-density weighted images with and without fat suppression. In this work, we focus on 4X acceleration of multi-coil data (same for fastMRI brain).

FastMRI Brain Dataset. [10] includes 67,558 images from 4,469 subjects for training and 20,684 images from 1,378 subjects for evaluation, including modalities of T1-weighted, T1-weighted pre-contrast, T1-weighted post-contrast, T2-weighted and T2 Fluid-attenuated inversion recovery images.

In-House Brain Dataset contains 584 images for evaluation, including five different gradient echo (GRE) contrasts. The data were collected with Institutional Reviews Board (IRB). We directly evaluate the networks trained on the fastMRI brain dataset.

3.2 Results

Qualitative Measure. Figure 2 illustrates examples of the sharpening results given by the compared methods on both public fastMRI and in-house datasets.

Table 1. Evaluation from 2 radiologists in a blind fashion over 3 knee and 3 brain cases from the fastMRI dataset. Ratings follow a 0–5 point scale, where 5 is the best and 0 is the worst. Results are shown in mean ± SD.

Method	Artifacts	Sharpness	Contrast-to-noise	Diagnostic confidence	Overall
Recon model 1	4.00 ± 0.95	4.00 ± 0.71	4.25 ± 0.40	3.75 ± 1.06	3.67 ± 0.98
Refinement	3.92 ± 0.87	3.88 ± 0.64	4.21 ± 0.40	3.71 ± 1.01	3.67 ± 0.98
cWGAN γ=0.01	3.75 ± 0.89	4.17 ± 0.58	4.33 ± 0.39	3.75 ± 1.01	3.71 ± 0.96
cWGAN γ=0.02	3.58 ± 0.95	4.33 ± 0.44	4.29 ± 0.45	3.79 ± 1.08	3.79 ± 0.96
InvSharpNet (bidirectional)	3.96 ± 0.92	4.21 ± 0.62	4.25 ± 0.26	**3.88 ± 1.13**	3.71 ± 0.96
InvSharpNet (backward)	**4.00 ± 0.88**	**4.67 ± 0.54**	**4.38 ± 0.43**	**3.88±1.13**	**3.88 ± 1.07**

The first column shows that the reconstructions given by recon model 1 look blurry compared to the ground truth images in the last column. As shown in the second column, training a refinement network in the forward direction produces almost identical images to the original reconstructions and fails to improve the visual quality. As well-documented in previous literature, training with the adversarial loss (cWGAN $\gamma = 0.01$) can improve the image sharpness, and using a stronger weight ($\gamma = 0.02$) can achieve further improvement. Using InvSharp-Net with bidirectional training achieved a similar level of sharpness enhancement as using cWGAN $\gamma = 0.01$. Finally, using InvSharpNet with backward training achieved even better sharpness than the bidirectional training. To better understand the visual quality improvement, we provide visualizations of k-space and image profile in Appendix Fig.A1. We also show a pathology case in Appendix Fig.A2.

The main advantage of using InvSharpNet instead of the cWGAN is the lower risk of introducing artifacts. As shown in Fig. 2 and Appendix Fig.A3, using generative models like cWGAN introduces artifacts (indicated by the yellow arrows) that were neither originally contained in the reconstructions nor contained in the ground truth, increasing the risk of incorrect medical diagnosis. Additionally, our results were evaluated from a clinical perspective using radiologists' ratings, which was considered as a key evaluation criterion in fastMRI competitions [9,14]. 2 radiologists examined the image quality of 6 selected cases (156 2D images) from the fastMRI knee and brain datasets in a blind fashion. The fully sampled images are given as rating references. The radiologists rated each image by artifacts, sharpness, contrast-to-noise ratio, diagnostic confidence and an overall score. The results are reported in Table 1, which shows that InvSharpNet with backward training outperforms other methods from all aspects. Although cWGAN models can also give higher sharpness scores than original reconstructions, they introduce artifacts that result in lower artifacts scores.

Quantitative Measure. Table 2 reports the commonly used evaluation metrics PSNR and SSIM. However, PSNR and SSIM are often degraded as sharpness improves due to the well-known perception-distortion tradeoff [3], making those metrics ineffective in evaluating our improvement. We observed that the image

Table 2. Quantitative comparisons using PSNR, SSIM and Contrast. Best scores are shown in bold. Underline indicates the second best contrast.

Method	fastMRI knee			fastMRI brain			in-house brain		
	PSNR	SSIM	Contrast	PSNR	SSIM	Contrast	PSNR	SSIM	Contrast
Recon model 1	38.9±2.8	.921±.043	.987±.008	40.2±2.2	.958±.015	.996±.002	**32.5±6.0**	.825±.175	.974±.034
Refinement	**39.1±2.7**	**.929±.039**	.984±.011	**40.6±2.3**	**.968±.014**	.994±.003	32.3±5.6	**.850±.165**	.964±.057
cWGAN γ=0.01	38.9±2.7	.927±.039	.990±.006	40.3±2.3	.967±.014	.996±.003	31.9±5.5	.848±.161	.972±.043
cWGAN γ=0.02	38.3±2.6	.920±.041	**.993±.004**	39.6±2.2	.963±.015	**.997±.002**	31.5±5.2	.840±.161	.980±.029
InvSharpNet(bi)	38.8±2.8	.922±.042	.989±.007	40.2±2.2	.961±.015	.997±.002	32.5±5.9	.835±.174	.977±.030
InvSharpNet(back)	38.5±2.7	.920±.043	.992±.005	39.4±2.1	.950±.017	.996±.002	32.4±5.7	.841±.170	**.981±.025**

sharpness is directly related to the contrast term in SSIM [23], so we also report it in Table 2. The refinement network gives the best PSNR and SSIM among all methods because it just focuses on minimizing the pixelwise and structural loss between the network's output and the ground truth. However, the contrast metric ranks the lowest for all datasets, indicating that high PSNR and SSIM scores do not necessarily correlate to good visual quality. Radiologists' ratings in Table 1 confirm this point: the refinement network provides images with the lowest sharpness and diagnostic confidence. On the other hand, although our InvSharpNet gives lower PSNR and SSIM than the refinement network, it provides images with better contrast and higher radiologists' ratings. Training InvSharpNet with a bidirectional strategy is a way to balance the trade-off between commonly used evaluation metrics and visual quality. A similar trade-off can also be observed when different values of γ were used for cWGAN.

We further demonstrate the effectiveness of our method using LPIPS [26], which measures images' high-level similarity and correlates well with human perceptual judgment (Table 3). InvSharpNet achieves better LPIPS on all three datasets compared to the reconstruction model and the refinement network, consistent with radiologists' ratings (Table 1) and the contrast metric (Table 2).

Generalizability. We also obtained results of sharpening the reconstructions based on recon model 2 in Fig. 3(a). Similar sharpness enhancement can be observed for reconstructions from recon model 2, which shows that InvSharpNet is a generalizable method. Evaluation scores in Appendix Table A1 further validate that InvSharpNet can improve the contrast of recon model 2 reconstructions.

Table 3. Quantitative comparisons using LPIPS (lower means more similar to GT).

Method	fastMRI knee	fastMRI brain	in-house brain
Recon model 1	0.078 ± 0.032	0.035 ± 0.015	0.067 ± 0.074
Refinement	0.089 ± 0.037	0.041 ± 0.018	0.078 ± 0.091
InvSharpNet(bi)	0.070 ± 0.029	**0.028 ± 0.013**	0.058 ± 0.069
InvSharpNet(back)	**0.068 ± 0.025**	**0.028 ± 0.012**	**0.055 ± 0.064**

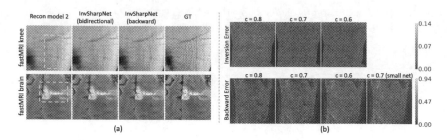

Fig. 3. (a) Generalizability. Sharpening results based on reconstructions from recon model 2. (b) Ablation studies on Lipschitz constants c and network sizes.

Lipschitz Constant. We compare three Lipschitz constants $c = 0.8, 0.7, 0.6$ by fixing the number of fixed-point iterations to 2 due to limited computation resources. Figure 3(b)(top) shows the inversion error defined as $E_{inv} = |I - S(S^{-1}(I))|$. A large inversion error means that a backward pass through the network is a poor approximation of the inverse of the forward pass, which could result in erroneous mapping learned from the backward training. $c = 0.8$ is a suboptimal choice as it gives an inversion error map in which the knee structure can clearly be observed, and $c = 0.7$ and 0.6 result in much smaller inversion errors. We then investigate how Lipschitz constant affects network's learning capability by showing the backward error as defined in Eq. 2 for one image example (Fig. 3(b)(bottom)). The backward error progressively increases as c is reduced from 0.8 to 0.6, implying a degradation of learning capability. To balance the inversion error and network's learning capability, we chose $c = 0.7$.

Network Size. A large network size is required to compensate for the Lipschitz constraint that undermines networks' learning capability. InvSharpNet contains roughly 5.4M parameters, and we justify this choice by comparing it with a smaller network containing 0.7M parameters. We show that when $c = 0.7$, using the small network results in a larger backward error (Fig. 3(b)(bottom)), indicating that the mapping is not learned as well as the larger model.

4 Conclusion

We propose a novel InvSharpNet that learns a blurring transform from the fully-sampled MRI images to the blurry reconstructions, which is inverted during inference to enhance the blurry input. Results show that InvSharpNet can improve image quality given by the existing reconstruction methods, providing higher diagnostic confidence for clinicians. The method can be extended to image denoising and super-resolution.

References

1. Antun, V., Renna, F., Poon, C., Adcock, B., Hansen, A.C.: On instabilities of deep learning in image reconstruction and the potential costs of AI. Proc. Natl. Acad. Sci. **117**(48), 30088–30095 (2020)

2. Behrmann, J., Grathwohl, W., Chen, R.T., Duvenaud, D., Jacobsen, J.H.: Invertible residual networks. In: International Conference on Machine Learning, pp. 573–582. PMLR (2019)
3. Blau, Y., Michaeli, T.: The perception-distortion tradeoff. In: Proceedings of the IEEE conference on computer vision and pattern recognition, pp. 6228–6237 (2018)
4. Chen, E.Z., Chen, T., Sun, S.: MRI image reconstruction via learning optimization using neural ODEs. In: Martel, A.L., et al. (eds.) MICCAI 2020. LNCS, vol. 12262, pp. 83–93. Springer, Cham (2020). https://doi.org/10.1007/978-3-030-59713-9_9
5. Duan, J., et al.: VS-Net: variable splitting network for accelerated parallel MRI reconstruction. In: Shen, D., et al. (eds.) MICCAI 2019. LNCS, vol. 11767, pp. 713–722. Springer, Cham (2019). https://doi.org/10.1007/978-3-030-32251-9_78
6. Jun, Y., Shin, H., Eo, T., Hwang, D.: Joint deep model-based MR image and coil sensitivity reconstruction network (Joint-ICNet) for fast MRI. In: Proceedings of the IEEE/CVF Conference on Computer Vision and Pattern Recognition, pp. 5270–5279 (2021)
7. Kingma, D.P., Dhariwal, P.: Glow: Generative flow with invertible 1×1 convolutions. Adv. Neural Inf. Process. Syst. **31**, 1–11 (2018)
8. Knoll, F., et al.: Deep-learning methods for parallel magnetic resonance imaging reconstruction: a survey of the current approaches, trends, and issues. IEEE Signal Process. Mag. **37**(1), 128–140 (2020)
9. Knoll, F., et al.: Advancing machine learning for MR image reconstruction with an open competition: Overview of the 2019 FastMRI challenge. Magn. Reson. Med. **84**(6), 3054–3070 (2020)
10. Knoll, F., et al.: fastMRI: a publicly available raw k-space and DICOM dataset of knee images for accelerated MR image reconstruction using machine learning. Radiol. Artif. Intell. **2**(1), e190007 (2020)
11. Li, W., et al.: Best-buddy GANs for highly detailed image super-resolution. arXiv preprint arXiv:2103.15295 (2021)
12. Malkiel, I., Ahn, S., Taviani, V., Menini, A., Wolf, L., Hardy, C.J.: Conditional WGANs with adaptive gradient balancing for sparse MRI reconstruction. arXiv preprint arXiv:1905.00985 (2019)
13. Menon, S., Damian, A., Hu, S., Ravi, N., Rudin, C.: Pulse: self-supervised photo upsampling via latent space exploration of generative models. In: Proceedings of the IEEE/CVF Conference on Computer Vision and Pattern Recognition, pp. 2437–2445 (2020)
14. Muckley, M.J., et al.: Results of the 2020 fastMRI challenge for machine learning MR image reconstruction. IEEE Trans. Med. Imaging **40**(9), 2306–2317 (2021)
15. Pezzotti, N., et al.: An adaptive intelligence algorithm for undersampled knee MRI reconstruction. IEEE Access **8**, 204825–204838 (2020)
16. Quan, T.M., Nguyen-Duc, T., Jeong, W.K.: Compressed sensing MRI reconstruction using a generative adversarial network with a cyclic loss. IEEE Trans. Med. Imaging **37**(6), 1488–1497 (2018)
17. Ronneberger, O., Fischer, P., Brox, T.: U-net: convolutional networks for biomedical image segmentation. In: Navab, N., Hornegger, J., Wells, W.M., Frangi, A.F. (eds.) MICCAI 2015. LNCS, vol. 9351, pp. 234–241. Springer, Cham (2015). https://doi.org/10.1007/978-3-319-24574-4_28
18. Schlemper, J., Caballero, J., Hajnal, J.V., Price, A.N., Rueckert, D.: A deep cascade of convolutional neural networks for dynamic MR image reconstruction. IEEE Trans. Med. Imaging **37**(2), 491–503 (2017)

19. Seitzer, M., et al.: Adversarial and perceptual refinement for compressed sensing MRI reconstruction. In: Frangi, A.F., Schnabel, J.A., Davatzikos, C., Alberola-López, C., Fichtinger, G. (eds.) MICCAI 2018. LNCS, vol. 11070, pp. 232–240. Springer, Cham (2018). https://doi.org/10.1007/978-3-030-00928-1_27

20. Sønderby, C.K., Caballero, J., Theis, L., Shi, W., Huszár, F.: Amortised map inference for image super-resolution. arXiv preprint arXiv:1610.04490 (2016)

21. Sriram, A., Zbontar, J., Murrell, T., Zitnick, C.L., Defazio, A., Sodickson, D.K.: Grappanet: combining parallel imaging with deep learning for multi-coil MRI reconstruction. In: Proceedings of the IEEE/CVF Conference on Computer Vision and Pattern Recognition, pp. 14315–14322 (2020)

22. Wang, P., Chen, E.Z., Chen, T., Patel, V.M., Sun, S.: Pyramid convolutional RNN for MRI reconstruction. arXiv preprint arXiv:1912.00543 (2019)

23. Wang, Z., Bovik, A.C., Sheikh, H.R., Simoncelli, E.P.: Image quality assessment: from error visibility to structural similarity. IEEE Trans. Image Process. **13**(4), 600–612 (2004)

24. Wang, Z., Simoncelli, E.P., Bovik, A.C.: Multiscale structural similarity for image quality assessment. In: The Thrity-Seventh Asilomar Conference on Signals, Systems & Computers, 2003. vol. 2, pp. 1398–1402. IEEE (2003)

25. Yang, G., Lv, J., Chen, Y., Huang, J., Zhu, J.: Generative adversarial networks (GAN) powered fast magnetic resonance imaging-mini review, comparison and perspectives. arXiv preprint arXiv:2105.01800 (2021)

26. Zhang, R., Isola, P., Efros, A.A., Shechtman, E., Wang, O.: The unreasonable effectiveness of deep features as a perceptual metric. In: Proceedings of the IEEE Conference on Computer Vision and Pattern Recognition, pp. 586–595 (2018)

Analyzing and Improving Low Dose CT Denoising Network via HU Level Slicing

Sutanu Bera[✉] and Prabir Kumar Biswas

Department of Electronics and Electrical Communication Engineering, Indian
Institute of Technology Kharagpur, Kharagpur, India
sutanu.bera@iitkgp.ac.in

Abstract. The deep convolutional neural network has been extensively studied for medical images denoising, specifically for low dose CT
(LDCT) denoising. However, most of them disregard that medical images
have a large dynamic range. After normalizing the input image, the difference between two nearby HU levels becomes minimal; furthermore,
after multiplying it with the floating-point weight vector, the feature
response becomes insensitive to small changes in the input images. As
a consequence, the denoised image becomes visually smooth. With this
observation, we propose to use HU level slicing for improving the performance of the vanilla convolutional network. In our method, we first use
different CT windows to slice the input image into a separate HU range.
Then different CNN network is used to process each generated input
slice separately. Finally, a feature fusion module combines the feature
learned by each network and produces the denoised image. Extensive
experiments with different state of the art methods in different training settings (both supervised and unsupervised) in three benchmark low
dose CT databases validates HU level slicing can significantly improve
the denoising performance of the existing methods.

Keywords: Low dose CT denoising · CT windowing · Dynamic range

1 Introduction

The resurgence of deep neural networks has created an alternative pathway for
medical image denoising via learning a non-linear function to map a noisy image
to its noise-free counterpart [1,3,13,14] . Recent works with both unsupervised
and supervised paradigm have demonstrated that neural networks can denoise
medical images of all modalities [4,8]. However, existing methods overlooked
one of the most elementary facts, that medical images have a large dynamic
range. For example, the dynamic range of computed tomography (CT) images
is 4096 HU (compared to 256 of the natural images). When we normalize the
large dynamic range image for feeding into the neural network, the difference

---

Supplementary Information The online version contains supplementary material
available at https://doi.org/10.1007/978-3-031-16446-0_56.

L. Wang et al. (Eds.): MICCAI 2022, LNCS 13436, pp. 593–602, 2022.
https://doi.org/10.1007/978-3-031-16446-0_56

between nearby HU levels or the intensity resolution becomes very small ($\approx 10^{-4}$). Again, convolutional neural networks mostly learn floating-point weights, so multiplying two small floating-point numbers further decreases the contrast in the latent feature space. As a result, the denoised output image exhibits a noticeable blurriness, and finer details present in the denoised image becomes imperceptible.

In this study, we first analyzed the effect of low intensity resolution of medical images in the CNN network concerning low dose CT (LDCT) denoising [2,12]. Next, we proposed a method to overcome this low intensity resolution issue. In our method, we first split the input LDCT image into different slices using HU level slicing and then feed those sliced images into the neural network instead of the full image. The slice images have a small dynamic range, so the contrast of the latent feature map remains adequate. For HU level slicing, we employ an unconventional CT windowing technique, where all HU values below/above the corresponding lower/higher range of CT window was set to 0. Next, we employed separate CNN networks of same architecture to extract features from each input slice. A novel feature fusion module is then used to combine the features learned by each CNN network. The integrated features are again back-projected to image space using a set of separate convolutional stems to produce slices of the output denoised image.

We experimented with three current state of art low dose CT denoising networks to analyze the effect of HU level slicing using three benchmark low dose CT databases, namely, TCIA Low Dose CT Image and Projection Data [7], the 2016 NIH-AAPM-Mayo Clinic low dose CT grand challenge database [6], and ELCAP Public Lung Image Database [10]. We found the proposed method can significantly improve the denoising performance of the existing methods. The denoised images also retain a visible sharpness compared to the earlier blurry images.

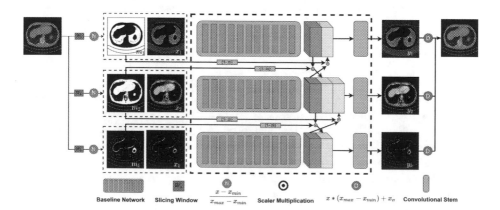

Fig. 1. Simplified illustration of the proposed method. Instead of feeding the original input image to the network, we proposed to feed slices (generated using CT windowing) of the input images to the network.

2   Method

We have given a visual illustration of the proposed method in Fig. 1. As seen, the input image is first passed through different HU slicing windows. The range of the slicing window depends on the number of slices used. For example, if we use 5 slices, then the range of the first slicing window is $[-1204, -400]$, the next window has the range $[-400\ 400]$ and so on. Here, the values outside the range of the window are set to 0. So, the output of the kth slicing window x_{w_k} is defind as

$$x_{w_k} = \left\{ x_{i,j} | x_{i,j} = \begin{cases} x_{i,j} & \text{if} \ \ W_{S_k} < x_{i,j} < W_{E_k} \\ 0 & \text{else} \end{cases} \right\}$$

Here, x is the input image, and $[W_{Sk}, W_{Ek}]$ is the range of the kth slicing window. The slicing window also produces a binary mask M_k, defined as below

$$M_k = \left\{ m_{i,j} | m_{i,j} = \begin{cases} 1 & \text{if} \ \ W_{S_k} < x_{i,j} < W_{E_k} \\ 0 & \text{else} \end{cases} \right\}$$

After k level of slicing we have $x_{w_1}, x_{w_2}, .. x_{w_k}$ slices, and $M_1, M_2, .. M_k$ binary mask. Next, each slice is normalized to the range [0,1] using the min-max normalization technique. The normalized slice is then fed to separate CNN networks. The output of the CNN network is a 3D feature map. Let $z_{w_1} \in \mathbb{R}^{C \times W \times H}$ be the output of latent feature map of the $\mathcal{F}_{w_1}$ network, i.e., $z_{w_1} = \mathcal{F}_{w_1}(x_{w_1})$. Likewise, there will be a k 3D feature map. Note, none of the networks has complete semantic knowledge about the input image. To efficiently reconstruct the boundary region of different slices and the pixel with values nearby to the extreme HU level of each window, a continuous information exchange between all the networks is required. We employed a future fusion module to achieve this seamless information flow. In the feature fusion module, one feature map is combined with the feature map of its two immediate windows as described below:

$$z_{w_i}^c = \left[(1 - M_i) \odot z_{w_i - 1}; z_{w_i}; (1 - M_i) \odot z_{w_i + 1} \right]$$

Here, $\odot$ is denotes element-wise multiplication with scalar term, $[a; b]$ indicates concatenation of feature map a and b. If i is 1 or k, then only next or previous feature map is combined with the current feature map in the fusion module. The combined feature map is fed to a convolutional stem layer in the next step that produced the denoised slice image $\hat{y}_{w_i}$, i.e., $\hat{y}_{w_i} = \mathcal{C}(z_{w_i}^c)$. Here, $\mathcal{C}$ is the convolution stem. In the final step the $\hat{y}_{w_i}$ is again denormalized to convert back to original HU range, and all the $\hat{y}_{w_i}$ are combined to produce the final output image $\hat{y}$.

Learning. Training all the networks jointly is a challenging problem. We used different strategies for different loss functions. For pixel-based loss functions (e.g., MSE loss, L1 loss), we employed the same CT windowing technique and min-max normalization to generate slices of the target image. The reconstruction loss is calculated between each pair of slices independently, i.e.,

$$L_{reconstruction} = L_{MSE}(\hat{y}_{w_1}, y_{w_1}) + L_{MSE}(x_{w_2}, y_{w_2}) + ... + L_{MSE}(x_{w_k}, y_{w_k})$$

This loss is back propagated to jointly train all the networks. Next, for other losses like adversarial or perceptual we computed the loss between x_N, and y_N. Where, x_N, and y_N is the normalized input and target image.

Network Architecture. We removed the last two convolutional layers of the vanilla denoising network (e.g., REDCNN [3], UNet [11]) and used it as $\mathcal{F}_{w_i}$. In our study, the architecture of each $\mathcal{F}_{w_i}$ is identical; however, the method can further optimize via adjusting the depth and width of the individual $\mathcal{F}_{w_i}$. We used two convolutional layers with the ReLU activation function to realize the convolutional stem.

3   Experimental Details

To validate the proposed method, we experimented with three state of the art low dose CT denoising method. Namely, 1. REDCNN [3], 2. SA-SNMP-GAN [1], 3. CycleGAN [5,15]. Among these methods, REDCNN and SA-SNMP-GAN are supervised methods, and CycleGAN is unsupervised methods. In REDCNN, MSE loss is used for training the network, whereas SA-SNMP-GAN is an adversarial loss based method. We used three publicly available low dose CT data sets to evaluate the proposed method as described below; we refer to them as D1, D2 and D3. **D1:** 2016 NIH-AAPM-Mayo Clinic Low Dose CT Grand Challenge Database **D2:** TCIA Low Dose CT Image and Projection Data **D3:** ELCAP Public Lung Image Database. The CNNs are implemented in python using the pytorch [9] library. A GeForce GTX 2080Ti GPU is used for acceleration. Other training details about training individual networks are given in the supplementary material.

4   Result and Discussion

4.1   Sensitivity Analysis

We first analyze the effect of the large dynamic range in the CNN network. We experimented with the REDCNN network on dataset D1 in this analysis. We first train a model (M1) using a normalized full range [0, 4095] input image. Next, we truncated the input image to the range [−160 240] range and normalized the truncated image in this range, and trained a model (M2) with this truncated data. Again, we normalized the input image in the entire HU range and truncated the image in the range corresponding to the HU value [−160 240] and trained a model (M3) with this data. Instinctively, the first and last cases have the same intensity resolution, whereas the second case has a higher intensity resolution. An objective comparison between the three models is given in Table 1.

Table 1. Objective evaluation of different trained network. The result are obtained by averaging the metric scores of all images from test set of dataset 1, using REDCNN network

Model	RMSE	PSNR	SSIM
M1	9.06	33.03	0.9011
M2	8.54	33.33	0.9115
M3	9.07	33.02	0.9011

Table 2. Ablation of number of slicing window used. The result are obtained by averaging the metric scores of all images from test set of dataset 1, using REDCNN nctwork

No of slice	2	3	4	5
RMSE	8.92	8.56	8.12	7.86
PSNR	33.10	33.23	33.31	33.46
SSIM	0.9017	0.9100	0.9110	0.9115

As shown in Table 1 the performance of the network increases significantly when we stretch the intensity resolution of the input image. In Fig. 2, we compared the denoising performance of these three networks visually. Here also, we can see that the sharpness of the denoised image has significantly boosted the output of M2, allowing the radiologist to understand the image content better. The splotchy artifact is much lower than the output of M1 and M3. Our analysis pinpoints that the intensity resolution plays a vital role in the deep CNN network, as only increasing the intensity resolution boosted the performance so much. It needs to be noted that both M2 and M3 used truncated data, so data truncation did not assist in performance boosting. Stretching intensity resolution through data truncation improves the denoising performance. However, training separate networks with different windowed CT images is impractical. We also found that the network entirely failed to remove noise if we changed the dynamic range during the test. The network considered noise as a signal due to intensity resolution mismatching and reproduced the original noisy image.

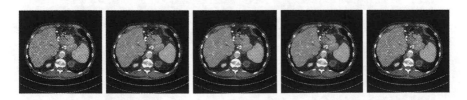

Fig. 2. Result of Denoising for comparison. From Left: LDCT, M1, M2, M3, NDCT. Viewers are encouraged to zoom for better view. The display window is [−140, 260].

The proposed HU level slicing significantly increases the intensity resolution of the input image feed to the network. Intuitively, increasing the no of the slicing window will increase the intensity resolution of each slice image. We experimented with the REDCNN network on dataset D1 to investigate the sensitivity of network performance on the addition in the number of slicing windows. As depicted in Table 2, the increase in the number of slicing windows used linearly increases the performance of the network; with five slicing windows, the PSNR is boosted by 0.40 dB.

Table 3. Objective comparison of different trained network. Here Method-1 indicate the original method, and Method-2 is the modified network with HU Level Slicing.

Method	D1			D2		
	PSNR	SSIM	RMSE	PSNR	SSIM	RMSE
REDCNN-1	33.03	0.9011	9.0623	40.81	0.9615	1.8623
REDCNN-2	**33.46**	**0.9115**	**7.8612**	**41.23**	**0.9679**	**1.7290**
SA-SNMP-GAN-1	31.26	0.9107	10.4601	39.44	0.9595	2.2009
SA-SNMP-GAN-2	**32.84**	**0.9231**	**9.5640**	**39.98**	**0.9515**	**2.3854**
CycleGAN-1	30.86	0.8860	11.2352	37.23	0.9351	3.1002
CycleGAN-2	**31.16**	**0.9007**	**10.2340**	**38.01**	**0.9452**	**2.7402**

4.2   Comparison with SOTA Method

Here we compare the effect of HU level slicing on different state of the art method. For every SOTA method, we first trained a model using the same training procedure mentioned in the respective literature and then trained another

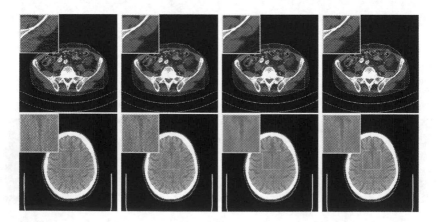

Fig. 3. Result of Denoising for comparison. From Left: LDCT, REDCNN-1, REDCNN-2, NDCT. Viewers are encouraged to zoom for better view.

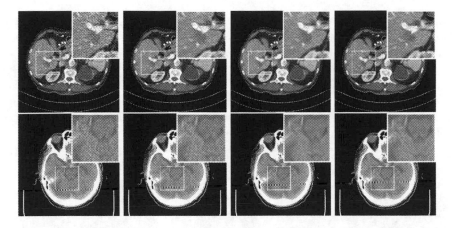

Fig. 4. Result of Denoising for comparison. From Left: LDCT, SA-SNMP-GAN-1, SA-SNMP-GAN-2, NDCT. Viewers are encouraged to zoom for better view.

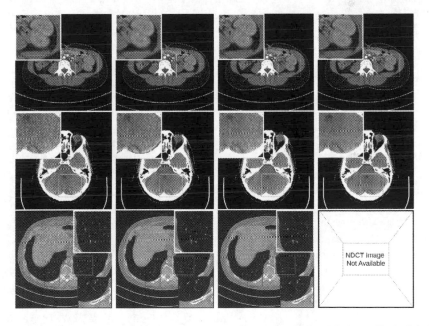

Fig. 5. Result of Denoising for comparison. From Left: LDCT, CycleGAN-1, CycleGAN-2, NDCT. Viewers are encouraged to zoom for better view.

model using the same training setting and loss function but employed the HU level slicing. We denote them as Method-1 and Method-2, respectively. Five level of slicing window is used to implement Method-2. Due to space limitations, we only showed the result on the head subset of the D2 dataset. The ground truth for D1 and D2 is available, so we used it for objective evaluation. Dataset D3 contain real low dose CT images of the Chest. As the ground truth image is not available, we used D3 for the qualitative assessment of the unsupervised Cycle-GAN method. We have collectively validated our method in LDCT images from 3 anatomical sites. The objective evaluation of different methods on D1 and D2 datasets is given in Table 3. As seen, the proposed HU level slicing significantly improved the denoising performance of every SOTA method. For example, PSNR is improved by 0.43 dB in REDCNN if we use HU level slicing in dataset D1. The same can be seen in dataset D2 also. Interestingly, our REDCNN-2 performed better than the model M2. Although the input data to both REDCNN-2 and M2 had higher intensity resolution. However, due to the data truncation, some input image information was missing in the input data of M2; as a result, the network performed lower than the optimal. Our proposed HU level slicing allows raising the intensity resolution without data truncation. Similar to the first two supervised methods, the proposed HU level slicing also helped in enhancing the performance of the unsupervised CycleGAN method. We compared the denoising performance of the modified REDCNN-2 network to the original REDCNN-1 network visually in Fig. 3. As shown, the contribution of the HU level slicing is not merely the PSNR or SSIM improvement, but the visual quality of the denoised image has been significantly enhanced. For example, in the abdomen image taken from dataset D1, the crispness of the denoised image is evident. We have also given the zoomed view of a sample region of the denoised image in the inset. From the zoom view, we can perceive the intensity resolution of the denoised image of the REDCNN-1 is very poor; many segments are blurry in the denoised image. The boundary line of the different organs is not clear. In the bottom row of Fig. 3, we have given an example denoised image of the head LDCT scan taken from dataset D2. We can see that the vanilla REDCNN-1 network's output still has a lot of residual noise left, and the overall appearance is blurry. In comparison, our REDCNN-2 has efficiently removed the noise from the LDCT image and maintained a sharp appearance. Next, we visually compared the denoising performance of the modified SA-SNMP-GAN-2 network to the original SA-SNMP-GAN-1 network in Fig. 4. We selected one sample location and gave the zoomed view in the inset. The noisy splotchy pattern is still present in the output image of vanilla SA-SNMP-GAN-2. These low magnitude variations are imperceptible to neural network weights because of the low-intensity resolution of the input image. In our method, the network effortlessly identified these variations and subsequently removed the noise. The same is also valid for the bottom row image taken from dataset D2. In Fig. 5 we have compared the denoising performance of the vanilla CycleGAN framework and the modified CycleGAN. We have shown the denoising performance on real low dose CT data in the bottom row. As evident, our method has significantly improved the visual quality of the denoised image in unsupervised settings also.

5   Conclusion

This study investigated one of the most disregarded issues of deep learning-based LDCT image denoising, i.e., the effect of a high dynamic range on CNN networks. To the best of our knowledge, this study is the first to analyse the above-mentioned. We have proposed a simple yet effective method to overcome the problem. The proposed HU level slicing can be used in any existing method to enhance the denoising performance. The extensive experiment on three low dose CT datasets containing images from three anatomical sites (i.e., head, abdomen, chest) validates that the proposed method can significantly improve the denoising performance of both supervised and unsupervised methods.

References

1. Bera, S., Biswas, P.K.: Noise conscious training of non local neural network powered by self attentive spectral normalized markovian patch gan for low dose ct denoising. IEEE Trans. Med. Imaging **40**(12), 3663–3673 (2021)
2. Brenner, D.J.: Radiation risks potentially associated with low-dose CT screening of adult smokers for lung cancer. Radiology **231**(2), 440–445 (2004)
3. Chen, H., et al.: Low-dose CT with a residual encoder-decoder convolutional neural network. IEEE Trans. Med. Imaging **36**(12), 2524–2535 (2017)
4. Gong, K., Guan, J., Liu, C.C., Qi, J.: Pet image denoising using a deep neural network through fine tuning. IEEE Trans. Radiat. Plasma Med. Sci. **3**(2), 153–161 (2019). https://doi.org/10.1109/TRPMS.2018.2877644
5. Li, Z., Huang, J., Yu, L., Chi, Y., Jin, M.: Low-dose CT image denoising using cycle-consistent adversarial networks. In: 2019 IEEE Nuclear Science Symposium and Medical Imaging Conference (NSS/MIC), pp. 1–3. IEEE (2019)
6. McCollough, C.H., et al.: Low-dose CT for the detection and classification of metastatic liver lesions: results of the 2016 low dose ct grand challenge. Med. Phys. **44**(10), e339–e352 (2017)
7. Moen, T.R., et al.: Low-dose CT image and projection dataset. Med. Phys. **48**(2), 902–911 (2021)
8. Moreno López, M., Frederick, J.M., Ventura, J.: Evaluation of MRI denoising methods using unsupervised learning. Front. Artif. Intell. **4**, 75 (2021)
9. Paszke, A., et al.: Pytorch: an imperative style, high-performance deep learning library. Adv. Neural Inf. Process. Syst. **32**, 1–12 (2019)
10. Reeves, A.P., Xie, Y., Liu, S.: Large-scale image region documentation for fully automated image biomarker algorithm development and evaluation. J. Med. Imaging **4**(2), 024505 (2017)
11. Ronneberger, O., Fischer, P., Brox, T.: U-Net: convolutional networks for biomedical image segmentation. In: Navab, N., Hornegger, J., Wells, W.M., Frangi, A.F. (eds.) MICCAI 2015. LNCS, vol. 9351, pp. 234–241. Springer, Cham (2015). https://doi.org/10.1007/978-3-319-24574-4_28
12. Su, A.W., et al.: Low-dose computed tomography reduces radiation exposure by 90% compared with traditional computed tomography among patients undergoing hip-preservation surgery. Arthroscopy J. Arthroscopic Related Surg. **35**(5), 1385–1392 (2019)
13. Wu, D., Gong, K., Kim, K., Li, X., Li, Q.: Consensus neural network for medical imaging denoising with only noisy training samples. In: Shen, D., et al. (eds.) MICCAI 2019. LNCS, vol. 11767, pp. 741–749. Springer, Cham (2019). https://doi.org/10.1007/978-3-030-32251-9_81

14. Yang, Q., et al.: Low-dose CT image denoising using a generative adversarial network with wasserstein distance and perceptual loss. IEEE Trans. Med. Imaging **37**(6), 1348–1357 (2018)
15. Zhu, J.Y., Park, T., Isola, P., Efros, A.A.: Unpaired image-to-image translation using cycle-consistent adversarial networks. In: Proceedings of the IEEE International Conference on Computer Vision, pp. 2223–2232 (2017)

Spatio-Temporal Motion Correction and Iterative Reconstruction of In-Utero Fetal fMRI

Athena Taymourtash[1], Hamza Kebiri[2,3], Ernst Schwartz[1],
Karl-Heinz Nenning[1,4], Sébastien Tourbier[2], Gregor Kasprian[5],
Daniela Prayer[1,5], Meritxell Bach Cuadra[2,3], and Georg Langs[1(✉)]

[1] Computational Imaging Research Lab, Department of Biomedical Imaging and
Image-Guided Therapy, Medical University of Vienna, Vienna, Austria
georg.langs@meduniwien.ac.at
[2] Medical Image Analysis Laboratory, Department of Radiology, Lausanne
University Hospital and University of Lausanne, Lausanne, Switzerland
[3] CIBM Center for Biomedical Imaging, Vaud, Switzerland
[4] Center for Biomedical Imaging and Neuromodulation, Nathan Kline Institute,
Orangeburg, NY, USA
[5] Division of Neuroradiology and Muskulo-Skeletal Radiology, Department of
Biomedical Imaging and Image-Guided Therapy, Medical University of Vienna,
Vienna, Austria

Abstract. Resting-state functional Magnetic Resonance Imaging
(fMRI) is a powerful imaging technique for studying functional development of the brain *in utero*. However, unpredictable and excessive movement of fetuses have limited its clinical applicability. Previous studies
have focused primarily on the accurate estimation of the motion parameters employing a single step 3D interpolation at each individual time
frame to recover a motion-free 4D fMRI image. Using only information
from a 3D spatial neighborhood neglects the temporal structure of fMRI
and useful information from neighboring timepoints. Here, we propose
a novel technique based on four dimensional iterative reconstruction of
the motion scattered fMRI slices. Quantitative evaluation of the proposed
method on a cohort of real clinical fetal fMRI data indicates improvement
of reconstruction quality compared to the conventional 3D interpolation
approaches.

Keywords: Fetal fMRI · Image reconstruction · Motion-compensated
recovery · Regularization

Supplementary Information The online version contains supplementary material
available at https://doi.org/10.1007/978-3-031-16446-0_57.

L. Wang et al. (Eds.): MICCAI 2022, LNCS 13436, pp. 603–612, 2022.
https://doi.org/10.1007/978-3-031-16446-0_57

1   Introduction

Functional magnetic resonance imaging (fMRI) offers a unique means of observing the functional brain architecture and its variation during development, aging, or disease. Despite the insights into network formation and functional growth of the brain, *in utero* fMRI of living human fetuses, and the developmental functional connectivity (FC), however, remain challenging. Since the fMRI acuisition takes several minutes, unconstrained and potentially large movements of the fetuses, uterine contractions, and maternal respiration can cause severe artifacts such as in-plane blurring, slice cross-talk, and spin-history artifacts that likely vary over time. Without mitigation, motion artifacts can considerably affect the image quality, leading to a bias of subsequent conclusions about the FC of the developing brain.

Standard motion correction approaches, including frame-by-frame spatial realignment along with discarding parts of data with excessive motion, have been adopted so far to address motion artifacts of *in utero* fMRI [9,16,19]. More recently, cascaded slice-to-volume registration [12] combined with spin history correction [4], and framewise registration based on the 2nd order edge features instead of raw intensities [10] were suggested. These studies used 3D linear interpolation of motion scattered data at each volume independently to reconstruct the entire time series. Since *in utero* motion is unconstrained and complex, the regular grid of observed fMRI volumes becomes a set of irregularly motion scattered points possibly out of the field-of-view of the reconstruction grid, which might contain gaps in regions with no points in close proximity. Therefore interpolation in each 3D volume cannot recover the entire reconstruction grid.

Here we propose a new reconstruction method that takes advantage of the temporal structure of fMRI time series and rather than treating each frame independently, it takes both the spatial and the temporal domains into account to iteratively reconstruct a full 4D in utero fMRI image. The proposed method relies on super-resolution techniques that attracted increasing attention in structural fetal T2-weighted imaging, aiming to estimate a 3D high-resolution (HR) volume from multiple (semi-)orthogonal low resolution scans [3,5,14]. In case of fMRI, orthogonal acquisitions are not available, instead the reconstruction of a 4D image from a single sequence acquired over time is desired (An illustration of the problem is shown in Fig. 1). Currently, existing single-image reconstruction methods are generally proposed for 3D structural MR images with isotropic voxels, while the effect of motion is implicitly modeled via blurring the desired HR image [13]. None of these methods have been tailored for 4D fMRI with high-levels of movement such as the fetal population.

Our contribution is threefold: (1) we develop a 4D optimization scheme based on low-rank and total variation regularization to reconstruct 4D fMRI data as a whole (2) we explicitly model the effect of motion in the image degradation process since it is the main source of gaps between interpolated slices; (3) we show the performance of our algorithm on the highly anisotropic *in utero* fMRI images. Experiments were performed on 20 real individuals, and the proposed method was compared to various interpolation methods.

2   Method

We first describe the fMRI image acquisition model and then its corresponding inverse problem formulation to recover a 4D artifact-free fMRI from a single scan of motion corrupted image, using low-rank and total variation regularizations.

2.1   The Reconstruction Problem

fMRI requires the acquisition of a number of volumes over time (fMRI time-series, bold signal) to probe the modulation of spontaneous (or task-related) neural activity. This activity is characterized by low frequency fluctuations ($<0.1\,\text{Hz}$) of bold signals and therefore temporal smoothing is often applied as a pre-processing step in fMRI analysis. We aim at estimating the motion-compensated reconstruction of fMRI time series ($\mathcal{X} \in \mathbb{R}^{\hat{B} \times \hat{K} \times \hat{H} \times N}$) from observed motion-contaminated fMRI volumes ($\mathcal{T} \in \mathbb{R}^{B \times K \times H \times N}$) that integrates temporal smoothing within a full 4D iterative framework. Both $\mathcal{X}$ and $\mathcal{T}$ are composed of N 3D volumes $\mathbf{X}_n, \mathbf{T}_n$ acquired over N timepoints. In MR image acquisition, a degradation process yields a low-resolution image from the latent high-resolution image:

$$\mathbf{T}_n = DSM_n\mathbf{X}_n + z \tag{1}$$

where D is a 3D downsampling operator, S is a 3D blurring operator, M is the set of estimated motion parameters (three rotation and three translation parameters for each slice $\mathbf{t}_{n,h} \in \mathbb{R}^{\mathbf{B} \times K}$ of the volume $\mathbf{T}_n$, estimated prior to optimization (Sect. 3.1)), and z represents the observation noise. The application of M_n in the model here is equivalent to transforming each slice by the motion followed by resampling them on a 4D regular grid. Successful recovery of $\mathcal{X}$ from the $\mathcal{T}$ not only ensures the compensation of motion but also smoother bold signals due to the implicit temporal structure present in the data. However, since the Eq. (1) is ill-posed, direct recovery of $\mathcal{X}$ is not possible without enforcing a prior. Hence, the reconstruction of the latent desired 4D image $\mathcal{X}$ is achieved by minimizing the following cost function based on the inverse problem formulation:

$$\min_{\mathcal{X}} \sum_{n=1}^{N} \|DSM_n\mathbf{X}_n - \mathbf{T}_n\|^2 + \lambda\Re(\mathcal{X}) \tag{2}$$

where $\Re(\mathcal{X})$ is a spatio-temporal regularization term, and λ balances the contributions of the data fidelity and regularization terms. We propose two regularization terms in this context, 4D low-rank for missing data recovery and total variation for preserving local spatial consistency.

4D Low-Rank Regularization. Rank as a measure of nondegenerateness of the matrix, is defined by the maximum number of linearly independent rows or columns in the matrix. Since self-similarity is widely observed in fMRI images, low rank prior has been successfully used in matrix completion of censored fMRI

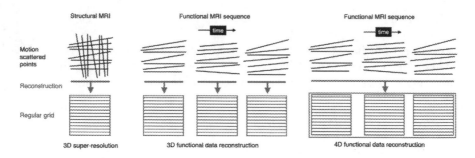

Fig. 1. Illustration of the image reconstruction using super-resolution technique. Oversampling exists in case of 3D structural MRI (left panel), however, there is not enough data for separate reconstruction of each 3D fMRI volume (middle panel). Here we propose to reconstruct the whole 4D fMRI at once using both spatial and temporal data structure (right panel).

time series [1]. Here we use low rank as a regularization term to help retrieve relevant information from all image regions. To compute the rank for a 4D image $\mathcal{X}$, we first unfold it into a 2D matrix along each dimension [6]. Specifically, suppose the size of $\mathcal{X}$ is $B \times K \times H \times N$, we unfold it into four 2D matrices $\{X_{(i)}, i = 1, 2, 3, 4\}$ with size of $B \times (K \times H \times N), K \times (B \times H \times N), H \times (B \times K \times N)$, and $N \times (B \times K \times H)$ where X(i) means unfold $\mathcal{X}$ along dimension i. Then we compute the sum of the singular values in each matrix for their trace norms $\|X_{(i)}\|_{tr}$. Finally, the rank of $\mathcal{X}$ is approximated as the combination of trace norms of all unfolded matrices [13]:

$$\Re_{rank}(\mathcal{X}) = \sum_{i=1}^{4} \alpha_i \|X_{(i)}\|_{tr} \tag{3}$$

where $\{\alpha_i\}$ are parameters satisfying $\alpha_i \geq 0$, and $\sum_{i=1}^{4} \alpha_i = 1$. By minimizing this term, we obtain a low-rank approximation of $\mathcal{X}$. The low rank regularization is applied in the entire 4D data retrieving useful information for the reconstruction task from both spatial and temporal domains.

Total Variation Regularization. Total variation (TV) is defined as integrals of absolute gradient of the signal. For a 4D functional image $\mathcal{X}$:

$$\Re_{tv}(\mathcal{X}) = \sum_{n=1}^{N} \int |\nabla \mathbf{X}_n| \, dbdkdh \tag{4}$$

where the gradient operator is performed in 3D spatial space. TV regularization has been largely adopted in image recovery because of its powerful ability in edge preservation [13,14]. Here, we use TV in 3D space instead of 4D space based on the notion that primarily the spatial neighborhood exhibits consistency and thus TV in temporal domain may not be effective.

Algorithm 1. 4D motion-compensated reconstruction of fMRI time series

---

Input: Single scan fMRI image $\mathcal{T}$, realignment parameters

Initialize: The desired $\mathcal{X}$ by resampling motion-transformed image $\mathcal{T}$ with linear interpolation. Set auxiliary variable $Y_i^{(0)} = 0, U_i^{(0)} = 0, i = 1, 2, 3, 4$

while $\left\| \mathcal{X}^k - \mathcal{X}^{k-1} \right\| / \left\| \mathcal{T} \right\| > \varepsilon$ **do**

Update $\mathcal{X}^k$ by using gradient descent:

$$\arg\min_{\mathcal{X}} \sum_{n=1}^{N} \left\| DSM_n \mathbf{X}_n^{(k-1)} - \mathbf{T}_n \right\|^2 + \sum_{i=1}^{4} \frac{\rho}{2} \left\| \mathcal{X}^{(k-1)} - Y_i^{(k-1)} + U_i^{(k-1)} \right\|^2 +$$
$$\lambda_{tv} \sum_{n=1}^{N} \int \left| \nabla \mathbf{X}_n^{(k-1)} \right| dbdhdk \tag{7}$$

Update $Y_i^{(k)}$ by using Singular Value Thresholding:

$$Y_i^{(k)} = fold_i \left[SVT_{\lambda_{rank}\alpha_i/\rho} \left(\mathcal{X}_{(i)}^{(k)} + U_{i(i)}^{(k-1)} \right) \right] \tag{8}$$

with $fold_i \left(Y_{i(i)} \right) = Y_i$

Update $U_i^{(k)} = U_i^{(k-1)} + \left(\mathcal{X}^{(k)} - Y_i^{(k)} \right)$ \hfill (9)

end while

2.2 Optimization

The proposed 4D single acquisition reconstruction is thus formulated as below:

$$\min_{\mathcal{X}} \sum_{n=1}^{N} \left\| DSM_n \mathbf{X}_n - \mathbf{T}_n \right\|^2 + \lambda_{rank} \mathfrak{R}_{rank} \left(\mathcal{X} \right) + \lambda_{tv} \sum_{n=1}^{N} \mathfrak{R}_{tv} \left(\mathbf{X}_n \right) \tag{5}$$

We employ the alternating direction method of multipliers (ADMM) algorithm to minimize the cost function in Eq. (5). ADMM has been proven efficient for solving optimization problems with multiple non-smooth terms [2]. Briefly, we first introduce redundant variables $\{Y_i\}_{i=1}^{4}$ with equality constraints $\mathcal{X}_{(i)} = Y_{i(i)}$, and then use Lagrangian dual variables $\{U_i\}_{i=1}^{4}$ to integrate the equality constraints into the cost function:

$$\min_{\mathcal{X}, \{Y_i\}_{i=1}^{4}, \{U_i\}_{i=1}^{4}} \sum_{n=1}^{N} \left\| DSM_n \mathbf{X}_n - \mathbf{T}_n \right\|^2 + \lambda_{rank} \sum_{i=1}^{4} \alpha_i \left\| Y_{i(i)} \right\|_{tr}$$
$$+ \sum_{i=1}^{4} \frac{\rho}{2} \left(\left\| \mathcal{X} - Y_i + U_i \right\|^2 - \left\| U_i \right\|^2 \right) + \lambda_{tv} \sum_{n=1}^{N} \int \left| \nabla \mathbf{X}_n \right| dbdkdh \tag{6}$$

We break the cost function into subproblems for $\mathcal{X}$, Y, and U, and iteratively update them. The optimization scheme is summarized in Algorithm 1.

3 Experiments and Results

3.1 Data

Data Acquisition: Experiments in this study were performed on 20 *in utero* fMRI sequences obtained from fetuses between 19 and 39 weeks of gestation. None of the cases showed any neurological pathology. Pregnant women were scanned on a 1.5T clinical scanner (Philips Medical Systems, Best, Netherlands) using single-shot echo-planar imaging (EPI), and a sensitivity encoding

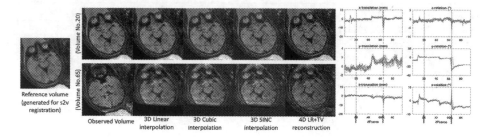

Fig. 2. Reconstruction of *in-utero* fMRI for a typical fetus, and the estimated slice-wise realignment parameters. When motion is small (volume No. 20) all interpolation methods recovered a motion compensated volume, and our approach resulted in a sharper image. In contrast, with strong motion relative to the reference volume (volume No. 65), single step 3D interpolation methods are not able to recover the whole brain, and parts remain missing, whereas the proposed 4D iterative reconstruction did recover the entire brain.

(SENSE) cardiac coil with five elements. Image matrix size was 144×144, with $1.74 \times 1.74\,\mathrm{mm}^2$ in-plane resolution, 3 mm slice thickness, a TR/TE of 1000/50 ms, and a flip angle of $90°$. Each scan contains 96 volumes obtained in an interleaved slice order to minimize cross-talk between adjacent slices.

Preprocessing: For preprocessing, a binary brain mask was manually delineated on the average volume of each fetus and dilated to ensure it covered the fetal brain through all ranges of the motion. A four dimensional estimate of the bias field for spatio-temporal signal non-uniformity correction in fMRI series was obtained using N4ITK algorithm [17] as suggested previously [11]. Intensity normalization was performed as implemented in mialSRTK toolkit [15]. Finally, motion parameters were estimated by performing a hierarchical slice-to-volume registration based on the interleaved factor of acquisition to a target volume created by automatically finding a set of consecutive volumes of fetal quiescence and averaging over them [12]. Image registration software package NiftyReg [7] was used for all motion correction steps in our approach. Demographic information of all 20 subjects as well as the maximum motion parameters estimated were reported in Supplementary Table S1.

3.2   Experimental Setting and Low-Rank Representation

We first evaluated to which extent *in utero* fMRI data can be characterized by its low-rank decomposition. The rapid decay of the singular values for a representative slice of our cohort is shown in Supplementary Figure S1. We used the top 30, 60, 90, and 120 singular values to reconstruct this slice and measured signal-to-noise ratio (SNR) to evaluate the reconstruction accuracy. The number of used singular values determines the rank of the reconstructed image. Using the top 90 or 120 singular values (out of 144), the reconstructed image does not show visual differences compared to the original image while it has a relatively high SNR (Fig. S1).

For the full 4D fMRI data of our cohort with the size of $144 \times 144 \times 18 \times 96$, four ranks, one for each unfolded matrix along one dimension is computed. Each is less than the largest image size 144. These ranks are relatively low in comparison to the total number of elements, implying *in utero* fMRI images could be represented using their low-rank approximations. We set $\alpha_1 = \alpha_2 = \alpha_3 = \alpha_4 = 1/4$ as all dimensions are assumed to be equally important, $\lambda_{rank} = 0.01$, $\lambda_{tv} = 0.01$ were chosen empirically. The algorithm stopped when the difference in iterations was less than $\varepsilon = 1e - 5$.

3.3   Evaluation of Image Reconstruction

A number of interpolation methods was employed to be compared with our reconstructed image including linear, cubic spline, and SINC interpolation. For each method, we applied the same realignment parameters as the ones used in our model, and in accordance with standard motion correction techniques, each 3D volumes of fMRI time series was interpolated separately. We quantified sharpness [8] of the average recovered image, standard deviation of bold signal fluctuations (SD) through-out the sequence, and the Structural Similarity Index (SSIM) which correlates with the quality of human visual perception [18]. Higher values of sharpness and SSIM, and lower values of SD are indicative of better recovery.

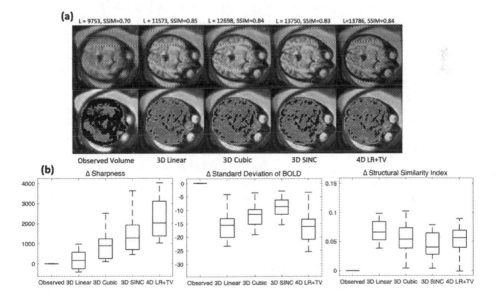

Fig. 3. Evaluation metrics for a typical fetus (a) and the whole cohort (b). Panel (a) shows an example slice in the average volume (top row) and voxel-wise standard deviation of the bold signal during fMRI acquisition. Higher Laplacian (sharpness) and SSIM, and lower standard deviation are indicative of better recovery. Panel (b) demonstrates these metrics in our fetal dataset.

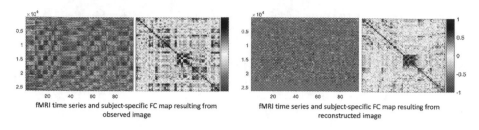

Fig. 4. Carpet plot and functional connectivity maps achieved for an example subject using the observed fMRI time series and the time series recovered by 4D iterative reconstruction.

Figure 2 shows, from left to right, the reference volume, two corresponding slices in the observed image, and the results of different reconstruction methods. Volume No.20 exhibits minor motion, volume No.65 exhibits strong motion. The motion estimate plots on the right show their respective time points. The figure shows the recovered slices of these two volumes using 3D linear, cubic, SINC, and the proposed 4D LR+TV method, respectively. In the case of excessive complex motion (30° out of the plane combined with in-plane rotation and translation), the 3D interpolation methods cannot recover the whole slice as they utilize information only from the local spatial neighborhoods. The reconstructed slice by the proposed 4D iterative reconstruction approach recovers the image information, is sharper, and preserves more structural detail of the brain. Figure 3 shows a qualitative and quantitative comparison of reconstruction approaches. Figure 3 (a) shows the average volume (top row), and the standard deviation of intensity changes over time (bottom row) for one subject. 4D reconstruction achieves sharper structural detail, and overall reduction of the standard deviation, which is primarily related to motion as described earlier. Although linear interpolation results in signals as smooth as the proposed method, severe blurring is observed in the obtained image by this approach. Figure 3 (b) provides the quantitative evaluation for the entire study population. The proposed method significantly ($p < 0.01$, paired-sample t-tests for each comparison) outperforms all comparison methods. The average gain of sharpness over the observed image is 2294 in our method compared to 1521 for 3D SINC, 959 for 3D Cubic, and 294 for 3D Linear, and the average reduction of SD relative to the observed image is -17 in our method compared to -9.34 for 3D SINC, -12.70 for 3D Cubic, and -16.50 for 3D Linear. The difference between linear interpolation and our approach did not reach the statistical significance level for SSIM ($p = 0.28$). In summary, 4D iterative reconstruction reduces standard deviation over time, while increasing sharpness and recovered structure, which the 3D approaches failed to achieve.

3.4 Functional Connectivity Analysis

Figure 4 illustrates the impact of the accurate motion correction and reconstruction for the analysis of functional connectivity (FC) in the fetal population.

The details of the pipeline employed for extracting subject-specific FC maps is explained in the supplementary material. When using the time series recovered by our proposed approach for FC analysis, the number of motion-corrupted correlations decreased significantly as visible in the *carpet plot* of signals, and the associated connectivity matrix.

4 Conclusion

In this work, we presented a novel spatio-temporal iterative 4D reconstruction approach for *in-utero* fMRI acquired while there is unconstrained motion of the head. The approach utilizes the self-similarity of fMRI data in the temporal domain as 4D low-rank regularisation together with total variation regularization based on spatial coherency of neighboring voxels. Comparative evaluations on 20 fetuses show that this approach yields a 4D signal with low motion induced standard deviation, and recovery of fine structural detail, outperforming various 3D reconstruction approaches.

Acknowledgment. This work has received funding from the European Union's Horizon 2020 research and innovation programme under the Marie Skłodowska-Curie grant agreement No 765148, and partial funding from the Austrian Science Fund (FWF, P35189, I 3925-B27), in collaboration with the French National Research Agency (ANR), and the Vienna Science and Technology Fund (WWTF, LS20-065). This work was also supported by the Swiss National Science Foundation (project 205321-182602). We acknowledge access to the expertise of the CIBM Center for Biomedical Imaging, a Swiss research center of excellence founded and supported by Lausanne University Hospital (CHUV), University of Lausanne (UNIL), Ecole polytechnique fédérale de Lausanne (EPFL), University of Geneva (UNIGE) and Geneva University Hospitals (HUG).

References

1. Balachandrasekaran, A., Cohen, A.L., Afacan, O., Warfield, S.K., Gholipour, A.: Reducing the effects of motion artifacts in fmri: a structured matrix completion approach. IEEE Trans. Med. Imaging **41**(1), 172–185 (2021)
2. Boyd, S., Parikh, N., Chu, E., Peleato, B., Eckstein, J., et al.: Distributed optimization and statistical learning via the alternating direction method of multipliers. Found. Trends® Mach. Learn. **3**(1), 1–122 (2011)
3. Ebner, M., et al.: An automated framework for localization, segmentation and super-resolution reconstruction of fetal brain mri. Neuroimage **206**, 116324 (2020)
4. Ferrazzi, G., et al.: Resting state fmri in the moving fetus: a robust framework for motion, bias field and spin history correction. Neuroimage **101**, 555–568 (2014)
5. Gholipour, A., Estroff, J.A., Warfield, S.K.: Robust super-resolution volume reconstruction from slice acquisitions: application to fetal brain mri. IEEE Trans. Med. Imaging **29**(10), 1739–1758 (2010)
6. Liu, J., Musialski, P., Wonka, P., Ye, J.: Tensor completion for estimating missing values in visual data. IEEE Trans. Pattern Anal. Mach. Intell. **35**(1), 208–220 (2012)

7. Modat, M., Cash, D.M., Daga, P., Winston, G.P., Duncan, J.S., Ourselin, S.: Global image registration using a symmetric block-matching approach. J. Med. imaging **1**(2), 024003 (2014)
8. Pech-Pacheco, J.L., Cristóbal, G., Chamorro-Martinez, J., Fernández-Valdivia, J.: Diatom autofocusing in brightfield microscopy: a comparative study. In: Proceedings 15th International Conference on Pattern Recognition, ICPR-2000, vol. 3, pp. 314–317. IEEE (2000)
9. Rutherford, S., et al.: Observing the origins of human brain development: Automated processing of fetal fmri. bioRxiv p. 525386 (2019)
10. Scheinost, D., et al.: A fetal fmri specific motion correction algorithm using 2nd order edge features. In: 2018 IEEE 15th International Symposium on Biomedical Imaging (ISBI 2018), pp. 1288–1292. IEEE (2018)
11. Seshamani, S., Cheng, X., Fogtmann, M., Thomason, M.E., Studholme, C.: A method for handling intensity inhomogenieties in fmri sequences of moving anatomy of the early developing brain. Med. Image Anal. **18**(2), 285–300 (2014)
12. Seshamani, S., Fogtmann, M., Cheng, X., Thomason, M., Gatenby, C., Studholme, C.: Cascaded slice to volume registration for moving fetal fmri. In: 2013 IEEE 10th International Symposium on Biomedical Imaging, pp. 796–799. IEEE (2013)
13. Shi, F., Cheng, J., Wang, L., Yap, P.T., Shen, D.: Lrtv: Mr image super-resolution with low-rank and total variation regularizations. IEEE Trans. Med. Imaging **34**(12), 2459–2466 (2015)
14. Tourbier, S., Bresson, X., Hagmann, P., Thiran, J.P., Meuli, R., Cuadra, M.B.: An efficient total variation algorithm for super-resolution in fetal brain mri with adaptive regularization. Neuroimage **118**, 584–597 (2015)
15. Tourbier, S., et al.: Automated template-based brain localization and extraction for fetal brain mri reconstruction. Neuroimage **155**, 460–472 (2017)
16. Turk, E.A., et al.: Spatiotemporal alignment of in utero bold-mri series. J. Magn. Reson. Imaging **46**(2), 403–412 (2017)
17. Tustison, N.J.: N4itk: improved n3 bias correction. IEEE Trans. Med. Imaging **29**(6), 1310–1320 (2010)
18. Wang, Z., Bovik, A.C., Sheikh, H.R., Simoncelli, E.P.: Image quality assessment: from error visibility to structural similarity. IEEE Trans. Image Process. **13**(4), 600–612 (2004)
19. You, W., Evangelou, I.E., Zun, Z., Andescavage, N., Limperopoulos, C.: Robust preprocessing for stimulus-based functional mri of the moving fetus. J. Med. Imaging **3**(2), 026001 (2016)

Deep Filter Bank Regression for Super-Resolution of Anisotropic MR Brain Images

Samuel W. Remedios[1(✉)], Shuo Han[2], Yuan Xue[3], Aaron Carass[3], Trac D. Tran[3], Dzung L. Pham[4], and Jerry L. Prince[3]

[1] Department of Computer Science, Johns Hopkins University, Baltimore, MD 21218, USA
samuel.remedios@jhu.edu
[2] Department of Biomedical Engineering, Johns Hopkins University School of Medicine, Baltimore, MD 21205, USA
[3] Department of Electrical and Computer Engineering, Johns Hopkins University, Baltimore, MD 21218, USA
[4] Center for Neuroscience and Regenerative Medicine, Henry M. Jackson Foundation, Bethesda, MD 20817, USA

Abstract. In 2D multi-slice magnetic resonance (MR) acquisition, the through-plane signals are typically of lower resolution than the in-plane signals. While contemporary super-resolution (SR) methods aim to recover the underlying high-resolution volume, the estimated high-frequency information is implicit via end-to-end data-driven training rather than being explicitly stated and sought. To address this, we reframe the SR problem statement in terms of perfect reconstruction filter banks, enabling us to identify and directly estimate the missing information. In this work, we propose a two-stage approach to approximate the completion of a perfect reconstruction filter bank corresponding to the anisotropic acquisition of a particular scan. In stage 1, we estimate the missing filters using gradient descent and in stage 2, we use deep networks to learn the mapping from coarse coefficients to detail coefficients. In addition, the proposed formulation does not rely on external training data, circumventing the need for domain shift correction. Under our approach, SR performance is improved particularly in "slice gap" scenarios, likely due to the constrained solution space imposed by the framework.

Keywords: Super-resolution · Filter bank · MRI

1 Introduction

Anisotropic magnetic resonance (MR) images are those acquired with high in-plane resolution and low through-plane resolution. It is common practice to acquire anisotropic volumes in clinics as it reduces scan time and motion artifacts while preserving signal-to-noise ratio. To improve through-plane resolution,

© The Author(s), under exclusive license to Springer Nature Switzerland AG 2022
L. Wang et al. (Eds.): MICCAI 2022, LNCS 13436, pp. 613–622, 2022.
https://doi.org/10.1007/978-3-031-16446-0_58

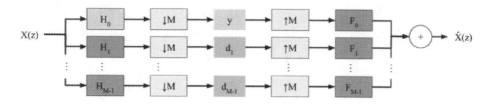

Fig. 1. The filter bank observation model. Both y and H_0 (green) are given and fixed. In stage 1, filters $H_1, \ldots, H_{M-1}$ and $F_0, F_1, \ldots, F_{M-1}$ (purple) are learned; in stage 2, a mapping from y to $d_1, \ldots, d_{M-1}$ (gold) is learned. (Color figure online)

data-driven super-resolution (SR) methods have been developed on MR volumes [1,2,7,12]. The application of SR methods to estimate the underlying isotropic volume has been shown to improve performance on downstream tasks [13].

For 2D multi-slice protocols, the through-plane point-spread function (PSF) is known as the slice profile. When the sampling step is an integer, the through-plane signals of an acquired MR image can be modeled as a strided 1D convolution between the slice profile and the object to be imaged [3,8,10]. Commonly, the separation between slices is equivalent to the full-width-at-half-max (FWHM) of the slice profile, but volumes can also be acquired where the slice separation is less than or greater than the slice profile FWHM, corresponding to "slice overlap" and "slice gap" scenarios, respectively.

Data-driven SR methods usually simulate low-resolution (LR) data from high-resolution (HR) data using an assumed slice profile [1,2,7,12], or an estimated slice profile according to the image data or acquisition [3]. In either case, SR methods are generally formulated as a classical inverse problem:

$$y = Ax, \tag{1}$$

where y is the LR observation, A is the degradation matrix, and x is the underlying HR image. Commonly, this is precisely how paired training data is created for supervised machine learning methods; HR data is degraded by A to obtain the LR y and weights θ of a parameterized function ϕ (e.g., a neural network) are learned such that $\phi_\theta(y) \approx x$. However, under this framework there is no specification of information lost by application of A; contemporary SR models train end-to-end and are directed only by the dataset.

In our work, we propose an entirely novel SR framework based on perfect reconstruction (PR) filter banks. From filter bank theory, PR of a signal x is possible through an M-channel filter bank with a correct design of an analysis bank H and synthesis bank F [11]. Under this formulation, we do not change Eq. 1 but explicitly recognize our observation y as the "coarse approximation" filter bank coefficients and the missing information necessary to recover x as the "detail" coefficients (see Fig. 1). For reference, in machine learning jargon, the analysis bank is an encoder, the synthesis bank is a decoder, and the coarse approximation and detail coefficients are analogous to a "latent space."

The primary contribution of this work is to reformulate SR to isotropy of 2D-acquired MR volumes as a filter bank regression framework. The proposed framework has several benefits. First, the observed low-frequency information is untouched in the reconstruction; thus, our method explicitly synthesizes the missing high frequencies and does not need to learn to preserve acquired low frequency information. Second, the downsampling factor M specifies the number of channels in the M-channel filter bank, constraining the solution space in tougher scenarios such as "slice gap" acquisition recovery. Third, the analysis filters of PR filter banks necessarily introduce aliasing which is canceled via the synthesis filters; therefore, we do not need to directly handle the anti-aliasing of the observed image. Fourth, our architecture has a dynamic capacity for lower-resolution images. The rationale behind the dynamic capacity is intuitive: when fewer measurements are taken, more estimates must be done in recovery and a more robust model is required. Fifth, our method exploits the nature of anisotropic volumetric data; in-plane slices are HR while through-plane slices are LR. Thus, we do not rely on external training data and only need the in-plane HR data to perform internal supervision. In the remainder of the paper, we describe this framework in detail, provide implementation details, and evaluate against a state-of-the-art internally supervised SR technique. We demonstrate the feasibility of formulating SR as filter bank coefficient regression and believe it lays the foundation for future theoretical and experimental work in SR of MR images.

2   Methods

The analysis bank H and synthesis bank F each consist of M 1D filters represented in the z-domain as H_k and F_k, respectively, with corresponding spatial domain representations h_k and f_k. As illustrated in Fig. 1, input signal $X(z) = \mathcal{Z}(x)^1$ is filtered by H_k, then decimated with $\downarrow M$ (keeping every M^{th} entry) to produce the corresponding coefficients. These coefficients exhibit aliasing and distortion which are corrected by the synthesis filters [11]. Reconstruction from coefficients comes from zero-insertion upsampling with $\uparrow M$, passing through filters F_k, then summing across the M channels.

Traditional design of M-channel PR filter banks involves a deliberate choice of a prototype low-pass filter H_0 such that modulations and alternations of the prototype produce the remaining filters for both the analysis and synthesis filter banks [11]. M is also chosen based on the restrictions of the problem at hand. However, for anisotropic 2D-acquired MRI, the slice profile *is* the low-pass filter and as such we have a fixed, given H_0. The separation between slices is equal to the FWHM of h_0 plus any further gap between slices. We denote the slice separation as M, corresponding to the number of channels in the PR filter bank. We use $A\|B$, read "A skip B", to denote a FWHM of A mm and slice gap of B mm and note that $M = A + B$. For this preliminary work, we assume A, B,

---

[1] $\mathcal{Z}(x)$ is the $\mathcal{Z}$-transform of x [11].

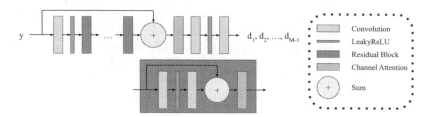

Fig. 2. This network architecture, used in the second stage of our algorithm, has the same structure for both the generator and discriminator but with different hyperparameters. All convolutional layers used a 3×3 kernel. The generator and discriminator used 16 and 2 residual blocks, respectively. The generator had $128 \times M$ features per convolutional layer while the discriminator had $64 \times M$ features per convolutional layer. The final convolution outputs $M - 1$ channels corresponding to the missing filter bank detail coefficients. The internal structure of the residual block is encapsulated in green. (Color figure online)

and M are all integer and, without loss of generality, assume that the in-plane resolution is $1\|0$.

Our goal is to estimate filters $H_1, \ldots, H_{M-1}$ and $F_0, \ldots, F_{M-1}$ and the detail coefficients $d_1, \ldots, d_{M-1}$ which lead to PR of x. We approach this problem in two stages. In stage 1, we approximate the missing analysis and synthesis filters, assuming there exists a set of filters to complete the M-channel PR filter bank given that H_0 and M are fixed and known ahead of time. These must be learned first to establish the approximate PR filter bank conditions on the coefficient space. Then, in stage 2, we perform a regression on the missing coefficients. Both of these stages are optimized in a data-driven end-to-end fashion with gradient descent. After training, our method is applied by regressing $d_1, \ldots, d_{M-1}$ from y and feeding all coefficients through the synthesis bank to produce $\hat{x}$, our estimate of the HR signal. The stage 2 coefficient regression occurs in 2D, so we construct our estimate of the 3D volume by averaging stacked 2D predictions from the synthesis bank from both cardinal planes containing the through-plane axis.

Stage 1: Filter Optimization. Previous works assumed the slice profile is Gaussian with FWHM equal to the slice separation [7,12]; instead, we estimate the slice profile, H_0, directly with ESPRESO[2] [3]. We next aim to estimate the filters $H_1, \ldots, H_{M-1}$ and $F_0, \ldots, F_{M-1}$. To achieve this, we learn the spatial representations $h_1, \ldots, h_{M-1}$ and $f_0, \ldots, f_{M-1}$ from 1D rows and columns drawn from the high resolution in-plane slices of y, denoted $\mathcal{D}_1 = \{x_i\}_{i=1}^{N}$. We initialize these filters according to a cosine modulation [11] of h_0, which is defined as

$$f_k[n] = h_k[n] = h_0[n]\sqrt{\frac{2}{M}} \cos\left[\left(k + \frac{1}{2}\right)\left(n + \frac{M+1}{2}\right)\frac{\pi}{M}\right],$$

for $k \in \{1, 2, \ldots, M - 1\}$. Accordingly, we initialize f_0 to h_0. We estimate $\hat{x}_i$ by passing x_i through the analysis and synthesis banks, then (since the entire

² https://github.com/shuohan/espreso2.

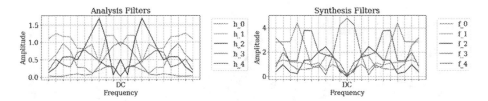

Fig. 3. Estimated PR filters from stage 1 for a single subject at 4∥1 resolution ($M = 5$) in the frequency domain. Note the amplitudes for analysis and synthesis banks are on different scales, DC is centered, and h_0 is estimated by ESPRESO [3].

operation is differentiable) step all filters except h_0 through gradient descent. The reconstruction error is measured with mean squared error loss and the filters are updated based on the AdamW [6] optimizer with a learning rate of 0.1, the one-cycle learning rate scheduler [9], and a batch size of 32 for $100,000$ steps.

Stage 2: Coefficient Regression. From stage 1, we have the analysis and synthesis banks and now want to estimate the missing detail coefficients given only the LR observation y. With the correct coefficients and synthesis filters, PR of x is possible. For this stage, we use 2D patches, in spite of the 1D SR problem, as a type of "neighborhood regularization". Let $\mathcal{D}_2 = \{x_i\}_{i=1}^N$, $x_i \in \mathbb{R}^{p \times pM}$; i.e., the training set for stage 2 consists of 2D $p \times pM$ patches drawn from the in-plane slices of y. The second dimension will be decimated by M after passing through the analysis banks, resulting in $y, d_1, \ldots, d_{M-1} \in \mathbb{R}^{p \times p}$. We use the analysis bank (learned in stage 1) to create training pairs $\{(y_i, (d_1, d_2, \ldots, d_{M-1})_i)\}_{i=1}^N$ and fit a convolutional neural network (CNN) $G : \mathbb{R}^{p \times p} \to \mathbb{R}^{p \times p^{M-1}}$ to map y_i to $(d_1, \ldots, d_{M-1})_i$. In this work, we set $p = 32$. Since this is an image-to-image translation task, we adopt the widely used approach proposed in Pix2Pix [4] including the adversarial patch discriminator.

Empirically, we found more learnable parameters are needed with greater M. Thus, our generator G is a CNN illustrated in Fig. 2 with 16 residual blocks and $128 \times M$ kernels of size 3×3 per convolutional layer. The discriminator D has the same architecture but with only 2 residual blocks and $64 \times M$ kernels per convolutional layer. Our final loss function for stage 2 is identical to the loss proposed in [4] and is calculated on the error in $(d_1, \ldots, d_{M-1})_i$. We use the AdamW optimizer [6] with a learning rate of 10^{-4} and the one-cycle learning rate scheduler [9] for $500,000$ steps at a batch size of 32.

3 Experiments and Results

Experiments. We performed two experiments to evaluate the efficacy of each stage in our approach. We randomly selected 30 T1-weighted MR brain volumes from the OASIS-3 dataset [5] to validate both stages and simulated LR acquisition via convolution with a Gaussian kernel with FWHM $\in \{2, 4, 6\}$ and slice gap $\in \{0, 1, 2\}$, yielding nine combinations of FHWM and slice gap in total.

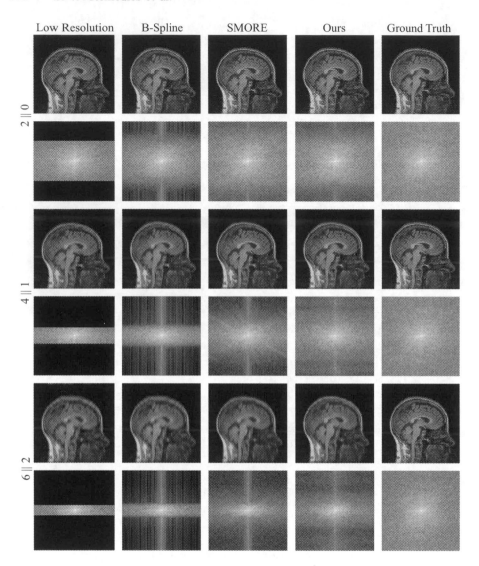

Fig. 4. Mid-sagittal slice for a representative subject at different resolutions and gaps for each method. The low resolution column is digitally upsampled with k-space zero-filling. $A\|B$ signifies a slice thickness of A mm and a gap of B mm. Fourier magnitude is displayed in dB on every other row. The top two rows correspond to $2\|0$ ($M = 2$) for the MR slice and Fourier space, the second two rows are for $4\|1$ ($M = 5$), and the bottom two rows are for $6\|2$ ($M = 8$).

Since $M = A + B$ for a scan of resolution $A\|B$, $M \in \{2, 3, 4, 5, 6, 7, 8\}$. For these experiments, the HR plane was axial while the cardinal LR planes were sagittal and coronal. We note that both stage 1 and stage 2 are trained for each LR volume separately as our proposed method does not use external training data,

Table 1. Mean ± std. dev. of volumetric PSNR values for stage 1 reconstruction of the 30 subjects. "Self" indicates a reconstruction of the input low-resolution volume on which the filter bank was optimized, while "GT" indicates reconstruction of the isotropic ground truth volume. (L-R), (A-P), and (S-I) are the left-to-right, anterior-to-posterior, and superior-to-inferior directions, respectively.

	Self (L-R)	Self (A-P)	GT (L-R)	GT (A-P)	GT (S-I)
2‖0	62.24 ± 0.97	60.19 ± 3.74	60.63 ± 0.56	59.59 ± 2.54	55.47 ± 4.69
2‖1	63.01 ± 4.91	62.25 ± 5.09	64.32 ± 0.63	59.49 ± 5.52	53.81 ± 6.50
2‖2	62.57 ± 1.59	57.93 ± 5.32	60.62 ± 1.34	59.31 ± 3.65	52.09 ± 4.34
4‖0	55.47 ± 3.81	52.36 ± 5.32	48.91 ± 4.65	48.77 ± 4.68	44.08 ± 4.78
4‖1	53.03 ± 1.54	50.31 ± 3.41	44.19 ± 1.57	45.65 ± 1.63	44.28 ± 2.14
4‖2	54.71 ± 2.61	51.08 ± 4.51	46.75 ± 2.83	46.39 ± 3.27	43.27 ± 2.80
6‖0	49.97 ± 1.07	40.18 ± 4.77	40.14 ± 1.35	41.04 ± 1.40	35.76 ± 3.19
6‖1	52.35 ± 0.55	45.69 ± 5.24	42.11 ± 0.84	42.74 ± 1.25	39.76 ± 3.47
6‖2	53.17 ± 3.17	49.11 ± 3.41	43.66 ± 4.12	44.87 ± 3.99	41.50 ± 2.29

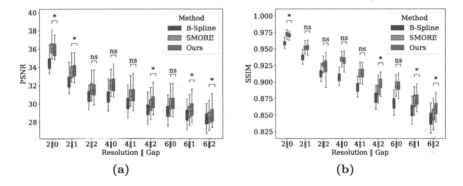

Fig. 5. Quantitative metrics PSNR in **(a)** and SSIM in **(b)**, computed over the 30 image volumes. Significance tests are performed between SMORE and our proposed method with the Wilcoxon signed rank test; * denotes p-values < 0.05; "ns" stands for "not significant".

but instead relies on the inherent anisotropy in the multi-slice volume (i.e., HR in-plane and LR through-plane data).

Stage 1 Results. We trained stage 1 using both cardinal 1D directions from in-plane data; that is, left-to-right (L-R) and anterior-to-posterior (A-P) directions. We then performed 1D reconstruction along these cardinal directions and collated all reconstructions into 3D volumes. In other words, this is an evaluation of self-auto-encoding. The mean volumetric reconstruction PSNR ± std. dev. across the 30 subjects is shown in Table 1. In addition to applying the learned filters to the LR image itself, we would also like to test the extent of signal recovery for the HR counterpart that is the ground truth (GT) of the

LR volume. Indeed, the coefficients generated by our learned analysis bank are what we will regress in stage 2, so a reconstruction of the GT is also shown in the right three columns of Table 1. This serves as a sort of "upper bound" on our super-resolution estimate and also answers the question of how well internal training generalizes to reconstruction of an isotropic volume.

We note that if we had attained PR filters, the PSNR would be ∞; our estimates fall short of this. Notably, reconstruction performance drops in the (S-I) direction; this is likely due to the fact that signals along this direction were not included in the training data. Additionally, an example of learned filters in the frequency domain for one resolution, 4∥1 ($M = 5$), is shown in Fig. 3. Recall that the fixed filter h_0 is the slice selection profile. We observe that our optimization approximated bandpass filters.

Stage 2 Results. To evaluate stage 2, we compared our method to two approaches which also do not rely on external training data: cubic b-spline interpolation and SMORE [12], a state-of-the-art self-super-resolution technique for anisotropic MR volumes. For a fair comparison and improving SMORE results, SMORE was trained with the same slice profile that we use (the ESPRESO estimate [3]) instead of a Gaussian slice profile used in the original paper.

Qualitative results are displayed in Fig. 4 of a mid-sagittal slice for a representative subject at 2∥0, 4∥1, and 6∥2. This subject is near the median PSNR value for that resolution across the 30 subjects evaluated in our experiments and for which SMORE outperforms our method at 2∥0, is on par with our method at 4∥1, and is outperformed by our method at 6∥2. Also shown in Fig. 4 is the corresponding Fourier space, and we see that our proposed method includes more high frequencies than the other methods. For quantitative results, PSNR and SSIM were calculated on entire volumes, as illustrated in box plots in Fig. 5.

4   Discussion and Conclusions

In this paper, we have presented a novel filter bank formulation for SR of 2D-acquired anisotropic MR volumes as the regression of filter-specified missing detail coefficients in an M-channel PR filter bank that does not change the low-frequency sub-bands of the acquired image. We would emphasize that our approach establishes a new theoretic basis for SR. In theory, these coefficients exist and give exact recovery of the underlying HR signal. However, it is unknown whether a mapping of $y \to (d_1, \ldots, d_{M-1})$ exists, and whether it is possible to find filters to complete the analysis and synthesis banks to guarantee PR. In practice, we estimate these in two stages: stage 1 estimates the missing analysis and synthesis filters towards PR and stage 2 trains a CNN to regress the missing detail coefficients given the coarse approximation y. According to our experiments, as the resolution worsens and slice gap increases our proposed method better handles the SR task than the competitive approach, validating the usefulness of our method for super resolving anisotropic MR images with large slice gaps. Future work will include: 1) deeper investigation into the limits of the training set in learning the regression; 2) the degree to which the mapping G

is valid; 3) more analysis of the super-resolved frequency space; and 4) develop methods to exactly achieve or better approximate PR. True PR filter banks should greatly improve the method, as Table 1 serves as a type of "upper bound" for our method; regardless of the quality of coefficient regression, even given the ideal ground truth coefficients, reconstruction accuracy would be limited. Furthermore, our work suffers two major shortcomings. First, our current assumptions are integer slice thickness and slice separation, which is not always true in reality. To address this, the use of fractional sampling rates with filter banks [11] may be a promising research direction. Second, our model in stage 2 scales the number of convolution kernels per layer by M. This induces a longer training and testing time when the image is of lower resolution. For reference, SMORE produced the SR volume in about 86 min on a single NVIDIA V100 regardless of the input resolution, but our proposed method produced the SR volume in 27 min for 2∥0, 85 min for 4∥1, and 127 min for 6∥2. Additionally, further investigation into improved regression is needed—a model which can better capture the necessary aliasing in the coefficient domain is vital for PR.

Acknowledgements. This material is supported by the National Science Foundation Graduate Research Fellowship under Grant No. DGE-1746891. Theoretical development is partially supported by NIH ORIP grant R21 OD030163 and the Congressionally Directed Medical Research Programs (CDMRP) grant MS190131. This work also received support from National Multiple Sclerosis Society RG-1907-34570, CDMRP W81XWH2010912, and the Department of Defense in the Center for Neuroscience and Regenerative Medicine.

References

1. Chen, Y., Shi, F., Christodoulou, A.G., Xie, Y., Zhou, Z., Li, D.: Efficient and accurate MRI super-resolution using a generative adversarial network and 3D multi-level densely connected network. In: Frangi, A.F., Schnabel, J.A., Davatzikos, C., Alberola-López, C., Fichtinger, G. (eds.) MICCAI 2018. LNCS, vol. 11070, pp. 91 99. Springer, Cham (2018). https://doi.org/10.1007/978-3-030-00928-1_11
2. Du, J., et al.: Super-resolution reconstruction of single anisotropic 3D MR images using residual convolutional neural network. Neurocomputing **392**, 209–220 (2020)
3. Han, S., Remedios, S., Carass, A., Schär, M., Prince, J.L.: MR slice profile estimation by learning to match internal patch distributions. In: Feragen, A., Sommer, S., Schnabel, J., Nielsen, M. (eds.) IPMI 2021. LNCS, vol. 12729, pp. 108–119. Springer, Cham (2021). https://doi.org/10.1007/978-3-030-78191-0_9
4. Isola, P., Zhu, J.Y., Zhou, T., Efros, A.A.: Image-to-image translation with conditional adversarial networks. In: CVPR (2017)
5. LaMontagne, P.J., et al.: OASIS-3: longitudinal neuroimaging, clinical, and cognitive dataset for normal aging and Alzheimer disease. medRxiv (2019)
6. Loshchilov, I., Hutter, F.: Decoupled weight decay regularization. arXiv preprint arXiv:1711.05101 (2017)
7. Oktay, O., et al.: Multi-input cardiac image super-resolution using convolutional neural networks. In: Ourselin, S., Joskowicz, L., Sabuncu, M.R., Unal, G., Wells, W. (eds.) MICCAI 2016. LNCS, vol. 9902, pp. 246–254. Springer, Cham (2016). https://doi.org/10.1007/978-3-319-46726-9_29

8. Prince, J.L., Links, J.M.: Medical Imaging Signals and Systems. Pearson (2015)
9. Smith, L.N., Topin, N.: Super-convergence: very fast training of neural networks using large learning rates. In: Artificial Intelligence and Machine Learning for Multi-domain Operations Applications, vol. 11006, p. 1100612. International Society for Optics and Photonics (2019)
10. Sønderby, C.K., Caballero, J., Theis, L., Shi, W., Huszár, F.: Amortised map inference for image super-resolution. arXiv preprint arXiv:1610.04490 (2016)
11. Strang, G., Nguyen, T.: Wavelets and Filter Banks. Wellesley - Cambridge Press (1997)
12. Zhao, C., Dewey, B.E., Pham, D.L., Calabresi, P.A., Reich, D.S., Prince, J.L.: SMORE: a self-supervised anti-aliasing and super-resolution algorithm for MRI using deep learning. IEEE Trans. Med. Imaging 40(3), 805–817 (2020)
13. Zhao, C., et al.: Applications of a deep learning method for anti-aliasing and super-resolution in MRI. Magn. Reson. Imaging 64, 132–141 (2019)

Towards Performant and Reliable Undersampled MR Reconstruction via Diffusion Model Sampling

Cheng Peng[1]([✉]), Pengfei Guo[1], S. Kevin Zhou[2,3], Vishal M. Patel[1], and Rama Chellappa[1]

[1] Johns Hopkins University, Baltimore, MD, USA
{cpeng26,pguo4,vpatel36,rchella4}@jhu.edu
[2] School of Biomedical Engineering and Suzhou Institute for Advanced Research Center for Medical Imaging, Robotics, and Analytic Computing and LEarning (MIRACLE), University of Science and Technology of China, Suzhou 215123, China
[3] Key Lab of Intelligent Information Processing of Chinese Academy of Sciences (CAS), Institute of Computing Technology, CAS, Beijing 100190, China

Abstract. Magnetic Resonance (MR) image reconstruction from under sampled acquisition promises faster scanning time. To this end, current State-of-The-Art (SoTA) approaches leverage deep neural networks and supervised training to learn a recovery model. While these approaches achieve impressive performances, the learned model can be fragile on unseen degradation, e.g. when given a different acceleration factor. These methods are also generally deterministic and provide a single solution to an ill-posed problem; as such, it can be difficult for practitioners to understand the reliability of the reconstruction. We introduce DiffuseRecon, a novel diffusion model-based MR reconstruction method. DiffuseRecon guides the generation process based on the observed signals and a pre-trained diffusion model, and does not require additional training on specific acceleration factors. DiffuseRecon is stochastic in nature and generates results from a distribution of fully-sampled MR images; as such, it allows us to explicitly visualize different potential reconstruction solutions. Lastly, DiffuseRecon proposes an accelerated, coarse-to-fine Monte-Carlo sampling scheme to approximate the most likely reconstruction candidate. The proposed DiffuseRecon achieves SoTA performances reconstructing from raw acquisition signals in fastMRI and SKM-TEA. Code will be open-sourced at www.github.com/cpeng93/DiffuseRecon.

1 Introduction

Magnetic Resonance Imaging (MRI) is a widely used medical imaging technique. It offers several advantages over other imaging modalities, such as providing high

---

Supplementary Information The online version contains supplementary material available at https://doi.org/10.1007/978-3-031-16446-0_59.

contrast on soft tissues and introducing no harmful radiation during acquisition. However, MRI is also limited by its long acquisition time due to the underlying imaging physics and machine quality. This leads to various issues ranging from patient discomfort to limited accessibility of the machines.

An approach to shorten MR scanning time is by under-sampling the signal in k-space during acquisition and recovering it by performing a post-process recon-struction algorithm. Recovering unseen signal is a challenging, ill-posed problem, and there has been a long history of research in addressing undersampled MR reconstruction. In general, this problem is formulated as:

$$y_{\text{recon}} = \arg\min_y \|\mathcal{MF}y - x_{\text{obs}}\| + \lambda R(y), \quad s.t. \quad x_{\text{obs}} = \mathcal{M}x_{\text{full}}, \quad (1)$$

where $x_{\{\text{full,obs}\}}$ denotes the fully-sampled and under-sampled k-space signal, $\mathcal{M}$ denotes the undersampling mask, and $\mathcal{F}$ denotes the Fourier operator. The goal is to find an MR image y such that its k-space content $\mathcal{MF}y$ agrees with x_{obs}; this is often known as the data consistency term. Furthermore, y_{recon} should fol-low certain prior knowledge about MR images, as expressed by the regularization term $R(*)$. The design of R is subject to many innovations. Lustig et al. [13] first proposed to use Compressed Sensing motivated ℓ_1-minimization algorithm for MRI reconstruction, assuming that the undersampled MR images have a sparse representation in a transform domain. Ravishankar et al. [16] applied a more adaptive sparse modelling through Dictionary Learning, where the transforma-tion is optimized through a set of data, leading to improved sparsity encoding. As interests grow in this field, more MR data has become publicly available. Con-sequently, advances in Deep Learning (DL), specifically with supervised learn-ing, have been widely applied in MR reconstruction. Generally, DL-based meth-ods [1,5–9,15,17,19,22,24,25,27] train Convolutional Neural Networks (CNNs) with paired data $\{y_{\text{und}}, y_{\text{full}}\} = \{\mathcal{F}^{-1}x_{\text{obs}}, \mathcal{F}^{-1}x_{\text{full}}\}$. Following the formulation of Eq. (1), data consistency can be explicitly enforced within the CNN by replac-ing $\mathcal{MF}y$ with x_{obs} [19]. The resulting CNN serves as a parameterized $R(*, \theta)$, and regularizes test images based on learned θ from the training distribution.

While supervised DL-based methods have led to impressive results, these methods generally train CNNs under specific degradation conditions; e.g., the under-sampling mask $\mathcal{M}$ that generates y_{und} follows a particular acceleration fac-tor. As a consequence, when the acceleration factor changes, the performances of various models often degrade significantly, making $R(*, \theta)$ less reliable in gen-eral. Furthermore, while the trained CNNs infer the most likely estimation of y_{full} given y_{und}, they do not provide possible alternative solutions. Since Eq. 1 is an under-constrained problem, y_{und} can have many valid solutions. The ability to observe different solutions can help practitioners understand the potential variability in reconstructions and make more robust decisions. As such, finding a stochastic R that is generally applicable across all x_{obs} is of high interest.

We leverage the recent progress in a class of generative methods called **dif-fusion models** [2,4,10,11,14,21], which use a CNN to perform progressive reverse-diffusion and maps a prior Gaussian distribution $\mathcal{N}$ to a learned image distribution, e.g. $p_\theta(y_{\text{full}})$. Based on a pre-trained θ, we propose to guide the iterative reverse-diffusion by gradually introducing x_{obs} to the intermediate results, as shown in Fig. 1. This allows us to generate reconstructions in the marginal distribution $p_\theta(y_{\text{full}}|x_{\text{obs}})$, where any sample $y_{\text{recon}} \sim p_\theta(y_{\text{full}}|x_{\text{obs}})$ agrees with the observed signal and lies on the MR image distribution $p_\theta(y_{\text{full}})$.

We make three contributions. (i) Our proposed **DiffuseRecon** performs MR reconstruction by gradually guiding the reverse-diffusion process with observed k-space signal and is robust to changing sampling condition using a single model. (ii) We propose a coarse-to-fine sampling algorithm, which allows us to estimate the most likely reconstruction and its variability within $p_\theta(y_{\text{full}}|x_{\text{obs}})$ while leading to an approximately 40× speed-up compared to naive sampling. (iii) We perform extensive experiments using raw acquisition signals from fastMRI [26] and SKM-TEA [3], and demonstrate superior performance over SoTA methods. In particular, DiffuseRecon outperforms supervised SoTA methods on specifically trained sampling conditions, which concurrent diffusion-based works are unable to do [2,11,21].

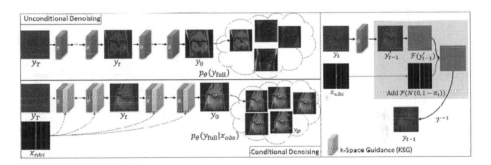

Fig. 1. DiffuseRecon gradually incorporates x_{obs} into the denoising process through a k-Space Guidance (KSG) module; as such, we can directly generate samples from $p_\theta(y_{\text{full}}|x_{\text{obs}})$. Visualizations are based on 8X undersampling.

2   DiffuseRecon

Background. Diffusion model [4,10,14] is a class of unconditional generative methods that aims to transform a Gaussian distribution to the empirical data distribution. Specifically, the forward diffusion process is a Markov Chain that gradually adds Gaussian noise to a clean image, which can be expressed as:

$$q(y_t|y_{t-1}) = \mathcal{N}(y_t; \sqrt{1-\beta_t}y_{t-1}, \beta_t\mathbf{I}); q(y_t|y_0) = \mathcal{N}(y_t; \sqrt{\bar{\alpha}_t}y_0, (1-\bar{\alpha}_t)\mathbf{I}), \quad (2)$$

where y_t denotes the intermediate noisy images, β_t denotes the noise variance, $\alpha_t = 1 - \beta_t$, and $\bar{\alpha}_t = \prod_{s=1}^t \alpha_s$. For simplicity, β_t follows a fixed schedule. When

T is sufficiently large, y_T is dominated by noise. A CNN model is introduced to gradually reverse the forward diffusion process, i.e. *denoise* y_t, by estimating

$$p_\theta(y_{t-1}|y_t) = \mathcal{N}(y_{t-1}; \epsilon_\theta(y_t, t), \sigma_t^2 \mathbf{I}), \tag{3}$$

where $\sigma_t^2 = \bar{\beta}_t = \frac{1-\bar{\alpha}_{t-1}}{1-\bar{\alpha}_t}\beta_t$ in this work. With fixed variance, ϵ_θ in Eq. (3) is trained by mean-matching the diffusion noise through an $\mathcal{L}_2$ loss. We follow [14] with some modifications to train a diffusion model that generates MR images.

After training on MR images y_{full}, ϵ_θ can be used to gradually transform noise into images that follow the distribution $p_\theta(y_{\text{full}})$, as shown in Fig. 1. We note that diffusion models generate images *unconditionally* by their original design. To reconstruct high fidelity MR images *conditioned* on x_{obs}, DiffuseRecon is proposed to gradually modify y_t such that y_0 agrees with x_{obs}. DiffuseRecon consists of two parts, k-Space Guidance and Coarse-to-Fine Sampling.

K-Space Guidance. We note that $R(*)$ is naturally enforced by following the denoising process with a pre-trained θ, as the generated images already follow the MR data distribution. As such, k-Space Guidance (KSG) is proposed to ensure the generated images follow the data consistency term. In a diffusion model, a denoised image is generated at every step t by subtracting the estimated noise from the previous y_t, specifically:

$$y'_{t-1} = \frac{1}{\sqrt{\alpha_t}}(y_t - \frac{1-\alpha_t}{\sqrt{1-\bar{\alpha}_t}}\epsilon_\theta(y_t, t)) + \sigma_t \mathbf{z}, \mathbf{z} \sim \mathcal{N}(0, \mathbf{I}). \tag{4}$$

For unconditional generation, $y_{t-1} = y'_{t-1}$, and the process repeats until $t = 0$. For DiffuseRecon, KSG gradually mixes observed k-space signal x_{obs} with y'_{t-1}. To do so, KSG first adds a zero-mean noise on x_{obs} to simulate its diffused condition at step t. The noisy observation is then mixed with y'_{t-1} in k-space based on the undersampling mask $\mathcal{M}$. This process is expressed as follows:

$$y_t = \mathcal{F}^{-1}((1-\mathcal{M})\mathcal{F}y'_t + \mathcal{M}x_{\text{obs},t}),$$
$$\text{where } x_{\text{obs},t} = x_{\text{obs}} + \mathcal{F}(\mathcal{N}(0, (1-\bar{\alpha}_t)\mathbf{I})). \tag{5}$$

The resulting y_{t-1} is iteratively denoised with decreasing t until y_0 is obtained, and $x_{\text{obs},0} = x_{\text{obs}}$. As such, y_0 shares the same observed k-space signal and achieves the data consistency term $\mathcal{M}\mathcal{F}y_0 = x_{\text{obs}}$. Since all generated samples fall on the data distribution $p_\theta(y_{\text{full}})$, KSG allows us to stochastically sample from the marginal distribution $p_\theta(y_{\text{full}}|x_{\text{obs}})$ through a pre-trained diffusion model. As demonstrated in Fig. 2a, we can observe the variations in y_0 with a given x_{obs} and determine the reliability of the reconstructed results. Furthermore, KSG is parameter-free and applicable to *any* undersampling mask $\mathcal{M}$ without finetuning.

Coarse-to-Fine Sampling. While sampling in $p_\theta(y_{\text{full}}|x_{\text{obs}})$ allows us to generate different reconstruction candidates, selecting the best reconstruction out of all candidates is a challenge. Since we do not have an analytic solution for $p_\theta(y_{\text{full}}|x_{\text{obs}})$, Monte-Carlo (MC) sampling can be used to estimate

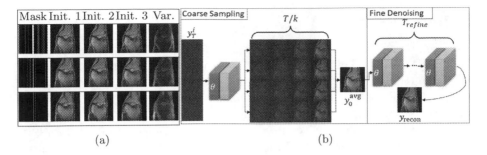

Fig. 2. (a) Visualizations on various under-sampled k-space signal ($8\times$, $16\times$, $32\times$, 1D Gaussian Mask). (b) To accelerate the sampling process for MC simulation, multiple coarse samples are generated using $\frac{T}{k}$ steps. These samples are averaged to y_0^{avg} and reintroduced to the denoising network for T_{refine} steps.

$\mathbb{E}(p_\theta(y_{\text{full}}|x_{\text{obs}}))$ in an unbiased way with sufficient samples. However, as sampling from a diffusion model already requires multiple steps, generating multiple samples is computationally costly. In practice, the denoising process can be accelerated by evenly spacing the $\{T, T-1, ..., 1\}$ schedule to a shorter schedule $\{T, T-k, ..., 1\}$ [14], where $k > 1$, and modifying the respective weights β, α based on k. However, the acceleration tends to produce less denoised results when k is large.

We propose a Coarse-to-Fine (C2F) sampling algorithm to greatly accelerate the MC sampling process without loss in performance. Specifically, we note that the diffusion noise that is added in Eq. (2) is zero-mean with respect to y_0, and can be reduced by averaging multiple samples. Since multiple samples are already required to estimate $\mathbb{E}(p_\theta(y_{\text{full}}|x_{\text{obs}}))$, we leverage the multi-sample scenario to more aggressively reduce the denoising steps. As shown in Fig. 2b, C2F sampling creates N instances of $y_T^{i,\frac{T}{k}} \sim \mathcal{N}(0, \mathbf{I})$ and applies denoising individually for $\frac{T}{k}$ steps based on a re-spaced schedule. The noisy results are averaged to produce $y_0^{\text{avg}} = \frac{1}{N}\sum_{i=0}^{N} y_0^{i,\frac{T}{k}}$. Finally, y_0^{avg} is refined by going through additional T_{refine} steps with ϵ_θ. To control the denoising strength in ϵ_θ, $\{T_{\text{refine}}, T_{\text{refine}} - 1, ..., 1\} \in \{T, T-1, ..., 1\}, T_{\text{refine}} \ll T$. The last refinement steps help remove blurriness introduced by averaging multiple samples and lead to more realistic reconstruction results. During the refinement steps, x_{obs} directly replaces k-space signals in the reconstructions, as is consistent with $\mathcal{MF}y_0^{i,\frac{T}{k}}$.

Compared to a naive approach which requires TN total steps to estimate $\mathbb{E}(p_\theta(y_{\text{full}}|x_{\text{obs}}))$, C2F sampling introduces an approximately k-time speed-up. Furthermore, while $y_0^{i,\frac{T}{k}}$ are noisy compared to their fully-denoised version $y_0^{i,T}$, their noise is approximately Gaussian and introduces only a constant between $Var(y_0^{i,\frac{T}{k}})$ and $Var(y_0^{i,T})$. As such, given a reasonable N, variance in $p_\theta(y_{\text{full}}|x_{\text{obs}})$ can still be estimated well from coarse samples.

3   Experiments

Dataset. In our experiments, we use two large knee MR datasets that contain raw, complex-value acquisition signals. FastMRI [26] contains 1172 subjects, with approximately 35 slices per subject and is split such that 973 subjects are used for training and 199 subjects are used for evaluation. SKM-TEA [3] contains 155 subjects, with approximately 160 slices per subject; 134 subjects are used for training, 21 subjects are used for evaluation. Single-coil data is used for both datasets. Undersampling masks $\mathcal{M}$ are generated by using the masking function provided in the fastMRI challenge with 6× and 8× accelerations. To avoid slices with little information, the first five and ten slices are removed from evaluation for fastMRI and SKM-TEA respectively. To accommodate methods based on over-complete CNNs, which require upsampling and a larger memory footprint, images from SKM-TEA are center-cropped to $\mathbb{R}^{448 \times 448}$.

Implementation Details. All baselines are implemented in PyTorch and trained with $\mathcal{L}_1$ loss and Adam optimizer. Following [6], a learning rate is set to 1.5×10^{-4} and reduced by 90% every five epochs; to ensure a fair comparison, U-Net [17] is implemented with a data consistency layer at the end. For DiffuseRecon, we follow [14] by using a cosine noise schedule and a U-Net architecture with multi-head attention as the denoising model. The model is modified to generate two consecutive slices; as such, the input and output channel sizes are 4, accounting for complex values. For C2F Sampling, $\{T, k, N, T_{\mathrm{refine}}\} = \{4000, 40, 10, 20\}$, which gives a $\frac{TN}{\frac{TN}{k} + T_{\mathrm{refine}}} \approx 39$ times speed-up compared to naive MC sampling.

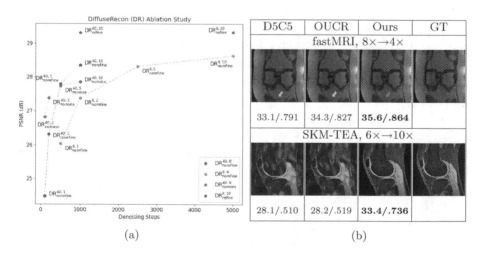

(a)   (b)

Fig. 3. (a) Ablation Study on DiffuseRecon with different parameters. (b) Visualizations on recovering from unseen acceleration factors.

Ablation Study. We examine the effectiveness of the following design choices:

- DiffuseRecon$_{\text{nonoise}}^{k,N}$: $\mathcal{MF}y_t'$ is directly replaced with x_{obs} in KSG instead of $x_{\text{obs},t}$; $k = \{40\}$ and $N = \{1, 2, 5, 10\}$ are tested.
- DiffuseRecon$_{\text{norefine}}^{k,N}$: a combination of $\{k, N\}$ are tested without the refining steps; specifically, $k = \{8, 40\}$ and $N = \{1, 2, 5, 10\}$.
- DiffuseRecon$_{\text{refine}}^{k,N}$: $T_{\text{refine}} = 20$ steps of further denoising is applied to the aggregate results from DiffuseRecon$_{\text{norefine}}^{k,N}$, $\{k, N\} = \{\{8, 40\}, 10\}$.

The PSNR comparisons are visualized in Fig. 3(a) and are made based on the middle fifteen slices for all subjects in the fastMRI's evaluation set. There are several interesting takeaways. Firstly, PSNR increases significantly with larger N for all instances, demonstrating the importance of multi-sample aggregation. We note that $k = 8$ applies 500 steps and yields sufficiently denoised results; as such, the low PSNR value for DiffuseRecon$_{\text{norefine}}^{8,1}$ is due to the geometric variability between sampled and groundtruth image. Secondly, when no gradual noise is added to x_{obs}, the reconstruction results are significantly better when $N = 1$ and worse when $N = 10$ compared to the proposed KSG; such a direct replacement approach is used in a concurrent work POCS [2]. This indicates that, while the clean x_{obs} introduced at $t = T$ helps accelerate the denoising process, the aggregate results do not estimate the ground-truth well, i.e. they are more likely to be biased. Finally, the refinement steps significantly remove the blurriness caused by averaging multiple samples. We note that performances are very similar for DiffuseRecon$_{\text{refine}}^{8,10}$ and DiffuseRecon$_{\text{refine}}^{40,10}$; as such, $k = 8$ leads to significant speed-up without sacrificing reconstruction quality.

Table 1. Quantitative volume-wise evaluation of DiffuseRecon against SoTA methods. Dedicated models are trained for 6× and 8× acceleration; model robustness is tested by applying $\{6\times, 8\times\}$ model on $\{10\times, 4\times\}$ downsampled inputs. All baselines achieved similar performance compared to the original papers.

Method	fastMRI				SKM-TEA			
	6×	8×	8×→4×	6×→10×	6×	8×	8×→4×	6×→10×
UNet [17]	29.79	28.89	30.67	21.98	31.62	30.47	32.06	24.34
	0.621	0.577	0.666	0.296	0.713	0.669	0.728	0.382
KIKI-Net [5]	29.51	28.09	30.18	22.31	31.67	30.14	32.20	24.67
	0.607	0.546	0.650	0.313	0.711	0.655	0.732	0.422
D5C5 [19]	29.88	28.63	30.90	23.07	32.22	30.86	32.99	25.99
	0.622	0.565	0.675	0.349	0.732	0.683	0.763	0.512
OUCR [6]	30.44	29.56	31.33	23.41	32.52	31.27	33.11	26.17
	0.644	0.600	0.689	0.371	0.742	0.696	0.766	0.516
DiffuseRecon	**30.56**	**29.94**	**31.70**	**27.23**	**32.58**	**31.56**	**33.76**	**28.40**
	0.648	**0.614**	**0.708**	**0.515**	**0.743**	**0.706**	**0.795**	**0.584**

Quantitative and Visual Evaluation. We compare reconstruction results from DiffuseRecon with current SoTA methods, and summarize the quantitative results in Table 1. KIKI-Net [5] applies convolutions on both the image and k-space data for reconstruction. D5C5 [19] is a seminal DL-based MR reconstruction work and proposes to incorporate data consistency layers into a cascade of CNNs. OUCR [6] builds on [19] and uses a recurrent over-complete CNN [23] architecture to better recovery fine details. We note that these methods use supervised learning and train dedicated models based on a fixed acceleration factor. In Table 1, DiffuseRecon is compared with these specifically trained models for acceleration factor of 6× and 8× in k-space. Although the model for DiffuseRecon is trained for *a denoising task* and has *not* observed any downsampled MR images, DiffuseRecon obtains top performances compared to the dedicated models from current SoTAs; the performance gap is larger as the acceleration factor becomes higher. To examine the robustness of dedicated models on lower and higher quality inputs, we apply models trained on 6× and 8× acceleration on 10× and 4× undersampled inputs, respectively. In these cases, the performances of DiffuseRecon are significantly higher, demonstrating that 1. models obtained from supervised training are less reliable on images with unseen levels of degradation, and 2. DiffuseRecon is a general and performant MR reconstruction method.

Visualization of the reconstructed images is provided in Fig. 3(b) and Fig. 4 to illustrate the advantages of DiffuseRecon. Due to limited space, we focus on the top three methods: D5C5 [19], OUCR [6], and DiffuseRecon. We observe that many significant structural details are lost in D5C5 and OUCR but can be recovered by DiffuseRecon. The errors in D5C5 and OUCR tend to have a vertical pattern, likely because the under-sampled images suffer from more vertical aliasing artifacts due to phase encoding under-sampling. As such, it is more difficult for D5C5 and OUCR to correctly recover these vertical details, and leads to blurry reconstructions under a pixel-wise loss function. DiffuseRecon, on the other hand, outputs realistic MR images that obey the distribution $p_\theta(y_{\text{full}}|x_{\text{obs}})$; it can better recover vertical details that fit the distribution of $p_\theta(y_{\text{full}})$. This is particularly pronounced in the 8× fastMRI results in Fig. 4, where the lost vertical knee pattern in D5C5 and OUCR renders the image highly unrealistic. Such an error is avoided in DiffuseRecon as each of its sample has a complete knee structure based on the learned prior knowledge. The uncertainty introduced by phase-encoding under-sampling is also captured by the variance map and demonstrates that exact placement of details may be varied. For more visualization and detailed comparisons, please refer to the supplemental material.

While DiffuseRecon holds many advantages to current SoTA methods, it does require more computation due to the multi-sampling process. The one-time inference speed is comparable to UNet [17] at 20 ms; however, DiffuseRecon performs 1000 inference steps. We note that 20 s per slice still yields significant acceleration compared to raw acquisitions, and there exists much potential in accelerating diffusion models [12,18,20] for future work. DiffuseRecon can also

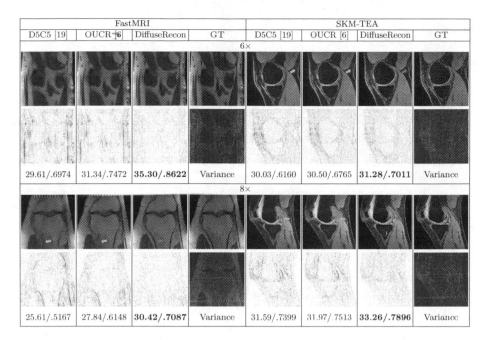

FastMRI				SKM-TEA			
D5C5 [19]	OUCR [6]	DiffuseRecon	GT	D5C5 [19]	OUCR [6]	DiffuseRecon	GT
6×							
29.61/.6974	31.34/.7472	**35.30/.8622**	Variance	30.03/.6160	30.50/.6765	**31.28/.7011**	Variance
8×							
25.61/.5167	27.84/.6148	**30.42/.7087**	Variance	31.59/.7399	31.97/.7513	**33.26/.7896**	Variance

Fig. 4. Visual comparison of DiffuseRecon with other SoTA reconstruction methods. Error maps are provided for reference.

be used in conjunction with deterministic methods, *e.g.*, when variance analysis is needed only selectively, to balance speed to performance and reliability.

4 Conclusion

We propose DiffuseRecon, an MR image reconstruction method that is of high performance, robust to different acceleration factors, and allows a user to directly observe the reconstruction variations. Inspired by diffusion models, DiffuseRecon incorporates the observed k-space signals in reverse-diffusion and can stochastically generate realistic MR reconstructions. To obtain the most likely reconstruction candidate and its variance, DiffuseRecon performs a coarse-to-fine sampling scheme that significantly accelerates the generation process. We carefully evaluate DiffuseRecon on raw acquisition data, and find that DiffuseRecon achieves better performances than current SoTA methods that require dedicated data generation and training for different sampling conditions. The reconstruction variance from DiffuseRecon can help practitioners make more informed clinical decisions. Future works include further acceleration of the inference process and examination into different MR sampling patterns.

References

1. Akçakaya, M., Moeller, S., Weingärtner, S., Uğurbil, K.: Scan-specific robust artificial-neural-networks for k-space interpolation (RAKI) reconstruction: database-free deep learning for fast imaging. Magn. Reson. Med. **81**(1), 439–453 (2019)
2. Chung, H., Chul Ye, J.: Score-based diffusion models for accelerated MRI (2021)
3. Desai, A.D., et al.: Skm-tea: a dataset for accelerated MRI reconstruction with dense image labels for quantitative clinical evaluation. In: Thirty-Fifth Conference on Neural Information Processing Systems Datasets and Benchmarks Track (Round 2) (2021)
4. Dhariwal, P., Nichol, A.: Diffusion models beat GANs on image synthesis. CoRR abs/2105.05233 (2021). https://arxiv.org/abs/2105.05233
5. Eo, T., et al.: KIKI-net: cross-domain convolutional neural networks for reconstructing undersampled magnetic resonance images. Magn. Reson. Med. **80**(5), 2188–2201 (2018)
6. Guo, P., Valanarasu, J.M.J., Wang, P., Zhou, J., Jiang, S., Patel, V.M.: Over-and-under complete convolutional RNN for MRI reconstruction. In: de Bruijne, M., et al. (eds.) MICCAI 2021. LNCS, vol. 12906, pp. 13–23. Springer, Cham (2021). https://doi.org/10.1007/978-3-030-87231-1_2
7. Guo, P., Wang, P., Zhou, J., Jiang, S., Patel, V.M.: Multi-institutional collaborations for improving deep learning-based magnetic resonance image reconstruction using federated learning. In: IEEE Conference on Computer Vision and Pattern Recognition, CVPR 2021, virtual, June 19–25, 2021, pp. 2423–2432. Computer Vision Foundation/IEEE (2021)
8. Hammernik, K., et al.: Learning a variational network for reconstruction of accelerated MRI data. Magn. Reson. Med. **79**(6), 3055–3071 (2018)
9. Han, Y., Sunwoo, L., Ye, J.C.: k-space deep learning for accelerated MRI. IEEE Trans. Med. Imaging **39**(2), 377–386 (2020)
10. Ho, J., Jain, A., Abbeel, P.: Denoising diffusion probabilistic models. In: Larochelle, H., Ranzato, M., Hadsell, R., Balcan, M., Lin, H. (eds.) Advances in Neural Information Processing Systems 33: Annual Conference on Neural Information Processing Systems 2020, NeurIPS 2020, 6–12 December, 2020, virtual (2020)
11. Jalal, A., Arvinte, M., Daras, G., Price, E., Dimakis, A.G., Tamir, J.I.: Robust compressed sensing MRI with deep generative priors. In: Ranzato, M., Beygelzimer, A., Dauphin, Y.N., Liang, P., Vaughan, J.W. (eds.) Advances in Neural Information Processing Systems 34: Annual Conference on Neural Information Processing Systems 2021, NeurIPS 2021, 6–14 December 2021, virtual, pp. 14938–14954 (2021)
12. Kong, Z., Ping, W.: On fast sampling of diffusion probabilistic models. CoRR abs/2106.00132 (2021). https://arxiv.org/abs/2106.00132
13. Lustig, M., Donoho, D., Pauly, J.M.: Sparse MRI: the application of compressed sensing for rapid MR imaging. Magnetic Resonance in Med. **58**(6), 1182–95 (2007)
14. Nichol, A.Q., Dhariwal, P.: Improved denoising diffusion probabilistic models. In: Meila, M., Zhang, T. (eds.) Proceedings of the 38th International Conference on Machine Learning, ICML 2021, 18–24 July 2021, Virtual Event. Proceedings of Machine Learning Research, vol. 139, pp. 8162–8171. PMLR (2021), http://proceedings.mlr.press/v139/nichol21a.html
15. Qin, C., Schlemper, J., Caballero, J., Price, A.N., Hajnal, J.V., Rueckert, D.: Convolutional recurrent neural networks for dynamic MR image reconstruction. IEEE Trans. Med. Imaging **38**(1), 280–290 (2019)

16. Ravishankar, S., Bresler, Y.: MR image reconstruction from highly undersampled k-space data by dictionary learning. IEEE TMI **30**(5), 1028–41 (2011)

17. Ronneberger, O., Fischer, P., Brox, T.: U-Net: convolutional networks for biomedical image segmentation. In: Navab, N., Hornegger, J., Wells, W.M., Frangi, A.F. (eds.) MICCAI 2015. LNCS, vol. 9351, pp. 234–241. Springer, Cham (2015). https://doi.org/10.1007/978-3-319-24574-4_28

18. Salimans, T., Ho, J.: Progressive distillation for fast sampling of diffusion models. In: International Conference on Learning Representations (2022)

19. Schlemper, J., Caballero, J., Hajnal, J.V., Price, A.N., Rueckert, D.: A deep cascade of convolutional neural networks for dynamic MR image reconstruction. IEEE Trans. Medical Imaging **37**(2), 491–503 (2018)

20. Song, J., Meng, C., Ermon, S.: Denoising diffusion implicit models. In: 9th International Conference on Learning Representations, ICLR 2021, Virtual Event, Austria, 3–7 May, 2021. OpenReview.net (2021)

21. Song, Y., Shen, L., Xing, L., Ermon, S.: Solving inverse problems in medical imaging with score-based generative models. In: International Conference on Learning Representations (2022). https://openreview.net/forum?id=vaRCHVj0uGI

22. Sriram, A., Zbontar, J., Murrell, T., Zitnick, C.L., Defazio, A., Sodickson, D.K.: Grappanet: combining parallel imaging with deep learning for multi-coil MRI reconstruction. In: 2020 IEEE/CVF Conference on Computer Vision and Pattern Recognition, CVPR 2020, Seattle, WA, USA, 13–19 June, 2020, pp. 14303–14310. Computer Vision Foundation/IEEE (2020)

23. Valanarasu, J.M.J., Sindagi, V.A., Hacihaliloglu, I., Patel, V.M.: KiU-Net: towards accurate segmentation of biomedical images using over-complete representations. In: Martel, A.L., et al. (eds.) MICCAI 2020. LNCS, vol. 12264, pp. 363–373. Springer, Cham (2020). https://doi.org/10.1007/978-3-030-59719-1_36

24. Wang, S., et al.: Accelerating magnetic resonance imaging via deep learning. In: 2016 IEEE 13th International Symposium on Biomedical Imaging (ISBI), pp. 514–517 (2016)

25. Yang, G., et al.: Dagan: deep de-aliasing generative adversarial networks for fast compressed sensing MRI reconstruction. IEEE Trans. Med. Imaging **37**(6), 1310–1321 (2018)

26. Zbontar, J., et al.: fastmri: an open dataset and benchmarks for accelerated MRI. CoRR abs/1811.08839 (2018)

27. Zhou, B., Zhou, S.K.: Dudornet: Learning a dual-domain recurrent network for fast MRI reconstruction with deep T1 prior. In: 2020 IEEE/CVF Conference on Computer Vision and Pattern Recognition, CVPR 2020, Seattle, WA, USA, 13–19 June, 2020, pp. 4272–4281. Computer Vision Foundation/IEEE (2020)

Patch-Wise Deep Metric Learning for Unsupervised Low-Dose CT Denoising

Chanyong Jung[1], Joonhyung Lee[1], Sunkyoung You[2], and Jong Chul Ye[1,3(✉)]

[1] Department of Bio and Brain Engineering, Korea Advanced Institute of Science and Technology (KAIST), Daejeon, Republic of Korea
jong.ye@kaist.ac.kr
[2] Department of Radiology, Chungnam National University College of Medicine and Chungnam National University Hospital, Daejeon, Republic of Korea
[3] Kim Jaechul Graduate School of AI, KAIST, Daejeon, Republic of Korea

Abstract. The acquisition conditions for low-dose and high-dose CT images are usually different, so that the shifts in the CT numbers often occur. Accordingly, unsupervised deep learning-based approaches, which learn the target image distribution, often introduce CT number distortions and result in detrimental effects in diagnostic performance. To address this, here we propose a novel unsupervised learning approach for lowdose CT reconstruction using patch-wise deep metric learning. The key idea is to learn embedding space by pulling the positive pairs of image patches which shares the same anatomical structure, and pushing the negative pairs which have same noise level each other. Thereby, the network is trained to suppress the noise level, while retaining the original global CT number distributions even after the image translation. Experimental results confirm that our deep metric learning plays a critical role in producing high quality denoised images without CT number shift.

Keywords: Low-dose CT denoising · Deep metric learning

1 Introduction

In computed tomography (CT), multiple X-ray projection images are obtained at various angles, which incurs considerable radiation exposure to a patient [3].

This study was approved by the institutional review board (IRB) of our institution, and the requirement for informed consent was waived. This study was supported by the National Research Foundation of Korea (NRF) grant NRF-2020R1A2B5B03001980, KAIST Key Research Institute (Interdisciplinary Research Group) Project, Field-oriented Technology Development Project for Customs Administration through NRF funded by the Ministry of Science & ICT (MSIT) and Korea Customs Service (NRF-2021M3I1A1097938). Sunkyoung You was supported by the Bio & Medical Technology Development Program of the NRF & funded by the MSIT (No. NRF-2019M3E5D1A02068564)
Joonhyung Lee is currently at VUNO Corp.

Supplementary Information The online version contains supplementary material available at https://doi.org/10.1007/978-3-031-16446-0_60.

In addition, for a temporal CT imaging to evaluate the pathologies of the ears especially for children, it is practical standard to use low-dose CT. Thus, low-dose CT reconstruction, which reduces the radiation dose for each projection while maintaining the image quality, is an important research topic.

Recently, deep learning approaches have become a main approach for low-dose CT reconstruction [4,17], which has resulted many commercially available products [9]. Furthermore, the difficulty of obtaining matched CT data pairs has led to exploring various unsupervised learning approaches [2,22]. In particular, image translation methodology is successfully employed for the low-dose CT noise suppression by learning the noise patterns through a comparison between the low-dose CT (LDCT) and high-dose CT (HDCT) distributions [7,16,20].

Despite the success, the approach is not free of limitation. In particular, for the real-world dataset, there often exists CT number shift between LDCT and HDCT dataset due to the different acquisition conditions. Hence, the networks often result the distortion in pixel values. Unfortunately, the change of the CT numbers has detrimental effects to the radiological diagnostic performance, since it is used as a diagnostic indicator [6]. Especially in the temporal bone CT scans which we are interested in this paper, the CT number supports the evaluation of a pathologies of the ear, such as an inflammation within the inner ear, and a cholesteatoma in early stage [1,5,13]. Wavelet-assisted approaches [7,8] partially address this problem by constraining the pixel value variations only in high-frequency subbands. However, even in the high-frequency image, there exists many important structural information, which can be altered during the image translation so that the localized CT number variation is unavoidable.

Recently, image translation methods utilizing patch-wise interaction have received significant attention [14,18]. By the contrastive loss, the mutual information (MI) between the patches are maximized, pulling positive pairs and pushing negative pairs. However, for denoising tasks, maximizing MI is not appropriate, since a preservation of noise pattern also contributes to the increase of MI.

Here, we propose a novel approach for the LDCT denoising, suggesting the pull-push mechanism for the denoising process by newly defined pairs and a metric. We set the positive pair as the patches from same location of noisy input and denoised output, which share anatomic structure. Also, the negative pair is set by the patches from different location of same image, which have same noise level. Thereby, the network is trained to maintain the structural information, and suppress the noise level. The experimental results on the synthetic noise dataset and a real-world dataset verify the effectiveness of the proposed method.

2   Method

2.1   Overview of the Proposed Method

In the proposed framework, we aim to learn the embedding space which focus on the anatomic structure features, and discards the noise features. In the training process, the image patches with same contents and different noise level will pull

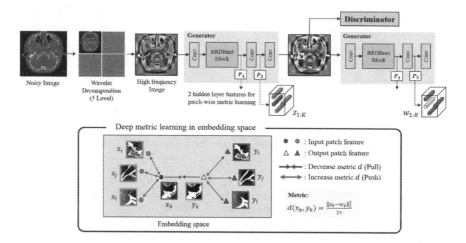

Fig. 1. Proposed deep metric learning for low-dose CT denoising. The positive pair x_k, y_k pull each other to decrease the metric d between them. x_i, x_j, x_l are pushed away $(i, j, l \neq k)$ from x_k, as they have same noise level and different contents. Likewise, y_i, y_j, y_l are pushed away from y_k.

each other, to learn the shared feature between them (i.e. anatomic structure). On the other hand, the image patches with same noise level and different contents will push each other, to suppress the network to learn the shared feature (i.e. noise). Deep metric is utilized for the pull and push between the image patches.

Specifically, as shown in Fig. 1, we first obtain a high-frequency image by a wavelet transform, and then exploit the patch-wise deep metric learning using the features of the image before and after the denoising process. Here, similar to [7,8], high frequency images are obtained by a wavelet decomposition, putting zeros at the low-frequency band, and then performing wavelet recomposition. This preprocessing preserves the low frequency image of input.

Then, the high-frequency images from the input and the output images are processed by shared feature extractors with projection heads to generate patch-by-patch latent vectors. In addition, as for the deep metric learning of these latent vectors, we propose a loss so that effective representation for the image generation can be obtained. The final denoised image is obtained by adding the generator output with low frequency image of input.

Here, we discuss the relation of our work with the contrastive learning. The goal of the contrastive loss as suggested in the related work [14] is to maximize the MI between the patches of input and output images. Hence, the negative pair is defined as the patches from input and output with different spatial location, to implement the sampling from marginal distributions. Then, the loss pushes the pairs with different noise level, which leads to different solution with our loss function. Both loss functions utilize the pulling and the pushing of the image patches, however, the objective and the pull-push mechanism of each loss are different. Therefore, we propose our work as deep metric learning which generalize the methods based on the pull-push mechanism.

2.2 Patch-Wise Deep Metric Learning

As shown in Fig. 1, we obtain the embedding space by the pull and push between the image patches. Let $x_k \in \mathcal{X}$ and $y_j \in \mathcal{Y}$ denote the image patches from the input and denoised output image, respectively, where the k, j are the indices for the patch locations, and $\mathcal{X}$ and $\mathcal{Y}$ are domains for LDCT and HDCT images. Also, let z_k and w_k are the L2 normalized embedding vectors for x_k and y_k. Then, we define the metric d as following:

$$d(x_k, y_k) = \frac{\|z_k - w_k\|_2^2}{2\tau} \tag{1}$$

where τ is the temperature parameter.

Using the defined metric d, we decrease the distance between the positive pairs, and make the negative pairs be far apart in the embedding space. We optimize the following metric loss $\mathcal{L}_m$ given as:

$$\mathcal{L}_m := \mathbb{E}_p\left[\exp(d(x_k, y_k))\right] - \mathbb{E}_{q_n}\left[\exp(d(x_k, x_j))\right] - \mathbb{E}_{q_o}\left[\exp(d(y_k, y_j))\right] \tag{2}$$

where p is the distribution for the positive pair, q_n is for the negative pair from the input image, and q_o is for the negative pair from the output image. Since $\|z_k - w_k\|_2^2 = 2 - 2z_k^\top w_k$, the loss function can be rewritten as:

$$\mathcal{L}_m := -\mathbb{E}_p[\exp(z_k^\top w_k/\tau)] + \mathbb{E}_{q_n}[\exp(z_k^\top z_j/\tau)] + \mathbb{E}_{q_o}[\exp(w_k^\top w_j/\tau)] \tag{3}$$

2.3 Network Architecture

Our generator architecture is shown in Fig. 2, where the generator G is composed of several blocks which are encoder network E and convolutional layers C_1, C_2:

$$G : x \in \mathcal{X} \mapsto \mathcal{Y}, \quad \text{where} \quad G(x) = (C_2 \circ C_1 \circ E)(x) \tag{4}$$

where $\circ$ denotes the composite function. The encoder network E is composed of convolutional layer followed by RRDBnet [19] architecture. Furthermore, we use two latent feature extractors:

$$F_1(x) = (P_1 \circ E)(x)$$
$$F_2(x) = (P_2 \circ C_1 \circ E)(x)$$

where P_1, P_2 are projection heads shown in Fig. 2.

Then, the overall loss function is given as:

$$\mathcal{L} = \mathcal{L}_{GAN} + \lambda_{idt}\mathcal{L}_{idt} + \lambda_m\mathcal{L}_m \tag{5}$$

where $\mathcal{L}_{GAN}, \mathcal{L}_{idt}$ and $\mathcal{L}_m$ are the GAN loss, identity loss and deep metric loss, respectively, and λ_{idt} and λ_m and denote their associated weighting parameters. As for the GAN loss $\mathcal{L}_{GAN}$, we use the LSGAN loss [12]:

$$\mathcal{L}_{GAN}(E, \{C_i\}, D) = \mathcal{L}_{GAN}(E, \{C_i\}) + \mathcal{L}_{GAN}(D) \tag{6}$$

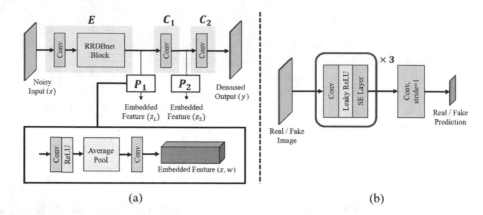

Fig. 2. Structure of the generator G and discriminator D. Two intermediate features of the G are used for deep metric learning. (a) G consists of feature extractor E, and convolutional layers C_1, C_2 and projection heads P_1, P_2. (b) D is composed of three repeated convolutional blocks.

where

$$\mathcal{L}_{GAN}(G) = \mathbb{E}_{x \sim P_X} \left[\| D(G(x)) - 1 \|_2 \right] \tag{7}$$

$$\mathcal{L}_{GAN}(D) = \mathbb{E}_{y \sim P_Y} \left[\| D(y) - 1 \|_2 \right] + \mathbb{E}_{x \sim P_X} \left[\| D(G(x)) \|_2 \right] \tag{8}$$

The identity loss is used to impose the reconstruction constraint for the target domain image on the network, thereby preventing any artifact of the output image caused by GAN loss. The idt loss $\mathcal{L}_{idt}$ is given as:

$$\mathcal{L}_{idt}(E, \{C_i\}) = \mathbb{E}_{y \sim P_Y} \left[\| (C_2 \circ C_1 \circ E)(y) - y \|_1 \right], \tag{9}$$

Finally, the deep metric loss $\mathcal{L}_m$ is composed of two terms, since we use two intermediate features as shown in Fig. 2

$$\mathcal{L}_m(E, C_1, \{P_i\}) = \mathcal{L}_{m,1}(E, P_1) + \mathcal{L}_{m,2}(E, C_1, P_2) \tag{10}$$

3   Experiments

We verify our method using two datasets. First, we use the publicly released CT dataset from the 2016 NIH-AAPM-Mayo Clinic Low Dose CT Grand Challenge dataset (AAPM), and the real-world temporal CT scan dataset. The real-world temporal CT scans are obtained at 100 kVp. Collimation is 128 mm × 0.6 mm, the pitch is set to 1, and the slice thickness is 0.6 mm. Reference mAs for low-dose and high-dose scans are 46 mAs and 366 mAs, respectively. H70s kernel for low-dose and H60s kernel high-dose scans are used. The dataset consists of 54 volumes of low-dose, and 34 volumes of high-dose scans. We split the low-dose data into two sets, a train set with 45 volumes and a test set with 9 volumes.

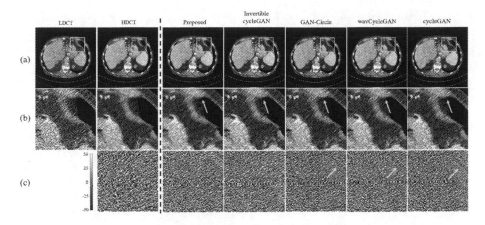

Fig. 3. Results from AAPM dataset. (a) CT images for the comparison, displayed with (−4150 HU, 210 HU). (b) Zoomed image for the comparison of fine structures. (c) Difference images of zoomed area subtracted by the low-dose images, displayed with (−450 HU, 50 HU).

Table 1. Quantitative metrics (PSNR, SSIM) to compare the performance with the previous methods on AAPM dataset.

	LDCT	Proposed	Invertible-cycleGAN	GAN-Circle	wavCycleGAN	cycleGAN
PSNR	33.300	**38.110**	37.855	37.795	37.736	37.673
SSIM	0.740	**0.875**	0.867	0.867	0.867	0.865

We compare our method with existing denoising methods based on the image translation framework, such as cycleGAN [23], wavCycleGAN [7], GAN-Circle [21] and Cycle-free invertible cycleGAN [11]. We measure PSNR, SSIM to compare the denoising performance for AAPM dataset. For temporal CT scans, the ground truth is not accessible. Hence, we measure the mean and standard deviation of pixels to investigate the CT number shift and denoising performance.

The method is implemented by the PyTorch [15] with two NVIDIA GeForce GTX 2080Ti GPU devices. The Adam optimizer [10] is used with $\beta_1 = 0.5$ and $\beta_2 = 0.999$. The learning rate is scheduled to be constant until the half of the total training epoch, and then linearly decreased to zero. The inputs for the network are randomly cropped images with size of 128×128. The projection heads downsample the features by the 2×2 pooling layer for temporal CT dataset. In case of AAPM dataset, the projection heads do not downsample the feature. The source code is available at: https://github.com/jcy132/DML_CT

Table 2. Quantitative comparison for the temporal CT data. The mean values of air and brain area shows the CT number shift problem between the LDCT and HDCT images. Our goal is to produce the outputs with similar mean with LDCT but low Std value.

| | Image patches with Homogeneous media | | | | Selected temopral region | | | | | |
| | Brain | | Air | | Soft Tissue | | Cavity | | Bone | |
	Mean	Std	Mean	Std	Mean	Std	Mean	Std	Mean	Std
LDCT	**35.02**	289.47	**-845.28**	132.82	**30.37**	285.97	**-775.71**	182.86	**1350.72**	344.54
HDCT	37.36	**48.62**	−972.29	**32.95**	N/A	N/A	N/A	N/A	N/A	N/A
cycleGAN	36.78	59.03	−968.14	40.12	38.06	52.89	−923.45	36.47	1389.07	116.46
WavCycleGAN	32.69	60.98	−852.94	33.13	49.71	58.43	−859.92	38.26	1375.65	156.43
GAN-Circle	39.43	49.23	−994.40	38.11	40.29	50.22	−925.42	36.50	1364.28	115.47
Invertible-cycleGAN	37.74	53.46	−846.87	33.47	44.44	54.44	−801.20	44.12	1384.13	111.81
Proposed	**35.05**	**49.06**	**−845.65**	**32.99**	**29.39**	**48.15**	**−777.63**	**33.65**	**1352.57**	**72.98**

3.1   AAPM Dataset

For AAPM dataset, the network was trained with learning rate 2e−4 with epoch 200. The wavelet decomposition is proceeded by level 6 using db3 wavelet filter. The batch size is 8, and the $\tau = 0.15$ for the metric d. $\lambda_{idt} = 5$ and $\lambda_m = 0.1$. We used 3112 images for training, and evaluated for 421 test images.

Figure 3 shows the visual quality of the output images. Compared to the previous works, the proposed method suppressed the noise level in the output image, while preserving the structures. The difference images indicates that the HU value is also well preserved during the denoising process of our method. Moreover, our method shows less distortion in pixel values, compared to the other methods which reveals the structures in the difference images. The quantitative result also supports the superiority of the proposed method. As shown in Table 1, the proposed method shows the best performance in PSNR and SSIM, which indicates the successful denoising performance compared to other methods.

3.2   Temporal CT Scans

For Temporal CT dataset, the networks are trained with learning rate 2e−4 with epoch 100. Wavelet decomposition is proceeded by level 5 with db3 wavelet filter. The batch size is 4, and the $\tau = 0.12$ for the metric d. $\lambda_{idt} = 5$ and $\lambda_m = 0.1$.

From the output and difference images in Fig. 4, we can see that the proposed method shows improved denoising output which has less distortion in the HU values. Also, the proposed method preserved the bone structure more than other methods. In contrast to our method, cycleGAN and GAN-Circle output the images with distorted HU values as shown in difference image. Since the methods translates the image to be similar to the target domain, it is vulnerable to the HU value shift problem caused by the different acquisition condition between the low-dose and high-dose scans. Despite the wavelet-domain processing, invertible-cycleGAN and wavCycleGAN produce the artifacts at the inner ear shown in the difference images in Fig. 4, which are undesirable for the temporal CT data with fine structures in the temporal region.

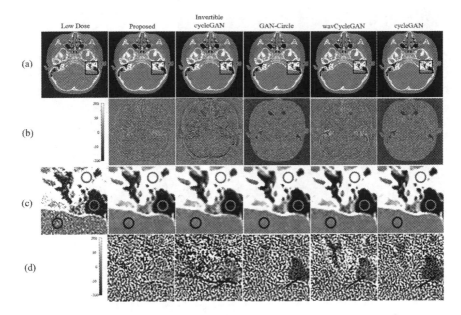

Fig. 4. Results from the temporal CT dataset. (a) CT images for the comparison, displayed with (−780HU, 820HU). (b) Difference images, displayed with (−200HU, 200HU). (c) Zoomed image for the temporal region. Colored circles are the selected regions for the quantitative evaluation. (d) Difference image for the zoomed images. Yellow arrows indicate the distortion of the CT numbers. (Color figure online)

For the quantitative evaluation of the methods, we compare the mean and standard deviation (Std) values of the pixels, to investigate the HU value shift and denoising performance. We proceed the quantitative evaluation in two different ways. First, we crop 60×60 sized 300 image patches with homogeneous media (i.e. air and brain), and obtain the average value of the mean and std. The CT number shift is investigated by the mean, and the denoising performance is compared by the std. Next, we compare the methods for the temporal region. We select the soft tissue, cavity and bone area, shown as yellow, blue and red circles in Fig. 4(c), respectively. Then, we measure the mean and std.

We present the results in Table 2. The proposed method shows the lowest Std values which indicate the successful denoising performance. Also, the mean values are similar to the LDCT, which verifies a robustness to the CT number shift problem of the real-world dataset. The cycleGAN and GAN-Circle show a vulnerability to the CT number shift problem. Specifically, the methods output the similar mean values with the HDCT, distorting the pixel values of the input image. The distortion is also observed for the mean values of the temporal region, which is coherent with Fig. 4. The wavCycleGAN and invertible-cycleGAN are somewhat robust to the CT number shift problem, since the methods utilize the high-frequency images. However, the CT number shift at the inner ear degrades the performance. The results for the temporal region in Table 2 reveal the distortion of the CT number and the degradation of the denoising performance, which is coherent with the difference images in Fig. 4.

4   Conclusion

In this paper, we developed a novel denoising methodology based on the patch-wise deep metric learning. In our framework, the patches sharing the same anatomic structure is used as positive pair, and patches which have similar noise level but different spatial information are considered as negative samples. By the push and the pull between the features in the embedding space, the network focuses on the anatomic information and neglect the noise features. The results verified that the proposed method is effective technique to improve the denoising performance without the CT number distortion.

References

1. Ahn, S.H., Kim, Y.W., Baik, S.K., Hwang, Yeon, J., Lee, I.W.: Usefulness of computed tomography hounsfield unit measurement for diagnosis of congenital cholesteatoma. J. Korean Radiol. Soc. **70**, 153–158 (2014)
2. Bai, T., Wang, B., Nguyen, D., Jiang, S.: Probabilistic self-learning framework for low-dose CT denoising. Med. Phys. **48**(5), 2258–2270 (2021)
3. Brenner, D.J., Hall, E.J.: Computed tomography - An increasing source of radiation exposure, November 2007. https://doi.org/10.1056/NEJMra072149. http://www.nejm.org/doi/abs/10.1056/NEJMra072149
4. Chen, H., et al.: Low-dose CT With a residual encoder-decoder convolutional neural network. IEEE Trans. Med. Imaging **36**(12), 2524–2535 (2017)
5. Thukral, C.L., Singh, A., Singh, S., Sood, A.S., Singh, K.: Role of high resolution computed tomography in evaluation of pathologies of temporal bone. J. Clin. Diagnostic Res. **9**, TC07–TC10 (2015)
6. Cruz-Bastida, J.P., Zhang, R., Gomez-Cardona, D., Hayes, J., Li, K., Chen, G.H.: Impact of noise reduction schemes on quantitative accuracy of ct numbers. Med. Phys. **46**(7), 3013–3024 (2019)
7. Gu, J., Yang, T.S., Ye, J.C., Yang, D.H.: CycleGAN denoising of extreme low-dose cardiac CT using wavelet-assisted noise disentanglement. Med. Image Anal. **74**, 102209 (2021)
8. Gu, J., Ye, J.C.: AdaIN-based tunable cycleGAN for efficient unsupervised low-dose CT denoising. IEEE Trans. Comput. Imaging **7**, 73–85 (2021)
9. Healthcare, G.: TrueFidelity CT. Technical white paper on deep learning image reconstruction. https://www.gehealthcare.co.kr/products/computed-tomography/truefidelity
10. Kingma, D.P., Ba, J.: Adam: a method for stochastic optimization. In: Bengio, Y., LeCun, Y. (eds.) 3rd International Conference on Learning Representations, (ICLR) 2015(May), pp. 7–9, 2015. Conference Track Proceedings. San Diego, CA, USA (2015). http://arxiv.org/abs/1412.6980
11. Kwon, T., Ye, J.C.: Cycle-free cyclegan using invertible generator for unsupervised low-dose CT denoising. IEEE Trans. Comput. Imaging **7**, 1354–1368 (2021)
12. Mao, X., Li, Q., Xie, H., Lau, R.Y., Wang, Z., Smolley, S.P.: Least squares generative adversarial networks. In: Proceedings of the IEEE International Conference on Computer Vision. vol. 2017-October, pp. 2813–2821. Institute of Electrical and Electronics Engineers Inc., December 2017. https://doi.org/10.1109/ICCV.2017.304. https://ieeexplore.ieee.org/document/8237566

13. Park, M.H., Rah, Y.C., Kim, Y.H., hoon Kim, J.: Usefulness of computed tomography hounsfield unit density in preoperative detection of cholesteatoma in mastoid ad antrum. Am. J. Otolaryngology **32**(3), 194–197 (2011)
14. Park, T., Efros, A.A., Zhang, R., Zhu, J.-Y.: Contrastive Learning for Unpaired Image-to-Image Translation. In: Vedaldi, A., Bischof, H., Brox, T., Frahm, J.-M. (eds.) ECCV 2020. LNCS, vol. 12354, pp. 319–345. Springer, Cham (2020). https://doi.org/10.1007/978-3-030-58545-7_19
15. Paszke, A., et al.: PyTorch: an imperative style, high-performance deep learning library. In: Wallach, H., Larochelle, H., Beygelzimer, A., d'Alché Buc, F., Fox, E., Garnett, R. (eds.) Advances in Neural Information Processing Systems 32, pp. 8026–8037. Curran Associates, Inc. (2019)
16. Sim, B., Oh, G., Kim, J., Jung, C., Ye, J.C.: Optimal transport driven cyclegan for unsupervised learning in inverse problems. SIAM J. Imag. Sci. **13**(4), 2281–2306 (2020)
17. Tang, C., et al.: Unpaired low-dose CT denoising network based on cycle-consistent generative adversarial network with prior image information. Computational and Mathematical Methods in Medicine 2019 (2019)
18. Wang, W., Zhou, W., Bao, J., Chen, D., Li, H.: Instance-wise hard negative example generation for contrastive learning in unpaired image-to-image translation. In: Proceedings of the IEEE/CVF International Conference on Computer Vision (ICCV), pp. 14020–14029, October 2021
19. Wang, X., et al.: ESRGAN: enhanced super-resolution generative adversarial networks. In: The European Conference on Computer Vision Workshops (ECCVW) (2018)
20. Yang, Q., et al.: Low-Dose CT image denoising using a generative adversarial network with wasserstein distance and perceptual loss. IEEE Trans. Med. Imaging **37**(6), 1348–1357 (2018). https://doi.org/10.1109/TMI.2018.2827462
21. You, C., et al.: CT super-resolution GAN constrained by the identical, residual, and cycle learning ensemble (GAN-circle). IEEE Trans. Med. Imaging **39**(1), 188–203 (2020)
22. Yuan, N., Zhou, J., Qi, J.: Half2half: deep neural network based CT image denoising without independent reference data 65(21), 215020, November 2020. https://doi.org/10.1088/1361-6560/aba939. https://doi.org/10.1088/1361-6560/aba939
23. Zhu, J.Y., Park, T., Isola, P., Efros, A.A.: Unpaired image-to-image translation using cycle-consistent adversarial networks. In: Proceedings of the IEEE International Conference on Computer Vision, vol. 2017, pp. 2242–2251. Institute of Electrical and Electronics Engineers Inc., December 2017. https://doi.org/10.1109/ICCV.2017.244

BMD-GAN: Bone Mineral Density Estimation Using X-Ray Image Decomposition into Projections of Bone-Segmented Quantitative Computed Tomography Using Hierarchical Learning

Yi Gu[1]([envelope]), Yoshito Otake[1], Keisuke Uemura[2], Mazen Soufi[1], Masaki Takao[3], Nobuhiko Sugano[4], and Yoshinobu Sato[1]

[1] Division of Information Science, Graduate School of Science and Technology, Nara Institute of Science and Technology, Ikoma, Japan
{gu.yi.gu4,otake,yoshi}@is.naist.jp
[2] Department of Orthopaedics, Osaka University Graduate School of Medicine, Suita, Japan
[3] Department of Bone and Joint Surgery, Ehime University Graduate School of Medicine, Matsuyama, Japan
[4] Department of Orthopaedic Medical Engineering, Osaka University Graduate School of Medicine, Suita, Japan

Abstract. We propose a method for estimating the bone mineral density (BMD) from a plain x-ray image. Dual-energy X-ray absorptiometry (DXA) and quantitative computed tomography (QCT) provide high accuracy in diagnosing osteoporosis; however, these modalities require special equipment and scan protocols. Measuring BMD from an x-ray image provides an opportunistic screening, which is potentially useful for early diagnosis. The previous methods that directly learn the relationship between x-ray images and BMD require a large training dataset to achieve high accuracy because of large intensity variations in the x-ray images. Therefore, we propose an approach using the QCT for training a generative adversarial network (GAN) and decomposing an x-ray image into a projection of bone-segmented QCT. The proposed hierarchical learning improved the robustness and accuracy of quantitatively decomposing a small-area target. The evaluation of 200 patients with osteoarthritis using the proposed method, which we named BMD-GAN, demonstrated a Pearson correlation coefficient of 0.888 between the predicted and ground truth DXA-measured BMD. Besides not requiring a large-scale training database, another advantage of our method is its extensibility to other anatomical areas, such as the vertebrae and rib bones.

Keywords: Generative adversarial network (GAN) · Radiography · Bone mineral density (BMD)

Supplementary Information The online version contains supplementary material available at https://doi.org/10.1007/978-3-031-16446-0_61.

1   Introduction

The measurement of bone mineral density (BMD) is essential for diagnosing osteoporosis. Although dual-energy X-ray absorptiometry (DXA) [1] and quantitative computed tomography (QCT) [2,3] are regarded as the gold standards for BMD measurement, there is a strong demand of developing simpler methods for measuring BMD, which provide opportunistic screening for the early detection of osteoporosis in patients without symptoms. To realize this, recent studies have focused on using deep learning to estimate BMD or diagnose osteoporosis from an x-ray image, which is a more widespread modality than DXA and QCT. These studies performed regression to estimate BMD or classification to diagnose osteoporosis, grading directly from x-ray images [4–7], some of which achieved high correlations with DXA-measured BMD, and grading using a large-scale training dataset. However, these methods do not provide the spatial density distribution of the target bone and do not leverage information from QCT. Furthermore, the critical requirement of a large-scale training database would limit the application of these methods when the target bone of BMD measurement extends to other anatomical areas (e.g., different positions of vertebrae, pelvis, sacrum, etc.).

From the viewpoint of processing x-ray images of bones, bone suppression is one of the main topics [8], enhancing the visibility of other soft tissues and increasing the diagnosis rate by machines and clinicians. These studies used a convolutional neural network, particularly a generative adversarial network (GAN) [9], to decompose x-ray images into bones and other soft tissues [8,10,11]. Because these studies focued on soft tissues, they did not address the quantitative evaluation of bone decomposition for BMD estimation. Despite the difficulty in GAN training, recent studies [12–14] were able to stabilize the training and reduce the demand for a large-scale database. While those studies inspired this study, we introduced the hierarchical learning (HL) method so that the small-area region of the target bone required for BMD estimation is decomposed accurately and stably even without requiring a large training dataset. Unlike the previous methods for BMD estimation from x-ray images [4–7], our method fully uses rich information from QCT in its training phase to estimate the density distributions in addition to BMD, that is, the average density within a specific clinically- defined region- of- interest (ROI). Furthermore, it can be applied to any ROI of any bone. In this study, we showed accuracy validations for the density distributions and BMDs estimated from x-ray images by comparing them with BMDs measured by DXA (hereafter "DXA-BMD"), QCT (hereafter "QCT-BMD"), and the average intensity of the ground truth 2D projections of bone-segmented QCT, respectively.

2   Method

2.1   Overview of the Proposed Method

Figure 1 shows the overview of the proposed method. An image synthesis model decomposes the x-ray image into the digitally reconstructed radiograph (DRR) of

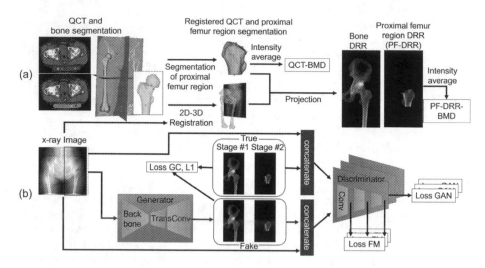

Fig. 1. Overview of the proposed method. (a) Construction of the training dataset consisting of the intensity calibration of CT [15], bone segmentation [16], 2D-3D registration to the x-ray image [17] and DRR generation by projecting QCT. (b) The network architecture of the proposed BMD-GAN.

the proximal femur region [hereafter "proximal femur region DRR (PF-DRR)"], whose average intensity provides the predicted BMD. Our BMD-GAN applies a hierarchical framework during the training in which the model is first trained to extract the pelvis and femur bones and then the proximal femur region in the subsequent stage. Figure 2 illustrates the relationship between x-ray images and BMDs in our patient dataset, demonstrating the challenge in the task of BMD prediction based on an x-ray image.

2.2 Dataset Construction

In this study, we constructed two datasets: 1) the stage-one dataset containing x-ray images; QCT; the 3D segmentation masks of the pelvis and femur, which were obtained by applying Bayesian U-net [16]; and bone DRR, which were created from QCT using 2D-3D registration [17] followed by projection with the 3D mask, and 2) the stage-two dataset containing x-ray images; QCT; the 3D mask of the proximal femur region, which is obtained by manually labeled bony landmarks defined in [18] by an expert clinician; and the PF-DRR. The construction procedure of the stage-two dataset followed [18]. The intensity-based 2D-3D registration using gradient correlation similarity metric and the CMA-ES optimizer [17] was performed on each patient's x-ray image and QCT. All x-ray images and DRRs were normalized into the size of 256×512 by central cropping and resizing. The aspect ratio of the original x-ray images varied from 0.880 to 1.228 (width/height). We first split them horizontally in half at the center. Then the side with the target hip was reshaped to a predefined image

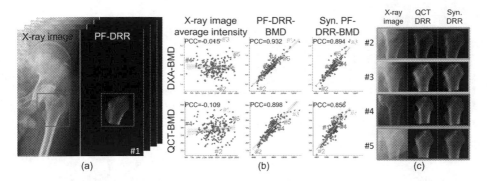

Fig. 2. Relationship between the intensities of the x-ray image, DRR, and BMD values in 200 patient datasets. (a) Paired (registered) dataset of x-ray image and DRR; (b) scatter plots showing the correlation of the average intensity of x-ray images, QCT DRR, and synthesized DRR with DXA-measured BMD and QCT-measured BMD; (c) proximal femur ROIs of four representative cases. ROIs #2 and #3 have similar x-ray intensity but significantly different BMD, whereas ROIs #4 and #5 have similar BMD but significantly different x-ray intensity. The synthesized DRRs correctly recovered the intensity of QCT DRR, regardless of the intensity of the input x-ray image.

size (256×512 in this experiment) by aligning the center of the image and cropping the region outside the image after resizing to fit the shorter edge of the width and height.

2.3 Paired Image Translation from an X-Ray Image to a PF-DRR

The GAN with conditional discriminators was used to train the decomposition model. We followed most settings used in Pix2PixHD [19] including the multi-scale discriminators and the Feature Matching loss (Loss FM in Fig. 1), among others. Instead of the ResNet Generator used in Pix2Pix [9] and Pix2PixHD [19], we adopted the state-of-the-art model HRFormer [20], which is a transformer-based model for segmentation to be the backbone of the generator, namely, HRFormer Generator. Instead of using the hierarchical structure of the generator used in Pix2PixHD [19], we applied the HL framework in which a two-stage training is used. In the first stage, the model is trained to decompose an x-ray image into the pelvis and femur bones; in the second stage, the target is transferred to the proximal femur region. In the training, we used the adversarial loss $\mathcal{L}_{\mathrm{GAN}}$, which is defined as

$$\mathcal{L}_{\mathrm{GAN}}(G, D) = \mathbb{E}_{(\mathbf{I}^{\mathbf{X}\mathbf{P}}, \mathbf{I}^{\mathbf{DRR}})}[\log D(\mathbf{I}^{\mathbf{X}\mathbf{P}}, \mathbf{I}^{\mathbf{DRR}})] + \mathbb{E}_{\mathbf{I}^{\mathbf{X}\mathbf{P}}}[\log(1 - D(\mathbf{I}^{\mathbf{X}\mathbf{P}}, G(\mathbf{I}^{\mathbf{X}\mathbf{P}}))],$$
$$(1)$$

where G, D, $\mathbf{I}^{\mathbf{X}\mathbf{P}}$, and $\mathbf{I}^{\mathbf{DRR}}$ are the generator, discriminator, x-ray image, and decomposed DRR, respectively. We denote $\mathbb{E}_{\mathbf{I}^{\mathbf{X}\mathbf{P}}} \triangleq \mathbb{E}_{\mathbf{I}^{\mathbf{X}\mathbf{P}} \sim p_{\mathrm{data}}(\mathbf{I}^{\mathbf{X}\mathbf{P}})}$ and $\mathbb{E}_{(\mathbf{I}^{\mathbf{X}\mathbf{P}}, \mathbf{I}^{\mathbf{DRR}})} \triangleq \mathbb{E}_{(\mathbf{I}^{\mathbf{X}\mathbf{P}}, \mathbf{I}^{\mathbf{DRR}}) \sim p_{\mathrm{data}}(\mathbf{I}^{\mathbf{X}\mathbf{P}}, \mathbf{I}^{\mathbf{DRR}})}$. Furthermore, we used the Feature Matching loss $\mathcal{L}_{\mathrm{FM}}$ proposed in [19], given by

$$\mathcal{L}_{\mathrm{FM}}(G, D) = \mathbb{E}_{(\mathbf{I}^{\mathbf{X_P}}, \mathbf{I}^{\mathbf{DRR}})} \sum_{i=1}^{T} \frac{1}{N_i} [\|D^{(i)}(\mathbf{I}^{\mathbf{X_P}}, \mathbf{I}^{\mathbf{DRR}}) - D^{(i)}(\mathbf{I}^{\mathbf{X_P}}, G(\mathbf{I}^{\mathbf{X_P}}))\|_1],$$

(2)

where $D^{(i)}$, T, and N_i denote the ith-layer feature extractor of discriminator D, the total number of layers, and the number of elements in each layer, respectively. We did not use a perceptual loss because a well-pretrained perceptual model is difficult to obtain under a limited dataset. We instead used a simple L_1 loss $\mathcal{L}_{L1}$ defined as

$$\mathcal{L}_{L1}(G) = \mathbb{E}_{(\mathbf{I}^{\mathbf{X_P}}, \mathbf{I}^{\mathbf{DRR}})} [\|\mathbf{I}^{\mathbf{DRR}} - G(\mathbf{I}^{\mathbf{X_P}})\|_1].$$

(3)

To maintain the consistency of the structure between the fake DRR $G(\mathbf{I}^{\mathbf{X_P}})$ and the true DRR $\mathbf{I}^{\mathbf{DRR}}$, we regularized the generator with the gradient-matching constraints proposed in [21], using the gradient correlation loss $\mathcal{L}_{GC}$ defined as

$$\mathcal{L}_{GC}(G) = \mathbb{E}_{(\mathbf{I}^{\mathbf{X_P}}, \mathbf{I}^{\mathbf{DRR}})} [NCC(\nabla_x \mathbf{I}^{\mathbf{DRR}}, \nabla_x G(\mathbf{I}^{\mathbf{X_P}})) + NCC(\nabla_y \mathbf{I}^{\mathbf{DRR}}, \nabla_y G(\mathbf{I}^{\mathbf{X_P}}))],$$

(4)

where $NCC(\mathbf{A}, \mathbf{B})$ is the normalized cross-correlation of $\mathbf{A}$ and $\mathbf{B}$, and ∇_x and ∇_y are the x and y components of the gradient vector, respectively. Thus, our full objective was defined as

$$\min_G \left(\lambda_{L1}\mathcal{L}_{L1}(G) + \lambda_{GC}\mathcal{L}_{GC}(G) + \lambda_{FM} \sum_{k=1,2,3} \mathcal{L}_{\mathrm{FM}}(G, D_k) \right.$$
$$\left. + \left(\max_{D_1, D_2, D_3} \sum_{k=1,2,3} \mathcal{L}_{\mathrm{GAN}}(G, D_k) \right) \right),$$

(5)

where the multi-scale discriminators D_1, D_2, and D_3 were used under three resolutions as in [19], and λ_{L1}, λ_{GC}, and λ_{FM} are the hyper-parameters that balance the importance of the terms. Both stage-one and stage-two training use the same loss functions. For the learning rate policy, we used the linear decay strategy used in Pix2Pix [9] in stage-one training and the stochastic gradient descent with warm restarts (SGDR) proposed in [22] in stage-two training.

Next, the average intensity of the predicted PF-DRR was calculated. Note that the pixels with an intensity equal to or larger than the threshold t were averaged in this study. We empirically defined $t = 1000$ in the experiment. The PF-DRR-average of all training datasets was linearly fitted to DXA-BMD and QCT-BMD to obtain the slope and intercept, which were used to convert the PF-DRR-average to the BMDs of the test dataset.

2.4   Generator Backbone

In the experiments, we compared the performance of two more models that were used for semantic segmentation as the backbone of generator–DAFormer [23] and HRNetV2 [24], namely, DAFormer Generator and HRNet Generator, respectively. Though these state-of-the-art models have been proven to have high performance in segmentation tasks, their ability to decompose images has not been thoroughly assessed. We tuned each backbone's learning rate, optimizer, weight decay, and epochs, including ResNet, DAFormer, HRNet, and HRFormer, separately.

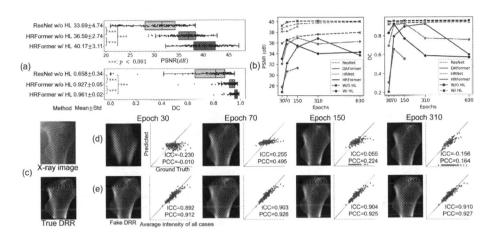

Fig. 3. Results of x-ray image decomposition. (a) Evaluation of image decomposition for ResNet (baseline) without HL, HRFormer without HL, and HRFormer with HL. (b) Convergence analysis of each backbone without and with HL. (c) The ROI of the input x-ray image and true DRR, and comparison of the training progress between (d) without HL and (e) with HL.

3   Experiments and Results

3.1   Experimental Materials, Setting, and Evaluation Metrics

Ethical approval was obtained from the Institutional Review Boards (IRBs) of the institutions participating in this study (IRB approval numbers: 21115 at Osaka University Hospital and 2021-M-11 at Nara Institute of Science and Technology). The constructed stage-one dataset contained 275 cases. Each case had an x-ray image, and its paired bone DRRs of the left and right sides were split by the vertical middle line, resulting in 525 image pairs after excluding the images with the hip implant. The constructed stage-two dataset contained 200 cases obtained retrospectively from 200 patients (166 females) who underwent primary total hip arthroplasty between May 2011 and December 2015.Each case has an x-ray image and its paired PF-DRR of one side with its ground truth DXA-BMD. The patients' age and T-scores calculated from the DXA-BMD of the proximal femur were 59.5 ± 12.9 years (range: 26 to 86) and -1.23 ± 1.55 (range: -5.68 to 4.47), respectively. The calibration phantom (B-MAS200, Kyoto Kagaku, Kyoto, Japan) [15], which is used to convert radiodensity [in Housunsfield units (HU)] to bone density (in mg/cm^3), contains known densities of hydroxyapatite $Ca_{10}(PO_4)_6(OH)_2$. All CT images used in this study were obtained by the OptimaCT660 scanner (GE Healthcare Japan, Tokyo, Japan); all x-ray images, which were scanned by the devices from FUJIFILM Corporation and Philips Medical Systems, were acquired in the standing position in the anterior-posterior direction; and all DXA images of the proximal femur were acquired for the operative side (Discovery A, Hologic Japan, Tokyo, Japan) to obtain the ground truth DXA-BMD. The evaluations in the following sections were performed on the stage-two dataset. Five-fold cross-validation was performed to investigate the effect of HL and compare the backbones. The ResNet Generator without HL was set as the baseline for evaluating the decomposition accuracy. Furthermore, We compared our best method with the conventional method proposed in [4], which directly regresses the BMD from the x-ray images, under our limited dataset.

To evaluate the performance on image decomposition, we used the peak signal-to-noise ratio (PSNR), multi-threshold dice coefficient (DC), intraclass correlation coefficient (ICC), and Pearson correlation coefficient (PCC) of the average intensity of the PF-DRR. To evaluate BMD estimation, we used ICC, PCC, mean absolute error (MAE), and standard error of estimate (SEE). Statistical significance was evaluated using the single-factor repeated measures analysis of variance model. P-values of less than were used to denote statistical significance.

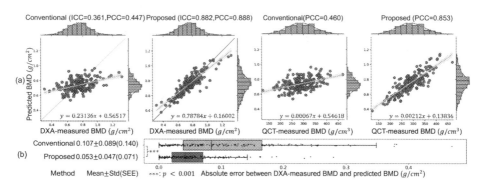

Fig. 4. Results of BMD estimation. (a) Correlation of the predicted BMD with DXA-BMD and QCT-BMD. (b) Boxplot of AE of the predicted BMD. The BMD predicted using the proposed method clearly shows a higher correlation with DXA-measured and QCT-measured BMDs and smaller absolute errors.

3.2   Results of X-Ray Image Decomposition

The decomposition accuracy of PSNR and DC is shown in Fig. 3(a), where significant improvement by HL was observed. The high performance of HRFormer Generator with HL in DC indicated the ability to maintain the silhouette of the decomposed structure, and the high PSNR suggested the superior capability of the quantitative decomposition compared with the same generator without HL and the baseline method. The representative cases in Fig. 2 also suggested the accurate recovery of the density distribution of PF-DRR despite the noise and variation of the overall intensity in the input x-ray image. Figure 3(b) shows the progress of training for each backbone with and without HL, in which the robust convergence was achieved consistently using HL even with few epochs. One case was randomly chosen to track the progress during training, which is shown in Fig. 3(d) and (e). The qualitative comparison demonstrated that the target region was well-formed in the early epoch using HL, suggesting the effectiveness of HL. A summary of the experimental results for all backbones is shown in Table 1; and a detailed comparison of decomposition results between HRFormer without and with HL can be found in supplemental video.

3.3 Results of BMD Estimation

A comparison of the BMD estimation performance between the conventional method [4], which uses a regression model, and the proposed HRFormer Generator with HL is shown in Fig. 4. The results suggest the failure of the conventional method, which achieved an ICC of 0.361 and PCC of 0.447 under the limited dataset. In contrast, the proposed method achieved high ICC and PCC of 0.882 and 0.888, respectively, demonstrating the effectiveness of the estimation strategy of the proposed method that extracts the density distribution of the target region of the bone. Furthermore, we evaluated the prediction error in terms of T-scores. The T-scores were calculated based on the mean and standard deviation of DXA-BMD for Japanese young adult women reported in the literature (proximal femur: 0.875 ± 0.100 g/cm^2 [25]). We found that the absolute error in T-score for HRFormer with HL was 0.53 ± 0.47. We additionally evaluated 13 cases whose repeated x-ray images (acquired in the standing and supine positions on the same day) were available. The coefficient of variation was $3.06\% \pm 3.22\%$ when the best model, HRFormer with HL, was used.

Table 1. Summary of the experimental results.

	Image decomposition accuracy				BMD estimation accuracy				
	mean PSNR	mean DC	ICC	PCC	mean AE	SEE	ICC	PCC	PCC wrt QCT
ResNet	30.688	0.658	−0.278	0.006	0.117	0.157	−0.024	−0.208	−0.130
+ HL	**39.105**	**0.952**	**0.866**	**0.894**	**0.057**	**0.074**	**0.872**	**0.879**	**0.818**
DAFormer	36.874	0.926	0.538	0.671	0.085	0.114	0.639	0.680	0.632
+ HL	**37.994**	**0.945**	**0.853**	**0.875**	**0.057**	**0.078**	**0.856**	**0.865**	**0.799**
HRNet	36.996	0.931	0.369	0.650	0.097	0.127	0.537	0.581	0.640
+HL	**39.971**	**0.958**	**0.883**	**0.920**	**0.057**	**0.074**	**0.870**	**0.878**	**0.843**
HRFormer	36.594	0.927	0.255	0.495	0.109	0.143	0.313	0.400	0.498
+ HL	**40.168**	**0.961**	**0.910**	**0.927**	**0.053**	**0.071**	**0.882**	**0.888**	**0.853**

3.4 Implementation Details

In implementing the methods for decomposing an x-ray image, we replaced the Batch Normalization and Instance Normalization with the Group Normalization [26], except for the Layer Normalization used in the Transformer. We used the structure of the Global Generator used in [19] for ResNet Generator. The HRNetV2-W48 [24] and HRFormer-B were used for HRNet Generator and HRFormer Generator, respectively. We set the λ_{L1}, λ_{GC}, and λ_{FM} to 100, 1, and 10, respectively. In the stage-one training for all generators, the initial learning rate and weight decay were 2e–4 and 1e–4, respectively. In the stage-two training, the initial learning rate and weight decay were 2e–4 and 1e–8, respectively, for the ResNet Generator; 5e–6 and 1e–2, respectively, for the DAFormer Generator; 1e–4 and 1e–4, respectively, for the HRNet Generator; and 1e–4 and 1e–2, respectively, for the HRFormer Generator. We used AdamW optimizer for all decomposition methods in both stages. For data augmentation, rotation (±25), shear (±8), translation (±0.3), scaling (±0.3), and horizontal and vertical flipping were used randomly. To implement conventional method [5] for BMD estimation, we followed most settings and training protocols, including the model structure, and data augmentation; however, the total number of epochs was set to 400, and we did not perform validation during training because we found that validation makes the performance worse under the limited dataset. Our implementation is available at https://github.com/NAIST-ICB/BMD-GAN.

4   Discussion and Conclusion

In this study, we proposed an HL framework for the image decomposition task, specifically focusing on the quantitative recovery of density distribution for small-area targets under a limited dataset. The HL reduced the demands of the dataset and had improved performance compared with conventional training. Furthermore, we experimentally compared the abilities of the generators with those of state-of-the-art backbones. With HL, all models showed significant improvement, and among them, the HRFormer Generator showed the best performance.

We proposed a BMD estimation method, leveraging the ability of the model to decompose an x-ray image into the DRR of the proximal femur region. The proposed BMD-GAN achieved high accuracy under the limited dataset where the conventional regression model-based method failed using the same dataset. By training using QCT data and x-ray images, the proposed method can target the BMD of any bone within the field of view of QCT and x-ray images (unlike previous methods based on training using BMD values and x-ray images). One limitation of this experiment was the use of QCT, which needs a special phantom in its image. However, some studies showed that BMD estimation had sufficient accuracy even using phantom-less CT data [2,18]. Our future work will include validation of training using phantom-less CT and the extension to other anatomical areas, such as the vertebrae and ribs. Furthermore, We plan to validate the performance of the proposed method using large-scale multi-institutional datasets.

References

1. Blake, G.M., et al.: Role of dual-energy X-ray absorptiometry in the diagnosis and treatment of osteoporosis. J. Clin. Densitometry **10**(1), 102–10 (2007)
2. Mueller, D.K., Kutscherenko, A., Bartel, H., Vlassenbroek, A., Ourednicek, P., Erckenbrecht, J.: Phantom-less QCT BMD system as screening tool for osteoporosis without additional radiation. Eur. J. Radiol. **79**(3), 375–381 (2011)
3. Aggarwal, V., et al.: Opportunistic diagnosis of osteoporosis, fragile bone strength and vertebral fractures from routine CT scans; a review of approved technology systems and pathways to implementation. Therap. Adv. Musculoskel. Dis. **13**, 1759720X211024029 (2021)
4. Hsieh, C.I., et al.: Automated bone mineral density prediction and fracture risk assessment using plain radiographs via deep learning. Nature Commun. **12**(1), 1–9 (2021)
5. Ho, C.-S., et al.: Application of deep learning neural network in predicting bone mineral density from plain X-ray radiography. Arch. Osteoporosis **16**(1), 1–12 (2021). https://doi.org/10.1007/s11657-021-00985-8
6. Jang, R., et al.: Prediction of osteoporosis from simple hip radiography using deep learning algorithm. Sci. Rep. **11**(1), 1–9 (2021)
7. Yamamoto, N., et al.: Deep learning for osteoporosis classification Using hip radiographs and patient clinical covariates. Biomolecules **10**(11), 1534 (2020)
8. Yang, W., et al.: Cascade of multi-scale convolutional neural networks for bone suppression of chest radiographs in gradient domain. Med. Image Anal. **35**, 421–433 (2017)
9. Isola, P., Zhu, J.Y., Zhou, T., Efros, A.A.: Image-to-image translation with conditional adversarial networks. In: Proceedings of the IEEE/CVF Conference on Computer Vision and Pattern Recognition, pp. 1125–1134 (2017)
10. Liu, Y., et al.: Automatic delineation of ribs and clavicles in chest radiographs using fully convolutional DenseNets. Comput. Methods Progr. Biomed. **180**, 105014 (2019)
11. Eslami, M., et al.: Image-to-images translation for multi-task organ segmentation and bone suppression in chest x-ray radiography. IEEE Trans. Med. Imaging **39**(7), 2553–2565 (2020)
12. Zhao, S., et al.: Differentiable augmentation for data-efficient GAN training. In: Conference on Neural Information Processing Systems (2020)
13. Zhang, H., Zhang, Z., Odena, A., Lee, H.: Consistency regularization for generative adversarial networks. In: International Conference on Learning Representations (2020)
14. Wu, Y.L., Shuai, H.H., Tam, Z.R., Chiu, H.Y.: Gradient normalization for generative adversarial networks. In: Proceedings of the IEEE/CVF International Conference on Computer Vision, pp. 6373–6382 (2021)
15. Uemura, K., et al.: Automated segmentation of an intensity calibration phantom in clinical CT images using a convolutional neural network. Int. J. Comput. Assist. Radiol. Surg. **16**(11), 1855–1864 (2021). https://doi.org/10.1007/s11548-021-02345-w
16. Hiasa, Y., Otake, Y., Takao, M., Ogawa, T., Sugano, N., Sato, Y.: Automated muscle segmentation from clinical CT using bayesian U-Net for personalized musculoskeletal modeling. IEEE Trans. Med. Imaging **39**(4), 1030–1040 (2020)
17. Otake, Y., et al.: Intraoperative image-based multiview 2D/3D registration for image-guided orthopaedic surgery: incorporation of fiducial-based C-arm tracking and GPU-acceleration. IEEE Trans. Med. Imaging **31**(4), 948–962 (2012)

18. Uemura, K., et al.: Development of an open-source measurement system to assess the areal bone mineral density of the proximal femur from clinical CT images. Arch. Osteoporosis **17**(1), 1–11 (2022). https://doi.org/10.1007/s11657-022-01063-3

19. Wang, T.C., et al.: High-resolution image synthesis and semantic manipulation with conditional GANs. In: Proceedings of the IEEE/CVF Conference on Computer Vision and Pattern Recognition, pp. 8798–8807 (2018)

20. Yuan, Y., et al.: HRFormer: high-resolution transformer for dense prediction. In: Conference on Neural Information Processing Systems, vol. 34, pp. 7281–7293 (2021)

21. Penney, G.P., et al.: A comparison of similarity measures for use in 2-D-3-D medical image registration. IEEE Trans. Med. Imaging **17**(4), 586–595 (1998)

22. Loshchilov, I., Hutter, F.: SGDR: stochastic gradient descent with warm restarts. In: International Conference on Learning Representations (2017)

23. Hoyer, L., Dai, D., Van Gool, L.: DAFormer: improving network architectures and training strategies for domain-adaptive semantic segmentation. In: Proceedings of the IEEE/CVF Conference on Computer Vision and Pattern Recognition (2022)

24. Wang, J., et al.: Deep high-resolution representation learning for visual recognition. IEEE Trans. Pattern Anal. Mach. Intell. **43**(10), 3349–3364 (2020)

25. Soen, S., et al.: Diagnostic criteria for primary osteoporosis: year 2012 revision. J. Bone Min. Metab. **31**(3), 247–257 (2013)

26. Wu, Y., He, K.: Group normalization. In: Proceedings of the European Conference on Computer Vision, pp. 3–19 (2018)

Measurement-Conditioned Denoising Diffusion Probabilistic Model for Under-Sampled Medical Image Reconstruction

Yutong Xie[1] and Quanzheng Li[2(✉)]

[1] Academy for Advanced Interdisciplinary Studies, Peking University, Beijing, China
[2] MGH/BWH Center for Advanced Medical Computing and Analysis and Gordon Center for Medical Imaging, Department of Radiology Massachusetts General Hospital and Harvard Medical School, Boston, MA, USA
li.quanzheng@mgh.harvard.edu

Abstract. We propose a novel and unified method, measurement-conditioned denoising diffusion probabilistic model (MC-DDPM), for under-sampled medical image reconstruction based on DDPM. Different from previous works, MC-DDPM is defined in measurement domain (e.g. k-space in MRI reconstruction) and conditioned on under-sampling mask. We apply this method to accelerate MRI reconstruction and the experimental results show excellent performance, outperforming full supervision baseline and the state-of-the-art score-based reconstruction method. Due to its generative nature, MC-DDPM can also quantify the uncertainty of reconstruction. Our code is available on github (https://github.com/Theodore-PKU/MC-DDPM).

Keywords: Measurement-conditioned · DDPM · Under-sampled · Accelerated MRI reconstruction

1 Introduction

Reconstruction from under-sampled measurements in medical imaging has been deeply studied over the years, including reconstruction of accelerated magnetic resonance imaging (MRI) [1,5–7], sparse view or limited angles computed tomography (CT) [8,22,24] and digital breast tomosynthesis (DBT). Most of works aim to obtain one sample of the posterior distribution $p(\mathbf{x} \mid \mathbf{y})$ where $\mathbf{x}$ is the reconstructed target image and $\mathbf{y}$ is the under-sampled measurements.

Recently, denoising diffusion probabilistic models (DDPM) [9,18], which is a new class of unconditional generative model, have demonstrated superior performance and have been widely used in various image processing tasks.

Supplementary Information The online version contains supplementary material available at https://doi.org/10.1007/978-3-031-16446-0_62.

DDPM utilizes a latent variable model to reverse a diffusion process, where the data distribution is perturbed to the noise distribution by gradually adding Gaussian noise. Similar to DDPM, score-based generative models [10,19] also generate data samples by reversing a diffusion process. Both DDPM and score-based models are proved to be discretizations of different continuous stochastic differential equations by [21]. The difference between them lies in the specific setting of diffusion process and sampling algorithms. They have been applied to the generation of image [4,14,21], audio [12] or graph [15], and to conditional generation tasks such as in in-painting [19,21], super-resolution [2,17] and image editing [13]. In these applications, the diffusion process of DDPM or score-based generative model is defined in data domain, and is unconditioned although the reverse process could be conditioned given certain downstream task. Particularly, the score-based generative model has been used for under-sampled medical image reconstruction [3,11,20], where the diffusion process is defined in the domain of image $\mathbf{x}$ and is irrelevant to under-sampled measurements $\mathbf{y}$.

In this paper, We design our method based on DDPM rather than score-based generative model because DDPM is more flexible to control the noise distribution. We propose a novel and unified method, measurement-conditioned DDPM (MC-DDPM) for under-sampled medical image reconstruction based on DDPM (Fig. 1 illustrates the method by the example of under-sampled MRI reconstruction), where the under-sampling is in the measurement space (e.g. k-space in MRI reconstruction) and thus the conditional diffusion process is also defined in the measurement space. Two points distinguish our method from previous works [3,11,20]: (1) the diffusion and sampling process are defined in measurement domain rather than image domain; (2) the diffusion process is conditioned on under-sampling mask so that data consistency is contained in the model naturally and inherently, and there is no need to execute extra data consistency when sampling. The proposed method allows us to sample multiple reconstruction results from the same measurements $\mathbf{y}$. Thus, we are able to quantify uncertainty for $q(\mathbf{x} \mid \mathbf{y})$, such as pixel-variance. Our experiments on accelerated MRI reconstruction show MC-DDPM can generate samples of high quality of $q(\mathbf{x} \mid \mathbf{y})$ and it outperforms baseline models and proposed method by [3] in evaluation metrics.

This paper is organized as follows: relevant background on DDPM and the under-sampled medical image reconstruction task is in Sect. 2; details of the proposed method MC-DDPM is presented in Sect. 3; specifications about the implementation of the application to accelerated MRI reconstruction, experimental results and discussion are given in Sect. 4; we conclude our work in Sect. 5.

2 Background

2.1 Denoising Diffusion Probabilistic Model

DDPM [9] is a certain parameterization of diffusion models [18], which is a class of latent variable models using a Markov chain to convert the noise distribution

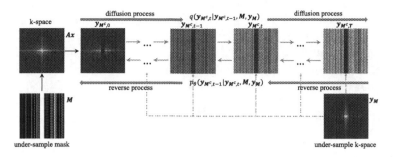

Fig. 1. Overview of the proposed method illustrated by the example of under-sampled MRI reconstruction. Diffusion process: starting from the non-sampled k-space $\mathbf{y}_{\mathbf{M}^c,0}$, Gaussian noise is gradually added until time T. Reverse process: starting from total noise, $\mathbf{y}_{\mathbf{M}^c,0}$ is generated step by step. The details of notations is presented in Sect. 3.

to the data distribution. It has the form of $p_\theta(\mathbf{x}_0) := \int p_\theta(\mathbf{x}_{0:T})\, d\mathbf{x}_{1:T}$, where $\mathbf{x}_0$ follows the data distribution $q(\mathbf{x}_0)$ and $\mathbf{x}_1, ..., \mathbf{x}_T$ are latent variables of the same dimensionality as $\mathbf{x}_0$. The joint distribution $p_\theta(\mathbf{x}_{0:T})$ is defined as a Markov chain with learned Gaussian transitions starting from $p(\mathbf{x}_T) = \mathcal{N}(\mathbf{0}, \mathbf{I})$:

$$p_\theta(\mathbf{x}_{0:T}) := p(\mathbf{x}_T) \prod_{t=1}^{T} p_\theta(\mathbf{x}_{t-1} \mid \mathbf{x}_t), \, p_\theta(\mathbf{x}_{t-1} \mid \mathbf{x}_t) := \mathcal{N}\left(\boldsymbol{\mu}_\theta(\mathbf{x}_t, t), \sigma_t^2 \mathbf{I}\right). \quad (1)$$

The sampling process of $p_\theta(\mathbf{x}_0)$ is: to sample $\mathbf{x}_T$ from $\mathcal{N}(\mathbf{0}, \mathbf{I})$ firstly; then, to sample $\mathbf{x}_{t-1}$ from $p_\theta(\mathbf{x}_{t-1} \mid \mathbf{x}_t)$ until $\mathbf{x}_0$ is obtained. It can be regarded as a reverse process of the diffusion process, which converts the data distribution to the noise distribution $\mathcal{N}(\mathbf{0}, \mathbf{I})$. In DDPM the diffusion process is fixed to a Markov chain that gradually adds Gaussian noise to the data according to a variance schedule $\beta_1, ..., \beta_T$:

$$q(\mathbf{x}_{1:T} \mid \mathbf{x}_0) := \prod_{t=1}^{T} q(\mathbf{x}_t \mid \mathbf{x}_{t-1}), \quad q(\mathbf{x}_t \mid \mathbf{x}_{t-1}) := \mathcal{N}\left(\alpha_t \mathbf{x}_{t-1}, \beta_t^2 \mathbf{I}\right), \quad (2)$$

where $\alpha_t^2 + \beta_t^2 = 1$ for all t and $\beta_1, ..., \beta_T$ are fixed to constants and their value are set specially so that $q(\mathbf{x}_T \mid \mathbf{x}_0) \approx \mathcal{N}(\mathbf{0}, \mathbf{I})$.

2.2   Under-Sampled Medical Image Reconstruction

Suppose $\mathbf{x} \in \mathbb{R}^n$ represents a medical image and $\mathbf{y} \in \mathbb{R}^m, m < n$ is the under-sampled measurements which is obtained by the following forward model:

$$\mathbf{y} = \mathbf{P}_\Omega \mathbf{A} \mathbf{x} + \boldsymbol{\epsilon}, \quad (3)$$

where $\mathbf{A} \in \mathbb{R}^{n \times n}$ is the measuring matrix and usually is invertible, $\mathbf{P}_\Omega \in \mathbb{R}^{m \times n}$ is the under-sampling matrix with the given sampling pattern Ω,[1] and $\boldsymbol{\epsilon}$ is the

---

[1] Assuming the sampling pattern Ω is $\{s_1, ..., s_m\} \subseteq \{1, ..., n\}$, the element of $\mathbf{P}_\Omega$ at position (i, s_i), $i = 1, ..., m$, is 1 and other elements are all 0.

noise. For example, $\mathbf{x}$ is an MR image, $\mathbf{A}$ is the Fourier transform matrix and $\mathbf{y}$ is the k-space. Under-sampled medical image reconstruction is to reconstruct $\mathbf{x}$ from $\mathbf{y}$ as accurate as possible. Assuming $\mathbf{x}$ follows a distribution of $q(\mathbf{x})$ and given $\mathbf{P}_\Omega$, according to Bayesian Formula, we can derive the posterior distribution as follows (usually $\mathbf{P}_\Omega$ is neglected):

$$q(\mathbf{x}\mid\mathbf{y},\mathbf{P}_\Omega)=\frac{q(\mathbf{x},\mathbf{y}\mid\mathbf{P}_\Omega)}{q(\mathbf{y})}=\frac{q(\mathbf{y}\mid\mathbf{x},\mathbf{P}_\Omega)\,q(\mathbf{x})}{q(\mathbf{y})}. \tag{4}$$

Therefore, the task of under-sampled medical image reconstruction is to reconstruct the posterior distribution.

3   Method: Measurement-Conditioned DDPM

Inspired by DDPM, we propose measurement-conditioned DDPM (MC-DDPM) which is designed for under-sampled medical image reconstruction. In this section, we formulate the MC-DDPM, including the diffusion process and its reverse process, training objective and sampling algorithm. For the convenience, we use new notations different from Eq. 3 to represent the under-sampled forward model:

$$\mathbf{y}_\mathbf{M}=\mathbf{MAx}+\epsilon_\mathbf{M}, \tag{5}$$

where $\mathbf{M}\in\mathbb{R}^{n\times n}$ is a diagonal matrix whose diagonal elements are either 1 or 0 depending on the sampling pattern Ω.[2] $\mathbf{y}_\mathbf{M}$ and $\epsilon_\mathbf{M}$ are both n-dimension vectors and their components at non-sampled positions are 0. The merit of the new notations is that we can further define $\mathbf{M}^c=\mathbf{I}-\mathbf{M}$ (the superscript c means complement) and $\mathbf{y}_{\mathbf{M}^c}=\mathbf{M}^c\mathbf{Ax}$ which represents the non-sampled measurements. In this paper, we assume $\epsilon_\mathbf{M}=\mathbf{0}$. Then, we have $\mathbf{y}_\mathbf{M}+\mathbf{y}_{\mathbf{M}^c}=\mathbf{Ax}$, i.e. $\mathbf{y}_\mathbf{M}+\mathbf{y}_{\mathbf{M}^c}$ is the full-sampled measurements. In addition, the posterior distribution of reconstruction can be rewritten as $q(\mathbf{x}\mid\mathbf{M},\mathbf{y}_\mathbf{M})$. Through this paper, the subscript $\mathbf{M}$ or $\mathbf{M}^c$ in notations indicates that only components at under-sampled or non-sampled positions are not 0.

The purpose of reconstruction task is to estimate $q(\mathbf{x}\mid\mathbf{M},\mathbf{y}_\mathbf{M})$. Since $\mathbf{y}_\mathbf{M}$ is known and $\mathbf{x}=\mathbf{A}^{-1}(\mathbf{y}_\mathbf{M}+\mathbf{y}_{\mathbf{M}^c})$, the problem is transformed to estimate $q(\mathbf{y}_{\mathbf{M}^c}\mid\mathbf{M},\mathbf{y}_\mathbf{M})$. Because $\mathbf{M}$ and $\mathbf{M}^c$ are equivalent as the condition, we can replace $q(\mathbf{y}_{\mathbf{M}^c}\mid\mathbf{M},\mathbf{y}_\mathbf{M})$ by $q(\mathbf{y}_{\mathbf{M}^c}\mid\mathbf{M}^c,\mathbf{y}_\mathbf{M})$. Based on this observation, we propose MC-DDPM which solves the reconstruction problem by generating samples of $q(\mathbf{y}_{\mathbf{M}^c}\mid\mathbf{M}^c,\mathbf{y}_\mathbf{M})$. MC-DDPM is defined in measurement domain, instead of image domain as usual DDPM, and is conditioned on the non-sampling matrix $\mathbf{M}^c$ and sampled measurements $\mathbf{y}_\mathbf{M}$. It has the following form:

$$p_\theta(\mathbf{y}_{\mathbf{M}^c,0}\mid\mathbf{M}^c,\mathbf{y}_\mathbf{M}):=\int p_\theta(\mathbf{y}_{\mathbf{M}^c,0:T}\mid\mathbf{M}^c,\mathbf{y}_\mathbf{M})\,d\mathbf{y}_{\mathbf{M}^c,1:T}, \tag{6}$$

---

[2] Specifically, $M_{i,i}=1$ if $i\in\Omega$. Otherwise its value is 0.

where $\mathbf{y}_{\mathbf{M}^c,0} = \mathbf{y}_{\mathbf{M}^c}$. $p_\theta \left(\mathbf{y}_{\mathbf{M}^c,0:T} \mid \mathbf{M}^c, \mathbf{y}_{\mathbf{M}} \right)$ is defined as follows:

$$p_\theta \left(\mathbf{y}_{\mathbf{M}^c,0:T} \mid \mathbf{M}^c, \mathbf{y}_{\mathbf{M}} \right) := p \left(\mathbf{y}_{\mathbf{M}^c,T} \mid \mathbf{M}^c, \mathbf{y}_{\mathbf{M}} \right) \prod_{t=1}^{T} p_\theta \left(\mathbf{y}_{\mathbf{M}^c,t-1} \mid \mathbf{y}_{\mathbf{M}^c,t}, \mathbf{M}^c, \mathbf{y}_{\mathbf{M}} \right),$$

$$p_\theta \left(\mathbf{y}_{\mathbf{M}^c,t-1} \mid \mathbf{y}_{\mathbf{M}^c,t}, \mathbf{M}^c, \mathbf{y}_{\mathbf{M}} \right) := \mathcal{N} \left(\boldsymbol{\mu}_\theta \left(\mathbf{y}_{\mathbf{M}^c,t}, t, \mathbf{M}^c, \mathbf{y}_{\mathbf{M}} \right), \sigma_t^2 \mathbf{M}^c \right),$$

where $\sigma_t^2 \mathbf{M}^c$ is the covariance matrix and it means the noise is only added at non-sampled positions because for all t the components of $\mathbf{y}_{\mathbf{M}^c,t}$ at under-sampled positions are always 0. If the conditions $(\mathbf{M}^c, \mathbf{y}_{\mathbf{M}})$ in equations above is removed, they degrade to the form of Eq. 1.

Similar to DDPM, the sampling process of $p_\theta \left(\mathbf{y}_{\mathbf{M}^c,0} \mid \mathbf{M}^c, \mathbf{y}_{\mathbf{M}} \right)$ is a reverse process of the diffusion process which is also defined in measurement domain. Specifically, the Gaussian noise is gradually added to the non-sampled measurements $\mathbf{y}_{\mathbf{M}^c,0}$. The diffusion process has the following form:

$$q \left(\mathbf{y}_{\mathbf{M}^c,1:T} \mid \mathbf{y}_{\mathbf{M}^c,0}, \mathbf{M}^c, \mathbf{y}_{\mathbf{M}} \right) := \prod_{t=1}^{T} q \left(\mathbf{y}_{\mathbf{M}^c,t} \mid \mathbf{y}_{\mathbf{M}^c,t-1}, \mathbf{M}^c, \mathbf{y}_{\mathbf{M}} \right), \tag{7}$$

$$q \left(\mathbf{y}_{\mathbf{M}^c,t} \mid \mathbf{y}_{\mathbf{M}^c,t-1}, \mathbf{M}^c, \mathbf{y}_{\mathbf{M}} \right) := \mathcal{N} \left(\alpha_t \mathbf{y}_{\mathbf{M}^c,t-1}, \beta_t^2 \mathbf{M}^c \right),$$

There are two points worthy of noting: (1) α_t, β_t are not restricted to satisfy $\alpha_t^2 + \beta_t^2 = 1$; (2) formally, we add $\mathbf{y}_{\mathbf{M}}$ as one of the conditions, but it has no effect on the diffusion process in fact. Let $\bar{\alpha}_t = \prod_{i=1}^{t} \alpha_i, \bar{\beta}_t^2 = \sum_{i=1}^{t} \frac{\bar{\alpha}_t^2}{\bar{\alpha}_i^2} \beta_i^2$, and we additionally define $\bar{\alpha}_0 = 1, \bar{\beta}_0 = 0$. Then, we can derive that:

$$q \left(\mathbf{y}_{\mathbf{M}^c,t} \mid \mathbf{y}_{\mathbf{M}^c,0}, \mathbf{M}^c, \mathbf{y}_{\mathbf{M}} \right) = \mathcal{N} \left(\bar{\alpha}_t \mathbf{y}_{\mathbf{M}^c,0}, \bar{\beta}_t^2 \mathbf{M}^c \right), \tag{8}$$

$$q \left(\mathbf{y}_{\mathbf{M}^c,t-1} \mid \mathbf{y}_{\mathbf{M}^c,t}, \mathbf{y}_{\mathbf{M}^c,0}, \mathbf{M}, \mathbf{y}_{\mathbf{M}} \right) = \mathcal{N} \left(\tilde{\boldsymbol{\mu}}_t, \tilde{\beta}_t^2 \mathbf{M}^c \right), \tag{9}$$

where $\tilde{\boldsymbol{\mu}}_t = \frac{\alpha_t \bar{\beta}_{t-1}^2}{\bar{\beta}_t^2} \mathbf{y}_{\mathbf{M}^c,t} + \frac{\bar{\alpha}_{t-1} \beta_t^2}{\bar{\beta}_t^2} \mathbf{y}_{\mathbf{M}^c,0}, \tilde{\beta}_t = \frac{\beta_t \bar{\beta}_{t-1}}{\bar{\beta}_t}$. In MC-DDPM, we assume that α_t is set specially so that $\bar{\alpha}_T \approx 0$, i.e. $q \left(\mathbf{y}_{\mathbf{M}^c,T} \mid \mathbf{y}_{\mathbf{M}^c,0} \right) \approx \mathcal{N} \left(0, \bar{\beta}_T^2 \mathbf{M}^c \right)$ is a noise distribution independent of $\mathbf{y}_{M^c,0}$.

Next, we discuss how to train MC-DDPM $p_\theta \left(\mathbf{y}_{\mathbf{M}^c,0} \mid \mathbf{M}^c, \mathbf{y}_{\mathbf{M}} \right)$. Firstly, let $p \left(\mathbf{y}_{\mathbf{M}^c,T} \mid \mathbf{M}^c, \mathbf{y}_{\mathbf{M}} \right) = \mathcal{N} \left(0, \bar{\beta}_T^2 \mathbf{M}^c \right)$ so that it is nearly equal to $q \left(\mathbf{y}_{\mathbf{M}^c,T} \mid \mathbf{y}_{\mathbf{M}^c,0} \right)$. Training of $p_\theta \left(\mathbf{y}_{\mathbf{M}^c,0} \mid \mathbf{M}^c, \mathbf{y}_{\mathbf{M}} \right)$ is performed by optimizing the variational bound on negative log likelihood:

$$\mathbb{E} \left[- \log p_\theta \left(\mathbf{y}_{\mathbf{M}^c,0} \mid \mathbf{M}^c, \mathbf{y}_{\mathbf{M}} \right) \right] \leq \mathbb{E}_q \left[- \log \frac{p_\theta \left(\mathbf{y}_{\mathbf{M}^c,0:T} \mid \mathbf{M}^c, \mathbf{y}_{\mathbf{M}} \right)}{q \left(\mathbf{y}_{\mathbf{M}^c,1:T} \mid \mathbf{y}_{\mathbf{M}^c,0}, \mathbf{M}^c, \mathbf{y}_{\mathbf{M}} \right)} \right]$$

$$= \mathbb{E}_q \left[- \log p \left(\mathbf{y}_{\mathbf{M}^c,T} \mid \mathbf{M}^c, \mathbf{y}_{\mathbf{M}} \right) - \sum_{t \geq 1} \log \frac{p_\theta \left(\mathbf{y}_{\mathbf{M}^c,t-1} \mid \mathbf{y}_{\mathbf{M}^c,t}, \mathbf{M}^c, \mathbf{y}_{\mathbf{M}} \right)}{q \left(\mathbf{y}_{\mathbf{M}^c,t} \mid \mathbf{y}_{\mathbf{M}^c,t-1}, \mathbf{M}^c, \mathbf{y}_{\mathbf{M}} \right)} \right] =: L.$$

Assuming that

$$\boldsymbol{\mu}_\theta \left(\mathbf{y}_{\mathbf{M}^c,t}, t, \mathbf{M}^c, \mathbf{y}_{\mathbf{M}} \right) = \frac{1}{\alpha_t} \left(\mathbf{y}_{\mathbf{M}^c,t} - \frac{\beta_t^2}{\bar{\beta}_t} \varepsilon_\theta \left(\mathbf{y}_{\mathbf{M}^c,t}, t, \mathbf{M}^c, \mathbf{y}_{\mathbf{M}} \right) \right), \tag{10}$$

Algorithm 1. MC-DDPM Training	**Algorithm 2.** MC-DDPM Sampling
1: **repeat**	1: Given $\mathbf{M}^c$ and $\mathbf{y_M}$
2: $\mathbf{x} \sim q(\mathbf{x})$, obtain $\mathbf{M}$ and $\mathbf{M}^c$	2: $\mathbf{y}_{\mathbf{M}^c,T} \sim \mathcal{N}\left(\mathbf{0}, \bar{\beta}_T^2 \mathbf{M}^c\right)$
3: $\mathbf{y_M} = \mathbf{MAx}, \mathbf{y}_{\mathbf{M}^c} = \mathbf{M}^c \mathbf{Ax}$	3: **for** $t = T, ..., 1$ **do**
4: $\varepsilon \sim \mathcal{N}(\mathbf{0}, \mathbf{M}^c)$	4: $\mathbf{z}_t \sim \mathcal{N}(\mathbf{0}, \mathbf{M}^c)$ if $t > 1$, else $\mathbf{z}_t = \mathbf{0}$
5: $t \sim \text{Uniform}(\{1, ..., T\})$	5: $\boldsymbol{\mu}_t = \boldsymbol{\mu}_\theta\left(\mathbf{y}_{\mathbf{M}^c,t}, t, \mathbf{M}^c, \mathbf{y_M}\right)$
6: $\mathbf{y}^c_{\mathbf{M},t} = \bar{\alpha}_t \mathbf{y}^c_{\mathbf{M},0} + \bar{\beta}_t \varepsilon$	6: $\mathbf{y}_{\mathbf{M}^c,t-1} = \boldsymbol{\mu}_t + \sigma_t \mathbf{z}_t$
7: Take gradient descent step on	7: **end for**
$\nabla_\theta \left\| \varepsilon - \varepsilon_\theta\left(\mathbf{y}^c_{\mathbf{M},t}, t, \mathbf{M}^c, \mathbf{y_M}\right) \right\|^2_2$	8: **return** $\mathbf{x} = \mathbf{A}^{-1}\left(\mathbf{y_M} + \mathbf{y}_{\mathbf{M}^c,0}\right)$
8: **until** converged	

and supposing $\mathbf{y}_{\mathbf{M}^c,t} = \bar{\alpha}_t \mathbf{y}_{\mathbf{M}^c,0} + \varepsilon, \varepsilon \sim \mathcal{N}\left(\mathbf{0}, \bar{\beta}_t^2 \mathbf{M}^c\right)$ (Eq. 8), after reweighting L can be simplified as follows:

$$L_{\text{simple}} = \mathbb{E}_{\mathbf{y}^c_{\mathbf{M},0}, t, \varepsilon} \left\| \varepsilon - \varepsilon_\theta\left(\bar{\alpha}_t \mathbf{y}^c_{\mathbf{M},0} + \bar{\beta}_t \varepsilon, t, \mathbf{M}^c, \mathbf{y_M}\right) \right\|^2_2, \varepsilon \sim \mathcal{N}(\mathbf{0}, \mathbf{M}^c), \quad (11)$$

where t is uniform between 1 and T. The details of derivation is in supplementary materials.

Algorithm 1 displays the complete training procedure with this simplified objective and Algorithm 2 shows the sampling process.

Since MC-DDPM can produce multiple samples of the posterior distribution $q(\mathbf{x} \mid \mathbf{y_M}, \mathbf{M})$, the pixel-variance can be computed by Monte Carlo approach which is used to quantify uncertainty of reconstruction.

4   Experiments

We apply MC-DDPPM to accelerated MRI reconstruction where $\mathbf{A}$ is 2d Fourier transform and $\mathbf{y_M}$ is the under-sampled k-space data. The specific design for $\varepsilon_\theta\left(\mathbf{y}_{\mathbf{M}^c,t}, t, \mathbf{M}^c, \mathbf{y_M}\right)$ in our experiments is given as follows:

$$\varepsilon_\theta\left(\mathbf{y}_{\mathbf{M}^c,t}, t, \mathbf{M}^c, \mathbf{y_M}\right) = \mathbf{M}^c f\left(g\left(\mathbf{A}^{-1}\left(\mathbf{y}_{\mathbf{M}^c,t} + \mathbf{y_M}\right), \mathbf{A}^{-1} \mathbf{y}_M\right), t; \theta\right), \quad (12)$$

where f is a deep neural network and $g(\cdot, \cdot)$ is the concatenation operation. Because MR image $\mathbf{x}$ is in complex filed, we use $|\mathbf{x}|$, the magnitude of it, as the final image. Pixel-wise variance is also computed using magnitude images.

4.1   Experimental Setting

All experiments are performed with fastMRI single-coil knee dataset [23], which is publicly available[3] and is divided into two parts, proton-density with (PDFS) and without fat suppression (PD). We trained the network with k-space data

---

[3] https://fastmri.org.

which were computed from 320×320 size complex images. We base the implementation of guided-DDPM [4] and also follow similar setting for the diffusion process in [4] but multiply β_t by 0.5 so that $\bar{\beta}_T \approx 0.5$. All networks were trained with learning rate of 0.0001 using AdamW optimizer. More details of experiments is in supplementary materials.

To verify superiority, we perform comparison studies with baseline methods (U-Net [16]) used in [23]. The evaluation metrics, peak signal-to-noise ratio (PSNR) and structural similarity index (SSIM), of score-based reconstruction method proposed in [3] are also used for comparison[4] since their experiments are conducted on the same dataset.

4.2   Experimental Results

We show the results of PD with $4\times$ (the first row) and $8\times$ (the second row) acceleration in Fig. 2. More results are shown in supplementary materials. We compare our method to zero-filled reconstruction (ZF) and U-Net. Since MC-DDPM can produce multiple reconstruction samples, we use the mean of 20 samples as the object for comparison. We observe that the proposed method performs best both in $4\times$ and $8\times$ accelerations, where we see virtually more realistic structures and less error in the zoomed-in image than ZF and U-Net. In the last column of Fig. 2, we show the standard deviation of the samples. As the acceleration factor is increased, we see that the uncertainty increases correspondingly. Quantitative metrics in Table 1 also confirm the superiority of our method. In the last two columns of Table 1, we compare MC-DDPM to the score-based reconstruction method proposed in [3]. Because the testing volumes are randomly selected both in our experiments and in [3], it is impossible to compare directly. As a substitution, we compare the enhancement of evaluation metrics which is computed by the result of proposed method subtracting the result of U-Net. Due to the experiments in [3] were conducted on the whole dataset (both PD and PDFS), we compute the average enhancement of PD and PDFS as our final result. Our method outperforms [3] by 3.62/0.077 ($4\times$) and 2.96/0.089 ($8\times$) in PSNR/SSIM.

We also explore the effects of sampling steps and number of samples on reconstruction quality, which are illustrated in Fig. 3 and Fig. 4. The two experiments are conducted on one volume of PDFS with $4\times$ and $8\times$ acceleration, and PSNR is computed on the mean of generated samples. We discover that: (1) even the sampling steps decrease to 250, PSNR only reduces a little; (2) the quality of the mean of samples is enhanced when the number of samples increases and seems to converge. Taking the efficiency into account, 20 samples with 250 sampling steps may be a good choice.

4.3   Discussion

It is very common in medical imaging that the measurement is under sampled to reduce the cost or dosage. Therefore, it is important to define the conditional

---

[4] They are provided in the paper of [3].

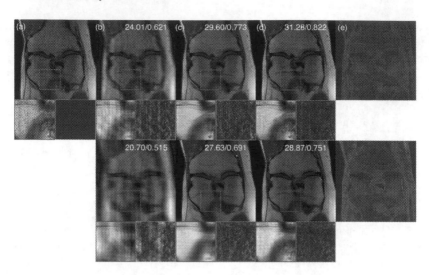

Fig. 2. Reconstruction results of 4× (the first row) and 8× (the second row) on PD data: (a) ground-truth, (b) zero-filled reconstruction, (c) U-Net, (d) the mean of samples generated by proposed method, (e) the standard deviation of the samples: range is set to [0, 0.2]. Blue box: zoom in version of the indicated red box. Green box: Difference magnitude of the inset. White numbers indicate PSNR and SSIM, respectively. (Color figure online)

Table 1. Quantitative metrics. Numbers in bold face indicate the best metric out of all the methods. The enhancement in the last two columns is computed based on U-Net.

		PD			PDFS			Enhancement	
		ZF	U-Net	Ours	ZF	U-Net	Ours	Score [3]	Ours
×4	PSNR	29.62	34.04	**36.69**	26.32	28.30	**33.00**	+0.06	**+3.68**
	SSIM	0.745	0.834	**0.905**	0.545	0.648	**0.735**	+0.002	**+0.079**
×8	PSNR	25.94	31.13	**33.49**	24.90	26.17	**31.75**	+1.01	**+3.97**
	SSIM	0.667	0.750	**0.862**	0.513	0.580	**0.702**	+0.028	**+0.117**

diffusion process in the measurement space for a reconstruction task. In this project, although our experiments are conducted using MR images, our method can be applied to other under-sampled medical image reconstruction tasks, such as limited angle or spare view CT Reconstruction. In our MC-DDPM, the variance schedule $\{\beta_t\}$ is an important hyper-parameter that is potentially related to the sampling quality and efficiency. Further investigation on hyper-parameter $\{\beta_t\}$ is planned in our future study.

The weakness of MC-DDPM is the relatively slow inference. It takes 10 s to generate one slice with 250 sampling steps on RTX 3090Ti. This limits the practical utilization of our method in some clinical settings. One defect of this work is that only one dataset, fastmri, was used. We will perform MC-DDPM to more datasets to verify the superiority in the future. Another defect is the assumption that ϵ_M in Eq. 5 is zero. When the noise is not zero, the theory, training, and inference will be more complicated but could be extended from the current method. In the near future, we aim to apply this method to cardiac MRI imaging and will solve the zero noise case at that time.

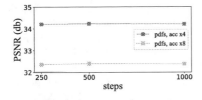

Fig. 3. Tradeoff between number of sampling steps vs. PSNR testing on one volume of PDFS.

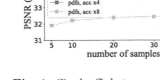

Fig. 4. Tradeoff between number of samples vs. PSNR testing on one volume of PDFS.

5 Conclusion

In this paper we present a novel and unified mathematical framework, MC-DDPM, for medical image reconstruction using under-sampled measurements. Our method applies diffusion process in measurement domain with conditioned under-sampling mask, and provides an estimate of uncertainty as output. The superior performance of our method is demonstrated using accelerated MRI reconstruction, although MC-DDPM should potentially work for other under-sampled medical image reconstruction tasks.

References

1. Aggarwal, H.K., Mani, M.P., Jacob, M.: MoDL: model-based deep learning architecture for inverse problems. IEEE Trans. Med. Imaging **38**(2), 394–405 (2018)
2. Choi, J., Kim, S., Jeong, Y., Gwon, Y., Yoon, S.: ILVR: conditioning method for denoising diffusion probabilistic models. arXiv preprint arXiv:2108.02938 (2021)
3. Chung, H., et al.: Score-based diffusion models for accelerated MRI. arXiv preprint arXiv:2110.05243 (2021)
4. Dhariwal, P., Nichol, A.: Diffusion models beat GANs on image synthesis. arXiv preprint arXiv:2105.05233 (2021)
5. Eo, T., Jun, Y., Kim, T., Jang, J., Lee, H.J., Hwang, D.: KIKI-net: cross-domain convolutional neural networks for reconstructing undersampled magnetic resonance images. Magn. Reson. Med. **80**(5), 2188–2201 (2018)
6. Hammernik, K., et al.: Learning a variational network for reconstruction of accelerated MRI data. Magn. Reson. Med. **79**(6), 3055–3071 (2018)
7. Han, Y., Sunwoo, L., Ye, J.C.: k-space deep learning for accelerated MRI. IEEE Trans. Med. Imaging **39**(2), 377–386 (2019)
8. Han, Y., Ye, J.C.: Framing U-Net via deep convolutional framelets: application to sparse-view CT. IEEE Trans. Med. Imaging **37**(6), 1418–1429 (2018)

9. Ho, J., Jain, A., Abbeel, P.: Denoising diffusion probabilistic models. arXiv preprint arXiv:2006.11239 (2020)
10. Hyvärinen, A., Dayan, P.: Estimation of non-normalized statistical models by score matching. J. Mach. Learn. Res. **6**(4) (2005)
11. Jalal, A., Arvinte, M., Daras, G., Price, E., Dimakis, A., Tamir, J.: Robust compressed sensing MRI with deep generative priors. In: Thirty-Fifth Conference on Neural Information Processing Systems (2021)
12. Kong, Z., Ping, W., Huang, J., Zhao, K., Catanzaro, B.: Diffwave: a versatile diffusion model for audio synthesis. arXiv preprint arXiv:2009.09761 (2020)
13. Meng, C., Song, Y., Song, J., Wu, J., Zhu, J.Y., Ermon, S.: SDEdit: image synthesis and editing with stochastic differential equations. arXiv preprint arXiv:2108.01073 (2021)
14. Nichol, A.Q., Dhariwal, P.: Improved denoising diffusion probabilistic models. In: International Conference on Machine Learning, pp. 8162–8171. PMLR (2021)
15. Niu, C., Song, Y., Song, J., Zhao, S., Grover, A., Ermon, S.: Permutation invariant graph generation via score-based generative modeling. In: International Conference on Artificial Intelligence and Statistics, pp. 4474–4484. PMLR (2020)
16. Ronneberger, O., Fischer, P., Brox, T.: U-Net: convolutional networks for biomedical image segmentation. In: Navab, N., Hornegger, J., Wells, W.M., Frangi, A.F. (eds.) MICCAI 2015. LNCS, vol. 9351, pp. 234–241. Springer, Cham (2015). https://doi.org/10.1007/978-3-319-24574-4_28
17. Saharia, C., Ho, J., Chan, W., Salimans, T., Fleet, D.J., Norouzi, M.: Image super-resolution via iterative refinement. arXiv preprint arXiv:2104.07636 (2021)
18. Sohl-Dickstein, J., Weiss, E., Maheswaranathan, N., Ganguli, S.: Deep unsupervised learning using nonequilibrium thermodynamics. In: International Conference on Machine Learning, pp. 2256–2265. PMLR (2015)
19. Song, Y., Ermon, S.: Generative modeling by estimating gradients of the data distribution. In: Advances in Neural Information Processing Systems, vol. 32 (2019)
20. Song, Y., Shen, L., Xing, L., Ermon, S.: Solving inverse problems in medical imaging with score-based generative models. arXiv preprint arXiv:2111.08005 (2021)
21. Song, Y., Sohl-Dickstein, J., Kingma, D.P., Kumar, A., Ermon, S., Poole, B.: Score-based generative modeling through stochastic differential equations. arXiv preprint arXiv:2011.13456 (2020)
22. Wang, J., Zeng, L., Wang, C., Guo, Y.: ADMM-based deep reconstruction for limited-angle CT. Phys. Med. Biol. **64**(11), 115011 (2019)
23. Zbontar, J., et al.: fastMRI: an open dataset and benchmarks for accelerated MRI. arXiv preprint arXiv:1811.08839 (2018)
24. Zhang, H., Dong, B., Liu, B.: JSR-Net: a deep network for joint spatial-radon domain CT reconstruction from incomplete data. In: ICASSP 2019–2019 IEEE International Conference on Acoustics, Speech and Signal Processing (ICASSP), pp. 3657–3661. IEEE (2019)

Orientation-Shared Convolution Representation for CT Metal Artifact Learning

Hong Wang[1], Qi Xie[2(✉)], Yuexiang Li[1(✉)], Yawen Huang[1], Deyu Meng[2,3,4], and Yefeng Zheng[1]

[1] Tencent Jarvis Lab, Shenzhen, People's Republic of China
{hazelhwang,vicyxli,yawenhuang,yefengzheng}@tencent.com
[2] Xi'an Jiaotong University, Xi'an, Shaan'xi, People's Republic of China
{xie.qi,dymeng}@mail.xjtu.edu.cn
[3] Peng Cheng Laboratory, Shenzhen, China
[4] Macau University of Science and Technology, Taipa, Macau

Abstract. During X-ray computed tomography (CT) scanning, metallic implants carrying with patients often lead to adverse artifacts in the captured CT images and then impair the clinical treatment. Against this metal artifact reduction (MAR) task, the existing deep-learning-based methods have gained promising reconstruction performance. Nevertheless, there is still some room for further improvement of MAR performance and generalization ability, since some important prior knowledge underlying this specific task has not been fully exploited. Hereby, in this paper, we carefully analyze the characteristics of metal artifacts and propose an orientation-shared convolution representation strategy to adapt the physical prior structures of artifacts, *i.e.*, rotationally symmetrical streaking patterns. The proposed method rationally adopts Fourier-series-expansion-based filter parametrization in artifact modeling, which can better separate artifacts from anatomical tissues and boost the model generalizability. Comprehensive experiments executed on synthesized and clinical datasets show the superiority of our method in detail preservation beyond the current representative MAR methods. Code will be available at https://github.com/hongwang01/OSCNet.

Keywords: Metal artifact reduction · Orientation-shared convolution · Rotation prior · Fourier series expansion · Model generalizability

1 Introduction

During the computed tomography (CT) imaging process, metallic implants within patients would severely attenuate X-rays and lead to the missing X-ray

Supplementary Information The online version contains supplementary material available at https://doi.org/10.1007/978-3-031-16446-0_63.

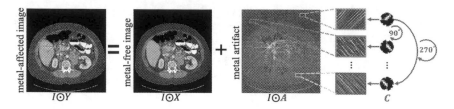

Fig. 1. Metal artifact A presents clear rotationally streaking structures, which can be represented by rotating each convolution filter C to multiple angles (*i.e.*, orientation-shared). Here Y, X, and I represent the metal-affected CT image, ground truth image, and non-metal region, respectively. Red pixels in Y and A are metallic implants. (Color figure online)

projections. Accordingly, the captured CT images often present streaking and shading artifacts [9,10,16], which negatively affect the clinical treatment.

Against this metal artifact reduction (MAR) task, many approaches have been proposed in the past few years. Traditional methods replaced the metal-corrupted region in sinogram domain with surrogates, which were estimated via different manners, *e.g.*, linear interpolation (LI) [7] and normalized MAR [13]. Recently, driven by deep learning (DL) techniques, some researchers exploited the powerful fitting capability of deep neural networks to directly reconstruct clean sinogram [3,5,8,14,25]. However, the estimated values in sinogram domain are not always consistent with the physical imaging geometry, which leads to the secondary artifacts in the reconstructed CT images. Furthermore, it is difficult to collect the sinogram data in realistic applications [9]. These limitations constrain the generality and performance of sinogram-based MAR approaches.

To loosen the requirement of sinogram, researchers proposed to train deep networks based on only CT images for the recovery of clean CT images [4,6,20]. Recently, some works simultaneously exploited sinogram and CT image [10,12,18, 19,21,24,26] to further boost the MAR performance. Nevertheless, the involved image domain-based network module of most methods is a general structure for image restoration tasks, which has not sufficiently encoded useful priors underlying this specific MAR task and made the network hardly interpretable.

To alleviate these issues, Wang *et al.* [16] proposed an interpretable MAR network named as DICDNet, which is integrated with the non-local repetitive streaking priors of metal artifacts A via a convolutional dictionary model as:

$$A = \sum_{s=1}^{S} C_s \otimes M_s, \tag{1}$$

where the filter C_s and the feature map M_s represent the local streaking patterns and the locations of artifacts, respectively; $\otimes$ denotes 2D convolution operator.

However, there is still some important and insightful prior knowledge not encoded by Eq. (1). Specifically, one of the most intrinsic priors is that along every rotation direction, the caused artifacts have similar streaking patterns, as shown in Fig. 1. Such inherent **rotationally symmetrical streaking (RSS)** prior structures are often caused by the rotationally scanning-based CT physical imaging process [9,25], and appear in diverse kinds of CT imaging-related artifacts. Besides, it should be noted that the RSS structure is specifically possessed by metal artifact A rather than the to-be-estimated clean CT image X. This fact implies that it would be useful and valuable to encode and utilize such RSS prior structure so as to distinguish metal artifacts from clean CT images.

To encode such inherent RSS prior structure, we seek to construct a novel convolutional dictionary model that shares filters among different angles. In other words, we aim to represent the metal artifact A along multiple directions by rotating each convolution filter C to multiple angles, as shown in Fig. 1. In this manner, we only need to learn the filter C along one angle, which can represent local patterns at different angles but with similar structures (*i.e.*, orientation-shared). Naturally, this helps reduce the number of learnable filters and improve the flexibility of network representation. However, the commonly-used discrete convolution filters can hardly be rotated to different angles with high precision. Thus, we adopt the filter parametrization method [22] and firstly propose an orientation-shared convolution representation model, which finely encodes the RSS prior of artifacts. Based on the proposed model, we construct an optimization-inspired network for artifact learning. Compared to current state-of-the-art (SOTA) MAR methods, our method can better reduce artifacts while more faithfully preserving tissues with fewer model parameters for representing artifacts, which are finely verified by experiments on synthetic and clinical data.

2 Preliminary Knowledge

Filter parametrization is an important strategy to achieve parameter sharing among convolution filters at different rotation angles. Since 2D discrete Fourier transform can be equivalently expressed as Fourier series expansion, it is natural to construct a Fourier-series-expansion-based filter parametrization method [22]. Specifically, to represent a discrete filter $C \in \mathbb{R}^{p \times p}$, we can discretize a 2D function $\varphi(x)$ by uniformly sampling on the area within $[-(p-1)h/2, (p-1)h/2]^2$, where h is the mesh size of images, and $\varphi(x)$ can be expressed as [2]:

$$\varphi(x) = \sum_{q=0}^{p-1} \sum_{t=0}^{p-1} a_{qt} \varphi_{qt}^c(x) + b_{qt} \varphi_{qt}^s(x), \tag{2}$$

where $x = [x_i, x_j]^T$ is 2D spatial coordinate; a_{qt} and b_{qt} are expansion coefficients; $\varphi_{qt}^c(x)$ and $\varphi_{qt}^s(x)$ are 2D basis functions. In conventional Fourier series, one can select the basis functions as:

$$\varphi_{qt}^c(x) = \Omega(x) \cos\left(\frac{2\pi}{ph}[q,t] \cdot \begin{bmatrix} x_i \\ x_j \end{bmatrix}\right), \quad \varphi_{qt}^s(x) = \Omega(x) \sin\left(\frac{2\pi}{ph}[q,t] \cdot \begin{bmatrix} x_i \\ x_j \end{bmatrix}\right), \tag{3}$$

where $\Omega(x) \geq 0$ is a radial mask function and $\Omega(x) = 0$ if $\|x\| \geq ((p+1)/2)h$. This facilitates the rotation operation [22].

Unfortunately, the Fourier bases (3) always present aliasing effect when $\varphi(x)$ is rotated. To alleviate this issue, Eq. (3) is revised in [22] as:

$$\varphi_{qt}^{c}(x)=\Omega(x)\cos\left(\frac{2\pi}{ph}[\mathcal{I}_p(q),\mathcal{I}_p(t)]\cdot\begin{bmatrix}x_i\\x_j\end{bmatrix}\right), \varphi_{qt}^{s}(x)=\Omega(x)\sin\left(\frac{2\pi}{ph}[\mathcal{I}_p(q),\mathcal{I}_p(t)]\cdot\begin{bmatrix}x_i\\x_j\end{bmatrix}\right),$$

(4)

where if $y \leq p/2$, $\mathcal{I}_p(y) = y$; otherwise, $\mathcal{I}_p(y) = y - p$.

3   Orientation-Shared Convolution Model for MAR

Clearly, the metals generally have extremely higher CT values than normal tissues. From Fig. 1, it is easily observed that for the MAR task, our goal is to reconstruct the clean tissues in the non-metal region from a given metal-corrupted CT image $Y \in \mathbb{R}^{H \times W}$, without paying attention to the learning in the metal region. Similar to [16], we define the decomposition model as:

$$I \odot Y = I \odot X + I \odot A,$$

(5)

where X and A are the unknown metal-free CT image and the artifact layer, respectively; I is a binary non-metal mask; $\odot$ denotes point-wise multiplication.

Clearly, estimating X from Y is an ill-posed inverse problem, and rationally utilizing prior knowledge can finely help constrain the solution space and better reconstruct clean images. To this end, we carefully analyze the physical priors of artifacts and accordingly formulate them as an explicit model. The prior model is then embedded into deep networks to regularize the extraction of artifacts.

Metal Artifact Modeling with Filter Parametrization. Specifically, since the CT imaging is generally performed in a rotationally scanning manner, metal artifacts generally present scattered streaking structures [9,10]. From Fig. 1, we can easily find that along every rotation angle, artifacts share similar streaking patterns. To encode such prior structures, we can rotate convolution filters to multiple angles so as to represent artifacts in different directions. To this end, we firstly propose a filter parametrization based convolutional coding model as:

$$A = \sum_{l=1}^{L}\sum_{k=1}^{K} C_k(\theta_l) \otimes M_{lk},$$

(6)

where L is the number of rotation angles; $\theta_l = 2\pi(l-1)/L$ is the l-th rotation angle; K is the number of convolution filters at each angle; $C_k(\theta_l) \in \mathbb{R}^{p \times p}$ is the k-th parametrized filter at angle θ_l, and it represents the streaking and rotated prior patterns of artifacts; M_{lk} is feature map reflecting the locations of artifacts.

From Eq. (6), one can easily find that metal artifacts in different orientations share the same set of filters as $C_k(\theta_l)(k = 1, \ldots, K)$ under orientation-variance freedom. This finely encodes the fact that metal artifacts in different directions share similar patterns. Compared to the conventional convolutional dictionary model (1) in [16], our proposed model (6) has two main merits: 1) Eq. (6) should be more accurate for representing artifacts than model (1), since it can ensure the RSS prior of artifacts (see Fig. 3 below); 2) The number of the learnable filters can be evidently reduced, which would benefit the learning of $C_k(\theta_l)$.

Specifically, for modeling $C_k(\theta_l)$, it is necessary to adopt a filter parametrization method with high representation accuracy. The work [22] has shown that the basis function in Eq. (4) can represent arbitrary filters with arbitrary angles. Based on this, we can parametrize every element in $C_k(\theta_l)$ as:

$$[C_k(\theta_l)]_{ij} = \varphi_k(T_{\theta_l} x_{ij}) = \sum_{q=0}^{p-1} \sum_{t=0}^{p-1} a_{qtk} \varphi_{qt}^c (T_{\theta_l} x_{ij}) + b_{qtk} \varphi_{qt}^s (T_{\theta_l} x_{ij}), \quad (7)$$

where T_{θ_l} is the rotation matrix with angle θ_l as $T_{\theta_l} = [\cos\theta_l, -\sin\theta_l; \sin\theta_l, \cos\theta_l]^T$; $x_{ij} = [x_i, x_j]^T = [(i - (p+1)/2)h, (j - (p+1)/2)h]^T$; $i = 1, \ldots, p$, $j = 1, \ldots, p$. $\varphi_{qt}^c(T_{\theta_l} x_{ij})$ and $\varphi_{qt}^s(T_{\theta_l} x_{ij})$ are rotated Fourier bases, and their definitions are in (4). The expansion coefficients a_{qtk} and b_{qtk} are shared among different rotations, which reflects the rotation symmetry of artifacts. Driven by the powerful fitting ability of convolutional neural network (CNN), we can automatically learn a_{qtk} and b_{qtk} from training data and then flexibly extract $C_k(\theta_l)$ (see Fig. 3).

Optimization Algorithm. By substituting Eq. (6) into Eq. (5), we can derive:

$$I \odot Y = I \odot X + I \odot (C \otimes M), \quad (8)$$

where $C \in \mathbb{R}^{p \times p \times LK}$ and $M \in \mathbb{R}^{H \times W \times LK}$ are stacked by $C_k(\theta_l)$ and M_{lk}, respectively. Clearly, given a metal-affected CT image Y, we need to estimate the artifact-removed CT image X and feature map M. Note that as explained in (7), C can be flexibly learnt from data. Then we adopt the maximum-a-posterior framework and formulate the optimization problem as:

$$\min_{M,X} \|I \odot (Y - X - C \otimes M)\|_F^2 + \alpha f_1(M) + \beta f_2(X), \quad (9)$$

where α and β are trade-off parameters; $\|\cdot\|_F$ is the Frobenius norm; $f_1(\cdot)$ and $f_2(\cdot)$ are regularizers representing the prior information of M and X, respectively. Similar to [16,18], we also adopt CNN to flexibly learn the implicit priors underlying M and X from training datasets. The details are given in Sect. 4.

To solve the problem (9), we can directly adopt the iterative algorithm in [16]. Specifically, by utilizing the proximal gradient technique [1] to alternatively update M and X, one can easily derive the following iterative rules as:

$$\begin{cases} M^{(n)} = \text{prox}_{\alpha\eta_1}\left(M^{(n-1)} - \eta_1 \nabla g_1\left(M^{(n-1)}\right)\right), \\ X^{(n)} = \text{prox}_{\beta\eta_2}\left(X^{(n-1)} - \eta_2 \nabla g_2\left(X^{(n-1)}\right)\right), \end{cases} \quad (10)$$

where $\nabla g_1\left(M^{(n-1)}\right) = C \otimes^T \left(I \odot \left(C \otimes M^{(n-1)} + X^{(n-1)} - Y\right)\right)$; $\nabla g_2\left(X^{(n-1)}\right) = I \odot \left(C \otimes M^{(n)} + X^{(n-1)} - Y\right)$; $\otimes^T$ is transposed convolution; η_1 and η_2 are step-sizes; $\text{prox}_{\alpha\eta_1}(\cdot)$ and $\text{prox}_{\beta\eta_2}(\cdot)$ are proximal operators, relying on the priors $f_1(\cdot)$ and $f_2(\cdot)$, respectively, and the detailed designs are presented in Sect. 4.

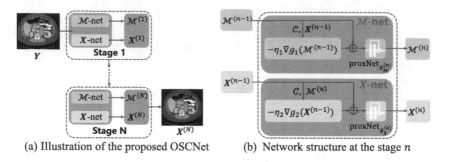

Fig. 2. (a) Illustration of our OSCNet. (b) At any stage n, the network sequentially consists of $\mathcal{M}$-net and $\boldsymbol{X}$-net, which are built based on the iterative rules (10).

4   Network Design and Implementation Details

Following DICDNet [16], we can easily build an optimization-inspired deep network by sequentially unfolding every computation step in (10) into the corresponding network module [17]. Specifically, as shown in Fig. 2, the proposed orientation-shared convolutional network (called OSCNet) contains N stages, corresponding to N optimization iterations. At each stage, OSCNet sequentially consists of $\mathcal{M}$-net and $\boldsymbol{X}$-net for optimizing $\mathcal{M}$ and $\boldsymbol{X}$, respectively. All the network parameters contain expansion coefficients $\{a_{qtk}, b_{qtk}\}_{q=0,t=0,k=1}^{p-1,p-1,K}$, stepsizes η_1 and η_2, and the weights of $\mathcal{M}$-net and $\boldsymbol{X}$-net as $\{\theta_{\mathcal{M}}^{(n)}, \theta_{\boldsymbol{X}}^{(n)}\}_{n=1}^{N}$, which are learnable in an end-to-end manner. At stage n, the network structure is:

$$\begin{cases} \mathcal{M}\text{-net: } \mathcal{M}^{(n)} = \text{proxNet}_{\theta_{\mathcal{M}}^{(n)}} \left(\mathcal{M}^{(n-1)} - \eta_1 \nabla g_1 \left(\mathcal{M}^{(n-1)} \right) \right), \\ \boldsymbol{X}\text{-net: } \boldsymbol{X}^{(n)} = \text{proxNet}_{\theta_{\boldsymbol{X}}^{(n)}} \left(\boldsymbol{X}^{(n-1)} - \eta_2 \nabla g_2 \left(\boldsymbol{X}^{(n-1)} \right) \right), \end{cases} \quad (11)$$

where consistent to DICDNet [16], $\text{proxNet}_{\theta_{\mathcal{M}}^{(n)}}(\cdot)$ and $\text{proxNet}_{\theta_{\boldsymbol{X}}^{(n)}}(\cdot)$ are ResNets with three $[Conv+BN+ReLU+Conv+BN+Skip\ Connection]$ residual blocks, representing the proximal operators $\text{prox}_{\alpha\eta_1}(\cdot)$ and $\text{prox}_{\beta\eta_2}(\cdot)$ in (10), respectively. Besides, since the formation of artifacts is complicated, we implement a ResNet after the last stage to further refine $\boldsymbol{X}^{(N)}$ [16]. It should be noted that the learnable parameter for representing filters is a common convolution layer for DICDNet but expansion coefficients for our OSCNet.

In such an optimization-inspired network design manner, our OSCNet is naturally integrated with the prior model (6). With the aid of such prior knowledge, OSCNet can achieve better model generalizability in artifact learning (see Sect. 5). Compared to most current MAR methods, which heuristically design deep networks, the physical meanings of every module in OSCNet, correspondingly built based on the iterative rules (10), are clearer. It is worth mentioning that OSCNet can be easily built by embedding the prior model (6) into the current SOTA framework [16]. This is friendly for model deployment in practices.

It is worth mentioning that as compared with DICDNet [16], the proposed OSCNet contains novel and challenging design: 1) Eq. (6) should be the first

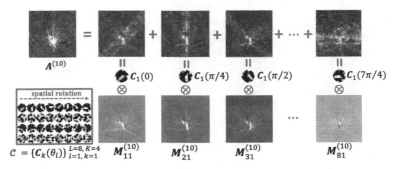

Fig. 3. Visualization of the model (6). $C_k(\theta_l)$, $M_{lk}^{(10)}$, and $A^{(10)}$ are convolution filters, feature map, and artifacts, respectively, extracted from the last stage of OSCNet. As seen, each filter in $\mathcal{C}$ can adaptively fit a local structure with different rotations.

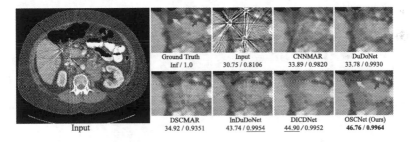

Fig. 4. Performance comparison on synthesized DeepLesion [23]. PSNR/SSIM is listed below each artifact-reduced CT image. Red pixels represent metallic implants.

orientation shared convolution coding model, which is hard to achieve without the filter parametrization strategy we adopt; 2) The OSC model is very suitable for encoding the rotational prior of artifacts ignored by DICDNet; 3) DICDNet is a special case of OSCNet ($L = 1$, $K = 32$). Such rotational design makes OSCNet outperform DICDNet obviously (See Sect. 5); 4) The OSC model would be used as a general tool for modelling any rotational structure, which is valuable.

Loss Function. The total objective function for training OSCNet is set as [16]:

$$\mathcal{L} = \sum_{n=0}^{N} \mu_n \boldsymbol{I} \odot \left\| \boldsymbol{X} - \boldsymbol{X}^{(n)} \right\|_F^2 + \lambda_1 \left(\sum_{n=0}^{N} \mu_n \boldsymbol{I} \odot \left\| \boldsymbol{X} - \boldsymbol{X}^{(n)} \right\|_1 \right) + \lambda_2 \left(\sum_{n=1}^{N} \mu_n \boldsymbol{I} \odot \left\| \boldsymbol{Y} - \boldsymbol{X} - \boldsymbol{A}^{(n)} \right\|_1 \right),$$
(12)

where $\boldsymbol{X}^{(n)}$ and $\boldsymbol{A}^{(n)}$ are the artifact-reduced image and the extracted artifact at the stage n, respectively; $\boldsymbol{A}^{(n)} = \mathcal{C} \otimes \mathcal{M}^{(n)}$; $\boldsymbol{X}$ is the ground truth CT image; λ_1, λ_2, and μ_n are trade-off parameters. Empirically, we set: $\lambda_1 = \lambda_2 = 5 \times 10^{-4}$, $\mu_N = 1$, and $\mu_n = 0.1$ $(n \neq N)$. $\boldsymbol{X}^{(0)}$ is initialized in the same manner to [16].

Training Details. OSCNet is implemented using PyTorch [15] and optimized on an NVIDIA Tesla V100-SMX2 GPU based on Adam optimizer with parameters $(\beta_1, \beta_2) = (0.5, 0.999)$. The learning rate is 2×10^{-4} and it is multiplied by 0.5

after every 30 training epochs. The number of total epochs is 200. The batch size is 16 and the patch size is 64×64. For a fair comparison, consistent to [16], $N = 10$, $p = 9$, $L = 8$, $K = 4$. The mesh size h in Eq. (4) is $1/4$ [22].

5   Experiments

Synthesized DeepLesion. Following [16,24], we can synthesize the paired X and Y for training and testing by utilizing 1,200 clean CT images from DeepLesion (mainly focusing on abdomen and thorax) [23] and 100 simulated metallic implants from [25]. All the CT images are resized to 416×416 pixels and 640 projection views are uniformly sampled in $[0°, 360°]$. The sizes of 10 testing metal masks are [2061, 890, 881, 451, 254, 124, 118, 112, 53, 35] in pixels. We take adjacent masks as one group for performance evaluation.

Synthesized Dental. For cross-body-site performance comparison, we collect clean dental CT images from [24] and adopt the simulation procedure [16,24] to synthesize paired X and Y for the evaluation of model generalization.

Clinical CLINIC-Metal. Besides, we collect the public metal-affected CLINIC-metal [11] (focusing on pelvic CT) for clinical evaluation. Consistent to [9,16], clinical metallic implants are roughly segmented with a threshold of 2,500 HU.

Evaluation Metrics. For synthesized data, we adopt PSNR/SSIM; For CLINIC-metal, due to the lack of ground truth, we provide visual results.

Baselines. We compare with traditional LI [7] and NMAR [13], DL-based CNN-MAR [25], DuDoNet [10], DSCMAR [24], InDuDoNet [18], and DICDNet [16].

Model Visualization. Figure 3 presents the convolution filter $C_k(\theta_l)$, feature map $M_{lk}^{(10)}$, and metal artifacts $A^{(10)}$ extracted by our OSCNet at the last stage. It is easily observed that C_k contains diverse patterns and is spatially rotated with angle $\frac{\pi}{4}(l-1), l = 1, 2, \cdots, 8$. Correspondingly, the extracted artifact layer $C_k(\theta_l) \otimes M_{lk}^{(10)}$ clearly shows rotated structures. The observation verifies the effectiveness of our OSCNet in the learning of RSS prior structures underlying the MAR task, which complies with the Fourier-series-expansion-based orientation-shared convolution prior model (6). Integrated with such prior regularization, OSCNet would recover CT images with better visual quality as shown below.

Experiments on Synthesized DeepLesion. Figure 4 shows the artifact-reduced CT images reconstructed by all comparing methods. Clearly, our OSC-Net better removes the artifacts while preserving the body tissues, especially around metallic implants. Compared to [16], the accurate embedding of rotation prior structures can indeed benefit the identification of metal artifacts. Table 1 lists the average quantitative results on synthesized DeepLesion. As shown, our OSCNet achieves the highest PSNR score for metals with different sizes. The

Table 1. Average PSNR (dB)/SSIM on synthesized DeepLesion [23].

Methods	Large Metal	$\longrightarrow$	Medium Metal	$\longrightarrow$	Small Metal	Average
Input	24.12/0.6761	26.13/0.7471	27.75/0.7659	28.53/0.7964	28.78/0.8076	27.06/0.7586
LI [7]	27.21/0.8920	28.31/0.9185	29.86/0.9464	30.40/0.9555	30.57/0.9608	29.27/0.9347
NMAR [13]	27.66/0.9114	28.81/0.9373	29.69/0.9465	30.44/0.9591	30.79/0.9669	29.48/0.9442
CNNMAR [25]	28.92/0.9433	29.89/0.9588	30.84/0.9706	31.11/0.9743	31.14/0.9752	30.38/0.9644
DuDoNet [10]	29.87/0.9723	30.60/0.9786	31.46/0.9839	31.85/0.9858	31.91/0.9862	31.14/0.9814
DSCMAR [24]	34.04/0.9343	33.10/0.9362	33.37/0.9384	32.75/0.9393	32.77/0.9395	33.21/0.9375
InDuDoNet [18]	36.74/0.9742	39.32/0.9893	41.86/<u>0.9944</u>	44.47/0.9948	45.01/<u>0.9958</u>	41.48/0.9897
DICDNet [16]	<u>37.19</u>/<u>0.9853</u>	<u>39.53</u>/**0.9908**	<u>42.25</u>/0.9941	<u>44.91</u>/<u>0.9953</u>	<u>45.27</u>/<u>0.9958</u>	<u>41.83</u>/<u>0.9923</u>
OSCNet(Ours)	**37.70**/**0.9883**	**39.88**/<u>0.9902</u>	**42.92**/**0.9950**	**45.04**/**0.9958**	**45.45**/**0.9962**	**42.19**/**0.9931**

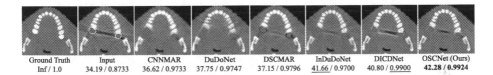

Ground Truth	Input	CNNMAR	DuDoNet	DSCMAR	InDuDoNet	DICDNet	OSCNet (Ours)
Inf / 1.0	34.19 / 0.8733	36.62 / 0.9733	37.75 / 0.9747	37.15 / 0.9796	<u>41.66</u> / 0.9700	40.80 / <u>0.9900</u>	**42.28 / 0.9924**

Fig. 5. Generalization comparison on synthesized Dental [24].

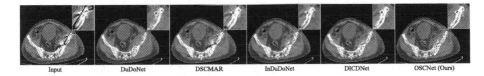

Input	DuDoNet	DSCMAR	InDuDoNet	DICDNet	OSCNet (Ours)

Fig. 6. Generalization comparison on CLINIC-metal [11].

experimental results finely verify the effectiveness of the prior model (6). Actually, DICDNet is exactly our backbone and represents ablation study.

Experiments on Synthesized Dental. Figure 5 compares the cross-body-site performances on synthesized Dental. As seen, there is still a black band in the CT image reconstructed by our method. The underlying explanation is that compared to the black-box network learning manner for artifact reduction, the explicit regularization on artifacts (*i.e.*, OSC model) would weaken the flexibility of artifact extraction to some extent. Even in this case, our method still obtains the best PSNR/SSIM for fine detail fidelity and shows better model generalizability. This is mainly attributed to the more accurate regularization, which can better help network distinguish artifact layer from body tissues and guarantee the detail fidelity. This would be more meaningful for clinical applications.

Experiments on CLINIC-Metal. Figure 6 provides the reconstruction results on CLINIC-metal. As seen, our proposed OSCNet outperforms other baselines on the removal of shadings and streaking artifacts, and more accurately recovers the bone areas, which demonstrates its better clinical generalization ability.

More experiments are provided in *supplementary material*.

6   Conclusion and Future Work

In this paper, against the metal artifact reduction task, we proposed an orientation-shared convolution model to encode the inherent rotationally symmetrical streaking prior structures of metal artifacts. By embedding such prior model into a current SOTA framework, we built an optimization-inspired deep network with clear interpretability. Comprehensive experiments on publicly available datasets have shown the rationality and effectiveness of our proposed method. However, there still exists some potential limitation, such as, metal segmentation might make tissues be wrongly regarded as metals and most MAR methods as well as our OSCNet would fail to recover image details. How to accomplish the joint optimization of automated metal localization and accurate metal artifact reduction deserves further exploration in the future.

Acknowledgements. This work was founded by the China NSFC project under contract U21A6005, the Macao Science and Technology Development Fund under Grant 061/2020/A2, the major key project of PCL under contract PCL2021A12, the Key-Area Research and Development Program of Guangdong Province, China (No. 2018B010111001), National Key R&D Program of China (2018YFC2000702), the Scientific and Technical Innovation 2030-"New Generation Artificial Intelligence" Project (No. 2020AAA0104100).

References

1. Beck, A., Teboulle, M.: A fast iterative shrinkage-thresholding algorithm for linear inverse problems. SIAM J. Imag. Sci. **2**(1), 183–202 (2009)
2. Cooley, J.W., Lewis, P.A., Welch, P.D.: The fast Fourier transform and its applications. IEEE Trans. Educ. **12**(1), 27–34 (1969)
3. Ghani, M.U., Karl, W.C.: Fast enhanced CT metal artifact reduction using data domain deep learning. IEEE Trans. Comput. Imaging **6**, 181–193 (2019)
4. Gjesteby, L., et al.: Deep neural network for CT metal artifact reduction with a perceptual loss function. In: Proceedings of the Fifth International Conference on Image Formation in X-ray Computed Tomography (2018)
5. Gjesteby, L., Yang, Q., Xi, Y., Zhou, Y., Zhang, J., Wang, G.: Deep learning methods to guide CT image reconstruction and reduce metal artifacts. In: Proceedings of the SPIE Conference on Medical Imaging: Physics of Medical Imaging, vol. 10132, p. 101322W (2017)
6. Huang, X., Wang, J., Tang, F., Zhong, T., Zhang, Y.: Metal artifact reduction on cervical CT images by deep residual learning. Biomed. Eng. Online **17**(1), 1–15 (2018)
7. Kalender, W.A., Hebel, R., Ebersberger, J.: Reduction of CT artifacts caused by metallic implants. Radiology **164**(2), 576–577 (1987)
8. Liao, H., et al.: Generative mask pyramid network for CT/CBCT metal artifact reduction with joint projection-sinogram correction. In: International Conference on Medical Image Computing and Computer Assisted Intervention, pp. 77–85 (2019)
9. Liao, H., Lin, W.A., Zhou, S.K., Luo, J.: ADN: artifact disentanglement network for unsupervised metal artifact reduction. IEEE Trans. Med. Imaging **39**(3), 634–643 (2019)

10. Lin, W.A., et al.: DuDoNet: dual domain network for CT metal artifact reduction. In: Proceedings of the IEEE/CVF Conference on Computer Vision and Pattern Recognition, pp. 10512–10521 (2019)
11. Liu, P., et al.: Deep learning to segment pelvic bones: large-scale CT datasets and baseline models. Int. J. Comput. Assist. Radiol. Surg. **16**(5), 749–756 (2021). https://doi.org/10.1007/s11548-021-02363-8
12. Lyu, Y., Lin, W.A., Liao, H., Lu, J., Zhou, S.K.: Encoding metal mask projection for metal artifact reduction in computed tomography. In: International Conference on Medical Image Computing and Computer Assisted Intervention, pp. 147–157 (2020)
13. Meyer, E., Raupach, R., Lell, M., Schmidt, B., Kachelrieß, M.: Normalized metal artifact reduction (NMAR) in computed tomography. Med. Phys. **37**(10), 5482–5493 (2010)
14. Park, H.S., Lee, S.M., Kim, H.P., Seo, J.K., Chung, Y.E.: CT sinogram-consistency learning for metal-induced beam hardening correction. Med. Phys. **45**(12), 5376–5384 (2018)
15. Paszke, A., et al.: Automatic differentiation in PyTorch. In: Advances in Neural Information Processing Systems Workshop (2017)
16. Wang, H., Li, Y., He, N., Ma, K., Meng, D., Zheng, Y.: DICDNet: deep interpretable convolutional dictionary network for metal artifact reduction in CT images. IEEE Trans. Med. Imaging **41**(4), 869–880 (2021)
17. Wang, H., Li, Y., Meng, D., Zheng, Y.: Adaptive convolutional dictionary network for CT metal artifact reduction. arXiv preprint arXiv:2205.07471 (2022)
18. Wang, H., et al.: InDuDoNet: an interpretable dual domain network for CT metal artifact reduction. In: International Conference on Medical Image Computing and Computer Assisted Intervention, pp. 107–118 (2021)
19. Wang, H., Li, Y., Zhang, H., Meng, D., Zheng, Y.: InDuDoNet+: a model-driven interpretable dual domain network for metal artifact reduction in CT images. arXiv preprint arXiv:2112.12660 (2021)
20. Wang, J., Zhao, Y., Noble, J.H., Dawant, B.M.: Conditional generative adversarial networks for metal artifact reduction in CT images of the ear. In: International Conference on Medical Image Computing and Computer Assisted Intervention, pp. 3–11 (2018)
21. Wang, T., et al.: Dual-domain adaptive-scaling non-local network for CT metal artifact reduction. In: de Bruijne, M., et al. (eds.) MICCAI 2021. LNCS, vol. 12906, pp. 243–253. Springer, Cham (2021). https://doi.org/10.1007/978-3-030-87231-1_24
22. Xie, Q., Zhao, Q., Xu, Z., Meng, D.: Fourier series expansion based filter parametrization for equivariant convolutions. arXiv preprint arXiv:2107.14519 (2021)
23. Yan, K., et al.: Deep lesion graphs in the wild: Relationship learning and organization of significant radiology image findings in a diverse large-scale lesion database. In: Proceedings of the IEEE Conference on Computer Vision and Pattern Recognition, pp. 9261–9270 (2018)
24. Yu, L., Zhang, Z., Li, X., Xing, L.: Deep sinogram completion with image prior for metal artifact reduction in CT images. IEEE Trans. Med. Imaging **40**(1), 228–238 (2020)
25. Zhang, Y., Yu, H.: Convolutional neural network based metal artifact reduction in X-ray computed tomography. IEEE Trans. Med. Imaging **37**(6), 1370–1381 (2018)
26. Zhou, B., Chen, X., Zhou, S.K., Duncan, J.S., Liu, C.: DuDoDR-Net: dual-domain data consistent recurrent network for simultaneous sparse view and metal artifact reduction in computed tomography. Med. Image Anal. **75**, 102289 (2022)

MRI Reconstruction by Completing Under-sampled K-space Data with Learnable Fourier Interpolation

Qiaoqiao Ding and Xiaoqun Zhang$^{(\boxtimes)}$

Institute of Natural Sciences & School of Mathematical Sciences & MOE-LSC & SJTU-GenSci Joint Lab, Shanghai Jiao Tong University, Shanghai 200240, China
{dingqiaoqiao,xqzhang}@sjtu.edu.cn

Abstract. Magnetic resonance imaging (MRI) acceleration is usually achieved by data undersampling, while reconstruction from undersampled data is a challenging ill-posed problem for data-missing and noisy measurements introduce various artifacts. In recent years, deep learning methods have been extensively studied for MRI reconstruction, and most of work treat the reconstruction problem as a denoising problem or replace the regularization subproblem with a deep neural network (DNN) in an optimization unrolling scheme. In this work, we proposed to directly complete the missing and corrupted k-space data by a specially designed interpolation deep neural networks combined with some convolution layers in both frequency and spatial domains. Specifically, for every missing and corrupted frequency, we use a $K-$ nearest neighbors estimation with learnable weights. Then, two convolution neural networks (CNNs) are applied to regularize the data in both k-space and image space. The proposed DNN structures have clear interpretability for solving this undersampling problem. Extensive experiments on MRI reconstruction with diverse sampling patterns and ratios, under noiseless and noise settings demonstrate the accuracy of the proposed method compared to other learning based algorithms, while being computationally more efficient for both training and reconstruction processes.

Keywords: MRI reconstruction · Deep learning · Compressed sensing · Learnable interpolation

1 Introduction

Magnetic resonance imaging (MRI) is a widely used medical imaging technique in clinical applications. However, the main drawback of MRI is the long acquisition time. In order to accelerate the imaging process, the k-space data can be undersampled by different ratio during the data collection procedure. This

Supplementary Information The online version contains supplementary material available at https://doi.org/10.1007/978-3-031-16446-0_64.

problem is closely related to compressed sensing, i.e., reconstructing the original image from limited Fourier measurements. The compressed sensing MRI (CS-MRI) reconstruction problem [16] can be formulated as

$$y = M \odot \mathcal{F}(x + \varepsilon) \tag{1}$$

where $\varepsilon = n_1 + in_2$, n_1 and n_2 are i.i.d normal distribution of mean zero and s.t.d. σ. Assume that the image $x \in \mathbb{R}^{M \times N}$ and the data $y \in \mathbb{C}^{M \times N}$, $\mathcal{F}$ is Fourier transform, M is a pointwise downsampling mask, and $\odot$ is the pointwise product operator. We define the sampled index set as $\Omega \subset \{1, \cdots M\} \times \{1, \cdots N\}$. Thus $M_{i,j} = 1$ if $(i, j) \in \Omega$ otherwise 0. The main task of CS-MRI is to reconstruct a high quality image x with under-sampled measurement y.

To solve such ill-posed problem, regularization methods with many different priors have been studied extensively, such as total variation (TV) [18], wavelet-based sparsity prior [5], nonlocal sparsity prior [14] and low-rank-based prior [6]. In recent years, deep learning methods have emerged in image restoration area as a prominent tool. Different network architectures, e.g., residual network [7], U-net [17] and generative adversarial network (GAN)/Wasserstein-GAN [23], were designed to process low quality images. Although these methods achieved superior performance in image restoration problems, it is still challenging to recover a high quality images when the training data set is limited and the data contain high level of noise. More recently, optimization unrolling with deep neural network (DNN) have been adopted in medical image reconstruction, such as learned primal dual and ADMM-Net. [1,2,12,15,20,24]. Based on the iterative procedure of optimization algorithm, these methods mainly have two blocks, the inversion block to preliminarily reconstruct an intermediate image and the denoising block to reduce the noises and artifacts. Unrolling methods learn an end-to-end inversion mapping from measurement to the target image [8,10] or the Plug-&-Play method replaces the denoising module with a pre-trained network in the iteration [15]. In traditional MRI reconstruction algorithms, data consistency in k-space is one of the most crucial term. Hence, many of learning methods [11,19,22] use the images as input and output of networks, and the reconstructed images are transformed to the k-space to enforce data consistency. Further, some learning based reconstruction techniques have been designed in Fourier domain. For example, in [13], the k-space data are updated at the masked positions with the measurements during the iteration. In [9], the Fourier domain data are recovered directly by a learnable interpolation kernels for sparse view CT Reconstruction. Different from most approaches, an end-to-end NN from k-space data to image is trained in [26] to represent Fourier transform, which requires a large amount of memory.

As the problem of MRI reconstruction essentially relies on how to complete and correct the missing/corrupted k-space data, this paper aims at developing a deep learning based Fourier interpolation method for MRI image reconstruction. More specifically, we proposed an interpolation scheme in k-space with adaptive interpolating weights trained with DNN. To evaluate the performance of the proposed method, we compare the results with zero-filling method (ZF) [3], TV-

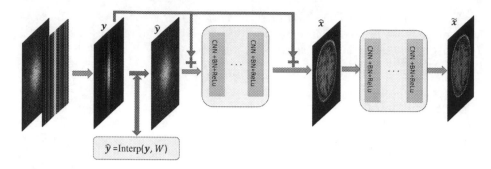

Fig. 1. Diagram of the Proposed method.

regularization-based method [16], ADMM-Net [20], ISTA-net [25] and an essentially plug-&-play methods in [15]. The experiments showed that the proposed method outperformed these methods by a prominent margin quantitatively and visually, while requiring much less training and testing time.

2   Method

In this paper, we proposed a learnable method for k-space data completion and filtering. The basic idea is to interpolate the missing Fourier coefficient using a weighted summation of its neighbors with adaptive weights. Specifically, for the k-space frequency $(i, j), i = 1, \cdots M, j = 1 \cdots N$, we define the $K-$ nearest neighbors set, from sampled index set Ω, as $N_{i,j}$. All the Fourier coefficients can be predicted by a weighted average of its K nearest neighbors $\{y_{i_k, j_k}\}_{k=1}^K$ for $(i_k, j_k) \in N_{i,j}$:

$$\hat{y}_{i,j} = \sum_{k=1}^K W_{i,j}(k) y_{i_k, j_k} \tag{2}$$

where $W_{i,j}(k)$ are learnable weights that are adaptive to different frequencies (i, j). We rewrite the interpolated frequencies vector in (2) as $\hat{y} := \text{Interp}(y, W)$.

With the initial interpolation, all Fourier coefficients are filled in k-space. We then apply convolution neural network (CNN) blocks, i.e. $\text{CNN}_1[\cdot, \theta_1]$ with parameter θ_1, to correct possible prediction errors arising in the interpolation/filtering stage. Specifically, we follow the thought of residual net and add the data y for the interpolation and CNN-based correction results. After the interpolation and CNN-based correction in Fourier domain, the image can be reconstructed by 2D inverse discrete Fourier transform (DFT). By inverse DFT, we obtain a reconstructed image and another CNN-based correction, $\text{CNN}_2[\cdot, \theta_2]$, is applied in image domain for refinement.

In summary, the resulting prediction of the image $\tilde{x}$ can be expressed as

$$\tilde{x} = \text{CNN}_2[\mathcal{F}^{-1}(\text{CNN}_1[\text{Interp}(y, W) + y, \theta_1] + y), \theta_2]. \tag{3}$$

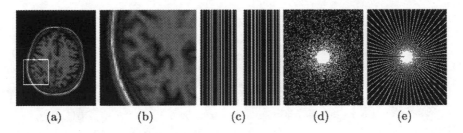

Fig. 2. (a) True Image. (b) ROI. (c) (d) (e) Three different types of sampling masks of sample ratio 20%. (c) 1D Gaussian. (d) 2D Gaussian. (e) radial lines.

We refer to Fig. 1 for the network diagram, where we denote $\hat{\boldsymbol{x}} = \mathcal{F}^{-1}(\text{CNN}_1[\hat{\boldsymbol{y}} + \boldsymbol{y}, \theta_1] + \boldsymbol{y})$. Let $\{\boldsymbol{x}^j, \boldsymbol{y}^j\}_{j=1}^J$ denote the training set with J training samples, where each $(\boldsymbol{x}^j, \boldsymbol{y}^j)$ denotes one pair of true image and k-space measurements. The network is trained by minimizing the following loss function

$$\mathcal{L}(\Theta) = \frac{1}{J} \sum\nolimits_{j=1}^{J} \mu \|\hat{\boldsymbol{x}}^j - \boldsymbol{x}^j\| + \|\tilde{\boldsymbol{x}}^j - \boldsymbol{x}^j\|_2^2, \tag{4}$$

where $\Theta := \{W, \theta_1, \theta_2\}$ denotes the whole set of NN parameters. The balancing parameters μ is set as 0.5 throughout all experiments.

Table 1. MRI reconstruction quantitative comparison (PSNR/SSIM) with ADNI.

Method	Noise	Rate	ZF	TV	ADMM-net	SCAE	SNLAE	GAN	ISTA-Net	Proposed	Difference
Radial	0%	20%	24.36/0.47	30.73/0.86	**32.31**/0.92	32.00/0.92	30.47/0.83	30.13/0.84	21.01/0.64	34.15/0.94	0.84/0.02
		25%	25.45/0.51	32.32/0.90	33.67/0.93	**33.94**/0.94	32.53/0.88	32.26/0.90	23.70/0.74	34.01/0.93	0.07/-0.01
		33%	27.25/0.56	34.60/0.94	35.27/0.94	36.37/0.96	**35.15**/0.92	34.49/0.94	28.05/0.86	34.67/0.91	-1.2/-0.05
	10%	20%	22.18/0.35	24.69/0.49	25.44/0.59	25.52/0.73	**25.98**/0.68	25.02/0.73	19.17/0.47	27.43/0.84	1.45/0.16
		25%	22.38/0.36	25.16/0.49	25.96/0.61	26.13/0.70	**26.38**/0.66	25.53/0.74	20.19/0.57	28.71/0.87	2.33/0.21
		33%	22.37/0.37	25.28/0.49	26.50/0.60	26.64/0.74	26.70/0.65	**26.71**/0.75	22.91/0.69	29.37/0.86	2.66/0.11
2D Gaussian	0%	20%	24.91/0.49	31.69/0.89	**33.81**/0.93	34.24/0.94	31.95/0.86	31.79/0.89	27.00/0.8	32.89/0.92	-1.35/-0.01
		25%	25.30/0.50	32.79/0.90	34.97/0.94	35.61/0.95	32.85/0.86	32.94/0.91	29.77/0.86	**35.31**/0.94	-0.29/-0.01
		33%	26.32/0.53	34.93/0.93	**36.31**/0.95	37.71/0.96	35.33/0.91	35.10/0.94	33.71/0.92	35.89/0.95	-1.8/-0.00
	10%	20%	22.37/0.37	24.97/0.51	25.42/0.61	25.90/0.73	**25.97**/0.67	25.78/0.75	21.67/0.57	27.93/0.84	2.03/0.11
		25%	22.38/0.36	24.92/0.49	25.84/0.60	26.06/0.74	26.15/0.67	**26.31**/0.75	23.78/0.66	28.33/0.83	2.02/0.08
		33%	22.37/0.37	24.91/0.47	26.14/0.56	26.38/0.72	26.41/0.62	**26.48**/0.76	24.87/0.71	28.53/0.87	2.06/0.11
1D Gaussian	0%	20%	22.78/0.61	25.22/0.75	28.53/0.85	**28.79**/0.87	28.73/0.86	27.21/0.81	28.65/0.85	30.77/0.92	1.98/0.05
		25%	23.06/0.62	25.77/0.76	28.99/0.87	29.37/0.88	29.06/0.86	27.47/0.82	**31.72**/0.92	32.18/0.90	0.46/-0.02
		33%	23.86/0.65	27.34/0.81	32.18/0.91	31.25/0.91	30.98/0.89	30.09/0.86	**32.73**/0.95	33.77/0.95	1.05/0.00
	10%	20%	20.72/0.27	22.38/0.39	22.59/0.40	22.22/0.61	**24.52**/0.60	22.76/0.67	23.17/0.67	26.37/0.82	1.85/0.22
		25%	20.37/0.26	22.25/0.37	22.98/0.44	22.72/0.63	24.39/0.56	23.32/0.69	**25.15**/0.75	26.58/0.83	1.43/0.08
		33%	20.37/0.28	22.59/0.37	23.96/0.47	23.75/0.62	24.98/0.58	23.93/0.70	**26.58**/0.79	28.14/0.85	1.56/0.06

3 Experiments

3.1 Results

In our experiments, the MRI images dataset is from ADNI1 (Alzheimer's Disease Neuroimaging Initiative) with Annual 2 Yr and 1.5T scanner, which can be directly downloaded from ADNI website[1]. After standard preprocessing and taking the same slice of 3D images, the dataset consist of 321 slices of size 192×160 (see Fig. 2(a)). We split the data into two parts: 300 slices used for training and 21 slices used for testing. There are three different sampling patterns, namely, 1D Gaussian mask, 2D Gaussian mask and radial mask, and three sampling rates (20%, 25%, 33%) are used for simulating the measurements. The three different types of mask with 20% sampling ratio are shown in Fig. 2(c), 2(d), 2(e). The MRI data were generated by (1), where the σ is set to 0 and 0.1 for noiseless and 10% noisy data.

Through the experiments, $K = 8$ is used for the number of neighborhood for every frequency. For an image of size $M \times N$, the learnable weights, $W^{M \times N \times K}$, are initialized with the normalized distance for every point and learned along with the parameters in CNN. The standard CNN blocks are stacked with the structure Conv→BN→ReLU. For all the Conv layers in the CNN, the kernel size is set as 3×3, and the channel size is set to 128. The block numbers of CNN are set to 15. The NN was implemented with PyTorch on a NVIDIA A100 GPU, and trained by Adam with the momentum parameter $\beta = 0.99$, the mini-batch size being 4, and the learning rate being 10^{-4}. The model was trained for 100 epochs. The convolution weights are initialized with constant matrices and the biases are initialized with zeros. Both peak signal to noise ratio (PSNR) and structural similarity index measure (SSIM) [21] are used for quantitative assessment of image quality. For performance evaluation, we compare our method with the simple zero-filling method (ZF) [3], TV-regularization-based method [16], ADMM-Net [20], a plug-&-play method in [15] with three different networks: SCAE, SNLAE, and GAN, and ISTA-Net [25]. See Table 1 for the quantitative comparison of different methods in terms of PSNR and SSIM. The best results

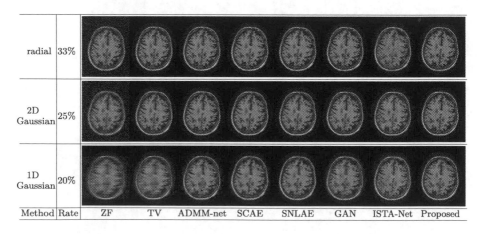

| Method | Rate | ZF | TV | ADMM-net | SCAE | SNLAE | GAN | ISTA-Net | Proposed |

Fig. 3. MRI reconstruction results from noiseless data with radial, 2D Gaussian, 1D Gaussian mask of sampling ratio 33%, 25% and 20% respectively.

---

[1] https://adni.loni.usc.edu/methods/mri-tool/mri-analysis/.

were emphasized in red and the second to the best results were marked in bold. The last column of Table 1 shows the difference between the proposed method and the best of comparison results. It can be seen that deep learning methods noticeably outperformed two non-learning methods, ZF and TV methods in most of cases. For 2D Gaussian mask and radial mask with 33% sample ratio, SCAE is the best performer when measurements are noise-free. In the presence of noise, the proposed method outperformed all the other methods in all settings by a noticeable margin.

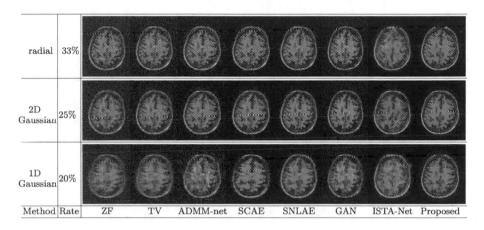

Fig. 4. MRI reconstruction results from 10% noisy data with radial, 2D Gaussian, 1D Gaussian mask of sampling ratio 33%, 25% and 20% respectively.

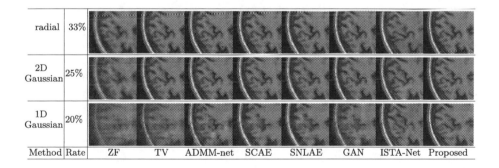

Fig. 5. Zoom-in results in Fig. 3.

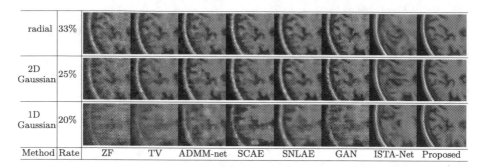

| Method | Rate | ZF | TV | ADMM-net | SCAE | SNLAE | GAN | ISTA-Net | Proposed |

Fig. 6. Zoom-in results in Fig. 4.

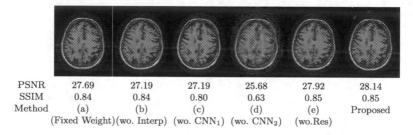

PSNR	27.69	27.19	27.19	25.68	27.92	28.14
SSIM	0.84	0.84	0.80	0.63	0.85	0.85
Method	(a)	(b)	(c)	(d)	(e)	Proposed
	(Fixed Weight)	(wo. Interp)	(wo. CNN_1)	(wo. CNN_2)	(wo.Res)	

Fig. 7. Reconstruction results of different NNs for ablation study.

In Fig. 3 and Fig. 4, we show the visual comparison of different methods on one noise-free and 10% noise case with different sampling patterns, respectively. Figure 5 and Fig. 6 demonstrate the zoomed region of interest (ROI) of boxes in Fig. 2(a) corresponding to Fig. 3 and Fig. 4 respectively. We can clearly see that less artifacts and noise present in our results. Thus, both quantitative and visual comparison showed the advantage of the proposed method over existing solutions to MRI reconstruction, especially in the present of noise.

We note that computational efficiency is another advantage of the proposed method. We compare the training and testing time of the proposed method with one unrolling optimization based method, ADMM-net. As the proposed method is a direct interpolation approach combined with FFTs, the proposed method is much more computational efficient than ADMM-net in both training and testing. In fact, in our experiments, the training time of ADMM-net and the proposed method are 11.5 h (hour) and 0.65 h respectively; for the reconstruction, it takes 0.58 s (seconds) and 0.045 s with ADMM-net and the proposed method respectively.

We further evaluated the proposed method on MICCAI 2015 grand challenge dataset BraTS [4] and compared with ISTA-net. Our numerical results show that our method outperforms ISTA-Net with a large margin. See Table 2 for the quantitative comparison and the visual comparison was included in supplementary material.

Table 2. MRI reconstruction quantitative comparison (PSNR/SSIM) with BraTS.

Noise	Method	0%			10%		
	Rate	33%	25%	20%	33%	25%	20%
Radial	ISTA-Net	24.57/0.81	20.05/0.69	19.98/0.69	21.38/0.72	18.95/0.63	17.08/0.58
	Proposed	39.41/0.98	35.62/0.96	33.41/0.95	29.53/0.92	29.13/0.90	27.70/0.88
2D Gaussian	ISTA-Net	26.75/0.89	25.00/0.78	23.36/0.80	22.26/0.76	22.53/0.73	18.49/0.65
	Proposed	36.36/0.97	36.05/0.97	34.90/0.96	29.21/0.91	28.92/0.90	28.20/0.89
1D Gaussian	ISTA-Net	27.03/0.93	23.95/0.91	24.18/0.87	21.61/0.81	21.97/0.80	21.82/0.74
	Proposed	31.87/0.95	30.68/0.92	31.03/0.92	26.63/0.85	25.85/0.83	26.54/0.85

We note that most of methods (such as ADMM-net, ISTA-Net) for MRI reconstruction are trained with 2D slices, including ours. In the supplementary file, we provided a comparison on reconstruction of whole 3D volume from BraTS, and it shows that the reconstruction quality still outperforms ISTA-Net. Visually, we observe much less artifacts along the slice direction, therefore we believe that our method can be directly used for 3D volume reconstruction for clinical practice.

3.2 Ablation Study

The ablation study conducted focuses on how the following four component impact the performance of image reconstruction: (1) the interpolation, learnable W vs. fixed Weight, (2) Fourier domain CNN-based correction, (3) image domain CNN-based correction and (4) the residual connection. In summary, we compare the performance of the proposed model with the following five models,

$$(a) \quad \tilde{x} = \text{CNN}_2[\mathcal{F}^{-1}(\text{CNN}_1[\text{Interp}(y, W_{fix}) + y, \theta_1] + y), \theta_2]$$

$$(b) \quad \tilde{x} = \text{CNN}_2[\mathcal{F}^{-1}(\text{CNN}_1[y, \theta_1] + y), \theta_2]$$

$$(c) \quad \tilde{x} = \text{CNN}_2[\mathcal{F}^{-1}(\text{Interp}(y, W)), \theta_2]$$

$$(d) \quad \tilde{x} = \mathcal{F}^{-1}(\text{CNN}_1[\text{Interp}(y, W), \theta_1])$$

$$(e) \quad \tilde{x} = \text{CNN}_2[\mathcal{F}^{-1}(\text{CNN}_1[\text{Interp}(y, W), \theta_1]), \theta_2].$$

Through the whole ablation study, all the different methods are trained by the same procedure on the same training dataset and tested on the same testing dataset. We tested on 10% noisy data downsampled by 1D Guassian mask with 33% sample ratio. See Fig. 7 for the comparison results by the different NNs. Based on 10-fold cross validation, it shows the proposed four components are essential for the high quality of reconstruction. Further, an ablation study for different size of neighborhood K was performed and these results were provided in supplementary file.

4   Conclusions

In this paper, we developed a deep learning method for MRI reconstruction by directly filling and filtering the missing and corrupted frequencies in k-space. The proposed NN structure is rather simple and has clear interpretation. The numerical results demonstrated the advantages on the efficiency and accuracy of this method with the comparison to other learning and non-learning based methods, especially in the presence of noise. The proposed method only involves one pair of FFT and IFFT, compared to multiple evaluations of forward and backward operators for unrolling and plug&play based methods. This results in an efficient scheme for both training and inference. The experiments on two datasets (ADNI and BraTS) showed the effectiveness of this network structure. We evaluate the performance on 3D volume and it show that our method can be still applied for 3D volume reconstruction for clinical practice.

Acknowledgment. This work was supported by Shanghai Municipal Science and Technology Major Project (2021SHZDZX0102) and NSFC (No. 12090024).

References

1. Adler, J., Öktem, O.: Learned primal-dual reconstruction. IEEE Trans. Med. Imaging **37**(6), 1322–1332 (2018)
2. Aggarwal, H.K., Mani, M.P., Jacob, M.: MoDL: model-based deep learning architecture for inverse problems. IEEE Trans. Med. Imaging **38**(2), 394–405 (2018)
3. Bernstein, M.A., Fain, S.B., Riederer, S.J.: Effect of windowing and zero-filled reconstruction of MRI data on spatial resolution and acquisition strategy. J. Magn. Reson. Imaging Off. J. Int. Soc. Magn. Reson. Med. **14**(3), 270–280 (2001)
4. Menze, B.H., et al.: The multimodal brain tumor image segmentation benchmark (BRATS). IEEE Trans. Med. Imaging **34**(10), 1993–2024 (2015)
5. Cai, J.F., Dong, B., Osher, S., Shen, Z.: Image restoration: total variation, wavelet frames, and beyond. J. Am. Math. Soc. **25**(4), 1033–1089 (2012)
6. Cai, J.F., Jia, X., Gao, H., Jiang, S.B., Shen, Z., Zhao, H.: Cine cone beam CT reconstruction using low-rank matrix factorization: algorithm and a proof-of-principle study. IEEE Trans. Med. Imaging **33**(8), 1581–1591 (2014)
7. Chen, H., et al.: Low-dose CT with a residual encoder-decoder convolutional neural network. IEEE Trans. Med. Imaging **36**(12), 2524–2535 (2017)
8. Ding, Q., Chen, G., Zhang, X., Huang, Q., Ji, H., Gao, H.: Low-dose CT with deep learning regularization via proximal forward-backward splitting. Phys. Med. Biol. **65**(12), 125009 (2020)
9. Ding, Q., Ji, H., Gao, H., Zhang, X.: Learnable multi-scale fourier interpolation for sparse view CT image reconstruction. In: de Bruijne, M., et al. (eds.) MICCAI 2021. LNCS, vol. 12906, pp. 286–295. Springer, Cham (2021). https://doi.org/10.1007/978-3-030-87231-1_28
10. Ding, Q., Nan, Y., Gao, H., Ji, H.: Deep learning with adaptive hyper-parameters for low-dose CT image reconstruction. IEEE Trans. Comput. Imaging **7**, 648–660 (2021). https://doi.org/10.1109/TCI.2021.3093003
11. Eo, T., Jun, Y., Kim, T., Jang, J., Lee, H.J., Hwang, D.: KIKI-net: cross-domain convolutional neural networks for reconstructing undersampled magnetic resonance images. Magn. Reson. Med. **80**(5), 2188–2201 (2018)

12. Hammernik, K., et al.: Learning a variational network for reconstruction of accelerated MRI data. Magn. Reson. Med. **79**(6), 3055–3071 (2018)

13. Hyun, C.M., Kim, H.P., Lee, S.M., Lee, S., Seo, J.K.: Deep learning for undersampled MRI reconstruction. Phys. Med. Biol. **63**(13), 135007 (2018). https://doi.org/10.1088/1361-6560/aac71a

14. Jia, X., Lou, Y., Dong, B., Tian, Z., Jiang, S.: 4D computed tomography reconstruction from few-projection data via temporal non-local regularization. In: Jiang, T., Navab, N., Pluim, J.P.W., Viergever, M.A. (eds.) MICCAI 2010. LNCS, vol. 6361, pp. 143–150. Springer, Heidelberg (2010). https://doi.org/10.1007/978-3-642-15705-9_18

15. Liu, J., Kuang, T., Zhang, X.: Image reconstruction by splitting deep learning regularization from iterative inversion. In: Frangi, A.F., Schnabel, J.A., Davatzikos, C., Alberola-López, C., Fichtinger, G. (eds.) MICCAI 2018. LNCS, vol. 11070, pp. 224–231. Springer, Cham (2018). https://doi.org/10.1007/978-3-030-00928-1_26

16. Lustig, M., Donoho, D., Pauly, J.M.: Sparse MRI: the application of compressed sensing for rapid MR imaging. J. Magn. Reson. Imaging Off. J. Int. Soc. Magn. Reson. Med. **58**(6), 1182–1195 (2007)

17. Ronneberger, O., Fischer, P., Brox, T.: U-Net: convolutional networks for biomedical image segmentation. In: Navab, N., Hornegger, J., Wells, W.M., Frangi, A.F. (eds.) MICCAI 2015. LNCS, vol. 9351, pp. 234–241. Springer, Cham (2015). https://doi.org/10.1007/978-3-319-24574-4_28

18. Rudin, L.I., Osher, S., Fatemi, E.: Nonlinear total variation based noise removal algorithms. Physica D **60**(1–4), 259–268 (1992)

19. Schlemper, J., Caballero, J., Hajnal, J.V., Price, A.N., Rueckert, D.: A deep cascade of convolutional neural networks for dynamic MR image reconstruction. IEEE Trans. Med. Imaging **37**(2), 491–503 (2017)

20. Sun, J., Li, H., Xu, Z., et al.: Deep ADMM-Net for compressive sensing MRI. In: Advances in Neural Information Processing Systems, vol. 29 (2016)

21. Wang, Z., Bovik, A.C., Sheikh, H.R., Simoncelli, E.P.: Image quality assessment: from error visibility to structural similarity. IEEE Trans. Image Process. **13**(4), 600–612 (2004)

22. Yang, G., et al.: DAGAN: deep de-aliasing generative adversarial networks for fast compressed sensing MRI reconstruction. IEEE Trans. Med. Imaging **37**(6), 1310–1321 (2017)

23. Yang, Q., et al.: Low-dose CT image denoising using a generative adversarial network with Wasserstein distance and perceptual loss. IEEE Trans. Med. Imaging **37**(6), 1348–1357 (2018)

24. Yang, Y., Sun, J., Li, H., Xu, Z.: ADMM-CSNet: a deep learning approach for image compressive sensing. IEEE Trans. Pattern Anal. Mach. Intell. **42**(3), 521–538 (2018)

25. Zhang, J., Ghanem, B.: ISTA-Net: interpretable optimization-inspired deep network for image compressive sensing. In: 2018 IEEE/CVF Conference on Computer Vision and Pattern Recognition (CVPR) (2017)

26. Zhu, B., Liu, J.Z., Cauley, S.F., Rosen, B.R., Rosen, M.S.: Image reconstruction by domain-transform manifold learning. Nature **555**(7697), 487–492 (2018)

Learning-Based and Unrolled Motion-Compensated Reconstruction for Cardiac MR CINE Imaging

Jiazhen Pan[1(✉)], Daniel Rueckert[1,2], Thomas Küstner[3],
and Kerstin Hammernik[1,2]

[1] Klinikum Rechts der Isar, Technical University of Munich, Munich, Germany
`jiazhen.pan@tum.de`
[2] Department of Computing, Imperial College London, London, UK
[3] Medical Image and Data Analysis (MIDAS.lab), University Hospital of Tübingen, Tübingen, Germany

Abstract. Motion-compensated MR reconstruction (MCMR) is a powerful concept with considerable potential, consisting of two coupled sub-problems: Motion estimation, assuming a known image, and image reconstruction, assuming known motion. In this work, we propose a learning-based self-supervised framework for MCMR, to efficiently deal with non-rigid motion corruption in cardiac MR imaging. Contrary to conventional MCMR methods in which the motion is estimated prior to reconstruction and remains unchanged during the iterative optimization process, we introduce a dynamic motion estimation process and embed it into the unrolled optimization. We establish a cardiac motion estimation network that leverages temporal information via a group-wise registration approach, and carry out a joint optimization between the motion estimation and reconstruction. Experiments on 40 acquired 2D cardiac MR CINE datasets demonstrate that the proposed unrolled MCMR framework can reconstruct high quality MR images at high acceleration rates where other state-of-the-art methods fail. We also show that the joint optimization mechanism is mutually beneficial for both sub-tasks, i.e., motion estimation and image reconstruction, especially when the MR image is highly undersampled.

1 Introduction

Cardiac magnetic resonance imaging (CMR) plays an essential role in evidence-based diagnostic of cardiovascular disease [16] and serves as the gold-standard for assessment of cardiac morphology and function [18]. High-quality cardiac

---

T. Küstner and K. Hammernik—Contributed equally.

Supplementary Information The online version contains supplementary material available at https://doi.org/10.1007/978-3-031-16446-0_65.

image reconstruction with high spatial and temporal resolution is an inevitable prerequisite for this assessment. Shorter scan times with higher spatio-temporal resolution are desirable in this scenario. However, this requires high acceleration rates which in turn is only achievable if sufficient spatio-temporal information linked by the cardiac motion is shared during reconstruction.

A large variety of CMR reconstruction methods have been dedicated to cope with cardiac motion during the reconstruction. They can be categorized into two sections: Implicit and explicit motion correction. Implicit motion correction during the reconstruction sidesteps the non-rigid cardiac motion estimation, which still remains one of the most challenging problems in CMR. Most research in this section focused either on exploiting spatio-temporal redundancies in complementary domains [14,30], enforcing sparseness/low-rankness along these dimensions [13,19,26], or improving the spatio-temporal image regularization in an unrolled optimization model [17,31]. Yet in this sense, motion is only implicitly corrected without knowing or estimating the true underlying motion.

Motion can also be explicitly corrected during the reconstruction by applying motion estimation/registration models. The work of Batchelor et al. [6] has pioneered the field of motion-compensated MR reconstruction (MCMR). It proposed the idea of embedding the motion information as an explicit general matrix model into the MR reconstruction process and demonstrated some successful applications in leg and brain reconstruction. However, in CMR, the respiratory and cardiac motion is much more complex and therefore a more sophisticated motion model is required. Some endeavours were made first in the field of coronary magnetic resonance angiography (CMRA) to compensate respiratory motion [7,9] in which non-rigid motion models based on cubic B-Splines were employed [15,21]. However, these conventional registrations require substantial computation times in the order of hours making the practical implementation of image reconstruction infeasible. More recently, learning-based registration methods [4,5,28] have been proposed, which leverage trained neural networks to accelerate the estimation in inference. In [29] these learned registrations are embedded into a CMRA reconstruction for an unrolled CG-SENSE optimization [27] with a denoiser regularizer [1]. However, MCMR has been rarely studied in the context of cardiac CINE imaging [8].

MCMR can be recast as two codependent and intertwined sub-optimization problems: Image reconstruction and motion estimation. This stands in contrast to methods in which only the MR image is optimized [7–9,29], whereas the motion is pre-computed and assumed to be fixed during the whole optimization process. A reliable reconstruction relies on precise motion estimation, while the accuracy of the motion prediction is subject to the quality of images. Odille et al. [23,24] introduced an iterative, alternating approach to solve this problem. Concurrently, [3,32] proposed to solve this joint optimization problem by leveraging variational methods. However, to the best of our knowledge, this problem has not been formulated and explored using deep learning-based approaches. Furthermore, as algorithm unrolling has been successfully applied in modern reconstruction approaches [1,11] by learning image regularization from data, the possibility to unroll the MCMR optimization with motion estimation networks has not been explored.

In this work, we introduce a deep learning-based and unrolled MCMR framework to reconstruct CMR images in the presence of motion. The highlights of the work can be summarized as follows: First, we propose an unrolled MCMR optimization process with an embedded group-wise motion estimation network [12]. A joint optimization between the image reconstruction and motion estimation is proposed, while the motion estimation is updated iteratively with the reconstruction progress. Second, in contrast to [7,8,29] our proposed approach does not require a pre-computed motion field, which is usually obtained from initial non-motion compensated reconstruction. Finally, instead of reconstructing only one frame by compensating motion from all frames to one target frame, our proposed method provides a motion-resolved image sequence in which all frames are motion-corrected. The proposed framework was trained and tested on in-house acquired 2D CINE data of 40 subjects and compared to state-of-the-art MCMR methods. The conducted experiments demonstrate that the proposed method outperforms the competing methods especially in high acceleration situations, concluding that embedding the dynamic motion into an unrolled MCMR can drastically improve the reconstruction performance.

2   Methods

Assume that $x^{(t)} \in \mathbb{C}^M$ is the t-th frame of the image sequence $x = [x^{(1)}, \ldots, x^{(N)}]$ with M pixels and $y^{(t)} \in \mathbb{C}^{MQ}$ denotes its corresponding t-th undersampled k-space data with Q coils. In the context of CMR, the MCMR of the whole MR sequence with N temporal frames can be formulated as

$$\min_{x,\mathbf{U}} \sum_{t_1=1}^{N} \sum_{t_2=1}^{N} \left\| \mathbf{A}^{(t_2)} \mathbf{U}^{(t_1 \to t_2)} x^{(t_1)} - y^{(t_2)} \right\|_2^2, \tag{1}$$

where $\mathbf{A}^{(t)}$ denotes the MR multi-coil encoding operator with $\mathbf{A}^{(t)} = \mathbf{D}^{(t)} \mathbf{F} \mathbf{C}$ for coil-sensitivity maps $\mathbf{C}$, Fourier transform $\mathbf{F}$ and the undersampling matrix $\mathbf{D}$. Based on the idea of [6], we build a motion matrix $\mathbf{U}^{(t_1 \to t_2)}$ representing the warping from the temporal frame t_1 to t_2, which is obtained from the estimated motion fields $u^{(t_1 \to t_2)}$ (introduced in Sect. 2.2).

In traditional MCMR [7,8,29], only the images x are optimized, whereas the motion is pre-computed from initial (non-motion compensated) reconstructed images just for once and assumed to be constant during the whole optimization process. However, motion estimation on the initial motion-corrupted and artifact-degraded images can be inaccurate, incurring error-propagation during the optimization. Therefore, a joint optimization as proposed in [24] for image x and motion $\mathbf{U}$ as described in Eq. 1 is desired.

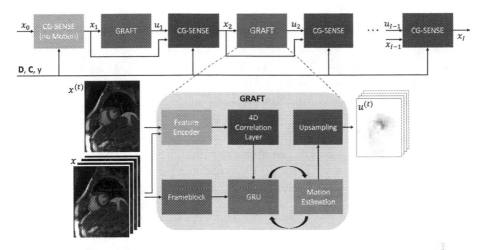

Fig. 1. The proposed unrolled MCMR framework. A dynamic joint optimization is performed between the image reconstruction in the CG-SENSE block and the motion correction from the motion estimator GRAFT. GRAFT is a group-wise motion estimation network leveraging the temporal redundancy to conduct a 1-to-N motion estimation. This estimation is carried out N times to accomplish an N-to-N motion correction for all temporal frames.

2.1   Motion-Compensated Image Reconstruction Framework

In this work we unroll the MCMR in Eq. 1 with a motion estimation network and apply the joint optimization between the image reconstruction and motion estimation. The framework is illustrated in Fig. 1. First, the zero-filled undersampled image sequence x_0 is fed to the conjugate gradient SENSE block [27] along with y, $\mathbf{C}$, and $\mathbf{D}$. The first SENSE block conducts a reconstruction without motion embedding. Afterwards, the reconstructed image sequence x_1 is passed to a motion estimation network (GRAFT, introduced in Sect. 2.2) as inputs and the first motion sequence u_1 comprising of all pairs of motion frames is predicted. This motion sequence is then applied to the input together with y, $\mathbf{C}$ and $\mathbf{D}$ in the next CG-SENSE block, while the previous reconstruction is used as a regularization. These CG-SENSE blocks solve Eq. 1 with an additional ℓ_2 regularization by the image from the previous step and output a motion-corrected image sequence with temporarily freezing $\mathbf{U}_{i-1}$ and x_{i-1}, following

$$x_i = \arg\min_x \sum_{t_1=1}^{N} \sum_{t_2=1}^{N} \left\| \mathbf{A}^{(t_2)} \mathbf{U}_{i-1}^{(t_1 \to t_2)} x^{(t_1)} - y^{(t_2)} \right\|_2^2 + \frac{1}{2\lambda} \left\| x - x_{i-1} \right\|_2^2. \quad (2)$$

This alternating scheme is carried out for I iterations. The motion estimation difficulty of GRAFT is alleviated gradually with the progress of this alternating scheme along with the image-quality improvement.

2.2   Motion Estimation Network

There exists various motion estimation approaches in the field of medical imaging. In this work, we select GRAFT [12] for motion estimation, which takes the full image sequence x together with the target frame $x^{(t)}$ as inputs to predict the motion sequence $u^{(t)} = \left[u^{(t \to 1)}, \ldots, u^{(t \to N)} \right]$ for all N frames. GRAFT is suitable to be embedded into our framework due to its accuracy, speed and efficiency.

Accuracy. An accurate motion estimation is the essential requirement for the unrolled MCMR framework. GRAFT contains a 4D correlation layer and iterative Gated Recurrent Unit (GRU) blocks to conduct precise motion predictions. It has shown superior results compared to conventional registration methods [12]. Furthermore, it is a group-wise estimation network considering all temporal frames and has a dedicated frameblock leveraging temporal redundancies to mitigate the impact of through-plane-motion. Because of this group-wise attribute, temporal coherence can be instilled during the training by appending temporal regularization in the loss function.

Speed. Since the motion registration is invoked at each iteration step and for all pairs of motion frames, a fast motion estimation method is required. The reconstruction of N frames involves N^2 motion predictions. In this context, traditional registration-based methods such as [15,34] require hours to perform N^2 calculations, rendering them impractical for our framework. In contrast, GRAFT only requires a few seconds to estimate the motion of all pairs.

Efficiency. For end-to-end learning over all iterative stages, the losses and gradients need to be accumulated. In the context that N^2 calculations (and for multiple iterations) are entailed, the training of large network architectures with more than 20 million trainable parameters [5,28] becomes infeasible due to their vast GPU memory footprint (>48 GB). In contrast, GRAFT has only 5 million trainable parameters circumventing the GPU overcharge problems.

In order to use GRAFT for motion estimation and integrate it in our unrolled framework we define the following loss function to train GRAFT:

$$
\mathcal{L}_i = \sum_{t_1=1}^{N} \sum_{t_2=1}^{N} \left\| \rho \left(\mathbf{U}_i^{(t_1 \to t_2)} x_{gt}^{(t_1)} - x_{gt}^{(t_2)} \right) \right\|_1
$$
$$
+ \alpha \sum_{t_1=1}^{N} \sum_{t_2=1}^{N} \sum_{d \in x,y} \left\| \nabla_d u_i^{(t_1 \to t_2)} \right\|_1 + \beta \sum_{t_1=1}^{N} \left\| \nabla_t u_i^{(t_1)} \right\|_1. \tag{3}
$$

The first term ensures data fidelity during the training. We warp the ground-truth frame $x_{gt}^{(t_1)}$ to the target ground-truth frame $x_{gt}^{(t_2)}$ using the motion $u_i^{(t_1 \to t_2)}$, which is predicted from GRAFT based on the previously reconstructed image x_{i-1}. It should be noted that we apply the ground-truth frame in the loss function to train GRAFT, so that GRAFT is forced to learn and extract genuine correlations from the undersampled images and that any motion falsely originating from image artifacts are not rewarded. The Charbonnier function $\rho(x) = (x^2 + 10^{-12})^{0.45}$ [25,33] is employed as the penalty function. Additional regularization terms for the spatial plane weighted by α and along the temporal axis weighted by β are included in the loss to mitigate estimation singularities and to ensure motion coherence in spatial and temporal domain. This loss is calculated after every unrolled motion estimation step with progressive exponential weight decay $\mathcal{L}_{total} = \sum_{i=1}^{I} \gamma^{I-i} \mathcal{L}_i$.

3   Experiments

Training was carried out on 35 subjects (a mix of patients and healthy subjects) of in-house acquired short-axis 2D CINE CMR, whereas testing was performed on 5 subjects. Data were acquired with 30/32/34 multiple receiver coils and 2D balanced steady-state free precession sequence on a 1.5T MR (Siemens Acra with TE = 1.06 ms, TR = 2.12 ms, resolution = 1.9 × 1.9 mm^2 with 8mm slice thickness, 8 breath-holds of 15 s duration). Image sequence size varies from 176 × 132 (smallest) to 192 × 180 (largest) with 25 temporal cardiac phases. A stack of 12 slices along the long axis was collected, resulting in 304/15 image sequence (2D+t) for training/test, while the apical slices without clear cardiac contour were excluded.

The proposed framework with GRAFT as the embedded motion estimator was trained on an NVIDIA A40 GPU with AdamW [20] (batch size of 1, learning rate 1e–4 and weight decay of 1e 5). The number of unrolled iterations is set to 3 during training, but this can be flexibly adapted during inference and iterations are stopped when the peak signal to noise ratio (PSNR) converges (PSNR increment < 0.1). The trainable weights of GRAFT are shared during the iterative optimization. The hyperparameters α, β, γ and λ were set to 10, 10, 0.6 and 2 respectively. Three trainings and tests were conducted separately on retrospectively undersampled images with VISTA [2] of R = 8, 12 and 16 acceleration without any prior reconstruction or prior motion correction as conducted in [7,8,29]. During the training and testing, raw multi-coil k-space data were used for the reconstruction. We compare the proposed approach with non-motion compensated CG-SENSE (N-CG-SENSE) reconstruction and with non-iterative MCMR methods. In the latter case, the motion is pre-computed from GRAFT [12] and Elastix [15] and set to be constant during the whole optimization process.

4   Results and Discussion

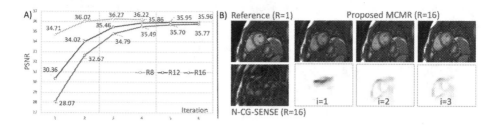

Fig. 2. Quantitative and qualitative results of proposed MCMR method. **A**) Performance measured by peak signal to noise ratio (PSNR) for increasing unrolled iteration numbers over all test subjects and temporal frames for retrospective undersampling with R = 8, 12 and 16. **B**) Qualitative image quality of the proposed MCMR at R = 16 over the first three iterations (i = 1,2,3) in comparison to the non-motion compensated CG-SENSE (N-CG-SENSE) at R = 16 and the fully-sampled reference image (R = 1).

Figure 2A reveals the relation between the estimation performance (indicated by averaged PSNR over all test subjects and temporal frames) and the unrolled iteration number of the proposed framework during inference for R = 8, 12 and 16. The reconstruction accuracy is improved with increasing iteration numbers for all three cases. The reconstruction for R = 12 and R = 16 benefit most from our framework and obtain a significant performance lifting for the first three iterations. The advantage of unrolling the motion estimator in the joint MCMR optimization process is qualitatively illustrated in Fig. 2B, in which the MR image is highly undersampled with R = 16. Not only is the image quality improved with the course of the iteration, but the motion estimator can also deliver more precise and detailed estimation by virtue of the higher quality image. A full qualitative analysis with R = 8 and 12 is shown in Supplementary Fig. S1. Furthermore, the motion estimation based on unprocessed and artifact-affected images (from high undersampling rates) is challenging. We also trained GRAFT without the proposed unrolled optimization framework [12] to generalize for motion estimation from images with different undersampling rates. However, training started to fail for accelerations R = 12 and beyond. In contrast, training difficulty is reduced if we embed GRAFT into the proposed joint optimization framework while the image quality is restored with the progress of the optimization. This makes GRAFT capable of estimating meaningful motion as showcased in Supplementary Fig. S1 for R = 12 and even for R = 16. Moreover, this mechanism also introduces a data augmentation process while more high-quality data is generated during training.

A comparison study of the proposed MCMR to N-CG-SENSE and CG-SENSE reconstruction with pre-computed motion based on GRAFT and Elastix is shown in Fig. 3. The training of GRAFT alone failed for R = 12 and 16, whereas motion estimation with Elastix for R = 16 was not conducted due to the poor

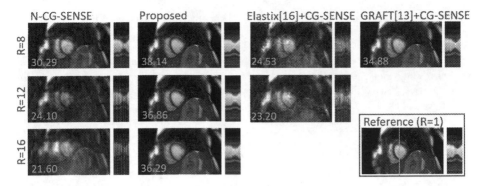

Fig. 3. Qualitative reconstruction performance of CINE CMR in spatial (x–y) and spatio-temporal (y–t) plane of non-motion compensated CG-SENSE (N-CG-SENSE), proposed MCMR at third iteration, CG-SENSE with pre-estimated motion from GRAFT and Elastix, for different acceleration rates R = 8, 12 and 16 in comparison to the fully-sampled (R = 1) reference. The selected superior-inferior (y-axis) is marked with a blue line in the reference image. The obtained PSNR in comparison to the fully-sampled reference is shown at the bottom left. The highly accelerated cases for Elastix/GRAFT + CG-SENSE did not converge therefore results are not shown. (Color figure online)

quality results collected at R = 12. The results are shown after the third iteration for the proposed MCMR, providing an optimal trade-off between time and performance. Our approach restores the undersampled MR sequence with high quality without artifacts in spatial and temporal domain. A quantitative analysis over all test subjects including reconstruction of all 25 temporal frames is shown in Table 1. Although the execution time of our approach is longer than the original GRAFT if the iteration is set > 1, an overall more precise reconstruction is achieved. Furthermore, the overall reconstruction is within acceptable clinical durations. The proposed MCMR enables to reconstruct an undersampled image with a much higher acceleration rate and offers the high flexibility to perform the reconstruction depending on different time/performance requirement.

The proposed MCMR framework also has some limitations: Currently, the proposed MCMR cannot guarantee that the estimated motion is diffeomorphic. The possibility to integrate the scaling and squaring layer [10] to ensure diffeomorphic motion estimation will be investigated in future work. Furthermore, we have not studied the interaction between our explicit motion correction framework with implicit motion correction (denoising) networks, which is also subject to future work. Moreover, we plan to evaluate the performance of our method on prospectively undersampled data in the future. Finally, the hyper-parameters applied in this work are estimated empirically and they might not be the optimal combination. Integration of the learnable hyper-parameters tuning [22] will be considered in our next step.

Table 1. Quantitative analysis of reconstruction for accelerated CINE CMR (R = 8, 12 and 16) using the proposed MCMR method, non-motion compensated CG-SENSE (N-CG-SENSE), GRAFT+CG-SENSE and Elastix+CG-SENSE. Peak signal-to-noise ratio (PSNR) and structural similarity index (SSIM) [35] are used to evaluate all test subjects. Their mean value, standard deviations are shown next to the respective methods execution times. The best results are marked in bold. The failed or inferior experiments are marked with 'N.A.'.

Acc R	Methods	SSIM	PSNR	Time (s)
8	Proposed MCMR	**0.943** (0.018)	**36.26** (2.22)	18.81 s
	GRAFT [12] + CG-SENSE	0.913 (0.019)	34.93 (1.80)	6.27 s
	Elastix [15] + CG-SENSE	0.645 (0.057)	25.04 (2.10)	4281 s
	N-CG-SENSE	0.821 (0.038)	30.80 (2.15)	1.37 s
12	Proposed MCMR	**0.932** (0.018)	**35.45** (2.00)	18.81 s
	GRAFT + CG-SENSE	N.A	N.A	6.27 s
	Elastix + CG-SENSE	0.568 (0.072)	23.51 (2.20)	4281 s
	N-CG-SENSE	0.637 (0.062)	24.40 (2.39)	1.37 s
16	Proposed MCMR	**0.927** (0.019)	**34.78** (1.86)	18.81 s
	GRAFT + CG-SENSE	N.A	N.A	6.27 s
	Elastix + CG-SENSE	N.A	N.A	4281 s
	N-CG-SENSE	0.531 (0.08)	21.736 (2.45)	1.37 s

5   Conclusion

In this work, we proposed a deep learning-based MCMR framework and studied it in CINE CMR imaging. We explored the possibility to unroll the MCMR optimization with a motion estimation network while a dynamic joint optimization between the reconstruction and the motion estimation is carried out. Although this idea is still at a nascent stage, its potential in high quality reconstruction of highly accelerated data can be appreciated. The conducted experiments against baseline methods showcased a rapid, more robust and more precise reconstruction of our proposed framework.

Acknowledgements. This work was supported in part by the European Research Council (Grant Agreement no. 884622).

References

1. Aggarwal, H.K., Mani, M.P., Jacob, M.: Model based image reconstruction using deep learned priors (MODL). In: IEEE International Symposium on Biomedical Imaging (ISBI), pp. 671–674 (2018)
2. Ahmad, R., Xue, H., Giri, S., et al.: Variable density incoherent spatiotemporal acquisition (VISTA) for highly accelerated cardiac MRI. Magn. Reson. Med. **74**(5), 1266–1278 (2015)

3. Aviles-Rivero, A.I., Debroux, N., Williams, G., et al.: Compressed sensing plus motion (CS + M): a new perspective for improving undersampled MR image reconstruction. Med. Image Anal. **68**, 101933 (2021)
4. Balakrishnan, G., Zhao, A., Sabuncu, M.R., et al.: An unsupervised learning model for deformable medical image registration. In: 2018 IEEE/CVF Conference on Computer Vision and Pattern Recognition, pp. 9252–9260 (2018)
5. Balakrishnan, G., Zhao, A., Sabuncu, M.R., et al.: Voxelmorph: a learning framework for deformable medical image registration. IEEE Trans. Med. Imaging **38**(8), 1788–1800 (2019)
6. Batchelor, P., Atkinson, D., Irarrazaval, P., Hill, D., et al.: Matrix description of general motion correction applied to multishot images. Magn. Reson. Med. **54**, 1273–1280 (2005)
7. Bustin, A., Rashid, I., Cruz, G., et al.: 3D whole-heart isotropic sub-millimeter resolution coronary magnetic resonance angiography with non-rigid motion-compensated prost. J. Cardiovasc. Magn. Reson. **22**(1) (2020)
8. Cruz, G., Hammernik, K., Kuestner, T., et al.: One-heartbeat cardiac cine imaging via jointly regularized non-rigid motion corrected reconstruction. In: Proceedings of International Society for Magnetic Resonance in Medicine (ISMRM), p. 0070 (2021)
9. Cruz, G., Atkinson, D., Henningsson, M., et al.: Highly efficient nonrigid motion-corrected 3D whole-heart coronary vessel wall imaging. Magn. Reson. Med. **77**(5), 1894–1908 (2017)
10. Dalca, A.V., Balakrishnan, G., Guttag, J., Sabuncu, M.R.: Unsupervised learning of probabilistic diffeomorphic registration for images and surfaces. Med. Image Anal. **57**, 226–236 (2019)
11. Hammernik, K., Klatzer, T., Kobler, E., et al.: Learning a variational network for reconstruction of accelerated MRI data. Magn. Reson. Med. **79**(6), 3055–3071 (2018)
12. Hammernik, K., Pan, J., Rueckert, D., Küstner, T.: Motion-guided physics-based learning for cardiac MRI reconstruction. In: Asilomar Conference on Signals, Systems, and Computers (2021)
13. Huang, W., Ke, Z., Cui, Z.X., et al.: Deep low-rank plus sparse network for dynamic MR imaging. Med. Image Anal. **73**, 102190 (2021)
14. Jung, H., Sung, K., Nayak, K.S., et al.: k-t FOCUSS: a general compressed sensing framework for high resolution dynamic MRI. Magn. Reson. Med. **61**(1), 103–116 (2009)
15. Klein, S., Staring, M., Murphy, K., et al.: Elastix: a toolbox for intensity-based medical image registration. IEEE Trans. Med. Imaging **29**(1), 196–205 (2009)
16. von Knobelsdorff-Brenkenhoff, F., Pilz, G., Schulz-Menger, J.: Representation of cardiovascular magnetic resonance in the AHA/ACC guidelines. J. Cardiovasc. Magn. Reson. **19**(1), 1–21 (2017)
17. Küstner, T., Fuin, N., Hammernik, K., et al.: CINENet: deep learning-based 3D cardiac CINE MRI reconstruction with multi-coil complex-valued 4D spatio-temporal convolutions. Sci. Rep. **10**(1), 1–13 (2020)
18. Lee, D., Markl, M., Dall'Armellina, E., et al.: The growth and evolution of cardiovascular magnetic resonance: a 20-year history of the society for cardiovascular magnetic resonance (SCMR) annual scientific sessions. J. Cardiovasc. Magn. Reson. **20**(1) (2018)
19. Liu, F., Li, D., Jin, X., et al.: Dynamic cardiac MRI reconstruction using motion aligned locally low rank tensor (MALLRT). Magn. Reson. Imaging **66**, 104–115 (2020)

20. Loshchilov, I., Hutter, F.: Decoupled weight decay regularization. arXiv preprint arXiv:1711.05101 (19) (2017)

21. Modat, M., Ridgway, G.R., Taylor, Z.A., et al.: Fast free-form deformation using graphics processing units. Comput. Methods Programs Biomed. **98**(3), 278–284 (2010)

22. Mok, T.C.W., Chung, A.C.S.: Conditional deformable image registration with convolutional neural network. In: de Bruijne, M., et al. (eds.) MICCAI 2021. LNCS, vol. 12904, pp. 35–45. Springer, Cham (2021). https://doi.org/10.1007/978-3-030-87202-1_4

23. Odille, F., Vuissoz, P., Marie, P., Felblinger, J.: Generalized reconstruction by inversion of coupled systems (GRICS) applied to free-breathing MRI. Magn. Reson. Med. **60**, 146–157 (2008)

24. Odille, F., Menini, A., Escanyé, J.M., et al.: Joint reconstruction of multiple images and motion in MRI: application to free-breathing myocardial t_2 quantification. IEEE Trans. Med. Imaging **35**(1), 197–207 (2016)

25. Pan, J., Rueckert, D., Küstner, T., Hammernik, K.: Efficient image registration network for non-rigid cardiac motion estimation. In: Haq, N., Johnson, P., Maier, A., Würfl, T., Yoo, J. (eds.) Machine Learning for Medical Image Reconstruction, pp. 14–24 (2021)

26. Poddar, S., Jacob, M.: Dynamic MRI using smoothness regularization on manifolds (SToRM). IEEE Trans. Med. Imaging **35**(4), 1106–1115 (2016)

27. Pruessmann, K.P., Weiger, M., Börnert, P., Boesiger, P.: Advances in sensitivity encoding with arbitrary k-space trajectories. Magn. Reson. Med. **46**, 638–651 (2001)

28. Qi, H., Fuin, N., Cruz, G., et al.: Non-rigid respiratory motion estimation of whole-heart coronary MR images using unsupervised deep learning. IEEE Trans. Med. Imaging **40**(1), 444–454 (2021)

29. Qi, H., Hajhosseiny, R., Cruz, G., et al.: End-to-end deep learning nonrigid motion-corrected reconstruction for highly accelerated free-breathing coronary MRA. Magn. Reson. Med. **86**(1), 1983–1996 (2021)

30. Qin, C., Duan, J., Hammernik, K., et al.: Complementary time-frequency domain networks for dynamic parallel MR image reconstruction. Magn. Reson. Med. **86**(6), 3274–3291 (2021)

31. Sandino, C.M., Lai, P., Vasanawala, S.S., Cheng, J.Y.: Accelerating cardiac cine MRI using a deep learning-based ESPIRiT reconstruction. Magn. Reson. Med. **85**(1), 152–167 (2021)

32. Schmoderer, T., Aviles-Rivero, A.I., Corona, V., et al.: Learning optical flow for fast MRI reconstruction. Inverse Probl. **37**(9), 095007 (2021)

33. Sun, D., Yang, X., Liu, M., Kautz, J.: PWC-Net: CNNs for optical flow using pyramid, warping, and cost volume. In: IEEE Conference on Computer Vision and Pattern Recognition (CVPR), pp. 8934–8943 (2018)

34. Vercauteren, T., Pennec, X., Perchant, A., Ayache, N.: Diffeomorphic demons: efficient non-parametric image registration. Neuro Image **45**(1), S61–S72 (2009)

35. Wang, Z., Bovik, A.C., Sheikh, H.R., Simoncelli, E.P.: Image quality assessment: from error visibility to structural similarity. IEEE Trans. Image Process. **13**(4), 600–612 (2004)

Accelerated Pseudo 3D Dynamic Speech MR Imaging at 3T Using Unsupervised Deep Variational Manifold Learning

Rushdi Zahid Rusho[1]([✉]) [ID], Qing Zou[2] [ID], Wahidul Alam[1] [ID],
Subin Erattakulangara[1] [ID], Mathews Jacob[2] [ID], and Sajan Goud Lingala[1,3] [ID]

[1] Roy J. Carver Department of Biomedical Engineering, The University of Iowa,
Iowa City, IA 52242, USA
rushdizahid-rusho@uiowa.edu
[2] Department of Electrical and Computer Engineering, The University of Iowa,
Iowa City, IA 52242, USA
[3] Department of Radiology, The University of Iowa, Iowa City, IA 52242, USA

Abstract. Magnetic resonance imaging (MRI) of vocal tract shaping and surrounding articulators during speaking is a powerful tool in several application areas such as understanding language disorder, informing treatment plans in oro-pharyngeal cancers. However, this is a challenging task due to fundamental tradeoffs between spatio-temporal resolution, organ coverage, and signal-to-noise ratio. Current volumetric vocal tract MR methods are either restricted to image during sustained sounds, or does dynamic imaging at highly compromised spatio-temporal resolutions for slowly moving articulators. In this work, we propose a novel unsupervised deep variational manifold learning approach to recover a "pseudo-3D" dynamic speech dataset from sequential acquisition of multiple 2D slices during speaking. We demonstrate "pseudo-3D" (or time aligned multi-slice 2D) dynamic imaging at a high temporal resolution of 18 ms capable of resolving vocal tract motion for arbitrary speech tasks. This approach jointly learns low-dimensional latent vectors corresponding to the image time frames and parameters of a 3D convolutional neural network based generator that generates volumes of the deforming vocal tract by minimizing a cost function which enforce: a) temporal smoothness on the latent vectors; b) l_1 norm based regularization on generator weights; c) latent vectors of all the slices to have zero mean and unit variance Gaussian distribution; and d) data consistency with measured k-space v/s time data. We evaluate our proposed method using in-vivo vocal tract airway datasets from two normal volunteers producing repeated speech tasks, and compare it against state of the art 2D and 3D dynamic compressed sensing (CS) schemes in speech MRI. We finally demonstrate (for the first time) extraction of quantitative 3D vocal tract area functions from under-sampled 2D multi-slice datasets to characterize vocal tract shape changes in 3D during speech production. Code: https://github.com/rushdi-rusho/varMRI.

Supplementary Information The online version contains supplementary material available at https://doi.org/10.1007/978-3-031-16446-0_66.

Keywords: Manifold learning · Dynamic 3D speech MRI ·
Unsupervised learning · Variational autoencoder · Accelerated MRI

1   Introduction

Dynamic magnetic resonance imaging of the upper-airway anatomy during speech production is a powerful tool to safely assess vocal tract shaping. It allows to resolve the kinematics of articulators (e.g. lips, tongue, velum, glottis, epiglottis), and has several application areas including understanding phonetics of language, assessing language disorders, informing treatment plans in oropharyngeal cancers [5,12,14,17]. However, a long standing challenge with MRI is its slow acquisition nature resulting in fundamental tradeoffs between the achievable spatio-temporal resolutions, spatial coverage, and signal-to-noise ratio. Approaches based on under-sampling the k-space v/s time (k-t) space coupled with model-based reconstruction have been proposed [2,4,6,10,13,15]. Notably, models exploiting l_1 norm sparsity under spatio-temporal finite differences [13], and low rank structure of the image time series, or both [4] have been applied. However, these assumptions breakdown while modeling rapid arbitrary speech motion patterns, and typically result in motion artifacts, and spatio-temporal blurring. 3D dynamic MRI for full vocal tract coverage is further challenging due to the need of encoding the extra spatial dimension. Current schemes are either restricted to image during sustained sounds (i.e. when the vocal tract motion is "frozen") [6,10], or does dynamic imaging at highly compromised spatio-temporal resolutions for slowly moving articulators (e.g. [11]).

In this work, we propose a novel unsupervised deep variational manifold learning approach to reconstruct a pseudo-3D dynamic speech dataset at a high native time resolution (of 18 ms) from sequential acquisition of sparse (k-t) measurements of multiple 2D slices. Our approach is inspired from the recent success of generative manifold models in free breathing ungated cardiac MRI [23,24]. In this paper, we systematically extend it to the problem of dynamic speech MRI. We jointly learn low-dimensional latent vectors corresponding to the image time frames and parameters of a 3D convolutional neural network (CNN)-based generator that generates volumes of deforming vocal tract by minimizing a cost function which enforce: a) temporal smoothness on the latent vectors; b) l_1 norm based regularization on generator weights; c) latent vectors of all slices to have zero-mean and unit variance Gaussian distribution, thus facilitating the slice alignment; and d) data consistency with measured k-space v/s time data.

Our approach has several advantages over state-of-the-art fast speech MRI schemes. **1)** In contrast to existing spatio-temporal models [2,4,13,15] that are limited to model rapid, and arbitrary speech motion patterns, we use an implicit motion resolved reconstruction strategy by exploiting the smoothness of the image time series on a manifold. This ensures distant image frames sharing the same vocal tract posture are mapped as neighbors on the manifold. **2)** In contrast to current 2D dynamic speech MRI approaches that reconstructs slices independently [2,13,15], resulting in full vocal tract motion to be out of synchrony across slices, we propose to jointly recover all the slices as a time aligned multi-slice 2D (or pseudo-3D) dataset. This ensures interpretation of full vocal tract organ motion in 3D, and allows for quantitative extraction of vocal tract area functions to characterize speech patterns. **3)** In contrast to existing model-based deep learning MRI reconstruction schemes that are reliant on fully sampled training datasets (e.g. [1,16]), our approach does not need to rely on training data, and reconstructs the image time series only from the measured under-sampled (k-t) data.

2   Methods

The overall framework of our proposed scheme for pseudo-3D dynamic speech MRI reconstruction is illustrated in Fig. 1. We propose to recover the time aligned multi-slice (or pseudo-3D) dynamic image time series dataset ($\mathbf{V}_{s,t}$) from sequentially acquired sparsely sampled spiral (k-t) space data ($\mathbf{y}_{s,t}$) of multiple 2D slices, where s and t respectively denotes the slice and time dimensions. Latent vectors ($l_{s,t}$) of sth slice and t^{th} frame are fed into a CNN-based generator ($\mathcal{G}_\omega$) which outputs ($\mathbf{V}_{s,t}$). These latent vectors capture the underlying vocal tract motion patterns, and are sampled from a time varying Gaussian probability distribution space with mean $\mu_{s,t}$ and diagonal covariance matrix $\mathbf{\Sigma}_{s,t}$. The operator ($\mathcal{F}_{s,t}$), selects s^{th} slice and t^{th} frame from ($\mathbf{V}_{s,t}$) and performs multi-coil Fourier undersampling operation. The loss function involves joint estimation of the generator parameters ω, latent vector space distribution parameters $\mu_{s,t}, \mathbf{\Sigma}_{s,t}$ subject to data consistency with the measured k-t space data [24]:

$$Loss(\omega, \mu_{s,t}, \mathbf{\Sigma}_{s,t}) = \mathcal{C}(\omega, \mu_{s,t}, \mathbf{\Sigma}_{s,t}) + \lambda_1 \|\omega\|_1 + \lambda_2 \sum_{s=1}^{M} \|\nabla_{s,t}(\mu_{s,t})\|_2^2; \quad (1)$$

$$C(\omega, \mu_{s,t}, \mathbf{\Sigma}_{s,t}) = \sum_{s=1}^{M} \sum_{t=1}^{N} \|\mathcal{F}_{s,t}(\mathcal{G}_\omega(l_{s,t})) - \mathbf{y}_{s,t}\|_2^2 + \sigma^2 K(l_{s,t}) \quad (2)$$

$$K(l_{s,t}) = \frac{1}{2} \left[-\log(\det(\mathbf{\Sigma}_{s,t})) - q + trace(\mathbf{\Sigma}_{s,t}) + \mu_{s,t}^T \mu_{s,t} \right] \quad (3)$$

M and N represents the total number of slices and time frames respectively. The second term in (1) penalizes the generator weight so that the training of generator is stable. The third term in (1) enforces the latent vectors to vary smoothly along time by penalizing its l_2 norm under the temporal gradient (∇_t) operation. The first term in (2) enforces consistency with the measured k-t data. The second term in (2) represents KL divergence between the distribution of latent vector $l_{s,t}$ and normal distribution with zero mean and unit covariance: $\mathcal{N}(\mathbf{0}, \mathbf{I})$, where $\mathbf{I}$ denotes the identity matrix. q in (3) indicates the dimension of the latent vector space (or the number of each latent vector components). The KL divergence term ensures the motion across all slices in $l_{s,t}$ are at the same scale. Note that the latent vectors have much lower dimension than the total number of pixels in an image time frame (e.g. $q = 20$ used in this work in comparison

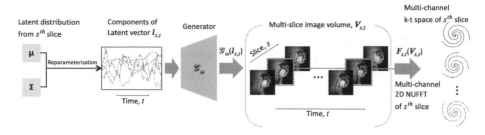

Fig. 1. The proposed pseudo-3D variational manifold speech MRI reconstruction scheme. Low dimensional latent vectors characterizing the motion patterns in the data set are jointly learnt along with the parameters of a 3D convolutional neural network based generator in an unsupervised manner subject to data consistency. The generator outputs a time aligned multi-slice (or pseudo-3D) image time series depicting the deforming vocal tract, and this is compared to the multi-channel multi-slice raw (k-t) space data via the Fourier under-sampling operator.

to $168 \times 168 = 28,224$ pixels in a spatial frame). The free parameters of the proposed variational manifold optimization are the regularization parameters λ_1, λ_2, σ, and need to be determined empirically.

3   Experiments and Results

3.1   In-vivo MRI Data Acquisition

Experiments were performed on a 3T GE Premier scanner using a custom 16 channel airway coil on two normal subjects producing a variety of speaking tasks. The subjects were scanned in accordance to our institute's review board protocol, and informed consent were obtained from the subjects prior to the study. Subjects were scanned while producing two different speech tasks: a) repetitions of interleaved consonants and vowel sounds by repeatedly uttering the phrase "za-na-za-loo-lee-laa", and b) repeated counting of numbers (1 to 5) at the subject's natural pace. A gradient echo based variable density spiral sampling with golden angle view ordering was used to sequentially (one after the other) acquire multiple 2D slices in the mid sagittal plane. Relevant sequence parameters were: Field of view (FOV in cm^2) = 20 × 20, flip angle = 5°, TR = 6 ms, spatial resolution (mm^2) = 2.4 × 2.4, slice thickness = 6 mm, number of slices = 10, spiral interleaves required for Nyquist sampling = 27, readout points = 335, readout duration = 1.3 ms, acquisition time per slice = 16.2 s; total scan time = 162 s. Raw k-t data from the ten slices were sorted at a time resolution of 18 ms/frame (i.e. 3 spiral interleaves/frame), and passed to the proposed variational manifold reconstruction pipeline.

We also compared our approach with two state-of-the-art dynamic upper airway MRI schemes: a) the 2D compressed sensing (2D CS) approach of [13] which reconstructs the above spiral 2D multi-slice data from each slice independently

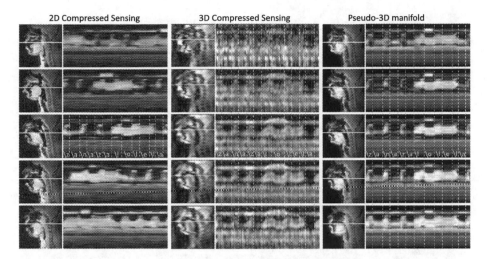

Fig. 2. Reconstruction evaluation: shown here are representative sagittal frames along with the image time profiles (cut through the white solid line) from 2D CS, 3D CS, and the proposed pseudo-3D manifold reconstructions on the speech task of repeatedly producing the phrase "za-na-za-loo-lee-laa". Note, 2D CS image time profiles are out of synchrony, and also exhibits temporal stair casing artifacts. 3D CS depict the vocal tract motion in synchrony across the slices, however contains significant unresolved alias energy. In contrast, the proposed pseudo-3D manifold approach recovers a time aligned dataset with high spatio-temporal fidelity.

via the l_1 sparsity based temporal finite difference constraint and b) a 3D compressed sensing (3D CS) scheme that employs 3D under-sampled acquisition on a Cartesian grid coupled with temporal finite difference constraint [7,9]. For the latter, we implemented an under-sampled Cartesian 3D GRE sequence where the ky-kz plane was prospectively under-sampled at an acceleration factor of 20 fold using a variable density spiral view order to achieve a time resolution of 40 ms [3]. Other sequence parameters were FOV (cm^3) = 20 × 20 × 6, flip angle = 5°, TR = 2 ms, image matrix size = 84 × 84 × 10; readout in the superior-inferior direction. For all of the proposed pseudo-3D manifold, 2D CS, and 3D CS schemes, prior to reconstruction, we coil compressed the raw k-t data into 8 virtual channels via a PCA based coil compression, and estimated coil sensitivity maps based on the time averaged data using the ESPIRiT algorithm [22].

3.2 Implementation of the Reconstruction Algorithms

In the proposed pseudo-3D manifold scheme, the CNN generator consisted of 2D convolution blocks followed by nonlinear activation and upsampling operations. At every time frame, the generator mapped the input latent vector of size $(1 \times 1 \times q)$ to an output 3D volume of size $(168 \times 168 \times 2M)$ for every time frame. The two channel generator output produced a real and imaginary components of the MR image. The generator weights were initialized randomly from a normal

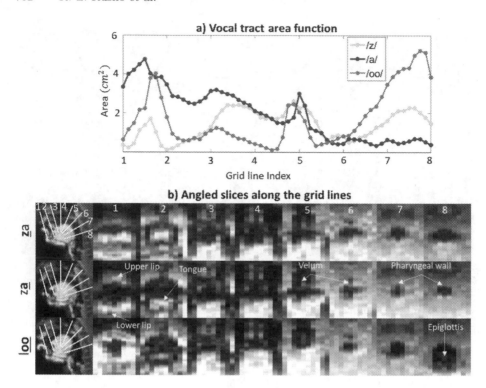

Fig. 3. Representative vocal tract area functions (VAFs) quantitating the vocal tract organ motion in 3D. (a) shows VAFs for representative time frames corresponding to the sounds of /z/ in /za/, /a/ in /za/, and /oo/ in /loo/. (b) shows the underlying vocal tract posture in 8 oblique cuts along the vocal tract airspace from the lips to the glottis. Note, how the shape change in the articulators (e.g. lips, tongue tip, tongue) modulate the vocal tract airspace opening, which is quantitated in the VAFs.

distribution. All activation functions prior to output layer were the leaky ReLU function, while the last layer had the *tanh* function. The generator has a parameter d in the network which controls the number of trainable parameters and we empirically set $d = 60$. The generator architecture is detailed in the supplementary material. We used an ADAM optimizer to solve (1). The free parameter λ_1 was set to 0.0001 and λ_2, σ were set to 1 based on empirical assessment of motion fidelity, particularly at the air tissue interfaces of the tongue tip, tongue base, and velum. Similarly, we empirically evaluated the reconstruction quality as a function of the size of the latent vectors ($q = 1, 2, 5, 15, 20$), and assessed spatio-temporal fidelity. Further details of parameter tuning are provided in the supplementary material. We optimized the network in two stages. In the first stage, we learnt only the generator parameters with a constant time series latent vector for 30 epochs, which resulted in capturing the overall structural anatomy of the upper-airway. In the second stage, both the generator parameters and the latent vector parameters were learnt for 53 epochs. If more epochs were executed, we observed the network to learn noise in the reconstructions, and therefore the stopping criterion was determined empirically by visual inspections of the reconstructions and also keeping most recent loss within 1.15 times that of previous iteration. We performed reconstruction in Python (version 3.9) with the PyTorch library using a CUDA (version 10.2) enabled machine: Intel(R) Xeon(R) Gold 6130 CPU, 2.10 GHz with a NVIDIA GeForce RTX 2080Ti GPU. The execution time of an epoch was approximately 110 s. The source code of this work can be found at https://github.com/rushdi-rusho/varMRI.

2D spiral CS reconstruction, and 3D Cartesian CS reconstruction both with temporal finite difference sparsity constraints were implemented in the Berkeley Advanced Reconstruction ToolBox (BART) computing environment [21] on the same machine above. The regularization parameter was set to 0.1, which was obtained using the approach of L curve optimization rule [13].

3.3   Vocal Tract Area Function (VAF) Extraction

The pseudo-3D dynamic image time series from the proposed variational manifold reconstruction were passed through a post-processing pipeline to extract the vocal tract area functions (VAFs) [19,20]. The VAFs quantify the area of the vocal tract airspace starting from the lips to the glottis (see Fig. 3). First, in the mid-sagittal orientation, an airway center line is first determined by a semi automatic air-tissue detection algorithm [8]. Next, grid lines perpendicular to the airway centerline are laid in the mid-sagittal plane, and oblique cuts corresponding to these grid lines are extracted from pseudo-3D image data at each time frame. A total of 8 grid lines were drawn equally spaced starting from the lips to the glottis along the vocal tract. The length of the angled slices were kept fixed to 30 pixels. From each of these angled oblique slices, we compute the airway area enclosed by articulator boundaries using a region growing algorithm [18]. Region growing was executed independently for each of the angled slices at each time frame and the corresponding seed points were automatically selected as intersection of the airway centerline in the mid-sagittal plane, and the oblique slices. We performed VAF evaluations in the MATLAB computing environment (version R2020b) on the same machine above.

4   Results

Figure 2 shows comparisons of the proposed pseudo-3D manifold reconstructions from representative 5 slices centered around the mid-sagittal slice against 2D CS multi-slice reconstructions, and matched slices from the 3D CS reconstruction. The figure shows the reconstructions corresponding to the repetitive speech task of uttering the phrase "za-na-za-loo-lee-laa". From the image time series of the 2D CS reconstructions, we observe a) out of synchrony of the articulatory motion patterns across slices, and b) classic finite difference related motion blurring artifacts manifesting as temporal stair casing (patchy artifacts along time). While the motion is in synchrony across slices in the 3D CS reconstruction, the images contain large amount of unresolved alias artifacts, and blurred air-tissue boundaries. In contrast, the proposed pseudo-3D manifold reconstructions depict time synchronized motion of the vocal tract across slices, crisp dynamic images with high spatial and temporal fidelity, and minimal artifacts.

Figure 3(a) shows representative VAFs for the sounds of /z in /za/, /a in /za/ and /o in /oo/. Figure 3(b) shows the corresponding angled oblique cuts along the vocal tract from the lips to glottis. Note, the subtle articular dynamics in 3D are well captured in these cuts. For example, the tongue tip hitting the alveolar ridge during the production of /z/ sound closes the vocal tract air space and is captured in oblique cut number 2 in the first row of Fig. 3(b). As another example, the wider opening in the vocal tract air-space between the back of the tongue and the pharyngeal wall just above the epiglottis (see oblique cuts at grid lines 7 and 8) during the production of /oo/ sound compared to the /aa/ sound is well depicted in the VAFs. Note these VAFs are time varying, and can reveal articulator interactions, and has potential to provide new insights to speech production.

5   Discussion and Conclusion

We proposed a novel pseudo-3D dynamic speech MRI reconstruction scheme that recovers time aligned multi-slice image time series from sequential acquisition of under-sampled (k-t) space measurements of multiple 2D slices. Using prospectively under-sampled in-vivo data from two speakers, we showed significant improvements against existing 2D and 3D dynamic CS approaches in terms of improved image quality and interpretation of complex speech motion in 3D. We showed for the first time extraction of 3D vocal tract area functions from under-sampled multi-slice 2D dynamic data.

In this work, we did not acquire subject's speech audio recordings during MRI data acquisition. A future scope would be to concurrently acquire such audio information, and leverage it in the latent vectors to further improve the acceleration for better image quality (e.g. improve the resolution along the slice direction). A recent review (e.g. [12]) laid out the spatial, temporal resolution requirements for various speech tasks based on consensus of several speech scientists, and linguists. With prospective under-sampling, we did not have a ground truth to compare the reconstructions against, and therefore our evaluation in this work was qualitative in terms of visually assessing the motion of the air-tissue interfaces, and alias artifacts. However, current researchers employ different strategies to address this lack of gold standard reference/ground truth issue. These strategies include a) constructing well-defined dynamic physical phantoms (e.g. representing vocal tract shaping), which may be imaged separately with a high resolution reference method such as dynamic CT, and b) seeking image quality ratings from expert end users (e.g. linguists, radiologists) to objectively assess spatial, temporal blurring, and alias artifacts. In the future, a more comprehensive analysis is needed in terms of image quality evaluation from expert end users (e.g. linguists, radiologists).

Acknowledgements. This work was conducted on an MRI instrument funded by NIH-S10 instrumentation grant: 1S10OD025025-01. We also acknowledge Yongwan Lim (University of Southern California, USA) for providing example code for vocal tract area function estimation.

References

1. Aggarwal, H.K., Mani, M.P., Jacob, M.: MoDL: model-based deep learning architecture for inverse problems. IEEE Trans. Med. Imaging **38**(2), 394–405 (2018)
2. Burdumy, M., et al.: Acceleration of MRI of the vocal tract provides additional insight into articulator modifications. J. Magn. Reson. Imaging **42**(4), 925–935 (2015)
3. Cheng, J.Y., Zhang, T., Alley, M.T., Lustig, M., Vasanawala, S.S., Pauly, J.M.: Variable-density radial view-ordering and sampling for time-optimized 3d cartesian imaging. In: Proceedings of the ISMRM Workshop on Data Sampling and Image Reconstruction (2013)
4. Fu, M., et al.: High-resolution dynamic speech imaging with joint low-rank and sparsity constraints. Magn. Reson. Med. **73**(5), 1820–1832 (2015)
5. Iltis, P.W., Frahm, J., Voit, D., Joseph, A.A., Schoonderwaldt, E., Altenmüller, E.: High-speed real-time magnetic resonance imaging of fast tongue movements in elite horn players. Quant. Imaging Med. Surg. **5**(3), 374 (2015)
6. Isaieva, K., Laprie, Y., Leclère, J., Douros, I.K., Felblinger, J., Vuissoz, P.A.: Multimodal dataset of real-time 2d and static 3d MRI of healthy French speakers. Sci. Data **8**(1), 1–9 (2021)
7. Javed, A., Kim, Y.C., Khoo, M.C., Ward, S.L.D., Nayak, K.S.: Dynamic 3-d MR visualization and detection of upper airway obstruction during sleep using region-growing segmentation. IEEE Trans. Biomed. Eng. **63**(2), 431–437 (2015)
8. Kim, J., Kumar, N., Lee, S., Narayanan, S.: Enhanced airway-tissue boundary segmentation for real-time magnetic resonance imaging data. In: International Seminar on Speech Production (ISSP), pp. 222–225. Citeseer (2014)
9. Kim, Y.C., Lebel, R.M., Wu, Z., Ward, S.L.D., Khoo, M.C., Nayak, K.S.: Real-time 3d magnetic resonance imaging of the pharyngeal airway in sleep apnea. Magn. Reson. Med. **71**(4), 1501–1510 (2014)
10. Lim, Y., et al.: A multispeaker dataset of raw and reconstructed speech production real-time MRI video and 3d volumetric images. Sci. Data **8**(1), 1–14 (2021)
11. Lim, Y., Zhu, Y., Lingala, S.G., Byrd, D., Narayanan, S., Nayak, K.S.: 3d dynamic MRI of the vocal tract during natural speech. Magn. Reson. Med. **81**(3), 1511–1520 (2019)
12. Lingala, S.G., Sutton, B.P., Miquel, M.E., Nayak, K.S.: Recommendations for real-time speech MRI. J. Magn. Reson. Imaging **43**(1), 28–44 (2016)
13. Lingala, S.G., Zhu, Y., Kim, Y.C., Toutios, A., Narayanan, S., Nayak, K.S.: A fast and flexible MRI system for the study of dynamic vocal tract shaping. Magn. Reson. Med. **77**(1), 112–125 (2017)
14. Miquel, M.E., Freitas, A.C., Wylezinska, M.: Evaluating velopharyngeal closure with real-time MRI. Pediatr. Radiol. **45**(6), 941–942 (2015)
15. Niebergall, A., et al.: Real-time MRI of speaking at a resolution of 33 ms: under-sampled radial flash with nonlinear inverse reconstruction. Magn. Reson. Med. **69**(2), 477–485 (2013)

16. Sandino, C.M., Lai, P., Vasanawala, S.S., Cheng, J.Y.: Accelerating cardiac cine MRI using a deep learning-based ESPIRiT reconstruction. Magn. Reson. Med. **85**(1), 152–167 (2021)
17. Scott, A.D., Wylezinska, M., Birch, M.J., Miquel, M.E.: Speech MRI: morphology and function. Phys. Med. **30**(6), 604–618 (2014)
18. Skordilis, Z.I., Toutios, A., Töger, J., Narayanan, S.: Estimation of vocal tract area function from volumetric magnetic resonance imaging. In: 2017 IEEE International Conference on Acoustics, Speech and Signal Processing (ICASSP), pp. 924–928. IEEE (2017)
19. Story, B.H., Titze, I.R., Hoffman, E.A.: Vocal tract area functions from magnetic resonance imaging. J. Acoust. Soc. Am. **100**(1), 537–554 (1996)
20. Story, B.H., Titze, I.R., Hoffman, E.A.: Vocal tract area functions for an adult female speaker based on volumetric imaging. J. Acoust. Soc. Am. **104**(1), 471–487 (1998)
21. Tamir, J.I., Ong, F., Cheng, J.Y., Uecker, M., Lustig, M.: Generalized magnetic resonance image reconstruction using the Berkeley advanced reconstruction toolbox. In: ISMRM Workshop on Data Sampling and Image Reconstruction, Sedona, AZ (2016)
22. Uecker, M., et al.: ESPIRiT–an eigenvalue approach to autocalibrating parallel MRI: where SENSE meets GRAPPA. Magn. Reson. Med. **71**(3), 990–1001 (2014)
23. Zou, Q., Ahmed, A.H., Nagpal, P., Kruger, S., Jacob, M.: Dynamic imaging using a deep generative SToRM (Gen-SToRM) model. IEEE Trans. Med. Imaging **40**(11), 3102–3112 (2021)
24. Zou, Q., Ahmed, A.H., Nagpal, P., Priya, S., Schulte, R., Jacob, M.: Variational manifold learning from incomplete data: application to multislice dynamic MRI. IEEE Trans. Med. Imaging (in press)

FSE Compensated Motion Correction for MRI Using Data Driven Methods

Brett Levac[✉], Sidharth Kumar, Sofia Kardonik, and Jonathan I. Tamir

The University of Texas at Austin, Austin, TX 78705, USA
{blevac,sidharth.kumar,sofia.kardonik,jtamir}@utexas.edu

Abstract. Magnetic Resonance Imaging (MRI) is a widely used medical imaging modality boasting great soft tissue contrast without ionizing radiation, but unfortunately suffers from long acquisition times. Long scan times can lead to motion artifacts, for example due to bulk patient motion such as head movement and periodic motion produced by the heart or lungs. Motion artifacts can degrade image quality and in some cases render the scans nondiagnostic. To combat this problem, prospective and retrospective motion correction techniques have been introduced. More recently, data driven methods using deep neural networks have been proposed. As a large number of publicly available MRI datasets are based on Fast Spin Echo (FSE) sequences, methods that use them for training should incorporate the correct FSE acquisition dynamics. Unfortunately, when simulating training data, many approaches fail to generate accurate motion-corrupt images by neglecting the effects of the temporal ordering of the k-space lines as well as neglecting the signal decay throughout the FSE echo train. In this work, we highlight this consequence and demonstrate a training method which correctly simulates the data acquisition process of FSE sequences with higher fidelity by including sample ordering and signal decay dynamics. Through numerical experiments, we show that accounting for the FSE acquisition leads to better motion correction performance during inference.

Keywords: Motion correction · Deep learning · Magnetic resonance imaging · Fast spin echo

1 Introduction

MRI is a powerful medical imaging modality due to its superb soft tissue contrast which can help in diagnosing various types of pathology. However, unlike imaging methods that use ionizing radiation such as CT, MRI is predominantly slow,

---

B. Levac and S. Kumar—Equal contribution.

Supplementary Information The online version contains supplementary material available at https://doi.org/10.1007/978-3-031-16446-0_67.

L. Wang et al. (Eds.): MICCAI 2022, LNCS 13436, pp. 707–716, 2022.
https://doi.org/10.1007/978-3-031-16446-0_67

and each MRI scan can take several minutes to acquire. This is because the MRI acquisition involves repeated application of signal excitation through radio-frequency (RF) pulses and signal reception using spatially varying magnetic field gradients. Due to physical limitations including signal decay, only a small number of measurements in k-space can be acquired in a single excitation, and a duration (called the repetition time, TR) must pass before the MRI signal resets to equilibrium or steady state. As a result, multiple excitations are needed to fully sample k-space. Patient motion during the scan therefore commonly occurs, and leads to degraded image quality [22]. If the degradation is not too severe the image might still be useful for clinical diagnosis. However, oftentimes, the motion is so severe that the image is nondiagnostic, and the scan needs to be repeated. It has been reported that motion-corrupted scans lead hospitals to incur nearly $365K in additional costs each year [22].

Due to the high associated cost, many methods have been proposed to mitigate and correct for motion [8]. A common approach to reduce motion is to modify the acquisition and change the sampling pattern and ordering so that the motion artifacts are incoherent, as is the case for non-Cartesian radial sampling [26]. Prospective motion correction during the scan is also possible using external sources such as respiratory bellows, nuclear magnetic resonance probes [7], optical and electromagnetic tracking [3], and wireless RF tones [16], or through self-navigators [4]. However, prospective motion correction in some cases reduces scan efficiency, as motion-corrupt measurements must be re-acquired with additional RF excitations. Retrospective motion correction is also popular [5,13], as it relies on computational processing during reconstruction in lieu of reducing scan efficiency.

Recently, data-driven approaches to retrospective motion correction have increased in popularity due to the rising success of deep learning and the availability of public MRI datasets with raw k-space [27]. These approaches are attractive as they do not require sequence modification, external hardware, or explicit knowledge of the motion information, and instead use a large corpus of training data to learn motion artifact removal. The motion removal can be posed as either supervised or self-supervised learning, in which a motion-corrupt image is "denoised" based on a motion-free reference. Many works that follow this paradigm simulate motion effects by corrupting k-space lines through linear phase augmentation and rotation [12].

When simulating motion artifacts for data driven motion correction, the ground truth k-space is divided into non-overlapping regions which are taken from different motion states of the underlying image. This structure of motion-corruption reflects the fact that in FSE scans the time between phase encode lines in different repetition times (TR) (inter-TR time) is much longer than the time between echoes in a single TR (intra-TR time) and thus motion is roughly simulated as being inter-TR and not occurring between lines in the same echo train. Many of the publicly available datasets are acquired using fast spin-echo (FSE) imaging [1,2,17,27], in which multiple k-space lines are rapidly acquired per RF excitation through the use of RF refocusing pulses. Therefore, the specific phase encode lines, their ordering, and signal decay modulation are all pre-determined by the acquisition parameters and the tissue relaxation parameters. In this setting it is often the case that when retrospectively applying motion to different lines of k-space the phase encode lines are grouped into non-overlapping subsets which are agnostic to the sampling pattern that was used to collect the data. This approach is fundamentally incorrect as it neglects the fact that signal decay is occurring within each echo train of the ground truth FSE image and thus training on such data will lead to inconsistent results when applying data driven methods to actual FSE data.

In this work, we propose a method for simulating synthetic motion artifacts that accounts for the echo ordering and signal decay present in FSE acquisitions, and we highlight the disparity in performance that occurs when training on simulated data that is agnostic to the acquisition parameters.

1.1   Related Works

In the case of retrospective motion correction with unknown motion, both physics and learning based methods have been proposed. Authors in [6] showed that by modeling the forward model of in-plane motion, an alternating minimization approach can be used to solve for both the parameterized motion model and the motion-free image. Similarly, authors in [10] proposed an algorithm to estimate the rotation and translation operator and used the estimated operator to remove the motion artifacts. Improving on that, the same authors used a convolutional network to first estimate the motion operator and then reconstruct the image with information and data consistency [9]. The work in [15] used image alignment to remove the motion artifacts by inputting multiple images to the network among which one has motion artifacts.

Authors in [19] used an Inception-ResNet based encoder-decoder network to correct motion artifacts, the motion generation method only uses two randomly generated motion states. Whereas [21] proposes a joint image and frequency space inter connected network to remove motion artifacts, the motion artifacts are simulated by drawing translation and rotation parameters from a uniform distribution. Authors in [12] used a Conditional Generative Adversarial Network (GAN) to correct motion-corrupt images which were generated using simulating translation and rotational motions. The considered motion model only used 2 or 3 motion events and the k-space data was acquired without considering the underlying scanning protocol.

2   Methods

MR Forward Model with Rigid Body Motion: Neglecting multiple coils and assuming Nyquist sampling, the forward model is as follows:

$$y = Fx + w, \quad w \sim \mathcal{N}(0, \sigma^2), \tag{1}$$

where x is the image to be reconstructed, F is the Fourier transform operator, y represents the k-space measurements for a particular scan, and w is additive white Gaussian noise. This model assumes that there is no motion during the scan. With the inclusion of motion, the forward model is as follows:

$$y = PFM(x) + w, \quad w \sim \mathcal{N}(0, \sigma^2). \tag{2}$$

Here, P is a sampling operator which takes non-overlapping k-space samples from each TR, and $M(\cdot)$ contains the linear motion operation for each TR. If the inverse problem is solved assuming no motion ($M = I$), then the solution will be a motion-corrupt.

MR Forward Model with Rigid Body Motion and Signal Decay: The forward model in (2) assumes that k-space is acquired at the same echo time which is only true for steady-state and spin-echo sequences where a single k-space line is collected in each excitation. However, nearly all clinical MRI exams employ FSE sequences in which multiple echoes are acquired per excitation, and each echo has a decay factor depending on T2 relaxation and the time when the echo is acquired. This gives rise to the well-known T2-blurring seen in FSE imaging, and can be interpreted as k-space filtering leading to spatially varying convolutions in image-space [23]. To account for this decay, the forward model is modified as follows:

$$y = PFM(h(TE, T2, PD)) + w, \quad w \sim \mathcal{N}(0, \sigma^2), \tag{3}$$

where

$$h(TE, T2, PD) = PDe^{\frac{-TE}{T2}}. \tag{4}$$

Here TE contains all the echo times at which the signal is being acquired, T2 is transverse relaxation time, and PD is the proton density. $h(\cdot)$ represents the exponential decay in the transverse magnetization as TE increases. For simplicity we neglect the effects of imperfect RF refocusing pulses and we assume complete T1 recovery, i.e. long TR, though these effects are easy to incorporate into the signal model [23] due to the differentiability of the extended phase graph algorithm [25].

2.1   Image Simulations

Ground Truth FSE Image: To correctly simulate the FSE sequence acquisition we first estimated T2 and Proton Density (PD) maps from multi-contrast brain MRI scanned at our institution with institutional board approval and informed consent (details about the protocol can be found in the supplementary materials section). Following the FSE example in [14], we simulated echo train lengths (ETL) of 16 and 8, and echo spacing of 12 ms, resulting in 16 (resp. 8) different echo images (Fig. 1) which depict how the signal changes during an FSE acquisition. To form our ground truth FSE image we used a center-out k-space acquisition ordering along the echo train axis, corresponding to PD contrast

Echo 1   Echo 2   Echo 16   FSE Image

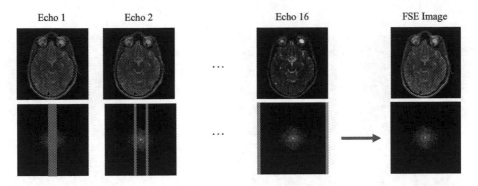

Fig. 1. Example of how ground truth FSE images were simulated using PD and T2 maps. Top row contains images generated using Eq. 3 at 16 different echo times with an echo spacing of 12 ms. The bottom row shows the respective k-space measurements collected and the sampling pattern used for each echo image to create the FSE image.

(Fig. 1). The non-overlapping k-space from each echo was combined into one k-space which was inverse Fourier transformed to make the ground truth image. A total of 18 TRs were acquired, corresponding to Nyquist rate sampling.

FSE Compensated Motion Simulation: To demonstrate the importance of accounting for the FSE effects, as proof-of-principle we simulated nine motion events evenly spaced every 2TR seconds. Each rotation angle was randomly chosen from a Normal distribution $\mathcal{N}(0,2)$ based on [12]. We then sampled k-space according to the particular motion state and echo time across the 18 TRs. The IFFT of this k-space resulted in a motion-corrupt image (See Supplementary Material for Simulation Outline). We emphasize that because this motion model used the same phase encode lines for each TR as was used to generate the ground truth image, the simulation correctly takes into account the relationship between the signal decay during the echo trains and the motion state for each TR.

FSE Agnostic Motion Simulation. To generate the FSE agnostic motion-corrupted images we simply took the FSE image (rightmost in Fig. 1), linearly segmented it into 9 disjoint regions of k-space (corresponding to two TRs each), and applied the same rotations we used previously (shown in Fig. 2). Although the angles of rotation remain the same in this method there is no acknowledgment of the temporal relationship found between lines captured in the same echo train for the true FSE acquisition and this is what ultimately causes this method of simulation to diverge from actual FSE scan data.

Motion Correction Network Training. To test the effect of the different motion models we trained two conditional GANs: the first model trained with our proposed FSE motion simulation, and the second trained using the FSE agnostic simulation. The input to the conditional GAN was the motion-corrupted image

712   B. Levac et al.

TR 1   TR 2   TR 18

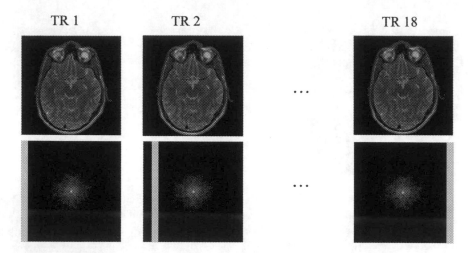

Fig. 2. Example naive motion-corrupted FSE images. The top row contains images which are rotated version of the GT FSE image. The bottom row depicts the sampling pattern in k-space for each TR. Note that there is no notion of signal decay or echo train ordering.

and the output was the motion-free FSE image. Additional information about the training can be found in the supporting information. Our conditional GAN approach was chosen as it is commonly used as the backbone for deep learning based motion correction methods [12]. We anticipate that more sophisticated methods would lead to similar overall conclusions.

We implemented image reconstruction using the BART toolbox [24] and motion correction networks using PyTorch; our code is publicly available[1]. Both models were trained using 819 paired images from the respective motion simulation method. We tested both models on data generated by properly simulating an FSE acquisition with motion and tracked both structural similarity index (SSIM) and normalized root mean square error (NRMSE) values to evaluate image quality and performance. The results for two different ETL values are summarized in Table 1.

3   Results and Discussion

Results. Table 1 shows the performance of both models when tested on simulated motion-corrupt FSE acquisitions. By training on simulated data which is agnostic to the actual acquisition parameters of an FSE sequence there is a significant drop in quantitative performance when compared to models trained and tested on FSE-aware models for motion-correction and this was observed for different ETL values. Figure 3 shows multiple motion correction examples

---

[1] https://github.com/utcsilab/GAN_motion_correction.

Table 1. Performance comparison of FSE agnostic vs. FSE aware motion correction on the test set for 2 different ETL values. For the ETL = 16 case, there are 18 repetition times and time between each echo was 12 ms. Whereas for the ETL = 8 case, there are 36 repetition times and time between each echo was 20 ms. For consistency, we simulated 9 motion states for both the cases.

ETL	16	16	8	8
Error metric	SSIM	NRMSE	SSIM	NRMSE
Input	0.554 ± 0.071	0.268 ± 0.058	0.659 ± 0.053	0.185 ± 0.047
FSE agnostic	0.730 ± 0.060	0.287 ± 0.040	0.885 ± 0.058	0.120 ± 0.025
FSE aware	$\mathbf{0.851 \pm 0.043}$	$\mathbf{0.215 \pm 0.039}$	$\mathbf{0.939 \pm 0.022}$	$\mathbf{0.119 \pm 0.016}$

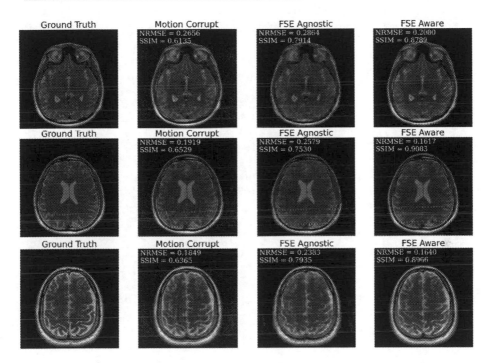

Fig. 3. Example motion artifact correction for 3 different slices. The first column is the ground truth, second column is for the motion-corrupt images, third column is for motion correction network trained on traditional motion simulation methods and the fourth column shows result for correct physics guided motion simulation methods.

chosen from the test set. All cases show a significant improvement in both quantitative and qualitative metrics when accounting for the FSE acquisition. The traditional simulation method does not properly account for the correct sampling of k-space, and therefore at test time it is not able to correct the motion artifacts.

Discussion. Many recent works that use deep learning for retrospective motion correction are trained with simulated motion-corruption. While spin-echo and steady-state sequences are only weakly dependent on the acquisition ordering, FSE acquisitions strongly depend on the data ordering. When this ordering is not correctly accounted for in simulation, there is an expected appreciable drop in performance at test time. This is important to consider as FSE is the backbone of clinical MRI and most publicly available raw MRI datasets are all FSE based. This bias is strongly related to other implicit data crimes arising from the misuse of public data for MRI reconstruction [20]. Fortunately, this problem is easily mitigated by accounting for the data ordering [15]. Another approach to circumventing the issue include unpaired training with experimentally acquired motion-corrupt data [11,18].

Further work is required to investigate the disparity in network performances on prospective motion corrupt data. While our model does not account for through-plane motion in 2D imaging, the model could be extended to 3D FSE acquisitions which have significantly longer ETLs and no through-plane motion.

4   Conclusion

When applying data driven methods to retrospective motion correction, simulation parameters are crucial. In particular, when training motion correction networks for FSE sequences the choice of sampling masks across echo trains and repetition times is key to ensuring that the correct artifact distribution is learned by the network to ensure best results at inference on experimentally acquired motion-corrupt data.

Acknowledgements. This work was supported by NIH Grant U24EB029240 and NSF IFML 2019844 Award.

References

1. Realnoisemri challenge. https://realnoisemri.grand-challenge.org/. Accessed 28 Feb 2022
2. Welcome to mridata.org! http://mridata.org/. Accessed 28 Feb 2022
3. Afacan, O., Wallace, T.E., Warfield, S.K.: Retrospective correction of head motion using measurements from an electromagnetic tracker. Magn. Reson. Med. **83**(2), 427–437 (2020)
4. Cheng, J.Y., et al.: Free-breathing pediatric MRI with nonrigid motion correction and acceleration. J. Magn. Reson. Imaging **42**(2), 407–420 (2015). https://doi.org/10.1002/jmri.24785. https://onlinelibrary.wiley.com/doi/abs/10.1002/jmri.24785
5. Coll-Font, J., et al.: Retrospective distortion and motion correction for free-breathing DW-MRI of the kidneys using dual-echo EPI and slice-to-volume registration. J. Magn. Reson. Imaging **53**(5), 1432–1443 (2021)
6. Cordero-Grande, L., Teixeira, R.P.A.G., Hughes, E.J., Hutter, J., Price, A.N., Hajnal, J.V.: Sensitivity encoding for aligned multishot magnetic resonance reconstruction. IEEE Trans. Comput. Imaging **2**(3), 266–280 (2016). https://doi.org/10.1109/TCI.2016.2557069

7. De Zanche, N., Barmet, C., Nordmeyer-Massner, J.A., Pruessmann, K.P.: NMR probes for measuring magnetic fields and field dynamics in MR systems. Magn. Reson. Med. **60**(1), 176–186 (2008). https://doi.org/10.1002/mrm.21624. https://onlinelibrary.wiley.com/doi/abs/10.1002/mrm.21624

8. Godenschweger, F., et al.: Motion correction in MRI of the brain. Phys. Med. Biol. **61**(5), R32–R56 (2016). https://doi.org/10.1088/0031-9155/61/5/r32

9. Haskell, M.W., et al.: Network accelerated motion estimation and reduction (NAMER): convolutional neural network guided retrospective motion correction using a separable motion model. Magn. Reson. Med. **82**(4), 1452–1461 (2019)

10. Haskell, M.W., Cauley, S.F., Wald, L.L.: Targeted motion estimation and reduction (TAMER): data consistency based motion mitigation for MRI using a reduced model joint optimization. IEEE Trans. Med. Imaging **37**(5), 1253–1265 (2018)

11. Isola, P., Zhu, J.Y., Zhou, T., Efros, A.A.: Image-to-image translation with conditional adversarial networks. In: Proceedings of the IEEE Conference on Computer Vision and Pattern Recognition, pp. 1125–1134 (2017)

12. Johnson, P.M., Drangova, M.: Conditional generative adversarial network for 3d rigid-body motion correction in MRI. Magn. Reson. Med. **82**(3), 901–910 (2019)

13. Kurugol, S., et al.: Motion-robust parameter estimation in abdominal diffusion-weighted MRI by simultaneous image registration and model estimation. Med. Image Anal. **39**, 124–132 (2017). https://doi.org/10.1016/j.media.2017.04.006. https://www.sciencedirect.com/science/article/pii/S1361841517300646

14. Layton, K.J., et al.: Pulseq: a rapid and hardware-independent pulse sequence prototyping framework. Magn. Reson. Med. **77**(4), 1544–1552 (2017). https://doi.org/10.1002/mrm.26235. https://onlinelibrary.wiley.com/doi/abs/10.1002/mrm.26235

15. Lee, J., Kim, B., Park, H.: Mc2-net: motion correction network for multi-contrast brain MRI. Magn. Reson. Med. **86**(2), 1077–1092 (2021)

16. Ludwig, J., Speier, P., Seifert, F., Schaeffter, T., Kolbitsch, C.: Pilot tone-based motion correction for prospective respiratory compensated cardiac cine MRI. Magn. Reson. Med. **85**(5), 2403–2416 (2021). https://doi.org/10.1002/mrm.28580. https://onlinelibrary.wiley.com/doi/abs/10.1002/mrm.28580

17. Menze, B.H., et al.: The multimodal brain tumor image segmentation benchmark (BRATS). IEEE Trans. Med. Imaging **34**(10), 1993–2024 (2014)

18. Oh, G., Lee, J.E., Ye, J.C.: Unpaired MR motion artifact deep learning using outlier-rejecting bootstrap aggregation. IEEE Trans. Med. Imaging **40**(11), 3125–3139 (2021). https://doi.org/10.1109/TMI.2021.3089708

19. Pawar, K., Chen, Z., Shah, N.J., Egan, G.F.: Suppressing motion artefacts in MRI using an inception-ResNet network with motion simulation augmentation. NMR Biomed. **35**, e4225 (2019)

20. Shimron, E., Tamir, J.I., Wang, K., Lustig, M.: Subtle inverse crimes: Naïvely training machine learning algorithms could lead to overly-optimistic results. arXiv preprint arXiv:2109.08237 (2021)

21. Singh, N.M., Iglesias, J.E., Adalsteinsson, E., Dalca, A.V., Golland, P.: Joint frequency and image space learning for Fourier imaging. arXiv preprint arXiv:2007.01441 (2020)

22. Slipsager, J.M., et al.: Quantifying the financial savings of motion correction in brain MRI: a model-based estimate of the costs arising from patient head motion and potential savings from implementation of motion correction. J. Magn. Reson. Imaging **52**(3), 731–738 (2020)

23. Tamir, J.I., et al.: T2 shuffling: sharp, multicontrast, volumetric fast spin-echo imaging. Magn. Reson. Med. **77**(1), 180–195 (2017)

24. Uecker, M., Tamir, J.I., Ong, F., Lustig, M.: The bart toolbox for computational magnetic resonance imaging. In: Proceedings of the International Society for Magnetic Resonance in Medicine, vol. 24 (2016)
25. Weigel, M.: Extended phase graphs: dephasing, RF pulses, and echoes - pure and simple. J. Magn. Reson. Imaging **41**(2), 266–295 (2015). https://doi.org/10.1002/jmri.24619. https://onlinelibrary.wiley.com/doi/abs/10.1002/jmri.24619
26. Zaitsev, M., Maclaren, J., Herbst, M.: Motion artifacts in MRI: a complex problem with many partial solutions. J. Magn. Reson. Imaging **42**(4), 887–901 (2015)
27. Zbontar, J., et al.: fastMRI: an open dataset and benchmarks for accelerated MRI. arXiv preprint arXiv:1811.08839 (2018)

Personalized dMRI Harmonization on Cortical Surface

Yihao Xia[1,2] and Yonggang Shi[1,2(✉)]

[1] Stevens Neuroimaging and Informatics Institute, Keck School of Medicine,
University of Southern California (USC), Los Angeles, CA 90033, USA
[2] Ming Hsieh Department of Electrical and Computer Engineering, Viterbi School of
Engineering, University of Southern California (USC), Los Angeles, CA 90089, USA
yshi@loni.usc.edu

Abstract. The inter-site variability of diffusion magnetic resonance imaging (dMRI) hinders the aggregation of dMRI data from multiple centers. This necessitates dMRI harmonization for removing non-biological site-effects. Recently, the emergence of high-resolution dMRI data across various connectome imaging studies allows the large-scale analysis of cortical micro-structure. Existing harmonization methods, however, perform poorly in the harmonization of dMRI data in cortical areas because they rely on image registration methods to factor out anatomical variations, which have known difficulty in aligning cortical folding patterns. To overcome this fundamental challenge in dMRI harmonization, we propose a framework of personalized dMRI harmonization on the cortical surface to improve the dMRI harmonization of gray matter by adaptively estimating the inter-site harmonization mappings. In our experiments, we demonstrate the effectiveness of the proposed method by applying it to harmonize dMRI across the Human Connectome Project (HCP) and the Lifespan Human Connectome Projects in Development (HCPD) studies and achieved much better performance in comparison with conventional methods based on image registration.

Keywords: Diffusion MRI · Harmonization · Cortical surface

1   Introduction

Diffusion MRI (dMRI) [1] is widely used for the in vivo and non-invasive investigation of brain connectivity. For large-scale imaging studies, it is often necessary to pool data across multiple sites for increasing statistical power [2]. However, the incompatibility of dMRI data across sites, owing to inter-site variations in the magnetic field strength, scanner vendor, and acquisition protocol, poses significant challenges for multi-site data aggregation [3,4]. The harmonization of dMRI data thus plays an important role in modern connectome imaging research.

This work was supported by the National Institute of Health (NIH) under grants RF1AG056573, RF1AG064584, R01EB022744, R21AG064776, R01AG062007, P41EB015922, P30AG066530.

According to observations in [5,6], the inter-site variability in dMRI is tissue- and region-specific, which implies that accurate alignment of brain anatomy is a key prerequisite in dMRI harmonization. For the harmonization of data from two different sites, in essence this requires the construction of two reference sets with comparable anatomy for each voxel to be harmonized. After that, various transformation models can be applied to remove scanner related differences. In [6], the ComBat method was used to harmonize the diffusion tensor imaging (DTI) by regressing out the site-specific factors voxel-wisely in a co-registered space. For the harmonization of diffusion weighted imaging (DWI), Mirzaalian et al. [5] utilized rotation invariant spherical harmonics (RISH) features as anchor features and the harmonization is conducted by linearly scaling spherical harmonic (SH) coefficients of dMRI signal. Following a similar framework, Huynh et al. presented a method of moments based harmonization approach [16]. Although, these harmonization frameworks demonstrate overall effectiveness in the reduction of site-wise variation, they all rely on conventional image registration to establish anatomical correspondences across subjects, which inevitably will suffer from significant misalignment of brain anatomy in cortical areas with high variability across population and hence result in degraded harmonization.

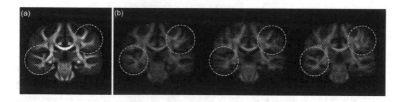

Fig. 1. Comparison between the anatomy of the individual subjects and the sample mean template: (a) the sample mean template of multiple FA images of HCP subjects and co-registered FA images of HCP subjects in (b)

Recent emergence of high resolution dMRI data from connectome imaging studies allows the analysis of cortical microstructure. The dMRI harmonization of gray matter (GM) in high resolution is thus an increasingly urgent problem. While, due to the geometric complexity of the cortex and the inter-subject variability, the dMRI harmonization of gray matter is hard to achieve for previous methods described above. As illustrated in the Fig. 1, the co-registration cannot properly build the anatomical correspondence across subjects, especially in the GM regions. This will no doubt lead to a highly undesirable scenario of harmonization based on reference voxels from drastically different anatomy and hence intensity distributions, which will confound the estimation of harmonization transformations. Alternatively, surface-based registration can alleviate some of this anatomy misalignment problem for dMRI harmonization, but it is still insufficient to resolve this challenge [14]. This is especially evident in association cortices where topographically different folding patterns are commonly present across subjects.

To robustly conduct dMRI harmonization of cortical gray matter in high resolution, we present a framework of personalized dMRI harmonization on the cortical surface by adaptively estimating the inter-site harmonization mappings. We integrated our personalized mechanism with the RISH based dMRI harmonization framework [15] for the dMRI harmonization across the Human Connectome Project (HCP) [8] and the Lifespan Human Connectome Projects in Development (HCPD) [9] studies. Our experiments demonstrate that the proposed method achieved better performance comparing with the conventional approach. Our main contributions include: (1) we proposed a surface based dMRI harmonization to improve the robustness of gray matter harmonization; (2) without relying on image or surface registration, we proposed a general local correspondence detection mechanism to enhance harmonization performance.

2   Method

The proposed dMRI harmonization framework is depicted in Fig. 2. The core of the personalized dMRI harmonization is the construction of local reference sets, which mitigates the anatomical mismatching problem by adaptively selecting corresponding locations according to geometric and biomedical features on the cortical surface. Then, site-specific templates could be reliably estimated in a personalized manner and used for the estimation of site-wise harmonization mapping.

2.1   Diffusion MRI Harmonization and Linear RISH Framework

Let's denote the dMRI datasets acquired from a source site (src) and a target site (tar) as $\mathcal{S}^{src} = \{S_i^{src}\}_{i=1}^{N^{src}}$ and $\mathcal{S}^{tar} = \{S_i^{tar}\}_{i=1}^{N^{tar}}$, where S represents diffusion MRI signal. The harmonization of dMRI is to mitigate the site-wise differences by mapping the dMRI data from the source site to the target one: $\hat{S}^{src} = \Psi(S^{src})$. Without explicitly paired scans from two sites for mapping estimation, the harmonization mapping can be determined by comparing the site-specific templates of diffusion representations such as the rotation invariant spherical harmonic (RISH) features [15]. With spherical harmonics, we can represent diffusion signal as $S \simeq \sum_{lm} C_{lm} Y_{lm}$, where Y_{lm} and C_{lm} are the spherical harmonics basis and corresponding coefficients of order l and degree m. The linear RISH based harmonization is conducted by scaling the spherical harmonic coefficients of the source site dMRI: $\hat{C}_{lm}^{src} = \Phi_l C_{lm}^{src}$, where Φ_l is the linear scale map. The harmonized data can be generated according to: $\hat{S}^{src} = \sum_{lm} \hat{C}_{lm}^{src} Y_{lm}$. The estimation of the mapping Φ_l relies on the estimation of the site-specific RISH templates: $\Phi_l = \sqrt{\frac{E_l^{tar}}{E_l^{src} + \epsilon}}$, where E_l^{tar} and E_l^{src} are the l-order's RISH templates for the target and source site, respectively.

2.2   Personalized dMRI Harmonization on Cortical Surface

The estimation of a site-specific template E is conducted by pooling the representative references of anatomical correspondence from multiple subjects:

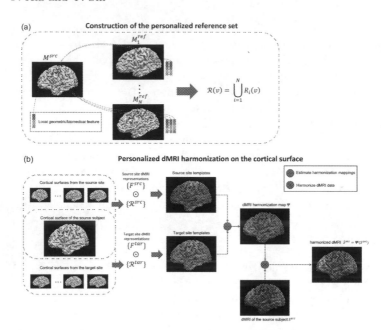

Fig. 2. Overview of personalized dMRI harmonization on the cortical surface. (a) illustrates the detection of inter-subject local correspondence and (b) shows the overall framework of personalized dMRI harmonization on the cortical surface

$E = G(\mathbf{F})$, where $\mathbf{F} = [F_1, \ldots, F_N]^T$ is a stack of dMRI representations. The co-registration is conventionally used to build the anatomical correspondence across subjects. However, being aware of the inter-subject variability in cortical folding, we aim to improve the performance of harmonization in gray matter regions by adaptively generating the inter-site dMRI mapping function for each subject from the source site (namely source subject) on the cortical surface. Locally, at a certain vertex v on the cortical surface of a source subject, we construct personalized reference sets $\mathcal{R}(v)^{src}$ and $\mathcal{R}(v)^{tar}$ for the source site and target site. Then the personalized dMRI representations, e.g. RISH features, can be estimated accordingly:

$$E(v) = \frac{1}{|\mathcal{R}(v)|} \sum_{v' \in \mathcal{R}(v)} F(v'), \tag{1}$$

where $F(v')$ is the local dMRI representation at vertex v' on the cortical surface of a reference subject and $|\mathcal{R}(v)|$ is the size of reference set.

Inter-subject Local Correspondence Detection on the Cortical Surface. For a real-valued function f on a Riemannian manifold M, the Laplace-Beltrami (LB) operator Δ_M is defined as: $\Delta_M f := div(grad\ f)$ with $grad\ f$ the gradient of f and div the divergence. At a vertex v on the manifold M, the LB embedding defined in [17] is a infinite-dimensional vector: $\mathcal{E}_M(v) = [\frac{\phi_1(v)}{\sqrt{\lambda_1}}, \frac{\phi_2(v)}{\sqrt{\lambda_2}}, \frac{\phi_3(v)}{\sqrt{\lambda_3}}, \dots]$, where λ_i and ϕ_i represent eigenfunction and eigenvalue of the LB operator. Given two surfaces M_1 and M_2, we can use the spectral distance: $d_g(v, w) = \|\mathcal{E}_{M_1}(v) - \mathcal{E}_{M_2}(w)\|_2$ for the corresponding vertex detection, where v and w are on surfaces M_1 and M_2 respectively. With the spectral distance defined in the context of the whole surface, we can only coarsely screen the corresponding vertices and narrow down the searching space. To refine the searching of corresponding vertices we examine the similarity of the local LB embedding. Within the LB framework, we construct the local LB embedding: $\mathcal{H}_{\mathcal{N}(k)}(v) = [\frac{\phi_1^{\mathcal{N}(k)}(v)}{\sqrt{\lambda_1^{\mathcal{N}(k)}}}, \sum_{i=2} \frac{\phi_i^{\mathcal{N}(k)}(v)}{\sqrt{\lambda_i^{\mathcal{N}(k)}}}]$, where $\mathcal{N}(k)$ is the k-ring patch with the center point at the vertex v. $\phi_i^{\mathcal{N}(k)}$ and $\lambda_i^{\mathcal{N}(k)}$ are the i-th eigenfunction and eigenvalue of the patch $\mathcal{N}(k)$. In this paper, we calculate the local LB embedding for $k = \{1, 3, 5, 7, 9\}$ and rearrange them into three group $\mathcal{K} = \{\{1, 3, 5\}, \{3, 5, 7\}, \{5, 7, 9\}\}$ to represent the geometric characteristics of different localities. Then, the local embedding distance is defined as follow:

$$d_l(v, w) = \min_{K \in \mathcal{K}} \max_{k \in K} \|\mathcal{H}_{\mathcal{N}(k)}(v) - \mathcal{H}_{\mathcal{N}(k)}(w)\|_1. \tag{2}$$

Besides the geometry of the cortical surface, the biomedical measurement such as cortical thickness could be employed to further regularize the construction of reference. The thickness difference between two locations can be defined as follow:

$$d_t(v, w) = \|T(v) - T(w)\|_1, \tag{3}$$

where $T(v)$ and $T(w)$ are the local cortical thickness.

Construction of Personalized Reference Sets. Equipped with the vertex-wise similarity measure, we can retrieve reliable references for any location v on the cortex surface of a source subject from a reference subject:

$$R(v) = \{w : w \in M^{ref}; d_l(v, w) \leq \theta_l \wedge d_t(v, w) \leq \theta_t\} \tag{4}$$

where M^{ref} is the cortical surface of the reference subject, θ_l is the local LB embedding distance threshold, and θ_t is the thickness difference threshold. The collection of the reference set for multiple subjects from a site (src or tar) forms the personalized reference set for that site:

$$\mathcal{R}(v) = \bigcup_i R_i(v). \tag{5}$$

3   Experiments and Results

3.1   Implementation Details

Our experiments focus on the dMRI harmonization between the HCP and HCPD studies. The MRI scans for HCP and HCPD subjects are acquired on a customized Siemens "Connectome Skyra" (100 mT/m) and 3T Siemens Prisma scanners (80 mT/m), respectively. We performed the harmonization on the single shell b-value = 3000 s/mm^2, which is overlapped across two studies. There are 90 and 46 directions in the selected shell for the HCP and HCPD studies, respectively. We followed the minimal preprocessing pipelines [10] for the distortion correction of dMRI [11] and generating the pial and white matter surface mesh [12]. From each dataset we selected 119 healthy subjects with well-matched age and genders for the cross-study dMRI harmonization, with 62 females and 57 males in HCP and 66 females and 53 males in HCPD. All selected subjects from each study were recruited as references for the site-specific template construction and harmonization mapping estimation. For the personalized dMRI harmonization on the cortical surface, we generated (left hemisphere and right hemisphere) gray matter surfaces which are the middle surfaces of the corresponding pial and white surfaces to reliably extract the dMRI signal of gray matter. The dMRI data were linearly interpolated onto these mesh surfaces to represent the gray matter dMRI. To construct the personalized reference sets at each query location, we empirically set the local LB embedding distance threshold $\theta_l = 0.2$ and the thickness difference threshold $\theta_t = 0.15$.

For comparison, we implement volume-based dMRI harmonization by following Linear RISH framework in [15]. The resolution of HCP data was downsampled from 1.25 mm to 1.5 mm isotropic to match HCPD's. We calculated five RISH templates of order $l = \{0, 2, 4, 6, 8\}$ in all harmonization tasks.

3.2   Results

Inter-subject Local Correspondence. The results of local correspondence detection on the cortical surface are illustrated in Fig. 3. One can see that for each query location (left in each subfigure) multiple locations with both geometric and anatomical similarity are detected (see mid and right in each subfigure). The corresponding parcels of cortex in Desikan-Killiany' cortical atlas [7] are used as references of anatomy (in yellow).

Distribution of DTI Features Before and After Harmonization. Figure 4 shows the density curve of fractional anisotropy (FA) and mean diffusivity (MD) on the cortical surface of all subjects before and after harmonization. Note that as we focus on the single shell dMRI harmonization, all DTI features are calculated from b = 3000 shell. It is observable that variability across HCP (red solid line) and HCPD (red dash line) datasets exists for both FA and MD features. Comparing with the volume-based harmonization (green solid and green dash lines), the surface-based harmonization (blue solid and blue dash lines) has supervisor performance as corresponding histograms have higher similarity to which of target site.

Jensen-Shannon Divergence of DTI Distributions. To quantitatively demonstrate the performance of harmonization, we measure the distribution differences in DTI features across sites by using the Jensen-Shannon divergence

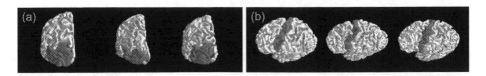

Fig. 3. Examples of inter-subject local correspondence detection at two typical locations. The query vertex (a red dot) on a source cortical surface (left) and corresponding reference sets (dots in red) of two reference subjects (middle and right) are shown in each subfigure. (Color figure online)

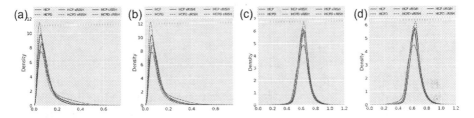

Fig. 4. FA and MD distributions before and after harmonization. The density curves for FA on left hemisphere, FA on right hemisphere, MD on left hemisphere, and MD on right hemisphere are shown in (a) (b) (c), and (d).

(JSD). Due to the lack of subject-wise correspondence across HCP and HCPD studies, we extend the Jensen-Shannon divergence to measure the subject-set divergence:

$$JSD(P\|\mathcal{Q}) = \inf_{Q \in \mathcal{Q}} (JSD(P\|Q)) \qquad (6)$$

where $JSD(P\|Q)$ is the JSD of distributions P and Q, $\mathcal{Q} = \{Q_i\}_{i=1}^{N_Q}$ is the distribution set. We computed the subject-set divergence between the DTI distribution of each harmonized subject from the *src* site and corresponding distributions of subjects from the *tar* set to reflect the performance of harmonization. A smaller JSD, indicating less inter-site variability, is preferred. The Jensen-Shannon divergences (magnified 1000 times) of DTI distributions across HCP and HCPD datasets for both left and right hemispheres (lh and rh) are summarized in Table 1. The results show that the volume-based harmonization can only mitigate the differences between datasets when harmonizing subjects from the HCPD study to HCP dataset (*HCP + HCPD vRISH*). In contrast, the proposed method can properly cope with both HCP harmonization task (*HCP cRISH + HCPD*) and HCPD harmonization task (*HCP + HCPD cRISH*). Further performance comparisons are conducted via paired Student's t-test, and the improvements achieved by our method over volume-based method are statistically significant (p $< 10^{-6}$) in all cases.

Table 1. Jensen-Shannon divergence of DTI distributions across HCP and HCPD studies.

Harmonization task	FA		MD	
	lh	rh	lh	rh
HCP + HCPD	3.69 ± 3.39	4.09 ± 3.60	5.98 ± 3.39	6.53 ± 4.17
HCP vRISH + HCPD	3.79 ± 2.03	4.98 ± 3.17	8.16 ± 3.88	18.80 ± 10.34
HCP cRISH + HCPD	**2.12 ± 0.82**	**2.19 ± 1.19**	**3.20 ± 1.55**	**2.86 ± 1.03**
HCP + HCPD vRISH	3.28 ± 2.84	3.15 ± 2.45	3.55 ± 1.95	4.16 ± 1.62
HCP + HCPD cRISH	**2.05 ± 0.90**	**1.80 ± 0.73**	**2.84 ± 1.30**	**2.62 ± 0.89**

Regional Coefficient of Variation of DTI Features. We investigated the effectiveness of harmonization on reducing the inter-site variation of regional DTI features. Figure 5 shows the FA and MD inter-site coefficient of variations (CoVs) for major cerebral cortex lobes. From the results we can find that the volume-based harmonization framework cannot reliably mitigate the inter-site CoVs of DTI features for lobes, such as left parietal and right occipital, in either harmonization task of *HCP vRISH + HCPD* or *HCPD vRISH + HCP*. By using the proposed method, the CoVs of both FA and MD reduce for all regions in both tasks.

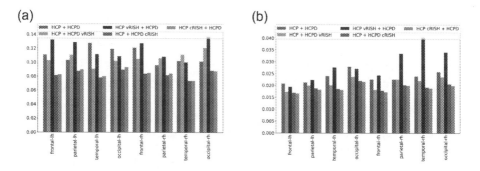

Fig. 5. FA and MD inter-site coefficient of variation.

4   Discussion and Conclusions

In the experiments, we focused on the harmonization of dMRI on the cortical surface, where the conventional registration methods cannot establish comparable anatomical correspondences across subjects. This anatomical misalignment dramatically increases the likelihood of failure in harmonization, as demonstrated in our experiments, which reaffirms the central role of anatomical correspondences in the site-wise harmonization. In this paper, we proposed a novel framework for dMRI harmonization on the cortical surface. By adaptively estimating the inter-site harmonization mappings according to underlying anatomical and biomedical information, our method outperformed the baseline framework. The proposed adaptive reference detection is a general mechanism and can be integrated into other harmonization framework to regularize the harmonization mapping estimation.

References

1. Basser, P.J., et al.: MR diffusion tensor spectroscopy and imaging. Biophys. J. **66**(1), 259–267 (1994)
2. Mueller, S.G., et al.: The Alzheimer's disease neuroimaging initiative. Neuroimaging Clin. N. Am. **15**(4), 869–877 (2005)
3. Vollmar, C., et al.: Identical, but not the same: Intra-site and inter-site reproducibility of fractional anisotropy measures on two 3.0T scanners. Neuroimage **51**(4), 1384–1394 (2010)
4. Zhu, T., et al.: Quantification of accuracy and precision of multi-center DTI measurements: A diffusion phantom and human brain study. Neuroimage **56**(3), 1398–1411 (2011)
5. Mirzaalian, H., et al.: Inter-site and inter-scanner diffusion MRI data harmonization. Neuroimage **135**, 311–323 (2016)
6. Fortin, J.P., et al.: Harmonization of multi-site diffusion tensor imaging data. Neuroimage **161**, 149–170 (2017)
7. Desikan, R.S., et al.: An automated labeling system for subdividing the human cerebral cortex on MRI scans into gyral based regions of interest. Neuroimage **31**(3), 968–980 (2006)
8. Van Essen, D.C., et al.: The WU-Minn human connectome project: an overview. Neuroimage **80**, 62–79 (2013)
9. Somerville, L.H., et al.: The lifespan human connectome project in development: a large-scale study of brain connectivity development in 5–21 year olds. Neuroimage **183**, 456–468 (2018)
10. Glasser, M.F., et al.: The minimal preprocessing pipelines for the Human Connectome Project. Neuroimage **80**, 105–124 (2013)
11. Andersson, J.L.R., et al.: A comprehensive Gaussian process framework for correcting distortions and movements in diffusion images. In: Proceedings of the 20th Annual Meeting of ISMRM, vol. 20, p. 91657 (2012)
12. Fischl, B.: Freesurfer. Neuroimage **62**(2), 774–781 (2012)
13. Cetin Karayumak, S., Kubicki, M., Rathi, Y.: Harmonizing diffusion MRI data across magnetic field strengths. In: Frangi, A.F., Schnabel, J.A., Davatzikos, C., Alberola-López, C., Fichtinger, G. (eds.) MICCAI 2018. LNCS, vol. 11072, pp. 116–124. Springer, Cham (2018). https://doi.org/10.1007/978-3-030-00931-1_14
14. Zhang, J., Shi, Y.: Personalized matching and analysis of cortical folding patterns via patch-based intrinsic brain mapping. In: de Bruijne, M., et al. (eds.) MICCAI 2021. LNCS, vol. 12907, pp. 710–720. Springer, Cham (2021). https://doi.org/10.1007/978-3-030-87234-2_67
15. Karayumak, S.C., et al.: Retrospective harmonization of multi-site diffusion MRI data acquired with different acquisition parameters. Neuroimage **184**, 180–200 (2019)
16. Huynh, K.M., et al.: Multi-site harmonization of diffusion MRI data via method of moments. IEEE Trans. Med. Imaging **38**(7), 1599–1609 (2019)
17. Rustamov, R.M.: Laplace-Beltrami eigenfunctions for deformation invariant shape representation. In: Symposium on Geometry Processing, vol. 257 (2007)

A Projection-Based K-space Transformer Network for Undersampled Radial MRI Reconstruction with Limited Training Subjects

Chang Gao[1]([✉]), Shu-Fu Shih[1], J. Paul Finn[1], and Xiaodong Zhong[2]

[1] University of California Los Angeles, Los Angeles, CA, USA
gaoc@ucla.edu
[2] MR R&D Collaborations, Siemens Medical Solutions USA, Inc.,
Los Angeles, CA, USA

Abstract. The recent development of deep learning combined with compressed sensing enables fast reconstruction of undersampled MR images and has achieved state-of-the-art performance for Cartesian k-space trajectories. However, non-Cartesian trajectories such as the radial trajectory need to be transformed onto a Cartesian grid in each iteration of the network training, slowing down the training process significantly. Multiple iterations of nonuniform Fourier transformation in the networks offset the advantage of fast inference inherent in deep learning. Current approaches typically either work on image-to-image networks or grid the non-Cartesian trajectories before the network training to avoid the repeated gridding process. However, the image-to-image networks cannot ensure the k-space data consistency in the reconstructed images and the pre-processing of non-Cartesian k-space leads to gridding errors which cannot be compensated by the network training. Inspired by the Transformer network to handle long-range dependencies in sequence transduction tasks, we propose to rearrange the radial spokes to sequential data based on the chronological order of acquisition and use the Transformer network to predict unacquired radial spokes from the acquired data. We propose novel data augmentation methods to generate a large amount of training data from a limited number of subjects. The network can be applied to different anatomical structures. Experimental results show superior performance of the proposed framework compared to state-of-the-art deep neural networks.

Keywords: Transformer network · MRI Reconstruction · Radial MRI

1 Introduction

Magnetic Resonance Imaging (MRI) has been widely used for non-invasive diagnosis due to its high resolution and excellent soft tissue contrast. However, its long acquisition time is a drawback and predisposes to artifacts due to patient movement. Undersampling is an efficient way to shorten the acquisition time but the undersampling process itself may produce artifacts and degrade image quality. In the past decades, methods such as compressed sensing (CS) use sparsity constraints to reconstruct images [1–3] but CS typically suffers from long computational time. The recent development of deep learning combined with CS acquisition schemes enabled fast acquisition and fast reconstruction and achieved state-of-the-art performance on Cartesian trajectories for MRI [4–6].

Enforcing k-space data consistency in deep learning-based CS reconstruction is straightforward and time-efficient for Cartesian trajectories, which only needs forward and inverse Fourier transforms between k-space and image space. However, for non-Cartesian trajectories, the non-Cartesian k-space needs to be gridded onto a Cartesian basis prior to Fourier transformation. Gridding is time-consuming and typically needs to be performed with each iteration of the network training and testing, which slows down the process profoundly and offsets the deep learning advantage of fast inference [7]. For this reason, a previous study employed a convolutional neural network (CNN) component with very few parameters and implemented a pretraining and fine-tuning strategy to train a radial reconstruction network [7], imposing limits on the application and performance of deep networks. Other work either used image-to-image networks [8–13] or gridded the radial k-space before the network training [14 16]. For image-to-image networks, the generated images may lack k-space data consistency and therefore compromise image fidelity [7]. Gridding non-Cartesian k-space before the network training can avoid the repeated gridding problem, but the network cannot learn to compensate for the gridding error [17]. In addition, the artifacts due to radial k-space undersampling manifest in the images as global streaks which are hard to remove in the image domain with local convolution kernels.

Inspired by the recent development of the Transformer network for handling long-range dependencies in sequence transduction tasks, we propose to use a projection-based k-space Transformer network to predict unacquired radial spokes from the acquired data. The Transformer network [18] has outperformed recurrent and convolutional neural networks in language translation [18], image generation [19] and image classification [20]. Previous works on vision Transformers proposed to crop the image and reshape the image patches to sequential vectors where each vector is a token [20]. However, cropping and reshaping the image will cut off the global streaking artifacts and make the network less effective at removing them.

Similar to the radial GRAPPA work [21], we aim to fill the missing radial spokes using the information from acquired ones. However, radial GRAPPA used local reconstruction kernels and a k-space center calibration region to utilize the multi-coil information. It cannot utilize the global k-space information and only works with radial spokes that are separated by the same angle. We propose to rearrange the radial k-space to sequential data based on the chronological order of acquisition and use the attention mechanism to learn the dependencies between the radial spokes.

To our knowledge, this work was the first to translate MRI k-space into sequential time-series data and to use the Transformer network for MRI raw data prediction and image reconstruction. We used the golden-angle stack-of-radial trajectory as an example to show the projection-based k-space Transformer network and its performance. Novel data augmentation methods were used to generate a large amount of training data from a limited number of subjects. The proposed network was generalized to test on various anatomical structures including the abdominal and pelvic regions.

2   Projection-Based K-space Transformer (PKT)

To demonstrate the concept of the proposed framework, a golden-angle-ordered radial k-space is shown as an example in Fig. 1(a). Starting from $0°$, each radial k-space spoke is rotated by a golden angle, which is approximately $111.25°$. The golden-angle acquisition ensures uniform coverage of the k-space for any arbitrary number of consecutive spokes so any newly acquired radial spoke is interleaved with the acquired ones. The spokes that are physically close (in azimuth angle) are dependent on each other. We hypothesize that the dependencies between each of the spokes can be learned by the attention modules in a Transformer network to predict unacquired spokes. We propose to rearrange the radial spokes based on the chronological order of acquisition and encode the temporal spoke index in the network. Note that the same concept can be extended to other non-Cartesian k-space trajectories such as the spiral trajectory or uniform-angle ordering.

2.1   The Overall Framework

Suppose there are 256 sampling points along each spoke, a fully-sampled radial k-space needs $256 * \pi/2 \approx 402$ spokes according to the Nyquist sampling requirement [2]. In this work we aim to achieve 4 times undersampling and thus set the number of spokes of the input to be 100 and the output has 300 new spokes to supplement the acquired ones. We propose to train 3 independent Transformer networks, each predicting 100 consecutive spokes of different angles.

As illustrated in Fig. 1(a), the undersampled radial k-space has 100 spokes $(p_i, p_{i+1}, ..., p_{i+99})$ (in black), where i is the spoke index of the first spoke in each sequential set of spokes. Transformers 1, 2 and 3 take the pre-processed radial spokes as input and predict unacquired k-space radial spokes independently and in parallel. Spokes $(p_{i+100}, p_{i+101}, ..., p_{i+199})$ (in blue), $(p_{i+200}, p_{i+201}, ..., p_{i+299})$ (in green) and $(p_{i+300}, p_{i+301}, ..., p_{i+399})$ (in orange) are the outputs of Transformers 1, 2 and 3, respectively. The corresponding spoke indices are encoded in the Transformer network to distinguish spokes at different angles. The input and 3 outputs are combined in the order of the spoke index to form a fully-sampled radial k-space. To reconstruct the final images, the radial k-space is nonuniformly fast Fourier transformed (NUFFT) using the Bart toolbox [22] and the

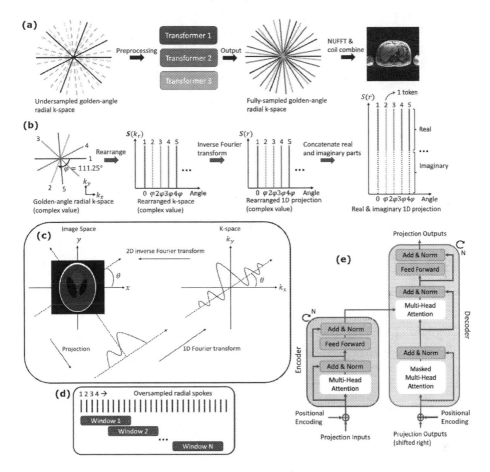

Fig. 1. (a) Overview of the proposed projection-based k-space transformer (PKT) network. (b) Illustration of the pre-processing of radial k-space. (c) The relationship between the image, projection and k-space. (d) Data augmentation method using over-sampling and sliding window approaches. (e) The Transformer network architecture.

images from different coils are combined using adaptive coil combination [23] using MATLAB R2021b (MathWorks).

Figure 1(b) shows pre-processing steps of radial k-space. For each single coil 2D slice, the golden-angle-ordered radial spokes are rearranged based on the chronological order of acquisition. Then each of the k-space spokes is inverse Fourier transformed to generate a projection vector at each angle. Figure 1(c) shows the relationship between the image, projection and k-space. The projection signals span the whole image compared to the centrally condensed k-space signals, so the network can better learn the image details and the reconstructed image is less sensitive to network errors. The real and imaginary parts of each complex-valued projection are concatenated to a single long vector prior to input to the network. Because the frequency encoding line (k_x) is typically 2 times oversampled, the complex-valued projection vector is of length 512 and the concatenated projection vector is of length 1024. The input and output are of size 1024×100 with each projection vector as a token in the network.

2.2   Data Augmentation

Generally, large training data are necessary to train deep learning networks, which can pose practical challenges. With the proposed k-space Transformer framework, several data augmentation methods were used to enlarge the training data size with limited subjects. The data augmentation methods used in this work include (1) acquisition from multiple anatomical regions (2) over-sampled 3D multi-coil acquisition and (3) a sliding window approach to generating more training data. Scanning from multiple anatomical regions not only enlarges the data size but also increases the data diversity and can help the generalization of the network on various anatomical images. Each 3D multi-coil acquisition is first inverse fast Fourier transformed (FFT) along k_z to generate multi-coil multi-slice 2D radial k-space. Because each slice has over-sampled k-space data, a sliding window approach was used to generate more training data from the same single-coil slice, as illustrated in Fig. 1(d). Each window contains 400 spokes and the step size is 200 spokes. Suppose n_{sub} subjects are acquired for training, n_{reg} anatomical regions for each subject, n_{slc} slices and n_{coil} coils for each 3D acquisition, and M spokes for each slice, the effective training data size DS will be:

$$DS = n_{sub} \times n_{reg} \times n_{slc} \times n_{coil} \times \lfloor M/400 \rfloor \tag{1}$$

where $\lfloor \rfloor$ represents the floor function.

2.3   Transformer Network

Considering the relatively long length of sequential radial spokes, the application of the Transformer network is expected to learn the long-range dependencies between the spokes. As shown in Fig. 1(e), the Transformer has an encoder-decoder structure. The encoder maps an input of the acquired radial spokes to sequential representations, which was used by the decoder to generate the sequential output. Each spoke is treated as a token in the network. At each step the decoder is auto-regressive, using the previously generated spokes to generate the next single spoke. The encoder consists of $N = 6$ identical stacks, each having a multi-head self-attention sub-layer and a fully connected feed-forward sub-layer. After each sub-layer, a residual connection [24] is implemented followed by layer normalization [25]. The decoder also has $N = 6$ identical stacks. In addition to the two sub-layers in encoder, the decoder has a third sub-layer, which learns the multi-head attention from the outputs. The output is offset by one position and is masked for each iteration so that the prediction for position *pos* depends only on the known outputs at positions smaller than *pos*.

The angle information of the radial spokes is highly correlated with their dependency. Therefore, positional encoding is implemented for the input and output to make use of the angle information. For a set of consecutive spokes $(k_1, ..., k_n)$ each having a length of d_{model}, the positional encoding is calculated using sine and cosine functions:

$$PE_{i_s,2j} = sin(i_s/10000^{2j/d_{model}})$$
$$PE_{i_s,2j+1} = cos(i_s/10000^{2j/d_{model}})$$

(2)

where i_s is the relative spoke index and $i_s \in \{0, 1, ..., 399\}$ and j is the dimension. The positional encoding is directly added to the input and output. Using this positional encoding strategy, consecutive input and output are not necessary which allows more flexibility for the network design. For example, when the input is $(k_1, ..., k_n)$, it is not necessary for the output to be $(k_{n+1}, ..., k_{2n})$ only, where $(k_m, ..., k_{m+n-1})$ is also feasible $(m > n)$. This strategy allows to train independent Transformers to predict spokes at different angles and combine all predictions and the input for the final reconstruction.

3   Experiments and Results

3.1   Dataset

The study was compliant with the Health Insurance Portability and Accountability Act and approved by the Institutional Review Board. With written informed consent from each subject, we acquired radial MRI data using a prototype golden-angle, gradient-echo stack-of-radial sequence from 17 healthy subjects in the abdomen, pelvis, thigh and leg (16 subjects on a 3T MAGNETOM Prisma[fit] and 1 subject on a 3T MAGNETOM Skyra, Siemens Healthcare, Erlangen, Germany). The sequence parameters were: 512 sampling points each spoke (with 2× oversampling along frequency encoding direction), 3500 spokes per partition and 32 partitions. For each subject, images were acquired at 3 regions on average and each acquisition had around 30 coils. The reference images were acquired with oversampling with 3500 radial spokes and were retrospectively downsampled to generate undersampled images.

We divided the data into training (8 subjects), validation (2 subjects) and testing (7 subjects) datasets. Because of the data augmentation strategies described in Sect. 2.2, although the number of subjects was relatively small in this study, the generated data size was considerably large, comprising 193536 training data, 61440 validation data and 11968 testing data.

3.2   Implementation Details

We used Mean-Squared-Error (MSE) loss, i.e. l_2 loss, to minimize the distance between the output and the ground truth:

$$\min_\theta L_{l_2}(\theta) = ||T_\theta(x) - y||_2^2$$

(3)

where θ represents the network parameters, T represents the Transformer, x is the input and y is the ground truth. Implementation and training of the proposed network were completed in Python 3.7.7 (Python Software Foundation) using the Pytorch library 1.8.1 [26] on a computer with three NVIDIA Quadro RTX 8000 GPUs. The networks were trained for 100 epochs with a batch size of 400. An Adam optimizer with $\beta_1 = 0.9$, $\beta_2 = 0.98$, and $\epsilon = 10^{-9}$ was used. The hyperparameters were $d_{model} = 1024$, 16 attention heads, dimensions of keys and values $d_k = 64$, $d_v = 64$, dropout $= 0.1$. The total training time was around 3 days. The reference data containing 400 spokes was regarded as the full k-space acquisition and was used to reconstruct the reference standard image.

3.3   Performance Evaluation

For quantitative evaluation, we used Normalized MSE (NMSE), peak signal-to-noise ratio (PSNR) and structural similarity index (SSIM) between the reconstructed images and the reference images. NMSE was also calculated for the projection data. All images were normalized by the 90th percentile before the assessment. Statistical differences between the proposed PKT and the baseline methods were assessed using a one-way ANOVA model [27] with the reconstruction method being the independent variable.

As representative state-of-the-art techniques, we also trained image-based U-Net [28], DenseUnet [29] and SEUnet [30] to compare with our proposed PKT network. DenseUnet used dense connections between U-Net layers and SEUnet added channel-wise attention modules to the U-Net. We reconstructed 2D images with 100 and 400 spokes as the input and output images, respectively. All network training were completed in Python 3.7.7 using the Pytorch library 1.8.1 on a computer with a NVIDIA V100 GPU. The initial learning rate was 0.0001 which was reduced with a factor of 0.7 if no improvement shown in 200 iterations. The training was stopped when the learning rate was below 1×10^{-6} or the max epoch number reached 100.

3.4   Results

The network generated k-space projection data is shown in Fig. 2(a). Representative abdominal and pelvis images of the proposed PKT compared with baseline reconstructions and the reference images are shown in Fig. 2(b) and (c), respectively. The proposed PKT successfully removed the streaking artifacts and improved signal-to-noise in the magnitude and phase abdominal images compared to the other reconstructions. Figure 2(c) shows that the PKT reconstruction can also be applied to the pelvis region to reduce streaking artifacts and noise.

The NMSE of all testing projection data is 0.0385±0.0497. Quantitative evaluations of the proposed PKT network compared with baseline reconstructions with respect to the reference images are shown in Table 1. The proposed PKT have a significantly lower NMSE ($p < .0001$) and significantly higher PSNR ($p < .0001$) and SSIM ($p < .0001$) compared to all other reconstructions. The

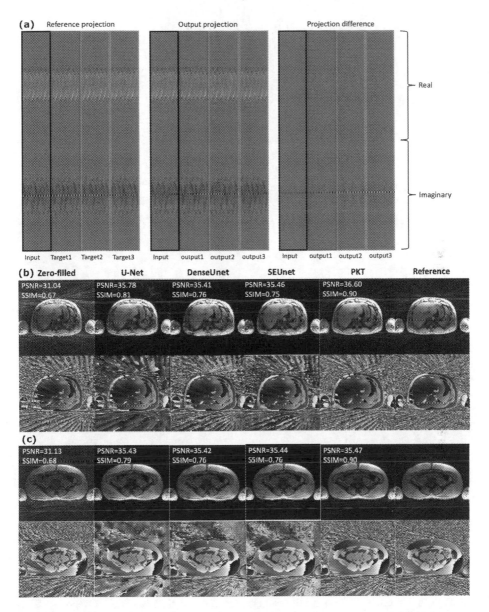

Fig. 2. (a) A representative comparison of the network outputs and the reference k-space projection data. (b) and (c) show representative images of the proposed PKT compared with baseline reconstructions along with the reference. Figure (b) shows an abdominal example and Fig. (c) shows a pelvis example. In both Figs. (b) and (c), the top row shows the magnitude images and the bottom row shows the phase images.

results indicate that the proposed PKT reconstructed images had fewer streaking artifacts and less noise compared to the other methods.

Table 1. Quantitative comparisons of the proposed PKT with baseline reconstructions. Values are reported as mean ± std across test subjects.

Methods	NMSE	PSNR	SSIM (%)
Zero-filled	0.1389 ± 0.0275	27.28 ± 2.10	59.19 ± 5.25
U–Net	0.0755 ± 0.0527	30.44 ± 2.87	71.81 ± 6.23
DenseUnet	0.0765 ± 0.0443	30.28 ± 2.87	67.20 ± 6.16
SEUnet	0.0759 ± 0.0447	30.34 ± 2.89	67.54 ± 6.45
PKT	$\mathbf{0.0456 \pm 0.0101}$	$\mathbf{32.13 \pm 2.26}$	$\mathbf{83.44 \pm 4.84}$

4   Conclusion

In this study, we propose to rearrange MRI radial projection to sequential time-series data and predict unacquired radial spokes using projection-based k-space Transformer (PKT) networks. We demonstrated PKT using golden-angle-ordered 3D radial data. Results showed PKT removed streaking artifacts and noise and had significantly better performance than other state-of-the-art deep learning neural networks. The novel data augmentation strategies in this study generated sufficient training data from a limited number of subjects by acquiring over-sampled multi-coil 3D data at various anatomical regions with the sliding window approach. We demonstrated that PKT could be applied to various anatomical structures including the abdominal and pelvic regions.

References

1. Lustig, M., Donoho, D.L., Santos, J.M., Pauly, J.M.: Compressed sensing MRI. IEEE Signal Process. Mag. **25**(2), 72–82 (2008)
2. Feng, L., et al.: Golden-angle radial sparse parallel MRI: combination of compressed sensing, parallel imaging, and golden-angle radial sampling for fast and flexible dynamic volumetric MRI. Magn. Reson. Med. **72**(3), 707–717 (2014)
3. Feng, L., Axel, L., Chandarana, H., Block, K.T., Sodickson, D.K., Otazo, R.: XD-GRASP: golden-angle radial MRI with reconstruction of extra motion-state dimensions using compressed sensing. Magn. Reson. Med. **75**(2), 775–788 (2016)
4. Yu, S., et al.: Deep de-aliasing for fast compressive sensing MRI. arXiv preprint arXiv:1705.07137 (2017)
5. Yang, G., et al.: DAGAN: deep de-aliasing generative adversarial networks for fast compressed sensing MRI reconstruction. IEEE Trans. Med. Imaging **37**(6), 1310–1321 (2017)
6. Quan, T.M., Nguyen-Duc, T., Jeong, W.K.: Compressed sensing MRI reconstruction using a generative adversarial network with a cyclic loss. IEEE Trans. Med. Imaging **37**(6), 1488–1497 (2018)

7. Kofler, A., Haltmeier, M., Schaeffter, T., Kolbitsch, C.: An end-to-end-trainable iterative network architecture for accelerated radial multi-coil 2D cine MR image reconstruction. Med. Phys. **48**(5), 2412–2425 (2021)
8. Hauptmann, A., Arridge, S., Lucka, F., Muthurangu, V., Steeden, J.A.: Real-time cardiovascular MR with SPATIO-temporal artifact suppression using deep learning-proof of concept in congenital heart disease. Magn. Reson. Med. **81**(2), 1143–1156 (2019)
9. Kofler, A., Dewey, M., Schaeffter, T., Wald, C., Kolbitsch, C.: Spatio-temporal deep learning-based undersampling artefact reduction for 2D radial cine MRI with limited training data. IEEE Trans. Med. Imaging **39**(3), 703–717 (2019)
10. Nezafat, M., El-Rewaidy, H., Kucukseymen, S., Hauser, T.H., Fahmy, A.S.: Deep convolution neural networks based artifact suppression in under-sampled radial acquisitions of myocardial T 1 mapping images. Phys. Med. Bio. **65**(22), 225024 (2020)
11. Fan, L., et al.: Rapid dealiasing of undersampled, non-Cartesian cardiac perfusion images using U-Net. NMR Biomed. **33**(5), e4239 (2020)
12. Shen, D., et al.: Rapid reconstruction of highly undersampled, non-Cartesian real-time cine k-space data using a perceptual complex neural network (PCNN). NMR Biomed. **34**(1), e4405 (2021)
13. Chen, D., Schaeffter, T., Kolbitsch, C., Kofler, A.: Ground-truth-free deep learning for artefacts reduction in 2D radial cardiac cine MRI using a synthetically generated dataset. Phys. Med. Bio. **66**(9), 095005 (2021)
14. Malavé, M.O., et al.: Reconstruction of undersampled 3D non-Cartesian image-based navigators for coronary MRA using an unrolled deep learning model. Magn. Reson. Med. **84**(2), 800–812 (2020)
15. Terpstra, M.L., et al.: Deep learning-based image reconstruction and motion estimation from undersampled radial k-space for real-time MRI-guided radiotherapy. Phys. Med. Biol. **65**(15), 155015 (2020)
16. El-Rewaidy, H., et al.: Multi-domain convolutional neural network (MD-CNN) for radial reconstruction of dynamic cardiac MRI. Magn. Reson. Med. **85**(3), 1195–1208 (2021)
17. Fessler, J.A.: On NUFFT-based gridding for non-Cartesian MRI. J. Magn. Reson. **188**(2), 191–195 (2007)
18. Vaswani, A., et al.: Attention is all you need. In: Advances in Neural Information Processing Systems, vol. 30 (2017)
19. Parmar, N., et al.: Image transformer. In: International Conference on Machine Learning, pp. 4055–4064. PMLR (2018)
20. Dosovitskiy, A., et al.: An image is worth 16x16 words: transformers for image recognition at scale. arXiv preprint arXiv:2010.11929 (2020)
21. Seiberlich, N., Ehses, P., Duerk, J., Gilkeson, R., Griswold, M.: Improved radial grappa calibration for real-time free-breathing cardiac imaging. Magn. Reson. Med. **65**(2), 492–505 (2011)
22. Uecker, M., Tamir, J.I., Ong, F., Lustig, M.: The BART toolbox for computational magnetic resonance imaging. In: Proceedings of the International Society for Magnetic Resonance in Medicine, vol. 24 (2016)
23. Walsh, D.O., Gmitro, A.F., Marcellin, M.W.: Adaptive reconstruction of phased array MR imagery. Magn. Reson. Med. Official J. Int. Soc. Magn. Reson. Med. **43**(5), 682–690 (2000)
24. He, K., Zhang, X., Ren, S., Sun, J.: Deep residual learning for image recognition. In: Proceedings of the IEEE Conference on Computer Vision and Pattern Recognition, pp. 770–778 (2016)

25. Ba, J.L., Kiros, J.R., Hinton, G.E.: Layer normalization. arXiv preprint arXiv:1607.06450 (2016)
26. Paszke, A., et al.: Automatic differentiation in pytorch (2017)
27. Howell, D.C.: Statistical methods for psychology. Cengage Learning (2012)
28. Ronneberger, O., Fischer, P., Brox, T.: U-Net: convolutional networks for biomedical image segmentation. In: Navab, N., Hornegger, J., Wells, W.M., Frangi, A.F. (eds.) MICCAI 2015. LNCS, vol. 9351, pp. 234–241. Springer, Cham (2015). https://doi.org/10.1007/978-3-319-24574-4_28
29. Xiang, L., et al.: Deep-learning-based multi-modal fusion for fast MR reconstruction. IEEE Trans. Biomed. Eng. **66**(7), 2105–2114 (2018)
30. Hu, J., Shen, L., Sun, G.: Squeeze-and-excitation networks. In: Proceedings of the IEEE Conference on Computer Vision and Pattern Recognition, pp. 7132–7141 (2018)

Scale-Equivariant Unrolled Neural Networks for Data-Efficient Accelerated MRI Reconstruction

Beliz Gunel[(⊠)], Arda Sahiner, Arjun D. Desai, Akshay S. Chaudhari,
Shreyas Vasanawala, Mert Pilanci, and John Pauly

Stanford University, Stanford, CA 94305, USA
{bgunel,sahiner,arjundd,akshaysc,vasanawala,pilanci,pauly}@stanford.edu

Abstract. Unrolled neural networks have enabled state-of-the-art reconstruction performance and fast inference times for the accelerated magnetic resonance imaging (MRI) reconstruction task. However, these approaches depend on fully-sampled scans as ground truth data which is either costly or not possible to acquire in many clinical medical imaging applications; hence, reducing dependence on data is desirable. In this work, we propose modeling the proximal operators of unrolled neural networks with *scale-equivariant* convolutional neural networks in order to improve the data-efficiency and robustness to drifts in scale of the images that might stem from the variability of patient anatomies or change in field-of-view across different MRI scanners. Our approach demonstrates strong improvements over the state-of-the-art unrolled neural networks under the same memory constraints both with and without data augmentations on both in-distribution and out-of-distribution scaled images without significantly increasing the train or inference time.

Keywords: MRI reconstruction · Scale-equivariance · Data-efficiency

1 Introduction

Magnetic resonance imaging (MRI) is a medical imaging modality that enables non-invasive anatomical visualization with great soft-tissue contrast and high diagnostic quality. Although the MRI data acquisition process can suffer from long scan durations, it can be accelerated by undersampling the requisite spatial frequency measurements, referred to as *k-space* measurements. As the k-space measurements are subsampled below the Nyquist rate, reconstructing the underlying images without aliasing artifacts from these measurements is an ill-posed

---

B. Gunel and A. Sahiner—Equal Contribution.

Supplementary Information The online version contains supplementary material available at https://doi.org/10.1007/978-3-031-16446-0_70.

problem. To tackle this, previous approaches have leveraged prior knowledge of the true underlying solution in the form of regularization – most notably enforcing sparsity in the Wavelet domain, referred to as *compressed sensing* [16]. However, these approaches suffer from long reconstruction times due to their iterative nature and can require parameter-specific tuning [15].

Unrolled neural networks [1, 24, 27, 28] have been shown to offer state-of-the-art reconstruction performance and faster reconstruction times compared to iterative methods, enabling higher acceleration factors for clinical applications. However, these approaches still depend on fully-sampled scans as ground truth data which is either costly or not possible to acquire in many clinical medical imaging applications; hence, reducing dependence on data, referred to as *data-efficiency*, is desirable. Towards the goal of improving data-efficiency, besides the prior proposals which leverage prospectively undersampled (unsupervised) data that currently lag in reconstruction performance [7,11], recent work has proposed designing data augmentation pipelines tailored to accelerated MRI reconstruction with appropriate image-based [10] or acquisition-based, physics-driven transformations [8,9]. Although helpful with data efficiency and robustness to certain distribution drifts, these approaches do not *guarantee* that the final reconstruction model satisfies the desired symmetries, introduced through the data augmentation transformations, at train or inference time – which may increase the existing concerns among clinicians around using data-driven techniques.

In this work, we propose modeling the proximal operators of unrolled neural networks with *scale-equivariant* convolutional neural networks (CNNs) in order to improve data-efficiency and robustness to drifts in scale of the images that could be caused by the variability of patient anatomies or change in field-of-view across different MRI scanners. We note that our method effectively encodes a lack of prior knowledge of the scale of the structures in the images, in addition to the lack of position knowledge encoded by the *translational equivariance* property of standard CNNs. Our approach *ensures* more stable behavior for our model under scale and position changes at inference time, as scale and translation equivariance get explicitly encoded into the network. Here, we demonstrate that (1) our approach outperforms state-of-the-art unrolled neural networks under the same memory constraints both with and without appropriate data augmentations on both in distribution and out-of-distribution scaled images with little impact on the train or inference time; (2) our method is empirically less sensitive to the step size initializations within the proximal updates in comparison to the state-of-the-art unrolled neural networks that are often tuned for each different dataset; (3) we depict a correlation between the fidelity of enforcement of scale equivariance, quantified by equivariance error (Eq. 10), and reconstruction performance. We note that this reinforces the utility of incorporating the scale symmetry into unrolled neural networks to improve reconstruction performance in a data-efficient manner. We test our method on publicly available mridata 3D fast-spin-echo (FSE) multi-coil knee dataset [19]. In order to promote reproducible research, we open-source our code, and will include experimental configurations along with trained models at https://github.com/ad12/meddlr.

2   Related Work

Data Augmentation for Accelerated MRI Reconstruction. Prior proposals designed transformations that leverage the natural symmetries of the accelerated MRI reconstruction problem in the form of data augmentation. Fabian et al. [10] proposed MRAugment, an image-based data augmentation pipeline. Desai et al. proposed a semi-supervised consistency framework for joint reconstruction and denoising [9], and later extended the denoising objective to a generalized data augmentation pipeline that enables composing a broader family of physics-driven acquisition-based augmentations and image-based augmentations [8].

Equivariant Networks. Cohen et al. [6] showed that encoding symmetries directly into the neural network architectures using group equivariant CNNs lead to data-efficiency with guaranteed equivariance to encoded symmetries at both train and inference time. Following this work, there has been considerable amount of work in this direction across different domains of machine learning including exploring roto-translational symmetries [5] and scaling symmetries [25, 26,33]. Within medical applications, prior proposals primarily focused on roto-translational symmetries for both classification & segmentation tasks [2,18,31, 32] and reconstruction tasks [3,4]. To the best of our knowledge, there has not been any prior work that explored scale equivariance in the context of accelerated MRI reconstruction or for any other type of inverse problem.

3   Background and Preliminaries

3.1   Accelerated MRI Reconstruction

We consider multi-coil MRI acquisition, which is a clinically-relevant setup where multiple receiver coils are used to acquire spatially-localized k-space measurements modulated by corresponding *sensitivity maps*. In this setup, scan times are accelerated by decreasing the number of samples acquired in k-space, referred to as *accelerated MRI reconstruction*. We represent the undersampling operation on acquired samples in k-space as a binary mask Ω. Overall, the multi-coil accelerated MRI problem can be written as

$$y = \Omega \boldsymbol{F} \boldsymbol{S} x^* + \epsilon = A x^* + \epsilon, \tag{1}$$

where y is k-space measurements, $\boldsymbol{F}$ is the matrix for discrete Fourier transform, $\boldsymbol{S}$ is the coil sensitivity maps, x^* is the underlying ground truth image, and ϵ is the additive complex Gaussian noise. Coil sensitivity maps are estimated to perform reconstruction in practice as they are often unknown and vary per patient [22]. $A = \Omega \boldsymbol{F} \boldsymbol{S}$ is the known *forward operator* during acquisition. Note that this problem is ill-posed in the Hadamard sense [12], which makes recovering the underlying image x^* impossible to recover uniquely without an assumption such as sparsity in a transformation domain as in compressed sensing [16].

3.2   Unrolled Proximal Gradient Descent Networks

For MRI compressed sensing, the ill-posed reconstruction problem can be addressed with a regularized least-squares formulation of the form

$$\hat{x} = \arg\min_{x} \|Ax - y\|_2^2 + \mathcal{R}(x), \qquad (2)$$

where $\mathcal{R}$ is some regularizer (originally proposed an ℓ_1 penalty in the Wavelet domain [16]). Problems of this form, where $\mathcal{R}$ is not necessarily smooth, are often solved with iterative optimization methods such as Proximal Gradient Descent (PGD). At iteration k, PGD operates as follows:

$$z^{(k)} = x^{(k)} - \eta_k \nabla_x \|Ax^{(k)} - y\|_2^2 \qquad (3)$$
$$x^{(k+1)} = \text{prox}_{\mathcal{R}}(z^{(k)}) \qquad (4)$$

with appropriately chosen step sizes η_k, and proximal operator $\text{prox}_{\mathcal{R}}(\cdot)$. The first step thus takes a gradient step to enforce consistency of the iterate $x^{(k)}$ with the measured signal in k-space y (data consistency), while the second step enforces the prior of regularizer $\mathcal{R}$ on $x^{(k)}$ (proximal step). It is known that following this procedure will provably solve Eq. (2) [21]. Choosing $\mathcal{R}$ requires strong a priori assumptions that may not hold in practice. Thus, with the recent success of deep learning approaches, it has been proposed to replace the proximal step with a data-driven supervised learning approach: a learned neural network [24]. In particular, one unrolls a fixed, small number of iterations K of Eqs. (3) and (4), and replaces each proximal step with a CNN, re-writing Eq. (4) with

$$x^{(k+1)} = f_{\theta_k}(z^{(k)}). \qquad (5)$$

The parameters $\{\theta_k, \eta_k\}_{k=1}^{K}$ are then trained in an end-to-end fashion over a dataset of undersampled k-space and ground-truth image pairs $\{y_i, x_i^*\}_{i=1}^{n}$ with some loss function $\mathcal{L}(\hat{x}_i, x_i^*)$, such as the pixel-wise complex-ℓ_1 loss $\|\hat{x}_i - x_i^*\|_1$. Such unrolled networks can outperform standard iterative compressed sensing methods, both in reconstruction quality and time [24]. One proposed explanation for the improved performance is that unrolled networks impose certain *priors* that are not captured by ℓ_1-Wavelet regularizers [17,23]. One such prior is that of *translation equivariance*, which we describe in the subsequent section.

3.3   Equivariance

We say that a function f is *equivariant* to a function g if

$$f(g(x)) = g(f(x)) \; \forall x \qquad (6)$$

Furthermore, we say f is equivariant to a *family* of functions $\mathcal{G}$ if Eq. (6) holds for all $g \in \mathcal{G}$. Standard convolutional layers are equivariant to the discrete translation group—if the input to a convolutional layer is translated in any direction, the corresponding output is the result of translating the original input's corresponding output. Thus, it is built into a CNN that translation does not affect the final output of the network (without pooling), thereby imposing an implicit prior on the nature of the functions that a CNN can learn. Note that in the context of unrolled proximal gradient descent networks, a translation equivariant proximal operator implies a translation invariant implicit regularizer $\mathcal{R}$ [3]. One may also desire to impose other priors through equivariance, as have been proposed with rotation-equivariant CNNs [6] and scale-equivariant CNNs [26].

4   Methods

4.1   Learned Iterative Scale-Equivariant Reconstruction Networks

We propose the use of *scale-translation equivariant* CNNs for unrolled proximal gradient descent networks, referred to as *unrolled neural networks*, for accelerated MRI reconstruction. *In particular, we enforce the prior that either scaling or translating the undersampled input in the image domain should correspond to a scaled and translated output ground truth image.* This scale-translation equivariance provides additional built-in priors to the network, which creates resilience to the changes of scale in the images that might stem from the variability of patient anatomies or change in field-of-view across different MR scanners. We thus replace the proximal step in Eq. (4) of the unrolled proximal gradient descent network as described in Sect. 3.2 with a scale-translation equivariant CNN as f_{θ_k} in Eq. (5), leaving the data consistency steps unchanged. We refer to scale-translation equivariance as *scale equivariance* throughout the text for brevity.

4.2   Implementation

We define the scale-translation group $H = \{(s,t)\} := S \rtimes T$ as the semi-direct product of the scale group S, which consists of scale transformations s, and the translation group T, which consists of translations t [26]. A scale transformation $L_{\hat{s}}$ of a function f defined on H is defined by scaling both the scale component and translation component of the arguments of f, i.e.

$$L_{\hat{s}}f(s,t) = f(s\hat{s}^{-1}, \hat{s}^{-1}t). \tag{7}$$

For a convolutional kernel w to be scale-translation equivariant for a specific scale s, we require, by Eq. (6),

$$L_s[f] \star w = L_s[f \star w_{s^{-1}}], \tag{8}$$

where $w_{s^{-1}}$ is w scaled by s^{-1}. To enforce scale equivariance, we follow [26] with an implementation of scale-equivariant convolutions for discrete scales with steerable filters. A convolutional filter is scale-*steerable* if an arbitrary scale transformation can be expressed as a linear combination of a fixed set of basis filters.

Each filter is expressed in terms of a B-dimensional *kernel basis*, where each basis filter is pre-calculated and fixed. For our case, we desire that the convolution to be equivariant to scaling an image by a single factor $a > 0$. We can then write our convolutional weights w as a linear combination of basis functions:

$$w = \sum_{i=1}^{B} v_i \psi_i^{(a)}, \tag{9}$$

where v_i is learned, and $\psi_i^{(a)}$ is a fixed basis filter which has been scaled by a factor of a^{-1}. This method has proven to provide scale equivariance, since convolving an image scaled x by a with a filter w is equivalent to convolving x with a filter w scaled by a^{-1} and then subsequently downscaled, by Eq. (8). In our work, we choose ψ to be the set of 2D Hermite polynomials with a Gaussian envelope, which has shown empirically to work well in image classification and tracking tasks, though other bases, such as Fourier or radial, may also be used [25,26]. We note that because these basis filters are based on continuous space and are then projected onto the pixel grid, the scale equivariance is not exact. This discrepancy between these two components for some function Φ, i.e.

$$\Delta = \frac{\|L_s[\Phi(f)] - \Phi(L_s[f])\|_2^2}{\|L_s[\Phi(f)]\|_2^2} \tag{10}$$

is defined as *equivariance error* of Φ. This error suggests that in many cases, exact equivariance is not possible to enforce due to the discrete spatial nature of convolutional kernels. However, using the projection onto the pixel grid as described, one may find close approximations to exact equivariance.

Table 1. Scale-Equivariant unrolled networks (Scale-Eq) outperform the state-of-the-art unrolled networks (Vanilla) both on in-distribution (None) and scaled images with scaling factor $a = 0.9$ (Scaled), both for zero-initialized and tuned step size initializations η_0 in the data-limited regime. Both Scale-Eq and Vanilla networks use appropriate scale data augmentations during training, as noted by $+$. Scale-Eq+ for tuned η_0 uses $B = 2$.

Model	η_0	Original		Scaled (a=0.9)	
		SSIM	cPSNR (dB)	SSIM	cPSNR (dB)
Vanilla+	Zero-init	0.864 (0.012)	35.77 (0.50)	0.919 (0.013)	39.03 (0.46)
Scale-Eq+		**0.900 (0.003)**	**36.44 (0.49)**	**0.944 (0.006)**	**40.45 (0.57)**
Vanilla+	Tuned	0.902 (0.008)	35.59 (0.40)	0.952 (0.004)	40.15 (0.41)
Scale-Eq+		**0.911 (0.008)**	**35.83 (0.46)**	**0.956 (0.001)**	**40.97 (0.65)**

5   Experiments and Results

We use the publicly-available mridata 3D fast-spin-echo (FSE) multi-coil knee dataset (http://mridata.org/) [19] of healthy patients to evaluate our approach.

Table 2. Comparison of Scale-Equivariant, Rotation-Equivariant, and Vanilla unrolled networks using the state-of-the-art data augmentation pipeline MRAugment [10] during training in the data-limited regime. Learned step sizes η_0 are zero-initialized for all networks; and Scale-Eq uses $B = 2$ for the order of the kernel basis. Scale-Eq-MRAugment outperforms other models, while Rotation-Eq-MRAugment outperforms Vanilla-MRAugment in cPSNR and does comparably in SSIM.

Model	SSIM	cPSNR (dB)
Vanilla-MRAugment	0.877 (0.016)	34.27 (0.31)
Scale-Eq-MRAugment	**0.909 (0.007)**	**36.37 (0.47)**
Rotation-Eq-MRAugment	0.873 (0.008)	36.30 (0.50)

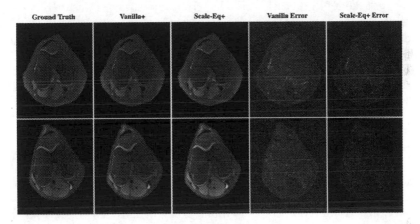

Fig. 1. Reconstruction examples comparing Vanilla+ and Scale-Equivariant+ on the middle slices of in-distribution test volumes. Error maps between the model reconstructions and ground truths demonstrate that Scale-Equivariant+ improves over Vanilla+.

We decode 3D MRI scans into a hybrid k-space $(x \times k_y \times k_z)$ using the 1D orthogonal inverse Fourier transform along the readout direction x so that all methods reconstruct 2D $k_y \times k_z$ slices. We estimate the coil sensitivity maps using JSENSE [34] as implemented in SigPy [20] with a kernel width of 8 and a 20×20 center k-space auto-calibration region. We use 2D Poission Disc undersampling with a 16x acceleration rate, a compressed sensing motivated sampling pattern for 3D Cartesian imaging that has been routinely implemented in the clinic at Stanford Hospital [29], for training and evaluation. We randomly partition the dataset into 4480 slices (14 volumes) for training, 640 slices (2 volumes) for validation, and 960 slices (3 volumes) for testing; and simulate a *data-limited regime* with limiting the training set to 320 slices (1 volume). We use magnitude structural similarity (SSIM) [30] and complex peak signal-to-noise ratio (cPSNR) in decibels (dB) to evaluate the quality of our reconstructions. We note that SSIM has shown to be a more clinically-preferred metric to cPSNR for quantifying perceptual quality of MRI reconstructions [14]. For all evaluated models, we train for 200 epochs, checkpoint every 10 epochs, and pick the best model based on validation SSIM; use the Adam optimizer [13] with its default parameters ($\beta_1 = 0.9$, $\beta_2 = 0.999$, base learning rate of 1e−3); open-source (blinded) our implementations, experimental configurations, and trained models in PyTorch version 1.8.1 (Fig. 1).

We follow [24]'s implementation for the state-of-the-art unrolled neural networks, referred to as *Vanilla*. For the rotation-equivariant unrolled network baseline, referred to as *Rotation-Eq*, we follow [3]'s work in our own implementation where we enforce equivariance to 90° rotations. For our scale-equivariant unrolled neural networks, referred to as *Scale-Eq*, we set the scale parameter $a = 0.9$ and consider the order of the kernel basis a hyperparameter and set it to $B = 3$, unless specified otherwise. All unrolled neural networks use 5 unrolled blocks where each proximal block consists of 1 residual block that includes convolutions with 96 channels, learnable step sizes η_k, and pixel-wise complex-ℓ_1 training objective.

We compare our method to baselines in the case where appropriate data augmentations are performed during training in order to demonstrate the practical utility of building equivariant networks *in addition to* the data augmentation based approaches. Specifically, we refer to Vanilla as Vanilla+ and Scale-Eq as Scale-Eq+ when scale data augmentations with a scaling factor of $a = 0.9$ are introduced with simple exponential augmentation probability scheduling [10]. In Table 1, we consider the cases where learnable step sizes (described in Eq. 3) are zero-initialized or tuned as a hyperparameter, and evaluate on both regular test slices and unseen scaled test slices with a scaling factor of $a = 0.9$ in the data-limited regime. Taking both target ground truth images and pre-computed coil sensitivity maps into account, the scaled setting simulates the scaling changes at inference time which might stem from the variability of patient anatomies or change of field-of-view across different MRI scanners in practice. We show that Scale-Eq+ outperforms Vanilla+ across all settings, overall considerably improving the data-efficiency of the network. We note that we keep the number of trainable parameters almost the same between Scale-Eq+ and Vanilla+ for fair performance comparison and demonstrate that Scale-Eq+ does not significantly increase the training or inference time over Vanilla+ in Table 3 (Supp.) to ensure practical utility. We include reconstruction examples along with error maps for Vanilla+ and Scale-Eq+ in Fig. 1. We empirically demonstrate in Table 2 (Supp.) that Scale-Eq is less sensitive than Vanilla to the learnable step size initializations that is often highly specific to the dataset and hence can require careful tuning.

In Table 2, we compare Vanilla, Rotation-Eq, and Scale-Eq using the state-of-the-art data augmentation pipeline MRAugment [10] in its default configuration specified in Table 1 (Supp.). We demonstrate that Scale-Eq-MRAugment outperforms Vanilla-MRAugment while Rotation-Eq-MRAugment outperforms Vanilla-MRAugment in PSNR and does comparably in SSIM. We clarify that we do not aim to argue that scale symmetry is more useful to encode than rotation symmetry here, in fact, we demonstrate that encoding scale symmetry is as helpful as encoding rotation symmetry, if not more. In Fig. 1 (Supp.), we depict a correlation between the fidelity of enforcement of scale equivariance, quantified by equivariance error (Eq. 10), and reconstruction performance in terms of SSIM. This further reinforces the utility of incorporating scale equivariance into unrolled networks to improve reconstruction performance in a data-efficient manner. Finally, in Table 4 (Supp.), we demonstrate that improvements for Scale-Eq+ over Vanilla+ increase as the dataset size decreases. This illustrates the utility of equivariance in data limited regimes.

6 Conclusion

We have proposed learned iterative scale-equivariant unrolled neural networks for data-efficient accelerated MRI reconstruction, demonstrating its utility in improving reconstruction performance in both in-distribution and out-of-distribution settings, even under cases of data augmentation during training. We thus demonstrate that encoding the lack of prior knowledge of the scale of the images can provide a more robust reconstruction network. Many other directions related to this work can be explored, such as applications to three-dimensional image recovery, or to other medical image tasks such as segmentation. One may also further explore the impact of particular transformation groups to which one may be equivariant, to encode multiple priors into various image processing tasks.

Acknowledgements. Beliz Gunel, Arda Sahiner, Shreyas Vasanawala, and John Pauly were supported by NIH R01EB009690 and NIH U01-EB029427-01. Mert Pilanci was partially supported by the National Science Foundation under grants IIS-1838179, ECCS- 2037304, DMS-2134248, and the Army Research Office. Arjun Desai and Akshay Chaudhari were supported by grants R01 AR077604, R01 EB002524, K24 AR062068, and P41 EB015891 from the NIH; the Precision Health and Integrated Diagnostics Seed Grant from Stanford University; National Science Foundation (DGE 1656518, CCF1763315, CCF1563078); DOD – National Science and Engineering Graduate Fellowship (ARO); Stanford Artificial Intelligence in Medicine and Imaging GCP grant; Stanford Human-Centered Artificial Intelligence GCP grant; Microsoft Azure through Stanford Data Science's Cloud Resources Program; GE Healthcare and Philips.

References

1. Aggarwal, H.K., Mani, M.P., Jacob, M.: MoDL: model-based deep learning architecture for inverse problems. IEEE Trans. Med. Imaging **38**(2), 394–405 (2018)
2. Bekkers, E.J., Lafarge, M.W., Veta, M., Eppenhof, K.A.J., Pluim, J.P.W., Duits, R.: Roto-translation covariant convolutional networks for medical image analysis. ArXiv abs/1804.03393 (2018)
3. Celledoni, E., Ehrhardt, M.J., Etmann, C., Owren, B., Schonlieb, C.B., Sherry, F.: Equivariant neural networks for inverse problems. Inverse Probl. **37**, 085006 (2021)
4. Chen, D., Tachella, J., Davies, M.E.: Equivariant imaging: learning beyond the range space. In: Proceedings of the IEEE/CVF International Conference on Computer Vision, pp. 4379–4388 (2021)

5. Cohen, T., Geiger, M., Köhler, J., Welling, M.: Spherical CNNs. ArXiv abs/1801.10130 (2018)
6. Cohen, T., Welling, M.: Group equivariant convolutional networks. In: International Conference on Machine Learning, pp. 2990–2999. PMLR (2016)
7. Darestani, M.Z., Heckel, R.: Accelerated MRI with un-trained neural networks. IEEE Trans. Comput. Imaging **7**, 724–733 (2021)
8. Desai, A.D., et al.: VORTEX: Physics-driven data augmentations for consistency training for robust accelerated MRI reconstruction. In: MIDL (2022)
9. Desai, A.D., et al.: Noise2Recon: a semi-supervised framework for joint MRI reconstruction and denoising. arXiv preprint arXiv:2110.00075 (2021)
10. Fabian, Z., Heckel, R., Soltanolkotabi, M.: Data augmentation for deep learning based accelerated MRI reconstruction with limited data. In: International Conference on Machine Learning, pp. 3057–3067. PMLR (2021)
11. Gunel, B., Mardani, M., Chaudhari, A., Vasanawala, S., Pauly, J.: Weakly supervised MR image reconstruction using untrained neural networks. In: Proceedings of International Society of Magnetic Resonance in Medicine (ISMRM) (2021)
12. Hadamard, J.: Sur les problèmes aux dérivées partielles et leur signification physique. Princeton Univ. Bull. 49–52 (1902)
13. Kingma, D.P., Ba, J.: Adam: a method for stochastic optimization. arXiv preprint arXiv:1412.6980 (2014)
14. Knoll, F., et al.: Advancing machine learning for MR image reconstruction with an open competition: Overview of the 2019 fastMRI challenge. Magn. Reson. Med. **84**(6), 3054–3070 (2020)
15. Lustig, M., Donoho, D., Pauly, J.M.: Sparse MRI: the application of compressed sensing for rapid MR imaging. Magn. Resona. Med.: Off. J. Int. Soc. Magn. Reson. Med. **58**(6), 1182–1195 (2007)
16. Lustig, M., Donoho, D.L., Santos, J.M., Pauly, J.M.: Compressed sensing MRI. IEEE Signal Process. Mag. **25**(2), 72–82 (2008)
17. Mardani, M., et al.: Neural proximal gradient descent for compressive imaging. Adv. Neural Inf. Process. Syst. **31** (2018)
18. Müller, P., Golkov, V., Tomassini, V., Cremers, D.: Rotation-equivariant deep learning for diffusion MRI. ArXiv abs/2102.06942 (2021)
19. Ong, F., Amin, S., Vasanawala, S., Lustig, M.: Mridata.org: an open archive for sharing MRI raw data. In: Proceedings of International Society for Magnetic Resonance in Medicine, vol. 26, p. 1 (2018)
20. Ong, F., Lustig, M.: SigPy: a python package for high performance iterative reconstruction. In: Proceedings of the ISMRM 27th Annual Meeting, Montreal, Quebec, Canada, vol. 4819 (2019)
21. Parikh, N., Boyd, S.: Proximal algorithms. Found. Trends Optim. **1**(3), 127–239 (2014)
22. Pruessmann, K.P., Weiger, M., Scheidegger, M.B., Boesiger, P.: Sense: sensitivity encoding for fast MRI. Magn. Reson. Med.: Off. J. Int. Soc. Magn. Reson. Med. **42**(5), 952–962 (1999)
23. Sahiner, A., Mardani, M., Ozturkler, B., Pilanci, M., Pauly, J.: Convex regularization behind neural reconstruction. arXiv preprint arXiv:2012.05169 (2020)
24. Sandino, C.M., Cheng, J.Y., Chen, F., Mardani, M., Pauly, J.M., Vasanawala, S.S.: Compressed sensing: from research to clinical practice with deep neural networks: shortening scan times for magnetic resonance imaging. IEEE Signal Process. Mag. **37**(1), 117–127 (2020)
25. Sosnovik, I., Moskalev, A., Smeulders, A.: DISCO: accurate discrete scale convolutions. arXiv preprint arXiv:2106.02733 (2021)

26. Sosnovik, I., Szmaja, M., Smeulders, A.: Scale-equivariant steerable networks. arXiv preprint arXiv:1910.11093 (2019)
27. Sriram, A., et al.: End-to-end variational networks for accelerated MRI reconstruction. In: Martel, A.L., et al. (eds.) MICCAI 2020. LNCS, vol. 12262, pp. 64–73. Springer, Cham (2020). https://doi.org/10.1007/978-3-030-59713-9_7
28. Sun, J., Li, H., Xu, Z., et al.: Deep ADMM-net for compressive sensing MRI. Adv. Neural Inf. Process. Syst. **29** (2016)
29. Vasanawala, S.S., et al.: Practical parallel imaging compressed sensing MRI: summary of two years of experience in accelerating body MRI of pediatric patients. In: 2011 IEEE International Symposium on Biomedical Imaging: From Nano to Macro, pp. 1039–1043 (2011)
30. Wang, Z., Bovik, A.C., Sheikh, H.R., Simoncelli, E.P.: Image quality assessment: from error visibility to structural similarity. IEEE Trans. Image Process. **13**(4), 600–612 (2004)
31. Weiler, M., Geiger, M., Welling, M., Boomsma, W., Cohen, T.: 3D steerable CNNs: learning rotationally equivariant features in volumetric data. In: NeurIPS (2018)
32. Winkels, M., Cohen, T.: 3D G-CNNs for pulmonary nodule detection. ArXiv abs/1804.04656 (2018)
33. Worrall, D.E., Welling, M.: Deep scale-spaces: equivariance over scale. ArXiv abs/1905.11697 (2019)
34. Ying, L., Sheng, J.: Joint image reconstruction and sensitivity estimation in SENSE (JSENSE). Magn. Reson. Med.: Off. J. Int. Soc. Magn. Reson. Med. **57**(6), 1196–1202 (2007)

DDPNet: A Novel Dual-Domain Parallel Network for Low-Dose CT Reconstruction

Rongjun Ge[1,4], Yuting He[2,4], Cong Xia[3], Hailong Sun[1], Yikun Zhang[2,4], Dianlin Hu[2,4], Sijie Chen[5], Yang Chen[2,4], Shuo Li[6], and Daoqiang Zhang[1(✉)]

[1] College of Computer Science and Technology, Nanjing University of Aeronautics and Astronautics, MIIT Key Laboratory of Pattern Analysis and Machine Intelligence, Nanjing, China
dqzhang@nuaa.edu.cn
[2] Laboratory of Image Science and Technology, School of Computer Science and Engineering, Southeast University, Nanjing, China
[3] Jiangsu Key Laboratory of Molecular and Functional Imaging, Department of Radiology, Zhongda Hospital, Medical School of Southeast University, Nanjing, China
[4] Key Laboratory of Computer Network and Information Integration (Southeast University), Ministry of Education, Nanjing, China
[5] Department of Radiology, Nanjing Medical University, Nanjing, China
[6] Digital Imaging Group of London, Department of Medical Imaging and Medical Biophysics, Western University, London, ON, Canada

Abstract. The low-dose computed tomography (CT) scan is clinically significant to reduce the radiation risk for radiologists and patients, especially in repeative examination. However, it inherently introduce more noise due to the radiation exposure. Nowadays, the existing LDCT reconstruction methods mainly focus on single domain of sinogram and image, or their cascade. But there still has limitations that the insufficient information in single domain, and the accumulation error in cascaded dual-domain. Though dual-domain can provide more information in reconstruction, how to effectively organize dual-domain and make complementary fusion still remain open challenges. Besides, the details inter-pixel in reconstructed LDCT is essential for structure maintenance. We propose a Dual-domain parallel network (DDPNet) for high-quality reconstruction from widely accessible LDCT, which is the first powerful work making parallel optimization between sinogram and image domains to eliminate the accumulation error, and fusing dual-domain reconstructions for complementary. DDPNet is constituted by three special designs: 1) a dual-domain parallel architecture to make joint mutual optimization with interactive information flow; 2) a unified fusion block to complement multi-results and further refine final reconstruction with triple-cross attention; 3) a pair of coupled patch-discriminators to drive the reconstruction towards both realistic anatomic content and accurate inner-details with image-based and inter-pixel gradient-based adversarial constraints, respectively. The extensive experiments validated on public available Mayo dataset show that our DDPNet achieves promising PSNR up to 45.29 dB, SSIM up to 98.24%, and MAE down to 13.54 HU in quantitative evaluations, as well as gains high-quality readable visualizations

L. Wang et al. (Eds.): MICCAI 2022, LNCS 13436, pp. 748–757, 2022.
https://doi.org/10.1007/978-3-031-16446-0_71

in qualitative assessments. All of these findings suggest that our method has great clinical potential in CT imaging.

Keywords: Dual-domain parallel network · Unified fusion block · Coupled patch-discriminators · Low-dose computed tomography

1   Introduction

Accurate reconstruction for low-dose computed tomography (LDCT) scan with noise reduction and structure maintenance is clinically significant in widely CT examination and diagnosis. As well known, CT scan is one of the most widely used medical imaging examination for inner anatomic structure visualization [1,2]. But its imaging principle with X-Ray radiation exposure causes potential risks of carcinogenesis and genetic damage for radiologists and patients, especially in repeative and follow-up examination. And LDCT is thus widely used according to "as low as reasonably achievable" (ALARA) principle for radiation risk reduction. But it still has obvious shortage of the increased noise, due to the decreased dose. As obviously shown in Fig. 1(a) vs. (b), LDCT is characterized with low signal-to-noise ratio compared to normal-dose computed tomography (NDCT), which causes challenge to read, especially for inexperienced radiologist. And in the enlarged region of Fig. 1(a), the vessel with red arrow pointed in NDCT is clear to be distinguished, but there exists difficulty for LDCT. Therefore, how to effectively make LDCT reconstruction in the more readable pattern with noise reduction and structure maintenance is of great contribution for clinical examination and diagnosis.

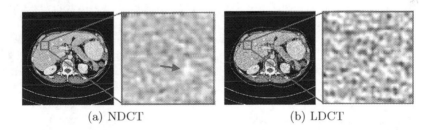

(a) NDCT   (b) LDCT

Fig. 1. The comparison between (a) NDCT and (b) LDCT. LDCT can effectively reduce the radiation risk, but get lower signal-to-noise ratio than NDCT. NDCT has more clear structure as the vessel with red arrow pointed, while LDCT causes difficulty. (Color figure online)

As far as we know, the existing methods for LDCT reconstruction can be mainly classified into three categories, that based on the single-sinogram domain, the single image-domain, and the dual-domain cascade, respectively. 1) Sinogram-domain based methods perform noise suppression on the projection data. Traditional methods either use filters [3,4] on the projection data to smooth the sinogram or make iterative reconstruction [5,6] based on priors. Deep-learning methods are used to conduct direct restorion from contaminated projection data. In [7], a deep convolutional neural network (CNN) with residual learning strategy is adopt to learn the difference between noisy and high-quality sinogram. [8] uses an attention residual dense network for LDCT sinogram denoising. 2) Image-domain based methods directly works on DICOM formatted LDCT images for pixel-to-pixel correction. In [9], a patch-based CNN is trained to transform low-dose CT images towards normal-dose CT images. [10] utilizes a residual encoder-decoder CNN to predict noise distribution in LDCT, aided by shortcut connections. [11] transfers a 2D trained network to accelerate the 3D denoising model. 3) Dual-domain cascade based methods process projection data and image data in a progressive way. [12] puts forward training sinogram-domain network firstly, and then training another image-domain network on the former result. In [13], sinogram-domain and image-domain networks are trained together in one step.

Discussion: But there still has limitations that the insufficient information in single-domain based methods, and the accumulation error in cascaded dual-domain based method. 1) For processing on single sinogram data, it can cause spatial resolution loss, and introduce new noise and artifacts, due to the sensitivity that small reconstruction error in sinogram causes unpredictable influence in image. And the sinogram data often behaves incomprehensible to human vision. 2) For processing on single image data, it has difficulty to model the noise distribution because the noise is caused by the back-projection from contaminated projection data. 3) For cascaded dual-domain processing, no matter training in two step or end-to-end, the accumulation error caused by the front sinogram network cannot be avoided, especially with the sensitivity inter domains. Although IDOL-Net [14] for CT metal artifact reduction adopts parallel structure between dual-domains, the information adjustment in inter-domain exchange is still ignored. Therefore, how to effectively organize the sinogram domain that contamination actually happens and the image domain that human vision directly comprehensible, and make complementary fusion, still remain open challenges. It is extremely crucial for LDCT reconstruction model design.

In this paper, we propose a novel Dual-domain parallel network (DDPNet) to make high-quality reconstruction with noise reduction and structure maintenance by fully and synergistically utilizing dual-domain information, from widely accessible LDCT. It promotes low-radiation risk in CT examination, and enable a more readable pattern for LDCT to get wider application potentials. The main contributions can be summarized as: 1) For the first time, a reliable dual-domain parallel solution is proposed to make parallel optimization between sinogram and image domains for eliminating the accumulation error, and fuse dual-domain reconstructions for complementary. 2) A novel Interactive Information Flow (IIF) mechanism is proposed across sinogram-domain stream and image-domain stream to make joint mutual optimization by introducing complementary information and establishing coherent constraint in dual-domain cross communication. 3) A new Unified Fusion Block is proposed at the end of the two domain streams to complement multi-reconstruction results and further refine final integrated reconstruction via our triple-cross attention. 4) A specially-designed gradient-based discriminator coupled with the image-based one is proposed to drive the reconstruction towards both the accurate inner-details and realistic anatomic content.

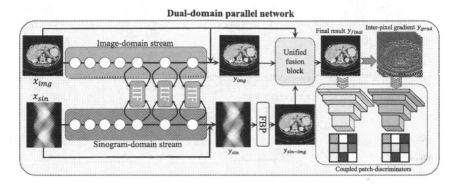

Fig. 2. DDPNet promotes LDCT reconstruction in a more readable pattern with noise reduction and structure maintenance, via 1) Dual-domain parallel architecture to make joint mutual optimization with IIF; 2) Unified fusion block to complement multi-results and further refine final reconstruction with triple-cross attention; 3) Coupled patch-discriminators to drive the reconstruction towards both realistic anatomic content and accurate inner-details with image-based and inter-pixel gradient-based adversarial constraints, respectively.

2   Methodology

As shown in Fig. 2, the proposed DDPNet is simultaneously performed on the both the image-domain data and signogram-domain data of LDCT to make a more readable pattern reconstruction with noise reduction and structure maintenance. Specifically, it is implemented with three designs: 1) The dual-domain parallel architecture (detailed in Sect. 2.1) uses IIF to connect the data-domain stream (denoted as R_{img}) and signogram-domain stream (denoted as R_{sin}) in cross. With IIF, the dual-domain information is frequently transferred to introducing complementary information and establishing coherent constraint. 2) The unified fusion block (denoted as U, detailed in Sect. 2.2) tails the dual streams to comprehensively integrate the results reconstructed from different domains. It use the triple-cross attention to refine the final result. 3) To drive the result more realistic and detailed, the coupled patch-discriminators work on both the image content (denoted as D_{img}) and inter-pixel gradient(denoted as D_{grad}).

In summarize, given the LDCT image-domain and sinogram-domain data as x_{img} and x_{sin}, the object of DDPNet can be formulated as:

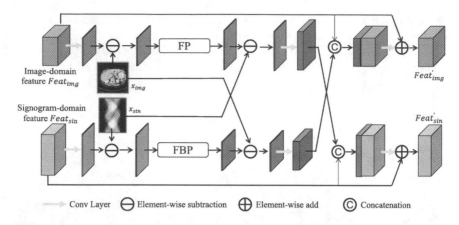

⤳ Conv Layer   ⊖ Element-wise subtraction   ⊕ Element-wise add   © Concatenation

Fig. 3. IIF connects sinogram-domain stream and image-domain stream to make joint mutual optimization by introducing complementary information and establishing coherent constraint in dual-domain cross communication.

$$\min_{\substack{R_{img} \\ R_{sig} \\ U}} \max_{\substack{D_{grad} \\ D_{img}}} \mathcal{L}_{DDPNet} = \mathcal{L}_{Recon}(R_{img}, R_{sin}, U) + \alpha\mathcal{L}_{Adv}(R_{img}, R_{sin}, U, D_{img}, D_{grad})$$

$$(1)$$

where $\mathcal{L}_{Recon}$ means loss function in reconstruction combined with L1 loss and Structural Similarity (SSIM) loss, and $\mathcal{L}_{Adv}$ represents adversarial loss.

2.1   Dual-Domain Parallel Architecture

The dual-domain parallel architecture creatively enables mutual optimization on both the image-domain and sinogram-domain of LDCT. Different from the existing dual-domain cascaded architecture, by using the IIF, it promotes the interactive collaboration between the two domain streams and avoid the front-back accumulation error.

As shown in Fig. 2, the special-designed **IIF** is embedded across the image-domain and sinogram-domain streams that both adopt Unet-similar structure with global residual connection modeling the difference between LDCT and NDCT. The detailed procedure of IIF can be seen in Fig. 3. 1) From the image domain, IIF decomposes the vision noise information, and introduce it to sinogram domain for enhancing the visual interpration. IIF first decodes the image-domain feature with convolution layer, and then makes subtraction with downsampled LDCT image for transforming into CT image space. It further utilizes the differentiable forward projection (FP) and the element-wise substraction between downsampled LDCT sinogram to transform the information obtained from the image domain into the sinogram domain. Finally, operations of convolution layers, concatenation and element-wise add refine the sinogram-domain feature together with the transformed image-domain information. 2) From the sinogram domain, IIF extracts the intrinsic noise distribution, and guides it image domain to complement imaging essential information. The implementation procedure is similar to 1), except that the differentiable filtered back-projection (FBP) replaces the FP to transform the extracted information from the sinogram domain into the image domain (Fig. 3).

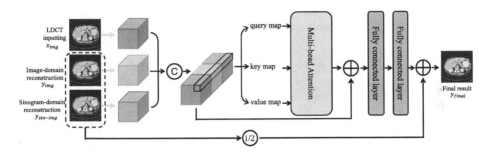

Fig. 4. Unified fusion block interactively complements multi-reconstruction results and refines final integrated reconstruction via our triple-cross attention

2.2   Unified Fusion Block

The unified fusion block robustly promotes the refined final reconstruction with the complementary advantages of dual-domain results, and enables self-adaptive integration.

As shown in Fig. 4, the unified fusion block develops the triple-cross attention among the reconstructions from the image-domain and sinogram domain streams, as well as the LDCT inputting. Cross attention is performed between image-domain and sinogram-domain results to deeply explore the dual-domain correlation for enhancing crucial information and mutually compensate reconstruction deficiency. Furthermore, the introduction of the LDCT inputting effectively enable an essential reference that can assess the dual-domain results in nature to guide the self-adaptive adjustment and fusion. The detailed composition of the unified fusion block includes: encoding the reconstructions from two streams and the LDCT inputting, and concatenating them together. Then linear operations are performed to generate query map, key map and value map. Multi-head attention is further conducted to learn more rich relation among reconstructions and inputting. And two fully connected (FC) layers are built to collate and map the information. It should be noted that the output of the last FC layer is added with the average of dual-domain reconstructions without LDCT inputting for avoiding additional noise, to gain the finally refined, unambiguous and accurate result.

Table 1. The quantitative analysis of the proposed method under different configurations. ("SD Net" and "ID Net" means reconstruction from single domain of sinogram and image, "+IIF" denotes adding IIF across SD Net and ID Net with average to fusion, "+UFB" represents using the unified fusion block to integrate multi results)

Method	SD Net	ID Net	+ IIF	+ UFB	**DDPNet**
MAE (HU)	19.27 ± 1.93	14.98 ± 1.65	14.21 ± 1.70	13.73 ± 1.60	**13.54 ± 1.63**
PSNR (dB)	43.35 ± 1.81	44.24 ± 1.59	44.95 ± 1.62	45.10 ± 1.49	**45.29 ± 1.43**
SSIM (%)	96.05 ± 1.14	97.70 ± 0.82	97.95 ± 0.078	98.07 ± 0.71	**98.24 ± 0.67**

2.3 Coupled Patch-Discriminators

The coupled patch-discriminators comprehensively enable multi adversarial constraints to guide the reconstructed result towards the realistic anatomic content and the accurate inner-details. With the rich experience granted from the determination on $N \times N$ real or fake matrix, discriminators intelligently assess the reconstruction weather fits the image content distribution with low noise and the inter-pixel gradients with structure preserving for driving the network to improve the reconstruction ability and cheat the discriminators.

The discriminators pair covers a image-based discriminator and a gradient-based one. The image-based one take the reconstructed image together with the prior-knowledge of LDCT image to make adversarial learning against the real data NDCT.

The gradient-based one conducts on the gradient map of the reconstruction, so that with the adversarial learning can deeply intemperate the inner-structure characteristics and rectify reconstruction direction. The gradient map is comprehensively calculated with four operators including $\begin{bmatrix} -1 & 0 \end{bmatrix}$, $\begin{bmatrix} -1 \\ 0 \end{bmatrix}$, $\begin{bmatrix} -1 & 0 \\ 0 & 1 \end{bmatrix}$ $\begin{bmatrix} 0 & -1 \\ 1 & 0 \end{bmatrix}$.

3 Experiments

3.1 Materials and Configurations

Experiments adopt thin slice CT from the dataset of "the 2016 NIH-AAPM-Mayo Clinic Low Dose CT Grand Challenge" to evaluate the performance. The dataset contains 5936 thin slice CT from 10 anonymous patients. We randomly divide the dataset into 5 patients' CT for training, 2 for validation, and 3 for testing. The net is implemented by Tensorflow, and performed on NVIDIA P100 GPU. Differential FP and FBP is achieved with Operator Discretization Library (ODL). Mean Absolute Error (MAE), SSIM and Peak Signal-to-Noise-Ratio(PSNR) are used to evaluate the performance.

Table 2. The quantitative analysis of the proposed method compared with the existing methods.

Method	RED-CNN	AttRDN	CLEAR	**DDPNet**
MAE (HU)	14.12 ± 2.02	21.47 ± 1.61	13.95 ± 1.77	$\mathbf{13.54 \pm 1.63}$
PSNR (dB)	44.69 ± 1.32	42.98 ± 1.52	44.90 ± 1.46	$\mathbf{45.29 \pm 1.43}$
SSIM (%)	97.83 ± 0.64	95.17 ± 2.68	97.86 ± 0.92	$\mathbf{98.24 \pm 0.67}$

3.2 Results and Analysis

Overall Performance. As the last column shown in Table 1 and Table 2, the proposed gains high-quality LDCT reconstruction with MAE down to 13.54 HU for information recovery, PSNR up to 45.29 dB for noise reduction, and SSIM up to 98.24% for structure maintenance.

Ablation Study. As can been from Table 1, the proposed DDPNet achieves error decreasement of 3.585 HU, as well as increasements of 1.5 dB PSNR, and 1.37% SSIM, in average, compared to the baseline of single domain networks SD Net and ID Net. It gets robust improvement with special-designed components: the IIF for inter-domain information cross-communication, the unified fusion block for interactively integrate the results from two domain streams, and the gradient-based discriminator coupled with the image-based on for both anatomic content and inner-details. Especially, IIF enables cross connection between two domains for learned information share, which promote obvious improvement for single domain.

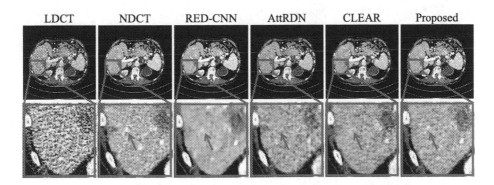

Fig. 5. Visual comparison with existing method, the proposed DDPNet effectively keep the tiny structure. The display window is $[-60, 200]$ HU. (Color figure online)

Comparison with Existing Methods. As shown in Table 2, the proposed DDPNet gains the best performance compared to the image-domain method RED-CNN [9], sinogram-domain method AttRDN [8], and the dual-domain cascade methods CLEAR [13], with error decreasement of 2.97 HU, as well as increasements of 1.10 dB PSNR and 1.29% SSIM, in average. Visually, the instance in Fig. 5 directly illustrates that the result from DDPNet can preserve tiny structure as can be seen in the enlarged ROI that even difficult to be distinguished in LDCT inputting, and structure preserving with details more easily identified as the vessel indicated by the red arrow, than the compared methods.

4   Conclusion

In this paper, we propose DDPNet, the first powerful work, make parallel optimization between sinogram and image domains to eliminate the accumulation error, and fusing dual-domain reconstructions for complementary, in LDCT reconstruction. DDPNet is innovatively built with 1) the novel dual-domain parallel architecture to make joint mutual optimization with interactive information flow; 2) the new unified fusion block to complement multi-results and further refine final reconstruction with triple-cross attention; 3) a pair of specially-designed patch-discriminators to drive the reconstruction towards both realistic anatomic content and accurate inner-details with image-based and inter-pixel gradient-based adversarial constraints, respectively. Extensive experiments with promising results from both quantitative evaluations and qualitative assessments reveal our method a great clinical potential in CT imaging.

Acknowledgements. This study was supported by the Fundamental Research Funds for the Central University (No. NS2021067), the National Natural Science Foundation (No. 62101249 and No. 62136004), the China Postdoctoral Science Foundation (No. 2021TQ0149), the Natural Science Foundation of Jiangsu Province (No. BK20210291).

References

1. Brenner, D.J., Hall, E.J.: Computed tomography—an increasing source of radiation exposure. New England J. Med. **357**(22), 2277–2284 (2007)
2. Pearce, M.S., et al.: Radiation exposure from CT scans in childhood and subsequent risk of leukaemia and brain tumours: a retrospective cohort study. Lancet **380**(9840), 499–505 (2012)
3. Manduca, A., et al.: Projection space denoising with bilateral filtering and CT noise modeling for dose reduction in CT. Med. Phys. **36**(11), 4911–4919 (2009)
4. Balda, M., Hornegger, J., Heismann, B.: Ray contribution masks for structure adaptive sinogram filtering. IEEE Trans. Med. Imaging **31**(6), 1228–1239 (2012)
5. Zhang, Y., Wang, Y., Zhang, W., Lin, F., Pu, Y., Zhou, J.: Statistical iterative reconstruction using adaptive fractional order regularization. Biomed. Opt. Express **7**(3), 1015–1029 (2016)
6. Geyer, L.L., et al.: State of the art: iterative CT reconstruction techniques. Radiology **276**(2), 339–357 (2015)

7. Ghani, M. U., Karl, W. C.: CNN based sinogram denoising for low-dose CT. In: Mathematics in Imaging. Optical Society of America (2018)

8. Ma, Y.-J., Ren, Y., Feng, P., He, P., Guo, X.-D., Wei, B.: Sinogram denoising via attention residual dense convolutional neural network for low-dose computed tomography. Nucl. Sci. Tech. **32**(4), 1–14 (2021). https://doi.org/10.1007/s41365-021-00874-2

9. Chen, H., Zhang, Y., et al.: Low-dose CT denoising with convolutional neural network. In: 14th International Symposium on Biomedical Imaging (ISBI 2017), pp. 143–146. IEEE, Melbourne (2017)

10. Chen, H., et al.: Low-dose CT with a residual encoder-decoder convolutional neural network. IEEE Trans. Med. Imaging **36**(12), 2524–2535 (2017)

11. Shan, H., et al.: 3-D convolutional encoder-decoder network for low-dose CT via transfer learning from a 2-D trained network. IEEE Trans. Med. Imaging **37**(6), 1522–1534 (2018)

12. Yin, X., et al.: Domain progressive 3D residual convolution network to improve low-dose CT imaging. IEEE Trans. Med. Imaging **38**(12), 2903–2913 (2019)

13. Zhang, Y., et al.: CLEAR: comprehensive learning enabled adversarial reconstruction for subtle structure enhanced low-dose CT imaging. IEEE Trans. Med. Imaging **40**(11), 3089–3101 (2021)

14. Wang, T., et al.: IDOL-net: an interactive dual-domain parallel network for CT metal artifact reduction. arXiv preprint arXiv:2104.01405 (2021)

Mapping in Cycles: Dual-Domain PET-CT Synthesis Framework with Cycle-Consistent Constraints

Jiadong Zhang[1], Zhiming Cui[1], Caiwen Jiang[1], Jingyang Zhang[1], Fei Gao[1], and Dinggang Shen[1,2(✉)]

[1] School of Biomedical Engineering, ShanghaiTech University,
Shanghai 201210, China
dgshen@shanghaitech.edu.cn

[2] Shanghai United Imaging Intelligence Co., Ltd., Shanghai 200230, China

Abstract. Positron emission tomography (PET) is an important medical imaging technique, especially for brain and cancer disease diagnosis. Modern PET scanner is usually combined with computed tomography (CT), where CT image is used for anatomical localization, PET attenuation correction, and radiotherapy treatment planning. Considering radiation dose of CT image as well as increasing spatial resolution of PET image, there is a growing demand to synthesize CT image from PET image (without scanning CT) to reduce risk of radiation exposure. However, most existing works perform learning-based image synthesis to construct cross-modality mapping only in the image domain, without considering of the projection domain, leading to potential physical inconsistency. To address this problem, we propose a novel PET-CT synthesis framework by exploiting dual-domain information (i.e., image domain and projection domain). Specifically, we design both image domain network and projection domain network to jointly learn high-dimensional mapping from PET to CT. The image domain and the projection domain can be connected together with a forward projection (FP) and a filtered back projection (FBP). To further help the PET-to-CT synthesis task, we also design a secondary CT-to-PET synthesis task with the same network structure, and combine the two tasks into a bidirectional mapping framework with several closed cycles. More importantly, these cycles can serve as cycle-consistent losses to further help network training for better synthesis performance. Extensive validations on the clinical PET-CT data demonstrate the proposed PET-CT synthesis framework outperforms the state-of-the-art (SOTA) medical image synthesis methods with significant improvements.

Keywords: Medical image synthesis · Dual-domain information · Cycle-consistent constraint

1 Introduction

Positron emission tomography (PET) are widely used in clinical for detection and diagnosis of various disease [11]. Specifically, the commonly used FDG-PET can

L. Wang et al. (Eds.): MICCAI 2022, LNCS 13436, pp. 758–767, 2022.
https://doi.org/10.1007/978-3-031-16446-0_72

reveal tissues' metabolic characteristics and thus potentially the disease status, i.e., for Alzheimer's disease [10,19]. Modern PET scanner is usually combined with computed tomographic (CT) for accurate PET attenuation correction and anatomical localization. In addition, CT image can also be used in radiotherapy treatment planning for cancer patients [5]. Considering radiation dose of CT image as well as increasing spatial resolution of PET image, there's a growing demand to synthesize CT image from PET image (without scanning CT, especially for patients who need multiple PET/CT scans within short time) to reduce risk of radiation exposure. The synthesized CT image can be used for anatomical localization, PET attenuation correction, and radiotherapy treatment planning.

Recently, deep learning has dominated state-of-the-art performance in various medical image synthesis tasks [15,18]. The key aspect of deep learning is to learn high dimensional non-linear mapping from the input to the output. Among all the deep learning methods, generative adversarial network (GAN) and its variations (such as p2pGAN [6] and CycleGAN [20]) are commonly used for synthesis tasks. However, for cross-modality image synthesis tasks, most existing works only exploit image domain information, and ignore the latent physical information in other domains (e.g., k-space and projection domain). Actually, the use of other domains can provide the latent physical relationship to help reconstruct more detailed structures for images in the image domain [7,13,14,17].

In this paper, we propose a dual-domain PET-CT synthesis framework to perform synthesis in both image and sinogram domains. To our best knowledge, it is the first time to exploit dual-domain information in cross-modality image synthesis tasks, especially for PET-CT synthesis. Specifically, we design an image domain network and a projection domain network to synthesize CT image and sinogram from their corresponding PET image and sinogram, respectively. The image domain and the projection domain can be connected with forward projection (FP) and filtered back-projection (FBP). To further help PET-to-CT synthesis task with structural consistency, we also design a secondary CT-to-PET synthesis task to cooperate with the main PET-to-CT task, for building a bidirectional mapping framework with several closed cycles. These closed cycles can serve as cycle-consistent losses to train all networks jointly for achieving better synthesis performance. Considering difficulty of jointly training these networks with possible unstable convergency, we further propose a two-stage training strategy, with dual-domain consistency and cycle consistency, to gradually build connections between PET and CT, between two domains, and between two synthesis directions. Extensive experiments conducted on real clinical PET-CT data demonstrate the effectiveness of our proposed framework with significant performance improvement, compared with state-of-the-art methods.

2 Method

2.1 Proposed Framework

As illustrated in Fig. 1, the proposed framework performs bidirectional synthesis within both image and projection domains via four networks, including

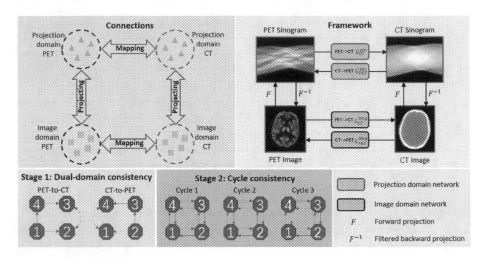

Fig. 1. The overview of our proposed dual-domain PET-CT synthesis framework. The 1st figure illustrates the connection between dual domains and two modalities. The 2nd figure illustrates the overall framework architecture. The 3rd figure illustrates dual-domain consistency in Stage 1. The 4th figure illustrates cycle consistency in framework in Stage 2.

PET-to-CT image synthesis network G_{CT}^{img}, CT-to-PET image synthesis network G_{PET}^{img}, PET-to-CT sinogram synthesis network G_{CT}^{sin}, and CT-to-PET sinogram synthesis network G_{PET}^{sin}. Each network is designed to learn a mapping across modalities (i.e., PET and CT) in respective image and projection domain. The image domain and the projection domain can be transformed by a forward projection (F) operation and a filtered back projection (F^{-1}) operation, respectively.

2.2   Training Strategy and Objectives

As shown in Fig. 1, four networks are designed in our proposed framework. Considering directly training all the networks is challenging due to large amount of network parameters and different network convergence properties, we propose a two-stage training strategy to optimize the framework, including dual-domain consistency (*Stage 1*) and cycle consistency (*Stage 2*). More specifically, Stage 1 aims to generate target images by dual-domain consistency (i.e., image domain and projection domain). Then, to further optimize the framework, Stage-2 with three cycles are proposed to ensure better information consistency between different domains and data modalities (i.e., PET and CT).

Stage 1: Dual-domain Consistency. As shown in Fig. 1, Stage 1 is designed to build mapping between two modalities by dual domains. We take PET-to-CT synthesis as an example. Given an input of PET image x_{PET}, we alternatively train the image domain network G_{CT}^{img} and the projection domain network G_{CT}^{sin} to generate target images in two domains (i.e., CT sinogram and CT image). A dual domain consistency is further employed to guarantee that they can promote each other to achieve overall better performance. To train the image domain network G_{CT}^{img}, we fix the parameters of the projection domain network G_{CT}^{sin} and use both ground-truth CT image and the output of projection domain network G_{CT}^{sin} as supervision. The loss function of training network G_{CT}^{img} can be defined as follows:

$$
\begin{aligned}
\mathcal{L}_{CT}^{img} = &\mathbb{E}_{x_{PET}, x_{CT}} || G_{CT}^{img}(x_{PET}) - x_{CT} ||_1 \\
&+ \lambda_1 \mathbb{E}_{x_{PET}} || G_{CT}^{img}(x_{PET}) - F^{-1}(G_{CT}^{sin}(F(x_{PET}))) ||_1,
\end{aligned}
\tag{1}
$$

where λ_1 is the hyper-parameter to balance the importance of the two terms. To train the projection domain network G_{CT}^{sin}, we fix parameters of the image domain network G_{CT}^{img} and use both ground-truth CT sinogram and the output of the image domain network G_{CT}^{img} as supervision. The loss function of training network G_{CT}^{sin} can be defined as follows:

$$
\begin{aligned}
\mathcal{L}_{CT}^{sin} = &\mathbb{E}_{x_{PET}, x_{CT}} || G_{CT}^{sin}(F(x_{PET})) - F(x_{CT}) ||_1 \\
&+ \lambda_2 \mathbb{E}_{x_{PET}} || G_{CT}^{sin}(F(x_{PET})) - F(G_{CT}^{img}(x_{PET})) ||_1,
\end{aligned}
\tag{2}
$$

where λ_2 is the hyper-parameter to balance the importance of the two terms. In this way, we can build the mapping between two modalities in dual domains by optimizing Eqs. 1 and 2 to a certain epoch.

Similarity, as for CT-to-PET synthesis task, we alternatively train the image domain network G_{PET}^{img} and the projection domain network G_{PET}^{sin}. The loss functions of training the two networks are defined as follows:

$$
\begin{aligned}
\mathcal{L}_{PET}^{img} = &\mathbb{E}_{x_{PET}, x_{CT}} || G_{PET}^{img}(x_{CT}) - x_{PET} ||_1 \\
&+ \lambda_3 \mathbb{E}_{x_{CT}} || G_{PET}^{img}(x_{CT}) - F^{-1}(G_{PET}^{sin}(F(x_{CT}))) ||_1,
\end{aligned}
\tag{3}
$$

$$
\begin{aligned}
\mathcal{L}_{PET}^{sin} = &\mathbb{E}_{x_{PET}, x_{CT}} || G_{PET}^{sin}(F(x_{CT})) - F(x_{PET}) ||_1 \\
&+ \lambda_4 \mathbb{E}_{x_{CT}} || G_{PET}^{sin}(F(x_{CT})) - F(G_{PET}^{img}(x_{CT})) ||_1,
\end{aligned}
\tag{4}
$$

where λ_3 and λ_4 are hyper-parameters to balance the importance of the two terms in the loss functions.

Stage-2: Cycle Consistency. Although the two modality mappings in the dual domains have been built in Stage 1, the cycle consistencies between two domains and two modalities are not guaranteed. Thus, as shown in Fig. 1, we design Stage 2 with three cycle-consistent losses, based on the intuition that, if we transform from one domain/modality to the other and back again, we should arrive at where we start. Specifically, we only train image domain networks (i.e., G_{CT}^{img} and G_{PET}^{img}) and fix the parameters of projection domain networks (i.e., G_{CT}^{sin} and G_{PET}^{sin}), due to two reasons. (1) The projection domain networks are well-trained in Stage 1. More importantly, they only serve as loss functions in the training stage, and will not be used in the testing stage. (2) Training four networks in Stage 2 will bring more computational costs with little benefit compared with the case of only training image domain networks.

In Stage 2, we also adopt an alternative training strategy. To train the network G_{CT}^{img}, we fix parameters of the other three networks. In addition, we also design one image domain cycle-consistent loss ($Cycle\ 1$) and two cross domain cycle-consistent losses ($Cycle\ 2$ and $Cycle\ 3$). Specifically, Cycle 1 denotes the cycle mapping between PET and CT images, and the trainable parameters are the same in the two direction mappings (i.e., PET-to-CT, or CT-to-PET). For example, we use a PET image as a starting point. First, the PET image goes through network G_{CT}^{img} to get a synthesized CT image, and then the synthesized CT image goes through network G_{PET}^{img} to obtain a reconstructed PET image. The reconstructed PET image is supposed to be as same as the input PET image. Moreover, two cross domain cycles are the cycles across image domain and projection domain in two directions. As for Cycle 2 of PET-to-CT mapping, we use a PET image as a starting point. First, the PET image goes through network G_{CT}^{img} to get a synthesized CT image. Then, the FP operator projects the synthesized CT image to a synthesized CT sinogram. And, the synthesized CT sinogram goes through network G_{PET}^{sin} to get a synthesized PET sinogram. Finally, the FBP reconstruct the PET image from the synthesized PET sinogram. The reconstructed PET image is also supposed to be as same as the input PET image. Thus, the loss function to train network G_{CT}^{img} can be described as follows:

$$
\begin{aligned}
\mathcal{L}_{CT} = {} & \mathbb{E}_{x_{PET},x_{CT}}||G_{CT}^{img}(x_{PET}) - x_{CT}||_1 \\
& + \xi_1 \mathbb{E}_{x_{PET}}||G_{PET}^{img}(G_{CT}^{img}(x_{PET})) - x_{PET}||_1 \\
& + \xi_2 \mathbb{E}_{x_{PET}}||F^{-1}(G_{PET}^{sin}(F(G_{CT}^{img}(x_{PET})))) - x_{PET}||_1 .
\end{aligned} \tag{5}
$$

As for Cycle 3 of CT-to-PET mapping, we use CT image as a starting point to train network G_{PET}^{img} by a cycle-consistent loss. The parameters of the other three networks are fixed at this cycle. The loss function can be described as follows:

$$
\begin{aligned}
\mathcal{L}_{PET} = {} & \mathbb{E}_{x_{PET},x_{CT}}||G_{PET}^{img}(x_{CT}) - x_{PET}||_1 \\
& + \xi_3 \mathbb{E}_{x_{CT}}||G_{CT}^{img}(G_{PET}^{img}(x_{CT})) - x_{CT}||_1 \\
& + \xi_4 \mathbb{E}_{x_{CT}}||F^{-1}(G_{CT}^{sin}(F(G_{PET}^{img}(x_{CT})))) - x_{CT}||_1 .
\end{aligned} \tag{6}
$$

In Eq. 5 and 6, the first term is the paired image reconstruction loss. The second and the third terms are the image domain cycle-consistent loss and the cross domain cycle-consistent loss, respectively. ξ_1, ξ_3 and ξ_2, ξ_4 are hyper-parameters to balance the importance of two cycle-consistent losses, respectively.

3   Experiments and Results

3.1   Dataset and Evaluation Metrics

To evaluate our method, we collected 65 paired brain PET and CT volumes from uEXPLORE PET/CT system. To increase the training samples and reduce the

Table 1. Quantitative comparison of our method with state-of-the-art PET-CT synthesis methods, in terms of SSIM ($\times 10^{-2}$) $\uparrow$, PSNR ([dB]) $\uparrow$ and NRMSE ($\times 10^{-2}$) $\downarrow$.

Task	PET-to-CT			CT-to-PET		
Method	SSIM	PSNR	NRMSE	SSIM	PSNR	NRMSE
U-Net [16]	95.8	35.1	16.0	91.6	33.5	28.2
RU-Net [9]	95.6	35.5	14.6	94.9	34.8	21.8
p2pGAN [3]	96.6	35.1	15.8	93.9	35.0	21.0
CycleGAN [4]	96.4	35.4	14.5	**95.8**	35.7	18.3
MedGAN [2]	97.0	35.7	14.0	90.9	35.8	19.7
Ours	**98.2**	**38.5**	**8.1**	93.8	**36.2**	**17.3**

dependence on GPU memory, we sample 20 slices of each volume in axial view with brain tissues. In this manner, the total training samples increase from 65 to 1300. In data pre-processing, all images are resampled to voxel spacing of $2.344 \times 2.344\,\mathrm{mm}^2$ with size of 128×128, and the intensity range is normalized to $[0, 1]$ by min-max normalization. We choose patient-wise 1000 samples as the training set, 60 samples as the validation set, and the resting 240 samples as the testing set.

Meanwhile, to measure quantitative results, we adopt three metrics (as typically adopted in synthesis tasks in the literature), including structural similarity index measurement (SSIM), peak signal-to-noise ratio (PSNR), and normalized root mean squared error (NRMSE).

3.2 Implement Details

In our proposed framework, we use RU-Net [9], which can capture global information, as image domain synthesis networks (i.e., G_{PET}^{img} and G_{CT}^{img}), and use Fully Connection Network (FCN) [12], which can keep most of detailed information, as projection domain networks (i.e., G_{PET}^{sin} and G_{CT}^{sin}). All experiments are conducted on PyTorch platform with one NVIDIA TITAN RTX GPU (24GB). We use the ADAM optimizer to optimize the four networks in all stages, and learning rates of Stage 1 and Stage 2 are 0.02 and 0.01, respectively. All hyperparameters (i.e., λ_1–λ_4 and ξ_1–ξ_4) are empirically set to 0.5. A total of 600 epochs are run for each method, and the best checkpoint model with the best evaluation performance is used as the final model to evaluate the performance on testing set.

3.3 Comparison with State-of-the-Art (SOTA) Methods

To demonstrate the effectiveness of proposed framework, we compare our method with five SOTA medical image synthesis methods, including U-Net [8], RU-Net [9], p2pGAN [1,3], CycleGAN [4] and MedGAN [2]. Note that CT-to-PET synthesis is the secondary task to help better complete the main PET-to-CT

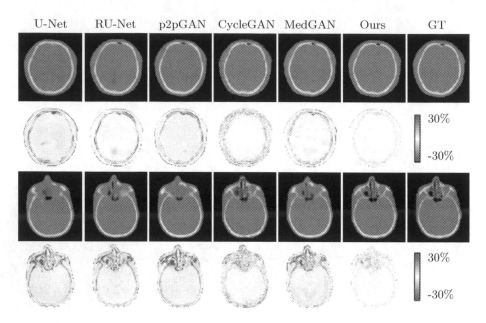

Fig. 2. Visual comparison of synthesized CT images by different methods on two typical samples. For each sample, the first row shows CT images, and the second row shows the corresponding error maps.

synthesis task, thus obtaining better trained image domain networks to achieve better synthesized PET images. Therefore, we show results of both the main task and the secondary task. Among all the comparison methods, only CycleGAN and our framework can jointly train the two tasks. Other methods are single-direction synthesis, and we have to train networks of different tasks independently.

The quantitative results are provided in Table 1, where our method achieves the overall best performance in terms of SSIM, PSNR, and NRMSE. For the main PET-to-CT synthesis task, compared to MedGAN with sub-optimal results, the improvements in SSIM, PSNR, and NRMSE are 1.2%, 2.8 dB, and 0.059, respectively. As the secondary task, we also get the best PET synthesis performance. Note that, as secondary task, CT-to-PET synthesis is designed to help the main PET-to-CT synthesis task, and thus its metrics are all lower than those obtained for the main PET-to-CT synthesis task.

Meanwhile, to further demonstrate the advantage of our method, we also provide qualitative results in Fig. 2. It can be seen that our method also achieves the best performance. As shown in Fig. 2, CT images synthesized by our method can successfully restore the skull structures with the most detailed information. Moreover, the difference map by our method has less blue color (i.e., less errors), demonstrating that our method can synthesize CT images matching well with the ground-truth CT images.

Table 2. Ablation study of different cycle-consistent constraints, in terms of SSIM ($\times 10^{-2}$) ↑, PSNR ([dB]) ↑ and NRMSE ($\times 10^{-2}$) ↓.

Tasks	PET-to-CT			CT-to-PET		
Method	SSIM	PSNR	NRMSE	SSIM	PSNR	NRMSE
Base	95.9	36.5	10.4	-	-	-
Base+S	98.1	37.3	9.7	93.1	36.0	17.2
Base+S+C1	98.1	37.8	8.7	93.2	36.1	17.6
Base+S+C2	**98.3**	37.8	8.9	93.2	36.1	**17.1**
Base+S+C1+C2	98.2	**38.5**	**8.1**	**93.8**	**36.2**	17.3

3.4 Ablation Study

To help the main PET-to-CT synthesis task, we also design a secondary CT-to-PET synthesis task and combine them into a bidirectional mapping framework with several closed cycles. To verify whether the secondary task can help the main task and also the effectiveness of the two cycle-consistent losses (i.e., image domain cycle-consistent loss, and cross domain cycle-consistent loss) in Stage 2, we perform an ablation experiment to compare the following five degenerated methods: 1) **Base**; 2) **Base + S**; 3) **Base + S + C1**; 4) **Base + S + C2**; 5) **Base + S + C1 + C2**, where **Base** denotes only using supervision loss in the main task, **S** denotes using the secondary task to help main task, and **C1** and **C2** denote the image domain cycle-consistent loss and cross domain cycle-consistent loss in Stage 2, respectively. The quantitative results are provided in Table 2.

As shown in Table 2, there is great improvement when using the secondary task to help the main task, indicating the necessity of employing the secondary CT-to-PET synthesis task. In addition, both **Base + S + C1** and **Base + S + C2** achieve superior results to **Base + S**, indicating that the image domain cycle-consistent constraint and the cross domain cycle-consistent constraint can consistently improve the synthesis tasks. Meanwhile, our final method (i.e., **Base + S + C1 + C2**) achieves the best performance. It shows that all designed cycle-consistent losses are effective in the synthesis tasks.

By comparing **Base** in Table 2 with RU-Net in Table 1, the SSIM and PSNR are increased with 0.3% and 1.0 dB, and NRMSE is decreased with 0.042, indicating the advantage of involving the projection domain information.

4 Conclusion

In this paper, we propose a novel dual-domain PET-CT synthesis framework. We use four networks to learn both image and sinogram with two synthesis directions. FP and FBP are also employed to connect image domain and projection domain together. We further propose a two-stage training strategy with dual-domain consistency and cycle consistency to help framework training with better synthesis performance. The experiments on clinical PET-CT dataset demonstrate significant improvement of our proposed method.

Acknowledgements. This work was supported in part by National Natural Science Foundation of China (grant number 62131015), Science and Technology Commission of Shanghai Municipality (STCSM) (grant number 21010502600), and The Key R&D Program of Guangdong Province, China (grant number 2021B0101420006).

References

1. Armanious, K., et al.: Independent attenuation correction of whole body [18 F] FDG-pet using a deep learning approach with generative adversarial networks. EJNMMI Res. **10**(1), 1–9 (2020)
2. Armanious, K., et al.: MedGAN: medical image translation using GANs. Comput. Med. Imaging Graph. **79**, 101684 (2020)
3. Bi, L., Kim, J., Kumar, A., Feng, D., Fulham, M.: Synthesis of positron emission tomography (PET) images via multi-channel generative adversarial networks (GANs). In: Cardoso, M.J., et al. (eds.) CMMI/SWITCH/RAMBO 2017. LNCS, vol. 10555, pp. 43–51. Springer, Cham (2017). https://doi.org/10.1007/978-3-319-67564-0_5
4. Dong, X., et al.: Synthetic CT generation from non-attenuation corrected pet images for whole-body pet imaging. Phys. Med. Biol. **64**(21), 215016 (2019)
5. Goitein, M., et al.: The value of CT scanning in radiation therapy treatment planning: a prospective study. Int. J. Radiat. Oncol.* Biol.* Phys. **5**(10), 1787–1798 (1979)
6. Isola, P., Zhu, J.Y., Zhou, T., Efros, A.A.: Image-to-image translation with conditional adversarial networks. In: Proceedings of the IEEE Conference on Computer Vision and Pattern Recognition, pp. 1125–1134 (2017)
7. Lin, W.A., et al.: DuDoNet: dual domain network for CT metal artifact reduction. In: Proceedings of the IEEE/CVF Conference on Computer Vision and Pattern Recognition, pp. 10512–10521 (2019)
8. Liu, F., Jang, H., Kijowski, R., Zhao, G., Bradshaw, T., McMillan, A.B.: A deep learning approach for 18 F-FDG pet attenuation correction. EJNMMI Phys. **5**(1), 1–15 (2018)
9. Liu, J., Kang, Y., Hu, D., Chen, Y.: Cascade ResUnet with noise power spectrum loss for low dose CT imaging. In: 2020 13th International Congress on Image and Signal Processing, BioMedical Engineering and Informatics (CISP-BMEI), pp. 796–801. IEEE (2020)
10. Luan, H., Qi, F., Xue, Z., Chen, L., Shen, D.: Multimodality image registration by maximization of quantitative-qualitative measure of mutual information. Pattern Recogn. **41**(1), 285–298 (2008)
11. Muehllehner, G., Karp, J.S.: Positron emission tomography. Phys. Med. Biol. **51**(13), R117 (2006)
12. Nie, D., et al.: Medical image synthesis with deep convolutional adversarial networks. IEEE Trans. Biomed. Eng. **65**(12), 2720–2730 (2018)
13. Shi, L., et al.: A novel loss function incorporating imaging acquisition physics for PET attenuation map generation using deep learning. In: Shen, D., et al. (eds.) MICCAI 2019. LNCS, vol. 11767, pp. 723–731. Springer, Cham (2019). https://doi.org/10.1007/978-3-030-32251-9_79

14. Sudarshan, V.P., Upadhyay, U., Egan, G.F., Chen, Z., Awate, S.P.: Towards lower-dose pet using physics-based uncertainty-aware multimodal learning with robustness to out-of-distribution data. Med. Image Anal. **73**, 102187 (2021)
15. Xiang, L., et al.: Deep embedding convolutional neural network for synthesizing CT image from T1-weighted MR image. Med. Image Anal. **47**, 31–44 (2018)
16. Xu, J., Gong, E., Pauly, J., Zaharchuk, G.: 200x low-dose pet reconstruction using deep learning. arXiv preprint arXiv:1712.04119 (2017)
17. Zhang, J., et al.: Limited-view photoacoustic imaging reconstruction with dual domain inputs based on mutual information. In: 2021 IEEE 18th International Symposium on Biomedical Imaging (ISBI), pp. 1522–1526. IEEE (2021)
18. Zhou, B., Zhou, S.K.: DuDoRNet: learning a dual-domain recurrent network for fast MRI reconstruction with deep T1 prior. In: Proceedings of the IEEE/CVF Conference on Computer Vision and Pattern Recognition, pp. 4273–4282 (2020)
19. Zhou, T., Thung, K.H., Zhu, X., Shen, D.: Effective feature learning and fusion of multimodality data using stage-wise deep neural network for dementia diagnosis. Hum. Brain Mapp. **40**(3), 1001–1016 (2019)
20. Zhu, J.Y., Park, T., Isola, P., Efros, A.A.: Unpaired image-to-image translation using cycle-consistent adversarial networks. In: Proceedings of the IEEE International Conference on Computer Vision, pp. 2223–2232 (2017)

Optimal MRI Undersampling Patterns for Pathology Localization

Artem Razumov, Oleg Y. Rogov, and Dmitry V. Dylov$^{(\boxtimes)}$

Skolkovo Institute of Science and Technology, Moscow, Russia
d.dylov@skoltech.ru

Abstract. We investigate MRI acceleration strategies for the benefit of downstream image analysis tasks. Specifically, we propose to optimize the k-space undersampling patterns according to how well a sought-after pathology could be segmented or localized in the reconstructed images. We study the effect of the proposed paradigm on the segmentation task using two classical labeled medical datasets, and on the task of pathology visualization within the bounding boxes, using the recently released fastMRI+ annotations. We demonstrate a noticeable improvement of the target metrics when the sampling pattern is optimized, *e.g.*, for the segmentation problem at ×16 acceleration, we report up to 12% improvement in Dice score over the other undersampling strategies.

Keywords: Scan acceleration · Pathology localization · Fast MRI

1 Introduction

With its excellent soft-tissue contrast and the absence of ionizing radiation, the value of Magnetic Resonance Imaging (MRI) in modern healthcare cannot be overstated. Yet, even today, this modality remains known for its long data acquisition times, requiring anywhere from 15 to 60 min to complete a single scan [12]. In lieu of the material-based and the hardware-based methods to accelerate MRI, another perspective to the challenge is offered by the field of *compressed sensing* [9,12,25]. The methodology entails an incomplete sampling of the raw k-space data that an MR machine can acquire, with the consequent digital compensation for the artifacts caused by the undersampling. To comply with the Nyquist-Shannon sampling theorem and to eliminate the appearance of the aliasing effects [42], the reconstruction models require incorporating additional *a priori* knowledge about the data (*e.g.*, via regularization [40,46]).

This paradigm has witnessed a recent explosive growth of interest following the publication of the open fastMRI dataset [22,29,43]. The deep learning community eagerly unleashed the available reconstruction methods, ranging from

---

Supplementary Information The online version contains supplementary material available at https://doi.org/10.1007/978-3-031-16446-0_73.

basic U-Net-like models [19], to those that incorporate specifics of the imaging process [31,35], to superresolution [5]. The deep learning methods proved superior to the classical reconstruction models in compressed sensing, ultimately resulting in their adoption by the MR industry [10].

Classical or deep-learning-based, the compressed sensing models proposed thus far have all had one optimization target at their core: *the quality of the reconstructed image*[1]. Although logical and intuitive, such an approach dismisses what happens to the reconstructed images further down the line – in the downstream image analysis and during the final decision-making. In our work, we aspired to reconsider the MRI k-space undersampling problem from the standpoint of the effect that the undersampling has on the ultimate outcome.

Specifically, we are motivated to find those undersampling patterns in k-space that optimize how well a certain object could be detected or localized in the reconstructed images (*e.g.*, the heart chambers in the popular ACDC dataset [6] or the brain tumor areas in BraTS [4]). We find the optimal undersampling patterns in k-space that maximize a target value function of interest in the segmentation and localization problems, proposing a new iterative gradient sampling routine universally suitable for these tasks. We also boost the visualization of the pathology predictions on the recently released fastMRI+ [44] dataset via the same undersampling paradigm.

It does not matter if the undersampling pattern ruins the look of the reconstructed image, *as long as it brings the ultimate benefit*, *e.g.*, improves the segmentation. What undersampling patterns can accomplish that?

Prior Work. MRI acceleration has become an intensively developing area over the past years [32]. Compressed sensing [20] and parallel imaging [13] methods prevail in a large cohort of publications along with dictionary-learning algorithms [24], advanced total variation [34] and tensor [16] methods, cross-sampling strategies [38], recurrent inference machines [23], and others. In these reconstruction-focused works, the optimization of the ultimate value function of interest to a clinical application, such as a Dice score, has been dismissed.

With the advent of deep learning [17,19,31,35,41] and the publication of the fastMRI benchmarks [22,43] the undersampling problem has experienced a resurgence. The latest articles report deep learning methods adaptation to k-space [17] and the use of image-to-image translation / superresolution models [5].

Of particular relevance to the results presented herein are the works that search for the optimal mask via the acquisition trajectory design [21], b-spline parametrization [39], and the works [1,14] that consider the value of using deep-learning algorithms on undersampled data for the MRI image processing. Noteworthy, these works either consider simplistic patterns (such as, central-weighted or the fixed fastMRI masks with, at best, a randomized side-band selection) or separate the reconstruction and the image analysis optimization problems into separate routines in their pipelines.

---

[1] Gauged quantitatively by a common metric, such as SSIM [26], or by perception [5].

Considered in this work are three popular datasets: ACDC [6], BraTS [27], fastMRI+ [43,44]. In-depth reviews [3] and [28] describe validation of MRI acceleration methods on BraTS and fastMRI datasets; and the review [37] covers state-of-the-art (SOTA) for the ACDC data.

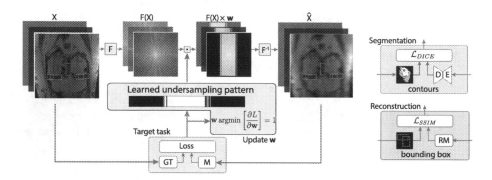

Fig. 1. Optimization of k-space undersampling patterns for object localization. GT is the ground truth, M is a baseline model, RM is a reconstruction model. Pathology can be localized either by segmentation or by reconstruction blocks on the right, depending on available annotation (contours or bounding boxes).

2   Methods

Using Fig. 1 for guidance, we begin by formulating the optimization problem for the undersampling pattern $\mathbf{w}$ in a vision task, performed by a differentiable model $S(\cdot)$:

$$\arg\min_{\mathbf{w}} \quad \mathbb{E}_X \left(L_{target}\big(S(\hat{X}_{\mathbf{w}}), Y\big)\right), \tag{1}$$

where L_{target} is a specific loss function determined by a target medical vision task, $\hat{X}_{\mathbf{w}}$ is a reconstructed MR image from the the undersampled k-space by pattern $\mathbf{w}$, and Y is the ground truth label for the dataset $\{(X,Y)\}^n$ of size $n \in \mathbb{N}$, and $X^{N \times N} \in \mathbb{R}$ is the fully-sampled image.

Finding such patterns $\mathbf{w}$, with acceleration factor $\alpha = \|\mathbf{w}\|_0 = N_s/N$, where N_s is the number of sampled columns in k-space, that minimize the target loss of interest L_{target}, will be the leitmotif of this work.

Segmentation. For the image segmentation, the Dice loss function is standard:

$$L_{\mathrm{DICE}}(Y, \hat{Y}) = 1 - \frac{2Y\hat{Y} + 1}{Y + \hat{Y} + 1}, \tag{2}$$

where $\hat{Y} = S(\hat{X}_{\mathbf{w}})$ is the predicted label. Given such loss and a desired acceleration factor α, the solution to (1) finds the so-called zero-filled [7] pattern $\mathbf{w}$ that will maximize the Dice score, without taking the image quality into account.

Algorithm 1: Iterative Gradients Sampling (IGS)

Data: X - MR images, Y - ground truth, $S(\cdot)$ - CNN model, $L_{target}(\cdot, \cdot)$ - target loss function, N - full sampling size, N_s - partial sampling size, $\mathbf{w}$ - k-space undersampling pattern.

Input: X, Y, N, N_s

Output: $\mathbf{w}$

1 $\mathbf{w} \leftarrow 0$;

2 $\mathbf{w}[\frac{N}{2}] \leftarrow 1$;

3 **for** $n \leftarrow 0$ **to** N_s **do**

4 $\quad \hat{X} \leftarrow F^{-1}(F(X) \cdot \mathbf{w})$;   7 $\quad i \leftarrow \arg\min_{i | \mathbf{w}[i]=0}(\frac{\partial L}{\partial \mathbf{w}})$;

5 $\quad \hat{Y} \leftarrow S(\hat{X})$;

6 $\quad L \leftarrow L_{target}(Y, \hat{Y})$;   8 $\quad \mathbf{w}[i] \leftarrow 1$

9 **end**

Result: Optimized pattern $\mathbf{w}$ for acceleration $\alpha = N_s/N$ w.r.t. model $S(\cdot)$.

Image Reconstruction. If instead of the contours, only the bounding boxes are available, one may attempt to find an optimal pattern to maximize the reconstructed image quality exactly within those boxes using conventional structural similarity (SSIM):

$$L_{\text{SSIM}} = -\frac{(2\mu_{X_i}\mu_{\hat{X}_i} + c_1) \cdot (2\sigma_{\hat{X}_i X_i} + c_2)}{(\mu_{X_i}^2 + \mu_{\hat{X}_i}^2 + c_1) \cdot (\sigma_{X_i}^2 + \sigma_{\hat{X}_i}^2 + c_2)}, \tag{3}$$

where c_1, c_2 are some coefficients and $\mu_{X_i}, \sigma_{X_i}, \sigma_{X_i\hat{X}_i}$ are the mean, the variance, and the covariance of the pixel intensities of the two images. For efficient whole image reconstruction, then, one can combine it with L1-Loss [31]:

$$L_{img}(X, \hat{X}_{\mathbf{w}}) = \kappa\, L_{\text{SSIM}}(X, \hat{X}_{\mathbf{w}}) + (1 - \kappa)\left\| X - \hat{X}_{\mathbf{w}} \right\|_1, \tag{4}$$

where $\kappa = 0.84$ (empirical). Within the bounding boxes $\mathbf{B} \in \{N_{boxes}, 4\}$, the minimization of L_{img} will highlight the regions of localized pathologies $\{x_0 : x_1, y_0 : y_1\}$ (such as those annotated in fastMRI+ [44]):

$$L_{box}(X, \hat{X}_{\mathbf{w}}) = \sum_{x_0, x_1, y_0, y_1}^{\mathbf{B}} L_{img}\left(X[x_0 : x_1, y_0 : y_1], \hat{X}_{\mathbf{w}}[x_0 : x_1, y_0 : y_1] \right). \tag{5}$$

2.1 Iterative Gradients Sampling

Inspired by [46], we propose to search for optimal $\mathbf{w}$ iteratively, starting from an initial filling $\mathbf{w}[\frac{N}{2}] = 1$. Next, the FFT is applied to image X, multiplied by $\mathbf{w}$, and the undersampled reconstruction is computed: $\hat{X} = F^{-1}(F(X) \cdot \mathbf{w})$. Then, $\hat{X}_{\mathbf{w}}$ becomes the input to the model $S(\cdot)$, generating a prediction $\hat{Y} = S(\hat{X}_{\mathbf{w}})$. Finally, we estimate the value of the target loss L_{target} for this pattern, and the position i of the $\mathbf{w}$ with the highest negative value is chosen, while the pattern is updated as $\mathbf{w}[i] = 1$:

$$i \leftarrow \underset{i|\mathbf{w}[i]=0}{\arg\min} \frac{\partial L_{target}}{\partial \mathbf{w}}. \tag{6}$$

This index is treated as the optimal position of the sampling pattern for the next transition (*i.e.*, adding 1 to its position). We, thus, obtain:

$$\mathbf{w}_{i+1} = \mathbf{w}_i + \mathbb{I}_{N,N} \left[\underset{j|\mathbf{w}_i[j]=0}{\arg\min} \left(\frac{\partial L_{target}}{\partial \mathbf{w}_i} \right) \right], \tag{7}$$

where $\mathbb{I}_{N,N}$ is the identity matrix, j is the index of the line in k-space, selected in $(i+1)$'th iteration. The gradient descend follows Eq. (7), yielding the sequence of lines joined as a final optimal pattern $\mathbf{w}$ for the target task (Algorithm 1).

To elaborate on the gradient calculation, the idea of IGS is to use the gradient descent on the undersampled pattern in order to optimize it. Noteworthy, the undersampled pattern is binary and cannot be trained by the gradient descent. Unlike [41], where the authors trained the estimation of each position in the undersampled vector, we iteratively estimate the gradients $\frac{\partial L_{target}}{\partial w_i}$ of the weights w and add them with some coefficient to the trained weights. Estimating the direction towards the optimal point in the parameter space allows for the shift in the direction of the gradient even for a binary pattern. Note that IGS is proposed as an intuitive way to tune the pattern; but other optimization methods, *e.g.*, LOUPE [2], can also work in the proposed framework.

3   Experiments

Datasets and SOTA k-space Acceleration Patterns. Experiments were carried out with publicly available MRI datasets[2]: ACDC [6], BraTS [27], and fastMRI [43] (fastMRI+ annotations from [44]).

Cardiac MRI data in ACDC includes slices from the left ventricle with a step of 5–10 mm. Train set: 100 subjects (1,188 slices). Test set: 50 subjects (514 slices). Ground truth contours for the cavities and myocardium are provided. The BraTS multi-modal data comprise MRI scans of the brain for different imaging protocols. Train set: 258 subjects (35,508 slices). Test set: 111 subjects (15,391 slices). Ground truth contours for gliomas (brain tumors) are provided. For BraTS and ACDC pre-processing, we follow the idea of using the inverse FFT to form a reconstruction dataset from the real-space image data [45]. Such methods became standard in the field of compressed sensing, when there is no raw k-space data available.

In the fastMRI subset, we took the original single-coil raw k-space data for the knee anatomy. Train set: 10,374 scans. Test set: 1,992 scans. We also used the authors' script to generate the default fastMRI patterns for acceleration, along with the fastMRI+ bounding box annotations for the knee pathologies [44].

---

[2] Refer to the original dataset descriptions for more details.

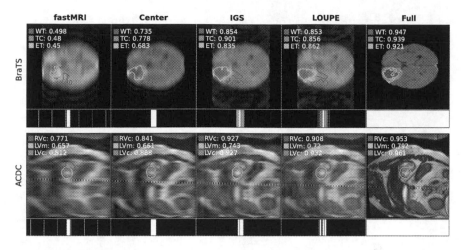

Fig. 2. *Top:* the whole (WT), the core (TC) and the enhancing (ET) tumor segmentation results on the BraTS data using U-Net 3D on undersampled images by different undersampling methods. *Bottom:* Cardiac structures in the ACDC dataset segmented by U-Net: left and right ventricular cavity (LVc, RVc) and the left ventricular myocardium (LVm). LOUPE is the optimization from [2].

Below, we compare our optimized undersampling patterns to the original fastMRI and the center-weighted (symmetric) masks and report p-values with the null hypotheses stating that the distribution of the metric values for the optimized patterns matches that of the Center pattern. Our primary acceleration factor of interest is ×16 (for a 256×256 images it implies N_s =16 lines), being somewhat of a challenging setting[3].

Implementation Details. Basic data pre-processing, the network training details, and the hyperparameters are summarized in the Supplementary material. The source code is available at https://github.com/cviaai/IGS/.

Results. The effect of the learned undersampling pattern on the reconstructed image and the segmentation quality (Dice score) is shown in Fig. 2 for various anatomies, with the quantitative comparison given in Table 2. The optimal k-space patterns are shown beneath the frames. Baseline reconstruction results are aggregated in Table 1 for BraTS and plotted against Dice score in Fig. 3 for ACDC data. Examples of the reconstructed images using the IGS optimization for fastMRI are shown in Fig. 4.

4   Discussion

Segmentation *vs.* Reconstruction. Fig. 3 illustrates the trade-off between segmentation quality (Dice score) and the image quality that one typically opti-

---

[3] The majority of fastMRI works, *e.g.*, consider ×4 and ×8 acceleration factors.

Table 1. Reconstruction metrics for × 4 acceleration.

	Pattern	F.M.	C.	Ours
fastMRI	SSIM	0.564	0.693	**0.700**
	PSNR	20.330	26.850	**26.861**
	NMSE	0.104	**0.029**	0.029
BraTS	SSIM	0.588	0.635	**0.678**
	PSNR	18.753	**20.969**	20.354
	NMSE	0.434	0.263	**0.268**

Note: F.M.: fastMRI pattern, C.: **Center** pattern.

Table 2. Segmentation results. Dice scores at ×16 acceleration.

		ACDC			BraTS		
	Model	RVc	LVm	LVc	WT	TC	ET
F.M.	M1	0.756	0.675	0.825	0.808	0.640	0.387
	M2	0.692	0.638	0.783	0.739	0.650	0.448
C.	M1	0.788	0.716	0.844	0.821	0.673	0.442
	M2	0.795	0.727	0.851	0.739	0.623	0.390
Ours	M1	**0.813**	**0.771**	**0.882**	**0.835**	0.690	0.468
	M2	0.790	0.749	0.859	0.787	**0.698**	**0.481**
Full	M1	0.868	0.865	0.931	0.873	0.726	0.575
	M2	0.899	0.891	0.941	0.888	0.792	0.623

Note: M1: U-Net [36], **ACDC** M2: Attention U-Net [30], **BraTS** M2: 3D U-Net [11]. **ACDC** p-value $= 0.0067$. **BraTS** p-value $= 0.0002$.

mizes in the reconstruction stage (SSIM) as the acceleration factor is varied from ×2 to ×26. It is evident that for the standard undersampling, the Dice and the SSIM metrics are almost linear. However, it starts to differ as the acceleration becomes extreme (×12 and above). The IGS-optimized Dice slows down its decay even though the quality of the reconstructed images becomes extremely low at this point, a direct consequence of the proposed optimization routine. **Center** and **fastMRI** patterns aim to improve the image quality instead, resulting in a similarly mediocre performance at moderate acceleration factors and with **fastMRI** patterns collapsing at the higher ones.

Brain Tumor Localization. In Table 2, the IGS sampling outperforms both **fastMRI** and **Center** sampling patterns when the goal is to localize the object of interest. U-Net + IGS sampling shows similar results to **ACDC** SOTA + IGS, and is significantly better than **BraTS** SOTA + IGS (p < 0.0002).

U-Net + IGS combination outperforms the other sampling and models on all tissue classes, except for several **BraTS** cases: here, U-Net 3D (M2) with IGS sampling segments ET and TC tissue classes better, which could be attributed to the way the small and the large volumetric details develop at such acceleration (×16). Notably, only our approach preserves the important image features at these scales[4] (Fig. 2), while the **Center** pattern dismisses the tumor core, as well as the fragments of the whole tumor borders. Similarly, the **fastMRI** pattern demonstrates inferior segmentation performance.

Cardiac Segmentation. For **ACDC** segmentation, U-Net with the proposed sampling also outperformed the other sampling patterns. Although SOTA models (U-Net with Attention [30]) demonstrate better performance on the fully sampled data, the ordinary U-Net shows better results with the IGS-undersampled

---

[4] Only those features that maximize the Dice score.

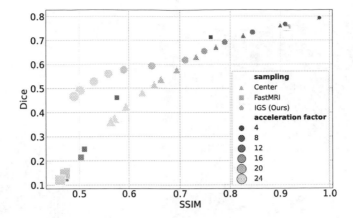

Fig. 3. Segmentation *vs.* **Reconstruction** for ACDC dataset. Measured Dice *vs.* SSIM at different acceleration factors. The size of the mark is proportional to acceleration factor. Note how our sampling boosts segmentation quality even when SSIM drops to the low values at moderate to high acceleration factors.

data. We speculate that the attention on the highly undersampled data limits the capacity of the SOTA model.

Knee Pathology Localization. The annotation provided in FastMRI+ [44], allows us to explore optimal patterns for localization of wanted MRI targets through optimized reconstruction within the bounding boxes. Such a problem statement is very relevant to clinical practice, as the exact contours of pathologies are more difficult (and more expensive) to obtain than the rough box regions. The obvious shortcoming of such an annotation approach is that the shapes and the sizes of the marked bounding boxes can vary greatly even for the same nosology, making the detection models hard to train when the annotation is scarce.

Instead, we considered the reconstruction loss term, set by Eq. (5), specifically for the bounding box regions, allowing us to optimize the pertinent sampling pattern in k-space for reconstructing those regions where the image quality matters the most. After the model learned to reconstruct the object for such local image enhancement, the localization of the pathology of interest became possible *with a simple ablation of the box loss* (see the cross-correlation difference map in Fig. 4). Although indirect, this method successfully highlights the pathology-prone areas in the image. Cropped pathology regions in Fig. 4 showcase how the optimized k-space undersampling mask enables visualization of the fine anatomic details exactly where it matters the most.

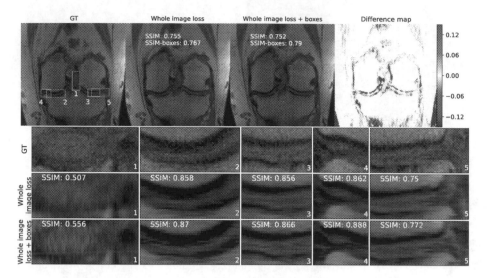

Fig. 4. *Top:* Reconstruction results for `fastMRI+` by Cascade U-Net at ×8 acceleration. *Bottom:* Cropped regions in the ground-truth bounding boxes. The heatmap highlights the pathology-prone areas (cross-correlation difference of the reconstructions with and without the box loss, see Supplementary Table S2).

5   Conclusions

To conclude, we proposed a new paradigm for accelerating MRI, where the undersampling of k-space occurs intelligently for the ultimate benefit of the localization task. The method holds promise to assist radiologists in detecting and localizing pathologies at low-field or high-speed imaging settings. A new iterative gradient sampling algorithm was shown to be capable of finding optimal undersampling patterns in several medical vision tasks and applications, with cardiac, neurological, and orthopedic utility confirmed herein. Remarkably, the learnt undersampling patterns could boost the target performance score by up to 12% (Dice metric) over the result obtained with the default `fastMRI` or with the center-weighted patterns.

Future research directions include adaptation of the undersampling strategy to 3D [39], application of the domain adaptation methods to the cross-task undersampling patterns [15,33], harnessing advanced MRI-specific image reconstruction metrics [18], and the study of the compound loss functions to optimize several medical vision objectives at once [8].

References

1. Aggarwal, H.K., Mani, M.P., Jacob, M.: MoDL: model-based deep learning architecture for inverse problems. IEEE Trans. Med. Imaging **38**(2), 394–405 (2019)
2. Bahadir, C.D., et al.: Deep-learning-based optimization of the under-sampling pattern in MRI. IEEE Trans. Comput. Imag. **6**, 1139–1152 (2020)

3. Bakas, S., et al.: Advancing the cancer genome atlas glioma MRI collections with expert segmentation labels and radiomic features. Sci. Data **4**(1) (2017)
4. Bakas, S., et al.: Identifying the best machine learning algorithms for brain tumor segmentation, progression assessment, and overall survival prediction in the brats challenge (2019)
5. Belov, A., Stadelmann, J., Kastryulin, S., Dylov, D.V.: Towards ultrafast MRI via extreme k-space undersampling and superresolution. In: de Bruijne, M., et al. (eds.) MICCAI 2021. LNCS, vol. 12906, pp. 254–264. Springer, Cham (2021). https://doi.org/10.1007/978-3-030-87231-1_25
6. Bernard, O., et al.: Deep learning techniques for automatic MRI cardiac multi-structures segmentation and diagnosis: is the problem solved? IEEE Trans. Med. Imaging **37**(11), 2514–2525 (2018)
7. Bernstein, M.A., King, K.F., Zhou, X.J.: Handbook of MRI Pulse Sequences. Elsevier Sci. & Techn. (2004)
8. Bespalov, I., Buzun, N., Dylov, D.V.: BRULÈ: Barycenter-regularized unsupervised landmark extraction. Pattern Recogn. **131**, 108816 (2022)
9. Candès, E.J., Romberg, J., Tao, T.: Robust uncertainty principles: exact signal reconstruction from highly incomplete frequency information. IEEE Trans. Inf. Theory **52**(2), 489–509 (2006)
10. Chaudhari, A.S., et al.: Prospective deployment of deep learning in MRI: a framework for important considerations, challenges, and recommendations for best practices. J. Magn. Reson. Imaging **54**(2), 357–371 (2021)
11. Çiçek, Ö., Abdulkadir, A., Lienkamp, S.S., Brox, T., Ronneberger, O.: 3D U-Net: learning dense volumetric segmentation from sparse annotation. In: Ourselin, S., Joskowicz, L., Sabuncu, M.R., Unal, G., Wells, W. (eds.) MICCAI 2016. LNCS, vol. 9901, pp. 424–432. Springer, Cham (2016). https://doi.org/10.1007/978-3-319-46723-8_49
12. Debatin, J.F., McKinnon, G.C.: Ultrafast MRI: Techniques and Applications. Springer, Heidelberg (1998). https://doi.org/10.1007/978-3-642-80384-0
13. Deshmane, A., Gulani, V., Griswold, M., Seiberlich, N.: Parallel MR imaging. J. Magn. Reson. Imaging **36**(1), 55–72 (2012)
14. Eo, T., et al.: KIKI-net: cross-domain convolutional neural networks for reconstructing undersampled magnetic resonance images. Magn. Reson. Med. **80**(5), 2188–2201 (2018). https://doi.org/10.1002/mrm.27201
15. Ganin, Y., Lempitsky, V.: Unsupervised domain adaptation by backpropagation. In: Bach, F., Blei, D. (eds.) Proceedings of the 32nd International Conference on Machine Learning, Proceedings of Machine Learning Research, vol. 37, pp. 1180–1189. PMLR, Lille, France, 07–09 July 2015
16. Guo, S., Fessler, J.A., Noll, D.C.: High-resolution oscillating steady-state fMRI using patch-tensor low-rank reconstruction. IEEE Trans. Med. Imaging **39**(12), 4357–4368 (2020)
17. Han, Y., Sunwoo, L., Ye, J.C.: k-space deep learning for accelerated MRI. IEEE Trans. Med. Imaging **39**(2), 377–386 (2020)
18. Kastryulin, S., Zakirov, J., Pezzotti, N., Dylov, D.V.: Image quality assessment for magnetic resonance imaging (2022). https://arxiv.org/abs/2203.07809
19. Knoll, F., et al.: Advancing machine learning for MR image reconstruction with an open competition: overview of the 2019 fastMRI challenge. Magn. Reson. Med. **84**(6), 3054–3070 (2020)
20. Liang, D., Ying, L.: Compressed-sensing dynamic MR imaging with partially known support. IEEE Eng. Med. Biol. Soc. **2010**, 2829–2832 (2010). https://doi.org/10.1109/IEMBS.2010.5626077

21. Liu, D., Liang, D., Liu, X., Zhang, Y.: Under-sampling trajectory design for compressed sensing mri. In: IEEE Eng. Med. Biol. Soc. **2012**, pp. 73–76. IEEE (2012)
22. Liu, R., Zhang, Y., Cheng, S., Luo, Z., Fan, X.: A deep framework assembling principled modules for CS-MRI: unrolling perspective, convergence behaviors, and practical modeling. IEEE Trans. Med. Imaging **39**(12), 4150–4163 (2020)
23. Lønning, K., et al.: Recurrent inference machines for reconstructing heterogeneous MRI data. Med. Image Anal. **53**, 64–78 (2019). https://doi.org/10.1016/j.media.2019.01.005
24. Lu, H., Wei, J., Liu, Q., Wang, Y., Deng, X.: A dictionary learning method with total generalized variation for MRI reconstruction. Int. J. Biomed **2016**, 1–13 (2016). https://doi.org/10.1155/2016/7512471
25. Lustig, M., Donoho, D., Pauly, J.M.: Sparse MRI: The application of compressed sensing for rapid MR imaging. Magn. Reson. Med. 58(6), 1182–1195 (12 2007). https://doi.org/10.1002/mrm.21391
26. Ma, Y., et al.: Low-dose CT image denoising using a generative adversarial network with a hybrid loss function for noise learning. IEEE Access **8**, 67519–67529 (2020)
27. Menze, B.H., et al.: The multimodal brain tumor image segmentation benchmark (BRATS). IEEE Trans. Med. Imaging 34(10), 1993–2024 (2015). https://doi.org/10.1109/TMI.2014.2377694
28. Muckley, M.J., et al.: Results of the 2020 fastMRI challenge for machine learning MR image reconstruction. IEEE Trans. Med. Imaging **pp** (2021). https://doi.org/10.1109/TMI.2021.3075856
29. Oh, G., et al.: Unpaired deep learning for accelerated MRI using optimal transport driven cycleGAN. IEEE Trans. Comput. Imag. **6**, 1285–1296 (2020)
30. Oktay, O., et al.: Attention U-Net: learning where to look for the pancreas. MIDL 2018 abs/1804.03999 (2018)
31. Pezzotti, N., et al.: An adaptive intelligence algorithm for undersampled knee MRI reconstruction. IEEE Access **8**, 204825–204838 (2020)
32. Pineda, L., Basu, S., Romero, A., Calandra, R., Drozdzal, M.: Active MR k-space sampling with reinforcement learning. In: Martel, A.L., et al. (eds.) MICCAI 2020. LNCS, vol. 12262, pp. 23–33. Springer, Cham (2020). https://doi.org/10.1007/978-3-030-59713-9_3
33. Prokopenko, D., Stadelmann, J.V., Schulz, H., Renisch, S., Dylov, D.V.: Unpaired synthetic image generation in radiology using GANs. In: Nguyen, D., Xing, L., Jiang, S. (eds.) AIRT 2019. LNCS, vol. 11850, pp. 94–101. Springer, Cham (2019). https://doi.org/10.1007/978-3-030-32486-5_12
34. Raja, R., Sinha, N.: Adaptive k-space sampling design for edge-enhanced DCE-MRI using compressed sensing. Magn. Reson. Imaging **32**(7), 899–912 (2014). https://doi.org/10.1016/j.mri.2013.12.022
35. Ramzi, Z., Ciuciu, P., Starck, J.L.: Benchmarking deep nets mri reconstruction models on the fastmri publicly available dataset. In: 2020 IEEE 17th International Symposium on Biomedical Imaging (ISBI), pp. 1441–1445 (2020)
36. Ronneberger, O., Fischer, P., Brox, T.: U-Net: convolutional networks for biomedical image segmentation. In: Navab, N., Hornegger, J., Wells, W.M., Frangi, A.F. (eds.) MICCAI 2015. LNCS, vol. 9351, pp. 234–241. Springer, Cham (2015). https://doi.org/10.1007/978-3-319-24574-4_28
37. Seo, B., et al.: Cardiac MRI image segmentation for left ventricle and right ventricle using deep learning. arXiv preprint arXiv:1909.08028 (2019)
38. Tamada, D., Kose, K.: Two-dimensional compressed sensing using the cross-sampling approach for low-field MRI systems. IEEE Trans. Med. Imaging **33**(9), 1905–1912 (2014)

39. Wang, G., Luo, T., Nielsen, J.F., Noll, D.C., Fessler, J.A.: B-spline parameterized joint optimization of reconstruction and k-space trajectories (BJORK) for accelerated 2D MRI. arXiv preprint arXiv:2101.11369 (2021)

40. Xiang, J., Dong, Y., Yang, Y.: FISTA-Net: learning a fast iterative shrinkage thresholding network for inverse problems in imaging. IEEE Trans. Med. Imaging **40**(5), 1329–1339 (2021)

41. Xuan, K., Sun, S., Xue, Z., Wang, Q., Liao, S.: Learning MRI k-space subsampling pattern using progressive weight pruning. In: Martel, A.L., et al. (eds.) MICCAI 2020. LNCS, vol. 12262, pp. 178–187. Springer, Cham (2020). https://doi.org/10.1007/978-3-030-59713-9_18

42. Ye, J.C.: Compressed sensing MRI: a review from signal processing perspective. BMC Biomed. Eng. **1**(1), 1–17 (2019)

43. Zbontar, J., et al.: fastMRI: an open dataset and benchmarks for accelerated MRI. arXiv preprint arXiv:1811.08839 (2018)

44. Zhao, R., et al.: fastMRI: Clinical pathology annotations for knee and brain fully sampled multi-coil MRI data. arXiv preprint arXiv:2109.03812 (2021)

45. Zheng, H., Fang, F., Zhang, G.: Cascaded dilated dense network with two-step data consistency for MRI reconstruction. In: Advances in Neural Information Processing Systems 32 (NeurIPS). Curran Associates (2019)

46. Zijlstra, F., Viergever, M.A., Seevinck, P.R.: Evaluation of variable density and data-driven k-space undersampling for compressed sensing magnetic resonance imaging. Investig. Radiol. **51**(6), 410–419 (2016)

Sensor Geometry Generalization to Untrained Conditions in Quantitative Ultrasound Imaging

SeokHwan Oh[1], Myeong-Gee Kim[1], Youngmin Kim[1], Guil Jung[1], Hyuksool Kwon[2], and Hyeon-Min Bae[1(✉)]

[1] Electrical Engineering Department,
Korea Advanced Institute of Science and Technology, 34141 Daejeon, South Korea
{joseph9337,hmbae}@kaist.ac.kr
[2] Department of Emergency Medicine, Seoul National University Bundang Hospital,
13620 Seong-nam, South Korea

Abstract. Recent improvements in deep learning have brought great progress in ultrasonic lesion quantification. However, the learning-based scheme performs properly only when a certain level of similarity between train and test condition is ensured. However, real-world test condition expects diverse untrained probe geometry from various manufacturers, which undermines the credibility of learning-based ultrasonic approaches. In this paper, we present a meta-learned deformable sensor generalization network that generates consistent attenuation coefficient (AC) image regardless of the probe condition. The proposed method was assessed through numerical simulation and in-vivo breast patient measurements. The numerical simulation shows that the proposed network outperforms existing state-of-the-art domain generalization methods for the AC reconstruction under *unseen* probe conditions. In in-vivo studies, the proposed network provides consistent AC images irrespective of various probe conditions and demonstrates great clinical potential in differential breast cancer diagnosis.

Keywords: Medical ultrasound · Domain generalization · Image reconstruction · Quantitative ultrasound imaging · Meta-learning

1 Introduction

Ultrasound (US) is a widely available medical imaging modality thanks to its cost-effective, real-time, and non-radiative nature. Although the conventional b-mode ultrasonography demonstrates high sensitivity in abnormal lesion detection, the tissue property cannot be characterized as the image offers only

---

Supplementary Information The online version contains supplementary material available at https://doi.org/10.1007/978-3-031-16446-0_74.

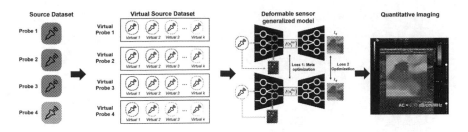

Fig. 1. Overall procedure of the sensor generalization training scheme.

operator-dependent qualitative information [1]. To overcome such clinical limitations, the need for quantitative ultrasound is increasing.

Quantitative ultrasound imaging has been developed to quantify the changes in tissue biomechanical properties caused by pathological changes. The quantitative ultrasonography has shown great potential in diverse clinical applications especially in differential cancer diagnosis [2–4]. In quantitative US, the reconstruction accuracy is highly dependent on the method of extracting relevant feature from radio-frequency (RF) signals [5,6]. Deep learning has shown great success in extracting features from the given data distribution and thus there have been increasing attempts to analyze RF signal via data-driven approaches. Recently, learning-based schemes have demonstrated great progress in quantitative US imaging [7,8].

While recent advances in deep learning have opened the possibility of novel quantitative US applications, there exists a crucial challenge when deployed in practice. Various degree of performance degradation is expected since the properties of US probes deployed in clinical field can be different from those under which quantitative US system is trained. Diverse level of dissimilarity exists between US probes including the number of sensor elements and pitch size. These differences in individual sensor geometry hinder quantitative US system from operating properly under *unseen* probe condition, and thus became an important research challenge [9].

In this paper, we propose a learning framework that improves the generality of the model to *unseen* probe conditions. Specifically, a data augmentation algorithm is introduced to generate virtual sensor geometry, and trains the NN under diversified probe conditions. We present a deformable sensor adaptation module that calibrates individual sensor geometry. We further demonstrate that the proposed model is better generalized through the meta-learning based optimization. The proposed framework is applied in attenuation coefficient (AC) image reconstruction, which is a promising biomarker for the diagnosis of cancer [4,6]. The framework is also applicable to a range of NN applications that suffer from diversity of measurement geometries including US elastography [10], and computed tomography (CT) reconstruction [11].

Table 1. Probe conditions of source and test dataset

Source dataset				Test dataset			
	$N_{element}$	Pitch-size[mm]	Width [cm]		$N_{element}$	Pitch-size	Width
$\mathbb{D}_{\mathbb{G}_1} \sim (x^{\mathbb{G}_1}, y)$	256	0.20	5.12	$\mathbb{D}_{T1} \sim (x^{\mathbb{G}T1}, y)$	192	0.23	4.42
$\mathbb{D}_{\mathbb{G}_2} \sim (x^{\mathbb{G}_2}, y)$	192	0.25	4.80	$\mathbb{D}_{T2} \sim (x^{\mathbb{G}T2}, y)$	128	**0.30**	3.84
$\mathbb{D}_{\mathbb{G}_3} \sim (x^{\mathbb{G}_3}, y)$	192	0.20	3.84	$\mathbb{D}_{T3} \sim (x^{\mathbb{G}T3}, y)$	**64**	**0.60**	3.84
$\mathbb{D}_{\mathbb{G}_4} \sim (x^{\mathbb{G}_4}, y)$	128	0.25	3.20				

2 Method

Figure 1 illustrates an overall procedure of the proposed sensor generalization learning scheme. RF signals, $x^{\mathbb{G}_i} \sim \mathbb{R}^{N_{elements} \times T}$ are obtained from plane waves with seven different incidence angles θ ranging between $-15°$ to $+15°$ at $5°$ intervals in multiple disparate sensor conditions $\mathbb{G}_i$. Here, $N_{elements}$ indicates the number of probe elements and T is discretized time indices. Data augmentation is applied to diversify the source dataset to numerous virtual sensor geometries. The meta-learned deformable sensor generalization network calibrates individual sensor conditions and generates an accurate AC image.

2.1 Synthetic Multi-sensor Dataset Generation

Diverse complex soft-tissue numerical phantoms are modeled and simulated as proposed in [8,12]. The organs and lesions y_j are modeled by placing 0–10 ellipses with radii of 2–30mm, at random positions on 50×50mm background with the biomechanical property that is set to cover general soft tissue characteristics [13]. Each y_j is measured with varying probe conditions $\mathbb{G}_i$, and compose source $(x^{\mathbb{G}_1}, x^{\mathbb{G}_2}, ..., x^{\mathbb{G}_i}, y) \sim \mathbb{D}$ and test $(x^{\mathbb{G}T_1}, x^{\mathbb{G}T_2}, ..., x^{\mathbb{G}T_i}, y^T) \sim \mathbb{D}_T$ dataset (Table. 1). We have simulated 8.85k phantoms for each source sensor geometry, and 0.5k for each test sensor geometry.

2.2 Data Augmentation

A virtual sensor geometry augmentation (VSG-aug) is proposed to generate RF signal $\hat{x}_j^{\mathbb{G}_i}$ measured in virtual domain of sensor geometry that is not provided in $\mathbb{D}$. Through the VSG-aug, a neural network (NN) is trained with a broader range of probe condition and is parameterized to better adapt to *unseen* sensor geometry. The VSG-aug algorithm is outlined in Algorithm 1. Hyper-parameters, sub-sample (α_{ss}) and sub-width (α_{sw}), are required for VSG-aug where each parameter adjusts the number of virtual transducer elements and width, respectively. During the training, each α_{ss} and α_{sw} are randomly generated in uniform distribution to create random probe conditions at each iteration (Fig. 2).

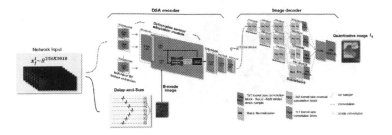

Fig. 2. Proposed DSG-net structure

2.3 Deformable Sensor Generalization Model

In this section, the architecture of the deformable sensor generalization network, referred to as a DSG-net, is presented. The network consists of two components: (a) a deformable sensor adaptive encoder extracting calibrated quantitative information under diverse sensor geometry and (b) an image decoder synthesizing an AC image.

Deformable Sensor Adaptive (DSA) Encoder. The DSA encoder is proposed to extract a generalized representation of quantitative feature $q \sim \mathbb{R}^{512 \times 16 \times 16}$ regardless of $\mathbb{G}_i$. The encoder performs convolutional operation, batch normalization, and ReLU activation function, which are proven as efficient components for extracting q from $x_j^{\mathbb{G}_i}$ [7,8] and includes a DSA module that calibrates individual sensor geometry through spatial deformation.

Deformable Sensor Adaptation Module. The DSA module is implemented from the idea that performance degradation caused by dissimilarity of each $\mathbb{G}_i$ can be resolved by finding a deformation field to calibrate measured RF data according to individual sensor geometry. The DSA module is based on convolutional operations, and learns a parameterized registration function $f(:)$. $f(:)$

Algorithm 1. Virtual sensor geometry augmentation

Input: Source training sample $(x_j^{G_i}, y_j) \sim \mathbb{D}_{\mathbb{G}i} \subset (x_j^{\mathbb{G}1}, x_j^{\mathbb{G}2}, ...x_j^{\mathbb{G}i}, y_j) \sim \mathbb{D}$
Output: Virtual training sample $(\hat{x}_j^{G_i}, y_j) \sim \hat{\mathbb{D}}_{\mathbb{G}i}$
Require: α_{ss} : *Sub-sample hyper-parameter*, α_{sw} : *Sub-width hyper-parameter*

1: Choose α_{ss} in uniform distribution $(0.5,1)$
2: **for** t in 1:T **do**
3:     $\bar{x}_j^{G_i}(:,t) \leftarrow x_j^{G_i}(round(\frac{1:\bar{n}_{element}}{\alpha_{ss}}),t)$
4: **end for**
5: Choose α_{sw} in uniform distribution $(0.7,1)$
6: **for** t in 1:T **do**
7:     $\hat{x}_j^{G_i}(:,t) \leftarrow \bar{x}_j^{G_i}(\frac{\bar{N}_{element}(1-\alpha_{sw})}{2} : \frac{\bar{N}_{element}(1+\alpha_{sw})}{2},t))$
8: **end for**

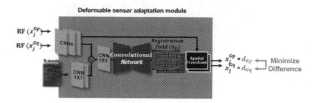

Fig. 3. DSA module

takes the sensory $x_j^{\mathbb{G}i}$ and the b-mode image $BM(x_j^{\mathbb{G}i})$ to generate displacement field $d_{\mathbb{G}i} = Identity + f(x_j^{\mathbb{G}i}, BM(x_j^{\mathbb{G}i}))$. $BM(x_j^{\mathbb{G}i})$ helps the DSA module to better recognize the individual $\mathbb{G}_i$ since the information about the probe geometry is contained in the relationship between $x_j^{\mathbb{G}i}$ and $BM(x_j^{\mathbb{G}i})$. Inspired by Voxelmorph [14], the spatial transformation [15] warps $x_j^{\mathbb{G}i}$ into deformed representation $x_j^{\mathbb{G}i} \circ d_{\mathbb{G}i}$. $f(:)$ is trained with a stochastic gradient descent algorithm objective to minimize the Euclidean distance between $x_j^{\mathbb{G}p} \circ d_{\mathbb{G}p}$ and $x_j^{\mathbb{G}l} \circ d_{\mathbb{G}l}$, where $\mathbb{G}_p \neq \mathbb{G}_l$. Namely, $f(:)$ learns $d_{\mathbb{G}i}$ that adjusts sensory data from diverse probe condition to have common sensory representation (Fig. 3).

Image Decoder. The image decoder translates compressed q to a higher resolution quantitative image $I_q \sim \mathbb{R}^{128 \times 128}$. The overall decoder architecture comprises parallel multi-resolution subnetwork to generate detailed I_q [12,16]. Each resolution subnetworks is responsible for generating quantitative image of corresponding resolutions $I_{q,\mathbb{R}} \sim \mathbb{R}^{R \times R}$, where $R \in \{16, 32, 64, 128\}$ denotes spatial resolution of the image. Finally, the subnetworks are concatenated into higher resolution representation, and I_q is generated via 1×1 convolution.

2.4   Meta-learned Spatial Deformation

In general, the data-driven approach can easily be over-fitted to trained condition. Recent studies in meta-learning have demonstrated that simulating virtual test scenarios during model optimization enhances the generalization of the NN to the actual *unseen* condition [17,18]. We propose meta-learned spatial deformation (MLSD) which improves the generalizability of the DSA module by optimizing f via the meta-learning scheme. Specifically, the source data $\mathbb{D}$ is allocated into meta-train $(\mathbb{D}_{\mathbb{G}_1}, ..., \mathbb{D}_{\mathbb{G}_{r-1}}, \mathbb{D}_{\mathbb{G}_{r+1}}, \mathbb{D}_{\mathbb{G}_i}) \sim \bar{\mathbb{D}}$ and meta-test $\mathbb{D}_{\mathbb{G}_r} \sim \tilde{\mathbb{D}}$ data. MLSD aims to train f on $\bar{\mathbb{D}}$, such that it generalizes to $\tilde{\mathbb{D}}$. At each iteration, the f is updated to f' with $\bar{\mathbb{D}}$ while regularzing f' to minimize loss $L_{DSA}(f - \beta \nabla_f, \bar{\mathbb{D}}, \tilde{\mathbb{D}}))$ (Eq. 3) on $\tilde{\mathbb{D}}$. The $L_{DSA}(f - \beta \nabla_f, \bar{\mathbb{D}}, \tilde{\mathbb{D}})$ adjusts f to be optimized towards a direction that can improve the accuracy of virtual *unseen* conditions. The MLSD enforces virtual train and test scenarios repeatedly so that the DSA module properly calibrates sensor geometry on actual *unseen* probe conditions without bias to $\mathbb{D}$. The proposed MLSD is presented in Algorithm 2.

Algorithm 2. Meta-learned spatial deformation

Input: $(x_j^{G_1}, x_j^{G_2}, ...x_j^{G_i}, y_j) \sim \mathbb{D}$
Initialize: DSG-net model parameter θ, DSA module paramter: f
Require: Hyper-parameter: $\beta, \lambda, \gamma = (1e^{-4}, 1e^{-4}, 1)$

1: **for** it in iterations **do**
2:      Split $\mathbb{D}$ and $\tilde{\mathbb{D}} \leftarrow \mathbb{D}$
3:      **Meta-train:** Loss $L_{DSA}(f, \bar{\mathbb{D}})$
4:      Update DSA parameter $f' = f - \beta\nabla_f = f - \beta\frac{\partial(L_{DSA}(f,\bar{\mathbb{D}}))}{\partial f}$
5:      **Meta-test:** Meta DSA Loss $L_{DSA}(f', \tilde{\mathbb{D}}, \tilde{\mathbb{D}})$
6:      **Meta-DSA Optimization:** $f = f - \lambda\frac{\partial((L_{DSA}(f,\bar{\mathbb{D}}))+\gamma L_{DSA}(f-\beta\nabla_f,\tilde{\mathbb{D}},\tilde{\mathbb{D}}))}{\partial f}$
7:      **Model Optimization:** $\theta = \theta - \lambda\frac{\partial L_{model}(f,\mathbb{D})}{\partial\theta}$
8: **end for**

Implementation Details. The objective function of the DSG-net is

$$\theta^* = \underset{\theta}{\text{argmin}} \ \mathbb{E}_{(x,y)\subset\mathbb{D}}[\|y - \theta(x))\|^2] + \sum_R[\|y_R - \theta_R(x))\|^2] + \epsilon\sum_{i=1}w_i^2, \quad (1)$$

where θ^* tries to minimize squared difference between the ground truth y, and the output $\theta(x)$ while each θ_R is regularized to progressively generate corresponding resolution image y_R. L_2 regularization ($\epsilon = 1e^{-6}$) is implemented to avoid overfitting [19]. The meta-objective function of the DSA module is denoted as

$$f^* = \underset{f}{\text{argmin}} \ \mathbb{E}_{(x^p,x^l,y)\subset\bar{\mathbb{D}},(x^r,y)\subset\tilde{\mathbb{D}}}[L_{DSA}(f, x^p, x^l) + L_{DSA}(f', x^p, x^r)], \quad (2)$$

$$L_{DSA}(f, x, y) = \|f(x) - f(y)\|^2, \quad (3)$$

where $L_{DSA}(f, x^p, x^l)$ is the Euclidean distance between deformed sensory from the aggregated meta-train domain ($\{x^p, x^q\} \subset \bar{\mathbb{D}}$), and $L_{DSA}(f', x^p, x^r)$ denotes the loss function from the meta-test domain ($\{x^r\} \subset \tilde{\mathbb{D}}$). The DSG-net was optimized with Adam ($lr = 1e^{-4}, \beta_1 = 0.9, \beta_2 = 0.999$) [20]. The NN is trained up to 150 epochs, which is determined based on the validation loss convengence. The NN is implemented using Tensorflow, accelerated with RTX Titan X GPU.

3 Experiments

The proposed method is assessed through numerical simulation and in-vivo studies. In in-vivo measurements, an ultrasound system (Vantage 64LE, Verasonics Inc., USA) is used with the linear probe with disparate sensor geometry (64ch, and 128ch of 5LE, Humanscan Inc., KR). The in-vivo study was approved by institutional review board of seoul national university bundang hospital (B-1910-570-301). The reconstruction accuracy is evaluated through peak signal to noise ratio (PSNR) and mean normalized absolute error (MNAE) metrics.

Table 2. Quantitative assessment result.

Ablation study				$\mathbb{D}_{T1}$		$\mathbb{D}_{T2}$		$\mathbb{D}_{T3}$	
	VSG -aug	DSA	MLSD	PSNR	MNAE	PSNR	MNAE	PSNR	MNAE
Base-line				21.24	0.0619	17.59	0.1152	15.78	0.1415
		✓		21.74	0.0591	19.18	0.0937	16.17	0.1385
		✓	✓	21.82	0.0590	19.76	0.0869	16.57	0.1314
	✓			21.19	0.0660	18.48	0.1036	17.68	0.1124
	✓	✓		22.03	0.0571	19.17	0.0935	17.72	0.1130
	✓	✓	✓	**22.20**	**0.0556**	**20.10**	**0.0811**	**18.27**	**0.1026**
Comparative study									
MTAE [21]		Multi-decoder		20.59	0.0726	17.00	0.1278	15.81	0.1464
+ VSG-aug				20.20	0.0751	18.13	0.1048	17.23	0.1171
MLDG [17]		Meta-learning		21.93	0.0579	19.16	0.0943	16.15	0.1398
+ VSG-aug				21.87	0.0612	19.44	0.0902	17.92	0.1088
EPI-FCR [22]		Episodic train		20.95	0.0693	17.87	0.1125	15.34	0.1545
+ VSG-aug				21.16	0.0670	19.37	0.0921	18.06	0.1084

3.1   Numerical Simulation

The performance of the proposed method is assessed with 0.5k representative test samples measured in three *unseen* probe conditions ($\mathbb{D}_{T1}, \mathbb{D}_{T2}, and \mathbb{D}_{T3}$ in Table 1). Considering the sensor geometry of the source dataset $\mathbb{D}$. $\mathbb{D}_{T1}$ shows within-distribution probe condition with $\mathbb{D}$. However, $\mathbb{D}_{T2}$ and $\mathbb{D}_{T3}$ can be considered as outlier conditions. The pitch-size of $\mathbb{D}_{T3}$ is outside the distribution of $\mathbb{D}$. In the case of $\mathbb{D}_{T3}$, both pitch-size and $N_{elements}$ are out-of-distribution condition. Hence, the image reconstruction is most difficult under $\mathbb{D}_{T3}$ condition. The proposed method is evaluated by performing comprehensive ablation studies using 5 different variants. The baseline model is trained with the aggregated $\mathbb{D}$. The NN trained with the VSG-aug method demonstrates 1.90 dB, and 25.8% enhance in PSNR and MNAE, respectively, in the reconstruction with $\mathbb{D}_{T3}$. The performance improvement is attributed to the fact that NN adapts to the out-of-distribution probe conditions by experiencing diverse virtual sensor geometry generated via VSG-aug. The accuracy of the AC image is enhanced by 9.7% through the use of the DSA scheme. In addition, the NN demonstrates prominent improvement when the DSA module is optimized with the MLSD. The study verifies that the generalisability of deformable adaptation scheme is enhanced through the MLSD. For further assessment of the method, the proposed model is compared with existing state-of-the-art domain generalization schemes. In the head-to-head comparison, the proposed method surpasses other domain generalization methods including the best prior method MLDG. In addition, the VSG-aug algorithm is applied to existing domain generalization models and demonstrates 11.8% improvement in the reconstruction of the *unseen* domain data (Table 2).

3.2   In-vivo Measurements

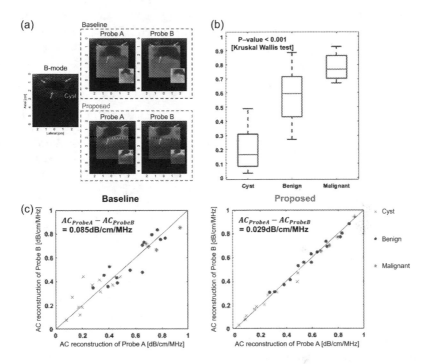

Fig. 4. Figure 4 In-vivo breast measurements. (a) AC reconstruction of the proposed and baseline model (b) Boxplot of the reconstructed AC of lesions. (p-value of Kruskal Wallis test < 0.001) (c) Consistency of AC reconstruction between different probe

In-vivo breast measurements are acquired from 29 breast subjects with cyst (n = 11), benign (n = 14), and malignant lesions (n = 4). Each measurement is obtained under two different probe conditions. Figure 4 presents reconstruction results of the proposed model, compared with ablated baseline. The proposed scheme demonstrates consistent AC reconstruction regardless of probe geometry. The shape and AC value of the lesion are better identified with the proposed NN, confirming the fact that the NN is well generalized to *unseen* sensor condition. Figure 4c compares the reconstructed AC of the breast leasions measured with the probe A and B. The proposed scheme clearly demonstrates that consistent AC reconstruction is achieved irrespective of probe elements (error rate = 1.9%). On the other hand, the ablated baseline demonstrates higher dependence on probe conditions (error rate = 5.7%). The cysts demonstrate the lowest AC value (0.257 ± 0.127 dB/cm/MHz), since the cyst is mostly composed of water with 0dB attenuation. The malignant lesions show higher AC (0.782 ± 0.110) than benign masses (0.571 ± 0.176), which agrees with the reported values [4]. As shown in Fig. 4, the proposed scheme is capable of identifying breast cancer irrespective of probe specifications from diverse manufacturers.

4   Conclusion

In this study, a single probe US system performing AC imaging under diverse probe specifications is presented. We implement a deformable sensor generalization network to calibrate individual probe conditions through spatial deformation of the sensory. The virtual sensor augmentation method synthesizes diverse probe geometry and demonstrates 26% enhancement for the reconstruction of out-of-distribution sensor geometry. The meta-learning scheme is applied in spatial deformation and improves the reconstruction accuracy by 10.2% in MNAE. In-vivo breast study demonstrates that the proposed scheme achieves consistent AC image reconstructions under disparate probe measurements. Through the study, we have shown that the NN has a potential in diagnosis of breast cancer. The proposed NN can be installed in any US system from diverse manufactures and provide accurate coherent AC images irrespective of the probe conditions.

References

1. Arribas, E.M., Whitman, G.J., De, B.N.: 2016 screening breast ultrasound: where are we today? Curr. Breast Cancer Rep. **8**, 221–9 (2016)
2. Goss, S.A., Johnston, R.L., Dunn, F.: Comprehensive compilation of empirical ultrasonic properties of mammalian tissues. J. Acoust. Soc. Am. **64**, 423–457 (1978)
3. Li, C., Duric, N., Littrup, P., Huang, L.: In vivo breast sound-speed imaging with ultrasound tomography. Ultrasound Med. Biol. **35**(10), 1615–1628 (2009)
4. Nam, K., Zagzebski, J.A., Hall, T.J.: Quantitative assessment of in vivo breast masses using ultrasound attenuation and backscatter. Ultras. Imaging. **35**, 46–61 (2013)
5. Sanabria, S.J., Ozkan, E., Rominger, M., Goksel, O.: Spatial domain reconstruction for imaging speed-of-sound with pulse-echo ultrasound: simulation and in vivo study. Phys. Med. Biol. **63**(21), 215015 (2018)
6. Rau, R., Unal, O., Schweizer, D., Vishnevskiy, V., Goksel, O.: Attenuation imaging with pulse-echo ultrasound based on an acoustic reflector. In: Shen, D., et al. (eds.) MICCAI 2019. LNCS, vol. 11768, pp. 601–609. Springer, Cham (2019). https://doi.org/10.1007/978-3-030-32254-0_67
7. Feigin, M., Zwecker, M., Freedman, D., Anthony, B.W.: Detecting muscle activation using ultrasound speed of sound inversion with deep learning. In: 2020 42nd Annual International Conference of the IEEE Engineering in Medicine and Biology Society (EMBC), pp. 2092–2095. IEEE (2020)
8. Oh, S.H., Kim, M.-G., Kim, Y., Kwon, H., Bae, H.-M.: A neural framework for multi-variable lesion quantification through B-mode style transfer. In: de Bruijne, M., et al. (eds.) MICCAI 2021. LNCS, vol. 12906, pp. 222–231. Springer, Cham (2021). https://doi.org/10.1007/978-3-030-87231-1_22
9. Wang, J., Lan, C., Liu, C., Ouyang, Y., Qin, T.: Generalizing to unseen domains: a survey on domain generalization. arXiv preprint (2021). arXiv:2103.03097
10. Ahmed, S., Kamal, U., Hassan., K.: SWE-Net: a deep learning approach for shear wave elastography and lesion segmentation using single push acoustic radiation force Ultrasonics, **110** (2021)
11. Shen, L., Zhao, W., Capaldi, D., Pauly, J., Xing, L.: A geometry-informed deep learning framework for ultra-sparse 3D tomographic image reconstruction. arXiv preprint arXiv:2105.11692 (2021)

12. Oh, S., Kim, M. -G., Kim, Y., Bae, H.-M.: A learned representation for multi variable ultrasound lesion quantification. In: ISBI, pp. 1177–1181. IEEE (2021)
13. Mast, T.D.: Empirical relationships between acoustic parameters in human soft tissues. Acoust. Res. Lett. Online 1(37), 37–43 (2000)
14. Balakrishnan, G., Zhao, A., Sabuncu, M.R., Guttag, J., Dalca, A.V.: Voxelmorph: a learning framework for deformable medical image registration. IEEE TMI (2019)
15. Jaderberg, M., Karen, S., Andrew, Z.: Jaderberg, M., et al.: Spatial transformer networks. In: NIPS, pp. 2017–2025 (2015)
16. Wang, J., et al.: Deep high-resolution representation learning for visual recognition. IEEE Trans. Pattern Anal. Mach. Intell. (2020)
17. Li, D., Yang, Y., Song, Y.Z., Hospedales, T.M.: Learning to generalize: meta-learning for domain generalization. In: AAAI (2018)
18. Balaji, Y., Sankaranarayanan, S., Chellappa, R.: Metareg: towards domain generalization using meta-regularization. In: NeurIPS, pp. 998–1008 (2018)
19. Krogh, A., Hertz, J.A.: A simple weight decay can improve generalization. In: Advances in Neural Information Processing Systems, pp. 950–957 (1992)
20. Kingma, D., Ba, J.: Adam: a method for stochastic optimization. In: ICLR (2014)
21. Ghifary, M., Bastiaan Kleijn, W., Zhang, M., Balduzzi, D.: Domain generalization for object recognition with multi-task autoencoders. In: Proceedings of the IEEE International Conference on Computer Vision, pp. 2551–2559 (2015)
22. Li, D., Zhang, J., Yang, Y., Liu, C., Song, Y.Z., Hospedales, T.M.: Episodic training for domain generalization. arXiv preprint arXiv:1902.00113 (2019)

A Transformer-Based Iterative Reconstruction Model for Sparse-View CT Reconstruction

Wenjun Xia[1], Ziyuan Yang[1], Qizheng Zhou[2], Zexin Lu[1], Zhongxian Wang[1], and Yi Zhang[1(✉)]

[1] Sichuan University, Chengdu 610065, China
yzhang@scu.edu.cn
[2] State Stony Brook University, New York, NY 11794, USA

Abstract. Sparse-view computed tomography (CT) is one of the primary means to reduce the radiation risk. But the reconstruction of sparse-view CT will be contaminated by severe artifacts. By carefully designing the regularization terms, the iterative reconstruction (IR) algorithm can achieve promising results. With the introduction of deep learning techniques, learned regularization terms with convolution neural network (CNN) attracts much attention and can further improve the performance. In this paper, we propose a learned local-nonlocal regularization-based model called RegFormer to reconstruct CT images. Specifically, we unroll the iterative scheme into a neural network and replace handcrafted regularization terms with learnable kernels. The convolution layers are used to learn local regularization with excellent denoising performance. Simultaneously, transformer encoders and decoders incorporate the learned nonlocal prior into the model, preserving the structures and details. To improve the ability to extract deep features during iteration, we introduce an iteration transmission (IT) module, which can further promote the efficiency of each iteration. The experimental results show that our proposed RegFormer achieves competitive performance in artifact reduction and detail preservation compared to some state-of-the-art sparse-view CT reconstruction methods.

Keywords: Computed tomography · Image reconstruction · Deep learning · Nonlocal regularization · Transformer

1 Introduction

X-ray computed tomography (CT) has been widely used and developed in medical applications because of its non-invasiveness, high efficiency and high resolution. However, the radiation risk is still one of the most important challenges of CT and results in the generally accepted ALARA (as low as reasonably achievable) principle in medical community. The radiation received by patients can be reduced by reducing the sampling views, which is called sparse-view CT. However, the reconstruction of sparse-view CT with classical filtered back-projection (FBP) tends to be seriously contaminated by the artifacts. Therefore, improving the image quality of sparse-view CT is always a hot topic,

L. Wang et al. (Eds.): MICCAI 2022, LNCS 13436, pp. 790–800, 2022.
https://doi.org/10.1007/978-3-031-16446-0_75

and a number of works have been proposed during the past decades [1–10]. However, the traditional methods are limited for clinical application due to the lack of robustness and generalization.

Recently, deep learning (DL) for CT imaging has attracted much attention. DL-based methods are data-driven and robust for different datasets. Researchers have proposed many post-processing DL methods for CT [11–18]. However, these methods lack the support of measured data, which can easily cause data inconsistency. To this end, iteration unrolling-based methods attract wide attention. For example, Chen *et al.* used CNNs to learn the regularization in the gradient descent algorithm [19]. [20] unrolled the primal-dual hybrid gradient (PDHG) algorithm into a learnable version. In [21], the authors found that the learned projector in the projected gradient algorithm can achieve better performance. He *et al.* plugged the denoised results obtained with the learned network back to the ADMM framework [22]. Similarly, [23] trained the networks to obtain the denoiser and plugged the denoised result into the momentum accelerated iterative scheme in a plug-and-play way. Xiang *et al.* unrolled FISTA algorithm with high convergence efficiency into neural network [24]. However, the main learnable structures of the above DL-based methods are all based on CNNs, which focus on the local receptive field and ignore nonlocal prior contained in CT images. A series of vision works have shown the importance of the nonlocal natures of images [25, 26].

In this paper, we propose a novel model based on learnable nonlocal regularization, which is called RegFormer. We unroll the gradient descent algorithm with fixed number of iterations into the neural network. In each iteration, we project the iterative result to the sinogram domain and calculate the projection correction with measured data. Instead of the commonly used back-projection, we use FBP to back-project the correction into the image domain. It has been proved that the replacement can accelerate the convergence of the IR algorithm [27, 28], which is significant for the unrolled neural network with a fixed number of iterations. Each iteration uses CNNs to extract local features to remove artifacts or leverage swin-transformer [29] to learn nonlocal regularization to recover details. The learned local regularization can effectively remove the noise and artifacts. Simultaneously, the learned nonlocal regularization can preserve the structures during artifact reduction. Meanwhile, we notice that each iteration in previous data-to-image methods is independent and lack communication. The input and output of each iteration are the iterative images, which are shallow pixel-level features. Therefore, the operation of the network to extract deep abstract features is limited in an iterative module, making it difficult for CNNs to extract deeper features. For neural networks, removing noise and obtain a smooth image is a relatively easy task, which will be completed in shallow layers, and restoring the details and structures is a more difficult task, requiring deeper convolutions. Therefore, the weak ability in extracting deep features will make the reconstruction over-smooth and lose details. To solve this shortcoming, we introduce an iteration transmission (IT) module. The intermediate feature maps of each iteration block will be transmitted and concatenated to the next iteration. IT module can improve the performance to extract deep features and obtain better visual performance. The main contributions of this paper can be summarized into twofold:

1. Learned local regularization with CNNs and nonlocal regularization with swin-transformer can achieve more general prior, which benefits the improvements of

unrolled IR network. The introduction of learned nonlocal regularization also brings better performance of structure and detail recovery.

2. IT module can connect the iterations to improve the deep feature extraction and structure preservation.

2 Methodology

2.1 Preliminary Knowledge

Considering a fan beam CT geometry with N_v scanning views and N_d detector elements, and the volume divided into a grid of $m \times n$, a general objective model for IR algorithm can be formulated as follows,

$$\min_x \tfrac{1}{2}\|Ax - y\|_2^2 + \lambda R(x), \tag{1}$$

where $y \in R^{M_1}$ ($M_1 = N_v \times N_d$) represents the measurement, $x \in R^{M_2}$ ($M_2 = m \times n$) denotes the vectorized CT image, $A \in R^{M_1 \times M_2}$ is the measurement matrix determined by the geometry and volume, and $R(x)$ stands for regularization term, balanced with the weight λ.

2.2 The Proposed RegFormer

To solve Eq. (1), the transpose of the system matrix A^T is usually involved. According to the recommendation of [27, 28], replacing A^T with the inverse transform of A (e.g., FBP) can achieve better convergence efficiency. Faster convergence is significant for optimization within a limited number of iterations. Then, a simple gradient descent algorithm to solve Eq. (1) can be formulated as:

$$x^{t+1} = x^t - \alpha^t A^\dagger \left(Ax^t - y\right) + \lambda^t \nabla_x R\left(x^t\right), \tag{2}$$

where α is the step size and α^t denotes its iteration-dependent version. $\nabla_x R\left(x^t\right)$ represents the gradient of $R(x)$ with respect to x at the point of x^t, which can be replaced with network module, and $A^\dagger$ denotes the pseudo-inversion of A, which can be implemented by FBP:

$$A^\dagger p = FBP(p) = B(h * p), \tag{3}$$

where h is the R-L filter and B denotes the back-projection matrix. Convolution and matrix multiplication are both linear operators and differentiable, making the gradient backpropagation of the proposed network feasible. As derived in [27], if it is satisfied that $\|I - \alpha A^\dagger A\| < 1$, the optimization can converge even if the replacement destroys the conjugate nature. And $\|I - \alpha A^\dagger A\|$ can provides smaller valuer than $\|I - \alpha A^T A\|$, which will result in faster convergence.

Iteration Block. To simultaneously learn local and nonlocal regularizations, we convert the iterations into two kinds of iteration blocks. As shown in Fig. 1, the local regularization is composed of three CNN layers. Local regularization iteration block can achieve good denoising performance, but it is easy to cause over-smooth and detail loss. To conquer this drawback, we introduce swin-transformer to learn the nonlocal regularization. In the nonlocal regularization iteration block, we use a convolution layer to obtain the pixel-level embeddings and feed the embeddings to two successive swin-transformer blocks. Each swin-transformer block consists of a window-based multi-head self-attention (WMSA) or shifted window-based MSA (SWMSA) module, followed by a two-layer multi-layer perceptron (MLP) with GELU function in between. After the windows are merged into feature maps and are subsequently fed into a convolution layer, we can obtain the single image feature map. The feature maps are all scaled with the layer normalization (LN) layer. (S)WMSA can learn the attention between pixel features in the window and then aggregate the pixel features according to the learned attention. Therefore, the nonlocal regularization iteration block not only focuses on locally adjacent pixels, but can also study relationship between any pixels in the window, and thus obtain the nonlocal regularization features.

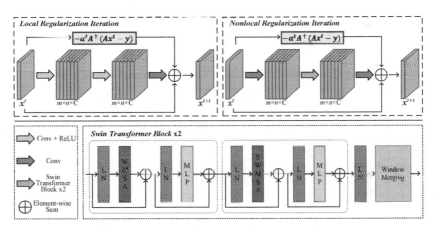

Fig. 1. The architecture of each iteration block.

Iteration Transmission. In current iteration unrolling-based CT reconstruction models, the feature maps between iterations are independent. The input and output of each iteration are both the iterative images, which are shallow pixel-level features. Therefore, the extraction of deep abstract features is limited in an iterative module. To establish communication between different iterations, an iteration transmission (IT) module is proposed. The module is shown in Fig. 2, and the structures other than convolution (including skip connection and fidelity term module) are omitted for simplicity. In Fig. 2, local and nonlocal regularization iteration blocks are merged and represented as parallel paths. The upper path corresponds to the local regularization iteration block, and the lower path is the nonlocal regularization iteration block. In our proposed local and nonlocal iteration blocks, there are two layers of C feature maps. We half the number of channels in the first layer and concatenate the feature maps with the message transmitted from the previous iteration. An additional convolution on the second feature maps obtains $C/2$ feature maps, which are the message transmitted to the next iteration. On the one hand, the proposed IT module can expand the network's depth and improve the network's performance. On the other hand, there is no convertion from deep features to pixel-level features in the whole IT path, so the proposed IT module can make the iterations connected, and extract deeper features to improve the ability of structure preservation.

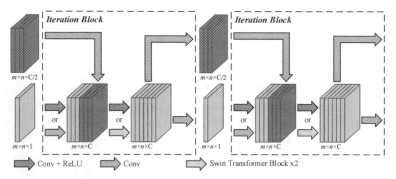

Fig. 2. The illustration of iteration transmission. The structures other than convolution are omitted.

Overall Architecture. The overall architecture of our proposed RegFormer is shown in Fig. 3. The inputs of the network are the under-sampled sinogram and corresponding FBP reconstruction. The network consists of alternate local iteration blocks and nonlocal iteration blocks. The iteration is fixed to N_t. Every two adjacent iteration blocks are connected with IT modules.

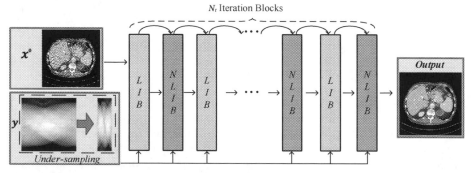

Fig. 3. The overall architecture of the proposed RegFormer. The network consists of alternate local iteration blocks (LIB) and nonlocal iteration blocks (NLIB). Feature maps are transmitted using the IT module between every two iterations.

3   Experiments

To evaluate the performance of our proposed RegFormer, the dataset "the 2016 NIH-AAPM-Mayo Clinic Low-Dose CT Grand Challenge" [30] was used. The dataset has

2378 full-dose CT images with a thickness of 3 mm from 10 patients. We randomly selected 600 images from 7 patients as the training set, 200 images from 1 patient as the validation set, and 200 images from the remaining 2 patients as the test set. The size of the images was 256×256. The projection data were simulated with the distance-driven method [31, 32] and fan-beam geometry.

The number of iteration blocks of RegFormer is set to $N_t = 18$. The feature maps have $C = 96$ channels. The parameter setup of swin-transformer blocks follows [26]. The sizes of the convolution kernel are 5×5 for the main iteration block and 3×3 for the IT module. Four state-of-the-art methods were used for comparison, including TGV [4], Uformer [33], FISTA-Net [24], LEARN [19]. In addition, to verify the advantage of inverse radon transform over back-projection, we replaced the back-projection in LEARN with FBP, which is referred to as LEARN+. All the deep learning methods were trained with AdamW optimizer [34] and 200 epochs. The learning rate was set to 1e-4 and gradually reduced to 0. The peak signal-to-noise ratio (PSNR) and structural similarity index measure (SSIM) were adopted to quantitatively evaluate the performance of different methods.

Figure 4 shows the results of an abdominal slice reconstructed using different methods with 64 projection view data. As an analytical reconstruction method, FBP requires sufficient data and the result suffers from severe artifacts. TGV is an IR algorithm based on handcrafted regularization. It can be seen from Fig. 4 that it often troubles the balance of artifact suppression and detail preservation. The results of Uformer, FISTA-Net and LEARN all suffered from obvious distortion. In particular, the result of Uformer loses many details while introducing structures that do not exist in the ground truth. The results of FISTA-Net and LEARN are severely over-smoothed. The MSE loss function makes FISTA-Net result has higher PSNR than TGV result, but also leads to its over-smoothness and worse SSIM score. In comparison, FISTA-Net can protect the details better than LEARN, but not as good as TGV. Overall, LEARN+ and RegFormer have overwhelming performance. For the blood vessel structures inside the liver that can be easily observed, LEARN+ and RegFormer also have better performances in the regions indicated by the blue arrows. In the magnified area indicated by the red box, it can be seen that RegFormer outperforms LEARN+ in terms of structure preservation as indicated by the red arrows, which show the advantage of nonlocal regularization.

To observe the numerical distribution of the results, we selected two relatively uniform and differently distributed representative ROIs indicated by blue boxes in Fig. 4(a). The box plots of the two regions from different reconstructions are presented in Fig. 5. In Fig. 5(a) ROI I, it can be seen that the box plots of different methods have a smaller interquartile range (IQR) than ground truth, which means that various methods smooth the image. In contrast, our proposed RegFormer has a closer IQR to the ground truth. Most methods have offset medians, indicating that their numerical distributions are biased. The box plot of RegFormer has the same median as the ground truth. In summary, in the ROI (a), the reconstruction of RegFormer has a more consistent numerical distribution with ground truth than other methods. The same conclusion can be reached in ROI (b).

Figure 6 shows the results of a thoracic slice reconstructed using different methods with 64 projection view data. There are severe artifacts in the FBP result. There are less artifacts in the TGV result, but it shows blocking effect. Deep learning-based

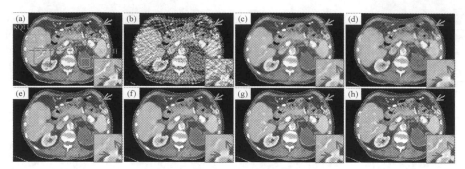

Fig. 4. Abdominal image reconstruction with 64 projection views by different methods. (a) Ground truth (PSNR/SSIM), (b) FBP (12.57/0.3146), (c) TGV (24.36/0.8200), (d) Uformer (23.36/0.7448), (e) FISTA-Net (25.91/0.7975), (f) LEARN (27.49/0.8431), (g) LEARN+ (31.57/0.8962) and (h) RegFormer (32.39/0.9164). The display window is [−160, 240] HU.

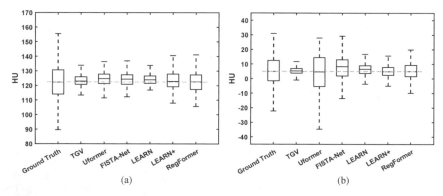

Fig. 5. Box plots for (a) ROI I and (b) ROI II indicated with blue rectangles in Fig. 4 (a).

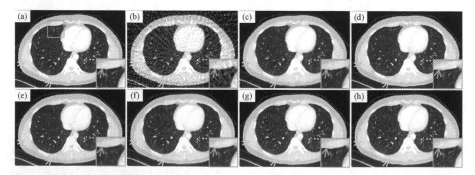

Fig. 6. Thoracic image reconstruction with 64 projection views by different methods. (a) Ground truth (PSNR/SSIM), (b) FBP (10.64/0.3053), (c) TGV (22.92/0.8421), (d) Uformer (22.22/0.7910), (e) FISTA-Net (24.74/0.8403), (f) LEARN (27.03/0.8976), (g) LEARN+ (31.28/0.9331) and (h) RegFormer (32.39/0.9414). The display window is [−1000, 200] HU.

methods have a stronger ability in artifact suppression. However, Uformer, FISTA-Net and LEARN miss some structure details indicated by the blue arrows, which are well maintained by LEARN+ and RegFormer. An ROI indicated by the red box is zoomed in and displayed at the bottom right. In the magnified ROI, it can be found that RegFormer outperforms LEARN in terms of structure preservation. In the region indicated by the red arrow, RegFormer maintains a higher contrast. Consistent with the visual inspection, RegFormer achieves better quantitative scores than other methods.

Figure 7 shows the noise power spectrum (NPS) maps of the thoracic reconstruction with different methods. It can be seen that LEARN+ and RegFormer have errors with lower energy than other methods. Especially in the low-frequency area, LEARN+ and RegFormer have smaller errors, indicating less structural errors.

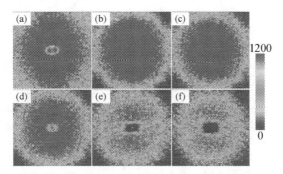

Fig. 7. NPS maps of thoracic reconstruction with 64 projection views by different methods. (a) TGV, (b) Uformer, (c) FISTA-Net, (d) LEARN, (e) LEARN+ and (f) RegFormer. The display window is [0, 1200] HU^2mm^2.

Table 1 shows the overall quantitative results of different methods on the whole testing set, and it can be seen that our proposed RegFormer has the best scores, followed by LEARN+.

Table 1. Quantitative results (mean over whole testing set) of different methods

	FBP	TGV	Uformer	FISTA-Net	LEARN	LEARN+	RegFormer
PSNR	11.98	24.47	23.45	26.34	28.21	32.92	**34.05**
SSIM	0.2769	0.8564	0.7911	0.8481	0.8874	0.9292	**0.9409**

4 Conclusions

In this paper, we propose a novel local-nonlocal regularization-based model for sparse-view CT reconstruction. Two innovations in our proposed RegFormer help to achieve better performance. There have been so many works showing that deep features are important for a variety of tasks. Independent iterations make the network extract only shallow features, which is insufficient to restore the detailed structure. The proposed IT module transmits features by establishing skip connections between iterations, which can extract both shallow and deep features. Additionally, the commonly used CNN can only focus on adjacent pixels, ignoring the nonlocal characteristics of CT images, which have been proved effective in previous studies. In this paper, we propose to use swin-transformer to extract features to learn nonlocal regularization. The nonlocal regularization expands the receptive field and improves the structure and detail preservation. As demonstrated in the experimental results, our proposed RegFormer outperforms the state-of-the-art methods in both qualitative and quantitative aspects. However, there are still some issues worthy of further study. Because the high memory consumption of transformer, the proposed RegFormer uses the architecture of alternative local regularization blocks and nonlocal regularization blocks, to ensure a sufficient number of iterations while introducing the learnable nonlocal regularization. Therefore, memory consumption is an important concern for the improvement of the proposed method. A potential future work is to reduce the memory consumption of transformer-based nonlocal regularization blocks for the extension of our proposed RegFormer to 3D reconstruction. In addition, the learnable parameters show better generalization than manually set parameters, which has been proved by the development of deep learning. So our another future work is to study whether the learned FBP filter can further improve the performance of the unrolling iteration scheme. Finally, the acquisition of paired data has always been an important concern in clinic. Therefore, we will study to incorporate our proposed RegFormer into an unsupervised training framework for clinical application.

Acknowledgements. This work was supported in part by Sichuan Science and Technology Program under Grant 2021JDJQ0024, and in part by Sichuan University 'From 0 to 1' Innovative Research Program under grant 2022SCUH0016.

References

1. Sidky, E.Y., Kao, C.-M., Pan, X.: Accurate image reconstruction from few-views and limited-angle data in divergent-beam CT. J. X-Ray. Sci. Technol. **14**(2), 119–139 (2006)
2. Sidky, E.Y., Pan, X.: Image reconstruction in circular cone-beam computed tomography by constrained, total-variation minimization. Phys. Med. Biol. **53**(17), 4777–4807 (2008)
3. Yu, G., Li, L., Gu, J., Zhang, L.: Total variation based iterative image reconstruction. In: Liu, Y., Jiang, T., Zhang, C. (eds.) CVBIA 2005. LNCS, vol. 3765, pp. 526–534. Springer, Heidelberg (2005). https://doi.org/10.1007/11569541_53
4. Niu, S., et al.: Sparse-view X-ray CT reconstruction via total generalized variation regularization. Phys. Med. Biol. **59**(12), 2997–3017 (2014)
5. Xu, Q., et al.: Low-dose X-ray CT reconstruction via dictionary learning. IEEE Trans. Med. Imaging **31**(9), 1682–1697 (2012)
6. Chen, Y., et al.: Bayesian statistical reconstruction for low-dose X-ray computed tomography using an adaptive-weighting nonlocal prior. Comput. Med. Imag. Graph. **33**(7), 495–500 (2009)
7. Ma, J., et al.: Iterative image reconstruction for cerebral perfusion CT using a pre-contrast scan induced edge-preserving prior. Phys. Med. Biol. **57**(22), 7519–7542 (2012)
8. Zhang, Y., et al.: Spectral CT reconstruction with image sparsity and spectral mean. IEEE Trans. Comput. Imaging **2**(4), 510–523 (2016)

9. Gao, H., Yu, H., Osher, S., Wang, G.: Multi-energy CT based on a prior rank, intensity and sparsity model (PRISM). Inverse Probl. **27**(11), 115012 (2011)
10. Cai, J.-F., et al.: Cine cone beam CT reconstruction using low-rank matrix factorization: algorithm and a proof-of-principle study. IEEE Trans. Med. Imaging **33**(8), 1581–1591 (2014)
11. Kang, E., Min, J., Ye, J.C.: A deep convolutional neural network using directional wavelets for low-dose X-ray CT reconstruction. Med. Phys. **44**(10), e360–e375 (2017)
12. Chen, H., et al.: Low-dose CT via convolutional neural network. Biomed. Opt. Exp. **8**(2), 679–694 (2017)
13. Chen, H., et al.: Low-dose CT with a residual encoder-decoder convolutional neural network. IEEE Trans. Med. Imaging **36**(12), 2524–2535 (2017)
14. Han, Y.S., Yoo, J., Ye, J.C.: Deep residual learning for compressed sensing CT reconstruction via persistent homology analysis, arXiv preprint arXiv:1611.06391 (2016)
15. Han, Y., Ye, J.C.: Framing U-Net via deep convolutional framelets: application to sparse-view CT. IEEE Trans. Med. Imaging **37**(6), 1418–1429 (2018)
16. Jin, K.H., McCann, M.T., Froustey, E., Unser, M.: Deep convolutional neural network for inverse problems in imaging. IEEE Trans. Image Process. **26**(9), 4509–4522 (2017)
17. Yang, Q., et al.: Low-dose CT image denoising using a generative adversarial network with wasserstein distance and perceptual loss. IEEE Trans. Med. Imaging **37**(6), 1348–1357 (2018)
18. Shan, H., et al.: 3-D convolutional encoder-decoder network for lowdose CT via transfer learning from a 2-D trained network. IEEE Trans. Med. Imaging **37**(6), 1522–1534 (2018)
19. Chen, H., et al.: LEARN: Learned experts' assessment-based reconstruction network for sparse-data CT. IEEE Trans. Med. Imaging **37**(6), 1333–1347 (2018)
20. Adler, J., Oktem, O.: Learned primal-dual reconstruction. IEEE Trans. Med. Imaging **37**(6), 1322–1332 (2018)
21. Gupta, H., et al.: CNN-based projected gradient descent for consistent CT image reconstruction. IEEE Trans. Med. Imaging **37**(6), 1440–1453 (2018)
22. He, J., et al.: Optimizing a parameterized plug-and-play ADMM for iterative low dose CT reconstruction. IEEE Trans. Med. Imaging **38**(2), 371–382 (2018)
23. Chun, I.Y., Huang, Z., Lim, H., Fessler, J.: Momentum-Net: fast and convergent iterative neural network for inverse problems. IEEE Trans. Pattern Anal. Mach. Intell. (2020)
24. Xiang, J., Dong, Y., Yang, Y.: FISTA-Net: learning a fast iterative shrinkage thresholding network for inverse problems in imaging. IEEE Trans. Med. Imaging **40**(5), 1329–1339 (2021)
25. Dosovitskiy, A., et al.: An image is worth 16x16 words: transformers for image recognition at scale, arXiv preprint arXiv:2010.11929 (2020)
26. Liu, Z., et al.: Swin transformer: hierarchical vision transformer using shifted windows. In: Proceedings of the IEEE/CVF International Conference on Computer Vision, pp. 10012–10022 (2021)
27. Gao, H.: Fused analytical and iterative reconstruction (AIR) via modified proximal forward–backward splitting: a FDK-based iterative image reconstruction example for CBCT. Phys. Med. Biol. **61**(19), 7187 (2016)
28. Chen, G., et al.: AirNet: Fused analytical and iterative reconstruction with deep neural network regularization for sparse-data CT. Med. Phys. **47**(7), 2916–2930 (2020)
29. Vaswani, A., et al.: Attention is all you need. In: Proceedings of Advances in Neural Information Processing Systems, vol. 30 (2017)
30. McCollough, C.: TU-FG-207A-04: overview of the low dose CT grand challenge. Med. Phys. **43**(6Part35), 3759–3760 (2016)
31. De Man, B., Basu, S.: Distance-driven projection and backprojection. In: Proceedings of IEEE Nuclear Science Symposium Conference Record, vol. 3, pp. 1477–1480 (2002)
32. De Man, B., Basu, S.: Distance-driven projection and backprojection in three dimensions. Phys. Med. Biol. **49**(11), 2463–2475 (2004)

33. Wang, Z., Cun, X., Bao, J., Liu, J.: Uformer: a general u-shaped transformer for image restoration, arXiv preprint arXiv:2106.03106 (2021)
34. Loshchilov, I., Hutter, F.: Decoupled weight decay regularization, arXiv preprint arXiv:1711.05101 (2017)

Correction to: RPLHR-CT Dataset and Transformer Baseline for Volumetric Super-Resolution from CT Scans

Pengxin Yu, Haoyue Zhang, Han Kang, Wen Tang, Corey W. Arnold, and Rongguo Zhang

Correction to:
Chapter 33 in: L. Wang et al. (Eds.): *Medical Image Computing and Computer Assisted Intervention – MICCAI 2022*, LNCS 13436, https://doi.org/10.1007/978-3-031-16446-0_33

In the originally published version of chapter 33, a footnote was missing. This has been included to confirm that both authors contributed equally to the contribution.

The updated version of this chapter can be found at
https://doi.org/10.1007/978-3-031-16446-0_33

Author Index

Printed in the United States
by Baker & Taylor Publisher Services